Lecture Notes in Computer Science 3795

Commenced Publication in 1973
Founding and Former Series Editors:
Gerhard Goos, Juris Hartmanis, and Jan van Leeuwen

Hai Zhuge Geoffrey C. Fox (Eds.)

Grid and Cooperative Computing – GCC 2005

4th International Conference
Beijing, China, November 30 – December 3, 2005
Proceedings

Volume Editors

Hai Zhuge
Chinese Academy of Sciences, Institute of Computing Technology
P.O. Box 2704-28, Beijing, China
E-mail: zhuge@ict.ac.cn

Geoffrey C. Fox
Indiana University, Community Grid Computing Laboratory
501 North Morton Street, Suite 224, Bloomington, IN 47404, USA
E-mail: gcf@indiana.edu

Library of Congress Control Number: 2005936339

CR Subject Classification (1998): C.2, D.4, I.2.11, H.4, H.3, H.5, K.6.5

ISSN 0302-9743
ISBN-10 3-540-30510-6 Springer Berlin Heidelberg New York
ISBN-13 978-3-540-30510-1 Springer Berlin Heidelberg New York

Springer is a part of Springer Science+Business Media

springeronline.com

Printed in Germany

Typesetting: Camera-ready by author, data conversion by Scientific Publishing Services, Chennai, India
Printed on acid-free paper SPIN: 11590354 06/3142 5 4 3 2 1 0

Preface

This volume presents the accepted papers for the 4th International Conference on Grid and Cooperative Computing (GCC 2005), held in Beijing, China, during November 30 – December 3, 2005. The conference series of GCC aims to provide an international forum for the presentation and discussion of research trends on the theory, method, and design of Grid and cooperative computing as well as their scientific, engineering and commercial applications. It has become a major annual event in this area.

The First International Conference on Grid and Cooperative Computing (GCC 2002) received 168 submissions. GCC 2003 received 550 submissions, from which 176 regular papers and 173 short papers were accepted. The acceptance rate of regular papers was 32%, and the total acceptance rate was 64%. GCC 2004 received 427 main-conference submissions and 154 workshop submissions. The main conference accepted 96 regular papers and 62 short papers. The acceptance rate of the regular papers was 23%. The total acceptance rate of the main conference was 37%.

For this conference, we received 576 submissions. Each was reviewed by two independent members of the International Program Committee. After carefully evaluating their originality and quality, we accepted 57 regular papers and 84 short papers. The acceptance rate of regular papers was 10%. The total acceptance rate was 25%.

We are pleased to thank the authors whose submissions and participation made this conference possible. We also want to express our thanks to the Program Committee members, for their dedication in helping to organize the conference and reviewing the submissions. We owe special thanks to the keynote speakers for their impressive speeches. We would like to thank the co-chairs Ian Foster and Tony Hey who provided continuous support for this conference.

Finally we would like to thank the China Knowledge Grid Research Group, especially Xiaofeng Wang, Jie Liu, Jin Liu, Chao He, and Liang Feng for their excellent work in organizing this conference.

October 2005 Hai Zhuge, Geoffrey C. Fox

Conference Committees

General Co-chairs

Ian Foster, University of Chicago, USA
Tony Hey, University of Southampton, UK

Program Committee Co-chairs

Hai Zhuge, Chinese Academy of Sciences, China
Geoffrey Fox, Indiana University, USA

Steering Committee

Andrew Chien, University of California at San Diego, USA
Hai Jin, Huazhong University of Science and Technology, China
Guojie Li, China Computer Federation, China
Zhiwei Xu, Chinese Academy of Sciences, China
Xiaodong Zhang, College of William and Mary, USA

Publicity Chair

Cho-Li Wang, University of Hong Kong, China

Program Committee Members

Mark Baker (University of Portsmouth, UK)
Yaodong Bi (University of Scranton, USA)
Rajkumar Buyya (The University of Melbourne, Australia)
Wentong Cai (Nanyang Technological University, Singapore)
Jiannong Cao (Hong Kong Polytechnic University, Hong Kong, China)
Guihai Chen (Nanjing University, China)
Guangrong Gao (University of Delaware Newark, USA)
Ning Gu (Fudan University, China)
Minyi Guo (University of Aizu, Japan)
Jun Han (Swinburne University of Technology, Australia)
Yanbo Han (Institute of Computing Tech., CAS, China)

Chun-Hsi Huang (University of Connecticut, USA)
Weijia Jia (City University of Hong Kong, Hong Kong, China)
Hai Jin (HuaZhong University of Sci.&Tech., China)
Francis Lau (Hong Kong University, Hong Kong, China)
Keqin Li (State University of New York, USA)
Minglu Li (Shanghai Jiao Tong University, China)
Qing Li (City University of Hong Kong, Hong Kong, China)
Xiaoming Li (Peking University, China)
Xiaola Lin (City University of Hong Kong, China)
Junzhou Luo (Southeast University, China)
Huaikou Miao (ShangHai University, China)
Geyong Min (University of Bradford, UK)
Jun Ni (University of Iowa, USA)
Lionel Ni (Hong Kong University of Science and Technology, Hong Kong)
Yi Pan (Georgia State University, USA)
Depei Qian (Xi'an Jiaotong University, China)
Yuzhong Qu (Southeast University, China)
Hong Shen (Japan Advanced Institute of Science and Technology, Japan)
Alexander V. Smirnov (St.-Petersburg Institute for Informatics and Automation of the Russian Academy of Sciences, Russia)
Xian-He Sun (Illinois Institute of Technology, USA)
Yuzhong Sun (Institute of Computing Technology, CAS, China)
David Taniar (Monash University, Australia)
Huaglory Tianfield (Glasgow Caledonian University, UK)
David W. Walker (Cardiff University, UK)
Shaowen Wang (University of Iowa, USA)
Jie Wu (Florida Atlantic University, USA)
Zhaohui Wu (Zhejiang University, China)
Nong Xiao (National University of Defense Technology, China)
Cheng-Zhong Xu (Wayne State University, USA)
Guangwen Yang (Tsinghua University, China)
Laurence Tianruo Yang (St. Francis Xavier University, Canada)
Zhonghua Yang (Nanyang Technological University, Singapore)
Xiaodong Zhang (NSF, USA and College of William and Mary, USA)
Weimin Zheng (Tsinghua University, China)
Wanlei Zhou (Deakin University, Australia)
Xinrong Zhou (Abo Akademi University, Finland)
Jianping Zhu (The University of Akron, USA)

Table of Contents

Session 2: Grid Middleware and Applications

Session 3: Knowledge Grid and Semantic Grid

Session 5: P2P Computing and Automatic Computing

Session 6: Performance Evaluation and Modeling

Session 7: Software Engineering and Cooperative Computing

Towards Global Collaborative Computing: Opportunities and Challenges of Peer to Peer Networks and Applications

Ling Liu

College of Computing Georgia Institute of Technology, USA
lingliu@cc.gatech.edu

Abstract. Collaborative computing has emerged as a promising paradigm for developing large-scale distributed systems. Peer to Peer (P2P) and Grid computing represent a significant step towards global collaboration, a fundamental capability of network computing. P2P systems are decentralized, self-organizing, and self-repairing distributed systems that cooperate to exchange data and accomplish computing tasks. These systems have transpired as the dominant consumer of residential Internet subscribers' bandwidth, and are being increasingly used in many different application domains. With rapid advances in wireless and mobile communication technologies, such as wireless mesh networks, wireless LANs, and 3G cellular networks, P2P computing is moving into wireless networking, mobile computing, and sensor network applications. In this keynote, I will discuss some important opportunities and challenges of Peer to Peer networks and applications towards global collaborative computing paradigm. I will first review the P2P research and development in the past few years, focusing on the remarkable results produced in P2P system scalability, robustness, distributed storage, and system measurements, the continued evolution of P2P systems, and how today's state-of-the-art developments differentiate from earlier instantiations, such as Napster, Gnutella, KaZaA, and Morpheus. Then I will discuss some important challenges for wide deployment of P2P computing in mission-critical applications and future computing environments.

References

1. Gedik, B. and Liu, L.: A Scalable Peer-to-Peer Architecture for Distributed Information Monitoring Applications. *IEEE Transactions on Computers*. 54(6) (2005) 767-782.
2. Gedik, B. and Liu, L.: PeerCQ: A Decentralized and Self-Configuring Peer-to-Peer Information Monitoring System. In: Proceedings of the 23rd International Conference on Distributed Computing Systems (ICDCS2003), Providence, Rhode Island USA, May 19-22, 2003. (Best Paper Award)
3. Ramaswamy, L., Gedik, B. and Liu, L.: A Distributed Approach to Node Clustering in Decentralized Peer-to-Peer Networks. *IEEE Transactions on Parallel and Distributed Systems* (TPDS), 16(9) (2005) 1-16.
4. Ramaswamy, L. and Liu, L.: FreeRiding: A New Challenge for Peer-to-Peer File Sharing Systems. In: Proceedings of the 36th HAWAII INTERNATIONAL CONFERENCE ON SYSTEM SCIENCES (HICSS-36) - Peer-to-Peer (P2P) Computing Track, Hilton Waikoloa Village, Big Island, Hawaii, January 6-9, 2003.

H. Zhuge and G.C. Fox (Eds.): GCC 2005, LNCS 3795, pp. 1 – 2, 2005.

5. Singh, A., Srivatsa, M., Liu, L. and Miller, T.: Apoidea: A Decentralized Peer-to-Peer Architecture for Crawling the World Wide Web. In: Proceedings of the ACM SIGIR workshop on Distributed IR. *Lecture Notes of Computer Science (LNCS) series*, Springer Verlag, Aug. 1, 2003.
6. Srivatsa, M. and Liu, L.: Vulnerabilities and Security Threats in Structured Overlay Networks: A Quantitative Analysis. To appear in the Proceedings of the 20th Annual Computer Security Applications Conference (ACSAC 2004), (IEEE Press). Tucson, Arizona, December 6-10, 2004.
7. Srivatsa, M. and Liu, L.: Countering Targeted File Attacks using LocationGuard. To appear in Proceedings of the 14th USENIX Security Symposium (USENIX Security), Baltimore, MD, 81-96, August 1 - 5, 2005.
8. Srivatsa, M. and Liu, L.: Securing Publish-Subscribe Overlay Services with EventGuard. To appear in Proceedings of ACM Computer and Communication Security (CCS 2005), Hilton Alexandria Mark Center, Alexandria, VA, USA, November 7-11, 2005.
9. Srivatsa, M., Xiong, L. and Liu, L.: TrustGuard: Countering Vulnerabilities in Reputation Management For Decentralized Overlay Networks. In: Proceedings of 14th World Wide Web Conference (WWW 2005), Chiba, Japan, May 10-14, 2005.
10. Srivatsa, M. Gedik, B. and Liu, L.: Scaling Unstructured Peer-to-Peer Networks with Multi-Tier Capacity-Aware Overlay Topologies. In: Proceedings of the Tenth International Conference on Parallel and Distributed Systems (IEEE ICPADS 2004), Newport Beach, California, July 7-9, 2004.
11. Xiong, L. and Liu, L.: PeerTrust: Supporting Reputation-Based Trust for Peer-to-Peer Electronic Communities. *IEEE Transactions on Knowledge and Data Engineering, Special issue on Peer to Peer Based Data Management*, 16(7) (2004) 843-857.
12. Zhang, J., Liu, L., Pu, C. and Ammar, M.: Reliable Peer-to-peer End System Multicasting through Replication. IEEE International Conference on Peer to Peer Computing (P2P 2004), Zurich, Switzerland, Aug. 25-27, 2004.
13. Zhuge, H.: The Future Interconnection Environment, *IEEE Computer*, 38 (4)(2005) 27-33.
14. Zhuge, H.: Exploring an Epidemic in an E-Science Environment, *Communications of the ACM*, 48(9)(2005)109-114.

Management of Real-Time Streaming Data Grid Services

Geoffrey Fox, Galip Aydin, Harshawardhan Gadgil, Shrideep Pallickara, Marlon Pierce, and Wenjun Wu

Community Grids Laboratory, Indiana University,
501 North Morton Street, Suite 224, Bloomington, IN 47404
{gcf, gaydin, hgadgil, spallick, marpierc, wewu}@indiana.edu

Abstract. We discuss the architectural and management support for real time data stream applications, both in terms of lower level messaging and higher level service, filter and session structures. In our approach, messaging systems act as a Grid substrate that can provide qualities of service to various streaming applications ranging from audio-video collaboration to sensor grids. The messaging substrate is composed of distributed, hierarchically arranged message brokers that form networks. We discuss approaches to managing systems for both broker networks and application filters: broker network topologies must be created and maintained, and distributed filters must be arranged in appropriate sequences. These managed broker networks may be applied to a wide range of problems. We discuss applications to audio/video collaboration in some detail and also describe applications to streaming Global Positioning System data streams.

1 Introduction

A growing number of applications involve real-time streams of information that need to be transported in a dynamic, high-performance, reliable, and secure fashion. Examples include sensor nets for both science and the military applications, mobile devices on ad-hoc networks, and collaborative applications. In the latter case the streams consist of a set of "change events" for a collaborative entity multicast to the participating clients. They could be the frames of audio-video streams, encoded changed pixels in a shared display, or high level semantic events such as signals of PowerPoint slide changes. Here we describe our research into ways of managing such streams, which we think are a critical component of both sensor nets and real time synchronous collaboration environments.

We develop real-time streaming technology assuming that the sources, sinks, and filters of these streams are Web or Grid services. This allows us to share the support technology between streaming applications and benefit from the pervasive interoperability of a service-oriented architecture. Further, this allows a simple model of collaborative Web and Grid services gotten by "just" sharing the input or output ports. As services expose their change by explicit messages (using what we call a message-based Model-View-Controller architecture [1]), it is much easier to make them collaborative than traditional desktop applications, in which events are often buried in the application. Traditional collaborative applications can be made service oriented with in particular a set of services implementing traditional H.323 functionality and interoperating with Access Grid and Polycom systems. This required development of

H. Zhuge and G.C. Fox (Eds.): GCC 2005, LNCS 3795, pp. 3 – 12, 2005.

an XML equivalent of the H.323 protocol [2]. Our other major motivation is the sensor networks of military, scientific and social infrastructure. These are well suited to a service architecture as exemplified by the US military Global Information Grid with its service-based Network Centric Operations and Warfare Architecture [3, 4].

We have developed general purpose, open source software to support distributed streams, described in Sec. 2. NaradaBrokering [5] forms a distributed set of message brokers that implement a publish-subscribe software overlay network. This environment supports multiple protocols (including UDP, TCP, and parallel TCP) and provides reliable message delivery with a scalable architecture.

Our architecture supports the interesting concept of hybrid streams where multiple "simple streams" are intrinsically linked: examples are linkages of a stream of annotation white boards with original audio/video stream [7] and the combination of lossless and lossy codec streams (using perhaps parallel TCP and UDP respectively) to represent a large dynamic shared display.

Several applications drive the development of our technology. These include collaboration services with audio, video, and shared display streams, as well as linkages of real-time Global Positioning System sensors to Geographical Information Systems implemented as Web services. Other examples include integration of hand-held devices to a Grid [6] and the linkage of annotations to video streams showing how composite streams can be supported for real-time annotation [7]. The first two applications are described in sections 4 and 5 and illustrate the need the high level session and filter infrastructure on top of the messaging infrastructure.

The messaging infrastructure supports the application services with their filters, gateways and sessions reflecting both collaborative and workflow functions. However we have found the need for a set of services that manage the messaging itself and so control broker deployment and quality of service. Section 3 describes the integration of the management of messaging and higher-level services.

2 NaradaBrokering: A Distributed Messaging Substrate

NaradaBrokering [5, 9] is a messaging infrastructure that is based on the publish/subscribe paradigm. The system efficiently routes messages [10] from the originators to the consumers that are interested in the message. The system places no restrictions on the size and the rate at which these messages are issued. Consumers can express their interests (or specify subscriptions) using simple formats such as character strings. Subscriptions may also be based on sophisticated queries involving XPath, SQL, or regular expressions. Support for these subscription formats enables consumers to precisely narrow the type of messages that they are interested in. The substrate incorporates support for enterprise messaging specifications such as the Java Message Service. The substrate also incorporates support for a very wide array of transports (TCP, UDP, Multicast, SSL, HTTP and ParallelTCP among others), which enable the infrastructure to be leveraged by entities in a wide variety of settings. To cope with very large payloads the system leverages ParallelTCP at the transport level and services such as compression and fragmentation to reduce individual message sizes. The fragments (compressed or otherwise) are reconstituted by appropriate services (coalescing and de-compression) prior to delivery to the application.

The most fundamental unit in NaradaBrokering is a message. A stream can be thought of as being composed by a series of messages, each with causal and ordering correlations to previous messages in the stream. The inter-broker latency for routing typical messages is around 1 millisecond. In a controlled cluster setting a single broker was found to support up to 400 UDP-based A/V clients concurrently with adequate latency [11]. Among the services most relevant for collaboration within the system are the following.

1. Support for a replay and recording services: The recording service is used to store messages reliably to the archival system. The recording is done in such a way that all events issued by the recording entity are stored in the order that they were published. The replay service facilitates the replay of these previously stored messages. The replay service support replays in multiple flavors. Entities may request replays based on sequencing information, timing information, content of the message or based on the topics that these messages were published to. In some cases one or more of the parameters can be combined in a single request.
2. Support for consistent global timestamps [12] through an implementation of the Network Time Protocol (NTP). This implementation ensures that timestamps at the distributed entities are within a few milliseconds of each other. This allows us to ensure that we can order messages based on these global timestamps. This is especially useful during replays when we can precisely determine the order in which messages should be released to the application.
3. Support for buffering and subsequent time-spaced release of messages to reduce jitters. The typical lower bound for time space resolution is a millisecond. However, we have also been able to successively time-space events in the order of several microseconds. By buffering and releasing messages we reduce the jitters that may have been introduced by the network.

More recently, we have incorporated support for Web Services within the substrate. Entities can send SOAP messages directly to the brokers that are part of the messaging infrastructure. We have incorporated support for Web Service specifications such as WS-Eventing, WS-ReliableMessaging, and WS-Reliability. Work on implementing the WS-Notification suite of specifications is currently underway. The implementation of these specifications also had to cope with other specifications such as WS-Addressing and WS-Policy that are leveraged by these applications. In addition to the rules governing SOAP messages and the implemented protocols, rules governing WS-Addressing are also enforced.

In our support for SOAP within NaradaBrokering we have introduced *filters* and *filter-pipelines*. A filter is smallest processing unit for a SOAP message. Several filters can be cascaded together to constitute a filter-pipeline. Here, the filters within a filter-pipeline can be dynamically shuffled and reorganized. The system allows a filter-pipeline to be registered for every role that the node (functioning as a SOAP intermediary) intends to perform.

Upon receipt of a SOAP message that is targeted to multiple roles (as indicated by the SOAP 1.2 role attribute) the corresponding filter-pipelines are cascaded so that the appropriate functions are performed. The SOAP message is first parsed to determine the roles that need to be performed. Next, we check to see if there are any pipelines registered for a specific role. The scheme allows developers to develop their own Filters and Filter-Pipelines and target them for specialized roles. For example, a developer may wish to develop a filter that performs message transformations between the competing notification specifications: WS-Eventing and WS-Notification. By providing an extensible framework for the creation of Filters and the registration of roles sophisticated applications can be built.

3 HPSearch: Managing Broker Networks and Service Grids

As discussed in the previous section, NaradaBrokering provides a software messaging infrastructure. In a related project, we have been developing HPSearch [14] as a scripting-based management console for broker networks and their services. At one end of the spectrum are services which help manage the messaging middleware, while at the other end are services that leverage capabilities of the middleware (WSProxy). The management of both sets of services is handled by a scripting medium that binds Uniform Resource Identifiers (URI) to the scripting language. By binding URI as a first-class object we can use the scripting language to manage the resource identified by the URI. We discuss these functions in detail below.

In order to deploy a distributed application that uses NaradaBrokering, the middleware must be setup and a broker network topology must be deployed. Broker network topology may also be changed at runtime using HPSearch by adding or deleting links between brokers. Once the middleware is setup, we leverage the broker network to deploy the distributed application.

To fulfill this requirement we have been developing a specialized Web Service called the Broker Service Adapter (BSA) that helps us deploy brokers on distributed nodes and setup links between them. The BSA is a Web Service that enables management of the middleware via WS-Management. Further, the BSA network is a scalable network that periodically restructures itself to achieve a tree based structure. A management engine simply sends the appropriate commands to the root BSA node which is then appropriately routed to the correct BSA. Errors and other conditions are similarly handled and notified to the management engine using WS-Eventing.

HPSearch uses NaradaBrokering to route data between components of a distributed application. This data transfer is managed transparently by the HPSearch runtime component, the Web Service Proxy (WSProxy) [14]. Thus, each of the distributed components is exposed as a Web Service which can be initialized and steered by simple SOAP requests. WSProxy can either wrap existing applications or create new data processing and data filtering services. WSProxy handles streaming data transfer using NaradaBrokering on behalf of the services thus enabling streaming data transfer for any service. The streaming data is enabled using NaradaBrokering middleware, a distributed routing substrate. Thus there are no central bottlenecks and failure of a broker node routes the data stream through alternate routes if available. Further, NaradaBrokering supports reliable delivery via persistent storage [13] thus enabling guaranteed delivery for data streams.

4 Global-MMCS: Audio and Video Stream Services and Management

Global-MMCS, as a service-oriented multimedia collaboration system, mainly processes multimedia streams: video, audio, whiteboards and so on. "Events" in video or audio are usually called video frames or audio samples. Generally speaking, there are a lot of similarities between multimedia streams and other data streams such as sensor data. All streaming data require significant Quality of Service (QoS) constraints and dynamic filtering. These are both particularly demanding and well-understood for multimedia streams for both communication and processing. Because of high bandwidth generated by raw multimedia bit-streams, complicated codecs must be used to compress the streams and transmit them over the Internet. Further, multimedia streams are typically used collaboratively and so stress the infrastructure needed to support the efficient software or hardware of multicasting required by the delivery of a given stream to multiple clients. Due to the diversity of collaboration clients supported by Global-MMCS, the services for multimedia streams need to adapt the streams to different clients. We note that many relevant web service specifications like those for reliable messaging and notification appear not well designed for scalable efficient multicast as needed by Global-MMCS. Thus we suggest that multimedia collaboration is an excellent proving ground for general streaming data grid infrastructure.

Streaming Filters: A media service or filter is a functional entity, which can receive one or multiple media streams, perform some processing, and output one or multiple media streams. Each service is characterized by a set of input and output stream interfaces and a processing unit. According to the number of fan-in and fan-out filters, they can be divided into three categories: one-in-one-out filters, multiple-in-one out filters, and one-in-multiple-out. In addition, there is a final "sink" filter category. We discuss each of these below.

One-In-One-Out filters implement the basic transformation operation. For instance, a filter can receive as input a video stream in YUV4:1:1 format, resize it and deliver the modified video as output. Each filter provides a very basic adaptation on a stream in an intermediate format. Complex stream transformations can be built by combining several basic filters and creating a filtering workflow pipeline. Below are examples of one-in-one-out filters:

Decoder/Encoder transcoder filters aim at compressing/uncompressing the data into a chosen intermediate format (e.g. RGB24, YUV4:1:1, Linear Audio). Common codecs include H.261, H.263, MPEG1, MPEG2, MPEG4, H.264, and RealMedia. Transcoding generates a new stream which is encoded in the format wanted by the user. For examples, if a RealPlayer user needs to receive a video encoded in H.261 RTP, a RealStream producer is needed to first decode the H.261 video and generate a new RealFormat stream. *Image-scaling filters* resize video frames, which is useful to adapt a stream for devices with limited display capacities. They are sometimes required to enable transcoding operations. For example MPEG videos may be transmitted in any size while H.261 videos require predefined sizes such as CIF, QCIF or SQCIF. *Color-space-scaling filters* reduce the number of entries in the color space, for example from 24 to 12 bits, gray-scale or black-and-white. *Frame-rate filters* can reduce the frame rate in a video stream to meet low-end clients like PDA. For example, we can discard B-frame or P-frame in a MPEG-4 video stream with 24 fps to create a new stream with a lower frame rate.

Multiple-In-One-Out filters, also known as *mixer filters*, combine multiple streams. A video mixer can create a mixed video streams resulting from several input sources. Each element of the resulting mixed video (typically displayed as a grid of images) results from an image-scaling adaptation of a particular stream. An audio mixer can create a mixed audio stream by summing up several input sources. Audio mixing is very important to those clients that can't receive multiple RTP audio streams and mix them. Video mixing service improves the visual collaboration especially for those limited clients that can only handle a single video stream. *Multiplexors//Demultiplexors* are used to aggregate/separate audio and video data in a multimedia stream. For instance, an MPEG multiplexor allows merging an MP3 audio and an MPEG-1 video in a MPEG2 stream. Multiplex and demultiplex are quite useful for guaranteeing stream synchronization in unpredictable network environments.

One-In-Multiple-Out filters, or *duplicator filters,* are used to replicate an output media stream. Duplication is useful when a stream has different targets with different requirements. In most cases, multiple simple media filters should be organized in a media filter chain. Filters can be either as simple as bit-stream parsing, or as complicated as decoding and encoding. Composite media services are usually acyclic computation graphs consisting of multiple filter chains.

There is also another type of bit-stream service, called *sink service*, which doesn't change bits in the stream. Examples of sink services include buffering and replaying services. These can buffer real-time multimedia streams in memory caches or disk storage, and allow users to reply or fast-forward these streams through RTSP session. Sink filters can handle single or multiple streams. When multiple streams flow into a sink entity, all the streams can be synchronized and replayed. Based on such a composite sink service, an annotation service can be developed. Through annotation, users can attach text and image streams to the original video and audio stream to convey additional meaning in collaboration.

Global-MMCS Workflow Management: There is substantial literature on Grid and Service-based workflow [16]. Unlike many of these systems, Global-MMCS's streaming workflow, especially conferencing workflow, is implicit and can be determined by the system at run time based on the specified (in XGSP) sinks and sources and their QoS. For example, when a PDA with limited network and processing capability wants to receive an H.261 encoded, 24 fps, CIF video stream, a customized workflow is need to transcode the H.261 stream to a JPEG picture stream or low-bitrate RealMedia Stream. An intelligent workflow engine can easily build a filter chain automatically based on the format description of the source stream and capability description of the PDA. Such an engine usually follows a graph search algorithm and tries to find a route from the graph node representing the format of the source stream to the destination node representing the format needed by the receiver.

No user involvement is needed for defining explicit workflow. Furthermore, in order to minimize the traffic and delay, most of one-in-one-out filter chain should be constrained in a single service container. One needs a distributed implementation to

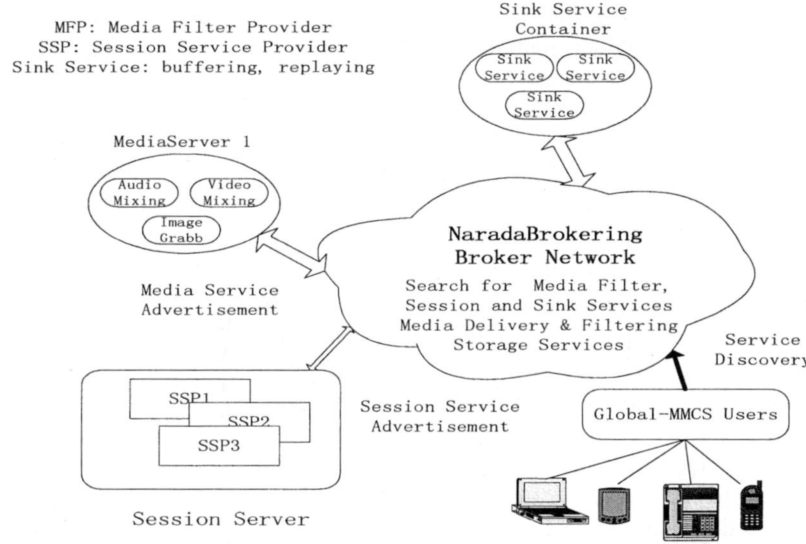

Fig. 1. Workflow and filters in GlobalMMCS

orchestrate multiple-in and multiple-out filters for different clients. Therefore the key issue in Global-MMCS media service management is how to locate the best service container based on streaming QoS requirement and make the service provider shared by participants in XGSP Sessions.

Session Management and NaradaBrokering Integration: As shown in Figure 1, NaradaBrokering can publish performance monitoring data in the form of XML on a topic which is subscribed to by the AV Session Server. From these performance data and broker network maps, the Session Server can estimate the delay and bandwidth between the service candidates and the requesting user. Based on the workload of the media service providers and estimated the performance metrics, the Session Server can find the best service providers and initiate a media service instance. Furthermore, the AV Session Server has to monitor the health of each media service instance. Through a specific NaradaBrokering topic, an active media service instance can publish status meta-data to notify the session server. If it fails to respond within a period of time, the AV Session Server restarts it or locates a new service provider and start a new instance. Note that the messaging infrastructure supports both TCP control and UDP media streams and their reliable delivery; the session can choose separate QoS for each type of stream.

Each session server may host limited numbers of active XGSP AV sessions. The exact number depends upon the workload and the computational power of the machine. The session initiator will firstly locate the right session provider to create a session service instance for a particular XGSP AV session. Then, this session server will locate the necessary media service resources on demand. In the current implementation, a default audio mixer is created to handle all the audio in the session.

Private audio mixers can be created on-demand for private sessions supporting subgroups in the session. Further, multiple video mixers can be created by the session server on the request of the client. An image grabber (thumbnail) service is created when a new video stream is detected in the session. Further, customized transcoding services can be created when a user sends a request to access particular streams. For example, a mobile client like PDA connected to Wi-Fi, which only has limited processing power wants to choose a 24 4-CIF MPEG-4 video; then a transcoding process pipeline consisting of frame rate adapter, video size down-sampler and color transformation, is needed to create this stream. Another example is an H.323 terminal, which can only handle H.261 and H.263 codecs, wants to display a MPEG-4 video, it will ask the session server to start a MPEG-4-to-H.261 transcoder.

Sink services like buffering, archiving and replaying services can also be initiated by real-time XGSP sessions. Buffering and archiving services store events into distributed cache and file storage attached to NaradaBrokering overlay networks. Once stream data flow into these "sinks", replaying service can pull the data flow out of the sinks and send to clients based on the RTSP request of the user. The events are accessed in an ordered fashion and resynchronized using their timestamps which have been unified using NaradaBrokers NTP service. The list with time-stamps of these archived and annotated streams is kept in the WS-Context dynamic meta-data service. Through the recording manager service, a component of AV session server, users can choose streams to be buffered and archived. And through replay and RTSP services, users can initiate RTSP sessions and replay those buffered streams. After the streams are buffered, users can add annotations to the streams and archive the new composite steams for later replay.

5 Supporting Real Time Sensor Grid Services

The basic services needed to support audio-video collaboration, such as reliable delivery, multicasting and replay, can also be applied to problems in real-time delivery of sensor grid data. In Fig. 2, we depict our work to develop filters on live Global Positioning System data. OCRTN, RICRTN, and SDCRTN represent GPS networks for Orange, Riverside, and San Diego Counties in Southern California. These stations are maintained by the Scripps Orbit and Permanent Array Center (SOPAC) and are published to an RTD server, where they are made publicly available. Data is published from these stations in the binary RYO format. By connecting a sequence of filters, we convert and republish the data as ASCII and as Geography Markup Language (GML) formatted data. The data can be further subdivided into individual station position measurements.

We are currently developing more sophisticated real-time data filters for data mining. Tools such as RDAHMM [17] may be used to detect state changes in archived GPS time signals. These may be associated with both seismic and aseismic causes. We are currently working to develop an RDAHMM filter that can be applied to real-time signals and link them in streaming fashion to the Open Geospatial Consortium standard services supporting integration of maps, features and sensors.

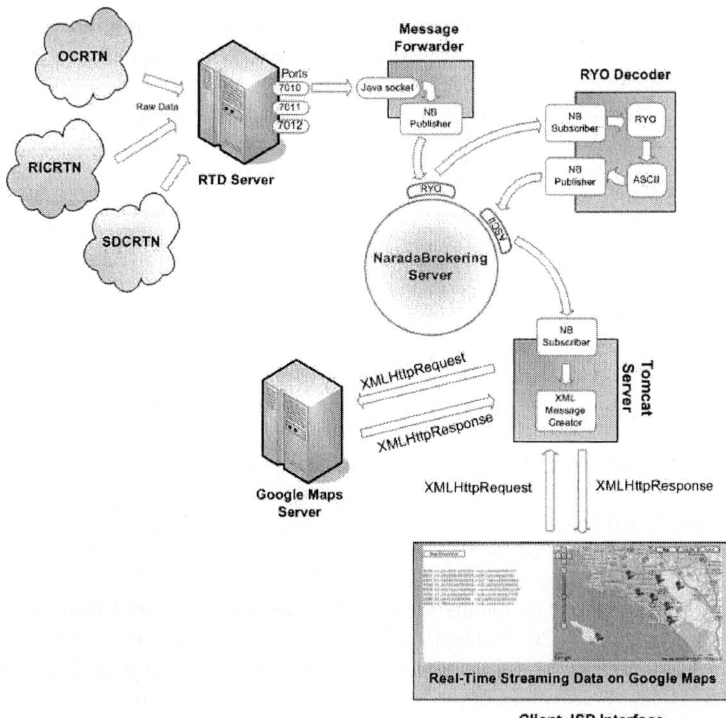

Fig. 2. Naradabrokering may be used to support filters of real-time GPS data

6 Future Work

Conventional support of SOAP messages using the verbose "angle-bracket" representation is too slow for many applications. Thus we and others are researching [6, 18] a systematic use of "fast XML and SOAP" where services negotiate the use of efficient representations for SOAP messages. All messages rigorously support the service WSDL and transport the SOAP Infoset using the angle bracket form in the initial negotiation but an efficient representation where possible for streamed data Another interesting area is structuring the system so that it can be implemented either with standalone services, message brokers and clients or in a Peer-to-Peer mode. These two implementations have tradeoffs between performance and flexibility and both are important. The core architecture "naturally" works in both modes but the details are not trivial and require substantial further research.

References

1. Qiu, X.: Message-based MVC Architecture for Distributed and Desktop Applications Syracuse University PhD March 2 2005
2. Wu, W., Bulut, H., Uyar, A., and Fox, G.: Adapting H.323 Terminals in a Service-Oriented Collaboration System. In special "Internet Media" issue of IEEE Internet Computing July-August 2005, Vol 9, No. 4 pages 43-50 (2005)

3. Fox, G., Ho, A., Pallickara, S., Pierce, M., and Wu, W.: Grids for the GiG and Real Time Simulations Proceedings of Ninth IEEE International Symposium DS-RT 2005 on Distributed Simulation and Real Time Applications (2005)
4. Birman, K., Hillman, R., and Pleisch, S.: Building Network-Centric Military Applications Over Service Oriented Architectures. In proceedings of SPIE Conference Defense Transformation and Network-Centric Systems (2005) http://www.cs.cornell.edu/projects/quicksilver/public_pdfs/GIGonWS_final.pdf
5. Fox, G., Pallickara, S., Pierce, M., and Gadgil, H.: Building Messaging Substrates for Web and Grid Applications. To be published in special Issue on Scientific Applications of Grid Computing in Philosophical Transactions of the Royal Society of London (2005).
6. Oh, S., Bulut, H., Uyar, A., Wenjun Wu, Geoffrey Fox Optimized Communication using the SOAP Infoset For Mobile Multimedia Collaboration Applications. In proceedings of the International Symposium on Collaborative Technologies and Systems CTS05 (2005)
7. For discussion, see http://grids.ucs.indiana.edu/ptliupages/presentations/DoDGrids Aug25-05.ppt
8. Aktas, M. S., Fox, G., and Pierce, M.: An Architecture for Supporting Information in Dynamically Assembled Semantic Grids Technical report (2005)
9. Pallickara, S. and Fox, G.: NaradaBrokering: A Middleware Framework and Architecture for Enabling Durable Peer-to-Peer Grids. Proceedings of ACM/IFIP/USENIX International Middleware Conference Middleware (2003).
10. Pallickara, S. and Fox, G.: On the Matching Of Events in Distributed Brokering Systems. Proceedings of IEEE ITCC Conference on Information Technology, Volume II (2004) 68-76
11. Uyar, A. and Fox, G.: Investigating the Performance of Audio/Video Service Architecture I: Single Broker Proceedings of the International Symposium on Collaborative Technologies and Systems CTS05 (2005)
12. Bulut, H., Pallickara, S., and Fox, G.: Implementing a NTP-Based Time Service within a Distributed Brokering System. ACM International Conference on the Principles and Practice of Programming in Java. (2004) 126-134.
13. Pallickara, S. and Fox, G.: A Scheme for Reliable Delivery of Events in Distributed Middleware Systems. In Proceedings of the IEEE International Conference on Autonomic Computing (2004).
14. Gadgil, H., Fox, G., Pallickara, S., Pierce, M., and Granat, R.: A Scripting based Architecture for Management of Streams and Services in Real-time Grid Applications, In Proceedings of the IEEE/ACM Cluster Computing and Grid 2005 Conference, CCGrid (2005)
15. Wu, W., Fox, G., Bulut, H., Uyar, A., and Altay, H.: Design and Implementation of a Collaboration Web-services system. Journal of Neural, Parallel & Scientific Computations, Volume 12 (2004)
16. Grid workflow is summarized in GGF10 Berlin meeting http://www.extreme.indiana.edu/groc/ggf10-ww/ with longer papers to appear in a special issue of Concurrency&Computation: Practice & Experience at http://www.cc-pe.net/iuhome/workflow2004index.html. See also Gannon, D. and Fox, G.: Workflow in Grid Systems.
17. Granat, R.: Regularized Deterministic Annealing EM for Hidden Markov Models, Doctoral Dissertation, University of California Los Angeles (2004)
18. Chiu, K., Govindaraju, M., and Bramley, R.: Investigating the Limits of SOAP Performance for Scientific Computing, Proc. of 11th IEEE International Symp on High Performance Distributed Computing HPDC-11 (2002) 256.

A QoS-Satisfied Interdomain Overlay Multicast Algorithm for Live Media Service Grid

Yuhui Zhao[1,2], Yuyan An[2], Cuirong Wang[3], and Yuan Gao[1]

[1] School of Information Science and Engineering,
Northeastern University,
Shenyang 110004, China
yuhuizhao@mail.neuq.edu.cn

[2] QinHuangDao Foreign Language Professional College,
066311, QinHuangDao, China

[3] Northeastern University at QinHuangDao,
066000, QinHuangDao, China

Abstract. We are developing a live media service Grid(LMSG) as an extensible middleware architecture for supporting live media applications in a grid computing environment. The LMSG service was provided by the service brokers nodes(SvBs) which are strategically deployed by Internet Service Providers (ISPs). This paper mainly presents a QoS-satisfied interdomain overlay multicast algorithm (QIOM), which is the key to organize the SvBs to build a QoS-aware multicast service tree and the most important part of LMSG middleware. It is an overlay based the multicast connection solution for live media relay in different ASes and can overcome the difficulties of Border Gateway Multicast Protocol. The simulation results show that the QIOM algorithms can effectively find and provide QoS-assured overlay services and balance the overlay traffic burden among the SvBs.

1 Introduction

Distributed collaboration based live media is an important class of Internet applications. Many educational and research institutions have begun to web cast lectures and seminars over the Internet, and distributed collaboration systems such as the Access Grid (AG) are increasingly popular. Although there are many web cast and distributed collaboration productions [1,2], several problems remain unsolved. First, they are lack of a QoS-awareness and scalability live media feasible delivery protocol which is fitted to the synchronous group communication. Second, there is not an efficient multicast model for ISP to benefit from the service providing. Third, applications that manage a production environment are difficult to build because the detailed knowledge of the environment is required. Forth, applications are often tightly coupled with the environment and cannot adapt well to changes. Furthermore, an application written for one environment cannot be easily reused in another environment.

H. Zhuge and G.C. Fox (Eds.): GCC 2005, LNCS 3795, pp. 13–24, 2005.

We are developing the live media service Grid (LMSG) to address the above challenges. LMSG aims to bring together large communities of users across networks to enable them to work together closely and successfully. The LMSG service was provided by the service broker nodes which are strategically deployed by ISPs and run the LMSG middleware. LMSG middleware is the key technology for supporting live media applications in a grid computing environment. It is to provide support for inter-active applications from atomic service components based on user's dynamic service requirements. LMSG provides a layer of abstraction between the audio/video environments and the applications, which provides abstractions and an API for managing entities in the environment without revealing the underlying details.

In this paper, we mainly discuss a QoS-satisfied Interdomain Overlay Multicast Optimizing Algorithm (QIOM), which is the key to organize the SvBs to build a QoS-aware multicast service tree and the most important part of LMSG middleware. It is an overlay based multicast connection solution for live media relay in different Ases and can overcome the difficulties of Border Gateway Multicast Protocol in IP level.

QIOM provides a novel probing scheme to achieve QoS-aware multicast service in a scalable and efficient fashion. The QIOM's features mainly include as follows. First, it provides multi-constrained statistical QoS assurances [3] for the distributed live media delivery services. Second, it achieves good load balancing in the SvBs to improve overall resource utilization and reduce the traffic cost among the ASes for ISP. Third, the interdomain multicast turns to feasible and this is the basic of synchronous interdomain group communication.

The rest of the paper is organized as follows. The related works are discussed in Section 2. In Section 3, we introduce Live Media Service Grid. Then, the basic idea of QoS-satisfied interdomain overlay multicast algorithm(QIOM) is described in Section 4. And a series of simulations and results are discussed in Section 5. Finally, we draw the conclusions in Section 6.

2 Relative Works

Recently, various overlay networks have been proposed, such as peer-to-peer data lookup overlay network[4, 5, 6, 7], locality-aware overlay networks [8], application-level multicast networks [9, 10], resilient overlay networks [11], and Internet Indirection Infrastructure [12]. The major difference between LMSG and the above work is that LMSG focuses on integrated collaboration live media service delivery rather than merely data transport or lookup. In doing so, LMSG tackles the challenge of scalable decentralized resource and QoS management while instantiating the composed service. The Opus project [13] proposed an overlay utility service that performs wide-area resource mapping based on the application's performance and availability requirements. Different from Opus that uses hierarchy, aggregation, and approximation for tracking global states, LMSG proposes on-demand states collection that is more suitable for at overlay structure and QoS-aware integrated service delivery. LMSG complements previous work by integrating interdomain resource management into dynamic cooperated services.

In IP layer, many protocols like BGMP[14], MASC[15] are still being investigated and tested for interdomain multicast. Their main objections include the protocol's complexity that makes implementation difficult and costly, and the limited multicast address space, and some additional shortcoming such as less QoS, security and billing. In contrast to IP multicast, QIOM is a QoS-awareness and scalability live media feasible delivery protocol which is fitted to the synchronous group communication. At the same time, it provides an efficient multicast model for ISP by deploying the service brokers to benefit from the service providing. By probing scheme, it can achieve QoS-aware multicast service in a scalable and efficient fashion.

3 The Live Media Service Grid (LMSG)

ISP needs a quality of service (QoS) ensured multicast service to save the resources and improve better service when more and more large-scale multimedia applications are emerging in the Internet. In order to provide the Live Media Service Grid(LMSG), it is necessary for ISPs to build a overlay service network by deploying the service brokers nodes. One or more SvBs are deployed in an Autonamous System(AS), the number depends on the needs of live media communication. This is different from IP multicast protocol. The SvBs run the LMSG middleware components which have efficient function for QoS management, live media organization and network accounting.

There are three tiers in the LMSG middleware framework. The top tier is called the Abstract Service Interface Layer, and composed of a manager and a set of agents, which is the interface of the application software. The second tier is called the Trans-action Service Layer, and composed of some function entities, which includes compo-nents of Authentication, Registration, Resource Discovery, Scheduling, Logging, audio and video etc. The substrate tier is the Overlay Multicast Layer, which is above the TCP/IP protocol; SvBs use the components to build a overlay network, to finish the QoS-aware live media deliveries. Figure 1 shows the tiers of LMSG.

Abstract Service Interface Layer is in charge of user's service requirements. The user can specify a service request using a function agent (*FA*) and a QoS requirement vector (Q_R). The FA specifies required service functions (F_i) and inter-service dependency and commutative relations. We use Q^{target}=[$<C^{q_1}, P^{q_1}>$, ..., $<C^{q_m}, P^{q_m}>$] to define the user's QoS requirements for the integrated service, where $<C^{q_i}, P^{q_i}>$ specifies the bound C^{q_i} and the satisfaction probability P^{q_i} for the metric q_i that represents a QoS metric such as delay and loss rate. Users can either directly specify the integrated service request using extensible markup language (XML) or use visual specification tools [11].

Transaction Service Layer consists of distributed live media services that are dynamically composed from existing service components. A live media service component (s_i) is a self-contained multimedia application unit providing certain functionality. Each service component has several input and output ports for receiving input messages and sending output messages, respectively. Each input port is associated with a message queue for asynchronous communication between service components. input quality requirements of the service component such as media format, frame rate, which is denoted by $Q^{in}=[{q_1}^{in}, ..., {q_d}^{in}]$; Output quality properties of the service component, denoted $Q^{out}=[{q_1}^{out}, ..., {q_d}^{out}]$. We describe an aggregate distributed live media service using a Directed Acyclic Graph called ServStreaming (λ). The nodes in the ServStreaming represent the service components and the links in the ServStreaming represent application-level connections called service link. Each service link is mapped to an overlay path by the Overlay Multicast Layer.

Overlay Multicast Layer consists of the service brokers — distributed overlay nodes (V_i) connected by application-level connections called overlay links (l_j). The overlay network topology can be formed by connecting each SvB node with a number of other nodes called neighbors via overlay links. For supporting large-scale live media communication to enhance scalability, the SvBs have a hierarchical architecture. The contiguous SvBs are grouped to form clusters, which in turn are grouped together to form super-clusters. And an end host could form a cluster with other end hosts close by. In the cluster, overlay multicast is used for efficient data delivery between the limited numbers of end users. The user clusters connect to the LMSG by the edge SvBs. Either the SvB or the user end, the LMSG middleware is the essential software. Each SvB can provide one or more multimedia service components.

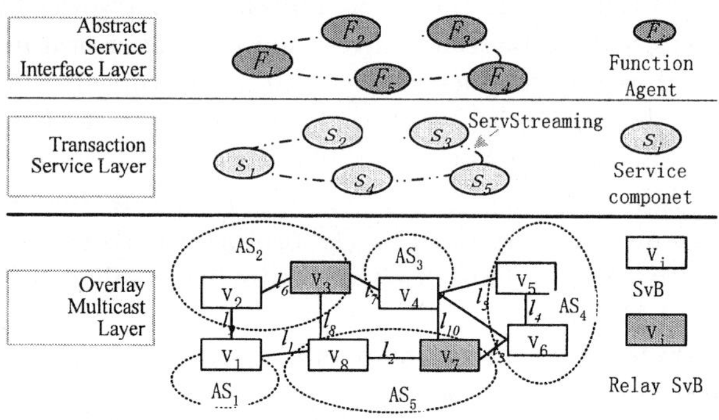

Fig. 1. The tiers of Live Media Service Grid

Each node V_i is associated with a statistical resource availability vector $<{r_1}^{v_i}, ..., {r_n}^{v_i}>$, where ${r_k}^{v_i}$ is a random variable describing the statistical availability for the $k'th$ end-system resource type (e.g. CPU, memory, disk storage). Each node v_i also maintains statistical bandwidth availability $b\omega^{l_j}$ for its adjacent overlay links l_j. For scalability, each node maintains the above histograms locally, which are not disseminated to other overlay nodes.

4 QoS-Satisfied Interdomain Overlay Multicast Algorithm

4.1 Problem Description

The function agent (*FA*) and QoS requirement vector (Q_R) in Abstract Service Interface Layer map to an overlay weighted directed acyclic graph G' in QIOM. For formalizing the QoS constraint for the overlay network between the ASes, we define the functions to do performance measurements among the SvBs, the function of the link delay as *Delay*: $E' \longrightarrow R^+$, *Delay*(l) denotes the delay of the packets passing the overlay link l, $l \in E'$. And the function of the performance of a node as *Perfo*: CPU⟶100%, *Perfo*(*SvB*) denotes the OccupyTime of the CPU of the SvB, SvB $\in V'$. To control the number of spawned probes, the probe carries a *probing budget* (β) that defines how many probes we could use for a composition request. The probing budget represents the trade-off between the probing overhead and composition optimality. Larger probing budget allows us to examine more candidate ServStreamings, which allows us to find a better qualified ServStreaming.

Let $M \in V'$ be a set of nodes involved in a group communication. M is called multicast group with each node V'_M, $V'_M \in M$, is a group member. Packets originating from a source node V'_s have to be delivered to a set of receiver nodes M - $\{V'_s\}$. A multicast tree $T(V'_M, E'_M)$ is a subgraph of G' that centers as c_i, $\forall\ c_i \in G'$, and spans all the nodes in M. The path from a source node V'_s to a receiver node V'_d in the tree T, is denoted by $PT(V'_s, V'_d)$, where V'_s, $V'_d \in M$.

The multicast tree should meet the following conditions:

$$\beta(SvB_i) \leq \gamma, \ \ and \ \ Perfo(SvB_i) \leq \tau, \ \forall\ SvB_i \in M \ \&\ SvB_i \in D_x \tag{1}$$

$$\min_{SvB_i \in M}(Perfo(SvB_1), Perfo(SvB_2), \ldots, Perfo(SvB_j)) \tag{2}$$

$$\min_{l_j \in P_t}(\sum_{j=1} Perfo(SvB_{l_j,i}), \ldots, \sum_{j=m} Perfo(SvB_{l_j,i})), \ \forall i,j,m \in N \tag{3}$$

$$\sum_{l \in P_T(V'_s, V'_d)} delay(l) \leq \Delta, \ \forall V'_s, V'_d \in M \tag{4}$$

$$|\sum_{l \in P_T(u,v)} delay(l) - \sum_{l \in P_T(x,y)} delay(l)| \leq \delta, \ \forall u,v,x,y \in M \tag{5}$$

where γ is the maximum of *probing budget*, τ is the maximum occupy time of the SvB's CPU, Δ is the maximum of delay, δ is the maximum of the delay variation between the any different l.

To quantify the load balancing property of an instantiated ServStreaming, we more define a resource cost aggregation metric, denoted by ψ^λ , which is the weighted sum of ratios between resource requirements of the SvB links and resource availabilities on the overlay paths. We use $C_{r_i}^{s_i}$ and $P_{r_i}^{s_i}$ to represent the resource requirement threshold and satisfaction probability of the service component s_i for the $i'th$ end-system resource type (e.g., CPU, memory, disk storage), respectively. Similarly, we use $C_{bw}^{l_i}$ and $P_{bw}^{l_i}$ to denote the required threshold and satisfaction probability for the network bandwidth on the service link l_i, respectively. The resource requirements of a service component depend on its implementations and the current workload. In contrast to the conventional data routing path, the resource requirements along a ServStreaming are no longer uniform due to the non-uniform service functionalities on the ServStreaming. Different service components can have different resource requirements due to hetero-geneous functions and implementations. The bandwidth requirements also vary among different service links since the value added service instances can change the original media content (e.g., image scaling, color filter, information embedding). We use $M_{ri}^{v_j}$ to denote *mean* availability of $i'th$ end-system resource type on the overlay node v_j . We use $M_{bw}^{\phi_i}$ to denote the mean availability of the bandwidth on the overlay path ϕ_i, which is defined as the minimum mean available bandwidth among all overlay links $e_i \in \phi$. The mean values can be calculated from the p.d.f.'s of the corresponding statistical metrics. Hence, the resource cost aggregation metric is ψ^λ defined as follows,

$$\psi^\lambda = \sum_{s_i,v_j \in \lambda} \sum_{k=1}^{n} W_k \frac{C_{r_i}^{s_i}}{M_{r_i}^{v_j}} + w_{n+1} \sum_{l_i,\phi_i \in \lambda} \frac{C_{bw}^{l_i}}{M_{bw}^{\phi_i}}, \quad here \sum_{k=1}^{n+1} w_k = 1, \ 0 \le w_k \le 1 \quad (6)$$

For w_k, $1 \le k \le n+1$ represents the importance of different resource types. We can customize ψ_λ by assigning higher weights to more critical resource types. The ServStreaming with smaller resource cost aggregation value has better load balancing property because the resource availabilities exceed the resource requirements by a larger margin.

4.2 Algorithm Suggestion

LMSG executes a QoS-satisfied Interdomain Overlay Multicast Algorithm (QIOM) to perform live media service. Given an aggregated service request, the source node invokes the QIOM algorithm, which includes major steps as following.

Step 1. The Initialization of Service Broker Probing
The source SvB first generates a QoS-requested probing message, called probe. The probe carries the information of Function Agent and the user's resource requirements. The probe can spawn new probes in order to concurrently examine multiple next-hop choices. If some terminal in AS_x belongs to a multicast group, then QIOM can select one or more adjacent SvBs as the multicast relay node, and the selecting SvB need to satisfy Expressions 1, which means only to select the free SvB as a relay node.

Step 2. Search for Candidate ServStreamings
The step's goal is to collect needed information and perform intelligent parallel searching of multiple candidate ServStreamings. We adopt the Probing ServStreamings to finish this.

Step 2.1: SvB QoS check and allocation. When a SvB receives a probe, it first check whether the QoS and resource values of the probed ServStreaming already violate the user's requirements using the Expressions 1 and 4. If the accumulated QoS and resource values already violate the user's requirements, the probe is dropped immediately. Otherwise, the SvB will temporarily allocate required resources to the expected application session. It will be cancelled after certain timeout period if the SvB does not receive a confirmation message. Thus, we can guarantee that probed available resources are still available at the end of the probing process.

Step 2.2: Derive next-hop node. After that, the SvB derives the next-hop service functions according to the dependency and commutative relations in the Function Agent. All the functions dependent on the current function are considered as next-hop functions. For each next-hop function F_k derived above, if there is an exchange link between F_k and F_l, F_l is also a possible next-hop function. The probing budget is proportionally distributed among next-hop functions.

Step 2.3: Check QoS consistency. Based on the service discovery results, the service node then performs QoS consistency check between the current SvB and next-hop candidate SvB. The QoS consistency check includes two aspects: (1) the consistencies between output QoS parameters Q_{out} of the current service component and input QoS parameters Qin of the next-hop service component; and (2) the compatibility between the adaptation policies of two connected SvBs. Unlike the IP layer network where all routers provide a uniform data forwarding service, the SvBs in the service overlay can provide different live media services, which makes it necessary to perform QoS consistency check between two connected service components. The process can use expression 6.

Step 3. Optimal selection and Setup multicast Tree service session The destination collects the probes for a request with certain timeout period. It then selects the best qualified ServStreaming based on the resource and QoS states collected by the probes. The destination sends an acknowledge message along the reversed selected ServStreaming to confirm resource allocations and initialize service components at each intermediate SvB. Then the application sender starts to send ap-plication data stream along the selected ServStreaming. If no qualified ServStreaming is found, the destination returns a failure message to the source directly.

The step of building the tree can be described more as follows.

Step3.1: the selected SvBs composed of the multicast group.

Step3.2: center as any node SvB_i in the multicast group, create a multicast tree T using Dijkstra Algorithm, compute the delay, if it satisfies the expression 4, then compute the delay variation, if it satisfies the expression 5, at last, the node is sent to the set of the center nodes.

Step3.3: in turn compute the cost order of the relating multicast tree l_j using expression 3.

Step3.4: In the set of the center nodes, in turn compute the order of the candidate center node using expression 2.

Step3.5: select the freest SvB as the center, and the relating tree as the current multicast tree, the others as candidates.

5 Performance Evaluations

5.1 Simulation Setup

We have implemented a session-level event-driven simulator to evaluate the performance of QIOM. The simulations are based on the Georgia Technology Internetwork Topology Model (GT-ITM) [16], which is used to generate the network topology. These topologies have 50 transit domain routers and 500-2000 stub domain routers. Each end host is attached to a stub router uniformly at random. To test the scalability of different schemes, we focus on large group sizes and vary the number of members in each group from 200 to 1000. When simulating the algorithms, the SvBs form a hierarchical topology. Each of the clusters in the hierarchy has an average of ten members — including subclusters or SvBs.

The dynamics of the overlay Multicasting is modeled as follows. The overlay multicasting request arrives at a random accSvB node according to a Poisson distribution with rate η. The destination domain is randomly chosen. The holding time of the overlay session is exponentially distributed with a mean of 2 min. Similar to [17], the offered load of the overlay routing request is defined as $\rho = (\eta * h/u * (\sum L_i))$, where h is the mean of overlay path hops (number of SvBs in the path), and u is the sum of the overlay link capacities in the corresponding overlay topology. During the process of simulation, we vary the value of to test QIOM's performance under different offered loads. The physical links' bandwidths during the simulation are randomly selected between 40 and 280 units with delay 2 ms, while the SvBs' capacities are uniformly set as 900 units. The non-overlay traffic occupies around 50 of each physical link's capacity. The non-overlay traffic varies its volume ±20% every 500 ms. The SvBs exchange their state information every 1000 ms. We assume that the error of available bandwidth measurement result is within ±10%. For each overlay routing request, we use QIOM to set up an overlay path connecting the source SvB and the destination SvB.

5.2 Simulation Results and Discussions

QoS-Satisfaction Ratio (QSR): Because of the unbalanced distribution of Internet traffic, in many situations, the shortest path-based routing protocol cannot provide a QoS-satisfied path connecting the source and destination domains. To quantify this factor, QSR is defined as

$$QSR = \frac{Number\ of\ QoS\ satisfied\ overlay\ paths}{Number\ of\ overlay\ request\ paths} \tag{7}$$

The results obtained for QIOM are compared with that of the shortest-path routing (SPR) algorithm, which refers to the shortest path in the overlay network, not in the IP layer. Fig. 2 shows the QSR of QIOM compared with SPR. From the figure, we can observe that QIOM can greatly improve the QSR. In addition to finding QoS-satisfying overlay paths, QIOM also helps in finding paths that are not affected significantly by the non-overlay traffic.

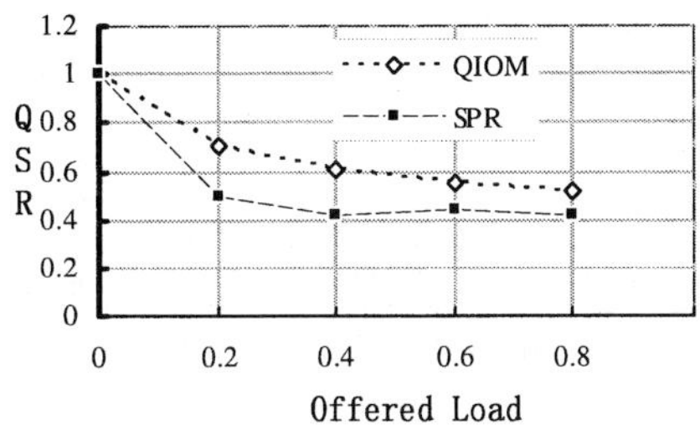

Fig. 2. QoS-Satisfaction Ratio and Offered Load comparison

Multicast tree cost: Multicast tree cost measures by the number of links in a multi-cast distribution tree. It quantifies the efficiency of multicast routing schemes. Application level multicast trees and unicast paths may traverse an underlying link more than once, and thus they usually have a higher cost than IP multicast trees. In Fig. 3, we plot the average tree cost of QIOM, NICE[18], and IP BGMP as group size increases from 100 to 900. As a reference, we also include the total link cost for unicast. Compared with the cost of unicast paths, NICE trees reduce the cost by 35%, QIOM trees reduce the cost by approximately 45-55%, and IP multicast BGMP trees save the cost by 68-80%. Clearly, the performance of QIOM is comparable to IP multicast. In addition, QIOM outperforms NICE in all cases, and their difference magnifies as group size is increased.

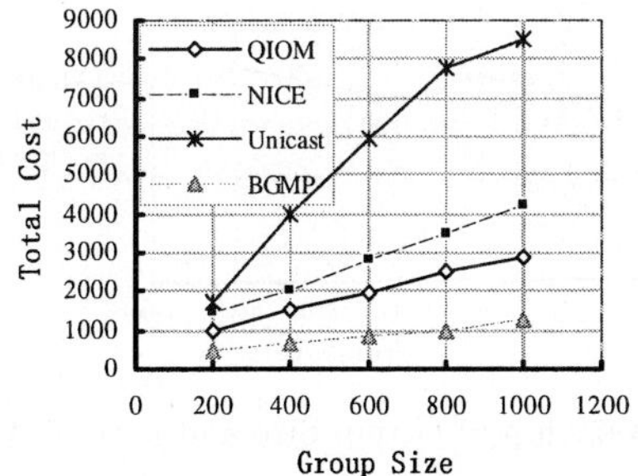

Fig. 3. The relationship of the Group size and tree cost

Average link stress: Link Stress is defined as the number of identical data packets delivered over each link. Fig. 4 shows the average link stress as the group size varies. IP multicast trees has the least link stress since only a single copy of a data packet is sent over each link. IP multicast maintains a unit stress since no duplicate packets are transmitted on the same link. QIOM trees exhibit average link stress between 1.2 and 1.6, whereas the average link stress of NICE trees is always higher than 2.00. For both QIOM and NICE, the link stress does not vary greatly with group size. However, unicast is not as scalable as QIOM and NICE, since its link stress keeps increasing when group size grows.

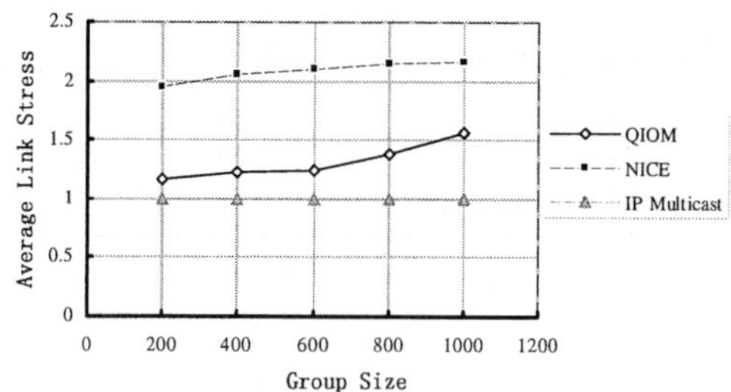

Fig. 4. The Group Size and average link stress

Average path length: Path Length is the number of links on the path from the source to a member. Unicast and shortest-path multicast schemes are usually optimized on this metric and thus have smallest path lengths. In simulation experiments, end hosts join the multicast group during an interval of 200 seconds. The results for average path length are shown in Fig.5. As expected, IP multicast has the shortest end-to-end paths. Additionally, the path lengths of QIOM trees are shorter than those of NICE trees on average. For instance, at group size of 1000, the average path lengths of QIOM and NICE trees are approximately 20 and 24, respectively.

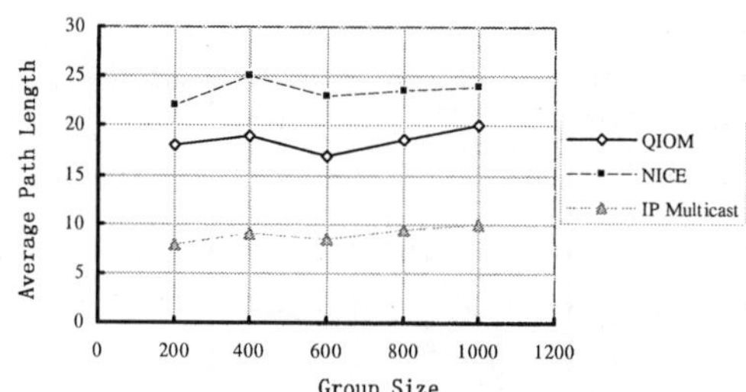

Fig. 5. The relationship of Group Size and average Length Length

6 Conclusions and Future Works

As an extensible middleware architecture, LMSG locates to provide the emerging large-scale live media applications and tries to build an overlay multicast service net-work for ISP. The LMSG service was provided by the service brokers nodes which are strategically deployed by ISPs. QIOM is the key to organize the SvBs to build a QoS-aware multicast service tree and the most important part of LMSG middleware. It is an overlay based the multicast connection solution for live media relay in different ASes and can overcome the difficulties of Border Gateway Multicast Protocol. The simulation results show that the QIOM algorithms can effectively find and provide QoS-assured overlay services and balance the overlay traffic burden among the SvBs, as well as the overlay links for live media service.

Our work is just beginning, only limited simulation has done, the suggestion needs to be tested in the distributed collaboration environment. It is necessary to do more optimize for more QoS problem during the process of looking for the multicast trees in the future.

Acknowledgements

This work is supported by the National Natural Science Foundation of China under grant No.60273078 and the Doctor Fund of Hebei under grant No.05547010D-3.

References

1. Machnicki, E., and Rowe, L.A. : Virtual director: Automating a webcast. In Proceedings of the SPIE Multimedia Computing and Networking 2002, Vol. 4673, San Jose, CA, January 2002
2. Perry, M., and Agarwal, D. : Remote control for videoconferencing. In Proceedings of the 11th International Conference of the Information Resources Management Association, Anchorage, AK, May 2000
3. Knightly, E., and Shroff, N.B. : Admission Control for Statistical QoS: Theory and Practice. IEEE Network, March 1999, 13(2):20-29
4. Rowstron, A., and Druschel, P. : Pastry: Scalable, distributed object location and routing for large-scale peer-to-peer systems. Proc. of IFIP/ACM International Conference onDistributed Systems Platforms (Middleware), November 2001
5. Stoica, I., Morris, R., Karger, D., Kaashoek, M.F., Balakrishnan, H. : Chord: A Scalable Peer-to-peer Lookup Service for Internet Applications. Proc. of ACM SIGCOMM 2001, San Diego, California, August 2001
6. Ratnasamy, S., Francis, P., Handley, M., Karp, R., Shenker, S. : A scalable content address-able network. Proc. of the ACM SIGCOMM 2001, San Diego, CA, August 2001
7. Kubiatowicz, D., Zhao, B.Y., and Joseph, A.D. : Tapestry: An infrstructure for fault tolerant wide-area location and routing. Technical Report UCB/CSD-0101141. U.C. Berkeley, April 2001
8. Harvey, N.J., Jones, M. B., Sarioiu, S., Theimer, M., and Wolman, A. : SkipNet: A Scalable Overlay Network with Practicaly Locality Properties. Proc. of the Fourth USENIX Sympo-sium on Internet Technologies and Systems (USITS '03), Seattle, WA, March 2003
9. Chu, Y., Rao, S.G., and Zhang, H. : A Case For End System Multicast. In Proc. of ACM SIGMETRICS, Santa Clara,CA, June 2000

10. Castro, M., Druschel, P., Kermarrec, A.M., and Rowstron, A. : SCRIBE: A large-scale and decentralised application-level multicast infrastructure. IEEE Journal on Selected Areas in Communication (JSAC), Vol. 20, No, 8, October 2000
11. Andersen, D., Balakrishnan,H.,Kaashoek, F., Morris. R. : Resilient Overlay Networks. In Proc. 18th ACM SOSP 2001, Banff, Canada, October 2001.
12. Stoica,I., D. Adkins, S. Zhuang,Shenker, S., and Surana, S. : Internet Indirection Infrastructure. Proc. of ACM SIGCOMM 2002, August 2002.
13. Braynard,R., Kostic,D., Rodriguez, A., Chase, J., and Vahdat, A. : Opus: an Overlay Peer Utility Service. Proc. of International Conference on Open Architectures and NetworkPro-gramming(OPENARCH), June 2002.
14. Thaler, D.: RFC 3913 - Border Gateway Multicast Protocol (BGMP): Protocol Specification, September 2004
15. Radoslavov, P., Estrin, D., Govindan, R., Handley, M., Kumar, S., Thaler, D. : RFC 2909 - The Multicast Address-Set Claim (MASC) Protocol, September 2000
16. GT-ITM: Modeling Topology of Large Internetworks [Online]. Available: http://www.cc.gatech.edu/projects/gtitm/
17. Shaikh,A., Rexford,J., and Shin, K. : Evaluating the overheads of source directed quality-of-service routing. Proc. 6th IEEE ICNP, Oct. 1998, pp. 42-51.
18. Banerjee, S., Bhattacharjee, B., and Kommareddy, C. : Scalable Application Layer Multicast. Proc. of ACM SIGCOMM '02, 2002.

Automated Immunization Against Denial-of-Service Attacks Featuring Stochastic Packet Inspection

Jongho Kim, Jaeik Cho, and Jongsub Moon

Center for Information Security Technologies (CIST),
Korea University
{sky45k, chojaeik, jsmoon}@korea.ac.kr

Abstract. Denial of Service attacks are easy to implement, difficult to trace, and inflict serious damage on target networks in a short amount of time. This model eliminates attack packets from a router using probability packet inspection as an automated defense against DoS. The detection module begins with an initial probability for inspecting packets. As an attack commences and the occupied bandwidth of the channel increases, the detection module optimizes the inspection probability.

1 Introduction

In recent years, information security has become and increasingly important aspect of network expansion. While novel security solutions have been employed to protect these infrastructures such as IDS, firewalls, VPN, ESM, and so on, many problems still remain unsolved. Prominent among these remaining threats are Denial of Service attacks.

Denial of Service attacks is easy to implement, difficult to trace, and inflict serious damage on target networks in a short amount of time. Over half of DoS attacks escalate within ten minutes [1], making it difficult for administrators to respond using manual defense mechanisms. Hence, there is a need to research automated defense systems that are capable of identifying and responding to these threats. One option is to monitor all packets, however this method is time consuming and inefficient. For one, DoS attacks to not occur frequently, and two, there is a risk that the filtering process will drop valid packets unnecessarily. Furthermore, the network equipment used to detect and filter attack packets could easily be overloaded and shut down in the case of a real attack.

In this paper we propose a more efficient automated defense model. This model removes inspects packets from a router using a stochastic packet inspection method as an automated defense against DoS. The detection module begins with an initial probability for inspecting packets; as an attack escalates and the occupied bandwidth of the channel increases, the detection module optimizes the inspection probability to balance network safety and quality of service.

2 Denial of Service Attacks

2.1 DoS Attack Trends

Traditional Denial of Service attacks, such as Ping of Death, exploited systems' inabilities to process irregular packets. Security patches were distributed that protected

H. Zhuge and G.C. Fox (Eds.): GCC 2005, LNCS 3795, pp. 25–34, 2005.

operating systems from these threats. Accordingly, Denial of Service attacks relying on single packet morphologies have become less and less common.

In February 2000, a Distributed Denial of Service (DDoS)[2] scheme attacked Yahoo, Ebay, and others using a system resource consumption method. This attack abused the fact that systems commit a great deal of resources to perform 3-way handshakes, reassemble fragmented packets, sustain half-open connections, and send *fragmented packet exception* messages.

In 2002, a new type of attack appeared: Distributed Reflective Denial of Service (DRDos)[3]. This technique strengthens weaknesses found in prior DoS attacks, offers more options and control to attackers, and neutralizes existing techniques for defending against DoS.

2.2 Existing Research on Defense Against Denial of Service Attacks

Approaches for defending against Denial of Service attacks can be divided into one of two categories: passive, such as attack detection [4,5], and active, which includes such tools as IP trace-back, traffic filtering, and packet filtering[11]. Because attack detection does not offer any defense in and of itself, this technique must be used in conjunction with attack response mechanisms. Likewise, IP trace-back methods such as PPM and ICMP trace-back [6,7] that search out and locate an attacker's position, are generally employed after an attack; they are more efficient as forensics tools rather than network defense mechanisms. Filtering is another option, however filtering every packet can cause the detection modules to overload and malfunction. Filtering based on traffic frequency analysis is an efficient isolation technique, but in the case of ingress filtering[8] this is only applied to certain packet fields. Source IP analysis, for example, is an option, however this is problematic against attacks such as DRDoS which use normal TCP servers to reflect and propagate attacks. Approaches such as ACC[9] and hop count filtering[10] are effective, but only when they can establish the path of routers traversed during the attack.

A truly effective defense against Denial of Service attacks must consist of an automated system which both systematically detects and eliminates attack packets, and is itself resistant to Denial of Service attacks.

3 Proposed Model

Our model removes attack packets from a router using stochastic packet inspection as an automated defense against DoS attacks. As long as no attack packets are detected, the detection module continues to inspect with a low initial probability. Once an attack packet is detected and the occupied bandwidth of the channel increases, the detection module increases the packet inspection probability.

3.1 Assumptions

First, we do not consider attacks that exceed the bandwidth of the external router. At present, there are no known methods for defending against attacks that exceed the bandwidth available between the internet service provider and the external router. To defend against this kind of attack, we would have to consider the service provider; however, these issues are not addressed in this paper.

Second, we assume that there is an interval between the arrival of the first attack packet and the peak of the attack. Although an attacker could select agents and issue the command to attack simultaneously, attack packets will arrive at different times. Therefore, we assume that it traffic attacking a target network will not reach its peak instantaneously.

Third, we assume that servers can process traffic below a certain acceptable bandwidth. The purpose of this paper is to present a defense against attacks that target exterior routers and consume internal network bandwidth. Efficient techniques for combating such system resource attacks exist, but are not included within the scope of this paper[12].

Fourth, we assume the existence of an efficient detection module. Methods for classifying attack packets are plentiful and well implemented [13, 14]. In this paper, we assume that such a module could classify normal and attack packets with ease.

3.2 Stochastic Packet Inspection

During a non-attack situation, this model inspects packets randomly with an initial probability (P_i). The detection module adjusts the inspection probability according to the bandwidth available.

Selection of Inspection Probability

From time t to $t+\Delta t$, if the module inspects packets with probability P_t, we can compute normal traffic (NT_t), attack traffic (AT_t), and total traffic (TT_t) at each time $t+\Delta t$.

$$NT_t(bps) = \frac{\sum_t^{t+\Delta t} \text{Length of inspected Normal Packets (bit)}}{P_t} \quad (1)$$

$$AT_t(bps) = \frac{\sum_t^{t+\Delta t} \text{Length of inspected Attack Packets (bit)}}{P_t} \quad (2)$$

$$TT_t(bps) = NT_t + AT_t \quad (3)$$

From time $t+\Delta t$, we can infer that the module will drop $P_t \bullet AT_t$ attack packet bits. Therefore, available bandwidth (ABW) on $t+\Delta t$ is calculated as shown below. Here PBW refers to the acceptable bandwidth on this channel.

$$ABW\text{(Available Bandwidth)} = PBW\text{(Acceptable Bandwidth)} - NT_t - (1-P_t) \bullet AT_t \quad (4)$$

If T is the minimum available bandwidth required for communication, then our goal is to maintain ABW at a larger value than or equal to T.

$$ABW \geq T \tag{5}$$

If we combine (4) and (5), following equation (6) and (7) are derived.

$$P_t \geq \frac{NT_t + AT_t - PBW + T}{AT_t} \tag{6}$$

$$P_t \geq 1 - \frac{PBW + T - NT_t}{AT_t} \tag{7}$$

The shape of equation (7) is shown in Figure 1. For example, if attack traffic is four times $PBW - NTt - T$, $(x = 4)$, then in order not to exceed the acceptable bandwidth, we must inspect no more than 75% of all packets. But we cannot know by how much the attack traffic will vary after $t + \Delta t$. Therefore this model calculates $P_{t+\Delta t}$ on $t + \Delta t$ based on the network environment between t and $t + \Delta t$. From equation (6), the following equations (8) and (9) are derived.

$$P_t = \frac{NT_{t-\Delta t} + AT_{t-\Delta t} - PBW + T}{AT_{t-\Delta t}} \tag{8}$$

$$P_{t+\Delta t} = \frac{NT_t + AT_t - PBW + T}{AT_{t-\Delta t}} \tag{9}$$

Equation (10) is derived using P_t from equation (8) and $P_{t+\Delta t}$ from equation (9).

$$P_{t+\Delta t} = \frac{TT_t + TT_{t-\Delta t} + P_t \bullet AT_{t-\Delta t}}{AT_t} \tag{10}$$

In the case of $AT_{t-\Delta t} > AT_t$, with each t, AT_t will become smaller, each $P_{t+\Delta t}$ will be smaller than the last P_t, available bandwidth (ABW) will increase, and no normal packet loss will occur.

In the case that $AT_{t-\Delta t} = AT_t$, the probability is appropriate, there will be no loss of normal packets, and the same probability will be applied in the period of $t + \Delta t$.

In the case of $AT_{t-\Delta t} < AT_t$, P_t is smaller than the probability required to achieve T, and there is a loss of normal packets. However, $P_{t+\Delta t}$ is adjusted to be larger than P_t.

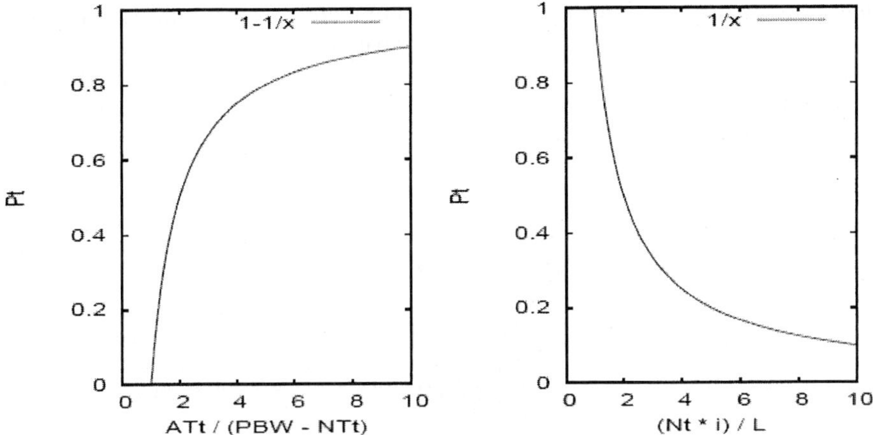

Fig. 1. Illustration of equation (7)

Fig. 2. Illustration of equation (11)

Selection of the Probability Adjustment Interval (Δt)

Using this approach, $P_{t+\Delta t}$ is the result of past traffic and current traffic and not a prediction of future traffic. However, in the event that the model calculates $P_{t+\Delta t}$ incorrectly, an adjustment can be made on $t+\Delta 2t$. Therefore appropriate selection of the interval (Δt) is important.

Limitation of Inspection Probability

From t to $t+\Delta t$, assume the total number of packets is N_t and the maximum number of packets that can be inspected by the detection module is L.

$$P_t < \frac{L}{N_t \bullet \Delta t} \tag{11}$$

For example, when P_t is 0.4, the model can inspect $2.5 \bullet L$ as many packets as in Figure 2. After that, the detection module is no longer able to inspect packets. In this case, the proposed model would pass excessive packets on to the server.

4 Methods and Experiments

For all experiments in this paper we apply the widely used NS-2 network simulator.

4.1 Test 1

Test 1 is a control experiment to determine the impact of an attack on a network not employing an attack detection module. The network used in this experiment is small than an actual network because of simulator resource and memory limitations.

Network topology was constructed as shown in Figure 3. Normal traffic is generated by a CBR agent and uses 25% of router-server bandwidth. Attack traffic is generated by an exponential agent that creates three times the traffic of an average router-server bandwidth. We did not apply the detection module to this experiment because we wanted to observe the impact of an attack on the network.

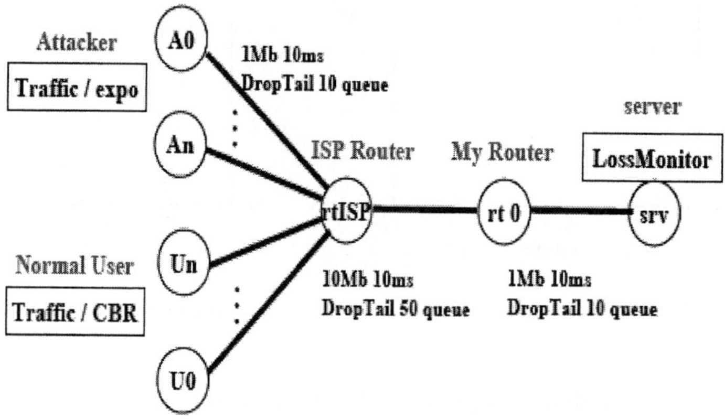

Fig. 3. Network topology of Test 1

4.2 Test 2

The normal and attack traffic and network topology in Test 2 are the same as those used in Test 1, however in this experiment, the attack detection module is installed on the router. The module inspects packets randomly and detects attack packets passing through the router. For this test we set $T = 0$, let L be infinite, and tested various values for P_t and Δt_k .

4.3 Test 3

Test 3 repeats Test 2 but limits the module L to 3000pps and 1500pps.

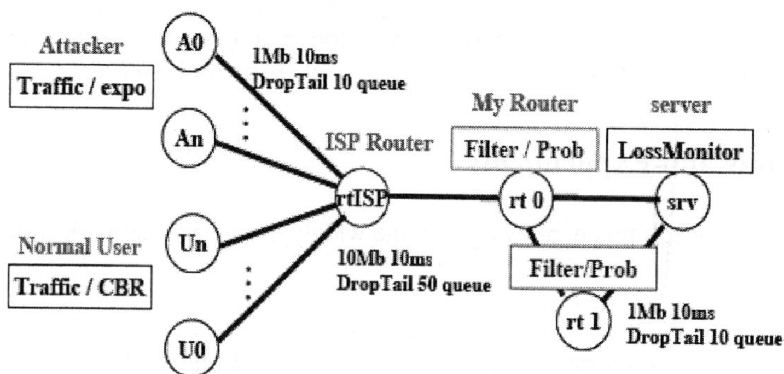

Fig. 4. Network Topology of Test 3

5 Experiment Results

5.1 Test 1 Results

The results of Test 1 are shown in Figures 5 and 6. Figure 5 shows the total traffic including normal and attack traffic. Figure 6 shows the change in traffic over the

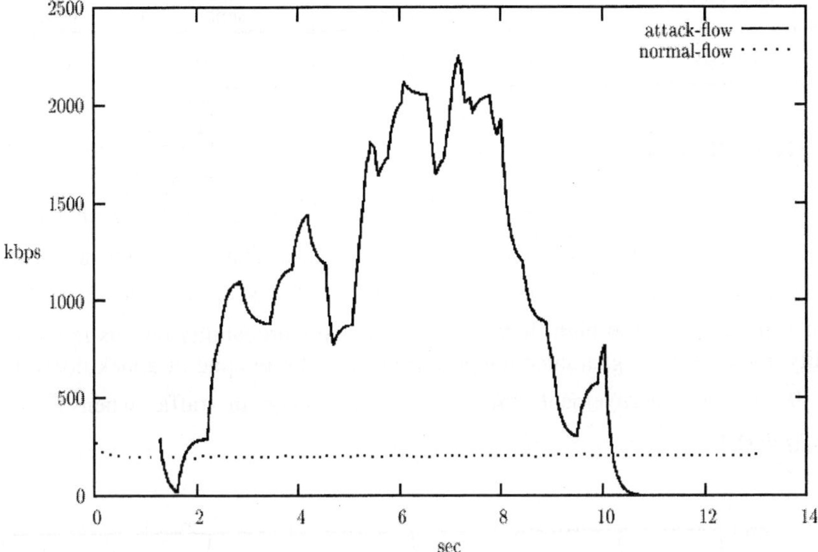

Fig. 5. Traffic change of $rtISP \sim rt0$

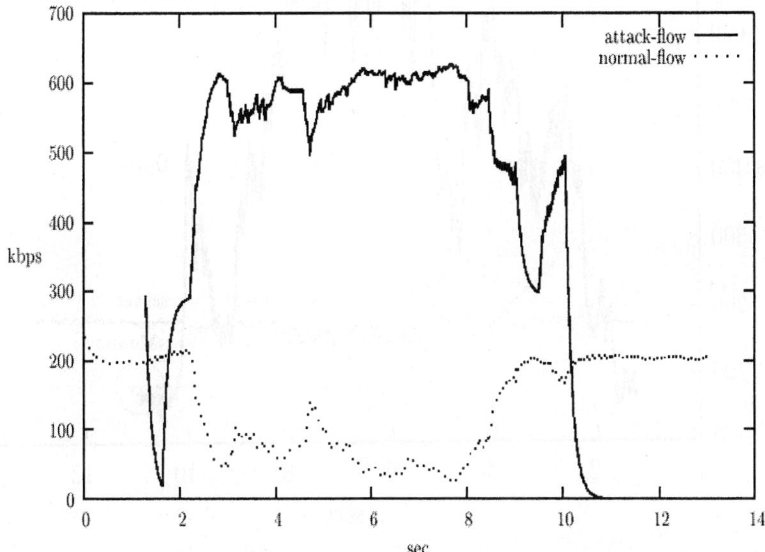

Fig. 6. Traffic change of $rt0 \sim srv$

router-server and displays the effect that attack traffic has on normal traffic. Table 1 shows that 40.33% of normal packets were lost because they were dropped from the router queue.

Table 1. Result of Test 1

Packet Attack	normal		Attack	
	Sent	loss	sent	Loss
3 Mbps	7788	40.33	33701	41.43

5.2 Test 2 Results

The results of Test 2 are shown in Table 2. When the initial probability (P_i) is set to 0.7, normal packet loss was below 1%. This indicates that it was not necessary to inspect all passing packets. When P_i was set to 0.1 and Δt was set to 0.5, the loss of normal packets was too high. It reason that module's probability returns initial probability when network guarantee temporarily bandwidth in spite of attack doesn't finish. It remains improvement. Figure 7 is the change in traffic when $P_i = 0.6$ and $\Delta t = 0.1$.

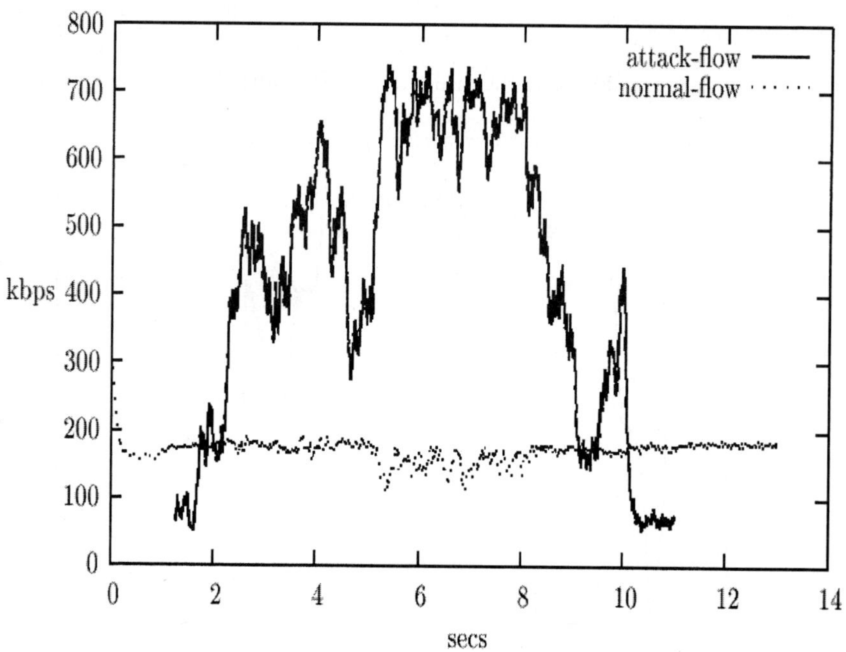

Fig. 7. Traffic change when $P_i = 0.6$, $\Delta t = 0.1$, and L is infinite

Table 2. Result of Test 2.(L = infinite)

Pi Δt(sec)	0.01	0.05	0.1	0.2	0.3	0.4	0.5	0.6	0.7	0.8
0.01	7.87	5.09	6.65	4.77	5.03	3.50	2.36	2.00	0.42	0.00
0.05	6.45	6.48	6.04	5.36	5.46	3.83	2.68	2.07	0.43	0.00
0.1	6.18	7.70	5.84	7.37	6.03	4.23	3.63	1.59	0.70	0.00
0.5	11.77	10.86	11.02	9.45	8.55	5.93	4.32	2.83	0.47	0.00
1.0	16.05	14.38	12.68	11.73	11.29	8.98	5.54	2.92	0.32	0.00
1.5	17.91	18.18	17.91	15.35	13.88	12.13	8.24	3.78	0.35	0.00

* loss of normal packet(%)

5.3 Test 3 Results

The results of Test 3 are shown in Tables 3 and 4. In Test 1, normal and attack agents generated a total of 41489 packets, an average of 3200 packets a second. Therefore,

Table 3. Test 3 Results (L = 3000)

Pi Δ*t*(sec)	0.01	0.05	0.1	0.2	0.3	0.4	0.5	0.6	0.7	0.8	0.9	1.0 (non-apply)
0.01	14.79	14.00	12.77	11.77	11.55	9.98	9.70	7.94	6.54	6.27	6.54	7.02
0.05	11.22	11.94	12.07	10.07	11.19	8.76	8.39	7.16	6.30	7.53	9.64	11.81
0.5	13.43	12.76	12.33	11.29	11.42	9.82	8.74	6.74	6.18	8.60	10.67	13.35
0.5	15.87	16.50	15.10	13.94	11.65	10.46	9.55	7.25	6.05	8.47	11.24	13.39
1.0	16.43	16.05	16.53	16.26	13.22	13.64	9.98	7.62	6.33	7.76	11.38	14.59
1.5	20.01	18.32	18.95	16.69	15.40	12.12	9.16	6.61	5.22	8.82	11.45	14.18

* Normal Packet loss(%)

Table 4. Test 3 Results (L=1500)

Pi *I*(sec)	0.01	0.05	0.1	0.2	0.3	0.4	0.5	0.6	0.7	0.8	0.9	1.0 (non-apply)
0.01	31.86	25.64	23.45	22.35	23.58	21.73	19.38	18.15	16.60	17.59	25.80	26.67
0.05	24.19	23.56	22.65	21.57	19.46	20.95	19.37	19.99	18.97	20.67	22.23	23.45
0.5	24.49	23.99	23.25	22.39	23.69	19.10	17.82	19.23	20.74	21.78	24.10	24.96
0.5	24.07	25.89	23.16	24.15	22.36	22.44	20.53	19.55	21.19	22.93	25.86	27.00
1.0	22.03	27.25	25.44	26.11	22.62	19.97	19.76	19.70	21.40	24.16	25.96	27.59
1.5	27.97	27.51	26.23	27.31	22.30	19.86	20.76	18.92	20.65	23.85	25.52	25.57

* Normal Packet loss(%)

when $L = 3000\,pps$, the attack slightly exceeded the module limits. However, when L was set to 1500pps, the attack exceeded module limits by a factor of two. In Test 3, when $L = 3000\,pps$, the module was most effective when $P_i = 0.7$. When $L = 1500\,pps$, the module was most effective when $P_i = 0.6$. For both 3000pps and 1500pps, the packet inspection probability was better than in the case when $P_i = 1.0$ (meaning that 100% of packets were inspected).

6 Conclusion

In this paper, we proposed and demonstrated the efficiency of a stochastic model for packet inspection as a defense against DoS attacks targeting network resources. In the future we hope to improve our model by using methods that maintain a certain constant probability as long as attack is underway, and as long as the network guarantees the appropriate bandwidth.

References

1. David Moore, Geoffrey Voelker, Stefan Savage, Inferring Internet Denial-of-Service Activity, Feb. 2001.
2. Lan.F. and S.H.Rubin and M.H.Smith and L.Trajovic. Distributed Denial of Service Attacks., IEEE International Conference on System, Man, and Cybernetics, 2000.
3. Steve Gibson, DRDoS, http://grc.com/doc/drdos/htm, Feb. 2002
4. S. Axelsson. Intrusion detection systems: A survey and taxonomy., Technicalrep ort, Depart. Of Computer Engineering, Chalmers University, 2000.
5. Tao Peng, Christopher Leckie, Kotagiri Ramamohanarao, Detecting Distributed Denial of Service Attack Using Source IP Address Monitoring
6. Michael T. Goodrich., Efficient Packet Masking for Large-Scale IP Traceback, CCS'02, November, 2002.
7. Steve Bellovin, Tom Taylor, ICMP Traceback Message, RFC 2026, Internet Engineering Task Force, 2003
8. P. Ferguson and D. Senie. Em Network ingress filtering: Defeating denial of service attacks which employ ip source address spoofing. In RFC 2827, 2001.
9. Kenjiro Cho, Ryo Kaizaki, Akira Kato, An Aggregation Technique for Traf.c Monitoring, IEEE Proceedings of the 2002 Symposium on Applications and the Internet, 2002
10. Cheng Jin, Haining Wang, Kang G. Shin, Hop-Count Filtering: An Effective Defense Against Spoofed DDoS Traffic, CCS'03, October, 2003.
11. Yih Huang J., Mark Pullen, Countering Denial-of-Service Attacks Using Congestion Triggered Packet Sampling and Filtering, 2001.
12. Chatree Sangpachatanaruk, Sherif M. Khattab, Taieb Znati, Rami Melhem, Daniel Moss, A Simulation Study of the Proactive Server Roaming for Mitigating Denial of Service Attacks., 2002.
13. Srinivas Mukkamala, Guadalupe Janoski, Andrew H. Sung, Intrusion Detection Using Neural Network and Support Vector Machine, IEEE, 2002.
14. Srinivas Mukkamala, Andrew H. Sung, Ajith Abraham, Intrusion Detection Using Ensemble of Soft Computing Paradigms, 2004.

Mobile-Agent-Based Web Service Composition*

Zhuzhong Qian, SangLu Lu, and Li Xie

State Key Laboratory for Novel Software Technology,
Department of Computer Science and Technology, Nanjing University, China
{qianzhuzhong, sanglu, xieli}@dislab.nju.edu.cn

Abstract. In this paper we propose a mobile-agent-based web service composition (MAWSC) model for the dynamic web service composition (WSC). As compared with the traditional WSC models, our model avoids bottleneck of data transfer by peer-to-peer approach. As it achieves the composition without a centralized control, there is no center needed and every WSC portal can offer services for a large quantity of clients. In MAWSC model, WSC client inputs the specification and the initial parameters through WSC portal; then, system creates mobile agents to achieve the task and return the final results back to the client. In this paper, we define "planning" to specify the logic actions of mobile agent so as to execute the WSC automatically. And we also give the process mapping rules to convert the specification of WSC to the planning, and the behavior matching algorithms to map the planning to the physical behaviors of agents.

1 Introduction

The Web Services Composition (WSC) is one of the basic aspects of the Service Oriented Computing[1]. WSC supports complex business process which expends the ability of the single web service and offers a way to reuse the software components. WSC uses a loosely coupled model to allow flexible composition of heterogeneous systems through the basic protocols of web services (SOAP[2], WSDL[3], and UDDI[4]).

Web services provide a common platform-independent framework that simplifies heterogeneous application integration. The composition of web services involves two issues[5], which are composition synthesis and orchestration. The former is concerned with synthesizing a new composite service, thus producing a specification of how to coordinate the component web services to obtain the composite service. The second issue is concerned with coordinating the various component web services according to some given specification. Our main focus in this paper is on the orchestration of the WSC.

Starting from the basic specifications for messaging and service description, several standards and approaches have been proposed recently for specifying the orchestration of the WSC. These languages include BPEL4WS (Web Service Business Process Execution Language for Web Services)[6], WSFL (Web Services Flow Language)[7], WSCI (Web Services Choreography Interface)[8], BPML (Business Process Modeling Language)[9], etc. For the purpose of a particular WSC, these standards provide syntax to specify that a port of one peer is linked to a port of another peer.

* This work is partially supported by the National Natural Science Foundation of China under Grant No.60402027 and the National Basic Research Program of China (973) under Grant No.2002CB312002.

H. Zhuge and G.C. Fox (Eds.): GCC 2005, LNCS 3795, pp. 35 – 46, 2005.

Using these standards, it is possible to build up a composite application wholly from already existing web services. However, this leads to a "hub-and-spoke" topology, where the central peer plays the role of mediator. Essentially, it is a centralized approach and has several shortcomings. Firstly, central peer has to control the execution of web services, and then, it becomes a performance bottleneck. Secondly, all the web services communicate with each other through the central peer, which results in the bottleneck of data transfer. Finally, even if the center is unavailable for a short time, WSC application will fail.

In order to overcome the problems of centralized approaches, it is necessary to adopt a distributed approach to realize WSC. In this paper, we propose a novel mobile-agent-based WSC (MAWSC) model which is a decentralized approach. We give a detailed description of the model including the architecture and the formal definition. The specific contributions of our research are as follows:

- We present the study on the properties of the mobile agent and argue that it is appropriate to realize WSC. And we give a detailed compare of our approach and the other related approaches.
- We describe the architecture of the agent and give the orchestration of the web services composition.
- The formal definition of mobile agent is presented, through which we establish the process matching rules to convert the specification of business process into a sequence of activities, namely "planning". Then, we give the behavior matching algorithms which map the logic "planning" into the physical behaviors of the agent.

This paper is organized as follows: section 2 presents the availability of using mobile agent technologies to realize WSC and gives a brief overview of the MAWSC model; section 3 gives the formal definition and the architecture of the mobile agent for WSC in our model; section 4 describes the process mapping rules; section 5 gives the behavior matching algorithms; section 6 discusses some related works and give a compare of our work and the prior work; finally, is the conclusion and the future work.

2 Mobile-Agent-Based Web Services Composition Model

2.1 Adoption of Mobile Agent

A mobile agent is a software component that has the ability to move from one host to another while preserving its state[10]. Now we adopt the mobile agent to achieve WSC, because it has the following characteristics which are benefit to the realization of decentralized WSC model.

- **Migration.** A mobile agent can migrate from one host to another carrying the information on. Essentially, this realizes the peer-to-peer communication mode between web services.
- **Local Access.** A mobile agent can migrate to the host and control the execution of the web service, so that there needn't another role to invoke the web service. During the execution of WSC, mobile agent itself is the controller of the execution. And it migrates from one host to another, consequently, there doesn't exist a host as the center peer.

Existing mobile agent systems also support clone as well as migration[11]. By clone, mobile agent itself creates new agents to achieve the WSC task in parallel. In this way, the execution of WSC is more effective.

2.2 Architecture of MAWSC Model

Our goal is to build a cooperative working environment that integrates web services on the pervasive networks, so that we can sufficiently utilize all kinds of the resources on the world. Figure 1 (a) shows the architecture of this model. There are three kinds of entities in MAWSC model: WSC portal, mobile agent, and web services. WSC client inputs the specification of WSC and the initial parameters through WSC portal. Then, system converts the specification into a sequence of the agent activities, called "planning", and creates a corresponding mobile agent to implement the task. After accomplishing the task, the agent returns back to the WSC portal and presents the result to the client.

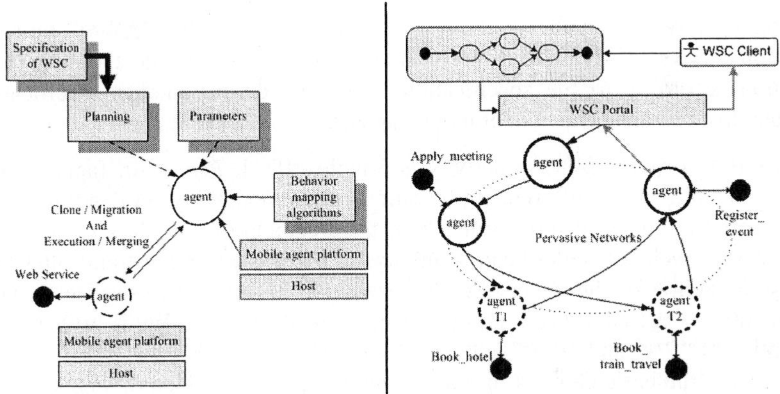

(a) Web Service Composition by mobile agent (b) Composition problem: travel service

Fig. 1. MAWSC model

(1) WSC portal. This is the interface to the WSC clients. The portal accepts the WSC specification and the initial parameters. Then, it converts the specification to the planning according to the process matching rules. Finally, a mobile agent is created to honor the WSC.

(2) Mobile agent. In this system, the mobile agent that achieves the composite web service is defined with three parts of descriptions: (1) a "planning" express the specification of the WSC, (2) parameters are the data flows in the process, (3) behavior matching algorithms decide the physical behaviors of the agents. We will give a detailed formal definition of the agent in section 4. As shown in Figure 1 (a), MAWSC needs the support of the mobile agent platform (e.g. IBM aglet platform[11]).

(3) Web service. This is the atomic function module and each achieves a sub task. Web services are passive in our model. The mobile agents invoke the related web services and transmit the parameters to them. During the execution, the agent monitors the web service, catching exceptions and collecting results.

Here is an example. Suppose a college student named Bob wants to go to Beijing to attend a meeting. He first applies for attending the meeting; then, books the train ticket and the hotel; finally, registers to the meeting. There are four single web services offering these functions, now we need to combine them into a new composite web service. In our model, WSC client inputs the request (a specification of WSC) and the parameters through the WSC portal. Then, the mobile agent is created to achieve the task. As shown in Figure 1 (b), the agent keeps moving to execute the required web services. During the executing, the agent replicates itself so that the "book_train_ticket" and "book_hotel" can be achieved in parallel. Before the "register_event" being executed, the two agents merge into one agent. After accomplishing the task, the agent returns the result.

3 Mobile Agent for WSC (WSC-MA)

3.1 Description of WSC-MA

Essentially, a WSC system is a kind of workflow system. In MAWSC model, the migration of the task is realized by agent. By judging the current state, the agent chooses an action according to the specification. Here, we define another specification – planning, to direct the behaviors of mobile agents.

Definition 1 Activity (A). An activity is 6-tuple <ID, I, *Pre*, *Post*, Input, Output>, where ID identifies the different specifications; I is a nonempty set denoting the web services offering the needed function; *Pre* is the precondition, which is a rule to decide whether some web service in I can be invoked; *Post* is a set of constraint rules, which specify the action of the agent after the execution of some web service; Input and Output refer to the parameters needed to implement the task. We'll give a detailed description of "*Pre*" and "*Post*" in the next section.

Activity is the basic element in process including the execution of web service and the behavior of agent. For each activity, any web services in I can be delegated to achieve the task. In our model, agent will pick one delegation a time. If the execution fails, another delegation will be picked.

Definition 2 Planning. A planning is a sequence of activities defined as $< (A)^{+} >$.

From the definition, we can see that a nonempty set of activities compose a planning. Essentially, in this sequence, *Pre*, execution of web service and *Post* appear alternately, which compose the workflow of composite process. While running, the agents are assigned to carry out the web service according to the planning. In MAWSC model, planning is very important which specifies the logic actions of mobile agent.

Definition 3 WSC-MA. A WSC-MA is a 5-ruple <ScopeNum, planning, A, DataBlock, ST>, where ScopeNum is an integer used to distinguish which agent scope it belongs to; the DataBlock stores a set of useful data, which is intermediate results or global parameters; ST is the status of the Agent, and it is an enumeration of {BEGIN, READY, WAITING, RUN, ABORT, TRANSITION}.

For one WSC process, maybe, there are several WSC-MAs to implement the task in parallel. We use ScopeNum to identify these WSC-MAs which belongs to the same group. ST refers to the status of WSC-MA. DataBlock is an important component during the running time. The variables in DataBlock reflect the current context of the composite process. The behavior of agent is mainly depended on the information.

3.2 Action Rules

As mentioned above, planning needs to describe the complex control flow corresponds to the procedural rules specified in the WSC specification. For example, when one agent finishes booking the train ticket and moves to the target host where to invoke the register service, it must make sure that there is another agent has finished booking hotel. Here we give the detailed definition of the action rules.

Definition 4 ***Pre.*** A *Pre* is a precondition rule defined as <Operator, A-Set >, where Operator is enumeration of {AND, XOR} which explains the relationship of the expression; A-Set is a nonempty set of activities, which should be completed before the execution of this activity.

Before the execution of the web service, a set of the related activities should be achieved first. There are mainly two reasons for WSC-MA waiting when it is ready. One is that some of the inputs required by the web service are outputs of some other web services, so that the WSC-MA has to wait for the intermediate results. Another reason is just follow the logic order of the WSC specification.

The two operators mean different control logic respectively. AND is the synchronization of the execution along the different path. Before WSC-MA invokes the web service, all the activities in A-Set should be finished. XOR is simple merge. One of activities being finished can trigger the web service. If there is only one activity in the A-Set, the operator is arbitrary and it indicates the sequence.

Definition 5 ***Post.*** The *Post* is defined as a set of rules < (Rule)*>. One Rule represents one succeeded branch of the process. Rule is a 2-tuple < Condition | ϕ , *A*> where a "Condition" is a logical expression which may be evaluated by the agent to decide whether a succeeded activity should be started.

The *Post* tells the agent what to do next, after the activity is completed in one host. *Post* is the logic transition of the activity, which enacts the behavior of agents. The basic construct of "sequence", "AND/OR-split" in workflow can be expressed.

3.3 Behaviors of WSC-MA

In MAWSC model, four basic physical behaviors of WSC-MA are defined: execution, merging, migration, and clone. These basic behaviors are the base of MAWSC and new behaviors also can be added in order to realize some special WSC applications.

(1) Execution. This behavior includes two steps: invoking a web service and collecting the results to the DataBlock.

(2) Merging. When the ST of an agent is WAITING, it means the WSC-MA is waiting for the complement of another activity. Once another WSC-MA arrives, the former WSC-MA checks the ScopeNum of incoming WSC-MA. If these two WSC-MA have the same ScopeNum, then a Merging operation takes place. This behavior corresponds to the "AND-join" and "XOR-join" in the workflow.

(3) Migration. After a WSC-MA completes the activity in one host it moves on achieving another activity. A migration indicates that the WSC-MA migrates to a certain host and access the web service locally. If the agent fails to migrate, it throws an exception and the ST of the agent turns to "ABORT".

(4)Clone. In this function, a WSC-MA is replicated. The input parameter is one of the rules in the *Post* of the primary WSC-MA. So any cloned WSC-MA only has one rule of *Post*. Suppose at one node in the process, a single thread is split into ***n*** threads, and then ***n*** agents are cloned to achieve these threads respectively. Each new agent has the same DataBlock and ST. After clone, the primary agent itself is destroyed.

3.4 Architecture of WSC-MA

We have designed WSC-MA to realize our approach and elide the description of mobile agent platform which is not the emphases of this paper.

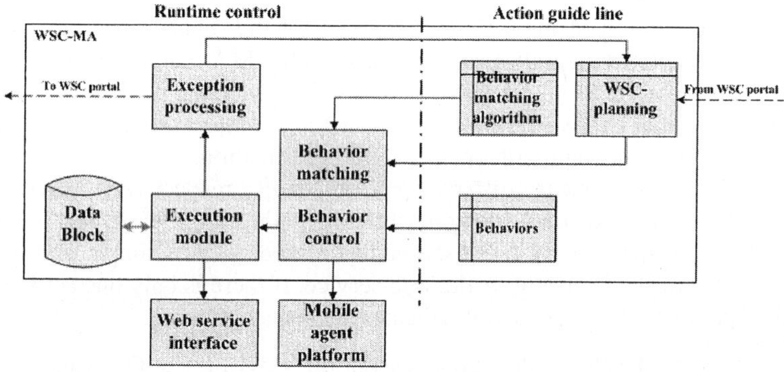

Fig. 2. Architecture of WSC-MA

WSC-MA is divided into two parts. As shown in Figure 2, the left part is the runtime control. According to the planning, behavior matching (detailed in section 5) convert the action of WSC-MA into the physical behaviors of WSC-MA. Then the behavior control module implements these behaviors. It calls the execution module to invoke the web service and transfers the instructions to the mobile agent platform. The execution module invokes the web service, collects the results and catches exceptions. The exception processing module calls the functions defined in the planning to handle the exception. If the exception is a fatal one, it sends a report to WSC portal and terminates the running.

The right part is the agent guide line. This part is preloaded before WSC-MA begins to achieve the task. It includes planning, behavior matching algorithms and behaviors. Changing the planning, we get the different WSC applications; while changing the behavior matching algorithms and behaviors, we get a new WSC-MA system used to some specific scenario. For example, we can import a new behavior of agent from MAFTM model[12], called "replication" and adds corresponding behavior matching algorithm. When there are more than one web services in set I (that is to say, there are several candidates to offer the same function), WSC-MA executes "replication", splitting into several WSC-MAs and accessing these web services respectively. Thus, this advanced MAWSC model is a fault tolerance WSC model.

4 Process Mapping Rules

In MAWSC model, we need to convert the input specification of WSC into planning. Literature [13] summarizes 20 workflow patterns and indicates that any complex process can be divided into these patterns. Consequently, so long as to define the mapping rules between the patterns and actions of WSC-MA, the specification can be converted to the planning. Among these patterns, there are 5 basic ones which closely match the definitions of elementary control flow concepts provided by the WfMC in [14]. For the limit of the space, we only give the 5 basic mapping rules.

Rule 1 Sequence. Suppose activity T_1 is enabled after the completion of activity T_2 (Figure 3(b)). Then T_2.*Post* and T_1.*Pre* are defined as Figure 3(a) shows.

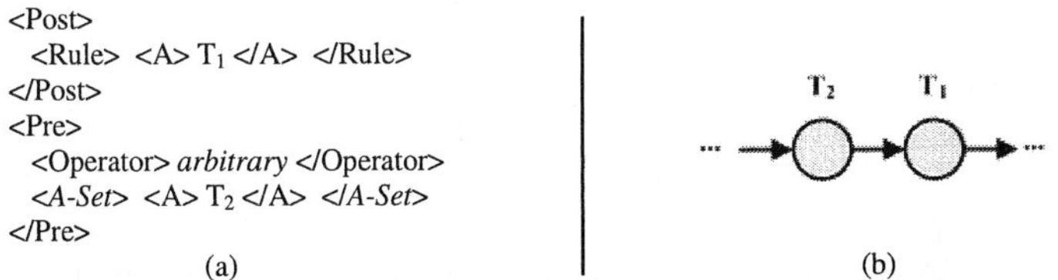

Fig. 3. Sequence

Rule 2 Parallel Split (AND-split). Suppose in the point of activity T_1, the single thread of control splits into multiple threads of control which can be executed in parallel and these thread are respectively started with T_2, T_3 ... (Figure 4(b)) Then, T_1.*Post* is defined in Figure 4(a)

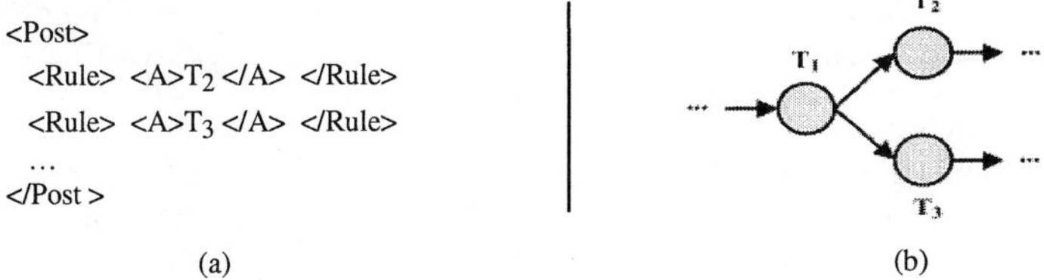

Fig. 4. Parallel split

Rule 3 Synchronization (AND-join). Suppose in the point of activity T_1, multiple parallel activities converge into one single thread of control, thus synchronizing multiple threads. And the activities before T_1 in these parallel activities are T_2, T_3... (Figure 5(b)) Then, T_1.*Pre* is defined in Figure 5(a).

```
<Pre>
  <Operator> "AND" </Operator>
  <A-Set>
      <A> T2 </A>
    <A> T3 </A>
    ...
  </A-Set>
</Pre>
```

(a)

(b)

Fig. 5. Synchronization

Rule 4 Exclusive Choice (XOR-split). Suppose in the point of activity T_1, according to the procedural rules, one of branches is chosen. These conditions are C_2, C_3 ... correspond to the branches started with T_2, T_3 ... (Figure 6(b)) Then, T_1.*Post* is defined in Figure 6(a).

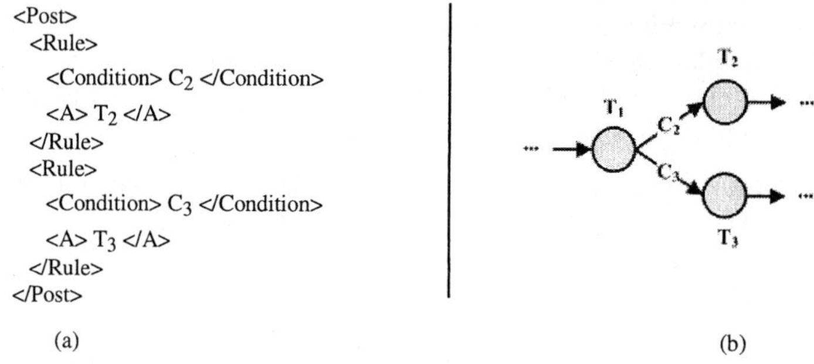

Fig. 6. Exclusive choice

Rule 5 Simple Merge (XOR-join). Suppose in the point of activity T_1, two or more alternative branches come together without synchronization. And the activities before T_1 in these parallel activities are T_2, T_3... (Figure 7(b)) Then, T_1.*Pre* is defined in Figure 7(a).

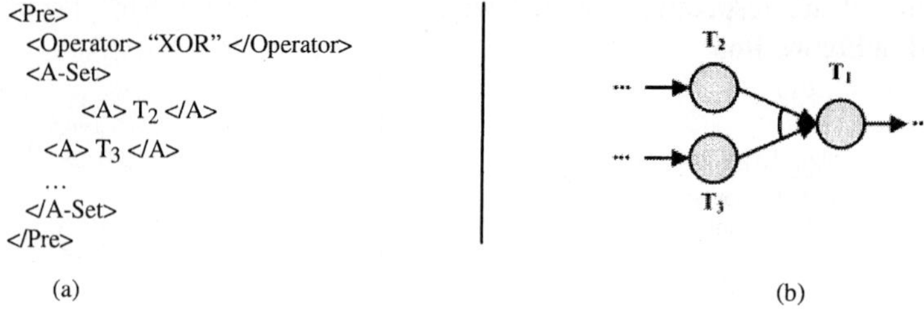

Fig. 7. Simple merge

The *Pre* and the *Post* always appear in pair, *Post* of the prior activity and the *Pre* of the successor compose of the relationship of these two activities. Note that in rule 2 and rule 4, we elide the *Pre* of the T_2 and T_3, clearly, their *Pre* should be T_1. Similarly, we elide the *Post* of the T_2 and T_3 in rule 3 and rule 5, their *Post* should be T_1.

5 Behavior Matching

WSC portal system converts the specification of WSC to the planning and creates WSC-MA to implement task. In this section we give "Pre2Behavior" and "Post2Behavior" to convert the action rules to the physical behaviors of WSC-MA.

```
Pre2Behavior () {
  Probe the existing WSC-MAs in this host
  If (this.SopeNum == Existing Agent.ScopeNum)
      If (this.A in ExistingAgent.Pre.A-Set) return;

  Switch (Operator){
    case XOR:
   case AND: {
     A-Set temp; this.ST == WAITING;
       temp = this.A.Pre.A-Set; delete this.A from temp;
      While (temp != empty) {
      Waiting for incoming agent ...
      If (AgentIncom.ScopeNum == this.ScopeNum)
        if (AgentIncom.A in temp){
          Delete Agent.A from temp; Merging (this, AgentIncom);
      }
      } This.ST == READY; U = choose( this.I); Execution (U);
   }
  }
}
```

Fig. 8. Algorithm of *Pre* to behavior

Figure 8 shows Pre2Behavior in which maps *Pre* to behaviors. Here "this" represents WSC-MA itself. Think about the following scenario. There are two activities T_1 and T_2 which are the priors of T_3 and the "operator" of the T_3.*Pre* is "XOR". That means whichever T_1 or T_2 has been completed, T_3 will be triggered. Suppose, after finishing the T_1, WSC-MA A_1 invokes the T_3 and gets the result migrating to the next host. Then, WSC-MA A_2 accomplishes T_2 and arrives, again it invokes the T_3. So T_3 is invoked twice. Respond to this problem, in this algorithm, the WSC-MA waits for the others until all the WSC-MAs arrive or overtime.

```
Post2Behavior() {
  RuleSet: set of Rule; RuleSet= this.A.Post;

  if (card(RuleSet) == 1) {
     check DataBlock to find out
     if (rule.Post == True) { Migration (rule.A); return; }
    else destroy this;
  }
  for each rule in RuleSet  { Clone (rule); }
  destroy this;
}
```

Fig. 9. Algorithm of *Post* to behavior

Figure 9 shows Post2Behavior, which converts the *Post* to the transition actions. Firstly, the WSC-MA with multiple succeeded activities is replicated by "Clone" and the cloned WSC-MA has single succeeded activity. That is to say, a WSC-MA with ***n*** succeeded activities will be replicated ***n*** times, creating ***n*** cloned ones with single activity. Then, these new WSC-MAs check the "condition" of the rule, deciding whether doing "Migration" or not. After the "Clone", the origin WSC-MA will be destroyed.

6 Related Work

Research on the orchestration of the WSC has mainly concentrated on the framework of the composition of web services.

In survey [15], three approaches to build composition services are discussed, which are *peer-to-peer*, *mediated* approach, and *brokered* approach. The widely used web services composition languages such as BPEL4WS, BPML, etc., is designed for specifying the behaviors of mediator service, namely central peer. The brokered approach is the expansion of the mediated approach. The central peer (the "broker") controls the other peers, but data can be passed between any pair of peers directly. This approach is embodied in GSFL[16] for scientific workflow and AZTEC[17] for telecommunications applications. It makes the central peer escape from the communication. However, mediated approach and brokered approach are both centralized approaches and have the shortcomings. The center peer becomes the bottleneck of performance and once it is down, the execution of the composite process will be failed. Furthermore, for the mediated approach, because both data and control flow passes through the center, the traffic on the network is heavy.

Compared with these two kinds of approaches, our WSC model is a decentralized orchestration model. In MAWSC model, the WSC portal is just an entrance of the WSC system; during the run time, the WSC-MA executes the WSC task according to the planning and need not a "central peer" to control the execution and the intermediate results are carried to service host directly. So our approach is in peer-to-peer mode and the bottleneck avoids. Another advantage is that even the client user is offline during the running time; the agent will keep on doing the WSC work.

Up to now, WSC systems based on agent also appears. In IG-JADE-PKSlib toolkit [18], four kinds of agents are defined. Among them, the Executor Agent (EA) is defined to implement the arrangements, and the JADE agent represents the web service. Essentially, this model is still a *mediated* approach; the mediator is composed of EA and the JADE agents. In [19], team-based agent is imported to achieve WSC; the team leader forms a team to honor a complex service. It is the typically broker architecture. Strictly speaking, the agents in these systems are not mobile agent; they only act as the connectors between the web services and the WSC control center.

In [20], Fuyuki Ishikawa presents a way to add description of the physical behaviors of agents to the integration logic based on BPEL, by which it tries to utilize the mobile agents to achieve the workflow of web service defined by BPEL. However, as mentioned above, BPEL is designed for centralized management. So, simply adding some actions of the agent to the BPEL is farfetched. Furthermore, [20] only explains the two kinds of the behaviors of agent and does not mention how the system works. In our model, we use the planning which is much more suitable to specify the behaviors of agent than use BPEL added with actions of agent and we also give the detailed orchestration of the execution of our model.

In [12], MAFTM is proposed, which is a mobile agent-based fault-tolerant model for WSC. However, as presented in the paper itself, MAFTM only describe the execution of the single mobile agent, and doesn't involve in the control of the composite web service. In section 3.4, we describe an advanced MAWSC model, which imports the fault-tolerant technologies of MAFTM. Consequently, MAFTM can be a module of WSC model, but itself is not a WSC model. In fact, in our model, WSC-MA executes the web services in set I (as mentioned in section 3.1, the web services in set I offer same function) one by one, until one of them executes successfully. This is also a policy of fault-tolerance. Compared with MAFTM, our approach is much simpler, while MAFTM works with good efficiency.

Anyway, MAWSC model is a novel WSC orchestration model, compared with the other WSC approaches, there are mainly three features:

- **Peer-to-peer Mode.** The migration of mobile agent realizes the communication between the web services directly. The network traffic is reducing.
- **Execution Independently.** There is no "center" controlling the execution of the WSC in MAWSC model. WSC-MA implements the task independently so that there is no bottleneck of performance and one WSC portal can provide WSC services to a large numbers of clients.
- **Extensibility.** The architecture of the WSC-MA is well extensible. By changing the physical behaviors and the corresponding matching algorithms, new features are easily added to WSC-MA. Beside the fault-tolerance technologies, we can add other behaviors (such as communication primitive, interoperability, etc.), so that WSC-MA can be used in some special application environment.

7 Conclusion and Future Work

In this paper, we present a novel web service composition model: MAWSC, which is based on mobile agents. This is a distributed WSC orchestration model. According to the model, the execution of WSC becomes more flexible and efficient. It avoids the dependence on the "central peer" and decreases the dependence on the traffic over network. So MAWSC model can directly utilize to pervasive network whose connection is relatively narrowness and instability. The project of cooperate office automation system we are developing now is just based on MAWSC model. There are two challenges in cooperate OA systems: (1) different kinds of client devices are used including PC, mobile phone, PDA, laptop, etc.; (2) large numbers of documents transfer. Adopting MAWSC model, we solve these two problems easily.

In section 4, we present five basic processing mapping rules, now we investigate the control patterns[13] of workflow in order to find some relationships between them and give unified mapping rules.

References

1. X. X. Ma, P. Yu, X. P. Tao, J. Lu: A Service-Oriented Dynamic Coordination Architecture and Its Supporting System. Chinese Journal of Computers, 4(2005) 467-477
2. M. Gudgin, M. Hadley, N. Mendelsohn, et al: SOAP Version 1.2 Part 1: Messaging Framework. W3C. (2003)
3. E. Christensen, et al: Web Services Description Language (WSDL) 1.1. W3C. (2001)
4. L. Clement, et al: UDDI Version 3.0.2:UDDI Spec Technical Committee Draft. W3C. (2004)

5. D. Berardi, D. Calvanese, G. D. Giacomo, et al: Automatic Composition of E-services That Export Their Behavior. In proceedings of International Conference of Service Oriented Computering 2003. Lecture Notes in Computer Science, Vol.2910. Springer-Verlag, Berlin Heidelberg (2003) 43-58.
6. T. Andrews, et al: Specification: Business Process Execution Language for Web Services Version 1.1. Microsoft, IBM, America (2003)
7. F. Leymann: Web Services Flow Language (WSFL) 1.0. IBM, America (2001)
8. A. Arkin, et al: Web Service Choreography Interface (WSCI) 1.0. W3C. (2002)
9. A. Arkin: Business Process Modeling Language. BPMI. (2002)
10. D. Milojicic. Mobile agent applications. IEEE Concurrency, 3(1999) 7-13.
11. M. Oshima, G. Karjoth, and K. Ono. Aglets specification. http://www.trl.ibm.com/aglets /spec11.htm. (1998)
12. W. Xu, B. H. Jin, J. Li, J. N. Cao: A Mobile Agent-Based Fault-Tolerant Model for Composite Web Service. Chinese Journal of Computers, 4(2005) 558-567.
13. W.M.P. van der Aalst, A.H.M. ter Hofstede, B. Kiepuszewski, A.P. Barros: Workow Patterns. Distributed and Parallel Databases, Kluwer Academic Publishers, USA. (2003) 5-51
14. WfMC: Terminology & Glossary, WFMC-TC-1011 issue 3.0. (1999)
15. R. Hull, M. Renedikt, V. Christophides, J. W. Su: E-Services: A Look Behind the Curtain. In proceedings of the 22nd ACM Symposium on Principles of Database Systems, California (2003) 1-14.
16. S. Krishnan, P. Wagstrom, G. von Laszewski. GSFL: A workflow framework for Grid services. Technical Report Preprint ANL/MCS-P980-0802, Argonne National Laboratory. (2002)
17. V. Christophides, R. Hull, G. Karvounarakis, A. Kumar, G. Tong, M. Xiong: Beyond discrete e-services: Composing session-oriented services in telecommunications. In Proceedings of Workshop on Technologies for E-Services (TES), Lecture Notes in Computer Science, Vol. 2193. Rome, Italy. (2001)
18. E. Martinez, Y. Lesperance: IG-JADE-PKSlib: An Agent-Based Framework for Advanced Web Service Composition and Provisioning. In Proceedings of Workshop on Web Services and Agent-based Engineering, New York, USA. (2004)
19. X. Fan, K. Umapathy, J. Yen, S. Purao: An Agent-based Approach for Interleaved Composition and Execution of Web Services. In proceedings of the 23rd International Conference on Conceptual Modeling, Shanghai, China. (2004)
20. F. Ishikawa et al: Mobile Agent System for Web Services Integration in Pervasive Networks. In Proceedings of International Workshop on Ubiquitous Computing. Miami, USA. (2004)38-47.

Trust Shaping: Adapting Trust Establishment and Management to Application Requirements in a Service-Oriented Grid Environment

E. Papalilo, T. Friese, M. Smith, and B. Freisleben

Department of Mathematics and Computer Science, University of Marburg, Hans-Meerwein-Str., D-35032 Marburg, Germany
{elvis, friese, matthew, freisleb}@informatik.uni-marburg.de

Abstract. In this paper, an approach for establishing and managing trust among the interaction partners (i.e. users, nodes and/or services) in a service-oriented Grid environment is presented. The approach is based on a flexible trust model and system architecture for collecting and managing multidimensional trust values. Both identity and behaviour trust of the interaction partners are considered, and different sources are used to determine the overall trust value of an interaction partner. A proposal for establishing the first trust between interaction partners is made, and the possibility to continuously monitor the partners' behaviour trust during an interaction is provided. The proposed trust architecture can be configured to the domain specific trust requirements by the use of several separate trust profiles covering the entire lifecycle of trust establishment and management.

1 Introduction

The Grid computing paradigm is aimed at providing flexible, secure, coordinated resource sharing among dynamic collections of geographically distributed collaborating individuals, institutions and resources [1]. In such a distributed and heterogeneous environment, trust is a major requirement for enabling collaboration among the interaction partners (i.e. users, nodes and/or services).

Azzedin et al. [2] have classified trust into two categories: identity trust and behaviour trust. Identity trust is concerned with verifying the authenticity of an interaction partner, whereas behaviour trust deals with the trustworthiness of an interaction partner.

The overall behaviour trust of an interaction partner can be built up by considering several factors, such as accuracy or reliability. These factors of behaviour trust should be continuously tested and verified. In this way, it is possible to collect a history of past collaborations that can be used for future decisions on further collaborations between interaction partners. This kind of experience can also be shared as recommendations to other participants.

Furthermore, the overall decision whether to trust an interaction partner or not may be affected by other non-functional aspects that cannot be generally determined for every possible situation, but should rather be under the control of the user when requesting such a decision. In addition, while the basic functionalities of two

H. Zhuge and G.C. Fox (Eds.): GCC 2005, LNCS 3795, pp. 47 – 58, 2005.

applications could be similar, differences in application behaviour could be caused by different domain specific trust requirements. Therefore, a trust system for a Grid environment should offer flexible and easy to use components that can be configured to the specific needs of a user on a per case basis.

In this paper, an approach that allows adapting trust establishment and management to user and application requirements in a service-oriented Grid environment is presented. The approach is based on a flexible trust model which includes identity and behaviour trust of the interaction partners and considers different sources to calculate the overall trust value for an interaction partner. A proposal for establishing the first trust between interaction partners is made, and the possibility to monitor the partners' behaviour trust during an interaction is provided. Finally, a system architecture for collecting and managing multidimensional trust values is proposed. It consists of two main components, a trust engine and a verification engine. The trust engine manages trust values and offers partner discovery and rating functionality to higher level applications. The verification engine handles the verification of Grid service results and other criteria (e.g. availability, latency etc.) and generates the necessary feedback for the trust engine regarding the partner. The proposed system architecture can be configured to the domain specific trust requirements by the use of several separate trust profiles covering the entire lifecycle of trust establishment and management.

The paper is organized as follows. Related work is discussed in section 2. In section 3, our trust model is introduced. In section 4, two sample application scenarios are discussed. Section 5 presents a system architecture supporting the proposed trust management model in a service-oriented Grid environment. Section 6 concludes the paper and outlines areas for future research.

2 Related Work

Trust is an important factor for establishing an interaction among participants in a collaborative computing environment, especially in virtual societies [3]. In the field of Grid computing, trust management has been discussed by Azzedin and Maheswaran [2] who separate the "Grid domain" into a "client domain" and a "resource domain". They define the notion of trust as consisting of identity trust and behaviour trust. Identity trust is considered only during the authentication and authorization process, and behaviour trust is limited to the abusive or abnormal behaviour of the entities during the collaboration. The authors present a formal definition of behaviour trust where for trust establishment among entities direct and indirect experiences together with a decay function that reflects the trust decay with time are considered. In their model, a recommender's trust is calculated at the end of a transaction, according to the directly accumulated experience.

Hwang and Tanachaiwiwat [4] propose a trust model based on the trust that Grid resources place to each others' identity. They make use of a central certification authority which bridges different PKI domains for cross-certification.

Goel and Sobolewski [5] present trust and security models for Grid environments using trust metrics based on e-business criteria. They offer a centralized and a distributed scheme for estimating trust among entities.

In [6], Thompson et al. examine the basis for the trust a relying party places on an identity certificate signed by a certification authority.

In [7], Lin et al. develop a trust management architecture for addressing security issues in Grid environments based on subjective logic. They use the belief, disbelief and uncertainty to weight the trustworthiness of the collaborating parties. Identity trust, although considered in the model, is implied to belong only to the authentication process, without offering any possibility to measure it. The authors deal with a general notion of behaviour trust that is established before a collaboration takes place among participants, using trust information from direct and recommenders' sources.

Quillinan et al. [8] propose to use trust management for establishing relationships between Grid administrators and users for automating administration tasks.

In [9], Jennings et al. develop a general trust model for agent-based virtual organizations. The authors make use of direct and indirect trust sources. A distinctive feature of their model is that recommendations coming from inaccurate sources are not given the same importance as those received from accurate sources. They suppose that the agents do not change their behaviour over time.

Finally, Tie-Yan et al. [10] propose a trust management model that supports the process of authentication between entities by considering their identity trust. Their model consists of two tiers. In the upper tier, trust among different virtual organizations is managed, and in the lower tier the trust among entities that belong to the same Grid domain or individuals is managed.

3 Establishing and Managing Trust in Grids

All approaches presented in the previous section have limitations. First, they only use part of the trust sources, more precisely only direct and indirect trust ([9] uses also prejudice), and either identity or behaviour trust. A collective characteristic is the lack of mutual verification of the partners involved in an interaction. An interaction is considered as successful only if an interaction partner *X* receives a response from an interaction partner *Y*. None of the proposals includes checks on the accuracy of the received responses. The trust models that manage identity trust involve a mutual verification of the identities of the collaborating partners at the beginning of the collaboration, but there still is the need for a continuous mutual verification strategy during the collaboration. This verification affects the behaviours of the partners involved and, as a result, influences their decision to continue the collaboration. Thus, there is a need for a flexible trust model whose properties reflect the requirements of Grid applications and the preferences and needs of their users. Our approach to achieve this goal in a service-oriented Grid environment is described in the following.

The following terminology is used in this section: A collaboration in a Grid takes places between interaction partners. An interaction partner is either a service provider (e.g. a node to host and provide a service, or a service instance running on the provider node) or a service consumer (e.g. a node that requests a service from a provider (which includes the request to deploy and perform a service at the provider), or a service instance running on the consumer node). There are two major aspects that influence the selection or acceptance of an interaction partner:

- The *identity* of the interaction partner or more specifically the trust that one can put in the credibility of the identity an interaction partner claims to have.
- The past *behaviour* of the interaction partner as an indicator for its future behaviour. This behaviour can be rated considering a multitude of dimensions, such as the accuracy of delivered results, actual costs compared to expected costs, availability of the service, response time, or fault and intrusion properties. Furthermore, the trust values might be different for different applications/services the interaction partner offers or requests.

In most cases, an interaction partner is not able to judge trustworthiness based on personal and direct experiences only. A socially inspired model using several dimensions of trust that builds on exchanges of experiences and recommendations is useful to decide whether to trust another interaction partner or not. In the following, a flexible trust model and system architecture for collecting and managing such multidimensional trust values are presented.

3.1 A Grid Trust Model

We assume that the probability for a successful future interaction among partners is closely related to the mutual trust values the partners assign to each other. These values vary in $[0,1] \subset \Re$, where 0 means that the other partner is not trusted at all or there are uncertainties due to the lack of information, and 1 means that it can be fully trusted and gives certainties on the success of the interaction that is going to take place. It is inherently clear that e.g. a service consumer will, for example, try to find the most trusted of all available providers for a given task to perform.

The trust T that an interaction partner X has for partner Y is influenced by both identity trust T^I and behaviour trust T^B:

$$T_X(Y) = T_X^I(Y) \cdot T_X^B(Y) \tag{1}$$

Although identity trust is part of the Grid authentication and authorization process, its value is nevertheless related to the overall trust value of a partner. It expresses the belief that the partner is who it claims it is. In a Grid environment, a participant is typically authenticated through a certification authority (CA) which could be: (a) a trusted and dedicated entity (e.g. Globus, IBM, etc.), (b) another participant in the environment, (c) the participant itself which could issue self-signed certificates.

To give an interaction partner X the possibility to determine the identity trust of an interaction partner Y, a collaboration subgraph is centred at X's CA. Similar to Erdös numbers [11], we define the degree of separation D of partner Y from partner X as the path length of the shortest certificate chain from X's CA to Y. Any partner who has no path to X's CA is said to have an infinite relationship with the centre of this "collaboration graph" and thus ∞ is assigned. A relationship is of first order (i.e. 1 assigned) between trusted and dedicated CAs like Globus, IBM, etc. In a well established Grid infrastructure, we do believe that all participants authenticated through CAs of first order are completely identified. In this case, if partner X needs to gather information regarding the identity trust of another partner Y, after establishing the degree of separation of partner Y with its CA, equation (2) can be used:

$$T_X^I(Y) = 1/D_{X,Y} \tag{2}$$

Participants can have different preferences and requirements for future interaction partners. Considering the relationship between quality of service (QoS) and trust [12], different QoS properties like availability of the service, accessibility of the service, accuracy of the response provided by the service, response time, cost of the services, security etc., can be considered and modelled as behaviour trust elements that a consumer uses to rate a provider. In a similar way, the total number of (concurrent) requests coming from a consumer or the size of the packets received from it can be considered as behaviour trust elements from the point of view of a provider.

Trust is a multidimensional value that can be derived from different sources. We distinguish between three of such sources. First, there is direct and personal experience from past collaborations with a partner. Second, there are recommendations from known sources (i.e. partners for which direct experiences exist). Finally, recommendations from other nodes/services in the Grid may be considered and then a path can be found using the known partners of known partners and so on. A collaboration graph similar to the one used in the determination of T^I can be constructed with a participant at its centre. Those three classes can be determined using the degree of separation from the participant (i.e. personal experience is a recommendation from a partner with D=0, all known partners are defined to have D=1 , and all unknown sources are identified by the value D>1).

Now assume that the trust based on direct experience of an interaction partner X with a partner Y is given by $T^B_{X,D=0}(Y)$. Each partner in the network can now calculate the weighted recommendations coming from the set of known partners N_k according to equation (3).

$$R_{X,D=1}(Y) = \sum_{k \in N_k} (T^B_{X,D=0}(k) \cdot T^B_{k,D=0}(Y)) \Big/ |N_k| \tag{3}$$

There are two strategies for calculating the total weighted recommendation coming from the set of unknown partners, either considering the experience values of each participant p_i along the shortest path $P=\{p_1,\ldots,p_D\}$between partner X and partner Y or taking only the experience of the participant in the path preceding partner Y into account. This value is weighted based on the degree of separation of this participant from partner X:

$$R_{X,D>1}(Y) = \sum_{u \in N_u} (\prod_{i=1}^{|P_u|} T^B_{p_{u,i},D=0}(p_{u,i+1})) \Big/ |N_u| \tag{4}$$

where $P_u=\{p_{u,1},\ldots,p_{u,D+1}\}$is the shortest path from X to Y with $p_{u,D}$ = u.

Equation (4) requires several subjective decisions in the determination of every partner's trust along the path, which are based on experience and - as we will see - based on several uncertainties regarding the evaluation of these experiences. Therefore, equation (5) represents a more prejudiced evaluation of the recommendations based on the idea that a more objective metric is needed to weight recommendations originating from unknown sources.

$$R^p_{X,D>1}(Y) = \sum_{u \in N_u} (T^I_X(u) \cdot T^B_{u,D=0}(Y)) \Big/ |N_u| \tag{5}$$

Users need the flexibility to weight the different sources for the total trust differently in different situations. For this purpose, we define the vector of all trust sources an interaction partner X may use for rating an interaction partner Y as:

$$T_X^S(Y) := (T_{X,D=0}^B, R_{X,D=1}, R_{X,D>1}, R_{X,D>1}^p) \tag{6}$$

Now, interaction partner *X* can calculate the resulting normalized trust to put into an interaction partner *Y* using a profile vector $\vec{P} \in [0,1]^4$:

$$\vec{P} = (w_{D=0}, w_{D=1}, w_{D>1}, w_{D>1}^p) \tag{7}$$

where the relative weights express direct experience (*D*=0), indirect experience of "known" sources (*D*=1), experiences of "unknown" sources (*D*>1) without prejudice and the last weight for experiences of "unknown" sources making prejudices on how they have gathered their experience with interaction partner *Y*. The weights can have values in [0,1].

Having defined the relative weights for the different sources, interaction partner *X* can calculate the resulting normalized trust to put into an interaction partner *Y*:

$$T_X^B(Y) = T_X^S \cdot P_X / \|P_X\| \tag{8}$$

The resulting trust value is only used in the decision to interact with a certain interaction partner *Y*. It does not affect the experience value, because this value only depends on the outcome of the subsequent interaction.

3.2 First-Trust Problem

Consider the situation when a user completely new to a Grid environment enters the network. He or she has no personal experience with any of the service providers, therefore all of the trust sources referenced in (3) are equal to 0. The usual strategies for selecting a partner do not apply in this situation. We distinguish two different basic strategies for "initializing" trust. One is a rather open approach to assign an initial trust value slightly above the minimal trust threshold to every partner, effectively giving the partner a chance to prove itself trustworthy without prior verification. We refer to this method as "warm start phase". In contrast, there might be scenarios in which a partner is tested by performing validation checks and deriving initial behaviour trust from these interactions. Obviously, this trust establishment phase through a "cold start" comes at a comparably high price.

The problem of establishing first trust may be seen both from a service consumer as well as a service provider point of view. We believe that a trust management environment for service-oriented Grids must be flexible enough to allow specification of the strategy to be used in either role and on an application basis. In addition to these two basic strategies, further strategies for first trust establishment may be specified in the system.

3.3 Verification Techniques

It might be desirable to verify that a particular partner stands up to an assumed or previously offered behaviour. The extent to which verification is performed may vary depending on application scenarios or various user requirements. Also, the need for verification of the partners' behaviour may arise in both roles (i.e. consumer or provider) of a service consumption scenario. Partners will continuously monitor the interaction process among each other, and in case of discovered anomalies in the behaviour of the other, the consumers and/or providers will reorganize their scheduling or access policies accordingly.

The different aspects of the partners' behaviour (e.g. availability, response time, accuracy, etc.) are criteria for developing verification strategies. In the following, we will only consider the *accuracy of the responses* coming from a service provider as an example and refer to this dimension as behaviour trust for brevity (note, however, that this is only one dimension of behaviour trust to be considered between partners).

The strategy to use for the verification of the accuracy of responses to be expected from one provider may vary depending on certain constraints such as the additional acceptable cost for performing the verification operations. The following verification strategies can be applied:

Challenge with known tasks. A service consumer may prepare a particular test challenge for which it knows the correct result. In this case, the consumer can directly verify if a service provider was able to calculate the correct response for this challenge. However, a malicious provider may be able to guess the correct answers to the set of challenges and thereby manipulate the behaviour trust assigned to it, as the computational resources of the consumer for test preparation may be very limited.

Best of n replies. A more feasible verification technique is similar to the one that is used by SETI@HOME (http://setiathome.ssl.berkeley.edu). The validity of the computed results is checked by letting different entities work on the same data unit. At the end, a majority vote establishes the correct response. This technique results in a significant increase of the total computational costs to solve a particular problem, since the overall workload is multiplied by the replication factor used to reassign subtasks. If there is a service charge collected by a service provider for every processed work unit, this also leads to a considerable increase of the overall cost.

Human in the loop. In some applications, it might be impossible to construct automatic verification or result rating modules. In such cases, it can still be helpful to involve human users in the process of verification. This technique relies on presenting the results to the user, offering the ability to directly express a value to be taken into the trust calculation.

In our approach, it is possible for each of the partners to develop their personalized trust preferences towards the interaction partners. These preferences include the initialization values that the user is willing to assign to each of the new partners, the selection of sources for getting trust information from (recommendations), the interaction partners the participant collaborates with and verification strategies for all the trust elements. The consumer may choose between verifying the accuracy of every single answer coming from the provider ("trust no one") or to verify the accuracy of only a part of the responses coming from the provider ("optimistic trust"). In order to minimize added costs, we propose to couple the frequency of this partial verification technique with the behaviour trust associated with a particular partner in the environment. This relationship is expressed by:

$$f = -((1 - V_{\min}) \cdot T_{last}^{B}) + 1 \tag{9}$$

where $V_{\min}$ is the minimal verification rate set by the consumer and T_{last}^{B} represents the trust value of a provider at a certain moment of time.

From the consumer side this means that for a non-trusted provider every single response is verified and for a fully trusted provider only a minimum of the responses coming from that specific provider has to be verified. The result of the verification operations will directly be used to alter the behaviour trust regarding accuracy.

4 Application Scenarios

We now present two cases, one from media sciences and one from medicine, to illustrate how different application requirements may arise depending on the field of application.

Grid Services for Video Cut Detection. An example from video content analysis is the process of identifying "cuts" in videos [13]. To identify such cuts, the video file is split and all parts are sent to a manager, which assigns the jobs (split video files) to remote services that will take care of the analysis and the identification of the cuts. After all the jobs have been processed, the resulting cut lists are merged together, some boundary processing takes place in the manager, and the user is notified that the work has been finished. Video analysis is a collaborative task with moderate security requirements and even moderate requirements on the accuracy of results. In this case, an open attitude accepting recommendations from strangers and requiring only occasional verification of the data returned from individual data processing services may be sufficient to satisfy the users of the application.

Grid Services for Medical Imaging. An example from medical imaging, is finding similar cases (images) in a set of mammograms [14] for diagnosis support. Images resulting from the mammography are passed to remote services representing image analysis algorithms which calculate similarities in image sets. These image analysis algorithms may be basically similar to those used in the identification of video cuts or in object recognition tasks within frames of video sequences. However, different standards are required in the medical scenario compared to the video application:

- The radiologist may be interested in simply performing standard image processing techniques on generated data sets without placing any special trust requirements on the interaction partners. A subset of images stored on a remote image server is retrieved, and viewing and analysis of image data on the local workstation is performed. Only occasional verification of the data returned from individual data processing services may be required.
- The analysis can be extended to the application of several different statistical analysis methods on data from multiple different studies to view the effects of a treatment method across a patient group. In this case, trusting the accuracy of the responses coming from the interaction partners is important. The radiologist may consider only own experience or recommendations from highly trusted sources for the selection of partners. A high frequency of verification of the data returned from the individual data processing services is required.

While the basic application is similar in both cases (i.e. applying a number of image processing algorithms to a set of images and merging the individual results), the domain specific trust requirements lead to different application behaviour .

Furthermore, the initialization of trust values in the above cases will vary. While it is feasible to assume a certain level of trust for new participants (assigning a positive initial trust value > 0 to them) in the video application, a more cautious behaviour is appropriate in the medical application (assigning a positive but small initial trust value ε to them).

Another interesting aspect in the trust calculation is the selection of trust sources. In the video application, the user has a very open attitude, accepting recommendations from other parties (even unknown sources) with a small bias against the less known recommenders and thus may choose a trust source vector of (1,0.5,0.25,0.25). This means that personal experience makes up 50% of the trust value, direct recommendation accounts for 25% and the more remote recommendation sources for 12.5% each. In the medical application, only highly trusted sources for the decision are desired, therefore the trust source vector could be (0.75,0.25,0,0) meaning that personal experience makes up 75% of the trust value, recommendations coming from directly known parties enter into the trust calculation with 25%, and other trust sources are disregarded.

As a verification strategy, a user may opt for verifying every result by choosing $V_{\min} = 1$ in the medical application, while in the video application only a moderate value of $V_{\min} = 0.3$ will be chosen, leading to a verification ratio of $1 - 0.7 \cdot T^{B}_{last}$.

5 System Architecture

A system architecture supporting trust management in service-oriented Grid applications is presented in Fig. 1. The system consists of two main components, the *trust engine* and the *verification engine*. The trust engine manages trust values and offers partner discovery and rating functionality to higher level applications, such as workflow engines or job scheduling systems. The verification engine handles the verification of Grid service results and generates the necessary feedback for the trust engine regarding the partner. For brevity, we will focus our discussion on the service consumer use of those platform components.

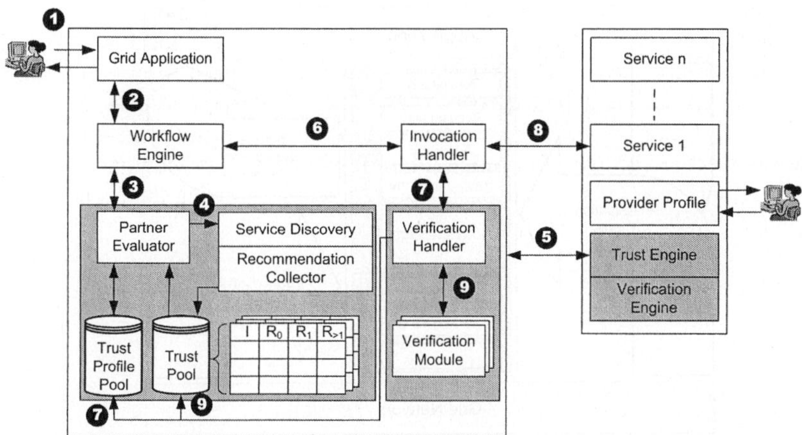

Fig. 1. Architecture of a grid system supporting our trust model

The user starts with specifying his or her trust requirements along with the input data to a trust enabled Grid application (step 1), which in turn uses the workflow engine of the local service-oriented Grid platform (step 2). To enable the selection of trusted services, the decision is made based on a rated list of potential partner services that is obtained from the trust engine (step 3). The trust engine uses its service discovery component to discover individual services (step 4) and to collect recommendations from other trust engines (step 5). These values are stored in the local trust pool to be used in subsequent interactions. The user specified trust profile is also stored in a trust pool for later reference and use by other components in the trust engine. The information gathered by the trust engine is now processed according to the user's trust profile specification and passed on to the workflow engine which then can use the partner services according to the rating generated by the trust engine.

Invocation of external services is then delegated to an invocation handler (step 6). The invocation handler consults the verification engine (step 7) to determine whether a call has to be replicated or redirected (e.g. to perform the best of n verification strategy). The verification engine considers the trust profile managed by the trust engine (step 7), allowing, for example, cost-trust-ratio relations to be taken into account. The resulting invocation is carried out at the selected partner services and results - both synchronous and asynchronous (notification) results - are then collected by the invocation handler (step 8) and verified through the verification engine, using a strategy and verification module consistent with the user supplied trust profile (step 9). The overall result of this process is then passed to the workflow engine that collects results for the application to present them to the end user.

The configuration of the trust engine by use of trust requirement profiles influences three phases during execution of an application workflow. These main phases are addressed by the three arrows in Fig. 2.

The initialization profile determines the influence and scope of factors for initializing the trust values to be used in an interaction. It allows to manually assign trust values to certain partners, as well as specifying how trust recommendations of partners are handled and weighted. This profile specifies the behaviour of the local platform in a situation that requires the establishment of first trust.

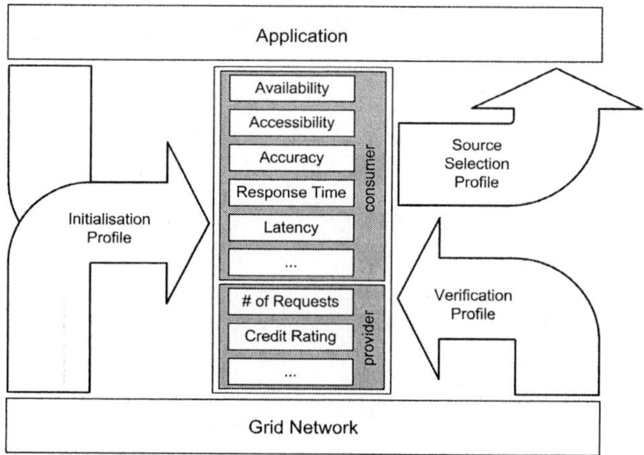

Fig. 2. Trust profile elements influencing the stored trust values and application decisions

The source selection profile determines the selection of behaviour trust dimensions (e.g. availability, accuracy) as well as trust sources (e.g. personal experience, recommendations from directly known partners) to determine a partner ranking according to the application needs. This allows a user to take accuracy trust recommendations from known partners into account with a higher weight than, for example, availability values (which might be caused by the different network locations) coming from the same partner.

The verification profile specifies which verification strategies are to be applied to the results of partner service invocations and the feedback parameters into the trust engine. In this profile, the user specifies how breaches of assumed service level agreements should influence the future interactions with a partner since they are fed back into the trust store for this application and partner service. This profile also dynamically determines the frequency of verification to allow a fine grained control over costs incurred by result verification.

6 Conclusions

In this paper, a flexible trust model and system architecture for collecting and managing multidimensional trust values have been presented. Both identity and behaviour trust of the interaction partners were considered, and different sources were used to determine the overall trust value of a partner. A proposal for establishing the first trust between interaction partners was made, and the possibility to monitor the partners' behaviour trust during an interaction has been provided. Our trust system can be configured to the domain specific trust requirements by the use of several separate trust profiles covering the entire lifecycle of trust establishment and management.

There are several areas of future work. First, the implementation of the proposed trust system architecture needs to be finished. Second, experiments involving a large number of participants in a Grid environment should be performed to evaluate the properties of our approach in real-life scenarios. Third, the system architecture should be extended and adapted to the needs of the service providers. Finally, further research will concentrate on increasing the security of the interaction among participants, especially message level security through using XML encryption.

Acknowledgements. This work is financially supported by Siemens AG (Corporate Technology), by DFG (SFB/FK 615, Teilprojekt MT), and by BMBF (D-Grid Initiative).

References

1. Foster, I., Kesselman, C., Tuecke, S.: The Anatomy of the Grid: Enabling Scalable Virtual Organizations. International J. on Supercomputer Applications 15 (2001)
2. Azzedin, F., Maheswaran, M.: Evolving and Managing Trust in Grid Computing Systems. In: Conference on Electrical and Computer Engineering, Canada, IEEE (2002) 1424-1429
3. Sabater, J., Sierra, C.: Review on Computational Trust and Reputation Models. Artificial Intelligence Review 24 (2005) 33-60

4. Hwang, K., Tanachaiwiwat, S.: Trust Models and NetShield Architecture for Securing Grid Computing. Journal of Grid Computing (2003)
5. Goel, S., Sobolewski, M.: Trust and Security in Enterprise Grid Computing Environment. In: Proc. of IASTED Int. Conf. on Communication, Network and Information Security, New York, USA (2003)
6. Thompson, M.R., Olson, D., Cowles, R., Mullen, S., Helm, M.: CA-Based Trust Model for Grid Authentication and Identity Delegation. Global Grid Forum CA Operations WG Community Practices Document (2002)
7. Lin, C., Varadharajan, V., Wang, Y., Pruthi., V.: Enhancing Grid Security with Trust Management. In: Proceedings of the IEEE International Conference on Services Computing (SCC), Shanghai, China, IEEE (2004) 303-310
8. Quillinan, T., Clayton, B., Foley, S.: GridAdmin: Decentralizing Grid Administration Using Trust Management. In: Third International Symposium on Parallel and Distributed Computing (ISPDC/HeteroPar), Cork, Ireland (2004) 184-192
9. Patel, J., Teacy, W.T.L., Jennings, N.R., Luck, M.: A Probabilistic Trust Model for Handling Inaccurate Reputation Sources. In: Proceedings of Third International Conference on Trust Management, Rocquencourt, France (2005) 193-209
10. Tie-Yan, L., Huafei, Z., Kwok-Yan, L.: A Novel Two-Level Trust Model for Grid. In: Proceedings of Fifth International Conference on Information and Communications Security (ICICS), Huhehaote, China (2003) 214-225
11. Erdös: Erdös Number Project. (2005) http://www.oakland.edu/enp/.
12. Ali, A.S., Rana, O., Walker, D.W.: WS-QoC: Measuring Quality of Service Compliance. In: Proceeding of the Second International Conference on Service-Oriented Computing Short Papers (ICSOC), New York, USA (2004) 16-25
13. Ewerth, R., Friese, T., Grube, M., Freisleben, B.: Grid Services for Distributed Video Cut Detection. In: Proceedings of the Sixth IEEE International Symposium on Multimedia Software Engineering, Miami, USA, IEEE (2004) 164-168
14. Amendolia, S., Estrella, F., Hassan, W., Hauer, T., Manset, D., McClatchey, R., Rogulin, D., Solomonides, T.: MammoGrid: A Service Oriented Architecture Based Medical Grid Application. In: Proceedings of the Third International Conference on Grid and Cooperative Computing, Wuhan, China (2004) 939-942

SVM Approach with CTNT to Detect DDoS Attacks in Grid Computing*

Jungtaek Seo[1], Cheolho Lee[1], Taeshik Shon[2], and Jongsub Moon[2]

[1] National Security Research Institute,
KT 463-1, Jeonmin-dong, Yuseong-gu, Daejeon,
305-811, Republic of Korea
{seojt, chlee}@etri.re.kr
[2] CIST, Korea University,
1-Ga, Anam-dong, Sungbuk-Gu, Seoul, Republic of Korea
{743zh2k, jsmoon}@korea.ac.kr

Abstract. In the last several years, DDoS attack methods become more sophisticated and effective. Hence, it is more difficult to detect the DDoS attack. In order to cope with these problems, there have been many researches on DDoS detection mechanism. However, the common shortcoming of the previous detection mechanisms is that they cannot detect new attacks. In this paper, we propose a new DDoS detection model based on Support Vector Machine (SVM). The proposed model uses SVM to automatically detect new DDoS attacks and uses Concentration Tendency of Network Traffic (CTNT) to analyze the characteristics of network traffic for DDoS attacks. Experimental results show that the proposed model can be a highly useful to detect various DDoS attacks.

1 Introduction

Over the last several years, a new breed of network worms such as *CodeRed*, *SQL Slammer*, and *Nimda* have launched widespread attacks on commercial web sites such as *Yahoo, CNN*, and *Amazon,* etc [1], [2], [3]. These incidents temporarily disable the network services or damage systems by flooding a huge number of network packets for several minutes or longer. These attacks are harmful to almost networked systems especially open resource sites such as computational grids, and it could well be the next wave of target. Thus, now more than ever, we need to provide a secure grid computing environment over the Internet.

Recently, many security models and systems are developed for secure Grid computing in encryption and authentication areas. However, there are rare researches on an availability area of grid computing even though malicious intrusions may easily destroy most of valuable hosts, network, and storage resources in the grids. The vulnerabilities of DDoS in grid computing arise from each grid's limited resources

* This work was supported by the Ministry of Information Communication, Korea, under the Information Technology Research Center Support Program supervised by the IITA.

H. Zhuge and G.C. Fox (Eds.): GCC 2005, LNCS 3795, pp. 59 – 70, 2005.

that can be exhausted by a sufficient number of users. Thus, most of flood attacks to exhaust resource (e.g., network bandwidth, computing power, and storage) of the victim are possible in grid [4].

In order to cope with the threat, there have been many researches on the defense mechanisms including various DDoS detection mechanisms [5], [6], [7]. However, the common shortcoming of the previous detection mechanisms is that they cannot automatically detect the new attacks.

To solve the problem, we adopt the Concentration Tendency of Network Traffic (CTNT) method and Support Vector Machine (SVM) method [8], [9], [10], [11]. In our earlier research, we presented CTNT method to analyze the characteristics of network traffic for the DDoS attacks [12]. CTNT monitors the ratio of a specific type of packets among the total amount of network packets, and compute TCP flag rate and Protocol rate. The result of analyzing network traffic using CTNT showed that there are predictable differences between normal traffic and DDoS attack traffic. In a normal situation, for instance, SYN and FIN are in the ratio of 1:1 and TCP and UDP traffic are in the ratio of 9:1. However, in an abnormal situation (e.g., SYN flooding, UDP flooding), these ratios are broken. Thus, CTNT is used good feature extraction method for SVM that is a machine learning algorithm. Using the traffic analyzing result as input feature of SVM, we were able to automatically generate effective DDoS detection rules. Our detection model showed a high degree of performance, and detected various DDoS attacks successfully.

We introduce related research in section 2, and explain CTNT in section 3. The background knowledge of SVM is discussed in section 4. In section 5, the experimental environment is introduced and the detection performance of SVM and other machine learning algorithms are tested and compared. Lastly, we mention the conclusion of this research and the direction of future work in section 6.

2 Related Work

There have been some researches to defend Grid environment from DDoS attacks. Xiang and Zhou introduce the vulnerability of grids to DDoS attack and propose distributed defense system to protect grids form DDoS attacks. The proposed system is built with protecting communication network, attack control system, intrusion surveillance system, and traceback system [4]. Hwang et al. proposed GridSec architecture. The architecture is built with distributed firewalls, packet filters, security managers, and intrusion detection and response system [13]. It adopts DHT-based overlay architecture as its backbone. Its overlay network maintains a robust virtual inter-networking topology. The GridSec system functions as cooperative anomaly and intrusion detection system. Intrusion information is exchanged by the overlay topology with confidentiality and integrity. The system reacts automatically to the malicious intrusions and attacks using the information.

Traditional defending mechanism against DDoS attacks includes defending, detecting, and reacting mechanism. Most of all, there have been many researches to detect the DDoS attacks since detecting the DDoS attacks is an essential step to defend

DDoS attacks [5], [6], [7]. When DDoS attacks occur, there is a big mismatch between the packet flows "to-rate" toward the victim and "from-rate" from the victim. Gil et al. propose the method that examines the disproportion between "to-rate" and "from-rate" in order to detect DDoS attacks [5]. Kulkarni et al. [6] presents DDoS detection methods based on randomness of IP spoofing. Almost DDoS attackers use IP spoofing to hide their real IP addresses and locations. Since spoofed IP addresses are generated randomly, this characteristic of randomness may be used to reveal the occurrence of DDoS attacks. Kulkarni's method uses *Kolmogorov complexity metrics* to measure the randomness of source IP addresses in network packet headers [14]. Wang et al. proposed the method that detects DDoS attack based on the protocol behavior of *SYN-FIN*(RST) pairs [7]. In the normal situation, the ratio of *SYN* and *FIN* is balanced because of the characteristic of the TCP 3-Way handshake. However, the ratio of *SYN* packet increases drastically during the SYN flooding attack. By monitoring sudden change of the ratio of *SYN* and *FIN*, the method detects SYN flooding attacks.

However, these approaches are based on the specific characteristics of the attacks such as a mismatch of "to-rate" and "from-rate", effect of IP spoofing, and unbalance of the ratio of *SYN* and *FIN* packet. Thus, these may not properly detect the attacks that use an undefined characteristic. For example, Gil's method is not applicable to detect attacks using IP spoofing since the method cannot discriminate legitimated packet and spoofed packet, and Wang's method is only applicable to SYN flooding attacks. On the other hand, the proposed detection model automatically generates detection rules using CTNT and SVM. The advantage of the proposed model will be discussed in the section 5.

3 Concentration Tendency of Network Traffic

In a normal situation, network traffic rate has specific characteristics. For example, SYN and FIN are in the ratio of 1:1 and TCP and UDP traffic are in the ratio of 9:1. However, in an abnormal situation such as SYN flooding and UDP flooding, these ratios are broken. Using these fact, CTNT method can effectively discriminate normal situation and abnormal situation. Thus, the traffic analysis result using CTNT method is good input feature of SVM. Details of the CTNT and the differences of normal traffic and attack traffic are explained in section 3.1 and 3.2.

3.1 Concentration Tendency of Network Traffic

The Internet provides the users with various types of network services such as WWW, E-mail, FTP, P2P, streaming services, and so on. However, network traffics which are found at endpoint servers have specific characteristics according to the services they provide. CTNT (Concentration Tendency of Network Traffic) is defined as a phenomenon that network traffics are mainly composed of one or more specific types of network packets. For instance, almost TCP packets have ACK flags in their headers during their connection sessions. Moreover, since the Internet has dominant network services such as WWW, E-mail, FTP which are dependent on specific network protocols, CTNT can be found on not only endpoint clients and servers but also core backbone networks [15].

To analyze network traffics on the Web servers in case that various types of DDoS attacks occur, we consider these CTNT as TCP flag rate and IP protocol rate [10]. They examine the occurrence rate of a specific type of packets within the stream of monitored network traffic. TCP flag rate is defined in the following equation.

$$R_{td}[F \; i \mid o] = \frac{\sum flag\,(F) \; in \; a\,TCP \; header}{\sum TCP \; packets} \tag{1}$$

TCP flag rate means the ratio of the number of a specific TCP flag to the total number of TCP packets. In the equation (1), a TCP flag '*F*' can be one of *SYN, FIN, RST, ACK, PSH, URG,* and *NULL*, and '*td*' is the time interval used to calculate the value. In this paper, we omit the time duration '*td*' when the interval is one. The direction of network traffic is expressed as '*i*' (inbound) and '*o*' (outbound).

$$R_{td}[[TCP|UDP|ICMP]\,i \mid o] = \frac{\sum[TCP|UDP|ICMP]\,packets}{\sum IP \; packets} \tag{2}$$

IP protocol rate is defined in equation (2). It means the ratio of specific Transport-Layer protocol (e.g. TCP, UDP, and ICMP) packets to total Network-Layer (IP) protocol packets.

3.2 Network Traffic Changes Under DDoS Attacks

In this section, we analyze normal Web traffic and DDoS attack traffic using the CTNT and show differences between them. Since web service is based on TCP connection, the number of HTTP requests in a TCP session (*R/C*: Requests per connection) and the number of TCP sessions simultaneously established (*SC*: Simultaneous Connection) are the key features of web traffic in terms of network traffic analysis. Thus, we can simulate various web traffic environments by adjusting these two features (*R/C* and *SC*).

In the experiments, we used *SPECweb99* as web traffic generating tool [16]. It sends HTTP requests to the Web server and receives HTTP replies from the Web server like the real Web browsers do. Fig. 1 shows the experimental results of *SPECweb99*. We changed *SC* to 5, 10, 50, 100, and 150, and *R/C* to 1, 2, 5, and 10. As a result, the experiments show that normal Web service traffic has a constant pattern with regardless of *SC*, *R/C*, and time. The resulting rate of *SYN* and *FIN* is almost identical. The other distinguishing result is that the rate of *ACK* is very high. It's because HTTP is based on TCP which is a connection-oriented protocol. These results show that network traffic of normal Web services has a specific pattern.

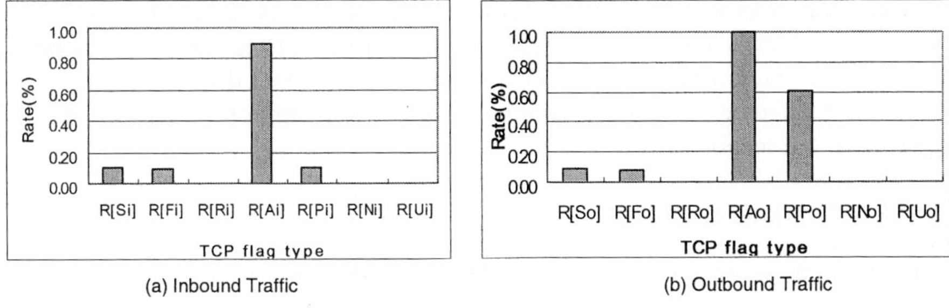

(a) Inbound Traffic (b) Outbound Traffic

Fig. 1. Web service traffic (average value) using *SPECweb99*

Fig. 2 shows the change of network traffic when a SYN flooding attacks occur. We generate Web service traffic during 72 seconds after 10th second from start the simulation, and a SYN flooding attack was generated during 40 seconds after 17th second from start the generation of the Web service traffic. As shown in Fig. 2-(a), the rates of *SYN* and *URG* increased to almost 1.0 and the rates of other flags, especially *ACK* rate, decreased to almost 0.0 during SYN flooding attacks.

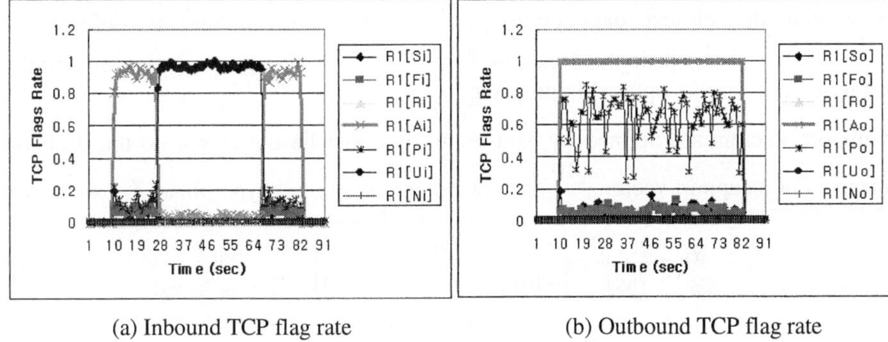

(a) Inbound TCP flag rate (b) Outbound TCP flag rate

Fig. 2. SYN flooding attacks against the Web server. Under SYN flooding attacks, the rates of *SYN* and *ACK* of inbound traffic change significantly.

Furthermore, we can also see big changes of network traffic during other types of DDoS attacks such as ICMP flooding attacks or UDP flooding attacks [8], [9].

4 Support Vector Machine

We have chosen Support Vector Machine (SVM) among various other machine learning algorithms as the focus of this paper. Support Vector Machine (SVM) is a learning machine that plots the training vectors in high-dimensional feature space, and labels each vector by its class. SVM classifies data by determining a set of support vectors, which are members of the set of training inputs that outline a hyper plane in feature space. The SVM is based on the idea of structural risk minimization, which minimizes the generalization error, i.e. true error on unseen examples. The number of free parameters used in the SVM depends on the margin that separates the data points to classes but not on the number of input features. Thus SVM does not require a reduction in the number of features in order to avoid over fitting [17]. Details of SVM are explained in section 4.1.

4.1 SVM for Categorization

In this section we review some basic ideas of SVM. Given the training data set $\{(x_i, d_i)\}_{i=1}^N$ with input data $x_i \in R^N$ and corresponding binary class labels $d_i \in \{-1,1\}$, the SVM classifier formulation starts from the following assumption. The classes represented by the subset $d_i = 1$ and $d_i = -1$ are linearly separable, where $\exists w \in R^N$, $b \in R$ such that

$$\exists w,b \quad s.t \quad \begin{Bmatrix} w^T x_i + b > 0 & for \ d_i = +1 \\ w^T x_i + b < 0 & for \ d_i = -1 \end{Bmatrix} \tag{3}$$

The goal of SVM is to find an optimal hyperplane for which the margin of separation , ρ , is maximized. ρ is defined by the separation between the separating hyperplane and the closest data point. If the optimal hyperplane is defined by $(w_0^T \cdot x) + b_0 = 0$, then the function $g(x) = w_0^T \cdot x + b_0$ gives a measure of the distance from x to the optimal hyperplane.

Support Vectors are defined by data points $x^{(s)}$ that lie the closest to the decision surface. For a support vector $x^{(s)}$ and the canonical optimal hyperplane g , we have

$$r = \frac{g(x^s)}{\|w_0\|} = \begin{Bmatrix} +1/\|w_0\| & for \ d^{(s)} = +1 \\ -1/\|w_0\| & for \ d^{(s)} = -1 \end{Bmatrix} \tag{4}$$

Since, the margin of separation is $\rho \propto \frac{1}{\|w_0\|}$. $\|w_0\|$ should be minimal to achieve the maximal separation margin. Mathematical formulation for finding the canonical optimal separation hyperplane, given the training data set $\{(x_i, d_i)\}_{i=1}^N$, solves the following quadratic problem

$$\begin{Bmatrix} \min \tau(\omega, \xi) = \frac{1}{2}\|w\|^2 + C\sum_{i=1}^{l} \zeta_i \\ s.t \quad d_i(w^T x_i + b) \geq 1 - \zeta_i \quad for \quad \zeta_i \geq 0, \quad i = 1, \ldots, l \end{Bmatrix} \tag{5}$$

Note that the global minimum of above problem must exist, because $\Phi(w) = \frac{1}{2}\|w_0\|^2$ is convex in w and the constrains are linear in w and b. This constrained optimization problem is dealt with by introducing Lagrange multipliers $a_i \geq 0$ and a Lagrangian function given by

$$L(w,b,\zeta,a,v)=\tau(w,\zeta)-\sum_{i=1}^{l}a_i\left[d_i(w_i^T x_i+b)-1+\zeta_k\right]-\sum_{i=1}^{l}v_i\zeta_i \tag{6}$$

which leads to

$$\frac{\partial L}{\partial w}=0 \Leftrightarrow w-\sum_{i=1}^{l}a_i d_i x_i=0 \quad (\therefore w=\sum_{i=1}^{l}a_i d_i x_i) \tag{7}$$

$$\frac{\partial L}{\partial b}=0 \Leftrightarrow \sum_{i=1}^{l}a_i d_i=0 \tag{8}$$

The solution vector thus has an expansion in terms of a subset of the training patterns, namely those patterns whose a_i is non-zero, called Support Vectors. By the Karush-Kuhn-Tucker complementarity conditions, we have,

$$a_i\left[d_i\left(w^T x_i+b\right)-1\right]=0 \quad for \quad i=1,\ldots,N \tag{9}$$

by substituting (7),(8) and (9) into equation (6), find multipliers a_i for which

$$\max\Theta(a)=\sum_{i=1}^{l}a_i-\frac{1}{2}\sum_{i=1}^{l}\sum_{i=1}^{l}a_i a_j d_i d_i\left\langle x_i\cdot x_j\right\rangle \tag{10}$$

$$s.t. \quad 0\le a_i\le c, \quad i=1,\ldots,l \quad and \quad \sum_{i=1}^{l}a_i y_i=0 \tag{11}$$

The hyperplane decision function can thus be written as

$$f(x)=\operatorname{sgn}\left(\sum y_i a_i\cdot(x\cdot x_i)+b\right) \tag{12}$$

where b is computed using (9).

To construct the SVM, the optimal hyperplane algorithm has to be augmented by a method for computing dot products in feature spaces nonlinearly related to input space. The basic idea is to map the data into some other dot product space (called the feature space) F via a nonlinear map Φ, and to perform the above linear algorithm in F, i.e nonseparable data $\{(x_i,d_i)\}_{i=1}^{N}$, where $x_i\in R_N$, $d_i\in\{+1,-1\}$, preprocess the data with,

$$\Phi: R^N\rightarrow\Theta(x) \quad where \quad N<<\dim(F) \tag{13}$$

Here w and $x_i$are not calculated. According to Mercer's theorem,

$$\left(\Phi(x_i)\cdot\Phi(x_j)\right)=K\left(x_j,x_j\right) \tag{14}$$

and $K(x, y)$ can be computed easily on the input space. Finally the nonlinear SVM classifier becomes

$$f(x)=\operatorname{sgn}\left(\sum_{i=1}^{l}a_i d_i K(x_i\cdot x)+b\right) \tag{15}$$

5 Experiments

5.1 DDoS Detection Process

Fig. 3 shows the overall composition of the DDoS detection process.

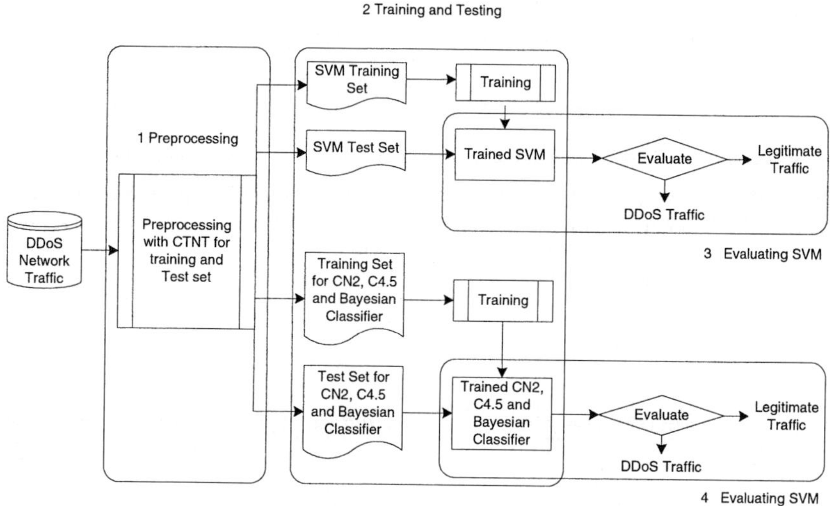

Fig. 3. Overall composition of DDoS detection process

It is composed of two steps. One is the preprocessing step, and the other is the training and testing step. In the preprocessing step, it captures raw network traffic from both DDoS and legitimate network traffics, and extracts features from the captured raw network traffic using CTNT method for each training and test set. For both training and testing, we used 10 features; $R_1[S_i]$, $R_1[F_i]$, $R_1[R_i]$, $R_1[A_i]$, $R_1[P_i]$, $R_1[U_i]$, $R_1[N_i]$, $R_1[TCP_i]$, $R_1[UDP_i]$, and $R_1[ICMP_i]$. In the training and testing step, they are trained by each machine using the training set. To train the machine, we classify input packets of the training set as *attack (-1)* and *normal (+1)*. Normal web traffic was categorized as *normal*, and the various DDoS attack traffic was categorized as *attack*. The trained machines evaluate test sets, and discriminate legitimate traffic and DDoS traffic. In the experiments, we used two different machine learning tools; mySVM [17] and ML v2.0 [18]. mySVM is used for SVM and ML v2. is utilized for CN2(the rule learning algorithm), C4.5(the tree learning algorithm), and Bayesian Classifier(the probabilistic learning algorithm).

5.2 Experimental Environment

Our traffic monitor was developed with the network packet capturing library *libpcap* [19]. It is divided into two modules. One is the module for capturing network traffic and calculating TCP flag rate and protocol rate from the monitored network, and the other is the DDoS attack detection module tuned by the support vector machine. The CTNT analyzer is located on the adjacent site of a target Web server and captures both inbound and outbound network traffic packets through an Ethernet hub, and then calculates TCP flag rate and protocol rate in every second.

Web clients are composed of four hosts using *SPECweb99* to generate normal web traffic toward an *Apache* web server [16]. *TFN2K* is use to generate DDoS attack traffic toward the web server [20]. *TFN2K* can generate various DDoS attacks such as TCP/SYN flooding attacks, UDP flooding attacks, ICMP flooding attacks and so on. All hosts in the simulated environment are Linux machines (Linux 2.4.18).

We collected network traffic for 100 seconds during training and testing. Web clients continually generated normal web traffic toward the web server, and various DDoS attacks occurred between the 25th and 75th seconds.

Table 1 shows the composition of the training set. The sizes of training sets were 400, 2,000, 4,000, 6,000, 8,000, 10,000, 12,000, 14,000, 16,000, and 18,000 for each feature. Each attack set was comprised of 5 different types of DDoS attacks (SYN, UDP, ICMP, TARGA3, MIX). For instance, in the case of T4, the *attack (-1)* class contained 60 traffic data for each type of DDoS attack, and 300 traffic data comprised the *normal (+1)* class. The number of test sets for performance testing was 10. Each test set contained the same amount of *attack* traffic and *normal* traffic.

Table 1. The composition of training set

Name	T1	T2	T3	T4	T5	T6	T7	T8	T9	T10
Attack	200	1,000	2,000	3,000	4,000	5,000	6,000	7,000	8,000	9,000
Normal	200	1,000	2,000	3,000	4,000	5,000	6,000	7,000	8,000	9,000
Total Size	400	2,000	4,000	6,000	8,000	10,000	12,000	14,000	16,000	18,000

5.3 Detection Performance Analysis

For each training set, we used dot and polynomial kernel with epsilon 0.01. The detection performance using SVM is shown in Fig. 4 and that using C4.5, CN2, and Bayesian Classifier is shown in Fig. 5.

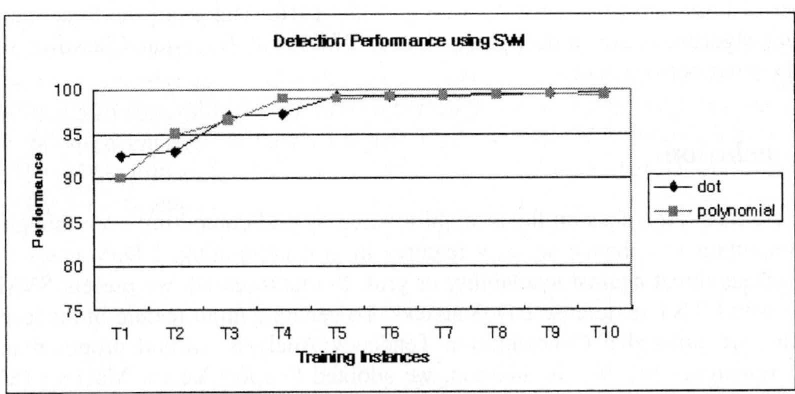

Fig. 4. Detection Performance using SVM. Polynomial kernel performed better than dot kernel. Overall performance was 99.5%.

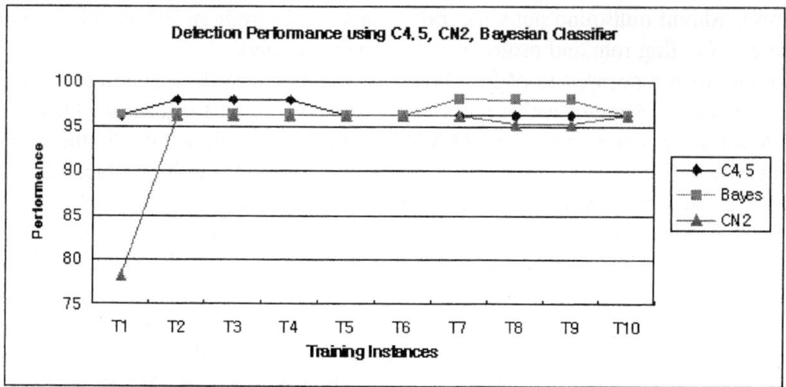

Fig. 5. Detection Performance using C4.5, CN2, and Bayesian Classifier. In our earlier research, Bayesian Classifier showed better performance. Overall performance was 97%.

Table 2. Performance of each training set with polynomial kernel

Name	T1	T2	T3	T4	T5	T6	T7	T8	T9	T10
Accuracy	0.950	0.965	0.990	0.990	0.991	0.992	0.994	0.995	0.993	0.994
Precision	0.978	0.969	0.994	0.993	0.997	0.995	0.996	0.998	0.998	0.998
Recall	0.920	0.960	0.985	0.986	0.985	0.988	0.991	0.991	0.998	0.990

As we can see in Fig. 4 and 5, SVM shows higher performance than CN2, C4.5, and Bayesian Classifier. In Figure 4, the detection performance is higher when more input data is used. When we used more than 8000 input data (T5), the overall detection performance is almost 100%. We used 1000 as capacity parameter and +0.01 as epsilon parameter which represents insensitivity value that prediction can deviate from the functional value without being penalized for both dot and polynomial kernel and degree 3 for polynomial kernel. Table 2 shows performance of each training set with polynomial kernel. In case of false alarm, our proposed scheme showed small number of false rate (below 0.5%). In Fig. 5, the performances of the three machine learning algorithms are almost same (below 97%), but Bayesian Classifier shows slightly better performance.

6 Conclusion

There are rare researches on the availability area of grid computing even though it is very important to enhance security features in grid computing. DDoS attack is the most serious threat against availability of grid. In this research, we present SVM approach with CTNT to defense DDoS attacks. To generate input feature of the learning machine, we utilized a Concentration Tendency Analysis method proposed in the earlier researches [8], [9]. In addition, we adopted Support Vector Machine (SVM) instead of CN2, C4.5 and the Bayesian Classifier to automatically generate detection rules in this research. Our studies reveal that SVM is the best choice for classification and SVM polynomial kernel is the best choice when compared to the others. We expect that our approach will be useful in providing an early detection of flooding attacks against grids.

However, our machine learning scheme does not have unsupervised feature. It may mean sometimes if our scheme meet a kind of unexpected situation, it is difficult it can work well or not. Thus, we need additional work using unsupervised learning method without pre-existing knowledge. In our future work, we will use other kernel function methods of SVM and various machine learning methods.

References

1. Garber, L.: Denial-of-Service Attacks Rip the Internet, IEEE Computer, vol. 33(4), (2000) 12-17
2. Houle, J.K., and Weaver, M.G.: Trends in Denial of Service Attack Technology, CERT Coordination Center, (2001)
3. Moore, D., Voelker, G.M., and Savage, S.: Inferring Internet Denial-of-Service Activity. In Proceedings of the 10th USENIX Symposium, (2001) 9-22
4. Xiang, Y., and Zhou, W.: Protect Grid from DDoS Attacks, Grid and Cooperative Computing, Lecture Notes in Computer Science(LNCS), Springer-Verlag, vol. 3251, (2004) 309-316
5. Gil, T.M, and Poletto, M.: MULTOPS: a data-structure for bandwidth attack detection, In Proceedings of the 10th USENIX Security Symposium, (2001) 23-38
6. Kulkarni, A.B., Bush, S.F., and Evans, S.C.: Detecting Distributed Denial-of-Service Attacks Using Kolmogorov Complexity Metrics. Technical report 2001CRD176, GE Research and Development Center, (2001)
7. Wang, H., Zhang, D., and Shin, K.G.: Detecting SYN Flooding Attacks, In Proceedings of IEEE INFOCOM – The Conference on Computer Communications, vol. 21, no. 1, (2002) 1530-1539
8. Lee, C., Noh, S., Choi, K., and Jung, G.: Characterizing DDoS Attacks with Traffic Rate Analysis, In Proceedings of the IADIS e-Society, vol. 1, (2003) 81-88
9. Noh, S., Lee, C., Choi, K., and Jung, K.: Detecting Distributed Denial of Service (DDoS) Attacks through Inductive Learning, Lecture Notes in Computer Science(LNCS), Springer-Verlag, vol. 2690, (2003) 286-295
10. Burges. C.: LA Tutorial on Support Vector Machines for Patter Recognition, Data Mining and Knowledge Discovery, Boston, 1588
11. Cristianini, N., Shawe-Taylor, J.: An Introduction to Support Vector Machines, Cambridge University (2000)
12. Seo, J., Lee, C., and Moon, J.: Defending DDoS Attacks using Network Traffic Analysis and Probabilistic Packet Drop, Grid and Cooperative Computing, Lecture Notes in Computer Science(LNCS), Springer-Verlag, vol. 3252, (2004) 390-397
13. Hwang, K., Kwok, Y., and Song, S.: GridSec: Trusted Grid Computing with Security Binding and Self –defense Against Network Worms and DDoS attacks, ICCS2005, Lecture Notes in Computer Science(LNCS), Springer-Verlag, vol. 3516, (2005) 187-195
14. Li, M., and Vitanyi, P.: An Introduction to Kolmogorov Complexity and Its Applications, Springer-Verlag, Section 7.6, (1997) 506-509
15. Paxson, V.: Growth Trends in Wide-Area TCP Connections, IEEE Network, vol. 8, (1994) 8-17

16. Standard Performance Evaluation Corporation. SPECweb99 Benchmark, available on-line: http://www.spec.org/osg/web99
17. Ruping S.: mySVM – a Support Vector Machine, University of Dortmund (2004)
18. Holder, L.: ML v2.0: Machine Learning Program Evaluator. available on-line: http://www-cse.uta.edu/~holder/ftp/ml2.0.tar.gz
19. Lawrence Berkeley National Labs Network Research Group. Libpcap
20. Packet Storm. Tribe Flood Network 2000 (TFN2K) DDoS tool, available on-line: http://packetstormsecurity.org/distributed/ TFN2k_Analysis-1.3.txt

Model Transformation Based Verification of Web Services Composition*

YanPing Yang[1], QingPing Tan[1], and Yong Xiao[2]

[1] School of Computer Science, National University of Defense Technology,
Changsha, P.R. China, 410073
yanpingyang@nudt.edu.cn
[2] National Lab of Parallel Distributed Processing,
Changsha, P.R. China, 410073
yongxiao@nudt.edu.cn

Abstract. Current Web services composition proposals, such as BPEL, BPSS, BPMN and WSCI, provide notations for describing the control and message flows in Web service collaborations. However, such proposals remain at the descriptive level, without providing any kind of mechanisms or tool support for verifying the composition specified in the proposed notations. In this paper, we present to analyze and verify Web services composition by using CP-nets. CP-nets combine the strengths of Petri nets with the expressive power of high-level programming and have sound mathematical semantics. These services composition proposals can be transformed by model transformation rules into CP-nets, which can be used to analyze the performance and to investigate behavioral properties by CP-nets specialized tools.

1 Introduction

Web services composition is an emerging paradigm for enabling application integration within and across organizational boundaries. Accordingly, a current trend is to express the logic of a composite web service using a business process modeling language tailored for web services. A landscape of such languages such as Business Process Modeling Language (BPML), Business Process Execution Language (BPEL) and Web service Choreography Interface (WSCI) has emerged and is continuously being enriched with new proposals from different vendors and coalitions. Practical experience indicates that the definition of real world Web services composition is a complex and error-prone process. However, all these proposals still remain at the descriptive level, without providing any kind of mechanisms or tool support for verifying the composition specified in the proposed notations.

Therefore, there is a growing interest for the verification techniques which enable designers to test and repair design errors even before actual running of the service, or allow designers to detect erroneous properties (such as deadlock and livelock) and formally verify whether the service process design does have certain desired properties (such as consistency with the conversation protocols of partner service).

* The paper is partially supported by the National Natural Science Foundation of China under Grant No.90104007, 60233020; the National High-Tech Research and Development Plan of China (863) under Grant No.2001AA113202, 2001AA113190, 2003AA001023.

H. Zhuge and G.C. Fox (Eds.): GCC 2005, LNCS 3795, pp. 71 – 76, 2005.

In this paper, we want to use Colored Petri Nets (CP-nets) [1] analysis and verification technique to raise the reliability of Web Services composition. CP-nets were formulated by Jensen [1] as a formally founded graphically oriented modeling language. CP-nets are useful for specifying, designing, and analyzing concurrent systems. In contrast to ordinary Petri nets, CP-nets provide a more compact way of modeling complex systems, which makes CP-nets a powerful language for modeling and analyzing industrial-sized systems. This is achieved by combining the strengths of Petri nets with the expressive power of high-level programming languages. Petri nets provide the constructions for specifying synchronization of concurrent processes, and the programming language provides the constructions for specifying and manipulating data values, and the latter point is very important to model business process.

Since Web service modeler may be unfamiliar with CP-nets, we provide translation rules of composition language into CP-nets and the techniques to analyze and verify them for investigating behavioral properties and techniques to simulate them to evaluate the performance of system.

The formal verification of Web Services composition based on transformation requires not only that the target model has the ability to verify the properties we need, but also that the transformation can transform the source model correctly and even effectively. So we verify the transformation itself based on some recognized criteria.

2 Analysis and Verification Approach

Fig.1 shows our analyses and verification approach. Web services composition description are translated into CP-nets, the input of Design/CPN (*http://www.daimi.au.dk/designCPN/*) or CPN tools (*http://www.daimi.au.dk/CPNtools/*), which are two outstanding tools with a variety of analysis techniques and computing tools for CP-nets. The formalization mainly concerns with the translation of composition specification into CP-net models. This is particularly important in discussions with Web services modelers unfamiliar with CP-nets.

The formal verification of Web Services composition based on transformation requires not only that the target model has the ability to verify the properties we need, but also that the transformation can transform the source model correctly and even effectively. So we verify the transformation itself based on the recognized criteria.

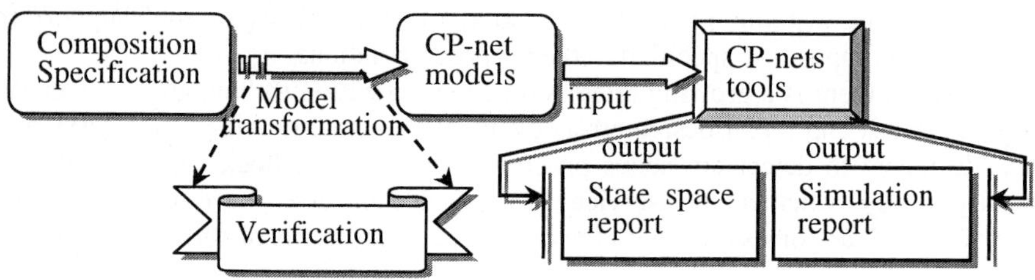

Fig. 1. Verification and analysis approach

CP-net models are executable. This implies that it is possible to investigate the behavior of the system by making simulations of the CP-net model. Simulations can well serve as a basis for investigating the performance of the considered system.
The state space method of CP-nets makes it possible to validate and verify the functional correctness of systems. The state space method relies on the computation of all reachable states and state changes of the system, and is based on an explicit state enumeration. By means of a constructed state space, behavioral properties of the system can be verified. The properties of CP-nets to be checked include boundness, deadlock-freedom, liveness, fairness, home, and application specific properties. The application specific properties are expressed as reachability of CP-nets. The properties of CP-nets mentioned above have their specific meaning in verifying Web services composition:

- ✓ Reachability – The possibility of reaching a given state. By formulate application specific properties as reachability of CP-net models, we can validate whether the models of the composition process can achieve the desired result.
- ✓ Boundness – The maximal and minimal number of tokens which may be located on the individual places in the markings. As the prototype of the composition process, if a place of it is *Control Place[14]*, then the number of tokens it contains is either o or 1, otherwise this indicates errors in the process. If a place of it is a *Message Place [14]*, then boundedness can be used to check whether the buffer overflows or not.
- ✓ Dead Transitions – The transitions which will never be enabled. There are no activities in the process that cannot be realized. If initially dead transitions exist, then the composition process is bad designed.
- ✓ Dead Marking – Markings having no enabled binding element. The final state of process instance is one of dead marking. If the number of dead markings reported by state space analysis tool is more than expected, then there must be errors in the design.
- ✓ Liveness – A set of binding elements remaining active. It is always possible to return to an activity if we wish. For instance, this might allow us to rectify previous mistakes.
- ✓ Home – About markings to which CP-net is always possible to return. It is always possible to return to a state before. For instance, to compare the results of applying different strategies to solve the same problem.
- ✓ Fairness – How often the individual transitions occur. Fairness properties can be used to show the execution numbers in each process. We can find the dead activity that will never be executed.
- ✓ Conservation – Tokens never destroyed. Certain tokens such as resources maintained in the system are never destroyed.

3 Verification of Transformation

The formal verification of Web Services composition based on model transformation requires not only that the target model language has the ability to verify the properties we need, but also that the transformation can transform the source model correctly and even effectively. In [12], the fundamental properties of a correct transformation are summarized as that the transformation should be complete, unique, syntactic correct, semantic correct and could terminate.

- ✓ Syntactic correctness, i.e., to guarantee that the generated model is a syntactically well–formed instance of the target language.
- ✓ Syntactic completeness is to completely cover the source language by transformation rules, i.e., to prove that there exists a corresponding element in the target model for each construct in the source language.
- ✓ Termination, i.e., to guarantee is that a model transformation will terminate.
- ✓ Uniqueness: As non-determinism is frequently used in the specification of model transformations, we also guarantee that the transformation yields a unique result.
- ✓ Semantic correctness: In theory, a straightforward correctness criterion would require to prove the semantic equivalence of source and target models. However, as model transformations may also define a projection from the source language to the target language with deliberate loss of information, semantic equivalence between models cannot always be proved. Instead we define correctness properties (which are typically transformation specific) that should be preserved by the transformation.

And for a transformation for verification, the performance requirement that the transformation should be effective should also be considered, i.e. the contents that need to be verified of the source model should be transformed to some properties of the target model that can be analyzed.

Because we transform the composition specification through traversing the xml document in a constructive way, the termination, completeness and uniqueness of the transformation can be easily proved. The syntactic correctness can be preserved by checking the generated nets against CP-net metamodel. For the verification technique of the semantic correctness and effectiveness of transformation, we propose to exploit Information Capacity presented in [16] to verify that there is no semantic information lost.

4 Related Works

Most of existing approaches [2-7] to verify business process are based on model checking techniques. Using Petri nets to model and verify business processes is another choice, and the discussion of the advantages and the disadvantages of the two approaches are out of scope.

For an overview of modeling business processes by means of Petri nets, we refer the reader to the work of Van der Aalst [8], Martens [9], Narayanan [10] and Stahl [11]. As we say above, because CP-nets combine the strengths of Petri nets with the expressive power of high-level programming languages, we claim that using the colored token of CP-nets to model different message and event type of business process are more natural. Table 1 shows the comparison between some existing approaches to business process verification.

Table 1. The comparison between some existing approaches to business process verification

Researchers	Specification	Formal Model	Tools	Transformation verification?
Koshkina	BPEL	Labelled Transition System	CWB[1]	No
Foster	BPEL	FSP-processes	LTSA toolkit[2]	No
Karamanolis	Abstract business process	FSP-processes	LTSA toolkit	No
Nakajima	WSFL	Promela	SPIN[3]	No
Koehler	Abstract business process	Nondeterministic Automata	NuSMV[4]	No
Stahl	BPEL	Petri net	LoLA[5]	No
Martens	BPEL	Petri net	Wombat4ws[6]	No
Narayanan	DAML-S	Petri net	KarmaSIM[7]	No
Our work	BPEL, WSCI	CP-nets	CPN tools[8]	yes

5 Conclusions

In this paper, we introduce an approach to verify and analyze Web Services composition based on transformation composition specification to CP-nets. These generated CP-net models can be analyzed, verified and simulated as prototypes of the former by many existing and specialized analysis and verification tools. As a correct transformation, we regard the semantic correctness and effectiveness as the fundamental requirement for transformation for verification, besides the completeness, uniqueness, termination and syntactic correctness.

We have analyze and verify the description written in BPEL (*http://www128.ibm.com/developerworks/library/ws-bpel/*) and WSCI (*http://ifr.sap.com/wsci/specification/wsci-spec-10.htm*) [13-15] using the approach reported in this paper. As future work, the back-annotation techniques from CP-nets are being considered.

References

1. K. Jensen: Colored Petri Nets Basic Concepts, Analysis Methods and Practical Use, Volume 1, 2 and 3, second edition. In: EATCS Monographs on Theoretical Computer Science. Springer-Verlag (1997).
2. H. Foster, S. Uchitel, J. Magee, and J. Kramer: Model-based verification of web service composition. In proceedings of the Eighteenth IEEE International Conference on Automated Software Engineering (ASE'03), IEEE Computer Society Press (2003)152-162.

---

[1] http://homepages.inf.ed.ac.uk/perdita/cwb
[2] http://www.doc.ic.ac.uk/jnm/book/ltsa/LTSA.html
[3] http://spinroot.com/spin/whatispin.html
[4] http://nusmv.irst.itc.it/
[5] http://www.mathematik.uni-kl.de/~lola/
[6] http://www.informatik.hu-berlin.de/top/wombat/
[7] http://www.ai.sri.com/daml/services/
[8] http://www.daimi.au.dk/CPNtools/

3. S. Nakajima: Verification of Web Service Flows with Model-Checking Techniques. In proceedings of the First International Symposium on Cyber Worlds (CW'02). IEEE Computer Society Press (2002) 378-385.
4. C. Karamanolis, D. Giannakopoulou, J. Magee, and S.M. Wheater: Model checking of workflow schemas. In proceedings of the 4th International Enterprise Distributed Object Computing Conference (EDOC'00). IEEE Computer Society Press (2000) 170-179.
5. W. Visser, K. Havelund, G. Brat, S. Spark, and F. Lerda: Model checking programs. In proceedings of the 15th IEEE International Conference on Automated Software Engineering (ASE 2000). IEEE Computer Society Press (2000) 203-232.
6. J. Koehler, G. Tirenni, and S. Kumaran: From business process model to consistent implementation: a case study for formal verification methods. In proceedings of the 6th International Enterprise Distributed Object Computing Conference (EDOC02). IEEE Computer Society Press (2002) 96-106.
7. M. Koshkina: Verification of business processes for web services. Master's thesis, York University, 2003.
8. W.M.P. van der Aalst: Verification of workflow nets. In: Pierre Azéma, Gianfranco Balbo (Eds.): Application and Theory of Petri Nets 1997. Lecture Notes in Computer Science, Vol. 1248. Springer-Verlag, Berlin Heidelberg New York (1997) 407-426.
9. A. Martens.: Distributed Business Processes -- Modeling and Verification by help of Web Services. PhD thesis, Humboldt-Universit¨at zu Berlin. Available at http://www. informatik. hu-berlin.de/top/download/documents/ pdf/Mar03.pdf. July 2003.
10. S. Narayanan and S. McIlraith: Analysis and simulation of Web services. In Special issue: The Semantic Web: an evolution for a revolution. Computer Networks: The International Journal of Computer and Telecommunications Networking, vol. 42, Elsevier North-Holland, Inc. New York (2003) 675-693.
11. Christian Stahl: Transformation von BPEL4WS in Petrinetze. Diplomarbeit, Humboldt-UniversitÄat zu Berlin, April 2004.
12. D. Varró, A. Pataricza: Automated Formal Verification of Model Transformations. In proceedings of Workshop on Critical Systems Development with UML (CSDUML 2003), Technische Universitat Munchen (2003) 63-78.
13. Y. Yang, Q. Tan, J. Yu, and F. Liu: Transformation BPEL to CP-Nets for Verifying Web services Composition. To appear in proceedings of the International Conference on Next generation Web services Practices (NWeSP'05), IEEE Computer Society Press (2005).
14. Y. Yang, Q. Tan, and Y. Xiao: Verifying Web Services Composition. To appear in proceedings of eCOMO workshop of the 24th International Conference on Conceptual Modeling (ER2005). Springer-Verlag Berlin Heidelberg New York (2005) 358-367.
15. Y. Yang, Q. Tan and Y. Xiao: Verifying Web Services Composition Based on Hierarchical Colored Petri Nets. To appear in proceedings of IHIS workshop of the 14th ACM Conference on Information and Knowledge Management (CIKM05). ACM (2005).
16. R. J. Miller, Y. E. Ioannidis, and R.Ramakrishnan: The Use of Information Capacity in Schema Integration and Translation. In: Rakesh Agrawal, Seán Baker, David A. Bell (Eds.): proceedings of the 19th Very Large Data Bases Conference. Morgan Kaufmann (1993) 120-133.

A Worm Behavioral Approach to Susceptible Host Detection

BaiLing Wang, BinXing Fang, and XiaoChun Yun

Research Center of Computer Network and Information Security Technology,
Harbin Institute of Technology, Harbin 150001, China
{wbl, fbx, yxc}@hit.edu.cn
http://www.hit.edu.cn

Abstract. A new detection approach based on worm behaviors for IDS anti-worm is presented. By the method, the susceptible hosts probed by worms can be detected, and then an immediate counter-attack to the susceptible host can be proposed. As a case study, a simulation on the IDS-based anti-worm counter-attacking the malicious worm is given, which shows the new containment is much more effective and bring less traffic to network than the traditional one. It can be used as a reference for Grid security infrastructure.

1 Introduction

Recent virus and worm outbreak, such as the *Slammer* worm in August 2003 and the *Sasser* worm in April 2004, have demonstrated that network computers continue to be vulnerable to new attacks. Security flaws still exist. First, software is often written in an unsecured manner. Also, when vulnerabilities are announced with corresponding software patches, many people are slow to apply patches to their computers for various practical reasons[1]. Weakly protected computers can be compromised, putting the entire community at risk, including secured computers that can still be impacted by the traffic effects of a worm outbreak. Besides, the non real-time characteristics of current defense approaches such as antivirus software render it highly ineffective against zero-day worms[2] (such as Witty, which appeared 1day after the exploited vulnerability was announced).

The worm will be the most thwart to Internet, to Grid[3], and to the P2P systems as P2P hosts are sharing data to the system[4]. A worm will struggle to find new holes, and the impact would be obvious in the information and knowledge age[5].

Castaneda proposed an IDS based anti-worm where an IDS or similar device intercept attack messages and counter-attacks[6]. Furthermore, an IDS-based anti-worm involves the use of dedicated intrusion detection sensors throughout the Internet, scanning suspected packets and identifying the sender and receiver for immunization. This scheme was proposed and simulated in [7] and [8]. But, in the traditional IDSs, there is a common fault that the sensors could only identify the infected hosts (the senders), and, after a patching worm occupying the victim, the IDS-based strike-back can only replace an infectious attempt monitored by an IDS, therefore limiting its effectiveness.

H. Zhuge and G.C. Fox (Eds.): GCC 2005, LNCS 3795, pp. 77 – 83, 2005.

Based on the worm behavior, we proposed a susceptible hosts detection approach for IDS-Based anti-worm, by which the intrusion detection sensors could not only identify the infected hosts (the senders), but the susceptible hosts (the receivers).

2 Susceptible Hosts Detection Approach for IDS-Based Anti-worm

The approach to the susceptible host detection problem introduced in this section relies on behavioral patterns of worms that reflect application communications typical of worms. It differs from those used in contemporary enterprise postures in two ways. The first characteristic of contemporary postures is the reliance on a particular type of signature-based intrusion detection. In the contemporary case, a signature is a regular expression known a prior (e.g., [9]). Most signatures deployed in current intrusion detection systems (IDSs) focus on detecting specific regular expressions in network packets. The use of a previously unknown version of an exploit will evade detection.

The behavioral detection approach contrasts from this form of signature-based detection. Besides looking for fixed regular expressions in payloads, the behavioral approach focuses on detecting patterns at a higher level of abstraction. Behavioral patterns can be used to detect the vulnerable hosts that worms try to attack, and then we can send out IDS-Based anti-worm to counter attack the vulnerable host.

2.1 Behavioral Detection Mechanism

The attribute of worms is evident in their communication patterns. In order to infect a victim an infected host must probe and exploit it in some way. That means the worm must send some data across the network that is engineered to force the victim to enable infection. The worm code itself also has to be placed on the victim (assuming it's not already present). Both of these events have a network footprint. The data must be sent from the infecting host to the victim, and the victim gets the worm code either from the infecting host or some other host on thc network. The property that the exploit (and possibly the worm code) is communicated from the infecting host to the target host is expressed as a link feature.

Definitions. If a worm sends out a request packet or every attempt to the target, just like the ICMP echo request, an **Event** e is created. For any event e, it includes the request e_{req} and the reply e_{res}. The event e arises when and only when the signatures of e_{req} and e_{res} are both detected. If e_{res} is null, the event e should be ignored.

Figure 1 shows a simplified communication pattern as a worm spreads from the infected node to the victim node, including an ICMP echo request and a reply followed by a TCP connection to port 135, just like the infection of worm Welchia. If either transaction in the communication is not completed or if the transactions are not in order, the infection does not spread. This communication consists of:

Event I:

- an ICMP echo request from a to b, followed by
- an ICMP echo reply from b to a, followed by

Event II:

- a TCP SYN from a to b, followed by
- a TCP SYN/ACK from a to b, followed by

Event III:

- an exploit and worm code from a to b.
- null

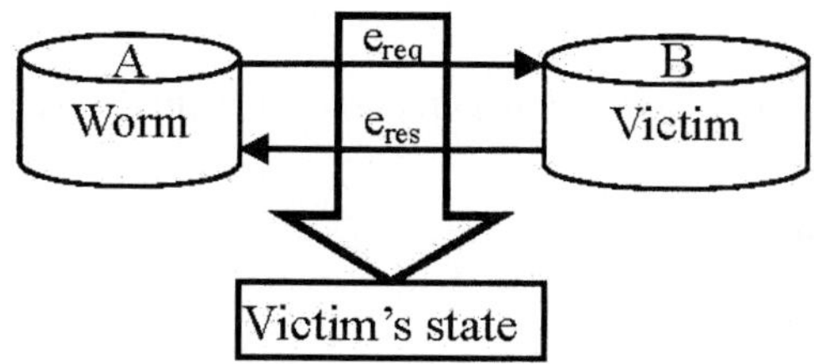

Fig. 1. Behavior detection mechanism: simplified worm behavior patterns including an ICMP echo request and a reply followed by a TCP connection to port 135

Suppose all the packets are intercepted by our probe. If event I is finished normally, the probe detects node B is online; if event II is finished normally, the probe detects TCP port 135 is open on node B; if event III is finished normally, the probe detects node B is attacked from node A. So based on the known worm behavior predicate, we can estimate the state of node B and the evolvement of the infection.

2.2 Worm Behavior Taxonomy

We class the worm behavior as scan behavior, attack behavior, control behavior, transmitting behavior and provoking behavior in one infection.

Scan Behavior: As the start of one infection, worm sends a series of scans to probe the target node to find whether the victim is online or whether the vulnerabilities exist on the victim. The request packet and the reply packet compose the worm scan behavior. For example, worm Welchia probes the victim by sending an ICMP request packet to detect whether the target is online.

Attack Behavior: Worm enters the victim by exploiting the vulnerable host, and the series of packets used in exploiting action compose the worm attack behavior. From the protocol point of view, the scan behavior and the attack behavior can be integrated into one behavior, for instance worm Nidma's scan behavior and attack behavior are integrated, but worm Welchia's aren't.

Control Behavior: After entering the vulnerable host, worm can control the victim by running shell command on the victim. The process transferring the commands from the worm to the victim is control behavior. The control behavior maybe arise in a new connection, for example, after entering the victim, worm MSBlaster connects the TCP port 4444 on the victim, and worm Welchia reverse connects the TCP port 707 on the attacker to create the control connection.

File Transfer Behavior: Worm often uses TFTP protocol to transfer worm code, attack tools and so on onto the victim, and the transfer process is file transfer behavior.

Some special examples like worm CodeRed don't have this behavior by integrating it into the attack behavior.

Provoke Behavior: The provoke behavior can let the worm copy on the victim in working state. For example, worm Nimda sends HTTP request "GET /scripts/Admin.dll HTTP/1.0" to provoke the worm copy, and worm Sasser and worm MSBlaster provoke the worm copy by sending the command through the control connection.

Sometimes, some of these behaviors is absent or incorporated, but the order can't be reversed.

Definitions. Suppose a behavior B is composed of n (n>0) events $E_n=\{e_1, e_2,\ldots e_n\}$, then:

Necessary Events Set:

$$\exists E_n'\left(E_n' \subseteq E_n\right)$$

$$\ni\left(\forall e \in E_n'\right)(B \rightarrow e) \wedge \forall e\left(\left(e \notin E_n'\right) \wedge \left(e \in E_n\right)\right)(B \mapsto e)$$

Optional Events Set:

$$\exists E_n''\left(\left(E_n' \subseteq E_n\right) \wedge \left(E_n' \cap E_n'' = \varnothing\right)\right),$$

$$\ni\left(\bigwedge_{e_i \in E_n'} e_i \bigwedge_{e_j \in E_n''} e_j \rightarrow B\right) \wedge \left(\left(\forall e_k \in E_n''\right)\left(\bigwedge_{e_i \in E_n'} e_i \bigwedge_{e_j \in E_n''-e_k} e_j \mapsto B\right)\right)$$

Optional Events Set Cluster:

$$\Gamma = \left\{E^* \mid E^* \text{is a Optional Events Set}\right\}$$

Behavior B arises if and only if all of events in necessary events set E_n' arise and all of events in optional events set E_n'' ($E_n'' \in \Gamma$) arise. E_n' is one and only, so if one of the events in E_n' is held back, the worm infection will not spread. Furthermore, let $E_S', E_A', E_C', E_T', E_P'$ denote the necessary events set of the scan behavior, the attack behavior, the control behavior, the file transfer behavior and the provoke behavior, then the necessary events set of the infection satisfies:

$$\xi = E_S' \cup E_A' \cup E_C' \cup E_T' \cup E_P' .$$

So if one of the events in ξ is held back, the worm infection will not spread.

Definitions. Suppose behavior B is composed of two events e_1 and e_2, and behavior B arises if and only if event e_1 and event e_2 both arise, then event e_1, event e_2 and behavior B is "AND" relation. By contraries, behavior B arises if one of the two events arises, event e_1, event e_2 and behavior B is "OR" relation. Fig. 2 is the expression of AND-OR relation in figure.

Extend the AND-OR relation to the whole infection process, it generates an AND-OR tree. From the AND-OR tree, we can find which node (event) is necessary, and which one is optional, and furthermore, we can conclude how to stop the infection by holding back one of the necessary evens.

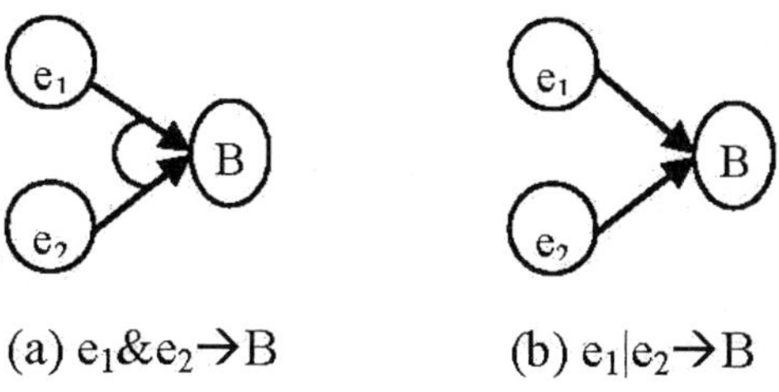

Fig. 2. AND-OR relation expression in figure

2.3 A Case Study on Worm Behavior Analysis

In this part, we will give an example of behavioral AND-OR tree as a case study. As we know, the infection process of worm Welchia is:

Scan Behavior: Sends an ICMP echo request, or PING, to check whether the constructed IP address is an active machine on the network.

Attack Behavior: Once the worm identifies a machine as being active on the network, it will either send data to TCP port 135, which exploits the DCOM RPC vulnerability, or it will send data to TCP port 80 to exploit the WebDav vulnerability.

Control Behavior: Creates a remote shell on the vulnerable host, which reconnects to the attacking computer on a random TCP port, between 666 and 765, to receive instructions.

Transfer Behavior: Launches the TFTP server on the attacking machine and instructs the victim machine to connect and download Dllhost.exe and Svchost.exe from the attacking machine. If the %System%\dllcache\tftpd.exe file exists, the worm may not download svchost.exe.

Provoke Behavior: Instruct the victim machine to run dllhost.exe.

So we can gain the followings:

$$\begin{cases} E_S' = \{s\}, E_S'' = \Phi \\ E_A' = \Phi, E_{A1}'' = \{a_1\}, E_{A2}'' = \{a_2\}, \\ \quad \Gamma_A = \{E_{A1}'', E_{A2}''\} \\ E_C' = \Phi, E_{C666}'' = \{c666\}, \cdots, E_{C765}'' = \{c765\}, \\ \quad \Gamma_C = \{E_{C666}'', E_{C667}'', \cdots E_{C765}''\} \\ E_T' = \{t_1, t_2\}, E_T'' = \Phi \\ E_P' = \{p\}, E_s'' = \Phi \end{cases}$$

The corresponding infection AND-OR tree is expressed as figure 3. So we can distinctly know which leaf (node) in the tree is necessary, and if we hold back these events, the infection will not spread.

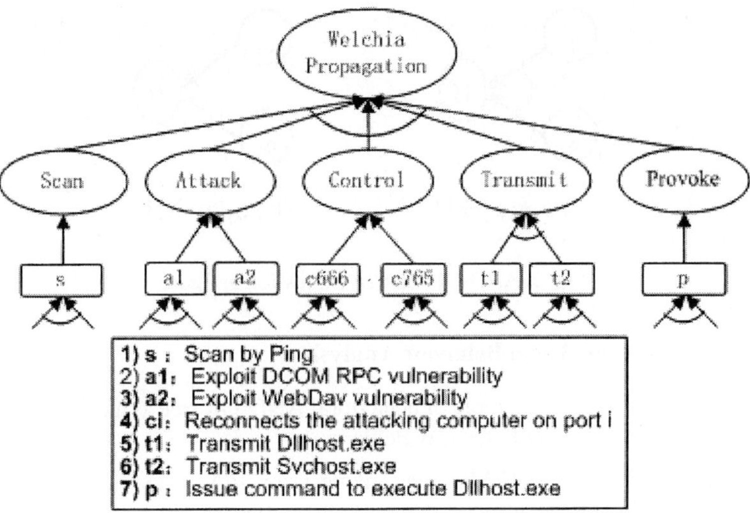

Fig. 3. Worm Welchia behavioral AND-OR tree

3 Simulation Experiments

We try to simulate a worm similar to the Code Red worm broke out on July 19th, 2001. Assume that the vulnerable population is N = 360,000, and the infected host number I_0 = 10 in the initial time. Suppose 25 percent of infected hosts will be detected by IDS

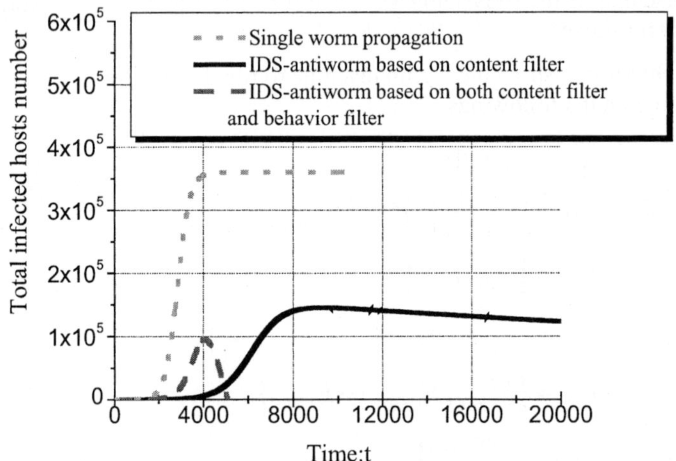

Fig. 4. Simulation of Code Red Propagation with different countermeasures. (Suppose 25 percent of the infected hosts will be detected by content-signature-based IDS sensors and 25 percent of the new probed susceptible hosts will be detected by behavior-signature-based IDS sensors. We also assume that the vulnerable population is N = 360, 000, and the infected host number I_0 = 10 in the initial time).

sensors and, if using the behavior-based detection technology, 25 percent of the new probed susceptible hosts will be detected per unit time. Referring to the mentioned above parameters, we simulate the propagation and plot it in Fig. 4.

There are three curves in Fig. 4 the single worm propagation without any countermeasure, the two worms' propagation under the countermeasure of content filter pattern and the propagation under the countermeasure of both the filter patterns. Comparing the curves, the one based on the IDS with both filter patterns is much better than that based on the IDS only with the content filter pattern.

4 Conclusions

The most significant contributions of this paper are the presentations of the worm behavior detection approach, which help IDS sensors to identify much more susceptible hosts. Based on the worm behavioral taxonomy, an IDS can affirm what state the susceptible hosts are in, and play its best card to attack and recover it.

However, the proposed anti-worms in their current forms have several unresolved issues and limitations, such as the legal issues, that are almost certain to cause serious deployment problems. In spite of these probably serious limitations, we proposed the susceptible hosts detection method based on worm behaviors. The techniques developed here would certainly be interesting to other researchers for studying future anti-worms and for inventing new techniques.

References

1. Thomas M. Chen: Trends in Viruses and Worms. The Internet Protocol Journal. Pages 23-33, Volume 6, No. 3, September 2003.
2. Levy, E. Approaching Zero, In IEEE Security & Privacy Magazine, Volume 2, Issue 4, pages 65-66. 2004.
3. Hwang, K., Kwok, Y.K., Song, S.S.: GridSec: Trusted Grid Computing with Security Binding and Self-defense Against Network Worms and DDoS Attacks. International Workshop on Grid Computing Security and Resource Management (GSRM'05)
4. Yu, W.: Analyze the Worm-based Attack in Large Scale P2P Networks, Proceedings of the Eighth IEEE International Symposium on High Assurance Systems Engineering (HASE'04). 2004
5. Zhuge, H., Shi, X.: Fighting Epistemology in Knowledge and Information Age, IEEE Computer, 36 (10) (2003) 114-116.
6. Castaneda, F., et al.: WORM vs. WORM: Preliminary Study of an Active Counter-Attack Mechanism. In Proceedings of ACM Workshop on Rapid Malcode (WORM'04), Oct 2004.
7. Mullen, T.: Defending your right to defend: Considerations of an automated strike-back technology. http://www.hammerofgod.com/strikeback.txt, October 2002.
8. Provos, N.: A virtual honeypot framework. CITI Technical Report 03-1, October 2003.
9. http://www.snort.org/.

A Dynamic Web Service Selection Strategy with QoS Global Optimization Based on Multi-objective Genetic Algorithm*

Shulei Liu, Yunxiang Liu, Ning Jing, Guifen Tang, and Yu Tang

College of Electronic Science and Engineering,
National University of Defense Technology,
ChangSha, HuNan, P.R. China
smartslliu@yahoo.com.cn

Abstract. Web Service selection is an important issue in dynamic Web Service composition. The existing approaches are QoS local optimization based. They cannot achieve global constraints and preferences set by user. In general, service selection with QoS global optimization is a NP-complete problem. So, we propose a model of Web Service selection with QoS global optimization and convert this NP-complete problem into a multi-objective optimization problem with constraints. Based on intelligent optimal theory of multi-objective Genetic Algorithm, we propose a strategy GODSS to realize Web Service selection with QoS global optimization.

1 Introduction

The emergence of Web services has led to more interest into Web service composition, and the process-driven composition of Web Services is emerging as a promising approach[1]. In this approach, the logic of Web Service's interactions is expressed as a process model[2] which is made up of service nodes, and each node must fulfill its own task. In Web, many Web Services may have same function, so it is very important to select specific service to form an executable service process.

The existing approaches on service selection of dynamic Web Service composition are almost QoS locally optimal based[3,4,5], and can not resolve the problem of Web Service selection with Qos global optimization, for example, finding an executable services process which is to be operated with ultra-low cost and ultra-short time on the condition of reliability exceeding 80% . To resolve the deficiency of the existing approaches, we propose a strategy GODSS (Global Optimization of Dynamic Web Service Selection) based on multi-objective Genetic Algorithm. We suppose that QoS parameters of each specific service are static when GODSS is running.

In section 2, we discuss related works; in section 3, we propose a model of Web Service selection with QoS global optimization; in section 4, we describe the steps of GODSS; section 5 discuss the use of GODSS in complex service composition process; section 6 draw some conclusions and make some expectations.

* This research is supported in part by the National High Technology Research and Development Program of China under grants No.2002AA134010 and No.2003AA135110.

H. Zhuge and G.C. Fox (Eds.): GCC 2005, LNCS 3795, pp. 84–89, 2005.

2 Relate Works

The majority of existing approaches on services selection[3,4,5] are locally optimal based. Although these approaches take QoS information of every service node into account, it cannot resolve the problem of QoS global optimization.

With regard to the problem of QoS global optimization, the existing works are relatively limited. In [2,6], each constraint parameter of QoS in service is linear weighted and converted into an objective function, and they make use of linear programming to resolve the problem of QoS global optimization in service composition. The solution of weighted sum is highly sensitive to the weights vector, and linear programming requires that objective functions and constraints are linear, to some extent practicability of this method is restricted.

3 Model of QoS Global Optimization in Service Selection

Let $G(N,E,W)$ to be a Directed Graph, N is set of vertexes, E is set of edges, W is weight of the edge. For popularity, we suppose all the weight parameters is plus.

Def 1.(Multi-Constraint and Multi-Objective Optimal Path, MCOOP). In $G(N,E,W)$, there is $k(k \geq 2)$ constraints $C_i(i=1,...,k)$, each path P from start vertex S to end vertex T has $m(m \geq 2)$ nonnegative measure rules $f_1,...,f_m$.The path P is a multi-objective optimal path with multi-constraints iff there is no another path P^*. When P and P^* are content with C_i, for each measure rule, $f_i(P) \succ= f_i(P^*)$, there is at least one rules i which meet $f_i(P) \succ f_i(P^*)$. $\succ=$ and $\succ$ respectively show non-inferior and priority relations between measure rules.

Def 2.(Service Node, *SN*). *SN* is an abstract concept, which only contains functional description and interface information instead of specified Web Service.

Def 3.(Service Group, *SG*). *SG* is composed of a set of services provided by different providers and having same (or similar) functions. The differences of the services in same *SG* are QoS.

Suppose a sequential services process model contain *m SN*, shown as following:

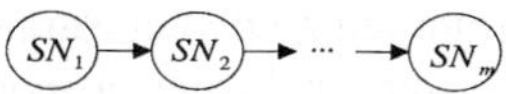

Fig. 1. Sequential Services Composition Process Model

SG_i corresponding to SN_i includes n_i services, $1 \leq i \leq m$. Each service in SG_i can be seen as the vertex of a graph; in order to analyze the problem of service selection, two virtual services S (start vertex) and T (end vertex) are added.

Def 4.(Services Composition Graph, *SCG*). If the service composition process model include *m SN*, the service group corresponding to SN_i is $SG_i(1 \leq i \leq m)$. $SCG=(N,E,W)$, where $N = SG_1 \cup ... \cup SG_m \cup \{S,T\}$, E is made up of three types of edges: ① edge $(S,u), \forall u \in SG_1$; ② edge $(v,T), \forall v \in SG_M$; ③ edge $(u,v), \forall u \in SG_i, \forall v \in SG_{i+1}, 1 \le i < m$ .The weight vector of edge $(u,v) \in E$ is QoS parameter vector of Web Service *v*. The *SCG* of Fig.1 shown as follows:

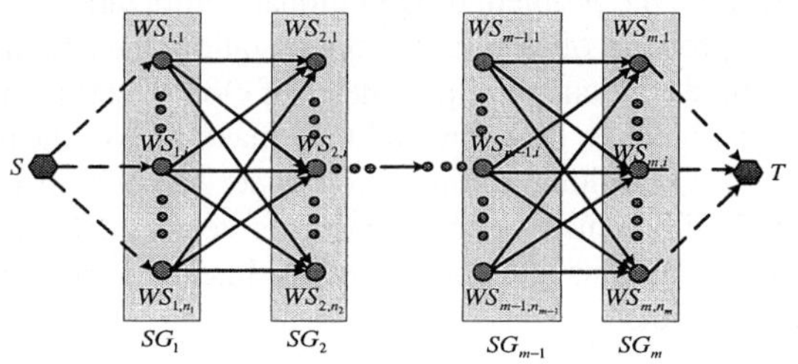

Fig. 2. SCG of Sequence Services Composition Process Model

Service dynamic selection with QoS global optimization refers to selecting a specific service from *SG* to construct an executable services process, on the precondition that the services process contents with specific QoS constraints, multi-objective functions are maximally optimized. One characteristic of multi-objective optimization is that the objective functions always collide with each other, improvement of some functions will decline the capability of other functions. Generally, there is no mutual minimal point among all the objective functions. According to the properties of multi-objective optimal, the problem of service selection with QoS global optimization can be converted into finding a set of multi-objective optimal paths satisfied QoS constraints from service *S* to *T*. In other words, it is a problem to find solutions of MCOOP in *SCG*. We propose GODSS to resolve this problem.

4 The Main Ideas and Description of GODSS

4.1 The Main Ideas and Model of GODSS

We suppose that each service contains four QoS parameters, which are Time(*T*), Cost(*C*), Reputation(*Rep*) and Reliability(*R*). *T* and *C* can be regarded as two objective functions, we hope that process model can be carried out with ultra-short *T* and ultra-low *C*. *Rep* and *R* can be regarded as two constraints. Suppose the service composition process is sequential (shown in Fig.1), a model of multi-objective service composition with multi-constraints can be depicted formally as follows:

$$MinF(P) = (\sum_{i \in P} T(i), \sum_{i \in P} C(i)) \tag{1}$$

In formula (1), path *P* has two constraints *Rep(P)* and *R(P)* :

$$\begin{cases} \mathrm{Re}\, p(P) = \sum_{i \in P} \mathrm{Re}\, p(i) \Big/ (m+1) \ge \mathrm{Re}\, p_0 \\ R(P) = \underset{i \in P}{Min} R(i) \ge R_0 \end{cases} \tag{2}$$

Where *m* is the number of *SN*; $Rep_0(R_0)$ means the lowest reputation(reliability).

Because the multi-objective optimization with constraints is more complex than absolute Pareto priority relation, we adopt the approach in [8] to distinguish relatively priority relation between different individual. In [8], the authors have proved that MCOOP is a NP-complete problem. As an intelligent optimal method, Genetic Algorithm has been extensively used in the solutions of NP-complete problems.

Based on above model and idea, we propose GODSS based on multi-objective Genetic Algorithm to realize the service selection with QoS global optimization. This strategy can ultimately produce a set of Pareto optimal paths satisfying the constraints. The user could select the best path in terms of specific requirement, in addition, the Pareto optimal paths which are not selected in the set of optimal paths can be regarded as spare schemes in case that the selected path can not be used.

4.2 The Description of GODSS

Suppose the composition process model is sequential, the steps of GODSS are shown as follows:

① Produce a set of initial composition paths satisfying constraints from start vertex *S* to end vertex *T*;
② Produce initial evolutional population;
③ *Repeat*
④ Assignment of individual adaptive value and maintenance of diversity;
⑤ Elitism;
⑥ Selection of prior individuals;
⑦ Crossover and mutation operation;
⑧ Yield new evolutional population;
⑨ *Until* (reach the predefined maximal generation)
⑩ Output the sets of Pareto optimal composition paths.

In these steps, initialized operation is carried out in step ①, we use DFS (deep first search) algorithm to produce a group of initial composition paths satisfied constraints from start vertex *S* to end vertex *T*.

Step ② map the composition path into individual of genetic space by means of fixed-length-integral coding. In this way, chromosome consists of service number, which corresponds to each service node in composition path by the calling order of the service. The first(last) gene of chromosome is always the start(end) vertex *S(T)*.

In step ④, we assign the adaptive value and keep the diversity of individuals. Based on Pareto sort, we make use of multi-objective functions to categorize the population. The strategy in common use for holding diversity is Niche[10], in this approach, share-function is used to restrict the selecting probability of similar individual, however Niche is very sensitive to σ_{share}, appreciably warp of σ_{share} will cause maximum divergence of the value of share-function. So, this paper adopted information entropy theory of Shannon to keep diversity of the population[7,11], it has no problems on evaluation and sensitivity of parameters..

In step ⑤, we update assistant population of next generation by using population P_1 and assistant population P_2, and copy the non-dominant solutions satisfied constraints from P_1 to P_2 ; if P_2 has dominated solutions, it will be deleted. If the number of individuals in P_2 exceeds the specified number, we use temporary sets to deal with this condition.

In step ⑥, we use Roulette Wheel to select prior individuals from P_1, and mixed individuals in P_2 with selected individuals from P_1, then, put the mixture into copulate pool.

In step⑦ and ⑧, we carry out crossover and mutation operations to produce new chromosomes as new population. We adopt the method of crossing two points to speed up astringency of GODSS. Because GODSS uses two virtual vertexes *S* and *T*, the location of mutation should not contain *S* and *T*, and mutation should be taken place in the scope of corresponding *SG*. The initial population is produced by DFS algorithm, so space searching ability is completely determined by crossover and variation operation, so crossover probability might(assumed) be 1, mutation probability might be 0.15.

5 Application of GODSS in Complex Service Composition Process

GODSS is not only suitable for sequential service composition but also suitable for other complex composition process. In [9], we proposed QoS assessment model for seven types of basic composition processes that based on reduction rules, most of complex composition processes are made up of these basic processes. QoS parameters of most complex service composition processes can be obtained by these rules repeating(details see [9]).

According to section 3, in GODSS application, the part relating to composition process only comprises creation of initial population and assignment of individual adaptive value. We can order each service node in composition process model to create initial population. Using the reduction rules described in [9], the complex service composition pattern can be reduced to a sequential pattern, and we can make use of the approach of calculating QoS parameters to substitute the formulas (1) and (2) in which objective functions and constraints are involved, then categorize, sort and calculate the individual adaptive value in turn. Then, we can use GODSS to get optimal service paths with QoS global optimization.

6 Conclusions

Web Service Selection is an important issue in dynamic Web Service Composition. To resolve the deficiency of the existing approaches, a strategy GODSS is proposed to realize the Web Service selection with QoS global optimization in dynamic Web Service composition.

Our research will be furthered in the future. For the time being, for lack of the service environment, we cannot carry out experiment for GODSS. Next, GODSS will be testified and improved in the real Web service environment provided by SIG (Spatial Information Grid, 863 project).

References

1. B. Benatallah and F. Casati, editors. Distributed and Parallel Database, Special issue on Web Services. Springer-Verlag, 2002
2. Liangzhao Zeng, Boualem Benatallah, Marlon Dumas. Quality Driven Web Service Composition, WWW2003
3. B. Benatallah, M. Dumas, Q. Z. Sheng, A. Ngu. Declarative Composition and Peer-to-Peer Provisioning of Dynamic Web Services, ICDE2002
4. YuTu Liu, Anne H.H.Ngu, LiangZhao Zeng. QoS Computation and Policing in Dynamic Web Service Selection. WWW2004
5. Yu Tang. Research on System Framework, Service Architecture and Service Composition Technology of Spatial Information Grid. PHD thesis. ChangSha: National University of Defense Technology,2004
6. Junfeng Zhao, Bing Xie, Lu Zhang, Fuqing Yang. A Web Services Composition Method Supporting Domain Feature, Chinese Journal of Computer, 2005, 28(4):731~738
7. Xun-Xue Cui, Chuang Lin. A Constrainted Quality of Service Routing Algorithm with Multiple Objectives, Journal of Computer Research and Development, 2004, 41(8): 1368~1375
8. M R Garey, D S Johnson. Computers and Intractability: A Guide to the Theory of NP-Completeness. New York: W H Freeman and Company,1979
9. ShuLei Liu, HaiQing Ren, GuiFen Tang, Ning Jing. QoS Model and Evaluation Methods for Dynamic Web Services Composition based Workflow. NDBC2005
10. Xiao-Ping Wang, Li-Ming Cao. Genetic Algorithms-Theory, Application and Software Implement. XiAn: XiAn Jiao Tong University Press, 2002, 74~76
11. J Kapur, H Kesavan. Entropy Optimization Principles with Application. San Diego: Academic Press, 1992

A Formal Model for Grid Service Deployment in Grid Service Mining Based on Installation Strategies*

Tun Lu, Zhishu Li, Chunlin Xu, and Xuemei Huang

School of Computer Science, Sichuan University,
Chengdu, P.R. China, 610064
lutun_scu@hotmail.com

Abstract. Grid Service Mining (GSM) is a user-oriented computing paradigm adopting the service-oriented architecture, in which users can expediently customize their computing tasks. Grid Service Deployment (GSD) is useful to deal with the growing complexity of interactions and diversity of co-ordinations between the transient and stateful grid services in GSM. Despite much work on the deployment process itself, the effect of GSD is not given much attention, especially from theoretical aspects. Hereby, in this paper we present a formal model for GSD in order to analyze dynamics of the GSM system in a consistent way. Four types of installation strategies are defined to determine how grid services of the same family are installed. Grid service compatibility is introduced to address issues of the safe and successful configuration of GSM system.

1 Introduction

Grid computing emerges as an effective technology to couple geographically distributed resources and solves large-scale computational problems in wide area networks [1]. Recent work [2,3,4] in grid computing field was centered around the concept of Grid Service, which is defined by the Open Grid Service Architecture (OGSA) [5], and is specified by Open Grid Service Infrastructure (OGSI) [6].

These standards and specifications provide foundation for the development of grid applications which facilitate scientists and researchers, but grid computing is currently far from reach for regular computer users. We've found that users want to customize their computing tasks in grid environments. Grid Service Mining (GSM) was presented and aims to let users retrieve the timely, accurate, comprehensive and relevant grid services from a variety of service sources according to users' requirements [7].

In GSM, user's applications are mostly the result of integrating grid services mined from different service domains or Virtual Organizations (VOs) [2]. In most cases, different grid services can be provided by different service producers and they can be used by different service consumers at the same time. Moreover, grid services can change rapidly and independently, which makes it difficult to manage the whole system in a consistent way. Grid Service Deployment (GSD) can effectively solve such issues. Much research work has been carried out on the deployment process [8, 9, 10, 11, 12].

* This work is supported by the National High Technology Research and Development 863 Program under Grant No. 2002AA144020.

H. Zhuge and G.C. Fox (Eds.): GCC 2005, LNCS 3795, pp. 90–95, 2005.

Different from the previous work, we focus on the effect of the process and present a formal model for GSD in order to analyze dynamics of the complicated GSM system. It defines four types of installation strategies to determine how grid services of the same family are installed. Grid service compatibility is introduced to address issues of safe and successful configuration of GSM system.

The remainder of the paper is organized as follows. In section 2, we give a brief review of GSM system. Then the formal model for GSD in GSM is discussed detailedly in section 3. In the end, conclusions are drawn in section 4 with future work given.

2 Brief Review of GSM

GSM is presented under the circumstance that users want to customize their computing tasks in grid computing systems. It is informally defined as: GSM is a user-oriented computing process adopting the service-oriented architecture, in which grid services distributed across the dynamical and multi-institutional virtual organizations can be organically and automatically located, acquired, and composed to form new services for the sake of meeting user's demands.

The GSM process is divided into three phases as service requirements analysis, service locating, and service composition. FGSM is a multi-agent framework for GSM [13], and its main parts such as GSM Portal, UBIR (User Behavior & Interests Repository), URA (User Requirement Analyzer), Service Searcher, and SC (Service Composer) are shown in Figure 1.

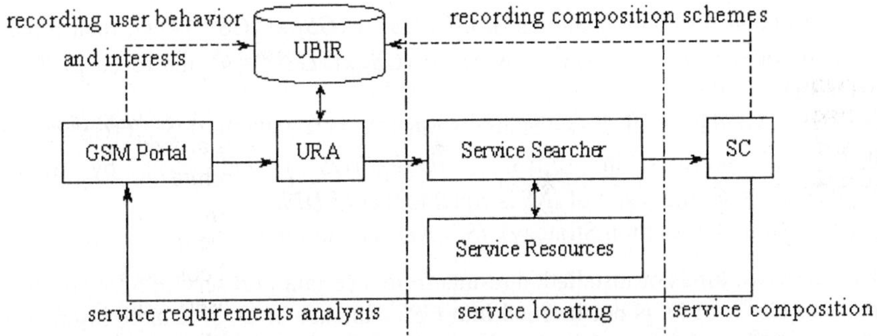

Fig. 1. FGSM: Framework for Grid Service Mining

3 Formal Model for Grid Service Deployment

All the activities related to the release, installation, activation, deactivation, upgrade, and removal of grid services, constitute a large and complex process that we refer to GSD. The formal model of GSD solves how the independently developed or provided, interacted sets of grid services evolve.

3.1 Problem Definition

A user submits a service application A_k to GSM system. If the set of services GS_k mined can realize functionalities of A_k, we denote this as *realize*(A_k, GS_k). Considering the general case, the GSM system at a certain time includes a finite set of service applications $SA^{Sys}=\{A_1, A_2,..., A_m\}$ submitted by users and a finite set of services $GS^{Sys}=\{S_1, S_2,..., S_n\}$ to realize SA^{Sys}.

Definition 1 (grid service family). A grid service family, written $GS_{F(i)}$, is a set of grid services. For $\forall S_i^p \in GS_{F(i)}$, p is a version number, and S_i^p is defined as the p-th version grid service of $GS_{F(i)}$.

Definition 2 (upgraded version). Let S_i^p and S_i^q be the grid services of $GS_{F(i)}$. If $p>q$, we say that S_i^p is an upgraded version of S_i^q.

When a user submit a new application A_k ($A_k \notin SA^{Sys}$) and A_k is inserted into SA^{Sys}, we called it the start of application A_k. When a service S_j^p ($S_j^p \in GS_k$) is installed in GS^{Sys}, we called it the installation of S_j^p. The installation of S_j^p is more complex, because it concerns how to install S_j^p into GS^{Sys}. The problem is how to install these services in GSM, and what are the conditions that can guarantee safe (no existing application is damaged) or successful (newly started applications work properly) configuration of different forms with the given $realize(A_k, GS_k)$.

3.2 Installation Strategies

Installation Strategy IS_j^p determines how grid service S_j^p is installed into GS^{Sys}. We've defined four kinds of installation strategies in FGSM:

(1) *DIS* (Direct Installation Strategy), $IS_j^p=DIS$: Directly insert S_j^p into GS^{Sys} as a new element.

(2) *TIS* (Total Installation Strategy), $IS_j^p=TIS$: If $(GS_{F(j)} \cap GS^{Sys}) \neq \Phi$, then replace all grid services in $(GS_{F(j)} \cap GS^{Sys})$ by S_j^p; if $(GS_{F(j)} \cap GS^{Sys}) = \Phi$, the result of *TIS* is equal to that of *DIS*.

(3) *INS* (Installation of New-version Strategy), $IS_j^p=INS$: If $(GS_{F(j)} \cap GS^{Sys}) \neq \Phi$, replace grid services in $\{S_j^r \mid S_j^r \in (GS_{F(j)} \cap GS^{Sys})$ and $p>r\}$ by S_j^p; if $(GS_{F(j)} \cap GS^{Sys}) = \Phi$, the result of *INS* is equal to that of *DIS*.

(4) *NIS* (None Installation Strategy), $IS_j^p=NIS$: Do nothing.

There are two kinds of installation results from a certain grid service S_j^p: a) S_j^p is inserted into GS^{Sys}; b) S_j^p is not inserted into GS^{Sys}. In case of a), S_j^p can be inserted directly into GS^{Sys} or can replace some grid services. If $IS_j^p=DIS$ or $(GS_{F(j)} \cap GS^{Sys}) = \Phi$, the installation outcome is that S_j^p is inserted directly into GS^{Sys}. If $(GS_{F(j)} \cap GS^{Sys}) \neq \Phi$ and $IS_j^p=TIS$, the installation outcome is that the grid services in $(GS_{F(j)} \cap GS^{Sys})$ are replaced by S_j^p. Or if $(GS_{F(j)} \cap GS^{Sys}) \neq \Phi$ and $IS_j^p=INS$, the installation outcome is that the grid services in $(GS_{F(j)} \cap GS^{Sys})$ are replaced by S_j^p. In case of b), if $IS_j^p=NIS$, or $(GS_{F(j)} \cap GS^{Sys}) \neq \Phi$, $IS_j^p=INS$ and $S_j^r \in (GS_{F(j)} \cap GS^{Sys})$ $(p<r)$, the installation outcome is that S_j^p is not inserted into GS^{Sys}.

3.3 Grid Service Compatibility

Grid service compatibility is introduced to embody relationship among various service versions of the same family.

Definition 3 (backward compatibility). Given *realize*(A_k, GS_k), GS_k' denotes the set in which S_i^r replace $\forall S_i^r \in GS_k (r>p)$. If *realize*($A_k$, GS_k'), we say that S_i^r is the backward compatibility (*BC*).

Definition 4 (forward compatibility). Given *realize*(A_k, GS_k), GS_k' denotes the set in which S_i^r replace $\forall S_i^r \in GS_k (r<p)$. If *realize*($A_k$, GS_k'), we say that S_i^r is the forward compatibility (*FC*).

We use *AC* to denote any kind of compatibility, i.e. $AC=\{BC, FC, BC \wedge FC\}$.

3.4 GSM System Configuration and Reconfiguration

GSM system configuration and reconfiguration describe the dynamic changes in evolving GSM system.

Definition 5 (GSM system configuration). (SA^{Sys}, GS^{Sys}) denotes GSM system configuration, where for $\forall A_s \in SA^{Sys}$ $(1 \leqslant s \leqslant m)$ *realize*(A_s, GS^{Sys}) meets.

Definition 6 (installation formula) A grid service installation formula is a triple (S_j^p, $Comp_j^p$, IS_j^p), which represents the grid service S_j^p with compatibility $Comp_j^p$ is installed by installation strategy IS_j^p.

Definition 7 (installation execution). Given *realize*(A_k, GS_k), an installation execution of A_k, denoted as SF_k, is a sequence of all GS_k's installation fomulas, in which the installation formula of every grid service is arranged in its corresponding order in GS_k.

Definition 8 (GSM system reconfiguration). Given *realize*(A_k, GS_k) and GSM system configuration (SA^{Sys}, GS^{Sys}), ($SA^{R\text{-}Sys}$, $GS^{R\text{-}Sys}$) denotes GSM system reconfiguration, where A_k ($A_k \notin SA^{Sys}$) is started in SA^{Sys} and every S_j^p ($S_j^p \in GS_k$) is installed in GS^{Sys}.

Sets $SA^{R\text{-}Sys}$ and $GS^{R\text{-}Sys}$ denote the set of grid service applications and the set of grid services after reconfiguration respectively.

Definition 9 (successful reconfiguration). Given GSM system reconfiguration ($SA^{R\text{-}Sys}$, $GS^{R\text{-}Sys}$), we said ($SA^{R\text{-}Sys}$, $GS^{R\text{-}Sys}$) a successful reconfiguration, if newly started A_k meets *realize*(A_k, $GS^{R\text{-}Sys}$).

Definition 10 (safe reconfiguration). Given GSM system reconfiguration ($SA^{R\text{-}Sys}$, $GS^{R\text{-}Sys}$), we said ($SA^{R\text{-}Sys}$, $GS^{R\text{-}Sys}$) a safe reconfiguration, if $\forall A_s \in SA^{Sys}$ $(1 \leqslant s \leqslant m)$ meets *realize*(A_s, $GS^{R\text{-}Sys}$).

Successful reconfiguration expresses that newly started applications work properly and safe reconfiguration expresses no existing application is damaged with the given *realize*(A_k, GS_k).

3.5 Some Theoretical Results

Five theoretical results are given out in below to help users to judge under what conditions the configuration is safe or successful. That's users most care.

Theorem 1. If any installation formula (S_j^P, $Comp_j^P$, IS_j^P) of SF_k has either of the following forms:

(a) (S_j^P, AC, DIS);
(b) (S_j^P, AC, TIS),

then the reconfiguration ($SA^{R\text{-}Sys}$, $GS^{R\text{-}Sys}$) is a successful reconfiguration.

Theorem 2. For any installation formula (S_j^P, $Comp_j^P$, IS_j^P) of SF_k, if S_j^P is not inserted into GS^{Sys} and (S_j^P, $Comp_j^P$, IS_j^P) meets either of the following conditions:

(a) (S_j^P, AC, NIS), $\forall S_j^q \in (GS_{F(j)} \cap GS^{Sys})$ is $BC \wedge FC$;
(b) (S_j^P, AC, INS), $\forall S_j^r \in (GS_{F(j)} \cap GS^{Sys})$ is BC,

then the reconfiguration ($SA^{R\text{-}Sys}$, $GS^{R\text{-}Sys}$) is a successful reconfiguration.

Proof: omitted.

Theorem 3. If any installation formula (S_j^P, $Comp_j^P$, IS_j^P) of SF_k has either of the following forms:

(a) (S_j^P, AC, DIS) ;
(b) (S_j^P, AC, NIS),

then the reconfiguration ($SA^{R\text{-}Sys}$, $GS^{R\text{-}Sys}$) is a safe reconfiguration.

Theorem 4. For any installation formula (S_j^P, $Comp_j^P$, IS_j^P) of SF_k, if S_j^P is inserted into GS^{Sys} and (S_j^P, $Comp_j^P$, IS_j^P) has either of the following forms:

(a) (S_j^P, $BC \wedge FC$,TIS) ;
(b) (S_j^P, BC, INS),

then the reconfiguration ($SA^{R\text{-}Sys}$, $GS^{R\text{-}Sys}$) is a safe reconfiguration.

Proof: omitted.

Theorem 5. If any installation formula (S_j^P, $Comp_j^P$, IS_j^P) of SF_k has the form (S_j^P, AC, DIS), then GSM system reconfiguration ($SA^{R\text{-}Sys}$, $GS^{R\text{-}Sys}$) is both success and safe reconfiguration.

Judging a reconfiguration safe or successful is a very complex problem. It concerns not only the installation strategies and service compatibility but also the tradeoff between preference of service providers and service consumers. System performance and the degree of service reuse are also important factors in the context. In despite of preliminary, the theoretical results presented above are enough for general cases.

4 Conclusions and Future Work

This paper has established a formal model for GSD to analyze and model the dynamic GSM system in a consistent way. We define four types of installation strategies to determine how grid services of the same family are installed. Forward and backward compatibility are introduced to express relations among various service versions. Moreover, four theorems give out conditions under which different forms of GSM configuration are safe (no existing applications are damaged) or successful (newly started applications work properly), or both safe and successful.

Our work is a preliminary theoretical foundation for GSD in GSM, and there are still many open problems. For example, in many cases service providers just provide service patches to update a service, then how do we modify the model? And efficient algorithms are needed to deploy the GSM system according to installation execution sequence. In the future, we will study these problems further. In addition, we'll also explore a more general model for grid computing systems.

Acknowledgement. Thanks specially associate professor Yunbo Wu, Ph.D. candidate Feng Yin and Hu Jin for their discussion, cooperation, and contribution.

References

1. Forster I. and Kesselman C.: The Grid2: Blueprint for a New Computing Infrastructure. Morgan Kaufmann Publishers, 2004.
2. Forster I., Kesselman C., Tuecke S.: The anatomy of the grid: Enabling scalable virtual organizations. Int. J. Supercomputing Applications, 2001, 15(3): 200-222.
3. Forster I., Kesselman C., Nick J. and Tuecke S.: Grid Services for Distributed System Integration. Computer, 2002, 35(6): 37-46.
4. Huang C.Q., Chen D.R., Hu H.L.: A grid service-based engineering computation architecture. In Proceedings of 28th Annual International Computer Software and Applications Conference, 2004.
5. Forster I., Kesselman C., Nick J. and Tuecke S.: The Physiology of the Grid: An Open Grid Services Architecture for Distributed Systems Integration. In Proceedings of the 5th Global Grid Forum Workshop (GGF5), Edinburgh, Scotland, July, 2002
6. Tuecke S., Czajkowski K., Forster I., Frey J., Graham S., Kesselman C., Maguire T., Sandholm T., Vanderbilt P., Snelling D.: Open Grid Services Infrastructure (OGSI) Version 1.0. Global Grid Forum Draft Recommendation, 6/27/2003.
7. Lu T., Li Z.S., Wu Y.B.: GSM: a new computing paradigm based on OGSA. Journal of Nanjing University of Science and Technology (Natural Science), 2005, 29(2): 149-152.
8. Talwar V., Milojicic D., Wu Q.Y., Pu C., Yan W., Jung G.Y.: Approaches for service deployment. IEEE Internet Computing, 2005, 9(2): 70-80.
9. Balsoy O., Jin Y., Aydin G., Pierce M., Fox G.: Automating metadata web service deployment for problem solving environments. Future Generation Computer Systems, 2005, 21(6): 910-919.
10. England D., Weissman J.: A stochastic control model for deployment of dynamic grid services. In Proceedings of the 5th IEEE/ACM International Workshop on Grid Computing, 2004.
11. Huang G., Wang M., Ma L.Y., Lan L., Liu T.C., Mei H.: Towards architecture model based deployment for dynamic grid services. IEEE International Conference on E-Commerce Technology for Dynamic E-Business, 2004.
12. Guan Z.J., Velusamy V., Bangalore P.: GridDeploy: A Toolkit for Deploying Applications as Grid Services. International Conference on Information Technology, 2005.
13. Lu T., Li Z.S., Xu C.L., et al: FGSM: a framework for grid service mining. Journal of Sichuan University (Engineering Science Edition), 2005, 37(2): 86-92.

A Grid Accounting Information Service for Site Autonomy

Beob Kyun Kim[1], Haeng Jin Jang[2], Tingting Li[1],
Dong Un An[1], and Seung Jong Chung[1]

[1] Dept. of Computer Engineering,
Chonbuk National University, South Korea
{kyun, duan, sjchung}@chonbuk.ac.kr,
pekingltt@yahoo.com.cn
[2] Korea Institute of Science and Technology Information
hjjang@kisti.re.kr

Abstract. Software, working in the Grid, must have extensibility and support site autonomy. And so does accounting software in the Grid. Architecture for grid accounting information collection and service which is designed for site autonomy is proposed. This architecture uses Globus Toolkit. To provide site autonomy in accounting information management, we use two kinds of information services. Site administrators can keep their autonomy by managing information service located in local administration domain. Portal administrators can have business relationships with each site by connecting their global information service to local information service.

1 Introduction

Grid computing represents the fundamental computing shift from a localized resource computing model to a fully-distributed virtual organization with shared resources [1][2][3][4]. And it virtualizes heterogeneous geographically disperse resources.

Major requirements for grid environments include extensibility and site autonomy. Accounting is one of obstacles that have impeded the widespread adoption of the Grid. Accounting systems try to keep track of resource usage and support resource consumption model [5]. The accounting information record must have end-to-end user identity, be extracted with minimum intrusion, and have a standard uniform structure. The architecture of accounting software must be flexible enough to allow for many deployment scenarios and leverage existing standards work and tools.

We design and implement the accounting information gathering and service system. Grid accounting information service is named as "AIService" and is based on OGSA. To provide end-to-end user identity of accounting information on each resource, we use a grid access control system, called PGAM [7]. By using PGAM, we can extract accounting information with minimum intrusion. There are two kinds of information services to make this architecture be more flexible and to provide site autonomy. Site administrators can keep their autonomy by managing information service in local domain. Portal administrators can have business relationships with each site by connecting their global information service to local one.

H. Zhuge and G.C. Fox (Eds.): GCC 2005, LNCS 3795, pp. 96 – 101, 2005.

2 Related Works

The area of Grid accounting has also been investigated by others [6][9][10]. Some of these have provided guidance in outlining the accounting information gathering system architecture.

GSAX [6] is an extensible OGSA accounting and logging framework. It is designed to provide a functionally modular accounting framework, to allow use of accounting at many levels of application and user understanding, to provide information at different levels of granularity, to integrate QoS and service-level agreements into the accounting framework, to be independent of any economic model, and to allow dynamic pricing stages. The implementation of accounting information gathering process is an implementation of monitoring block of this framework.

DGAS (DataGrid Accounting System) model, developed by DataGrid Project [9], envisions a whole new economic Grid market, where supply and demand of Grid resources work in unison to strive towards equilibrium where all resources are fully utilized to the lowest possible price. The Home Location Register acts as a local bank branch managing the fund status of a subset of Grid users and resources. But, DataGrid employs a centralized resource broker intercepting all jobs within the Grid. Such centralized solutions are not in agreement with the decentralized nature of the Grid.

3 Design of Accounting Information Gathering System

Designed and implemented system uses the globus toolkit as its default middleware which is the most widely adopted grid middleware. But, the globus toolkit is lack of end-to-end user identity.

3.1 Identity in Globus Toolkit

Globus toolkit comprises a set of components that implement basic services for resource management, information service, data management, grid security, etc. The gatekeeper is a simple component that responds to a request by doing three things: performing mutual authentication of user and resource, determining a local user name for the remote user, and starting a job manager which executes as that local user and actually handles the request. Normally, when a request for access is received, the gatekeeper attempts to find the corresponding local username in the "grid-mapfile."

```
"/O=Grid/O=Globus/OU=chonbuk.ac.kr/CN=hdg" gw1
"/O=Grid/O=Globus/OU=chonbuk.ac.kr/CN=dgs" gw2
"/O=Grid/O=Globus/OU=chonbuk.ac.kr/CN=kyun" gw2
"/O=Grid/O=Globus/OU=chonbuk.ac.kr/CN=duan" gw3
```

Fig. 1. An example of "grid-mapfile"

In the original syntax of this file, several certificate subjects can be mapped to one local username. But, this mechanism cannot guarantee end-to-end user identity: who is the owner of local process or job, if there are several certificate subjects mapped to one local username. If the site administrator wants to trace the usage, he must deploy other monitoring or tracing tool which is implemented by kernel programming.

3.2 PGAM

To provide end-to-end user identity, we adopted PGAM. It uses only 1-to-1 mapping of certificate subject and local username. But 1-to-1 mapping can cause a heavy load on the site administrator and local system. So, PGAM implements template account mechanism [11] to reduce the burden of administrator and local system.

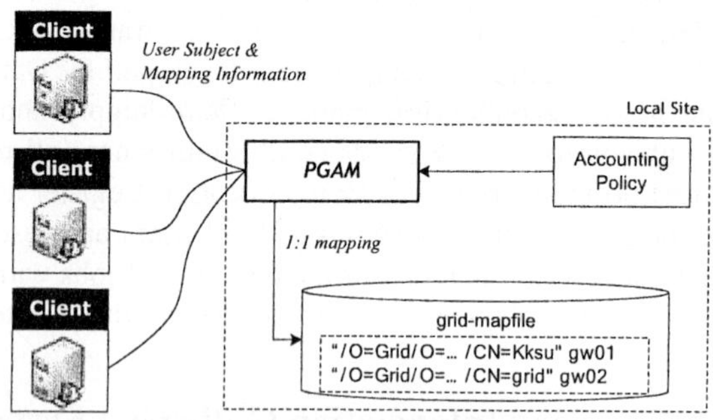

Fig. 2. Function of PGAM

When a grid user requests a right for access to local resource with his credential and personal information and job specification, PGAM handles interaction from client. It logs all the record during operation and enforces local resource management policies. By using PGAM, we can provide end-to-end user identity to each activity in local system.

3.3 Grid Accounting Information Service Architecture

Each module in this architecture works independently from each other. They interchange their information with OGSI-compliant interfaces [12]. Accounting information is extracted with minimum intrusion and follows a standard uniform structure.

Each local system gathers local accounting information, transforms into grid-aware accounting information, and reports to LAITS (Local Accounting Information Tracking Service). Accounting information is gathered from existing accounting software's log with minimum intrusion. By help of PGAM, local information is transformed into a grid-aware uniform accounting information structure which follows Usage Record [8] of UR-WG in GGF. And it is reported to LAITS using common interface *LAITC*.

Usually, one domain (like VO) can have more than one LAITS. The administrator of LAITS is responsible for management and usage of all the accounting information in LAITS. Information can be used for various purposes by local site policy.

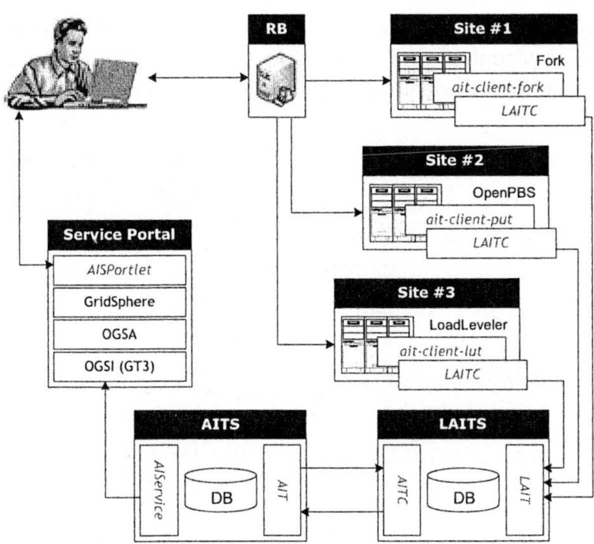

Fig. 3. Architecture for grid accounting information service

LAITS reports its records to AITSs which have business relationship. LAITS can have relationships to multiple AITSs. Each AITS provides few functions that focus on efficient management and analysis of global grid-aware accounting information and on analysis. *AIService,* located in AITS, is an OGSI-compliant service and may provide information service to portal service.

We developed the grid accounting information service portal by using GridSphere portal framework. GridSphere portal allows users to customize their workspace by adding and removing portlets as needed. Portlets are defined as visual components that can be assimilated into portal web pages. *AISPortlet* gets information from *AIService* and provides it to grid users.

3.4 Heterogeneity of Accounting Information Records

Accounting in the grid environment is very different from that in the traditional computing environment, because the concept of the user is different from the traditional local user and the format of accounting data of each system is different from each other. Accounting information in the grid environment is not produced by the local user but by the grid user. The format and meaning of accounting information produced by OpenPBS is different from that produced by LoadLeveler. To build an accounting information service, which incorporates heterogeneous systems, each gathered accounting information must be transformed into a standard format. In this paper, we choose Usage Record, suggested by UR-WG in GGF, as a standard format. It is represented in an XML format and intended to be a common exchange format.

3.5 Accounting Information Interactions

Each accounting information record is expressed an XML document following Usage Record and is identified globally by having '<urwg:RecordIdentity>' as its field.

Local accounting information gathering modules (ait-client-*) report in real-time. LAITS reports its accounting information to AITS in periodically. If AITS need an un-reported accounting information, it can request this information asynchronously.

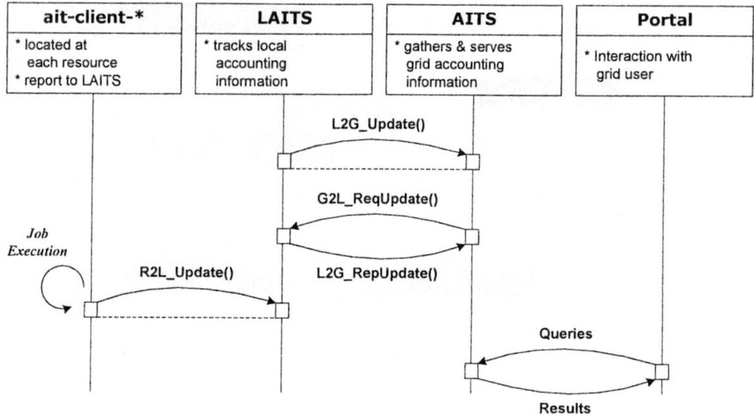

Fig. 4. Accounting information interactions

4 Implementation

We implemented this system in the following environments. For the portability of this system, Java is selected. We use MySQL for DBMS. We tested this system on resources provided by KISTI(Korea Institute of Science and Technology Information) and CBNU(Chonbuk National University, South Korea).

http://tea04.chonbuk.ac.kr:8080 - GridSphere Portal - Microsoft Internet Explorer

파일(F) 편집(E) 보기(V) 즐겨찾기(A) 도구(T) 도움말(H)

```
:Identity>
ocalUserId>globus</urwg:LocalUserId>
obalUserDN>/C=KR/O=KISTI/OU=Grid/CN=Globus</urwg:GlobalUserDN>
rIdentity>
```

RecordId	CreateTime	GlobalUserDN	CPUDuration	NodeCount	Queue
eros01.gridcenter.or.kr@eros01.gridcenter.or.kr	2004-06-28 16:19:02	/C=KR/O=KISTI/OU=Grid/CN=Globus	00:00:00	1	workq
3.eros01.gridcenter.or.kr@eros01.gridcenter.or.kr	2004-06-28 16:19:01	/C=KR/O=KISTI/OU=Grid/CN=Globus	00:00:00	1	workq
4.eros01.gridcenter.or.kr@eros01.gridcenter.or.kr	2004-06-28 16:19:00	/C=KR/O=KISTI/OU=Grid/CN=Globus	00:00:00	1	workq
0.eros01.gridcenter.or.kr@eros01.gridcenter.or.kr	2004-06-28 16:15:44	/C=KR/O=KISTI/OU=Grid/CN=Globus	00:00:00	1	workq
5.eros01.gridcenter.or.kr@eros01.gridcenter.or.kr	2004-06-28 16:19:01	/C=KR/O=KISTI/OU=Grid/CN=Globus	00:00:00	1	workq
	2004-06-	/C=KR/O=KISTI/OU=Grid/CN=Globus	00:00:00	1	workq

완료 인터넷

Fig. 5. AISPortlet(a portlet for grid accounting information service)'s table view

Figure 5 shows a table view of *AISPortlet*. We developed this portlet to show the original grid accounting information in XML format and to show as table and to show a chart.

5 Conclusion and Future Works

In this paper, we designed and implemented the grid accounting information service. This system follows the GSAX framework and the accounting information is formatted so that it follows Usage Record suggested by UR-WG in GGF. And we developed its service as an OGSI-compliant service.

To provide extensibility and site autonomy, two kinds of information service is developed. LAITS gathers accounting information produced within local domain. AITS gathers accounting information from LAITSs to provide accounting information service and mine new information.

References

1. I. Folster, C. Kesselman, and S. Tuecke, "The Anatomy of the Grid: Enabling Scalable Virtual Organizations", *The International Journal of High Performance Computing Applications*, vol. 15, no. 30, pp. 200-222, 2001.
2. Global Grid Forum, http://www.ggf.org
3. The Globus Alliance, http://www.globus.org
4. Grid Forum Korea, http://www.gridforumkorea.org
5. M. Melani, "Thinking about Accounting," http://sdm.lbl.gov/srm-wg, September, 2004.
6. A. Beardsmore, K. Harley, S. Hawkins, S. Laws, James Magowan, and A. Twigg, "GSAX: Grid Service Accounting Extensions," http://www.doc.ic.ac.uk/~sjn5/GGF/rus-wg.html, Resource Usage Service WG, Global Grid Forum, September, 2002.
7. B. K. Kim et al, "A Study on Access Control System for Site Autonomy in Grid Environment," *The KIPS Transactions: Part A*, vol. 12-A, no. 2, April, 2005.
8. Usage Record, http://forge.gridforum.org/projects/ur-wg
9. The DataGrid Project, http://eu-datagrid.web.cern.ch/eu-datagrid
10. Sebastian Ho, "GridX System Design Documentation", Bioinformatics Institute, 2002
11. Thomas J. Hacker, Brian D. Athey, "Account Allocations on the Grid", Center for Parallel Computing University of Michigan, 2000
12. S. Tuecke et al, "Open Grid Services Infrastructure (OGSI)", (draft), GGF, 2003
13. B. K. Kim, D. U. An, S. J. Chung, and H. Jang, "Grid Accounting Information Gathering System with Access Control", *APWeb 2005, 7th Asia-Pacific Web Conference, Lecture Notes in Computer Science*, Springer, vol. 3399, pp. 845-850, 2005.

A KPN Based Cooperative Composition Model of Services

Xiuguo Zhang[1,2], Weishi Zhang[1], and Jinyu Shi[1]

[1] Department of Computer Science and Technology, Dalian Maritime University, Dalian 116026, China
zhangxg@newmail.dlmu.edu.cn
{teesiv, sjy1967}@dlmu.edu.cn
[2] College of Information and Electrical Engineering, Shandong University of Science & Technology, Qingdao 266510, China

Abstract. KPN (Kahn Process Network) is a model of computation based on dataflow and commonly used for describing a set of cooperative processes that communicate with each other by means of dataflow. In this paper, we propose a KPN based cooperative composition model of services called CCM. The corresponding mapping mechanism of KPN to CCM is presented. CCM model aims at reducing unanticipated circumstances and uncooperative cases of services in service composition and improving chances of composition success. The data description and service description techniques adopted in CCM model is introduced in detail. Based on CCM model, a cooperative composition framework of services is designed. Finally a case study is presented to show how to describe cooperative service processes in CCM model.

1 Introduction

Service-Oriented Architecture (SOA)[1] is a kind of new distributed application architecture. It is being promoted in the industry as the next evolutionary step in software architecture to help IT organizations meet their ever more complex set of challenges. In this architecture, all functions are defined as independent services with well-defined interfaces which can be called in defined sequences to compose new services. Service composition is the process of creating new services from a set of services. In reference [2], service composition approaches are classified as standard based syntactic approach and ontology based semantic approach. Syntactic approach describes and composes services based on XML, such as BPEL4WS[3], WSFL[4]. Semantic approach composes services based on ontology and relies on the use of AI planning techniques to automatically search, orchestrate, compose and execute services, the typical representations are DAML-S[5] and CoSMoS[6]. Both of the two approaches provide orchestrate process in which the dataflow and control flow are choreographed as service composition plan. For example, BPEL4WS itself is a kind of process description language and DAML-S includes the concept of process model in its service model class. But the plans of each approach are all designed manually and none adopts a standard process schema that enables composition process automation.

H. Zhuge and G.C. Fox (Eds.): GCC 2005, LNCS 3795, pp. 102–110, 2005.

This paper proposes a cooperative composition model of services based on process schema. In this model, KPN(Kahn Process Network)[7,8] model is used to model dataflow distribution among services. KPN is a model of computation based on dataflow and commonly used for describing a set of cooperative processes that communicate with each other by means of dataflow. The purpose of using KPN to model interactions among services is to reduce unanticipated circumstances and uncooperative cases of services in service composition and improve chances of composition success.

This paper is structured as follows: Section 2 is the introduction to KPN. Section 3 presents a KPN based cooperative composition model of services called CCM, including data description and service description techniques adopted in this model. Section 4 discusses the basic implementation framework of CCM. In Section 5, we provide a case to show CCM model does work. Section 6 concludes the paper.

2 Introduction to KPN

KPN(Kahn Process Network)[7, 8] is a model of computation based on dataflow and commonly used for developing media- and signal-processing applications. A strong aspect of KPNs is that they make (task-level) parallelism and communication in an application explicit, which means that they are very suitable for execution on distributed architectures. Figure 1 shows the KPN process network model.

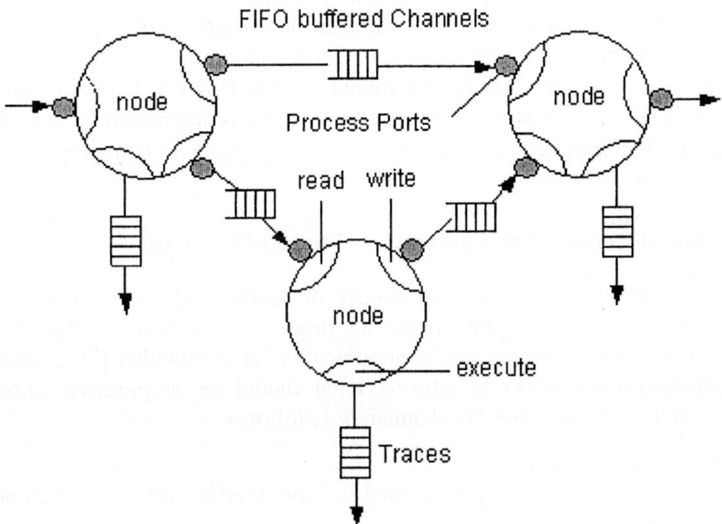

Fig. 1. KPN Process Network Model

In KPN model, nodes represent computations (processes) and arcs represent totally ordered sequences of data (commonly called tokens). Kahn process networks connect nodes. Each node communicates with others using FIFOs (unbounded containers of data tokens between two processes). An autonomous process is associated with each node. Nodes have ports and each port is linked to at most one other port through a unidirectional unbounded FIFO queue. Processes are allowed to read from an input port and are allowed to write to an output port. The read operation is blocking and the write operation is non-blocking. When tokens available on every input the process will execute. The read(), write() and execute() operations of a process form a trace. Kahn semantics guarantee a causal relation between input events and output events; incoming events do never influence previously generated output events. Furthermore, KPNs have a straightforward, unambiguous semantics and they are fully compositional. Thus, KPNs facilitate the reuse of application models, which is becoming increasingly important for reducing the design time of new products and services.

3 KPN Based Cooperative Composition Model of Services

As to a service, the basic ideas are as follows: (1) service is provided by component. A component service is a network service. Network service is individual component, which can be distributed within a network environment. A component service is described as a service interface used to provide service and a set of operations. A Service interface consists of a number of ports. Input and output data of service are transmitted via input and output ports of service interface; (2) a service can be either primitive or composed. Primitive service is the least unit of component service and represents the component implementation with concrete component technology. The composite service is composed by sub-services and their interconnections. Sub-services are connected via distributed data flows and control flows; (3) service execution will produce data and data flows are formed among services at runtime. The execution order of services is determined by data flows distribution and control flows of services; (4) dynamic service composition is supported at runtime, i.e., component services can be combined at runtime to provide an enhanced service as a single, self-contained entity.

3.1 KPN Based Cooperative Composition Model of Services

KPN based cooperative composition model of services consists of services and dynamic interactions among them. A service process network is a collection of service nodes which are connected and communicate over unbounded FIFO queues. We provide mapping mechanism to convert KPN model to cooperative composition model of services. The mapping mechanism is as follows:

- Node get mapped to service
- Input-output port of a node get mapped to input-output port of a component service interface
- FIFO channels get mapped to communication resources
- Read(), write(), execute() operations get mapped to readdata(), writedata() and service() events of a service node respectively
- Traces get mapped to service control queue which consists of events of service nodes.

We named the KPN based cooperative composition model of services CCM which is shown in Figure 2.

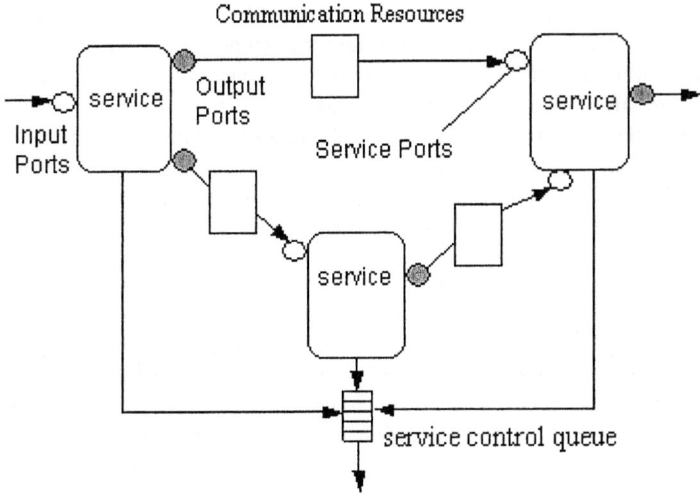

Fig. 2. KPN Based Cooperative Composition Model of Services (CCM)

In CCM, we define the events of service nodes to enable services to communicate with each other. The main events are as follows:

- **init().** This event is used to initialize a service and prepare the necessary resources at runtime. It invokes readdata() event to read input data from FIFO queue and convert XML documents of RDF format to general data types and allocate them to operation parameters in the logical order of service operations.
- **service().** This event is used to execute an initialized service. It invokes write-data() event to convert output results of service of general data type to XML document of RDF format and put it into FIFO queue.
- **stop().** This event unconditionally terminates a running service and releases system resources involved with this service.
- **flowxml().** This event is used to transmit data token saved in FIFO queue from a service port to another service port.
- **readdata().** This event reads input data from FIFO queue and converts XML documents of RDF format to general data types.
- **writedata().** This event converts output results of service of general data types to XML document of RDF format and puts it into FIFO queue.

3.2 Data Description of CCM

There are two kinds of data in CCM. One is the input and output data of service operations and the other is the data transmitted among component services. The data types of input and output data of service operations are general data type (e.g. integer, float, string) and some more sophisticated data structures. As to the format of data transmitted among component services, we use RDF (resource Description Framework) standard to describe it. XML syntax is used for RDF in this model. RDF is a framework for describing and interchanging metadata. It is a general-purpose language for representing information in the Web. We provide conversion mechanism of XML document for RDF to general data types and vice versa. This benefits the allocation of input data of XML syntax to operation parameters of service.

Making use of RDF to describe input and output data of service will benefit the distribution of dataflow in the web. It is convenient for data exchange between component services developed with different component technology by means of the uniform RDF standard. The type of data transmitted among component services is denoted by the type symbol "DATAxml" in this paper.

3.3 Service Description of CCM

A component service comprises the following aspects: input and output ports, input and output data, service operations, sub-services and the interactions among sub-services. The description of a service should cover every aspect of the service.

In CCM, we define service description language CCML to describe services and dynamic interactions among services. The basic format of CCML is as follows:

```
service service_name{
   //describing ports of input and output
   input:
      port <port 1 name>, <port 2 name>, …;
   output:
      port <port 1 name>, <port 2 name>, …;
   //describing data of input and output
      DATAxml <data 1 name>, <data 2 name>, …;
   //describing service operations
         //input data of service is impliedly bound to parameters of operations by ac-
      tual order of operations
         //output data of service is impliedly bound to return results of operations by
      actual order of operations
      <return type> operation 1 name (<parameter 1 type> <parameter 1 namc>,
            <parameter 2 type> <parameter 2 name>, ...);
      <return type> operation 2 name (<parameter 1 type> <parameter 1 name>,
            <parameter 2 type> <parameter 2 name>, ...);
         ……;
      //defining instances of sub-service
      <definition of sub-service>;
     //describing service composition
<invoking events of services to compose sub-services into mega-service>
```

4 KPN Based Cooperative Composition Framework of Services

Based on CCM model discussed above, we designed a cooperative composition framework of services. Figure 3 shows this framework. KPN based cooperative composition framework of services consists of four components: (1) KPN based cooperative orchestrator of services; (2) service composition engine; (3) service adapter; (4) service container.

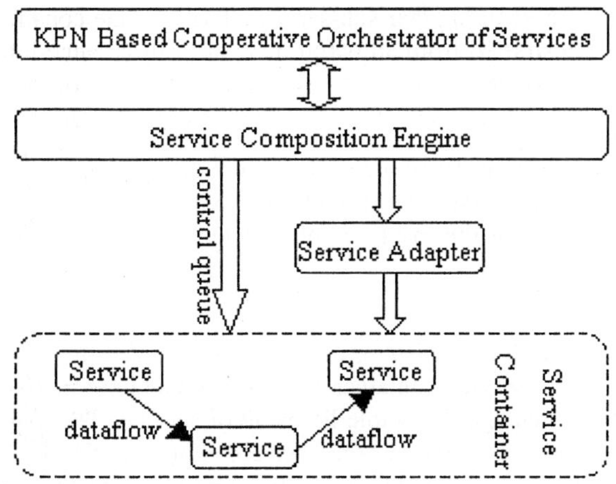

Fig. 3. KPN Based Cooperative Composition Framework of Services

(1) KPN based cooperative orchestrator of services

KPN based cooperative orchestrator of services is a visual modeling tool which is used to model cooperative composition model of services (CCM). The CCM consists of services and dynamic interactions among them. The corresponding CCM model is stored as .ccm extension file. This tool provides functions to convert CCM model to CCML description format. In a CCM model, the round rectangles denote services and small ellipses on them denote input and output port of services. The white ellipse is input port and the grey ellipse is output port. Arrowhead between services denotes the direction of data flows between services and the marker on arrowhead denotes actual input and output data of service. In section 5, we'll present an application case of CCM model.

(2) Service composition engine

Service composition engine is the scheduler of CCMs. It loads and parses .ccm files and selects appropriate service from service repository to service container dynamically via scheduling events of service control queue in the order by which they are modeled. Service repository is used to store component services implemented with different component technologies. As to the issues of service selecting and service repository, we'll discuss them in another paper. Service composition engine also takes charge of managing input and output data flows among services and allocating them to service operations. Composite service is a mega-service composed of sub-services and interconnections among them. For example, in Figure 3, the dashed round rectangle denotes a composite service that is composed by three sub-services. To a composite service, dataflow is transparent. Service composition engine explicitly passes dataflow to each sub-service. In the execution process of .ccm models, data are transmitted between services via input and output ports of services interface. Data flowing from one service interface to another is named interface binding. There are three cases of interface binding. The first one is called In-In binding, i.e., data are transmitted from an input port of service interface to an input port of sub-service. The second one is called Out-In binding, i.e., data are transmitted from an output port of a sub-service interface to an input port of another sub-service. The last one is called Out-Out binding, i.e., data are transmitted from an output port of a sub-service interface to an output port of service interface.

(3) Service adapter
A service component may be implemented with different component technology. Service adapter is used to adapt the different service interfaces provided by different service components before the instances of selected services are loaded into service container.

(4) Service container
Services have lifecycle that consists of three stages: initialization, running and termination. Services runs in service container and service container invokes corresponding events of services to manage the whole lifecycle of service. The main lifecycle management events invoked by service container are init(), service() and stop(). Meanwhile, service container also provides transaction operations of service instances.

5 Case Study: Application of CCM to a Concrete Scenario

Figure 4 shows a simple ship information query system which is modeled with KPN based cooperative orchestrator of services.

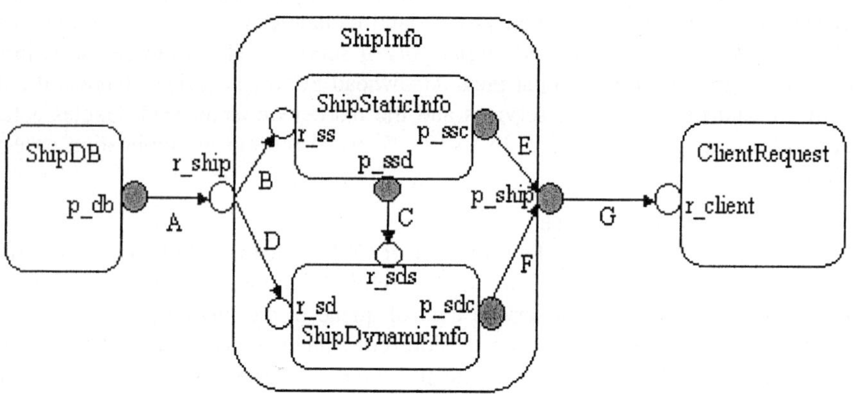

Fig. 4. CCM Model of A Ship Information Query System

The whole system consists of five services: ShipDB, ShipInfo, ShipStaticInfo, ShipDynamicInfo and ClientRequest. ShipInfo is a nested service composed of two sub-services that are ShipStaticInfo and ShipDynamicInfo. The basic business process of this system is as follows. ClientRequest service requests the entire ship information from ShipInfo service containing static and dynamic information of ship. Ship static information is provided by ShipStaticInfo and dynamic information provided by ShipDynamicInfo. ShipDynamicInfo needs static information from shipStaticInfo to finish its query. Eventually ShipInfo obtains query information from ShipDB.

ShipInfo is a composite service composed of two primitive services. In the following section we'll describe ShipInfo using CCML language.

```
service ShipInfo{
intput:
  port r_ship;
output:
  port p_ship;
DATAxml A, G;
string getCbbhByCoor(double wdmin, double wdmax, double jdmin, double jdmax);
string getStaticShipInfo(string cbbh);
string getDynamicShipInfo(string cbbh);
string getDynamicLastInfo(string cbbh);
Instance ShipStaticInfo SSInfo;
Instance ShipDynamicInfo SDInfo;
flowxml(B, r_ship, SSInfo.r_ss);
   //flowing dataflow B from port r_ship to SSInfo.r_ss
SSInfo.init(); //initializing ShipStaticInfo sub-service
<C|E>=SSInfo.service(B);
   //running SSInfo sub-service instance, producing C and E dataflow
flowxml(C, SSInfo.p_ssd, SDInfo.r_sds);
   //flowing dataflow C from port SSInfo.p_ssd to SDInfo.r_sds
flowxml(D, r_ship, SDInfo.r_sd);
   //flowing dataflow D from port r_ship to SDInfo.r_sd
SDInfo.init();
   //initializing ShipDynamicInfo sub-service F=SDInfo.service(D)□
      //running SDInfo sub-service instance, producing F dataflow
flowxml(E, SSInfo.p_ssc, p_ship);
   //flowing dataflow E from port SSInfo.p_ssc to p_ship
flowxml(F, SDInfo.p_sdc, p_ship);
   // flowing dataflow F from port SDInfo.p_sdc to p_ship
}
```

6 Conclusions

KPN based cooperative composition model of services improves chances of composition success to some extent. The composed system can meet requirements of end users via selecting and composing services on demand. The ongoing work is developing a prototype system of CCM based cooperative composition framework to verify the feasibility and practicability of CCM model. The prototype system consists of four main components, i.e., KPN based cooperative orchestrator of services, service composition engine, service adapter and service container.

Acknowledgements

This research is partially supported by the National High Technology Development 863 Program under Grant No. 2004AA116010.

References

1. Kishore Channabasavaiah, Kerrie Holley, Edward M. Tuggle, Jr., Migrating to a service-oriented architecture, Part 1, http://www-900.ibm.com/developerWorks/cn/webservices/ws-migratesoa/index_eng.shtml, 16 December 2003.
2. Muhammad Adeel Talib, Yang Zongkai and Qazi Mudassar Ilyas, "Modeling the Flow in Dynamic Web Services Composition", Information Technology Journal 3 (2): 184-187, 2004
3. Tony Andrews et al. Business Process Execution Language for Web Services (BPEL4WS) 1.1. Online: http://www-106.ibm.com/developerworks/webservices/library/ws-bpel, May 2003.
4. F. Leymann. Web Services Flow Language (WSFL 1.0), 2001. w-4.ibm.com/software/solutions/webservices/pdf/WSFL.pdf.
5. David Martin et al. DAML-S(and OWL-S) 0.9 draft release. Online: http://www.daml.org/services/daml-s/0.9/, May 2003.
6. Keita Fujii, Tatsuya Suda, Dynamic Service Composition Using Semantic Information, http://icsoc.dit.unitn.it/abstracts/A155.pdf
7. Twan Basten1, Jan Hoogerbrugge2, Efficient Execution of Process Networks, http://www.ics.ele.tue.nl/~tbasten/papers/eepn.pdf
8. Hylke W. van Dijk, Henk J. Sips, Context-Aware Process Networks, http://www.pds.ewi.tudelft.nl/pubs/papers/capn_ijes2005.pdf

A Layered Architecture of Service Organization in AegisGrid*

Li Liu, Zhong Zhou, and Wei Wu

School of Computer Science and Engineering, Beihang University,
Beijing 100083, P.R. China
{liuli, zz, wuwei}@vrlab.buaa.edu.cn

Abstract. In AegisGrid, a special Architecture of Service Organization is required to organize large-scale services. According to the characteristics of AegisGrid, this paper provides a layered architecture of service organization, AG-SOA, solving the key problems in large-scale services' architecture. It also describes the method of classification of services. Methods and critical algorithm are provided for service registry and service discovery. Experiment shows that AG-SOA is an architecture that fits the characteristics of large-scale services organizing and the dynamic properties of the services in AegisGrid, and costs less in service registry and service discovery.

1 Introduction

In recent years, many researchers have attempted to adopt Grid technology into HLA to improve the scale and efficiency of distributed interactive simulation. AegisGrid[1] is based on HLA and Grid technology, aiming at providing an accordant and seamless Grid Computing Environment for distributed interactive simulation application. It integrates various complicated and heterogeneous resources in WAN, and provides them to users following OGSA[2] rules. The services in AegisGrid are distributed in different parts. They are in various types and dynamically transferred with time's transformation. The simulation services should be reusable and the service architecture is required to be robust.

In the research of service architecture, Globus realizes Globus resource allocation manager (GRAM) and math directory service[3], and organizes services in grid in form of virtual organization. Nowadays, UDDI[4] of Web Service in Internet realizes central service entity description, registry and discovery, and fits various services. However, it manages services in centralization which is unable to solute large-scale service in AegisGrid. In addition, robustness is absent. In VegaGrid[5], it uses the layered virtual machine model and routing-Transferring resource discovery model which transfer resource requests one by one from service demander to service provider. It is robust but does not organize the services with the rule of OGSA. The ontology-based model for Grid Resource Publication and Discovery (GRPD)[6] is a two-level registry mechanism. It is supposed that under the large-scale Grid system, the "index" nodes are used to discover services in each VO, and the user must know the GSH of the Service they

* This paper is supported by the National Grand Fundamental Research 973 Program of China under the grant No. 2002CB312105.

H. Zhuge and G.C. Fox (Eds.): GCC 2005, LNCS 3795, pp. 111 – 116, 2005.

request for. But in AegisGrid and other kind of Grid, users do not certainly know the GSH of the service they ask for, but only know what the kind of services they need.

This paper provides a layered architecture: AG-SOA. It designs layered classification for services, service registry and unregistry methods and critical algorithm based on AG-SOA. Users do not need to know GSH that the specific service needs by using this service organization architecture, they only need to provide the type of service. AG-SOA will accomplish the whole specific procedure without users' participation. At the same time, AG-SOA service organization architecture supports the dynamically join of other virtual system.

2 AG-SOA

In AG-SOA, the services is classified into two logical layers, global_class_service and local_class_service, which means classified in grid range and in each virtual organization (VO) according to the service types. Each global_class_service bears the uniform GlobelClass_ID that each service solely belongs to. All the services of different resources do not bear intersection. Different VO may have different classification method. The service name and LocalClass_ID map are required in each VO. Therefore it is convenient for a VO to join current AegisGrid, the service do not need to be classified again, but only need to correspond the LocalClass to the GlobalClass that the user can query the services in this VO. This structure supports other VO which bears the same structure could be added into AegisGrid only need a corresponding service router added to the SR network.

AG-SOA's topological structure includes two logical layers. The upper one is service router layer, and the lower one is virtual organization (VO) layer. The mechanism of service router is similar with that of the IP router, but the information saved and sent by service router (SR) is the information of all services in grid. In each SR, the mapping between various global_class_services and service symbols has been recorded. Each SR maps a virtual architecture for each service in this virtual architecture registry in tree structure according to classification. SR uses binary search method for service search to increase efficiency.

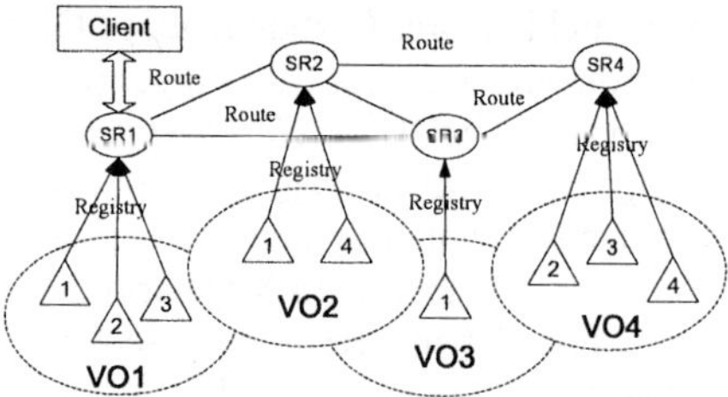

Fig. 1. AG-SOA topological structure

VO1 to VO4 are four Virtual Organizations of AegisGrid. SR1 to SR2 are the corresponding service router of them. The number in the triangle expresses different global_class_services. This structure supports that other VO which has the same structure could be added into AegisGrid withing a corresponding service router added to the SR network. Instead of simple information service of VO in general Grid, SR processes services by classification. Ordinary VO only searches services, and the user is required to distinguish the classification of services. SR could transmit services automatically to default router if it couldn't found the needed services itself. AG-SOA could organize large-scale Grid services by multi-layered distributed structure. If some parts of VO get fault, the whole gird environment could still run well.

To describe the service registry and discovery method, the definitions and rules have been defined, and the expression used is also explained as following.

Definition 1: definite the AG-SOA as a diagram has weight lines, G= (V, E), the number of node is V = n, and the number of the lines is E = m. V is the gather of SR node, E is the gather of line that connect the SR network. Each line i weigh Wi, Wi is the time cost on searching. S is the number of global_class_services, L is the number of local_class_services in on VO, and R is the number of services in Grid. The max weigh of the longest line in figure G is marked as Wmax.

Definition 2: service attributes include service name, producer, issuance time and relational operators. That is service attribute=<name, producer, time, operator>.

Rule 1: in each VO, service belonging to same LocalClass must belong to the same GlobalClass, but the service belonging to same GlobalClass does not surely belong to the same LocalClass.

Rule 2: the priority of service matching is: GlobalClass_ID, LocalClass_ID, service attributes.

The expressions used in this paper is as following:

Neighbors(a):gather of neighborSR of SR_a.

GCS(a): contraction of global_class_service, gather of global_class_service in SR_a, element of this gather is the group include service S and $GlobalClass_m$ that S is belonged to.

LCS(a,i): contraction of local_class_service, gather of local_class_service registry to $VOProxy_i$ in VO_a, element of this gather is the group include service S and $LocalClass_n$ that S is belonged to.

LtoG(a){ $G \times L, G \in GCS\{\}, L \in LCS\{\}$ }: mapping function of LocalClass to GlobalClass in VO_a, each VO has exclusive mapping function.

VOPRX (a): contraction of VOProxy, gather of VOProxy that registryed to VO_a.

NextSR(a) : transmitting gather of SR_a computed after receive service S search information, element of it is the group includes service S, the goal neighberSR SR_b and distance d_s between SR that has S and SR_a. SR_b in NextSR(a) is element of Neighbors(a).

Distance(S,a): distance from $SR_{a\,t}$ to SR that has service S.

3 Service Registry Method

In the SR network layer of AG-SOA, the SR map is initialized by the configuration file, which is a standard document in accordance with XML format. According to the function of SR, the service router updating algorithm of the AG-SOA is depicted as following:

Step 1:

IF Service $S \in$ GlobleClassm registry to VO_a $VOProxy_i$ THEN

IF GlobleClassm $\in$ GCS(a) THEN do not need update SR Table;

ELSE $VO_a VOProxy_i$ send registry message to SR_a;

GCS(a).add(S,$Service\_id_m$);

VOPRX(a).add($VOProxy_i$);

SR_a SR Table Distance(S,a) = 0; //Because service S registry in SR_a 's VO_a, so distance is zero.

Go to Step 5;

Step 2:

IF Service $S \in$ GlobleClassm registry to VO_a $VOProxy_i$ THEN

$VOProxy_i$ send unregistry message to SR_a;

IF VO_a中 $\forall S' \notin$ GlobleClassm THEN

GCS(a).del($Service\_id_m$);

VOPRX(a).del($VOProxy_i$);

Go to Step 5;

Step 3: worked as follow when the topology structure changed dynamically

IF new SR_b join to SR network THEN

Send update message to $\forall SR_r \in$ NeighberSR(b)

//update message include GCS(b)& Neighber(b) information of SR_b

IF neighberSR SR_r receive update message THEN

Neighber(r).add(SR_b);

GCS(b).add(S, S,$Service\_id_m$); // $\forall$(S,Service_idm) $\in$ GCS(r)

NextSR(b).add(S,SR,d); //IF $S \in SR_r$, d_s=1; IF $S \notin SR_r$, d_s= d_s +1;

IF old SR_a quit from SR network THEN

SR_a send quit message to $\forall SR_r \in$ NeighberSR(a);

NextSR(r).del(SR_a);

GCS(r){} = GCS(r){} - GCS(a){};

Go to Step 5;

Step4:

IF Distance(S, a) in SR Table changed, and NextSR(a) do not change THEN change the item of Distance(S, a) in SR Table, do not add new item to record the service S information, so that the number of the SR Table item will not endless.

Step 5:

IF SR Table of SR_a changed, THEN send update information to SR in NeighberSR(a). Ask them to replace the SR Table. The times of extending is limited by the scale of the AG-SOA to prevent infinite extending. As the extending of information, all the SR Table in AegisGrid have been updated.

After extending with several times, all the SRs in AG-SOA have kept all the GlobalClass information. The number of SRs is much few than that of VOProxy, therefore the service information may extend to the whole Grid in a short time.

4 Service Discovery Method

In this paper, the service discovery match algorithm in AG-SOA help users find the service they request. The algorithm is as following:

Step1: SR_a received user service request, search LtoG(a) to match the service S with $GlobalClass_m$.
Step2:

IF $\exists GlobleClass_m \in GCS(a)\{\}$, Go to Step 3.

IF $\exists GlobleClass_m \in NextSR(a)\{\}$, Go to Step 4. ELSE return that there do not have service S in AegisGrid.

Step3: send search service S information to $VOProxy_i$ that have $GlobalClass_m$. Search the localClassTable ensure the $LocalClass_n$ match S.

IF $\exists LocalClass_n \in LCS(a)\{\}$, THEN search S in $VOProxy_i$,

IF $VOProxy_i$ is organized in tree structure, match the LocalClassn with the digit of and the layer to fix on the point where S is, and return the result to user. End searching.
Step4: Service S is on other SR, search the NextSR(a) to find SR_r have minimize $Distance_s$. Send the service request to SR_r, Go to Step 2.

5 Experiments and Analysis

Two experiments have been designed using the architecture described in section 2 to evaluate the efficiency of service registry and service discovery in AG-SOA. Without knowing the delay of network we use the hops from the section starting node to the final node that all SRs had received the update information to scale the efficiency of the services updated. The first experiment simulated the implementation of services update in SR network. The SR network adopted the symmetrical topology, the neighbor node number of each node in this topology is the same (we use four here). In the experiment we used thread class to simulate nodes, we use six computers to simulate 1000-5000 nodes, measure the update rate that after update information come from the section starting node. We test the service discovery matching algorithm in

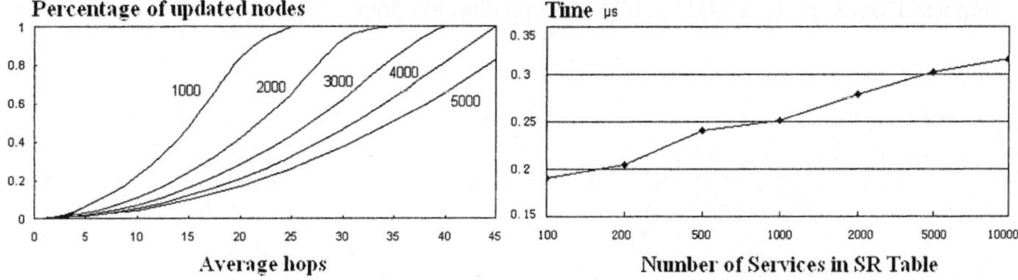

Fig. 2. SR network average updating probability

Fig. 3. SR Table searching time

AG-SOA from two aspects, the service matching and information transmitting. It is to measure the service matching time of SR Table and simulate the service searching hops.

In Fig 2 we can see SR network shows good updating effect with the symmetrical topology. The diffused speed is tolerable. Fig 3 shows that, the service matching time increased tardily when the service number is less than 10000. As the result showed in first experiment, we can see that average service searching hop is not changed with the node number in Grid, it is according to the rate of goal node of the network.

6 Summary

This paper addresses the key problems of services organization in AegisGrid. The layered Architecture of Services Organization AG-SOA has been developed for large-scale organization of services. The paper describes the method of classification of services, and provides methods and critical algorithm of service registry and service discovery. The experimental results demonstrate that AG-SOA is suitable for large-scale organization of services and adapts the dynamic properties of the services in AegisGrid. Experiment shows that the cost of service registry and service discovery is low. We plan to do our research on the load balancing and fault tolerance of Aegis-Grid.

References

1. W Wu, Z Zhou, SF Wang, et al. Aegis: A simulation grid oriented to large-scale distributed simulation. GRID AND COOPERATIVE COMPUTING GCC 2004, PROCEEDINGS 413-422, 2004.
2. I Foster, C Kesselman, J Nick, S Tuecke. The Physiology of the Grid: An Open Grid Services Architecture for Distributed Systems Integration. Open Grid Service Infrastructure WG, Global Grid Forum, June 22, 2002.
3. I Foster, C Kesselman, J Nick et al. Grid services for distributed systems integration. IEEE Computer, 2002,35(6):37~46
4. UDDI.org, 2000.http//www.uddi.org
5. FP Dong, YL Gong, W Li, L Cha. Research on Resource Discovery Mechanisms in Grid. Journal of Computer Research and Development, 2003, 12.1749~1755
6. L Cao, ML Li, H Rong, JS Huang. An Ontology-Based Model for Grid Resource Publication and Discovery. GCC2004,LNCS 3251,pp.448-455,2004

A Multi-agent Framework for Grid Service Workflow Embedded with Coloured Petri Nets*

Zhengli Zhai[1], Lei Zhou[2], Yang Yang[1], and Zhimin Tian[1]

[1] School of Information Engineering,
University of Science and Technology Beijing, China
{Zhaizhl@163.com}
[2] Shijiazhuang University of Economics,
Shijiazhuang, China

Abstract. The dynamics of Grid calls for flexible and adaptive workflow systems. This paper integrates Web Services and intelligent resource allocation mechanism (through Agent technologies) to Grid Services Workflow System embedded with Coloured Petri Nets (CPNs). The cooperation of Agents and CPNs enhances the adaptability of the framework. We discuss how Web Services can be located and the services provided by them can be invoked. We also discuss how the Agents and Web Services can co-exist to create highly flexible and dynamic Grid Services Workflow System. Finally this paper shows how our framework can be used to achieve adaptability from process, resource and task perspectives through an example of airline ticket service system.

1 Introduction

WfMSs [1] are increasingly being used to manage business processes associated with distributed global enterprises for benefits such as automation, coordination and collaboration between entities. However, existing commercially available WfMS does not offer sufficient flexibility for distributed organizations in Grid. These systems have rigid, centralized architectures that do not adapt to the dynamically changing circumstances of Grid [2].

In the past, WfMS was used in well-defined activities where the processes tend to be more established and stable. But at present WfMS may be used in more diverse business processes or in processes involving human interactions. In such situations, it is not always possible to predict in advance all the parameters.

We construct a distributed network of agents that can adapt to the dynamics of Grid. It is adaptable in the following ways: 1) from the process perspective, the process model can be changed dynamically; 2) from the resource perspective, the choosing particular resource could be done at run time according to the history data; 3) from individual task point of view, in order to take advantage of web services that are available in an intranet as well as in the Internet, our system provides mechanisms to integrate and use these Web Services.

---

* This work is supported by National Natural Science Foundation of China (No.90412012).

H. Zhuge and G.C. Fox (Eds.): GCC 2005, LNCS 3795, pp. 117 – 122, 2005.

2 Related Work

2.1 Coloured Petri Nets

CPNs [3] are used to model workflow systems due to their sound mathematical foundation, rich analysis techniques and the fact that they have been used extensively for modeling distributed systems. CPN Tools [4] are used here to design and execute the models. CPNs consist of the following basic elements:

- Tokens, which are typed data values.
- Places, which are typed locations that can contain zero or more tokens.
- Transitions, which represent actions whose firing can change the number, location and value of tokens in the places connected to them. Sometimes a transition may associate a guard (for example [a=True,b=True] in Fig. 2), which is a Boolean expression, to define an additional constraint that must be satisfied for the transition to be enabled.
- Arcs, which connect places and transitions. An arc can have associated inscriptions, which are Java expressions whose evaluation to token values affects the enabling and firing of transitions.

2.2 Agent Systems

Some commonly accepted characteristics of agent system are: reactivity, autonomy, collaborative behavior, adaptivity and mobility [5]. There are several benefits of using multi-agent systems for building complex software [6]. For example, multi-agent systems can offer a high level of abstraction and encapsulation. Multi-agent systems offer a distributed and open architecture. Because agents are independent, every agent can decide by itself what is the best strategy for solving a particular problem.

Agent technology has been used in the context of WfMS. In some cases the agents fulfill particular roles that are required by different tasks in the workflow, the existing workflow is used to structure the coordination of these agents, for example, Nissen [7] designed a set of agents to perform activities associated with the supply chain process in the area of e-commerce. In other cases, the agents have been used as part of the infrastructure associated with the WfMS itself, these agents provide an open system with loosely coupled components, which provides more flexibility than the traditional systems [8].

2.3 Web Services

Web Services are software components available in the Internet; they provide certain services of interest for some of the tasks associated with a process model. For example, the process model associated with the travel plan of a tourist depends upon the weather conditions.

Buhler et al. [9] integrate agent-based workflow systems with web services, BPEL4WS is used as a process model and this model is converted to a Petri net. The problem with this approach is that the demonstration system developed by them so far does not support some simple constructs of BPEL4WS. However, in our system the process model is described using a CPN that can be directly executed. Our system does not require the conversion of a BPEL process into a Petri net process.

3 Multi-agent Framework Integrated with Web Services

Our framework consists of seven agents that provide the functionality to control the workflow (see Fig. 1); in addition, there is an UDDI Server that is used to invoke external Web Services.

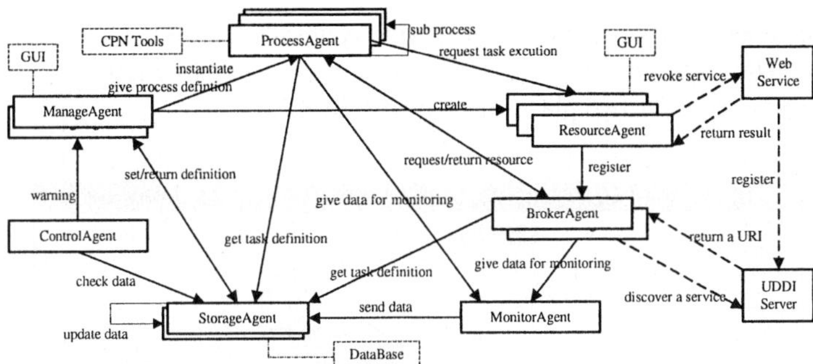

Fig. 1. Architecture of the agent based workflow system

The ManageAgent provides all functionality the workflow manager needs such as creation and deletion of tasks, instantiation of new process instances and creation of ResourceAgents. The workflow process models are executed by the ProcessAgent throuth the CPN engine. For each work case a new ProcessAgent is created. A transition in a CPN represents the task that has to be performed. The ProcessAgent assigns this task to a ResourceAgent. Each resource in the system has its own ResourceAgent and gets registered to at least one of the BrokerAgents that allocate the resources to the process. The StorageAgent manages the persistent data that is needed, for instance the definition of tasks, roles and processes and the monitored data. The MonitorAgent gathers these data and sends them to StorageAagent. The ControlAgent provides the feedback mechanism required for process re-engineering, it continuously looks for abnormalities to the criteria specified by the human manager and sends warning messages to the ManageAgent and also logs these messages.

Our framework supports adaptability from process, resource and task perspectives.

For each work case, a new process agent is created and an appropriate CPN model is instantiated. While the workflow system is running, there might be a scenario where requires a new CPN model. In this case there are several possible actions can take place. The choice depends on the scope of the change requested and the degree it has to be applied to the existing work cases. If the change has to be applied to new work cases that are waiting in the queue to be processed, then we can easily instantiate the ProcessAgent with the modified model instead of the old model. However, if the proposed change in the process should be applied to the running instances, we can transfer the state of the running instance to the new model by making use of one agent for each work case.

The resource adaptability is achieved by the run time binding of the ResourceAgent to the BrokerAgent and allocating resources to perform a task dynamically. A resource may register its availability and the roles it can perform at any time.

The tasks specified in the model can invoke a suitable Web Service. Task perspective deals with the atomic activities specified in the process model such as 'billing' task associated with a airline ticket service.

4 An Example of Airline Ticket Service System

We choose an example of airline ticket service system to illustrate the functionality of the system. The CPN model of it is shown in Fig. 2, in this Figure, all places are STRING type except for two places tagged with BOOL.

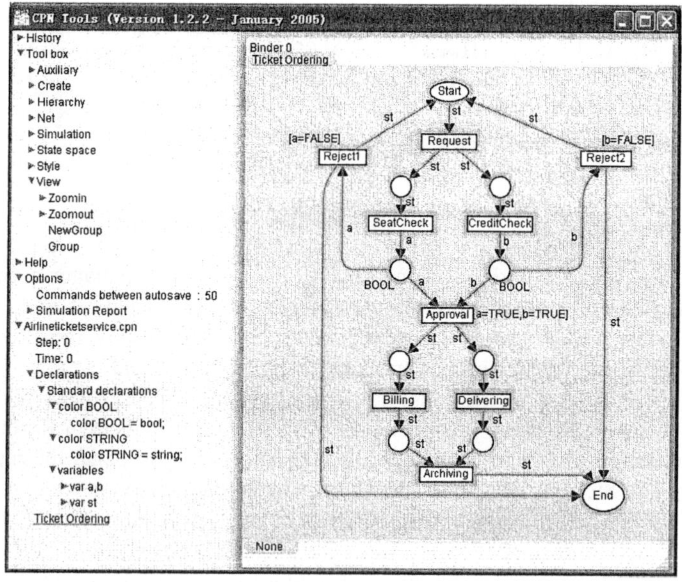

Fig. 2. The snapshot of the simulation of airline ticket service system

After a request for ordering ticket arrives, the system firstly checks seat's availability and whether the credit rating of the customer is satisfactory. The credit checking activity is available as an external Web Service, which can be invoked by ResourceAgent. If the credit of the customer is below the purchasing limits, the order is rejected. Otherwise the execution continues to the next task. Credit and seat's availability checks are done in parallel to speed up the process and the results are then evaluated. The guard associated with transition **Approval** represents that transition Approval can enable only when the results of credit and seat's availability checks both are **true**. After transition **Approval** is fired, the delivering of the ticket and the sending of the bill are done in parallel. Finally the results of delivering and billing activities are archived to be able to follow up possible complaints.

4.1 Intelligent Resource Allocation

Assume that a request for ticket arrives. The first step is the creation of a new ProcessAgent and getting all task definitions. Then the newly created ProcessAgent starts executing the work case by putting a job token in the place called **Start** (see Fig. 2). This activates the transition **Request**.

Fig. 3 shows how the resource is allocated depending on the history data. The ProcessAgent requests the BrokerAgent to return a resource that can perform the task. The BrokerAgent firstly finds the list of all resources that can perform the task from the StorageAgent. Then, depending upon the history data for this task, it chooses the resource that can perform this task in the least amount of time.

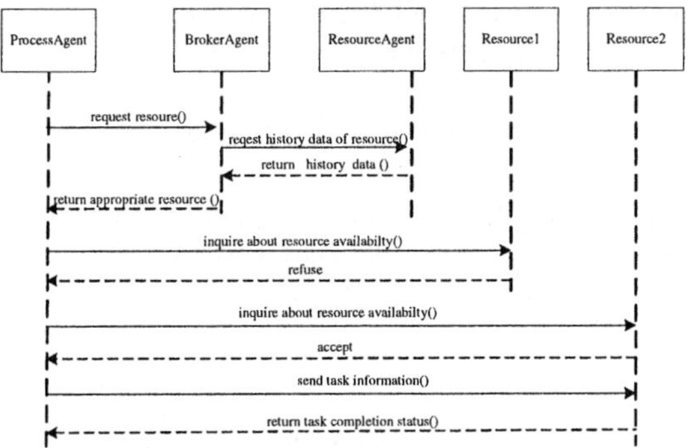

Fig. 3. Sequence diagram of allocating resource to task

If BrokerAgent cannot allocate a resource it will send the ProcessAgent a message that it failed to allocate a resource and the ProcessAgent has to decide how to handle this. After the resource executes the task and returns the result of the task, the CPN Tools engine continues executing the CPN model. This process continues for the remaining tasks based on the model.

4.2 Dynamic Discovery and Invocation of Web Services

There are scenarios in a workflow model where certain services are available in the Internet. For example, the credit of the customer can be checked using a Web Service. So, the workflow system has to support mechanisms by which this can be accomplished.

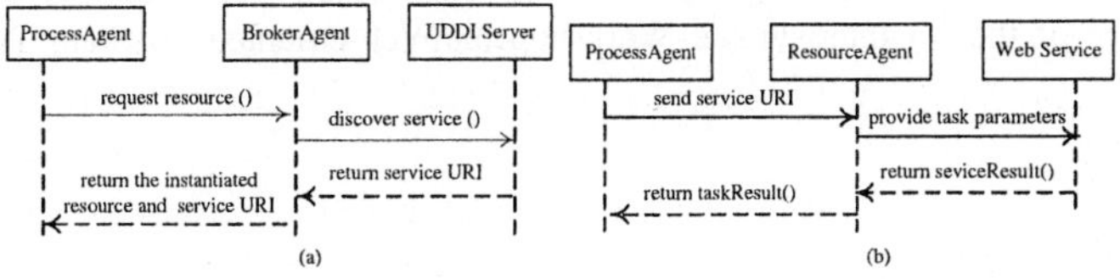

Fig. 4. Sequence diagram for (a) discovery and (b) Invocation of Web Services

Fig. 4 shows how our framework discovers and invokes Web Services dynamically. Task parameters are specified by the WSDL definition of the service interface. The ResourceAgent parses the corresponding WSDL document and invokes the Web Service.

After the results of Web Service are returned to the ProcessAgent. The ProcessAgent then decides where the token in the CPN has to be placed, i.e., if the credit is low, then the work case is rejected or else it proceeds to the execution of the next task by enabling the **Approval** transition.

5 Conclusion

In this paper, we employ a distributed network of software agents that can adapt to dynamically changing circumstances in Grid. Through an example, we have shown how the framework allocates resources based on history data and how it can discover and invoke the Web Services dynamically. All these make the architecture suitable to dynamically changing Grid environment.

Our future work is to examine the model's properties such as liveness, soundness, reachability, etc. by using CPN Tools's analysis Toolbox.

References

1. S. Meilin, et al., "Workflow Management Systems: A Survey". In Proceedings of IEEE International Conference on Communication Technology. Beijing, China, 1998.
2. J. Shepherdson, S. Thompson, B. Odgers, "Cross Organisational Workflow Coordinated by Software Agents". In Proceedings of WACC Workshop on Cross-Organisational Workflow Management and Coordination. 1999. San Francisco, USA, 1999.
3. K. Jensen, "Coloured Petri Nets – Basic Concepts, Analysis Methods and Practical Use, Vol. 1: Basic Concepts" (2nd Edition), Heidelberg, Berlin: Springer-Verlag, 1996.
4. CPN Tools, http://www.daimi.au.dk/CPNTools
5. J. Bradshaw, "An Introduction to Software Agents". In Software Agents, J. Bradshaw, Editor, Cambridge: MIT Press, 1997.
6. M. Wooldridge, "Intelligent Agents". in Multiagent Systems, G. Weiss, Editor, Cambridge: MIT Press, 1999.
7. M. Nissen, "Supply Chain Process and Agent Design for E-Commerce". In [33]rd International Conference on System Sciences, Hawaii, 2000.
8. M. Wang, H. Wang, "Intelligent Agent Supported Flexible Workflow Monitoring System". In Proc. of [14]th International Conference on Advanced Information Systems Engineering, Toronto, 2002.
9. P. Buhler, J. Vidal, "Integrating agent services into BPEL4WS defined workflows". In Proceedings of the [4]th International Workshop on Web-Oriented Software Technologies, 2004.

A New United Certificate Revocation Scheme in Grid Environments*

Ying Liu, Sheng-rong Wang, Jing-bo Xia, and Jun Wei

Telecommunication Engineering Institute, Air Force Engineering University, Xi'an, shaanxi, 710077, P.R. China
{yying_liu, sr_wan, jingbo_xia, weijun}@126.com

Abstract. This paper analyses security drawbacks of traditional certificates revocation in GSI. And we bring forward a new united certificate revocation scheme. In our scheme, one-way hash chains, novel multiple certificates and CRLs shared mode are proposed to improve the revocation mechanism. So partial functions of CA are distributed to other Grid nodes, congestion and single-point failure is avoided in Grid environments. The certificates issued by different CAs could carry out mutual authentication, and users can verify the validity of certificates without retrieving the revocation information from the CA which issues the certificates. To study the performance, three classical revocation schemes are used to compare with our united revocation scheme in the experiments. Simulation results and analysis show that the peak request value of united revocation is lower than other three schemes and the peak bandwidth value is narrower and the risk is reduced.

1 Introduction

The Globus Toolkit has emerged as the dominant middleware for Grid deployments worldwide. The Grid Security Infrastructure (GSI) [1] is the portion of the Globus Toolkit that provides the fundamental security services needed to support Grids. The CRL-based mechanisms adopted in GSI require the certificate verifier to obtain the revocation information from a third party server. This could bring a heavy burden to applications and result in bottle-neck and single-point failure.

Many efforts have been devoted to improve the efficiency of certificates revocation. Kocher [2] proposed Certificate Revocation Trees (CRTs). Gassko, Gemmell and MacKenzie [3] proposed EFECTS (Easy Fast Efficient Certification System) that combines the best properties of certificates and CRTs. Rivest [4] proposed an agent based approach that employs on-line "suicide bureaus" to issue "certificates of health" for certificates. But these approaches above could not solve bottle-neck and single-point failure problems perfectly in Grid environments.

In this paper, a new united certificate revocation scheme based on one-way hash chains, multiple certificates and CRLs shared mode is brought out. This scheme contributes to certificates revocation in the following aspects: (1) CA is nor necessary when a certificate needs revoke; (2) the problem of single-point failure and CA's cross

* This research is supported by Shaanxi Provincial Natural Science Foundation of China under Grant No. 2004F14.

H. Zhuge and G.C. Fox (Eds.): GCC 2005, LNCS 3795, pp. 123 – 128, 2005.

authentication can be solved better; (3) communications congestions are avoided and real-time of certificates revocation is ensured.

The rest of this paper is organized as follows: Section 2 introduces traditional X.509 public key certificates revocation in GSI. A new united certificate revocation scheme is proposed in Section 3. Experimental results of the united revocation scheme are discussed in Section 4. Section 5 is conclusions and future work.

2 Traditional Certificates Revocation in GSI

The GSI uses public key cryptography as the basis for its functionality. A central concept in GSI authentication is the certificates. Every user and service on the Grid is identified via a certificate, which contains information to identifying and authenticating the user or service.

GSI supports certificates revocation lists (CRLs). CRL is a list of certificates that have been revoked before the predetermined expiration date. There are several reasons why a certificate need be revoked and placed on a CRL. For instance, the private key specified in the certificates might have been leaked or the user specified in the certificates may no longer have authority to use it.

When verifying a certificate, user examines the relevant CRLs to make sure it has not been revoked yet. CRL is maintained by a CA, and it provides information about revoked certificates which are issued by that CA. CRLs only list current certificates, since expired certificates could not be accepted in any case; when a revoked certificate's expiration date occurs, the certificates must be removed from the CRLs.

Although CRLs are maintained in a distributed manner, there must be central repositories for CRLs, such as, network sites containing the latest CRLs from many organizations. So, this certificate revocation approach has two disadvantages in Grid environments as follows: (1) This revocation mechanisms require all the certificates verifiers to obtain the revocation information from a trusted third party to check the status of a public-key certificate. That may place a heavy burden of processing, communication and storage on the CA as well as the trusted parties, which might be unaffordable to applications with limited computational and/or network capability. (2) The dynamic joining and exiting of Grid nodes could result in single-point failure of overall system, and different certificates from different CAs must be affirmed by cross authentication, so much CAs' authentication would slow the velocity of Grid service and add complexity to Grid applications.

3 The United Certificate Revocation Scheme

There are two conditions for certificates revocation: firstly, the private key corresponding to the public key in the certificates may be lost or leaked; secondly, the certification contract may be terminated or the certificates holder's status and abilities described in certificates may change or have been cancelled by the manager.

Next, we put forward a new revocation mechanism of X.509 public key certificates. By using one-way hash chains, it can make certificates invalidate temporarily or timelessly without CA's participation in the first condition above. Then, multiple certificates and CRLs shared mode are used to reduce the Peak request value in the second one.

3.1 New Certificates Based on One-Way Hash Chains

The definition of a one-way hash function is given in [5]. A hash chain of length N is constructed by applying a one-way hash function H( ) recursively to an initial seed value s.

We divide the maximum lifetime of a certificate into short periods. The certificates could expire at the end of any period, the expiry under the control of the certificates owner or his manager. The certificates verifiers can check the validity without retrieving the revocation information from the CA. Hence this revocation scheme is simpler without incurring any security penalty. A one-way hash chain is constructed by recursively applying an input string to a one-way hash function, which can be denoted as $H_i(r) = H(H_{i-1}(r))$ $(i = 1, 2,\ldots)$, where $H_0(r) = r$ is the root of the hash chains.

For getting a certificate, the user of Grid firstly generates a pair of keys on one Grid node: SK_1 – private key ; PK_1– public key. Then, define the certificates parameters: T – maximum lifetime ; D – starting valid date ; L – time period for refreshing validity of the certificate. Suppose $j = T/L$ is an integer. The refreshing points are denoted as $D_1 = D+L$, $D_2 = D+2*L\ldots$, $D_j = D+j*L$ and generate a one-way hash chain $H_i(r) = H(H_{i-1}(r))$ $(i = 1,2, \ldots, j)$, where $H_0(r) = r$ and r is a random number known only to user. Finally, user send $(PK_1, D, H_j(r), j, L)$ to the CA.

CA authenticate user's request and generate a certificate (U, PK, D, Hj(r), j, L). Compared with an ordinary public-key certificate, the new certificate contains extra data $(H_j(r), j, L)$ as described in Fig.1.

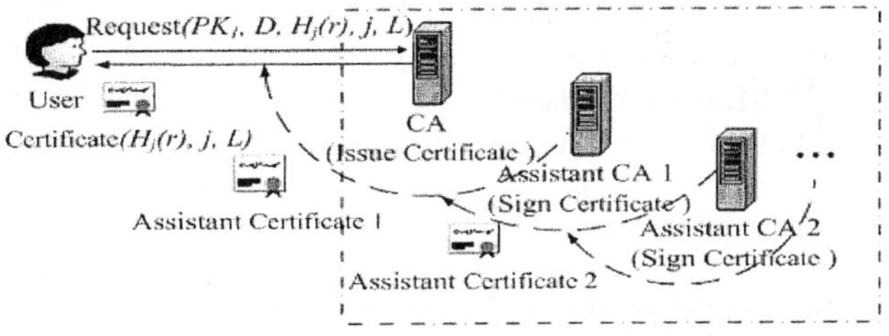

Fig. 1. One-way hash chains and multiple certificates

User should release $H_{j-1}(r)$ to initialize the validity of certificate after received it from CA. If user wants to revoke the certificate for some reasons, he can do so by stopping release of hash values, thus the certificate will expire soon at the next refreshing point. The user could even temporarily invalidate certificate, and refresh certificate later if necessary by releasing the corresponding hash value. For certificate revocation in the first condition that mentioned at the beginning of this section, CA is not needed. So it will reduce CA's burden and overhead.

3.2 Description of Multiple Certificates

In order to solve the problems of single-point failure and CA's cross authentication, we put forward novel certificates, called multiple certificates. For issuing multiple certificates, several CAs constitute a virtual organization (VO). Other members of the VO sign the content of certificates according to appointed order when one CA issue it, and generate a assistant certificate that includes the content of original one and the CA's signature for it. For example, User sends his request for a certificate to the CA, as showed in Fig.1. If CA authenticates the request, it will issue the certificate. At the same time, assistant CA 1 also sign it and generate assistant certificate 1 and assistant CA 2 sign assistant certificate 1 and generate assistant certificate 2. So, we only need either assistance certificate verify the validity of the certificate when the validity is required but there is without direct communications with CA that issues it.

3.3 CRLs Shared Mode

For Grid applications, there are large numbers of users and resources. Each of them holds a certificate. When their certificates must be revoked, enormous CRLs will be brought to CA. CA's server will be a bottle-neck for the whole system, network delay will increase and users cannot get the certificate revocation information in time. In addition, because the nodes of Grid are dynamic, it must assure all nodes reliable to obtain the latest CRLs even list server is disabled at a particular time. According to characteristics of Grid, we bring out the CRLs shared mode.

Each Grid node downloads CRLs from CA's directory server, and issues it as the form of Grid services. The node finds and obtains latest CRLs from other nodes or CAs according to the algorithm as follows:

```
1. Check local cache for current CRL
2. If (no CRL or not CRL valid) then
3.   Check for current CRL in nearby nodes
4.   If (no valid CRL in peers) then
5.     Get current CRL from CA's directory server
6.   Else
7.     use CRL from nodes
8. Else
9.   use CRL in local cache
```

CAs use own personal key to sign CRLs, and the verifiers affirm that CRLs are not tampered by authentication the signature with CAs' public key.

4 Experiments and Analysis

In order to study the performance of the proposed scheme, we have run some experiments through simulation. The simulated environments are conducted on a Grid environment consisting of eight Lenovo E3 workstations, an IBM X455 server and a Lenovo T630 server. The two servers simulate two CAs that have sustaining business to issue and manage certificates.

Fig. 2 shows the result of the simulation for an example environment with 10000 users, 25 certificate validations per end entity per day, CRL updates per 60 minutes, and a revocation rate of 10% of all certificate per year.

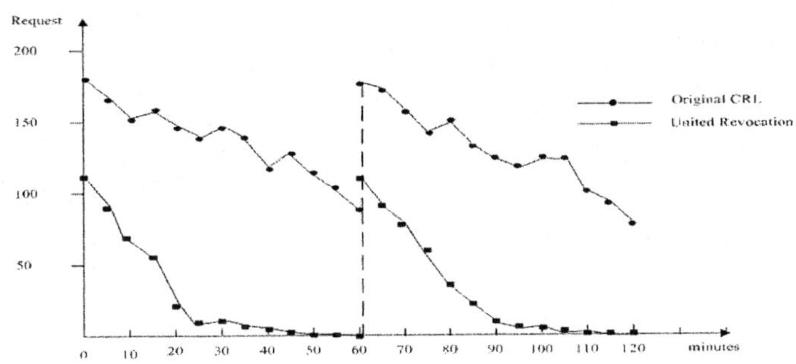

Fig. 2. Result of the simulation

As shown in the figure3, our proposed United Revocation scheme performed much better compare to the original CRL scheme. Requests per minute are reduced obviously.

Next, we calculate the peak request value, CRLs size and peak bandwidth value to analyze the performance of the scheme. At the same time, we calculate these parameters of Original CRL, Delta-CRL [6] and Segment-CRL [7] schemes as a contrast. The results are shown in Table 1.

Table 1. Comparison of four revocation schemes

Parameters	Original CRL	Delta CRL	Segment CRL	United Revocation
peak request value (r/s)	52.10	52.10	52.10	10.92
CRLs size(KB)	1318	196	330	1318
Peak bandwidth value (Mbps)	537	501	135	112
Risk	high	low	high	low

The assumption and constraints are specified as follows: There are 4,500,000 users, each of which has a certificate; on average, every user has 10 request everyday. Request rate obey an exponential distribution; CA revokes 4500 certificates everyday, issuance cycle of CRL is 24 hours; period of certificates validity is 365 days.

Because the setting with 8 connected nodes share in the CA's burden and the users can revoke their certificates based on one-way hash chains without CA's participation in some circumstances, the peak request value of united revocation is only 20.96% of other three approaches. Although the size of CRLs in our scheme isn't smaller than others, the peak bandwidth value is narrower. And with the multiple certificates, the problems of single-point failure and CA's cross authentication are solved.

5 Conclusions and Future Work

In this paper, we introduce a new united certificate revocation scheme in Grid environments. The certificates are issued on base of one-way hash chains, users can carry out certificates revocation autonomously rather than CA to control them. CRLs shared mode and multiple certificates are also adopted in our scheme. So partial functions of CA are distributed to other Grid nodes, congestion and single-point failure can be avoided. The certificates issued by different CAs may carry out mutual authentication, and users verify the validity of certificates without visiting CAs which issued the certificates and real-time of certificates revocation can be ensured. Our future work is to implement and test the scheme cooperating with the Shaanxi Digital Certificate Authority of China.

References

1. Welch, V.: Security for Grid Services. Twelfth International Symposium on High Performance Distributed Computing (HPDC-12). IEEE Press (2003)
2. Kocher, P.: On Certificate Revocation and Validation. Proceedings of Financial Cryptography 98. Lecture Notes in Computer Science, Vol. 1465. Springer-Verlag, Anguilla BWI (1998) 172-177
3. Gassko, I., Gemmell, P. S., MacKenzie, P.: Efficient and Fresh Certification. Proceedings of Public Key Cryptography (PKC) 2000. Lecture Notes in Computer Science, Vol. 1751. Springer-Verlag, Melbourne Australia (2000) 342-353
4. Rivest, R.: Can We Eliminate Certificate Revocation Lists. Proceedings of Financial Cryptography 98. Lecture Notes in Computer Science, Vol. 1465. Springer-Verlag, Anguilla BWI (1998) 178-183
5. Berson, T.A., Gong , L., Lomas, T.M.A.: Secure, Keyed, and Collisionful Hash Functions. Technical Report. SRI-CSL-94-08. SRI International (1994)
6. Cooper, D.: A More Efficient Use of Delta-CRLs. Security and Privacy (2000) 190-202
7. Andre, A., Mike, J., Steve, L.: Selecting revocation solutions for PKI. Proceedings of The Fifth Nordic Workshop on Secure IT Systems (NORDSEC 2000). Reykjavik Iceland (2000) 360-376

A Novel Secure Routing System in Overlay Environment

Han Su and Yun Wang

Department of Computer Science & Engineering, Southeast University,
Lab of Computer Network and Information Integration, MOE,
Nanjing, 210096, P.R. China
sukerhan@seu.edu.cn

Abstract. Routers are effective building blocks for Internet. It is almost impossible to modify router software only for applications. How to satisfy applications' specific requirements of communication is a big problem. Now more and more systems begin to place application oriented routing service on overlay networks. This paper compares several overlay routing systems based on route number and brings forward a novel routing system based on trust model. System design principles are discussed and system simulation performance is analyzed. The results show that the system is able to provide secure routing service to applications in the case of vicious nodes.

1 Introduction

Routers are effective building blocks for Internet. With more and more routing demands appearing, such as multicast, QOS etc, traditional network routing functions are no longer satisfying. Due to high expenses and difficulties of deployment, it is almost impossible to modify router software only to meet several applications' demands. Many researchers begin to place these functions on overlay networks. Overlay network systems can be divided into two categories based on appointed route number, i.e. single-path systems and multi-path systems. This paper will provide a novel multi-path routing system in overlay environment. The contributions of the paper are on one hand trust concept is introduced to overlay routing service, on the other hand dynamic and random route selection helps to improve system security.

The rest of paper is constructed as following. Section 2 compares routing models in overlay environment. A novel multi-path routing system in overlay environment based on trust model is proposed and described in Section 3. In Section 4, simulation performance of possibility of vicious node appearing, vicious node removal and vicious node affections are analyzed. Section 5 is a paper summary.[1]

2 Overlay Routing Service

Overlay network technique aims to provide better solutions for problems such as routing problem with consideration of requirements from applications. [4]

[1] The research work is partially supported by 973 Program project (No. 2003CB317004), NSFC project (No. 60273038).

H. Zhuge and G.C. Fox (Eds.): GCC 2005, LNCS 3795, pp. 129 – 135, 2005.

2.1 Single-path Overlay Routing Systems

One of such systems is RON [5], which is a probe-based reactive routing protocol. RON uses link state protocol and obtains total network topology by exchanging routing information among each other. RON periodically sends probes to determine the availability, latency, and loss rate of route connecting nodes in overlay. When a probe is lost, the related node sends an additional string of up to four probes with one-second interval in order to determine if a remote host is down. Routes are selected based on average loss rate over last probes. RON is always used to construct an overlay in large areas with fixed peer number and network topology.

2.2 Multi-path Overlay Routing Systems

(1) Replicated Packets

In this mode, a source peer sends packets by primary route and backup route simultaneously. If packet loss occurs in primary route, the lost packets can be recovered from another route. In Reference 6, each packet is sent twice. The first packet is sent directly over the Internet, and the second one is sent through a randomly chosen. In this mode, a source peer sends packets by primary route and backup packets along another route simultaneously. If packet loss occurs in primary route, the lost packets can be recovered from another route. In Reference 6, each packet is sent twice. The first packet is sent directly over the Internet, and the second one is sent through a randomly chosen intermediate node on overlay. This solution will achieve fault tolerance routing, while extra resource assumption is obvious.

(2) Backup Routes

Every peer in Reference 7 and 8 maintains more than two backup routes. System sends probes to determine the availability of primary route. If there is something wrong with primary route, a sender will transmit packets along backup routes. Communication delay is greater.

Recent works on multi-path routing overlay systems pay more attention to selecting irrelevant routing routes. These systems always require fixed network topology and peer numbers, which guarantee network stability.

3 Trust-Based Multi-path Routing System

In this section, we put forward a trust-based multi-path routing system. We think it is quite common that there are some vicious nodes in Internet. If they appear in an overlay route, it means that information message may not arrive to its destination according to predefined specifications. Trust is a concept to evaluate to what degree a node in Internet is able to behave as it is required. Trust is presented as a value between 0 and 1. A node's trust value with 1 stands for that it is absolutely trustful, otherwise distrustful with 0. With a trust value between 0 and 1, a node behaves sometimes well and sometimes bad. Higher a trust value is, more trustful a node is. Each node in the system maintains a trust vector for all its related nodes. We assume that all intermediate nodes a packet passes are recorded in one of the packet format fields.

3.1 Vicious Behavior Determination

(1) Receiver Mode

We take the following scenario into consideration. A sender uses MD5 to make a MIC to a packet and encrypts it. After getting the packet, the receiver authenticates the packet integrity to determine if there is a juggle node in the route. If yes, the receiver could not tell which node it is. A simple solution is that the receiver updates the trust vector of its previous node in the route, and so on. Every node in the route updates the trust vector of its previous node.

(2) Sender Mode

A receiver will return an ACK to a sender after receiving packets successfully. If the sender does not receive the ACK in a period of time, it demonstrates some nodes in the route fail due to unexpected behavior. Note that network link failures are out of our consideration in this paper. The sender then updates the trust vector of its next node in the route and so on. Every node in the route updates the trust vector of its next node.

3.2 Trust Value Computing

A trust vector [9] is used to describe trust degree of a node in the viewpoint of the other node. A trust vector is a binary vector with a length of 8 or 16 bits. Value 1 represents a successful packet exchange and value 0 represents a failure. Suppose that a trust vector about node A in node B is 11101000. If the next transmission is successful, the trust vector is evolved to 11110100, otherwise 01110100.

With trust vector, trust value for A by B can be computed. Trust value has a range of -1 to 3. Initially trust value is 0. Trust value changes according to its trust ratio, which is the ration of number of 1 in trust vector and vector length. To denotes trust value before updates, Tn for trust value after updates, and Tr for trust ratio.

$$cTn = \alpha\, To + Tr + \beta \qquad (1)$$

Here α denotes the weight factor, which is from 0 to 1. β is the adjusting factor, which is 1, 0 or -1. The default value of β is 0. In addition, we define $\theta 1$ and $\theta 2$ the threshold values ($0<\theta 1<\theta 2<1$). If $Tr < \theta 1$, the trust ratio is too small, β should be -1. On the other hand, if $Tr > \theta 2$, β is 1.

Table 1. Relationship of To, θ1 and θ2

To	-1	0	1	2	3
θ1		40%	30%	20%	10%
θ2	70%	80%	90%	100%	

Trust value plays an essential role in next hop selection. A node with higher trust value will be selected with higher probability. We denote Ps as the probability of a node to be selected. In our system, Ps = (Tn+1)/10.

3.3 Routing Strategies Based on Trust Value

We assume that all the nodes in the system are fully connected. In transferring a packet, a node looks up its routing table and finds all potential nodes for next hop. All its neighboring nodes except its previous node for the packet are under consideration. The rules for node selection are:

(1) If there are some neighboring nodes' trust values higher than 1, all such nodes are potential nodes;
(2) If there is no neighboring node's trust value higher than 1 and there are neighboring nodes with trust value of 0, all such nodes are potential nodes;
(3) If all neighboring nodes are with trust value of -1, the node reports access unavailable and disperses the information.

If potential node set is not null, a node in the set is selected randomly. The packet is transferred to the appointed node as its next hop. Otherwise, a NACK is returned to the packet's sender according to its routing information contained in the packet.

The procedure goes on till the packet arrives at its destination. If an error occurs in the route and the destination has not received the packet, the sender will try to transmit the packet by another node in potential node set. The procedure fails till no potential node is available. An exception report informs applications.

4 System Properties Analysis

4.1 Security Analysis

(1) Preventing wiretapping nodes

Before sending a message, a sender encrypts it and divides it to several fragments. Then the sender transmits them along different routes to its destination. After receiving all the fragments, the receiver assembles them together and decrypts them. Even if a vicious node of wiretapping may get some fragments, and decrypt some of them fortunately, it is difficult for him to get to know the whole message. Multi-path strategy can be great beneficial as to avoid this kind of vicious nodes.

(2) Anonymity

A sender selects a relay node randomly from its routing table to transfer packets to a receiver. Thanks to the protocol packet format, every node in a route knows its previous relay node. A sender's ID is concealed from all relay nodes. Only the receiver knows about it. Even a vicious node of wiretapping could not ascertain sender's ID unless it decrypts a packet. System achieves sender anonymity and prevents intrusions from route tracking.

(3) Preventing juggling nodes

A receiver will inform a packet's source node as soon as it finds that a packet is polluted. The source node may retransmit a packet in two ways. One way is that a sender retransmits the packet directly to the destination without any relay node in overlay. The other way is that a sender retransmits the packet along another route in overlay. If we use the first method when a vicious node juggles continually, sender anonymity will be destroyed. Practically, when a juggling event is detected, sender retransmits a packet along another route. If a packet has not been transmitted correctly after three times, the first method will be used.

(4) Preventing routing failure nodes

Routing failure nodes are those who do not perform routing function correctly including routing redirection and other ill routing nodes. A receiver will return an ACK to corresponding sender after receiving a packet successfully. If a sender does not receive ACK in a period of time, the sender will retransmit packets along another route. Practically, we may not distinguish an overlay routing failure from network link failure.

In our system, after a period of trust computing and route selecting, the number of juggling nodes and routing failure nodes decreases obviously in selected routes.

4.2 System Simulation Performance

Suppose that a total number of nodes in an overlay is n. In our simulation test, n equals 100. Further assume that average route length is k, and the total number of vicious nodes is m. Vicious nodes cover juggle nodes and routing failure nodes. Senders and receivers are all good nodes.

4.2.1 Ratio of Vicious Nodes Appearing In a Route

Initially the possibility of routes covering no vicious nodes is:

$$\prod_{i=0}^{k} \frac{n-m-2-i}{n-2-i} \tag{2}$$

The possibility of routes including at least one vicious node is:

$$1-\prod_{i=0}^{k} \frac{n-m-2-i}{n-2-i} \tag{3}$$

With progress of packet exchange and trust computing, the possibility of routes including vicious nodes decreases dramatically as shown in Fig.1 and Fig.2.

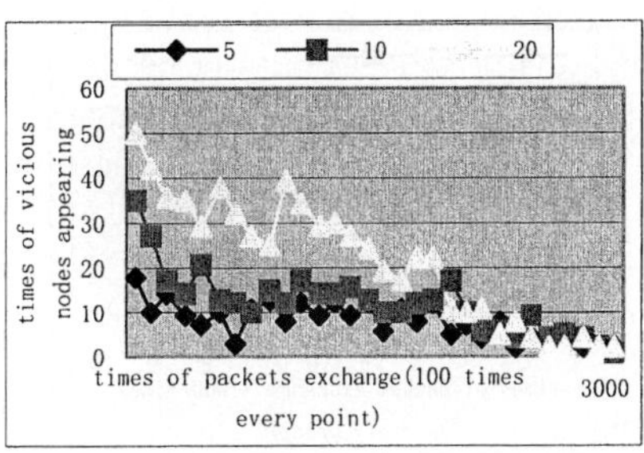

Fig. 1. Possibility tests with always vicious nodes

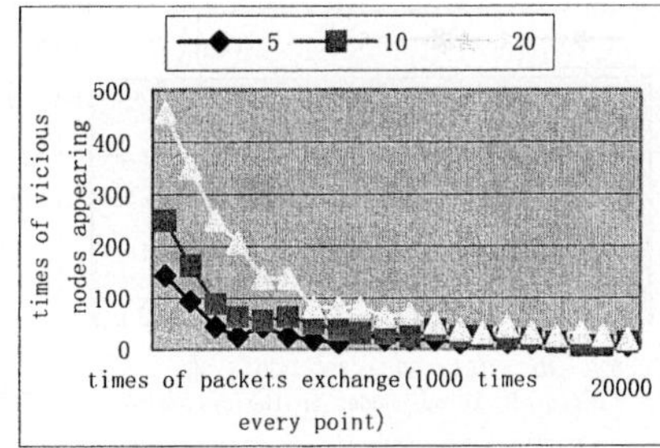

Fig. 2. Possibility tests with occasionally vicious nodes

Fig.1 and Fig.2 both show the test results of a system with 5, 10 and 20 vicious nodes respectively. The different simulation condition for Fig.1 and Fig.2 lies on vicious nodes' behavior. Fig.1 is with always vicious nodes that destroy passing packets and their transmissions every time. Fig.2 is with occasionally vicious nodes that behave well sometimes and misbehave themselves sometimes.

Fig.1 tells us that after 3000 packet exchange, the possibility of vicious nodes appearing in a route decreases to 5% of the number in beginning. The situation in Fig.2 is more difficult. After 20000 packet exchanges, the possibility of vicious nodes appearing in a route decreases to 5% of the number in beginning.

In our simulation test, the ratio of vicious nodes that are not correctly evaluated is below 5%, and the ratio of normal nodes evaluated as vicious nodes by mistake is below 2%. This is because the system cannot precisely tell which node is a vicious node in a route when route failure appears. Every node in a route takes the responsibility for route failure no matter it is a normal or vicious node. In addition, it is almost impossible to remove all vicious nodes. We can use cryptology technology to restrain these remained vicious nodes.

4.2.2 Affections of Vicious Nodes

If vicious nodes appear in a route for a packet transmission, it is more likely that the packet will be retransmitted. In order to determine the affections of vicious nodes on packet transmission times, a simulation test is designed. Test results are shown in Fig.3 and Fig.4, where t stands for packet retransmission times of a packet.

Fig.3 shows the relationship between vicious node ratio in a system and packet retransmission times with different average route length of 4, 6 and 8. The curve illustrates that packet retransmission times go up with higher vicious node ratio in a system and higher average route length. If vicious node ratio is greater than 25%, packet retransmission times exceed 3. It means a sender will retransmit packets directly to its destination and sender anonymity may be destroyed.

Fig.4 tells us the relationship between packet retransmission times and trust computing progress with 5, 10 and 20 vicious nodes in a system respectively in the case that average route length is 6. The curve shows the trend that packet retransmission times decrease obviously with trust computing progress.

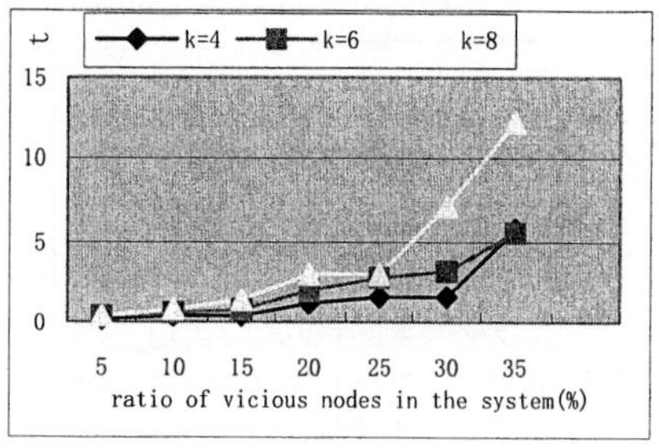

Fig. 3. Relationship between vicious node ratio and packet retransmission times

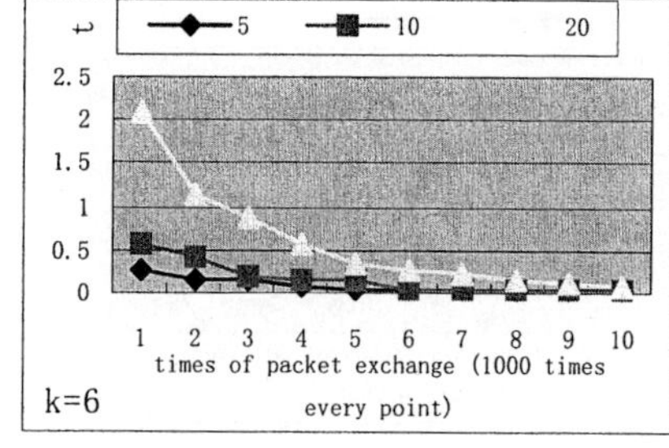

Fig. 4. The influence of trust model on packet retransmission times

6 The Conclusion

This paper compares overlay routing systems in existence and provides a novel overlay routing system providing secure multi-path routing service. Unlike present multipath systems, this system is based on trust model. Using the trust model and multipath strategy, vicious node number decreases obviously in selected routes. We plan to simulate the system in a larger area and evaluate its performance in the near future.

References

1. S. Sherry, G Meyer. RFC2092: Protocol Analysis for Triggered RIP. January 1997 http://rfc2092.x42.com
2. Y. Rekhter, T. Li. A Border Gateway Protocol 4 (BGP-4), RFC 1771, March 1995 http://www.scit.wlv.ac.uk/rfc/rfc17xx/RFC1771.html
3. A Akella, J Pang. A Comparison of Overlay Routing and Multi homing Route Control. Proc. ACM SIGCOMM 2004 Conference (Taormina, Sicily, Italy).
4. D Andersen, A Snoeren, Best-Path vs. Multi-Path Overlay Routing. In Proc. ACM SIGCOMM Internet Measurement Conference, (Miami, FL), (October. 2003.)
5. D Andersen, H Balakrishnan, M Kaashoek. Resilient Overlay Networks. In Proc. 18th ACM SOSP (Banff, Canada, October 2001), 131-145.
6. A Snoeren, K Conley, D Gifford. Mesh Based Content Routing Using XML. In Proc. 18th ACM SOSP(Banff, Canada, October 2001), 160–173.
7. B Zhao, L Huang, A Joseph. Exploiting Routing Redundancy Using a Wide-area Overlay. Technical Report UCB/CSD 2002.12, November 2002 , http://www.cs.ucsb.edu/~ravenben/tapestry/html/fault.html
8. D Zhu, M Gritter. Feedback Based Routing. In Proc. ACM HotNet-I Workshop 2002, (Princeton, NJ, USA, October 2002), 71 – 76
9. U Ersin, R Mark. A Reputation-Based Trust Management System for P2P Networks. ACM International Conference on Information and Knowledge Management, 2001.Atlanta, 65-73.

A Semantic Metadata Catalog Service for Grid

Kewei Wei, Ming Zhang, and Yaping Zhu

School of Electronics Engineering and Computer Science, Peking University, Beijing 100871, China
{wkw, mzhang, zhuyaping}@db.pku.edu.cn

Abstract. Metadata is the information that describes the most important feature of an object. In recent years, metadata plays a more and more important role in data intensive applications. In this paper, we propose a semantic metadata catalog service, Semantic MCS. Semantic MCS has a well-organized data management model and supports the query mechanism using Ontology inference. Furthermore, we discuss the main problems that we met in real Grid applications. We propose a framework of metadata interoperation to resolve the problem of the services interoperability. And we propose a dynamic framework for metadata management for the rapid changing metadata in Grid.

1 Introduction

In recent years, coordination and cooperation become more and more important in scientific research. Consequently, "Grid" technology is emerging as a new important field. The problem underlies the "Grid" concept is coordinated resource sharing and problem resolving in dynamic, multi-institutional virtual organizations[1]. Grid computing requires a mass of resources, which are of diverse form; therefore, it is a tough task to describe them in a uniform structured method. Besides, people who are working on different research areas have different knowledge background; as a result, they would give different description to the same resource, which renders it more difficult to make the "right" decision among thousands of resource candidates.

Metadata is the information that reflects the characteristic of a resource. Any property that can distinguish resources could be metadata, such as URI and resource owner. Metadata is able to represent the content, capacity and semantic of an object. Moreover, Metadata has the natural relationship with semantic web technologies. Semantic annotation is a kind of metadata and is used in Ontology reasoning.

In Grid, Metadata services exist in many forms:

Information Service is the metadata service that focuses on resource's status. Monitoring and Discovery System (MDS)[2] and R-GMA[3] are implementations of Information Service. Both of MDS and R-GMA are trying to support a more flexible metadata schema. Service Registry is another form of metadata services. Universal Description, Discovery and Integration (UDDI) registry is a typical example.

Besides these specific metadata services, there are several generic metadata catalog services:

Metadata Catalog (MCAT)[4] is a part of the Storage Resource Broker (SRB) from SDSC. MCAT is designed as a central catalog for the metadata of data files. It supports logical name space that is independent from the physical name space.

H. Zhuge and G.C. Fox (Eds.): GCC 2005, LNCS 3795, pp. 136 – 142, 2005.

Metadata Catalog Service (MCS)[5] is a project from USC. MCS is designed as a part of Grid infrastructure and follows the standards of Web Services. It is built upon other Grid Services, such as GSI and DAI.

However, none of the services that we have introduced can make use of the semantic information in metadata. In this paper, we made the following contributions:

- We develop a generic semantic metadata catalog services.
- We propose a dynamic framework for metadata management that focuses on the rapid changing metadata in Grid.
- We propose a framework of metadata interoperation that support the metadata interoperability.

2 Semantic Metadata in Grid

The information that can be processed by computer consists of three layers[6]: data, information and knowledge[7]. Metadata is "data about data"; therefore, metadata belongs to the "Information" layer. Semantic metadata contains richer semantic information than traditional metadata.

In order to find out the requirements of semantic metadata services, we will discuss the relationships between semantic metadata and Ontology in each stages of semantic metadata management in Grid. The entire semantic metadata lifecycle consists of five parts:

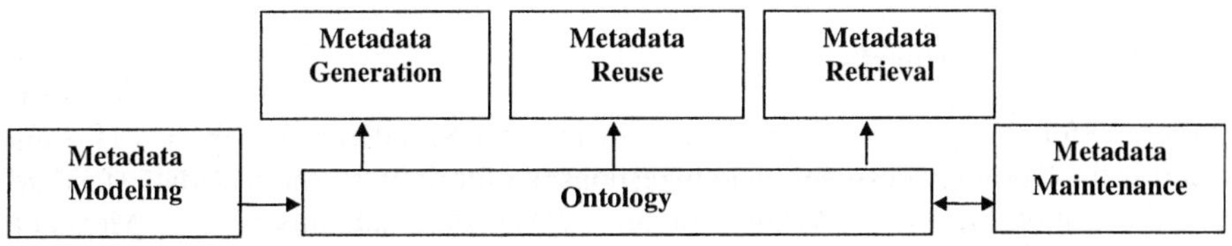

Fig. 1. The lifecycle of metadata

- Metadata modeling

Metadata is the property and abstract of resource. In Grid environment, there are complicated relationships between resources and resources properties, which can be described using Ontology. Ontology creation is the basic building block of metadata modeling. The Ontology used for semantic metadata consists of two categories: metadata definition and value Ontology. Metadata definition is the metadata standard of resources, such Dublin Core. Value Ontology contains the concept that is used as metadata value.

- Metadata generation

The resources' type that is used in Grid computing differs in thousands of ways, and resources have their own methods for metadata generation. No matter which the metadata generation method is used or what the metadata definition is followed, the metadata catalog must fit the metadata's schema and can find out the semantic information in it. The logical inference technology will help us to enrich the semantic information.

- Metadata reuse

Metadata reuse is to bridge the gap between the creator and the user of metadata. In traditional computing, metadata is generated for the resource owner or limited users in some institutions, while, in grid computing, metadata will be used for any user. Therefore, metadata must be understood by those who have totally different research backgrounds. The biggest challenge is sharing knowledge at different levels in all kinds of scenarios. In order to exchange information and knowledge between VOs, an open framework of metadata interoperation is required.

- Metadata retrieval

Metadata retrieval is the key problem of metadata problem. As mentioned before, logical reasoning can infer more information based on existed knowledge and information. So the main challenge is to use the richer information contained in semantic metadata. On the other hand, the process metadata retrieval must be efficient to answer the requestor in a reasonable time.

- Metadata maintenance

Metadata maintenance is the process of updating, annotating and refining metadata. Metadata in Grid changes along with the status of its corresponding resource; therefore, metadata has its own lifetime. Semantic metadata catalog service must update metadata before it expires.

3 Semantic Metadata Catalog Service

3.1 Semantic MCS Interface

There are four categories of users of Semantic MCS: 1)Domain expert - Domain expert is the Ontology designer, who is responsible for defining the metadata standard and the Ontology for a certain domain. 2)Metadata administrator - Metadata administrator is responsible for inserting, updating, deleting and organizing metadata. 3)Metadata consumer - Metadata consumer uses the metadata directly, who has the "read" right to metadata. 4)Other service - These services are other Semantic MCSs, which need to federate with each other. This requires the metadata interoperability.

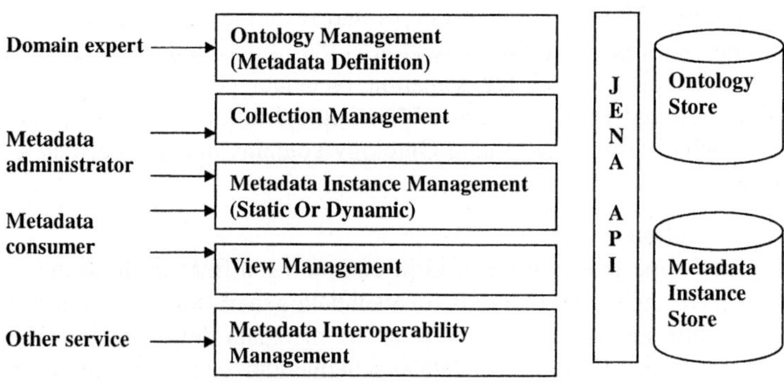

Fig. 2. Semantic MCS Interface

For these users, Semantic MCS should provide the following interfaces:

- Ontology management

Ontology management interface is provided for domain experts to create and refine domain Ontology. Metadata definition is a special kind of Ontology, which defines the metadata standard. In our system, we have designed a Grid resource Ontology. Our Ontology is based on the work of GLUE Schema[8] from EUDataGrid, CIM[9] from DMTF and Network Performance Hierarchy[10] from NM-WG.

- Metadata instance management

In Semantic MCS, semantic metadata is represented in RDF, and Ontology is represented in OWL[11]. We store metadata instance and Ontology in a central RDF repository and use JENA API to manipulate the store.

- Collection/View management

The collection/view concept is used in most metadata catalog system, such as MCAT and MCS. Metadata needs good organization for each type of users. Collections are a set of data items or other collections. This allows for defining authorization in a scalable way. For metadata consumer, they can aggregate the metadata that interest them into a view.

- Metadata interoperability management

In grid environment, it is impossible to manage all resources' information by a single center service. In order to coordinate these services, Semantic MCS must offer metadata interoperability so that lots of Semantic MCSs are able to collaborate well in Grid.

3.2 Dynamic Metadata Management Framework

In Grid environment, because of the status of rapid changing resources, lots of metadata have short lifetime. And it will make mistake if the "expired" metadata is used in resource selection. Whether the metadata stored in Semantic MCS is useful depends on the characteristics of resource and when the metadata is registered into catalog.

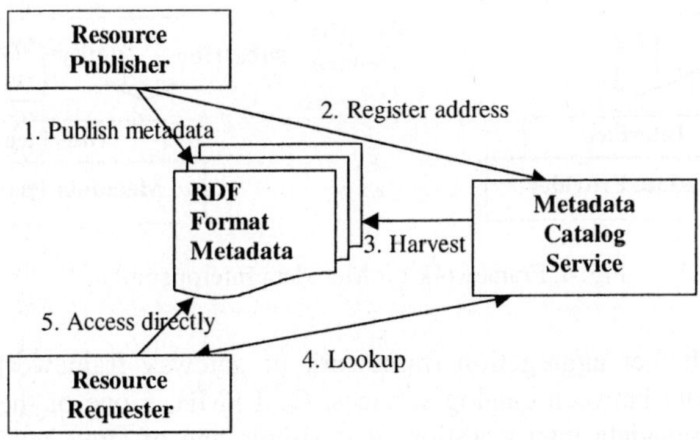

Fig. 3. Dynamic Metadata Management Framework

In our dynamic framework for metadata management, resource owner publish their resource metadata in a RDF format document, which is a dynamic document (e.g. a dynamic webpage), because its contents change as the status of the resource changes. Then it registers the address of the document into a Semantic MCS. The address may be a URL, a WS-Address, and so on. Due to the difference of the resource changing frequency, resource publisher needs to tell Semantic MCS what the estimated metadata lifetime is. Semantic MCS is responsible for retrieving the metadata according to the estimated lifetime, and cached these metadata. When some resource requester sends their request to service, the service returns and ranks the result according to the cached metadata. The result contains the address of original metadata document and the cached "metadata", including a time stamp. The requester then accesses these metadata documents directly to get the latest status of the metadata.

The main benefits of this framework are: 1)Resource owner publishes resources' status to MCS and consumer in a RDF document, so not only Semantic MCS, but also other services can access it in a uniform way. 2)RDF has a free schema; it is not necessary to register the structure of metadata. With the aid of Ontology, consumer and producer can get agreement with the syntax and semantic of these metadata. 3)Because the "cached metadata" may indicate which resources has low probability to match the request, the number of the resources that need to contact directly is declined.

3.3 The Framework of Metadata Interoperation

In grid environment, it is impossible to manage all resource's information by a single center service; therefore, we should create metadata catalog services for all kinds of VOs respectively. It brings up the issue how to coordinate these services. There are two possible approaches. The first is to aggregate these services into a center services by an aggregation protocol. MDS is an example of this framework. And the second is to use a gateway service. The gateway is responsible for selecting the service for users when they submit their request. In this framework, all metadata catalog services are independent. These two frameworks can be used together.

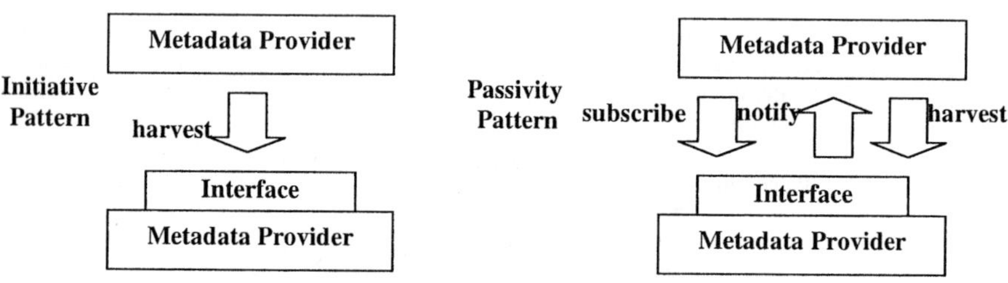

Fig. 4. Framework for Metadata Interoperation

No matter whether aggregation framework or gateway framework, we need to exchange metadata between catalog services. OAI-PMH is one of the most popular frameworks of metadata interoperation. It is simple and of "low barrier". However, OAI-PMH lacks in synchronization mechanism. We improved it to propose our framework of metadata interoperation framework between metadata catalogs.

There are two roles in the framework: metadata provider and metadata consumer. Metadata provider must expose an interface to publish the metadata to other services. Metadata consumer can harvest metadata from provider through the interface. The exchanged metadata is also transferred in a RDF document. The harvest is based on time stamp. That is, metadata consumer can get all public metadata in the catalog of metadata provider whose updating time is ahead of the time stamp. The published metadata is organized via view, so metadata consumer is able to limit the harvest metadata in a view.

And there are two scenarios in the framework: passivity and initiative. In passivity pattern, provider just implements the publishing protocol, and consumer can harvest the metadata after it gets the authentication. In initiative pattern, provider need offer a subscribe interface. Firstly, consumer subscribes via the interface, the subscription including consumer's address and the trigger threshold. When the number of the updated (including new inserted) items reach the threshold, provider will notify the consumer, and consumer begin harvesting.

The benefits of the framework are: 1)Because the framework extends OAI-PMH, it inherited all benefits of OAI-PMH. Its publishing interface is simple and easy for implementation. It supports the segmentation transfer when the network burden is heavy. 2)The exchanged information is also represented in RDF, so not only Semantic MCS but also other services can use it. 3)The subscription/notification mechanism makes it possible to synchronize the metadata between different VOs.

4 Conclusion and Future Works

In this paper, we describe a metadata catalog service, Semantic MCS, which supports the semantic metadata management in the Grid. We describe the requirements that occur on the lifecycle of semantic metadata. We propose an interfaces design of a semantic metadata catalog service. And for the problem of metadata interoperability and dynamic metadata management, we give our solution.

In our work, we make use of semantic information; however, users must specify the knowledge that is required by the reasoning process. We are currently studying how to select the right knowledge automatically.

Acknowledgements. Our work is supported by the National Natural Science Foundation of China under Grant No. 90412010 and ChinaGrid project of the Ministry of Education, China.

References

1. Ian Foster, Carl Kesselman, and Steven Tuecke, The Anatomy of the Grid: Enabling Scalable Virtual Organizations, International J. Supercomputer Applications, 15(3), 2001
2. MDS, http://www.globus.org/mds/
3. R-GMA, R-GMA: Relational Grid Monitoring Architecture, www.r-gma.org/
4. MCAT - A Meta Information Catalog, www.sdsc.edu/dice/Software/SRB/mcat.html

5. Ewa Deelman, et al, Grid-Based Metadata Services, 16th International Conference on Scientific and Statistical Database Management (SSDBM04), 21-23 June 2004 Santorini Island Greece
6. Keith G Jeffery, Knowledge, Information and Data, 1999
7. David De Roure, Nicholas R. Jennings and Nigel R. Shadbolt, The Semantic Grid: A Future e-Science Infrastructure, 2004
8. GLUE Schema, http://www.cnaf.infn.it/~sergio/datatag/glue/
9. CIM, http://www.dmtf.org/standards/cim/
10. GGF Network Measurements Working Group, A Hierarchy of Network Performance Characteristics for Grid Applications and Services, 2004
11. OWL, http://www.w3.org/2001/sw/WebOnt/

An ECA-Rule-Based Workflow Management Approach for Web Services Composition*

Yi Wang, Minglu Li, Jian Cao, Feilong Tang, Lin Chen, and Lei Cao

Department of Computer Science and Engineering, Shanghai Jiao Tong University, Shanghai 200030, China
{wangsuper, li-ml, cao-jian, tang-fl, chenling, lcao}@cs.sjtu.edu.cn

Abstract. Composing autonomous Web services to achieve new function, is receiving more and more attention in recent years in several computer science communities. The workflow model is the most important part in Web services composition. However, the existing approaches have difficulties in the process because their complexity. In this paper, we have developed an ECA (Event-Condition-Action)-rule-based workflow management system (EWMS) for Web service composition, which can help users compose Web services conveniently. We also use an image processing application to validate the feasibility and efficiency of our system.

1 Introduction

More and more interesting services are moving online and the web is being fast transformed into a service oriented environment where software components are available online in the form of Web services. The service oriented environment, we called service grid, brings up the emerging need of services composition, which means composing different services to a more complex and useful service that can provide new functions to achieve the users' needs.

Several approaches have been proposed and investigated to solve the problem of Web services composition. DAML-S[1] is a part of DARPA Agent Markup Language project that aims at making Web services computer-interpretable, which means being described with sufficient information to enable automated Web services discovery, invocation, aggregation into a process, and execution monitoring. Some people also use Petri net[2] or extended Petri net[3] to describe the model of Web services composition. The recently released Business Process Execution Language for Web Services (BPEL4WS)[4] supports business process coordination among multiple parties and enables modeling of long-running interactions between business processes. However, the use of these solutions needs too much modeling knowledge. They are much complicated for the end users.

In this paper, we present an ECA-rule-based workflow management system to enable users to construct and instantiate workflow models for composition of Web

* This work is supported by the 973 program (2002CB312002) of China, ChinaGrid program of MOE of China and the ShanghaiGrid project from the Science and Technology Commission of Shanghai Municipality (03dz15027).

H. Zhuge and G.C. Fox (Eds.): GCC 2005, LNCS 3795, pp. 143 – 148, 2005.

services easily, without having to interact with individual services composed. There are at least three good reasons for using ECA rule for Web services workflow modeling and analysis: It is easily understood by end-users, it can express complicated logical relationship of Web services, and it fits in with graphic realization.

The rest of this paper is organized as follows. Next section redefines some definitions of ECA rule. Section 3 introduces the framework of our workflow management system—EWMS. A modeling example for Web services composition is discussed in Section 4. The last Section concludes the whole paper and points out some future works briefly.

2 Related Definitions for ECA Rule

Event-Condition-Action (ECA) rule is put forward in the research field of active database[5]. For the purpose of using ECA rule in our system, we will redefine some basic definitions of ECA rule.

Definition 1. Event presents a function that map time to boolean value and can be presented as follows:

$$E : T \rightarrow \{\text{ True }, \text{False}\}$$

$$E(t) = \begin{cases} \text{True, if Event of E kind happen at the time of t} \\ \text{False, others} \end{cases}$$

Event can be differed as atomic event and composite event.

Definition 2. Atomic event means the one that can be detected directly by the workflow management system, such as the initialization, start, end, overtime, abortion and error of an activity.

Definition 3. A composite event is the composition of atomic events and other composite events through composing operators. Two basic composing operators are as follows:

- AND: e1 AND e2 means e1 and e2 both happened.
- OR: e1 OR e2 means at least one of e1 and e2 happened.

Definition 4. Object means workflow control data and workflow related data, includes XML document, other document, object variable and inherent variable. Here, object variable can be bound with the element in a document by using a query tree such as XPath, inherent variable can be seemed as independent variable defined by user.

Definition 5. Condition presents the limitation of the relationship among objects or relationship of objects and constants defined by processor designer.

Definition 6. Action means the actual operation based on the navigation of ECA rule. In EWMS, An action means doing an activity.

Definition 7. Activity is a term of workflow. An activity is a software application or a procedure set executed in order to accomplish a mission. In EWMS, we defined the activity types such as start, end, invoking Web service, delay, setting value, transferring XML document, etc.

Definition 8. ECA rule is a triple R=<E, C, A>, where E is an event set to trig the rule and events can be atom or composite, C is the condition set to reflect the status of the system and environment and will be evaluated when the rule is triggered by its event, and A is the action set that is executed when the rule is triggered and its condition is satisfied. An ECA rule states that if E happens and the condition set C can be satisfied then all the actions of A will be executed.

3 Framework of EWMS

We have realized an ECA rule-based workflow management system, called EWMS for composing Web services which is the part encircled by dashed lines in Fig.1, containing workflow design tool, workflow database, workflow engine, adapter and workflow monitor.

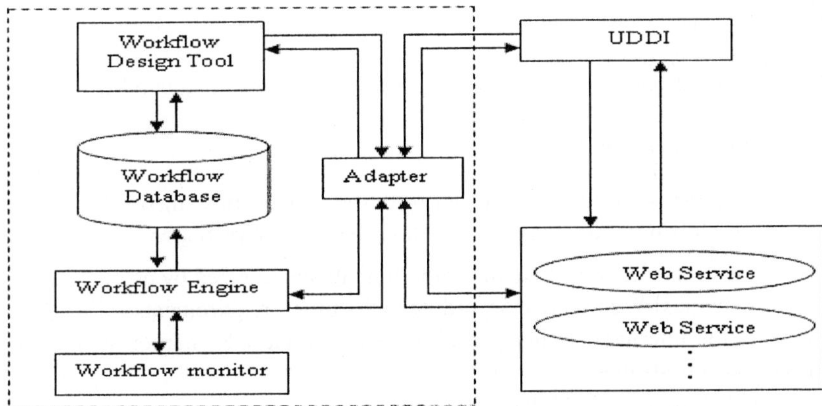

Fig. 1. Framework of EWMS

Workflow design tool provide users with a graphical design environment to model different processes as workflows. The design tool uses different icon to present different element of a workflow model.

Workflow database is a bridge of workflow design tool and workflow engine in EWMS. It mainly stores three kinds of data. Modeling data present the relationship of the elements in a workflow model and their location information in the workflow design tool to ensure the workflow model can be repainted in the design tool. Process data record the information of a workflow process running in the workflow engine. It can help the users to analyze the real executive process of a workflow. System data, includes the data can be used by both design tool and engine, such as the addresses of Web services.

Workflow engine is the most important component in EWMS. When a workflow is instantiated, the engine creates the process data, most of time, just copies the workflow data except the workflow model elements' location in the design tool. Then, the engine executes the process in term of ECA rules of the process.

Adapter is the connecting point of workflow design tool, workflow engine and Web service parts. Through the adapter, design tool can find and select compatible Web services for a specific workflow, and get their location, operation and argument information from UDDI registry center, as well as engine can bind and invoke the Web services to realize a workflow process.

Workflow monitor supervises the real-time information of workflow engine, such as the process number executed in the engine, the user number, etc.

4 Implementation

To invalidate the feasibility and efficiency of our system, we design and execute a process of an image processing, which needs the support from three different image processing services. Reverse service takes charge of reversing the color of every pixel of an image, Smooth service is used to smooth an image, and Sharpen service can sharpen an image. An image database was also created to save the original and processed images. The services can get the image ID from an input XML document, read the image from image database, process the image, save the processed image to the database, and finally return the processed image ID through an output XML document.

4.1 Design of Workflow Model

Now, we used the workflow design tool to design a workflow model for an image processing, as shown in Fig. 2. The model described the following workflow:

- use reverse service to reverse the color of an image selected by user,
- choose the next Web service according to the user's requirements,
- process the intermediate image with smooth service OR sharpen service as the user's selection, and
- return the final processed image.

The right side of Fig. 2 is a graphic design panel to show the flow of the model. Icon is the symbol of the activity to invoke a Web service, means the activity of setting value to an object, ↗ means control flow, ●, ◐ and ◑ indicate three different logic nodes, i.e., and-and, and-or , and or-and nodes respectively, they can express the logic relation of the conditions and the actions. For example, and-or node means the logic relation of conditions is AND, and the relation of actions is OR.

The left side of Fig. 2 is a navigating tree of the model. We can find following objects: six XML document related with the Web services; two inherent variables-choice means the user's decision of which services to be executed, and OutputImageID means the ID of final processed image; six object variables binding with the image ID in the six XML document, e.g. InputImageID binds with the image ID in the input XML document of reverse service-ReverseInputXML through the XPath "/INPUT/PARAMETER/VALUE". In order to transfer the intermediate result, we use setting value activity, e.g. activity RevToSmo set the value of object variable SmoothInputID with the value of ReverseOutputID. Because of the binding relationship, the input XML document of smooth service will get the image ID from the output XML document of reverse service. We also use setting value activity to set the output image ID.

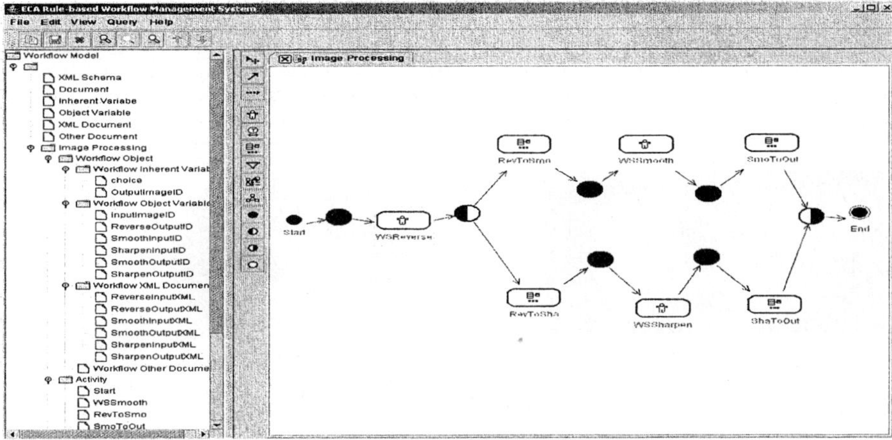

Fig. 2. Image Processing Model

4.2 Instantiating and Result

We use a simple JSP page to submit input values needed by the model, start the workflow engine and observe the executing result. We choose two executing paths to the process, and get different result, shown in Fig. 3 and Fig. 4 respectively.

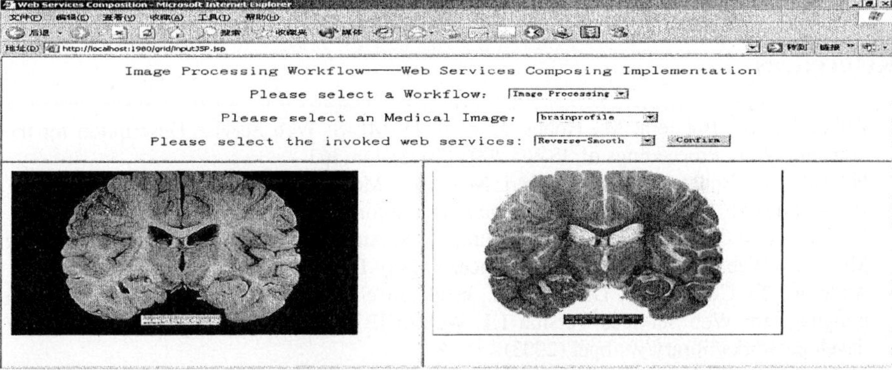

Fig. 3. Image Processing Result A

In the two instances, we select the same brain image as the input image, which is shown in the left-side of the two figures, and select the same workflow process which has been shown in Fig. 2 to be executed. Then, we choose two different executing paths for the two instances, one is invoking Reverse and Smooth services sequently, the other is invoking Reverse and Sharpen services sequently. We get two different output images which are shown in the right-side of the two figures. This example validates the feasibility and efficiency of our system.

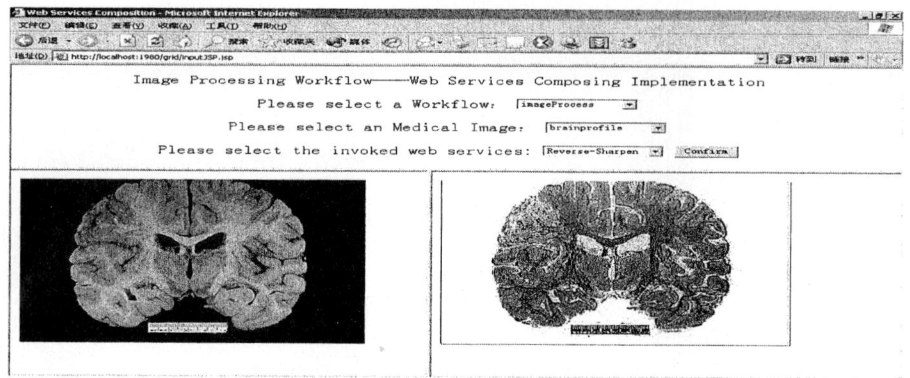

Fig. 4. Image Processing Result B

5 Conclusions and Future Work

Web services composition provides methods for service-oriented cooperation and receives much attention. We have proposed an ECA rule-based workflow approach and developed a system to implement the idea. The experiment results proved the feasibility of our system. In near future, we will extend it to compose kinds of applications, including grid services, COM component, etc. We are also planning to revise our design tool for the use of the agent technology.

References

1. Ankolekar, A., Burstein, M., Hobbs, J., et al: DAML-S: Web Service Description for the Semantic Web. Proceedings of ISWC 2002 (2002) 348-363
2. Hamadi, R., Benatallah, B.: A Petri Net-based Model for Web Service Composition. Proceedings of ADC 2003, Workshop on Planning for Web Services (2003) 191-200
3. Yu Tang, Luo Chen, Kai-Tao He, Ning Jing: SRN: An Extended Petri-Net-Based Workflow Model for Web Service Composition. Proceedings of ICWS 2004 (2004) 591-599
4. Andrews, T., Curbera, F., Dholakia, H., et al: Specification: Business Process Execution Language for Web Services Version 1.1. Web of IBM Corporation. http://www.ibm.com/developerworks/library/ws-bpel (2003)
5. McCarthy, D. R., Dayal, U.: The Architecture of An Active Database Management System. Proc. ACM-SIGMOD 1989 Int'l Conf. Management of Data, Portland, Oregon (1989) 215-224

An Efficient Password Authentication Schemes Without Using the Server Public Key for Grid Computing

Eun-Jun Yoon and Kee-Young Yoo*

Department of Computer Engineering, Kyungpook National University,
Daegu 702-701, Republic of Korea
Tel.: +82-53-950-5553; Fax: +82-53-957-4846
ejyoon@infosec.knu.ac.kr, yook@knu.ac.kr

Abstract. In the Grid computing environments, it should be guaranteed that efficient and secure password-authentication key-exchange technologies needed for users and servers and ensure that resources and data not provided by an attacker. In 2004, Chang et al. proposed a secure, efficient, and practical password authentication scheme without using the server public key. The current paper presents more efficient password authentication scheme that does not use the server public key and that can simply update user passwords without additional message transmission.

Keyword: Security, Grid computing, Password authentication.

1 Introduction

Grid technology enables complex interactions among computational and data resources. To be deployed in production computing environments, Grid, however, needs to implement additional security mechanisms. In Grid systems, it should be guaranteed that stronger authentication needed for users and servers and ensure that resources and data not provided by an attacker. Recent compromises of user and server machines at Grid sites have resulted in a need for efficient and secure password authentication key exchange technologies. In 2004, Chang et al. [1] proposed a secure, efficient, and practical password authentication scheme without using the server public key. However, the current paper presents a more efficient password authentication scheme that does not use the server public key. The computational cost of the proposed scheme is more efficient than Chang et al.'s scheme. Furthermore, in contrast to Chang et al.'s protected password change scheme, the proposed protected password change scheme can simply update user passwords without a complicated process.

The remainder of this paper is organized as follows: Section 2 briefly reviews Chang et al.'s schemes. The proposed scheme is presented in Section 2, while Section 3 and 4 discusses the security and efficiency of the scheme. Final conclusions are given in Section 5.

* Corresponding author.

H. Zhuge and G.C. Fox (Eds.): GCC 2005, LNCS 3795, pp. 149–154, 2005.

2 Review of Chang et al.'s Schemes

This section briefly reviews Chang et al.'s schemes. Some of the notations used in this paper are defined as follows:

- U, S, E: client, trusted server and attacker, respectively.
- id: public user identity of client.
- pw: secret and possibly weak user password.
- T, K: timestamp and secret key of server.
- p, q: large prime numbers p and q such that $q|p-1$.
- g: generator with order q in the Galois field $GF(p)$, in which Diffie-Hellman problem is of hard.
- r_1, r_2: session-independent random exponents $\in [1, q-1]$ chosen by client and server, respectively.
- sk: shared session key computed by client and server.
- $flow[i]$: data transmitted in the i-th step.
- $E(pw, m), E_1(pw, m)$: symmetric encryption scheme of message m with pw.
- $E(sk, m), E_2(sk, m)$: symmetric encryption scheme of message m with sk.
- $H(\cdot)$, $||$: strong one-way hash function and concatenation symbol.

Protected Password Transmission Scheme: In Chang et al.'s protected password transmission scheme, the server stores $ID, E_2(K, pw)$ for each client in the database.

(1) $U \rightarrow S$: $id, T, E_1(pw, g^{r_1} \bmod p)$
U chooses a random number r_1 and computes $E_1(pw, g^{r_1} \bmod p)$. Then, U sends the computation result with id and the timestamp T to S as a login request.

(2) $S \rightarrow U$: $E_1(pw, g^{r_2} \bmod p), E_2(sk, H(flow[1]))$
S uses pw to retrieve $g^{r_1} \bmod p$. S generates a random number r_2 and computes the session key $sk = (g^{r_1})^{r_2} \bmod p$. Thereupon, S computes $E_1(pw, g^{r_2} \bmod p)$ and $E_2(sk, H(flow[1]))$, and sends the results to U.

(3) $U \rightarrow S$: $id, E_2(sk, H(flow[2]))$
U uses pw to retrieve $g^{r_2} \bmod p$ and computes the session key $sk = (g^{r_2})^{r_1} \bmod p$. Then, U authenticates S by checking whether the decryption result of $E_2(sk, H(flow[1]))$ with the session key sk is equal to the hash value of the data sent by himself/herself in Step (1). If it holds, U computes and sends $E_2(sk, H(flow[2]))$ with id to S.

(4) $S \rightarrow U$: *Access granted or denied*
S decrypts $E_2(sk, H(flow[2]))$ and compares the result with the hash value of the transmitted data in Step (2). S will grant U the access right if it holds.

Protected Password Change Scheme: The steps of Chang et al.'s protected password change scheme are almost the same as those of the password transmission scheme, except for an additional password change request in Step (3).

(1) $U \rightarrow S$: $id, E_1(pw, g^{r_1} \bmod p)$
(2) $S \rightarrow U$: $E_1(pw, g^{r_2} \bmod p), E_2(sk, H(flow[1]))$
(3) $U \rightarrow S$: $id, E_2(sk, H(flow[2])), E_2(sk, (pw'||T))$
U sends id, $E_2(sk, H(flow[2]))$ and $E_2(sk, (pw'||T))$ to S, where pw' is the new password chosen by U.
(4) $S \rightarrow U$: *Access granted or denied*
S decrypts $E_2(sk, (pw'||T))$ with the session key sk to get U's new password pw' and T. S compares the timestamp T with the transmitted one in $flow[1]$ to authenticate U.

3 Proposed Scheme

This section proposes new efficient password authentication scheme. In the proposed scheme, the server stores $ID, E(K, pw)$ using a server's secret key K for each user in the database to overcome server data eavesdropping [3] by the method introduced in [1]. For simplicity, we omit $(\bmod p)$ from expressions.

Protected Password Transmission Scheme: The proposed protected password transmission scheme works as follows.

(1) $U \rightarrow S$: $id, E(pw, g^{r_1})$
U chooses a random number r_1 and computes $E(pw, g^{r_1})$. Then, U sends the computation result with id to S as a login request.
(2) $S \rightarrow U$: $g^{r_2}, H(sk, g^{r_1})$
After receiving a login request, S uses pw to retrieve g^{r_1}. S generates a random number r_2 and computes the session key $sk = (g^{r_1})^{r_2}$. Thereupon, S computes g^{r_2} and $H(sk, g^{r_1})$, and sends the results to U.
(3) $U \rightarrow S$: $id, H(sk', g^{r_2})$
U computes the session key $sk' = (g^{r_2})^{r_1}$ and authenticates S by checking whether $H(sk, g^{r_1}) = H(sk', g^{r_1})$ holds. If it holds, U computes $H(sk', g^{r_2})$ and sends it with id to S.
(4) $S \rightarrow U$: *Access granted or denied*
S computes the hash value $H(sk, g^{r_2})$ using its own copies of sk and g^{r_2} and determines whether $H(sk, g^{r_2}) = H(sk', g^{r_2})$ holds or not. If it holds, S will grant U access. After mutual authentication between U and S, $sk = sk' = g^{r_1 r_2}$ is used as the session key.

Protected Password Change Scheme: The protected password change scheme allows U to change its old password pw to a new password pw'. The proposed protected password change scheme is much the same as the protected password transmission scheme, except for Steps (1) and (4). The proposed protected password change scheme is works as follows:

(1) $U \rightarrow S$: $id, E(pw, (pw'||g^{r_1}))$
U chooses a random number r_1 and a new password pw', and computes $E(pw, (pw'||g^{r_1}))$. Then, U sends the computation result with id to S as a login request.

(2) $S \to U$: $g^{r_2}, H(sk, g^{r_1})$
(3) $U \to S$: $id, H(sk', g^{r_2})$
(4) $S \to U$: *Access granted or denied*
S computes the hash value $H(sk, g^{r_2})$ using its own copies of sk and g^{r_2} and determines whether $H(sk, g^{r_2}) = H(sk', g^{r_2})$ holds or not. If it holds, S will grant U access and replaces $E(K, pw)$ with $E(K, pw')$. After mutual authentication between U and S, $sk = sk' = g^{r_1 r_2}$ is used as the session key.

4 Security Analysis

This section provides the proof of correctness of the proposed scheme. Here, seven security properties [2,3,4]: replay attack, password guessing attack, server data eavesdropping, server spoofing attack, denial of service attack, mutual authentication, and perfect forward secrecy should be considered for the proposed scheme.

(1) **Replay attacks:** If E intercepts $id, E(pw, (pw'||g^{r_1}))$ sent by U in Step (1) and uses it to impersonate U when sending the next login message. However, for a random challenge, the g^{r_1} separately generated by U is different every time, and the replay of U's old login message in Step (1) is encrypted under the U's password. Therefore, the proposed scheme can resist replay attacks.
(2) **Password guessing attacks:** Because detectable and undetectable on-line guessing attacks can be prevented by letting the server take appropriate intervals between trials, weak passwords with low entropy are easily guessed by off-line guessing attacks. To avoid this problem, there must be no verifiable information on passwords in message exchanges. In the proposed scheme, the password pw is protected by U's random integer g^{r_1}. As such, no one can reveal the pw from U's login message $\{id, E(pw, g^{r_1})$ without knowing U's random integer g^{r_1}. If the attacker wants to guess U's password, he/she first guesses a password pw^* and then finds g^{r_1} by decrypting $E(pw, g^{r_1})$. However, E has to break the discrete logarithm problem and Diffie-Hellman problem to find g^{r_1} in Step (1). Hence, without knowing g^{r_1}, E cannot verify the correctness of the guessed password by checking $pw = pw^*$ in Step (1). Therefore, the proposed scheme can resist password guessing attacks.
(3) **Server data eavesdropping:** Servers are always the target of attacks. E may acquire $E(K, pw)$ stored in S. However, without knowing S's secret key K, E cannot forge a login request to pass the authentication, as pw is hidden in $E(K, pw)$ using S's secret key, thus, the correctness of the guessed password pw^* cannot be verified by checking $pw^* = pw$. Therefore, the proposed scheme can resist server data eavesdropping.
(4) **Server spoofing attacks:** The proposed scheme uses shared password pw by U and S to ensure that only the real S can decrypt U's login message $E(pw, g^{r_1})$. Only the real S can obtain g^{r_1} from U's login message. After verifying the identity of U, S then sends g^{r_2} and $H(sk, g^{r_1})$ to U to achieve mutual authentication. Therefore, the proposed scheme can resist server spoofing attacks.

(5) **Denial of service attacks:** The denial of service attacks prevents or inhibits the normal use or management of communications facilities. This attack may act on a specific user. For example, an adversary may perform this attack to cause the server to reject the login of a specific user. In the proposed password change scheme, U's new password pw' is also encrypted using U's current password pw in Step (1). Therefore, E is unable to choose a random number to replace pw'. Additionally, S updates replaced new password pw' only if the computed hash value $H(sk, g^{r_2})$ is equivalent to the received $H(sk', g^{r_2})$. However, E cannot compute this session key sk' in hashed value $H(sk', g^{r_2})$ because of the discrete logarithm problem, Diffie-Hellman problem, and a secure one-way hash function. Therefore, the proposed password change scheme is simple and can resist denial of service attacks.

(6) **Mutual authentication:** Mutual authentication means that both the client and server are authenticated to each other within the same protocol, while explicit key authentication is the property obtained when both implicit key authentication and key confirmation hold. As such, the proposed scheme uses the Diffie-Hellman key exchange algorithm to provide mutual authentication, then the key is explicitly authenticated by a mutual confirmation session key sk.

(7) **Perfect Forward secrecy:** Perfect forward secrecy means that if a long-term private key (e.g. user password or server private key) is compromised, this does not compromise earlier session keys. In password authentication with key distribution, forward secrecy is a highly desirable security feature. In the proposed scheme, since the Diffie-Hellman key exchange algorithm is used to generate a session key $g^{r_1 r_2}$, forward secrecy is ensured, as an adversary with a compromised U's password pw is only able to obtain the g^{r_1} and g^{r_2} from an earlier session. In addition, it is also computationally infeasible to obtain the session key $g^{r_1 r_2}$ from g_1^r and g_2^r, as it is a Diffie-Hellman problem. Therefore, the proposed scheme provides perfect forward secrecy.

5 Performance Analysis

The performance comparison between Chang et al.'s password authentication scheme [1] and our proposed password authentication scheme are shown in Table 1. Because the protected password change scheme needs additional computation to transmit the new password pw', the number of symmetric encryption and symmetric decryption moves in Chang et al.'s and our proposed scheme are shown as a/b in Table 1, where a denotes the number needed in the protected password transmission scheme, and b denotes the number needed in the protected password change scheme.

Chang et al.'s protected password change scheme requires a total of 5 times symmetric encryption and 5 times symmetric decryption, but our proposed password change scheme only requires total 1 symmetric encryption and 1 symmetric

Table 1. Comparisons of computation costs

Computation type	Chang et al.'s [1]		Proposed	
	User	Server	User	Server
Modular exponential	2	2	2	2
Symmetric encryption	2/3	2/2	1/1	0/0
Symmetric decryption	2/2	2/3	0/0	1/1
Hash operation	2	2	2	2
Timestamp	Required		Not Required	

decryption. Other computation costs are equal with Chang et al.'s scheme. Moreover, unlike the Chang et al.'s scheme, the proposed scheme does not require a timestamp. Thus, our proposed password authentication scheme is more efficient than Chang et al.'s scheme.

6 Conclusions

The current paper presented a new efficient password authentication scheme without using the server public key. The computational costs of the proposed scheme are more efficient than Chang et al.'s scheme. In contrast to Chang et al.'s protected password change scheme, the proposed protected password change scheme can simply update user passwords without additional message transmission.

Acknowledgements

This research was supported by the MIC (Ministry of Information and Communication), Korea, under the ITRC (Information Technology Research Center) support program supervised by the IITA (Institute of Information Technology Assessment).

References

1. Chang, Y.F., Chang, C.C., Liu, Y.L.: Password Authentication Without the Server Public Key. IEICE Transactions on Communications. Vol. E87-B. No. 10. (2004) 3088-3091
2. Menezes, A.J., Oorschot, P.C., Vanstone, S.A.: Handbook of Applied Cryptograph. CRC Press. New York. 1997
3. Yang, C.C., Chang, T.Y., Li, J.W.: Security Enhancement for Protecting Password Transmission. IEICE Transactions on Communications. Vol. E86-B. No. 7. (July 2003) 2178-2181
4. Lin, C.L., Hwang, T.: A Password Authentication Scheme with Secure Password Updating. Computers & Security. Vol. 22. No. 1. (2003) 68-72

Certificate-Driven Grid Workflow Paradigm Based on Service Computing

Wanchun Dou[1,2,3], S.C. Cheung[3], Guihai Chen[1,2], and Shijie Cai[1,2]

[1] State Key Laboratory for Novel Software Technology
[2] Department of Computer Science and Technology, Nanjing University, Nanjing, China, Post Code 210093
[3] Department of Computer of Computer Science, Hong Kong University of Science and Technology, Hong Kong
douwc@nju.edu.cn

Abstract. Taking advantage of the application paradigm of web service, a general paradigm of service computing is discussed for underlying workflow execution based on collaborative operation. In line with the scenario of service computing, a certificate-driven workflow application paradigm based on service computing is discussed under grid environment in form of virtual organization. The details engaged in the certificate-driven grid workflow paradigm are listed to demonstrate its execution. The conclusion is presented at last.

1 Introduction

Workflow technology has long been considered as an essential technique to integrate distributed and often heterogeneous applications and information systems. It aims to improve the effectiveness and productivity of business processes by supporting business process reengineering or realizing full or partial automation of a business process [1,2]. Generally, the traditional workflow system is often enacted inside an organization. With the advent of e-commerce, business processes involving business-to-business and business-to-customer activities usually span across multiple organizations. Additionally, more and more complex problems engaged in engineering or science domain are processed relying on collaborative work implemented by more than one organization on Internet. As a tendency, workflow management systems (WfMSs) are being increasingly deployed to deliver e-business transactions across organizational boundaries. The large-scale collaborative design or e-Science enacted in distributed environment has presented some issues challenging the traditional workflow technologies [3,4]. The organization-across interactions among activities or processes will lead a complex flow relationship. Accordingly, how to enhance a workflow system into a fundamental support mechanism underlying organization-across workflow application poses a challenge in workflow research and attracts increasing attentions [4].

Satisfying the web-based workflow application requirements, one promising technique is web service to realize support for cross-organizational processes [5]. The challenges of building B2B applications have driven rapid innovation in Web-based application in the last few years. In this paper, the sub-workflow deployed inside a

H. Zhuge and G.C. Fox (Eds.): GCC 2005, LNCS 3795, pp. 155–160, 2005.

constituent organization is degraded into a workflow segment upon the hybrid workflow system. The paper concentrates on a certificate-driven grid workflow paradigm based on service computing. The paper is organization as follows. In section 2, a service computing paradigm is analyzed based on the basic concepts of web service. In section 3, a certificate-driven grid workflow paradigm is explored. At last, we give the conclusion and point out future work.

2 Basic Concepts Related to Service Computing

With recent advances in pervasive devices and communication technologies, there are increasing demands in workflow application for ubiquitous access to networked services. These services extend supports from Web browsers on personal computers to handheld devices and sensor networks. Taking advantage of the distributed technologies such as the CORBA, mobile agents, and web service [5], the web-based workflow segments could be orchestrated by RPC (Remote Procedure Call), message passing, RMI (Remote Method Invocation) or Applet invoked by service agent. Despite great interests and improvement in technology in this area, complicated technical issues and organizational challenges remain to be solved.

Generally, the concept of service computing could be interpreted from narrow sense and general sense. In narrow sense, it could be instantiated into web service with concrete application in practice. WSDL, UDDI, QoS, and XML characterize the technologies of web service. Moreover, there are often three roles engaged in web service application, i.e. a service provider, a service requestor, and a service registry [5]. From the organizational-across workflow point of view, the service invocation could be characterized by three phases:

1 How to efficiently discover and locate required web services (enacted by a third-party)
2 How to organize the required web service into ad-hoc or collaborative workflow system
3 How to facilitate the interoperability of heterogeneous web services

Fig.1 illustrates the scenario of a typical web application from the first topic [6]. This paper concentrates on exploring the second topic listed above. In technology

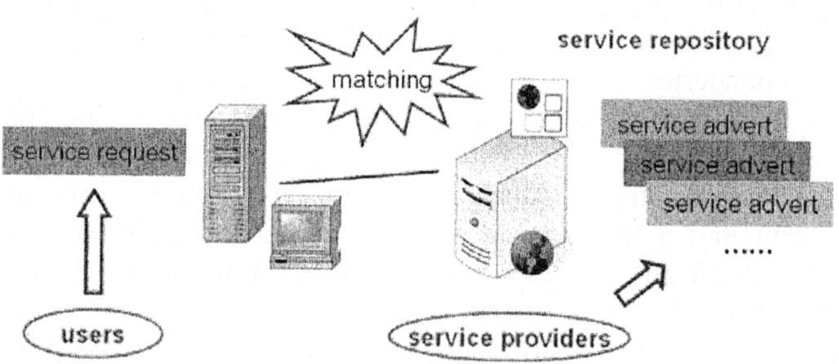

Fig. 1. The scenario of a typical web application based on efficiently discovering and locating required web services

point of view, Web service represents a black-box functionality that can be reused without worrying about how the service is implemented. In this paper, the concept of service computing has a generic meaning that concentrates on a framework supporting task execution, while not middleware's structuring. By defining a binding agreement or contract between two parties, workflow pattern is setup in Client/Server mode. Quality of Service (QoS) becomes an important factor in workflow management. During workflow execution, individual enterprises will centralize on achieving their business goals according to their task with a self-governing fashion.

In general sense, the service computing is a novel computing paradigm that underlies the collaboration under distributed environment based on service paragigm. Organization, team, or group provides contribution each other according to some contracts set down in advance or according to the needs during task execution. The general sense of service computing could be formalized as bellows:

$$\text{Service-computing} = \text{service} + \text{computing}$$

Where, service are composed of object and subject of service, content of service, quality of service, et ac, which could be presented in simplified formalization as Service = {object, content, quality, ... }; Computing is treated as a kind of behavior or activity that are implemented with certain goal by consuming some resource, exploiting some tools, and taking advantage of some helps (services) from its collaborators, which could be presented in simplified formalization as Computing = {behavior, resource, tool, goals,...}.

In this general sense of service computing, the service computing concentrates on the service mode, service supervision, quality of services, and service direction, on the consumption that the service relation has been set up. Additionally, the role of service provider and service requestor could be switched frequently. Typically, peer-to-peer system is an application paradigm with frequent roles switching with server and client.

3 A Certificate-Driven Workflow Application Paradigm Under Grid Environment

According to the rational explored in section 2, a service-based workflow system can be characterized as sequences of service invocations that could provide autonomous services. The autonomous services could be treated as task-oriented processing [7]. At the stage of modeling an organization-across workflow, the concept of control flow is exploited to prescribe the service relation among organization with a temporal dependency. During workflow execution, control flow is instantiated into a logical switching according to an scheduled temporal logic among activities. In this section, a certificate-driven and organization-across workflow system will be explored as a case study, with service computing perspective based on the security mechanism deployed in grid computing. Grid computing focus on facilitates the sharing of computer resources and services with a certificate mechanism in form of virtual organization. In our case study, service is deployed by granting certificate to facilitating resource access. Here, the resource is mainly the data resource or other computing resource such as CPU, et ac. Now, virtual organization has been brought into grid-based application as one of the key concepts, and the practice of grid-based E-Science, for example, is often enabled by virtual organization [4]. Under grid environment, servers supporting workflow application are decentralized (duplicated) throughout the virtual organization and the distributed servers are controlled by a centralized authority (headquarters); Accordingly, some basic features of virtual organization could be drawn out from those literatures:

1 Lifetime of cooperative is limited;
2 Organization-across collaboration;
3 Access to a wide range of specialized resources during collaboration;
4 Task- or goal-driven autonomous processes;
5 Role-based communication, et ac.

Generally, logical execution relationship prescribed in organization-across workflow model depicts the visited and the visiting workflow segment. If the supporting resource or service host are also initiated by workflow engine, the workflow segments in organization level will take little care of the issues of workflow management and centralizes on its inside-execution in self-governing way in practice. Grid-oriented workflow would be an *ad hoc* workflow system that centralizes on globally distributed and large-scale resource sharing. Workflow inside virtual organization becomes one of the important enabling technologies supporting grid applications [7].

In accordance with those characteristics listed above, a prototype of certificate-driven automatic workflow system will be explored supporting grid-oriented workflow implementation, upon which the time model discussed in section underlie the implementation of logical control in resource access and the validity of certificate is just determined by the relation of temporal dependency of service invocation. The typical scenario of grid-oriented workflow system can be illustrated as follows:

1 Server-level or proxy-level workflow segments delegate their certificate granting to workflow engine;
2 Invocation of services and functions among workflow segments are awakened through certificate granted by workflow engine;
3 The period of certificate's validity reflects the lifetime of cooperative, and guarantees the QoS in time;
4 Workflow segments are task- or goal-driven autonomous process and the workflow engine play the part of nerve center in workflow system.

Here, grid-oriented workflow execution is initiated by server-based workflow engine that control workflow execution by navigating the workflow specifications according to pre-defined workflow model. Fig.2 demonstrates the enactment of the prototype in service computing paradigm. Some details indicated by the arrow diagram are depicted as follows.

Step1: Proxy-based workflow segment hand over the routines of certificate release to workflow engine that acts as the certificate authority in later workflow executed. User and service identified via a certificate that contains information vital to identifying and authenticating the user or service.

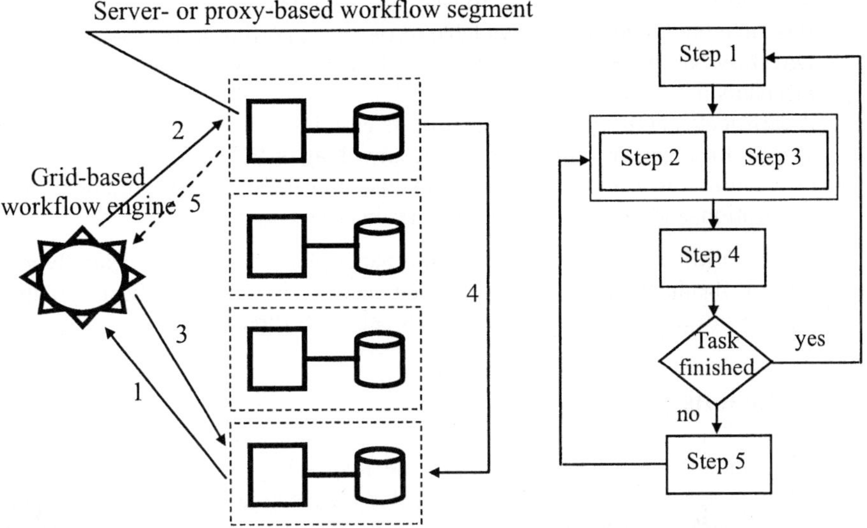

Fig. 2a. Performance Analysis of a Grid-Oriented and Certificate-Driven Workflow System

Fig. 2b. Flow Diagram of Logical Execution in Accordance with Fig.2.a

Fig. 2. A Grid-Oriented and Certificate-Driven Workflow System in Self-Governing Fashion

Step2: According to the pre-defined workflow model and the executed stage of a task, the workflow engine invokes process service through certificate granting for some resource access. Process segment or activity is wakened by the certificate. Accordingly, the validity of the certificate indicates the executed time of the task.

Step3: After granting a certificate, a duplicated content of the certificate is sent to the resource or service host for identifying and authenticating the future logging or visiting.

Step4: According to the certificate and its security level, the certificate holder could get the access to the needed resource or invoke some service across the borders of different security domains in order to achieve the local goals.

Step5: If a task is not finished in the period of validity, the resource access is forbidden, the actor must apply for an added time and then repeat step 2 after granted. Otherwise, the task is finished in the scheduled time. Please note that this step is needed if there has an unexpected requirement during workflow execution in resource access or service invoking across the borders of different security domains.

The invocating process among these steps is certificate-driven. The lines indicate those steps listed above with arrow demonstrated in Fig.2, respectively. In concise way, the logical execution of the steps listed above can be formalized as shown in Fig.2.b. For achieving the object, the grid-oriented workflow engine demonstrated in Fig.2 should contain some basic items related to service definitions as below:

1 Workflow model oriented toward web-based application
2 Resource pool indexing the available resource supporting workflow execution
3 Directory-based resource location mechanism and workflow peer location mechanism
4 A certificate authority (CA) for certificate granting
5 Trigger mechanisms initiated by service invoking or ECA rules.
6 Delegation capability supporting dynamic process data transportation, agent application, and other proxy-based issues in access control.

Note that workflow engine discussed in this paper plays the part of a centrally managed security mechanism by taking over the security issue in certificate granting, those routines are carried out among workflow segments directly.

4 Conclusions

For current state-of-the-art, how to enhance the adaptability of a workflow system in organization-across application is the key factor for meeting ever-changing requirements of business applications. The approach presented in this paper underlies the organization-across workflow based on service computing paradigm. For future research, we will apply the service-computing paradigm to the implementation of dependable, adaptive and web-service oriented workflow system.

Acknowledgement. This paper is based on the Project 60303025 supported by NSFC, and Jiangsu Provincial NSF research funds (No. BK2004411 and No. BK2005208). Besides, it is partially supported by a grant of the Research Grants Council of Hong Kong (Project No. HKUST6167/04E).

References

1. J.Q.Li, Y.S.Fan, and M.C.Zhou.Timing Constraint Petri nets and Their Application to Schedulability Analysis of Real-Time System Specifications. IEEE Transactions on System, Man, and Cybernetics-Part A:System and Humans, 2003, 33(2):179-193.
2. E.A.Stohr and J.L.Zhao. Workflow Automation: Overview and Research Issues. Information System Frontiers, 2001, 3(3):281-296.
3. Dickson K.W.Chiu, S.C.Cheung, et al. Workflow View Driven Cross-Organization Interoperability in a Web Service Environment. Information Technology and Management, 2004, 5(3-4):221-250.
4. D.D.Roure and J.A.Hendler. E-Science: The Grid and the Semantic Web. IEEE Intelligent Systems, 2004, 19(1):65-71.
5. Steve Graham, et al. Building Web Services with Java™: Making Sense of XML, SOAP, WSDL, and UDDI. Sams Publishing, Dec.12, 2001.
6. Chang Xu, S.C. Cheung, Xiangye Xiao, Semantic Interpretation and Matching of Web Services, Proceedings of the 23rd International Conference on Conceptual Modeling (ER 2004), Shanghai, P.R. China, Nov 2004.
7. M.Bubak, et al. Workflow Composer and Service Registry for Grid Applications. Future Generation Computer Systems, 2005, 21(1):79-86.

Dynamic-Role Based Access Control Framework Across Multi-domains in Grid Environment*

Ying Chen, Shoubao Yang, and Leitao Guo

Computer Science Department, University of Science and Technology of China, Hefei 230026, P.R. China
{ychen34, syang, ltguo}@mail.ustc.edu.cn

Abstract. To improve system scalability and restrain cheat, which are two important aspects in resource sharing gird environment, a dynamic-role based access control framework is proposed in this paper. This framework imports trust model, proposes "conversion parameter" and dynamic-role to resolve the problems of access control across multi domains. Simulation results show that it can realize access control easily, prohibit malicious behavior of entities, and improve the scalability of the system. An implementation is also shown in this paper.

1 Introduction

With the development of grid computing[1] system, resource-sharing has become more and more important, along with which the security problems can not be neglected. Trust management[3] and access control[4] are both used to guarantee the security of the grid applications. For the sake of the convenience of access control, entities in the grid are often divided into many domains. So the main issues of access control focus on problems of scalability in domains and negotiating the access control policy among domains.

Role-based Access Controls (RBAC)[2], as a widely used access control method, imports the conception "role", which is the base of the framework proposed in this paper, to bring more flexibility. In traditionally RBAC, no good scheme is proposed to constraint cheat. So concept of dynamic-role is proposed that users' roles can change in correspondence with their behavior. The trust model proposed in this paper mainly adopts global-trust model for intra-domain, while partial-trust model[5] for inter-domain, and imports conversion factor to implement role conversion among domains, so that it can accomplish the objective to realize intra/inter domain access control with security.

An access control framework based on central server Authentication and Authorization Center (AAC), with trust management introduced, is proposed in this paper, which can improve the scalability of system, prohibit malicious behaviors, and convert the access control privileges conveniently among different domains.

---

* This paper is supported by the National Natural Science Foundation of China under Grant No.60273041 and the National '863' High-Tech Program of China under Grant No. 2002AA104560.

H. Zhuge and G.C. Fox (Eds.): GCC 2005, LNCS 3795, pp. 161 – 165, 2005.

This paper is organized as follows: intra/inter domain access control policy is introduced in section2, simulations and implementations are shown in section 3; conclusions and future works are depicted in section 4.

2 Dynamic-Role Based Access Control Across Multi-domains

Figure 1 shows the framework of intra-domain access control. Set reputation for each user, a certain scope of which is mapped to a role. When a user needs to access resources in the domains: (1) he interacts with AAC with his id and password, and the resource he needs. AAC queries database to determine his role, and sends back user certificate. (2) The user accesses the resource with the certificate. (3)(4) When the interaction is over, the user and the resource make rank for each other respectively. When an entity's reputation has been changed to a certain degree, TMS modifies the entity's role to change its privileges.

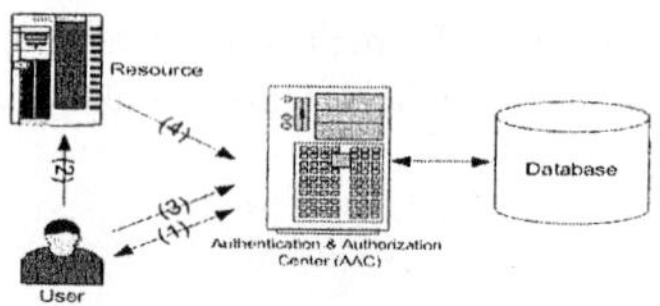

Fig. 1. Framework of Intra-Domain Access Control

When computing reputations, following aspects must be considered: the reputation of submitter itself; the satisfaction from the same submitter should be considered only once in case of it ranks multiple times for entity to debase its reputation; ranks submitted recently should be emphasized because one entity may behavior well at beginning to gain good reputation, and then act maliciously.

Let $rank(i,j)^k$ denote the ranks made by entity i to j at their k^{th} interaction, $-1 <= rank(i,j)^k <= 1$. Negative value means dissatisfaction with this interaction, positive, satisfied. Let $Sat(i,j)^k$ denote the satisfied degree made by i to j in their k^{th} interaction, p(u,i)denote the other participating peer in u's i^{th} interaction, then entity u's reputation can be defined as equation 1 (if the total interaction times are n):

$$Reputation_u = \frac{\sum_{i=1}^{n} Sat(p(u,i),u)^i * Reputation_{p(u,i)}}{n} \tag{1}$$

where

$$Sat(i,j)^{n+1} = rank(i,j)^{n+1} * 50\% + Sat(i,j)^n * 50\% \tag{2}$$

Since policies in different domains are different, role of one user in his own domain should be distinguished from those in other domains. Conversion parameter (CP, $-1 <= CP <= 1$) is introduced to make the conversion: let CP from domain A to B be CP(A,B), then reputation of user in domain A multiply CP(A,B) is his corresponding reputation in domain B to determine his role in B. An inter-domain access control framework is shown in figure2: AAC (X) is AAC of domain X.

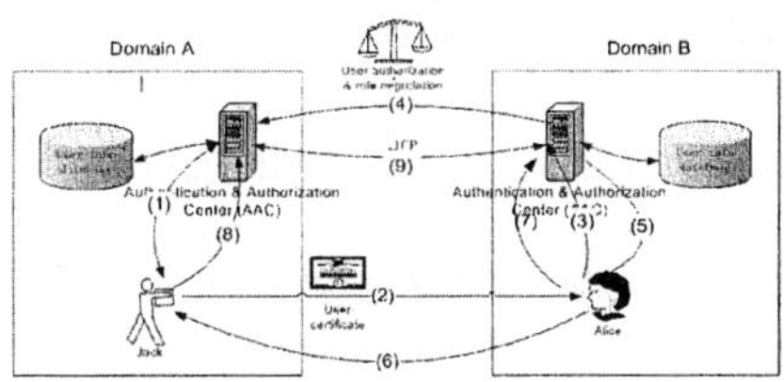

Fig. 2. Inter-Domain Access Control Framework

Jack is a user from A, when he wants to use resources in B provided by Alice, he：(1) interacts with AAC(A) to get his certificate. (2)Jack interacts with Alice to apply for resources, showing his user certificate; (3)Alice submits the certificate to AAC(B). (4)AAC(B) authenticates user certificate to AAC(A), and figures out Jack's role in B according to CP(A,B). (5)AAC(B) judges Jack's requirement, and sends back the result to Alice. (6)Alice sends back the result to Jack. If permitted, service is provided. (7)(8)Alice and Jack submit ranks to their home AAC respectively, which modifies CP. (9)AAC(A) and AAC(B) exchange the influence on its counterpart's CP so they can modify their reputations.

Considering the above interaction in domain B, AAC(B) maintains a CP for each domain. Let $p(A,i)$ denote the other participating peer in domain A's i^{th} interaction with B, $Sat(u,A)^i$ denote u's satisfaction with entity from A in the ith times. Let Jack and Alice's interaction be the nth times from A to B. After this interaction,

$$CP(A,B)^n = \frac{CP(A,B)^{n-1} * (n-1) + Sat(p(A,n),A)^n * Reputation_{p(A,n)}}{n} \quad (3)$$

so ΔCP(A,B) can be expressed as:

$$\Delta CP(A,B) = \frac{Sat(p(A,n),A)^n * Reputation_{p(A,n)} - CP(A,B)^{n-1}}{n} \quad (4)$$

AAC(B) sends ΔCP(A,B) to AAC(A), and receives ΔCP(B,A) from it. AAC(B) computes and modifies Alice's reputation as equation 5:

$$Reputation_{Alice} = Reputation_{Alice} + \sum_{i \in B} reputation_i \times \Delta CP(B,A) \quad (5)$$

where $Repatation_{Alice}$ at left represents new reputation of Alice, and $Repatation_{Alice}$ at right means the old one. If new $Repatation_{Alice}$ is more than 1, then $Repatation_{Alice}$ =1. If $Repatation_{Alice}$ is less than -1, Alice is banished out of B. It is the same in domain A.

There are many advantages to do like this: first, since user's behavior will influence CP of his domain, AAC will have to be more careful when choosing users to access other domains. Quality of interactions will be ensured and penalty will be made to low reputation users. Second, exchanging ΔCP between AACs can let AAC know the behavior of users from home domain, but prohibit AAC from getting his CP to other domain by ΔCP.

3 Simulations and Implementation

To confirm equation 1, we consider entity A with reputation 0.5, which has 50 times of ranks already. It interacts with entity B, who makes multiple negative ranks to AAC for A. Line 1 in figure 3 shows A's reputation in non-debasing scheme. It can be seen that, the more malicious ranks, the lower A's reputation.

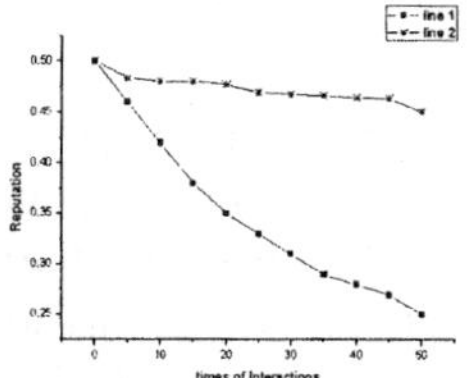

Fig. 3. Comparison of Non-Debasing and Debasing Scheme

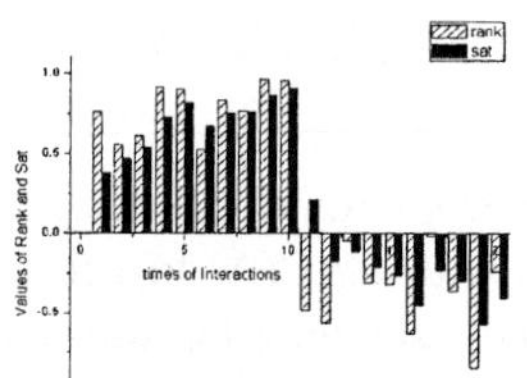

Fig. 4. the Influence of Rans Submitted recently on Satisfactory

To estimate the influence of ranks submitted recently on satisfactory, we simulate an entity C: it always behaves well at its first ten interactions, and then starts malicious behavior. As shown in figure 4, column 1 means ranks from C's partners, and column 2 means satisfactory of them. X-coordinate is times of interactions and Y-coordinate is the values of ranks and Satisfactory from users. It is can be seen in figure 4 that C's reputation has dropped off deeply since its first malicious activity, which proves effectively that the scheme of "recently ranks weight more" works well.

In the inter-domain access control, to affirm the relationship among "ranks of user by resource-CP-users' reputation", considering a domain A with 100 entities whose reputations distribute from -1 to 1 randomly. Jack, a user from A, whose reputation is 0.5, interacts with a resource provider in B named Alice whose reputation is 0.8. And there are 20 interactions between A and B before. Then we can see how rank from Alice influences on Jack's reputation by CP in figure5.

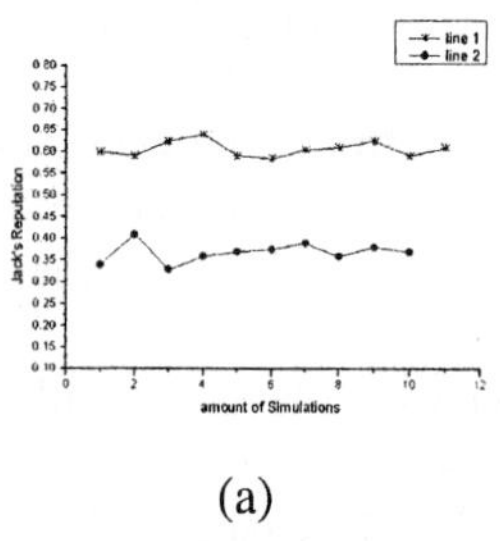

(a)

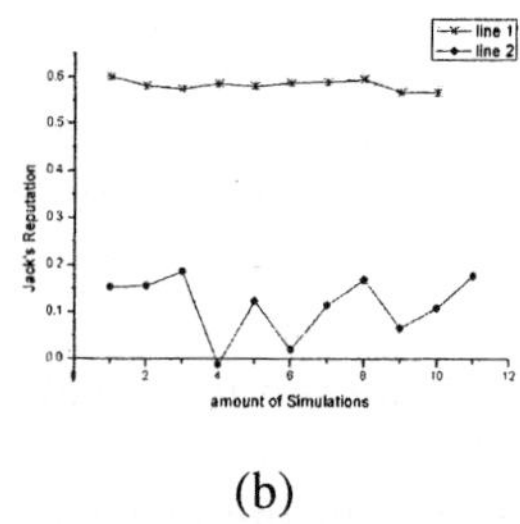

(b)

Fig. 5. the Influence on Jack's reputation of ranks from Alice

Suppose CP(A, B) in (a) is 0.5, if rank from Alice is 0.8, then ⊿CP(A,B)is 0.0067, and Jack's new reputation will be line 1 in (a); if rank from Alice is 0.4, then ⊿CP(A,B)is -0.0086, and Jack's new reputation will be line2 in (a). Similarly, suppose CP(A,B) in (b) is 0.2, rank from Alice is 0.4 brings up Jack's new reputation like line1 in (b)(⊿CP(A,B)is 0.0057); rank from Alice is -0.4 brings up Jack's new reputation like line2 in (b) (⊿CP(A,B is -0.0248). From (a) and (b) we can see that: (1) Ranks higher than CP(A, B) will increase Jack's reputation, while ranks lower than CP(A,B) will decrease Jack's reputation. Jack' behavior influences his reputation by influencing ⊿CP(A,B. (2) Little change of CP(A,B) will cause much change of Jack's reputation. By this way malicious behavior will be prohibited better in inter-domain access control.

The model of "dynamic-role based access control frame" has been implemented shown in figure 6. The main modules are as follows: Portal**:** a module that can provide users with dynamic service list, and interact with users. User-Role-Conversion Module: realizes policy negotiating inter-domains and roles' conversion. Service Access Control Module: realizes the mapping of reputation-role-privileges. Reputation Management Module: accepts ranks from entities, computes and modifies their reputations.

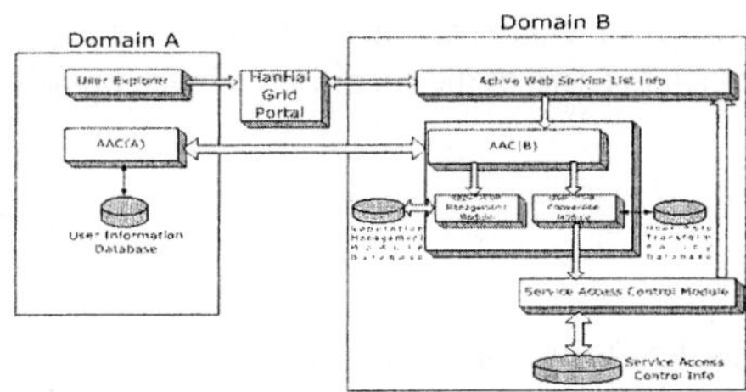

Fig. 6. Implementation Modules of Dynamic-Role Based Access Control

4 Conclusions and Future Works

Dynamic-RBAC policy is proposed in this paper to solve the problems of security of resource sharing. It modifies user's role and related privileges dynamically by his behavior; and can get more exact reputations. In the future, multi-AAC will be set to solve the problem of single point of failure.

References

1. Foster, I., Kesselman, C. and Tuecke, S.: The Anatomy of the Grid: Enabling Scalable Virtual Organizations. International Journal of High Performance Computing Applications, 15 (3). 200-222. 2001
2. Butler, R., Engert, D., Foster, I., Kesselman, C., Tuecke, S., Volmer, J. and Welch, V.: A National-Scale Authentication Infrastructure. IEEE Computer, 33 (12). 60-66. 2000
3. M. Blaze, J. Feigenbaum, J. Lacy: "Decentralized trust management". Proc. of 1996 IEEE Symposium on Security and Privacy, pages 164–173, 1996
4. http://httpd.apache.org/docs/1.3/howto/auth.html
5. A. Abdul-Rahman: "Supporting Trust in Virtual Communities". In Proceedings Hawaii International Conference on System Sciences 33, Maui, Hawaii, 4-7 January 2000

An Automatic Policy Refinement Mechanism for Policy-Driven Grid Service Systems*

Bei-shui Liao and Ji Gao

Institute of Artificial Intelligence, Zhejiang University, Hangzhou 310027, China
baiseliao@zju.edu.cn, gaoji@mail.hz.zj.cn

Abstract. Currently, the management of grid services is becoming increasingly complex. To resolve this complexity problem, autonomic computing and policy-based multi-agent technology have been proposed as promising methods. However, there are many challenges to be resolved. Among them, policy refinement is a great problem that hampers the development of policy-based system. To cope with this issue, this paper presents a policy refinement mechanism based on recipes. Recipes define possible refinement alternatives for each abstract policy. And the policy refinement engine automatically refines the policies by choosing the refinement branch in terms of the conditions of each branch.

1 Introduction

In recent years, with the development of grid services [1,2], more and more large-scale and cross-organizational information systems are established. However, the management of these open, dynamic, and heterogeneous grid service systems is becoming increasingly complex. In order to treat this challenging problem, many research efforts have been made. Among them, autonomic computing [3,4,5] and policy-driven agent system [6,7] are promising examples. Due to the dynamic nature of virtual organization (VO), the policy-driven system will play an important role. As we know, from the users' perspectives, there are two desirable functionalities of the grid service systems within VO environment. First, specific virtual organizations should be formed quickly by dynamically organizing distributed partners to resolve the specific problems, according to high-level business requirements. And if the requirements vary at run time, the system is able to take these changes into consideration, and then modify the system's configurations to meet the new requirements. Second, the stakeholders of resource consumers or providers should be enabled to influence the behaviors of the underlying components at run time in terms of their real-time preferences and requirements. To meet these demands, policy-driven multi-agent system is an ideal candidate, as formulated in [6, 7, 8]. However, there are many challenges to be coped with to make the framework proposed in [8] more practical and intelligent. One of them is how to automatically refine high-level abstract policies to low-level concrete policies. In [8], human designers who model the policies are in charge of this part of work, which is a great problem that hampers the practical use of policy-driven system. So, our

* This work is supported by the National Grand Fundamental Research 973 Program of China under Grant No.2003CB317000.

H. Zhuge and G.C. Fox (Eds.): GCC 2005, LNCS 3795, pp. 166 – 171, 2005.

ultimate objective is to make automated refinement of policies a reality based on policy refinement templates (recipes), and this paper is the initial work.

Until now, only few researchers have devoted their attention to policy refinement, e.g., Bandara [9] and Beigi [10] et al. In paper [9], the authors presented an approach to policy refinement that allows the inference of the low-level actions that satisfy a high-level goal by making use of existing techniques in goal-based requirements elaboration and the Event Calculus. This method is useful to make policy refinement automatic, but it requires that the policy-regulated objects are predetermined and specific, which often can't be met in the VO environment where the participants are dynamic. Paper [10] proposed three types of policy transformation approaches such as transformation using static rules, transformation by policy table lookup, and transformation using case based reasoning. Among them, the static rules based approach is the simplest and most efficient one, and is useful when the application context is static. But when the business requirements and application environment are dynamic, it is infeasible. So, as for dynamic VO environment, in which participating agents may join or leave at run time, we need a more flexible mechanism for policy refinement. This paper proposes a method that extends the rule-based method with dynamic characteristics, called recipe-based mechanism. Recipes defined at design-time consist of all possible refinement schemes under different conditions. Then, under run-time environment, a policy-refinement engine automatically produces specific refined policies according to the real-time conditions.

This paper is organized as follows. Section 2 proposes a recipe-based policy refinement mechanism, in which the policies, the definition of recipes and the principle of policy refinement engine are formulated respectively. Section 3 is conclusions.

2 Policy Refinement Mechanism

As proposed in [8], there are three levels of policies, i.e., abstract policies, concrete policies, and enforceable policies, in which enforceable policies are distributed to specific agents who are obliged to fulfill them, while concrete policies defined the duties and rights of roles will be enforced by role-enacting agents. When an agent enacts a role by negotiation and signing a contract, it will be obliged to fulfill the contract (the details of negotiation and contract-based cooperation are out of the range of this paper and are presented another paper [11]), thus enforce the concrete policies indirectly.

Now, the problem is how to automatically refine the abstract polices to concrete or enforceable ones. Due to the dynamic nature of virtual organization, the policy refinement mechanism should be context-aware. First, the mechanism should be flexible enough to reflect the environment variations. Second, the mechanism should be simple and efficient enough to ensure the process of policy refinement within tolerant time limit. We propose a recipe-based refinement mechanism to treat this problem, as shown in figure 1.

Central to this mechanism is the recipe-based approach. The idea of this approach is inspired by the styles of human treating complex problems. As we know, when a person deals with a complex problem, he should first have the knowledge about how to achieve it. This knowledge is not static, specific program to be executed, but a template that defines possible plan steps. Which branch of plan steps is chosen at run time depends on the real time conditions. In this paper, we take recipes as templates of policy refinement. Each recipe defines all possible refinement plan steps of an abstract policy. Conditions of the plan steps that reflect the state of application context and environment are the basis for refinement engine's decision-making. As to a specific abstract policy, the refinement engine reasons about the abstract policy according to related recipes and the real-time context of the VO, and brings about concrete policies or enforceable policies. In this way, the outcomes of the refinement not only meet the goal of abstract policy, but also reflect the status of the underlying environment.

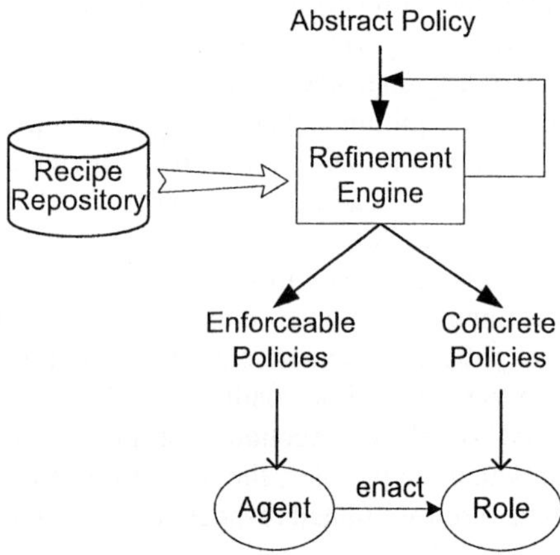

Fig. 1. Recipe-Based Policy Refinement Mechanism

Policy Definition. In this system, we extend the policy definition presented in our previous papers. The *Behavior* of a policy subject [6] is extended to *Processing*. There are three types of *Processing,* including abstract goals (prefixed by "$"), enforceable goals, and activities. Abstract goal can't be realized directly, and should be mapped to enforceable goals. We distinguish three levels of policy, including abstract policy (also prefixed by "$"), concrete policy, and enforceable policy. When a policy has one or more abstract goals, we call it abstract policy. Abstract policy is directly derived from business requirements. Concrete policy is refined from abstract policy. Its subject and target are roles of a VO. Enforceable policy is specific to individual agents and can be enforced by related agents. Now, we need an approach to refine an abstract policy to concrete policies or enforceable ones. In the following, we first give the definition of policy, and then formulate the policy refinement mechanism. The abstract policies, concrete policies and enforceable policies are specified in a unified form, as defined in the following in the form of EBNF[1].

[1] In EBNF, terminals are quoted; non-terminals are bold and not quoted. Alternatives are either separated by vertical bars (|) or are given in different productions. Components that can occur at most once are enclosed in square brackets ([…]); components that can occur any number of times(including zero) are enclosed in braces ({…}). Whitespace is ignored in the productions here.

```
Policy    ::= 'Policy(' ['$'] PolicyID Modality  [Trigger]
              Subject {Processing} [Target]
              [Constraint]')'
Modality::= 'A⁺' | 'A⁻'| 'O⁺' | 'O⁻'
Trigger ::= 'Trigger(' AgentMentalState| TimeEvent ')'
Subject ::= 'Subject(' Role | AgentID ')'
Processing::= 'Processing(' ['$']Goal| Activity')'
Target     ::= 'Target(' Role | AgentID ')'
Constraint ::= 'Constraint(' LogicalExpression ')'
```

According to this definition, there are four kinds of policy (expressed by *modality*): positive authorization (A^+), negative authorization (A^-), positive obligation (O^+) and negative obligation (O^-). When a policy is abstract, it is prefixed with a symbol '$'. In each policy, there is a *PolicyID* that is globally unique to identify a policy, a *Trigger* that denotes the triggering conditions of a policy, and a *Constraint* that expresses the applicable conditions of a policy. In addition, the *Subject* and *target* of a policy can be a role or an agent, expressed by *Role* and *AgentID* respectively. Finally, *Processing* is the means taken by a policy subject. A *Processing* can be an abstract goal, an enforceable goal, or an activity, in which abstract goal is prefixed with a symbol '$'.

Recipe Definition. The refinement of abstract policies to concrete or enforceable ones is carried out by means of recipes, which are designed offline by system designer. A recipe is defined **in the form of EBNF** as follows.

```
Recipe    ::='Recipe('RecipeID AbstractPolicyID
             {PlanStep |'Loop(' PlanStep ')'}')'
PlanStep::= '(←' PolicySet [Condition] ')'|
              {'(←'PolicySet [Condition]')'}|
              '(←' 'Return(error)' Condition ')'')'
PolicySet::= Policy |'(' ('sequence'|'Concurrence') '('
              {'←'Policy [Condition] }|{Policy}')'')'
Condition::= 'Condition(' LogicalExpression ')'
```

In this definition, a recipe is composed of a *RecipeID* that identifies a recipe, an *AbstractPolicyID* that specifies the abstract policy to be refined, and some plan steps that defines possible refinement schemes of an abstract policy. In each plan step, there are a *PolicySet* and a *Condition*. When a *Condition* is satisfied, the related *PolicySet* is selected.

Policy Refinement Engine. As shown in figure 1, policy refinement engine (PRE) transforms abstract policies to concrete policies or enforceable policies with the support of recipes. When an abstract policy is put into a PRE, the PRE will select a recipe whose abstract policy ID (AbstractPolicyID) matches that of this abstract policy. And then, a policy refinement scheme will be produced according to the recipe and the conditions within each plan step. The PRE makes decisions by checking the conditions of each plan step, and forms a policy refinement scheme. In PRE, there is an algorithm for policy refinement. Let RCP be a set of available recipes; AP be a set of abstract policies to be refined; A and NA be lists for storing on-going refinement policies and non-abstract policies respectively; T be a tree to record the refinement scheme of an abstract policy; p be an abstract policy to be refined. Formally, the algorithm is defined as follows.

Step1 Let A={p}, NA=∅, T.ROOT=p;
Step2 Take p out of the list A, and let p_0=p;
Step3 If p_0 is not an abstract policy, push it into the list NA and GOTO Step7;
Step4 If $\exists r_i \in$ RCP, such that r_i.AbstractPolicyID=p_0.PolicyID, then Input(r_i); else Return error and GOTO Step9;
Step5 If $\exists c_k \in r_i$.PlanStep.Condition = TRUE, then Output(c_k, PolicySet); else Return error and GOTO Step9;
Step6 Let the policies of PolicySet from Step5 be p_0's Children, adding to the tree T, and meanwhile push them into the list A;
Step7 Take the first element (denoted as f) out of A, if A≠∅ then Let p_0=f, GOTO Step3, else GOTO Step8;
Step8 Output T;
Step9 Stop.

In this algorithm, we adopt a width-first approach. At the first, an abstract policy (p) is refined to several sub-policies. Then, if there are some abstract policies among these sub-policies, the abstract policies are further refined to sub-sub-policies respectively. And then, if there are some abstract policies among these sub-sub-policies, the refinement will continue, until all policies are concrete or enforceable.

3 Conclusions

Policy-based management (PBM) is an important technology for simplifying the management of grid service systems. As a key part of PBM, policy refinement is still a challenging issue to be resolved. In light of the recipe-based idea, this paper presented a mechanism for automatic policy refinement. The contributions of this paper are two-fold. First, we proposed a notion of policy refinement recipe, which can not only express all possible refinement alternatives of a specific high-level policy, but also reflect the runtime context by conditions within plan steps. Second, a novel policy refinement mechanism and its reasoning algorithm are presented. By this mechanism, an abstract policy can be refined to different sets of policies under various real-time contexts, thus human administrator can only focus on defining high-level policies, without worrying about the underlying details. Compared to the mechanisms proposed by other works [9,10] mentioned in section 1, our method have the following advantages. On the one hand, in our policy definition, the subject and target of policy can be roles, which are mapped to specific agents at run-time by a mechanism proposed in the paper [8], so the specification and refinement of policies can meet the demands of VO environment where the participants are dynamic. On the other hand, the conditions within a recipe reflect the context of dynamic environment, thus our approach is more flexible and powerful than traditional static rule based methods [10].

References

1. I.Foster, C. Kesselman, S. Tuecke. The Anatomy of the Grid: Enabling Scalable Virtual Organizations. *International J. Supercomputer Applications*, 15(3), 2001.
2. I. Foster, C. Kesselman, J. Nick, S. Tuecke.The Physiology of the Grid: An Open Grid Services Architecture for Distributed Systems Integration. Open Grid Service Infrastructure WG, Global Grid Forum, June 22, 2002.
3. Jeffrey O. Kephart and David M. Chess.The Vision of Autonomic Computing. IEEE Computer, 36(1):41--52, 2003
4. Bei-shui Liao, Ji Gao, Jun Hu, Jiujun Chen. A Model of Agent-Enabling Autonomic Grid Service System. In proceedings of GCC 2004, LNCS 3251, pp.839-842, 2004
5. Bei-shui Liao, Ji Gao, Jun Hu, Jiujun Chen. A federated multi-agent system: Autonomic Control of Web Services.In Proceedings of the Third International Conference on Machine Learning and Cybernetics, pp.1-6 vol.1, 2004
6. Bei-shui Liao, et al. A Policy-Driven Multi-Agent System for OGSA-Compliant Grid Control. In the proceedings of 2004 IEEE International Conference on System, Man and Cybernetics: 5525-5530
7. Bei-shui Liao, Ji Gao. Dynamic Self-Organizing System Supported by PDC-Agents. Journal of Computer-Aided Design & Computer Graphics, to appear
8. Bei-shui Liao, et al. Ontology-Based Conceptual Modeling of Policy-Driven Control Framework: Oriented to Multi-agent System for Web Services Management. In: C.-H. Chi and K.-Y. Lam(Eds): AWCC2004, LNCS 3309, pp. 346-356, 2004
9. A. K. Bandara, et al. A Goal-based Approach to Policy Refinement. In Proceedings of 5th IEEE Workshop on Policies for distributed Systems and Networks (Policy 2004) 229-239
10. Beigi, M., Calo, S., Verma, D., "Policy Transformation Techniques in Policy-based Systems Management", in proc of 5th IEEE International Workshop on Policies and Distributed Systems and Networks, IEEE, 2004, pp 13-22
11. Beishui Liao, Ji Gao.A Model of Multi-agent System Based on Policies and Contracts. Proceedings of 4th International Central and Eastern European Conference on Multi-Agent Systems (CEEMAS'05), 15-17 September 2005, Budapest, Hungary, LNAI, Springer Verlag.

Grid Services Adaptation in a Grid Workflow*

Wencai Guo, Yang Yang, and Zhengli Zhai

School of information engineering, University of Science and Technology Beijing,
Beijing 100083, P.R. China
wc_guo@yahoo.com.cn

Abstract. At present the grid workflow is a focus topic in the research on grid technologies, but few approaches are provided for designing and checking the grid services adaptation in a workflow, especially in a formal way. As a mobile process algebra, Pi-Calculus is suitable tool for modeling and analyzing distributed, concurrent and dynamic system, such as grid workflow. Addressing the protocol level deadlock, a grid service adaptor is proposed with the Pi-Calculus based Grid Services Deadlock Eliminating algorithm. Through analyzing the experiment results the algorithm proves to be available and useful for service adaptation. As a conclusion the future research work is also discussed.

1 Introduction

In the recent years, Grid technologies are getting increasingly popular and have developed quickly to a degree of maturity. Grid is a distributed environment that enables flexible, secure, coordinated resource sharing, among dynamic collections of individuals and institutions. The benefits of embracing Web services on Grid have been recently realized in the Open Grid Services Architecture [1], which defines a service-oriented architecture for Grid systems. One of the compelling reasons for the acceptance of the web service model as the basis of Grid services is their ability to combine existing services into new ones, i.e. through workflow, in which its participant is usually a Web service or Grid service and its engine coordinates the execution order of tasks.

In the studies of grid workflow, some architectures have been provided, such as GSFL [2], OCGSA [3] and CCA [4]. But a major limitation of these architectures is that they do not present suitable means for describing and reasoning on the concurrent behavior of interacting service oriented systems. Indeed while these platforms provide convenient ways to describe the service interfaces and service data, they offer a quite low-level support to describe the concurrent behavior of service. For instance, system developers would like to determine beforehand whether the inclusion of a third-party service may introduce a deadlock into the application under development. In order to rigorously verify properties of system consisting of large numbers of dynamically interacting services, a formal description of the interactive behavior of services is needed.

Our present goal is to make use of a fair amount of work [5][6][7][8] currently available on the behavioral descriptions of components and web services at the

* This work has been supported by National Natural Science Foundation of China (No.90412012).

H. Zhuge and G.C. Fox (Eds.): GCC 2005, LNCS 3795, pp. 172 – 177, 2005.

protocol level, in order to apply many of such theoretical results to the practical field of the grid services. In particular, in this paper we show how the grid workflow can be checked whether two or more grid services are compatible to interoperate or not, and if not, whether the specification of adaptors that mediate between them can be automatically generated.

2 Protocol Level Grid Services Adaptation

In a grid workflow application, multi grid services have to coordinate to work according to certain rules, but all the service compositions are based on the successful message exchange between them. Otherwise, the service deadlock will happen. For instance, when a grid service S_1 sends a message to invoke a synchronous method on another service S_2, S_1 will block waiting for the method to complete. If S_2 attempt to call S_1 (invoke a callback) while S_1 is waiting for the original method to complete, then each party will be waiting for the other. This is a kind of deadlock. The same situation could occur if a callback handler attempted to call a synchronous method on its caller.

Protocol level adaptation [13] can be seen as an interoperability adjustment that deals just with the partial order between the services' exchanged methods, and the blocking conditions that rule the availability of the services. Of course it does not cover all the semantic aspects of services, but it is not weighed down with the heavy burden of semantic checks. At the protocol level the problems can be more easily identified and managed, and practical (tool-based) solutions can be proposed to solve them.

In OGSI [12], although any grid service has the common NotificationSource/ NotificationSink interface, its message sequence order is distinct due to its inherent behaviors or semantics, which results in the possible protocol mismatching between interactive grid services. As a solution, we propose a grid service adaptor (also a grid service instance) to realize the mapping between heterogeneous service protocols and then to eliminate the possible deadlocks.

3 Grid Services Adaptor

In figure 1, a grid service adaptor is located between two services. It is created by grid workflow coordinator and responsible for receiving or sending all the required messages of these two services in a deadlock free way. As a critical component, adaptor specification plays important role in protocol level grid service adaptation.

In order to describe an adaptor specification, a grid service is re-defined in following style:

GridService *ServName* = {
    signature *input and output actions*
    protocol *messages sequencing*
}

The **signature** interface of a grid service declares a set of input and output actions, that is, the set of messages sent and received by the service, representing the methods that the service offers and invokes, the values or exceptions returned, etc. Both input and output actions may have parameters, representing the data exchanged in the communication.

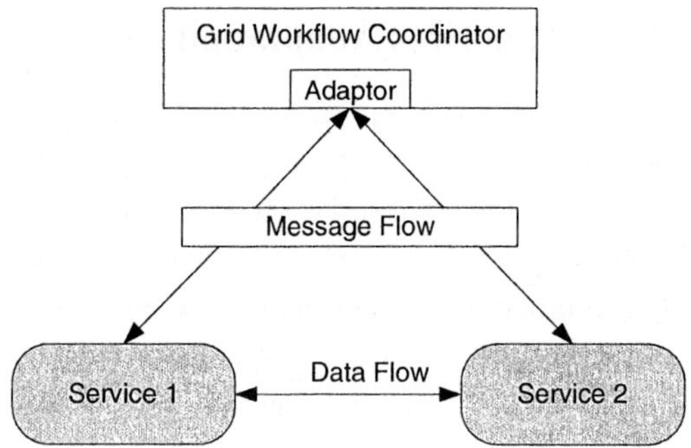

Fig. 1. Grid Services Adaptor

The **protocol** description of a service consists of sequenced messages, which reflects the essential aspects of the finite interactive behavior that a service may show to its environment in part. Compared with CCS[10], CSP[11] or other process algebra theories, the pi-calculus[9], allowing link names to be sent and received as values, is a very expressive notation for describing the behavior of grid services in applications with changing interconnection topology.

As an example, we assume a book borrowing service, *Library*, has been deployed in a library web and one student broker service, *Student*, sends a request for borrowing some book after passing the login authentication. Via Pi-Calculus, the service specification can be described as following:

GridService $Student = \{$

  signature $Book\_request!()$, $reply?(answer)$;

  protocol $Book\_request!().reply?(answer).0$

$\}$

GridService $Library = \{$

  signature $Lib\_Query?()$, $Ack!()$, $Confirmation!()$;

  protocol $Lib\_Query?().\ Ack!().\ Confirmation!().0$

$\}$

where the parameter *answer* is a data value either representing a confirmation or a refusal from a borrowing service.

Hence, we represent an adaptor specification by a mapping that establishes a number of rules relating actions and data of two services. For instance, the mapping expressing the intended adaptation for the previous example consists of the following three rules:

$$
\begin{aligned}
MA = \{ request!() &\diamond Query?(), Ack!();\\
reply?(''Confirmed'') &\diamond Confirmation!();\\
reply?(''Refused'') &\diamond Refusal!() \}
\end{aligned}
$$

where the messages in the left refer to the *Student* service, while those in the right refer to the *Library* service. The intended meaning of the first rule is that whenever the student outputs a request message, the borrowing service must eventually input one *Query* message, and output one *Ack* message. The rest rules have the similar meaning.

Given a mapping *MA* and the interaction pattern *P* and *Q* of two services, a concrete adaptor is generated by means of a fully automated procedure. Intuitively speaking, such an adaptor will be a component-in-the-middle *A* such that: 1) the parallel composition *P|A|Q* will not deadlock, and 2) *A* will satisfy all the action correspondences and data dependencies specified by *MA*.

For such goals, the adaptor *A* is formed by eliminating gradually all the possible deadlocks that may occur in the evolution of the system.

4 A Pi-Calculus Based Grid Service Deadlock Eliminating Algorithm (PGSDE)

For removal of grid service deadlocks in a grid workflow, a Pi-Calculus based grid service deadlock eliminating algorithm is proposed in this section. The description of the algorithm is as following:

```
Input: a grid workflow W ;
Output: the complete adaptor specifications;
List all involving grid services of W, the amount of
them is n;
Adaptor A= 0;  bool isDeadlock = false; int i=0;
While (n>0){
  Select service(i);
  List all the messages required by activities;
  Perform the service protocol via pi-calculus;
  Find its partner services and produce all mappings MA
between them;
  while ( isDeadlock) {
    Reconstruct and expanded A[i] ;
    To check its correctness by theorems
    of Pi-calculus;
  }
  Output the adaptor A[i];
  n = n-1; i = i+1;
}
return all the adaptors
```

In this algorithm, all the adapters among the involved grid services in workflow *W* are produced by exhaustively eliminating possible deadlocks.

5 Performance of PGSDE Algorithm

Up to now, fewer studies on grid service adaptation are performed and less experiment results are reported in literatures. As an optional comparison, we choose web service composition method, Keyword-based Service Composition Method (KSCM) [14], to compare with PGSDE algorithm.

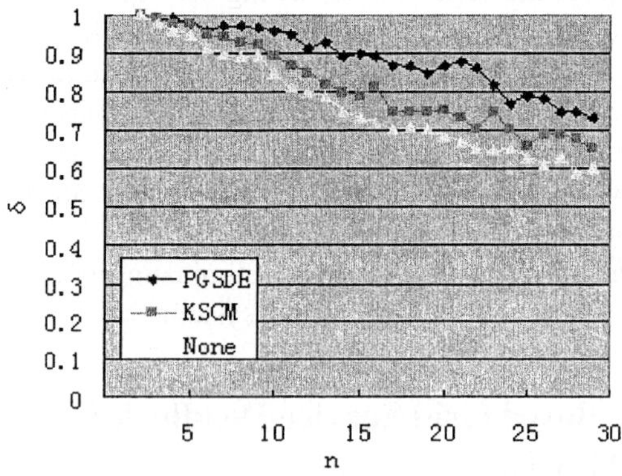

Fig. 2. Performance Comparison among PGSDE, KSCM and none adaptation

We define successful service adaptation rate δ as performance data. δ is defined as:

$$\delta(w) = \frac{Succ\_Message(n)}{Total\_Message(n)} \tag{1}$$

where w is the tested workflow application which is executed by the services numbered n, range over 2 to 30 , and messages numbered range over 10 to 300 . *Succ_Message(n)* and *Total_Message(n)* are defined as the number of successful message and the total service message required by n services in w.

Figure 2 gives a performance comparison among PGSDE, KSCM and none adaptation in grid workflow applications, which indicates that PGSDE is obviously better than the other two methods when the number of grid services in a workflow is more than 10. And we can also conclude that the number of failure requests increases with the increasing service number in a same workflow.

6 Conclusion

In order to reduce the deadlocks among services when a heterogeneous service is included, it's necessary to adapt the protocol interaction between the service and the existing ones. So a service adaptor in this paper is presented to meet such demands in concurrent, distributed and dynamic grid environment through eliminating protocol mismatching between services with a Pi-Calculus based deadlock eliminating algorithm (PGSDE). The analysis of PGSDE performance proves the adaptor is available and effective.

But in real world, such as in e-Commerce or e-Government fields, the service workflow process is more complicated, which results in more difficulties to describe and refine it in process modeling. Such complexities are from two basic properties of grid service: 1) the status of any service is dynamic during its execution, and 2) a service may play multiple roles in practice. Moreover, as stated in [15], flows in the future Internet environment can involve more rich semantics. Therefore, addressing these issues the future work should be extended to establish a flexible and robust semantics-rich adaptor, such as adaptor reconstruction once it fails to work properly.

References

1. Foster, I., Kesselman, C., Nick, J. and Tuecke, S.: The Physiology of the Grid: An Open Grid Services Architecture for Distributed Systems Integration. Globus Project, 2002. http://www.globus.org /research/papers /ogsa.pdf.
2. Wagstrom, P., Krishnan, S. and von Laszewski:, G.: GSFL: A Workflow Framework for Grid Services. In Supercomputing Conference (SC 2002).
3. Amin, K., Nijsure, S., von Laszewski, G.: Open Collaborative Grid Service Architecture (OCGSA). http://www1.bcs.org.uk/ DocsRepository/03700/3789/amin.htm, December 2002.
4. Govindaraju, M., Krishnan, S., Kenneth Chiu, Slominski, A. etc.: Merging the CCA Component Model with the OGSI Framework. Proceedings of CCGrid2003. The 3rd International Symposium on Cluster Computing and the Grid, http://www.extremeindiana.edu/ xcat/publications/xcatogsi.pdf, May 2003.
5. Bracciali, A., Brogi, A., Turini, F.: 2001. Coordinating interaction patterns. In: ACM Symposium on Applied Computing (SAC'2001). ACM Press.
6. Brogi, A., Canal, C., Pimentel, E., Vallecillo, A.: Formalizing Web Service Choreographies. WS-FM 2004 Preliminary Version. 2004.
7. Zhuge, H.: Component-based Workflow Systems Development. Decision Support Systems, 35(4)(2003)517-536.
8. Bracciali, A., A. Brogi and C. Canal, A formal approach to component adaptation. Journal of Systems and Software, 74(2005)45-54.
9. Milner, R., Parrow, J., and Walker, D.: A calculus of mobile processes, parts i and ii. Journal of Information and Computation, 100:1-77,1992.
10. Milner, A.J.R.G.: A Calculus of Communicating Systems. Lecture Notes in Computer Science, Volumn 92, Springer-Verlag,1980.
11. Hoare. C. A. R.: Communication Sequential Processes. International Series in Computer Science. Prentice Hall, 1985.
12. Tuecke, S., Czajkowski, K., Foster, I., Frey, J., Graham, S., Kesselman, C., Maguire, T., Sandholm, T., Vanderbilt, P. and Snelling, D.: Open Grid Services Infrastructure (OGSI) version 1.0. Technical report, Open Grid Services Infrastructure WG, Global Grid Forum, 2002.
13. Yellin, D.M., Strom, R.E.: Protocol specifications and components adaptors. ACM Transactions on Programming Languages and Systems 19 (2), 292–333.
14. Thakkar S.: Dynamically composing Web services. Proceedings of AAAI Workshop on Intelligent Service Integration , Edmonton , Alberta , Canada , 2002 , 1-7
15. Zhuge, H.: The Future Interconnection Environment. IEEE Computer, 38 (4)(2005) 27-33

BlogGrid: Towards an Efficient Information Pushing Service on Blogspace

Jason J. Jung[1,2], Inay Ha[1], and Geun-Sik Jo[1]

[1] School of Computer Engineering, Inha University,
253 Yonghyun-dong, Incheon, Korea 402-751
j2jung@intelligent.pe.kr, inay@eslab.inha.ac.kr,
gsjo@inha.ac.kr
[2] INRIA Rhone-Alpes,
655, avenue de l'Europe, Montbonnot St. Martin,
38334 Saint-Ismier cedex, France

Abstract. With increasing concerns about the personalized information space, users have been posting various types of information on their own blogs. Due to the domain-specific properties of blogging systems, however, searching relevant information is too difficult. In this paper, we focus on analyzing the user behaviors on blogspace, so that the channel between two similar users can be virtually generated. Eventually, social grid environment can be constructed on blog organization. We therefore propose a BlogGrid framework to provide the information pushing service without any user intervention.

1 Introduction

Many kinds of personalized information spaces have been developed. As a representative example, a blog (originally Weblog) is a Web application presented as a web page consisting of periodic posts, normally in reverse chronological order [8]. Since Jorn Barger coined this idea in 1997, the usage of blogs has been spread from individual diaries to arms of political campaigns, media programs and corporations, and from the writing of one occasional author to the collaboration of a large community of writers [4]. More importantly, each blogger can make explicit connections with others such as families, friends, and colleagues. Through these social activities, indeed, bloggers can organize communities in a form of blogs. In summary, we note two main features of blogs, as follows.

- **Personal content management.** Bloggers can create and manage various forms of contents such as personal history, commentaries, and photos.
- **Information propagation by social activities.** Along with the social links, they can have access to the other's blogs. It is similar to browsing the hypertext documents.

However, we have faced on two serious problems. Firstly, a large amount of information on blogspace is overwhelming to users. It means that bloggers are getting more overloaded to search relevant information. The blog-tracking company Technorati, Inc., reports almost 4.2 million Weblogs worldwide as of October 2004, up from about one million a year earlier. And a 2003 Pew/Internet survey estimated that more than 53 American adults, or 44\% of Internet users, had used the Internet to

H. Zhuge and G.C. Fox (Eds.): GCC 2005, LNCS 3795, pp. 178 – 183, 2005.

publish their thoughts, respond to others, post pictures, share files, and otherwise contribute to the content available online [8].

Second problem, which is much more serious than a former, is that most of communities tend to be organized by the private relations between bloggers, e.g., nepotism. Not only the community policy for protecting the privacy of members but also the isolation of social structure causes the information flows on blogsphere to be limited.

In this paper, we exploit the grid computing paradigm, which is capable of supporting a efficient framework of information sharing between heterogeneous sources, to blogspaces and bloggers. Thereby, each blogger's behaviors should be captured and analyzed to extract what topics he is (or they are) interested in and, more exactly, what he has been trying to search. On this grid environment for information sharing on blogsphere, called BlogGrid, each user can be provided with information pushing service. This service consists of three steps, which are construction of latent channels, organization of transparent communities, and information pushing. The goal of this service is efficient information diffusion on blogsphere. It means that a certain information should be delivered to the bloggers who have been looking for that information as quickly as possible, regardless of the social distances and topologies.

2 Modeling Behaviors on Blogspace

We assume that each action taken by bloggers have implicit meaning and be able to be applied to extract useful information. In order to model behaviors on blogspace, we need to thoroughly note the roles of blogspaces and bloggers. Blogspaces are divided into personal and community space [7]. Each user is able not only to possess his own personal blogspace, but also to take part in community blogspaces as a member. Due to the particular purposes, bloggers conduct the following behaviors.

- Linking with others. It is to establish a social network such as families, friends, and colleagues. More importantly, in order to share information about a particular topic, people can organize a community and actively participate it.
- Posting articles. It is the most basic action on blogspaces. As taking this action, bloggers can input various types of information and enrich blogspaces. This action explicitly represents the corresponding blogger's preferences. For example, he is probably interested in "music", because he has been posting articles about recital schedules and musical instruments.
- Navigating. In order to get relevant information within a blog system, people can visit other blogspaces. Bloggers can navigate the other blogspaces by the following two methods. i) Random browsing. Bloggers can "randomly" jump into other blogspaces. In fact, this has been the only way to deal with nepotism problem. ii) Accessing to neighbors on social network. By referring to the list of neighbors, bloggers easily move into their blogs.
- Responding. Bloggers can respond to a certain article while navigating blogspace. Their responses like personal opinions, sympathies, antipathies, or even apathy are express as the following two ways: i) *Comment.* A blogger can leave his responses which consist of short text sentences. More than a comment can be serially and continuously attached to each post article. ii) *Trackback.* In contrast to comments,

it allows a blogger to see who has seen the original post and has written another entry concerning it. It works by sending a `ping' between the blogs, and therefore providing the alert. Trackback typically appears below a blog entry and shows a summary of what has been written on the target blog, together with a URL and the name of the blog. Since implemented by Movable Type, most blogging systems have adopted trackback mechanism as generic function.

Not only free-text sentence but also numeric rating format (e.g., from 0 to 5) and voting format (e.g., "Yes" or "No") can be applied to reflect the corresponding blogger's interests and opinions.

Another interesting feature is that the responding can be nested. It means that bloggers can respond to a certain comment already attached to articles.

Above all, a community blogspace is supposed to utilize categories and manage them. This category is very similar to simple taxonomies and topic hierarchies. Examples of such categories are "Music> Blues>", "Computer Science> Artificial Intelligence>", and "Conference> Grid Computing> GCC>". It makes every articles posted in his blogspace well-organized and semantically annotated.

Most importantly, bloggers have concerned on dealing with the difficulties of navigating blogspaces. Thereby, in this paper, we have focused on extracting behavioral patterns of responses, rather than analyzing free texts posted on the user's blogspace.

A blogger finally is modeled with his own preference information extracted from his behaviors on blogspaces. It is represented as a set of hierarchical topics, which is derived from particular bloggers' categories. Suppose that user A attach his comments to blogspaces B which are annotated to a set of categories C_A

$$C_A = \{[c_1, w_{c_1}], [c_2, w_{c_2}], \ldots, [c_n, w_{c_n}]\} \tag{1}$$

$$w_{c_i} = \frac{|c_i|}{n} \tag{2}$$

where n is the total number of different categories and w_{ci} is the weight value of i-th category c_i. The summation of weight values is equal to one for normalization.

3 Information Pushing on BlogGrid

Information should be pushed to the bloggers who are looking for it. This service is simply composed of two main processes; organization of latent communities and recommendation by facilitator agent.

3.1 Transparent Organization of Latent Communities

In order to construct latent communities, a group of bloggers who are interested in same topics should be obtained. As measuring the similarity between two bloggers, we can infer their relationship and make a decision whether they should be participated in a same community together or not. Especially, this task should be transparently done, which means it has to be performed without user's intervention and realization. Simple scheme for measuring the similarity between two users A and B is based on the equation

$$Sim(A,B) = H[C_A, C_B, \cap_{k=1}^{K}\{\tilde{o}(C_A, C_B)\}] \tag{3}$$

where the function $\tilde{o}$ is to obtain the K common elements from both sets. And the notation H indicates several heuristic functions that systems can apply to quantitating the similarities between two users.

In this paper, we want to utilize three difference heuristic functions, mentioned in [5], to compare two random sets. Derived from the previous equation, we formulate these heuristic ways, as shown in the following equations

$$H[A,B,C] = \frac{|C|}{\max(|A|,|B|)} = \max_{i=1}^{|C|}(W_{c_i}) = \frac{\sum_{i=1}^{|C|} w_{c_i}}{|C|} \tag{4}$$

where C is $A \cap B$. While the first one in Equ.4 simply expresses the minimum ratio of the common categories, the others use the weight value of each category. Second one in Equ.4 simply chooses the category of which weight value is maximal, and the last computes the average weight value of common categories.

3.2 System Architecture of BlogGrid

Along with the estimated information channel, the relevant pieces of information should be pushed actively. Information pushing service proposed in this paper is remote and asynchronous because this is based on web environment and information about a participant's interests extracted from his own behaviors. The whole system architecture consists of two main parts, which are a facilitator located between the users and the client-side blogspace browser that communicates with the facilitator. We embed autonomous and proactive agent module into this system. Every communication between agents is conducted, regardless of user's interventions. Also, while browsing blogspaces to search information, users can be "implicitly" recommended from the facilitator in the following two ways:

- By querying specific information for the facilitator. After the information about a particular topic is requested, the facilitator can determine who has the maximum weight value of that topic by scanning his yellow pages.
- By broadcasting new information of like-minded bloggers from the facilitator. Every time a user responds a new comment, this fact, after normalization, is sent to the facilitator. Users thereby can obtain information related to the common concepts in their own preferences from neighbors.

Each blogger needs personal agent module. This agent initializes and manages the preference of the corresponding blogger based on blogspace repository. Through personal agents' reporting responding activities of bloggers, the facilitator agent can automatically generate queries and recommendations.

4 Experimental Results

For evaluating our system, we have conducted preliminary experimentation. First of all, ten people were invited to participate to navigate BlogGrid environment. Before starting experiment, they claimed their own preferences, by referring to "Entertainment" directory in Yahoo directory service (http://dir.yahoo.com/). We asked them to post information relevant to their preferences.

After testing bed was prepared, these ten bloggers were linked with at most two acquaintances for constructing social networks, and they conducted two-week BlogGrid experimentation. During first one week, bloggers were allowed to browse other blogspaces and respond posts by leaving comments and trackbacks without BlogGrid's recommendation. Next one week, BlogGrid supported them to easily exchange information.

The issue for evaluation is how accurately BlogGrid recommended information to each blogger. We measured the ratio of the number of posts by BlogGrid's recommendation to the total number of posts. With human evaluation by interviewing with bloggers,

- Six bloggers, $User_2$ (35.3%), $User_3$ (31.7%), $User_4$ (28.1%), $User_6$ (37.5%), $User_8$ (36.7%), and $User_{10}$ (23.9%) were fully satisfied
- Two bloggers, $User_1$ (26.2%) and $User_9$ (15.6%) were partially satisfied
- One blogger, $User_5$ (28.1%) were partially unsatisfied
- One blogger, $User_7$ (7.5%) were fully unsatisfied

with BlogGrid's recommendations. Roughly, 80% of bloggers rated BlogGrid as a useful system to them. $User_6$ has shown the largest ratio level, which means he was been most effectively helped by BlogGrid. Particularly, $User_5$ judged BlogGrid to be negative. We found out his preference is very diverse, so that his ratio showed relatively high.

5 Concluding Remarks and Future Work

As the concerns about blogspace is ever-increasing, efficient information delivering function is desperately necessary. We were motivated to enhance this primitive blogspace with cooperative computing paradigm.

Therefore, this paper proposes that BlogGrid system is capable of helping bloggers, by analyzing and recognizing user activity and interests. Bloggers can get information pushing service with BlogGrid's recommendation, which consists of mainly two steps; i) organization of transparent communities and ii) information pushing by facilitator.

We developed BlogGrid system by using Blojsom libraries and Borland Delphi software. BlogGrid browser's graphic user interface can visualize the communications and relationships between bloggers. More importantly, facilitator of BlogGrid is capable of

1) Investigating the factors which influence relationships.
2) Drawing out implications of the relational data.
3) Making recommendations to improve communications.

Through simple experimentation, we have shown that a relatively large part of bloggers were satisfied with this service.

References

1. Athanasiadis, I.N., Mitkas, P.A.: Social influence and water conservation: an agent-based approach. Computing in Science & Engineering **7**(1) (2005) 65-70
2. Blojsom: http://wiki.blojsom.com/wiki/display/blojsom/About+blojsom.
3. Cayzer, S.: Semantic blogging and distributed knowledge management. Communications of ACM **47**(12) (2004) 47-52
4. Dekker, A.H.: A Category-Theoretic Approach to Social Network Analysis. Electonic Notes in Theoretical Computer Science **61** (2002) 21-33
5. Jung, J.J., Lee, K.-S., Park, S.-B., Jo, G.-S.: Efficient Web Browsing with Semantic Annotation: a Case Study of Product Images in E-Commerce Sites. IEICE Transactions on Information and Systems **E88-D**(5) (2005) 843-850
6. Kleinberg, J.: Authoritative sources in a hyperlinked environment. Journal of the ACM **46**(5) (1999) 604-632
7. Nardi, B.A., Schiano, D.J., Gumbrecht, M., Swartz, L.: Why We Blog. Communications of ACM **47**(12) (2004) 41-46
8. Rosenbloom, A.: The Blogosphere. Communications of ACM **47**(12) (2004) 31-33
9. Zhuge, H.: Semantics, Resource and Grid. Future Generation Computer Systems **20**(1) (2004) 1-5

Research of Security Architecture for P2P Network Based on Trust Management System*

Zhang Dehua[1,2], Yuqing Zhang[2], and Yiyu Zhou[1]

[1] College of Electronics and Engineering,
National University of Defense Technology,
410073, Changsha, Hunan, China
[2] National Computer Network Intrusion Protection Center, GSCAS,
100039, Beijing, China
{zhangdh, zhangyq}@nipc.org.cn

Abstract. The P2P network and its applications have the characters of dynamic and self-management, so the existing technologies do not solve the security issues of P2P network appropriately. In this paper, we describe new techniques that overcome many of the cited difficulties. We propose a new security architecture named SAP2P to address the security problems in P2P network. The core of SAP2P is based on a trust management named ExSPKI that establishes the trust relationships between peers. This architecture is adapted to the features of P2P network.

1 Introduction

The P2P network has the unique characteristics of dynamic topology and autonomy, these characteristics lead to security problems that are not addressed by existing security technologies for distributed system. For example, the peers in P2P network that want to share resources and communicate with others need to establish security trust relationships each other, the trust relationships do not mean authentication only but also authorization and delegation which can not be expressed by PKI certificates or Kerberos tokens. The existing technologies consider establishing trust relationship as performing authentication that makes the ID band to a public key and they describe the security policy using the IDs. But in the P2P network, the ID of a peer is often a random number without practice meaning. Finally, the peers in P2P network may use different methods to complete access control, so the access control technology used in P2P network should be interoperate with them.

In this paper, we describe new techniques that overcome many of the cited difficulties. We propose a new security architecture named SAP2P to address the security problems in P2P network[6][7]. The core of SAP2P is based on a trust management named ExSPKI that establishes the trust relationships between peers. This architecture is adapted to the features of P2P network.

* This work is supported by National Natural Science Foundation of China under Grant 60373040 and National "863" Program Grant 2003AA142150.

H. Zhuge and G.C. Fox (Eds.): GCC 2005, LNCS 3795, pp. 184–189, 2005.

2 Trust Relationship in the P2P Network

Building the trust relationship between users is the foundation of the security in all the distributed systems[2]. There are two main existing methods of building the trust relationship. One is called tree of trust, the other is called web of trust. The typical implementation being widely used of these two methods are PKI and PGP.

The two implementations all establish the binding of the users ID and its public key. But in the P2P network ID is always a random number with no meanings which is mainly used for search in the P2P network. So it is not useful of building trust relationship only binding the ID and the public key. We will give the definition of the trust relationship in P2P network following.

Definition 1(Trust relationship in P2P network) : In the P2P network the trust relationship between A and B that we say A trust B means B can complete authentication, authorization and delegation instead of A.

In our definition we add three items in trust relationship. They are

- Authentication: which means confirm a user's identity in the P2P network.
- Authorization: which means give the right of implementing some operations to other peers
- Delegation: which means the transfer of the trust relationships.

We think in the P2P network the trust relationship should include the items above, and the existing definition only binding ID to public key is not suitable in the P2P network.

3 Trust Model Based on ExSPKI

ExSPKI is the trust management system we designed to be used in the P2P network, Which is similar with SPKI[3]. Here we can treat ExSPKI as SPKI.

This section presents the proposal of a trust model using the trust management system ExSPKI. The proposed trust model is based on the concept of a Peer Group, which emphasize the grouping of principals with common trust relationship. The

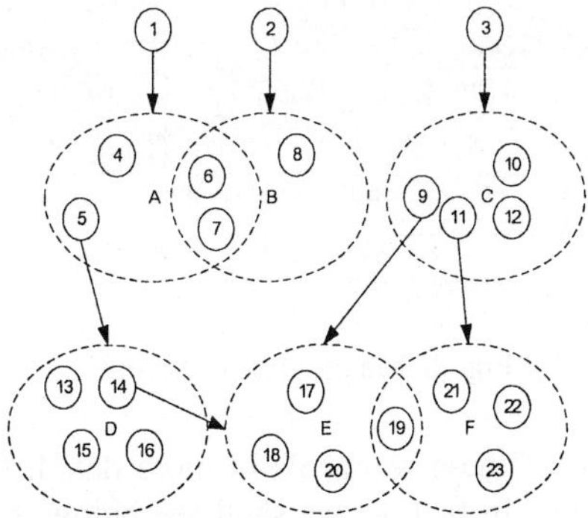

Fig. 1. The trust model based on group

purpose of a group is to establish a security environment through the service provided by the group.

The trust model is shown in figure 2. The dots are peers and the dashed circles are groups. In this model the group is equal to the trust relation defined above. The peer are not must stay in a group. But every group must have a creator. In this trust model every peer is identified with his public key. The group is declared use ExSPKI certificate.

In this trust model, there are two types of trust relationship. On is called the initial trust, the other is implicit trust. The initial trust is established used the method off line as Kerberos do. The implicit trust is found out using our trust management system ExSPKI. In the figure 2, peer 1, peer5, peer14 and peer17 can establish a trust chain.

The process to find the implicit trust is completed with several protocols. We will explain them below.

4 The Security Architecture of P2P Network

The peer in the P2P network serves as both client and server. So we design the peer to be composed with two function modules in which one is manage the local security and the other is responsible for communicate with other peers. The components are : user proxy, authorization Sever, Group Sever, Discovery Sever, authentication Sever, Resource Sever.

In our architecture, there are communications among the components. We describe these communications with protocols. The protocols and their processes are described in figure 2.

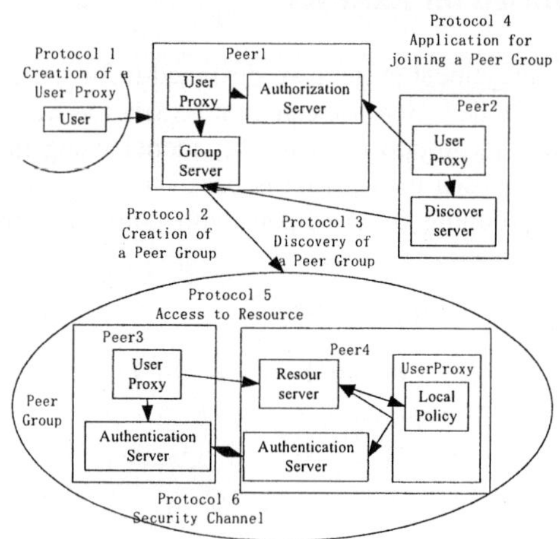

Fig. 2. The protocol of SAP2P

We now describe each of these protocols in more detail. Our descriptions do not talk about specific methods. In fact, as we shell see below, our implementation uses the JAVA programming interface to achieve independence from any specific security technology.

4.1 User Proxy Creation Protocol

A user could enable a proxy to act on her behalf by giving the proxy the appropriate credentials like [7](e.g., a password or private key). In our architecture the public key is represented the user. So we give the proxy the user's key pair that is loaded to the computer where user-proxy runs by the user. In this paper, how the user get the key pair is beyond the scope of the problem (the possible solutions include self-signed certificates).The actual process of user proxy creation is summarized in Protocol 1.

1. The user gains access to computer from which the user-proxy is to be created, using whatever form of local authentication is placed on that computer.
2. The user run a P2P application (active a peer in the network)
3. A user proxy process is created and the user's key pair is loaded.

In our architecture, the user-proxy uses the user's key pair directly. So the protection of the private key is essential job.

4.2 Peer Group Creation Protocol

As we have said above, the peers should be dispersed into many partitions. Here we define these partitions to be peer groups. The trust relationship and the peer group are related. It is well understood that the peers with the same trust relationships will compose a group. Protocol 2 defines the process by which this can be accomplished.

1. User-proxy issues the group declaration .
2. User add the contents of the items in the declaration
3. Add the signature of the conditions
4. Issues the declaration in the P2P network.

Here we do not appoint how to publish the declaration of the group concretely. It is because there are different methods in different P2P network, like DHT and broadcast. It is decided by the real environment where the P2P applications run. We treat the declaration of a group as a special resource. This resource is similar with the seed in the file-sharing application like Gnutella.

So the declaration can be published like other resource seeds in the P2P network.

4.3 Discovering the Peer Group Protocol

A peer who wants to join a group should find it out firstly. The discovery of the group is the same as finding the trust relationship in the P2P network. We can find the group according to the items in the declarations. Protocol 3 describes the steps:

1. The user-proxy lunches a discovery request in the P2P network with an index of one of the items in the declaration.
2. The P2P network do with this request according to the implementation of the mechanism of resource discovery
3. A response will be return to the peer when the group is found or after an interval the user defined there is no response which means the group is not existed.
4. The peer will cash the declaration of the group.

The discovering of the peer group mainly uses the function providing by the P2P network. A good arithmetic is DHT[8] which has the high research efficacy and time delay.

4.4 Joining the Group Protocol

The process that a peer joins a group is also the process that confirms the relationship between the applier and the creator of the group. The protocol is the core of the architecture. Through the protocol, the peers in the P2P network can establish a trust network which is the foundation of P2P security. Protocol 4 gives more details of the progress.

1. The applicant gets the declaration and initializes the peer group.
2. The user-proxy get the conditions to be the member of the group
3. The user-proxy user the ExSPKI arithmetic to construct the certificate link.
4. the user-proxy start the group membership service and give the certificate link and request as parameter. The every certificate and request are singed
5. The group membership service will verify the certificate link and the conditions. If the certificate link is correct. Then creator will give the applicant an ExSPKI certificate to show the membership.

4.5 Access Resource Protocol

Access resource protocol can make the user to access the resource in the group he joins. We assume peer A and B are all in the same group. The process of protocol 6 is described in detail below:

1. Every peer will announce in the group the resource he wants to share with others. It is common process in P2P network, as the seed is published in Freenet.
2. When A wants to access some resources, A can first search the announcement to find the owner of the resource.
3. Peer A will give the request and his credential of the group to the Peer B
4. Peer B will give peer A an ACK or the conditions A should accorded to.

The process is similar with the process of group creation. But there are different here. The announcement of the resource does not include the conditions because it is good to reduce the data used to transform in the network and the security policy is control by each peer themselves.

4.6 Security Channel Protocol

This protocol is a reverse of SSL[1]. What is different to SSL is that the peer use the credential got from the group creator. A session key is created and exchange between the two peers. Using this session key, the security channel is established.

In this protocol, the credential is the ExSPKI certificate which the creator of the group gives to the applicant. So only the peers in the same group can establish the security channel. This makes the group to be a security environment in the P2P network. And the protocol is under the control of local security policy.

5 Conclusions

We have described a security architecture for P2P network. This architecture is immediately useful and, in addition, provides a firm foundation for investigations of more sophisticated mechanism. Our architecture addresses most of the requirements introduce in Section 3. We have also implement the architecture based on JXTA[4]. We will give the standard API of the architecture next step.

References

[1] SSL http:// www.openssl.org/

[2] Matt Blaze, Joan Feigenbaum, and Jack Lacy. Decentralized Trust Management. In Proceedings of the 1996 IEEE Symposium on Security and Privacy, pages 164-173. IEEE Computer Society Press, 1996.

[3] Carl Ellison, Bill Frantz, Butler Lampson, Ron Rivest, Brian Thomas, and Tatu Ylonen. SPKI Certificate Theory. IETF RFC 2693, September 1999.

[4] Bernard Traversat, Mohamed Abdelaziz, Mike Duigou, Jean-Christophe Hugly, Eric Pouyoul and Bill Yeage, Sun Microsystems, Inc. Project JXTA Virtual Network. October 28, 2002.

[5] Zhang Dehua, Zhang YuQing. A Survey of P2P Network Security Issues Based on Protocol Stack, Progress on Cryptography, 25 Years of Cryptography in China, pages 209-216, Shanghai, China.

[6] Zhang Yuqing , Zhang Dehua. Authentication and Access Control in P2P Network. Grid and Cooperative Computing , GCC2003, pages 468-470, Shanghai ,China.

[7] I. Foster , C. Kesselman, G. Tsudik, S. Tuechk : A Security Architecture for Computational Grids, 5th ACM Conference on Computer and Communication Security Conference, 1998

[8] STOICA, I., MORRIS, R., LIBEN-NOWELL, D., KARGER,D. R., KAASHOEK, M. F., DABEK, F., AND BALAKRISHNAN,H. Chord: a scalable peer-to-peer lookup protocol for internet applications. IEEE/ACM Trans. Netw. 11, 1 (2003), 17.32.

A Time-Frame Based Trust Model for Grids

Woodas W.K. Lai and Kam-Wing Ng

Department of Computer Science and Engineering,
The Chinese University of Hong Kong,
Shatin, N.T., Hong Kong
+852-2609-8440
{wklai, kwng}@cse.cuhk.edu.hk

Abstract. A Grid is a virtual resource framework[1,2] which provides the ability to access, utilize, and manage a variety of heterogeneous resources among multiple domains. However, selecting appropriate resources within such a distributed Grid environment is a complex and difficult task. In recent years, trust models have been proposed[4,5], but most of them do not deal with the temporal issue of trust. In this paper, we aim to extend the trust model with a novel data structure called Time-Frame which can store temporal information regard-ing to the trust involved. With the Time-Frame structure, we can evaluate the resources accurately by means of the available temporal information.

1 Introduction

A Grid[1,2] is a large-scale distributed computing system. It aims to encourage the sharing of computational, storage and other resources among multiple domains. Trust is a sociological topic that exists in the human society. An important practical example of trust and reputation is eBay[6] (www.ebay.com), most likely the largest online auction site. After each transaction, buyers and sellers can rate each other and the overall reputation of a participant is computed as the sum of these ratings over the last six months. The eBay example does illustrate the use of trust. However, one may argue that why eBay only takes the last six months' transaction into account, but not a longer period, say, one year. We will further discuss this issue in the coming sections. In this paper, we try to present a data structure called Time-Frame. Time-Frame can be used to extend the Trust model so as to enhance the capability and accuracy. Due to the limited space, we focus on the Time-Frame structure and its operations only in this paper. If you want to look into the detail of what trust and reputation are, please refer to the reference[3].

2 Discussion on Trust

2.1 Temporal Issues

Trust and Reputation are usually based on the past transactions of the entities. History can tell how well a resource has behaved. Analogously, in human society,

H. Zhuge and G.C. Fox (Eds.): GCC 2005, LNCS 3795, pp. 190–195, 2005.

we always look into someone's history in order to evaluate whether we should trust him or not. However, to have a fair view on a particular entity, one should study the whole history pertaining to that entity. In the Grid context, it would mean that each entity should store all the past transactions in order to get a more accurate trust evaluation. But this induces huge storage consumption. However, with reasonable storage consumption, it would be beneficial if we can take as many past transactions as we could into consideration when we have to decide whether to trust an entity or not. Our novel data structure, Time-Frame, uses a logarithmic scale structure in order to store the temporal information of a resource. Meanwhile, as mentioned in [4], trust decays with time. Therefore, in our trust model, more weight will be given to the re-cent history.

2.2 Temporal Failure Locality

If a resource fails to fulfill the request submitted, there could be lots of reasons behind the failure, like outage, system failure or network failure, etc. In reality, failures would take time to recover. Therefore, if we continue to request for service just after a failure has immediately occurred, most likely our request will lead to another failure again as the problem would probably not have been resolved yet. In this paper, we name this phenomenon "Temporal failure locality". Obviously, Trust models should take this phenomenon into account so as to enhance accuracy.

3 Time Frame

The existing trust models need further enhancements. In section 2, some discussions were presented. Unfortunately, the existing trust models cannot address all the mentioned issues and this further motivates the evolution. Each Time-Frame represents a period of time. The design of the Time-Frame structure is based on the fact that people are often interested in recent changes at a fine granularity, but long term changes at a coarse granularity. Figure 1 shows such a Time-Frame structure. The Time-Frame structure is constructed based on a logarithmic time scale. Suppose the current Time-Frame holds the transactions in the current quarter. Then the remaining slots are for the last quarter, the last two quarters, 4 quarters, 8 quarters, 16 quarters, etc., growing at an exponential rate of 2. According to this model, with one year of data and the finest precision at a quarter, we will need $\log2(365*24*4)+1 =$ around 16 Time-Frames. It is very space-efficient.

In each time frame, two numbers will be stored with respect to the time period specified. They are the number of successful transactions and the number of unsuccessful transactions in that specified time period.

In addition, in a Time-Frame structure, intermediate buffer frames need to be maintained. These intermediate frames will replace or be merged with other Time-Frames when they are full. Figure 2 shows the Time-Frame structure with intermediate buffer frames which exist at each level except for level 0. Moreover,

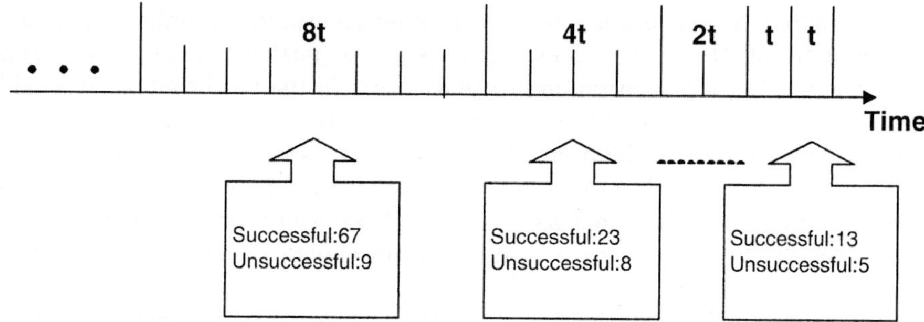

Fig. 1. Time frame with logarithmic partition

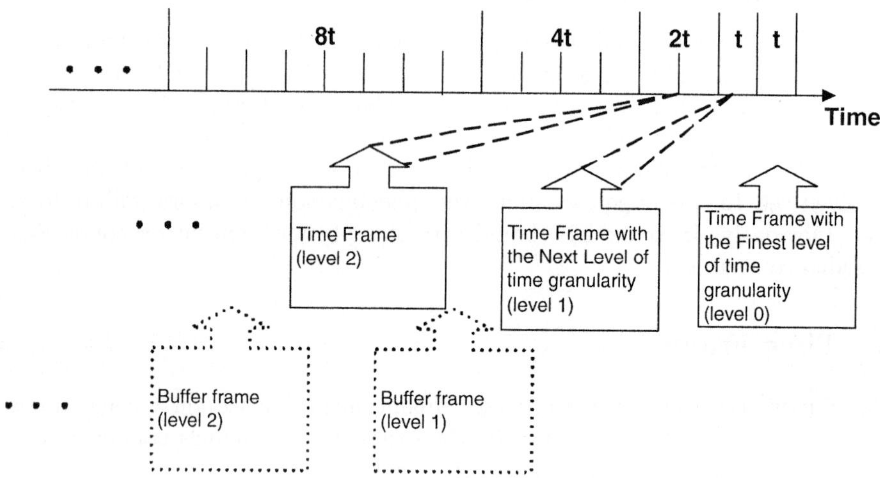

Fig. 2. Time-Frame structure with buffer Time-Frame

as only one Time-Frame buffer is needed at any granularity level, the size of the Time-Frame structure can grow no larger than $2\lceil \log_2(N) \rceil + 2$ where N is the number of quarter-based batches seen for the Time-Frame structure.

3.1 Time-Frame Updating

First of all, the stream of transactions is broken up into fixed sized batches (quarter-based). Besides, one Time-Frame structure will be used to maintain the transaction history of one resource domain. Consider a client domain A continues to interact with a resource domain R. In domain A, a Time-Frame structure will then be maintained for resource domain R.

The first quarter transaction history between R and A will be kept in the level-0 time frame. After that, when the next quarter transaction history comes, the content of the level-0 time frame will be shifted to the level-1 time frame and the recent quarter transaction history will be kept in the level-0 time frame.

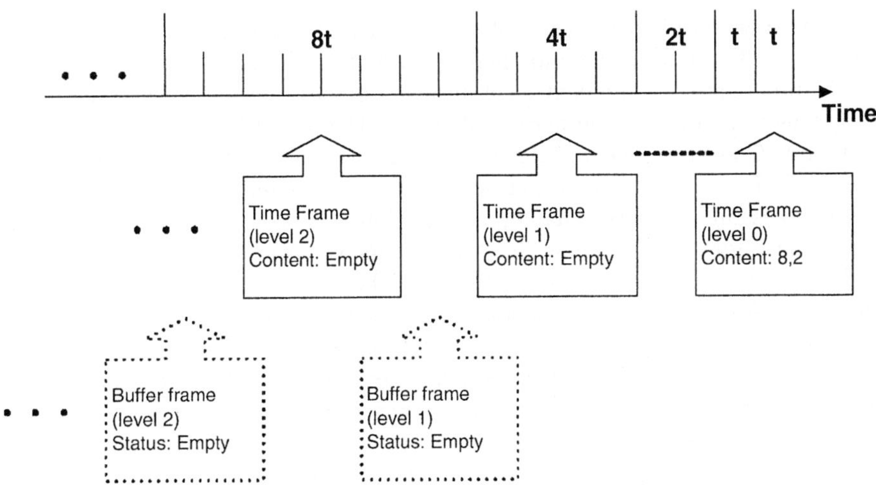

Fig. 3. Time-Frame structure after the first quarter transaction

Later on, when another next quarter transaction history comes, again, the content of the level-0 time frame will always be shifted to the level-1 time frame. However, the level-1 time frame is already occupied and it needs to be shifted upwards too. For the Time-Frame whose level is greater than zero, if it wants to be shifted to the next level, it should always check whether the buffer Time-Frame at its level is being occupied or not. There will be two different cases. If the buffer time frame at that level is not occupied, the content of that Time-Frame should be placed in the buffer Time-Frame. Instead, if the buffer time

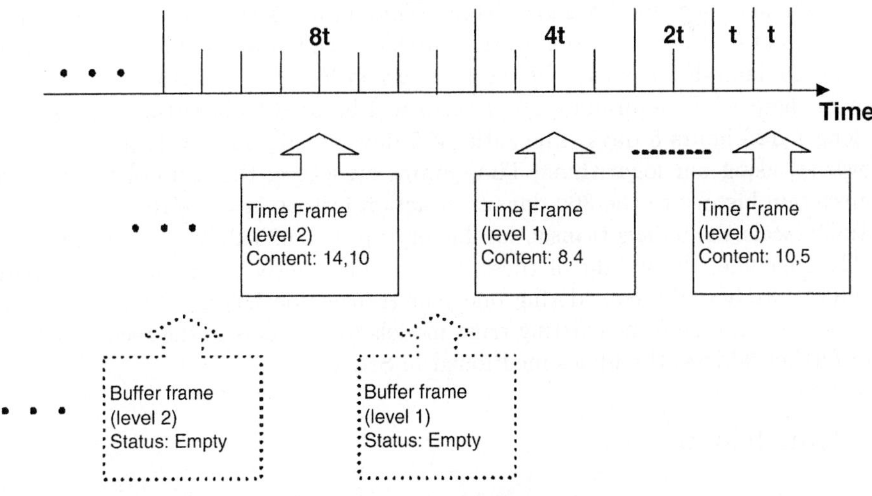

Fig. 4. Final Time-Frame structure

frame at that level is occupied, the content of that Time-Frame will be merged with the buffer time frame and then be shifted to the next level. This process will be propagated to the next level until the highest level Time-Frame.

Let us take an example here to illustrate the updating of the Time-Frame structure. Consider a client domain A continues to interact with a resource domain R. In the first quarter period, 10 transactions have been performed and 8 are successful. The first quarter information will be kept in the level-0 time frame and Figure 3 shows how the Time-Frame structure looks like.

In the next quarter, 14 transactions have been performed and 6 of them are successful. After that, 12 transactions have been performed and 8 of them are successful. The interaction continues and 15 transactions have been performed and 10 of them are successful in next quarter. Figure 4 shows the final Time-Frame structure for the previous 1-hour transactions.

The Time-Frame structure will be updated continuously according to the above discussion when the next quarter information arrives.

4 Analysis with Time-Frame

With the Time-Frame structure, the transaction history of a domain will now be stored in different Time-Frame partitions. Each Time-Frame represents a period of time. However, the length of the period is not equal for all the Time-Frames. Instead, they are in logarithmic scale. Logarithmic scale Time-Frame helps to give more weight to the recent history than the ancient history. However, the terms ancient and recent are not absolute, they are somehow related to the computing environment, such as the transaction rate is high or not. In general, as a Grid task can last for a few days to be completed and recorded, therefore, we assume that the recent 5-day's activities are the most important for a resource domain to be evaluated.

To evaluate how good our logarithmic Time-Frame structure is in giving bias to the recent 5-days transaction history, we have the following analysis. Consider we use 16 Time-Frames to hold the transaction history for 8216 hours 1 year. Out of these 16 Time-Frames, 10 of them will be used to hold the time period of length 128 hours 5 days. The ratio of 5 days to 365 days $= 5/365 = 0.014$. However, using our logarithmic Time-Frame structure, the ratio of the 5-days transaction history to the 365-days transaction history is $= 10/16 = 0.625$. We actually scale the 5-days transaction history up by $0.625/0.014 = 44.6$ times.

To conclude, the weight of these recent 5-days activities is more than half when we are actually considering one-year transaction history. This feature of Time-Frame can help the existing trust models to give bias to the recent history and further address the issues mentioned in Section 2.

5 Conclusion

Nowadays, many resources are available through the Internet. To select the best out of these resources, it is not a simple issue but relies on trust and reputation.

However, the existing trust models do not address the temporal issues of trust as mentioned in Section 2. Therefore, Time-Frame, a novel data structure, is introduced in this paper. Time-Frame can be integrated into the existing trust models so as to enhance the capability and accuracy.

References

1. Ian Foster, The Grid: A New Infrastructure for 21st Century Science, Physics Today, Febru-ary 2002.
2. Ian Foster, Carl Kesselman, and Steve Tuecke, The Anatomy of the Grid, Enabling Scalable Virtual Organizations, International Journal of Supercomputer Applications, 2001.
3. Alfarez Abdul-Rahman, Stephen Hailes Supporting Trust in Virtual Communities. In Proceedings Hawaii International Conference on System Sciences 33, Maui, Hawaii, 4-7 January 2000.
4. Farag Azzedin and Muthucumaru Maheswaran, "Evolving and Managing Trust in Grid Computing Systems," Proceedings of the 2002 IEEE Canadian Conference on Electrical Computer Engineering.
5. Farag Azzedin and Muthucumaru Maheswaran, Integrating Trust into Grid Resource Man-agement Systems, Proceedings of the International Conference on Parallel Processing (ICPP'02).
6. "ebay," Web Page. [Online]. Available: http://www.ebay.com.

Application of Control Engineering Methods to Congestion Control in Differentiated Service Networks

F. Habibipou, M. Khajepour, and M. Galily

Iran Telecom research Center, Ministry of ICT, Tehran, Iran
m.galily@gmail.com

Abstract. In this paper, an application of one of the interesting methods in control engineering, i.e. sliding mode control, to congestion control and avoidance in differentiated services network is presented. To this end, the traffic is divided into three classes: Premium, Ordinary and Best Effort traffic. The Premium and Ordinary traffic are controlled using the proposed robust sliding mode control strategy, but the Best Effort traffic is uncontrolled. Simulation results of the proposed control action demonstrate the effectiveness of the controller in providing robust queue management system.

1 Introduction

Diff-Serv architecture will try to provide QoS by using differentiated services aware congestion control algorithms. Recently several attempts have been made to develop congestion controllers [1-3], mostly using linear control theory. Despite these efforts, the design of congestion controllers whose performance can be analytically established and demonstrated in practice is still a challenging unresolved problem. It should also be mentioned that, even for the present Internet architecture, network congestion control remains a critical and high priority issue, and is unlikely to disappear in the near future. Furthermore, if we consider the current utilization trends, congestion in the Internet maybe come unmanageable unless effective, robust, and efficient methods for congestion control are developed.

Sliding mode control systems (SMCS) have started in Russia by many researches, like Barbashin [4] and Utkin [5]. Due to its excellent invariance and robustness properties, Sliding mode control has been developed into a general design method and extended to a wide spectrum of system types including multivariable, large-scale, infinite-dimensional and stochastic systems. The ideas have successfully been applied to many control problems [6,7]. In this paper, we will make use of SMC to congestion control in differentiated services networks. Using the proposed robust control action, congestion control in Premium and Ordinary classes is performed.

2 Dynamic Network Model

In this section, a state space equation for M/M/1 queue is presented. The model has been extended to consider traffic delays and includes modeling uncertainties then three classes of traffic services are introduced in a Diff-Serv network.

H. Zhuge and G.C. Fox (Eds.): GCC 2005, LNCS 3795, pp. 196–201, 2005.

2.1 Fluid Flow Model

A diagram of a sample queue is depicted in Fig.1. Let $x(t)$ be a state variable denoting the ensemble average number in the system in an arbitrary queuing model at time t. Furthermore, let $f_{in}(t)$ and $f_{out}(t)$ be ensemble averages of the flow entering and exiting the system, respectively.
$\dot{x}(t) = dx(t)/dt$ can be written as:

$$\dot{x}(t) = f_{in}(t) - f_{out}(t) \tag{1}$$

Equation of this kind of model has been used in the literature, and is commonly referred to as fluid flow equation [22-24]. To use this equation in a queuing system, C and λ have been defined as the queue server capacity and average arrival rate respectively. Assuming that the queue capacity is unlimited, $f_{in}(t)$ is just the arrival rate λ. The flow out of the system, $f_{out}(t)$, can be related to the ensemble average utilization of the queue, $\rho(t)$, by $f_{out}(t)=\rho(t)C$. It is assumed that the utilization of the link, ρ, can be approximated by the function $G(x(t))$, which represents the ensemble average utilization of the link at time t as a function of the state variable. Hence, queue model can be represented by the following nonlinear differential equation [3]:

$$\dot{x}(t) = -CG(x(t)) + \lambda \tag{2}$$

Utilization function, $G(x(t))$, depends on the queuing system under study.If statistical data is available, this function can be empirically formulated. This, however, is not generally the case and $G(x(t))$ is normally determined by matching the results of steady state queuing theory with (2). M/M/1 has been adopted in many communication network traffics. In this model input and service rates both have Poisson distribution function. For M/M/1 the state space equation would be [3]:

$$\dot{x}(t) = -C\frac{x(t)}{1 + x(t)} + \lambda \tag{4}$$

The validity of this model has been verified by a number of researchers [3].

2.2 System Structure and Controller Mechanism

Consider a router of K input and L output ports handling three differentiated traffic classes mentioned above. At each out port a controller has been presented to handle different classes of traffic flows entering to that port. An instance of the controller is illustrated in Fig. 2. The incoming traffic to the input node includes different classes of traffic. The input node then separates each class according to their class identifier tags and forwards the packets to the proper queue. The output port could transmit packets at maximum rate of C_{server} to destination where

$$C_{server} < C_p + C_r + C_b \tag{6}$$

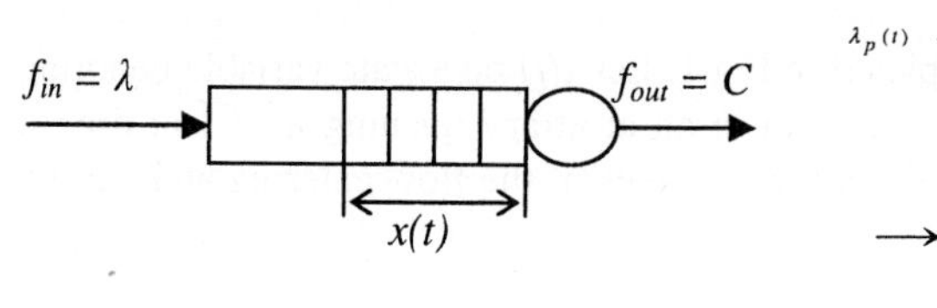

Fig. 1. Diagram of sample queue

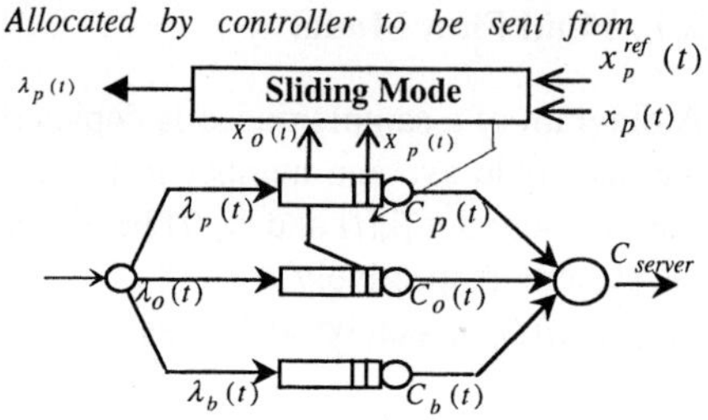

Fig. 2. Control strategy at each switch output port

2.3 Premium Control Strategy

Premium traffic flows needs strict guarantees of delivery. Delay, jitter and packet drops should be kept as small as possible. The queue dynamic model can be as:

$$\dot{x}_p(t) = -C_p(t)\frac{x_p(t)}{1 + x_p(t)} + \lambda_p(t) \tag{6}$$

The control goal here is to determine $C_p(t)$ at any time and for any arrival rate $\lambda_p(t)$ in which the queue length, $x_p(t)$ is kept close to a reference value, $x_p^{ref}(t)$, specified by the operator or designer. So in (6), $x_p(t)$ would be the state to be tracked, $C_p(t)$ is the control signal determined by the congestion controller and $\lambda_p(t)$ is the disturbance.

The goal here is to allocate minimum possible capacity for the premium traffic to save extra capacity for other classes of traffic as well as providing a good QoS for premium flows. Note that we are confined to control signals as

$$0 < C_p(t) < C_{server} \tag{7}$$

In other words the assigned premium capacity must always be less than the maximum server capacity C_{server}. This constraint would make the controller design more difficult.

2.4 Ordinary Control Strategy

In the case of ordinary traffic flows, there is no limitation on delay and we assume that the sources sending ordinary packets over the network are capable to adjust their rates to the value specified by the bottleneck controller. The queue dynamic model is as follows

$$\dot{x}_o(t) = -\frac{x_o(t)}{1 + x_o(t)}C_o(t) + \lambda_o(t - \tau) \tag{8}$$

Where, τ denotes the round-trip delay from bottleneck router to ordinary sources and back to the router. The control goal here is to determine $\lambda_o(t)$ at any time and for any allocated capacity $C_o(t)$ so that $x_o(t)$ be close to a reference value $x_o^{ref}(t)$ given by the operator or designer. There are two important points that must be considered, first, $C_o(t)$ is the remaining capacity, $C_o(t)=C_{server}-C_p(t)$ and would be considered as disturbance which could be measured from the premium queue. In our controller scheme we would try to decouple the affect of $C_o(t)$ on the state variable $x_o(t)$, and the another point is that λ_o is limited to a maximum value λ_{max} and no negative λ_o is allowed i.e.

$$0 <= \lambda_o(t) <= \lambda_{max} <= C_{max}.$$

2.5 Best-Effort Traffic

As mentioned in the previous section, best effort traffic has the lowest priority and therefore could only use the left capacity not used by Premium and Ordinary traffic flows. So, this class of service is no-controlled.

3 Sliding Mode Congestion Controller Design

In this section, the controller for the congestion control objective is described above. We have made the following assumptions for controller design throughout this paper:

$$C_{max} = 300000 \text{ Packets Per Second}$$
$$\lambda_{max} = 150000 \text{ Packets Per Second}$$

In addition at first is assumed there is not any delay in system ($\tau = 0$). In this system two controllers are designed for premium and ordinary systems. For both premium and ordinary classes, the sliding surface has been selected as follows:

$$s = x(t) - x_{ref}(t) \tag{9}$$

In sliding surface the following condition should be satisfied:

$$\dot{s} = 0 \tag{10}$$

So,

$$\dot{x}(t) - \dot{x}_{ref}(t) = 0 \tag{11}$$

From (4) the main part of control law for premium and ordinary system achieved as follows respectively:

$$C_p(t) = \frac{-\lambda_p + \dot{x}_{ref}(t)}{\left(-\frac{x(t)}{1+x(t)}\right)} \tag{12}$$

$$\lambda_o(t) = \frac{x(t)}{1+x(t)} C(t) + \dot{x}_{ref} \tag{13}$$

In addition sliding mode control has a *signum* part. So (12), (13) can be rewritten as follows:

$$C_p(t) = \frac{-\lambda_p + \dot{x}_{ref}(t)}{\left(-\frac{x(t)}{1+x(t)}\right)} + k_1 sign(s(t)) \tag{14}$$

$$\lambda_o(t) = \frac{x(t)}{1+x(t)} C(t) + \dot{x}_{ref} + k_2 sign(s(t)) \tag{15}$$

k_1 and k_2 for both systems are determined using trial and error. To reach a chattering free action, a *tangent hyperbolic* is used instead *signum* function. So, the control input for both systems are as follows:

$$C_p(t) = \frac{-\lambda_p + \dot{x}_{ref}(t)}{\left(-\frac{x(t)}{1+x(t)}\right)} + 100000 \tanh(s(t)) \tag{16}$$

$$\lambda_o(t) = \frac{x(t)}{1+x(t)} C(t) + \dot{x}_{ref} - 100000 \tanh(s(t)) \tag{17}$$

The simulation results are depicted in Figs. 3 and 4 for premium traffic, and in Figs. 5 and 6 for ordinary traffic. As it can be seen the results are satisfactory.

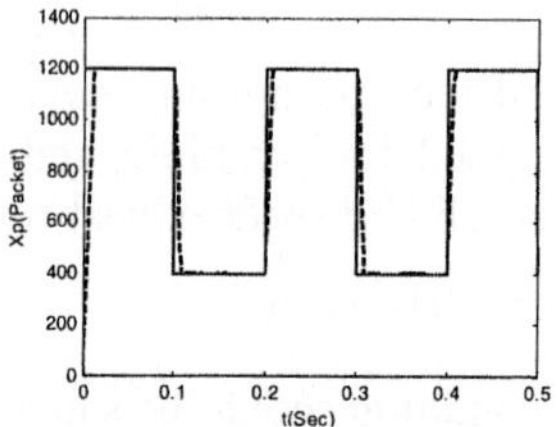

Fig. 3. $x_p^{ref}(t)$ and $x_p(t)$

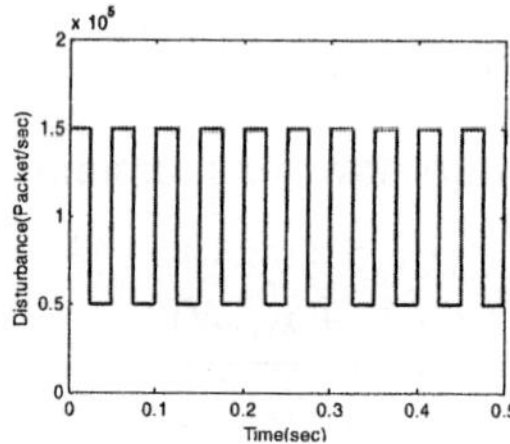

Fig. 4. Input rate of Premium's buffer

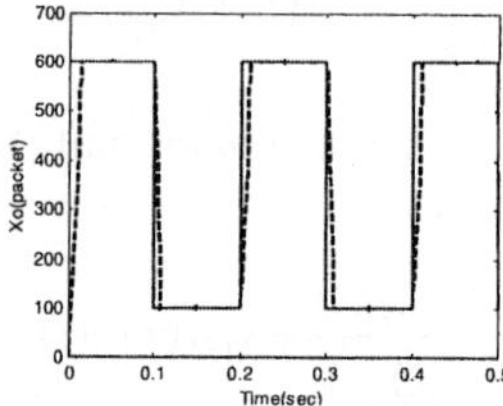

Fig. 5. $x_o^{ref}(t)$ and $x_o(t)$

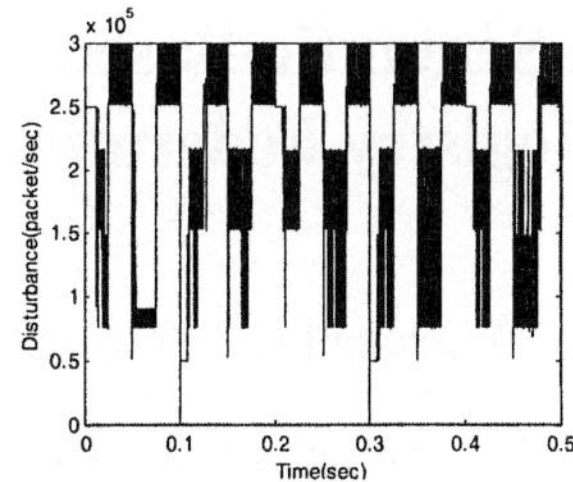

Fig. 6. Input rate of Ordinary's buffer

4 Conclusion

In this paper, sliding mode Controller was applied to congestion control in Differentiated-Services networks. A differentiated-services network framework was assumed and the control strategy was formulated for three types of services: Premium Service, Ordinary Service, and Best Effort Service. The proposed sliding mode control action demonstrated robust performance against round trip time delay and uncertainty. Some computer simulations showed good and satisfactory performance for the proposed controller.

References

1. Benmohamed L. and Yang Y.T.,: A Control-Theoretic ABR Explicit Rate Algorithm for ATM Switches with Per-VC Queuing, *Infocom 98*, 1998.
2. Kolarov and Ramamurthy G.,: A control theoretic approach to the design of an explicit rate controller for ABR service, *IEEE/ACM Transactions on Networking*, October 1999.
3. Pitsillides A.and Ioannou P.,: Non-linear Controllers for Congestion Control in Differentiated Services Networks, *TR-99-1, Dept. Computer Science, University of Cyprus*, 2001
4. Barbashin E. A. and Geraschenko E.I.,: On speeding up sliding modes in automatic control systems. *Differentzialniye Uravneniya, Vol. 1*, 25-32, 1965.
5. Utkin, V. I.,: Sliding modes in control optimization. New York, *Springer- Verlag,* 1992.
6. Stepanenko, Y. and Su, C.,: Variable structure control of robot manipulator with nonlinear sliding manifolds. *INT. J. Control,* 58(2), 285-300, 1993.
7. Xu, J.-X. and Cao, W.-J.,: Synthesized sliding mode control of a single-like flexible robot. *Int. J. control* 73(3), 197-209, 2000.

Research on Semantic-Based Web Services Registry Federation*

Bing Li[1], Fei He[2], Wudong Liu[1], KeQing He[1], and Jin Liu[1]

[1] The State Key Lab. of Software Engineering, Wuhan University, Wuhan 430072, China
[2] Major in Computer Science, Graduate School of Science and Engineering, Waseda University, Tokyo, 169-8555, Japan
libing@sklse.org

Abstract. Meta modeling is an effective approach to implement interoperability among distributed and heterogeneous information sources on Web. MMFI (Framework for Metamodel Interoperability) is a set of meta objects and Metamodel constructs to be used in the development a metamodel in actual implementation of information registry and repository. As a scalable solution to requirements of semantic interoperation between heterogeneous and autonomous Web services registries, we provide an ontological metamodeling approach to combine MMFI with technologies from the federated information management to create an architecture for Web services registry federation. A software component service registry prototype system implemented based on these methods is introduced.

Keywords: Web service registry, ontological metamodeling, federated information management.

1 Introduction

With the development of computer networks, sharing and utilization of accumulated information resources are difficult to be retrieved, shared and utilized on account of dynamic, heterogeneous and autonomous characteristics of these distributed resources[1]. That makes it necessary to constructs federated virtual organizations across organizations and individuals via open and interoperable network service. Web Service (WS) has brought enormous revolution to the existent Web application pattern. As a result, the Websites will no longer stay in a passive position [2]. With the help of standardized data formats and protocols such as SOAP, UDDI, WSDL and etc., WS provides a middleware platform to integrate existent applications and business procedure into the compound application in a kind of loosely collaboration. However, the semantic interoperability of WS registration limits more automatic and intelligent interoperation [3].

* This work was supported by the National Natural Science Foundation of China under Grant 60373086, the Provincial Natural Science Foundation of Hubei under Grant 2005ABA123, 2005ABA240 and Open Foundation of SKLSE under Grant No. 2003-03.

H. Zhuge and G.C. Fox (Eds.): GCC 2005, LNCS 3795, pp. 202 – 207, 2005.

Presently, there are several common or user defined registration standards for the WS registration such as UDDI and ebXML [4, 5, 6]. Comprehensive service publishing and discovery require a more compatible and scalable infrastructure to integrate information from multiple distributed, heterogeneous and autonomous registration repositories and keep the information integrity and consistency in different registration repositories at the same time. Therefore, we propose the WS registration federation built on the basis of semantic interoperability so that users to different registration systems can publish and discover each other's registration information transparently.

The research on federated information management has already been around for about 20 years. The federated information system was defined as the next generation information integration infrastructure to cover the need for online real time information integration of the trans-enterprise virtual organization [7, 8]. A kind of scalable federated data management architecture based on CORBA was proposed in [9]. However, CORBA integration does not go up to the height of semantic, and not fit for the need of loosely coupled service collaboration in the Web environment. In addition, various registered objects are not limited to structured database object. The traditional federated data model integration should be greatly challenged.

Standardization is base of the network application. From 2003, ISO SC32 has organized to realize the information registering in semantic Web repository's MMFI (Framework for Metamodel Interoperability) standardization project [10]. By our research, we found that the ontological metamodeling method works well with the WS platform and becomes the core mechanism of the semantic Web Service. A scalable WS registration federation that combines ontological metamodeling method with federated information management technique can extend the WS platform.

2 Architecture of the Web Service Federation

2.1 MMFI

A Web based environment is faced with transorganizational complex systems that need to share and interchange various complex business objects. Only if we extract and analyze the metamodel, meta data and meta service, are we able to conceal the semantic and structural heterogeneity effectively, accomplish automatic integration transparently.

MMFI provides a framework for meta data registration by integrating meta data registration standards at the meta model level. MMFI is composed of 3 parts now, namely, the core model of MMFI, MMFI for ontology registration and MMFI for mapping [11]. Figure 1 illustrates the architecture of MMFI. The Core metamodel directs other parts. There is correlation between the ontology registration and the metamodel for mapping.

MMFI Core Model is the core part of MMFI. It provides common description mechanism for entire metamodel framework [12]. MMFI Core Model is constructed by integrating MOF (Meta-Object Facility) and the international standard for meta data registrationISO11179 (MDR).

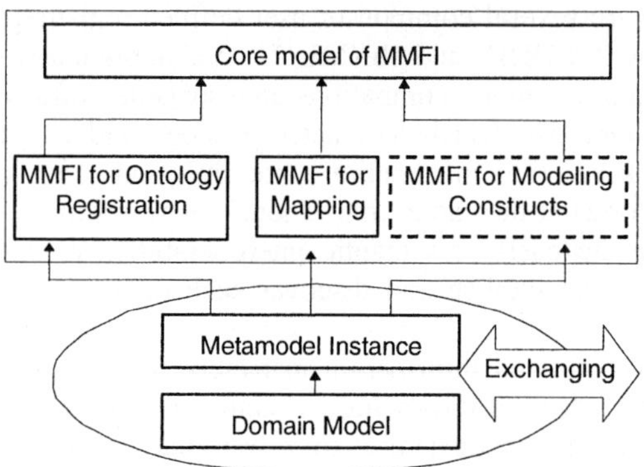

Fig. 1. Architecture of MMFI(citing from [12])

MMFI for Ontology registration inherits from the Core Model, and mainly used for providing a common metamodel framework for ontology registration so that ontology (especially classifying pattern) definition from every metamodel could be unified [10]. As the ontology is predominant in knowledge representation, it is a model rich in semantic. At the same time, ontology is also the basis for the semantic Web service, and the OWL (Web Ontology Language) under developing is one of the important standards.

2.2 Web Service Registration Federation Architecture Based on MMFI

Service registration in Web environment has its own characteristics in distribution, heterogeneity, autonomy and dynamics. Among them, the distribution problem is mainly caused by the huge size of the Web and its loose relation as well as the balancing problem in logic; heterogeneity focuses on the semantic heterogeneity; autonomy is manifested in the design and execution autonomy; dynamics need to solve the scalability and evolution problem of the overall system throughout its lifecycle. To treat all these, we proposed a WS registration federation architecture based on metamodel interoperability framework. This system is divided into 3 layers: the federation management layer, local agent layer and the member system layer (shown in Figure 2).

(1) Federation management layer. Federation management layer is the core of the system. It provides the registered semantic mapping between registered members and the mapping between registered models. Ontology server maintains federation ontology, and federation ontology provides the mappings between different registered ontology to ontological metamodeling. The contents include properties concerning WS registration and relations between registrations; thus, realizing the semantic mapping between different registered members. When the member system changes in the federation, ontology server is responsible for updating the federation ontology. As a result, the semantic interoperability of dynamic service publishing and discovery of the heterogeneous member systems in the Web environment is solved.

Because of the structural complexity of the WS registered objects, a global registration metamodel providing mapping between different registered models is needed. The mapping metamodel provides interoperability assurance at metamodel level for different WSs to compose a complex WS. The mapping mechanism between registered structures can adopt techniques in federation data management.

(2) Local agent layer. Local agent layer carries out the communication mechanism between federation management layer and registered member systems. A local agent not only works as query agent with the identity of system user and accomplishes the query transformation between different information models, but also maintains the registration ontology of registered member ontology and implements the registered ontology's semantic description of WS. In addition, if global transactions are needed in the registered member system, a local agent is also responsible for transaction management in order to ensure the serializability and semantic integrity control of global transaction. Because the local updating of registered member system will affect the integrity of the global information, the local agent has to sense and monitor local operations, and report the updates to the federation management layer in time; it assumes the validity checking, authentication and access control operations and works as the security agent in the information transformation process.

(3) Member system layer. Every member system is an autonomous field, which has its own local users and follows its usual working process. When a user need to deal with WS publishing or discovery in the registration federation, he will become a global user and his registration request will be accepted and processed by local global agents.

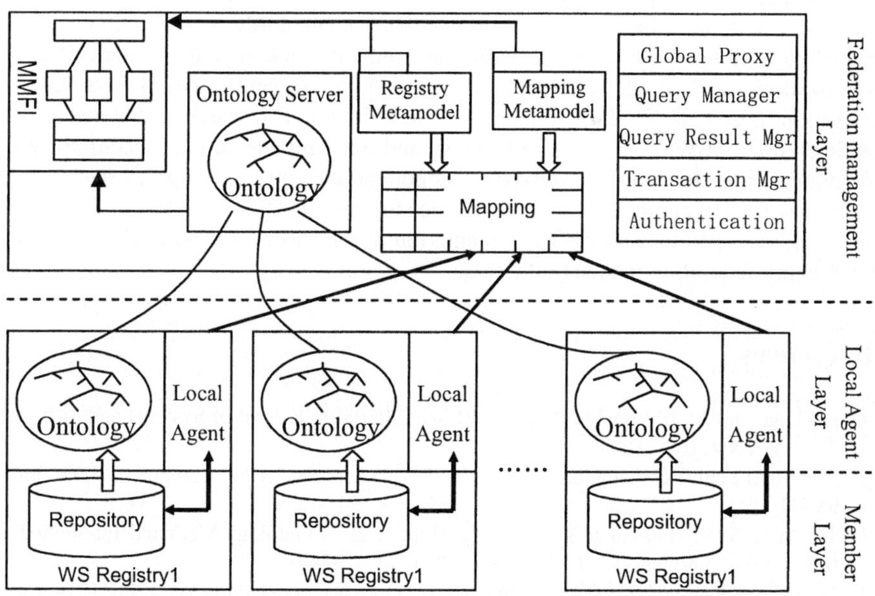

Fig. 2. Web Services Registry Federation based on MMFI

3 Software Component Web Service Registry Federation

To verify the architecture and runtime mechanism, we first develop a software component repository platform (WHCRP) [13] as the base of further software component service registry federation. The system is based on J2EE architecture, and the messages delivered between client and server adopts SOAP.

The system is made up of client side and server side. Client side is responsible for providing client with flexible, convenient registering, searching interface. SOAP subsystem is responsible for packaging messages from client into SOAP format and transferring them to server side through Internet. The response from the server is also interpreted by the SOAP subsystem. Server side is made up of SOAP dispatcher, ontology server, query manager, metadata register manager, repository manager, etc. Several kinds of interfaces are provided by the repository including database, file system, WS. Repository is made up of database and files system, with the database responsible for persisting metadata and file system for files relating to software component.

We construct a common software component ontology based on the analysis and abstraction. The software component ontology is a consistent knowledge representation including software component's attribute, object, relationship, constrains, etc. For now, WHCRP implements the interoperability with ebXML registry and repository.

4 Summary

This paper deals with the cross point research between data management and software engineering, synthesizing newest research result from both fields. It proposes combining federated data management and theory of ontological metamodeling to settle the problem results in distribution, semantic heterogeneity, and dynamic organization of WSs. It describe a framework of semantics-based WS registry federation, based on the ISO standardized MMFI. Some research and development has been done in Web service's registering and management in the field of software component. We construct the software component attributes ontology to registry and classify software component, verifying the support from MMFI for WS registry. Future works will focus on the implementation of our theory and method to construct WS registry federation in different fields.

References

1. H.Zhuge and J.Liu, Flexible Retrieval of Web Services, Journal of Systems and Software, 70 (1-2) 2004, 107-116.
2. Christoph Schlueter Langdon. The State of Web Services. IEEE Computer, 2003, 36(7): 93~94
3. Tse-Ming Tsai, Han-Kuan Yu, Hsin-Te Shih, et al. , Ontology-Mediated Integration of Intranet Web Services. IEEE Computer, 2003,36(7): 63~71
4. OASIS. UDDI Version 3.0.1vv[EB/OL], http://uddi.org/pubs/uddi-v3.0.1-20031014.htm
5. OASIS. ebXML Registry Services Specification v2.5 [EB/OL]. http://www.oasis-open.org/committees/regrep/ documents/2.5/ specs/ebrs-2.5.pdf

6. OASIS. ebXML Registry Information Model v2.5[EB/OL]. http://www.oasis-open.org/committees/ regrep/documents/2.5/specs/ebrim-2.5.pdf
7. Philip Bernstein, Michael L. Brodie, Stefano Ceri, et al. The Asilomar Report on Database Research. SIGMOD Record, 1998, 27(4): 74~80
8. S.Abiteboul, R. Agrawal, Phil Bernstein, et al. The 2003 Lowell DatabaseResearch Self-Assessment Meeting[EB/OL], http://research.microsoft.com/~gray/lowell
9. Bing Li, Zhengding Lu, Weijun Xiao, Ruixuan Li, et al. An Architecture for Multidatabase Systems Based on CORBA and XML. In: Tjoa A. Min, Wagner Roland eds, Proc of 12th International Workshop on Database and Expert Systems Applications (DEXA 2001): 32~37, Oakland: IEEE Computer Society press, 2001.
10. Keqing He. Information Technology – Framework for Metamodel Interoperability-- Part-3: Metamodel Framework for Ontology Registry. ISO/IEC JTC1, Tech Rep: ISO/IEC 19763-3, 2004
11. Horiuchi Hajime. Information Technology--Framework for Metamodel Interoperability-Reference Model. ISO/IEC JTC1, Tech Rep: ISO/IEC 19763-1, 2003
12. Obayash Masaharu. Information Technology--Framework for Metamodel Interoperability-Core Model. ISO/IEC JTC1, Tech Rep: ISO/IEC 19763-2, 2003
13. Bing Li, Keqing He, Jin Liu et al. Building Interoperable Software Components Repository based on MMF. In: Proc of 3rd International Workshops on Grid and Cooperative Computing (GCC 2004):, 2004. 67~74

A Proxy-Based Dynamic Inheritance of Soft-Device

Jia Bi[1,2,3], Yanyan Li[1,2], Yunpeng Xing[1,2], Xiang Li[1,2], and Xue Chen[1,2]

[1] Institute of Computing Technology, Chinese Academy of Sciences, China
{bj, liyy, ypxing}@kg.ict.ac.cn
[2] Graduate School of Chinese Academy of Sciences
[3] Oracle, China Development Center, China

Abstract. Soft-device is a promising infrastructure of next-generation distributed system. Soft-devices are configurable and adaptive software virtual mechanism, providing services to each other and to other virtual roles according to the content of the resources and related configuration information. In order to aggregate and reuse the existing soft-devices for more complex applications, this paper proposes a dynamic inheritance mechanism of soft-devices. By taking into account the novel characteristics of soft-devices, this approach provides flexible and effective inheritance modes, which overcomes the limitation of traditional local inheritance. It will play an important role in future interconnection environment.

1 Introduction

Inheritance mechanism has been investigated in software engineering and artificial intelligence [1, 2, 3, 4, 5]. The Knowledge Grid is an intelligent sustainable internet application environment that enables people or virtual roles to effectively capture, publish, share, and manage explicit knowledge resources [6, 8, 9].

Soft-devices are configurable and adaptive software virtual mechanism, representing distributed network software and devices. It takes the advantages of the active and intelligent features of the intelligent agents, the semantic-based features of the semantic web, the advantages of the Knowledge Grid, and the configurable feature of general-purpose computers [7, 10, 12, 13]. This paper implements soft-device inheritance.

Based on the notion and mechanism introduced in [7, 11], a soft-device comprises six components, which can be defined as a six tuple:

$$SD = < C, K, D, W, E, I >$$

Where *C*, *K*, *D*, *W*, *E*, *I* respectively denotes the container, knowledge base, detector, built-in workflows, explainer, and interface.

2 Inheritance Mechanism of Soft-Device

2.1 Dynamic Single Inheritance

Let Loc1= Loc3 Loc1<>Loc2 and ΔSD is unchangeable. The definition of the dynamic inheritance becomes:

$$SD1(t, Loc1) = SD2(t, Loc2) \oplus \Delta SD(Loc1)$$

H. Zhuge and G.C. Fox (Eds.): GCC 2005, LNCS 3795, pp. 208–213, 2005.

This type of inheritance is named as dynamic single inheritance. Because each child soft-device inherit only one parent soft-device, there are only one proxy resource in the soft-device, namely Np2=1. Because ΔSD is local increment, there are no proxy resource in it, namely Np3=0. The corresponding operations of components are defined as followings:

$$SD1(t, Loc1).C = SD2(t, Loc2).C \oplus \Delta SD(Loc1).C$$
$$=< \{\mathrm{Re}c2_1(t, Loc2), \cdots, \mathrm{Re}c2_{Nr2}(t, Loc2), \Delta \mathrm{Re}c_1(Loc1), \cdots, \Delta \mathrm{Re}c_{Nr3}(Loc1)\}, \{\mathrm{Pr}o2_1(t, Loc2)\} >$$
$$SD1(t, Loc1).K = SD2(t, Loc2).K \oplus \Delta SD(Loc1).K$$
$$= \{Rul2_1(t, Loc2), \cdots, Rul2_{Nr2}(t, Loc2), \Delta Rul_1(Loc1), \cdots, \Delta Rul_{Nr3}(Loc1)\}$$
$$SD1(t, Loc1).D = SD2(t, Loc2).D \oplus \Delta SD(Loc1).D = SD2(t, Loc2).D \mid \Delta SD(Loc1).D = NewD$$
$$SD1(t, Loc1).E = SD2(t, Loc2).E \oplus \Delta SD(Loc1).E = SD2(t, Loc2).E \mid \Delta SD(Loc1).E = NewE$$
$$SD1(t, Loc1).W = SD2(t, Loc2).W \oplus \Delta SD(Loc1).W$$
$$= \{wf2_1(t, Loc2), \cdots, wf2_{Nw2}(t, Loc2), \Delta wf_1(Loc1), \cdots, \Delta wf_{Nw3}(Loc1)\}$$
$$SD1(t, Loc1).I = SD2(t, Loc2).I \oplus \Delta SD(Loc1).I$$
$$= \{Ser2_1(t, Loc2), \cdots, Ser2_{Ns2}(t, Loc2), \Delta Ser_1(Loc1), \cdots, \Delta Ser_{Ns3}(Loc1)\}$$

Because of the dynamic and local facets, the dynamic single inheritance has not the transfer characteristic compared with traditional inheritance mode.

The operation of single inheritance of soft-devices results in abstraction hierarchies that take the form of tree or more generally directed acyclic graph (DAG). Because of remote inheritance, a soft-device may inherit his child soft-device, which generates circular inheritance. Thus, in order to void circular inheritance, a soft-device can not inherit his child.

We define function IsOne to mean whether two soft-devices is the same one. If the result is true, the two soft-devices is exactly the same one, or else they are two soft-devices. It is easy to judge, because soft-devices are registered on a site, and they have the unique id.

$$IsOne(SD1, SD2) = \begin{cases} ture \\ false \end{cases}$$

Consider that SD1 will inherit SD2. The following algorithm judge whether there are circular inheritance.

```
Algorithm
    If (IsOne(SD1,SD2)= true)
    then return there exists circular inheritance
    else
    {       Put child soft-devices of SD1 in a Queue.
            while (Queue is not empty)
            {       Pop a soft-device SD from Queue,
                    if (IsOne(SD,SD1)=true )
                            then return there exist circular inheritance,
                            else Put child soft-devices of SD1 in a Queue.
            }
            Return There are not circular inheritance.
    }
```

2.2 Dynamic Multiple Inheritance

Let Loc1<>Loc2, Loc2<>Loc3, Loc1<>Loc3, the inheritance is dynamic multiple inheritance. We can change the definition as follows:

$$SD1(t, Loc1) = SD2(t, Loc2) \oplus SD3(t, Loc3)$$

We can consider SD2 is the parent soft-device and the SD3 is the incremental part, or SD3 is the parent soft-device and SD2 is the incremental part. The operation is the same.

We can easily expand the definition to multiple inheritances.

$$SD5(t, Loc5) = SD1(t, Loc1) \oplus SD4(t, Loc4)$$

$$SD5(t, Loc5) = (SD2(t, Loc2) \oplus SD3(t, Loc3)) \oplus SD4(t, Loc4)$$

Because the $\oplus$ operation has the law of exchange and combine, the equation can be written as follows:

$$SD5(t, Loc5) = SD2(t, Loc2) \oplus SD3(t, Loc3) \oplus SD4(t, Loc4)$$

2.3 Dynamic Characteristic of Inheritance

The parent soft-device change dynamically, and the child soft-device can change correspondingly. This section discusses the machine of realization.

In the moment *t*, the soft-device satisfies the following equation:

$$cSD(t, Loc1) = pSD(t, Loc2) \oplus \Delta SD(Loc1)$$

In the next moment t+1, $pSD(t, loc2) \rightarrow pSD(t+1, loc2)$, namely $pSD(t, loc2) =< pC(t,\ loc2),\ pK(t,\ loc2),\ pD(t,\ loc2),\ pE(t,\ loc2),\ pW(t,\ loc2),\ pI(t,\ loc2) > \rightarrow$ pSD(t+1, loc2)=<pC(t+1, loc2), pK(t+1, loc2), pD (t+1,loc2), pE (t+1,loc2), pW (t+1,loc2), pSD(t+1, loc2)=<pC(t+1, loc2), pK(t+1, loc2), pD (t+1,loc2), pE (t+1,loc2), pW (t+1,loc2), pI(t+1,loc2)> $cSD(t+1, Loc1) = pSD(t+1, Loc2) \oplus \Delta SD(Loc1)$.

According to the definition of $\oplus$ operation, the cSD should be:

$$cSD(t+1, Loc1).C =< \{p\,\mathrm{Re}\,c_1(t+1, Loc2), \cdots, p\,\mathrm{Re}\,c_{Nr2}(t+1, Loc2), \Delta\,\mathrm{Re}\,c_1(Loc1), \cdots, \Delta\,\mathrm{Re}\,c_{Nr3}(Loc1)\}, \{\mathrm{Pr}\,o2_1(t+1, Loc2)\} >$$

$$cSD(t+1, Loc1).K = \{pRul_1(t+1, Loc2), \cdots, pRul_{Nu2}(t+1, Loc2), \Delta Rul_1(Loc1), \cdots, \Delta Rul_{Nu3}(Loc1)\}$$

$$cSD(t+1, Loc1).D = NewD(t+1, Loc1)$$

$$cSD(t+1, \mathrm{Loc1}).\mathrm{E} = \mathrm{NewE}(t+1, \mathrm{Loc1})$$

$$\mathrm{cSD}(t+1, \mathrm{Loc1}).\mathrm{W} = \{pwf_1(t+1, Loc2), \cdots, pwf_{Nw2}(t+1, Loc2), \Delta wf_1(\mathrm{Loc1}), \cdots, \Delta wf_{Nw3}(Loc1)\}$$

$$\mathrm{cSD}(t+1, \mathrm{Loc1}).\mathrm{I} = \{pSer_1(t+1, Loc2), \cdots, pSer_{Ns2}(t+1, Loc2), \Delta Ser_1(Loc1), \cdots, \Delta Ser_{Ns3}(Loc1)\}$$

Because Pro is local mirror of pSD, in the moment *t*+1

$$\mathrm{Pr}\,o(t+1, loc1) = pSD(t+1, Loc2)$$

The child soft-device is

$$cSD(t+1) =<< \Delta SD.C, \Pr o(t+1) >, \Delta SD.K, NewD, NewE, \Delta SD.W, \Delta SD.I >$$

This means the parent soft-device change, we only need change the proxy, the other components don't change.
$pSD(t+1, loc2)$ has three status:

(1)Stop. $pSD(t+1, loc2)$ stops server for others. pSD informs his child soft-devices and disable them.
(2)Limited Change. The interface component of pSD does not change, namely $pI(t+1, loc2) = pI(t, loc2)$ .Because the interface does not change, the proxy of the pSD doesn't change, and his child soft-devices needn't change.
(3)Change. The interface component of pSD changes, namely $pI(t+1, loc2) \neq pI(t, loc2)$. Its child soft-devices need change correspondingly. There are three possibilities:

- Servers increase. $pSD(t+1, loc2)$ provides more services, namely $pI(t, loc2) \subset pI(t+1, loc2)$. Servers increasing do not affect the child soft-devices, and the child soft-devices get the new proxy of pSD.
- Servers decrease. $pSD(t+1, loc2)$ provides less services, namely $pI(t+1, loc2) \subset pI(t, loc2)$. Servers decreasing may make the child soft-devices work incorrectly, if the child soft-devices use its servers.
- Servers change. $pSD(t+1, loc2)$ changes some services, namely $(\exists Ser_i \in pI(t+1, loc2) \wedge Ser_i \notin pI(t, loc2)) \wedge (\exists Ser_j \in pI(t, loc2) \wedge Ser_j \notin pI(t+1, loc2))$.

3 Implementation

The architecture of inheritance is shown in the Fig.1.

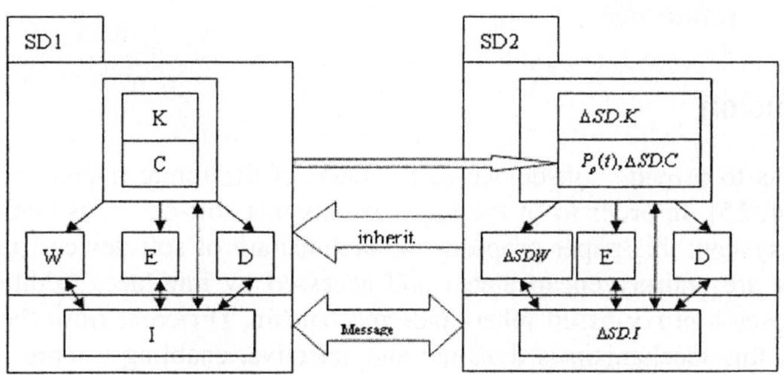

Fig. 1. Architecture of inheritance

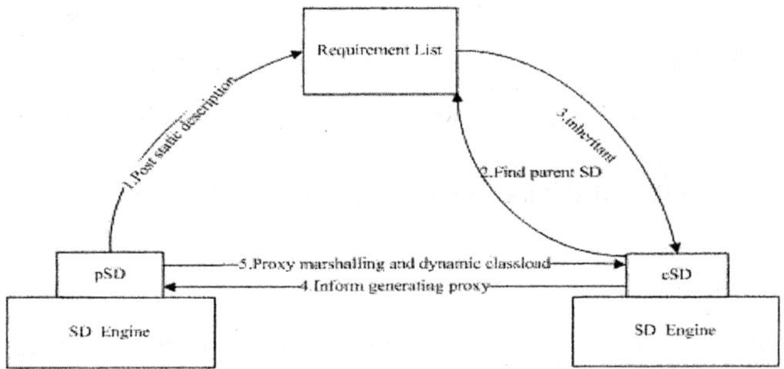

Fig. 2. The process of inheritance

Fig. 2 describes the process of inheritance, where the requirement list plays the same role as in [7].

The process of dynamic inheritance is described in detail as follows:

Step1. The owner post static description of his soft-device on the requirement list.

Step2. The other one search the requirement list, and find the soft-device which he requires.

Step3. According the static description of parent soft-device, add incremental part, and then form the static description of child soft-device.

Step4. The static description of child soft-device is parsed to form dynamic instance of the child soft-device by the generator. At the same time, parent soft-device and child soft-device establish the message pipe. The process of building dynamic instance of the child soft-device includes the following three steps.

Step4.1. The child soft-device informs the parent soft-device generate proxy of its.

Step4.2. The parent soft-device marshals the proxy, and sends it to child soft-device.

Step4.3. The child soft-device unmarshals the proxy, and dynamic loading in the container component of child soft-device.

Step4.4. The each part of constitutes the corresponding component of the child soft-device.

4 Conclusion

Our vision is to provide soft-device as the basis of the future interconnection environment [14, 15]. In order to fit the requirements that soft-device is deployed in the distributed system, this paper proposes the architecture of soft-devices, in which the soft-devices are entirely encapsulated and accessed by interface. Additionally, this paper proposes a proxy-based inheritance mechanism. Different from the traditional inheritance, this mechanism is dynamic and selective, enabling a more flexible and effective inheritance in different scenarios.

References

1. Booch, G. Object Oriented Design with Applications. Redwood City, Calif.: Benjamin/ Cummings Pub. Co., 1991.
2. Horty, J.F., Thomason, R.H., and Touretzky, D.S. A Skeptical Theory of Inheritance in Nonmonotonic Semantic Networks. *Artificial Intelligence*, 42 (1990) 311-348.
3. Taivalsaari, A. On the Notion of Inheritance. *ACM Computing Surveys*, 28, 3 (1996) 438-479.
4. Tamma, V.A.M. and Bench-Capon, T.J.M. Supporting Inheritance Mechanisms in Ontology Representation, *EKAW 2000*, LNAI, 1937 (2000) 140-155.
5. Zhuge, H. Inheritance Rules for Flexible Model Retrieval, *Decision Support Systems*, 22 (4) (1998) 383-394.
6. Zhuge, H. A Knowledge Grid Model and Platform for Global Knowledge Sharing, *Expert Systems with Applications*, 22 (4) (2002)313-320.
7. Zhuge, H. Clustering Soft-Devices in Semantic Grid, *IEEE Computing in Science and Engineering*, 4 (6) (2002) 60-62.
8. Zhuge, H. China's E-Science Knowledge Grid Environment, *IEEE Intelligent Systems*, 19(1) (2004) 13-17.
9. Zhuge, H. The Knowledge Grid, *World Scientific Publishing Co.*, 2004.
10. Zhuge, H. Resource Space Grid: Model, Method and Platform, *Concurrency and Computation: Practice and Experience*, 16 (14) (2004) 1385 – 1413.
11. Zhuge, H. Soft-Device Inheritance in the Knowledge Grid, *Springer LNCS*, 3505 (2005) 62-78.
12. Zhuge, H. Semantic Grid: Scientific Issues, Infrastructure, and Methodology, *Communications of the ACM*. 48(4) (2005)117-119.
13. Zhuge, H. and Xing, Y. Integrity Theory for Resource Space Model and Its Application, Keynote at WAIM2005, *Springer LNCS* 3739(2005)8-24.
14. Zhuge, H. The Future Interconnection Environment, *IEEE Computer*, 38(4) (2005) 27-33.
15. Zhuge, H. Exploring an Epidemic in an E-Science Environment, *Communications of the ACM*, 48(9) (2005)109-114.

Temporal Logical-Based Web Services Architecture Description

Yuan Rao

Department of Automation, Tsinghua University, Beijing, 100084, China
UFIDA Software Co. Ltd., Beijing, 100085, China
yuanrao@163.com

Abstract. The formalized definitions about service and service-oriented architecture were proposed on the basis of the temporal logical language XYZ/E. The whole web services architecture and the stepwise refinement process were formally described, where the web service architecture could be divided into four sub-processes to be concretely realized by stepwise refinement programming. In addition, the liveness and the security of system also had a semantic characteristic of composition during the process of service refinement under this architecture, which is described by XYZ/ADL language to provide a formalized foundation in theory for web service reusing and composition.

1 Introduction

With the popularization of web service application [1], especially for the advancement of web service reuse and composition techniques, how to guarantee the verification of service reachability, liveness and correctness in the process of service deployment and state transition have become a bottleneck to influence further development about web service applications. The formalized description, semantic analysis and verification about web services architecture are effective methods [2].

This paper introduces XYZ/ADL, a kind of ADL based on the temporal logical language XYZ/E[3], to describe and analyze the property and process of web services architecture (WSA), which can provide the security and liveness of system architecture by top-down stepwise refinement description method.

2 Basic Conceptions and Definition

Definition 1: (Service) Service is an autonomic software module with independent function, which is composed of one or more agents and encapsulates data packages and processes among different agents [4] with standard interface description by WSDL. The message communication between services can utilize SOAP protocol, which provides syntax and semantic support for heterogeneous distributed computing environment. The syntax about service is presented as follow:

Service ::=ServiceName [ServiceDecPart] = = [Agent] [WherePart]
ServiceDecPart==[IntefaceDecPart][FunctionDecPart][ComputationDecPart]
IntefaceDecPart ::= %PORT [port, ..., port]

H. Zhuge and G.C. Fox (Eds.): GCC 2005, LNCS 3795, pp. 214–219, 2005.

Port ::= PortName [PortDec] == [DataType][PortBehavior]
FunctionDecPart ::= FunctionName [Function_specification]
ComputationDecPart ::= ComputationName [Computation_specification]
Agent :: = AgentName [AgentDec] = = [Package][process]

Where, the package and the process in agent can be considered the refinement of interfaces, functions and computing declaration parts in service.

Definition 2: Service-Oriented Architecture (SOA) is a distributed software system framework that is composed of some Service Role Objects (SRO) and some connection methods. The SRO means the different functional roles in the process of service invocation and communication, which can be connected together by different connection methods based on the standard protocols to form an application style. The SOA can be defined as follow:

SOA::=SOA_InstanceName = = [[SRO[Service]]Connector][WherePart]

3 The Formalized Description for Web Service Architecture

3.1 Formalized Description and Refinement of Web Service Architecture

There are some differences between SOA and Web service architecture [5]. The former one is a conception mode and faces to business application, which leaves out the concreted details of network deployment methods and the specific implementation of communication protocols. The latter one is a concrete software development mode and faces to technique framework, which is an instantiation of SOA. The WSA is illustrated in Fig. 1 and the formally definition is described as follows:

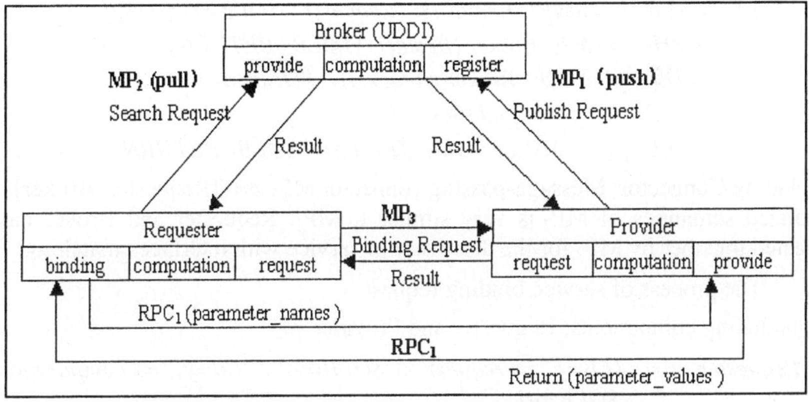

Fig.1. Web Services Architecture Formalization Framework

WSA::=Web-Service-Architecture==[[SRO[Service];] Connector][WherePart]
ServiceRoleObject:: = %ROLE [Requester, Provider, Broker]
Connector:: = %CONN [MP_1, MP_2, MP_3, RPC_1]
WherePart:: = □ (Safety ∧ Liveness ∧ Correctness)

The refinement process about WSA is showed as follow:

(1) The process of service registration and publication

Including components：Provider and Broker

$Provider==[LB=y=>reques \wedge \$OLB=y_1;\ LB=y_1=>computation \wedge \$OLB=e]$
$Broker==\ [LB=v=>provide \wedge \$OLB=z]$
$request == [LB=r=>MP_1.Provider\ (Request(WSDL)\ ) \wedge \$OLB=r_1;$
$LB=r_1=>MP_1.Broker\ (Result) \wedge \$OLB=RETURN]$
$provide == [LB=p=>MP_1Broker\ (Request(WSDL)) \wedge \$OLB=p_1;$
$LB=p_1=>register(WSDL)\ \wedge\ \$OLB=p_2;LB=p_2=>MP_1.Provider\ \ (Result)$
$\wedge \$OLB=RETURN]$

Including connector: Message-passing connector MP_1 == || [Provider; Broker]. The formalized semantics of MP_1 can be expressed as follow:

$$\frac{\{P\}\,_{\Gamma}[Provider\ ;\ Broker]\{Q(u/w)\}}{LB = y \wedge P \Rightarrow \Diamond\ \ (Q \wedge \$O\ LB = v)}$$

Where, P denotes Pre-assertion and Q denotes Post-assertion, $P \rightarrow \Diamond Q$ (u/w) means all the 'w' values can be replaced by 'u' under the Pre-assertion condition. The sender and receiver of message are Provider and Broker, respectively. Both of them can be connected by MP_1 and can execute the message requirement in parallel method.

(2) The process of service discovery

Including components: Requester and Broker

$Requester==[LB=y'=>request \wedge \$OLB=y_1';LB=y_1'=>computation \wedge \$OLB=u]$
$Broker==\ [LB=w=>provide \wedge \$OLB=z]$
$request == [LB=r'=>MP_2.\ Requester\ (Request) \wedge \$OLB=r_1';$
$LB=r_1'=>MP_2.Broker\ (Result) \wedge \$OLB=RETURN]$
$provide == [LB=p'=>MP_2.Broker\ (Request) \wedge \$OLB=p_1';$
$LB=p_1'=>\ computation \wedge \$OLB=p_2';$
$LB=p_2'=>MP_2.\ Provider\ (Result) \wedge \$OLB=RETURN]$

Including Connector: Message-passing connector MP_2 == ||[Requester; Broker]. The formalized semantics of MP_2 is very similar to MP_1. Requester and Broker can be connected together by MP_2 for the discovery of service with interfaces matching.

(3) The process of service binding request

Including components: Requester and Provider

$Requester\ ==\ [LB=y''=>request\ \wedge\ \$OLB=y_1'';\ LB=y_1''=>computation\ \wedge$
$\$OLB=u]$
$Provider==\ [LB=v=>provide \wedge \$OLB=k]$
$request == [LB=r''=>MP_3.\ Requester\ (Request) \wedge \$OLB=r_1'';$
$LB=r_1''=>MP_3.Broker\ (Result) \wedge \$OLB=RETURN]$
$provide\ ==\ [LB=p''=>MP_3.\ Provider\ (Request)\ \wedge\ \$OLB=p_1'';\ LB=p_1''=>$
$computation \wedge \$OLB=p_2'';$
$LB=p_2''=>MP_3.\ Provider\ (Result) \wedge \$OLB=RETURN]$

Including Connector: Message-passing connector MP_3 == || [Requester; Provider]. The service Requester and Provider can be connected together by MP_3 for the binding requirement of service.

(4) The process of remote service call

Including components: Requester and Provider

Requester == [LB=y ∧ Binding (Requester; Provider) =>call ∧ $OLB=$y_1$;*
LB=y_1=>computation ∧ $OLB=u]*

Provider== [LB=v'=>provide ∧ $OLB=k']

call == [LB=r=> Requester.RPC_1 (parameter_names) ∧ $OLB=$r_1$*;*
LB=r_1=> Provider.RPC_1 (parameter_values) ∧ $OLB=RETURN]*

provide == [LB=p=> Provider.RPC_1 (parameter_names) ∧ $OLB=$p_1$;*
LB=p_1=> computation ∧ $OLB=$p_2$*;*
LB=p_2=>Provider.RPC_1(parameter_values) ∧ $OLB=RETURN]*

Including Connector: RPC_1, the formalized semantics of RPC_1 can be expressed as follow:

$$\frac{\{P\}\ RPC_1\ \{Q\}}{LB = y^* \wedge P \Rightarrow \Diamond\ (Q\ \wedge \$O\ LB = w)}$$

Where, P and Q denote the Pre-assertion and Post-assertion in RPC_1 process, respectively. Requester and Provider can be connected by RPC_1 for remote service invoked and data transfer in certain SOAP channel.

3.2 The Properties of Web Services Architecture

Definition 5: Liveness means that the system can reach to the stop state whenever there is a certain input with per-condition P_{in} under a certain state of system architecture. It can be defined as follow:

$$Liveness\ ::= [LB=start\ \wedge P_{in} => \Diamond(LB=stop)]$$

Definition 4: Security means that there must be certain output values as soon as the system reaches to the stop state, when system provided certain input values, i.e. pre-condition P_{in}, at any possible state of architecture. Its formalized definition is expressed as follow:

$$Safety\ ::= [LB=start\ \wedge P_{in} => \Box(LB=stop \rightarrow Q_c)]$$

Property 1: The liveness of web service architecture can be comprised by the liveness of the four processes above-mentioned, which means that the liveness of web service architecture can be realized by stepwise refinement in the process of service execution process mentioned above. Its formalized description is expressed as follow:

$$Liveness_{WSA}==\Box\ (Liveness_{MP1} \wedge Liveness_{MP2} \wedge Liveness_{MP3} \wedge Liveness_{RPC1})$$

The semantics of the liveness about four processes above-mentioned can be unified described as follow:

$$\frac{\{P_{in}\}[\ MP_1 \mid MP_2 \mid MP_3 \mid RPC_1]\{Q_c\}}{LB=start\ \wedge P_{in} => \Diamond(Q_c\ \wedge \$OLB= stop)}$$

Property 2: The security of web service architecture is composed of the security of the four processes above-mentioned, which means that the security of web service architecture can also be realized by stepwise refinement in the process of service execution process above- mentioned. Its formalized description is expressed as follow:

$$Safety_{WSA} == \Box\ (Safety_{MP1} \wedge Safety_{MP2} \wedge Safety_{MP3} \wedge Safety_{RPC1})$$

The semantics of the security about four processes above-mentioned can be unified described as follow:

$$\frac{\{P_{in}\}[\,MP_1 \mid MP_2 \mid MP_3 \mid RPC_1]\{Q_c\}}{LB=start \wedge P_{in} => \Box(LB=stop \rightarrow Q_c)}$$

3.3 Analysis

Web services provided service-driven and service component-composed software architecture under the loosely coupled and distributed environment. The formalized description and refinement of web service architecture indicate that the properties of system, such as liveness and security, can be composed of the properties of sub-processes in semantic composition method. In addition, a new solution for software reusing is provided under the process of stepwise refinement of web service architecture, which solves the critical problems about software components reusing, such as the existence, discovery and usability (i.e. interoperability) of service components. From the viewpoint of software architecture, the style of web service architecture is a kind of heterogeneous style of software architecture that is composed of some different sub-style in a certain temporal sequence relationship. While the properties of the liveness and the security all depended on these sub-styles of web service architecture, especially in parallel processing of service or the reusing and composing of service. Therefore, it is important for developing a system based on the service reuse and composition to design a perfectly software architecture.

4 Conclusion

The automatic assembly of the software module is an important goal and mechanism for software producing and reusing on the larger scale. Software architecture provides the theoretical foundation and realization framework for realizing this goal. Reference [6] indicated that the larger scale software reusing would not be successful without the detailed analysis and design of the system architecture, components and connection methods. This paper proposes the formal definitions about service, compositional service and service-oriented architecture based on the basic conception of temporal logical language XYZ/E. The web service architecture is described and refined by stepwise in XYZ/ADL method. In addition, the web service architecture could be divided into four sub-process by stepwise refinement for realization. The properties of the liveness, the correctness and the security in WSA also have a characteristic of semantic composition, which has been proven by an abstract model of service state transition with XYZ/ADL language. All these work provide a formally theoretical guidance for web services reusing and composition.

References

1. U. Ogbuji, The Past, Present and Future of Web Services, http://www.webservices.org /index.php/article /articleview/663/
2. Zhang GQ, Sun M, Comparison and Analysis of Temporal Logic, Journal of YUZHOU University (Nat. Scien. Edit, in Chinese), 1999 Vol. 16(2), p.15-18;
3. Zhu XY, Tang ZS, A temporal logic-based software architecture description language XYZ/ADL, Journal of Software (in Chinese), 2003, 14(4):713~720.
4. Tang ZS, et al., Temporal Logic Programming and Software Engineering, Beijing: Science Press, 1999/ 2002 (in Chinese).
5. Guo L., Tang ZS, An Overview Towards the Semantics of XYZ/E Object-Oriented Programs, Journal of Software (in Chinese), 2003, Vol. 14 (3) : 356-361.
6. *Griss, M.L.,* Architecting for large-scale systematic component reuse, Proceedings of the 1999 International Conference on Software Engineering, May 1999, p.615-616.

The Design and Implementation of GIS Grid Services*

Wen-jun Li, Yong-ji Li, Zhi-wei Liang, Chu-wei Huang, and Ying-wen Wen

Department of Computer Science, Sun Yat-sen University,
Guangzhou 510275, P.R. China
lnslwj@zsu.edu.cn

Abstract. This paper illustrates a GIS (Geographic Information Systems) application integration framework, which utilizes GIS Grid services (GGS) to enable large-scale resource sharing and better reusing of legacy systems. Considering the fundamental requirements of GGS, a design with sophisticated interfaces which enables explicit state semantics is proposed as a major contribution of this study. In addition, a prototype system of GGS based on legacy systems and web services is developed. Furthermore, the implementations are evaluated in a grid service selector environment proposed in another paper of this project.

1 Introduction

The development of GIS software architecture is always keeping its pace with the progress of computing technology, and profoundly affected by Internet and Web. GIS Web service, as the new generation of GIS applications based on Internet, is a kind of SOA which has already become the focus of distributed computing, resulting in a rising tide for B2B enterprise applications and e-governments to share geo-spatial information and spatial analysis services. GIS Grid service (GGS), combining grid technology with Service Oriented Architecture (SOA), is a natural evolution of GIS Web service. From our point of view, GGS are more suitable for GIS application integration. The most attractive advantage of Grid services is large-scale resource sharing [1]. In addition to supports on integrating GIS data and services, GGS also enables sharing of dynamic resources, such as high-performance computers, high-capacity storages, heterogeneous sensors and devices (including GPS, RS and CDMA/GSM).

The rest of this paper is organized as follows. Section 2 provides a brief survey of the research closely related to our work. In section 3, we introduce our integration framework for GIS applications. And section 4 illustrates the design and implementation of our prototype system of GGS. Furthermore, evaluation of our prototype system will be provided in section 5. The final section will put forward the conclusions and introduce the future works of our project.

2 Related Works

Although great development has been obtained both in the fields of GIS and Grid Computing, yet the combination of these two areas is still relatively new, calling for

* Supported by the Industrial Research Projects of the Science and Technology Plan of Guangdong Province, P.R. China, under Grant No. 2003A1030403.

H. Zhuge and G.C. Fox (Eds.): GCC 2005, LNCS 3795, pp. 220–225, 2005.

more attention and research. In [2], it is proposed that grid computing technologies should serve as the network infrastructure for geo-science applications. Another two papers [3, 4] aim to better resource sharing by employing high performance computing network technology, but both focused on the middleware technology, rather than the wrapping of legacy systems and the Enterprise Application Integration.

3 Integration Framework for GIS Applications

The conceptual overview of the architecture of our integration framework is shown in Fig 1. To be emphasized, grid services serve as the abstraction of any resources within the distributed environment, or rather, the VO. The top of the framework is the application layer including a virtual GIS grid portal and various GIS-based enterprise applications, which are running with the support of a grid service container, a component-based runtime environment. The bottom of the framework lie various implementations of GGS, named as legacy systems, including component GIS implemented by different programming languages, WMS-compatible and Non WMS-compatible Web Services, etc, the details of which have been encapsulated by the unified form of grid services. After the encapsulation, GGS can enjoy the various services provided by the grid service container, including a kind of Service Selector proposed in another paper of our project [5], which is used for selecting the current best services in a dynamic GGS Virtual Organization (VO) according to the combination of time-dependent QoS.

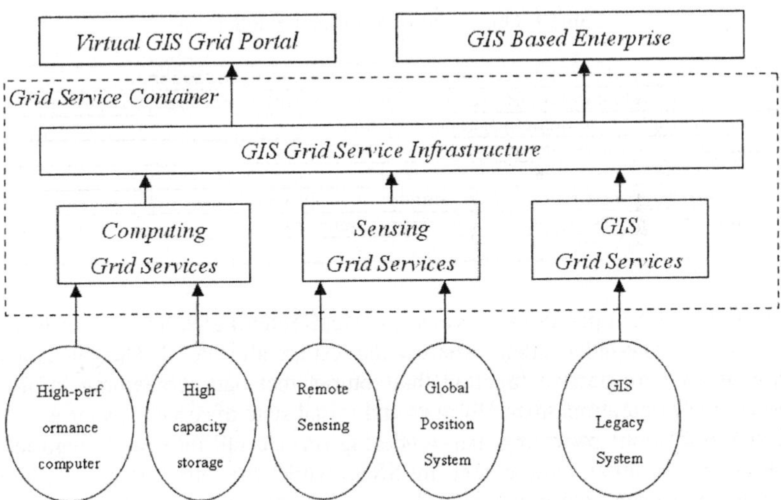

Fig. 1. Integration framework for GIS application

4 Design and Implementation of GGS

4.1 Requirements

In contrast to the statelessness of GIS Web Services, GIS Grid services are designed as stateful services in that they are exposed with explicit state semantics via their interfaces. In distributed computing environment, clients have to transfer GIS data across network themselves if the servers providing GIS services do not support stateful service instances. This will increase the network load and inconvenience of client-side programming. As a result of the rapid development of GIS, together with the Information Technology, more and more abundant implementations of similar interfaces will be provided. As far as GGS is concerned, famous for its uniform interface semantics, a unified interface ought to be provided to enable the clients to employ the Selector based on dynamic QoS to select an appropriate version from redundant GIS service implementations according to their QoS, which are published through service data.

4.2 Map Rendering Interface

WMS [6] published by OGC defines an HTTP based web service interface, which captures some basic requirements when involving map rendering service. Unfortunately, it is defined as a HTTP based web service that no states are exposed to clients. Client-side programs become involved in HTTP protocol and version negotiation with WMS servers, etc. In addition, WMS-compatible servers do not preserve the states such as Spatial Reference System (SRS), extent, layers, so that they cannot provide state-dependent operations such as enlarging maps and selecting region. As a result, clients have to manage complex states and cope with much low-layered logic like coordinates transformations, and cannot concentrate on business logic, which are more important in enterprise applications.

Table 1. Operations of MapRenderingService

`MapRenderingServiceMeta getCapabilities( updateSequence)`
`Response getFeatureInfo(queryLayers, point, infoType, layers)`
`RenderingConfig getRenderingConfig()`
`MapResult displayExtent(extent, SRS, option)`
`MapResult displayRectangle(corner1, corner2, option)`
`MapResult pan (startPoint, endPoint, option)`
`MapResult zoom (center, zoomRate, option)`
`MapResult moveTo(center, option)`

Table 1 shows the operations provided by MapRenderingService. The getCapabilities operation is state-independent, whereas the rest are all stateful. The getCapabilities operation is an introspective function that returns metadata, containing information such as layer configuration, image formats and initial state of service instance.

The five operations providing map-rendering service fall into two categories. The displayExtent operation uses extent in SRS, while the other four operations -- displayRectangle, pan, zoom and moveTo -- use extent in client-screen coordinates, which are the major improvement to WMS, following the flow below: First the service instance updates the current state according to the parameter option prior to others, then it calculates the new extent corresponding to the current client-screen region, finally the map rendering according to the new state and the new envelope are returned. Operations defined by WMS do not return the new envelope, yet still it has to be included in the results because the returned image ought to fit into the scale of SRS, even if the extent computed with the parameters passed by client may not. Clients should update the extent according to the returned envelope.

Client-side programs gain some benefits from MapRenderingService compared to WMS. The map rendering operations with client-screen coordinates as parameters do make client-side programming more convenient, free from GIS algorithms such as coordinate transformation, scale adjustment and complex states management, which enables the programmer to concentrate on business logic.

4.3 Implementation of Adapters

There are various kinds of GIS legacy systems running on various platforms and implemented by different languages, such as component-based products implemented in Java or Microsoft .Net, WMS-compatible Web Service, Non WMS-compatible Web Service, etc. The LegacyMapService in Fig 2 is a stateless interface that all kinds of legacy systems should implement. MapRenderingServiceImpl uses the LegacyMapService and manages the states of the service instances to implement the MapRenderingService interface. The LegacyMapServiceFactory, following GoF's Factory design pattern [7], creates implementations for different legacy systems of the LegacyMapService interface. The implementation details of MapRenderingService for each kind of legacy system are quite easy and left out.

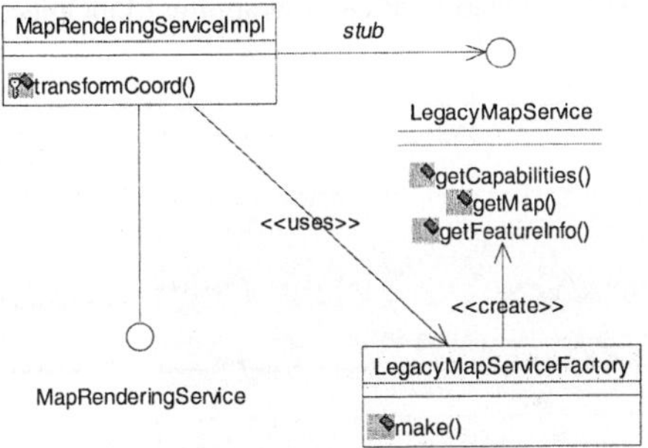

Fig. 2. Adapters for GIS legacy systems

This design isolates the state management and coordinates transformation, so MapRenderingServiceImpl does not depend on any GIS products. Under our integration framework, all kinds of legacy systems can be easily wrapped as GGS, with the subtle workload to implement the stateless interface LegacyMapService and register to the LegacyMapServiceFactory. As a result of the uniform interfaces with explicit semantics, GGS can conveniently employ the facilities provided by the grid service container, especially the Selector mechanism mentioned above.

5 Experimental Evaluations

In terms of the evaluation of the implementation of GIS grid services based on the wrapping of legacy systems, this paper focuses mainly on performance. It is quite obvious that the performance will be inevitably influenced because of the additional wrapping of grid services. As a result, hereby, this study will concentrate on the loss of performance after the wrapping.

Two kinds of Map Rendering Grid Services are tested in our simulation, respectively based on MapObjects, known as a component GIS, and a web service provided by Intergraph, known as a WMS-compatible GIS web service. In our evaluation, the differences in efficiency between direct invocation and that after wrapping are presented with massive tests.

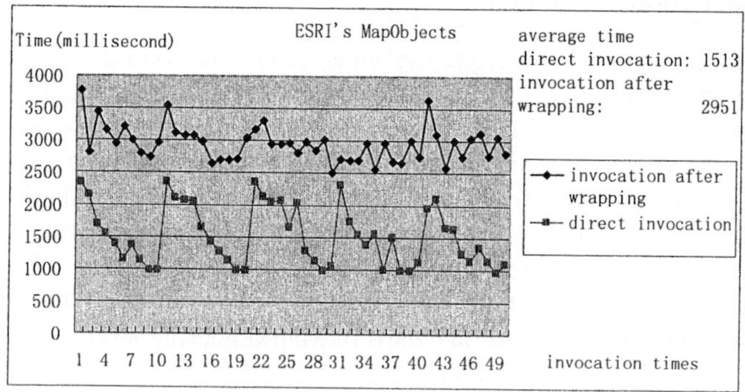

Fig. 3. Evaluation of GGS wrapping MapObjects

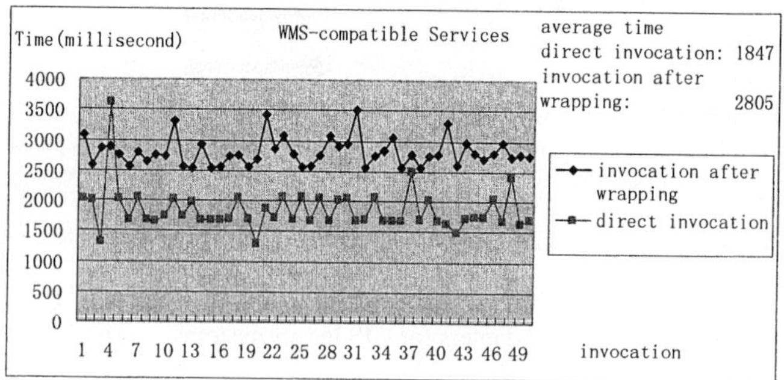

Fig. 4. Evaluation of GGS wrapping WMS Services

From Figure 3, showing the time needed by the MapObjects Component GIS and the relative GIS Grid service, a zigzag-distributed curve of response time is presented, because of the change of the layers every 10 times of invocation. The curve of GIS grid service is comparably smooth, because of the pre-loading and caching techniques employed in the implementation, which is based on the stateful transient instances in grid service, one of the remarkable advantages. While in Figure 4, which evaluates the performance of WMS-compatible web service and the grid service after wrapping, the curves are both quite smooth, with only a little fluctuation due to the load of network transport. The additional time is rather subtle when a complicated operation, especially GIS process, is requested, which is the very operation needed in daily life and enterprise decision-making.

6 Conclusion and Future Work

Thanks to Grid Service, the integration framework for GIS application proposed in the paper provides an easy way to integrate GIS data, spatial analysis, high-performance computers, high-capacity storages and heterogeneous sensors, etc. GGS encapsulating these resources provides a promising way of large-scale sharing, together with the load balancing mechanisms and the supports to QoS.

Our ongoing research is to define ontology of GGS and help client to determine which services can be viewed as equivalent, to further improve the resource sharing and load balancing in this integration framework.

References

1. I. Foster, and C. Kesselman (eds.), The Grid: Blueprint for a New Computing Infrastructure, Morgan Kaufmann, 1999.(book)
2. Thomas H. Hinke, Grid Technology as a Cyberinfrastructure for Earth Science Applications, Earth Science Technology Conference (ESTC), Crowne Plaza Cabaña, Palo Alto, CA, USA, June 2004, http://www.esto.nasa.gov/conferences/estc2004/papers/a3p1.pdf
3. Luo Jiancheng, Zhou chenghu, Cai Shaohua. The Design of Middleware-Based Grid-GIS. Geo-Information Science, 2002,(3):17-25.
4. Fang Jinyun, He Jianbang. Architecture of Grid GIS and Its Implementation Techniques. Geo-Information Science,2002,(4):36-42.
5. Wen-jun Li, Dan Chen, Yong-ji LI, Zhi-wei LIANG, and Gao-feng JI. GIS Grid Services Load Balancing Based on Dynamic Resource Discovery. In Proc. the 8th International Symposium on Future Software Technology (ISFST 2004), Xi'An, China, Nov. 2004
6. OpenGIS Consortium. OGC Web Map Service Interface. Version 1.1.1, Reference Number OGC 03-109r1, January 2004
7. E. Gamma, R. Helm, R. Johnson, and J. Vlissides, Design Patterns: Elements of Reusable Object-Oriented Software, Addison-Wesley, 1995.

The Minimization of QoS Deviation in Grid Environment*

YongZhong Zhang, Yinliang Zhao, FangFang Wu, and ZengZhi Li

Department of Computer Science and Technology Xi'an Jiaotong University, 710049 xi'an, china
zhyzh39@163.com, zhaoy@mail.xjtu.edu.cn

Abstract. In this paper, we link the issue of service pools' sizes allocation scheme with QoS requirement and formulize the problem of minimizing the QoS deviation of service requests in the grid environment by optimally allocating the service pool's size of each service class. The optimally allocating service pools' sizes scheme is solved by Lagrangian optimization approach. The simulation results show the efficiency of optimal service pools' sizes allocation scheme.

1 Introduction

In grid environment, different service pools' servers provide different services to widely distributed user communities. Users submit different service class's requests with different QoS requirement. The system distributes those service requests among the servers, attempting to meet the QoS requirement of all service classes' requests.

The arrival rate of each service class's request varies severely, can lead to temporary oversubscription of some services, underutilization of others. In such situations, in order to guarantee the QoS requirement of requests, it could be advantageous to reallocate the service pool size of each service class. The question that arises in that context is how to minimize the QoS deviation of service requests by optimally allocating the service pool's size of each service class.

In this paper, we link the issue of service pools' sizes allocation with QoS requirement and provide the optimal service pools' sizes allocation scheme, to our known, the problem has not been presented and solved in this way before. Palmer[1] consider the cost of switching servers from one service class to another. A number of papers [2][3][4] have focused on QoS based service selection and management, but none of them addressed the topic of minimizing QoS deviation. The issue of minimizing QoS deviation in shared data centers was studied by Chandra in [5]. They try to optimally allocate the resources for each application to minimize the QoS deviation and the close-form solution to optimal resource scheme that only considers the allocating resource proportion for each application. But, in this paper, we focus on the grid which has thousands of servers. The problem of minimizing QoS deviation in the grid is solved by the optimal service pools' sizes allocation and the service pools' sizes allocation scheme for minimizing QoS deviation is provided by Lagrangian optimization approach.

* This work is supported by the National High-Tech Development 863 program of China under Grant NO .2004AA111110.

H. Zhuge and G.C. Fox (Eds.): GCC 2005, LNCS 3795, pp. 226–231, 2005.

The rest of the paper is organized as follows: Section 2 presents the system architecture; Section 3 shows the problem definition; Section 4 discusses the optimal service pools' sizes allocation scheme; Section 5 evaluates the efficiency of our scheme by simulation. A brief conclusion is drawn at Section 6.

2 System Architecture

The grid architecture is composed of multi servers and one front-end. The front-end is used for dispatching all incoming service requests, and servers are used for processing service requests. All servers in the grid are connected using high network.

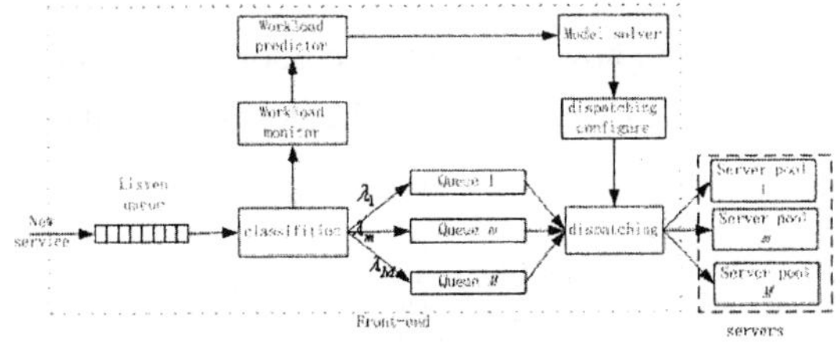

Fig. 1. The grid architecture

Figure 1 depicts the general system model that we consider. All incoming service requests are queued onto the listen queue. The classification dequeues service requests from the listen queue. In classification model, different service classes are classified by service URL, and service requests with different class are sent to corresponding queue. Dispatching model uses round robin algorithm and sends a request to servers which is allocated to service Pool of that service class. Workload monitor collects information about arrival rate and service time of each service class's requests during any time interval. Workload predictor predicts mean arrival rate and service time of each service class in next time interval using history data, and sends the predicted value to Model solver. At the end of each time interval, Model solver computes the allocating service pool's size of each service class, and lastly send the result to scheduling configure model. Scheduling configure model reconfigures scheduling information of each service class in scheduling table using computing result.

3 Problem Definition

Consider a grid consisting of N servers (possibly geographically distributed) and M service class, split into M service pools of sizes $n_1, n_2, \ldots, n_M$, where $\sum n_i = N$. Pool i is dedicated to a queue of services class $i (i=1, \ldots, M)$. Different service types may have different quality of service (QoS) requirements. Examples of service classes may include short web page accesses, long database searches, streamed media, etc. Note, in this paper, we use service delay as QoS metric, and the communication delay is ignored. Assuming that n_i servers is allocated to pool i, according to queue theory, we can get:

$$d_i = 1/(u_i - \lambda_i) = 1/(1/s_i - \lambda_i / n_i) = s_i n_i / (n_i - s_i \lambda_i) \le \bar{d}_i \, . \tag{1}$$

Table 1. Denotations

s_i	The service time of Service class *i* requests in one server
λ_i	The arrive rate of service class *i* requests in the grid
n_i	The number of servers in service pool *i*
u_i	The service rate of Service class *i* request in one server
$\overline{d}_i$	The requirement delay of service class *i*
d_i	The mean delay of service class *i*

The formula (1) can be written:

$$n_i \geq s_i \lambda_i \overline{d}_i /(\overline{d}_i - s_i) \,. \qquad (2)$$

From formula (2), we can know, if the service pool's size n_i of each service class i is no less than $s_i \lambda_i \overline{d}_i /(\overline{d}_i - s_i)$, the mean requirement delay time $\overline{d}_i$ of service class i will be met. Thus, if $\sum_{i=1}^{M} s_i \lambda_i \overline{d}_i /(\overline{d}_i - s_i) \leq N$, we get:

$$n_i = N \times \frac{s_i \lambda_i \overline{d}_i}{\overline{d}_i - s_i} / \sum_{i=1}^{M} \frac{s_i \lambda_i \overline{d}_i}{\overline{d}_i - s_i} \,. \qquad (3)$$

In the formula (3), the service pool's size n_i of each service class can guarantee the QoS requirement of each service class's requests.

If $\sum_{i=1}^{M} s_i \lambda_i \overline{d}_i /(\overline{d}_i - s_i) \geq N$, in this scenario, the server's resources of the grid cannot guarantee the target delay of all service classes. The expression $s_i n_i /(n_i - s_i \lambda_i) > \overline{d}_i$ exists.

We need optimize service pools' sizes allocation to guarantee the minimal QoS deviation of all service classes. The QoS deviation of an service class grows as its delay time deviates from the requirement's delay $\overline{d}_i$. This QoS deviation function can be represented as follows:

$$F_i(d_i) = (d_i - \overline{d}_i)/\overline{d}_i \,. \qquad (4)$$

In this scenario, the QoS deviation grows linearly when the observed delay time exceeds the specified requirement $\overline{d}_i$. The gird goal then is to assign n_i servers to each service type, such that the total system-wide QoS deviation, i.e., the total grid QoS deviation function is minimized.

$$F = \sum_{i=1}^{M} F(d_i) \,. \qquad (5)$$

Subject to:

$$\sum_{i=1}^{M} n_i = N \,. \qquad (6)$$

$$s_i \lambda_i < n_i \leq s_i \lambda_i \overline{d}_i /(\overline{d}_i - s_i) \qquad i = 1, \cdots, M \,. \qquad (7)$$

In the constraint(7), $n_i > s_i \lambda_i$ protects servers from overload, and $n_i \leq s_i \lambda_i \overline{d}_i /(\overline{d}_i - s_i)$ guarantees the value of $F_i(d_i)$ (see formula(4)) is large than 0.

4 Optimal Service Pools' Sizes Allocation Scheme

Based on formula (5) ,(6) and (1), we can construct the following Lagrange equation:

$$L(\{n_i\},\alpha)=\sum_{i=1}^{M}(\frac{s_i n_i}{n_i - s_i\lambda_i}-\bar{d}_i)/\bar{d}_i - \alpha(\sum_{i=1}^{M} n_i - N) \tag{8}$$

Set the partial derivative of L in Eq. (8) to zero, i.e.,

$$\partial L/\partial n_i = 0 \quad \forall i = 1,\cdots,M \ . \tag{9}$$

And

$$\partial L/\partial\alpha = 0 \ . \tag{10}$$

Using formula (9) and (10), we get:

$$\bar{n}_i = s_i\lambda_i + (N - \sum_{i=1}^{M} s_i\lambda_i)\times s_i\sqrt{\frac{\lambda_i}{\bar{d}_i}} / \sum_{i=1}^{M} s_i\sqrt{\frac{\lambda_i}{\bar{d}_i}} \ . \tag{11}$$

If every pool's size $\bar{n}_i$ meets the constraint (7), this scenario explains the formula (5) has the minimal value under the constraint (7), so $n_i = \bar{n}_i$. Else if exit the dissatisfied $\bar{n}_i$, this scenario explains the formula (5) does not have the minimal value under the constraint (7). We use two facts as foundations to solve this scenario: (1) the QoS deviation function (see formula (4)) is larger than 0; (2) the QoS deviation function monotonously decreases under increasing n_i. According to foundations we should adjust the pool's size n_i:

$$n_i = \begin{cases} s_i\lambda_i\bar{d}_i/(\bar{d}_i - s_i) & \bar{n}_i \geq s_i\lambda_i\bar{d}_i/(\bar{d}_i - s_i) \\ s_i\lambda_i + (N - \sum\limits_{\{i|\bar{n}_i \geq \frac{s_i\lambda_i\bar{d}_i}{\bar{d}_i - s_i}\}} \frac{s_i\lambda_i\bar{d}_i}{\bar{d}_i - s_i} - \sum\limits_{\{i|\bar{n}_i < \frac{s_i\lambda_i\bar{d}_i}{\bar{d}_i - s_i}\}} s_i\lambda_i)\times s_i\sqrt{\frac{\lambda_i}{\bar{d}_i}} / \sum\limits_{\{i|\bar{n}_i < \frac{s_i\lambda_i\bar{d}_i}{\bar{d}_i - s_i}\}} s_i\sqrt{\frac{\lambda_i}{\bar{d}_i}} & otherwise \end{cases} \ . \tag{12}$$

So the optimal allocating service pools' sizes scheme is solved.

5 Simulations

We demonstrate the efficacy of scheme using a simulation study. We first present our simulation environment, and then results.

5.1 Simulation Environment

In simulation environment of the grid, the grid consists of 1000 web servers, and each web server is homogeneous. C++sim toolkit[6] is used to build simulation of the grid , which support server element, such as queues, processes, stream, scheduler etc., and can provide us the necessary abstractions for implementing simulation. The prediction and optimization module are written using C++, those codes are invoked directly from the simulator for pools' sizes allocation.

The number of service classes is 3, and the proportion of three service classes' arrive rates is 6:3:1, and the requirement delay of service class is 20ms, 250ms, and 3000ms respectively. We assume the executing time of the service requests with the same service class is uniform distribution. The executing time of service requests with service class 1 are uniform random number in [5, 15], the service class 2 in [50, 150], and the service class 3 in [500, 1500]. The arrival process of service request destined for the grid was modeled by Poisson distribution.

Under each aggregative arrival rate, the test includes two phases which are divided by time interval (5 minutes). In the first phase, the data is collected by workload monitor; in the second phase, Workload predictor predicts arrival rate and service time of each service class by methods which is presented in [5], and the pools' sizes are adjusted using scheme we introduced, and then the service delay time is collected.

5.2 Result

The Proportional Service Pools' Sizes Allocation (P-SPSA) scheme is a natural way to allocate servers in a grid, and it results in the pools' sizes assigned to class i as below:

$$n_i = \lambda_i s_i / \sum_{j=1}^{M} \lambda_i s_i \ .$$

We compare P-SPSA scheme with Service Pools' Sizes Allocation for the minimizing QoS deviation (MQD-SPSA) scheme. Table 2 lists the allocated service pool's size of each service class. Under different aggregative arrival rate, because the proportion of the arrival rates of the three service classes is the same, the service pool's size of each service class is the same using the P-SPSA scheme, but the service pool's size of each service class is different using MQD-SPSA.

Table 2. The allocated service pool's size of each service class

Aggregative Arrival rate	P-SPSA			Q-SPSA		
	1	2	3	1	2	3
4000	44	221	735	57	236	707
5000	44	221	735	60	250	690
6000	44	221	735	65	238	697
7000	44	221	735	49	226	725

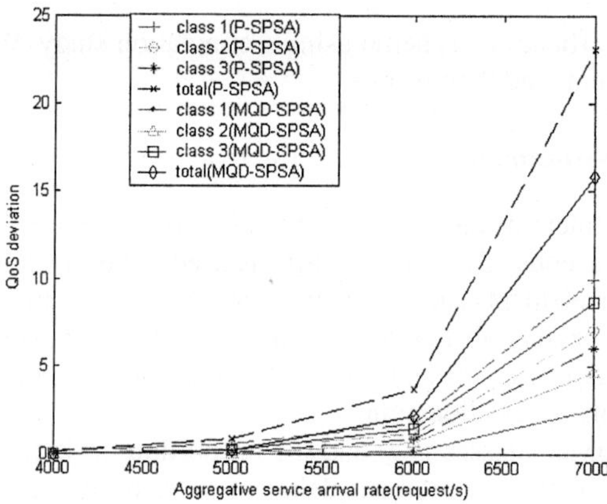

Fig. 2. The QoS deviation of different service class

The figure 2 shows the QoS deviation of different service class and the total service requests when using MQD-SPSA, P-SPSA schemes. It can be seen that QoS deviation of total service requests reduces using the MQD-SPSA scheme. MQD-SPSA scheme compares with the P-SPSA scheme, the QoS deviation of total service requests reduces 46%, the QoS deviation of the service class 1 reduces 300%, the QoS deviation of the service class 2 reduces 52.2%, and only the QoS deviation of the service class 3 increases 30%. It shows that MQD-SPSA optimizes the QoS deviation of grid system.

6 Conclusions

In this paper, we link the issue of service pool's sizes allocation with the QOS requirement and explore the problem of the minimal QoS deviation in the grid by optimally allocating service pools' sizes. The simulation results demonstrate that MQD-SPSA scheme can succeed in implementing the minimization of QoS deviation under different aggregative service request rate.

References

1. M.Fisher, C.Kubicek, and P.McKee, et al. Dynamic Allocation of Servers in a Grid Hosting Environment. In Proceedings of the Fifth IEEE/ACM International Workshop on Grid Computing (Grid '04), Pittsburgh, Pennsylvania, November, 2004.
2. Daniel A. Menascé, E. Casalicchio. QoS in Grid Computing. IEEE Internet Computing, 8(4), July/August 2004.
3. Rashid Al-Ali, Omer Rana and David Walker. G-QoSM: A Framework for Quality of Service. In e-Science AHM03 Proceedings, Nottingham UK, September 2003.
4. S. Kalepu, S. Krishnaswamy, and S. W. Loke. Verity: A QoS Metric for Selecting Web Services and Providers. In Proc. of the First Web Services Quality Workshop, Rome, Italy, Dec. 2003. IEEE Computer Society
5. A.Chandra, W. Gong, et al. Dynamic Resource Allocation for Shared Data Centers Using Online Measurements. In Proceedings of the Eleventh International Workshop on Quality of Service (IWQoS 2003), Berkeley, Monterey, CA, Springer. pp. 381-400.
6. C. Little and D. L. McCue. Construction and Use of a Simulation Package in C++. Newcastle University, Department of Computing Science, Technical Report No. 437, July 1993.

The Research on MPC-WS, a Web Service for the Simulation of Metal Powder Compaction Process*

Puqing Chen[1,**], Kejing He[2], Zhaoyao Zhou[1], and Yuanyuan Li[1]

[1] College of Mechanical Engineering, South China University of Technology, Guangzhou, 510640, P.R. China
[2] Guangdong Key Laboratory of Computer Network, South China University of Technology, Guangzhou, 510640, P.R. China

Abstract. Compaction is a nonlinear procedure commonly used to form powder material. Simulating the compaction process is often time-consuming. In this paper, a parallel computation system for the simulation of metal powder compaction process was established on a Linux cluster that consists of 32 IBM eServer xSeries machines connected over 1 Gb Ethernet. Test problem of the compaction of a gear was simulated. Density distribution as well as other useful results was obtained. Performance of the system was evaluated with different parallel schema used. It shows that four processors produce maximum time saving. Efficiency tends to decline if parallel scale exceeds the limit. Incoming network traffic of the master node was measured for two different cases where eight and ten processors are employed respectively. It shows that when the number of processors increases, more network traffic is created, which decreases the platform's efficiency. An MPC-WS that can choose approximate number of processors for user jobs and serve user requests concurrently was offered.

1 Introduction

Compaction is a commonly used procedure to form powder material into a specified shape. Various factors, including mechanical properties of the powder, die-wall friction and punch-movements, etc. have influence on the procedure and then the quality of the products. Traditionally, trial-and-error method is used in the design of the dies and processing parameters, which spends much time and fund in repeatedly making, testing and modifying the design, and is more and more difficult to match the rapidly changing demand of the market. Numerical simulation is promising to substitute the old design style for it enables the testing process to be conducted virtually in computers, therefore saves the time and fund in each cycle. However, in order to apply this technology in industry, some problems have to be solved.

Firstly, mechanical behavior of powder material must be modeled. Powder material is quite different from normal solids. It deforms under very slight forces, gets denser during compaction and its properties change along with the density. Models for solid

* Foundation item: Project (CG2003-GA005) supported by China Education and Research Grid (China Grid).

** Correspondence: Puqing Chen, Postdoctoral researcher; Tel: +86-20-87112933; E-mail: chpq2000@gmail.com

H. Zhuge and G.C. Fox (Eds.): GCC 2005, LNCS 3795, pp. 232–237, 2005.

materials cannot be used. Although some models have been presented for powder material, it is still controversial which one reflects the material best.

Secondly, as nonlinear material, large deformation and changing contact conditions are involved in the process, iterative algorithm is necessary to solve the problem. For three-dimensional problems, the simulation is often time-consuming. The emergence of grid technologies that can aggregate heterogeneous and distributed resources dynamically provides a new solution for accelerating the design progress [1].

Thirdly, since most of the designers are engineers with various technical backgrounds, such as metallurgy, ceramic production, medicine manufacturing, etc., the simulation platform must have a friendly user-interface for them. Preferably, it should be highly interactive and simulation results should be visualized to facilitate further analysis.

This paper focuses on the simulation of metal powder compaction, which is a common procedure in powder metallurgy industry. Parallel computation of the forming process of the powder was conducted and the performance of the computational cluster was benchmarked. All the metal powder compaction process has been wrapped as a web service called MPC-WS and a web-based user interface is provided to users for friendly interaction.

2 Theoretical Basis

Compaction of metal powder is often operated at room temperature. Under such circumstances, metal powder can be considered as a kind of time-independent, elasto-plastic and compressible material. Quite a few models have been presented for such kind of material [2~9]. Some of them are characterized by an ellipsoidal yield surface, such as Kuhn's, Green's, Shima's and Doraivelu's etc. The yield surface can be expressed with the following equation:

$$AJ'_2 + BJ_1^2 = 1 \tag{1}$$

The constitutive relation is

$$d\sigma_{ij} = D_{ijkl}^{ep} d\varepsilon_{kl} \tag{2}$$

where

$$D_{ijkl}^{ep} = D_{ijkl}^{e} - D_{ijkl}^{p} \tag{3}$$

And D_{ijkl}^{p} can be derived from the yield equation, with associated flow rule assumed.

$$D_{ijkl}^{p} = \frac{D_{ijmn}^{e} \dfrac{\partial f}{\partial \sigma_{mn}} D_{rskl}^{e} \dfrac{\partial f}{\partial \sigma_{rs}}}{\dfrac{\partial f}{\partial \sigma_{ij}} D_{ijkl}^{e} \dfrac{\partial f}{\partial \sigma_{kl}} + \rho\left(E_B J_1^{\,2} + E_A J_2{}'\right) \dfrac{\partial f}{\partial \sigma_{ij}} \delta_{ij}} \tag{4}$$

When powder gets denser, the yield surface also changes. This relationship can be represented by the dependency of *A* and *B* on the relative density ρ, written as $A(\rho)$ and $B(\rho)$.

3 Parallel Simulation System and Performance Analysis

The MPC (metal powder compaction) application simulates the compaction process in powder metallurgy manufacturing. The application uses MSC.Marc, a commercial FEA code, as numerical solver. The problem was split into sub-domains. Inter-domain communications are achieved through the message-passing interface (MPI) [10].

Test problem is the compaction of a gear. The finite element model involves 8580 elements, 11129 nodes and 33387 DOFs. The computation was run on an SMP cluster that consists of 32 IBM eServer xSeries servers connected with 1Gb Ethernet. Every

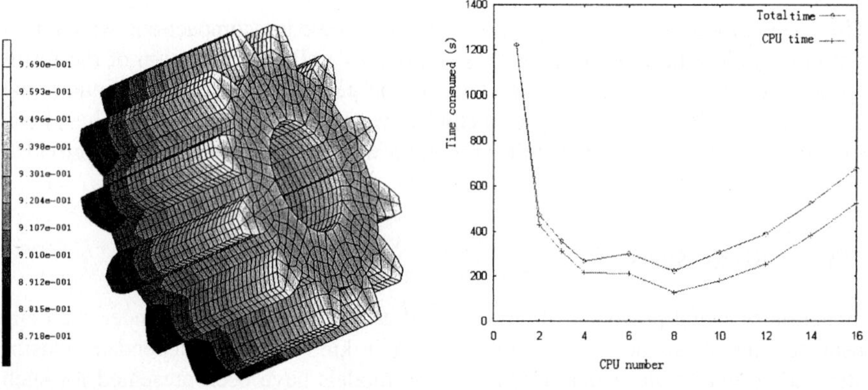

Fig. 1. Relative density distribution in the green part, obtained in simulation

Fig. 2. Time consumed by the computation with different number of processors used

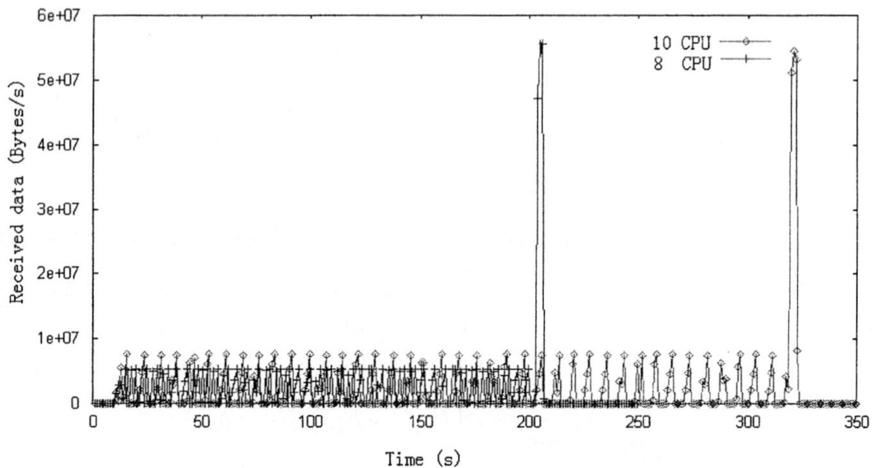

Fig. 3. Network traffic measured on the master node when 8 and 10 processors are used in the computation

server has dual xeon 2.0GHz processors, 1GB memory and Fedora Core 2 operating system installed. Relative density distribution in the green compact obtained in the simulation was shown in Fig. 1.

To analyze the performance of the parallel computation platform, the computation was conducted repeatedly, with the processor number and domain number range from 1 to 16, to see the relationship between the parallel scale and computation efficiency.

Fig. 2 shows the relation between processor number and the time consumed in each time of computation. Against the single-processor case, prominent time saving was observed in double processor case. Increasing the processor number, the computation time decreases more. However, the tendency reaches a limit when eight processors were employed. More processors cause less efficiency when parallel scale extended beyond that limit.

Fig. 3 shows the network traffic of the master node during two times of computation, with eight and ten processors used respectively. Comparison between the two cases indicates that when the number of processors increases, the network traffic increases too. Therefore, although more processors were allocated in the computation, total efficiency declined. The peak value at the end of the simulation indicates that the master node gathered some data just after the whole computation was completed.

4 MPC-WS

From Fig. 2, we can see that decrease of the execution time of a single job is nonlinear with respect to the increase of the number of processors. However, the system achieve its best speedup when there are about 4 to 12 processors participated in the simulation. Thus, rather than offering many processors to a single job, we prefer to provide a MPC-WS which can chose approximate number of processors for users' jobs and serve users' requests concurrently.

The backend metal powder compaction process was converted into MPC-WS by creating a Web service wrapper. The wrapper acts as an intermediary for the MPC application by exposing a Web service interface to users. The function of the Web service wrapper at a very high level is to wait for Simple Object Access Protocol

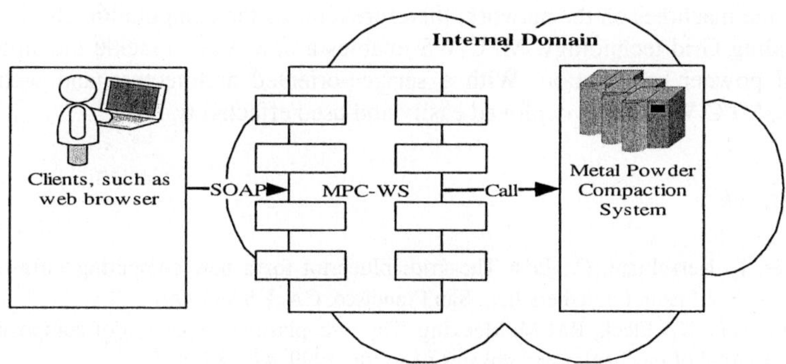

Fig. 4. MPC-WS serves as a intermediary between clients and backend MPC system

(SOAP) calls and then call the metal powder compaction system with appropriate input files. Fig. 4 illustrates the role of MPC-WS in the system.

4.1 Input Generation

The simulation software accepts input data as an ASCII file that contains the elements, node coordinates, forces and other job parameters. Most web services that wrap legacy systems often require users to prepare and upload the input files, hence hamper the system's interactivity. Herein, the web service overcomes this problem by analyzing the parameter values obtained from web pages and generating formatted input file from the values by itself.

4.2 XML Schema for Standardizing MPC-WS's Input

To simplify the invocation of the Web service, so that the clients need only pass the required parameters to the methods rather than the complete input files, we designed an XML schema that defines all the information about the MPC-WS's XML input. The XML Schema contains details such as the element names, sequences, and default values. So, if the web interface creates SOAP messages based on the schema, it is guaranteed to be in functional compliance with the backend MPC system.

4.3 Web-Based Interface

An interactive web-based interface for simplify the use of our system was also developed. The interface sends user's input to MPC-WS and displays the compaction progress in the browser periodically.

5 Conclusion

On parallel computation platform, metal powder compaction process was simulated. Density distribution of the green part was obtained. With the help of the parallel computation platform, much time saving was obtained in the simulation process. However, if too much processors are allocated in the computation, communication increases between the machines on the network, therefore reduces the computation efficiency.

Coupling Grid technology, MPC-WS enables a new way to tackle the simulation of metal powder compaction. With a service-oriented architecture and web-based interface, MPC-WS can be deployed easily and used effectively.

References

1. Foster, I., Kesselman, C., Eds: The grid: blueprint for a new computing infrastructure. Morgan Kaufmann Publishers Inc., San Francisco, CA, USA (1999)
2. B Storakers, NA Fleck, RM McMeeking. The viscoplastic compaction of composite powders. Journal of mechanics and physics of solids. 1999, 47: 785~815
3. Pia Redanz. Numerical modeling of the powder compaction of a cup. Eur. J.Mech. A/Solids 1999,18:399 ~ 413.

4. H.A. Kuhn, C.L. Downey. Deformation characteristics and plasticity theory of sintered powder materials. International Journal of Powder Metallurgy. 1971, 7(1): 15~25
5. R.J. Green. A plasticity theory for porous solids□Int. J. Mech. Sci. Pergamon Press. 1972, 14: 215-224
6. Shima Susumu, Oyane M. Plasticity theory for porous metallurgy. International Journal of Mechanical Sciences. 1976, 18(6): 285 ~ 291
7. S.M. Doraivelu, H.L. Gegel, J.S. Gunasekera, J.C. Malas, J.T. Morgan, J.F. Thomas, Jr. A new yield function for compressible P/M materials. International Journal of Mechanical Sciences. 1984, 26: 527~535
8. Hyoung Seop Kim, Dong Nyung Lee. Power-law creep model for densification of powder compacts. Materials Science and Engineering. 1999, A271: 424~429
9. P.Q. Chen, W. Xia, Z.Y. Zhou, W.P. Chen, Y.Y. Li. Three-dimensional finite element analysis of metal powder compaction. Materials Science Forum. 2004, 471~472: 201~205
10. Karonis, N.T., Toonen, B., Foster, I.: MPICH-G2: A grid-enabled implementationof the message passing interface. Journal of Parallel and Distributed Computing, 63 (2003): 551–563

Towards a Framework for Automatic Service Composition in Manufacturing Grid

Lei Zhang[1], Weizheng Yuan[1], and Wei Wang[2]

[1] Advanced Manufacturing Engineering Institute, School of Mechatronic Engineering, Northwestern Polytechnical University, Xi'an, 710072, China
{npuzhanglei, yuanwz}@sina.com
[2] School of Optic and Electronic Engineering, Xi'an Institute of Technology, Xi'an, 710032, China
wangwei.nwpu@163.com

Abstract. In order to realize automatic service composition in Manufacturing Grid (MG), a framework based on manufacturing domain-specific ontology (MGOnto) is proposed. MGOnto integrates three existing manufacturing ontologies, and represented in First Order Logic and Rules respectively. The framework consists of five core and three supporting services. It can reuse previously processed workflows in local repository and compose new workflows from services MG wide, by automatic service chaining which uses a MGOnto based backward recursive algorithm. A test bed is implemented and experiments on the example of an airfoil rib verify the feasibility of the framework.

1 Introduction

Manufacturing Grid (MG) is a kind of new paradigm of contemporary manufacturing system, by which inter-organizationally distributed manufacturing resources can be integrated, shared, discovered, and aggregated to implement complex manufacturing tasks in a Service Oriented Architecture (SOA) environment. Some works have been done with regard to framework, resource discovery [1] and scheduling [2] of MG. However, these works are limited to a manual or somewhat semi-automatic mechanism. Contributions from Semantic Grid (SG) [3] and Semantic Web (SW), such as SWSF [4] in SWSI, WSMO in SDK, are promising solutions for automatics of MG.

Considering the differences between MG and Computing Grid, Information Grid in resources and applications, this work focuses on a manufacturing domain specific ontology (named as MGOnto) supported framework and mechanism for automatic MG service composition, on the basis of the work done by Shalil Majithia et al [5].

2 The Infrastructure of MGOnto

MGOnto is designed on the basis of the works of PSL [4], TOVE [6], STEP [7] and SWSF, as shown in Fig.1. TOVE ontology focuses on manufacturing domain-specific terminology and the corresponding semantics. PSL Out Core provides manufacturing process specification ontology. STEP has defined a semi-structured ontology for representation and exchange of product data. They fabricate the manufacturing

H. Zhuge and G.C. Fox (Eds.): GCC 2005, LNCS 3795, pp. 238 – 243, 2005.

domain-specific ontology. The ontology is expressed in two forms: FOL and Rules, which specializes in description and reasoning of ontology respectively. SWSL-FOL (based on FOL) and SWSL-Rules (based on logic-programming, i.e. Rules) are employed as the languages to express the ontology, which are the two sub-languages of Semantic Web Services Language (SWSL) developed by the SWSF initiative [4]. Before the ontology can take effect in MG, a concept model of MG is defined and formalized, which is the ontology for MG services. As a result, the MGOnto is fabricated and expressed in two forms: First-order Logic Ontology for MG (FLOMG) and Rules Ontology for MG (ROMG), according to the two sub-languages of FOL and Rules. FLOMG and ROMG share the same manufacturing domain-specific ontology, and ROMG is a counterpart translation from FLOMG.

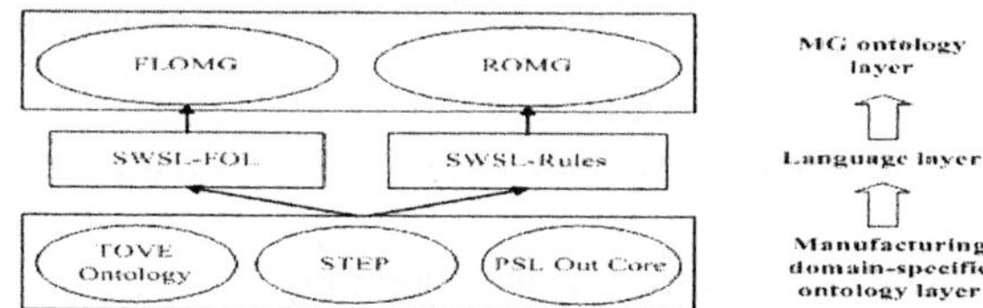

Fig. 1. The infrastructure of MGOnto

FLOMG is a complete axiomatization given in FOL used primarily to present the ontology of MG service concepts. ROMG is systematically translated from FLOMG, and is used to support the use of MGOnto in reasoning and execution environments.

3 The Framework Architecture

As shown in Fig. 2, the automatic task of service composition plays the role of producing reserved workflows under certain user goals. It is dynamically and automatically done by local workflow (i.e. service flows composted previously) reuse and new workflow composition. The WFMS is the bootstrap entrance and puts together the framework, which consists of five core and three supporting services: AWFC, CWFC, AWF-M&RS, CWF-M&RS, QoS-R&RS, LWFR, R&CS, and the ROMG service.

AWFC and CWFC coordinate abstract and concrete workflow composition respectively. The AWF-M&RS can match a goal with previously processed abstract workflows in LWFR and select out the ones or chains of abstract workflow complying

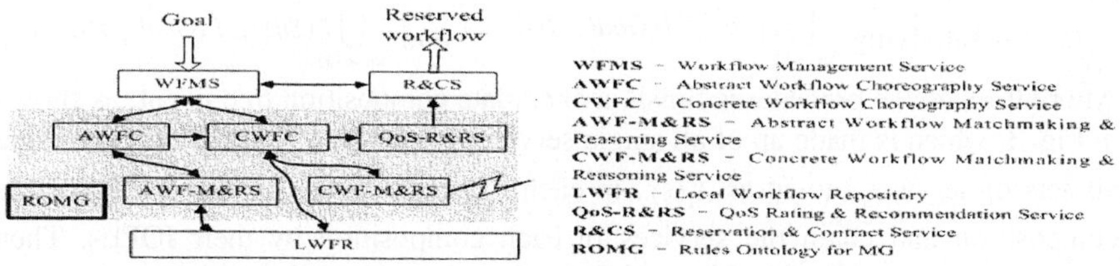

Fig. 2. The framework architecture based on ROMG of MGOnto

with the whole or a conjunction of atomic parts of the goal. The CWF-M&RS is similar, except that it matches and chains concrete services MG wide. The QoS-R&RS evaluate and rate all possible compositions for a goal according to user-specific Quality of Service (QoS). Here, QoS is a combination of Time, Quality (of a product or service), Cost, Service (value-added pre and post services), Environment (indices related to health), Knowledge (technology assurance), Location, and a weight (importance or power) for each. The R&CS supports high-level reservation and contract, since there may be material flows and pre-positive time for service prepare. The LWFR is a local repository that stores the relation of triples (goal, abstract workflow, concrete workflow). Considering that service location plays a very important role in service selection for a specific user, this repository is designed to be local to an organization and only service the local matchmaking. The ROMG provides the framework with full-fledged and pervasive domain-specific ontology used for reasoning.

4 Methodology of Automatic Service Composition

4.1 The Algorithm for Automatic Service Chaining

Automatic service chaining undertakes the search, matchmaking and chaining issues of automatic service composition. In the framework, it is the core capability of the AWF-M&RS and the CWF-M&RS, which act on the ROMG for reasoning. Here, a backward recursive algorithm for automatic chaining is studied. Given the IOPEs of a goal, the algorithm for concrete service chaining is as follows:

- For a goal with its IOPEs noted as $Goal\_IOPEs$, find a set of single MG services $G(S)=\{S_{g1},S_{g2},\cdots,S_{gm}\}$, which satisfies that for each $S_{gi}, i=1,2,\cdots,m$, $O(S_{gi})=O(Goal\_IOPEs)$ and $E(S_{gi})=E(Goal\_IOPEs)$. $O(*)$ and $E(*)$ are the sets of output and effect of *, respectively.
- For each S_{gi} in $G(S)$, find a set of service set $A=\{A_1(S), A_2(S), \cdots, A_k(S)\}$, which satisfies that for each element (also a set) $A_j(S)\in A, j=1,2,\cdots k$, $I(S_{gi})-\bigcup_{Sn\in Aj(S)}O(Sn)\subseteq I(Goal\_IOPEs)$ and $P(S_{gi})-\bigcup_{Sn\in Aj(S)}E(Sn)\subseteq P(Goal\_IOPEs)$, and for any $Sn_1, Sn_2\in A_j(S), Sn_1\neq Sn_2$, $O(Sn_1)\cap O(Sn_2)=\varnothing$, $E(Sn_1)\cap E(Sn_2)=\varnothing$. $I(*)$ and $P(*)$ are the sets of input and precondition of *, respectively.
- For each $A_j(S)\in A, j=1,2,\cdots k$, recursively execute the second step (i.e. the previous step) until the result set of discovered services $A=\varnothing$, or exists a set $A_j(S)\in A$ satisfying $\bigcup_{Sn\in Aj(S)}I(Sn)\subseteq I(Goal\_IOPEs)$ and $\bigcup_{Sn\in Aj(S)}P(Sn)\subseteq P(Goal\_IOPEs)$.
- After all recursive procedures finish, a candidate composition tree is got, as shown in Fig. 3, which is made up of all single services (noted as S_g) in the first layer and all sets of services (noted as $A_j(S)$) in each recursive layer. Expand each feasible composition and chain the services in each composition by their IOPEs. Then structured chains of the feasible workflows that can achieve the goal are got.

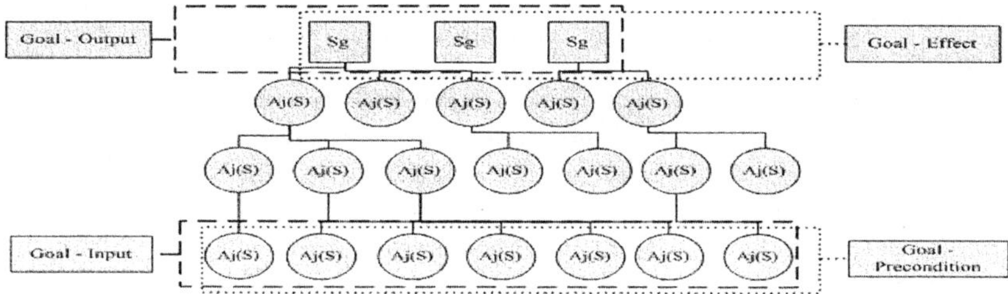

Fig. 3. Candidate tree illustration of automatic MG service chaining

ROMG is essential to matching IOPEs intelligently, in order to find those services that can help to achieve the goal but will be excluded by exact matching. The algorithm of abstract workflow chaining is similar, except that it treats abstract workflows as single services and only operates on the local repository.

4.2 The Algorithm for Automatic Service Composition

A goal is firstly handed over to AWFC by WFMS. The AWFC then resorts to AWF-M&RS to search LWFR (by the backward recursive algorithm discussed in section 4.1). The goal may be completely matched by single or chain (a chain is composed into one workflow immediately by AWFC) abstract workflows, or only some atomic parts (independent atomic sub-chains) of the goal do. The matching results are integral and partial matched abstract workflows respectively. All the matched results are supposed to be caught, composed, cached and passed to CWFC for implementation.

CWFC draws all concrete workflows according to the matched abstract workflows from LWFR, and the integral concrete workflows are passed to QoS-R&RS as candidates. The comprehensive index of each element in QoS is counted for each candidate, and those satisfying each threshold specified in the goal are transferred to R&CS for pre-reservation. This is to verify that every service in a concrete workflow is available and valid. Eligible and sorted concrete workflows are presented to the end user for reservation. Eventually, one of the candidates that is selected and confirmed by the end user is reserved and contracts are made by the R&CS.

If there are no eligible concrete workflows got at last, or the AWFC does not get any integral matched abstract workflows, the CWFC turns to considering the partial ones and MG wide services. Partial matched workflows are passed to the CWF-M&RS. Then the CWF-M&RS chains services from services MG wide and the partial matched workflows (by the backward recursive algorithm discussed in section 4.1). The result of chaining made up of integral concrete workflows is passed to QoS-R&RS as candidates. The following steps are then the same as discussed above: QoS evaluation by the QoS-R&RS, pre-reservation, incoming end user confirmation and reservation by the R&CS. Eligible concrete workflows along with their corresponding abstract workflows (abstracted reversely from the concrete ones) and the goal are loaded into the LWFR as triples for reuse.

The algorithm discussed above now is shown in Fig. 4 in a descriptive syntax.

```
Auto_composition(well_ formed_ goal)
{   referring to ROMG ://all the procedure refer to ROMG as reasoning base
    reservation_flag = " unreserved" ://flag
    AWFC_Result = AWFC( AWF-M&RS( well_ formed_ goal )):
    CWFC_Result = CWFC( AWFC_Result ); //retrieve concrete workflows from LWFR
    if( integral_workflows_in( CWFC_Result ) ≠ null )
    {   feasible_concrete_workflows = QoS-R&RS( integral_workflows_in( CWFC_Result ));
        eligible_concrete_workflows = R&CS_pre-reservation( feasible_concrete_workflows ):/pre-reservation
        present to end user GUI
        workflow = user_selection;
        if ( workflow ≠ null )
        {   R&CS( workflow ) :
            reservation_flag = " reserved" ;
        }; //reservation
    };
    if(reservation_flag ≠ " reserved" )
    {   //chaining concrete workflows among MG services and part chained workflows (treated as services)
        feasible_concrete_workflows = CWF-M&RS( MG_search_handler, part_workflows_in( CWFC_Result ) );
        eligible_concrete_workflows = R&CS_pre( feasible_concrete_workflows )://pre-reservation
        LWFR( eligible_concrete_workflows , AWFC(eligible_concrete_workflows), goal):/*loaded eligible
                                                        triples into the LWFR for reuse*/
        present to end user GUI
        workflow = user_selection;
        if ( workflow ≠ null )
            R&CS( workflow ) ; //reservation
    };
}
```

Fig. 4. The algorithm for automatic service composition

5 Implementation and Evaluation

We build our test bed on an Enterprise MG (EMG) we have just finished in a military airplane corporation. The EMG consists of 12 nodes running Globus Toolkit 3.9, more than 470 MG resources, MGOnto represented in OWL-S, and a matchmaking and reasoning service using DQL/JTP server (powered by the Java Theorem Prover package). The services of the framework and three algorithms discussed in section 4 are implemented and integrated into the EMG as Java plug-ins. Since OWL-S based on OWL is a subset of SWSL-Rules, we leave the ontology of EMC unchanged.

We experimented on an example: composite a workflow automatically for the machining and assembly of a rib used in airfoil, under specific IOPEs, and also satisfying specific QoS. We know that there are 4 workshops, 16 machining tools (16 corresponding services) in 5 sorts with different QoS can be utilized to achieve the goal, and the number of atomic processes in possible workflows varies from 2 to 5.

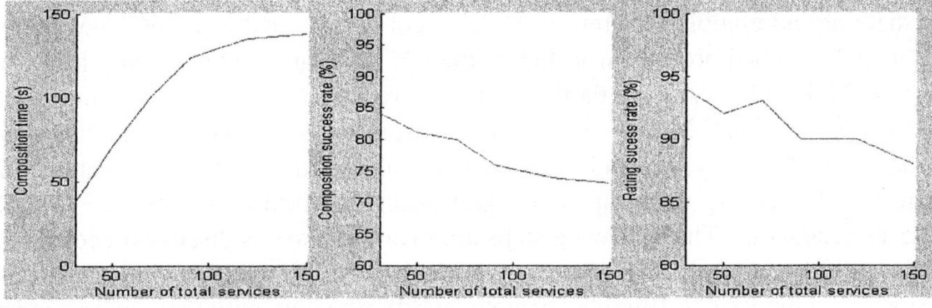

Fig. 5. The composition time (left), composition success rate (middle) and rating success rate (right) with the number of useful services is 16

For convenience, the QoS here only includes time, quality, cost. The IOPEs are as follow:

Input - numeric 3D drawing (filetype: STEP), Bill of Material (filetype: tabulate).
Prediction - rough materials corresponding to the BOM (armor plate, bolt).
Output - message of accomplishment.
Effect - assembled rib, part delivery, part certificate, QoS satisfied.

We caught the composition time, composition success rate and rating success rate (according to QoS) each time changing the condition by adding unrelated services from 20 to 120, with 14 unrelated services at the beginning. Results in Fig.5 show that the performance of the framework is relatively good and acceptable for MG.

6 Conclusions

Automatic service composition is a core automatic task for MG, and researches up to now have not put forward an efficient solution. In this work, a novel manufacturing domain-specific ontology based framework, along with the algorithms are studied. MGOnto is designed to provide the framework with a full-fledged manufacturing domain-specific ontology. The framework can reuse previously processed workflows in the local repository and compose new workflows from services MG wide, automatically by reasoning on ROMG. A test bed is implemented and evaluated from three perspectives. Results of experiments on an actual example have shown that the framework and its algorithms have good performance and are feasible for MG.

References

1. Lilan Liu, Tao Yu, Zhanbei Shi, Minglun Fang. Resource Management and Scheduling in Manufacturing Grid. (Eds.): GCC 2003, LNCS3032-3033, 2003.
2. Zhanbei Shi, Tao Yu, and Lilan Liu: MG-QoS: QoS-Based Resource Discovery in Manufacturing Grid. (Eds.): GCC 2003, LNCS 3033, pp. 500–506, 2004.
3. David De Roure. The Semantic Grid: Past, Present, and Future. A. Gómez-Pérez and J. Euzenat (Eds.): ESWC 2005, LNCS 3532, p. 726, 2005.
4. Steve Battle, Abraham Bernstein, Harold Boley et al. Semantic Web Services Framework (SWSF). http://www.daml.org/services/swsf/1.0/overview/. 2005.5
5. Shalil Majithia, David W.Walker, W.A.Gray. Automated Composition of Semantic Grid Services. Proceedings of the UK e-Science Programme All Hands Meeting 2004, held 1-3 September 2004 in. Nottingham, UK, pages 363-370.
6. Gruninger, M., Atefi. Ontologies to Support Process Integration in Enterprise Engineering. Computational and Mathematical Organization Theory, Vol. 6, No. 4, p. 381-394.
7. ISO TC184/SC4. STEP Overview. http://www.tc184-sc4.org/SC4%5FOpen/SC4%5FWork%5FProducts%5FDocuments/STEP%5F%2810303%29/. 2005

Characterizing Services Composeability and OWL-S Based Services Composition

Zhonghua Yang[1], Jing Bing Zhang[2], Jiao Tao[1], and Robert Gay[1]

[1] Information Communication Institute of Singapore,
School of Electrical and Electronics Engineering,
Nanyang Technological University, Singapore 639798
[2] Singapore Institute of Manufacturing Technology,
71 Nanyang Drive, Singapore 638075
eZhYang@ntu.edu.sg

Abstract. Grid has emerged as a new paradigm for integration within dynamic virtual enterprises. Given a service-oriented Grid environment, more complex, value-added sophisticated services and applications can be built via service composition. In this paper, we discuss Grid services composition by leveraging Semantic Web services standards and technology, especially OWL-S. The characterization of service composeability is presented in the context of OWL-S. The techniques for constructing the Web/Grid service composer are described, and the focus is placed on composition engine and OWL-S Matcher.

1 Introduction

Grid systems and applications aim to integrate, virtualize, and manage resources and services within distributed, heterogeneous, dynamic "virtual organizations (VOs)". In the recent years, there is the alignment of Grid technology to Web services, and a *Grid services* is defined as *a Web service* that is designed to operate in a Grid environment and meets the requirements of the Grid(s) in which it participates. The early definition that a Grid service is a service that implements the GridService portType of OGSI is now considered deprecated. Web services are assumed widely shared and available in the community. One of the primary benefits of service oriented architecture (SOA) is the ability to compose applications, processes, or more complex services from other less complex services. This activity is called *service composition.* Service composition is emerging as the technology of choice for building cross-enterprise applications on the Web. Given the well-defined (and well-described) interfaces, loose-coupling, and Web standard-based interaction protocols between services, a complex value-added service or process can be dynamically constructed out of available Web services as needed.

In this paper, we present a Semantic Web services based approach to Grid service composition. Service semantics is represented in OWL-S. Based on OWL-S, we characterize the composeability of Web/Grid services on which OWL-S based grid services composition is presented, and a OWL-S based Web/grid services composer is described, focusing on composition engine and OWL-S matcher.

H. Zhuge and G.C. Fox (Eds.): GCC 2005, LNCS 3795, pp. 244–249, 2005.

2 Composeability of Web Services

Composeability of Web services refers to the ability that participant services can actually work together as expected. In a sense, composeability of Web services is the extent to which two services are related in a way that they can be assembled to offer a value-added service.

In view of service composition, it is necessary to decide when one Web service *matches* what we want. It is well known that these characterization of a function or a software component cannot be determined by its signature alone. Web services composition needs to characterize the dynamic behavior, i.e., semantics, of each Web service.

There are different kinds of semantic matches. While *exact match* between services (or between service and requirements) appears the best choice, many flavors of relaxed match may also serve the purpose. In the remainder of this section, we attempt to characterize matches based on semantics. This characterization requires the semantic description of Web services in OWL-S [1]. OWL-S is a OWL-based Web service ontology, which supplies Web service providers with a core set of markup language constructs for describing the properties and capabilities of their Web services in unambiguous, computer-interpretable form. There are two aspects of behavior that can be described in OWL-S: the information transformation represented by *inputs* and *outputs* and the state change produced by the execution of the service, represented by *preconditions* and *effects*. This together is known as IOPE.

Inputs and outputs are named and typed using either OWL-S ontologies (classes or properties) or data types that XML Schema provides. OWL-S allows the specification of the set of conditions under which the outputs or the effects may result. In addition, OWL-S process ontology allows to associate conditions with outputs and effects because a service's outputs and effects are often predicated on some observable characteristic of the system.

The following characterization is based on OWL-S IOPE description of services.

Definition 1 (Inputs-Match).

$$match_{inputs}(A, B) = A_{inputs} \Leftrightarrow B_{inputs}$$

Service A is said inputs-matched with service B if and only if each input of service B has corresponding matched partner in service A's inputs.

If Service C is looking for a service B for composition, any advertised service A that is input-matched with B can be used. Because we do not have the precondition term, there is no guarantee that the preconditions of the advertised service actually holds, so we may have to provide an additional "wrapper" to establish the required precondition before we invoke the advertised service. The Guarded Inputs-Match takes into account the required preconditions.

Definition 2 (Guarded Inputs-Match).

$$match_{guarded-inputs}(A, B) = A_{inputs} \Leftrightarrow B_{inputs} \wedge A_{pre} \Rightarrow B_{pre}$$

Service A is said Guarded inputs-matched with service B if and only if each input of service B has corresponding matched partner in service A's inputs under the same or weak precondition.

Definition 3 (Outputs-Match).

$$match_{outputs}(A, B) = A_{outputs} \Leftrightarrow B_{outputs}$$

Service A is said outputs-matched with service B if and only if each output of service B has corresponding matched partner in service A's outputs.

If Service C is looking for a service B for composition, any advertised service A that is output-matched with B can be used.

Definition 4 (Guarded outputs-Match).

$$match_{guarded-outputs}(A, B) = A_{outputs} \Leftrightarrow B_{outputs} \wedge B_{effects} \Rightarrow A_{effects}$$

Service A is said Guarded outputs-matched with service B if and only if they are output matched under the same or stronger effects.

The characterization of input-match and output-match is useful and brings flexibility for service composition. For example, sometimes we are unable to find an exactly matched service, we can find a service which is the combination of input-matched service and an output-matched service.

Definition 5 (Exact-IO-Match).

$$match_{exactIO}(A, B) = match_{inputs}(A, B) \wedge match_{outputs}(A, B)$$

If two services A and B produce the same outputs when supplying the same inputs, then two service A and B have the equivalent behavior in terms of their inputs and outputs.

A more complex service can be composed of from service C, D, and B, if we are looking for a service that has inputs of service D and outputs of C. In this case, the service B is "exact IO matched" with what we are looking for.

Definition 6 (Exact IOPE Match).

$$match_{iope}(A, B) = match_{exactIO}(A, B) \wedge A_{pre} \Leftrightarrow B_{pre} \wedge A_{effect} \Leftrightarrow B_{effect}$$

Service A is said IOPE-matched with service B if and only if each aspect of IOPE of service B's description has corresponding matched partner in service A's IOPE.

IOPE matched two services (one advertised and one requested) are essentially equivalent and thus completely interchangeable. Anywhere that one service is used, it could be replaced by the other with no change in observable behavior.

Exact IOPE match or Equivalence is a strong requirement. Sometimes a weaker match is "good enough."

Definition 7 (PlugIn match).

$$match_{plugIn}(A, B) = A_{output} \subset B_{output}$$

An advertised service A subsumes a requested service B if and only if outputs of B are the subset of outputs of service A.

This match acknowledges that there is a weaker relation between tw services. In other words, the advertised service A could be plugged in place of the requested service B [4,2]. For example, a service that provides (any type of ...) "Books" could be of use for another service that expects "Computer Books".

In some cases, the plugIn relation only holds for values of the input allowed by the precondition. The guarded plug-in match adds A_{pre} as an assumption (or "guard") to exclude such cases.

Definition 8 (Guarded PlugIn match).

$$match_{GuardedplugIn}(A, B) = match_{plugIn}(A, B) \wedge A_{pre}$$

An advertised service A plug in matched with a requested service B under precondition of service A.

Definition 9 (subsume match).

$$match_{subsume}(A, B) = B_{output} \supset A_{output}$$

A service B subsumes match an advertised service A if and only if outputs of B are the superset of outputs of service A.

If a service B subsumes a service A, then the provider of service A does not completely fulfill the request for service B. The requester may use the provider to achieve its goals, but it likely needs to modify its plan or perform other requests to complete its task.

Similar to guarded plugIn match, we have the guarded subsume match.

Definition 10 (Guarded subsume match).

$$match_{Guardedsubsume}(A, B) = match_{subsume}(A, B) \wedge A_{pre}$$

A requested service B subsumes an advertised service A under precondition of service A.

In some cases, we are more concerned with the relation between the preconditions and effects of services. This is Pre/Effect matches which relate the preconditions of each service and the effects of each service.

Definition 11 (PE match).

$$match_{PE}(A, B) = B_{pre} \Leftrightarrow A_{pre} \wedge A_{effect} \Leftrightarrow B_{effect}$$

A service B is PE matched with any advertised service A if and only if both services produce the equivalent effects under equivalent preconditions.

Definition 12 (PlugIn PE match).

$$match_{PlugIn-PE}(A, B) = B_{pre} \Rightarrow A_{pre} \wedge A_{effect} \Rightarrow B_{effect}$$

A service B is PlugIn PE matched with any advertised service A whose precondition is weaker (to allow at least all of the conditions that B allows) and whose effects is stronger (to provide a guarantee at least as strong as B).

Often, we are concerned with only the effects of services; thus, a useful relaxation is to consider only the effect part of the service description. Most preconditions could be satisfied by adding an additional check before consuming the service.

Definition 13 (Effect match).

$$match_{effect}(A, B) = A_{effect} \Leftrightarrow B_{effect}$$

A service B is effect matched by any advertised service A if and only if both services present the equivalent effects.

Definition 14 (PlugIn Effect match).

$$match_{pluginеffect}(A, B) = B_{pre} \Rightarrow A_{pre} \wedge match_{effect}(A, B)$$

A service B is plugIn effect matched by any advertised service A whose precondition is weak and both services present the equivalent effects.

We have characterized the composeability of a service by defining a variety of matches. Which match is most appropriate for composition will depend on the particular situation. Clearly, the choice of match depends on the context in which the match is used: how strong of a guarantee is needed about the relation between the two services in terms of their semantic description (for OWL-S, IOPE)? While an exact match appears attractive, a various weak form of match may be found serving the purpose.

3 Semantic-Enhanced Grid Services Composition

Based on our characterization of services composeability, we present a composer of Web/Grid services which are described using Web services upper ontology OWL-S. The architecture of the composer (SWSC) is shown in Figure 1. The composer consists of the following main components: *OWL-S services repository, Composition engine:* The composition engine actually accomplishes the composition based on the requirements from service consumer in terms of service capability represented as OWL-S IOPE. *OWL-S matcher* OWL-S Matcher plays the role of matchmaking between requested service capability and advertised service capability in the repository, and the matcher relies on the OWL Inference engine to perform semantic-based matchmaking. *OWL-S API library* [3]. It is a convenient programming library for implementing OWL-S based composer.

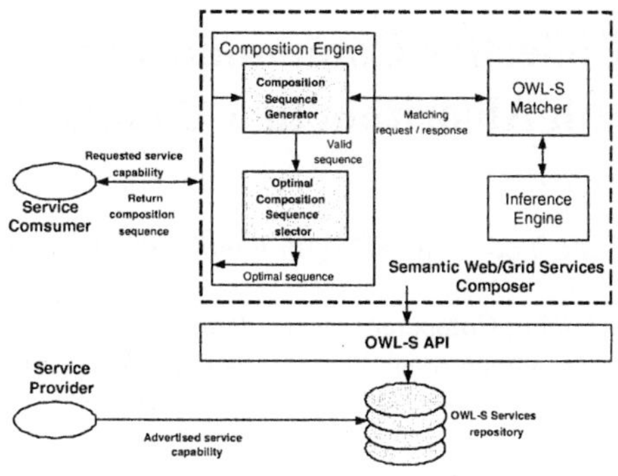

Fig. 1. Architecture for Grid services composition based on OWL-S

4 Conclusion

In this paper, we have discussed Grid services composition by leveraging Semantic Web services standards and technology, especially OWL-S. The characterization of service composeability is presented in the context of OWL-S. It is expected that this characterization facilitates more effective Grid service composition. A business process driven approach is briefly discussed to derive IOPE-based requirements of service provision. The techniques for constructing the Web/Grid service composer are described. Based on IOPE-based requirements, service composition is gradually generated with a forward or backward chaining of services.

References

1. David Martin, Mark Burstein, and Jerry Hobbs *et al.* *OWL-S: Semantic Markup for Web Services.* W3C Member Submission, 22 November 2004.
2. Massimo Paolucci, Takahiro Kawamura, Terry R. Payne, and Katia Sycara. Semantic Matching of Web Services Capabilities. In *Proceedings of the First International Semantic Web Conference, LNCS 2342*, pages 333–347. Springer-Verlag, 2002.
3. Evren Sirin. OWL-S API. The MINDSWAP Group, University of Maryland, http://www.mindswap.org/2004/owl-s/api/index.shtml, 2005.
4. Amy Moormann Zaremski and Jeannette M. Wing. Specification Matching of Software Components. *ACM Transactions on Software Engineering and Methodology (TOSEM)*, 6(4):333–369, October 1997.

An Efficient Collective Communication Method Using a Shortest Path Algorithm in a Computational Grid

Yong Hee Yeom, Seok Myun Kwon, and Jin Suk Kim*

School of Computer Science, University of Seoul,
90 Cheonnong-dong, Dongdaemun-gu, Seoul, Korea
jskim@venus.uos.ac.kr

Abstract. In a computational grid, collective communication methods are inefficient because of heterogeneous network's features on wide area network. In this paper, we propose the efficient MPI(Message Passing Interface)'s collective communication method in a computational grid on wide area network. The SPPT(Shortest-Path-based Process Tree) algorithm is our proposed algorithm that creates the dynamic-process-tree based on latency information to communicate with each process for efficient collective communication. The experiment shows that the performance of MPI broadcast operation implemented by the SPPT algorithm is higher about 50% and 15% than the Flat-Tree and the HLOT algorithms, respectively, in a grid network which has relatively high latency links.

1 Introduction

A grid computing system is constructed by existing networks and distributed computing technologies. However, a grid computing system uses heterogeneous nodes and networks which differ from previous distributed computing using homogeneous nodes and networks. Therefore, there are new problems (delay of message passing, inefficient task allocation, difficulty of reliable grid-component development, etc. caused by heterogeneous resources) that must be solved. In this paper, we solve a problem that is the delay of message passing caused by heterogeneous network's features in a computational grid. Most of message passing methods in a computational grid [8] are used to operate parallel processing for calculation. Thus many researchers use MPI(Message Passing Interface) libraries for parallel processing in grid environment.

MPI's Collective operations are constructed by collective communication methods that include several point-to-point communications. MPI applications communicate with each node concurrently by these collective communication methods. Previous MPI libraries' collective communication methods are supported by layered algorithms that consider homogeneous network's features. But these collective communication methods are inefficient in a computational grid because grid networks are heterogeneous [3, 14]. Therefore, efficient collective communication methods to increase MPI applications' performance are needed in a computational grid. In this paper, we propose an efficient collective communication method based on shortest path algorithm for MPI libraries in a computational grid.

* Corresponding author.

H. Zhuge and G.C. Fox (Eds.): GCC 2005, LNCS 3795, pp. 250–261, 2005.

This paper is organized as followed: Section 2 presents the general concepts of grid-enabled MPI libraries, MPI libraries' topology algorithms for collective communication methods, and the network information measurement. Section 3 presents the proposed algorithm and the comparison between the proposed algorithm and previous algorithms. Section 4 presents experimental results. Finally the conclusion is given in Section 5.

2 Related Works

2.1 MPI Libraries and Collective Communication Method

Favorite MPI libraries for a computational grid are MPICH-G2 [10] and MPICH-GX [1]. And MPI library for wide are network is MagPIe [3].

MPICH-G2 is the MPI library which extends MPICH to grid-enabled MPICH. MPICH-G2 supports topology-aware collective operations for heterogeneous networks. Topology-aware strategy is the layered communication methods based on performance asserting wide are network, local area network, intra-machine TCP, and vendor-supplied MPI. They are distinguished by user's specific RSL(Resource Specification Language) description, and then multi-level topology is constructed.

MPICH-GX is the MPI library that extends MPICH-G2 to grid-enabled MPI with higher performance than MPICH-G2. MPICH-GX supports private IP and efficient collective operations. In MPICH-G2, processes communicate with each others based on IP addresses. MPICH-G2 cannot support private IP clusters by the nature. However, MPICH-GX supports private IP to handle the NAT(Network Address Translation) service. Back-end(slave) nodes in different clusters directly communicate with each others. And MPICH-GX has efficient collective operations for a grid network when if the high latency occurs between the root and the other nodes.

MagPIe is the MPI library that extends MPICH-G2 for wide area network. MagPIe supports the minimum message transmission. For the minimum message transmission, MagPIe has a coordinate nodes within each cluster. Coordinate nodes avoid the overlapped message transmission. And MagPIe has the ability to minimize the overhead of message transmission.

Basically, MPI libraries have collective operations that are broadcast, gather, scatter, reduce [9]. For improving the performance of collective operations on wide area network, efficient collective communication methods are needed. Previous related studies [1, 3, 10] show that performance can be achieved by following two approaches: Firstly, constructing multi-level topology with topology-aware methods. Secondly, constructing process tree within each level. Figure 1 shows multi-level topology and process-tree algorithms within each level.

Multi-level topology divides networks, which processes communicate with each others directly, into several levels. A process which communicates with other processes in same level sends or receives messages efficiently. Figure 1-(a) shows that MagPIe has two levels; WAN and LAN. Figure 1-(b) shows that MPICH-G2 has four levels; WAN, LAN, intraTCP, and vendorMPI. Figure 1-(c) shows that MPICH-GX has five levels including GSN(Grid Scale Network) level.

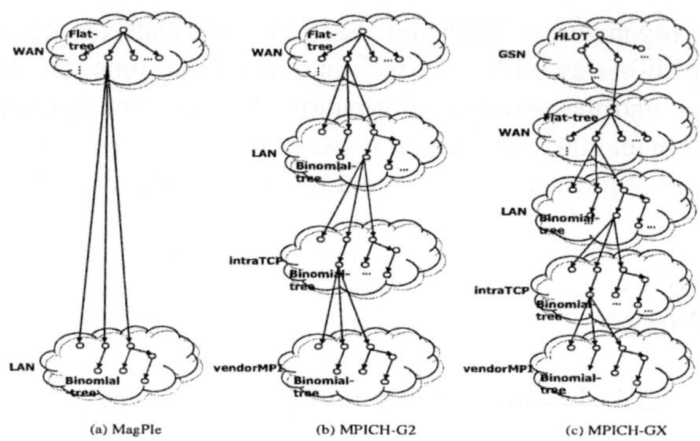

Fig 1. Multi-level topology and process trees in each MPI library

Above all of grid-enabled MPI libraries have multi-level topology approach to construct tree of processes. In each level, a specific tree should be constructed to efficiently communicate with each process. Therefore a process tree in each level is well constructed by considering network's features. The network's parameters of constructing a process tree are link's bandwidth, hop, latency, etc.

Figure 1-(a) shows that MagPIe's process trees are Flat-Tree in WAN level and Binomial-Tree in LAN level. MagPIe constructs a process tree in WAN level to avoid high latency links and overlapped message transmission. Figure 1-(b) shows that MPICH-G2's process trees are Flat-Tree in WAN level, Binomial-Tree in LAN, intraTCP, and vendorMPI levels. Basically MPICH-G2 does not use the network's features for constructing multi-level topology. Figure 1-(c) shows that MPICH-GX's process trees are HLOT(Hierarchical Latency Optimal Tree) in GSN level, Flat-Tree in WAN level, and Binomial-Tree in other levels. GSN level is the level for existing high latency links in wide area network. The HLOT is dynamically constructed from latency information to avoid message transmission through high latency links.

As a grid network is wide area network, previous related studies [1, 2, 3, 5] imply following characteristics to design efficient collective communication methods.

1. The network information is dynamically and radically changed in a grid network.
2. The most considerable parameter is latency in a grid network.
3. Links are bidirectional among grid nodes.

The first characteristic is common state due to the nature of distributed computing resources, especially heterogeneous networks. Because a grid network is composed of heterogeneous networks, there is frequent network traffic more than homogeneous network. The second characteristic is that the latency affects the total communication time when transferring a message from one process to another in a grid network. When LogP model [4], that o_s(sending overhead), o_r(receiving overhead), g(gap), and l(latency) are considered, applies a grid network, o_s, o_r, and g are ignorable due to the nature of wide area network. Therefore l is the most considerable parameter in a grid network. The third characteristic is that the latency is not two-way delay but one-way delay. In a grid network, a difference between uplink and downlink delays is larger than homogeneous network due to the ADSL, satellite, routing policy, etc.

Figure 2 shows a grid network and the network information. Figure 2-(a) shows that a grid network is constructed by a set of nodes into the single virtual organization. Figure 2-(b) shows that the network information is latencies among them in Figure 2-(a).

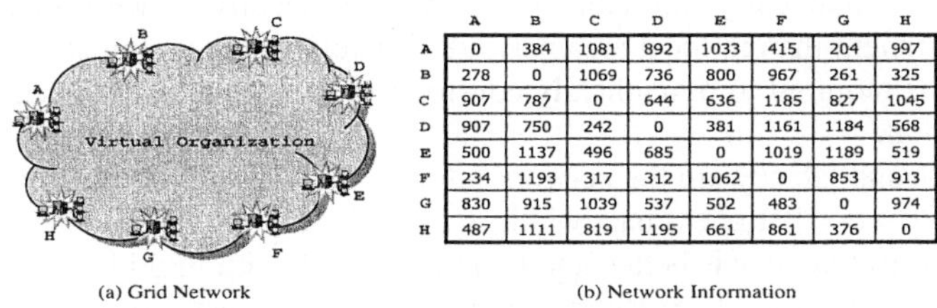

	A	B	C	D	E	F	G	H
A	0	384	1081	892	1033	415	204	997
B	278	0	1069	736	800	967	261	325
C	907	787	0	644	636	1185	827	1045
D	907	750	242	0	381	1161	1184	568
E	500	1137	496	685	0	1019	1189	519
F	234	1193	317	312	1062	0	853	913
G	830	915	1039	537	502	483	0	974
H	487	1111	819	1195	661	861	376	0

(a) Grid Network (b) Network Information

Fig. 2. Grid network and the network information in terms of latencies

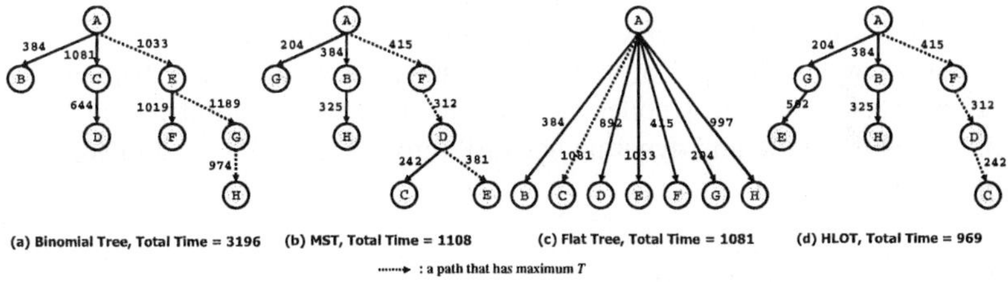

(a) Binomial Tree, Total Time = 3196
(b) MST, Total Time = 1108
(c) Flat Tree, Total Time = 1081
(d) HLOT, Total Time = 969
: a path that has maximum T

Fig. 3. Process trees in each algorithm when broadcasting a message

Process trees from each algorithm are static or dynamic shapes. Flat-Tree and Binomial-Tree are static shapes. MST(Minimum Spanning Tree) and HLOT are dynamic shapes. Therefore MST and HLOT need the network information to construct process trees.

Figure 3 shows process trees and the total completion time (*T*) to broadcast a message about each algorithm for Figure 2-(b). *T* is the maximum sum of weights of links over path. The Binomial Tree algorithm minimizes o_s and o_r in local area network. Therefore the Binomial Tree algorithm is good performance in local area network. But it does not fit in wide area network because o_s and o_r are ignorable in wide area network. The MST in Figure 3-(b) shows that it minimizes total costs of all links. But, one path may be a long way and links are unidirectional. The Flat-Tree algorithm in Figure 3-(c) shows that it maximizes the overlapping of communication when used non-blocking model. In previous related studies [2, 3, 6, 7], the Flat-Tree algorithm was regarded as an optimal algorithm in wide area network. The HLOT algorithm in Figure 3-(d) shows that it has both advantages of maximizing the parallelism of the Flat-Tree algorithm and minimizing communication cost of the MST algorithm. The HLOT algorithm performs in wide area network which has high latency links to avoid them. Therefore it has better performance than the Flat-Tree algorithm in wide area network which has high latency links.

2.2 Measurement of the Network Information

Previous process trees for collective communication are static shapes which are constructed by static network topology. Therefore process trees in each level of multilevel topology are all the same. But static process trees are inefficient because network status is dynamically and radically changed. Especially, in wide area network, it is better inefficient than in local area network. Therefore measurement of the network information is required to dynamically construct process trees for efficient collective communication.

Bandwidth and latency are the network information that is dynamically changed. In previous MPI related studies, bandwidth is used for the QoS(Quality-of-Service) of MPI libraries. But latency is better important than bandwidth in grid network [3].

In a grid system, the MDS(Metacomputing Directory Service) supports the information of resources. But the MDS does not support the dynamic network information. Many researchers are going to discuss the measurement of the network information in a grid network [13].

The next best way to measurement the network information in a grid network is using assistant systems. The NWS(Network Weather Service) is a distributed system that has agents in each grid nodes to measure the network information [11]. The NWS measures the static and dynamic network information. It is used to support QoS in a grid system.

3 The Proposed Algorithm

In this paper, we use the Dijkstra's shortest path algorithm [15] to construct process trees for efficient collective communication. Figure 4 shows the pseudo-code of our proposed SPPT(Shortest-Path-based Process Tree) algorithm. The first stage in Figure 4 selects edges about all nodes using the Dijkstra's shortest path algorithm. But shortest path tree does not have communication sequence. Also it is not necessary to have selected all edges in each node. The second stage in Figure 4 selects necessary edges from shortest path tree. And the last stage in Figure 4 sorts selected edges by maximum path.

```
Algorithm : SPPT (Shortest-Path-based Process Tree)

  Input :
    W[][] : 2-d latency matrix
    NID : my_node(process) ID

  Output :
    SPPT_NID : a list of selected edges in each node
-----------------------------------------------------------------
    SPPT_NID = ()
I.  SPT = A set of edges from Shortest Path Tree (W[][])
II. if (NID != root) {
      1) SPPT_NID = SPPT_NID + e
         (e : a edge in SPT, that a node can send a message to my node)
    }
    2) SPPT_NID = SPPT_NID + E
       (E : a subset of edges in SPT, that my node can send a message
            to others)
III. sort edges in SPPT_NID by the accumulated weights of edges from my_node
     to leaf nodes via my_node
```

Fig. 4. Pseudo-code of the SPPT algorithm

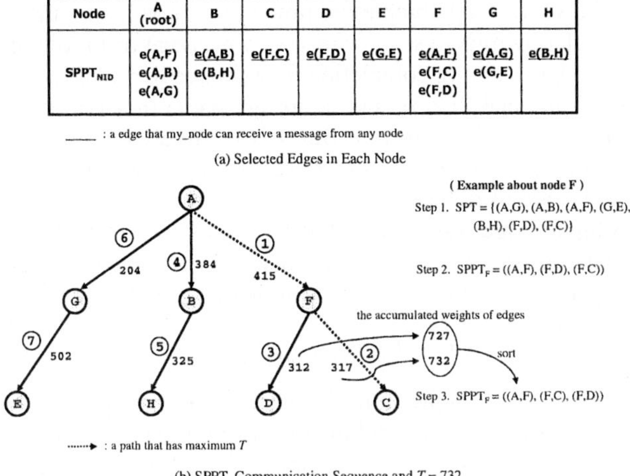

Node	A (root)	B	C	D	E	F	G	H
$SPPT_{NID}$	e(A,F) e(A,B) e(A,G)	e(A,B) e(B,H)	e(F,C)	e(F,D)	e(G,E)	e(A,F) e(F,C) e(F,D)	e(A,G) e(G,E)	e(B,H)

Fig. 5. Broadcasting a message by the SPPT algorithm with the network information in Fig. 2

Figure 5 shows selected edges in each node, SPPT, communication sequence, and *T* about broadcasting a message. Figure 5-(a) shows that root node(A) only sends a message, but other nodes firstly receive a message from their adjacent parent node, then secondly send messages to their adjacent child nodes. Figure 5-(a) also shows that each node does not have all edges. Figure 5-(b) shows that the SPPT is a shortest path tree. And communication sequence is that nodes send or receive a message from a path with maximum *T* to next maximum path. Therefore the SPPT algorithm has both advantages of the parallelism of message transmission and minimizing communication cost *T*. It is enabled that collective communication by the SPPT algorithm is efficient in a grid network which has high latency links.

For example, if the SPPT algorithm is applied to node F, the SPT in first step is {(A,G), (A,B), (A,F), (G,E), (B,H), (F,D), (F,C)}. The $SPPT_F$ in second step is ((A,F), (F,D), (F,C)). To broadcast a message with maximum path, the third step sorts the $SPPT_F$ by the accumulated weights of edges from node F to leaf nodes via node F. Therefore the $SPPT_F$ is ((A,F), (F,C), (F,D)).

In order that the SPPT algorithm has smaller *T* than other algorithms, we will apply the SPPT algorithm to LogP model. Equation (1) and (2) show equations when broadcasting a message [14].

$$T = \sum_{i=0}^{n-1} Max\ T_{pi}, \quad where \quad n = number \ of \ processes \tag{1}$$

$$T_{pi} = \begin{cases} 0 & , \ if \ i = 0 \\ T_{pj} + (c-1)(t_{so} + t_g) + l_{ji} + t_{ro} & , \ otherwise \end{cases} \tag{2}$$

j : parent's index of the i-th process
T_{pj}: delivery time from the root process to j
c : number of child nodes of j
t_{so}: time of sending overhead
t_g: time of sending gap
t_{ro}: time of receiving overhead
l_{ji}: directed latency from j to i

Equation (1) shows the total completion time (T) to broadcast a message. Equation (2) shows the completion time to send or receive a message from root process to process i. In Equation (1), the sum of completion times is due to the blocking model.

As we described in Section 2, o_s and o_r are ignorable in a grid network. Thus, t_{so} and t_{ro} in Equation (2) can be removed. But g is relatively considerable. If the message size is increased, g is increased too. However, in grid-enabled MPI applications, collective operations are used to send or receive sub-results for calculation. In a grid system, other techniques are used to transfer huge data; FTP or NFS. Therefore g can be fixed as a relatively small constant, and then t_g in Equation (2) can be removed. Consequently, Equation (3) shows the total completion time in a grid network.

$$T = Max\,(L_j + l_{ji}) \tag{3}$$

Equation (3) shows that L_j is the sum of latencies from root process to process i via other processes. When applying algorithms to Equation (3) except the Binomial Tree algorithm in Figure 3, the Flat-Tree algorithm is $T = Max(l_{0i})$ because all processes directly communicate with each others. The MST and the HLOT algorithms are same to Equation (3). The MST algorithm selects process i to minimize l_{ji}. The HLOT algorithm selects process i to minimize l_{ji} and satisfy the condition, $(L_j + l_{ji}) < l_{0i}$. Thus, the HLOT algorithm's T is smaller than or equal to the Flat-Tree algorithm's T. But, the condition, $(L_j + l_{ji}) < l_{0i}$, has a disadvantage. It only compares $(L_j + l_{ji})$ with l_{0i}, in spite that it may be exist smaller path than l_{0i}. Therefore the HLOT algorithm's T may be larger than the MST algorithm's T. In our proposed SPPT algorithm, it always guarantees that L_j is minimum sum of latencies and its path is optimal. Thus, Li also minimum sum of latencies and its path is optimal when selecting a shortest path from process j to process i directly. But the MST and the HLOT algorithms do not always construct optimal trees that its T are smaller than or equal to the Flat-Tree, the MST, and the HLOT algorithms.

In terms of algorithms' time complexity, the Flat-Tree algorithm shows $O(n)$. The MST algorithm (Prim's algorithm) [16] shows $O(n^2 log(n))$. The HLOT algorithm shows more than $O(n^2 log(n))$ due to the greedy approach. But the SPPT algorithm shows $O(n^2 + nlog(n)) = O(n^2)$.

The SPPT algorithm also has other functions for implementing a collective communication of MPI broadcast operation. It is also an efficient method for improving the performance of MPI broadcast operation.

4 Simulation and Experimental Result

We divide it into two parts to evaluate the performance of the SPPT algorithm for MPI broadcast operation. Firstly, we analyze previous algorithms including the SPPT in simulation. Secondly, we examine MPI broadcast operation implemented by algorithms including the SPPT.

4.1 Simulation for Algorithms

To evaluate the performance of algorithms in terms of T, we use our simulator implemented by C language. Firstly, simulator generates the network information in terms of latencies among grid nodes. Secondly, simulator creates process trees about each algorithm. Lastly, simulator calculates T about each algorithm.

Figure 6 shows three cases of the network information in a grid network. Figure 6-(a) is the "Completely Symmetric Case" that latencies between uplink and downlink are same. Figure 6-(b) is the "Approximately Symmetric Case" that latencies between uplink and downlink are approximately same. Figure 6-(c) is the "Asymmetric Case" that latencies between uplink and downlink are not same. In our simulator, these three cases are generated.

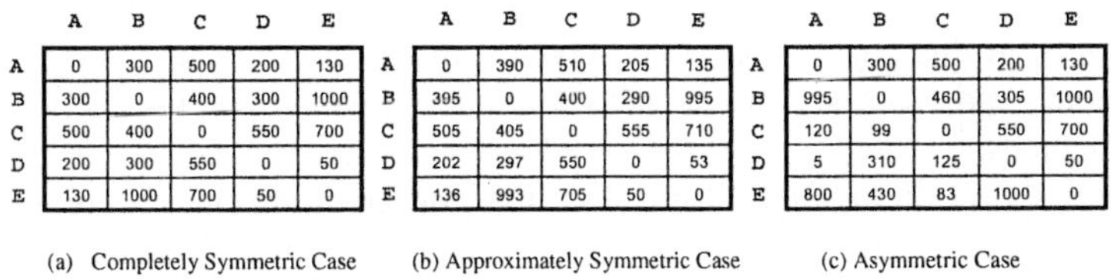

	A	B	C	D	E
A	0	300	500	200	130
B	300	0	400	300	1000
C	500	400	0	550	700
D	200	300	550	0	50
E	130	1000	700	50	0

(a) Completely Symmetric Case

	A	B	C	D	E
A	0	390	510	205	135
B	395	0	400	290	995
C	505	405	0	555	710
D	202	297	550	0	53
E	136	993	705	50	0

(b) Approximately Symmetric Case

	A	B	C	D	E
A	0	300	500	200	130
B	995	0	460	305	1000
C	120	99	0	550	700
D	5	310	125	0	50
E	800	430	83	1000	0

(c) Asymmetric Case

Fig. 6. Three cases of the network information

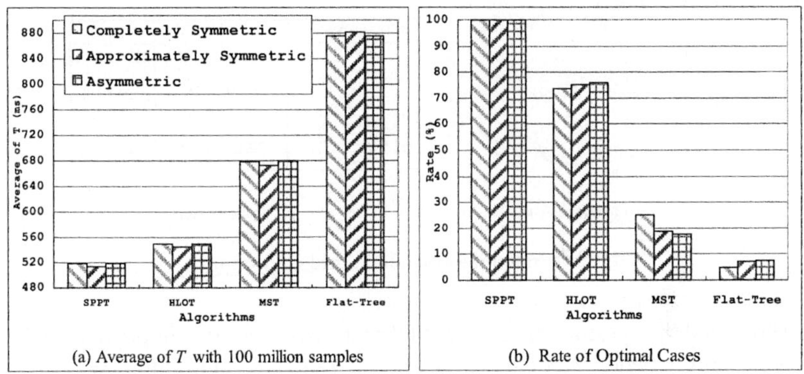

(a) Average of T with 100 million samples

(b) Rate of Optimal Cases

Fig. 7. The performance of algorithms in terms of the average of T

We assume that latencies are randomly generated between 1ms and 1000ms. In wide area network, latencies are at least ten times larger than latencies in local area network. With a hundred million samples of the network information, we calculate the average of T about each algorithm. Figure 7 shows the performance of algorithms in terms of the average of T. Figure 7-(a) shows that the performance of the SPPT algorithm is better than HLOT, MST, and Flat-Tree algorithms by about 5.6%, 23.6%, and 37.3%, respectively. These results are because SPPT algorithm is always optimal. Figure 7-(b) shows the rate of creating optimal process trees in a hundred million samples. The SPPT algorithm always creates optimal process trees by 100%. But HLOT, MST, and Flat-Tree algorithms create optimal process trees by about 74.7%, 24.1%, and 6.6%.

4.2 Performance Evaluation for MPI Broadcast Operations in Testbed

To evaluate the performance of MPI broadcast operations in a real grid environment, we use the Globus Toolkit and MPICH-GX. MPICH-GX already has the Flat-Tree and the HLOT algorithms in GSN level and WAN level, respectively. And MPICH-GX operates the Flat-Tree algorithm when the network information is not supported in GSN level. Thus, we implement MPI broadcast operation by the SPPT algorithm in GSN level.

In MPICH-GX, NWS is used to collect the network information. But, when high latencies exist in a network, NWS's agents are fault to communicate with each others. Thus, in this paper, file-based network information replaces NWS's network information. And, to test various network environments, we use network traffic control methods.

Figure 8 shows the testbed information in a grid environment. Figure 8-(a) shows that the testbed has 8 grid nodes which are front-end nodes in each cluster. It is because we do not test algorithms in LAN, intraTCP, and vendorMPI levels. Figure 8-(b) shows the information of each node.

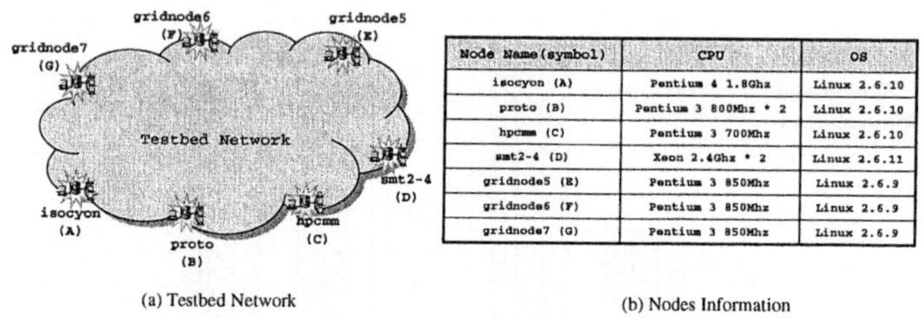

Node Name(symbol)	CPU	OS
isocyon (A)	Pentium 4 1.8Ghz	Linux 2.6.10
proto (B)	Pentium 3 800Mhz * 2	Linux 2.6.10
hpcmm (C)	Pentium 3 700Mhz	Linux 2.6.10
smt2-4 (D)	Xeon 2.4Ghz * 2	Linux 2.6.11
gridnode5 (E)	Pentium 3 850Mhz	Linux 2.6.9
gridnode6 (F)	Pentium 3 850Mhz	Linux 2.6.9
gridnode7 (G)	Pentium 3 850Mhz	Linux 2.6.9

(a) Testbed Network (b) Nodes Information

Fig. 8. Testbed information in grid environment

To show that the performance of MPI broadcast operation implemented by the SPPT algorithm is better than the HLOT and the Flat-Tree algorithms, we firstly test in a specific network sample. A specific network sample is generated by network traffic control method. And then we operate the OL_i test [12]. The OL_i test is the method to evaluate the performance of MPI broadcast operation in a computational grid. The result of the OL_i test is the maximum time that takes to complete a communication with each other.

Example 1: We assume that latencies are randomly generated between 5ms and 100ms. Firstly, we select a specific network sample in case that the algorithmic performance of the SPPT algorithm is better than others. Figure 9 shows a specific network sample and processes trees created by each algorithm. Figure 9-(a) shows that the network information is "Completely Symmetric Case" and some latencies are too larger than others. In Figure 9-(a), there are some latencies because randomly generated latencies are bidirectional. Figure 9-(b), (c), and (d) shows that the algorithmic performance of the SPPT algorithms is better than others.

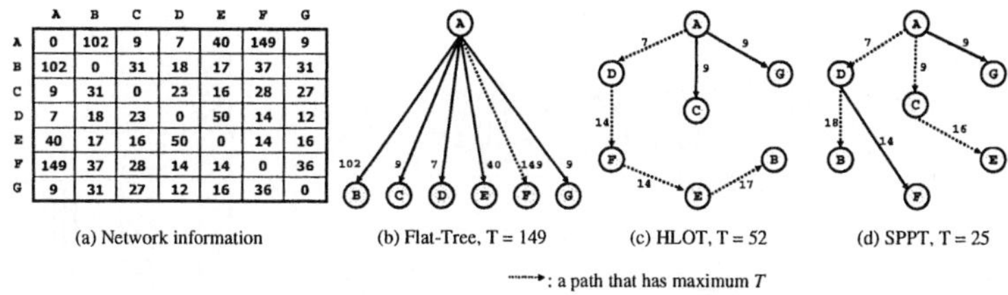

	A	B	C	D	E	F	G
A	0	102	9	7	40	149	9
B	102	0	31	18	17	37	31
C	9	31	0	23	16	28	27
D	7	18	23	0	50	14	12
E	40	17	16	50	0	14	16
F	149	37	28	14	14	0	36
G	9	31	27	12	16	36	0

Fig. 9. A specific network sample and process trees

Secondly, we control the network traffic with a specific network sample. Lastly, we operate the OL_i test to each MPI broadcast operation. Figure 10 shows the result of the OL_i test, repeately until 150 times, in case that the message size is 2 bytes. Figure 10-(a) shows that the performance of MPI broadcast operation by the SPPT algorithm is reliable and valid. Figure 10-(b) shows the performance of MPI broadcast operation by the SPPT algorithm is better than the Flat-Tree and the HLOT algorithms by about 72.3% and 37.8%, respectively. Figure 10-(c) shows the result of the OL_i test by increasing the message size. In Figure 10-(a), as increasing the message size, the performances of MPI broadcast operation by the SPPT algorithm are reliable and good.

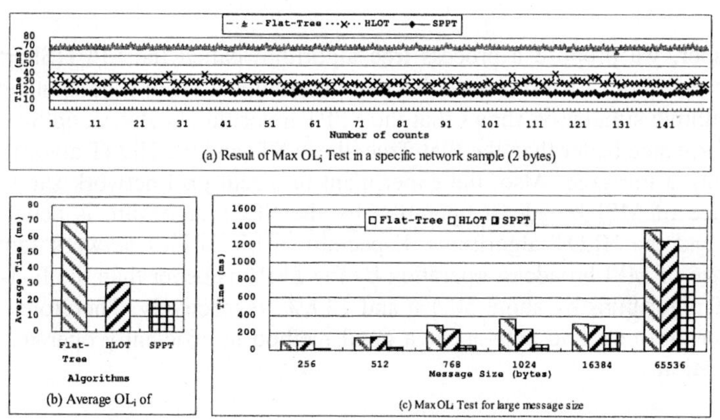

Fig. 10. The result of OL_i test with a specific network sample, message size = 2 bytes

In Example 1, MPI broadcast operation by the SPPT algorithm is better performance than others. But this is the specific case that process trees by the Flat-Tree and the HLOT algorithms are not optimal. Thus, we have to test in various network samples generally.

Figure 11 shows the performance of algorithms in various network samples. The number of samples is 150 and all samples are completely different cases. The message size is 2 bytes. Figure 11-(a) shows that performances of MPI broadcast operations by the SPPT and the HLOT algorithms are better than the Flat-Tree algorithm, and the performance of MPI broadcasting operation by the SPPT algorithm is

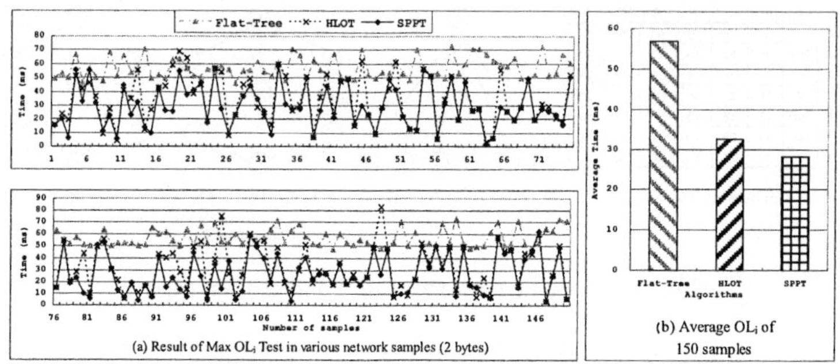

Fig. 11. The result of OL_i test with various network samples

nearly equal to the HLOT algorithm. Figure 11-(b) shows the average time of 150 samples. In Figure 11-(b), the performance of MPI broadcast operation by the SPPT algorithm is better than the Flat-Tree and the HLOT algorithms by about 50.4% and 13.8%, respectively.

5 Conclusion

In this paper, we propose a process tree algorithm called the SPPT(Shortest-Path-based Process Tree) for efficient collective communication in a computational grid. The algorithmic simulation shows that the SPPT algorithm is always optimal, and has good performance better than the Flat-Tree, the MST, and the HLOT algorithms when broadcasting a message. Also, the experiment in a real grid network shows that the performance of MPI broadcast operation by the SPPT algorithm is better than the Flat-Tree and the HLOT algorithms. Especially, with various network samples, the performance of MPI broadcast operation by the SPPT is better than the Flat-Tree and the HLOT algorithms by about 50.4% and 13.8%, respectively. Therefore, using the SPPT algorithm in a grid network is a good method to efficiently operate collective communication.

Acknowledgement

The author would like to thank K. L. Park at the Yonsei University for his comments.

References

1. K. L. Park, H. J. Lee, O. Y. Kwon, S. W. Park, and S. D. Kim: Design and Implementation of a Dynamic Communication MPI Library for the Grid, International Journal of Computers and Applications, vol. 26, no. 3, pp. 165-172, 2004.
2. M. Bernaschi and G. Iannello: Collective Communication Operations: Experimental Results vs. Theory, Concurrency: Practice and Experience, vol 10, no. 3, pp. 359-386, 1998.

3. T. Kielmann, R. F. H. Hofman, H. E. Bal, A. Plaat, and R. A. F. Bhoedjang: MagPIe: MPI's Collective Communication Operations for Clustered Wide Area Systems, Proc. of Symposium on Principles and Practice of Parallel Programming, pp. 131-140, 1999.
4. D. Culler, R. Karp, D. Patterson, A. Sahay, K. E. Schauers, E. Santos, R. Subramonian, and T. Von Eicken: LogP: Towards a Realistic Model of Parallel Computation, Proc. of Symposium on Principles and Practice of Parallel Programming, pp. 1-13, 1993.
5. A. Alexandrov, M. F. Lonescu, K. E. Schauser, and C. Scheiman: LogGP: Incorporating Long Messages into the LogP Model – One Step Closer Towards a Realistic Model for Parallel Computation, Proc. of Symposium on Parallel Algorithms and Architectures, pp. 95-105, 1995.
6. I. Foster and N. Karonis: A grid-enabled MPI: Messaging Passing in Heterogeneous Distributed Computing Systems, Proc. of Supercomputing, pp. 46, 1998.
7. N. Karonis, B. de Supinski, I. Foster, W. Gropp, E. Lusk, and J. Bresnahan: Exploiting Hierarchy in Parallel Computer Networks to Optimize Collective Operation Performance, Proc. of the International Parallel and Distributed Processing Symposium, pp. 377-386, 2000.
8. I. Foster and C. Kesselman: Globus: A Metacomputing Infrastructure Toolkit, International Journal of Supercomputer Applications, vol. 11, no. 2, pp. 115-128, 1997.
9. Message Passing Interface Forum: MPI: A Message-Passing Interface Standard, International Journal of Supercomputer Applications, vol. 8, no 3/4, pp. 165-414, 1994.
10. N. Karonis, B. Toonen, and I. Foster: MPICH-G2: A Grid-Enabled Implementation of the Message Passing Interface, Journal of Parallel and Distributed Computing, vol. 63, no. 5, pp. 551-563, 2003.
11. R. Wolski, N. Spring, and J. Hayes: The Network Weather Service: A Distributed Resource Performance Forecasting Service for Metacomputing, Journal of Future Generation Computting Systems, vol. 15, no. 5-6, pp. 757-768, 1999.
12. B. de Supinski and N. Karonis: Accurately Measuring MPI Broadcasts in a Computational Grid, Proc. of 8th IEEE Symp. on HPDC-8, pp. 29-37, 1999.
13. B. Lowekamp, B. Tierney, L. Cottrell, R. Hughes-Jones, T. Kielmann, and M. Swany: A Hierarchy of Network Performance Characteristics for Grid Applications and Services, GWD-C Internal Draft, Network Measurements Working Group, Global Grid Forum, 2003.
14. K. L. Park, H. J. Lee, Y. J. Lee, O. Y. Kwon, S. Y. Park, H. W. Park, and S. D. Kim: An Efficient Collective Communication Method for Grid Scale Networks, International Conference on Computational Science, LNCS, vol. 2660, pp. 819-828, 2003.
15. E. Dijkstra: A Note on Two Problems in Connection with Graphs, Numerische Mathematik, vol. 1, pp. 269-271, 1959.
16. R. C. Prim: Shortest Connection Networks and Some Generalizations, Bell System Technical Journal, vol. 36, pp. 1389-1401, 1957.

MAG: A Mobile Agent Based Computational Grid Platform

Rafael Fernandes Lopes, Francisco José da Silva e Silva, and Bysmarck Barros de Sousa

Departamento de Informática, Universidade Federal do Maranhão,
Av. dos Portugueses, s/n, Campus do Bacanga, CCET,
CEP 65085-580, São Luís - MA, Brazil
{rafaelf, fssilva}@deinf.ufma.br, bysmarck@gmail.com

Abstract. In recent years, Grid computing has emerged as a promising alternative to the integration and sharing of multi-institutional resources. However, constructing a Grid middleware is a complex task. Developers must address several design and implementation challenges, such as: efficient management and allocation of distributed resources, dynamic task scheduling, high scalability and heterogeneity, fault tolerance, efficient mechanisms for collaborative communication among Grid nodes, and security issues.

MAG (Mobile Agents for Grid Computing Environments) explores the agents paradigm as a way to overcome several of these challenges. MAG middleware executes Grid applications by dynamically loading the application code into a mobile agent. The MAG agent can be dynamically reallocated to Grid nodes though a transparent migration mechanism, as a way to provide load balancing and support for non-dedicated nodes. MAG middleware also includes mechanisms for providing fault tolerance and support for mobile clients. This paper describes MAG architecture, implementation and performance issues.

1 Introduction

Grid computing allows the integration and sharing of computers and computing resources, such as software, data and peripherals, in corporate networks and among these networks, stimulating cooperation among users and organizations, creating dynamic and multi-institutional environments, providing and using the resources in order to improve common or individual goals [6]. Through the Grid infrastructure it is possible to execute a large number of applications, such as: distributed super-computing applications (e.g. simulation of complex physical processes like climatic modeling), high throughput (e.g. cryptographic problems resolution), on demand applications (e.g. medical instrumentation applications and requests for software use), data intensive applications (e.g. weather forecast systems) and collaborative applications (e.g. collaborative and educational projects).

H. Zhuge and G.C. Fox (Eds.): GCC 2005, LNCS 3795, pp. 262–273, 2005.

However, constructing a Grid middleware is a complex task. Developers must address several design and implementation challenges, such as: efficient management and allocation of distributed resources; dynamic task scheduling according to distributed resources availability. Task allocation should not be static, since it must consider the dynamic nature of Grid environments. This requires transparent code mobility, as a way to promote load balancing and support for non-dedicated Grid nodes; the task scheduler may take into consideration the historic use of Grid nodes, as a way to preview resource availability, improving task allocation and minimizing the cost of application reallocations; the existence of fault tolerance mechanisms, since that Grid nodes, in general, are not dedicated to the execution of Grid applications, and do not comprise a controlled environment; support for high scalability and great heterogeneity of software and hardware components; efficient mechanisms for collaborative communication among Grid nodes; protection and security mechanisms must be available to provide secure communication channels between the middleware components, authenticate the application code downloaded to Grid nodes, and access control mechanisms for accessing distributed resources.

The mobile agents paradigm exhibits great adequacy for the development of a Grid infrastructure because of some intrinsic characteristics, such as:

1. *Cooperation*: agents have the ability to interact and cooperate with other agents; this can be explored for the development of complex communication mechanisms among Grid nodes;
2. *Autonomy*: agents are autonomous entities, meaning that their execution goes on without any or with little intervention by the clients that started them. This is an adequate model for submission and execution of Grid applications;
3. *Heterogeneity*: several mobile agent platforms can be executed in heterogeneous environments, an important characteristic for better use of computational resources among multi-institutional environments;
4. *Reactivity*: agents can react to external events, such as variations on resources availability;
5. *Mobility*: mobile agents can migrate from one node to another, moving part of the computation being executed and providing load balancing among Grid nodes;
6. *Protection and Security*: several agent platforms offer protection and security mechanisms, such as authentication, cryptography and access control.

The MAG project (*Mobile Agents Technology for Grid Computing Environments*), currently being developed at the Computer Science Department of the Federal University of Maranhão (DEINF/UFMA), main goal is the development of a free software infrastructure based on mobile agents technology that allows the resolution of computationally intensive problems in computational Grids.

This paper describes MAG architecture, implementation and some performance issues. It is organized in the following sections: Section 2 describes MAG architecture and its application execution mechanism. Section 3 presents the support for fault tolerance and transparent migration, while Section 4 describes the architecture for supporting Grid clients using mobile devices. Section 5 shows some performance analysis and on Section 7 we drove conclusions obtained from the work performed and describe its next steps.

2 MAG Architecture

The MAG project uses the Integrade Grid middleware as the foundation for its implementation, adding a new application execution mechanism based on mobile agents, as well as a set of new services.

Integrade[8] is a Grid middleware being developed by the Mathematics and Statistics Institute at the University of São Paulo (IME/USP), the Federal University of Mato Grosso do Sul (UFMS) and by the Pontifícia Universidade Católica of Rio de Janeiro (PUC/RIO). Integrade is structured in clusters organized in a hierarchical way. A cluster is defined as an autonomous unit inside the Grid, since it has all the components necessary for it to work independently. The components of the Integrade architecture are [8]: Application Submission and Control Tool (ASCT), a graphical user interface that allows users, to submit applications to be executed on the Grid; Application Repository (AR) stores the applications to be executed on the Grid; Local Resource Manager (LRM) is a component that runs in each cluster node, collecting information about the state of resources such as memory, CPU, disk and network usage. It is also responsible for instantiating applications scheduled to the node; Global Resource Manager (GRM) manages the cluster resources by receiving notifications of resources usage from the LRMs, and runs the scheduler that allocates tasks to nodes based on resources availability. Integrade adopts the BSP model for execution of parallel computations, using the BSPLib library from the Oxford University as reference.

MAG architecture was designed to be a natural extension of the Integrade middleware, allowing the execution of native applications as well as applications written in Java. Native applications are executed directly above Integrade. Among them, there are parallel applications that follows the BSP model. Java applications are executed above the MAG layer, through the mobile agents paradigm. Figure 1 shows the layers that comprise the MAG architecture.

The MAG layer supplies an application execution mechanism through mobile agents and adds new services to the Integrade platform, such as the use of mobile computing devices as Grid clients, fault tolerance, and migration of application executions among Grid nodes.

The JADE layer (Java Agent Development Framework) is a framework used for building multi agent systems. It is compliant to FIPA[1] specification.

The upper layers use the CORBA distributed objects technology, using many services provided by this middleware such as the trading service. At last, the operating system layer may be variable, since MAG is platform independent.

[1] *Foundation for Intelligent Physical Agents* - non-profit organization aimed at producing standards for the interoperation of heterogeneous software agents. Available in: *http://www.fipa.org/*

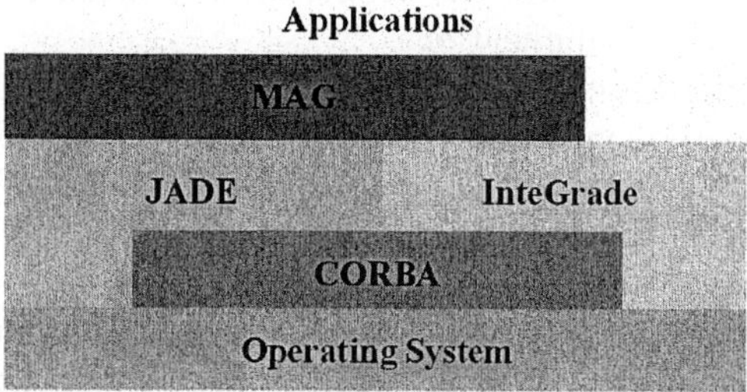

Fig. 1. Layers architecture of the MAG grid middleware

2.1 MAG Application Execution

To provide the execution of Java applications through mobile agents paradigm, MAG incorporates two new components to the original Integrade architecture: `MagAgent` and `AgentHandler`.

`MagAgent` is a mobile agent responsible for executing applications in the Grid. For each application execution, a `MagAgent` is created. It downloads the application bytecode from the application repository and dynamically instantiates it using the reflection mechanisms provided by the Java platform. An `AgentHandler` runs in every Grid node that can execute MAG applications. It maintains the container of agents executing in the node and is also responsible for creating an `MagAgent` in response to an application execution request. It interacts with Integrade components, making the agent paradigm transparent to the Integrade

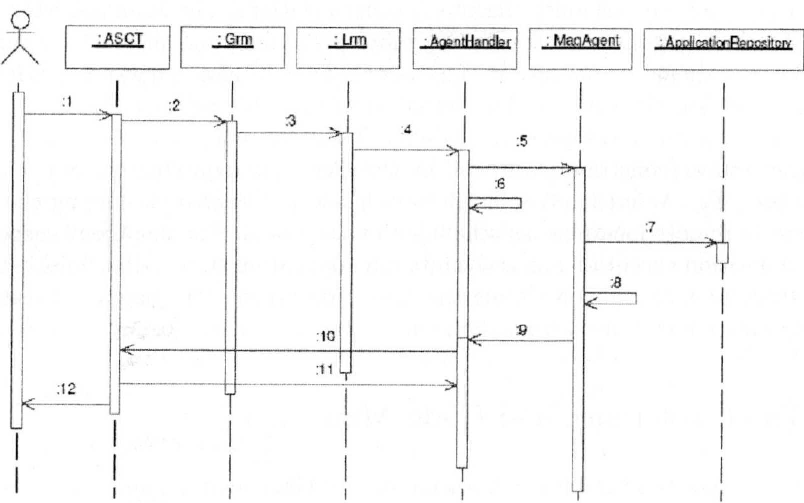

Fig. 2. Sequence diagram "execution of applications in the grid"

middleware. Figure 2 illustrates the cooperation between Integrade and MAG components for executing applications.

An user requests the execution of an application (1) through the ASCT interface. The application must have been previously registered in the application repository. The ASCT forwards the request to the GRM (2), which executes its scheduling algorithm in order to select an available node. The GRM then forwards the request to the selected LRM (3).

If the application to be executed is native, the LRM executes the application without any MAG intervention. However, if it is a Java application, the request is forwarded to the local `AgentHandler` (4). The `AgentHandler` creates a new `MagAgent` (5) and stores its reference (6) for future communications. During the creation process, the `AgentHandler` passes to the `MagAgent` the identification of the application to be executed, as well as the input data and parameters.

The `MagAgent` uses this identification to request the application bytecode from the repository (7), saving it in the local filesystem. It then dynamically instantiates the application bytecode and starts its execution in an independent thread (8).

The `MagAgent` notifies the local `AgentHandler` whenever the application finishes its execution (9). The notification is forwarded to the ASCT that originated the request (10), which collects the execution results (11, 12).

2.2 Releasing Grid Nodes

One of the MAG/Integrade design goal is to exploit the idle time of resources that comprise the computing infrastructure. The GRM schedules tasks to be executed in a node whenever the node remains idle for a certain time period. However, if an user requires to use the node, the machine's resources must be released and the Grid computations must migrate to other locations. The `AgentHandler` verifies which `MagAgents` are consuming more processing and memory resources, and selects them for migration. The `AgentHandler` also request the GRM a list of available Grid nodes. The selection of available nodes is based on several criteria such as resources availability (CPU, memory, and disk space) and the preferences/constraints imposed by the user that requested the application execution. The `AgentHandler` notifies each selected `MagAgent`, forcing the migration to remote locations, as scheduled by the GRM. The `MagAgent` suspends the application execution and transmits the application state. After finishing the state transference and completing the migration process, the `MagAgent` restarts the application execution from the point it was interrupted before migration.

3 Fault Tolerance and Code Migration

Fault tolerance is an essential characteristic for Grid environments. As the Grid acts as a massively parallel system, the loss of computation time must be avoided. In fact, the likelihood of errors occurring may be exacerbated by the fact that many Grid applications will perform long tasks that may require several days of computation[19]. Thus, a fault tolerance mechanism is not a feature, but a requirement.

Several challenges must be faced for the construction of such mechanism: since the Grid aggregates an enormous amount of hardware and software components, the probability of failures increase proportionally to the system size; the elements that compose the Grid are extremely heterogeneous, which can lead to failures in the interactions among them; detecting failures in a complex system, such as the Grid, is not only difficult, but difficulties arise to identify the root cause of the problem[15]; Grid nodes are unstable, since in general they are not dedicated to the execution of Grid applications, and do not comprise a controlled environment.

If a Grid node fails, all the applications being executed on the node will also fail, causing the loss of all computations performed up to the moment of the failure. The fault tolerance mechanism must avoid this waste of computational resources and also be totally transparent to the application user.

3.1 Fault Tolerance in MAG

The current MAG implementation has a basic infrastructure to provide dependability to Grid applications. Each component was developed as a mobile agent forming a multi agent community responsible for providing fault tolerance to Grid applications. The current version treats only nodes crash failures. In the future, we aim to provide support for other failure models.

The fault tolerance in MAG is based on the checkpoint approach, where the execution state of applications is periodically saved into a stable storage (a repository that must survive to all system failures). Thus, if a node failure happens, all computations running in that node can be recovered from they last checkpoints.

The MAG fault tolerance mechanism is composed of three software agents: `StableStorage`, `AgentMap`, and `AgentRecover`. The `StableStorage` acts as the stable storage of the system. Its current implementation is centralized and it must be executed on the cluster manager node. The `AgentMap` provides the mapping between applications and their execution nodes. This mapping is dynamic, since in MAG, application agents can migrate as resources availability varies. It stores control information (class name, execution id and the node name where the agent is acctually running) relative to the applications that are being executed on the Grid as XML files. The last component of the MAG fault tolerance mechanism is the `AgentRecover`, an agent responsible for manage the recovery process. Figure 3 shows the interactions among the fault tolerance components.

When an application agent is created or migrated, the agent must register its location in the `AgentMap` (1). During the application execution, the agent periodically capture and saves the application state on the `StableStorage` (2). If a node A fails (3), the GRM detects the failure (4)and instantiates a new `AgentRecover` (5), requesting to it the recovery of node A. The `AgentRecover` initiates the process, consulting the `AgentMap` (6) to discover what agents were executing in node A at the moment of the crash. The `AgentRecover` finds a

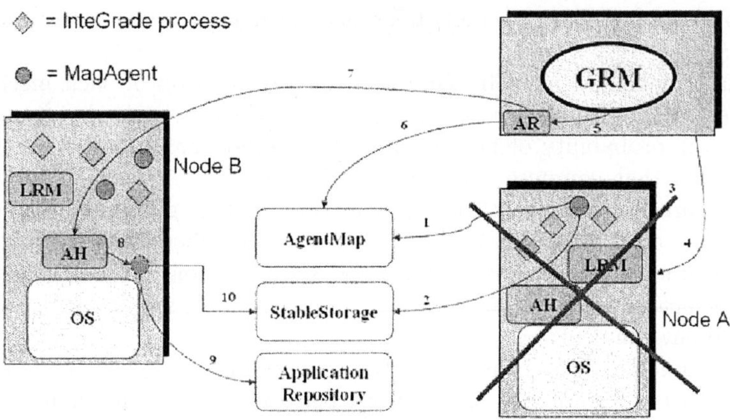

Fig. 3. MAG Recovery Process

new node (B) where the crashed computations will be restored using the GRM. It passes a list of agents (7) to be recovered to the `AgentHandler` running in the new node. This `AgentHandler` recreates the agents, informing them which crashed computations must be recovered (8). Each agent requests the application bytecode to the `ApplicationRepository` (9), and its last checkpoint from the `StableStorage` (10), resuming a failed job from its pre-failure state.

3.2 MAG Support for Code Migration

Since MAG executes Java applications using mobile agents, a suitable mechanism for capturing and reestablishing of Java threads state must be implemented, in order to provide fault tolerance to nodes failures. Unfortunately, Java does not provide sufficient mechanisms for capturing the computation state. The Java serialization mechanism only allows the saving of code and values of object members. Java classes cannot access intern and native information of the Java Virtual Machine (e.g. program counter and call stack), necessary to save the full execution state[12] of a Java thread.

During the last years, several techniques were developed for artificially gathers the information required to fully capture the state of Java threads. They can be classified in four basic approaches [12,13]: modification of the virtual machine, instrumentation of the application bytecode, instrumentation of the application source code, and modification of the *Java Platform Debugger Architecture* (JPDA).

MAG adopts the instrumentation of the application bytecode for its transparent migration mechanism. This mechanism is based on a modified version of the Brakes[20] framework, developed at the Katholieke Universiteit Leuven, Belgium, by the Distributed systems and computer Networks (DistriNet) research group.

The standard version of the Brakes framework is called "Brakes-serial". This version does not allow the execution of concurrent threads and cannot be used by MAG, given that in JADE each agent is executed as a thread of the container process.

Brakes has also other version, called "Brakes-parallel", that allows the execution of concurrent threads but it was developed as a proof-of-concept system, without any optimizations for real-world use. It is an unoptimized add on of the first prototype, and has a much higher overhead. This higher overhead is caused by a set of new components that was added to the serial version.

Given the above limitations, we decided to reuse in MAG only the Brakes bytecode transformer . We modified the original transformer in order to store state information inside each object, as member attributes instead of using Brakes components, reducing the overhead caused by the "Brakes-parallel" version. This modified version of Brakes was called MAG/Brakes.

4 Pervasive Grid

The use of mobile computing devices on many different areas grows in importance and availability of services, from the simplest assistance of personal activities to Internet and corporate access. Portable (or mobile) computing devices, such as laptops, PDA's (Personal Digital Assistants), and intelligent phones (SmartPhones) have become very common. The access to computer Grids by mobile device users presents several research challenges, such as: [16]: the introduction of mobile devices amplifies the necessity the management of heterogeneous resources comprising the computing infrastructure, since portable devices are highly heterogeneous in terms of resource properties such as CPU power, memory and storage limitations, display resolution and color depth. [11]; wireless communication technologies present smaller bandwidth, higher error rates, high variations on communication quality as the user moves around, and periods of disconnection and intermittent connectivity; software developers for mobile computing environments must decide how different components of the Grid middleware and applications should be mapped: on mobile device (front-end) or on fixed Grid nodes (back-end). This mapping must take into consideration aspects like processing capacity, energy consumption (due to batteries limitations), resources requirements and others [14].

We are currently developing the software infrastructure that will allow Grid access by mobile device clients. In this case, the Grid acts as an extension to the limited resources provided by portable devices. In the future, we also plan to investigate the use of mobile devices as Grid nodes (providing computing resources to the Grid). Our prototype architecture is based on the client/agent/server model described by Pitoura et. al [17]. This architecture are is composed by four components: Mobile Application Submission and Control Tool (MASCT), a component that allow users of mobile devices to submit applications to be executed on the Grid, as well as receive the results of requested computations; Mobile Local Resource Manager (MLRM), responsible for monitor the wireless connection state of mobile devices connected to the Grid, and notifies the MASCT about significant variations, making it context aware. Agent (Proxy) is a component responsible for making mobile devices, and the problems related to wireless communication, transparent to the other Grid components. It receives application execution requests from mobile users and forwards them to be executed on the Grid; Web Application Submission and Control Tool (WASCT) is a web interface to used to request the execution of applications and to collect its execution results.

5 Performance Analysis

In this section we present a performance analysis of the impact of MAG architecture on the Grid nodes. We evaluated the impact of the `AgentHandler` using as metric the relative use of the CPU usage.

We performed the tests using a single cluster composed by 3 computers with the following configuration: Intel Pentium 4 processor with 2.8 GHz and 1 GB of RAM memory running Linux 2.6.10, interconnected by a 100 Mbps Ethernet local network. One machine was running the GRM, another one the LRM, `AgentHandler` and the applications (`MagAgents`), and the last one the application submission tool (ASCT).

The experiment consisted of submitting the system to a load of 800 applications executions, gathering at every 10 secs the values of the used metric. During the whole experiment, we collected 2500 observations. The application submitted was an implementation of the Fibonacci algorithm with an input of 45. We developed a small application in C for gathering the data and modified the ASCT in order to generate the application execution requests. To simulate a real environment, we generated pseudo random time intervals between each application submission, using an inverse exponential distribution. We calculated the following statistics about the collected data: average, standard deviation, mode, median and confidence interval of 0,95.

Table 1. AgentHandler Processor Usage

Average	Standard Deviation	Median	Max. Value	Mode	Confidence Interval
0,086114	0,523206	0,000000	7,142900	0,000000	[0,065604 ; 0,106623]

Table 1 presents the results for the AgentHandler component. As we can see, the average of processor usage is close to 0%. The median confirms this, suggesting that at least half of the values, when ordered, are not greater than 0%. The standard deviation value presents only a small variability. We can conclude that the AgentHandler has little impact on the processor usage. We can conclude, by analyzing the results collected from the experiments, that the CPU consumption generated by the `AgentHandler`, responsible for applications execution, is very small and can be, for most cases, neglected.

6 Related Work

The benefits of integrating and sharing multi-institutional computational resources has stimulated many research on Grid projects, with different objectives, implementation issues, target applications, and computing infrastructure. Globus[5] aims to build software services that allow applications to run in a Grid composed by computers in geographically dispersed domains, adopting the OGSA (Open Grid Service Architecture) standard for the implementation of its services; Legion[10] has as philosophy the construction of a computational Grid system based on the object paradigm and aims to provide services that promote the illusion of one single virtual machine to its users. OurGrid[1] provides a Grid middleware that forfeits supporting arbitrary applications in favor of supporting only Bag-of-Tasks applications (parallel applications whose tasks are independent of each other). Condor[18] emphasizes the use of shared resources that remain idle for a significant amount of time, such as workstations, to execute high throughput computations. An important distinction between MAG and the above projects is that we make extensive use of the agent paradigm as a way to overcome some challenges cited in Section 1.

Other research projects suggest the use of agents to provide Grid services, such as resource management, service discovery, and task scheduling. MAIS [9] is the information and reservation component of CLUMAKE, a middleware kit for dynamic cluster management. CLUMAKE goal is to offer an environment for creating ad-hoc clusters composed of mobile devices. In MAIS, mobile and stationary agents interact in order to provide task scheduling and decentralized resource management. The ARMS project [2] proposes an agent based resource management system. Each agent represents a Grid resource, such as a computer. The agents are responsible for the publication and discovery of Grid resources and are hierarchically arranged in order to facilitate searches. ACG [3] represents resources and services as agents. It uses a Grid Service Manager (GSM) to register and search for available services. The communication mechanism used by ACG is based on TuplaSpace [4]. A major difference between MAG and the above projects is that MAG uses the agents paradigm not only to develop the Grid middleware components, but also to execute applications.

CoordAgent [7], like MAG, proposes a Grid middleware based on mobile agents, providing mechanisms for application execution, transparent code migration, and fault-tolerance. Both, MAG and CoordAgent, execute C/C++ and Java applications. They also allows the execution of parallel and regular (a single application copy executes all computations) applications. CoordAgent adopts MPI as the programming model for parallel applications while MAG uses BSP. In MAG, the BSP programming model is currently available only for C/C++ applications. CoordAgent uses the HTTP protocol for agent migration and communication, while MAG follows the FIPA standard, which provides compatibility with all FIPA compliant agent platforms. The CoordAgent migration mechanism uses the source code instrumentation approach for gathering the state of running applications. MAG uses bytecode instrumentation, which does not requires the application source code. The bytecode approach normally imposes less space and time overhead to application execution.

7 Conclusions and Future Directions

Considering some intrinsic characteristics of the mobile agents paradigm, such as cooperation, autonomy, reactivity, and mobility we can conclude that this paradigm can potentially simplify the development of a Grid infrastructure. As a proof of concept, this paper described MAG, a Grid middleware that explores the mobile agent paradigm as a way to overcome several of the described challenges.

MAG executes Grid applications by dynamically loading the application code into a mobile agent. The MAG agent can be dynamically reallocated to Grid nodes though a transparent migration mechanism, as a way to provide load balancing and support for non-dedicated nodes. MAG also provides fault tolerance mechanisms to Grid applications.

This paper described the software infrastructure being implemented on MAG that will allow Grid access by mobile device clients. In this case, the Grid acts as an extension to the limited resources provided by portable devices.

Some future directions of the MAG project are: we intend to investigate adaptive approaches to the fault tolerance mechanism, in order to provide dynamic and efficient mechanisms for detection and the recovery of faults. We intend to develop a distributed version of this component, avoiding the single point of failure and bottleneck created by the centralized one; we plan to investigate the use of mobile devices as Grid nodes, providing computing resources to the Grid; we plan to develop services to store and access large volumes of distributed data as well as data publishing and discovery.

References

1. N. Andrade, W. Cirne, F. B., and P. R. Ourgrid: An approach to easily assemble grids with equitable resource sharing. In *Proc. of the 9th Workshop on Job Scheduling Strategies for Parallel Processing*, June 2003.
2. J. Cao, S. A. Jarvis, D. J. Kerbyson, and G. R. Nudd. "arms: An agent-based resource management system for grid computing". *"Scientific Programming 10"*, "2002".
3. L. "Chunlin and L. Layuan. "an agent-based approach for grid computing". In *"Parallel and Distributed Computing, Applications and Technologies, 2003. PDCAT'2003. Proc. of the Fourth International Conference"*, pages "608–611", "Aug" "2003".
4. L. Chunlin, L. Zhengding, L. Layuan, and Z. Shuzhi. "a mobile agent platform based on tuple space coordination". *"Journal of Advances in Engineering Software, Elsecier, UK"*, "33/4":"215–225", "May" "2002".
5. I. Foster, C. Kesselman, and S. Tuecke. The Anatomy of the Grid: Enabling Scalable Virtual Organizations. *Lecture Notes in Computer Science*, 2150, 2001.
6. I. Foster, C. Kesselman, and S. Tueke. The anatomy of the grid: Enabling scalable virtual organizations. *International Journal of Supercomputing Applications*, 2001.
7. M. Fukuda, Y. Tanaka, L. F. Bic, and S. Kobayashi. A mobile-agent-based pc grid. *IEEE Computer*, 2003.
8. A. Goldchleger, F. Kon, A. Goldman, M. Finger, and G. C. Bezerra. Integrade: Object-oriented grid middleware leveraging idle computing power of desktop machines. *Concurrency and Computation: Practice & Experience. Vol. 16, pp. 449-459*, 2004.

9. D. Grigoras, C. Mulcahy, and R. Mcinerney. "the anatomy of a mobile agent information system for dynamic enviroments". *"Proc. of the International Conference on Parallel Computing in Eletriacal Engineering (PARELEC'02) IEEE"*, "2002".
10. A. S. Grimshaw, M. J. Lewis, A. J. Ferrari, and J. F. Karpovich. Architectural support for extensibility and autonomy in wide-area distributed object systems. Technical report, Proc. of the 2000 Network and Distributed System Security Symposium (NDSS2000), February 2000.
11. A. Helal, B. Haskell, J. Carter, R. Brice, D. Woelk, and M. Rusinkiewicz. *Any Time, Anywhere Computing.* Kluwer Academic Publishers, 1999.
12. T. Illmann, F. Kargl, T. Krueger, and M. Weber. Migration in Java: problems, classifications and solutions. In *MAMA'2000*, Wollongong, Australia, 2000.
13. T. Illmann, T. Krueger, F. Kargl, and M. Weber. Transparent migration of mobile agents using the Java Platform Debugger Architecture. In *Lecture Notes in Computer Science*, volume 2240, page 198, Jan 2001.
14. J. Jing, A. Helal, and A. Elmagarmid. Client-server computing in mobile enviroments. *ACM Computing Surveys, 31:2*, 1999.
15. R. Medeiros, W. Cirne, F. Brasileiro, and J. Sauvé. Faults in Grids: Why are they so bad and What can be done about it? In *Grid Computing, 2003. Proceedings. Fourth International Workshop*, pages 18–24, Nov. 2003.
16. T. Phan, L. Huang, and C. Dulan. Challenge: Integrating mobile wireless devices into the computational grid. *In Proc. of the 8th ACM International Conference on Mobile Computing and Networking (MobiCom'02), 271-278 Atlanta-GA, USA*, 2002.
17. E. Pitoura and G. Samaras. *Data Management for Mobile Computing.* Kluwer Academic Publisher, 1998.
18. D. Thain, T. Tannenbaum, and M. Livny. Condor and the grid. In F. Berman, G. Fox, and T. Hey, editors, *Grid Computing: Making the Global Infrastructure a Reality.* John Wiley & Sons Inc., December 2002.
19. P. Townend and J. Xu. Fault Tolerance within a Grid Environment. *In Proceedings of AHM2003*, page 272, 2003.
20. E. Truyen, B. Robben, B. Vanhaute, T. Coninx, W. Joosen, and P. Verbaeten. Portable support for transparent thread migration in java. In *ASA/MA*, 2000.

Experiences in Running Workloads over Grid3

Catalin L. Dumitrescu[1], Ioan Raicu[1], and Ian Foster[1,2]

[1] Computer Science Department, The University of Chicago,
5801 S. Ellis Ave., Chicago, IL, 60637
cldumitr@cs.uchicago.edu

[2] Mathematics and Computer Science Division, Argonne National Laboratory,
9700 S. Cass Ave., MCS/221, Argonne, IL, 60439
foster@mcs.anl.gov

Abstract. Running workloads in a grid environment is often a challenging problem due the scale of the environment, and to the resource partitioning based on various sharing strategies. A resource may be taken down during a job execution, be improperly setup or just fail job execution. Such elements have to be taken in account whenever targeting a grid environment for execution. In this paper we explore these issues on a real grid, Grid3, by means of a specific workload, the BLAST workload, and a specific scheduling framework, GRUBER - an architecture and toolkit for resource usage service level agreement (SLA) specification and enforcement. The paper provides extensive experimental results. We address in high detail the performance of different site selection strategies of GRUBER and the overall performance in scheduling workloads in Grid3 with workload sizes ranging from 10 to 10,000 jobs.

1 Introduction

Grid3 represents a multi-virtual organization that sustains production level services required by various physics experiments. The infrastructure is composed of more than 30 sites and 4500 CPUs, over 1300 simultaneous jobs and more than 2TB/day. The participating sites are the main resource providers under various conditions. We consider in this paper that all these sites are governed by various usage SLAs [3]. We distinguish here between "resource *usage* policies" (or SLAs) and "resource *access* policies." Resource access policies typically enforce authorization rules. In contrast, resource usage SLAs govern the *sharing* of specific resources among multiple groups of users. Once a user is permitted to access a resource via a resource access policy, then the resource usage policy steps in to govern *how much* of the resource the user is permitted to consume. GRUBER focuses on computing resources such as computers, storage, and networks; owners may be either individual scientists or sites; and VOs are collaborative groups, such as scientific collaborations.

In this paper, we focus on the problems that can occur in Grid3, because various elements affect workload execution times. We measure the impact by means of *average resource utilization*, *average response time*, *average job completion*, *average job re-planning* (Replan), *workload completion time* (Time), and *job completion gain* (Speedup) [1]. We present our detailed results for scheduling BLAST workloads over one of the largest US grid, the Grid3 [3] environment.

H. Zhuge and G.C. Fox (Eds.): GCC 2005, LNCS 3795, pp. 274–286, 2005.

2 Goals

Running various size workloads over Grid3 can become a challenging problem when resources are shared by a large user community. For most environments, even short periods of overloading can decrease the performance the users get from the system. In any grid context, such overloading scenarios can be only partial as a grid is a large composition of resources spread in various administrative domains. Here we try to identify some of the main challenges users may face when submitting workloads in such environments and to provide also some simple means for improving their achieved performance. We assume in our scenario that various sites are used at particular times and we are interested in measure how well the overall performance maintains over larger time intervals.

2.1 Resource Providers and Consumers

Grid3 is composed of resources provided based on various usage SLA [1],[17]. Further, resources are aggregated at the VO level and provided on similar usage SLA means to groups and users. Our usage SLA scheduling framework, GRUBER, deals with two classes of entities: resource providers and resource consumers. A physical site is a resource provider; a VO is a consumer (consuming resources provided by a site) and a provider (providing resources to users, groups or workload types). We assume that each provider-consumer relationship is governed by an appropriate SLA.

2.2 Usage SLA-Based Resource Sharing

The entire grid environment is described as follows:

- A grid consists of a set of resource provider *sites* and a set of *submit hosts.*
- Each site contains a number of processors and some amount of disk space.
- A three-level hierarchy of *users*, *groups*, and *VOs* is defined, such that, each user is a member of one group, and each group is a member of one VO.
- Users submit jobs for execution at submit hosts. A job is specified by four attributes: VO, Group, Required-Processor-Time, Required-Disk-space.
- A *site policy statement* defines site usage SLAs by specifying the number of processors and amount of disk space that the site makes available to each VOs.
- A *VO policy statement* defines VO usage SLAs by specifying the fraction of the VO's total processor and disk resources (i.e., the aggregate of contributions to that VO from all sites) that the VO makes available to different groups.

We note that this model is one of resource sub-allocation: resources are owned by sites, which apportion them to VOs. VOs in turn apportion their "virtual" resources to groups. Groups could, conceptually, apportion their sub-allocation further, among specific users. Without loss of generality, we simplify both this discussion and our implementation by sub-allocating no further than from VOs to groups.

3 Environment Settings

The execution environment is based on the VDS toolkit developed in the GriPhyN project context. The specific technicalities are as follows.

3.1 Euryale as Concrete Planner

Euryale [9] is a complex system aimed at running jobs over a grid, and in special over Grid3 [3]. The approach used by Euryale is to rely on the Condor-G capabilities to submit and monitor jobs at sites. It takes a late binding approach in assigning such jobs to sites. In addition, Euryale allows a simple mechanism for fault tolerance by means of job re-planning when a failure is discovered.

During a workload execution, DagMan executes the Euryale's pre- and post-scripts, the heart of Euryale concrete planner, which also contain the Euryale's execution logic. The prescript calls out to the external site selector, rewrites the job submit file, transfers necessary input files to that site, registers transferred files with the replica mechanism, and deals with re-planning. The postscript file transfers output files to the collection area, registers produced files, checks on successful job execution, and updates file popularity. To run things in the grid, Euryale needs knowledge about the available resources, or sites. An important feature of Euryale is its capacity to invoke external site selectors in job scheduling, such as our resource broker, GRUBER [18].

3.2 GRUBER as Resource Broker

GRUBER is the main component that we used for the site selection. It is composed of four principal components, as we now outline [18]. The *GRUBER engine* represents the main component of the architecture. It implements various algorithms for detecting available resources and maintains a generic view of resource allocations and utilizations.

The *GRUBER site monitoring component* is one of the data providers for the GRUBER engine. This component is optional and can be replaced with various other

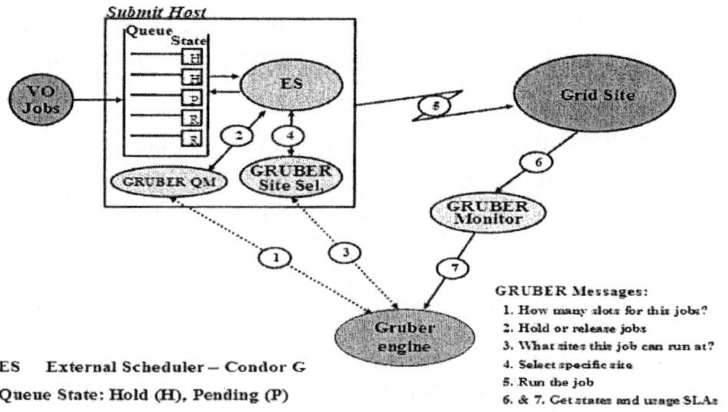

Fig. 1. GRUBER Architecture

grid monitoring components that will provide similar information, such as MonaLisa [10] or Grid Catalog [3]. So far, we are unaware of any complete replacement. *GRUBER site selectors* are tools that communicate with the GRUBER engine and provide answers to the question: "*which is the best site at which I can run this job?*". Site selectors can implement various task assignment policies, such as random assignment (*G-RA*), round robin (*G-RR*), least used (*G-LU*), or last recently used (*G-LRU*) task assignment policies. We note that one can use just the GRUBER engine and site selectors, without the GRUBER queue manager. This option makes GRUBER only a site recommender, without having the capacity to enforce any usage SLA expressed at the VO level, while enforcing the usage SLA at the site level by means of removing a site for an already over-quota VO user at that site.

3.3 Disk Space Considerations

Disk space management introduces additional complexities in comparison to job management [18]. For the experiments in this paper, we have extended GRUBER to deal with multiple resource issues and describe here in more detail our work. If an entitled-to-resources job becomes available, it is usually possible to delay scheduling other jobs, or to preempt them if they are already running. In contrast, a file that has been staged to a site cannot be "delayed," it can only be deleted. Yet deleting a file that has been staged for a job can result in livelock, if a job's files are repeatedly deleted before the job runs. As a consequence, a different approach has been devised. As a concrete example, a site can become heavily loaded with a one VO jobs and because of which other jobs are either in the local queue in an idle state waiting for their turn. But this does not stop the submission of more jobs. As a result, there may be lots of other input data on the site and the disk used space will keep on growing. On the other hand, the other jobs are not getting their turn to actually finish and delete their files. The rate of input data being copied over to the site is higher than the rate of completion of jobs, making the disk space to get full.

So far, we have considered a UNIX quota-like approach. Usually, quotas just prevent one user on a static basis from using more than his hard limit. There is no adaptation to make efficient use of disk in the way a site CPU resource manager adapts to make efficient use of CPU (by implementing more advanced disk space management techniques). More precisely, for scheduling decisions a list of site candidates that are available for use by a VO i for a job with disk requirements J, in terms of provided disk space, is built by executing the following logic.

for each site s **in** site list G **do**
  # Case 1: *over-used site by* VO_i
  if $IA_i > IP_i$ for VO i at site s
    next
  # Case 2: *un-allocated site*
  else
    if $\Sigma_k(IA_k) < s.TOTAL - J$ **&&**
        $IA_i + J < IP_i$ **then**
      add (s, S)
return S

with the following definitions:

S = Site Set
k = index for any VO != VO_i
IP_i = Instantaneous Usage SLA for VO_i
IA_i = Instantaneous Resource Usage for VO_i
TOTAL = upper limit allocation on the site

The set of disk-available site candidates is combined with the set of CPU-available site candidates and the intersection of the two sets is used for further scheduling decisions.

4 Experimental Results

We first introduce the metrics [18] that we used to evaluate the alternative strategies, and then introduce our experimental environment, and finally present and discuss our results.

4.1 Metrics

We use five metrics to evaluate the effectiveness of workload performance execution.

- **Comp:** the percentage of jobs that complete successfully.

$$\textbf{Comp} = \textbf{(Completed Jobs)} / \#_{jobs} * 100.00$$

- **Replan:** the number of performed replanning operations.
- **Util:** average resource utilization, the ratio of the per-job CPU resources consumed (ET_i) to the total CPU resources available as a percentage:

$$\textbf{Util} = \Sigma_{i=1..N} ET_i / (\#_{cpus} * \Delta t) * 100.00$$

- **Delay:** average time per job (DT_i) that elapses from when the job arrives in a resource provider queue until it starts:

$$\textbf{Delay} = \Sigma_{i=1..N} DT_i / \#_{jobs}$$

- **Time:** the total execution time for the workload.
- **Speedup:** the serial execution time to the grid execution time for a workload.
- **Spdup75:** the serial execution time to the grid execution time for 75% of the workload.

All metrics are important: an adequate environment will both maximize delivered resources and meet owner intents. For example, Table 1 presents a simple case scenario in which several VOs have various SLAs, resource requests, and resource utilizations at a particular resource provider. The column names have the following meanings:

- **Target:** the usage SLA for the consumer at the resource provider, as a percentage of site capacity.
- **Current:** the current utilization for the consumer at the provider, as a percentage.
- **Demand:** the current resource demand from the consumer for the provider, as a percentage (it cannot be less than **Current**).
- **Level:** how our criteria is met (OK when **Current** = MIN (**Target, Demand**)).

Table 1. Usage SLAs in our Scenario

VO	Target	Current	Demand	Level
USCMS	60	50	50	OK
USATLAS	20	15	30	Under
IVDGL	10	10	100	OK
LIGO	5	3	3	OK
SDSS	5	22	50	Over

4.2 Experiment Settings

We used a single job type in all our experiments, the sequence analysis program BLAST. A single BLAST job has an execution time of about 40 minutes (the exact duration depends on the CPU), reads about 10-33 kilobytes of input, and generates about 0.7-1.5 megabytes of output: i.e., an insignificant amount of I/O. We used these BLAST workloads in three different sets of workload configuration: (1) small workloads of 10, 50, and 100 jobs that get scheduled at once; (2) medium workloads of 500 to 1000 jobs that are submitted in several steps in order to honor the VO usage SLAs; and (3) large workloads of 10k jobs.

Table 2. Grid3 CPU Allocations on July 9, 2004

Site Name	# of CPUs	VO Allocations (in %)		
		iVDGL	Atlas	USCMS
T2cms0.sdsc.edu	76	0.62	24.74	0.40
nest.phys.uwm.edu	305	0.00	7.28	0.00
uscmsb0.ucsd.edu	3	11.68	11.68	11.68
xena.hamptonu.edu	1	25.00	25.00	25.00
garlic.hep.wisc.edu	101	3.01	3.01	3.01

We performed all experiments on Grid3, which comprises around 30 sites across the U.S., of which we used 15. Each site is autonomous and managed by different local resource managers, such as Condor, PBS, or LSF. Each site enforces different usage policies which are collected by the GRUBER site monitor. For example, Table 1 gives CPU allocations per VO on five Grid3 sites on July 9, 2004 as collected through the GRUBER site monitor. We submitted all jobs within the iVDGL VO, under a VO usage policy that allows a maximum of 600 CPUs. Furthermore, we submitted each individual workload under a separate iVDGL group, with the constraint than no one group can get more than 25% of iVDGL CPUs, i.e., 150.

We also configured GRUBER to employ a replanning policy, by which a starving job was removed after a predefined time interval (20 minutes here) and resubmitted for rescheduling. If a job was submitted unsuccessfully 10 times or it was reported as application level "failure" by a site, then it is considered a failure. All submissions were performed without withholding or setting any special priorities at sites, practically GRUBER had to find resources while all workloads ran in parallel. The VO usage SLA limited the submitting group to approximately 150 jobs at a time.

Regarding the site selectors, they were already introduced by Dumitrescu et al. [18] and used in a similar fashion. In a nutshell, G-RA represents GRUBER random assignment site strategy, G-RR represents GRUBER round robin site strategy, G-LU represents GRUBER least used site assignment strategy, and G-LRU represents least recently used site strategy [18].

4.3 Small Workload Results

Table 3 shows the results for the 1x10 jobs workloads. In the ideal case, these values are: Comp=100, Replan=0, Util=1.25, Delay=0, Time=3000, and Speedup=10. As can be seen, the speedup is 2.5 to 3.5 times smaller due to the probability of a jobs ending on sites with a local resource manager that do not behave as expected. The job starvation was "detected" after a time interval comparable with the execution time (20 minutes vs. 40 minutes). However, 75% of the jobs do complete in a time interval closer to the ideal case of a speedup of 10.

Table 3. Results and 90% Confidence Intervals of Four Policies for 1x10 workloads

	G-RA	G-RR	G-LU	G-LRU
Comp(%)	100	100	100	100
Replan	34.1 ± 5.51	47.5 ± 9.26	8.6 ± 1.83	13.6 ± 2.18
Util (%)	0.36 ± 0.05	0.31 ± 0.07	0.55± 0.10	0.50 ± 0.04
Delay (s)	3262 ± 548	4351 ± 824	1162 ± 376	801 ± 313
Time (s)	12436 ± 1191.4	13966 ± 2208.8	8787±158	7653 ± 205.9
Speedup	2.33 ± 0.25	2.21 ± 0.35	3.6 ± 0.6	3.46 ± 0.45
Spdup75	3.72 ± 0.59	3.46 ± 0.51	5.32± 0.67	5.66 ± 0.55

Table 4 shows the results for the 1x50 jobs workloads. In the ideal case, these values are: Comp=100, Replan=0, Util=6.25, Delay=0, Time=3000, and Speedup=50. The same situation as before was encountered in this set of experiments: several jobs starved and their execution time affected the overall speedup. The speedup of 75% of the jobs instead is more than the half of the ideal speedup, proving that most of the jobs do complete close to the optimal time.

Table 4. Results and 90% Confidence Intervals of Four Policies for 1x50 workloads

	G-RA	G-RR	G-LU	G-LRU
Comp(%)	100	100	100	100
Replan	35 ± 14	51.1 ± 28	48.8 ±10.8	78.8 ± 9.51
Util (%)	1.18 ± 0.25	1.44 ± 0.27	1.89 ±0.43	1.76 ± 0.18
Delay (s)	1420 ± 713	583 ± 140.4	653.8 ±202	1260 ± 528.7
Time (s)	8035 ± 990.4	9654 ± 603.5	8549 ±898	9702 ± 1247.3
Speedup	16.35 ± 1.17	14.12 ± 0.90	15.16 ±2.42	12.76 ± 0.71
Spdup75	30.84 ± 5.70	35.36 ± 2.79	35.41 ±2.48	24.36 ± 2.28

Table 5 shows the results for the 1x100 jobs workloads. In the ideal case, these values are: Comp=100, Replan=0, Util=12.50, Delay=0, Time=3000, and Speedup=100. Again, similarly to the 1x50 workloads, the execution performance is half for 75% of the workloads and drops for the entire workload.

Table 5. Results and 90% Confidence Intervals of Four Policies for 1x100 workloads

	G-RA	G-RR	G-LU	G-LRU
Comp(%)	100	100	100	100
Replan	228.7 ± 21	39.9 ± 13.8	124.7 ± 17	230 ± 20.3
Util (%)	2.86 ± 0.30	3.48 ± 0.59	3.51 ± 0.7	1.87 ± 0.46
Delay (s)	1691 ± 198	529 ± 92.67	640 ± 93.4	1244 ± 387.9
Time (s)	10350 ± 565.9	9013 ± 1025.1	9716±1130	7507 ± 2325.1
Speedup	22.43 ± 1.55	30.15 ± 3.43	28.02 ± 5.4	19.24 ± 1.56
Spdup75	47.38 ± 3.24	77.19 ± 3.26	73.54 ± 2.0	35.86 ± 3.72

4.4 Medium Workload Results

Table 6 shows the results for the 1x500 jobs workloads. Here, in the ideal case, the values are: Comp=100, Replan=0, Util=25.00, Delay=3600, Time=3000, and Speedup=150. The size of the workloads makes the execution performance to increase, and practically almost match the ideal speedup for the 75% of the workload and be only half for the overall workload.

Table 6. Results and 90% Confidence Intervals of Four Policies for 1x500 workloads

	G-RA	G-RR	G-LU	G-LRU
Comp(%)	100	100	100	100
Replan	925 ± 103.5	816 ± 245.6	680 ± 139.3	1024 ± 154.2
Util (%)	34.04 ± 4.55	33.19 ± 2.39	30.3 ± 4.7	25.41 ± 5.6
Delay (s)	9202 ± 1716.8	6700 ± 816.6	6169 ± 407	9125 ± 6117.8
Time (s)	28116 ± 2881	24225 ± 035.9	21362 ±1250	20434 ± 4100
Speedup	67.32 ± 5.6	60.22 ± 3.26	63.12 ±3.41	51.77 ± 5.94
Spdup75	98.43 ± 8.7	111.69 ± 9.81	113.2 ±8.82	101.48 ± 10.05

4.5 Large Workload Results

Next, we report on previous results were we used a more aggressive scheduling approach. In this approach, the number of retries was limited to five versus ten job retries. Also, in these measurements some of the sites were not properly configured and jobs failed immediately. These workloads provide also insights about GRUBER's scalability. Our results are captured in Table 7. Round-robin and random-assignment prove to achieve the best performance. The lower completion rates are explained by the number of low number of retries (5) and the missing of BLAST environment configuration at a few sites. All these factors are also an explanation for the lower performance achieved in these cases.

Table 7. Results of Four GRUBER Strategies for 1x1k workloads

	G-RA	**G-RR**	**G-LU**	**G-LRU**
Comp(%)	97	96.7	99.3	85.6
Replan	1396	1679	1326	1440
Util (%)	12.85	12.28	14.56	10.63
Delay (s)	49.07	53.75	50.50	54.69
Time (s)	29484	37620	33300	80028
Speedup	140.3$^+$	113.1$^+$	122$^+$	101.4$^+$
Spdup75	173.5	159.3	161.4	127.8

Further, in the 10k workloads, the completion rates drop even more, as the probability of failures increases linearly with the number of jobs (GRUBER maintains a constant load on the available sites).

Table 8. Results of Four GRUBER Strategies for 1x10K workloads

	G-RA	**G-RR**	**G-LU**	**G-LRU**
Comp(%)	91.75	91.88	77.88	73.58
Replan	18000	23900	27718	24350
Util (%)	24.3	23.3	20.0	17.6
Delay (s)	86.63	85.17	89.01	90.45
Time (s)	226k	260k	295k	349k
Speedup	137$^+$	145.4$^+$	134$^+$	98.3$^+$
Spdup75	156.2	163	139.6	98.3$^+$

The results in Table 9 are the means across the four submitters. We see some interesting differences from Table 7. G-LU's completion rate drops precipitously, presumably for some reason relating to greater contention. The total execution times for G-RA and G-LU increase, although more runs are required to determine the significance of these results.

$^+$ Results for incomplete workloads.

Table 9. Results of Four GRUBER Strategies for 4x1K workloads

	G-RA	G-RR	G-LU	G-LRU
Comp(%)	98.2	98.7	91.7	87.9
Replan	1815	1789	2409	1421
Util (%)	13.51	14.02	11.52	11.05
Delay (s)	66.62	64.41	63.96	68.97
Time (s)	40356	37800	48564	48636
Speedup	77.3^{+}	74.1^{+}	71^{+}	60^{+}
Spdup75	105.6	102.9	93.8	82.4

4.6 Failure Analysis

While for the small and medium workloads the number of failures was null, for large workloads the completion rates vary as can be observed from the tables in subsection 4.5. The motivations for these failures are in most cases the small number of retries used during these tests (5 instead of 10), the temporary failure of the RLS server used to stage in and out data (overloading issues), in a few cases due to DagMan failure in managing jobs (application bugs), and gatekeepers overloading. Most of these errors were reported and fixes were performed or are expected in the future for the signaled problems.

Also, we have to note that Grid3 performance in executing BLAST workloads has already increased between the first set of experiments (large workloads) and the second ones (small and medium workloads). Either individual sites had undergone hardware upgrades or the job assignment policies to individual computing nodes became more job requirements aware (avoiding node overloads).

5 Statistical Analysis

While previous results provide useful insight about how Grid3 performs in executing workloads when GRUBER is the steering mechanism, further analysis is required to identify how the scheduling strategies have performed comparatively. Fig. 2 presents the speedup performance over all runs and the confidence intervals at 90%. Note the small confidence intervals for all runs, which express low standard deviation and the strength of our results across the runs and configurations.

Further, we use the T-test to correlate the results of these experiments. The T-test is usually used for comparing the results of two alternative approaches with the claim that the results are significantly different. For comparison means, we use tournament trees and T-tests as comparison operator. These results are captured in Table 10. The null hypothesis and alternative hypothesis that we set up to conduct the t-test are:

- H_0 (null hypothesis): any given two runs have comparable performance;
- H_a (alt. hypothesis): prove H_0 is false; two runs do not have same performance.

The null hypothesis is the one that we want to reject as not being true, while the alternative hypothesis is the one that we want to accept as being true. Our alternative

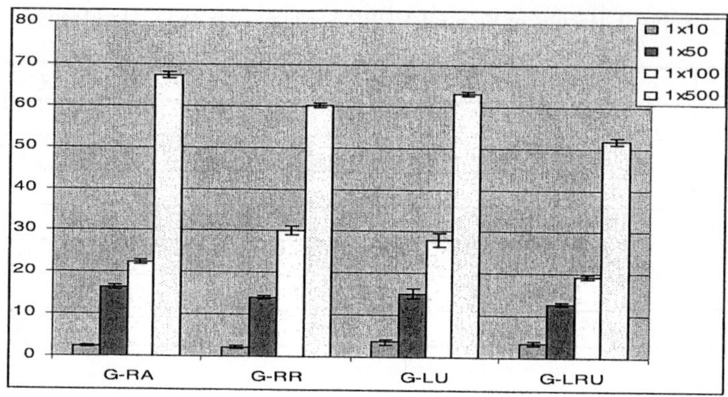

Fig. 2. Speedup Comparisons among Workloads

hypothesis is two sided since we test that the runs are just different, which implies either < or >; we essentially test 2 * P (t > critical_value) to be less than 0.05. The goal is to obtain a probability that the t value will be greater or less than the critical value. The p value needs to be less than 0.05 for the results to be statistically significant, which implies that H_a is true with 95% confidence for the corresponding comparisons; the lower the p value, the better the confidence. If a p value cannot be found that is less than 0.05, then the sample space is not statistically significant, and hence more samples must be obtained.

Table 10. Tournament Tree (T-tests) Results

	G-RA vs. G-RR	G-LU vs. G-LRU	G-RA vs. G-LU
1x10	0.09 (?)	0.17 (?)	0.0005 (T)
1x50	0.0005 (T)	0.0005 (T)	0.0005 (T)
1x100	0.0005 (T)	0.0005 (T)	0.0005 (T)
1x500	0.0005 (T)	0.0005 (T)	0.0005 (T)

The results from Table 10 show that for all workloads other than the smallest one, the results are statistically significant with at least a 99.95% confidence. Regarding the smallest workload of 1x10 (for which we had 10 sample runs), the number of samples in our experiment do not seem to be enough, and hence more experiments would have to be performed for the 1x10 workload.

6 Related Work

There are several other production workloads running over Grid3, such as the QuarkNet Project, SDSSCoAdd, GADU, or fMRIDC. While these workloads are important from the GriPhyN project point of view, they offer little elements for comparisons with the work described here. Firstly, these workloads are run mostly for their results and not for measuring various Grid3 execution capacities. The closest one is the SDSS/CoAdd workload in scope; however we do not have information to date about various metrics [20]. Besides the iVDGL workloads running over Grid3, there are other challenge problems solved. For example, the ATLAS "VO" and applications focus on Monte Carlo simulation of the physics processes that will occur in high energy proton collision at LHC; SDSS runs various problems related to galaxy clusters identification or pixel-level analysis of astronomical data, etc. [3].

7 Conclusions

Running workloads in grid environments is often a challenging problem due the scale of the environment and to the resource participation based on various sharing strategies. A resource may be taken down during job execution, be improperly setup or just fail job execution. Such elements have to be taken in account when targeting a grid environment.

In this paper we explored some of the issues that occur on a real grid, namely Grid3, by means of a specific workload, the BLAST workload, and a specific scheduling framework, GRUBER - an architecture and toolkit for resource usage service level agreement (SLA) specification and enforcement. During these experiments we faced various problems as described above, as well as quantified what performance a grid user should expect. In addition, we observed for our brokering mechanism that for medium workloads, G-RA performs best with a 90% confidence interval, while G-LU performed best for smaller workloads. We also note that G-LRU performed worst for all tested workloads.

References

1. Dumitrescu, C. and I. Foster, "Usage Policy-based CPU Sharing in Virtual Organizations", in *5th International Workshop in Grid Computing*, 2004.
2. Foster, I., C. Kesselman, and S. Tuecke, "The Anatomy of the Grid: Enabling Scalable Virtual Organizations", in *International Journal of Supercomputer Applications*, 2001.
3. Foster, I., et al., "The Grid2003 Production Grid: Principles and Practice", in *13th International Symposium on High Performance Distributed Computing*, 2004.
4. Dan, A., C. Dumitrescu, and M. Ripeanu, "Connecting Client Objectives with Resource Capabilities: An Essential Component for Grid Service Management Infrastructures", in *ACM International Conference on Service Oriented Computing (ICSOC'04)*, NY, 2004.
5. Altair Grid Technologies, LLC, *A Batching Queuing System*, Software Project, 2003.
6. Irwin, D., L. Grit, and J. Chase, "Balancing Risk and Reward in a Market-based Task Service", in *13th International Symposium on High Performance Distributed Computing*.
7. IBM, *WSLA Language Specification, Version 1.0.* 2003.
8. Pearlman, L., et al., "A Community Authorization Service for Group Collaboration", in *IEEE 3rd International Workshop on Policies for Distributed Systems and Networks*.
9. Voeckler, J., et al, "Euryale: Yet another Concrete Planner", Virtual Data Workshop, Presentation, 2004.
10. Legrand, I.C., et al. "MonALISA: A Distributed Monitoring Service Architecture", in *Computing in High Energy Physics*, La Jolla, CA, 2003.

11. Ludwig, H., A. Dan, and B. Kearney. "Cremona: An Architecture and Library for Creation and Monitoring WS-Agreements", in *ACM International Conference on Service Oriented Computing (ICSOC'04)*, NY, 2004.
12. Cluster Resources, Inc., *Maui Scheduler*, Software Project, 2001-2005.
13. Henry, G.J., *A Fair Share Scheduler.* AT&T Bell Laboratory Technical Journal, 1984.
14. Kay, J. and P. Lauder, "A Fair Share Scheduler", University of Sydney, AT&T Bell Labs.
15. In, J., P. Avery, R. Cavanaugh, and S. Ranka, "Policy Based Scheduling for Simple Quality of Service in Grid Computing", in *International Parallel & Distributed Processing Symposium (IPDPS)*, New Mexico, '04.
16. Buyya, R., "GridBus: A Economy-based Grid Resource Broker", The University of Melbourne, 2004, Melbourne.
17. Dumitrescu, C. and I. Foster, "GangSim: A Simulator for Grid Scheduling Studies", in *Cluster Computing and Grid (CCGrid),* 2005, Cardiff, UK.
18. Dumitrescu, C., and I. Foster, "GRUBER: A Grid Resource SLA Broker", Euro-Par, 2005, Lisbon, Portugal.
19. Dumitrescu, C., I. Foster and I. Raicu, "A Scalability and Performance Measurements of a Usage SLA based Broker in Large Environments", iVDGL/GriPhyN Tech-Report, 2005.
20. Avery, P. and I. Foster, "GriPhyN Project Description", http://www.griphyn.org.
21. Dumitrescu, C., Wilde, M., and Foster, I., "A Model for Usage Policy-based Resource Allocations in Grids", in *IEEE/Policy Workshop*, 2005, Stockholm, Sweden.
22. Zhuge, H., The Future Interconnection Environment, IEEE Computer, 38 (4)(2005) 27-33.

An Efficient Network Information Model Using NWS for Grid Computing Environments*

Chao-Tung Yang[1,**], Po-Chi Shih[1,2], Sung-Yi Chen[1], and Wen-Chung Shih[3]

[1] High-Performance Computing Laboratory, Department of Computer Science and Information Engineering, Tunghai University, Taichung, 40704 Taiwan, R.O.C.
ctyang@thu.edu.tw

[2] Department of Computer Science, National Tsing Hua University, Hsinchu, 30013 Taiwan, R.O.C.
shedoh@gmail.com

[3] Department of Computer and Information Science, National Chiao Tung University, Hsinchu 300, Taiwan, R.O.C.
gis90805@cis.nctu.edu.tw

Abstract. Grid computing technologies enable large-scale aggregation and sharing of resources via wide-area networks focused on sharing computational, data, and other resources to form general-purpose services for users. In this paper, we address network information gathering and focus on providing approximate measurement models for network-related information using Network Weather Service (NWS) for future scheduling and benchmarking. We propose a network measurement model for gathering network-related information including bandwidth, latency, forecasting, error rates, etc., without generating excessive system overhead. We consider inaccuracies in real-world network values in generating approximation values for future use.

Keywords: Network information, NWS, Globus, Grid computing, Bandwidth.

1 Introduction

Grid computing is commonly used by scientists and researchers to solve complex problems in parallel and distributed paradigm [1, 2, 3, 4, 5, 12, 13]. A key issue in Grid computing environments is providing a centralized interface that enables users to make use of various resources easily. Grid computing technologies includes many elements such as user authentication, job description, information gathering, job scheduling, and resource dispatching. In this work, we concerned with information gathering. Without precise information, no scheduling strategy or algorithm will work well.

* The authors would like to acknowledge the National Center for High-Performance Computing for sponsoring the Taiwan UniGrid project, under the national project "Taiwan Knowledge Innovation National Grid". This work is supported in part by National Science Council Taiwan, under grants no. NSC93-2213-E-029-026, NSC94-2213-E-029-002, and NSC93-2119-M-002-004.

** Corresponding author.

H. Zhuge and G.C. Fox (Eds.): GCC 2005, LNCS 3795, pp. 287 – 299, 2005.

In this paper we report on using the Globus Toolkit [6, 7, 10] to build a grid environment. Globus is a commonly used middleware for constructing grid environments and providing development tools. Its main advantage is that it supplies a good security model with a provision for hierarchically collecting information about the grid.

Regardless of grid type, bandwidth management is a question of manipulating numerous variables to support systems and maximizes grid performance [15]. As grid computing becomes popular, there is a need to manage and monitor available resources worldwide, as well as a need to convey these resources to people for everyday use. Network bandwidth is crucial when work is distributed around groups of machines, especially when jobs require heavy communication. To understand why managing bandwidth is so critical, we need to analyze what affects overall grid performance.

The Globus Information Service, Monitor and Discover Service (MDS), provides good system-related information support on CPU speeds, CPU loading, memory utilization, etc., but no network-related information support [5, 12]. Therefore, we make use of the open-source program NWS for providing network information.

Network Weather Service (NWS) can measure point-to-point network bandwidth and latency that may be important for grid scheduling and load balancing [9, 11]. NWS detects all network states during time periods selected by the user. Because this kind of site-to-site measurement results in $N(N\text{-}1)$ network measurement processes, the time complexity is $O(N^2)$. Our network model focuses on solving the problem of reducing this time complexity without losing too much precision.

In this paper, we focus on providing approximate measurement models for network-related information using NWS for future scheduling and benchmarking. We first propose a network measurement model for gathering network-related information including bandwidth, latency, forecasting, error rates, etc., without generating excessive system overhead. We then consider inaccuracies in real-world network values in generating approximation values for future use.

This paper is organized as follows. We give a background review of NWS and Globus in Section 2. In Section 3 we describe our measurement model and research questions. In Section 4 we report on a grid computing environment constructed in three Taiwan schools using the Globus Toolkit, and experimental results and discussion are presented. We conclude this study in Section 5.

2 Background Review

2.1 Globus Project

The Globus Toolkit is an open source software toolkit used for building Grid systems and applications [10]. It is being developed by the Globus Alliance and many others all over the world. A growing number of projects and companies are using the Globus Toolkit to unlock the potential of grids for their causes. The Globus Toolkit has become an actual standard for Grid middleware to handle these four kinds of services:

- Resource management: Grid Resource Allocation & Management (GRAM)
- Information Services: Monitoring and Discovery Service (MDS)

- Security Services: Grid Security Infrastructure (GSI)
- Data Movement and Management: Global Access to Secondary Storage (GASS) and GridFTP.

GRAM is designed to provide a single common protocol and API for requesting and using remote system resources, by providing a uniform, flexible interface to local job scheduling systems. The Grid Security Infrastructure (GSI) provides mutual authentication of both users and remote resources using GSI (Grid-wide) PKI-based identities. GRAM provides a simple authorization mechanism based on GSI identities and a mechanism to map GSI identities to local user accounts.

MDS is designed to provide a standard mechanism for publishing and discovering resource status and configuration information. It provides a uniform, flexible interface to data collected by lower-level information providers. It has a decentralized structure that allows it to scale, and it can handle static (e.g., OS, CPU types, and system architectures) or dynamic data (e.g., disk availability, memory availability, and loading). A project can also restrict access to data by combining GSI (Grid Security Infrastructure) credentials and authorization features provided by MDS.

GridFTP [3] is a high-performance, secure, and reliable data transfer protocol optimized for high-bandwidth wide-area networks. The GridFTP protocol is based on FTP, the highly-popular Internet File Transfer protocol.

2.2 Network Weather Service

The Network Weather Service, though not targeted on clusters, is a distributed system that periodically monitors and dynamically forecasts the performance that various network and computational resources can deliver over a given time interval. The service operates a distributed set of performance sensors (network monitors, CPU monitors, etc.) from which it gathers system condition information. It then uses numerical models to generate forecasts of what the conditions will be for a given time period. It also uses mathematical models to forecast each condition and the Mean Absolute Error (MAE) and Mean Square Error (MSE) rates. NWS is a widely used measurement tool for Grid environments. Studies on topics, such as load balancing, scheduling, brokering, replica selection, etc., are available [9, 11].

3 Network Information Model

We constructed a network measurement model to solve a complete point-to-point network measurement problem. Consider the twelve-node grid environment shown in Figure 1. The lines linking the nodes represent site-to-site network measurement. A "node" or "site" here represents a single machines or a personal computer. This model is often used for local grids or cluster environments when the scale is not too large. In large-scale grid environments this kind of architecture results in excessive bandwidth overhead. In order to reduce the total number of times of NWS measurement, we proposed the "domain" concept shown in Figure 2 to partition the network measurement environment.

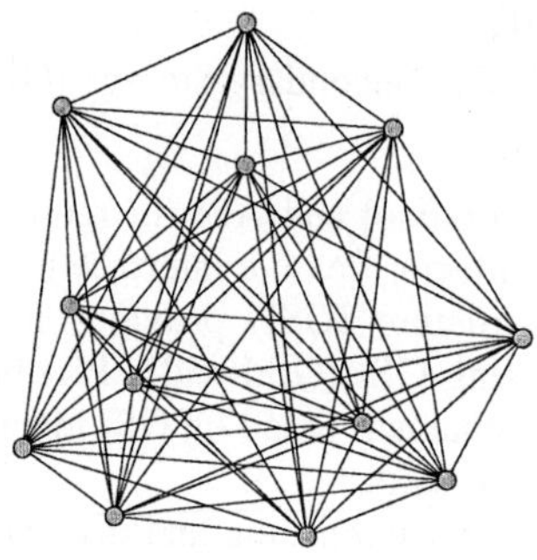

Fig. 1. Network measurement model

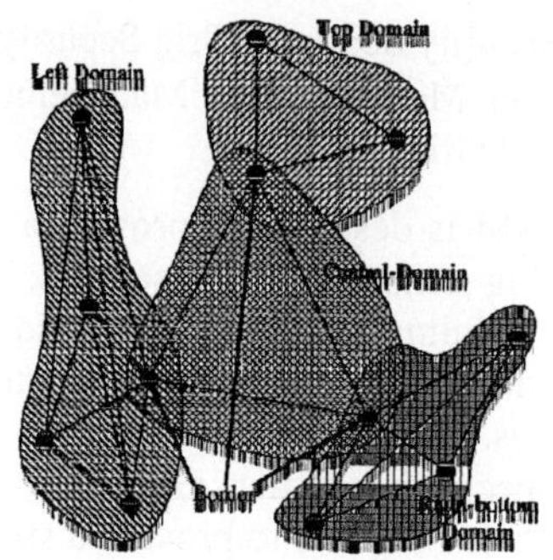

Fig. 2. Domain-based network measurement model

In our domain-based model, we define several hosts as a domain ("host" means the same as "node" and "site"). Figure 2 shows three domains, one with 5 hosts at left, one with 3 hosts on top, and one with 4 hosts at right-bottom. They are linked by "borders" that form a central domain. We thus need only pairwise measurements within domains. Domain-to-domain data is measured by the central-domain, considerably reducing the number of measurements required.

Our domain-based model looks like the clique of NWS seemingly, but they are not in same level. The Clique co-operates with token passing skill and it is a bottom level component built in NWS. Our model is on top of all. Hence, its advantages include reducing the number of experiments conducting. Our main idea is to predict some links that are lost in our model. We will discuss several types of cases about prediction technique related to our model later. Now we can extend existing group models and consider how to construct domain-based models from geographical and real bandwidth perspectives.

We separate schools or organizations into domains on the basis of geography. Hosts in each domain are thought of as tightly coupled, and it is convenient for each domain to control and maintain its hosts. The domains may each use a different network infrastructure: Fast Ethernet, Gigabit, or InfiniBand. This design ensures that local fluctuations won't affect the entire grid system. Some questions about the model remain:

- how to select a representative host in each domain to form a central domain without loss of generality?
- how to accurately evaluate host-to-host network information lost in the domain model?

About the first question, we should discuss about what is a representative border in a domain. In our model, a job may be submitted cross different domains. In this case, we will consider the bandwidth between each border to decide where we should submit our jobs (we focus on parallel jobs). The host with the worst bandwidth will encumber the total execution time. Therefore the representative border must be the one which has the worst bandwidth.

Here we discuss how to select borders. One way is to conduct an all-pair network test and select the worst one in each domain. However, this may not work in a real grid environment because the organizations owning the domains may each control their hosts according to different policies. Another way is to let domain administrators select borders according to network topology or architecture (maybe select the host in the deepest topology away from the router who connects to WLAN). These two methods are not smart and not scalable, so we propose an alternative way to select borders.

1. When the Grid is first being built up, pick some domains (perhaps 2~4 if the total number of domains is more than that) to start with. Then, perform one of the above ways to select borders and save them in a border list.
2. The other domains (not selected in step one) should select a border one by one according to network topology, or test all hosts in each domain against each border in border list to select one and add to the list. We take Figure 3 for example. The top and right domains have already selected their borders by step 1. Now we take left domain to perform step 2.We perform network tests to know the bandwidth of R_1, R_2, … , R_5 and T_1, T_2, … ,T_5. Then select the one who has the minimal bandwidth (minimize R_n+T_n for n = 1 to 5)
3. Repeat step 2 until every domain has found a best border.

This simplifies construction complexity to avoid all pair network testing and makes the grid environment scalable for adding new domains. When a new domain will join the existing grid, only step 3 need be performed.

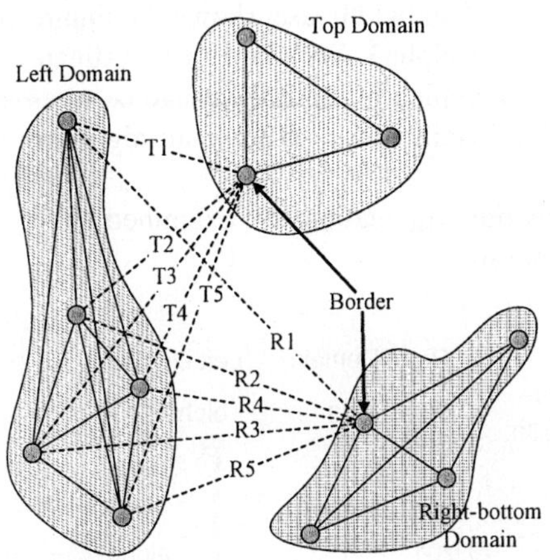

Fig. 3. Border selection diagram

About the second question, in order to obtain the all-pair network values lost in out model, we use a few measured values from NWS to estimate the lost value.

Figure 4 shows an example of a network estimation model. The line connecting alpha1 and lz01 is part of the central-domain, which we called the *Bridge* in our experimental environment. The solid lines mean that our domain model has gotten the network information; the dotted lines are examples of many lines our model has not measured, so we use an evaluation model to calculate them. The following notation is used throughout this paper.

- B_in_{avg}: average inner-domain bandwidth (Mbits/sec)
- B_out_{avg}: average outer-domain bandwidth (Mbits/sec)
- P_{flu}: amplitude of bandwidth fluctuation (%)
- N_{flu}: number of times of bandwidth fluctuation detected
- P_{vaflu}: valid fluctuation rate (%)
- *Use:* Boolean value signifying whether-bandwidth has been used
- $Lij(k)$: the kth inner-domain measurement value counted backward from node i to node j.

B_in_{avg} and B_out_{avg} are obtained by averaging historical bandwidth values. N_{flu} traces network fluctuations over given time periods ignoring pulses and bandwidth noise. Our algorithm will detect the bandwidth value of last N_{flu} times similar to a sliding window. P_{vaflu} shows how much percentage of bandwidth fluctuation occurred during N_{flu} times, which is treated as actual bandwidth use (*Use*). $L_{ij}(k)$ is the latest k^{th} value measured by NWS. We give a default values that P_{flu} = 30%, N_{flu} = 10, time period = 5 second (achieved by setting NWS sensor period), and P_{vaflu} = 80% through our experiment.

We employ our algorithm in three separate cases to consider possible bandwidth usage patterns.

Case 1

Assume the inner domain bandwidth use shown in Figure 5. The bandwidth use occurred between alpha2 to alpha3. We want to investigate that how it affects our target bandwidth. This is complex because the usage between alpha2 and alpha3 may not affect the bridge bandwidth much. We use an algorithm to calculate the target bandwidth.

Left domain bandwidth fluctuation is examined first, ignoring pulses and bandwidth noise fluctuations:

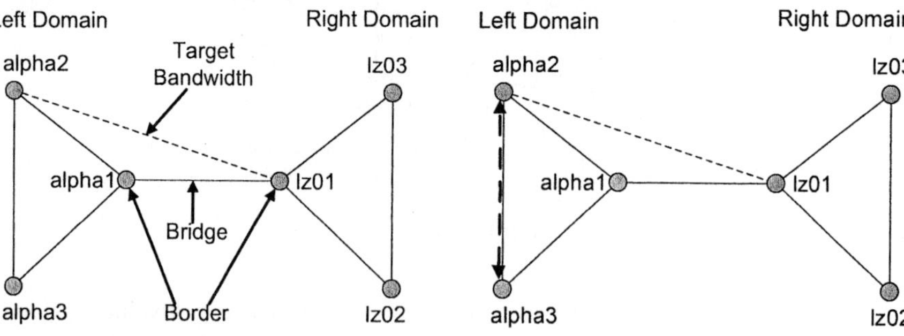

Fig. 4. Network estimate model

Fig. 5. Bandwidth usage in Case 1

$$Use = \texttt{CountIf}(\frac{|L_{ij}[k]-B\_in_{avg}|}{B\_in_{avg}} > P_{flu}) > (N_{flu} \times P_{vaflu}),\ k = 1, \ldots, N_{flu},\ \forall ij \text{ in left domain.} \quad (1)$$

The function **CountIf** is used to count the times if the condition in brackets is true. $\frac{|L_{ij}[k]-B\_in_{avg}|}{B\_in_{avg}}$ is the percentage of bandwidth down. $N_{flu} \times P_{vaflu} = 8$ is set as our default value. For example, the formula *Use* is true if the percentage of bandwidth down large than 30% is more than 8 times over last 10 network values measured by NWS. The remaining bandwidth usage is then calculated by ignoring the maximal and minimal bandwidth values via sorting L_{ij} list.

$$B_{rem} = \frac{\sum_{k=2}^{N_{flu}-1} L_{ij}[k]}{N_{flu}-2} \quad (2)$$

Finally, the target bandwidth is calculated as follows:

$$B_{tar} = \frac{B_{rem}}{B\_in_{avg}} \times B\_out_{avg} \times \alpha \quad (3)$$

The symbol α here indicates a value converted from internet bandwidth to LAN and is used throughout this paper.

Case 2

We assumed that bandwidth use occurs within organizations but not with other members of the domain (machine pc1), as shown in Figure 6. Figure 7 shows the general topology of network architecture. The network transfer will go through the top switch. So we claim that the target bandwidth almost follows bridge bandwidth.

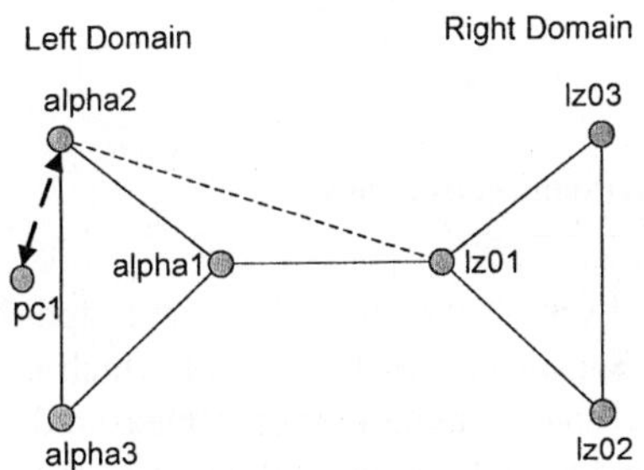

Fig. 6. Bandwidth usage in Case 2

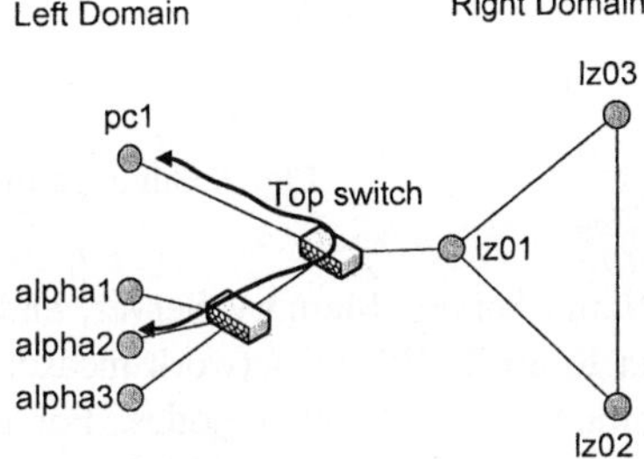

Fig. 7. Topology for Case 2

Case 3

We assumed that bandwidth use occurs between two domains, as shown in Figure 8. Bandwidth use between alpha2 and lz03 will affect the available bridge bandwidth. So we claim that the target bandwidth almost follows bridge bandwidth just like Case 2.

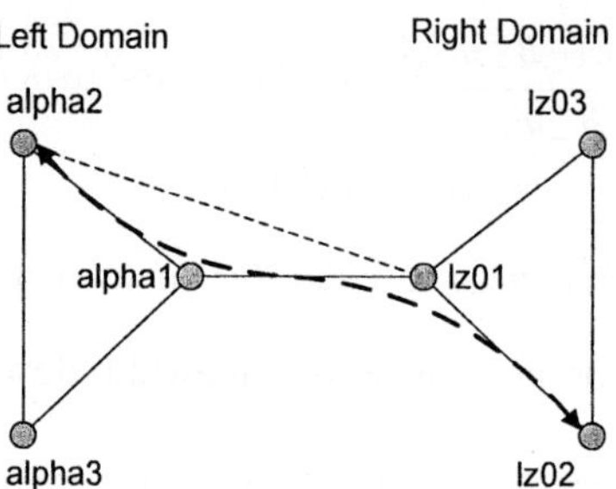

Fig. 8. Bandwidth usage in Case 3

4 Experimental Results

We set up the two domains shown in Figure 9 for experimentation using our grid testbed. The alpha domain with four hosts is situated at the THU HPC laboratory, and the lz-domain, also with 4 hosts, is at the LZ senior high school. We installed and set up NWS on each node and configured the domains appropriately. The servers alpha1 and lz01 were used as border nodes and connected to the other nodes in their respective domains. Both domains have 100MB fast Ethernet capacity.

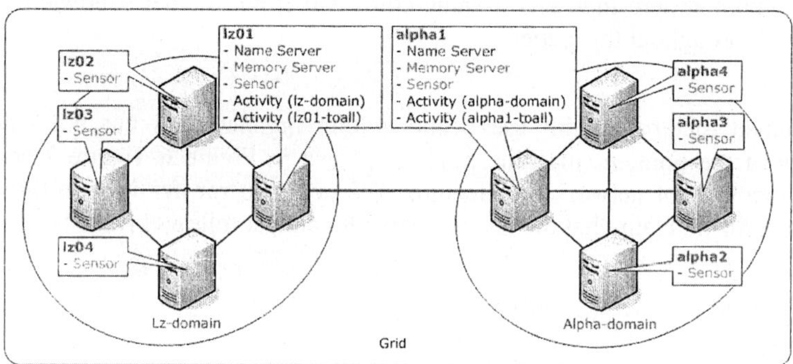

Fig. 9. Our experimental environment overview

Name Server, Memory Server, and Sensor were installed on lz01 and alpha1 in order to use NWS for network measurement. Sensor is used to monitor which nodes communicate with other nodes. For example, the lz-domain sensor measured link information between nodes in the lz-domain and stored the measurements in the lz01 Memory Server. The lz01-toall sensor measured link information between the border nodes lz01 and alpha1 and stored the results in the lz01 Memory Server.

We used the Java CoG Kit [8] to implement the GUI as shown in Figures 10, 11, and 12. Our application can connect with the grid system by using the Java CoG kit. The key characteristics include:

- GridProxyInit, which creates a limited-life proxy for authorized users to access grid resources.
- GridConfigureDialog, which uses the CoG Kit UITool to enable users to configure the number of process and the grid server host name.
- GridJob, which creates GramJob instances. This class represents a simple gram job, allowing submitting jobs to a gatekeeper, canceling them, sending signal commands, and registering and unregistering callbacks.
- GetRSL, RSL provides a common interchange language for describing resources. The various Globus Resource Management architecture components manipulate RSL strings to perform their management functions in cooperation with the other system components. GetRSL combines RSL strings.
- JobMonitor, uses two parameters, Gridjob and RSL to start GlobusRun and monitor the job process.
- GlobusRun is a factory method for creating and exporting credentials, and submitting jobs to the grid server and receiving the responses from it.

We also developed some APIs for our system. For example, ProxyDestroy, which destroys CA files to protect the grid system from the application site we can configure the machinefile for the grid system.

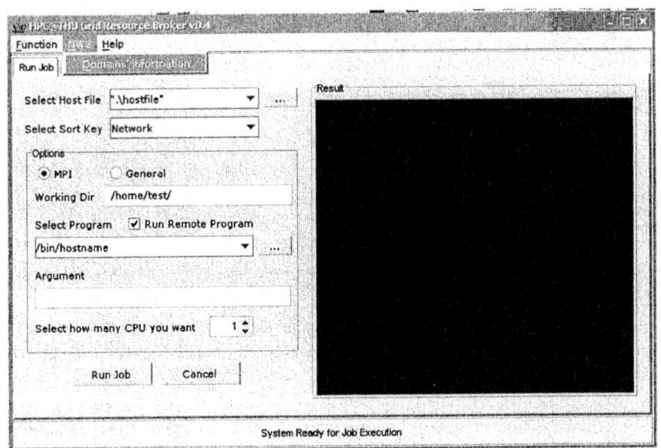

Fig. 10. Domain information is used to show network information

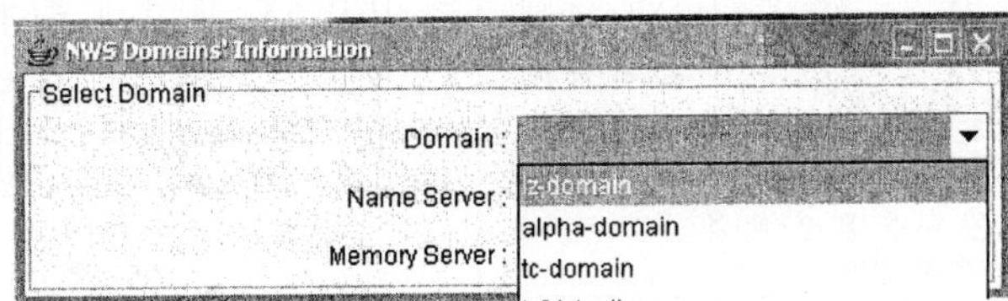

Fig. 11. lz-domain is selected

Select Domain

Domain : lz-domain

Name Server : lz01.lzsh.tcc.edu.tw

Memory Server : lz01.lzsh.tcc.edu.tw

Domain Information

name : lz-domain

host : lz01.lzsh.tcc.edu.tw:8060

period : 30

member 0 : lz01.lzsh.tcc.edu.tw:8060

member 1 : lz02.lzsh.tcc.edu.tw:8060

member 2 : lz03.lzsh.tcc.edu.tw:8060

member 3 : lz04.lzsh.tcc.edu.tw:8060

Records

lz01.lzsh.tcc.edu.tw:8060	lz02.lzsh.tcc.edu.tw:8060		lz03.lzsh.tcc.edu.tw:8060		lz04.lzsh.tcc.edu.tw:8060	
Bandwidth (Mbits/sec) :	1102600530	43.57447	1102600530	43.80749	1102600530	43.51660
Latency (ms) :	1102600530	0.38900	1102600530	0.53000	1102600530	0.44600
lz02.lzsh.tcc.edu.tw:8060	lz03.lzsh.tcc.edu.tw:8060		lz04.lzsh.tcc.edu.tw:8060		lz01.lzsh.tcc.edu.tw:8060	
Bandwidth (Mbits/sec) :	1102600533	44.87999	1102600533	43.66156	1102600533	55.88233
Latency (ms) :	1102600533	0.56700	1102600533	0.48300	1102600533	0.34300
lz03.lzsh.tcc.edu.tw:8060	lz04.lzsh.tcc.edu.tw:8060		lz01.lzsh.tcc.edu.tw:8060		lz02.lzsh.tcc.edu.tw:8060	
Bandwidth (Mbits/sec) :	1102600496	43.87347	1102600496	56.04960	1102600496	51.98176
Latency (ms) :	1102600496	0.55800	1102600496	0.34200	1102600496	0.55800
lz04.lzsh.tcc.edu.tw:8060	lz01.lzsh.tcc.edu.tw:8060		lz02.lzsh.tcc.edu.tw:8060		lz03.lzsh.tcc.edu.tw:8060	
Bandwidth (Mbits/sec) :	1102600531	55.45674	1102600531	44.61266	1102600531	52.25115
Latency (ms) :	1102600531	0.35200	1102600531	0.51000	1102600531	0.50200

Fig. 12. Detailed information provided by the GUI

The symbol "~" is used below to indicate connection speed. For example, lz01~alpha1 is the connection speed between lz01 and alpha1. We transferred an 800MB file from alpha2 to alpha3 to simulate bandwidth usage. We observed five links, including three links in the alpha-domain, and one bridge lz01~alpha1. However, the last one lz01~alpha2 is not shown in our model, which was added for experimental comparison. Figure 13 clearly shows that alpha2~alpha3 did not affect lz01~alpha1. Therefore, to evaluate lz01~alpha2 (not shown in our network model), we had to observe the connection speed inside the alpha domain. Figure 14 shows the

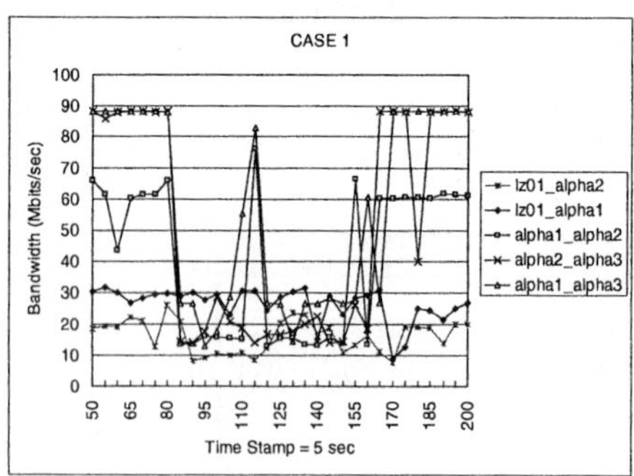

Fig. 13. Experimental result for transferring an 800MB file from alpha2 to alpha3

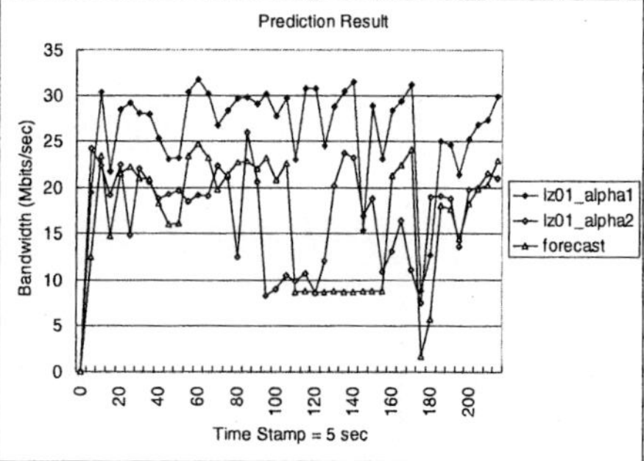

Fig. 14. Experimental results comparing actual bandwidth with our algorithm prediction

prediction result of our algorithm. The curve of target bandwidth fits the actual bandwidth as our expectation. But there exists some delay caused by N_{flu} times sliding window detection period. So we summarize that our algorithm can predict the network behavior with a little delay.

Case 2

In this case, the 800MB file was transferred from alpha2 to an external server called pc1, as shown in Figure 15. The connection speeds shown for lz01~alpha1 and alpha1~alpha2 were obtained by NWS; besides, lz01~alpha2 was measured for comparison. In this case, the curve of lz01~alpha1 is almost the same as lz01~alpha2. This result fits our claim that the target bandwidth goes with the border bandwidth.

Case 3

In this case, the 800MB file was transferred from alpha2 to lz02. The connection speed between lz01~alpha1 shown in Figure 16 was obtained using NWS. The others were measured for experimental comparison. The situation of lz01~alpha2 can be substitute with lz01~alpha1 by experiment result. The situation of alpha1~lz02 can be substituted with alpha1~lz01 by the two situation above, and lz02~alpha2 can be substituted with lz01~alpha1. The experimental result confirms the inference above.

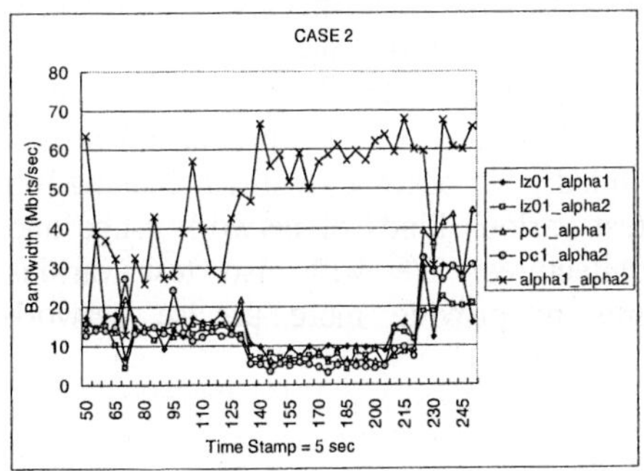

Fig. 15. Experimental results for transferring an 800MB file from alpha2 to the pc1

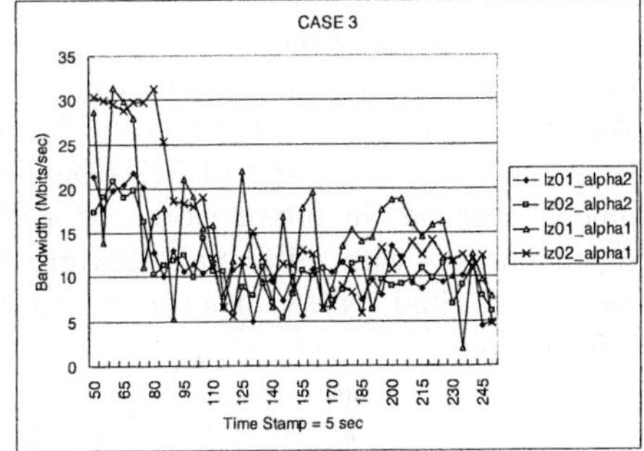

Fig. 16. Experimental results for transferring an 800MB file from alpha2 to lz02

Through the above three experiments, we can summarize the result under 3 cases. Case 1: the target bandwidth can be predicted by our algorithm within acceptable error and delay. Case 2: the bridge bandwidth can be use to substituted with target bandwidth. Case 3: almost likes Case 2.

The second experiment tested NWS measurement values for various packet (frame) sizes. There exists an inaccuracy problem with NWS. We want to know if we can improve the accuracy by adjusting some setting of NWS. The most effective parameter is the packet size used by NWS sensor. The results of varying packet sizes shown in Figures 17 and 18 indicate that the measured bandwidth increased as packet size increased and approached the maximum bandwidth. Our test indicated that a 512-Kbits packet size is most suitable, which can avoid wasting too much bandwidth in our grid environment.

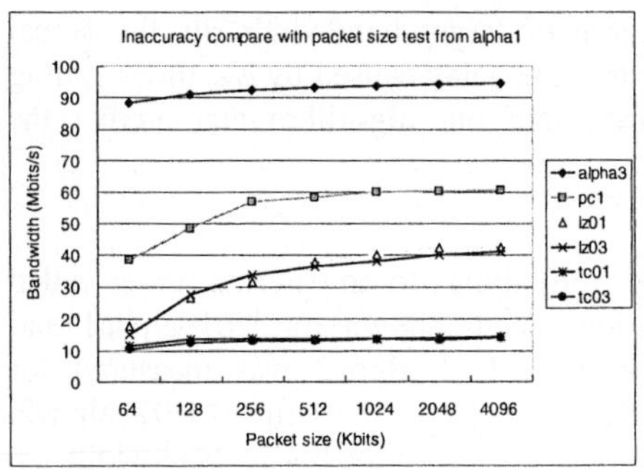

Fig. 17. NWS measurement value testing from alpha1

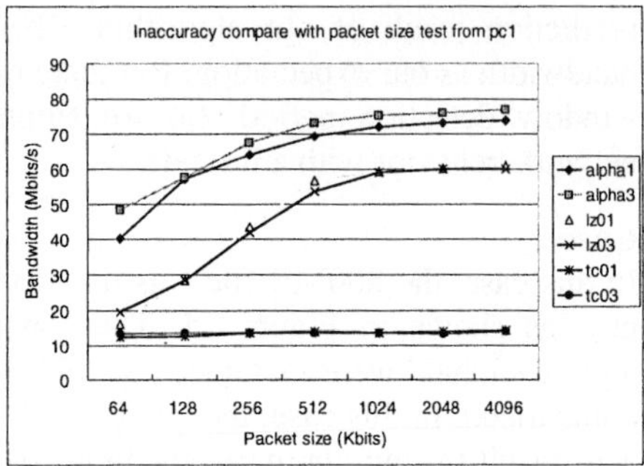

Fig. 18. NWS measurement value testing from pc1

5 Conclusion

We constructed a domain-based model to investigate reducing network measurements. We also proposed an algorithm to evaluate point-to-point network bandwidth without measuring. Finally we considered inaccuracies in real-world network values by generating approximation values for future use. The results show that our algorithm was useful in calculating target bandwidths in Cases 1, 2, and 3. We also compared the influence of different packet sizes. The experimental results showed that a packet size of 512-Kbits provided good accuracy without causing too much overhead. In future work, we will test various kinds of network usage and organizations with different network architectures. We will also test various parameters and NWS inaccuracy measures to provide more precise network information.

References

1. B. Allcock, J. Bester, J. Bresnahan, A. L. Chervenak, I. Foster, C. Kesselman, S. Meder, V. Nefedova, D. Quesnal, S. Tuecke. "Data Management and Transfer in High Performance Computational Grid Environments." *Parallel Computing*, 28(5):749-771, May 2002.
2. B. Allcock, S. Tuecke, I. Foster, A. Chervenak, and C. Kesselman. "Protocols and Services for Distributed Data-Intensive Science." *ACAT2000 Proceedings*, pp. 161-163, 2000.
3. W. Allcock, J. Bester, J. Bresnahan, A. Chervenak, L. Liming, S. Meder, S. Tuecke. "GridFTP Protocol Specification." *GGF GridFTP Working Group Document*, September 2002.
4. I. Foster, C. Kesselman, S. Tuecke. "The Anatomy of the Grid: Enabling Scalable Virtual Organizations." *Int. J. of Supercomputer Applications and High Performance Computing*, 15(3), pp. 200-222, 2001.
5. I. Foster, C. Kesselman, "Globus: A Metacomputing Infrastructure Toolkit," *Intl J. Supercomputer Applications*, 11(2), pp. 115-128, 1997.
6. Global Grid Forum, http://www.ggf.org

7. IBM Redbooks, "Introduction to Grid Computing with Globus", http://www.redbooks.ibm.com/redbooks/pdfs/sg246895.pdf
8. Java CoG Kits, http://www.cogkit.org/
9. Network Weather Service, http://nws.cs.ucsb.edu/
10. The Globus Alliance, http://www.globus.org/
11. R. Wolski, N. Spring and J. Hayes, "The Network Weather Service: A Distributed Resource Performance Forecasting Service for Metacomputing," *Future Generation Computer Systems*, 15(5-6):757-768, 1999.
12. Chao-Tung Yang, Chuan-Lin Lai, Po-Chi Shih, and Kuan-Ching Li, "A Resource Broker for Computing Nodes Selection in Grid Environments," *Grid and Cooperative Computing - GCC 2004: Third International Conference, Lecture Notes in Computer Science*, Springer-Verlag, Hai Jin, Yi Pan, Nong Xiao (Eds.), vol. 3251, pp. 931-934, Oct. 2004.
13. Chao-Tung Yang, Po-Chi Shih, Kuan-Ching Li, "A High-Performance Computational Resource Broker for Grid Computing Environments," *Proceedings of the International Conference on Advanced Information Networking and Applications (AINA 2005) INA'2005 The First International Workshop on Information Networking and Application*, vol. 2, pp. 333-336, Tamkang University, Taipei, Taiwan, March 28-30, 2005.
14. X. Zhang, J. Freschl, and J. Schopf, "A Performance Study of Monitoring and Information Services for Distributed Systems", *Proceedings of 12th IEEE International Symposium on High Performance Distributed Computing (HPDC-12 '03)*, pp. 270-282, August 2003.
15. H. Zhuge, "The Future Interconnection Environment," *IEEE Computer*, 38(4): 27-33, 2005.

Flexible Temporal Consistency for Fixed-Time Constraint Verification in Grid Workflow Systems

Jinjun Chen and Yun Yang

CICEC – Centre for Internet Computing and E-Commerce,
Faculty of Information and Communication Technologies,
Swinburne University of Technology,
PO Box 218, Hawthorn, Melbourne, Australia 3122
{jchen, yyang}@ict.swin.edu.au

Abstract. To verify fixed-time constraints in grid workflow systems, the consistency and inconsistency conditions have been defined in the conventional work. However, in this paper, we argue that although the conventional consistency condition is reasonable, the conventional inconsistency condition is too rigorous and covers several different situations. These situations which are handled conventionally by the same exception handling should be handled differently for cost saving. Therefore, we divide the conventional inconsistency into *weak consistency, weak inconsistency and strong inconsistency* and treat the conventional consistency as *strong consistency*. Correspondingly, we discuss how to verify them. Especially, for the weak consistency, we present a method on how to adjust it to the strong consistency. For the weak inconsistency, we analyse why it can be handled by simpler and more economical exception handling. The final comparison and discussion further demonstrate that our research can achieve better cost effectiveness than the conventional work.

1 Introduction

Grid workflow systems are supposed to support modelling, redesign and execution of large-scale sophisticated e-science and e-business processes in many complex scientific and business applications such as climate modelling, astrophysics, international finance and insurance [1, 2, 3, 12, 19]. A grid workflow normally contains many computation or data intensive activities and the dependencies between them [3, 6, 15]. The activities are implemented and executed by corresponding grid services. And the dependencies define activity execution orders and form four basic control structures: sequential, parallel, selective and iterative [3]. The whole working process of a grid workflow system can be divided into three stages: build-time stage, run-time instantiation stage and run-time execution stage. At the build-time stage, grid workflow specifications are defined by some grid workflow definition languages such as Grid Services Flow Language (GSFL), Abstract Grid Workflow Language (AGWL), Service Workflow Language (SWFL) and Grid Workflow Execution Language (GWEL) [3, 11, 15, 16]. At the run-time instantiation stage, grid workflow instances are created, and especially grid services specified in the build-time definition documents are discovered by an instantiation service that is a high-level grid service [3, 16]. At the

H. Zhuge and G.C. Fox (Eds.): GCC 2005, LNCS 3795, pp. 300–311, 2005.

run-time execution stage, the grid workflow instances are executed, and the execution is coordinated between grid services by the grid workflow engine. The grid workflow engine is also a high-level grid service, hence automatically grid aware [3, 15, 16].

To control the temporal correctness of the grid workflow specification and execution, fixed-time constraints are often set at build-time [4, 10, 18]. A fixed-time constraint at an activity is an absolute time value by which the activity must be completed. For example, a climate modelling grid workflow must be completed by the scheduled time [1], say 8:00pm, so that the weather forecasting can be broadcasted at a later time, say 10:30pm, on the same day. Here, 8pm is a fixed-time constraint. After the fixed-time constraints are set, the temporal verification is conducted at the above three stages to check whether they are consistent. At the run-time execution stage, some checkpoints are selected for conducting the temporal verification because it is inefficient to do so at all activity points [5, 6, 7, 18].

According to the literature, [10] uses the modified Critical Path Method (CPM) to calculate temporal constraints and is one of the very few projects that consider temporal constraint reasoning at both build-time and run-time. [18] presents a method for dynamic verification of absolute deadline constraints and relative deadline constraints. [20] proposes a timed workflow process model with considering the flow time, the time difference in a distributed execution environment and consistency checking combining the exact run-time duration and the estimated build-time duration. [5] represents our work on discussing the checkpoint selection and the integration of the different stage temporal verification to improve the temporal verification efficiency.

However, the inconsistency condition defined in the above conventional work and some of our previous work such as [4] is too rigorous although the consistency condition is reasonable. To distinguish with the related concepts to be presented later by us, we rename the consistency and the inconsistency defined in the conventional work as CC (*Conventional Consistency*) and CI (*Conventional Inconsistency*) respectively. However, in Section 3, we will see that CI actually covers several different situations. By separating them, we can treat them differently while the conventional work treats them by the same exception handling. Consequently, a significant handling cost can be saved. Therefore, in this paper, we divide CI into three states: WC (*Weak Consistency*), WI (*Weak Inconsistency*), and SI (*Strong Inconsistency*) and for integrity we treat CC as SC (*Strong Consistency*). The specific definitions and explanation of the four states will be given in Section 3. Correspondingly, we investigate how to verify them, and develop a method on how to utilise the mean activity time redundancy and the temporal dependency between fixed-time constraints to adjust WC so that statistically it can still be kept as SC. For WI, we discuss why it can rely on simpler and less costly exception handling than SI. The final quantitative comparison shows that our research can achieve better cost effectiveness than the conventional work.

The remainder of the paper is organised as follows. Section 2 describes a timed grid workflow representation. Section 3 details SC, WC, WI and SI. Section 4 discusses the verification of SC, WC, WI and SI. Section 5 presents a WC adjustment approach. Section 6 further shows the benefits of our work through a comparison and discussion. Section 7 concludes our contributions and points out the future work.

2 Timed Grid Workflow Representation

Based on the directed graph concept, a grid workflow can be represented by a grid workflow graph, where nodes correspond to activities and edges correspond to dependencies between activities, called flows [8, 10]. As far as the time is concerned, an activity is similar to a flow. Therefore, we use term "activity" to refer to the real activity as well as the flow and will not distinguish them if not explicitly mentioned. We borrow some concepts from [4, 10, 18] such as the maximum or minimum duration as a basis to represent the time attributes. We denote the ith activity of a grid workflow as a_i, the expected time that the specification of grid workflow *gw* comes into effect as $Cie(gw)$. For each a_i, we denote its maximum duration, minimum duration, run-time start time, run-time end time and run-time completion duration as $D(a_i)$, $d(a_i)$, $S(a_i)$, $E(a_i)$ and $Rcd(a_i)$ respectively. $D(a_i)$ and $d(a_i)$ can be obtained based on the past grid workflow execution history collected by the grid workflow systems. $Rcd(a_i)$ covers the queuing delay, set-up delay, synchronisation delay, network latency and so on caused at a_i. If there is a fixed-time constraint at a_i, we denote it as $FTC(a_i)$, its value as $ftv(a_i)$.

In addition, we introduce mean duration to each activity. And at a_i, we denote it as $Mean(a_i)$. The activity mean duration means that statistically the activity can be completed around its mean duration. According to [13, 17], we can apply some stochastic models such as poisson distribution or exponential distribution to obtain the mean duration for each activity. Normally, we have $d(a_i) \le Mean(a_i) \le D(a_i)$.

If there is a path from a_i to a_j $(i \le j)$, we denote the maximum duration, minimum duration, mean duration, run-time real completion duration between them as $D(a_i, a_j)$, $d(a_i, a_j)$, $Mean(a_i, a_j)$ and $Rcd(a_i, a_j)$ respectively [10, 18]. For convenience, we consider one execution path in the grid workflow without losing generality. As to a selective or parallel structure, for each branch, it is an execution path. For an iterative structure, from the start time to the end time, it is still an execution path. Therefore, for the selective/parallel/iterative structure we can also apply the results achieved from one execution path. Correspondingly, between a_i and a_j, $D(a_i, a_j)$ is equal to the sum of all activity maximum durations, and $d(a_i, a_j)$ is equal to the sum of all activity minimum durations, and $Mean(a_i, a_j)$ is equal to the sum of all mean durations.

There is a difference between $Mean(a_i)$ and $D(a_i)$. We define it as the mean activity time redundancy.

Definition 1. The mean activity time redundancy of a_i is defined as the difference between its maximum duration and its mean duration, namely $D(a_i)-Mean(a_i)$.

3 CC and CI vs SC, WC, WI and SI

The definitions of CC and CI in the conventional work can be summarised as follows.

Definition 2. At the build-time stage, $FTC(a_i)$ is said to be of CC if $D(a_1, a_i) \le ftv(a_i)-Cie(gw)$, and is said to be of CI if $ftv(a_i)- Cie(gw) < D(a_1, a_i)$.

Definition 3. At the run-time instantiation stage, $FTC(a_i)$ is said to be of CC if $D(a_1, a_i) \le ftv(a_i) - S(a_1)$ and is said to be of CI if $ftv(a_i)- S(a_1) < D(a_1, a_i)$.

Definition 4. At the run-time execution stage, at checkpoint a_p which is either before or at a_i $(p \leq i)$, $FTC(a_i)$ is said to be of CC if $Rcd(a_1, a_p)+D(a_{p+1}, a_i) \leq ftv(a_i)-S(a_1)$, and is said to be of CI if $ftv(a_i)-S(a_1) < Rcd(a_1, a_p)+ D(a_{p+1}, a_i)$.

The CC conditions in Definitions 2, 3 and 4 are reasonable because we should try to keep a fixed-time constraint consistent and with such conditions we can get to the largest extent where we can ensure the consistency of a fixed-time constraint. For clarity, in this paper, we treat CC as SC.

Now considering CI, we take Definition 4 as an example to analyse why its condition is too rigorous. In Definition 4, if $ftv(a_i)-S(a_1) < Rcd(a_1, a_p)+D(a_{p+1}, a_i)$, $FTC(a_i)$ will be treated as CI and the exception handling is triggered. However, at the run-time execution stage, the activity completion duration is uncertain. Therefore, there could be some time redundancy by the succeeding activities after a_i. With this time redundancy, some situations of CI may be able to be adjusted to SC without triggering the exception handling that normally causes some extra cost. For those that cannot be adjusted to SC, the specific difference between $ftv(a_i)-S(a_1)$ and $Rcd(a_1, a_p)+D(a_{p+1}, a_i)$ could vary depending on the system load. It may be bigger or smaller. For the smaller ones, we can trigger the simpler exception handling that may adjust and compensate fewer activities and hence save more cost. For the bigger ones, we can leave it for the more complicated exception handling as that in the conventional work.

In summary, we should divide CI into three different situations. The first one can be adjusted to SC with the possible time redundancy without triggering any exception handling. The second one can be treated by simpler and less costly exception handling. The third one has to be treated by more complicated exception handling as in the conventional work. Correspondingly, we divide CI into WC, WI and SI. We now give the specific definitions of them and SC.

Definition 5. At the build-time stage, $FTC(a_i)$ is said to be of SC if $D(a_1, a_i) \leq ftv(a_i)-Cie(gw)$, WC if $Mean(a_1, a_i) \leq ftv(a_i)-Cie(gw) < D(a_1, a_i)$, WI if $d(a_1, a_i) \leq ftv(a_i)-Cie(gw) < Mean(a_1, a_i)$, and SI if $ftv(a_i)-Cie(gw) < d(a_1, a_i)$.

Definition 6. At the run-time instantiation stage, $FTC(a_i)$ is said to be of SC if $D(a_1, a_i) \leq ftv(a_i)- S(a_1)$, WC if $Mean(a_1, a_i) \leq ftv(a_i)- S(a_1) < D(a_1, a_i)$, WI if $d(a_1, a_i) \leq ftv(a_i)- S(a_1) < Mean(a_1, a_i)$, and SI if $ftv(a_i)- S(a_1) < d(a_1, a_i)$.

Definition 7. At the run-time execution stage, at checkpoint a_p which is either before or at a_i $(p \leq i)$, $FTC(a_i)$ is said to be of SC if $Rcd(a_1, a_p)+D(a_{p+1}, a_i) \leq ftv(a_i)-S(a_1)$, WC if $Rcd(a_1, a_p) + Mean(a_{p+1}, a_i) \leq ftv(a_i)-S(a_1) < Rcd(a_1, a_p)+D(a_{p+1}, a_i)$, WI if $Rcd(a_1, a_p)+d(a_{p+1}, a_i) \leq ftv(a_i)-S(a_1) < Rcd(a_1, a_p)+Mean(a_{p+1}, a_i)$, and SI if $ftv(a_i)-S(a_1) < Rcd(a_1, a_p)+d(a_{p+1}, a_i)$.

For clarity, we further depict CC & CI and SC, WC, WI & SI in Fig. 1.

Fig. 1 clearly depicts the difference between CC & CI and SC, WC, WI & SI. We now further explain SC, WC, WI and SI. We take the run-time execution stage as an example. The corresponding explanation for the other two stages is similar.

- At checkpoint a_p, if $Rcd(a_1, a_p)+D(a_{p+1}, a_i) \leq ftv(a_i)-S(a_1)$, it means $FTC(a_i)$ can be kept if the succeeding activities can be completed by their respective maximum durations. Since the maximum duration of an activity is carefully set and mostly should be kept, we define this state as SC.

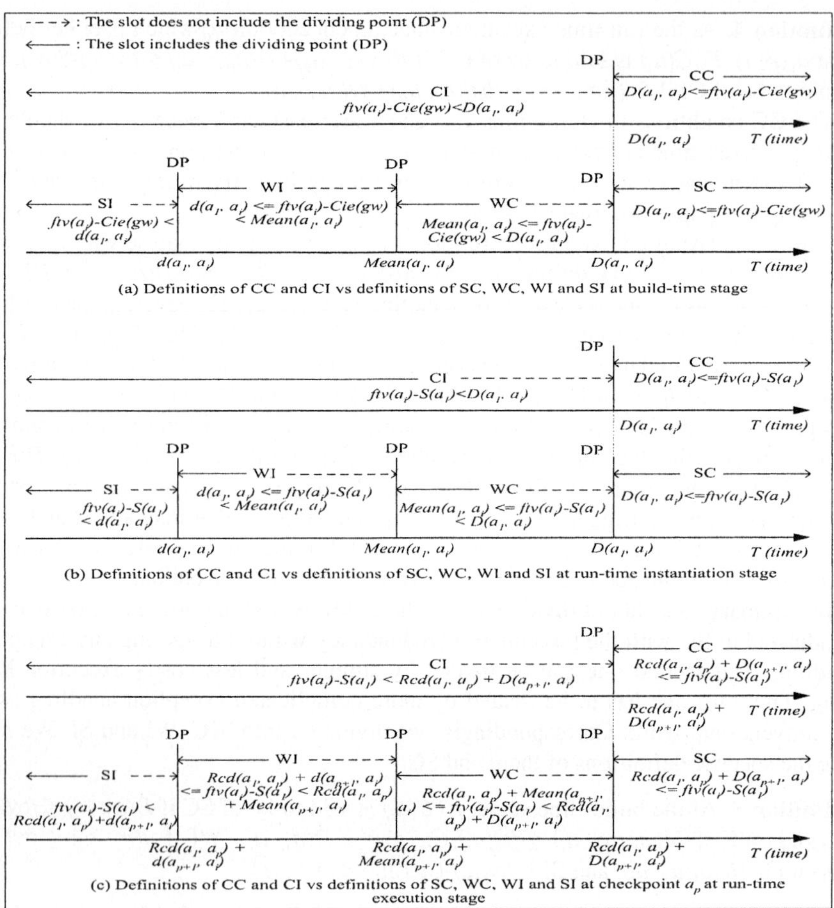

Fig. 1. Definitions of CC and CI vs definitions of SC, WC, WI and SI

- If $Rcd(a_l, a_p)+Mean(a_{p+1}, a_i) \leq ftv(a_i)\text{-}S(a_l) < Rcd(a_l, a_p)+D(a_{p+1}, a_i)$, it means that if the succeeding activities take their respective maximum durations to complete, $FTC(a_i)$ will be violated. But if they just take about the mean durations or less, $FTC(a_i)$ can still be kept. Since statistically, an activity takes about its mean duration to complete, we define this state as WC. It means that with the control of the succeeding activity execution based on the activity mean duration, $FTC(a_i)$ can still be kept as SC.
- If $Rcd(a_l, a_p) + d(a_{p+1}, a_i) \leq ftv(a_i)\text{-}S(a_l) < Rcd(a_l, a_p) + Mean(a_{p+1}, a_i)$, it means that if the succeeding activities take their respective mean durations or more to complete, $FTC(a_i)$ will be violated. However, if the succeeding activities take about their respective minimum durations to finish, $FTC(a_i)$ can still be kept. According to the setting of the mean and minimum durations, this means that statistically, for most cases, $FTC(a_i)$ is difficult to be kept, and only for fewer cases such as those where all succeeding activities can finish by their respective minimum durations, $FTC(a_i)$ can be kept. Therefore we define this state as WI.

- If $ftv(a_i)$-$S(a_1) < Rcd(a_1, a_p)$+$d(a_{p+1}, a_i)$, it means that even if all succeeding activities can be completed by their respective minimum durations, $FTC(a_i)$ still cannot be kept. According to the setting of the minimum durations, this means that mostly $FTC(a_i)$ cannot be kept. Therefore, we define this state as SI.

According to the above explanation, we need not do anything for SC as in the conventional work. Unlike the conventional work which treats WC, WI and SI by the same exception handling, we should treat them differently. For WC, we should investigate how to adjust it to SC using the possible time redundancy. For WI, compared to SI, it has smaller time deficit to recover to SC and there are more cases where it could still be kept like SC. Therefore, we can use simpler and more economical exception handling. However, how simple and economical exception handling should be triggered is beyond the scope of this paper because it is not a part of temporal verification and is often related to some other overall aspects of the whole grid workflow systems such as QoS (Quality of Service) [14]. For SI, we leave it for the more sophisticated and costly exception handling as in the conventional work [14].

4 Temporal Verification of SC, WC, WI and SI

At the build-time stage, to verify SC, WC, WI and SI, for each fixed-time constraint $FTC(a_i)$, we firstly compute $Mean(a_1, a_i)$, $d(a_1, a_i)$ and $D(a_1, a_i)$. Then, we compare them with $ftv(a_i)$-$Cie(gw)$. According to the comparison results and Definition 5, we can judge whether $FTC(a_i)$ is of SC, WC, WI or SI.

At the run-time instantiation stage, some extra activities such as temporal data transfer activities may be added to the grid workflow specification. In addition, the real start time of a grid workflow, $S(a_1)$, is instantiated by the grid workflow engine and may be different from the build-time expected time $Cie(gw)$. Therefore, we need to re-verify the fixed-time constraints. Hence, we need to re-compute $Mean(a_1, a_i)$, $d(a_1, a_i)$ and $D(a_1, a_i)$, and compare them with $ftv(a_i)$-$S(a_1)$. According to the comparison results and Definition 6, we can judge whether $FTC(a_i)$ is of SC, WC, WI or SI.

At the run-time execution stage, the grid workflow instances are executed and consequently, we will get the specific activity completion duration. Because the activity completion duration varies, we also need to re-verify the fixed-time constraints at selected checkpoints [5, 18].

Along with the grid workflow execution, at checkpoint a_p, before the execution of a_p, all fixed-time constraints are of either SC or WC because according to Section 3, for WI and SI, we already trigger their respective exception handling to change them to SC or WC. Therefore, at checkpoint a_p, after the execution of a_p, we verify the previous SC and WC fixed-time constraints. For a previous SC or WC fixed-time constraint, say $FTC(a_i)$ $(p \leq i)$, we compute $Rcd(a_1, a_p)$ and $D(a_{p+1}, a_i)$. In addition, we compute $Mean(a_{p+1}, a_i)$. Then, according to Definition 7, we compare $Rcd(a_1, a_p) + D(a_{p+1}, a_i)$ and $Rcd(a_1, a_p) + Mean(a_{p+1}, a_i)$ with $ftv(a_s)$-$S(a_1)$. According to the comparison results, we can judge whether it is of SC, WC, WI or SI.

Based on the above discussion, we can further derive some specific verification algorithms. However, due to the space limit, we simply omit them.

5 WC Adjustment

Suppose $FTC(a_i)$ is of WC, to adjust it to SC, at the build-time stage, we have to compensate a time deficit: $D(a_1, a_i)$-$[ftv(a_i)$-$Cie(gw)]$. At the run-time instantiation stage, the time deficit is $D(a_1, a_i)$-$[ftv(a_i)$-$S(a_1)]$. And at the run-time execution stage, at checkpoint a_p, the time deficit is $Rcd(a_1, a_p)+D(a_{p+1}, a_i)$-$[ftv(a_i)$-$S(a_1)]$. Because in real world grid workflow systems, there are often a lot of grid workflows in one grid workflow systems, we perform WC adjustment in a statistical way by utilising the mean activity time redundancy specified in Definition 1. In addition, according to the discussion in [4, 6], all fixed-time constraints are nested one after another and hence have temporal dependency on their setting and temporal consistency. By the temporal dependency, we can use the previous WC adjustments to facilitate the current one. Therefore, we will incorporate the temporal dependency into the time deficit allocation to improve its efficiency.

We take the run-time execution stage as an example to discuss the time deficit allocation as the corresponding discussion for the build-time and the run-time instantiation stages is similar. At checkpoint a_p, we can only allocate the time deficit to the succeeding activities between a_{p+1} and a_i because all activities before a_p have already completed and those after a_i have nothing to do with the consistency of $FTC(a_i)$. We denote the time deficit quota to be allocated to a_j between a_{p+1} and a_i by $FTC(a_i)$ as $rdq_i(a_j)$, and the time deficit quota that a_j is holding as $dq(a_j)$. Since statistically the activity with a bigger mean activity time redundancy has more time to compensate the time deficit, we allocate the time deficit to a_j based on the proportion of its mean activity time redundancy $D(a_j)$-$Mean(a_j)$ out of the overall mean time redundancy of all activities between a_{p+1} and a_i. Correspondingly, if there is only one WC fixed-time constraint, say $FTC(a_i)$, we have:

$$rdq_i(a_j) = (Rcd(a_1, a_p) + D(a_{p+1}, a_i) - [ftv(a_i) - S(a_1)])\frac{D(a_j) - Mean(a_j)}{\sum_{l=p+1}^{i}[D(a_l) - Mean(a_l)]} \quad (p+1 \le j \le i) \qquad (1)$$

To be able to apply formula (1), we must ensure $rdq_i(a_j) \le D(a_j)$-$Mean(a_j)$. Otherwise, the available time for a_j to complete is less than its mean duration $Mean(a_j)$. Therefore, statistically, for most cases, the allocation will probably lead to new WC or WI or SI, which means (1) should not be used. Theorem 1 below supports this point.

Theorem 1. At the run-time execution stage, for WC fixed-time constraint $FTC(a_i)$, if we allocate the time deficit to activity a_j between a_{p+1} and a_i according to formula (1), then, we have: $rdq_i(a_j) \le D(a_j)$-$Mean(a_j)$.

Proof: To prove $rdq_i(a_j) \le D(a_j)$-$Mean(a_j)$, according to (1), we only need to prove $Rcd(a_1, a_p)+D(a_{p+1}, a_i)$-$[ftv(a_i)$-$S(a_1)] \le \sum_{l=p+1}^{i}[D(a_l) - Mean(a_l)] = \sum_{l=p+1}^{i} D(a_l) - \sum_{l=p+1}^{i} Mean(a_l)$ $= D(a_{p+1}, a_i) - Mean(a_{p+1}, a_i)$, namely $Rcd(a_1, a_p) + Mean(a_{p+1}, a_i) \le ftv(a_i)$-$S(a_1)$. Because $FTC(a_i)$ is of WC, according to Definition 7, we do have $Rcd(a_1, a_p) + Mean(a_{p+1}, a_i) \le ftv(a_i)$-$S(a_1)$. Therefore, the theorem holds. ∎

If there are more than one WC fixed-time constraints, because they are nested one after another [4, 6], they have some activities in common. For such activities, they will undergo multiple time deficit allocations. Therefore, we have to investigate how to conduct the time deficit allocation for multiple fixed-time constraints together. Based on formula (1), Theorem 1 and the temporal dependency between fixed-time constraints [4, 6], we derive a systematical time deficit allocation approach for multiple WC fixed-time constraints. For convenience, we name the approach as FCTDA (Fixed-time Constraint Time Deficit Allocation). To detail FCTDA, we set a variable, *Maxftv*, that is equal to current maximum one of all allocated time deficits. And we also suppose that the current WC fixed-time constraint of *Maxftv* is $FTC(a_k)$. Correspondingly, *Maxftv* is equal to $Rcd(a_1, a_p)+D(a_{p+1}, a_k)-[ftv(a_k)-S(a_1)]$.

In detail, **FCTDA is:** *at checkpoint* a_p, *for the first WC fixed-time constraint, we use formula* (1) *to allocate its time deficit and set it to Maxftv. From the second WC fixed-time constraint onwards, for each one, say* $FTC(a_i)$, *we compare Maxftv with its time deficit, namely* $Rcd(a_1, a_p)+D(a_{p+1}, a_i)-[ftv(a_i)-S(a_1)]$. *If* $Rcd(a_1, a_p)+D(a_{p+1}, a_i)-[ftv(a_i)-S(a_1)] \leq Maxftv$, *we directly use the previous time deficit allocations and need not conduct the time deficit allocation for* $FTC(a_i)$. *Otherwise, we firstly compute the difference between Maxftv and the time deficit of* $FTC(a_i)$, *namely* $Rcd(a_1, a_p)+D(a_{p+1}, a_i)-[ftv(a_i)-S(a_1)] - Maxftv$. *Secondly, we allocate the difference to activities between* a_{k+1} *and* a_i $(p\leq k<i)$. *Specially, for each activity between* a_{k+1} *and* a_i, *say* a_j, *we use* (2) *below to compute* $rdq_i(a_j)$. *Then, we compare* $rdq_i(a_j)$ *with* $dq(a_j)$. *If* $dq(a_j)$ *is less, we set* $rdq_i(a_j)$ *to* $dq(a_j)$. *Otherwise, we need not do anything. Thirdly, we update Maxftv with the time deficit of* $FTC(a_i)$, *namely* $Rcd(a_1, a_p)+D(a_{p+1}, a_i)-[ftv(a_i)-S(a_1)]$.

$$rdq_i(a_j) = (Rcd(a_1,a_p)+D(a_{p+1},a_i)-[ftv(a_i)-S(a_1)]-Maxftv)\frac{D(a_j)-Mean(a_j)}{\sum_{l=k+1}^{i}[D(a_l)-Mean(a_l)]} \quad (p\leq k;\ k+1\leq j\leq i) \qquad (2)$$

We can further derive the working algorithm of FCTDA. However, due to the space limit, we simply omit it here.

To be able to use FCTDA, we must answer four questions: 1) "Why we need not conduct the time deficit allocation for $FTC(a_i)$ if *Maxftv* is more than or equal to the time deficit of $FTC(a_i)$?"; 2) "Based on FCTDA, can we ensure $rdq_i(a_j) \leq D(a_j)-Mean(a_j)$?". Otherwise, FCTDA should not be used as it may incur new WC, WI or SI; 3) "After all time deficit allocations finish, can we ensure $dq(a_j)\leq D(a_j)-Mean(a_j)$?"; 4) "After all time deficit allocations finish, can every WC fixed-time constraint be adjusted to SC?". To answer these questions, we derive Theorems 2, 3, 4, 5 below.

Theorem 2. At checkpoint a_p, for WC fixed-time constraint $FTC(a_i)$, if $Rcd(a_1, a_p)+D(a_{p+1}, a_i)-[ftv(a_i)-S(a_1)] \leq Maxftv$, the previous WC adjustments are enough for $FTC(a_i)$ to change to SC.

Proof: To adjust $FTC(a_i)$ to SC, we have to compensate the time deficit $Rcd(a_1, a_p)+D(a_{p+1}, a_i)-[ftv(a_i)-S(a_1)]$. *Maxftv* is the maximum one of the previously allocated time deficits. Because $Rcd(a_1, a_p)+D(a_{p+1}, a_i)-[ftv(a_i)-S(a_1)] \leq Maxftv$, the current time deficit of $FTC(a_i)$ has already compensated by the previous maximum time deficit allocation. Therefore, the previous WC adjustments are enough for $FTC(a_i)$ to change to SC. Hence, the theorem holds. ∎

Theorem 3. In FCTDA, after we use formula (2) to compute $rdq_i(a_j)$, we still have: $rdq_i(a_j) \leq D(a_j)\text{-}Mean(a_j)$.

Proof: To prove Theorem 3, we borrow some conclusions from [4, 6] about the temporal dependency between fixed-time constraints. According to [4, 6], the temporal dependency means that the fixed-time constraints are dependent on each other in terms of their settings and verification because they are nested one after another. Correspondingly, given two WC fixed-time constraints $FTC(a_k)$ and $FTC(a_i)$ ($k<i$), we have $Mean(a_{k+1}, a_i) \leq ftv(a_i)\text{-}ftv(a_k)$. The detailed discussion and deducing process can be referred to [4, 6]. To avoid repetition, we do not address them here again.

Now, we prove Theorem 3. To prove $rdq_i(a_j) \leq D(a_j)\text{-}Mean(a_j)$, according to formula (2), we only need to prove $Rcd(a_1, a_p)+D(a_{p+1}, a_i)\text{-}[ftv(a_i)\text{-}S(a_1)] - Maxftv \leq \sum_{l=k+1}^{i} [D(a_l) - Mean(a_l)]$. Since $Maxftv = Rcd(a_1, a_p)+D(a_{p+1}, a_k)\text{-}[ftv(a_k)\text{-}S(a_1)]$, we actually only need to prove $\sum_{l=k+1}^{i} Mean(a_l) \leq [ftv(a_i)\text{-}S(a_1)]\text{-} [ftv(a_k)\text{-}S(a_1)]$, namely $Mean(a_{k+1}, a_i) \leq ftv(a_i)\text{-}ftv(a_k)$. However, in the above paragraph, we do have $Mean(a_{k+1}, a_i) \leq ftv(a_i)\text{-}ftv(a_k)$. Therefore, the theorem holds. ▮

Theorem 4. At checkpoint a_p, if we use FCTDA to conduct the time deficit allocation for every WC fixed-time constraint that covers a_p, then, finally, we have: $dq(a_j) \leq D(a_j)\text{-}Mean(a_j)$.

Proof: According to FCTDA, $dq(a_j)$ is equal to the maximum deficit quota allocated to a_j by all WC fixed-time constraints. According to Theorems 1 and 3, any deficit quota allocated to a_j is less than or equal to $D(a_j)\text{-}Mean(a_j)$. Therefore, the maximum one must also be less than or equal to $D(a_j)\text{-}Mean(a_j)$, namely $dq(a_j) \leq D(a_j)\text{-}Mean(a_j)$. Hence, the theorem holds. ▮

Theorem 5. At checkpoint a_p, after we use FCTDA to allocate all time deficits for all WC fixed-time constraints that cover a_p, the final time deficit quotas of activities between a_{p+1} and a_i are enough for all WC fixed-time constraints to change to SC.

Proof: Considering a WC fixed-time constraint, say $FTC(a_i)$, for any a_j between a_{p+1} and a_i, after all time deficit allocations finish, according to FCTDA, we have $rdq_i(a_j) \leq dq(a_j)$. This means that at a_j, by taking $dq(a_j)$, $FTC(a_i)$ can get more time to compensate its time deficit than by its own deficit allocation. Because $FTC(a_i)$ can switch to SC even only based on its own deficit allocation, based on multiple allocations, $FTC(a_i)$ can be easier to switch to SC. Hence, the theorem holds. ▮

Obviously, Theorems 2, 3, 4 and 5 answer the four questions respectively. Therefore, we can use FCTDA to conduct the time deficit allocation so that statistically, every WC fixed-time constraint can still be kept as SC.

6 Comparison and Discussion

The conventional fixed-time constraint verification work treats WC, WI and SI as CI with the same exception handling. However, in this paper, by separating them, we can handle them differently. For WC, by deploying FCTDA, WC can still be kept as SC without triggering any exception handling. For WI, we can resort to simpler and less costly exception handling. Since in the real world every exception handling normally causes some cost such as compensating some completed activities [14], our four-state approach can be more cost effective than the conventional two-state approach.

We can further conduct the corresponding quantitative analysis so that we can obtain a specific picture of how our four-state approach is more cost effective than the conventional two-state one. However, due to the space limit, we simply outline the quantitative analysis process. We consider a complex climate modelling grid workflow which must be time constrained for the weather forecasting [1]. Then, if we denote the difference in the total exception handling cost between the conventional work and our research as $DIFF_{total}$, at the run-time execution stage, we have (3) below.

$$DIFF_{total} = CXN[P+(M-1)Q]+CXQ\frac{N(N+1)}{2}+C(X-Y)MP+C(X-Y)Q\frac{M(M-1)}{2} \quad (3)$$

Here, C is the mean activity exception handling cost; N is the mean number of WC; M is the mean number of WI; P is the number of activities covered by the first fixed-time constraint; Q is the mean distance between two adjacent fixed-time constraints; and X and Y are the mean weights for the numbers of activities addressed by the exception handling conducted by the conventional work and by our research respectively. With some specific values where P=10, Q=5, X=1/2, Y=1/3, and C is equal to 1 cost unit, N can change from 0 to 20 and M can change from 0 to 10, we list corresponding $DIFF_{total}$ in Fig. 2 below. The selection of such specific values does not affect our analysis because what we want is the trend of how $DIFF_{total}$ is changing related to N and M.

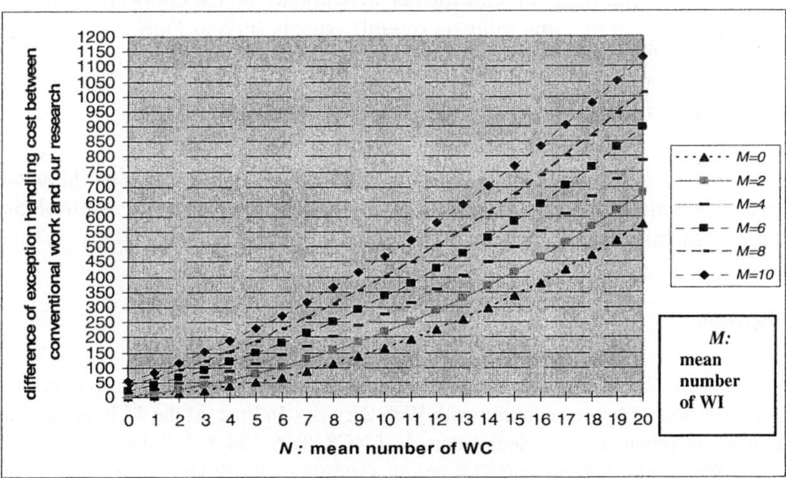

Fig. 2. Change trend of the exception handling cost difference between the conventional work and our research by mean WC number N and mean WI number M

According to Fig. 2, we can see that with N increasing, $DIFF_{total}$ is increasing. This means that the more WC, the more exception handling cost our research can save. We can also see that with M increasing, $DIFF_{total}$ is also increasing. This means that the more WI, the more exception handling cost our research can save. In summary, the bigger number of WC or WI, the more cost our research can save. Hence, statistically, our research can achieve better cost effectiveness than the conventional work.

7 Conclusions and Future Work

In this paper, based on the analysis of CC (*Conventional Consistency*) and CI (*Conventional Inconsistency*) conditions defined in the conventional work, and the run-time uncertainty of the activity real completion duration in grid workflow systems, we have introduced four states to a fixed-time constraint. They are SC (*Strong Consistency*), WC (*Weak Consistency*), WI (*Weak Inconsistency*), and SI (*Strong Inconsistency*). Correspondingly, we have discussed how to verify them. Furthermore, for WC, we have developed a method on how to use the mean activity time redundancy and the temporal dependency between the fixed-time constraints to adjust it so that statistically, it can still be kept as SC without triggering any exception handling. For WI, we have analysed the reason why it can be treated by simpler exception handling than that used by the conventional work. Finally, we have conducted the quantitative comparison which has further demonstrated that our four-state approach can achieve better cost effectiveness than the conventional two-state one. Since in grid workflow systems, the activity completion duration is highly uncertain and normally every exception handling causes some handling cost, by deploying our four-state approach and the corresponding results, we can make the temporal verification more applicable to dynamic grid workflow systems.

With these contributions, we can further investigate the exception handling for WI with the consideration of some relevant overall aspects such as QoS.

Acknowledgements

The work reported in this paper is partly supported by Swinburne Vice Chancellor's Strategic Research Initiative Grant 202-2004, and by the National Natural Science Foundation of China under grant No.60273026 and grant No.60273043.

References

1. D.Abramson, J.Kommineni, J.L.McGregor and J.Katzfey. An Atmospheric Sciences Workflow and its Implementation with Web Services. In Proc. of the 4th International Conference on Computational Science, Part Ⅰ, LNCS 3036, 164-173, Poland, 2004.
2. J.Cao, S.A.Jarvis, S.Saini and G.R.Nudd. GridFlow: Workflow Management for Grid Computing. In Proc. of the 3rd IEEE/ACM International Symposium on Cluster Computing and the Grid (CCGrid 2003), 198-205, Tokyo, May 2003.
3. D.Cybok. A Grid Workflow Infrastructure. In Proc. of Workflow in Grid Systems Workshop in GGF10, Berlin, Germany, Mar. 2004.

4. J.Chen and Y.Yang. Temporal Dependency for Dynamic Verification of Temporal Constraints in Workflow Systems. In Proc. of the 3rd International Conference on Grid and Cooperative Computing, Springer-Verlag, LNCS 3251, 1005-1008, Oct. 2004.
5. J.Chen, Y.Yang and T.Y.Chen. Dynamic Verification of Temporal Constraints on-the-fly for Workflow Systems. In Proc. of the 11th Asia-Pacific Software Engineering Conference (APSEC2004), IEEE CS Press, 30-37, Busan, Korea, Nov./Dec. 2004.
6. J.Chen and Y.Yang. Temporal Dependency for Dynamic Verification of Fixed-date Constraints in Grid Workflow Systems. In Proc. of the 7th Asia Pacific Web Conference, Springer-Verlag, LNCS 3399, 820-831, Mar. 2005.
7. J.Chen and Y.Yang. An Activity Completion Duration based Checkpoint Selection Strategy for Dynamic Verification of Fixed-time Constraints in Grid Workflow Systems. In Proc. of the 2nd International Conference on Grid Service Engineering and Management, Springer-Verlag, LNI, to appear (accepted on June 8, 2005).
8. S.Chinn and G.Madey. Temporal Representation and Reasoning for Workflow in Engineering Design Change Review. IEEE Transactions on Engineering Management, 47(4), 485-492, 2000.
9. E.Deelman, J.Blythe, Y.Gil, C.Kesselman, G.Mehta and K.Vahi. Mapping Abstract Complex Workflows onto Grid Environments. Journal of Grid Computing, 1(1), 9-23, 2003.
10. J.Eder, E.Panagos and M.Rabinovich. Time Constraints in Workflow Systems. In Proc. of the 11th International Conference on Advanced Information Systems Engineering (CAiSE'99), Springer Verlag, LNCS 1626, 286-300, June 1999.
11. T.Fahringer, S.Pllana and A.Villazon. A-GWL: Abstract Grid Workflow Language. In Proc. of the 4th International Conference on Computational Science, Part III, Springer Verlag, LNCS 3038, 42-49, Krakow, Poland, June 2004.
12. I.Foster, C.Kesselman, J.Nick and S.Tuecke. The Physiology of the Grid: An Open Grid Services Architecture for Distributed Systems Integration. In Proc. of the 5th Global Grid Forum Workshop (GGF5), Edinburgh, Scotland, July 2002.
13. B.Ha, J.Bae and S.Kang. Workload Balancing on Agents for Business Process Efficiency Based on Stochastic Model. In Proc. of the 2nd International Conference on Business Process Management, LNCS 3080, 195-210, June 2004.
14. C.Hagen and G.Alonso. Exception Handling in Workflow Management Systems. IEEE Transactions on Software Engineering, 26(10), 943-958, 2000.
15. Y.Huang. JISGA: A JINI-BASED Service-Oriented Grid Architecture. The International Journal of High Performance Computing Applications, 17(3), 317-327, 2003.
16. S.Krishnan, P.Wagstrom and G.V.Laszewski. GSFL: A Workflow Framework for Grid Services. Technical Report, Argonne National Laboratory, Argonne, U.S.A., 2002.
17. Z.Liu. Performance Analysis of Stochastic Timed Petri Nets Using Linear Programming Approach. IEEE Transactions on Software Engineering, 11(24), 1014-1030, 1998.
18. O.Marjanovic and M.E.Orlowska. On Modeling and Verification of Temporal Constraints in Production Workflows. Knowledge and Information Systems, 1(2), 157-192, 1999.
19. D.R.Simpson, N.Kelly, P.V.Jithesh, P.Donachy, T.J.Harmer, R.H.Perrott, J.Johnston, P.Kerr, M.McCurley and S.McKee. GeneGrid: A Practical Workflow Implementation for a Grid Based Virtual Bioinformatics Laboratory. In Proc. of the UK e-Science All Hands Meeting 2004 (AHM04), 547-554, Sept. 2004.
20. H.Zhuge, T.Cheung and H.Pung. A Timed Workflow Process Model. The Journal of Systems and Software, 55(3), 231-243, 2001.

An Adaptive Scheduling Algorithm for Molecule Docking Design on Grid

Yan-Li Hu, Liang Bai, Wei-Ming Zhang, Wei-Dong Xiao, and Zhong Liu

Sch. of Information System & Management, National Univ. of Defense Technology, 410073 Changsha, China
smilelife1979@hotmail.com, xabpz@163.com, wmzhang@nudt.edu.cn, wilsonshaw@vip.sina.com, phillipliu@263.net

Abstract. Grid provides a promising platform for the efficient execution of drug molecular docking design. Scheduling such applications is challenging for the heterogeneity, autonomy, and dynamic adaptability of grid resources. Assuming resource owners have a preemptive priority, we propose an adaptive algorithm of jobs scheduling based on time balancing strategy, which solves parallel molecular docking task by using the idle resources in the Grid. A mathematical model is developed to predict performance, which also considers systems with heterogeneous machine utilization and heterogeneous service distribution. According to the time balancing policy, ligands are partitioned into several subtasks and scheduled. The expected value of molecular docking completion time is predicted with performance model. To get better parallel computing performance, an optimal subset of heterogeneous resources with the shortest parallel executing time of tasks can be selected with the algorithm.

Keywords: Molecular docking, ligand, receptor, Grid, time-balancing, jobs scheduling.

1 Introduction

Drug molecular docking design on grid is receiving increased attention. The Smallpox Project by IBM uses grid computing to screen millions of potential anti-smallpox drugs[1]. D2OL project[2] improves the cost and overall efficiency of evaluating potential drug candidates necessary to address general health concerns. The drug discovery grid (DDG) utilizes the distributed resources to implement the efficient drug-design applications[3]. Grid can provide super distributed computing power transparently and satisfy these applications effectively.

It is important to study molecular docking theoretically. Up to now, most systems devoted to solve this so called "protein docking problem" include DOCK, the system of Connolly detecting critically shaped points, the geometric hashing systems of Norel et al. and Fischer et al, a system computing the critical points in an octree-representation of protein surfaces, or most recently a system matching possible donors and acceptors in its initial step[4].

Scheduling in grid is complicated, usually NP-complete hard. Some work has been done in the past, and many algorithms have been proposed, such as Min-min, Hybrid Remapper (HR), Sufferage and etc. Min-min[5-6] heuristic, which schedules

H. Zhuge and G.C. Fox (Eds.): GCC 2005, LNCS 3795, pp. 312 – 322, 2005.

independent tasks statically in batch mode, assigns tasks with the overall minimum completion time to the corresponding computational nodes according to priority. The hybrid remapper[7-9] improves a statically initial scheduling by remapping to reduce the overall execution time based on a mixture of runtime and expected values. Sufferage[10] heuristic, which schedules independent tasks dynamically in heterogeneous computing environments, defines sufferage value as the difference between its best minimum completion time and its second-best minimum completion time. And tasks with high sufferage value take precedence.

The purpose of this study is to analyze the nature of molecular docking so that we are able to schedule such jobs efficiently. Partitioning and scheduling policies for molecular docking jobs are developed based on the analytical model, which are targeted to utilize the abundant computing cycles available on the network to provide high computing power. Experimental results show that the scheduling algorithm is effective.

This paper is organized as follows: in section 2, the nature of molecular docking design is analyzed. In section 3, an analytical model for estimating molecular docking completion time in a non-dedicated distributed computing environment is developed. The analytical model is carefully examined and evaluated in Section 4. Effects of different factors on molecular docking completion time are examined. And optimal partitioning of molecular docking jobs based on time balancing strategy is discussed. And an algorithm based on time-balancing strategy, TBBS for short, is proposed. The results are tested in simulation experiments in Section 5. Finally, conclusions are given in Section 6.

2 Molecular Docking Technology

The procedure of binding ligand molecules to a specific place on a protein receptor is commonly called docking. Molecular docking design involves screening millions of molecules of chemical compounds in a small molecule database, CDB (chemical database) to identify those that are potential drugs[11-12]. Current estimates place the number of "druggable"genes at 5-10,000, with each gene encoding for around ten proteins, with two to three percent considered high value targets [13].

The ligands of high-affinity with proteins appear to conform closely to the shape of the binding cavity, maximizing the hydrophobic contribution to binding, and to interact at a number of hydrogen bonding sites. The optimal binding mode may thus involve the ligand forming hydrogen bonds at key hydrogen-bonding sites, accompanied by hydrophobic surface area burial.

Molecular docking design helps scientists explore how two molecules, such as a drug and an enzyme or protein receptor, fit together. It is our goal to use Grid technologies to provide cheap and efficient solutions to the process.

Molecular docking design is composed of one parallel phase with ligands evaluated independently, no communication or synchronization requirements among evaluations till the final synchronization, which occurs when all of the jobs are completed. In order to accomplish high throughput, we partition molecular docking task into subtasks and assign them to available computing resources according the capacity in order to minimize the completion time.

3 A Scheduling Model for Molecular Docking Design on Grid

In this section, we describe the application scenario for scheduling molecular docking jobs, and develop an optimal performance modeling.

3.1 Application Model

Grid resources are of heterogeneity, autonomy, and dynamic adaptability. Without loss of generality, we describe the capacity of computational nodes with CPU performance mainly and define it as traffic intensity. And the same, we use CPU busy rate to describe the load of computational nodes mainly.

Definition 1. Traffic intensity of node *k* is the rate of the average number of arrival jobs with the average number of processed jobs on node *k*, labeled as ρ_i.

We assume that there are *N* nodes which are idle or light-loaded in the grid, their loads are L_1,L_2,, ⋯, L_n, and traffic intensity ρ_1, ρ_2, ⋯, ρ_n respectively. The molecular docking design requires a total processing time *W*. The primary concern in a heterogeneous environment is how to partition ligand molecules and allocate the subtasks to nodes to achieve maximum performance.

3.2 Performance Modeling

We use *Tk* to present the total time required to finish parallel subtask *k* at node *k*, whose processing time is w_k. Assuming *m* nodes are used for parallel computing, the molecular docking completion time *T* can be expressed as:

$$T = \max\left\{T_k \middle| k = 1, 2, \cdots, m\right\} . \quad (1)$$

T is a continuous random variable. Assuming probability density function is *f(t)*, the expected value of the molecular docking completion time within time *t* can be expressed as:

$$E(T) = \int_{w}^{t} tf(t)\, dt . \quad (2)$$

However, it is difficult to find the exact distribution of the server busy time based on the existing result in probability[14]. So we approximate molecular docking completion time with subtasks completion time.

As mentioned above, the molecular docking task is partitioned into *m* subtasks and allocated to corresponding computational nodes. In this partition pattern, we define the expected value of the parallel task completion time $ECT(T)^m$ as:

$$ECT(T)^m = \max\left\{ECT(T_k) \middle| k = 1, 2, \cdots, m\right\}. \quad (3)$$

The expected value of the molecular docking completion time is different for different partition pattern. So $ECT(T)^m$ comprises the set of the expected value of the molecular docking completion time. It is expected to partition the molecular docking task rightly, and minimize the expected value of the molecular docking completion time. So a mathematical model is developed to predict performance as follows:

$$\min\{\max_{k=1}^{m}[ECT\left(T_k\right)]\}\text{, where } m = 1, 2, \cdots, N . \quad (4)$$

4 A Time-Balancing Based Scheduling Algorithm for Molecular Docking Design

In this section, we deduct formulas for molecular docking completion time. Firstly, we derive simple formulations to predict subtask completion time. Secondly, aiming to minimizing the molecular docking completion time, we propose time-balancing partition strategy, which balances the expected value of subtask completion time. Thirdly, methods are suggested to improve the efficiency of partition by reducing partition and prediction spending. Finally, a time balancing based scheduling algorithm, TBBS for short, is proposed.

4.1 Subtask Completion Time at a Single Node

Given a node is idle when the subtask arrives at the node and the number of interruptions of the subtask encountered during the procession is *S*, the parallel completion time *Tk* at node *k* can be expressed as:

$$T_k = X_{k1} + I_{k1} + X_{k2} + I_{k2} + \cdots + X_{ks} + I_{ks}^{-} + \varepsilon . \quad (5)$$

As defined above, S is the total number of interruptions that occur during the processing of the subtask due to the arrival of one or more sequential jobs. X_{ki}, I_{ki}, $i=1, \cdots, S$ represents the computing time consumed by the subtask and the sequential jobs respectively. ε is the execution time of the last parallel process that finishes the subtask. We have

$$w_k = X_{k1} + X_{k2} + \cdots + X_{ks} + \varepsilon . \quad (6)$$

The arrival and processing preemptively of the owners\` local jobs influence *Tk* heavily. In order to analyze this quantitatively, we have assumptions as:

Assumption 1. The arrival of the owner's local jobs in different time is statistically independent of each other.

Assumption 2. The arrival of the owner's local jobs increases steadily.

Assumption 3. The owner node process can be treated as a *M/G/1* queuing system with arrival rate λ and service rate μ, so $\rho_k = \lambda / \mu$.

Based on probability and queuing theory, we have:

Theorem 1. The total number of interruptions *S* on the owner node *k* follows a Poisson distribution with parameter λw_k, and the expected value of *S* is $E(S) = \lambda w_k$.

Theorem 2. The expected value of the owner's local job completion time *Ik* on the node *k* is $E(Ik) = 1/(\mu - \lambda)$..

Based on theorem 1 and theorem 2, we have:

$$E\left(T_k\right)=\sum_{s=0}^{\infty} P\left(S=s\right)E\left(T_k \middle| S=s\right)=w_k\left(1+\frac{\lambda}{\mu-\lambda}\right)=\frac{1}{1-\rho_k}w_k . \tag{7}$$

The expected value of parallel subtask completion time includes the waiting time in the job queue and the execution time of the subtask at node k. The waiting time mainly depends on the completion time of other tasks before the subtask, namely the load of node k. So we have:

$$ECT\left(T_k\right)=L_k+E\left(T_k\right)=L_k+\frac{1}{1-\rho_k}w_k . \tag{8}$$

4.2 Time-Balancing Strategy

We can minimize the parallel task completion time in formula (4) if the load, traffic intensity, and demand of the subtask on node k are all known. The load and traffic intensity are related with the state of the node k, and can be measured easily. Then the key is the partition of the parallel task.

Theorem 3. Assume that molecular docking task is partitioned into m subtasks and allocated to corresponding computational nodes, then in this partition pattern the expected value of the molecular docking completion time $ECT(T)^m$ is the minimum if the same expected value of subtask completion time can be reached at different nodes with consideration of resource capacity.

Definition 2. Time balancing strategy is to partition molecular docking task into subtasks such that the same expected value of subtask completion time can be reached at different nodes with consideration of resource capacity.

Time balancing strategy shortens the arrearage for the final synchronization when the subtasks completion time is different and the early-finished ones have to wait for the late ones.

4.3 Molecular Docking Design Partition Based on Time-Balancing Strategy

4.3.1 Molecular Docking Design Partition Based on Time-Balancing Strategy

Let a be the value of the same expected value subtask completion time, we have

$$ECT\left(T_k\right)=E\left(T_k\right)+L_k=a . \tag{9}$$

The total demand of the molecular docking design W is:

$$\Sigma_{k=1}^{m} E\left(T_k\right)\left(1-\rho_k\right)=W . \tag{10}$$

From (9), (10), we have:

$$E\left(T_k\right)=\frac{W+\sum_{k=1}^{m} L_k\left(1-\rho_k\right)}{m\left(1-\overline{\rho}\right)}-L_k \text{, where } \overline{\rho}=\frac{1}{m}\Sigma_{k=1}^{m}\rho_k . \tag{11}$$

Hence, from (7), (11), the parallel subtask processing time w_k can be calculated.

We find that in some partition pattern, the expected value of parallel subtask completion time is only related with the molecular docking demand under certain circumstances, such as extremely low traffic intensity and zero loads. And for the given system parameters, the molecular docking completion time will increase when the total demand of molecular docking design increases. These are consistent with the simulated experimental results[14].

And we also find that the larger *m* does not expected value the better performance, for $\Sigma_{k=1}^{m} \rho_k$ and $\Sigma_{k=1}^{m} L_k \left(1-\rho_k\right)$ will increase when *m* increases, and $E(T_k)$ is not linear with *m* with consideration of resource capacity and load.

Time balancing strategy is focused on balancing the expected value subtask completion time at nodes in every partition pattern. It finds some partition pattern, which minimizes the expected value of molecular docking completion time.

4.3.2 Partition Improvement

There are *N* idle or light-loaded nodes in grid, which are in increasing order of the load. If two nodes have the same load, the one with higher capacity is in front of the other. So we have Theorem 4.

Theorem 4. Assume that there are *N* available resources, which are in increasing order of the load, $L_1 \leqslant L_2 \leqslant \cdots \leqslant L_n$, and the molecular docking task is partitioned from the lightest node firstly. It must be true that $ECT(T)^m \leqslant ECT(T)^{m+1}$ if the expected value of the molecular docking completion time between preceding *m* nodes is less than the load of the $m+1$ node, namely $ECT(T)^m \leqslant L_{m+1}$.

So it is not necessary to partition between all available nodes to achieve the minimum molecular docking completion time according to theorem 4. If the expected value of the molecular docking completion time between preceding $m(m<N)$ nodes is less than the load of the $m+1$ node, the partition procedure for the molecular docking design will end, for the expected value of the molecular docking completion time in the latter partition pattern is not less than $ECT(T)^m$, namely:

$$ECT\left(T\right)^m \leq ECT\left(T\right)^i \qquad \left(i = m+1,\cdots,N\right). \tag{12}$$

4.4 A Time-Balancing Based Scheduling Algorithm for Molecular Docking Design

Based on the above analytical model, we propose a time balancing based scheduling algorithm, TBBS for short. Tasks are gathered into meta-task to schedule in batch mode in TBBS algorithm, and they may be remapped.

Assume that the *ith*-scheduling event happens at τ_k, both the new arrival tasks and the tasks which have not yet executed are gathered into Meta-Task *M*. All available resources form Res-Set *R*, and all expected values of molecular docking completion time comprise ECT-Set *E*. Assuming the state of nodes are the same as is described in Section 2, then TBBS algorithm is as follows:

```
Algorithm TBBS(Meta-Task M, Res-Set R, ECT-Set E)
  Begin
    getMetaTask(M);
    collect resource state info from Grid Information
    Service;
    getAvaliableResources(R);
    while (M≠Φ)
      for each (T∈M)
        for (m=1; m<=N; m++)
          ECT(T)^m=calculateECT(T, m, R(T, m));
          if ECT(T)^m≤L_m+1
            ECT(T)=getMinECT(E, R(T, m));
            UpdateResInfo(R);
            break;
          else
            InsertECTSet(ECT(T)^m, E);
        end for
      end foreach
      T_min =min(ECT(T));
      Assign T_min to R(T_min, m) to process;
      M=M-{ T_min };
    endwhile
  end.
```

Assume that the average size of meta-task is L, and the average size of available resource is N, then TBBS algorithm has asymptotic complexity of $O(L^2n), 1\leq n\leq N$. The complexities of Min-min algorithm and Sufferage algorithm are $O(L^2N)$ and $O(kLN)$, $1\leq k\leq L$ respectively.

5 Simulation Experimental Analysis

Virtual screening experiment based on the desktop grid by Andrew A. Chien is well-known[15]. In this section, we examine the effects of TBBS algorithm through simulation experiment of that. Protein receptor is Enzyme Inhibitors, and ligands come from the Cambridge Structural Database, which is the world repository of small molecule crystal structures[16]. Simulation results will be compared with Min-min algorithm and Sufferage algorithm.

Without loss of generality, we assume that the arrival rate of the owner local job sequence is $\lambda=1$. The parameters are shown in table 1.

Table1. Parameters setting of virtual screening

Num of candidate molecules	Num of available computational nodes	Traffic intensity
5000	94	0.05~0.90

We implement 50 groups simulation. And in every group, 5000 candidate molecules are included to form the virtual screening set.

The amount of data required for each molecular evaluation is small – basically the atomic coordinates of the molecules – and the essential results are even smaller, a binding score. Hence, the communication time is extremely lower than the computing time. Without loss of generality, the communication time is not considered[14].

In Fig.1, sets of simulation outcome examples for molecular docking completion time are shown. TBBS algorithm costs about 346 hours to finish the virtual screening averagely, Sufferage algorithm 372 hours averagely and Min-min algorithm 384 hours averagely.

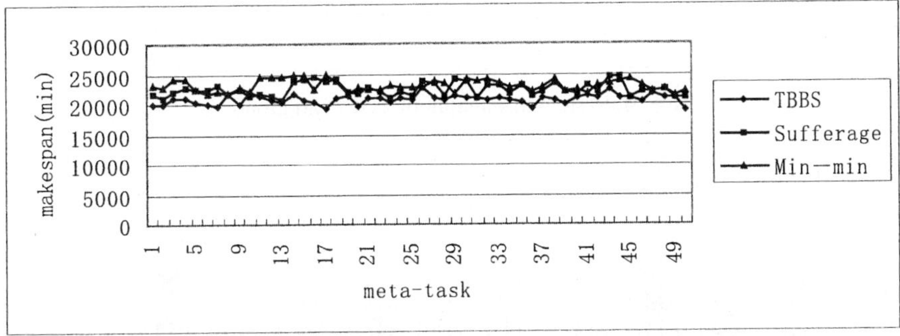

Fig. 1. Simulation for molecular docking completion time

We analyze the experiment results statistically, calculating the system throughput of every group as shown in following figs:

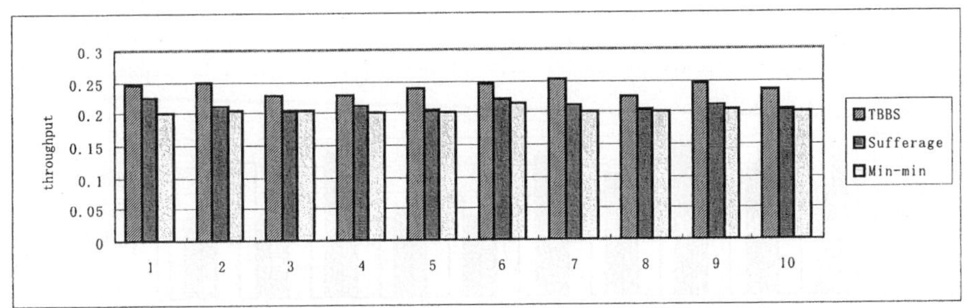

Fig. 2. System throughput of 1st -10th group

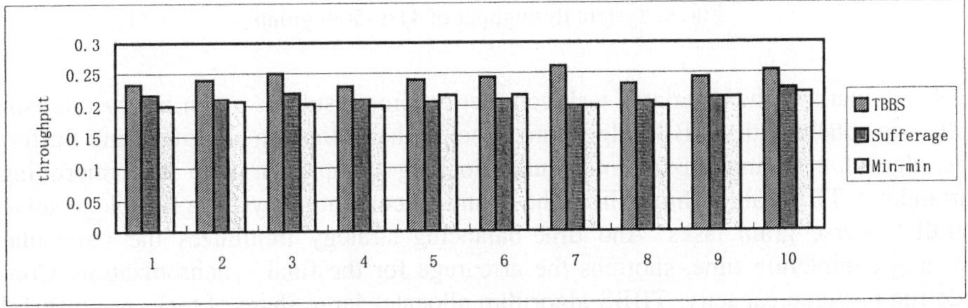

Fig. 3. System throughput of 11th -20th group

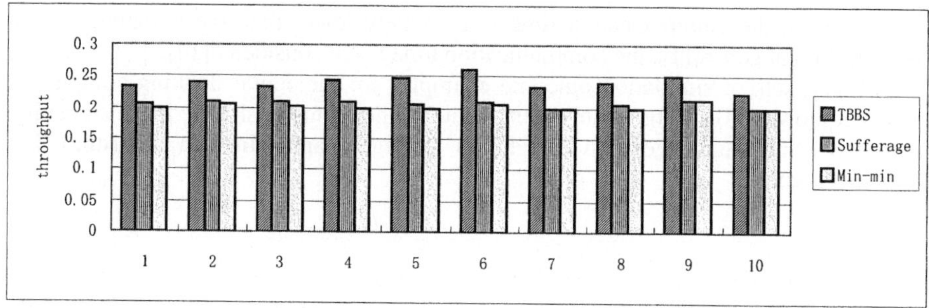

Fig. 4. System throughput of 21st -30th group

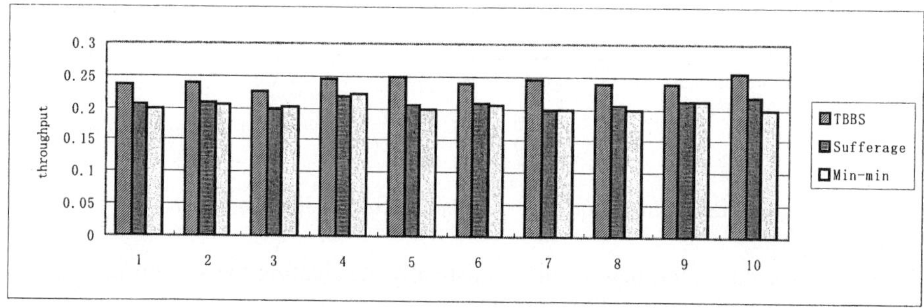

Fig. 5. System throughput of 31st -40th group

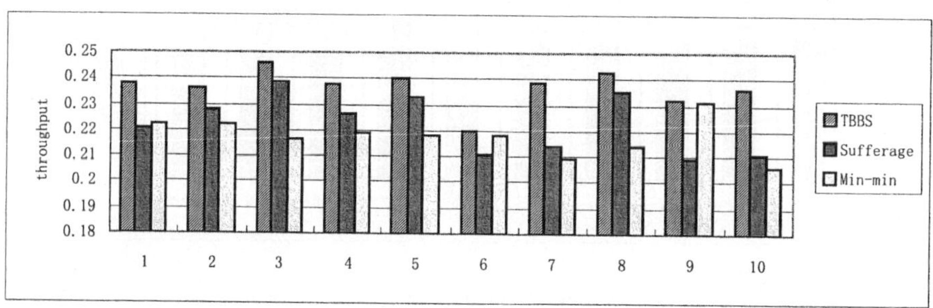

Fig. 6. System throughput of 41st -50th group

A summary of the simulated task completion time results is given below. Statistically, we conclude that TBBS algorithm is better than Min-min algorithm and Sufferage algorithm in minimizing molecular docking completion time and improving throughput. TBBS algorithm utilizes the abundant computing cycles available to solve parallel coarse grain tasks. And time-balancing strategy minimizes the molecular docking completion time, shortens the arrearage for the final synchronization. Considering resource capacity, TBBS algorithm allocates large share of tasks to powerful resources.

6 Conclusion

Drug molecular docking design on grid is receiving increased attention, which is usually over very large sample spaces. Grid can provide super distributed computing power transparently and satisfy these applications effectively. Scheduling such applications is challenging for the heterogeneity, autonomy, and dynamic adaptability of grid resources.

In this paper, we present a performance model to study molecular docking design scheduling in a non-dedicated environment. Based on this model, we propose time-balancing strategy for molecular docking task partition. Finally, an efficient scheduling algorithm based on time-balancing strategy, TBBS algorithm for short, is proposed. TBBS algorithm utilizes idle resources in the grid to solve the molecular docking task. To maximize performance, an optimal subset of heterogeneous resources with the shortest parallel executing time of tasks is selected with the efficient algorithm. TBBS algorithm partitions and schedules molecular docking task to minimize the expected completion time, which assigns large share of task to powerful resources and improve the throughput of system. It sorts resources according to their capacity and reduces the times of partition to improve the efficiency of scheduling. Experimental results show that TBBS algorithm is more efficient than Min-min and Sufferage algorithm, which may provide a practical solution for molecular docking design on grid.

Acknowledgments

This work is supported in part by the National Natural Science Foundation of China under Grant No. 70271004, and in part by the Natural Science Foundation of HuNan Province under Grant No. 03JJY3110.

References

1. Grant McFadden. The smallpox research project. http://www.grid.org/projects/smallpox, 2004
2. E Bonnie. The Drug Design and optimization Lab. http://www.d2ol.com/dOL/download_instructions.html, 2004
3. ZHANG Jun, CHANG Yan, XIE Xiang-Hui and etc, Realization of Multi-Level Parallel Load-Balance P2P Computation in the DDG, Journal of Computer Research and Development, Vol. 41, No. 12,Dec. 2004.
4. Friedrich Ackerman, Grit Herrmann, Stefan Posch. Estimation and filtering of potential protein-protein docking positions. Bio-informatics, Vol.14, No.2, pp196-205, 1998
5. Tracy D. Braun, Howard Jay Siegek, Noah Beck. A Comparison of Eleven Static Heuristics for Mapping a Class of Independent Tasks onto Heterogeneous Distributed Computing Systems. Journal of Parallel and Distributed Computing. 2001.810-837
6. Tracy D. Braun, Howard Jay Siegel, et al. A Comparison Study of Static Heuristics for a Class of Meta-tasks on Heterogeneous Computing Systems. Journal of Parallel and Distributed Computing. 2002.723-751

7. M Maheswaran. S Ali. et al. Dynamic Matching and Scheduling of a Class of Independent Tasks onto Heterogeneous Computing Systems. Proceedings of the 8th IEEE Heterogeneous Computing Workshop(HCW`99), IEEE Computer Society Press,1999, pp30-44
8. M Maheswaran, H J Siegel. A Dynamic Matching and Scheduling Algorithm for Heterogeneous Computing Systems. Proceedings of the 7th IEEE Heterogeneous Computing Workshop(HCW`98), IEEE Computer Society Press,1998, pp57-69
9. M. Maheswaran, S. Ali, H. et al. Dynamic mapping of a class of independent tasks onto heterogeneous Computing systems. Journal of Parallel and Distributed Computing. Vol. 59, No. 2, Nov. 1999, pp. 107–131
10. Henri Casanova, Arnaud Legrand. Heuristics for Scheduling Parameter Sweep Applications in Grid Environments. 2003.609-630
11. R. Buyya, K. Branson, J. Giddy, and D. Abramson. The Virtual Laboratory: Enabling On-Demand Drug Design with the World Wide Grid, In Proceedings of the IEEE International Symposium on Cluster Computing and the Grid, May 21-24, 2002.
12. R. Buyya, K. Branson, J. Giddy, and D. Abramson. The Virtual Laboratory: Enabling Molecular Modeling for Drug Design on the World Wide Grid In Proceedings of the IEEE International Symposium on Cluster Computing and the Grid, May 12-15, 2003.
13. A. A. Chien, B. Calder, S. Elbert, and K. Bhatia, Entropia: architecture and performance of an enterprise desktop grid system, Journal of Parallel and Distributed Computing, Vol. 63, No. 5, pp. 597--610, 2003.
14. Linguo Gong, Xian-He Sun, Senior Member, IEEE, and Edward F. Watson. Performance Modeling and Prediction of Nondedicated Network Computing. IEEE Transaction on Computers, Vol. 51, No. 9, September 2002
15. Ian Foster, Carl Kesselman,The Grid2:Blueprint for a New Computing Infrastructure. Publishing House Electronics Industry. 2004.10
16. H Kubinyi. Burger`s medicinal chemistry and drug discovery. In: M E Wolff ed, Principles and Practice, Vol 1. News York: John Wiley &Sons, 1995. 497~571

XML-Based Digital Signature Accelerator in Open Mobile Grid Computing

Namje Park[1], Kiyoung Moon[1], Kyoil Chung[1],
Seungjoo Kim[2], and Dongho Won[2]

[1] Information Security Research Division, ETRI,
161 Gajeong-dong, Yuseong-gu, Daejeon, 305-350, Korea
{namjepark, kymoon, kyoil}@etri.re.kr
[2] School of Information and Communication Engineering, Sungkyunkwan University,
300 Chunchun-dong, Jangan-gu, Suwon-si, Gyeonggi-do, 440-746, Korea
skim@ece.skku.ac.kr, dhwon@dosan.skku.ac.kr

Abstract. As Grid technology evolves it is becoming evident that the inclusion of mobile devices in a Grid environment will benefit both the Grid and mobile network communities. Many mobile devices, however, have limits on their computational resources that make it difficult to achieve this goal. The goal of this paper is to investigate how well the most limited wireless devices can make use of grid security services. This paper describes a novel security approach on fast mobile grid services based on current mobile web services platform environment using XML signcryption mechanism.

1 Introduction

Grid is the umbrella that covers many of today's distributed computing technologies. Grid technology attempts to support flexible, secure, coordinated information sharing among dynamic collections of individuals, institutions, and resources. This includes data sharing but also access to computers, software and devices required by computation and data-rich collaborative problem solving. So far the use of grid services has required a modern workstation, specialized software installed locally and expert intervention. In the future these requirements should diminish considerably. One reason is the emergence of grid portals as gateways to the Grid. Another reason is the 'web services' boom in the industry. The use of XML as a network protocol and an integration tool will ensure that future grid peer could be a simple wireless device [2, 3].

Mobile communications represent one potential new area where Grid technology may be applied. In parallel with the evolution of Grid computing, mobile communications technology has developed to the stage where wireless networks are now becoming commonplace in the home environment. The potential for new applications based around the convergence of mobile devices and Grid technology is now becoming apparent to both the research and business communities [2, 3].

Furthermore, open mobile grid service infrastructure will extend use of the grid technology or services up to business area using web services technology. Therefore differential resource access is a necessary operation for users to share their resources securely and willingly. Therefore, this paper describes a novel security approach on fast mobile grid services based on current mobile web services platform environment using XML signcryption mechanism.

H. Zhuge and G.C. Fox (Eds.): GCC 2005, LNCS 3795, pp. 323–333, 2005.

2 Emerging Technologies and Background

2.1 Open Mobile Grid Architecture and XML Protocols

The XML protocol-based Web Services interfaces were initially promising as a communication method between wireless devices and back-end servers. A prime candidate for wireless Grid applications is the new Open Grid Services Architecture (OGSA) model used in the Globus Toolkit 3 [10]. Wrapping the existing Grid middleware with XML interfaces holds the promise of providing a universal solution also to wireless devices. As it happens the XML multipurpose protocol stack can be reused over and over again, while the protocol implementation and payload can be described with Web Service Description Language (WSDL) in plain text. However given account to the limited memory constraints, Web Services technology is likely too heavy for first generation MIDP devices. The fact remains, that Web Service protocol implementations such as kSOAP weigh 41 kilobytes i.e. over 30 percent of standard application memory of low-end MIDP device whereas more lightweight protocols such as kXML-RPC requires only 24 kilobytes. The overhead of Simple Object Access Protocol message parsing in light J2ME-based wireless devices has also been studied and the results show 2-3 times slower response times compared to a proprietary protocol that communicates with a proxy client that utilizes Web Services on behalf of the wireless client. The upper scale of MIDP devices is quickly changing and highend mobile phones will provide as large memory footprints as 16Mb. Mobile Web Services is a future technology trend addressed by Microsoft, Open Mobile Alliance and the Parlay Group [11].

2.2 The Performance Problem of XML

XML-based messaging is at the heart of the current grid based on web services technology. XML's self-describing nature has significant advantages, but they come at the price of bandwidth and performance. XML-based messages are larger and require more processing than existing protocols such as RMI, RMI/IIOP or CORBA/IIOP: data is represented inefficiently, and binding requires more computation. For example, an RMI service can perform an order of magnitude faster than an equivalent web service-based grid. Use of HTTP as the transport for Web Services messages is not a significant factor when compared to the binding of XML to programmatic objects.

Increased bandwidth usage affects both wired and wireless networks. Often the latter, e.g. mobile telephone network, have bandwidth restrictions allotted for communication by a network device. In addition, larger messages increase the possibility of retransmission since the smaller the message, the less likely it will be corrupted when in the air. Increased processing requirements affects network devices communicating using both types of networks (wired and wireless). A server may not be able to handle the throughput the 'network' demands of it. Mobile phone battery life may be reduced as a device uses more memory, performs more processing and spends more time transmitting information. As the scale of Web Services usage increases, these problems are likely to be exacerbated.

Fast grid services attempts to solve these problems by defining binary-based messages that consume less bandwidth and are faster and require less memory to be processed. The price for this is loss of self-description. Fast grid service is not an attempt to replace XML-based messaging. It is designed to be an alternative that can be used when performance is an issue.

2.3 XML Signature Acceleration - XML Signcryption

XML signcryption structure and schema has been proposed. Shown below is the XML signcryption XML document.

```
<?xml version="1.0" encoding="UTF-8"?>
<XML_Signcryption>
<SignedInfo>
<CanonicalizationMethod Algorithm/>
 <SignatureMethod Algorithm/>
 <EncryptionMethod Algorithm/>
<Reference URI>
 <DigestMethod1 Algorithm/>
 <DigestMethod2 Algorithm/>
 <DigestValue/>
 </Reference>
 </SignedInfo>
 <SigncryptionValue> </SigncryptionValue>
 <Rvalue> </RValue>
 <Svalue> </Svalue>
 </XML_Signcryption>
```

Fig. 1. Basic Architecture of Proposed XML Signcryption

The root element XML signcryption is the fundamental element of the XML documents. Within the root element are contained various other elements such as signed info and the Signcryptionvalue, Rvalue and Svalue [6, 7]. The SignedInfo element contains the information about the signcryption methodology used. It described about the implementation details about signcryption. Within the signed info element there are other elements such as CanonicalizationMethod Algorithm, SignatureMethod Algorithm, EncryptionMethod Algorithm and Reference URI. The CanonicalizationMethod indicates the method that is used for canonicalization. The canonical method allows the use of different characters in the XML document. For example, if there are white spaces in the xml document, these are removed because of the XML canonicalization method used.

The signatureMethod element indicates the signature element used in the signcryption process. EncryptionMethod is the encryption method that is used in the signcryption process. In our example, the algorithm used is DES. The element Reference indicates the link of the file that is being signcrypted. It contains the path of the file that is being signcrypted. The reference URI also contains the different Hashing algorithms that are being used in the signcryption process. In our implementation, we are using MD5 and SHA1.

As indicated in sections above, the result of signcryption are three values, namely c, r and s. these three values are required by the system to create the plain text from these messages. When signcryption is performed on a data, the output is a signcryption value. Signcryption requires different digest functions. The description of the hash functions and also the different parameters required for encryption. The encryption method that is used for signcryption is also shown in the XML document. This information is also shown in the canonicalization method is used to embed a document in another document. Using Xpath filtering, an appropriate file is opened so that the file is opened using the application specified.

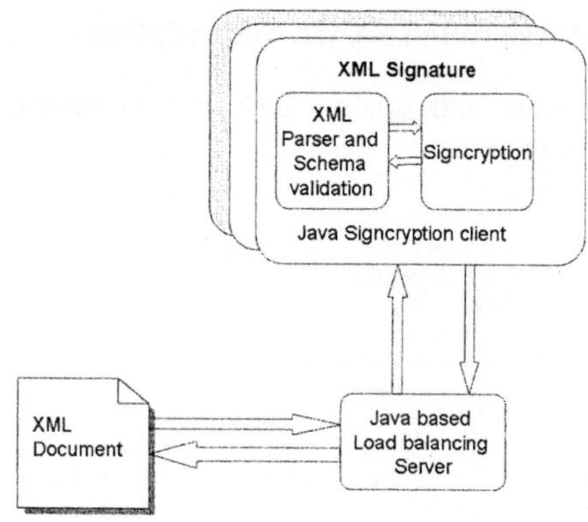

Fig. 2. Architecture for XML-based Signature Acceleration

Signcryption technique has two different variations. These variations are Shortened Digital Signature Standard 1 [6, 7] and Shortened Digital Signature Standard 2. Using JCE based crypto library, Signcryption will be programmed using verification to [6, 7, 9].

XML signcryption schema is shown above. The schema is required to validate the received XML message for its integrity. A part of the XML signcryption module is to create a technique where in badly formed XML documents need to be removed. Survey shows that a lot of attacks on XML servers are due to the fact that the XML documents created are not properly formed. The hardware-based solutions perform this additional task. The software-based module also needs to check the validity of the schema before the document is passed onto the next stages for verification.

The schema defines the various attributes and the elements that are required in a XML document. These attributes declare the feature of the XML document. The Id the element possesses and Multipurpose Internet Mail Extensions (MIME) so as to allow non-textual message to be passed can be incorporated into the XML document. The mode in which thc signcryption has occurred, Type specifies a built-in data type.

```
<element name="XML_Signcryption" type="SigncryptionType"/>
  <complexType name="SigncryptionType">
   <sequence>
     <element ref="SignedInfo"/>
   <element ref="SignatuereMethod"/>
   <element ref="EncrptionMethod" />
   <element ref="Reference" minOccurs="0"/>
    </sequence>
       <attribute name="Id" type="ID" use="optional"/>
       <attribute name="MimeType" type="MIME" use="optional"/>
       <attribute name="Mode" type="MODE" use="required"/>
   <attribute name="Type" type="TYPE" use="required"/>
   <attribute name="Encoding" type="CODING" use="optional"/>
  </complexType>
</element>
```

Fig. 3. XML-Signcryption Schema , root element

The XML signcryption schema and is being used with Java Crypto Extensions and SAX parser to create a XML signcryption module. As the signcryption algorithm is faster compared to other signature algorithms, because of its reduced computation, the system is faster. This system introduces faster processing and also provides an additional feature of encryption along with the signature. Hence, the XML signcryption not only performs the integrity of the XML document, but also performs the confidentiality of the system. This additional facility is provided to the system with faster execution time.

The proposed XML signcryption test environment, as shown in figure 6, an XML document is parsed and schema is validated using SAX parser. After the XML document is validated, the information is passed to signcryption module. The signcryption components can verify/generate the signature for an XML document.

3 The Mobile Grid Security Infrastructure

Web services can be used to provide mobile security solutions by standardizing and integrating leading security solutions using XML messaging. XML messaging is referred to as the leading choice for a wireless communication protocol and there are security protocols for mobile applications based upon it. Among them are the follows. SAML is a protocol to transport authentication and authorization information in an XML message. It could be used to provide single sign on web services. XML signatures define how to digitally sign part or all of an XML document to guarantee data integrity. The public key distributed with XML signatures can be wrapped in XKMS (XML Key Management Specification) formats. XML encryption allows applications to encrypt part or all of an XML document using references to pre-agreed symmetric keys. The WS-Security, endorsed by IBM and Microsoft, is a complete solution to provide security to web services. It is based on XML signatures, XML encryption, and an authentication and authorization scheme similar to SAML (Security Assertions Markup Language). When a mobile device client requests access to a back-end application, it sends authentication information to the issuing authority. The issuing authority can then send a positive or negative authentication assertion depending upon the credentials presented by the mobile device client. While the user still has a session with the mobile applications, the issuing authority can use the earlier reference to send an authentication assertion stating that the user was, in fact, authenticated by a particular method at a specific time. As mentioned earlier, location-based authentication can be done at regular time intervals, which means that the issuing authority gives out location-based assertions periodically as long as the user credentials make for a positive authentication.

CVM (Certificate Validation Module) in XKMS system perform path validation on a certificate chain according to the local policy and with local PKI (Public Key Infrastructure) facilities, such as certificate revocation (CRLs) or through an OCSP (Online Certificates Status Protocol). In the CVM, a number of protocols (OCSP, SCVP, and LDAP) are used for the service of certificate validation. For processing the XML client request, certificate validation service from OCSP, LDAP (Lightweight Directory Access Protocol), SCVP (Simple Certificate Validation Protocol)

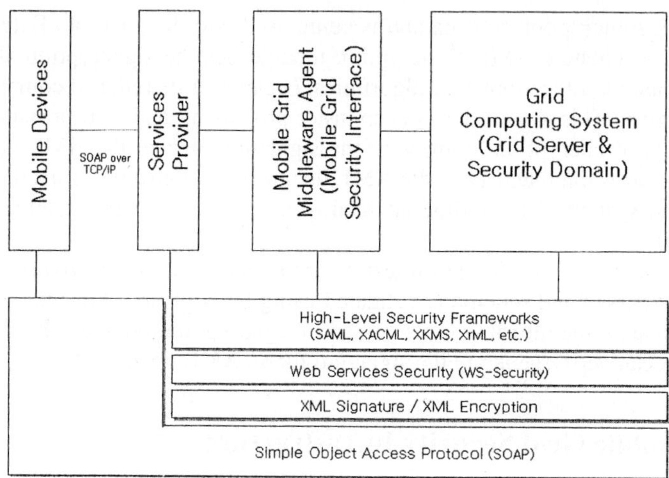

Fig. 4. Security Architecture for Open Mobile Grid Middleware

protocols in XKMS based on PKI are used. The XKMS client generates an 'XKMS Validate' request. This is essentially asking the XKMS server to go and find out the status of the server's certificate. The XKMS server receives this request and performs a series of validation tasks e.g. X.509 certificate path validation. Certificate status is determined. XKMS server replies to client application with status of the server's certificate and application acts accordingly. Using the OCSP protocol, the CVM obtained certificate status information from other OCSP responders or other CVMs. Using the LDAP protocol, the CVM fetched CRL (Certificate Revocation List) from the repository. And CA (Certificate Authority) database connection protocol (CVMP;CVM Protocol) is used for the purpose of that the server obtains real-time certificate status information from Cas [3, 4, 5]. The client uses OCSP and SCVP. With XKMS, all of these functions are performed by the XKMS server component [8, 10]. Thus, there is no need for LDAP, OCSP and other registration functionality in the client application itself.

4 Implementation Prototypes

In this architecture we are adopting a security-oriented approach currently conforming to the OGSA specification and using the Globus Toolkit 3 implementation. In the near future we plan to migrate to the newest WS specification and take advantage of the latest WSDL that will provide a lot of enhancements for Grid service development. Components of the grid security are XML security library, service components API, application program. Although message service component is intended to support XML applications, it can also be used in order environments where the same management and deployment benefits are achievable.

The figure for representing testbed system architecture of service component is as follows figure 5. We use testbed system of windows PC environment to simulate the

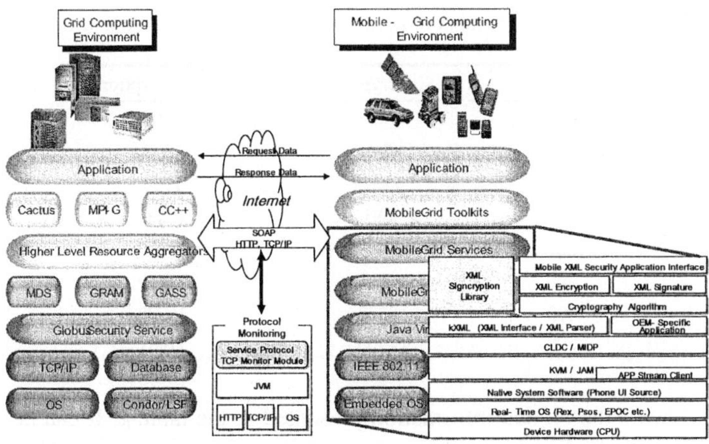

Fig. 5. XML Signcryption Component for Open Mobile Grid Services

processing of various service protocols. The protocols have been tested on pentium 3 and pentium 4 PCs. It has been tested on windows 2000 server, windows XP.

Java 2, Micro Edition (J2ME) is a set of technologies and specifications developed for small devices like smart cards, pagers, mobile phones, and set-top boxes. J2ME uses subset of Java 2, Standard Edition (J2SE) components, like smaller virtual machines and leaner APIs. J2ME has categorized wireless devices and their capabilities into profiles: MIDP (Mobile Information Device Profile), PDA and personal. MIDP and PDA profiles are targeted for handhelds and personal profile for networked consumer electronic and embedded devices. As the technology progresses in quantum leaps any strict categorization is under threat to become obsolete. It is already seen that J2ME personal profile are being used in high-end PDAs such as pocketPCs and mobile communicators. We will concentrate on the most limited category of wireless J2ME devices that use MIDP. Applications that these devices understand are Midlets. Typically maximum size of a Midlet varies from 30-50kbs and user can download four to six applications to his mobile phone. Midlet is a JAR-archive conforming to the Midlet content specification [2].

The server is composed server service component of mobile grid platform package. And the message format is based on Specification of W3C (World Wide Web Consortium). XML signcryption based technique that has been under study. Signcryption is a technique that provides both confidentiality and integrity by performing both the techniques of encryption and signature at reduced costs.

5 Simulative Network Performance Evaluation

As explained in section 2, the signcryption technique has been developed and tested against other signature systems. Table 1 below shows the time taken for the generating signcryption plotted against the number of iterations [12].

Table 1. Total time taken vs. number of iterations for both Signcryption and Unsigncryption

	Signcryption	Unsigncryption
Iterations	Ms	Ms
1	891	1672
10	1157	1906
100	3391	8125
200	6390	13890
300	8219	19109
400	10328	26078
500	12468	31437

Figure 6 shows the plotted information presented in the table 1. It can be seen that the time taken for verification of the signature takes a longer time than the generation of the signcryption value itself.

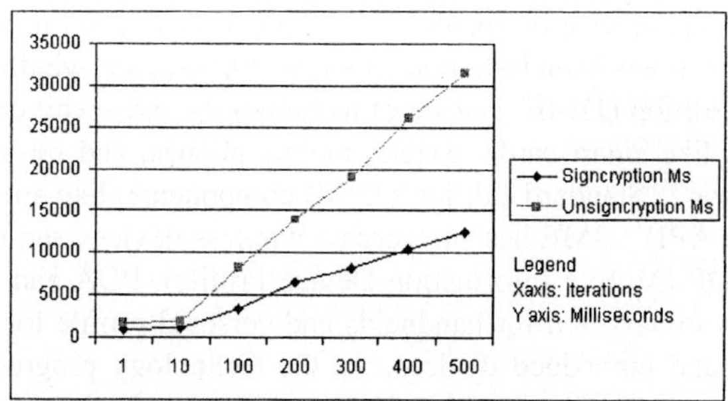

Fig. 6. Time taken plotted against number of iterations for Signcryption and Unsigncryption

Table 2 shows the time taken per iteration versus the number of iterations. Figure 7 shows in the information in a graphical form. It can be noticed that as the number of iterations increase the amount of time taken per iteration decreases significantly.

Table 2. Total time taken vs. Number of iterations for Signcryption and Unsigncryption

	Signcryption	Unsigncryption
Iterations	Ms/iteration	Ms/iteration
1	891	1672
10	115.7	190.6
100	33.91	81.25
200	31.95	69.45
300	27.40	63. 70
400	25.82	65.195
500	24.936	62.874

In the case of Unsigncryption the time taken per iteration is much more than the time taken for signcryption. The process provides both confidentiality and integrity at relatively lesser speed and lesser time as compared to other signature techniques.

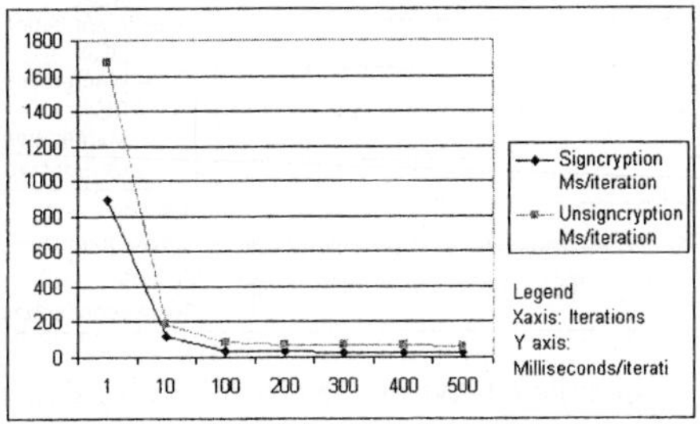

Fig. 7. Time taken plotted against number of iterations for Signcryption and Unsigncryption

5.1 Comparison Among the Signature Techniques

The different techniques discussed above has been tested and compared. The figure 8 shows the time taken per iteration for signature generation. It can be noticed that the time taken for signcryption decreases steadily as the number of iterations are increased. For one iteration, the time taken for signcryption is higher than other signature techniques. But as the number of iterations decrease, the performance of signcryption is comparable with the other techniques. But as the signcryption embodies both signature and encryption, signcryption would be recommended [12,13].

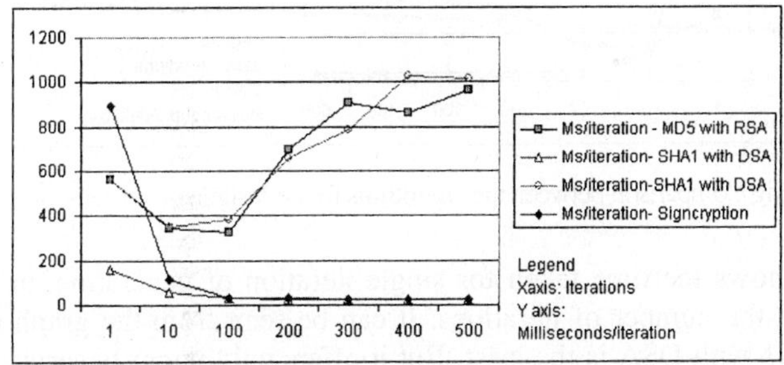

Fig. 8. Comparison between the algorithms for signature generation

It can be noted that the best performance in signature verification is performed by SHA1 with DSA. Figure 9 shows the comparison between the time taken per iteration versus number of iterations for signature verification for the signature algorithms discussed. It can be seen that the time taken for Unsigncryption is high for single iteration than compared to others. But as the time increases, the time taken for iteration decreases but is higher than the other techniques.

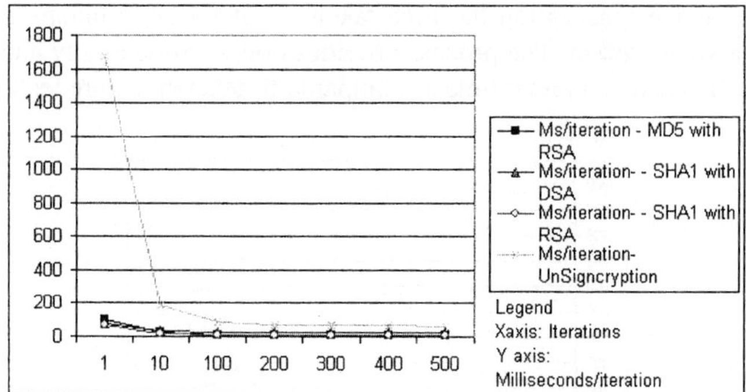

Fig. 9. Showing Comparison between the algorithms for signature verification

The time taken per iteration is not significantly lower in case of verification, but is significant in the case of signature generation except for signcryption. If the primary concern is integrity, then the ideal solution to use would be to use SHA1 with DSA. However if the concern is for both integrity and for confidentiality then signcryption would be an ideal solution to use. This can be demonstrated by figure 10.

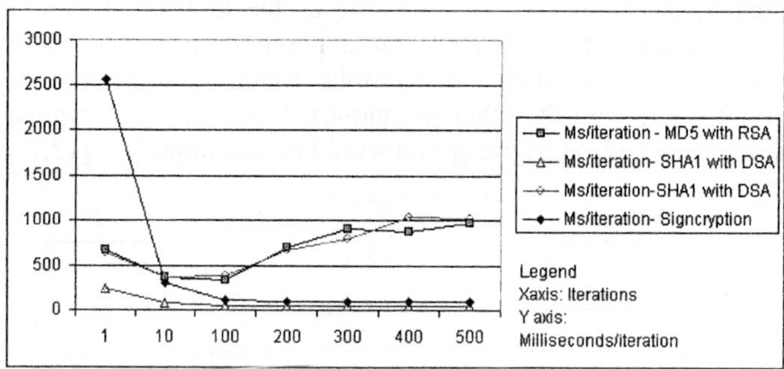

Fig. 10. Showing Comparison between the algorithms for both signature generation and verification

Figure 10 shows the time taken for single iteration of generation and verification plotted against the number of iterations. It can be seen from the graph that the time taken for SHA1 with DSA is the least. But it offers only integrity services. Signcryption offers both confidentiality and integrity and performs well when the numbers of iterations are used.

6 Conclusion and Further Works

Mobile grid services are so attractive that they can cover all walks of life. However, current grid is growing slower than expected. Many problems like accuracy, privacy, security, customer requirement have to be addressed. It should be understood that there is no single universal solution to grid. Signcryption technique allows simultaneous processing of encryption-decryption and Signature. It has been proved that the use of signcryption decreases the processing time by 58%. Signcryption is being programmed using the field theory. Signcryption technique is very efficient as it uses only a single exponentiation for both encryption and signature.

We propose a novel security approach on fast mobile grid services based on current mobile web services platform environment using XML signcryption mechanism. Our approach can be a model for the future security system that offers security of open mobile grid security.

The further works are follows: the new problems may arise for introduction of secure mobility of grid services. These problems include protocol compatibility, security of mobile service and complexity of programming, etc. Our further works are to consummate protocol extension, implement the secure mobile agent's replant to Grid, and deeply research and implement secure mobile agent control mechanisms in grid environment.

Acknowledgement

The first author would like to thank Yuliang Zheng, Ph.D. of the University of North Carolina at Charlotte for his encouragement and assistance.

References

1. Mika Tuisku: Wireless Java-enabled MIDP Devices as peers in Grid Infrastructure. Helsinki Institute of Physics. CERN
2. Ye Wen: Mobile Grid Major Area Examination. University of California (2002)
3. E. Faldella and M.Prandini: A Novel Approach to On-Line Status Authentication of Public Key Certificates, in Proc. the 16th Annual Computer Security Applications Conference (2000)
4. Yuichi Nakamur, et. Al.: Toward the Integration of web services security on enterprise environments. IEEE SAINT '02 (2002)
5. Diana Berbecaru, Antonio Lioy: Towards Simplifying PKI Implementation, Client-Server based Validation of Public Key Certificates. IEEE ISSPIT (2002) 277-281
6. Joonsang Baek, et. Al.: Formal Proofs for the security of signcryption, PKC'02 (2002) 80 - 98
7. Y. Zheng: Digital signcryption or How to Achieve Cost(Signature & Encryption) << Cost(Signature) + Cost(Encryption) , Advances in Cryptology -- Crypto'97. Lecture Notes in Computer Science, Vol. 1294. Springer-Verlag (1997) 165-179
8. Jang Hyun Baek, et. Al.: An Efficient Two-Step Paging Strategy Using Base Station Paging Agents in Mobile Communication Networks. ETRI Journal, Vol.26, No.5 (2004) 493-496
9. Proposed Fedral Information Proceeding standard for Digital Signature Standard(DSS), Fedral Register. Vol. 56. (1991)
10. I. Foster and C. Kesselman. Globus: A metacomputing infrastructure toolkit. International Journal of Supercomputer Applications, 11(2), 1997.
11. Miika Tuisku: Wireless Java-Enabled MIDP Devices as Peers in a Grid Infrastructure. Lecture Notes in Computer Science, Vol. 2970. Springer-Verlag (2004) 273-281
12. Seunghun Jin, et. Al.: Cluster-Based trust Evaluation Scheme in Ad hoc Network. ETRI Journal, Vol.27, No.4 (2005) 465-468
13. Yuliang Zheng, et. Al.: Research on Software-based XML Signature Acceleration. Project of ETRI, Vol. 1 (2004) 22-35

Experiences on Parallel Replicated Discrete-Event Simulation on a GRID

Ángel Perles, Antonio Martí, Francisco Rodríguez, Juan José Serrano, and Miguel A. Mateo

Dept. of Computer Engineering, Universidad Politécnica de Valencia, 46022, Valencia, Spain
{aperles, amarti, prodrig, jserrano, mimateo}@disca.upv.es}

Abstract. Concurrent and distributed simulation has proven its value reducing the time researchers spend in simulation model validation and execution. Our research group has developed distributed simulation tools applicable to any discrete-event simulator. PVM was used before as distributed execution environment, but the use of PVM is not transparent for final users. On the other hand, GRID frameworks are being used successfully to distribute execution of applications. Once a GRID framework is installed and configured, it is very easy to use for any user so we thought that GRID frameworks could be a better base system than PVM for our distributed simulation tool. The experience presented in this paper shows that GRID frameworks offer an environment that is easier to exploit, while providing similar efficiency than the PVM version used previously.

1 Introduction

Discrete-event simulation models are necessary for the design and evaluation of a wide range of technologies. In our case we apply this technique to the design of real-time digital systems, industrial LANs, GRID printing evaluation, memory cache for real-time systems, etc.

But actual systems and future designs are growing in complexity, so equivalent simulation models require a lot of computer time in order to get output results statistically valid. Many researchers suffer the long response times executing these simulation models.

A lot of research work is being carried out in order to improve the response time of simulators by using parallel and distributed simulation techniques. A main work line develops the possibility of decomposing the simulation model into sub-models that can be executed concurrently. The main problem of this approximation consists the need to maintain the logical consistency of the event list [1,2]. The use of such distributed simulation techniques require a great decomposition effort and model tuning, and it can be a good approach when the simulator is the final product itself (i.e. a world-wide airport management simulator).

An alternative to the distributed simulation technique consists in executing several copies of the simulation model in parallel. This approach can be used to improve the response time taking advantage of the "statistical parallelism", that is, the fact that

H. Zhuge and G.C. Fox (Eds.): GCC 2005, LNCS 3795, pp. 334 – 344, 2005.

samples of statistical information are generated at higher rates. Some authors [3,4,5,6] propose tools that attempt to benefit of this method in different ways.

We developed a tool [3] devoted to benefit of the second approach. The idea is to spawn concurrent copies of a classic sequential simulation program and monitor them to extract statistical information of selected output variables. This tool use the idle time of a lot of heterogeneous workstations at university laboratories and research centers to run simulation experiments from many users concurrently. It provides a general form of monitoring and controlling simulations also, allowing its application to any commercial or public discrete-event simulator (it has been applied on SMPL [7] and CSIM [8] simulation models). Its easy application avoids the learning curve of a new simulation language and focuses the effort on the model itself.

This tool was developed as a distributed application working under PVM 3.4 [9] and permits the incorporation of Unix and Windows computers into an heterogeneous parallel virtual machine. It worked well but required an important system administrator effort in order to configure appropriately the environment (specific user accounts with restricted privileges for model execution, NFS shared filesystems, etc.), required enumeration of specific machines to be incorporated to the virtual machine, and it had poor fault-tolerant characteristics.

We thought that a GRID framework [10] could provide a valid way to minimize these problems, so we decided to migrate the tool to a GRID solution such as Globus Toolkit 4 [11]. The use of facilities to run PVM legacy code on that environment (i.e. on the PVM universe of a Condor scheduler) was early discarded because it does not eliminate the problems described before.

This paper presents the result of this experience that can be extrapolated to other applications that work in a similar way. Next section introduces some concepts of discrete-event simulation and the parallelization approach used. Then, next section describes the parallel tool design. Finally, we conclude summarizing our experience about the migration.

2 Parallel Replications Algorithm

2.1 Discrete-Event Simulation Basics

Discrete-event modelling is a paradigm based on the specification of the system response to discrete events produced at given instants of time. Running a discrete-event simulation model consist in processing such events in an ordered manner. Events are ordered in occurrence time and the "simulated time" evolves according the "occurrence time" of the next event. An event processing produces a change of the model state and can produce new events to be processed in the future.

The objective of such discrete-event models can be different, for example: to know better the behaviour of a system, to obtain average estimates of performance, to guide in the election of configurations, etc.

Events generated in a discrete-event simulation can be taken from a trace of real systems or generated statistically. In the second case, the researcher has to deal with an statistical output analysis problem, being the main ingredient for the simulation a good random number generator to produce a correct probabilistic distribution of events [12].

Assuming that the simulation model uses random numbers as its input, the output of the model is a response to such input, being samples of an unknown population. In our case we are interested on the estimation of the mean value of a sample *E[X]* (or expected value) of an output variable (called also a point estimator). However, the only way to achieve this (mathematically) is with an infinite sample of values, which it is not possible with a limited amount of computer time. The best we can offer is an estimation of the true value *E[X]* in a given confidence interval $\left(\overline{X}-H,\overline{X}+H\right)$ where there is a high probability of containing *E[X]*.

Most of the cases, the measure of interest is the mean value of an output value. This variable can represent a discrete (i.e. time of service of a customer) or a continuos (i.e. queue length at the cinema) time stochastic process. For a discrete time variable, the simulation produces a sequence of N samples $X_1 \ldots X_N$ with mean $\overline{X}$ and variance s^2,

$$\overline{X}=\sum_{i=1}^{N}\frac{X_i}{N} \qquad s^2=\sum_{i=1}^{N}\frac{(X_i-\overline{X})^2}{N-1} \tag{1}$$

These values must be statistically qualified by means of a confidence interval at a given confidence level. This is not a completely solved statistical problem. There are different approaches to solve it [13], each one with its advantages and drawbacks, but always with doubts about the validity of the result. Popular methods are: replications, batch-means, regeneration, autoregression, spectral and standardized time-series.

2.2 Parallel Replications Approach

Our tool, called "Cluster Simulation Experimenter" (CSX), can use different statistical output analysis techniques, but our main effort has been on the independent replication method. This method proposes that we can run k replications of a simulation program using independent input random streams to compute a sample mean.

This is the theoretical support of the replication method: let be the sample mean of the observations of some output variable for the j-th replication. These observations can be regarded as realizations of independent and normally distributed random variables. Then we can compute an estimator of the true mean *E(X)* using these k sample means as,

$$\overline{\overline{X}}=\frac{\sum_{j=1}^{k}\overline{X}_j}{k} \tag{2}$$

In order to obtain an asymptotically valid $(1-\alpha)x100\%$ confidence interval for the grand mean we can apply the equation,

$$\overline{\overline{X}}\pm t_{1-\alpha/2,k-1}\sqrt{\frac{S_k^2}{k}} \tag{3}$$

where S_k^2 is the variance of sample means and t is the Student distribution.

The sequential and classic replication method consists of running fixed size simulations and test if they have been reached the required confidence interval at a given confidence level. If the replications are too short, starting another simulation execution of longer will be needed. On the other hand, if they are too long, the results will be unnecessarily more accurate, wasting computer resources and increasing the response time. The difficulty to predict the number of replications and their respective lengths has motivated the development of alternative methods, some of then named before.

The problem of the sequential scheme of the replication method can be avoided by using parallel techniques. There are two different ways to apply parallelism in his case: running fixed size replications in parallel until the wished confidence interval is achieved [4] or keep running a fixed low number of replications until they produce the needed confidence interval.

We have developed our tool using this second option because it seems to be statistically more robust on the assumption of independence hypothesis and normal distribution of the output variable. In [14] it is established the asymptotic superiority of a few long replications relative to a large number of shorter replications it is established.

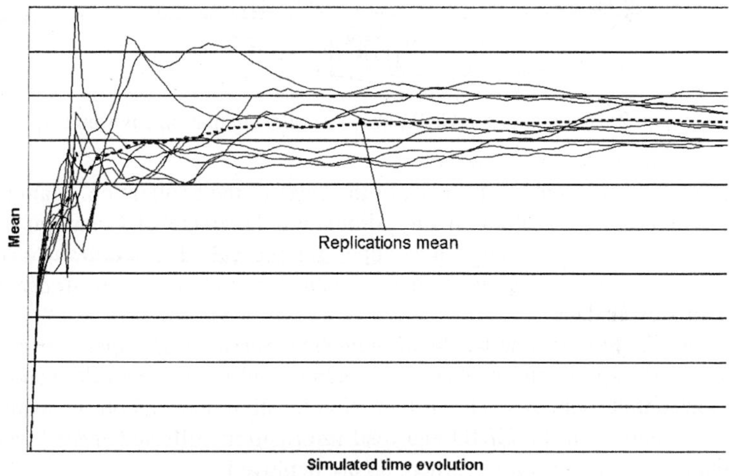

Fig. 1. Example of the evolution of $\overline{X}$ of a set of replications

The replication method of CSX consists in the execution of a fixed set of independent replications and obtaining as they change their size, maintaining the replications running until the confidence interval is achieved. Figure 1 shows an example of the evolution of $\overline{X}$ for N replications as simulated time evolves. This is a typical behaviour where a simulation model departs from a non-natural state (called transient phase) and converges to the true mean value at infinite. The grand mean $\overline{\overline{X}}$ is shown as a dashed line.

3 Parallel Simulation Tool Design

Figure 2 shows the design of a CSX environment in operation. This is outlined as a set of distributed web services working under the Globus Toolkit 4 [5].

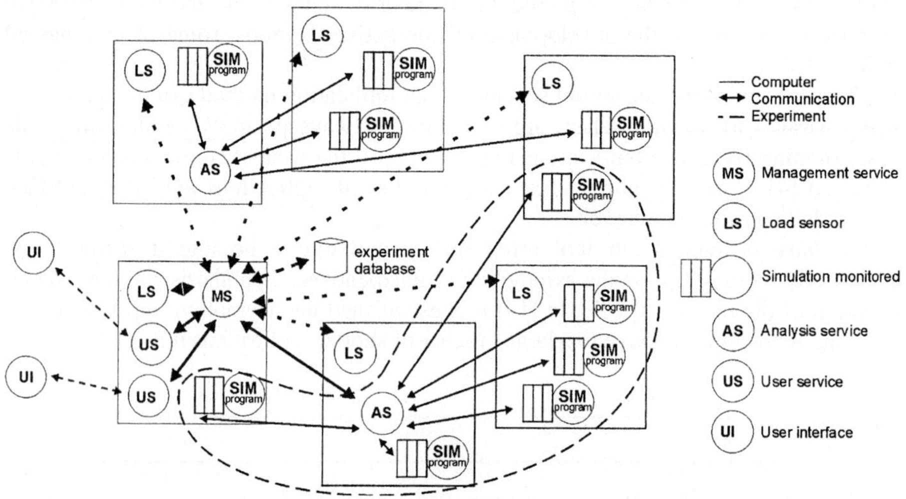

Fig. 2. Diagram of the GRID-based parallel simulation environment

There is a different service for each of the tasks of the application. Main element is a simulation program written in any simulation language and manipulated to be spawned and controlled through a wrapper service called *Simulation Service* (*SS*). Replications are a set of *SS* whith their statistical output sent to an *Analysis Service* (*AS*) that processes data.

Main coordination is done by the *Management Service (MS)*, that is responsible of maintaining the experiment database (executables and processing rules) and to decide where to instantiate services. The instantiation location depends on the availability of registered resources in the GRID and load information collected from *Load Sensors* (*S*) available on active machines where *SS* are deployed.

User Service (*US*) instances manages access and rights of users to send and control their experiments.

Next subsections give some highlights about the design of the tool.

3.1 Adapting Legacy Simulations

The parallel simulation tool CSX has been designed to manage and extract information of classic sequential simulation models. The simulation model is a program developed in any standard simulation language (SMPL, QNAP, CSIM, SIM++, DEVS *, etc.); CSX requirements imply that such a program has to be modified to integrate it as a *SS*.

The modification technique has been developed in order to achieve objectives such as:

- Maximum transparency. Minimal modifications to the simulation model.
- External control. To avoid doing explicit the type of control and the nature and type of the statistical analysis applied.
- Dual behaviour. To make possible a non-monitored execution of the program so that it can be executed as a normal sequential simulation, helping the design and debugging stage of the model.
- Minimal overhead. To use instrumentation techniques that produce minimal overhead to the execution of the program.

These objectives have been achieved by injecting a special event in the simulator event queue [15]. This technique is transparent to the user, which only needs to introduce some modifications to the source code and link it with a set of CSX-supplied libraries. Source code snippet below shows an example of the modifications required in a CSIM M/M/1 queue simulation model.

```
/* /M/M/1 example for CSIM */
#include <csim.h>
// CSX added header file, specific for CSIM
#include <csx_csim.h>

FACILITY f;
double Ta, Ts;

main (int argc, char *argv[])
{
   // input variables controlled by CSX
   csx_gpdouble(argc,argv,"Ta",&Ta,1.0);
   csx_gpdouble(argc,argv,"Ts",&Ts,0.5);

   sim();
}

sim()
{
   create("sim");
   f=facility("center");

   while (simtime()<5000.0) {
      hold(exponential(Ta));
      customer();
   }

   report();
   terminate();
}

customer()
{
   create("customer");
   use(f,exponential(Ts));
   terminate();
}
```

This simulation model represents a fifo queue server. The time required to serve a customer demand is a function of the *Ts* input parameter. Customer arrives to the server queue's at a rate function of *Ta*.

The "`csx_csim.h`" header file defines prototypes of CSX functions an overloads (using C preprocessing directives) some of the CSIM functions. Input parameters of the simulation model, *Ta* and *Ts*, should be managed by CSX, for example, `csx_gpdouble()` CSX function (get double parameter) let to obtain input parameters from command line for a non-monitored execution, and from a web services in monitored mode. Output variables of the model (mean customer service time, mean queue length, etc.) are collected automatically and sent to the *AS*.

These CSX libraries use a three-tier design that isolates each aspect of the instrumentation. Figure 3 shows a diagram: the main layer is the "SIM manager" whose function is to collect information of the simulation model and to coordinate specific layers for a given simulator and given communications system. In the figure, the "SMPL interface" layer transforms SMPL calls to specific "SIM manager" functions and conversely. The "GRID interface" layer transacts the interactions between the "SIM manager" and the distributed computation system.

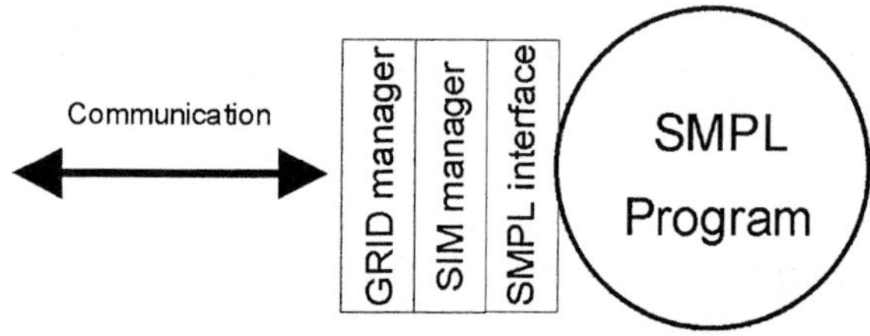

Fig. 3. Three-tier libraries used to adapt different simulation languages

A replication in this context is the execution of a copy of a simulation model, modified to incorporate CSX calls, in a computer through the instantiation of a *simulation service* (*SS*). Computers on the grid available to perform simulations are recognized because they have registered this *SS*. When the instantiation is requested, a workspace of the simulation is created, the file of the executable is transferred to the workspace through GRIDFtp service, and the executable is initiated using Globus *fork()* GRAM service.

Replication receives its initial configuration and posterior reconfigurations through the *SS* instance wrapper.

Every time a sample of statistical data is available (mean and variance of a preconfigured number of samples), the data is coded using XML (libxml2) and sent to an *analysis service* (*AS*) instance.

3.2 Analysis Service

The *Analysis service* (*AS*) is responsible of processing statistical data received from its subordinated replications. It decides the end of the simulation based on the precision of the measure of interest and a set of stopping criteria [15]. An AS service instantiation can be developed for different statistical output analysis methods. We normally apply the analysis method explained before.

If a replication fails (due to a network problem, a computer shutdown, etc.) the experiment can continue using the statistical data of the rest of replications; simply it is necessary adjust formula (3). But if an *AS* fails, an important amount of computer time may be lost. Computers that perform the *AS* task do not have important requirements of CPU power or memory, so they are elected from the point of view of reliability.

The replication method of CSX consists in the execution of a fixed set of independent replications and obtaining sample means as they change their size, maintaining the replications running until the confidence interval is achieved.

Each replication runs until a specified point (number of collected samples or simulated time), sends the required statistical information to the *AS*, and continues simulating without waiting a decision of the *AS*.

This approach avoids an important problem of the classic parallel execution of replications: the duration of the simulation. This time is, al least, the sum of the execution times of the slower replication in each checkpoint. In [16] it is established that the execution times of replications are identical independent (i.i.d.) exponentially distributed random variables with mean 1. We solve the duration problem allowing each replication to run as fast as possible sending, asynchronously, statistical information to the analyzer monitor service, a continuing its work, thus avoiding synchronization delays. The analyzer can save statistical information and process the next checkpoint when it has information of all replications.

Figure 4 is an example with 3 replications (R1, R2 and R3) and an *AS* monitor (M); in the X axis is represented the wall clock time evolution, replications and AS can be running or idle, arrows represent main flow of information. AS processes statistical information when it receives the corresponding statistical data of all replications at a given checkpoint.

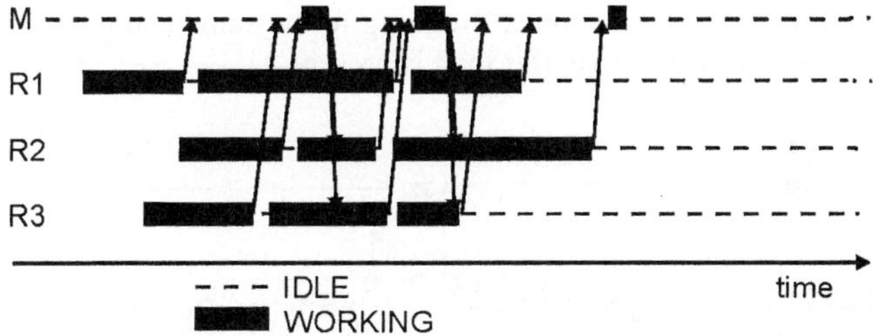

Fig. 4. Optimal utilization of computational resources avoiding the synchronization effect in the output analysis phase at each checkpoint

3.3 Load Balancing

The parallel simulation environment can be running simulation experiments of various users at a time, and each simulation experiment is a set of replications, so especial care must be considered in load balancing.

The only difference between replications of a simulation model is the input of random seed and, asymptotically speaking, the mean time of execution should be the same. The main factor that influences replication response time is the machine speed. When parallel replications or similar method is used for the analysis of output data, it is necessary to have measures of all implied replications to calculate the confidence intervals; any delay collecting a measure implies a global delay in obtaining the results.

All computers where the *Simulation Service* is deployed include a *Load Sensor* that monitors CPU load and main memory usage. This information is periodically sent to the *Management Service (MS)* that decides which machines are used for each new set of replications.

Due to the architecture heterogeneity of the machines employed in the GRID, it is difficult to know in advance what the simulation time is when executing a *SS* in a given machine using load information exclusively. Our approach has been to provide a performance index that lets to classify the different machines that compose the GRID.

When the *Simulation Service* is deployed in a machine, a special SMPL simulation model is executed in the machine to calculate the events per millisecond (roughly equal to the speed of simulation) achieved for this particular simulation model when 100% of the CPU time is used without interference from other tasks. The fact those replications are similar in behaviour let us assume that their speed will be proportional to that index. This index is part of the *Simulation Service* information saved in the GRID registry service.

Dynamic load balancing techniques where considered in the previous PVM version, but they are not available in the current GRID implementation. The idea could be extrapolated to other GRID based computer intensive problems however. In our case it is necessary to know the performance of every replication in execution, and this is achieved recording the number of simulation events per millisecond processed in each replication and attaching this information with each sample of output variables sent.

Based on the information of processed events and the current simulated time, it is possible to estimate the response time needed to reach a given point of the time in the simulation. It is also possible to determine if it could be convenient to transfer the load to other machines to balance the response time. Figure 5 represents an example of the "simulation performance" of two quasi-identical replications (only change the random number generator seed utilized) running in the same computer and the effect on their performance if interactive user load is present.

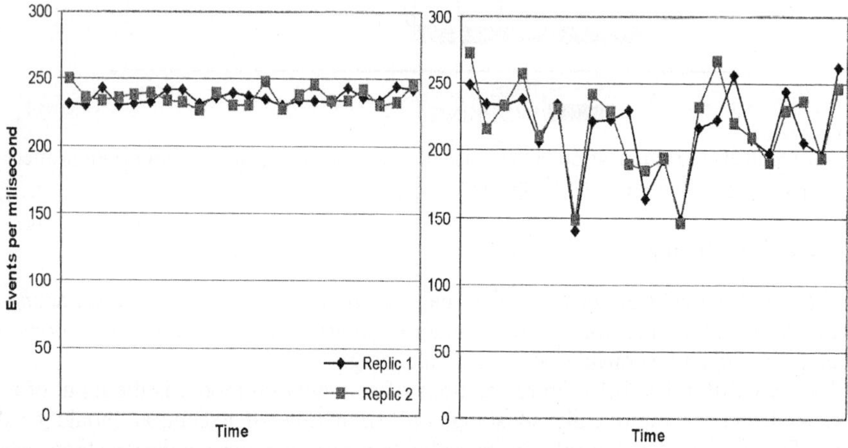

Fig. 5. Simulation speed of two replications of the same model running in a computer (left). The effect of interactive user load on the replications speed (right).

3.4 User Service

To access the GRID based parallel simulation tool we use a *User Service* (*US*) instance. This *US* must be deployed in a reliable computer because it also maintains the experiment database (simulation executables, experiment definitions, etc.).

Two different types of user applications may interact with a *US* instance actually: a command line version that lets the researcher to specify the experiments definition in a script based manner, and a visual interface version. Figure 6 shows a screenshot of the output results of a running set of replications.

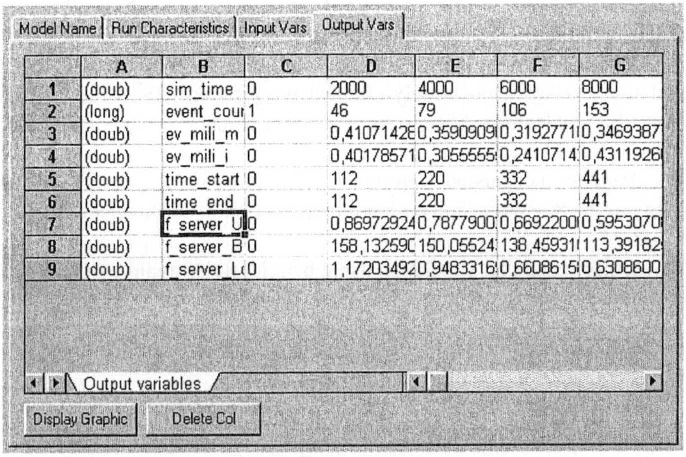

Model Name | Run Characteristics | Input Vars | Output Vars

	A	B	C	D	E	F	G
1	(doub)	sim_time	0	2000	4000	6000	8000
2	(long)	event_cour	1	46	79	106	153
3	(doub)	ev_mili_m	0	0,4107142E	0,3590909	0,3192771	0,3469387
4	(doub)	ev_mili_i	0	0,4017857	0,3055555	0,2410714	0,4311926
5	(doub)	time_start	0	112	220	332	441
6	(doub)	time_end	0	112	220	332	441
7	(doub)	f_server_U	0	0,86972924	0,7877900	0,6692200	0,5953070
8	(doub)	f_server_B	0	158,13259C	150,05524	138,45931	113,39182
9	(doub)	f_server_L	0	1,17203492	0,9483316	0,6608615	0,6308600

Output variables

Display Graphic | Delete Col

Fig. 6. Screenshot of the visual interface

4 Conclusions

We have successfully ported our PVM based parallel simulation tool to the Globus Toolkit. As we expected, now it is easier to benefit from computers where desired services has been deployed without dealing with cumbersome lists of machines because GRID MDS service let us to circumvent this problem.

We detected an increment in the size of communicated data between processes of about five times. This was expected because web services require a self-defined XML message, and PVM uses XDR coding. Our application is very CPU intensive and its asynchronous design minimizes interprocess communication dependencies, so this problem is not important. But it can be an important drawback if very intense communications are required [17].

We also expected less effort of the system administrator installing and maintaining the GRID environment compared with PVM. Installation of Globus has been problematic and difficult to maintain however. The cause seems to reside in the nature of research platform of the toolkit. Another problem has been the lack of "commodity grid" software for C similar to the ones available for Java that facilitates the grid-based software development.

As main conclusion, if we plan to develop a new distributed application from scratch and there are no special communications requirements, web services based GRID should be considered as convenient candidate. Also, we should take in consideration that communication frameworks are in evolution actually, and we can expect new advances and approaches [18].

References

1. Fujimoto, R. M.: Parallel and distributed simulation systems. John Wiley (2000)
2. Zarei, B. A taxonomic review of parallel discrete event simulation. Proceedings of the 12th European Simulation Symposium. (2000) 61-76
3. Perles, A., Martí, A., Serrano, J.J. Clustered simulation experimenter: A tool for concurrent simulation execution on loosely coupled workstations. Proceedings 13th European Simulation Multiconference. Society for Computer Simulation International. (1999) 207-214
4. Lin, Y-B. Parallel independent replicated simulation on a network of workstations. Proceedings of the 8th Workshop on Parallel and Distributed Simulation (PADS'94). **24** 1 (1994) 73-80
5. Yau, V. Automating parallel simulation using parallel time streams. ACM Transactions on Modeling and Computer Simulation. **9** 2 (1999) 171-201
6. Rego, V. J., Sunderam, V. S. Experiments in concurrent stochastic simulation: The EcliPSe paradigm. Journal of Parallel and Distributed Computing. **14** 1 (1992) 66-84
7. MacDougall, M. H. Simulating Computer Systems. The MIT Press, Cambridge, Massachusetts. (1987)
8. User's guide: CSIM18 Simulation Engine. Mesquite Software, Inc. (1998)
9. Geist, A., Beguelin, A., Dongarra, J., Jiang, W., Manchek, R., Sunderam, V. PVM3 user's guide and reference manual. Technical Report ORNL/TM-12187, Oak Ridge National Laboratory. (1994)
10. Foster, I., Kesselman, C., Tuecke, S. The anatomy of the grid: enabling scalable virtual organizations. Int. J. Supercomp. Appl. **15** 1 (2001) 115-128
11. The Globus Project. http://www.globus.org
12. L'Ecuyer, P. Some recomendable uniform random number generators. Proceedings of the 13th European Simulation Multiconference. **2** (1999) 185-190
13. Law A. M., Kelton W. D. Simulation Modeling and Analysis. Ed. McGraw-Hill. (2000)
14. Glynn, P. W. Some new results on the initial transient problem. Proceedings of the 1995 Winter Simulation Conference. (1995) 165-170
15. Perles, A. Técnicas para el aprovechamiento de redes de computadores heterogéneos en la ejecución paralela de modelos de simulación por eventos discretos. Ph.D Thesis. Universidad Politécnica de Valencia. (2003)
16. Bhavsar, V. C., Isaac, J. R. Design and analysis of parallel Monte-Carlo algorithms. SIAM Journal on Scientific and Statistical Computing. **8** (1987) 73-95
17. Migliardi, M., Kurzyniec, D., and Sunderam, V. S. Standards Based Heterogeneous Metacomputing: The Design of HARNESS II. Proceedings of the 16th international Parallel and Distributed Processing Symposium (HCW2002). 304
18. Zhuge, H. The Future Interconnection Environment. IEEE Computer. **38** 4 (2005) 27-33

Towards an End-User Programming Environment for the Grid

Chengchun Shu[1], Haiyan Yu[2], Lijuan Xiao[1], Haozhi Liu[1], and Zhiwei Xu[2]

[1] Graduate School of the Chinese Academy of Sciences,
Beijing, 100039, P.R. China
{shuchengchun, xiaolijuan, liuhaozhi}@software.ict.ac.cn
[2] Institute of Computing Technology, Chinese Academy of Sciences,
Beijing, 100080, P.R. China
{yuhaiyan, zxu}@ict.ac.cn

Abstract. For end users, building applications with current Grid programming paradigms still remains a difficult and time-consuming task by dealing with excessive low-level details of provided APIs. We present a high-level application description language called Grid Service Markup Language (GSML) and its supporting development environment, to facilitate end-user programming in an approach that applications could be visually composed by well-defined software components in an event-driven fashion. Core constructs of GSML language, *Pipe*, *Event*, *Target*, and *EventSet*, are developed to address the complexity of dynamic interaction behaviors of grid applications. By raising the level of abstraction as well as simplifying the programming model, GSML allows end users to build grid applications easily with improved productivity.

1 Introduction

The Grid promises to aggregate and coordinate a collection of geographically distributed resources into a relatively seamless computing framework, and then allows the developments of applications of unprecedented scale and innovative nature that solve problems unable to be solved before. However, the Grid environment is inherently parallel, distributed, heterogeneous and dynamic, in terms of both their natures and performances, which requires new application tools and programming environments that enable efficient aggregation and composition of the diverse resources and services.

It is widely agreed that Grid programming is more complex than sequential and distributed programming. It not only requires managing the inherently dynamic and heterogeneous computing environment, but also needs to deal with flexible and dynamic composition of resources and services with a memory and latency/bandwidth hierarchy. Currently there are a variety of available technologies [1, 2, 3] for building Grid applications including Grid-enabled MPIs, Middlewares, Problem Solving Environments (PSEs) and Portals. Grid end users, the highest percentage of Grid users, are application users (e.g. biologists, chemists, meteorologists) who use Grid as part of their daily work but may not have professional background on computer programming. For them, building Grid application remains a difficult and time-consuming task with current Grid programming paradigms. To build new applications, end users need to work with details of low-level APIs provided by current Grid technologies,

H. Zhuge and G.C. Fox (Eds.): GCC 2005, LNCS 3795, pp. 345–356, 2005.

which requires a high learning curve for them. For example, users must have extensive knowledge of XML, SOAP and Web Services when developing applications based on service-oriented Grid platforms like Globus Toolkit 4 [19] and OMII [20]. These technical details often divert user's attention from application-specific programming tasks, resulting in increased cost and complexity that is hard to be afforded by users.

This paper presents Grid Service Markup Language (GSML), an end-user programming environment for the Grid. The whole environment consists of three parts: GSML language, GSML Composer and GSML Browser. GSML language is a generic, easy-to-use, but flexible and expressive Grid programming language which simplifies the development of Grid applications. Its core idea is to solve a problem by orchestrating interactions between inherently parallel, distributed and high-level components. GSML language characterizes asynchronous event-driven model, recursive Pipe definition, flexible Pipe development and easy development. GSML Composer is a visual programming environment supporting the development GSML applications in an intuitive way. For Grid users, especially for the non-programmer or novice programmers, the more visual programming [21] could be easier to be understood and utilized. GSML Browser provides convenient execution environment for GSML applications, which are XML documents automatically generated by GSML Composer or manually written by end users. By GSML, users need not build the application from the scratch but integrate many read-to-use components as needed. These components have already encapsulated low-level and labor-sensitive coding works, and therefore the high-level abstractions provided by GSML make the programming task easier even for nonprofessional programmers, and thus improve the productivity.

This paper is organized as follows. Section 2 discusses the background of our research and other related work. Section 3 presents the overview of GSML programming environment. Section 4 presents more detailed GSML Language design and implementation, while Section 5 covers the details of GSML Composer and GSML Browser. Several examples are demonstrated in Section 6. Section 7 presents a simple qualitative evaluation of GSML. We outline items for future work and conclude the paper in Section 8.

2 Background and Related Work

In our VEGA Grid [11] project, two Grid programming environments are proposed: Abacus [12] and GSML. GSML is a high-level programming environment for the non-professional end users, while Abacus is a lower-level service-oriented programming language for Grid developers.

Currently most of the Grid programming models are evolved from the traditional parallel and distributed programming models. Representative efforts on grid programming environment include Grid-enabled MPI projects such as MPICH-G2 [4] and MPI_Connect [5], network-enabled servers such as Netsolve [6] and Ninf [7], frameworks such as Cactus [15], component-based technologies such as CCAT [8], and problem solving environment such as Java CoG Kit [9]. There are some useful tools for efficient building of grid portals such as Hotpage [13] and GPDK [14]. GrADS [10] is a global Grid compilation system which optimizes a Grid application to maintain highest overall performance when employed resources change. These technologies address the complexity of Grid programming in lower-level than GSML. They often requires users to work with excessive low-level details of Grid architectures and protocols.

GRID superscalar [16] explores the idea of detecting implicit parallelism, forwarding of data and read/write conflicts resolution from superscalar processor designs. It can detect the inherent parallelism of the Grid applications written in sequential fashion and perform concurrent task submission. GRID superscalar focuses on improving system performance by exploiting the parallelism and other optimizations, while GSML aims to hide low-level details and complexity of Grid programming from end users and improve productivity of Grid programming. GSML only guarantees that the inherently parallel and concurrent components function correctly even in distributed environment no matter how the actual messages interacts.

There are a number of XML-based languages targeting the interaction among software components, services and even users. Microsoft's XAML [17] (Extensible Application Markup Language) is a language used to describe UI contents and behaviors in XML-based markup language. XUL (XML User Interface Language) is used for creating rich dynamic user interface in Mozilla browser and related applications. BPEL [18] (Business Process Execution Language) is an XML language for specifying business processes by orchestrating web services. BPEL explicitly deals with the functional aspects of business processes: control flow (branch, loop, parallel), asynchronous conversations and correlation, non-determinism and long-running, nested units of work, faults and compensation. While BPEL deals with composition and orchestration of Web services, GSML tries to cover more general and diverse Grid resources. Unlike BPEL, GSML does not differentiate control flow and data flow explicitly.

3 GSML Overview

3.1 System Model

Conceptually, GSML model is divided into three sub layers (Figure 1): GSML Resource layer, GSML Logic Layer and GSML UI Layout Layer. The lowest GSML Resource Layer provides resource abstractions. The resources can be desktop applications (e.g. Excel, Matlab, Web Browser), Web Services, Grid resources and services. Though the resources and services are inherently heterogeneous and dynamic, all of them are encapsulated into components with uniform interfaces: they receive target messages from, and send event messages to the surroundings. The components run concurrently and asynchronously and they interact with each other only by messages. GSML Logic Layer defines the interactions between these components. The interactions between components are modeled as a collection of event messages from components and target messages to components. The event messages in one interaction are synchronized. When all the synchronized event messages are sent out, the target messages in the interaction are sent to the destination components. GSML UI Layout Layer defines the layout of all components displayed in GSML Browser. A GSML application defines which components are used and how the interactions between components are organized. It also defines how the components with UIs are displayed. Figure 1 illustrates an example model for travel application. This GSML application contains five components (i.e. Input, AirlineService, BusService, Hotel-Service, Travel and TravelResult) and three interactions.

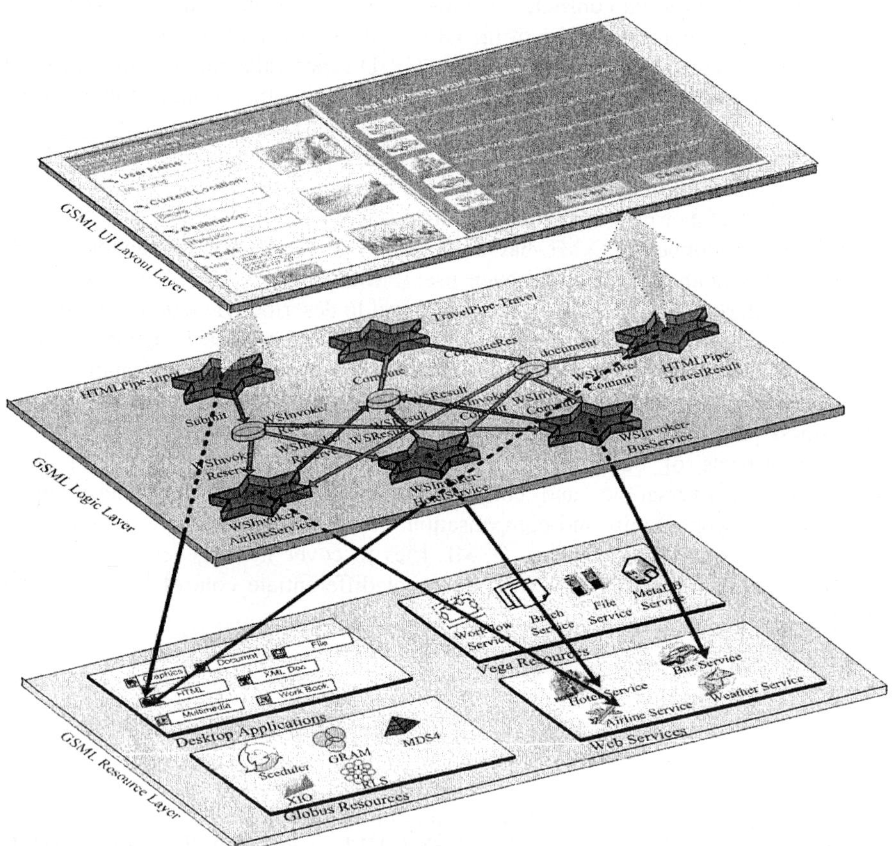

Fig. 1. An example model for travel application

3.2 Overview

As an end-user programming environment for Grid, GSML provides abstractions over the real Grid environment to insulate end users from the complexity of building a Grid application. GSML defines four basic constructs for system model: Pipe, Event, Target and EventSet, which correspond to component, event message, target message and interaction respectively. The challenge of GSML is to keep it accessible for the non-professional users but flexible and expressive enough. In addition to high-level abstraction, and portable, interoperable XML-based messages and Grid application descriptions, key GSML design features are as follows:

Asynchronous event-driven model: In GSML applications, runtime Pipes operate on their own logic concurrently, independently, and asynchronously. They only interact through messages with each other when expected Events are triggered. Because it is the most close and natural programming model for such applications, the asynchronous event-driven model can more precisely and easily express the Grid applications that solve problems by composition of the parallel and heterogeneous resources through interactions. Moreover, Grid applications can be more adaptive to the dynamic computing environment because this model essentially specifies the relative message dependencies rather than the absolute ones during actual interactions.

Recursive Pipe definition: A Pipe can be either a simple encapsulation of the resource, or a composite Pipe which is essentially a GSML application with exposed interfaces. Through the exposed interfaces, composite Pipes can receive incoming Target messages from, and send outgoing Event messages to the surroundings. Functionally composite Pipes and simple Pipes are the same. The recursive definition benefits GSML in many ways. Firstly, it is one of the means of abstraction [22] which provides a mechanism of constructing more complex Pipes on the top of existing Pipes. Secondly, it enables GSML language to support modular style programming that decomposes a complex application into several smaller modules which are reused in any applications.

Flexible Pipe: A Pipe is flexible both in its design and implementation because it is only required to provide uniform interfaces. Pipes can be designed and implemented on top of any Grid programming models (e.g., Middlewares, PSEs etc.) in any languages supporting sockets (e.g. C/C++, Java and Perl). Pipes can be local or remote, coarse-grained or fine-grained.

Easy development and execution: A GSML program defines required Pipes, their interactions and UI layout. End users program GSML application on the abstractions such as Pipes, and messages, insulating from all low-level details. Furthermore, GSML Composer presents a visual programming environment where end users can build applications by selecting ready-to-use components and organizing the interactions and layout in intuitive way. To execute the GSML application, GSML Browser loads and parses the GSML document, and initializes the runtime environment for the execution, as easy as run HTML applications in Web browsers.

4 GSML Language

GSML Language is an XML-based language for gluing modules of a grid application in an event-driven way. It includes four kinds of basic constructs: Pipe, Event, Target, EventSet.

4.1 Basic Concepts

Application. A GSML application is a Grid application. It consists of a collection of Pipes and the interactions between Pipes.

Definition 1. *Application* = (*Ps*, *ESs*), where 1) *Ps* is a set of Pipes, *Ps* = {p_i | p_i is a Pipe included}; 2) *ESs* is a set of EeventSets, *ESs* = {es_i | es_i is a EventSet describing a interaction}.

Pipe. A Pipe is a component with uniform interfaces. It can either be a simple Pipe which is an encapsulation of resource or service, or be a composite Pipe which is essentially a GSML application. A simple Pipe is defined as a tuple of a typename, target message types and event message types.

Definition 2. *Pipe* = *Pipe_s* | *Pipe_c*, where 1) *Pipe_c* is a composite Pipe, *Pipe_c* = *Application* = (*Ps*, *ESs*); 2) *Pipe_s* is a simple Pipe, *Pipe_s* = (*Pn*, *ETs*, *TTs*), *Pn* is the name of Pipe, *ETs* = {et_i | et_i is an event message type}, *TTs* = {tt_i | tt_i is a target message type}.

EventSet. An EventSet represents one interaction between Pipes. It contains a collection of target messages and event messages.

Definition 3. *ES* = (*Es*, *Ts*), where *Es* is a set of event messages, *Es* = {e_i | e_i is an event message}; *Ts* is a set of target messages, *Ts* = {t_i | t_i is a target message}.

Event. An Event represents an event message which is sent by Pipes for notification of responses or state changes. It is made up of a tuple of a source Pipe, and an event message type.

Definition 5. *Event* = (*source*, *MessageType*), where *source* is the source Pipe which sends out the Event; *MessageType* is where the message information is stored.

Target. A Target represents a target message which is send to Pipes for request during an interaction. It is made up of a tuple of a destination Pipe, a condition and an target message type.

Definition 5. *Target* = (*destination*, *condition*, *MessageType*), where *destination* is the message's destination; *MessageType* contains the message information; *condition* is a Boolean statement which servers branch functionality.

MessageType. A MessageType contains messages information for both event and target message types. A MessageType is made up of a name and a set of parameters. Each parameter in the set of parameters is a name-value pair.

Definition 6. *MessageType* = (*Mn*, *ParameterSet*), where *Mn* is a string name for the MessageType; *ParameterSet* = {*parameter* | *parameter* is one parameter in the MessageType}, *parameter* = (*name*, *value*).

4.2 Programming

A GSML application consists of definitions of Pipes, interactions and layout. Interactions are specified using construct EventSet; and each EventSet contains event messages and target messages which are expressed using construct Event and Target. The GSML browser provides simple layout functionality that places each Pipe with UI in a a region specified by two-dimensional coordinates. Construct EventSet and GSML document are means of combination. Construct EventSet is used to combine Events and Targets into an interaction; GSML documents group all the constructs, layout and other information (e.g. namespaces) into GSML applications. GSML documents are in XML-based syntax. Like a HTML document, a GSML document contains Header part and Body part. Header part contains information such as the title string. Body part provides the core application logic and layout. Figure 2 is an example GSML program for the travel application in Section 3.

```
<?xml version="1.0" encoding="utf-8"?>
<gsml xmlns="http://gsml.ict.org" xsi:schemaLocation="http://gsml.ict.org GSML.xsd">
<head><title>untitled</title></head>
<body>
    <row><cell>
      <pipe id="Input" type="HTMLPipe">
      <eventset>
            <event source="Input" type="Submit"/>
            <target destination="AirlineService" type="WSInvoke" />
            <paras><para>
            <name>parameters</name><value>$(Input.Submit.src),$(Input.Submit.dst)</value>
            </para>
            <para><name>protocol</name><value>axis</value></para>
            <para><name>operationName</name><value>Reserve</value></para>
            ......</paras>
            </target>
            <target destination="HotelService" type="WSInvoke" />
            ......</target>
            <target destination="BusService" type="WSInvoke" />
            ......</target>
      </eventset>
      ......
      </pipe>
      <pipe id="AirlineService" type="WSInvoker" />
      <pipe id="BusService" type="WSInvoker" />
      <pipe id="HotelService" type="WSInvoker" />
      <pipe id="Travel" type="TravelPipe" />
    </cell></row>
    <row><cell>
      <pipe id="TravelResult" type="HTMLPipe" />
    </cell></row>
</body>
</gsml>
```

Fig. 2. Example GSML program for the travel application described in Figure 1

5 GSML Toolkits

5.1 GSML Composer

To support the development of GSML applications, GSML Composer integrates heterogeneous resources into a visual programming environment where end users can visually select Pipes and specify the interactions between Pipes.

GSML Composer is made up of three parts: Repositories Area, Edit Area and Properties Area. Repositories Area lists all the integrated resources encapsulated in Pipes. Currently two classes of resources are available in the prototype system: generic Pipes and instanced Pipes. An instanced Pipe is a special instance of generic Pipe because it contains instance information unavailable for generic Pipes. For example, each UDDI Web Service Pipe in UDDI Mapper represents a web service which is dynamically discovered using UDDI protocol and contains instance information such as the URI, operations, ports and parameter of the discovered web service. Instanced Pipes discover the resource and figure out instance information which can hide the low-level details from end users. Edit Area is where end users visually and intuitively select Pipes, and organize the EventSets and messages. In Properties Area, end users can adjust the parameters of Pipes, Targets, Events, and specify Pipes' layout.

GSML Composer generates the GSML document for the GSML application and can directly launch the GSML Browser to run the application.

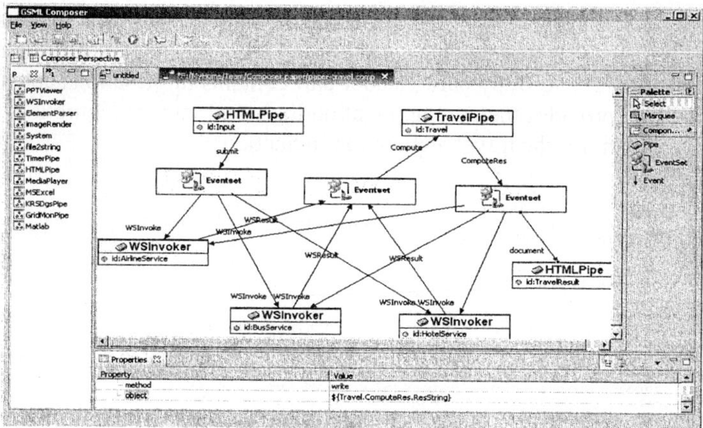

Fig. 3. A GSML Composer snapshot

5.2 GSML Browser

GSML Browser provides the runtime execution environment for GSML applications. It is made up of three parts: GSML Parser, Pipe Manager and Event Manager. To run a GSML application, first GSML Parser parses the GSML document after it is loaded, then all the Pipes in the document are initiated by Pipe Manager, and Event Manager opens its TCP socket and waits for Event messages from all the Pipes in the application. If any Event is ready on the socket, Event Manager reads, parses and checks it with the application interactions, and triggers Target messages if any interaction synchronization is satisfied.

Because GSML applications aggregate resources including desktop applications such as Excel, and need more interactive execution environment than Web Browser, GSML Browser generates and renders all Pipes' UI results locally and has no dependency on servers. Therefore, the execution of GSML applications has no centralized server bottleneck. Moreover, installing required Pipe libraries and jar files for GSML Browser is simple, and PCs are powerful to run lightweight Pipes whose main task is to serve the message requests and forward heavy task to the underlying resources themselves. To sum up, this design provides better scalability.

6 Application Examples

In Figure 4, four application examples are demonstrated. Example A demonstrates a resource information monitor which uses TimerPipe to retrieve and update the monitored host's resource statistics information periodically. Example B integrates desktop applications Web Browser, ftp client and MediaPlayer seamlessly to form a digital library system. Example C demonstrates the synchronization of PowerPoint slides and video materials in an E-learning scenario. Example D builds a collaboration platform by integrating Web Browser, Excel and VideoCap Pipes. Table 1 lists the number of Pipes used and the number of lines of application for each example.

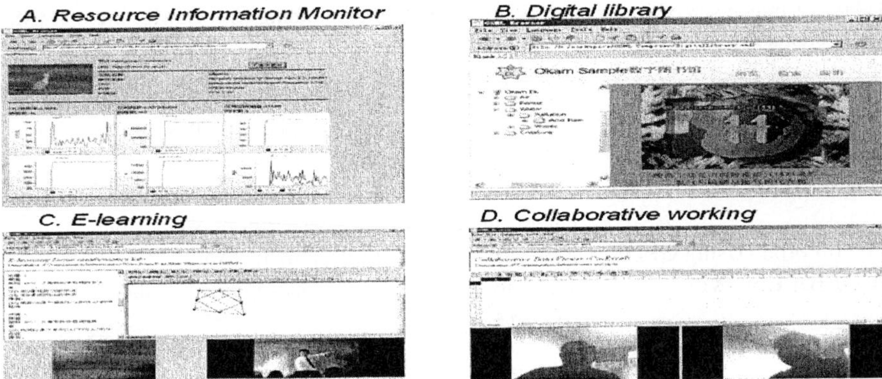

Fig. 4. GSML applications Examples

Table 1. Statistics of Application Examples

	Example A	Example B	Example C	Example D
# of Pipes used	4	4	5	7
# of lines of source code	98	80	93	112

7 Evaluation

GSML provides high-level abstraction and hides complexity of low-level details for Grid end users. However, it also makes some tradeoffs. For example, it does not deal with controls over the resources scheduling as in GRID superscalar. In this section, we make the qualitative evaluation of GSML by looking at its knowledge requirement for development, flexibility & expressiveness, and productivity improvement.

Development. Table 2 lists the knowledge requirement of programming using different programming paradigms. End users of GSML programming require knowledge of XML syntax, GSML constructs, Pipe functionalities and message parameters. The requirement is actually no more than Static HTML programming. Unlike other Grid programming paradigms such as Web Portal (using GPDK) and CORBA CoG kits, GSML insulates end users from low-level details such as APIs and protocols which is inaccessible to high percentage of Grid end users. Moreover, GSML Composer provides visual programming and development environment for end users with which they need not deal with boring and error-prone XML syntax and they can benefit from facilities such as instanced Pipes. For most of the application changes, end users should only modify some parameters of Pipes or messages. Even if new Pipes and interactions are needed, the modification can be done in several minutes. Above advantages are mostly contributed to high-level abstractions and visual programming environment.

Table 2. Comparison of Knowledge requirements of programming with GSML, Static HTML, Web Portal and CORBA CoG Kits

	Knowledge Requirement
GSML	XML Syntax; GSML Constructs; Pipe functionality; Message parameters
Static HTML	HTML syntax; HTML tags; tag attributes; component functionalities; JavaScript or VBScript
Web Portal (Using GPDK)	HTML; Servlet; GPDK API; Java
CORBA CoG Kits	CORBA; CoG API; Component functionalities; C/C++

Flexibility and Expressiveness. The flexibility and expressiveness of GSML can be studied in combinational layer and functional layer. GSML builds application by aggregating and composing ready-to-use components whose interfaces are organized by end users. In combinational layer, flexibility and expressiveness exclude those of Pipes and refers to the capability gained by means of combinations. One obvious result is that the combinational expressiveness and flexibility are no more than finite-state machine [11]. However, the whole story of GSML is determined by the functional flexibility and expressiveness. They exceed those of GPDK and CoG Kits because the combinational expressiveness and flexibility are complemented by Pipes which are essentially flexible and expressive.

Productivity. GSML enhances productivity in two ways. First, GSML features easy development and convenient execution. Second, GSML separates several concerns of Grid applications. GSML is responsible for specifying application logic, layout and interactions over ready-to-use components. Pipe development is responsible to encapsulate services and resources into components. The effort of Pipe development is amortized by reusing the available Pipes in different GSML applications. Compared with other programming paradigms, GSML builds Grid applications with lower requirements and less effort.

8 Future Work and Conclusion

For end users, building Grid applications remains a difficult and time-consuming task with current Grid programming technologies. This paper proposes Grid Service Markup Language (GSML) to address the complexity of Grid programming and enable end users to efficiently develop and execute Grid applications. GSML is distinguished by its simplified and component-based programming model as well as an event-based communication pattern among components. A visual programming environment is implemented to integrate heterogeneous resources and support intuitive applications development by dragging and dropping components. GSML Brower provides an efficient and scalable execution environment for GSML applications. By raising the level of abstraction as well as simplifying the programming model, GSML allows end users to build grid applications easily with improved productivity.

As part of our future work, we will continue to investigate the mechanism of composite Pipes, which is crucial to support the construction of complex applications. Currently the composition mechanism is implemented in an ad-hoc way that a particular Target named "Parent" stands for a Pipe's parent. A better approach is to introduce new constructs that are more comprehensible for end users. Another topic is to the remote Pipe framework that allows GSML to seamlessly integrate Pipes running in remote machines. Furthermore, we plan to investigate a theoretical and formal analysis of GSML language with focus on its semantics and expressiveness.

Acknowledgements

This work is supported by China's National Basic Research and Development 973 Program (Grant No. 2003CB317008, 2005CB321807) and National 863 Hi-Tech R&D Plan (Grant No. 2004AA104330).The authors are very grateful for these sponsors and other anonymous referees' comments.

References

1. C. Lee, S. Matsuoka, D. Talia, A. Sussman, M. Mueller, G.Allen, and J. Saltz, A Grid Programming Primer. Technical Report, Global Grid Forum Programming Model Working Group, August, 2001.
2. D. Laflorenza, Grid programming: some indications where we are headed. Parallel Computing, Vol. 28 (2002) 1733-1752
3. G. Fox, D. Gannon, M. Thomas, Overview of Grid Computing Environments. In Grid Computting: Making the Global Infrastructure a Reality. Hohn Wiley and sons Ltd, Chichester (2003) 543-554
4. I. Foster, N. T. Karonis, A grid-enabled MPI: Message passing in heterogeneous distributed computing systems. In SC'98, Orlando, FL, (1998)
5. G.E. Fagg, K.S. London, J.J. Dongarra, MPI_Connect: managing heterogeneous MPI applications interoperation and process control. Recent Advances in Parallel Machine and Message Passing Interface. Lecture Notes in Computer Science, Springer (1998) 93-96
6. H. Casanova, J. Dongarra, NetSolve: A network server for solving computational science problems. The International Journal of Supercomputer Applications and High Performance Computing, Vol. 11 (1997) 212-223
7. S. Sekiguchi, M. Sato, H. Nakada, S. Matsuoka, U. Nagashima. Ninf: Network-based information library for globally high performance computing. Parallel Object-Oriented Methods and Applications (1996) 39-48
8. R. Armstrong, D. Gannon, A. Geist, K. Keahey, S. Kohn, L. Mcinnes, S. Parker, B. Smolinski, Toward a Common Component Architecture for High Performance Scientific Computing. High Performance Distributed Computing Conference (1999)
9. G.V. Laszewski, J.Gawor, P. Lane, N. Rehn, M. Russel, Features of the Java Commodity Grid Kit. Concurrency and Computation: Practice and Experience, Vol. 14 (2002) 1365-1394
10. F. Berman, A. Chien, K. Cooper, J. Donarra, I. Foster, D. Gannon, et al, The GrADS Project: Software Support for High-Level Grid Application Development. International Journal of High Performance Computing Applications (JHPCA), Vol. 15 (2001) 327-344

11. Z. Xu, W. Li, L. Zha, H. Yu, D. Liu, Vega: A Computer Systems Approach to Grid Computing. Journal of Grid Computing (2004) 109-120
12. X. Wang, L. Xiao, W. Li, H. Yu, Z. Xu, Abacus: A Service-Oriented Programming Language for Grid Applications. In SCC2005 (2005)
13. M. Pierce, C. Youn, G. Fox, The Gateway Computational Web Portal: Developing Web Services for High Performance Computing. International Conference Computational Science (ICCS 2002), Amsterdam, Netherlands (2002)
14. Jason Novotny, The Grid Portal Development Kit. Concurrency and Computation: Practice and Experience, Vol. 14, Grid Computing environments Special Issue 13-15 (2002) 1129-1444
15. G. Allen, T. Goodale, G. Lanfermann, T. Radke, E. Seidel, W. Benger, et al, Solving Einstein's equations on supercomputers. IEEE Computer, Vol. 32 (1999)
16. R.M. Badia, J. Labarta, R. Sirvnet, J.M. Perez, J.M. Cela, R. Grima, Programming Grid Applications with GRID superscalar. Journal of Grid Computing, Vol. 1 (2003) 151-170.
17. D. Esposito, A first look at writing and deploying apps in the next generation of windows. Microsfot MSDN Magazine, Vol. 19 (2004) 1~8
18. X. Fu, T. Bultan, J. Su, Analysis of Interacting BPEL Web Services. Proceeding of the 13th International World Web Conference (WWW'04), USA, ACM Press (2004)
19. GT4 Primer. http://www.globus.org/toolkit/docs/4.0/key/GT4_Primer_0.6.pdf
20. OMII. http://www.omii.ac.uk/
21. M. M. Burnett, Visual Programming. Encyclopedia of Electrical and Electronics Engineering. John Wiley & Sons, (1999)
22. H. Abelson, G. J. Sussman, J. Sussman, Structure and Interpretation of Computer Programs. The MIT Press, (1996)

TCP/IP Offload Engine Module Supporting Binary Compatibility for Standard Socket Interfaces

Dong-Jae Kang[2], Kang-Ho Kim[1], Sung-In Jung[1], and Hae-Young Bae[2]

[1] Interne Server Group, Digital Home Research Division, ETRI,
161 Gajeong-dong, Yusung-gu, Daejeon, South Korea
{djkang, khk, sijung}@etri.re.kr
[2] Dept. of Computer Science and Information Engineering, INHA University,
253 Yonghyeon-dong, Nam-gu, Incheon, South Korea
hybae@inha.ac.kr

Abstract. TCP/IP is the most commonly used protocol to communicate among servers, especially, it is used in a wide range of applications in GRID evironment. Unfortunately, Data transmission through TCP/IP places a very heavy burden on host CPUs. And it hardly makes another job to be processed. So, TOE(TCP/IP Offload Engine) is considered in many servers. But, most of TOE modules tend to not support binary compatibility for standard socket interfaces. So, it has problems that existing applications should be modified and recompiled to get advantage of TOE device. In this paper, to resolve upper problems, we suppose design and implementation of TOE module supporting binary compatibility for standard socket interfaces. Also, it can make a usage of multiple TOEs and NICs simultaneously.

1 Introduction

In GRID environment, many researches to reduce TCP/IP processing overhead have performed until now. Data transmission through TCP/IP places a very heavy burden on host CPUs and it hardly makes another job to be processed. TOE(TCP/IP Offload Engine) is suggested to resolve upper problems. But, most of TOE modules tends to not support binary compatibility for standard socket interfaces. So, it has problems that existing applications should be modified and recompiled to get advantage of TOE device.

In this paper, we suppose design and implementation of TOE module to support TOE devices efficiently. TOE is dedicated device embedding TCP/IP protocol stack and TOE module is software installed in kernel for supporting TOE device. Suggested TOE module supports binary compatibility for standard socket interfaces, so it allows that existing socket applications can use TOE devices without modification or recompilation. Consideration in design and implementation is as below.

- All standard socket interfaces should be supported over TOE devices.
- Binary compatibility for standard socket interfaces should be supported
- Multiple NICs and TOE devices can be used simultaneously.
- Architecture should support a layered design so as to easily support multiple offload technologies.
- Zero-copy should be supported to remove unnecessary memory copies.

H. Zhuge and G.C. Fox (Eds.): GCC 2005, LNCS 3795, pp. 357–369, 2005.

Through usage of TOE module, the large number of host CPU cycles spent on TCP/IP processing could be put to much better use by systems and applications.

In the Chapter 2, we will explain about related work, OSF, and network architecture in Linux. And design and implementation of supposed TOE module is described in chapter 3. In chapter 4, we will test our software and analyze the result. Finally, summarize the contents of this paper and describe future works to be done.

2 Related Works

2.1 Offload Socket Framework (OSF)

The researches about architecture for using network accelerators has been performed until now and OSF is representative one of them.[2][8] OSF is a framework that supports TOE and InfiniBand devices with existing NICs in communication.

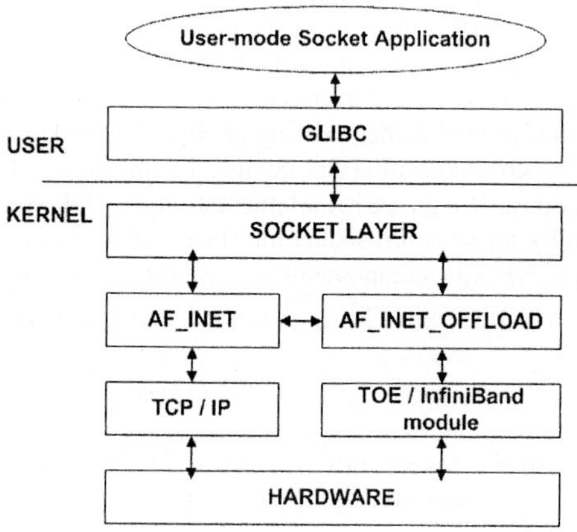

Fig. 1. Architecture of OSF

Fig.1 shows architecture of OSF. It adds new network address family, AF_INET_OFFLOAD, to supports TOE and InfiniBand devices. But, Adding new network address family has a problem that existing application should be modified and recompiled to use the new devices. Domestic research, KSOVIA[8], has a similar architecture. So, it has similar problems.

2.2 Supporting Standard Socket Interfaces

The researches on supporting standard socket interfaces over network devices, like as TCP/IP Offload Engine, VIA and IB(Infini Band) and so on, has achieved until now, and the examples for it are OSF(Offload Socket Framework) in aboard and KSOVIA in domestic and so on. The object of them gives usage convenience to users and supports high-performance transmission of data traffic. Like this, Supporting standard socket interfaces needs modification of user interface or kernel. Possible ways for it are as below.

- Modifying user-level libraries implementing socket interfaces, like as glibc.
- Adding new address family, AF_XXX, and implementing it's protocol stack
- Changing the Linux loader to transparently hook into the socket and file I/O calls from user-mode.
- Use the call intercept methods employed in strace(1) and ltrace(1) to modify the behavior of network calls transparently to application

Most current design and implementations accept adding new address family, because it can be implemented easily under current Linux architecture. But, it has a defect that can not support binary compatibility for socket interfaces.

3 TOE Module

In this chapter, we describe about design and implementation of TOE module supporting binary compatibility for standard socket interfaces. First of all, we investigate whole architecture and explain details of each layer.

3.1 Architecture of TOE Module

TOE module is consists of three-layers, TOE Socket Switching Layer(TSSL), TOE Offload Protocol Layer(TOPL) and TOE Device Driver Layer(TDDL) as showed in Fig.2.

TSSL determines whether socket API call by application is switched to existing INET or TOPL protocol stack. And it is located over TCP/IP layer. TOPL calls

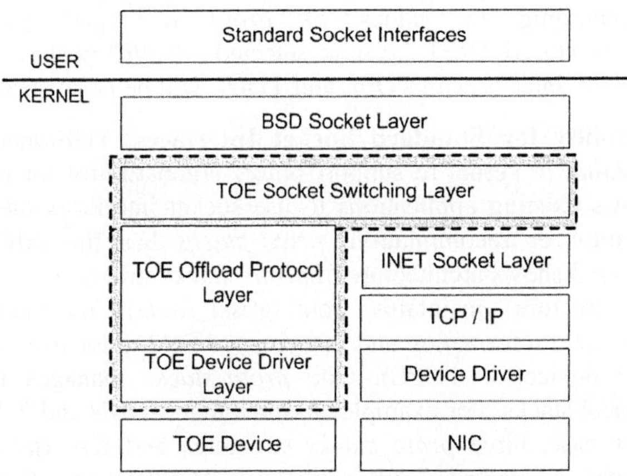

Fig. 2. Architecture of TOE module

adequate interfaces of TDDL according to request from TSSL, and it is similar level with INET protocol stack. Zero-copy between application buffer and memory on TOE device is implemented here. TDDL has role that transmits request from TOPL to TOE device, and manage communication between kernel module and TOE device. TOE module described upper is as like Fig.2. It is the part marked by dotted line.

3.2 Main Data Structure

Main data structures for TOE module are *struct tssl_inet_sock*, *struct net_proto_family* and *struct proto_ops*. *tssl_inet_sock* is extended socket structure for our software, and it classifies protocol stacks under TSSL. It has existing *struct inet_sock* structure as a first member variable and has many additional fields for TOE module. *net_proto_family* and *proto_ops* are existing data structure. *net_proto_family* is the structure that has protocol family identifier(PF_INET) and CREATE function pointer for TSSL. *net_families[]* is the array structure that is referenced on creating new socket and located on BSD socket layer. *proto_ops* is consists of function pointers for TSSL socket interfaces. All sockets after TOE module is loaded have this pointer, and it allows TSSL to use INET or TOPL protocol.

Besides upper described data structures, there is important one, *struct proto_stacks*. It is a routing table for directing to INET and TOPL, and is core structure to support binary compatibility for standard socket interfaces without defining new protocol family. Details of it are explained in next chapter.

3.3 TOE Socket Switching Layer(TSSL)

In this chapter, we explain main issues in TSSL, it is the layer that allows application using AF_INET protocol family to use TOE module without modification and recompiling. When application calls socket interface, the control flow is transmitted to BSD socket layer and functions in BSD layer call *tssl_XXX* interface in TSSL to determine where it switches to. Interfaces in TSSL takeover control flow to INET or TOPL layer according to values of *proto_stack* and port in socket structure(*tssl_inet_sock*). If INET layer is selected, TCP/IP protocol stack will be processed. Otherwise, interfaces in TOPL and TDDL will be performed.

Binary Compatibility for Standard Socket Interfaces. TOE module maintains *proto_stacks* structure in kernel to support binary compatibility for standard socket interfaces, it allows existing applications to use socket interfaces over TOE device without modification or recompilation. *proto_stacks* has the information about protocol stacks. Fig. 3 shows architecture of *proto_stacks* structure.

proto_stacks structure maintains routing(*tssl_route*) information, network interface(*tssl_interface*) information and *interface_id* field to identify normal NIC(for INET) and TOE device(for TOPL). One *proto_stacks* manages information of independent protocol stacks. For example, Assume that 3-NICs and 2-TOE devices is in a host. In this case, three *proto_stacks* structures and five *tssl_interfaces* and *tssl_route* structures are created. 3-NICs use same TCP/IP protocol stack in kernel. But 2-TOEs use different one that embedding to itself. So, the number of *proto_stacks* structure, one for 3-NICs and two for 2-TOEs, is three. The *proto_stacks* for 3-NICs has three couple of *tssl_interface* and *tssl_route* structures for information of each NIC. The pointer for this *proto_stacks* is member variable of *tssl_inet_sock* and it is referred when control flow should be divided.

Let's investigate about switching to INET or TOPL when applications call socket interface. Generally, protocol stack to be performed is selected when BIND function is called. It binds a socket to special IP address. If BIND is finished, *proto_stacks* related to bound IP address(for NIC or TOE) is allocated to current socket. After this process is completed, all requests for the socket is performed through allocated proto_stack information. But, most applications call BIND function with INADDR_ANY option, So, we should define selection priority on NICs and TOEs in a host.

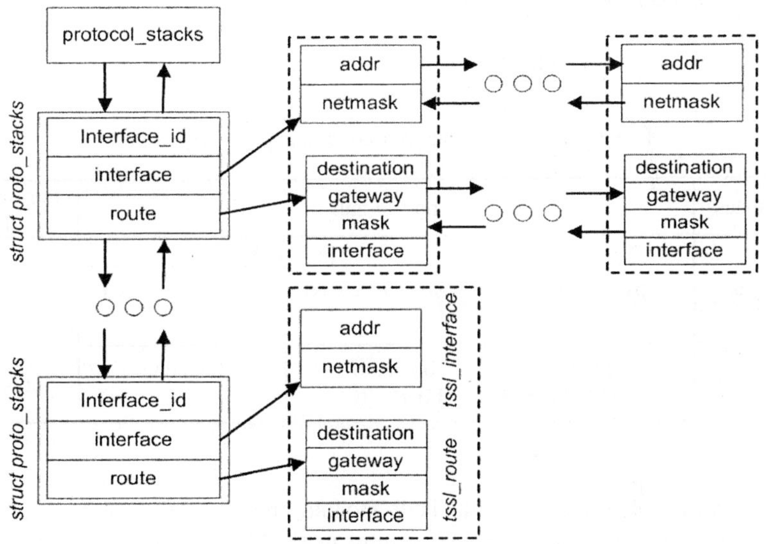

Fig. 3. Architecture of *proto_stacks* structure

If socket call is requested, *proto_stacks* and port in *tssl_inet_sock* structure is referred to select protocol stack to be performed. Table 1 depicts socket bind status according to port and *proto_stacks* value. Let's consider the case of data transmission. In the case of "Not bound" in Table 1, TSSL executes BIND with INADDR_ANY option. And, if the status is "binded to INADDR_ANY", performs SEND or RECEIVE operation against all available protocol stacks registered in *proto_stacks*. A first protocol stack that transmission operation is executed successfully is selected and it is used first for transmission in next time. If only one TOE or NIC is used, the system will operate as a NIC or TOE dedicated system. Like as described upper, TOE module supports binary compatibility for standard socket interfaces through maintaining local routing table, *proto_stacks*, instead of defining new protocol family.

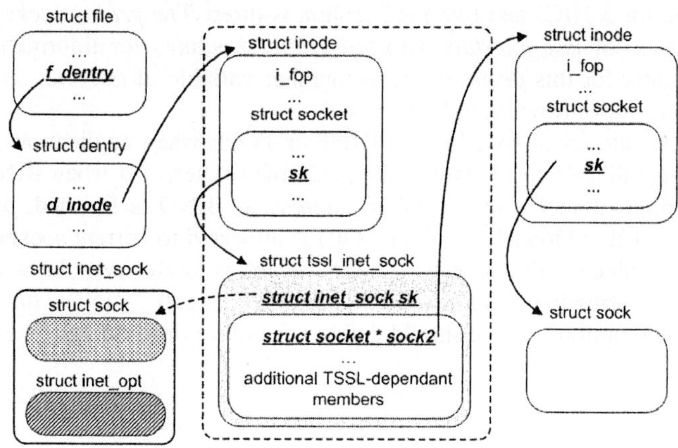

Fig. 4. Socket structure for TOE module

Table 1. Socket bind status according to port and ps value

port status	port != null			Port == null
ps status	ps == null	ps != null		*
		Interface_id == NIC	*Interface_id* == TOE	
bind status	bound to INADDR_ANY	bound to Local NIC	bound to TOE	not bound

ps : *proto_stacks*

Creation and Release of Socket. TOE module creates additional sock structure except existing INET sock for itself(structures marked by dotted line in Fig. 4). Two sockets is needed in our software, one is for INET, another is for TSSL and TOPL. So, in tssl_create function, both op_create for TOPL and inet_create for INET are executed. First socket for TOE and second socket for INET is created sequentially(one has struct sock, another has struct tssl_inet_sock instead of normal sock structure). And second socket is linked by first one. Socket for TSSL and TOPL maintains function pointers(tssl_stream_ops) for TOE kernel module and socket for INET has one(inet_stream_ops) for TCP/IP protocol stack. When socket is released, we should release two sockets like as creation.

Transmission of Data. In this section, we describe data transmission in case of using TOE and NIC simultaneously. Data transmission is performed when interfaces like as *send*, *sendto*, *sendmsg*, *recv*, *recvfrom* and *recvmsg* are called. The code below presents pseudo code of tssl_sendmsg.

If socket was bound to special IP address, *tssl_sendmsg* calls SEND function of equivalent protocol stack(if the IP address is for NIC, calls *inet_sendmsg* for INET, otherwise, *op_sendmsg* for TOPL). If socket was not bound yet, first, allocates a available port number by executing *get_port* function. After it, performs BIND with INADDR_ANY option. Anyhow, if the status of socket has INADDR_ANY, TSSL performs SEND operation against all available protocol stack registered in *proto_stacks* structure until it is successful. Finally, first successful protocol stack is used in current data transmission. Determination for socket status is based on Table 1. RECEIVE has the same control flow with SEND. Below pseudo codes, *dst_addr*, *dst_port* and *send_ps* fields maintains the information of most recently used protocol stack that was performed successfully. And it is for more rapid execution of data transmission in next time.

```
BEGIN tssl_sendmsg(Socket, Msg, Size, Scm)
        SET tsslsk to sk member of Socket
        SET Addr to Source Address of Socket
        IF Port of Socket is zero THEN /* not bound */
                CALL get_port with INET Socket
                SET tsslsk->src_port to new port value
                SET Addr to INADDR_ANY
                FOR each TOE in proto_stacks
                        CALL bind with new port value
                END FOR
        END IF
        IF Addr is Specail IP THEN /*bound to Special IP*/
                IF Addr is NIC's address THEN
                        CALL sendmsg for INET
                ELSE IF Addr is TOE's address THEN
                        CALL sendmsg for TOPL
                END IF
        ELSE IF Addr is INADDR_ANY THEN
                /* bount to INADDR_ANY */
                IF Dest Address of Msg is tsslsk->dst_addr THEN
                        CALL sendmsg for send_ps->interface_id
                ELSE THEN
                        FOR each proto_stacks
                                IF ps->interface_id is NIC THEN
                                        CALL sendmsg for INET
                                ELSE IF ps->interface_id is TOE THEN
                                        CALL sendmsg for TOPL
                                END IF
                                IF sendmsg is successful THEN
                                        SET send_ps, dst_addr, dst_port to current
values
                                        CALL return
                                END IF
                        END FOR
                END IF
        END IF
        CALL return
END tssl_sendmsg
```

3.4 TOE Offload Protocol Layer(TOPL)

TOPL is the layer that is designed to offload TCP/IP processing from host to TOE device. It links the requests from TSSL to TDDL. It's main role is that it controls interrupt from TOE device and supports zero-copy function between application buffer and device.

Control Flow in TOPL. Fig. 5 shows process sequence in TOPL. Socket creation or release call inserts or deletes a socket to/from the list in Fig. 5.

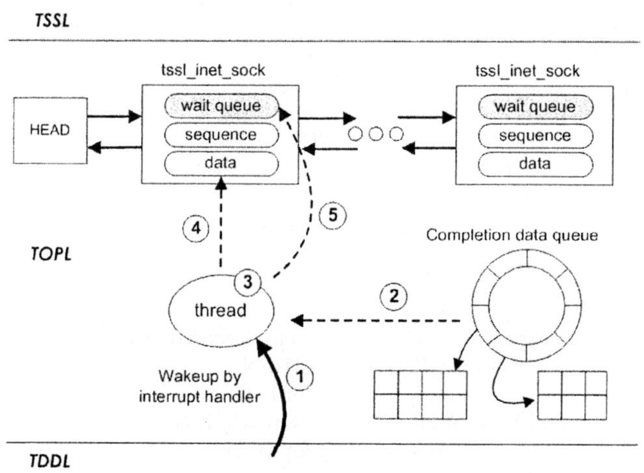

Fig. 5. Control flow in TOPL

Commands from TSSL are transmitted to TDDL through TOPL, and it is registered to doorbell in device. Equivalent process becomes to sleep status waiting for completion of command. When processing is complete, TOE device issues interrupt. The control flow after interrupt is as below.

1. Interrupt handler wakes up thread in TOPL.
2. Thread gets completed result data form completion data queue.
3. Thread investigates equivalent socket in the list based on socket ID and sequence number in result data.
4. Allocates result data to selected socket.
5. Wakes up process related with the socket.

If upper execution is completed, process returns to TSSL.

Zero-copy between Application Buffer and Device. We support zero-copy function between application and TOE device to remove unnecessary data copies in kernel. It is implemented as DMA by transmitting physical address of application buffer to device. Generally, target device has limitation that a N byte-aligned address should be used. Fig. 6 depicts data exchange for zero-copy.

The virtual address of application buffer is transformed to physical address in page unit when data transmission command is called. And it is allocated to *sg_list* structure for transmitting to TOE device. If the address is not *N* byte-aligned, not-aligned area is copied to kernel memory for transforming it as *N* byte-aligned address. After this, it is converted to physical address and allocated to *sg_list*. If all physical addresses of application buffer are allocated to *sg_list*, it is transmitted to TOE device through TDDL.

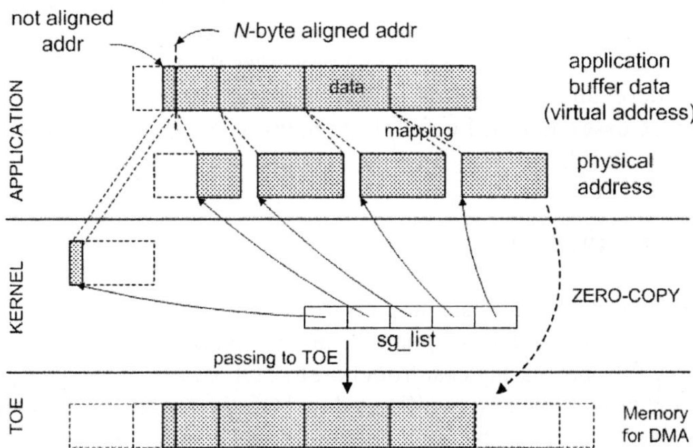

Fig. 6. Zero-copy between application buffer and TOE device

3.5 TOE Device Driver Layer(TDDL)

TDDL is the layer that communicates with TOE device through doorbell mechanism. It has important role to exchange messages between kernel and device and processes the hardware interrupt.

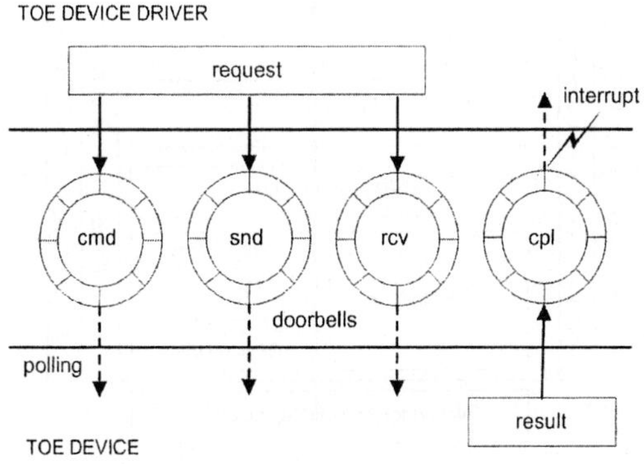

Fig. 7. Usage of doorbells in TDDL

TDDL uses four circular queues, those are doorbells, to communicate with TOE device. Doorbells are located in TOE device and shared between kernel and device by pre-defined address mode. Fig. 7 shows usage of doorbells in kernel. In figure, a solid arrows represent that command is added to doorbell and a dotted ones mean that command is extracted from doorbell.

In Fig. 7, Requests for data transmission is registered to *snd* or *rcv* doorbell and the rest requests are added to *cmd* doorbell by TDDL. Commands registered to doorbells are processed by TOE devices and the results are added to *cpl* doorbell by TOE device. Each doorbell shares head and tail register between kernel and device.

The number of registered command is computed by them. TDDL registers commands to doorbells and TOE device inquires into each doorbell continuously. If command was added, TOE device gets and processes it. After this, TOE registers the result to *cpl* doorbell and informs of kernel by interrupt. Hardware interrupt is occurred in three cases, doorbell is full, one request is completed, pre-defined number of request is completed.

4 Test and Evaluation

In this chapter, we test and evaluate performance of TOE module and analyze the result. The aim of TOE module supports the binary compatibility for socket interfaces and offloads TCP/IP processing cost from host to TOE device.

So, we tested how much cost is offloaded to TOE device and how much additional cost was imposed on kernel by TOE module. Maybe, main additional cost comes from creation and maintenance of new socket structures. Fig.8 shows test method for system.

Until now, most existing TOE module is targeted to specific devices, and its known performance is about TOE device rather than TOE module. So, it is no meaning to compare performance of supposed TOE module and that of others.

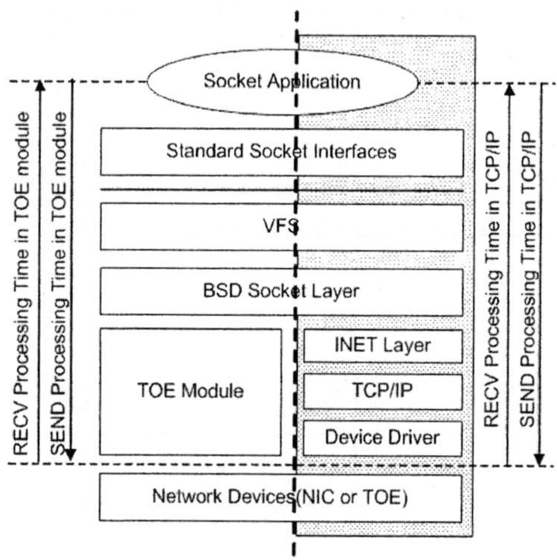

Fig. 8. Testing method of TOE module

Therefore, in this paper, the test is performed about processing time between kernel TCP/IP and TOE module as like Fig.8. we had measured processing time from application to device driver layer to get cost required in kernel. We had used Intel pentium IV-2.6G CPU, 128M system memory and linux(fedora core II) kernel-2.6.8.1

4.1 Comparison of Cost for Transmission

We tested how much cost from system is offloaded to TOE device by measuring the cost of data transmission in the system with TOE module and without it. To measure pure cost in kernel, we divided control flow by two parts. One part is from application to network device driver, another one is from interrupt(device driver) to application. So, sum of two costs is what we want to acquire.

Fig. 9 represents the processing time of data transmission through protocol stack, INET and TOPL, in kernel. The left graph is for SEND, and the right one is for RECEIVE call. In the left figure, the average processing time for SEND through INET required 83.2 usec, average processing time through TOPL was 46.2usec. Therefore, the result says that TOE module can offload nearly 44.5 percents of the

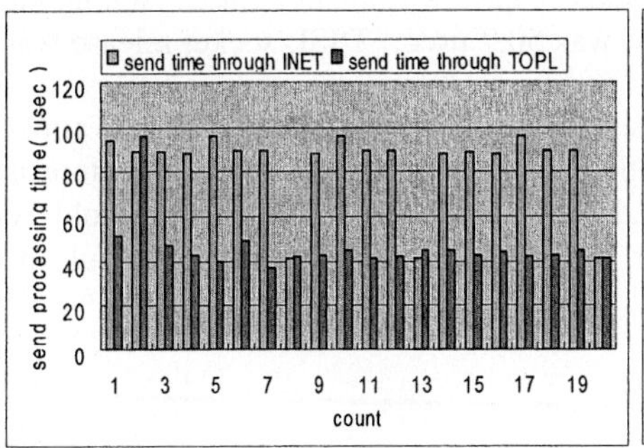

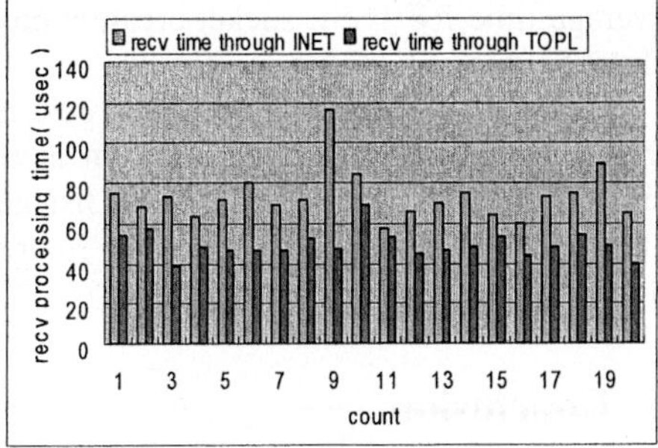

Fig. 9. Comparison of data transmission cost through INET and TOPL(left figure - cost for SEND, right figure - cost for RECEIVE)

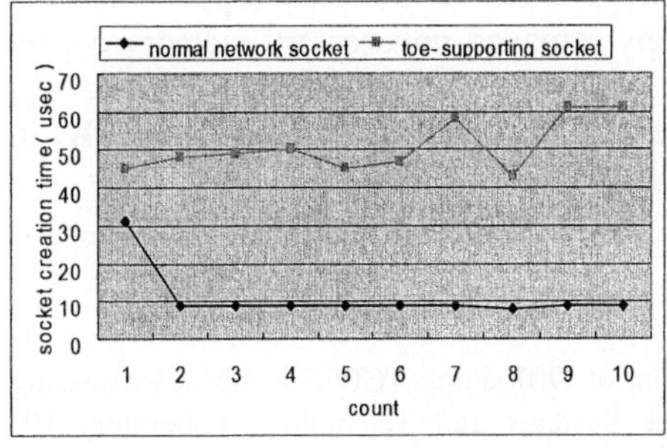

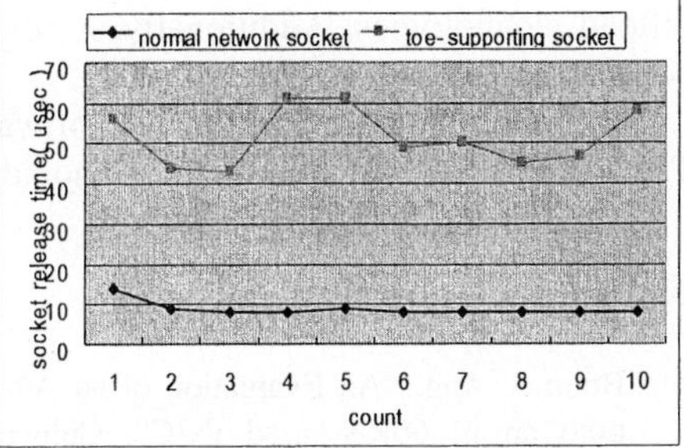

Fig. 10. Comparison of Cost for Socket creation and release (right figure– socket creation, left figure-socket release)

processing cost in SEND to TOE device. The right figure shows kernel processing costs in INET and TOPL protocol stack, when RECEIVE is called. The average processing time through INET was about 73.3usec and 49.2usec was required in the TOPL. Therefore, the result shows that TOE module can offload about 32.9 percents of the TCP/IP processing cost in RECEIVE. As like the result, TOE module can offload about 30~40 percents of TCP/IP processing time in kernel to TOE device in the case of data transmission.

So, through usage of TOE module, the large number of host CPU cycles spent on TCP/IP processing could be put to much better use by systems and applications instead. And it will make host system more available in processing TCP/IP protocol.

4.2 Comparison of Cost for Socket Creation and Release

TOE module creates and maintains additional socket structure except existing network socket. So, additional cost is required in maintenance for it.

In this section, we measured and analyzed the cost of creation and release for normal network socket and TSSL socket. It was performed in application level and based on application response time. Fig. 10 shows socket creation and release cost in the system with TOE module and without it. The average time for normal socket creation was about 11.1usec and normal socket release was about 8.8usec. While, the average time for TSSL socket creation cost was 50.7 usec, TSSL socket release was about 51.4usec.

Therefore, TSSL socket creation cost is 4.57 times and release cost is 5.84 times than normal socket cost. The reason of upper result is that new socket structure is created and maintained, additional list and new values in TSSL socket should be allocated and deleted and so on. In future, optimization for TOE module should be done to reduce upper additional cost.

5 Conclusion

Supposed TOE module supported binary compatibility for standard socket interfaces over TOE devices. Also, multiple NICs and TOE devices can be used simultaneously. So, it allows existing applications to get advantage of TOE device without modifying and recompiling. And it is designed as multi-layers so as to easily support multiple offload technologies. Additionally, Zero-copy removed unnecessary memory copies between application and kernel in TOPL.

In future, we will optimize our software to reduce additional cost, especially, in TSSL socket management. And we should consider about taking over IPv6.

References

1. Boon S. Ang, "An Evaluation of an Attempt at Offloading TCP/IP Protocol Processing onto an i9 60RN-based iNIC", Computer Systems and Technology Laboratory HP Laboratories, 2001.
2. Intel, "Architectural Specification Offload Sockets Framework and Sockets Direct Protocol (SDP) High Level Design", IBM Software Architecture, infiniband.sourceforge.net , 2002.

3. Jeffrey C. Mogu,l, "TCP Offload is a Dumb Idea Whose Time Has Come. Proceedings of HotOS IX", The 9th Workshop on Hot Topics in Operating Systems, USENIX, 2003.
4. "Advantages of a TCP/IP Offload ASIC", Adaptec, Inc, 2002.
5. Hardware Platform Research Team, "Doorbell Mechanism for Network Protocol Acceleration Hardware version1.0", Digital Home Division, ETRI, 2004. 10.
6. Hardware Platform Research Team,"Specification of TOE Software", ETRI, 2004.
7. System SW Research Team, "OS Subsystem Kernel Block Specification ver1.0", ETRI, 2003.
8. J.-S. Kim, K. Kim, S.-I. Jung, and S. Ha, "Design and Implementation of a User-level Sockets Layer over Virtual Interface Architecture", Concurrency and Computation, Practice and Experience, Volume 15, Issue 7-8, 2003.
9. M. Blumrich, K. Li, R. Alpert, C. Dubnicki, E. Felten and J. Sandberg, "Virtual Memory Mapped Network Interface for the SHRIMP Multicomputer", in Proceeding 21st Annual Int. Symp.Comp. Arch., IEEE/ACM, apr, 1994 , pp 142-153.
10. H.K. Jerry Chu, Vivek Kashyap, "Transmission of IP over InfiniBand", Internet Draft, IETF, January, 2005.
11. Gary R. Wright and W. Richard Stevens, "TCP/IP Illustrated", Volume 2-The Implementation, Addison-Wesley, 1995.
12. David Mosberger, Larry L. Peterson and Sean O'Malley, "Analysis of Technique to Improve Protocol Processing Latency", Proc of Conference on Applications, Technologies, Architectures, and Protocols for computer communications(SIGCOMM'96), August, 1996.
13. Jeff Chase, Andrew Gallatin and Ken Yocum, "End-System Optimization for High-Speed TCP", June, 2000.(http://www.cs.duke.edu/ari/publications/publications.html)
14. C. Dalton, G. Watson, D. Banks, C. Calamvokis, A. Edwards, and J. Lumley, "Afterburner: Architectural Support for High Performance Protocols", IEEE Network Magazine, 7(4), 1995.
15. J. Brustoloni, "Interoperation of Copy Avoidance in Network and File I/O", In Proc. INFOCOM 99, mar. 1999.
16. T. von Eicken, A. Basu, V. Buch, and W. Vogels, "U-Net: A User-Level Network Interface for Parallel and Distributed Computing", Proc. 15th ACM symposium on Operating system Principles, 1995.

A Hybrid Parallel Loop Scheduling Scheme on Grid Environments*

Wen-Chung Shih[1], Chao-Tung Yang[2,**], and Shian-Shyong Tseng[1,3]

[1] Department of Computer and Information Science, National Chiao Tung University, Hsinchu 30010, Taiwan, R.O.C.
{gis90805, sstseng}@cis.nctu.edu.tw

[2] High-Performance Computing Laboratory, Department of Computer Science and Information Engineering, Tunghai University, Taichung 40704, Taiwan, R.O.C.
ctyang@thu.edu.tw

[3] Department of Information Science and Applications, Asia University, Taichung 41354, Taiwan, R.O.C.
sstseng@asia.edu.tw

Abstract. Effective loop-scheduling can significantly reduce the total execution time of a program on grid environments, especially for loop-intensive applications. This paper describes a two-phased method, named HPLS (Hybrid Parallel Loop Scheduling), to dynamically schedule loop iterations of a program on grid environments. In the first phase, most of the workload is dispatched to each node for execution according to its performance. Then, some well-known self-scheduling scheme is utilized to schedule the remaining workload. Experimental results showed that in most cases our approach could produce more efficient scheduling than previous schemes on our testbed grid. In addition, the results suggest that our approach is suitable for loop scheduling on grid environments.

Keywords: Loop scheduling, self-scheduling, grid computing, Globus, NWS.

1 Introduction

Much attention has been directed to grid computing since it is an inexpensive and promising alternative to parallel computing [9, 10, 11]. Simply speaking, grid computing extends traditional parallel and distributed computing by utilizing computers on the Internet to compute [1]. As in parallel and distributed systems, loop scheduling is a central issue in grid computing environments because effective loop-scheduling can significantly reduce the total execution time of a program on grid environments, especially for loop-intensive applications.

Previous work [15] proposes some useful self-scheduling schemes, which are applicable to PC-based cluster and grid computing environments. Nevertheless, the performance of this approach depends on the appropriate choice of scheduling

* This work was supported by National Science Council of the Republic of China under Grant No. NSC93-2752-E-009-006-PAE.

** Corresponding author.

H. Zhuge and G.C. Fox (Eds.): GCC 2005, LNCS 3795, pp. 370–381, 2005.

parameters. Besides, it estimates node performance only by CPU speed, which is one of the factors affecting node performance. In [7, 16], an enhanced scheme, which dynamically adjusts scheduling parameters according to system heterogeneity, is proposed. In [8], a class of loop self-scheduling for heterogeneous clusters was proposed. Nevertheless, it did not consider the influence of network bandwidth.

In this paper, we propose a general approach called HPLS (Hybrid Parallel Loop Scheduling). This approach utilizes performance functions to estimate the performance ratio of each node. Previous work in [7, 16] and this paper are all inspired by the α self-scheduling scheme presented in [15]. However, this work has different viewpoints and unique contributions. First, our method is a generalized approach, which is designed to be suitable for general grid environments, not just for extremely heterogeneous environments. Second, we put great emphasis on accurate estimation of node performance, rather than dynamical adjustment of scheduling parameters as in [7, 16], to achieve effective loop scheduling. Besides, simulated execution time and networking bandwidth are taken into consideration for estimation of node performance, which is not found in previous work. Finally, we have implemented three types of applications on a testbed grid to verify our approach.

The rest of this paper is organized as follows. In section 2, the background about parallel loop self-scheduling is reviewed. In section 3, we define our model and describe our approach. Next, our system configuration is specified and experimental results on three types of application programs are also presented in section 4. Finally, the concluding remarks are given in the last section.

2 Review of Loop Self-scheduling Schemes

Parallel loop scheduling schemes can be classified into two approaches: static scheduling and dynamic scheduling. The former makes scheduling decisions at compile time. Therefore, it is not suitable for grid environments where performance of each node could fluctuate dramatically, which might result in serious degradation of overall performance.

In this paper we focus on self-scheduling schemes, which are a large class of dynamic loop scheduling schemes. A good review of self-scheduling has been presented in [8]. Basically, these schemes address how to partition all workload into chunks, which are then dispatched to each idle slave node. To reduce scheduling overhead and achieve load balancing, the list of chunk sizes tends to be a decreasing-order list. Some well-known self-schemes are listed as follows.

- Pure Self-Scheduling (PSS) [13]
- Chunk Self-Scheduling (CSS) [13]
- Guided Self-Scheduling (GSS) [14]
- Factoring Self-Scheduling (FSS) [12]
- Trapezoid Self-Scheduling (TSS) [17]

Table 1 shows the different chunk sizes for a loop with the number of iterations being 1024 and the number of processors being 4.

Table 1. Sample partition size

Scheme	Sample partition size
PSS	1, 1, 1, 1, 1, 1, 1, 1, 1, ...
CSS(125)	128, 128, 128, 128, 128, 128, 128, 128, 128, ...
GSS	256, 192, 144, 108, 81, 61, 46, 34, 26, ...
FSS	128, 128, 128, 128, 64, 64, 64, 64, 32,...
TSS	128, 120, 112, 104, 96, 88, 80, 72, 64, ...

In [15], the authors revise known loop self-scheduling schemes to fit extremely heterogeneous PC cluster environments. An approach is proposed to partition loop iterations by two phases and it achieves good performance. It partitions $\alpha\%$ of workload according to their performance weighted by CPU clock in the first phase and the rest $(100-\alpha)\%$ of workload according to some well-known self-scheduling scheme in the second phase. Their experiments are conducted on a cluster environment with six nodes and the fastest computer is 6 times faster than the slowest ones in CPU-clock cycle. Many various α values are applied to the matrix multiplication and a best performance is obtained with α being 75.

3 Our Approach: HPLS (Hybrid Parallel Loop Scheduling)

Traditional static scheduling incurs less scheduling overhead, but might suffer from load unbalancing. In contrast, dynamic scheduling can achieve load balancing while it might incur excessive scheduling overhead. Our hybrid method tries to include the advantages of the two approaches while avoiding their disadvantages. In this section, the concept of performance ratio is described first. Then, we present the algorithm of our scheme.

3.1 Performance Ratio

We propose to partition $\alpha\%$ of workload according to the performance ratio of all nodes, and the remaining workload is dispatched by some well-known self-scheduling scheme. Using this approach, we do not need to know the real computer performance. However, a good performance ratio is desired to estimate performance of nodes accurately.

To estimate the performance of each slave node, we define a performance function (*PF*) for a slave node j as

$$PF_j(V_1, V_2, \ldots, V_M) \tag{1}$$

where V_i , $1< i <M$, is a variable of the performance function. In more detail, the variables could include CPU speed, networking bandwidth, memory size, etc. In this paper, our *PF* for node *j* is defined as

$$PF_j = w_1 \times \frac{1/T_j}{\sum_{\forall node_i \in S} 1/T_i} + w_2 \times \frac{B_j}{\sum_{\forall node_i \in S} B_i} \tag{2}$$

where

- S is the set of all grid nodes.
- T_i is the execution time (sec.) of node i for some application program, such as matrix multiplication.
- B_i is the bandwidth (Mbps) between node i and the master node.
- w_1 is the weight of the first term.
- w_2 is the weight of the second term.

The performance ratio (*PR*) is defined to be the ratio of all performance functions. For instance, assume the *PF*'s of three nodes are 1/2, 1/3 and 1/4. Then, the *PR* is 1/2 : 1/3 : 1/4; i.e., the *PR* of the three nodes is 6 : 4 : 3. In other words, if there are 13 loop iterations, 6 iterations will be assigned to the first node, 4 iterations will be assigned to the second node, and 3 iterations will be assigned to the last one.

3.2 Our Algorithm

Our algorithm is also a two-phased scheme and the skeleton of the algorithm is borrowed from [15]. In phase one, the performance ratio of slave nodes is estimated by experimental simulation and NWS tools [4, 6]. Then, we partition $\alpha\%$ of workload according to the performance ratio of all slave nodes, and the remaining workload is dispatched by some well-known self-scheduling scheme. The algorithm of our approach is described as follows.

Module MASTER

```
Initialization
Collect execution time and NWS information
Calculate performance ratio of all slave nodes
r = 0;
for (i = 1; i < number_of_slaves; i++) {
   partition •% of loop iterations according to the
performance ratio;
   send data to slave nodes;
   r++;
}
Master does its own computation work
Partition (100-•)% of loop iterations into the task
queue using some known self-scheduling scheme
Probe for returned results
Do {
     Distinguish source and receive returned data
     If the task queue is not empty then
           Send another data to the idle slave
           r -- ;
       else
           send TAG = 0 to the idle slave
} while (r > 0)
Finalization
END MASTER
```

Module SLAVE

```
Initialization
Probe if some data in
```

```
  While (TAG > 0) {
       Receive initial solution and size of subtask work
and compute to fine solution
       Send the result to the master
       Probe if some data in
  }
  Finalization
  END SLAVE
```

4 Experimental Results

To verify our approach, a testbed grid is built, and three types of application programs are implemented with MPI (Message Passing Interface) to be executed on this testbed. To begin with, our grid environment is illustrated, and terminologies for our programs are described. Next, performance of our scheme is compared with that of other static and dynamic schemes on this grid, with respect to matrix multiplication, Mandelbrot and circuit satisfiability. Based on experimental results in this section, we could conclude that our HPLS got performance improvement on static scheduling schemes and previous self-scheduling schemes for most cases.

4.1 Hardware Configuration and Terminology

We have built a testbed grid by the following middleware:

- Globus Toolkit 3.0.2 [5]
- Mpich library 1.2.6 [3]

This grid consists of one master and three domains, and its hardware configuration is shown in Table 2. In this experiment, the performance function and the performance ratio are the same as in Section 3. Besides, w_1 is assigned as 1 and w_2 is

Table 2. Hardware configuration

Master			
Host	CPU Type	CPU Speed	RAM
hpc	Intel Xeon™	2.4GHz	
Cluster 1			
Host	CPU Type	CPU Speed	RAM
hpc09	AMD Athlon™ XP	2.4GHz	1G
hpc10	AMD Athlon™ XP	2.4GHz	1G
hpc11	AMD Athlon™ XP	2.4GHz	1G
Cluster 2			
Host	CPU Type	CPU Speed	RAM
gridhit0	Intel Pentium™ 4	2.8GHz	512MB
gridhit1	Intel Pentium™ 4	2.8GHz	512MB
Cluster 3			
Host	CPU Type	CPU Speed	RAM
alpha1	AMD™ MP	2.4GHz	1G
alpha2	AMD™ MP	2.0GHz	1G

assigned as 0.5. Furthermore, T_i for node i is obtained by executing matrix multiplication for matrix size 512×512, while B_i for node i is obtained by NWS statistics [4, 6]. The resulting performance ratio is shown in Figure 1. For example, a node with faster processing speed (node 6, gridhit1) does not necessarily perform better than a node which has larger memory size (node 8, alpha2). This justifies our proposal of performance functions.

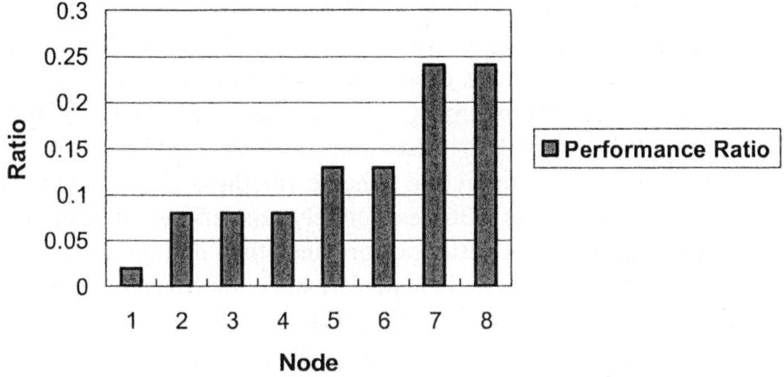

Fig. 1. Performance ratio of 8 processors for our testbed grid

We have implemented three categories of application programs in C language, with message passing interface (MPI) directives for parallelizing code segments to be processed by multiple CPU's. For readability of experimental results, the description of our implementation for all programs is listed in Table 3. In this paper, the scheduling parameter α is set to be 50 for all hybrid schemes, except for the schemes by [16], of which α is dynamically adjustable according to cluster heterogeneity.

Table 3. Description of our implementation for all programs

AP	Name	Description	Reference
AAA=mat: Matrix Multiplication AAA=man: Mandelbrot AAA=sat: Circuit Satisfiability	AAAstat	Static scheduling	[13]
	AAAgss	Dynamic scheduling (GSS)	[14]
	AAAngss0	Fixed α scheduling + GSS	[15]
	AAAngss2	Adaptive α scheduling + GSS	[16]
	AAAhgss	Our hybrid scheduling + GSS	
	AAAfss	Dynamic scheduling (FSS)	[12]
	AAAnfss0	Fixed α scheduling + FSS	[15]
	AAAnfss2	Adaptive α scheduling + FSS	[16]
	AAAhfss	Our hybrid scheduling + FSS	
	AAAtss	Dynamic scheduling (TSS)	[17]
	AAAntss0	Fixed α scheduling + TSS	[15]
	AAAntss2	Adaptive α scheduling + TSS	[16]
	AAAhtss	Our hybrid scheduling + TSS	

4.2 Application 1: Matrix Multiplication

The matrix multiplication is a fundamental operation in many numerical linear algebra applications [15]. This operation derives a resultant matrix by multiplying two input matrices, A and B, where A is a matrix of m rows by p columns and matrix B is one of p rows by n columns. The resultant matrix is one of m rows by n columns.

First, execution time on the grid for GSS group is investigated. Figure 2(a) illustrates execution time of static (matstat), dynamic (matgss) and our hybrid scheme (mathgss), with input matrix size 512×512, 1024×1024 and 1536×1536 respectively. Experimental results show that our hybrid scheduling scheme got better performance than static and dynamic ones. In this case, our scheme for input size 1536×1536 got 2% and 23% performance improvement over the static one and the dynamic one respectively. Figure 2(b) illustrates execution time of previous hybrid schemes (matngss0 and matngss2) and our hybrid scheme (mathgss), with input matrix size 512×512, 1024×1024 and 1536×1536 respectively. Experimental results show that our hybrid scheduling scheme got better performance than matngss2. In this case, our scheme for input size 1536×1536 got 10% performance improvement over matngss2.

Next, execution time on the grid for FSS group is investigated. Figure 3(a) shows that our scheme for input size 1536×1536 got 10% performance improvement over the static one. Figure 3(b) shows that our scheme for input size 1536×1536 got 18% performance improvement over matnfss2.

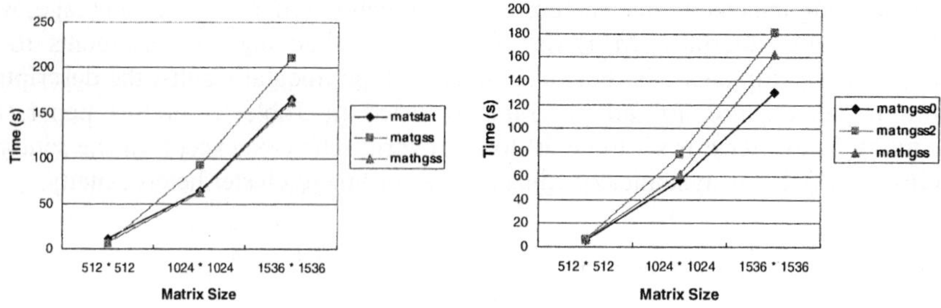

Fig. 2. Matrix multiplication execution time on the grid for GSS group schemes. (a) Static, dynamic and our hybrid scheme; (b) hybrid schemes: matngss0, matngss2 and our mathgss.

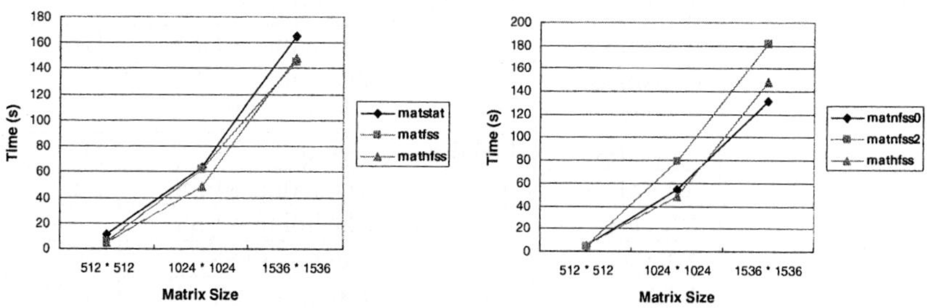

Fig. 3. Matrix multiplication execution time on the grid for FSS group schemes. (a) Static, dynamic and our hybrid scheme; (b) hybrid schemes: matnfss0, matnfss2 and our mathfss.

Finally, execution time on the grid for TSS group is investigated. Figure 4(a) sows that our scheme for input size 1536×1536 got 17% performance improvement over the static one. Figure 4(b) shows that our scheme for input size 1536×1536 got 1% and 26% performance improvement over matntss0 and matntss2 respectively.

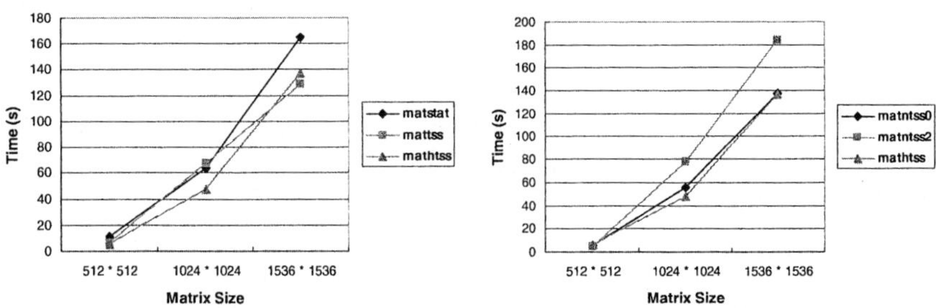

Fig. 4. Matrix multiplication execution time on the grid for TSS group schemes. (a) Static, dynamic and our hybrid scheme; (b) hybrid schemes: matntss0, matntss2 and our mathtss.

4.3 Application 2: Mandelbrot

The Mandelbrot set is a problem involving the same computation on different data points which have different convergence rates [2]. This operation derives a resultant image by processing an input matrix, A, where A is an image of *m* pixels by *n* pixels. The resultant image is one of *m* pixels by *n* pixels.

First, execution time on the grid for GSS group is investigated. Figure 5(a) illustrates execution time of static (manstat), dynamic (mangss) and our hybrid scheme (manhgss), with input image size 64×64, 128×128 and 192×192 respectively. Experimental results show that our hybrid scheduling scheme got better performance than static and dynamic ones. In this case, our scheme for input size 192×192 got 90% and 5% performance improvement over the static one and the dynamic one respectively.

Figure 5(b) illustrates execution time of previous hybrid schemes (manngss0 and manngss2) and our hybrid scheme (manhgss), with input image size 64×64, 128×128 and 192×192 respectively. Experimental results show that our hybrid scheduling scheme got better performance than manngss2. In this case, our scheme for input size 192×192 got 16% performance improvement over manngss2.

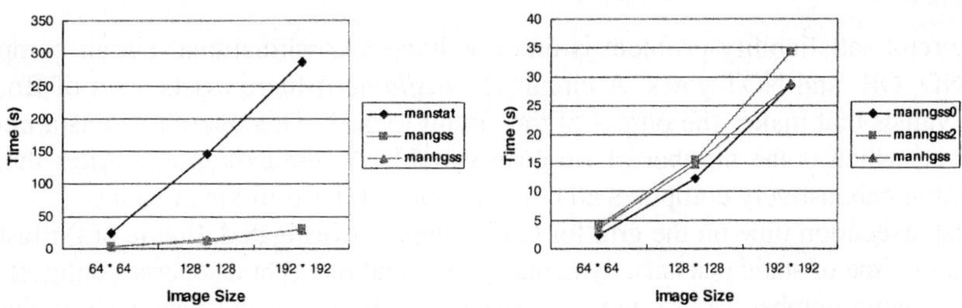

Fig. 5. Mandelbrot execution time on the grid for GSS group schemes. (a) Static, dynamic and our hybrid scheme; (b) hybrid schemes: matngss0, matngss2 and our mathgss.

Next, execution time on the grid for FSS group is investigated. Figure 6(a) shows that our scheme for input size 192×192 got 93% and 27% performance improvement over the static one and the dynamic one respectively. Figure 6(b) shows that our scheme for input size 192×192 got 1% and 28% performance improvement over mannfss0 and mannfss2 respectively.

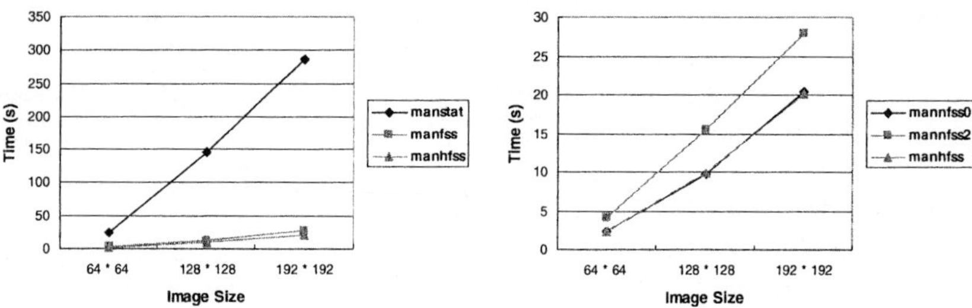

Fig. 6. Mandelbrot execution time on the grid for FSS group schemes. (a) Static, dynamic and our hybrid scheme; (b) hybrid schemes: matnfss0, matnfss2 and our mathfss.

Finally, execution time on the grid for TSS group is investigated. Figure 7(a) shows that our scheme for input size 192×192 got 93% and 11% performance improvement over the static one and the dynamic one respectively. Figure 7(b) shows that our scheme for input size 192×192 got 42% performance improvement over manntss2.

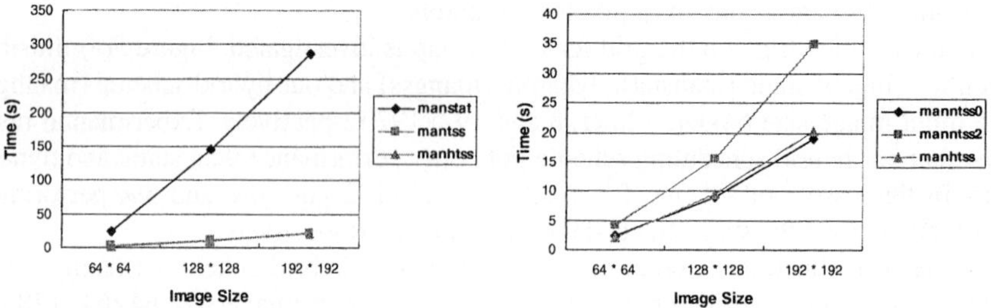

Fig. 7. Mandelbrot execution time on the grid for TSS group schemes. (a) Static, dynamic and our hybrid scheme; (b) hybrid schemes: matntss0, matntss2 and our mathtss.

4.4 Application 3: Circuit Satisfiability

The circuit satisfiability problem is one involving a combinational circuit composed of AND, OR, and NOT gates. A circuit is *satisfiable* if there exists a set of Boolean input values that makes the output of the circuit to be 1. This operation gets a number as input, which is the number of Boolean variables in the expression. After that, the algorithm exhaustively computes all combinations of these Boolean values.

First, execution time on the grid for GSS group is investigated. Figure 8(a) illustrates execution time of static (satstat), dynamic (satgss) and our hybrid scheme (sathgss), with input variable number 14, 15 and 16 respectively. Experimental results show that our hybrid scheduling scheme got better performance than the static one. In this case, our scheme for input size 16 got 63% performance improvement over the static one.

Figure 8(b) illustrates execution time of previous hybrid schemes (satngss0 and satngss2) and our hybrid scheme (sathgss), with input size 14, 15 and 16 respectively. Experimental results show that our hybrid scheduling scheme got better performance than satngss2. In this case, our scheme for input size 16 got 32% performance improvement over satngss2.

Next, execution time on the grid for FSS group is investigated. Figure 9(a) shows that our scheme for input size 16 got 65% performance improvement over the static one. Figure 9(b) shows that our scheme for input size 16 got 8% and 25% performance improvement over satnfss0 and satnfss2 respectively.

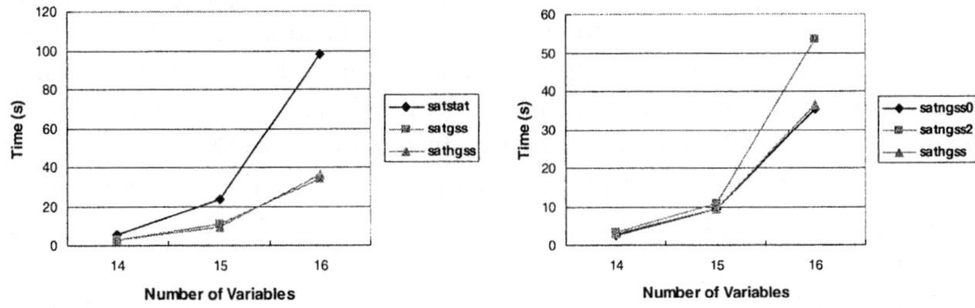

Fig. 8. Circuit Satisfiability execution time on the grid for GSS group schemes. (a) Static, dynamic and our hybrid scheme; (b) hybrid schemes: matngss0, matngss2 and our mathgss.

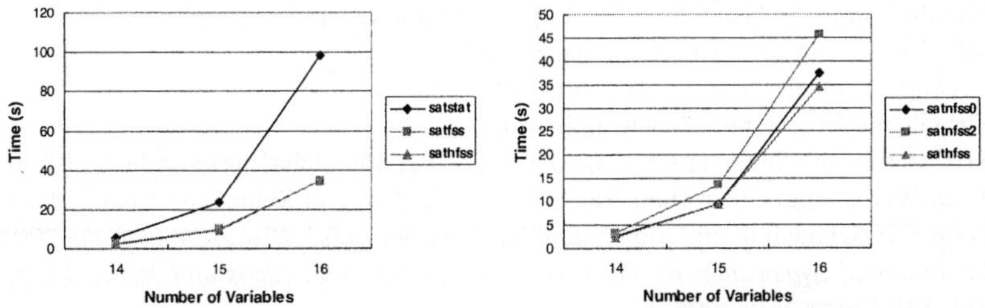

Fig. 9. Circuit Satisfiability execution time on the grid for FSS group schemes. (a) Static, dynamic and our hybrid scheme; (b) hybrid schemes: matnfss0, matnfss2 and our mathfss.

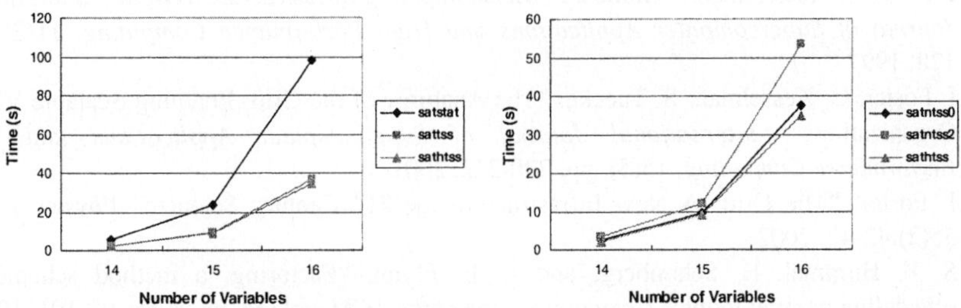

Fig. 10. Circuit Satisfiability execution time on the grid for TSS group schemes. (a) Static, dynamic and our hybrid scheme; (b) hybrid schemes: matntss0, matntss2 and our mathtss.

Finally, execution time on the grid for TSS group is investigated. Figure 10(a) shows that our scheme for input size 16 got 65% and 6% performance improvement over the static one and the dynamic one respectively. Figure 10(b) shows that our scheme for input size 16 got 7% and 35% performance improvement over satntss0 and satntss2 respectively.

5 Conclusions

In this paper, we have proposed a hybrid approach, which combines the advantages of static and dynamic loop scheduling schemes, and have compared it with previous algorithms by experiments for three types of application programs on our grid environment. In each case, our approach can obtain performance improvement on previous schemes. Besides, our approach is less sensitive to α values than previous schemes; in other words, it is more robust. In our future work, we will implement more types of application programs to verify our approach. Furthermore, we hope to find better ways of modeling the performance function, incorporating more status information.

References

1. Introduction to Grid Computing with Globus, http://www.ibm.com/redbooks/
2. Introduction to the Mandelbrot Set, http://www.ddewey.net/mandelbrot/
3. MPICH-G2, http://www.hpclab.niu.edu/mpi/
4. Network Weather Service, http://nws.cs.ucsb.edu/
5. The Globus Project, http://www.globus.org/
6. THU Bandwidth Statistics GUI, http://140.128.101.150/alpha1hpc09gridhit0lz01tc01.png
7. Kuan-Wei Cheng, Chao-Tung Yang, Chuan-Lin Lai, and Shun-Chyi Chang, "A Parallel Loop Self-Scheduling on Grid Computing Environments," *Proceedings of the 2004 IEEE International Symposium on Parallel Architectures, Algorithms and Networks*, pp. 409-414, KH, China, May 2004.
8. A. T. Chronopoulos, R. Andonie, M. Benche and D.Grosu, "A Class of Loop Self-Scheduling for Heterogeneous Clusters," *Proceedings of the 2001 IEEE International Conference on Cluster Computing*, pp. 282-291, 2001.
9. I. Foster, C. Kesselman., "Globus: A Metacomputing Infrastructure Toolkit," *International Journal of Supercomputer Applications and High Performance Computing*, 11(2):115-128, 1997
10. I. Foster, C. Kesselman, S. Tuecke. "The Anatomy of the Grid: Enabling Scalable Virtual Organizations." *International Journal of Supercomputer Applications and High Performance Computing*, 15(3), pp. 200-222, 2001.
11. I. Foster, "The Grid: A New Infrastructure for 21st Century Science," *Physics Today*, 55(2):42-47, 2002.
12. S. F. Hummel, E. Schonberg, and L. E. Flynn, "Factoring: a method scheme for scheduling parallel loops," *Communications of the ACM*, vol. 35, no. 8, pp. 90-101, 1992.
13. H. Li, S. Tandri, M. Stumm and K. C. Sevcik, "Locality and Loop Scheduling on NUMA Multiprocessors," *Proceedings of the 1993 International Conference on Parallel Processing*, vol. II, pp. 140-147, 1993.

14. C. D. Polychronopoulos and D. Kuck, "Guided Self-Scheduling: a Practical Scheduling Scheme for Parallel Supercomputers," *IEEE Trans. on Computers*, vol. 36, no. 12, pp 1425-1439, 1987.
15. Chao-Tung Yang and Shun-Chyi Chang, "A Parallel Loop Self-Scheduling on Extremely Heterogeneous PC Clusters," *Journal of Information Science and Engineering*, vol. 20, no. 2, pp. 263-273, March 2004.
16. Chao-Tung Yang, Kuan-Wei Cheng, and Kuan-Ching Li, "An Efficient Parallel Loop Self-Scheduling on Grid Environments," *NPC'2004 IFIP International Conference on Network and Parallel Computing*, *Lecture Notes in Computer Science*, Springer-Verlag Heidelberg, Hai Jin, Guangrong Gao, Zhiwei Xu (Eds.), vol. 3222, pp. 92-100, Oct. 2004.
17. T. H. Tzen and L. M. Ni, "Trapezoid self-scheduling: a practical scheduling scheme for parallel compilers," *IEEE Transactions on Parallel and Distributed Systems*, vol. 4, no. 1, pp. 87-98, 1993.

A Conceptual Modeling Approach to Virtual Organizations in the Grid*

William Song[1] and Xiaoming Li[2]

[1] Computer Science, University of Durham, UK
[2] School of Information Technology, Peking University, China

Abstract. One of the key problems with virtual organizations in the context of the (Semantic) Grid is we don't know how to describe the components used in virtual organizations because they appear to be dynamic, dispersed, transient, type-vague (or we don't know their types), heterogeneous, semantically informal, and disorderly. The existing semantic modeling approaches lack effective modeling facilities for modeling virtual organization components. Our observations were suggesting focusing on the following aspects: First, we should model both static resources and dynamic states of a virtual organization. Second, we should build up the virtual organizations with abundant static resource. Third, we should combine the semantic modeling with the users' requirements description for virtual organizations due to its importance. In this paper, we analyze the current situation of the virtual organization research and propose our experimental semantic description model for virtual organizations. We also present the design architecture for the *Realcourse* application.

1 Introduction

Current researches on the World Wide Web and the Grid, as well as Web Services, have come to a consensus issue. That is, how to extract and represent semantics for the web information and the Grid recourses. As known to us, the W3C (the World Wide Web Consortium) provides standards/recommendations for information exchange and interoperation, such as RDF(S) [5, 8], and the Grid community provides an infrastructure for resource sharing and cooperation, i.e. OGSA [3]. The interoperability and collaboration requires common understanding of information/data and resources and the understanding requires canonical and well-formed semantic description. The semantic description for the Web and Grid resources is used both for human and machine to understand each other.

The Grid is an emerging platform to support on-demand "virtual organizations" for coordinated resource sharing and problem solving on a global scale [4]. The virtual organization is seen as "a temporary alliance of contracted individuals or companies linked together by information and communication technologies, which assembles for the purpose of a specific business task" [6, 7]. In the Grid computing environment, there are many resources, e.g., courses, lectures, articles, presentation slides, demonstration videos, training systems, and testing papers in the area of online teaching/learning, which we call nodes. These nodes are connected to each other,

* The work is partially supported by the NSF project (90412010).

H. Zhuge and G.C. Fox (Eds.): GCC 2005, LNCS 3795, pp. 382–393, 2005.

exchanging information, sharing their resources, and collaborating on certain tasks. Usually, for a given task, a collection of nodes can be temporarily and dynamically organized together to form a virtual organization, while each node in the organization plays different role and performs different activity and these nodes should coordinate and cooperate so that the different roles and activities are integrated for achieving the assigned goal.

1.1 Related Issues

The "virtual organizations" has been considered to play an important role in a variety of applications of the Web and Grid communities. It is necessary to discuss and clarify some basic concerns of virtual organizations.

Time dimension. A virtual organization has a life cycle, noted as vo[t_{begin}, t_{end}]. It is created upon a requirement at time t_{begin}. When all the tasks of the virtual organization finish, the virtual organization itself will dissolve at time t_{end}. The lifecycle of a virtual organization provides a mechanism that the resources can be dynamically added to the organization when required and released when not used anymore. Similarly, any component or task in a VO has also a starting time and ending time. Of course, the begin time of any component or task is greater than that of the VO and the end time of any component or task is less than that of the VO.

Workflow. A virtual organization is an organization of task-driven, resource-based, and workflow-managed. Traditional workflow model concerns the execution dependence between tasks [12]. It also concerns the dependence between resources available for the VO and time sequence dependence. A workflow model for the VO represents a series of states and their transitions. In other words, at time t_k, VO_{tk} is a set of states, noted as S_{tk}, with pre-conditions and post-conditions, noted as $PreC_{tk}$ and $PostC_{tk}$ respectively, to form a triple set $<S_{tk}, PreC_{tk}, PostC_{tk}>$. Here the pre-conditions, $PreC_{tk}$, and the post-conditions, $PostC_{tk}$, indicate the required inputs to and the expected outputs from the states S_{tk}. In the life cycle of a VO, a series of states and their transition flows form a state-transition graph.

Resources. Resources are considered to be the most fundamental components [10]. All the activities or tasks carried on in a VO are the process of requesting, comparing, selecting, consuming, integrating and releasing resources. We define two types of resources: sharable and non-sharable. A resource is sharable if it can be used or consumed in more than one task or component at the same time. Such resources are as electronic games, electronic documents, and digital movies. A resource is non-sharable if it can only be used in one task at a time. For example, CPU, memory, and printer are non-sharable resources. In this paper, we only consider the sharable resources because to provide better semantic description to them is more important in the context of the VO. A resource is apparently associated to some actions, such as resource requesting and resource releasing. Therefore, the life cycle of a resource is associated with an action, denoted as Act(Res, t_k), meaning that an action Act is on the resource Res at the time t_k. There are two actions, called resource requesting and resource releasing, stipulating the begin time t_{begin} and the end time t_{end} of the resource. All other actions on this resource at the time t_k, Act(Res, t_k), must follow $t_{begin} < t_k < t_{end}$.

Unlike the interdependence between the workflow states where one state's output is the input to another state (logic dependence), the interdependence between the resources is of semantics, for example, in the relation between Lecture One and Lecture Two. Most of the time, this kind of semantic dependence may not be of time order. Therefore, it is difficult to completely and exactly capture this kind of interdependence relationship between the resources in advance.

Roles and access control. A VO involves various actors (both human beings and machine agents) and different actors play different roles and therefore possess different access rights. Since accesses are given to either resources or processes, the resources and processes will be described with access rights (metadata for access rights). In this paper, we will not consider in detail how to semantically depict the access rights of resources and processes. However, the semantic description of various resources implicitly implies a hierarchy of access rights. For example, a student, not allowed to view a test paper, will not be able to access the test paper resource and the model answers to the test paper as well.

Task and task hierarchy. We define a high level task to be a goal for building up a virtual organization. That is, the description of this high level task is to describe what demand or goal that an end-user expects to meet, such as "to study the Semantic Web". Therefore it is natural that this task will be decomposed into a number of subtasks. Using the decomposition operation, we create a hierarchical structure for tasks. The tasks that cannot be further decomposed are called leave tasks. Each leaf task corresponds to and consumes a set of resources. The process of task decomposition supports forming the workflow of the virtual organization.

1.2 Overview

The paper is organized as follows. In the next section we propose the system architecture for the virtual organization system design, where we briefly discuss various components and their functions in the system. In section 3 we discuss and clarify some basic concepts for virtual organization through the example "virtual course", where we focus on the description of resource, by defining the metadata models for logic resource description and task description and the ontology model for the conceptual description of resources in virtual organizations. In section 4, we discuss the resource storage structure in servers and the task decomposition process in the context of the *Realcourse* application. Finally in section 5 we conclude the paper by discussing our next research work.

2 System Architecture

The system architecture proposed to the virtual organization design consists of two major components: the Task Analysis (TA) component and the Resource Management (RM) component, see Fig. 1.

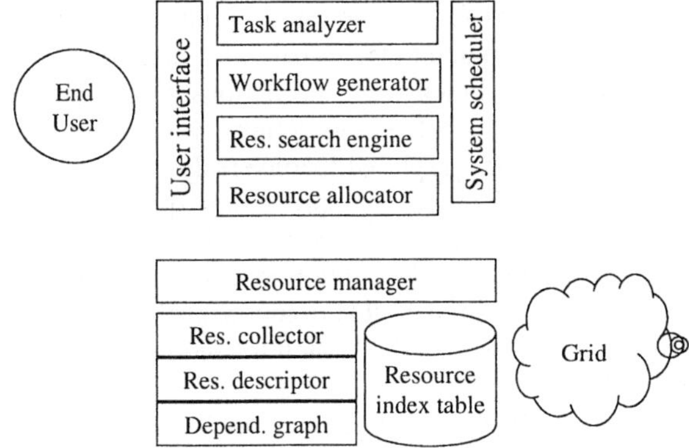

Fig. 1. The system architecture for building a virtual organization

In the Resource Management (RM) component, there are three major function blocks, i.e., the resource collection block, the resource description block, and the resource interdependence graph, and two supporting function blocks: the resource management block and the resource indexing repository. The recourse management block coordinates the functions of the other function blocks, provides an interface to the servers and the resources in the servers, and connects to the Task Analysis component. The resource index table (RIT) saves the results from the resource collection and description blocks, provides a structured organization for the resources, and manages various queries to the resources. The three main function blocks are described below.

Resource collector (RC) block finds and collects all the resources, which are related to a given task, from a distributed environment, extract the contextual information for each resource, and generate for the first round a resource index table.

Resource descriptor (RD) block uses the proposed semantic model for virtual organizations and the extracted resource description information, form a structured, resource associated graph, and generate for the second round a semantic richer resource index repository.

In general, any pair of resources possesses a certain kind of relationships, for example, sequence in time, difference in position, semantic similarity, and so on. The resource interdependence graph (RIG) provides a very general semantic relationship between two resources if they have a certain semantic association. For instance, two resources, "XML course" and "advanced XML course", may have a semantic similarity relation between them. In this case, one resource, when it is not available, may be replaced by the other because they are semantically similar.

In the Task Analysis (TA) component, there are four main function blocks and two assistant blocks. The assistant blocks, User interface (UI) and System scheduling (SS), deal with the interactions with the end users, such as user queries, obtaining user preferences, and presenting the VO results, and respectively the internal event management and task (workflow) scheduling. The rest four function blocks are explained below.

Task analyzer (TA) block is to take in a task (in the form of user initial requirements), analyze the task and decompose it into a set of subtasks in the form of object-action pairs. The actions serve to the generation of workflow and the objects serve to the Resource Search Engine to form search formulation.

Workflow generator (WG) block uses the actions to produce a state-transition graph, which represents a flow of events/actions with pre-conditions and post-conditions. The state-transition graph will conversely be used to check the user requirements and will require the users to improve their queries accordingly.

Resource search engine (RSE) block receives the objects stated in the tasks, formulate them according to the semantic description model for resources, and finally send the queries to the RM component. The RM component then returns a set of relevant resources and the RSE performs an exact match to find the resource set which better meet the demand.

Resource allocator (RA) block will map the resources from the resource set, the result of the RSE, to the actions and objects in the workflow graph, and generate a resource mapping table (RMT).

3 Semantic Modeling for Virtual Organizations

Undoubtedly, semantics is extremely important in successfully building up a virtual organization and using it. Therefore we discuss where we should make semantic modeling in the context of virtual organizations. Firstly, user demands are very often expressed in a very informal way. So the semantic description model should be able to describe the user demands in a formal manner with less semantic loss. Secondly, resources and components are already stored and described in the Grid. However, their semantics is usually buried in their representation structures and connotations. The semantic description model should be able to capture richer semantics out from the structures and the domain experts' expressions. Thirdly, the model should be able to provide a uniform expression for them. The uniform expression requires the semantic model to be sufficiently general to accommodate various modeling approaches with different semantic foci and precise enough to be able to describe most of the details. The Entity Relationship Approach (ER) [1] and Resource Description Framework (RDF) [8] are currently two main modeling approaches. In this paper we propose a variant schema of ER and RDF, where we adopt the advantage of both modeling approaches.

3.1 Basic Concepts

The main concept to be discussed is "resource". Here we distinguish two kinds of resources, i.e., physical resources and logical resources. A physical resource is an object physically existing in a server, for example, CPU time. A typical property of such physical resources is its status, e.g., whether it is on or off (connected or disconnected to the internet). Usually a physical resource has, as its attributes, a name, an identifier, an access address, a size, etc.

A logical resource is a logical representation of an object. It usually represents a set of distributed physical resources. A logical resource has, as its attributes, a name, an address, a type, and other metadata such as subject. In a virtual organization, a resource refers to a logical one if not explicitly specified. A logical resource usually has a relationship with another logical resource, for example, having the same subject or being similar.

A virtual organization is a set of interrelated resources, which are from different servers. A virtual organization is usually involved in a number of logic structures. On the server side, each server provides a set of physical resources assumedly forming a logical structure, which contributes to the virtual organization. For example, the virtual course "Protégé" includes, as parts of the course, a demo system from Stanford and a series of tutorials from Manchester.

The logic structure for the set of resources on the server side is based on a semantic modeling method, which has two sub-models: metadata model and ontology model.

3.2 Semantic Description Models

There are many resources available on the Grid but most of them are less described and structured. The resources, such as electronic documents, images, movies, sounds, and their interrelations and links, all are overwhelmingly complicated. As the number of resources available on the Grid is explosively growing, this complexity must be managed. Semantic modeling is an effective means to manage complexity in resource information construction. Semantic models can help us to understand the web resources by simplifying some of details [2, 9] and to represent main features and main structures of information and its management.

Physical resources. As we previously described, each server provides a set of physical resources and a virtual organization consists of resources from many servers. Therefore, a collection of servers supporting the virtual organization to operate is denoted to be $S = \{s_1, s_2, \ldots, s_m\}$. Each server contains a collection of resources, denoted to be $R = \{R_1, R_2, \ldots, R_m\}$, where $R_i = \{r_1, r_2, \ldots, r_n\}$ is the resources in the server s_i and r_j is a single resource.

(Physical resource) A physical resource description is defined to be a quintuple: $r_j = \{\mathbf{id}, \mathbf{name}, \mathbf{type}, \mathbf{p}, \mathbf{s}\}$, where **id** is the internal representation of the resource; **name** is the name of the resource; **type** is the type of the resource, **p** is the physical location, i.e., the path of the resource from the server root; and **s** is the name of the server holding the resource.

The **type** element is an important element for defining a resource. The types contain e.g., multimedia types, textual types, and executable file type. A multimedia type can be mpg, rm, etc. A textual type can be doc, ppt, etc.

For the path (physical location) **p**, we assume a hierarchical structure to be used to organize all the resources in a server. For each resource, there is a path, **p**, from the server root down to the folder directly containing the resource. In this tree structure, a non-leave node is a folder (represented by its name). The root node is the server, **s**, and the leave nodes are the resources. For example, the physical resource description for the resource Lect1.ppt, see the Fig 2, is as follows: {**id**: #sw-lecture-1; **name**: lect1; **type**: ppt; **p**: hudson/public/course/CS/Web Tech/Semantic Web; **s**: hudson;}.

Maintaining this hierarchy aims at acquiring the genuine and natural information of how the users organize and manage their resources. Usually a name the user gives to a resource contains a certain meaning.

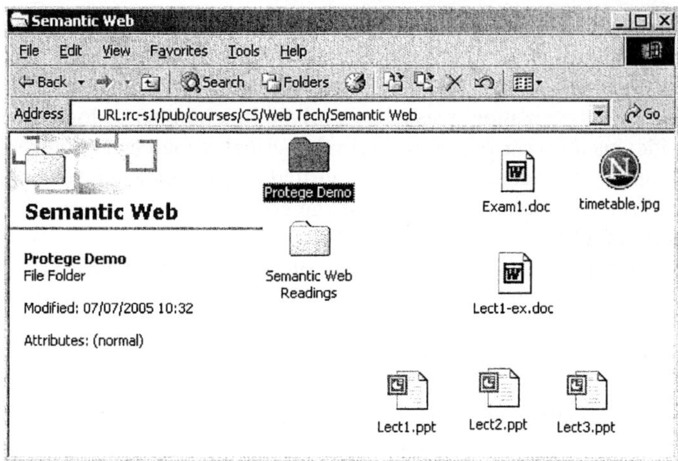

Fig. 2. The folder contains the resources for the Semantic Web course

Metadata model. As we know, the major purpose to create a virtual organization is to find a suitable set of interrelated resources to fulfill the requirements of a given task. Therefore the semantic model should target at resource description, resource integration, and requirement description. The semantic description for resources includes a metadata model and an ontology model.

The metadata model for the logic resource description is a set of normalized metadata, which can identify and describe the resources in VO. In the metadata model, each metadata represents a resource attribute. In our application domain (i.e. the *Realcourse*), the metadata model contains these attributes: subjects (associating with its ontology model), title, description, author, logic relation, length, etc. All the attributes for physical resource description are naturally included in the metadata model.

(Logic resource) A metadata model for a logic resource, **r**, is defined to be a binary <r-id, r-attr>, where r-id is the internal representation of the resource (the same as in the physical resource definition) and r-attr is a list of attributes, which are described as follows:

- **Subject:** topic of the content of the resource. This topic is the reasonably smallest concept, i.e., the leaf node in the ontology
- **Title**: the name of the resource
- **Description:** an account of the content of the resource, usually in natural language
- **Author:** the responsible one for the content of the resource. We also use creator or owner instead of author.
- **Logic relation:** the relations of the resource with other resources. The relations are collected from the Resource Interdependence Graph (RIG), see Chapter 2, which was previously defined by the domain experts.
- **Length:** the play time for the resource.

In the following we use an example (self-explanatory) to illustrate the metadata model for the resource <#sw-lecture-1, r-attr>, where r-attr = {**Subject**: Semantic

Web; **Title**: lecture 1; **Description**: This is the first lecture for the semantic Web course, mainly introducing some basic concepts and discussing background knowledge; **Author**: William; **Logic relations**: *pre-req*(XML, Internet Tech), *post-req*(Metadata model, Semi-structured data); **Length**: 60 min}.

In a virtual organization, tasks are the major components, which realize the end users' requirements, construct workflows for the requirements, and allocate and assembly the resources. In other words, the tasks represent and formulate the users' demands and requirements at one end and deliver the basic services and consume the resources at the other end. It is obvious that the decomposition operation is a most fundamental one on the tasks. By applying the decomposition operation, the tasks form a tree structure, which supports to construct and schedule workflows for the virtual organization.

(Task) A metadata model for a task, **t**, is defined to be a binary <t-id, t-attr>, where t-id is the internal representation of the task **t** and t-attr is a list of attributes, which are described as follows:

- **<t_{begin}, t_{end}>:** this is a pair of time units to indicate the beginning and the end of the task. So it delimits the life cycle of the task.
- **Description:** a natural language description of the task.
- **Resource set:** a set of resources from various servers, to be consumed by the task.
- **Roles:** a number of actors that play various roles in performing the task, e.g., task trigger, task subject, etc.
- **Decomposition:** this is an operation on the task. The result is a set of subtasks.
- **Rules**: a set of rules, stipulating inputs to and outputs from the task.

In the following we illustrate the task metadata model with an example, see Fig. 3. In the example, the task #012 starts at 16:30 and finishes at 17:30, lasting for one hour which matches the length of the consumed resource lect1.ppt. The task also consumes other two resources lect1-ex (exercises for lecture one) and demo-pres#2 (the second demo presentation, which is located in the folder Protégé Demo, see Fig. 2). This task is further decomposed into three subtasks: #0121, #0122, and #0123. The task is triggered by the outputs of the tasks #011 and #01 and followed by the task #013.

Ontology model. The ontology model is a special structure for a set of resources, where only a special relationship between resources is maintained, for example, the generalization (is-a) relationship. From the point of view of concepts, an ontology model is a tree, where all the nodes are concepts. There is one special node, called the root, which is the most general concept in the tree.

----

t-id: #012
<t_1, t_2>: 16:30-17:30
description: this task is to take the lecture 1 and read some materials.
resource set: lect1.ppt, lect1-ex, demo-pres#02
roles: triggers <#011, #01>, followers <#013, #121>
decomposition: <#0121, #0122, #0123>
rules: <inputs, outputs>

Fig. 3. The example of the tasks

The purpose of defining an ontology model is to provide a referencing conceptual framework for a virtual organization, which we use to reason about, e.g., whether two resources (teacher A and lecturer B) belong to the same concept. The ontology model also supports resource search, formulating search queries for the RSE function block, and resource-task match, refer to Chapter 2.

Following is a widely accepted definition for the ontology. The ontology is defined to be a quintuple: concept (the concept itself), properties (all the relationships of the concept with other concepts and the attributes of the concept), axioms (rules and constraints on the concept), value domains and nominal (names or terms for the concept). However, based on our investigation on the application domain, we redefine the ontology to better accommodate the features of the *Realcourse* (the virtual course).

(Ontology model) An ontology model for the resources is defined as follows:

Concept: a concept name is used to represent the concept of a resource.

Properties: a set of properties of the concept, e.g., location of the resource, difficulty level.

Constraints: the constraints on the concept of the resource, e.g., *disjoint* (A, B), *overlapping* (A, B) where A and B are two concepts.

Relationships: the semantic relations between two concepts, e.g., *similar* (A, B).

Internal structure: *subClassOf, partOf*. This forms an ontology tree for the concept of the resource.

In the following we illustrate the ontology model through describing the course Web Technology Course, see Fig. 4.

Concept: Web Technology Course (in short, WT)
Properties: location(WT) = "dcs/courses/CS/WT/WT1", difficulty(WT) = "beginner"
Constraints: disjoint(WT, OS), overlapping(WT, DB), where OS and DB are the course resources Operating Systems and Database Systems.
Relationships: relevant(WT, programming), similar(WT, Internet Tech)
Internal structure: WT(XML(X1), Web Engineering(WE1), Semantic Web(SW1, SW2), Web Services(WS1))

Fig. 4. An ontology model for description of the resource Web Technology Course

4 A *Realcourse* Case

University Course Online (in short, the *Realcourse*), composed of 20 servers, is a Course service supported by a collection of physical servers distributed on CERNET all over China [11]. Besides the servers that share the single URL, there are more than 800 hours of quality course services available. These services are from different universities, uploaded to different servers with a permanent backup copy created in a server other than the original one, and flow from one server to another. If one server is down, its duty is automatically taken up by some other server. In this circumstance, each server provides a number of resources for a course (usually all the resources required for a course are in one server). However, with the fast growing of the capacity of resources and variation of courses, it will be difficult and unreasonable for one server to contain all the required resources for a "single" course.

We use a metadata model to provide semantic description for resources and courses. Other than the elements which are similar to the Dublin Core elements, the metadata model also provides description for the tasks which form various workflows to realize the virtual organization for the *Realcourse*. The description for a course is more complicated. For example, a course may consist of a lot of resources. These resources include some training materials such as video clips and sound clips, a dozen of presentations (in PPT or PDF form), many research papers, articles, standards specifications documents, and other textual materials, some tools with user manuals and reference books.

4.1 Logic Structure for the "Virtual Course"

In the following, we briefly illustrate the content of the structure of virtual courses in a server and the process of task decomposition. See Fig. 5.

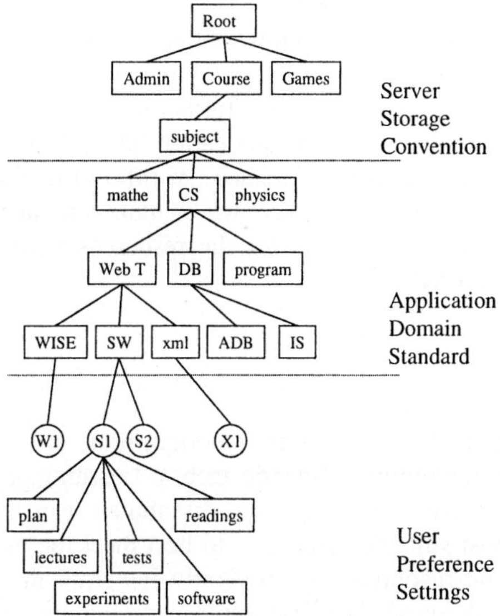

Fig. 5. The example shows the resources in a server for various courses

A server, providing various resources about learning materials, can be described as a tree structure, which has three layers in building up it, i.e., server storage convention, application domain standard, and user preference settings. We assume that the server storage convention maintains a similar structure for all the files and folders, like in a Unix system. For each resource, as an item of descriptive information, we need the path from the root (e.g., the server name) to the physical object name.

However, semantic richer information comes from the lower layers, i.e., the application domain standard (e.g., library subject category) and the user settings, where the latter contains more informal semantics. In the reality, we can obtain this kind of ontology from any standard body. For example, an ordinary library subject category (LSC) is this kind of ontology model for learning purpose. The user settings provide more semantic connotations for the concepts of resources but they are quite informal. Currently we manage this part manually. For example, the users need to prepare a resource interdependence graph (RIG) to provide semantic relationships between the resources.

4.2 Task Decomposition Process

Assume that an objective for a virtual organization is "to build up a course on Semantic Web from the existing courses" with a set of requirements "for beginners", "in English/Chinese", "12 hours long", and "self-testing". We take the objective as the first, very general task, T0. Then T0 is decomposed into two subtasks: subject search T10 ("Semantic Web") and attribute match T11 (attributes). Using the ontology in the system, we find *subClassOf*("Semantic Web", "Web Technology") and *similar*("Semantic Web", "Advanced Information Systems"). Then T11 is decomposed into the following subtasks: resource search T20, task-resource match T21, task scheduling T22, and attribute tuning T23.

The task T20, resource search, attempts to find all the resources available in the ontology internal structure. The task T21, task-resource match, collects the found resources and matches them to the subtasks (further decomposition may be needed for better matches.) and generate a resource allocation table. The task T22 is to arrange all the tasks and form an executive sequence (workflow) in time order. Finally the task T23, attribute tuning, checks whether two or more similar resources are serving the same task. If so, the requirements for the resources need further analysis and users' interference is required.

5 Conclusion

The 'Virtual organization' has become an important issue in many application areas, such as semantic grid computing, semantic web, e-Learning, e-Government, and e-Business. To make best use of the resources distributed over the Grid environment, we need to find the most suitable resources, to best meet the users' requirements, to most effectively use the resources, to efficiently integrate the resources to form a virtual organization on demand. The first step toward the above mentioned objective is to use a semantic model for resource description. In this paper we proposed a metadata model for resource description and for task description. We also proposed an ontology model for resource conceptual description.

We use the *Realcourse* as a testing application to build up a virtual course, which aims to realize some important aspects of a virtual organization, including semantic extraction and modeling from resources, ontology design and use.

When developing the semantic models, we find that a further investigation on the behavior of the tasks for resource management is crucial. Our next step is to formalize the semantic model for virtual organization resources so that a deeper analysis of various tasks and their internal features and structures is very important. In addition, we will develop an automatic task development and analysis mechanism based on the *Realcourse* to support the virtual course design.

References

1. Chen P.: The Entity-Relationship Model - Toward a Unified View of Data. ACM Transaction on Database Systems 1, 1 (1976) 9-36
2. Conallen J.: Modeling Web Application Architectures with UML, Communications of the ACM, Vol. 42, No. 10 (1999)
3. Foster I, Kesselman C, Nick J, and Tuecke S.: The physiology of the grid: open grid services architecture for distributed systems integration, GGF4 (2002)
4. Gobel C and de Rouce D.: The Grid: an application of the semantic web, SIGMOD Record Vol. 31 No. 4, ACM (2002)
5. Horrocks I,: DAML+OIL: a reason-able web ontology language, in the Proceedings of EDBT (2002)
6. "ICENI Virtual Organisation Management", London e-Science Centre, UK (2001)
7. Introna L, Moore H, Cushman M.: The Virtual Organisation – Technical or Social Innovation? Lessons from the Film Industry, Working Paper Series 72, Department of Information Systems, London School of Economics and Political Science, UK (2002)
8. Klyne G and Carroll J.: Resource Description Framework (RDF): Concepts and Abstract Syntax, W3C, http://www.w3.org/TR/rdf-concepts/ (2004)
9. Song W.: Semantic Issues in the Grid computing and Web Services, in the Proceedings of International Conference on Management of e-Commerce and e-Government, Nanchang, China (2003)
10. Song W and Li X.: Semantic Modeling for Virtual Organization: A Case for Virtual Course, to appear in Advances in Information Systems Development - Bridging the Gap between Academia and Industry, (eds.) Nilsson A. and Gustas R., Springer (2005)
11. Zhang J-Y and Li X-M.: The Model, Architecture and Mechanism Behind *Realcourse*, the Proceedings of International Symposium on Parallel and Distributed Applications (2004).
12. Zhuge, H.: Component-based workflow systems development, Decision Support Systems, Vol. 35, Elsevier (2003) 517-536

Incorporating Data Movement into Grid Task Scheduling

Xiaoshan He and Xian-He Sun

Department of Computer Science, Illinois Institute of Technology,
Chicago, Illinois, 60616, USA
{hexiaos, sun}@iit.edu

Abstract. Task Scheduling is a critical design issue of distributed computing. The emerging Grid computing infrastructure consists of heterogeneous resources in widely distributed autonomous domains and makes task scheduling even more challenging. Grid considers both static, unmovable hardware and moveable, replicable data as computing resources. While intensive research has been done on task scheduling on hardware computing resources and on data replication protocols, how to incorporate data movement into task scheduling seamlessly is unrevealed. We consider data movement as a dimension of task scheduling. A dynamic data structure, Data Distance Table (DDT), is proposed to provide real-time data distribution and communication information. Based on DDT, a data-conscious task scheduling heuristics is introduced to minimize the data access delay. A simulated Grid environment is set up to test the efficiency of the newly proposed algorithm. Experimental results show that for data intensive tasks, the dynamic data-conscious scheduling outperforms the conventional Min-Min significantly.

1 Introduction

Grid computing provides a seamless access to immerse network resources, such as high-performance computers and networks, or otherwise unavailable data files. The widely available network resources, however, are geographically distributed, heterogeneous, and under autonomous administration domains. Task scheduling is a vital issue of Grid computing, and, on the other hand, many technical challenges need to be addressed before an efficient task scheduling strategy can be developed. In this study, incorporating data movement and replication into task scheduling is proposed. Consequently, a light-weighted dynamic adjustable strategy for integrating data movement delay with task execution scheduling is introduced. A scheduling heuristic, which treats data as one dimension of the quality of service, is derived to address the issue of data-conscious task scheduling of Grid computing.

Intensive research has been conducted in parallel and distributed task scheduling [1, 2, 3]. Task scheduling can be classified as parallel scheduling, where the tasks may be from the same application and have inherent dependence relations, and metatask scheduling, where the tasks are independent from each other [4, 5, 6]. Current Grid scheduling research has been focusing on metatask scheduling. We will focus on metatask scheduling in this study as well. There are two categories of modes of metatask: Online mode and batch mode. Online mode schedules a task upon its arrival whereas batch mode schedules the tasks periodically after a fixed time period.

H. Zhuge and G.C. Fox (Eds.): GCC 2005, LNCS 3795, pp. 394–405, 2005.

Batch mode is a better choice for busy systems. Among various batch mode scheduling heuristics, the Min-Min is the most frequently used heuristic. In this work, we consider data movement as a factor of QoS requests, and we extend Min-Min to integrate the dynamic adjustment of data access cost, thus achieving a better scheduling of Grid tasks.

Data has been recognized as an important resource of Grid computing. Some recent works have addressed data movement in task scheduling. Current research is developed along two directions: allocate the task to where the data is, and move the data to where the task is. Researches on integrating data movement with task scheduling seamlessly, however, is rare. Xsufferage [7] considers the data location in task scheduling. It finds the "site-level sufferage value" to avoid unnecessary data replication. For each task and each site, the function f computes the minimum completion times of the task over the hosts in the site. This minimum is called site-level completion time. For each task, f returns the difference between the second minimum and the minimum site-level completion time. The difference is called site-level sufferage value. Xsufferage allocates task close to data in order to reduce data movement, but does not incorporate the data movement into the scheduling.

Other scheduling heuristics for data-intensive tasks include [8]. [8] tries to statistically predict the data request and get data ready before it is called. It schedules data movement based on its prediction, and a decoupling strategy is proposed to separate data movement scheduling from task scheduling. Within the decoupled framework, data movements are operated in a decoupled, asynchronous process on the basis of observed data access patterns and load. [8] contributes to data usage prediction and moves the data to where the task is, but tries to schedule data and task separately. In this study, we intend to incorporate data movement into task scheduling. We use a newly introduced data structure to measure the dynamic data movement cost, and integrate this cost into an extended Min-Min scheduling heuristics. We dynamically adjust data replica based algorithm to get data ready on under-utilized sites, before possible load imbalance occurs.

The organization of this paper is as follows. In section 2, the Grid scheduling model deployed in this study is introduced. Then, a dynamic adjusting strategy for moveable resources is proposed in section 3. Section 4 introduces a simulated Grid environment. In section 5, the experimental results are presented and discussed. We conclude this study in section 6.

2 The Scheduling Model in Grid

The Grid considered in this study is composed of a number of non-dedicated hosts and each host is composed of several computational resources, which may be homogeneous or heterogeneous. To simulate the computational hosts, we represent each host with three local parameters for the utilization, arrival rate, and standard deviation of service time, respectively. These parameters are the recorded average performance of the computing hosts. The host set is the set of available hosts in the Grid:

$$Hosts = \{H_1, H_2, ..., H_m\} \tag{1}$$

Each host in Hosts is composed of the processor sets P_m available in H_m, and the data Set D_m available in H_m.

$$H_m = P_m \cup D_m \tag{2}$$

where D_m is the set of all the data sets available in S_m

$$D_m = \bigcup_{d_n\_is\_on\_host\_m} d_n \tag{3}$$

The metatask to be scheduled is composed of a set of independent tasks that is to be executed remotely: $M = \{T_1, T_2, \ldots, T_l\}$. For each of those independent tasks T_i, it has a set of independent subtasks: $T_i = \{t_{i1}, t_{i2}, \ldots, t_{ij}\}$. t_{ij} denotes the subtask j of task T_i. I_{ij} denotes the input data requested by the subtask j of task T_i. Therefore, the input data requested by task i is I_i:

$$I_i = \bigcup_{j=1}^{|T_i|} I_{ij} \tag{4}$$

A scheduler allocates tasks by selecting the "best" match from a pool of available resources. Before moving to the scheduling heuristics, let us first review some terms and definitions [5, 6].

The expected execution time ET_{ij} of task t_i on machine m_j is defined as the amount of time taken by m_j to execute t_i given that m_j has no load when t_i is assigned. The expected completion time CT_{ij} of task t_i on machine m_j is defined as the wall-clock time at which m_j completes t_i (after having finished any previously assigned tasks). Let m be the total number of the machines in the H/C suite. Let K be the set containing the tasks that will be used in a given test set for evaluating heuristics in the study. Let the arrival time of task t_i be a_i, and the beginning time of t_i be b_i. From the above definitions, $CT_{ij} = b_i + ET_{ij}$. Let CT_i be CT_{ij}, where machine j is assigned to execute task i. The makespan for the complete schedule is then defined as $max\{t_i \in K\}$ (CT_i). Makespan is a measure of the throughput of the heterogeneous computing system. The objective of Grid scheduling is to minimize the makespan. It is well known that the problem of deciding on an optimal assignment of tasks to resources is NP-complete. Heuristics are developed to solve the NP-complete problem. In this paper, we mount dynamic data adjusting to task scheduling heuristics to achieve efficient Grid task scheduling.

A *scheduling hole* is defined as an idle period of a host between two busy periods. Scheduling holes may be a result of the mismatching of resources and tasks, e.g. the idle host is not qualified to execute waiting tasks. For tasks with data requests, a host without the requested data has to wait for the qualified tasks, so it may cause idling. Meanwhile, tasks that need to access critical data have to wait in the waiting queue to access the data, which even more likely lead to scheduling holes. Integrating data movement with task scheduling will reduce the scheduling holes and, therefore, maximize the host utilization and achieve a better makespan.

3 Dynamic Adjusting Strategy for Moveable Resources

In Grid task scheduling, we not only are concerned with the availability of those hardware static resources, but also with moveable software resources, such as data that reside in a host. For this type of the resource, the load imbalance resulted from resource constraints could be alleviated by adjusting the resource attributes of the hosts. In this section, we intend to investigate those moveable resources, such as data replica, as one dimension of QoS. A dynamic adjusting strategy for such problems is proposed to address the QoS scheduling in data-intensive applications.

In a Grid environment, if a data is only statically available in one host, the executions of tasks that request the data are restricted to that host. Thus, an undesirable congestion brought by data requests from tasks occurs on the host with the critical data. To avoid such congestion, we could leverage the data distribution of the hosts. We define the data whose replica is requested by tasks as a QoS in the system as critical data. The critical data could be replicated to other hosts, so that more hosts are able to provide a certain level of QoS. However, we have to be aware that the replication of data needs communication cost. A model is proposed to implement the scheduling strategy that decides if the replication is worthwhile by evaluating if the cost of the communication surpasses the computation delay brought by scheduling congestion. We have made the assumption that the replicated data we referred to here are the input data that are read-only. Such cases occur in the application, such as gene comparison, etc.

3.1 Data Distance Table

To make the leverage between communication cost of the data replication and the queuing time for the host with data, we have to formulize the information of data replica placement of the hosts and the communication cost of each data replication. A dynamic *data distance table* (DDT), is generated to record the information.

The *data distance* represents the distance between data copy d_n and host H_m. The *data distance* decides the communication cost of replicating data d_n to host H_m. *Data distance* is defined as:

$$dist_{nm} = \begin{cases} 0 & \text{if } d_n \in D_m \\ \dfrac{\min(rep\_time\_mk)}{rep\_time\_std} & \text{if } d_n \notin D_m \end{cases} \tag{5}$$

So, if data n is in host m, then $dist_{ij}$ will be 0. If data n is not in host m, then $dist_{ij}$ will depend on the communication time from host m to the nearest host k that has data n. The communication cost of data replication is normalized by a standard communication time, which is chose as the shortest path between any two hosts. To reflect the real time Grid data distribution, the table is updated once a replication of data happens. Therefore, the data replica placement and the communication cost of replication are represented by a dynamic data distance table, which may look like:

Table 1. A sample data distance table

	h_1	h_2	h_3	h_4
d_1	0	1.2	2	0
d_2	1.5	0	1.5	3
d_3	0	3	0	1.5
d_4	4	2	2	0

A row in the table represents a dataset's distances to each host. A column in the table represents the distance of different datasets to a host. The value of each entry $dist_{ij}$ depends on both the replica of data n and host m, and the communication cost of data *n* to host *m*.

The DDT not only provides the information of data distribution, but also the real time network performance. It enables the calculation of communication cost to be independent from the scheduling heuristic, and thus makes the scheduling heuristic light-weighted. In the heuristic presented in the next subsection, the replication decision is made based on the DDT. DDT is updated periodically based on the data distribution, and the network performance. By looking up the DDT, the nearest data are located, so that the heuristic is well informed when making data replication decision. Hence, a light-weighted data-conscious scheduling heuristic is achieved.

3.2 A Data-Conscious Scheduling Heuristic

We have to leverage the communication cost of a data replication with the queuing time of the task in the host with critical data. Intuitively, a data replication can be considered when 1) the communication time can overlap with computing time; and 2) the communication time is less than the data access queuing time on the host with data. However, we have to consider other factors, such as processing overhead and the data update cost.

If we do not replicate the data, undesirable scheduling holes may exist on the receiver hosts due to the data access delay. If we replicate the data at the execution time of tasks, the scheduling holes may also appear, resulting from the data replication delay. Since the scheduling holes could be filled by executing tasks that do not need the critical data, the detriment brought by scheduling holes varies in different situations. So it is necessary to make a tradeoff between the detriment brought by scheduling holes and computation time gain.

However, if the extra copy of the data is created, extra communication cost will be paid for the data replication. The extra communication cost includes the notification of the modification and another round of sending data. A straightforward way to compromise is to compare the two makespan brought by scheduling with and without data replication. If the scheduling with data replication results in a smaller makespan, we replicate the critical data. Otherwise, we do not replicate.

In our heuristics, the replication of datasets should take place when replication of some datasets could bring a shorter makespan of the metatask. The source host of the dataset to be replicated should be an over-loaded host, a host that is queued while scheduling holes exist at other hosts due to the queuing delay. We select a threshold of the queue to decide the time to replicate. Here in our algorithm, we select the threshold as 0. This means we will test to see if we need replication once there are tasks in the queue. As the complexity of the algorithm is low, we trade the computation cost of scheduling heuristic for less cost on waiting for the data.

Based on these considerations, we propose our data-conscious scheduling heuristic in Figure 1, where MCT denotes the Minimum Completion Time of the current metatask according to the scheduling.

```
While there are tasks to be scheduled
   For each task i in M but not run yet
         For all H_m in Hosts
             Compute MCT_im.
         Endfor
         MCT_i0 = min (MCT_im)
         If subtask t_ij needs any data d_n in set I_i
             For all H_m in Hosts
                Compute MCT'_im based on copying nearest
            copy of data_j to m by looking up
                the DDT
             Endfor
             MCT'_i0 = min (MCT'_im)
             If MCT'_i0 < MCT_i0
                 Copy data_j from host 1 to host r
      MCT_min = MCT'_i0
             Else
                 MCT_min = MCT_i0
          Else
               MCT_min = MCT_i0
   Endfor
   Schedule MCT_min
Endwhile
```

Fig. 1. Data-conscious Scheduling Heuristic

In the data-conscious scheduling heuristic, we consider the matching of the data request and data replica between the tasks and hosts based on the conventional Min-Min. Similar to Min-Min, the data-conscious scheduling heuristic computes MCT_{im}, the minimum completion times of each task on all the hosts at the start. Then, we get the MCT_{i0} according to the Min-Min heuristic. Instead of selecting the task/host pair, we take a test on all the tasks that request data in the metatask: For each task i with data request $data_j$, firstly, compute the MCT'_{im} based on the replication of $data_j$ for all the m hosts available using the information provided by dynamic *data distance table (DDT)*. Secondly, among the m data replications, algorithm finds the one with the minimum completion time MCT'_{i0}. If MCT'_{i0} is less than the minimum completion time before the replication MCT_{i0}, we make the data replication that result in MCT'_{i0}, and set it as MCT_{min}. Otherwise, we do not make the replication. By repeating the same process as we described on all the tasks, we get a group of data replications and the minimum completion time MCT_{min} for each task. We schedule the data replication, if necessary, and the task/host pair that results in minimum MCT_{min}. The scheduling process will be repeated till all tasks are scheduled. The data-conscious scheduling heuristic will be executed at every scheduling event.

3.3 A Sample Scenario

Tables 2 and 3 give a scenario in which the data-conscious scheduling heuristic outperforms the Min-Min. It shows the expected execution time of four tasks on two hosts. The hosts are assumed to be idle in the beginning. In this particular case, the Min-Min heuristic gives a makespan of 11, whereas the data-conscious scheduling heuristic gives a makespan of 9. Figures 2 and 3 give a pictorial representation of the assignments made for the case in Table 2 and 3.

Table 2 shows the four tasks with their data requests. The entry of required data indicates the data d that is requested by task *i*. Task 4 does not have data request, so it is x. The execution time of the four tasks is assumed to be the same on the two hosts. Table 3 shows the data distribution on two hosts. In this case, data 1, 2, 3 initially reside in host 1, and data 4 is in host 2. The communication cost of data replication is assumed to be 1.

Table 2. The data request of 4 tasks

Task	Execution Time	Required Data
t_1	4	1
t_2	5	2
t_3	2	3
t_4	3	x

Table 3. The data distribution on 2 hosts

Machine	Data Hosted
1	1, 2, 3
2	4

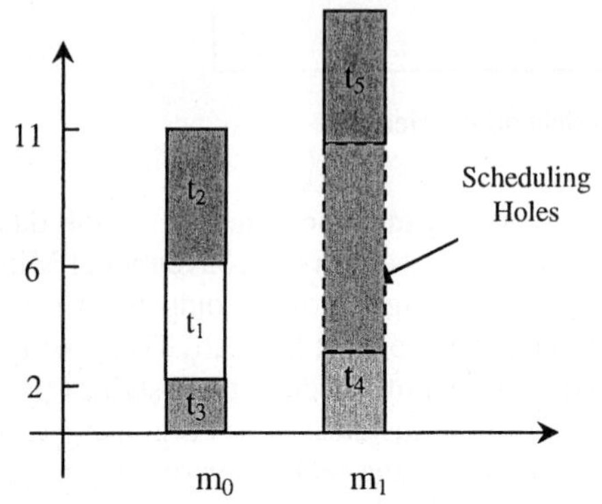

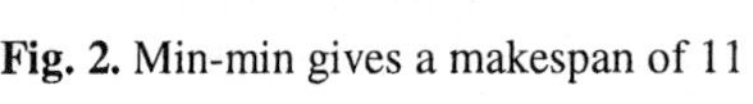

Fig. 2. Min-min gives a makespan of 11

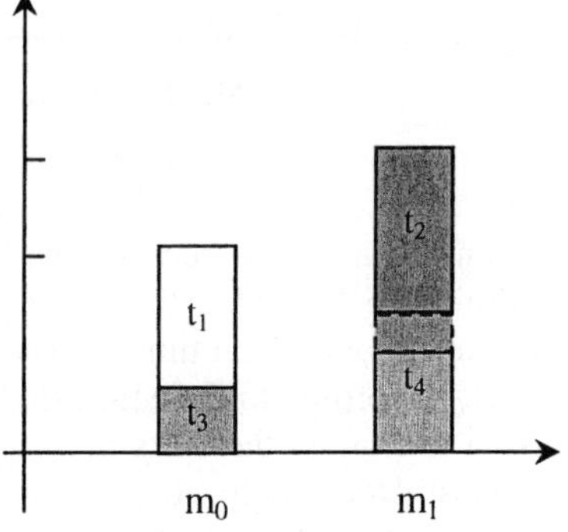

Fig. 3. Data-conscious scheduling heuristic gives a makespan of 9

4 Implementation Details

The goal of implementing the simulation model is to demonstrate the efficiency of our dynamic adjusting strategy. The model consists of a simulated Grid environment and a scheduler that implements different scheduling strategies. The system is illustrated in Figure 4.

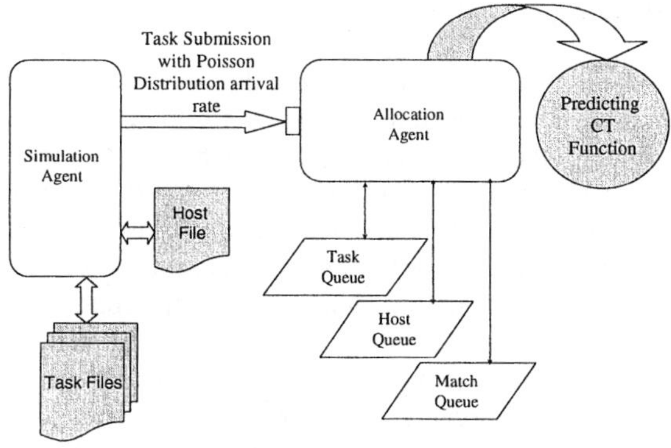

Fig. 4. The scheduling model in a simulated Grid environment

Task Attributes. For each task, the attributes of the task include interarrival time, number of subtasks, data request, and the workloads of the subtasks. The task arrival rate follows the Poisson distribution. The number of the subtasks is generated to randomly fall from 1 to 20. The data request is generated according to different request ratios. The workloads of the subtasks are generated randomly between 1000 and 2000.

Machine Attributes. For each set of machines, the attributes of the machine include number of workstations (or computing nodes), replica of the data, and the information of each workstation, which includes the utilization, arrival rate, and standard deviation of service time. Each data initially has only one copy in the system. Data sizes vary from 0 to 5, and 20 to 40 unit sizes in two experiments. The network speeds between hosts are set to vary from 0 to 1.

5 Experimental Results

5.1 Experiments Overview

We have developed a simulator to compare the performance of the data-conscious scheduling heuristic and the general Min-Min [9] under the same load conditions representing a wide variety of system states. In this simulator, we fix the parameters of the hosts during all these simulations with four data request and distribution scenarios. In addition, we compare the scheduling performance under different communication cost of the data replication. The metric of the comparison is the makespan of the tasks.

Based on the analysis above, the experimental evaluation of the scheduling algorithm is performed in two parts. In the first part, the data-conscious scheduling heuristics and the general Min-Min heuristics will be compared in four data request and distribution scenarios, respectively, with smaller data set size, and thus smaller communication cost. In the second part, the effect of the scheduling frequency will be discussed using a larger data size, thus, larger communication cost, which is averagely about four times as much as in the first experiment.

5.2 Host and Task Setup

As we mentioned before, all configurations about the hosts remain the same during all the simulations. The four non-dedicated networks are settled as follows. Each network has 20 workstations and the local parameters, such as *util*, *arri* and *serstd*, are generated randomly in given scope, such as *util* is from 0.0 to 1.0, arriving rate is from 0.01 to 0.15 and *serstd* is about 25. This setup makes this Grid non-dedicated and heterogeneous. For the data status, we assume there are 60 different data on four hosts. Initially, there is only on copy for each data. The distribution of the data on four hosts varies in the four scenarios. In scenarios (a) and (b), the distribution of the data is uneven. Host 1 has 30 data whereas the host 2, 3, and 4 each has 10 data. In scenarios (c) and (d), the data is evenly distributed. All four hosts have 15 data.

A hundred independent tasks are created based on Poisson distribution. Each task has randomly 1-20 subtasks and each subtask has randomly 1000-2000 work demand. The running time interval is one time unit. For data request, we assume each task requests exactly one data or requests none. The data requests of 100 tasks vary in the four scenarios. In scenarios (a) and (c), the data request percentage from tasks is 50%, whereas in scenarios (b) and (d), the data request percentage from tasks is 35%. Based on the actual world, the four different scenarios simulated are shown in Table 4:

Table 4. The four scenarios of data request and distribution

Scenarios	Date Request Task %	Data Distribution on the 4 Hosts
a	50%	30, 10, 10, 10
b	35%	30, 10, 10, 10
c	35%	15, 15, 15, 15
d	50%	15, 15, 15, 15

5.3 The Comparison Based on Smaller Data Size

For each scenario presented in the previous section, we compare the performance of the general Min-Min with the data-conscious scheduling heuristics. For each scenario, we create the 100 tasks 100 times independently and get the average makespan by two algorithms 100 times. The data size is randomly between 0 to 5 unit sizes. Figure 5 and Table 5 show the comparison. The data is in unit size.

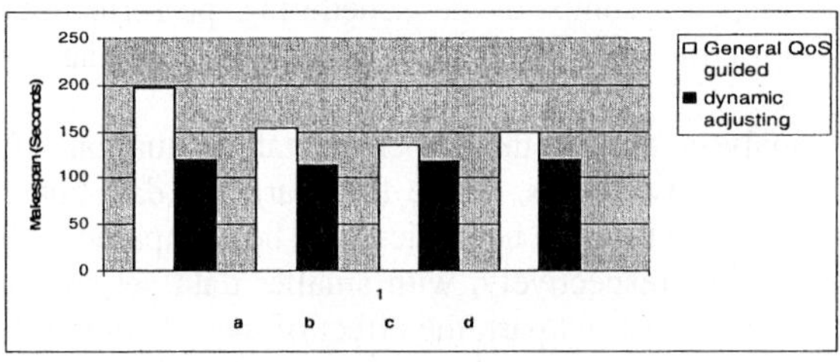

Fig. 5. The comparison based on data size of 0 to 5 unit size

As shown in Figure 5, for all four scenarios the dynamic adjusting scheduling heuristics for data-intensive task outperforms the general Min-Min heuristics. The makespan using data-conscious scheduling heuristics can be as much as 46.02% shorter than that using the general Min-Min. For scenario (a), where the tasks that request the data contribute 50% of the metatask and the data are unevenly distributed, the performance gain reaches as high as 38.57%. For scenario (b), where the tasks that request data are in lower density (35%), a satisfactory performance gain of 25.46% is acquired. For scenario (c), where only 35% of the tasks request data and the data distribution becomes even, the performance gain of the data-conscious scheduling heuristics is relatively small, i.e., 13.21% better than the general Min-Min. Finally, in scenario (d), the data request rate of tasks becomes 50% with all data evenly distributed on the hosts, and the performance gain is 19.70%.

5.4 The Comparison Based on Larger Data Size

The size of the data plays an important role in the efficiency of the data-conscious scheduling heuristics, since the larger the data size is, the larger the communication cost is. If the communication cost is too high, we would be less likely to overlap the communication of the data by the computation of execution of other tasks.

In this subsection, we compare the performance of the general Min-Min heuristics with the data-conscious scheduling heuristic under different data sizes. The data sizes are randomly generated between 20 to 40 unit sizes. For each scenario, we create the 100 tasks 100 times independently and get the average makespan by two algorithms 100 times. Table 5 and Figure 6 show the comparison. The data is in unit size.

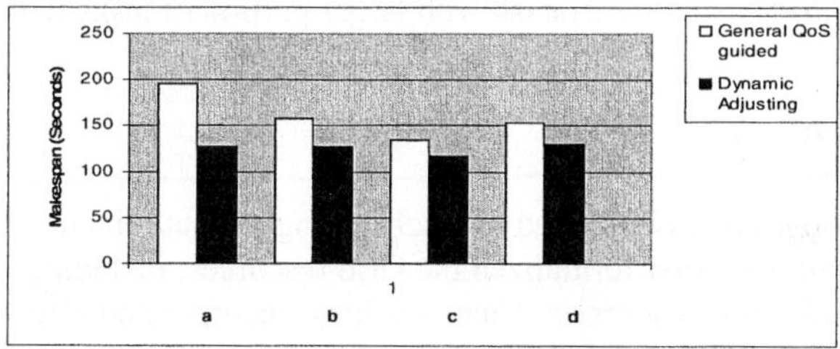

Fig. 6. The comparison based on data size of 20 to 40 unit size

As shown in Figure 6, for all four scenarios the general Min-Min heuristic is outperformed by data-conscious scheduling heuristics. The best performance gain of the data-conscious scheduling heuristics over general Min-Min can be as much as 33.20%. For scenario (a), where the tasks that request the data contribute 50% of the metatask and the data are unevenly distributed, the performance gain reaches as high as 33.20%. For scenario (b), where the tasks that request data are in lower density (35%), a satisfactory performance gain of 18.24% is acquired. For scenario (c), where only 35% of the tasks request data and the data distribution becomes even, the performance gain of the data-conscious scheduling heuristics is relatively small, i.e., 12.96% better than the general Min-Min. Finally, in scenario (d), the data request rate of tasks becomes 50% with all data evenly distributed on the hosts, and the performance gain is 13.95%.

Table 5. The experiment result of the comparison

Scenarios	Gain (0-5)	Gain (20-40)	Date Request Task %	Data Distribution on the 4 Hosts
a	38.57%	33.20%	50%	30, 10, 10, 10
b	25.46%	18.24%	35%	30, 10, 10, 10
c	13.21%	12.96%	35%	15, 15, 15, 15
d	19.70%	13.95%	50%	15, 15, 15, 15

Table 5 shows the performance gain of the comparison. The green parts in the table show the performance gains of the four scenarios, according to different data sizes. The first column is measured based on the relatively smaller data sizes that are randomly between 0 to 5 unit sizes. The second column is measured based on the relatively larger data sizes that are between 20 and 40 unit size.

From the table, we can conclude that our dynamic adjusting heuristics outperforms the general Min-Min. Especially, when the data is not evenly distributed, our dynamic adjusting strategy greatly reduces the makespan of a metatask. This is because our dynamic adjusting strategy can dynamically replicate the data among hosts. Hence, it is able to alleviate the load balance caused by the improper distribution data replica. Further, the metatask with a larger portion of tasks with data requests will benefit more from our dynamic adjusting strategy. The reason is that the denser the tasks with data request (constraints), the more likely hosts are to be imbalanced with load. Our strategy performs real-time adjusting on the data replica distribution. Therefore, it results in better makespan on metatask with larger portion of tasks with data request.

6 Conclusion

In this study, we have investigated the scheduling of data-intensive tasks in Grid environments. We have first formulized the Grid resources, including static resources, as well as the movable resources. Then, we have incorporated data movement into Grid task scheduling. The scheduling holes caused by the data access delay have been reduced through integrating data movement into the traditional Min-Min scheduling heuristics. By replicating the data, a tradeoff has been made between the communication cost and load balance of the hosts. The lack of administration-level information in a Grid computing environment has been redeemed by the newly introduced dynamic data distance table (DDT) data structure, which provides the sufficient real-time information for the data replication decision making. A dynamic adjusting scheduling heuristics has been proposed.

To verify our scheduling heuristics, a simulation architecture of Grid environment has been introduced. The simulation is composed of two parts: the simulation agent generates the task and host information, whereas the allocation agent executes the scheduling algorithms. We have carried out a series of experiments based on the simulation environment. Experimental results show that the new data-conscious dynamic adjusting scheduling heuristics outperforms the general Min-Min significantly for data intensive application, especially when the critical data are unevenly distributed.

Acknowledgments

This research was supported in part by national science foundation under NSF grant EIA-0130673, ANI-0123930, and by Army Research Office under ARO grant DAAD19-01-1-0432.

References

1. Buyya, R., Murshed, M., Abramson, D.: A Deadline and Budget Constrained Cost-Time Optimization Algorithm for Scheduling Task Farming Applications on Global Grids. 2002 Intl. Conference on Parallel and Distributed Processing Techniques and Applications (PDPTA'02), Las Vegas, Nevada, USA, (2002)
2. Casanova, H., Legrand, A., Zagorodnov, D., Berman, F.: Heuristics for Scheduling Parameter Sweep applications in Grid environments. Proceedings of the 9th Heterogeneous Computing workshop (HCW'2000) 349-363.
3. Raman, R., Livny, M., Solomon, M.: Matchmaking: Distributed Resource Management for High Throughput Computing. Proceedings of the Seventh IEEE International Symposium on High Performance Distributed Computing, July 28-31, 1998, Chicago, IL
4. T. D. Braun, H. J. Siegel, N. Beck, L. Boloni, M. Maheswaran, A. I. Reuther, J. P. Robertson, M. D. Theys, and B. Yao: A taxonomy for describing matching and scheduling heuristics for mixed-machine heterogeneous computing systems. IEEE Workshop on Advances in Parallel and Distributed Systems (1998) 330-335.
5. M. Maheswaran, S. Ali, H. J. Siegel, D. Hensgen, and R. Freund, ``Dynamic mapping of a class of independent tasks onto heterogeneous computing systems," 8th IEEE Heterogeneous Computing Workshop (HCW '99), San Juan, Puerto Rico (1999) 30-44
6. Pinedo, M.: Scheduling: Theory, Algorithms, and Systems, Prentice Hall, Englewood Cliffs, NJ (1995)
7. Henri Casanova, Graziano Obertelli, Francine Berman and Rich Wolski, "The AppLeS Parameter Sweep Template: User-Level Middleware for the Grid", Proceedings of the Super Computing Conference (SC'2000), (2000)
8. Kavitha Ranganathan and Ian Foster. “Decoupling Computation and Data Scheduling in Distributed Data Intensive Applications”. International Symposium for High Performance Distributed Computing (HPDC-11), Edinburgh, July 2002.
9. Xiaoshan He, Xian-He Sun, and Gregor von Laszewski, "QoS Guided Min-Min Heuristic for Grid Task Scheduling", Journal of Computer Science and Technology, Special Issue on Grid Computing, 18(4), 2003.

An Integration of Global and Enterprise Grid Computing: Gridbus Broker and Xgrid Perspective

Marcos Dias de Assunção[1,2], Krishna Nadiminti[1], Srikumar Venugopal[1], Tianchi Ma[1], and Rajkumar Buyya[1,2]

[1] Grid Computing and Distributed Systems Laboratory
[2] NICTA Victoria Laboratory,
Department of Computer Science and Software Engineering,
The University of Melbourne,
Parkville Campus, Melbourne, VIC 3010, Australia
{marcosd, kna, srikumar, tcma, raj}@cs.mu.oz.au
http://www.gridbus.org

Abstract. In this work, we present two perspectives of Grid computing by using two different Grid middleware as examples: an Enterprise Grid using Xgrid and a Global Grid with Gridbus. We also present the integration of Enterprise and Global Grids by proposing the integration of Gridbus Broker with diverse enterprise Grid middleware including Xgrid, PBS, Condor and SGE. The sample performance results demonstrate the usefulness of this integration effort.

1 Introduction

Improvements in communication and computing technology have led to the possibility of aggregating diverse, globally distributed, computing and storage resources to form what is now commonly known as Grid [1]. In order to provide users with such a seamless computing environment as the Grid, the middleware for Grid systems need to solve several challenges originating from the inherent features of the Grid, such as heterogeneity [21].

Grids can be classified in two ways, according to their architecture and presence. Considering their presence, we can define two main categories: global Grids and enterprise Grids. These two categories have varying characteristics and are suitable for different scenarios. Global Grids are established over the public Internet, are characterized by a global presence, comprise of highly heterogeneous resources, present more sophisticated security mechanisms, focus on single sign-on and are mostly batch-job oriented [10]. Enterprise Grids consist of resources spread across an enterprise and provide services to users within that enterprise and are managed by a single organization [12]. They can be deployed within large corporations that have a global presence though they are limited to a single enterprise [13]. Such Grids are more concerned with cycle stealing from unused desktops within enterprises and security mechanism design is not as difficult as it is for global Grids since they are mostly established within the borders of a single organization [11].

Although these Grids present different functions and abilities, organizations are moving towards using both the heterogeneous computing and storage capabilities of global Grids along with the utility maximization offered by enterprise Grids. For

H. Zhuge and G.C. Fox (Eds.): GCC 2005, LNCS 3795, pp. 406–417, 2005.

example, a company may want to fetch data from a data repository shared by academic and enterprises but leverage its infrastructure by processing the data on its own enterprise Grid. Organizations may also want to go beyond their Grids to share resources with new partners when their applications require computing resources that surpass what their own Grids can offer [12]. In this way, by using extra resources offered by other partners they can improve their performance as well as increasing their agility. We need middleware to integrate global and enterprise Grids in order to enable such scenario.

Integration of global and enterprise Grid middleware is motivated by offering a uniform API that helps users to write applications for all kind of Grid middleware. In this paper, we present how this was achieved by extending Gridbus Broker [2] to support four different middlewares: Xgrid [4], PBS [15], Condor [14] and SGE [16]. Xgrid is a Grid technology that provides means to build Grids of Mac OS X based computers. PBS is a batch queuing system that provides controls over initiating or scheduling execution of batch jobs. SGE provides distributed resource management software for wide ranging requirements from compute farms to Grid computing. Similarly, Condor supports high throughput computing on collections of distributed computing resources. As a case study, we present the process of integrating Xgrid with Gridbus Broker in detail.

The remainder of this paper is organized as follows. Section 2 presents a discussion about middleware and the positioning of the broker in integrating enterprise and global Grids. We also discuss in detail the characteristics of the Apple's Xgrid technology and justify why we chose to integrate the broker with this middleware. We demonstrate how we have been developing interfaces to different middleware in Section 3. In Section 4, we present how to implement an interface between the Gridbus Broker and Xgrid as a case study. Section 5 presents some experiments demonstrating the usability of the interface. We describe related work in Section 6. Finally, Section 7 presents future work and concludes the paper.

2 Grid Middleware and Background Technologies

During the last few years, research communities have proposed and developed several middlewares for Grid computing that each address issues such as security, uniform access, dynamic discovery, aggregation and quality-of-service differently. Although there have been efforts of standardizing various middleware interfaces and functions [22], they still present some distinguishing characteristics that need to be tackled individually. A layered view for Grid architecture is commonly adopted [21].

The *Fabric* layer provides resources for which the shared access is mediated. Components of the fabric layer interface provide specific functions and services that are used by operations in the upper layers. *Low-level* middleware offers services such as remote process management, co-allocation of resources, storage access, information registration and discovery and security. These services abstract the complexity and heterogeneity of the fabric level by providing a consistent method for accessing distributed resources [5]. *User-level* middleware uses the uniform interfaces provided by the low-level middleware to provide higher-level abstractions and services [6]. Several *applications* have been developed on top of these layers by using Grid-enabled languages and utilities.

Nowadays, Grid technologies are available for UNIX based OSes and Windows, while Xgrid is an intent to construct Grids of Mac computers. Moreover, there is a great intent in integrating such enterprise Grid technologies with global Grids so that enterprises can maximize their utility and tap into resources across several organizations. The user level middleware and tools such as a broker play an important role in this scenario. Considering these factors, we can perceive that providing a broker for these technologies, that facilitates the aggregation, selection and scheduling of applications in different technologies, is essential.

The Gridbus Broker supports computational and data Grid applications [2] and its architecture has an emphasis on simplicity, extensibility and platform independence. The main design principles of the broker include:

- Assume nothing about the environment: It is just assumed that low-level middleware is able to provide an interface to submit and monitor a job.
- Client-centric design: the broker does not depend on metrics provided by the resources. No software, besides the middleware itself, needs to be installed on resource side.
- Extensibility is the key: the broker is extensible in many ways. We can implement support for new middleware; new information sources can be added; and the XML-based language used to specify jobs and resources is highly extensible.

2.1 The Xgrid Architecture

Xgrid's architecture is similar to other desktop middleware systems such as Condor, and consists of the following components: agents, clients and the controller [9]. In the normal flow of execution, clients originate and submit jobs to the controller; they are split into tasks by the controller and sent on to agents. The agents execute tasks and return results to the controller, which collects them and reports to the client.

Some features provided by Xgrid include [8]: (a) easy Grid configuration and deployment; (b) straightforward and flexible job submission; (c) Kerberos single sign-on and password based authentication; (d) hides complex issues such as data distribution, job execution, and result aggregation from the user; (e) uses open standards; and (f) provides tools for the customization of the job submission process;

Some ongoing research projects are currently using Xgrid. For example, the Xgrid at Stanford is a project from Stanford University [7] and aims at harnessing processing cycles from computers from all over the world. The purpose is to *modelize* the conformational changes of the beta 2 adrenergic receptor, and have a better understanding of its pharmacology.

3 Interface to Different Enterprise and Global Grid Middleware

In order to integrate a different middleware into the broker, an actuator specific to that middleware needs to be implemented; it is responsible for dispatching and monitoring the job. This is done by extending two classes: `ComputeServer` and `JobWrapper`. The implementation of the `JobWrapper` class implements methods necessary for job submission to a resource by using the corresponding middleware, while `ComputeServer` provides means to query the job execution status and discover server's properties.

Interfaces to diverse middleware were implemented, and are summarized in Table 1. Currently, we have implemented adaptors for heterogeneous middleware systems, namely Fork (for forking jobs on local UNIX-like systems), Xgrid, PBS (Portable Batch System), SGE (Sun N1 Grid Engine) and Condor. As we know, PBS, SGE and Condor are all technically mature and widely-adopted computational management middleware for clusters and LAN-based distributed systems. They can link nodes to follow their particular structure so that optimizations could be carried on the managed domain, in order to achieve respective goals. The broker will abstract these irregular structures into general computational resources, while keeping the benefit and autonomy of each middleware.

Conceptually, the middleware implementation works in three "spaces" (Fig. 1). A space is defined as the execution environment, including paths and user accounts. The user space is where users start the broker, as well as the source of all input files and the destination of all output files. The driver working space is a client node (or head node) of the target middleware. The broker provides a dispatcher to control remotely the data and behaviors in the driver working space. The dispatchers also provide the functionality of staging files between the two spaces. The dispatchers are based on some remote logon channels. Currently we have implemented local (meaning the broker itself sits in the driver working space) and SSH (Secure Shell) dispatchers. There exists another space called the middleware inner working space, which is maintained by the middleware systems, on their executing nodes. Also the middleware systems have their own mechanism to stage files and data between the inner working space and their client nodes (that is, the driver working space).

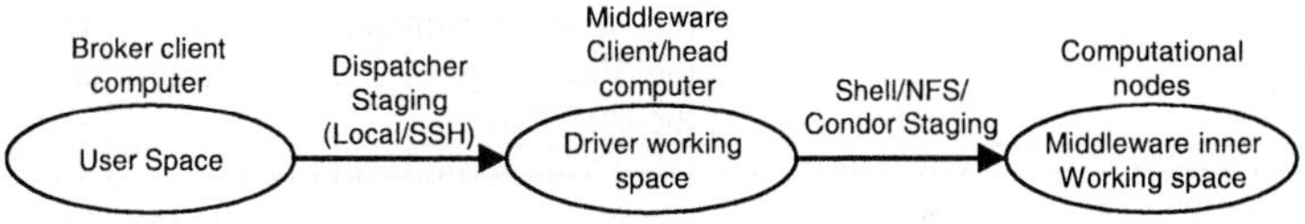

Fig. 1. The three spaces

There is also similar mechanism provided by the Globus Toolkit [20] (by implementing a driver to incorporate middleware with the GRAM service). As stated earlier, Gridbus broker has been designed to support coordinated use of Grid resources that are accessible via Globus or other services. The Gridbus broker aims to provide an environment that scales and supports full utilization of all types of local and remote resources (desktops, supercomputers and clusters). Therefore, we have extended our Gridbus broker so that it can support scheduling of applications on local and remote resources irrespective their access interfaces (e.g., direct access using local interfaces, SSH-based remote access, or PKI/Globus-based access). This is especially useful in case of Xgrid as to the best of our knowledge there is no Globus-based access to Xgrid resources. Thus, our integration solution supports uniform and simultaneous use of local and remote resources regardless their access interfaces or mechanisms.

Table 1. Characteristics of the interfaces for different middleware

Middl.	File Stage-In	File Stage-Out	Execute Job	Query Job Status
Fork	Use symbolic links to avoid an additional copy	Move the output files to the specified directory	Encapsulate the execution and process ID reflection commands into a shell script, then directly execute it, get the process ID from the script's standard output.	Analyze "ps -a" command and obtain the status
Condor	Similar to Fork for NFS. Otherwise, specify the files to-be-staged-in in the condor script	Similar to Fork for NFS. Otherwise, specify the files to-be-staged-out in the condor script	Encapsulate the submission of the condor script into another shell script. Also the shell script is responsible for analyzing the output of the "condor_submit" command while reflecting the condor PID	Analyze the output of the "condor_q" command (executed as a shell script)
SGE	Same as Fork in an NFS system.	Same as Fork in an NFS system.	Explore the suitable queue using a Fork job. Then customize a SGE script for submitting job into the best queue. Another script is responsible for executing the "qsub" command to submit the SGE script and get the SGE PID	Analyze the output of the "qstat" command (executed as a shell script)
PBS	Same as Fork in an NFS system.	Same as Fork in an NFS system.	Find best queue by using a Fork job. Then customize a PBS script for submitting job to the best queue. Another script is executes the "qsub" command to submit the PBS script as well as getting the PBS PID	Analyze the output of the "qstat" command (executed as a shell script)
Xgrid	Copy files to Xgrid input directory.	Move the output files to the specified directory.	Uses Xgrid command line to submit a job. Xgrid ID is used to query job status, redirect output files and delete the job after it was been completed.	Analyze the "xgrid –job status/attributes" command.

Fig. 2 shows a state machine indicating the flow for the broker dispatching jobs to a middleware system. The main steps include file stage-in/out, job execution and job status query. In most cases, we generate a new shell script to interact with the middleware. For different middleware, the driver can adapt to local shell command interfaces. The next sections show how this happens for each middleware.

For the Fork adaptor, it creates symbolic links for stage-in and moves files for stage-out. The driver creates a new process calling the shell script to do the file staging, then execute the job and redirect the stdout and stderr streams to specified files and stages these files back right after their creation. The process ID of the job is reflected in the stdout stream, which is parsed by the broker. The process ID is the job handle. After the job submission, the broker queries job status by analyzing the output of a "ps –a" (for listing all the processes in UNIX-like systems) command. If the job is active or pending, its status can be obtained from the "ps" output, otherwise, the broker parses the stderr stream to determine whether the job has been successfully finished (if there is nothing in the stderr) or failed. If the job is finished, the output files generated by the job are staged back to the broker side.

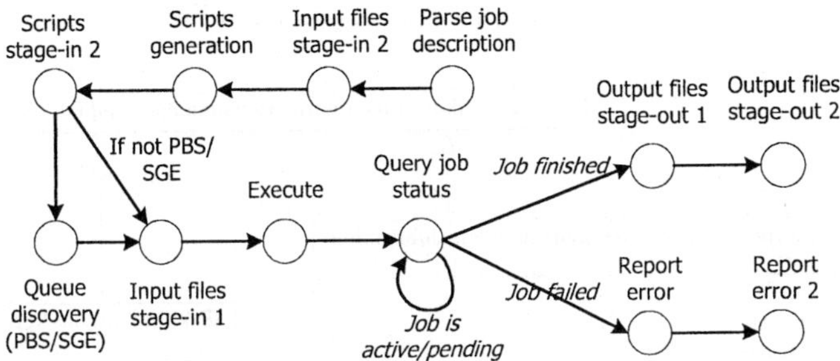

Fig. 2. State machine of the driver flow. For Stage-In and Stage-Out: 1 represents between the user space and driver working space. 2 represents between the driver working space and middleware inner working space.

For PBS and SGE driver, it will not stage the input files between the driver working space and the middleware inner working space, because they are configured to share the same NFS. Nevertheless, the execution scripts describing the job configuration need to be staged to the correct directory specified by the middleware and all file attributes have to be updated so that the files could be accessible under the middleware execution environments. In addition, after the execution, the location of output files (also specified by the middleware) is given to the dispatcher. In PBS/SGE, the computational resources are further partitioned into queues. In our current implementation, the user can either specify the queue(s) to be used by the job submission or let the broker select the most suitable one from all the available queues. In the second case, the broker submits a queue discovery job (marked as a Fork job) prior to the PBS/SGE job in order to select the "best queue". Then the PBS/SGE job is submitted to the specified or selected queue by another job submission shell script by running "qsub" (the job submission interface) to submit the execution script to PBS/SGE. The job handle is set as the PBS PID or SGE PID, which is retrieved from the output of the job submission script. The broker queries the job status by running the command "qstat" through a shell script and analyzing the stdout stream.

With the Condor driver, the staging of both the input and output files is handled automatically by Condor. The adaptor needs to specify all the files in the Condor execution script (needed by Condor for describing the job configuration). Then the adaptor generates a shell script to submit the execution script to Condor and retrieves the Condor PID, which is the job handle for Condor jobs. After the job submission, the broker queries the job status using a shell script by running "condor_q". The *standard* Condor universe provides the feature of checkpointing and process migration. However, as a requirement, the job must be re-linked to the Condor library using "condor_compile", which is unpractical for most jobs without the source code. Therefore, the broker submits the job into a universe called "vanilla".

4 Design and Implementation for Xgrid

As discussed beforehand, the scheduler in Gridbus broker does not assume anything about the diverse middleware that may be utilized by users. Two classes have to be implemented so that the broker is able to submit jobs to different middleware, which are `ComputeServer` and `JobWrapper` as described in Fig. 3.

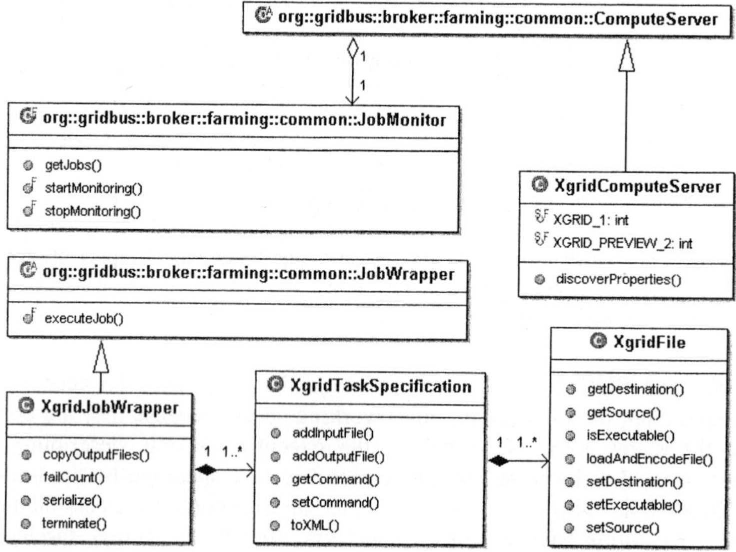

Fig. 3. Class diagram of the Xgrid adaptor

Gridbus Broker aims at being platform independent and client-centric. Following this approach, we assumed that the broker can be installed on a computer under a different operating system from Mac OS X, while it submits jobs to Xgrid. To the best of our knowledge, at the present there is no Xgrid API for Windows or UNIX class operating systems. Therefore, we proceed according to the following steps:

- The user performs the job submission using Gridbus Broker informing it of the scripts or commands to be executed on the remote node as well as the necessary input files.
- The submission is carried out using the command line application on an Xgrid client. Since Xgrid's local working directory is specified, and all files contained in this directory will be compressed into a file that is sent to the controller. The results will be available in the local working directory when the job execution is finished. The broker node can use this node directly if it is being run natively on the same node, or via SSH when it is running on a remote node and possibly under a different operating system.
- Once the job completes in Xgrid, the broker copies the files back from the Xgrid client node to the broker node.

A ComputeServer in the broker represents a resource. To implement an interface to a new middleware one has to extend this class and implement the methods responsible for discovering properties of the resource and for querying the job status, by using the tools specific to the corresponding middleware. For Xgrid, a ComputeServer represents a cluster of Mac computers.

While each middleware has its own representation of a job, the broker uses its own generic representation. The XgridJobWrapper class converts the job description from the broker representation to the Xgrid specific representation and submits it. In the broker, a job can consist of tasks such as SUBSTITUTE, COPY and EXECUTE. The copy tasks may represent input files that are required by the job or files that have to be copied back after the job has been completed.

The Xgrid Version 1.0 accepts XML documents containing serialized input files, description of commands to be executed, arguments. Since the interface was implemented to work for both Technical Preview 2 and 1.0 versions of Xgrid, the input files are copied as a single XML document for version 1.0, and as separate files for the Technical Preview 2 version. When the job is submitted, a job ID is obtained from Xgrid, which is used to monitor the job execution.

5 Performance Evaluation

To evaluate the interfaces to Xgrid, we conducted several experiments. This section describes results of experiments we carried out for (a) Xgrid and (b) combined use of SGE and PBS resources.

5.1 The Xgrid Testbed and Results

For the evaluation of the integration of Xgrid and its usage via Gridbus Broker, we have used a cluster composed of Mac OS X computers located in the Howard Florey Institute for Neuroscience at the University of Melbourne. This cluster has 13 nodes that are connected by a Fast Ethernet LAN. Each node has two Power PC processors of 1.8GHz. The Xgrid Technical Preview 2 is installed on this cluster, which is a beta version of Xgrid. Since version 1.0 of Xgrid requires an upgrade of the operating system on all nodes to version 10.4 of Mac OS X and the computers are used for other purposes such as mail and web servers, we are unable to install Xgrid version 1.0 on this cluster at the moment. For future experiments, we aim at using version 1.0, which is a stable production release.

For validating our integration with Xgrid, we have used a sample of application for the jobs submitted to our testbed. The jobs consist of an executable file that is copied to the Xgrid client node. This application generates 16,000 digits for PI and takes about 12 seconds to be executed on the head node of the Xgrid cluster. This application creates an output file of 16KB with the digits and no stdout. In this way, the files that are copied back are this output file, the standard output that is of size 0 and stderr that will be of size 0 in case of success.

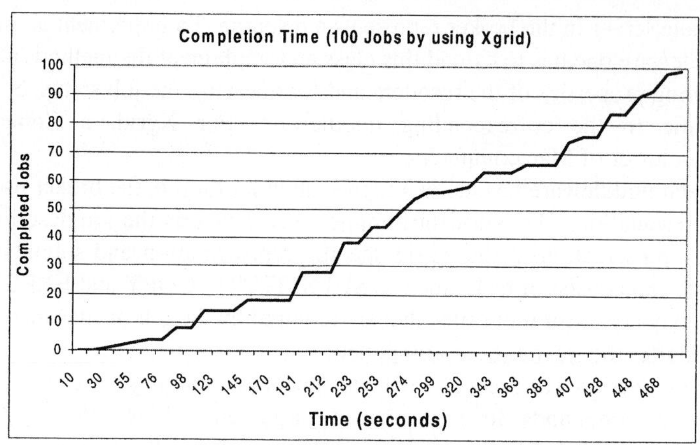

Fig. 4. Execution time (100 jobs by using Xgrid TP2)

The scenario evaluated with Xgrid was the execution of a parameter-sweep application of 100 jobs described using XPML (The XML-based parametric modeling language supported by the Gridbus Broker). During the execution, we measured how many jobs were completed over the execution time. Fig. 4 presents the results of this evaluation. In this experiment, 99 out of 100 jobs were successfully completed. For some unknown reason, the Xgrid command line application hangs sometimes. Hence, it results in an increase of the time the job takes to execute.

We evaluated the round trip time for job submission for Xgrid when using SSH from a computer in the same local area network. The round trip time can present some variation since often users have been utilizing the network for other purposes, and according to these results, all the jobs will have increase in the execution time of about 1 second in the testbed's local area network.

5.2 The PBS/SGE Testbed and Results

We have used two clusters in this evaluation. The first one, the same as the above, is composed of Mac OS X machines located within the Howard Florey Institute for Neuroscience at the University of Melbourne, but SGE was used to manage its resources. The second cluster, called Manjra, is composed of 12 Linux nodes with 2.40GHz Intel Pentium 4 CPUs and 512MB of memory and it is located in another building (GRIDS Lab) at the University of Melbourne. We used PBS to manage Manjra's resources. The job submission to PBS was done using SSH/SCP and the results are presented in Fig. 5. Since the second cluster is running a different operating system (Linux) and as the executables are not portable between Mac OS X operating system and Linux, we implemented the PI calculator described previously as a Java application. On the head computer in the cluster managed by SGE this application takes around 3-5 minutes to finish its execution by using Java 1.4.

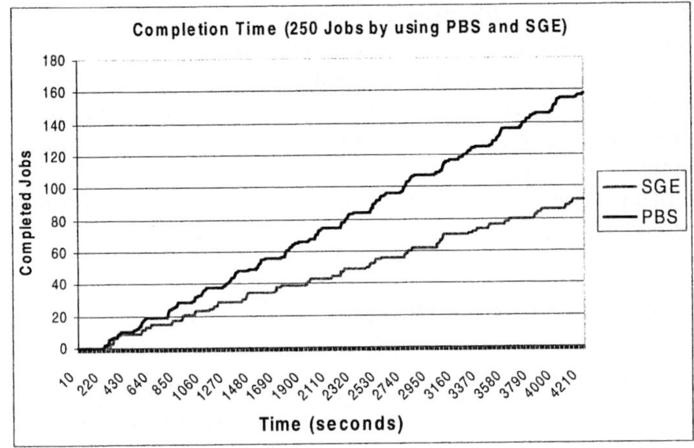

Fig. 5. Execution time (250 jobs by using SGE and PBS)

As presented in the last graph, the interface for PBS presented a better performance compared to SGE. PBS executed 158 out of 250 jobs, whilst SGE executed 92 jobs. The Xgrid experiments were carried out by using an executable application for Mac OS X. We are satisfied with the results even though this release presents some issues such as failing of job submission. We plan to carry out experiments by utilizing the version 1.0.

6 Related Work

There exist some works aiming at integrating the middleware described in this paper with other technologies. For instance, pools of resources managed by Condor can be integrated with other Condors pools by setting up the manager of a cluster to accept requests from another manager. Such an approach is commonly called a flock of Condors [17]. In this case, a pool *B* will send jobs to a pool *A* if the local resources are unavailable or in use.

TrellisWeb [18] provides an interface to a placeholder scheduling that addresses resource scheduling and allocation, single log on and access control. The system is integrated with PBS, SGE and IBM's LoadLeveler and applies these tools in a metacomputing scenario. However, this work does not contemplate integration with global Grid middleware such as Globus and Unicore.

Grid(Lab) Grid Application Toolkit (GAT) [19] presents an architecture in which common APIs sit between Grid applications and diverse Grid middleware. The main goal of GAT is providing Grid programmers with a uniform interface to different middleware and services, such as data catalog, data replication, data movement, Globus Grid Services and Globus 2.X and 3.X Pre WS. By providing such an API, GAT aims at enabling the easy development of "Grid-aware" applications. This API targets the development of portals and can therefore enable a range of Grid applications. Although this project shares many characteristics with our approach, it is not targeted towards at integrating the API with enterprise middleware.

Our integration differs still from the works mentioned above in that Gridbus broker does not provide the integration with only one toolkit, seen with the flock of Condors, but instead integrates several enterprise and global Grid middleware. Furthermore, the Gridbus Broker provides a uniform interface that users can utilize to specify their parameter sweep applications by using an XML-based parametric modeling language as well as Grid portals. The scheduler in Gridbus Broker is middleware independent and can be set to optimize user-supplied parameters such as deadline and budget.

7 Conclusions and Future Works

Gridbus project provides a broad range of tools and aims at leveraging Grid technologies for different platforms. Through its broker, Gridbus targets to provide a common interface and API for users to develop their applications for enterprise and global Grids.

We have developed interfaces to integrate different middleware with the Gridbus Broker. By integrating such technologies with the broker, we aim at leveraging global Grids. Users can use their Macs as well as other computers via integration with other systems.

We also present some experiments that demonstrate the usability of the interface for Xgrid, SGE and PBS. Our experiments consisted of running a parameter sweep application. A description about how to implement interfaces for other middleware was provided along with the results of the experiments that were carried out.

As future work, we propose to adapt the Gridbus interface to Xgrid make use of the BEEP protocol to communicate directly with the Xgrid controller, avoiding using the Xgrid command line application to submit jobs and monitor results. By doing so, we can collect more information about nodes in the Grid and the jobs submitted to Xgrid. We also aim at carrying out tests for the interfaces for other middleware described in this paper.

References

1. Ian Foster, Carl Kesselman, and Steve Tuecke. The anatomy of the grid: Enabling scalable virtual organizations. *International J. Supercomputer Applications*, 15(3), 2001.
2. Srikumar Venugopal, Rajkumar Buyya, and Lyle Winton. A grid service broker for scheduling distributed data-oriented applications on global grids. In *Proceedings of the 2nd workshop on Middleware for grid computing*, pages 75–80, New York, USA, 2004.
3. Jim Almond and Dave Snelling. Unicore: uniform access to supercomputing as an element of electronic commerce. *Future Gener. Comput. Syst.*, 15(5-6):539–548, 1999.
4. David A. Kramer and Matthew MacInnis. Utilization of a local grid of mac os x-based computers using xgrid. In *HPDC*, pages 264–265. IEEE Computer Society, 2004.
5. Parvin Asadzadeh, Rajkumar Buyya, Chun Ling Kei, Deepa Nayar, and Srikumar Venugopal. *High Performance Computing: Paradigm and Infrastructure*, chapter Global Grids and Software Toolkits: A Study of Four Grid Middleware Technologies. ISBN: 0-471-65471-X. Wiley Press, New Jersey, USA, June 2005.

6. Rajkumar Buyya and Srikumar Venugopal. The gridbus toolkit for service oriented grid and utility computing: An overview and status report. In *Proceedings of the First IEEE International Workshop on Grid Economics and Business Models (GECON 2004)*, ISBN 0-7803-8525-X, pages 19–36, Seoul, Korea, April 2004. IEEE Press.
7. Blane Warrene. Stanford University Lab builds an xgrid. Macnews: Hardware, Aug. 2004.
8. Stuart Bowness. Xgrid and cross platform grid computing. 440 project report, University College of the Fraser Valley, April 2005.
9. Xgrid: High performance computing for the rest of us. Apple Developer Connection, March 2005.
10. Ahmar Abbas. *Grid Computing: A Practical Guide to Technology and Applications*. Charles River Media, Hingham, Massachusetts, first edition edition, 2004. ISBN: 1-58450-276-2.
11. Geoffrey Fox and David Walker. e-science gap analysis. UK e-Science Technical Report Series, June 2003.
12. Enterprise grid alliance reference model v1.0. Enterprise Grid Alliance, April 2005.
13. Ian Baird. Grids in practice: a platform perspective. MIDDLEWARESpectra, June 2003. www.middlewarespectra.com/grid.
14. The condor project homepage. http://www.cs.wisc.edu/condor/.
15. Openpbs: The portable batch system software. Veridian Systems, Inc., Mountain View.
16. Sun grid engine (sge): A cluster resource manager. http://gridengine.sunsource.net/.
17. Ali Raza Butt, Rongmei Zhang, and Y. Charlie Hu. A self-organizing flock of condors. In *SC '03: Proceedings of the 2003 ACM/IEEE conference on Supercomputing*, page 42, Washington, DC, USA, 2003. IEEE Computer Society.
18. Christopher Pinchak, Paul Lu, Jonathan Schaeffer, and Mark Goldenberg. The canadian internetworked scientific supercomputer. In *17th Annual International Symposium on High Performance Computing Systems and Applications (HPCS)*, pages 193–199, Sherbrooke, Quebec, Canada, May 2003.
19. Gabrielle Allen, Kelly Davis, Tom Goodale, Andrei Hutanu, Hartmut Kaiser, Thilo Kielmann, AndreMerzky, Rob Van Niewpoort, Alexander Reinefeld, Florian Schintke, Thorsten Schutt, Ed Seidel, and Brygg Ullmer. The Grid Application Toolkit: Toward Generic and Easy Application Programming Interfaces for the Grid. *Proceedings of the IEEE*, 93(3):534–550, March 2005.
20. Ian Foster and Carl Kesselman. Globus: A metacomputing infrastructure toolkit. *Intl J. Supercomputer Applications*, 11(2):115–128, 1997.
21. Mark Baker, Rajkumar Buyya, and Domenico Laforenza. Grids and grid technologies for wide-area distributed computing. *International Journal of Software: Practice and Experience (SPE)*, 32(15):1437–1466, December 2002.
22. Global Grid Forum. http://www.ggf.org, 2005.

Design and Implementation of a Middleware for Hybrid Switching Networks*

Yueming Lu, Yuefeng Ji, and Aibo Liu

The School of Telecommunications Engineering ,
Beijing University of Posts and Telecommunications Beijing,
P. O. Box 128, Beijing, 100876, China
{ymlu, jyf}@bupt.edu.cn, aiboliu@263.net

Abstract. As circuit-based switching is efficient to transmit bulk datasets in data intensive applications, we proposed a middleware for hybrid switching networks. The middleware and our hybrid switching network interconnect distributed computational communities and satisfy the demands of various transmissions. The measurements on the ION test-bed and simulations show that the middleware supports traditional transmission functionalities and is efficient to transmit bulk datasets.

1 Introduction

The Internet is too slow to allow efficient use of remote resources for distributed computing and computational grids. Applications, such as NSF's e-science[1], HEP projects at CERN[2], interactive HDTV and e-health, need huge amount of bandwidth between a limited number of hosts[3].

GLIF[4] is a consortium which develops the Global Lambda Grid for the advancement of scientific collaboration. Moreover, Starlight and Eurolight are well known optical grids for high performance computing. Two national UK HPC services performed through a collaboration of Uklight, Netherlight, Starlight, and Internet2, and won SC2003 bandwidth challenges[5].

However, the optical networks for high performance computing are weak in the switching technologies and lack of middleware for optical network. For example, The packet-based switching technology is limited in high-bandwidth required applications, while the optical switching (e.g. the optical burst switching (OBS) [6]and automatic switched optical network (ASON)[7]) is slow start in transmitting short messages. Regarding the middleware, the legacy TCP is inefficient in transmitting bulk datassets over a high bandwidth*latency lightpath. Till now, no sophisticated middleware within hosts would handle the GMPLS[8]-based signaling and control messages.

As a result, we propose a middleware for hybrid switching based on our ION test-bed (ASON-based). Trails and simulations for the middleware are to test the performance of the middleware and know how fast to transmit bulk datasets.

---

* This work is jointly supported by the National Science Fund for Distinguished Young Scholars (No. 60325104), National 863 Program (No. 2005AA122320), the Grand Key Science and Technology Research Program of MOE (No.0215), the SRFDP of MOE (No.20040013001), P. R. China. Thanks for the great helps.

H. Zhuge and G.C. Fox (Eds.): GCC 2005, LNCS 3795, pp. 418 – 423, 2005.

2 ION Test-Bed

The ION test-bed is shown in Fig.1, where the high performance computers (HPCs) have two interfaces: traffic interface and UNI signaling interface[9]. The traffic interface(Gigabit Ethernet, GE) connects to the transmission plane of the ION and the UNI signaling interface(Fast Ethernet, FE) connects to the control plane of ASON. The UNI signaling interface is out-of-fiber here, because ASON nodes don't support in-band signaling from routers.

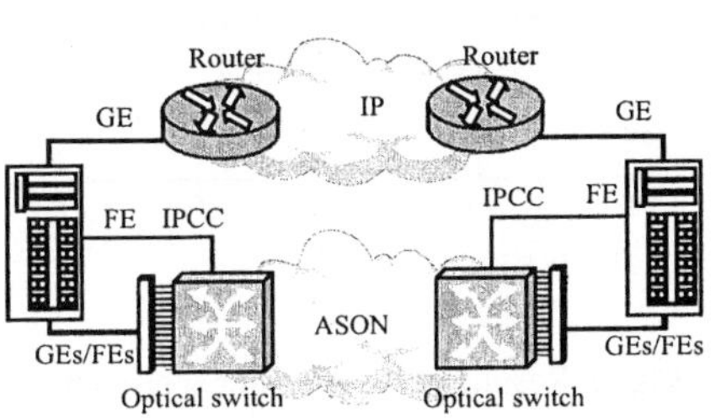

Fig. 1. The ION test-bed

As ASON support dynamic bandwidth provisioning, new access equipments begins to mapping traffic to various bandwidths. For example, Ethernet frames in the MSTP (Multi-service Transmission Platform) or OXC can be mapped to SDH circuits (i.e. Ethernet circuits) and lightpaths(i.e. Ethernet lightpaths)[10].

3 Impact of the Signaling

As a signaling packet reaches an intermediate node, the node will delay the transmission of the signaling packet when the node checks and reserves resources. Hence, we measured the average delay t_n = 2.3 ms of the transmission at the node. But the delay of transmission on Ethernet depends on the throughput from the sender to the receiver. That is other traffics may affect the transmission delay of the signaling packet.

The DCN[11] (data communication network) for signaling is Ethernet of 1Mbps-100Mbps or ECC (embedded control channel) [12]of 192Kbps-576Kbps. In order to know performance of signaling, we measured round trip times (RTTs) of signaling sessions. Let B_i and Bt_i denote bandwidth and throughput of the *i*th link along a path respectively, where $B_i > Bt_i$. Hence, the RTT (*rtt*) of a signaling session is: $rtt \approx 2*((n-1)t_n+l/(Bt_1+Bt_2+\ldots+Bt_{n-1}))$, where the l denotes the size of the signaling packet.

Here we had started two experiments. The first experiment was taken to measure RTTs when only one signaling packet traversed on a DCN, where the DCN is an Ethernet of 100Mbps with bandwidth utilization of 85%. Results of the first experiment were illustrated in Fig.2. As we can see, Fig.2 showed the curve of *rtt*, where the $Bt_1 \approx B_1$ *85%.Therefore the *rtt* varied mostly depending on how many nodes as well as links which has various bandwidths. The second experiment was taken to see how other traffics affected the *rtt*. We retransmitted a signaling packet 6 times along the same path which included 5 nodes and 4 links. At the third and fourth times, random traffics were injected into the signaling network. The results in the Fig.5 showed the third and fourth *rtt* increased about 60ms compared with the ordinary values of the first and second *rtt*. That is effects of other traffics lead the *rtt* not predictable.

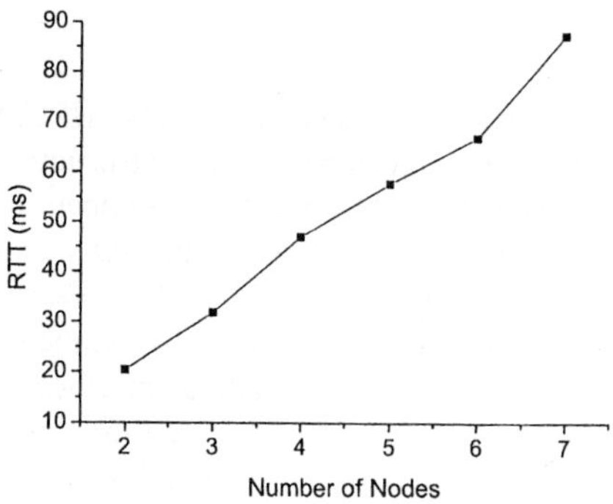

Fig. 2. Results of the first experiment

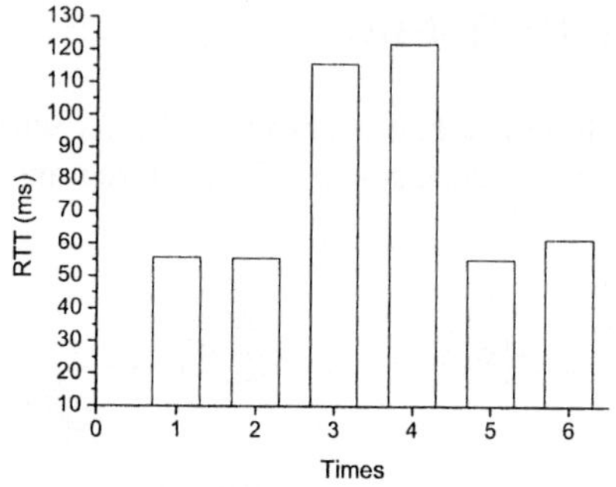

Fig. 3. Results of the second experiment

4 Why Need Hybrid Switching

The packet-based switching is weak in QoS support, but it is flexible in short message transmission. For example, the RTT for transmitting a short message may approach 100 ms, but establishing an end-to-end Ethernet circuit may last 1 second. Regarding bulk data transmission, transmission of 1 Terabytes data over the Internet may take 1 year while the same data requires a throughput of 10 Gbit/s for delivery within 2 hours.

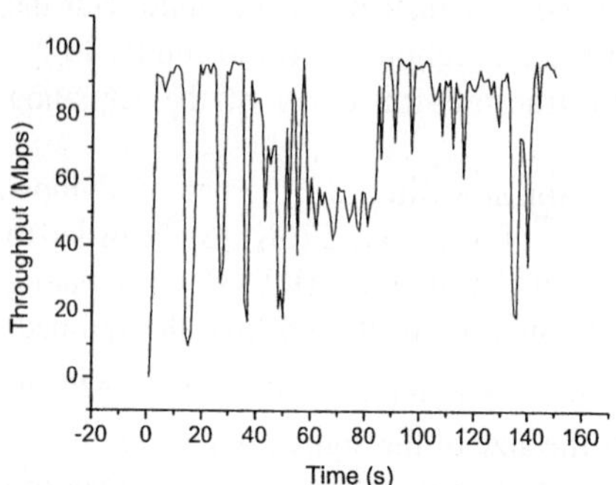

Fig. 4. Transmission over the packet-based switching network

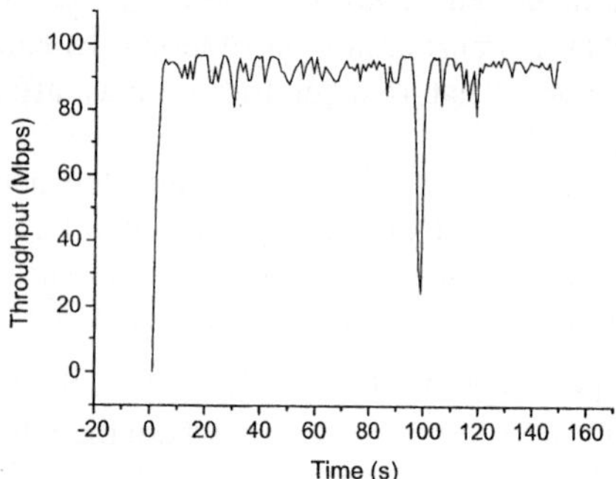

Fig. 5. Transmission over the circuit-based switching network

In order to compare the throughput over packet-based switching networks with over circuit-based networks, we measured the performance of transmissions on the ION test-bed. The transmission over packet-based switching network (the IP switching/routing network) is illustrated in Fig.4, where the bandwidth*latency of the network was 100Mbps*0.5ms. The result showed that the throughput was dynamic, depended on the situation of the packet-based switching network, and can't be estimated. The transmission over the circuit-based network is illustrated in Fig.5, where the throughput was stable. The transmission of bulk datasets over the ION test-bed had two modes. One was the disk-to-disk mode. The transmission of the disk-to-disk mode would have breaks (e.g. 1 second, see Fig.5) for disk operations. Another was memory-to-memory mode where the transmission had no breaks.

Therefore, packet-based switching and circuit-based switching should be integrated in one system in order to offer various services for different transmissions, especially in data intensive applications.

5 Impact of the Middleware

The transmission of optical networks is characterized as high bandwidth (e.g. 10Gbps) and long latency (e.g. 50 ms). The legacy TCP's sliding window flow control mechanism often leads to burst packet traffic and low throughput. The default window size for legacy TCP is 16K or 32K bytes. It is inadequate for high bandwidth and long latency links. For example, for a RTT of *rtt* s on a *B* Mbps link, if the receiver has a *w* KB window, the maximum throughput will be $Bt = w/rtt$. If the $rtt = 50$ ms, $w = 16$KB and $B = 1000$Mbps, $Bt = 2.56$ Mbps. To reach full bandwidth on this link, the receiver needs to have a window of $w=B*rtt = 6.25$MB.

Recently more efforts are focused on rate-based TCPs[12] over the high bandwidth* latency optical networks for bulk data transmission in data intensive applications. The throughput of legacy TCP without the enhancements is up to 20Mbps over a high bandwidth* latency Ethernet lightpath. Tests have seen GridFTP to achieve 512Mbs , Tsunami at 700Mbs, FAST achieved 930Mbs from CERN to SLAC. None of the above protocols can fully utilize OC-192 links[3].

The ITCP is designed for provisioning of dynamical bandwidth on the ION test-bed and transmitting bulk datasets for data intensive applications. Therefore the functionalities of the ITCP are required to estimate bandwidth for transmission depending on data size and acceptable delay from the request of applications, invoke the ASON's dynamic provisioning service (from ION test-bed) via a UNI-C, pre-calculate the TCP window size that the ITCP expect to send in rate-based protocol and the timing between segments in that window, and control the transmission of segments in rate-based protocol.

The ION test-bed is limited in long latency transmission due to lack of long distance WDM systems. Note that the transmission of the TCP for Windows XP only achieves 200Mbps over GE interface. Therefore we simulated high bandwidth*latency for the ITCP and the extended TCP with the help of the NS2. Fig. 6 showed the throughput of the extended TCP where the sliding window was dynamic with the bandwidth*latency of 1Gbps*30ms. The throughput of the ITCP is shown in Fig.7, where the window size is pre-calculated. The throughput of the extended TCP was dynamic (from 200Mbps to 700Mbps) while the throughput of the ITCP was much stable (about 650Mbps). Because end-to-end circuit-based bandwidth is stable, low packet loss and QoS guaranteed, the ITCP which is a rate-based TCP is recommended to transmit bulk data in data intensive applications.

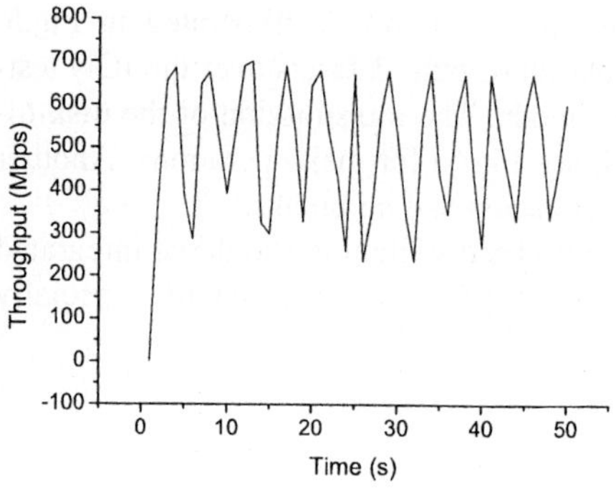

Fig. 6. Throughput of the extended TCP

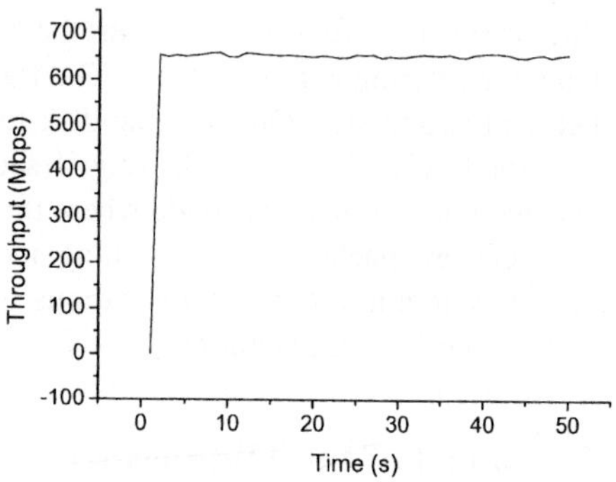

Fig. 7. Throughput of ITCP

6 Middleware for Hybrid Switching Network

The middleware for hybrid switching network provides functional inter-operation between applications and the ION test-bed. Fig.8 shows the structure and organization of the middleware. Here, the extended TCP and the ITCP are independent modules from which applications choose proper services for their special needs. The ITCP is an enhanced module based on rate-based protocol, specially developed for the transmission of bulk data in data intensive applications on the ION test-bed. The difference between the extended TCP and the ITCP is that the ITCP has additional features which can calculate transmission bandwidth for applications based on the data size and acceptable delay, control the window size of the ITCP, inject congestion control policies, and invoke the services from the ION test-bed via UNI-C. That is applications have another choose to transmit their data on optical network directly via the ITCP.

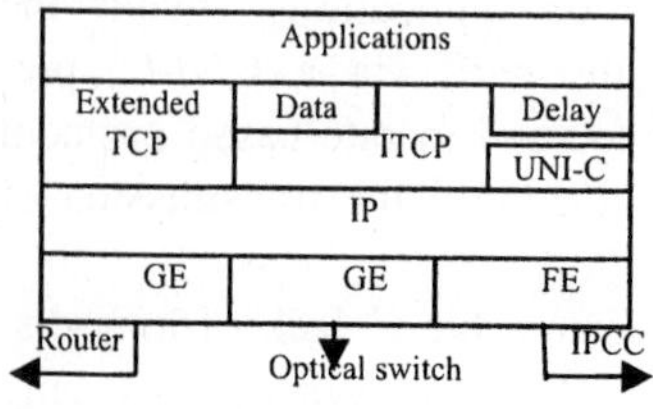

Fig. 8. Architecture of the middleware

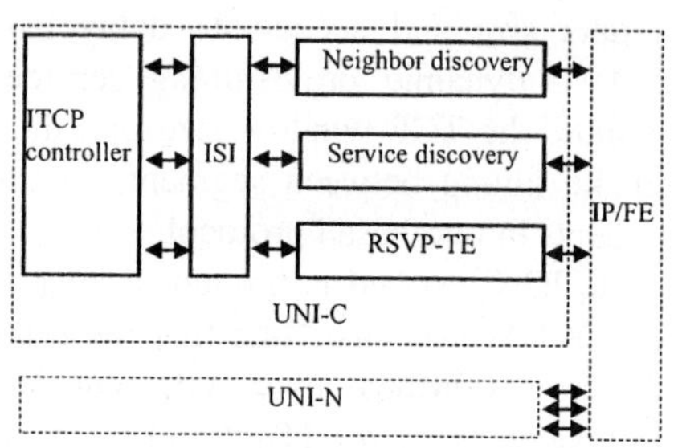

Fig. 9. Architecture of UNI-C

The ION test-bed is designed to establish dynamic connectivity and provide bandwidth (e.g. VC-4 and light-path) between hosts connected to the optical network. The interfaces between hosts and the ION test-bed are based on the UNI specification. The middleware of the client (e.g. host) is to fulfill the service request, neighbor auto-discovery and service auto-discovery.

The organization and functions of the UNI-C is shown in Fig. 9. Here, the neighbor discovery is a software module for maintaining the FE link with the ION test-bed and verifying local port connectivity. The service discovery is another software module by which host obtains information about available services from the ION test-bed and the ION test-bed obtains information about the host. The RSVP-TE is the signaling by which host invokes services from the ION test-bed and maintains connections. These modules are fundamental middleware centrally controlled by the ITCP controller via the ISI (internal signaling interface).

7 Conclusion

The circuit-based switching is efficient to transmit bulk datasets but is slow in the beginning. However, the hybrid switching and middleware which integrate the packet-based switching and circuit-based switching are highly recommended to interconnect distributed computing communities in order to transmit both short messages and bulk datasets. The middleware for the hybrid switching must integrate the traditional middleware, and support rate-based protocols and control messages.

References

1. Harvey B. Newman, Mark H. Ellisman, John A. Orcutt: Data Intensive E-Science Frontier Research. Special Issue, Communications of the ACM, Blueprint for the Future of High Performance Networking (2003) 68-77
2. CERN: The CERN Grid Deployment group: http://it-divgd. web.cern.ch/it-div-gd/ (2003)
3. Grid High Performance Networking Research Group: Optical Network Infrastructure for Grid. http://forge.gridforum.org/projects/ghpn-rg/ (2002)
4. Cees deLaat, Kees Neggers: The Global Lambda Integrated Facility (GLIF). 4th Annual Global LambdaGrid Workshop, Nottingham, UK (2004)
5. SC2003: http://www.sc-conference.org/sc2003/ (2003)
6. E. Van Breusegem, et al.: An OBS Architecture for Pervasive Grid Computing. The IEEE Global Telecommunications Conference (Globecom), Dallas Texas (2004)
7. ITU-T: Architecture for the automatically switched optical network (ASON). G.8080/Y.1304 (2001)
8. Peter Ashwood-Smith, et al.: Generalized Multi-Protocol Label Switching (GMPLS) Architecture. draft-ietf-ccamp-gmpls-architecture-01.txt (2001)
9. Optical Interworking Forum: User Network Interface (UNI) 1.0 Signaling Specification. http://www.oiforum.com/public/documents/OIF-UNI-01.0.pdf (2001)
10. ITU-T: Generic framing procedure. G.7041 (2003)
11. ITU-T: Architecture and specification of data communication network. G.7041 (2003)
12. D. Katabi, M. Handley, C. Rohrs: Internet Congestion Control for High Bandwidth Delay Product Network. In Proceedings of ACM SIGCOMM 2002, Pittsburgh (2002)

A Dynamic Grid Workflow Model Based On Workflow Component Reuse

Jian Cao[1], Yujie Mou[1], Jie Wang[2], Shensheng Zhang[1], and Minglu Li[1]

[1] Department of Computer Science, Shanghai Jiaotong University, 200030, Shanghai, P.R. China
{cao-jian, sszhang, li-ml}@cs.sjtu.edu.cn
[2] Department of Civil and Environment Engineering, Stanford University, Stanford, CA 94305, USA
{jiewang}@stanford.edu

Abstract. A grid workflow is regarded as a fundamental service in a grid environment. To design a user friendly end-to-end grid workflow model is generally a challenging task for general users. In this paper, we propose the concept of grid workflow component, which can be created and then reused to construct the grid workflow model dynamically. This paper firstly presents a framework for dynamic grid workflow. Then the grid workflow component model, which consists of a semantic sub-model and a syntactic sub-model, is defined. Next the methodologies for reusing grid workflow component, especially its search strategy and assembling patterns, are discussed in the paper.

1 Introduction

Grid, which can provide a virtual organization with capabilities to solve problems cooperatively, is put forward to meet increasingly critical collaborative requirements [1]. As a new distributed computing infrastructure, the grid-computing paradigm is extending its role as a high performance-computing environment and has been showing deep impacts on human life and the society [2].

To make these complex grid applications easily accessible to many potential users outside the specific scientific community is a great challenge [3]. Workflow has been used to describe and to control the logic and data flows among grid services so that the burdens for end users to set up a preparatory grid applications are greatly reduced or even eliminated. Although workflow technology in business management applications has been maturing [4], we can't simply integrate a business workflow system into a grid environment without the necessary modification of current architecture of a workflow system. The fact that a grid workflow is much more dynamic than a business workflow is a critical issue to be solved.

In this paper, we proposed the concept of grid workflow component to support dynamic grid workflow construction and execution. With its semantic and syntax models defined, a grid workflow component can be defined and reused to construct dynamic grid workflow model. This paper is organized as follows. Section 2 presents a framework for dynamic grid workflow environment based on grid workflow component reuse. The definition of grid workflow component is discussed in detail in Section 3. Section 4 explains how to reuse the grid workflow component to support

H. Zhuge and G.C. Fox (Eds.): GCC 2005, LNCS 3795, pp. 424 – 429, 2005.

dynamic grid workflow. Related works are discussed in Section 5. Finally, Section 6 summarizes the paper and points out several directions for future works.

2 A Framework for Dynamic Grid Workflow

Figure 1 shows a framework for a dynamic grid workflow. A workflow designer can design, annotate and publish the grid workflow model through the portal as a grid workflow component in the grid environment. Workflow users can first retrieve the grid workflow components, then compose and apply them to solve the problem through the portal. The composed grid workflow model will be executed by the grid workflow execution services. These services make use of the grid workflow model to access the proper grid resources for fulfilling the tasks.

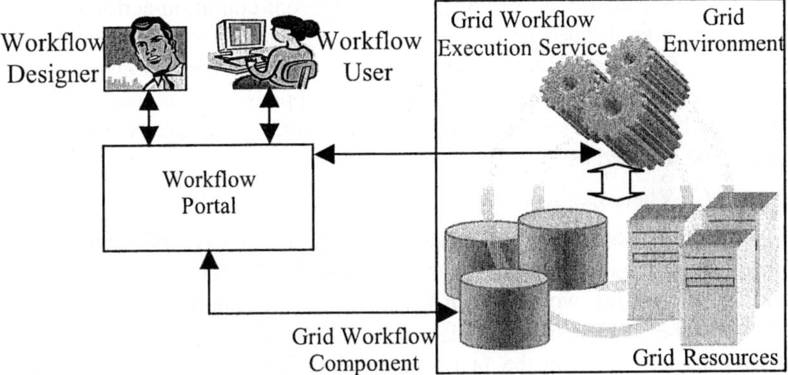

Fig. 1. A Framework for Dynamic Grid

As a key element in the framework, a grid workflow component represents a reusable building block for a problem solving process. Section 3 and Section 4 provide detail discussions about it.

3 The Model of Grid Workflow Component

A grid workflow component can be defined as *<Function, QoS, WorkflowModel ApplicationDomain>*. *Function* denotes what kinds of problem can be solved and what objectives are to be reached by applying this workflow component. *QoS* defines which performance levels this workflow can achieve. Tasks and their relationships are defined in *WorkflowModel*. The *ApplicationDomain* depicts which area this workflow can be applied to. Among four elements of the definition, *Function* and *QoS* constitute the semantics of a sub-model. The *WorkflowModel* describes the syntax of the sub-model of a grid workflow, which can be executed by a certain workflow engine.

The semantic model is composed of *Function* and *QoS* descriptions. For a function, there must exist a verb $v \in \mathrm{VE}$ (a verb set) and an object $o \in \mathrm{OA}$ (an object set) expressed in the domain ontology. The object designates an entity operated by the function. Another component of a function is the way, which is represented by a set of attribute and its value couple, i.e., w_i=<at_i, v_i>. The way specifies the means to provide a function and its attributes come from the attribute set defined for the verb in the domain ontology. There are two relationships to be defined for any function, i.e., generalization and decomposition relationships. A function f can be decomposed into several sub-functions, i.e., $f=\{f_1, f_2, \ldots, f_m\}$ and each sub-function $f_i=SubOf(f)$ (i=1, 2, …, m) will contribute to the partial fulfillment of f. In order to avoid the concept confusion, $verb(f_i)$ must be different from $verb(f)$.

A *QoS* is represented by a set, whose elements are pairs of *QoS* index and its value, i.e., {<QoSIndex, Value>}. A QoS index may be the attributes defined for the verb in the domain ontology or general indexes defined for the workflow, such as execution time, reliability, cost, etc.

In order to support a dynamic grid workflow construction, the syntactic model of the grid workflow component is defined based on event-condition-action (ECA) rules. An ECA rule can be defined as $R_{eca}=<e, C_{on}, A_c>$, where e is an event to trigger the rule, C_{on} is the condition set to reflect the status of the system and environment, and A_c is the action set. An ECA rule states that if e happens and the condition set C_{on} is satisfied then this rule will be fired and all the actions of A_c are executed. An ECA rule can also be denoted as:

On e If C_{on} Then A_c

Events can be composed using the composite operators such as AND and OR.

A grid workflow model is defined as $GridWorkflowModel=<T_t, RA>$, where T_t is the task set of a grid workflow; RA represents relationships among the tasks. $RA=DF\cup LF$, where DF and LF are data flow set and the logic flow set respectively. A data flow is derived from the fact that the data is produced or read by different tasks. A logic flow defines the ordering relationships among tasks and also the state transition relationships in a task.

The content of each task in the model can be specified by a concrete operation, a grid workflow component or a requirement specification. The operation can be a predefined action (for example, data format transformation) or a service invocation. In the case where a specific grid workflow component is defined as the content of a task, when the state of the task is changed to "ready", the grid workflow component will be instantiated as a sub-workflow of this task. The requirement specification of a task can be defined as $<Function_{re}, QoS_{re}>$. The definition of $Function_{re}$ is similar to the related concept of semantic model of the grid workflow component. The QoS requirement includes a set of quality constraints and an evaluation scheme.

4 Grid Workflow Component Reuse

In order to satisfy the requirements, we should firstly choose appropriate grid workflow components. Several strategies are provided to support selection; they include a search strategy, an evaluation strategy, a refinement strategy and a decomposition strategy. Whenever a required grid workflow component cannot be found in the existing environment, a new grid workflow component can be designed and implement on demand. Those grid workflow components that are available to end users should be allowed to be assembled into a workflow model in the ways of sequential composition, parallel composition or complex composition. In this section, these strategies are discussed.

4.1 Grid Workflow Component Selection

1. Search Strategy

Since each grid workflow component is annotated with a semantic model, its search process is a relatively simple process comparing with a general Web Service discovery process [5]. We use description logic [6] to represent functional requirement and functions provided by each grid workflow component as follows:

$$FunctionRequirement \equiv hasVerb \ni verb(Function_{re}) \cap hasObject \ni Object(Function_{re})$$

2. Other Strategies

(1)Evaluation Strategy: After a set of qualified grid workflow components are found, we should choose the best one from them. We employ a fuzzy synthesis evaluation method to fulfill this goal. The total evaluation value for a specific grid workflow component is calculated by summarizing weighted evaluation values of QoS indexes.

(2) Refinement Strategy: The selected grid workflow component may need refinement to adapt to the context. The refinement can become very complex since it is a knowledge intensive process. Currently we provide an editor to allow users to revise the workflow model. But it is possible to provide some even better intelligent supports. For example, we can design a computer understandable guideline to remove, add and merge the workflow model according to the context information.

(3) Decomposition Strategy: In a grid workflow component, a task can also be decomposed if it is an abstract one. In order to decompose it, we can also apply the search strategy and add the selected workflow component as it's sub-workflow. If we can't find any appropriate workflow, we can also design a sub-workflow for it.

4.2 Grid Workflow Component Assemble

When the grid workflow components found can only fulfill partially functional requirements, we should assemble them together to see if the combined functionalities of the components could fulfill all the requirements. There are basically two kinds of composition involved: the logic composition and data flow composition.

There are three main logic composition patterns for a logic composition:

(1) Parallel Composition: If the functions of two selected grid workflow components complement each other and they also have no any data association relationship, we can apply parallel composition pattern. Suppose a workflow model is WM_1, and the other one is WM_2. We can add an ECA rule as follows to assign the parallel composition relationship:

On StartOf(WM_1) Then Initialize(WM_2)

(2) Sequential Composition: The sequential composition pattern is applied to the situation where two grid workflow components each can only achieve part of functional requirement. These two components have some input output data interaction relationships. In this pattern, we should determine the order that the workflows must follow. It is determined by identifying whose results are the sources of another component. We can assign sequential composition relationship by adding an ECA rule as follows:

On EndOf(WM_1) Then Initialize (WM_2)

(3) Complex Composition: The other composition modes are categorized into complex composition pattern, which include additive, disjunctive and conjunctive models. They can also be realized by applying ECA rules.

Besides a logic flow composition, the composition of a data flow should also be carried out whenever necessary. It might be necessary to make some terminology adjustments of maps before their composition. The domain ontology is adopted to support the name unification in our framework. When a grid workflow component is registered into the environment, we should define the transforming rules for local data of the workflow component to the domain ontology.

5 Related Works

In order to support dynamic workflow construction, some researchers investigate applying AI technologies to automatically generate a grid workflow model [3][7][8]. All these methods assume the goals and decision rules can be predefined accurately, but in reality it is very difficult, if not possible [9], to implement a complete rule set a priori. Our assumption is that human intervention is inevitable in implementing a practical system. Therefore, we provide a reuse methodology, which includes the steps for end users to design and execute services on demand.

With an increasing number of scientists begin to make use of existing workflow construction tools to design their experimental grid services, as demonstrated in *my*-Grid project of UK e-Science plan, the issues related to semantic description, publishing and discovery of workflows are also investigated [10]. In our approach, the semantic model of a grid workflow component consists of straightforward functional and QoS descriptions. We also apply a description logic reasonner, which is guided by different matching criteria, to support component search. In addition, our syntactic model for a grid workflow is based on the ECA rule; composing workflow components can be achieved by simply adding more ECA rules.

6 Conclusions

This paper discusses how to reuse the grid workflow components to support dynamic grid workflow. Our model is not directly based on current industry standards such as BPEL4WS, but rather on our preparatory technologies that has some unique properties for dynamic workflow composition. As a result, extra tools need to be developed to support this new concept and the related framework. So far we have developed several basic tools to support the grid workflow. More tools will be developed in the future.

Acknowledgements

This work is partially supported by "SEC E-Institute: Shanghai High Institutions Grid", Chinese High Technology Development Plan (No.2004AA104340), Chinese Semantic Grid Project (2003CB317005) and Chinese NSF Project (No.60473092).

References

1. Foster, I., Kesselman, C., Tuecke, S., The Anatomy of the Grid: Enabling Scalable Virtual Organization, International Journal of Supercomputer Applications, Vol. 15(3), 2001, pp200-222
2. Foster, I., Kesselman, C., et. al., The Anatomy of the Grid: Enabling Scalable Virtual Organizations, International Journal of Supercomputer Applications, Vol. 15(3), 200-222, 2001
3. Yolanda Gil., Ewa Deelman, Jim Blythe, et. al., Artificial Intelligence and Grids: Workflow Planning and Beyond, IEEE Intelligent Systems, 2004.1, pp26-33
4. http://www.wfmc.org
5. Daniela Damm, Farshad Hakimpour, Andreas Geppert, Translating and Searching Service Descriptions Using Ontologies, J.Eder and M.Missikoff (Eds.): CAiSE 2003, LNCS 2681, pp.308-323, 2003
6. Horrocks, U.Sattler and S. Tobies. Practical Reasoning for Expressive Description Logics, In H. Ganzinger, D. McAllester, and A. Voronkov, Editors, Proceedings of LPAR'99, Lecture Notes in Artificial Intelligence, Springer, 1999, Vol. 1705, pp161-180
7. Aiello M., Papazoglou, M., Yang, J., A Request Language for Web-Services Based on Planning and Constraint Satisfaction, Lecture Notes in Computer Sciences, 2002, 2444: 76-85
8. McIlraith, S., Son, T., Adapting Golog for Composition of Semantic Web Services, Proceeding of the International Conference on the Principles of Knowledge Representation and Reasoning (KRR'02), 2002.4, pp 482-496
9. Kim, J., Gil, Y., Towards Interactive Composition of Semantic Web Services, 2004 AAAI Spring Symposium, Technical Report SS-04-06, http:// www.isi.edu /ikcap / scec/papers/ AAAI-Symp-04-Kim-Gil. pdf, 2004.6
10. Tom Oinn, Matthew Addis, Justin Ferris, et.al, Taverna, Lessons in Creating a Workflow Environment for the Life Sciences, http://twiki.mygrid.org.uk/twiki/ pub/Mygrid/ WorkflowAtGGF/taverna-ccpe.pdf. 2004

Coordinated Placement and Replacement for Grid-Based Hierarchical Web Caches

Wenzhong Li, Kun Wu, Xu Ping, Ye Tao, Sanglu Lu, and Daoxu Chen

State Key Laboratory for Novel Software Technology,
Department of Computer Science and Technology, Nanjing University,
P.R. China 210093
lwz@dislab.nju.edu.cn

Abstract. Web caching has been well accepted as a viable method for saving network bandwidth and reducing user access latency. To provide cache sharing on a large scale, hierarchical web caching has been widely deployed to improve the scalability of content dissemination through the World Wide Web. In this paper, we present GHC, a grid-based hierarchical web caching architecture, for constructing efficient cache hierarchy in Grid environment. Basing on the GHC architecture, we also proposed HCPR algorithm, which is a novel coordinated placement and replacement algorithm for hierarchical web caching scheme. The principle of HCPR algorithm is to improve cache usage, to cache hot document close to clients so as to minimize the number of hops to locate and access Web documents. The simulation study shows that the HCPR algorithm has higher cache hit ratio and lower access latency compared with the traditional hierarchical caching algorithms.

1 Introduction

Cooperative web caching has been recognized as one of the effective solutions to alleviate web service bottlenecks, reduce bandwidth consumption, access latency, as well as server load. There are basically two types of cooperative architecture-Hierarchical and Distributive. With hierarchical caching [1], caches are placed at multiple levels of the network. With distributed caching, caches are only placed at the bottom levels of the network and there are no intermediate caches [2]. There are two important issues to cooperative caching: object location and object placement/replacement. Object location focuses on finding nearby copies of objects [3]. Object placement/replacement attempts to solve the problem of making storage decisions and coordinating object replacement. Efficient coordinated object placement and replacement algorithms have been widely studied in [2].

Grid computing has emerged as the next major distributed computing platform [4]. Data grid addresses the problem of storage and data management, network-intensive data transfers and data caching and replication, while maintaining high reliability and availability of the data. Web caching Grid [5] uses grid caches to achieve load balancing among multiple Web servers, in which remote servers in a Grid may function as caches when request rates are high and quality of service (QoS) for response times are in danger of degradation. GCaching [6], a Grid-based cooperative caching system, organizes a set of distributed caching proxy servers to form a "caching pool" for large-scale distributed caching data sharing.

H. Zhuge and G.C. Fox (Eds.): GCC 2005, LNCS 3795, pp. 430–435, 2005.

This paper addresses the issue of coordinated placement and replacement for grid-based hierarchical web caches. The remainder of this paper is organized as follows. Section 2 present the grid-based hierarchical web caching architecture called GHC. In Section 3, we introduce HCPR algorithm. In Section 4, we evaluate the performance of HCPR algorithm by means of synthetic simulation. Finally, we conclude this paper in Section 5.

2 GHC: A Grid-Based Hierarchical Web Caching Architecture

Web caching sharing was first proposed in the context of the Harvest [1] project. The basic idea of Harvest system is to have a series of caches hierarchically arranged in a tree-like structure and to allow those caches to leverage from each other when an object request arrives and the receiving cache do not have that object. Hierarchical architecture is widely deployed for large-scale web caching sharing.

Web caches need to be arranged in a hierarchical structure due to the hierarchical nature of the Internet. In the Grid context, Hierarchical discovery scheme is used for resource registration, querying and sharing among multiple virtual organizations (VOs). A Grid-based hierarchical Web caching architecture called GHC is presented in Fig. 1. In this architecture, web caches are arranged in a hierarchical tree-like form, which allow caches sharing and coordinating among VOs. The leaf nodes correspond to the end users. User requests travel from a given leaf node towards the root node, until the requested document is found. If the requested document cannot be found even at the root level, the request is redirected to the web server containing the document.

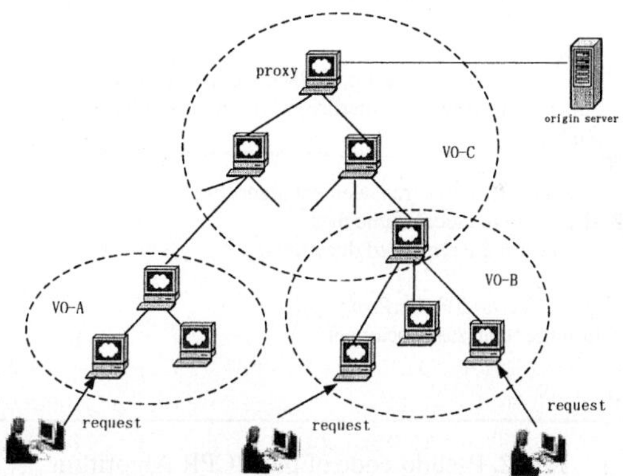

Fig. 1. The GHC Architecture

3 HCPR: A Hierarchical Web Caching Placement and Replacement Algorithm

In the traditional hierarchical web caching, requests are first received at the leaf caches and are routed upwards until they reach a cache that stores a copy of the requested document. If the document is not found at any cache level, the root cache contacts directly the origin server. When the requested document is found, it is sent on the reverse path to the client, and each cache on this path gets to store a local copy of the document so as to service future requests. Such traditional hierarchical web caching algorithm is known as LCE (Leaving Copies Everywhere) algorithm, which has been considered as a de facto behavior.

One remarkable disadvantage of LCE is documents redundancy [7]. Basing on the GHC architecture, we present a history-based hierarchical caching replacement algorithm called HCPR. The principle of HCPR algorithm is to improve cache usage, to cache data close to clients and to minimize the number of hops to locate and access Web documents.

```
Procedure to be invoked on reference to document p at time t:
If p does not exist in the HIST table
then
insert p to the HIST table;
HIST(p,1)=0;
end if
For i=2 to K do  HIST(p, i)=HIST(p, i-1)   od
HIST(p, 1)=t;
If be a leaf node  then      //leaf node replacement algorithm
if p is already in the local cache then
            return the requested document;
else
    request_forward(FatherProxy, p);
    if p is fetched from the origin server  then
                               //select replacement document ;
       min=t
       for all document q in the local cache do
            if HIST(q,K)<min then
                 victim_document=q ;
                 min=HIST(q,K) ;
            end if
       od
               cache document p, replace victim_document ;
       document_upgrade(fatherProxy, victim_document)
    end if;
end if
else       // non-leaf node replacement algorithm
if p is already in the local cache then
            return the requested document;
else
    request_forward(FatherProxy, p);
    return the requested document;
end if
end if
```

Fig. 2. Pseudo-code of the HCPR Algorithm

HCPR algorithm uses documents reference history information for caching placement and replacement decision. The basic idea of HCPR algorithm is placing the most frequently referenced documents in the leaf node of the hierarchy. The less frequently a document is referenced, the higher level it is placed. HCPR Algorithm tries to avoid redundancy by placing documents in a "bottom-up" manner. Documents are first cached at the bottom level caches (leaf nodes). When the bottom level reaches the cache predetermined limits, documents are replaced according to their reference history. By using a page upgrade process, the replaced document from level m cache is brought to its upper level cache.

Suppose that r_1, r_2, ..., r_n are the requests for Web documents as logged at the time units t_1, t_2, ..., t_n, respectively. Basing on the idea of [8], the reference history record of document *x* is defined as follows:

$$\mathrm{HIST}(x,k) = \begin{cases} t_i & \text{if there are exactly k - 1 references between times } t_i \text{ and } t_n \\ 0 & \text{otherwise} \end{cases}$$

Here t_i denotes the time of the first of the last *k* references to *x*. HIST(x , k) is a time metric which defines the time of the past *k*-th reference to document *x*.

In the GHC architecture, each caching proxy runs HCPR algorithm. Figure 2 presents the HCPR algorithm in pseudo-code.

When caching replacement occurs, the less frequently referenced document is replaced. The replaced document will be "upgraded" to its father proxy. The pseudo-code of document upgrade process is presented in Figure 3.

```
Procedure to be invoke on receiving a document upgrade request:
p=the document to be upgraded;
If p does not exist in the HIST table then
    insert p to the HIST table;
    HIST(p,1)=0;
end if
For i=2 to K do  HIST(p, i)=HIST(p, i-1)  od
HIST(p, 1)=t;
if p is already in the local cache then
      return;
else
      //select replacement document
        min=t;
        for all document q in the local cache do
              if HIST(q,K)<min then
                     victim_document=q;
                     min=HIST(q,K);
              end if
        cache document p, replace  victim_document ;
        if not reaches the root level
          document_upgrade(fatherProxy, victim_document) ;
end if
```

Fig. 3. Pseudo-code of Document Upgrade Process

4 Synthetic Simulations

In order to evaluate the performance of the HCPR algorithm, we conduct simulations using synthetically generated Zipf-like document popularity distributions [9] to model client request. Let N be the total number of web pages in the universe. Let $p(i)$ be the probability of requesting the *i*th most popular document. We assume that $p(i)$, defined for i=1, 2, …, N, has a "cut-off" Zipf-like distribution given by $P(i) = \frac{C}{i^{\alpha}}$, where $C = (\sum_{i=1}^{N} \frac{1}{i^{\alpha}})^{-1}$.

In our simulation, we follow the network model presented in [10]. We model the network topology as a full Q-ary tree with L levels. An origin server resided outside the hierarchy is considered to be at a conceptual level L+1. A request travels from a leaf cache towards the location of the hit. If a request hits in the l-level cache, the hops of fetching the document are defined to be l-1.

Two metrics are used to evaluate our algorithm: cache hit ratio and Average Access Distance (AAD). Cache hit ratio is defined by the ratio of the number of hits in the cache hierarchy to the total number of user requests. AAD denotes the average hops to fetch a document.

For all the case studies in this paper, we set L=3, Q=4 and N=100000. For the reference history, we set K=2. We assume all documents have the same size. We also assume the total storage capacity is S unit sized documents, equally allocated to the n caches of a hierarchy with each cache taking S/n units of storage. We study the performance of HCPR algorithm under Zipf-like distribution, with α=0.7, 0.8 and 0.9. Figure 4 to Figure 9 present the cache hit ratio and average access distance for the HCPR and LCE algorithms under different α value.

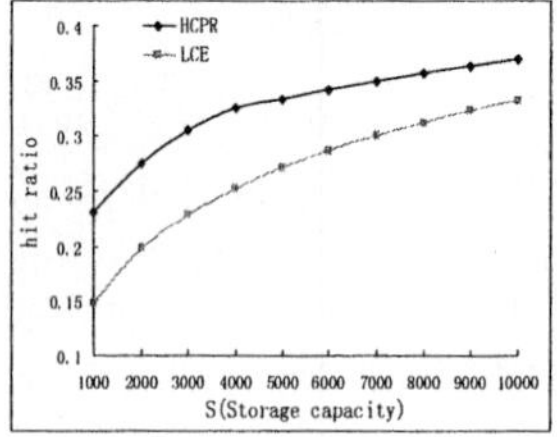

Fig. 4. Cache hit ratio for LCE and HCPR, under Zipf-like (0.9) requests. N=100000, L=3, Q=4.

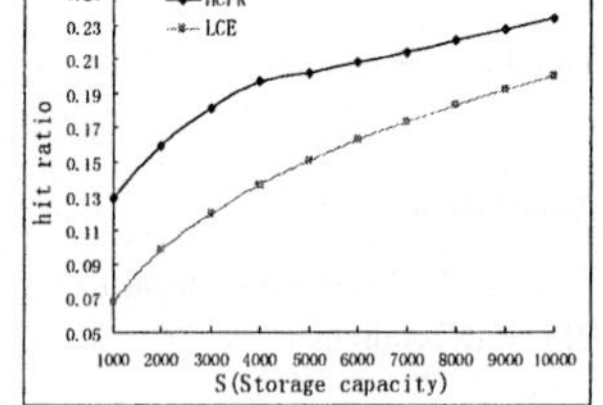

Fig. 5. Cache hit ratio for LCE and HCPR, under Zipf-like (0.8) requests. N=100000, L=3, Q=4.

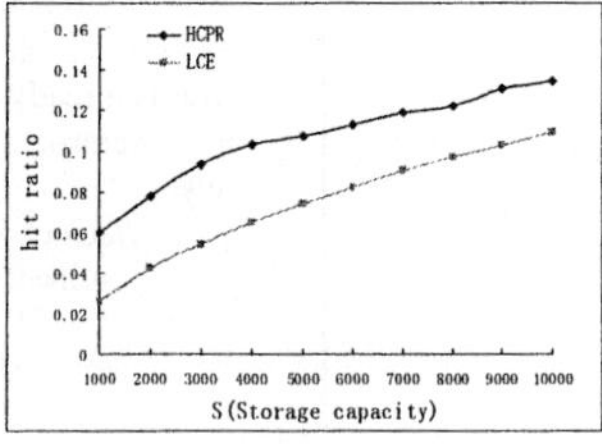

Fig. 6. Cache hit ratio for LCE and HCPR, under Zipf-like (0.7) requests. N=100000, L=3, Q=4.

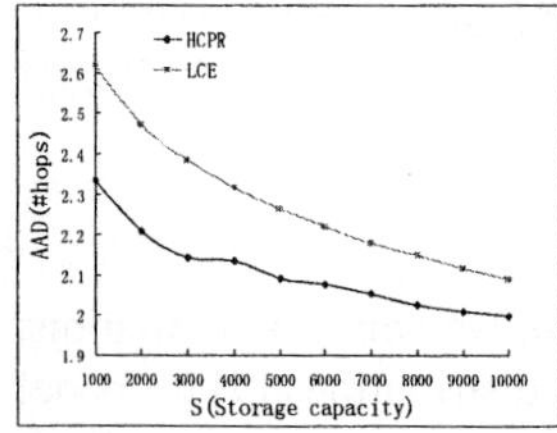

Fig. 7. Average Access Distance for LCE and HCPR, under Zipf-like (0.9) requests. N=100000, L=3, Q=4.

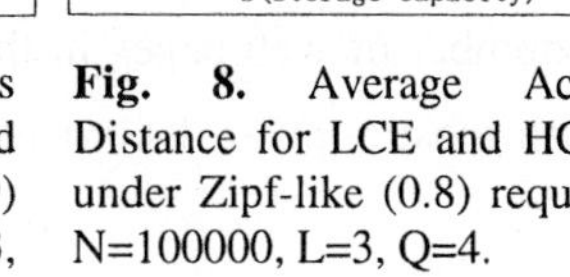

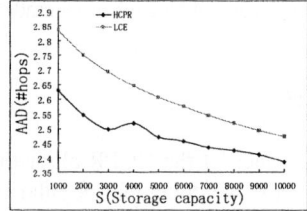

Fig. 8. Average Access Distance for LCE and HCPR, under Zipf-like (0.8) requests. N=100000, L=3, Q=4.

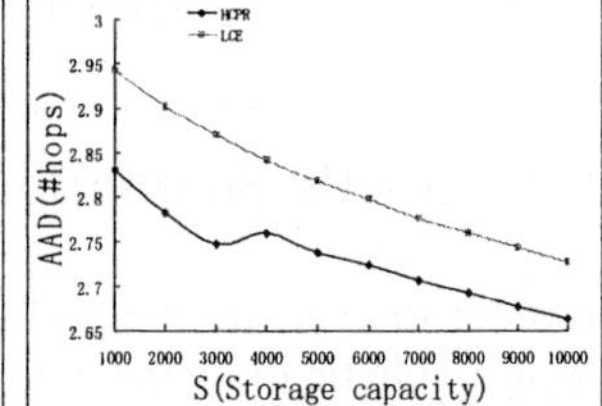

Fig. 9. Average Access Distance for LCE and HCPR, under Zipf-like (0.7) requests. N=100000, L=3, Q=4.

The simulation study shows that the HCPR algorithm has higher cache hit ratio and lower access latency compared with the traditional hierarchical caching algorithm.

5 Conclusions

Hierarchical web caching has been widely deployed to improve the scalability of content dissemination for large scale caches sharing. In this paper, we present a grid-based hierarchical web caching architecture called GHC. Basing on GHC architecture, we present HCPR algorithm which is a novel coordinated placement and replacement algorithm for hierarchical web caching. The simulation study shows that the HCPR algorithm outperforms the traditional LCE algorithm.

Acknowledgement

This work is partially supported by the National Natural Science Foundation of China under Grant No.60402027; the National High-Tech Research and Development Program of China (863) under Grant No.2004AA112090; the National Basic Research Program of China (973) under Grant No.2002CB312002.

References

1. A. Chankhunthod, P.B. Danzig, C.Neerdaels, et al "A Hierarchical Internet Object Cache," Usenix'96, 1996.
2. M.R. Korupolu and M.Dahlin, "Coordinated Placement and Replacement for Large-scale Distributed Caches," In *Proc. of the IEEE Workshop on Internet Applications*, 1999.
3. H. Zhuge, J. Liu, L. Feng, et al "Query Routing in a Peer-to-Peer Semantic Link Network," *Computational Intelligence*, 21(2): *pp*197-216, 2005.
4. I.Foster, C.Kesselman, "The Grid, BluePrint for a New Computing Infrastructure," San Francisco, Morgan Kaufmann Publisherd Inc, 1999
5. Catherine H.Crawford, Daniel M.Dias, Arun K.Iyengar, et al "Commercial Applications of Grid Computing", IBM Research Division, Thomas J.Watson Research Center, 2003
6. LI Wen-Zhong, GU Tie-Cheng, et al "GCaching: A Grid-Based Cooperative Caching System", *Journal of Computer Research and Development*, 41(12): *pp*2211-2217, 2004.
7. Nikolaos Laoutaris, Sofia Syntila and Ioannis Stavrakakis, "Meta Algorithms for Hierarchical Web Caches," In *IEEE International Performance Computing and Communications Conference (IEEE IPCCC)*, 2004
8. E.J. O'Neil, and G. Weikum. "The LRU-K Page Replacement Algorithm for Database Disk Buffering," In *Proc. of the 1993 ACM Sigmod International Conference on Management of Data*, *pp*297-306, 1993.
9. L. Breslau, P. Cao, L. Fan, et al "Web caching and Zipf-like Distributions: Evidence and Implications." In *Proc. of IEEE INFOCOM'99*, *pp*126-134, New York, USA, 1999.
10. P. Rodriguez, C.Spanner, and E.W.Biersack, "Web Caching Architectures: Hierarchical and Distributed Caching," In *Proc. of WCW*, 1999.

A XML-Based Composition Event Approach as an Integration and Cooperation Middleware

Gang Xu, JianGang Ma, and Tao Huang

Technology Center of Software Engineering, Institute of Software,
Chinese Academy of Sciences, Beijing 100080, P.R. China
{xugang, mjg, tao}@otcaix.iscas.ac.cn

Abstract. Content-based Pub/Sub systems are gaining increasing popularity as an integration and cooperation middleware supporting large-scale distributed applications, especially for Grid. However, existing content-based Pub/Sub systems mainly focus on the "one-to-one" event matching, not on the composite event matching. The composite event matching enables application components to express more interest in the occurrence of event composite patterns. In this paper, we present a XML-based composite event model that consists of the temporal logical model and the event composite pattern. Based on the composite event model, a subscription language (EXML-QL) is introduced by extending XML-QL to support the XML-based composite event computing. Finally, in terms of the peculiarities of the subscription language, a composite event matching process is presented and analyzed.

1 Introduction

As a loose coupling and scalable integration middleware, content-based Pub/Sub systems are gaining increasing popularity in the area of large-scale distributed applications, such as Grid [1]. However, existing content-based Pub/Sub systems only support the single event matching and lose the ability to express the more interests of event composite patterns. For example, in Grid information integration, information formatted as XML must be delivered timely, which raises the potential need that the users only receive relevant information under certain event conditions, not the whole huge XML data.

To solve this problem, we propose a XML-based composite event model and its subscription language. The composite event model describes the temporal relationship of composite events and the event forwarding patterns. At the same time, its subscription language supports the composite operations on XML events.

2 Composite Event Model

The composite event model of content-based Pub/Sub systems consists of the event temporal logic models and the event composite patterns. The event temporal logic models describe the time sequence relationship of events in distributed environment; the event composite patterns describe the event forwarding patterns.

H. Zhuge and G.C. Fox (Eds.): GCC 2005, LNCS 3795, pp. 436–442, 2005.

2.1 Temporal Logic Model

In distributed environments, we use a two-part interval timestamp to illustrate events, rather than a single conventional timestamp due to network delays or radio transmission lag. In terms of the characteristics of interval timestamps, the temporal logic relation definition is defined as follows:

Definition 1: $t=[t^s,t^f]$ denotes an interval timestamp of events, where t^s denotes the time at which publishers release events; t^f denotes the time at which Pub/Sub systems receive events. Temporal logic relation is $T-Logic \in \{<,\prec,\supset,\cup\}$, where "$<$" denotes the total order relation, "$\prec$" denotes the partial order relation. Temporal logic relations meet the following formal relations: $t_i < t_q \Leftrightarrow t_i^f < t_q^s$; $t_i \prec t_q \Leftrightarrow (t_i^s < t_q^s < t_i^f) \vee (t_i^f < t_q^f)$; $t_i \supset t_q \Leftrightarrow (t_i^s < t_q^s < t_i^f) \vee (t_q^f < t_i^f)$; $t_i \cup t_q \Leftrightarrow [\min(t_i^s,t_q^s), \max(t_i^f,t_q^f)]$.

2.2 Event Composite Patterns

Event composite patterns illustrate different event matching and forwarding approaches. According to the relation of the matched content and the forwarded content and the relation of the in-degree and the out-degree of Pub/Sub systems, we define the event composite patterns as follows:

Definition 2: Event composite operator: $Composite\text{-}Operator \in \{\xrightarrow{=},\xrightarrow{\approx},\xrightarrow{\supset},\xrightarrow{\subset}\}$, where "$\xrightarrow{=}$" denotes "forwarding pattern" that is correspondent to the "one-to-one" event matching, namely it resolves a single input event matching and forwards this single event. "$\xrightarrow{\approx}$" denotes "triggering pattern" that is correspondent to one of the "many-to-one" event matching. For the "triggering pattern", Boolean evaluating the temporal logic relations of several input events is the pre-condition. The events that be forwarded may be arbitrary input events. "$\xrightarrow{\supset}$" denotes "splitting pattern" that is correspondent to the "one-to-many" event matching pattern. Other than matching the single input event, the "splitting pattern" is required to have the capability of select the particular part of the event's content, forwarding the selected contents to one or several subscribers. "$\xrightarrow{\subset}$" denotes "merging pattern" that is correspondent to the other of the "many-to-one" event matching pattern. The "merging pattern" needs to merge several events distributed over the temporal sequence into a single event, and further forward this merged event.

3 Composite Event Subscription Language

In Pub/Sub systems, information providers publish information in the form of events, information consumers subscribe to events by subscription languages, and Pub/Sub systems deliver the published events to all interested subscribers. Events and subscription languages are an interactive entity. In other words, what form of events decides the form of subscription languages; what form of subscription language also decides the form of events.

Without loss of generality, we define an XML-event as below:

Definition 3: an XML event is a tri-tuple: XML-event=(element, attribute, structure), where elements and attributes have name, type and value, attributes belong to certain elements, structures restrict the structural relations of elements, such as parent, sibling, ancestor.

We further define the temporal operators in the events as the following:

Definition 4: Temporal operator: T-Operator∈ {":", ";", "||", "⊥", "∇"}, where ":" denotes the concatenation event that follows the partial order relation and overlaps in time, such as e_1:e_2; ";" denotes the sequence event that follows the complete order relation and doesn't overlap in time, such e_1;e_2; "||" denotes the parallelization event that matches two events in parallel, and succeeds only if both are matched. Any order is allowed and events overlap in time, such as $e_1 || e_2$; "⊥" denotes the timing event that matches a event within a give interval, such as $(e_1 \perp e_2)e_3$; "∇" denotes the alternation event that is satisfied if either e_1 or e_2 is matched, such as $e_1 \nabla e_2$.

In the environment of the unrestricted context, Pub/Sub systems may match several input events and not all input events may be meaningful to the event forwarding. For example, for the sequence event and the triggering operator $(e_1;e_2 \xrightarrow{\approx} e_3)$, the several events of e_3 may be matched after e_1 happened and before e2 happens. So, we need to further define parameter contexts to designate which event to be used.

Definition 5: Parameter-Context ∈ {Recent, Exclusive, Globe}, where "Recent" represents only the most recent input event is used; "Exclusive" represents only the events that happen after the terminating event is matched are used, "Globe" represents the events that happen after the initiating event is matched are used.

It is easy to prove that the synthesis of temporal logic evaluations and parameter contexts is the fairness assertion of the composite event temporal logic.

```
WHERE<$><author><firstname>$fn</>
        <lastname>$ln</>
      </>
      <title>$t</>
      </>IN"www.a.b.c/bib.xml"
CONSTRUCT<OutputXML>
<person ID=PersonID($fn,$ln)>
        <firstname>$fn</>
        <lastname>$ln</>
        <publicationtitle>$t</>
        </>
        </>
```

Fig. 1. An XML-QL example

3.1 Composite Event Subscription Language EXML-QL

In the section, we extend XML-QL to be a composite event subscription language EXML-QL (Event XML-QL). XML-QL itself is a declarative "relational complete" query language and is simple enough that it can be optimized [2]. XML-QL is suitable for extracting data from existing XML documents and constructing new XML documents. In the aspect of constructing new XML documents, XML-QL utilizes nested queries to support the structure hierarchy of XML data and use Skolem functions to control how the result is grouped. A XML-QL example is given in Fig. 1.

In the example, variable names are preceded by $ to distinguish them from string literals. The "WHERE" clause contains the content needed to be matched and extracted. The "CONSTRUCT" clause constructs a XML document whose root element is a <person> element. Among the "CONSTRUCT" clause, PersonID is a Skolem function that can produce a new tag for each new ($fn, $ln).

Though XML-QL has many advantages in constructing XML documents, it can't satisfy the need of composite event subscription languages as follows:

- In Pub/Sub systems, detecting events is based on the content of events, so it is impossible to name events in advance.
- In XML-QL, if omitting "IN" clauses, the XML matching sections for different events can't be distinguished.
- XML-QL doesn't contain the time concept, so it doesn't support the temporal logic evaluation.
- XML-QL doesn't support the event composite patterns.

Based on the existing function of XML-QL, we further define EXML-QL by adding the time operators and the composite operators, using the "block-variable" substituting the "IN" clauses in XML-QL to support the composite event subscription. EXML-QL is defined as follows:

Definition 6: EXML-QL is a extended XML-QL language for the composite event subscription: EXML-QL={#Block-variable} ∪ {T-Operator} ∪ {Composite-Operator} ∪ {XML-QL}, where # is the prefix of block variables, T-Operator is the time operators, Composite-Operator is the composite operators.

So, we change the grammar of XML-QL as the following.

- EXML-QL::=(Function | Query | CompositeCondition)<EOF>;
- CompositeCondition::=Block-variable | T-Operator | EP;
- Condition::=Pattern BindingAs* '#' Block-variable | Predicate.

Fig. 2 is a simple EXML-QL example. This example contains two block variables #P and #T representing the <person> element and the <orderpayer> element from the different events. In the end of the "WHERE" clause, we add the temporal operators and utilize the block variables referencing to events to build the temporal logic relations of discrete events. This temporal logic relation in the example is a sequence event, namely the event #P weekly follows the event #T. The "CONSTRUCT" clause uses the content of the event #P to construct a new output XML event.

```
WHERE<person>
    <name></>ELEMENT_AS $n
    <personnumber>$pn</>
  </>#P
  <orderpay>
    <pay>finished</>
    <deliver>ok</>
    <pn>$pn</>
  </>#T
#T;#P
CONSTRUCT<result><pn>$pn</>$n</>
```

Fig. 2. An example of EXML-QL

4 Composite Events Matching

4.1 Composite Events Matching

Based on EXML-QL, matching composite events has the following characteristics:

- Decomposing the "WHERE" clause into a set of block variables and implementing the XML event matching.
- Based on the temporal logic built from the block variables, the temporal logic relations are evaluated on the matched events.
- Transforming the XML events that satisfy the temporal logic relation into the naming XML document, furthermore transforming EXML-QL into XML-QL and using XML-QL interpreters to construct new output XML events.

In the process of matching XML events, we convert block variables to Finite State Machines (FSM). The events that drive the execution of the matching are generated by the XML parser. In the execution model, a subscription is considered to match a XML event when the final state of its FSM is reached. We construct a main element index table that indexes all the subscriptions. The main elements are the root elements in block variables. The matching process is based on the "Push" mechanism, namely XML event are used to match subscriptions. For each parsing event, we implemented three functions to deal with the element start tag, the element end tag and the element internal data. Firstly, the main element index table is checked to match the root element in block variables; secondly, other element nodes are performed three checks: the name check, the level check and the predicate check. The name check makes sure that the parsing element name equals the name of the node. The level check makes sure that the level of the element appeared in the XML event matches the level of element in EXML-QL. The predicate check makes sure that the values of the element and attribute satisfy the evaluation of the matching predicates.

For the "WHERE" clauses that may contain the temporal logic, we construct event graphs to evaluate the composite event temporal logic. An event graph is a rooted, directed acyclic graph whose each node has an out-degree edge and two in-degrees edges and is labeled by a time operator. The terminal output of the whole event graph is "true" or "false" representing whether the XML event is triggered or not, or whether a new XML event is constructed or not. The non-terminal outputs of event graph are the union calculation of the time of the two input events. Besides, each node is appended a parameter context to restrict the selection of input events.

In the process of constructing new XML events, currently we only utilize the existing XML-QL interpreter and do the following change:

- transforming EXML-QL into XML-QL;
- Naming the XML events that satisfy the content matching and the temporal logic evaluation and input these named XML events into XML-QL interpreter;
- XML-QL interpreter constructs new output XML events.

4.2 Performance Analysis

Fig.3 is the result of calculating the matching rate of the sequence event. In the matching rate experiment, we restrict the EXML-QL only contains one sequence temporal operator and construct a new output event in the "CONSTRUCT" clause. The number of subscription is 500; the whole number of Block variable is 1000. We have the 500 input XML events that are divided into ten groups of XML events, where only four groups meet the subscriptions. Each group of XML event has the same 50 XML event. The 500 input XML events are inputted in an average time interval way. Fig. 3 shows the event matching rate depends on the event input sequence and the matching rate increased when the number of the accumulated events increased.

In calculating the matching time of the sequence event, we restrict the EXML-QL only contains one sequence temporal operator, does not contain the "CONSTRUCT" clause and uses the event composite pattern operator to point out the event that is need to be forwarded. The number of block variables in each subscription is two; the number of subscriptions is from 500 to 10,000. Fig. 4 shows the result of the experiment that denotes the matching time is mostly proportional to the number of input events.

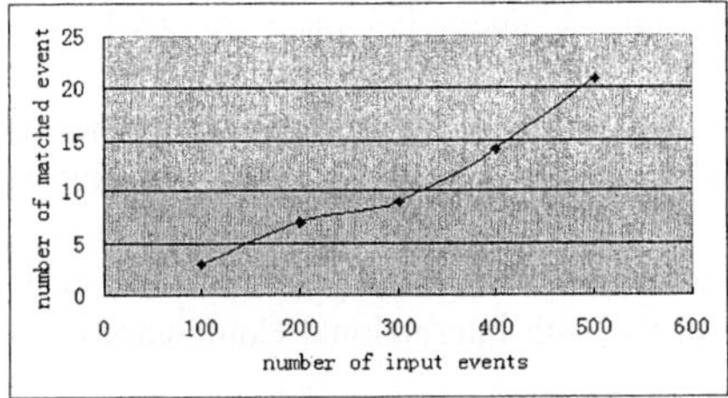

Fig. 3. Results of matching rates

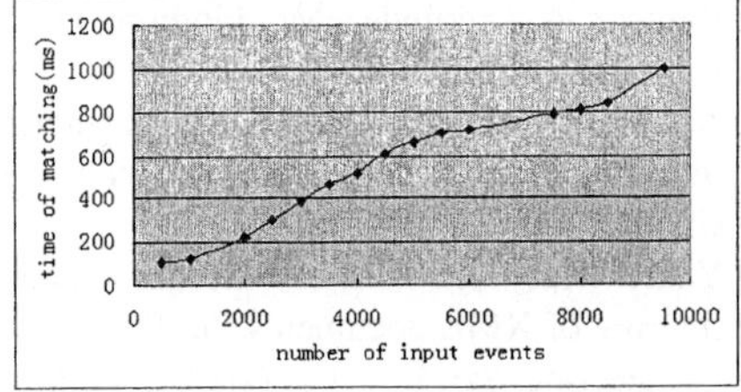

Fig. 4. Results of matching time

5 Related Works

Currently, XML-based Pub/Sub systems are mainly XFilter [3], YFilter [4], XTrie [5] and WebFilter [6]. They adopt XPath as subscription languages to performing efficient filtering of XML documents for large-scale information dissemination systems. XPath has more expressive capability for user interests than XML-QL, but XPath has not ability to construct new XML document. Compared to EXML-QL, XML-QL can't support composite event operations.

The researches of composite events mainly focus on active databases. Snoop was to design an expressive composite event specification language with powerful temporal support [7]. Peter discussed composite event detection in distributed environments [8]. Compared to this paper, it emphasizes particularly on the topological structure analysis of composite event detection in distributed environments and don't make reference to composite patterns such as splitting and merging.

6 Conclusions

We present the study of XML-based composite event matching approach, an important problem in next-generation, scalable content-based Pub/Sub systems. We introduce the temporal logical model to describe the temporal relationship of events in distributed environments and the event composite pattern to describe the different forwarding and triggering patterns. Based on composite event model, a description language (EXML-QL) is presented by extending XML-QL. Finally, according to the peculiarities of the subscription language, the process of matching composite events is presented and further analyzed.

Acknowledgements. This work is partially supported by the Chinese National "973" Key Research Program (2002CB312002, 2002CB312005), the Chinese National "863" High-Tech Program (2001AA113010, 2001AA414020, 2001AA414330).

References

1. Zhuge H.: China's E-science knowledge grid environment. IEEE Intelligent Systems 1 (2004) 13-17
2. Deutsch A., Fernndez M., Florescu D.: XML-QL: A query language for XML. Http://www.w3.org/TR/NOTE-xml-ql/, 1998
3. Altinel M., Franklin M. J.: Efficient filtering of XML document for selective dissemination of information. In: Proceedings of 26th International Conference on Very Large Data Bases, Cario, Egypt (2000) 53-64
4. Yanlei Diao, Peter Fisher, Michael J. Franklin, Raymond T.: Yfilter: efficient and scalable filtering of XML documents. In: Proceedings of the 18th International Conference on Data Engineering, San Jose, CA (2002) 341-342
5. Chan C. Y., Felber P., Garofalakis M., Rastogi R.: Efficient filtering of XML documents with XPath expressions. The VLDB Journal 4 (2002) 354-379
6. Pereira J., Fabret F., Llirbat F., Jacobsen H. A., and Shasha D.: WebFilter: A high throughput XML-based Publish and Subscribe system. In: Proceedings of 27th International Conference on Very Large Data Bases, Roma, Italy (2003) 1101-1104
7. Chakravarthy S., Mishra D.: Snoop: An expressive event specification language for active databases. Techinical Report UF-CIS-TR-93-007, Department of Computer and Information Science, University of Florida, Florida (1993)
8. Peter R. Pietzuch, Brian Shand, Jean Bacon: Composite event detection as a generic middleware extension. IEEE Network 1 (2004) 44-55

An Infrastructure for Grid Job Monitoring

Cuiju Luan, Guanghua Song, and Yao Zheng

College of Computer Science, and Center for Engineering and Scientific Computation, Zhejiang University, Hangzhou, Zhejiang, 310027, P.R. China
{cuijuluan, yao.zheng}@zju.edu.cn
ghsong@cs.zju.edu.cn,

Abstract. As a part of an ongoing project titled MASSIVE, we have designed and implemented the MASSIVE Monitoring System (MMS) to monitor grid jobs. MMS is able to work on multiple sites and support multiple users. In addition to grid jobs, MMS is capable of monitoring and steering file operations. The Job Register Code (JRC) is adopted to map a job to its processes, and used to decide whether a user can access the monitoring information or steer the jobs. MMS supports top-down start-up of the monitoring components, which can ensure the components at their places.

1 Introduction

Getting the idea from power grid, people expect the computational grid to hide the complexity as much as possible. Therefore, for understanding the grid operation, failure detection and performance optimization, monitoring is essential. There are various grid entities to be monitored, such as grid infrastructure and running jobs.

In a grid environment such as MASSIVE [1], when a job is submitted to the grid, there will be three basic steps to be performed, which include file operations before executing the application, execution of the application, and file operations after executing the application. In order to monitor the whole job, the file operations must be monitored besides the application execution.

The MMS is able to monitor and steer file operations and job execution. It can also deal with the job executed on multi-resources. The rest of this paper is arranged as follows. Section 2 introduces related works. Section 3 presents the MMS architecture, while Section 4 details the problems for job monitoring in the MASSIVE. We analyze the monitoring and steering of file operations in Section 5. Finally, we conclude with a summary of our work and an outline of our plans for further research in Section 6.

2 Related Works

There are a few tools developed by different research communities, which feature in application monitoring in the grid. The representative application monitors include CrossGrid/OCM-G, GrADS/-Autopilot, DataGrid/GRM, mercury, NetLogger, etc. All of them can monitor the applications, but few of them can monitor file operations. The MMS can provide the information about the performance and fault detection against file operations, and can also steer the file operations.

H. Zhuge and G.C. Fox (Eds.): GCC 2005, LNCS 3795, pp. 443 – 448, 2005.

In some cases, the jobs in the grid will be submitted to more than one site, which demands that the monitoring system can monitor the jobs running on multiple resources. But not all of the above monitors can do this, such as OCM-G [2].

To monitor the jobs in the grid, there must be some mechanism to map the jobs at the client sides to their processes at the server sides. The Mercury authors proposed a solution in [3] by creating a new temporary user account on the machines for each job. This solution is of several advantages. However, it is not easy to be implemented, because all the jobs will run at the local grid user accounts after passing the authentication with the Globus toolkit. In [4], the authors make the application self-register in the monitoring system in a bottom-up fashion. But the application has to be edited to register itself in this method and all the monitoring components must be at their place. In the MMS, the JRC (Job Register Code) is used to find the processes for the job in a secure way.

3 MMS Architecture

The architecture of the MMS is based on the Grid Monitoring Architecture (GMA) [5] proposed by the Global Grid Forum (GGF). Due to the large scale and distributed feature of the grid, the MMS adopts the distributed and hierarchy structure, which is shown in Fig. 1. The main components of the MMS are Local Monitors (LM), Site Monitors (SM), Node Monitors (NM), Job Register Tables (JRT), and sensors that are not presented in Fig. 1. The others are all grid services participating in the job execution except AP, which represents the application running on the target system.

An NM runs on each node, on which there are processes of the application running. It collects information from processes and transfers them back to the SM on the same site. It can steer the processes according to the commands received from the SM.

There is an SM on each site, to which the job is submitted. The SM accepts the requests from the LMs and distributes them to appropriate NMs on the same site. After receiving the information from the NMs, it forwards them to the LMs.

The LM resides on the client side. It can query or subscribe to the SMs for information about the running jobs, and can send the commands to the SMs to steer the executing of the jobs. It also can control the file operations.

The JRT stores the information of mappings between the JRC and the JVT, where JRC is the job register code provided by the client to register the jobs, and the JVT is the job vector table storing the information about the jobs running on which nodes of the site and what their processes IDs are. It is used for the consumers to find the producers and will be discussed further in Section 4.

There are several non-MMS components in Fig. 1. The MMS will interact with them during the monitoring process. The Job Scheduler allocates the resources to the jobs according to the requirements of the jobs and the information of the resources. It provides the information about the current job running on which sites to the MMS. The Job Executor is responsible for submitting the jobs described in RSL [6] to the JobManagers on the remote resources to be executed. So it registers the jobs with their JRCs. The File Controller and the JobManager will be introduced in the next session.

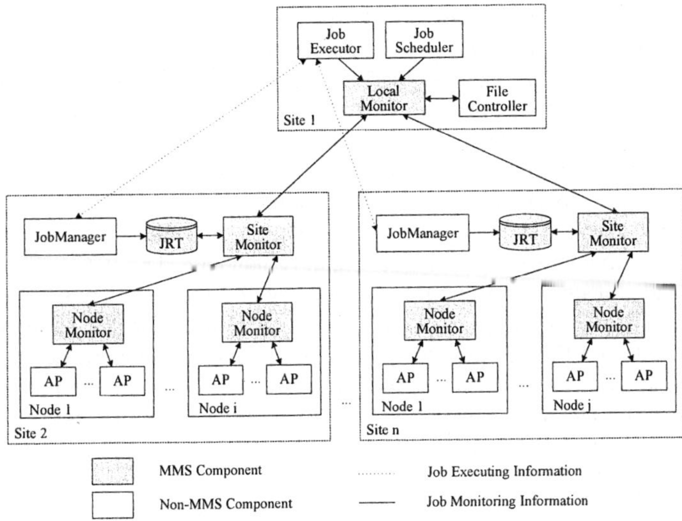

Fig. 1. The MMS architecture

4 Job Monitoring in the MASSIVE

4.1 Job Monitoring with MMS in the MASSIVE

Almost all the jobs in the MASSIVE involve the file operations, such as transferring files, deleting files, creating folders, etc. If one of the operations fails, the job cannot be executed successfully. Moreover, if the file is very large, the transferring performance will affect the whole performance of the job obviously. Therefore, the monitoring of the file operations is necessary.

Because the grid is dynamic, the performance of file transferring is also. Therefore, one mode of file transferring cannot be always the optimization. It is significant to change the transferring dynamically. The MMS provides this function, so the user can steer the file transferring according the monitoring views to improve the performance.

In the MMS, the LM is used to monitor the file operations. The LM gets the information about file operations from the File Controller, which is responsible for various operations related to files. Furthermore, the LM can control the file operations by sending the commands to the File Controller.

4.2 Mapping a Job to Its Processes

Given all the components related to the monitoring system, there should be some mechanism for the consumers to find the producers. The SM can be regarded as the agent between LM and NM. The LM and NM need not to know about each other, they communicate through SM. Therefore, SM should know which nodes the job is running on and what the process IDs are. In MMS, the JRT is used to do this.

The JRT is Job Register Table, which stores the Job Register Code (JRC) and its corresponding Job Vector Table (JVT). The JRC is supplied by the LM and used to identify the job. The JVT stores the (hostname, process ID) pairs, which indicate which nodes the processes of the job is running on and what their IDs are. The JRT is filled by the JobManager, which is a grid service in Globus Toolkit 2.4 and is edited to complete the above function.

The JRC is provided by the client to register its job in the monitoring system, and it will be used by the LM to monitor the jobs submitted to the remote sites. Its format is userID@hostname:jobID, where userID denotes who owns this job, hostname indicates from which resources the job is submitted, and jobID is a random number with nine digits to identify a job uniquely at the client side. The JRC is constructed by the client and transferred to the JobManagers of the target systems as an attribute specified in RSL. By translating the job description, the JobManager gets the JRC. Getting the JRC and JVT of the same job, the JobManager will store them in JRT.

At the client side, the LM can get the information about where the job is submitted to from the Job Scheduler. When querying the monitoring information, the LM will create and send the JRC with the query command to the SMs of the resources scheduled to the job. Then the SMs will search the JRTs for the JVTs of the job with the JRC. With the JVTs, the SMs get the (hostname, process ID) pairs. Thereby, the SMs find the NMs that can monitor the processes belong to the job.

4.3 Startup of SM and NM

In the MMS, there are problems about how to start up the SMs and the NMs, and how to ensure the NMs available on the nodes.

The SM is permanent. It can be started as the other grid services. The JobManager can start it also. In the latter case, before the JobManager creating the JVT for the job, it can check if the SM is running on the site and start it if the answer is negative.

The NMs can be started by the SM. Before the SM querying the processes information, it can examine whether the LM is on. If there is no LM available, the SM can create one on the node and leave it there to work on.

Thereby, the MMS adopts top-down start-up to start the monitoring components, which can ensure the components at their place whenever needed. By this method, the two problems described above can be solved at the same time. Therefore, the monitoring can be carried out for the subsequent jobs even if the SMs or NMs abort abnormally.

4.4 Security in the MMS

The MASSIVE components and services use Globus GSI security model and the user certificates for authentication. All the authenticated and authorized users can access the information of the infrastructure. So the GSI is enough. But to the monitoring information of the job, only the owner can access. Moreover, the MMS is a multi-user system and it handles various jobs, so the access control is needed besides the GSI.

The JRC is used to judge whether the user is the owner of the job. When the user uses the JRC, of which the format is userID@hostname:jobID, to query the monitoring information or send the control commands, the SM will check if the connection comes from the host of the hostname and if his ID is userID. Only the passed user can access the monitoring information or steer the jobs.

5 Analyses of File Operation Monitoring and Steering

In this section, we will analyze the monitoring and steering of the file operations to illustrate the suitability, flexibility and validity of the MMS.

The application in the experiments is structural analysis of a crank. To ease the experiments the job will be submitted to a cluster from a desktop PC. The input data are several mesh files and one parameter file detailing the solving process and method. They should all be transferred to the cluster before the job execution.

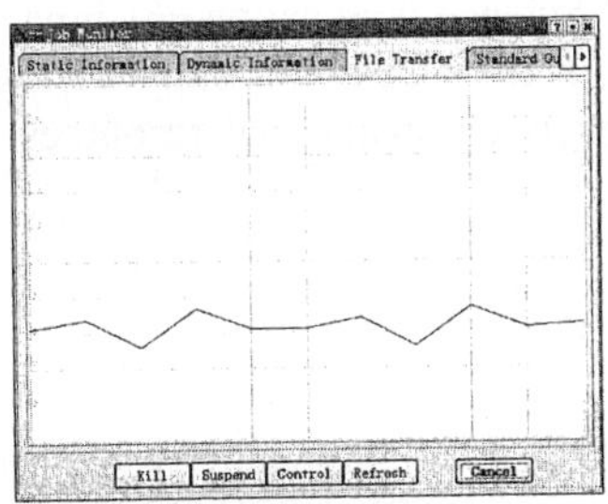

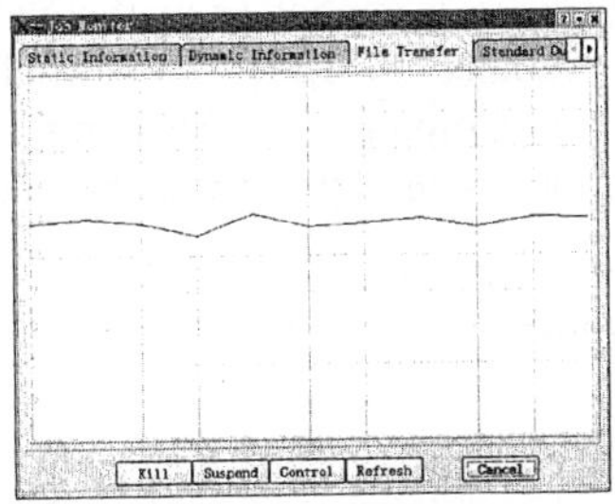

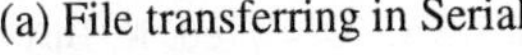

(a) File transferring in Serial (b) File Transferring with Parallelism of 4

Fig. 2. The monitoring views without change of parallelism during the file transferring

In the first set of experiments, all the files were transferred in the same mode and no changes were made during the files transferring. The monitoring views are presented in Fig. 2, where (a) and (b) are the performance views with parallelism of 1 and 4, respectively. The performance of (b) is better than (a), which indicates that the efficiency of the file transferring in parallel is better than in serial.

In the second set of experiments, the mode of file transfer was changed during the transferring. The corresponding monitoring views are presented in Fig. 3, where (a) and (b) are the performance views of parallelism changing from 1 to 4 and 8, respectively. Both views indicate that increasing the parallelism improves the performance of file transfer by about 37.5% and 44%, respectively.

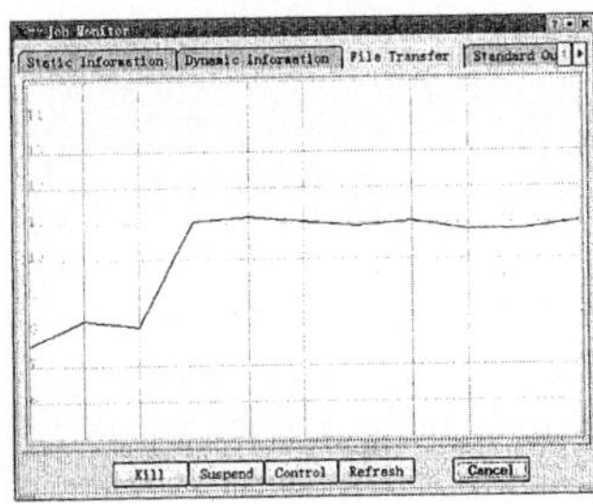

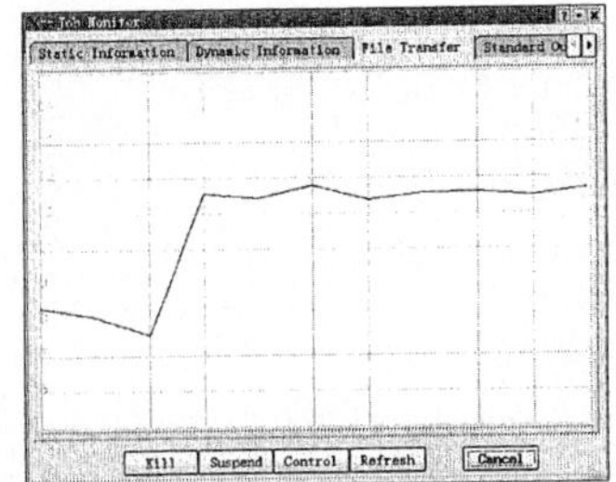

(a) Parallelism changing from 1 to 4 (b) Parallelism changing from 1 to 8

Fig. 3. The monitoring views with change of parallelism during the file transferring

6 Conclusions and Future Work

In this paper we presented the MMS – a scalable and efficient monitoring system for the grid jobs. We have shown that the MMS supports multiple sites. It can monitor and control the file operations that are normally essential for the execution of the grid jobs.

Presently, we have implemented a prototype for the MMS. On extending the types of the sensors, we will deploy it in a grid project and adopt more suitable tools to use the monitoring information.

This work is supported by the National Natural Science Foundation of China under grant Number 90412014. We would like to thank the Center for Engineering and Scientific Computation, Zhejiang University, for its computational resources, with which the research project has been carried out.

References

1. Yao Zheng, Guanghua Song, Jifa Zhang, Jianjun Chen: An Enabling Environment for Distributed Simulation and Visualization. Proceedings of the 5th IEEE/ACM International Workshop on Grid Computing (Grid 2004) (Pittsburgh, USA, 2004), (ed. R. Buyya), IEEE Computer Society, Los Alamitos, California (2004) 26-33
2. Bartosz Balis, Marian Bubak, Marcin Radecki, Tomasz Szepieniec, Roland Wismüller: Application Monitoring in CrossGrid and Other Grid Projects. Proc. Second European Across Grids Conference, AxGrids 2004, Nicosia, Cyprus (2004) 212-219
3. Zoltán Balaton, Gábor Gombás: Resource and Job Monitoring in the Grid. Proc. of EuroPar'2003 Conference, Klagenfurt, Austria (2003) 404-411
4. Bartosz Balis, Marian Bubak, Wodzimierz Funika, Tomasz Szepieniec, Roland Wismüller: An Infrastructure for Grid Application Monitoring. Proceedings of the 9th European PVM/MPI Users' Group Meeting on Recent Advances in Parallel Virtual Machine and Message Passing Interface, September 29-October 02 (2002) 41-49
5. B. Tierney, R. Aydt, D. Gunter, W. Smith, M. Swany, V. Taylor, R. Wolski: A Grid Monitoring Architecture. http://www.ggf.org/documents/GFD/GFD-I.7.pdf
6. Resource Specification Language, http://www-fp.globus.org/gram/rsl.html

Grid Enabled Master Slave Task Scheduling for Heterogeneous Processor Paradigm

Ching-Hsien Hsu, Tai-Lung Chen, and Guan-Hao Lin

Department of Computer Science and Information Engineering
Chung Hua University, Hsinchu, Taiwan 300, R.O.C.
chh@chu.edu.tw

Abstract. Efficient task scheduling is an important issue on system performance of computational grid. In this paper, we present an efficient method for dispatching tasks to heterogeneous processors in master slave environment. The main idea of the proposed technique is first to allocate tasks to processors that with lower communication overheads. Improvement of this approach is that average turnaround time can be minimized. The proposed model can also be applied to map tasks to heterogeneous cluster systems in grid environments in which the communication costs are various from clusters.

1 Introduction

One of the virtues of high performance computing is to integrate massive computing resources for accomplishing large computation problems. The use of master slave cluster of computers as a platform for high-performance and high-availability computing is mainly due to their cost-effective nature. The master slave tasking is a simple and widely used technique. Figure 1 shows an example of the master slave paradigm. One master node connects to n slave nodes. A pool of independent tasks are dispatched by master processor and be processed by the n slave processors. Communication between master and slave nodes is handled through a shared medium (e.g. bus) that can be accessed only in exclusive mode. Based on master-slave architecture, Olivier Beaumont *et al.* [1, 2] presented a method on master-slave paradigm to forecast the quantity of tasks each processor needs to receive in a period of time. In their implementation, intuitionally, fast processor receives more tasks in the proportional distribution policy. Tasks are also prior allocated to faster slave processors and expected higher system throughput could be obtained.

In this paper, an efficient method for scheduling homogeneous tasks to heterogeneous processors in master slave environment is presented. The main idea of the proposed technique is first to allocate tasks to processors that with lower communication overheads. A significant improvement of this approach is that average turnaround time can be minimized. The second advantage of the proposed approach is that system throughput can be increased by dispersing processor idle time.

The rest of this paper is organized as follows. Section 2 introduces the research architecture and defines notation used in this paper. Section 3 assesses the new scheduling algorithm of the master-slave model. The performance comparisons and experimental results are discussed in section 4. Finally, section 5 makes conclusions.

H. Zhuge and G.C. Fox (Eds.): GCC 2005, LNCS 3795, pp. 449–454, 2005.

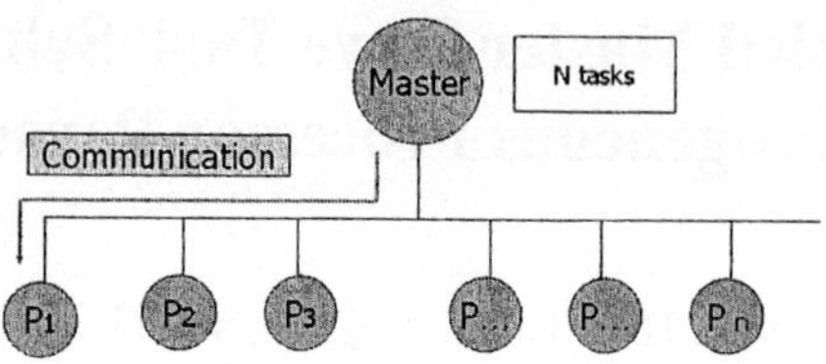

Fig. 1. The Master-Slave paradigm

2 Preliminaries

In this section, we first introduce the basic concept and models of this paper. Then, we define notations and terminologies that will be used in later sections.

2.1 Research Architecture

We revisit several characteristics that were introduced by Beaumont *et al.* [1, 2]. Based on the master slave paradigm demonstrated in figure 1, this paper conforms to the following assumptions.

- Heterogeneous processors: all processors have different computation speed.
- Identical tasks: all tasks are of equal size.
- Non-preemption: tasks are considered to be atomic.

Exclusive communication: communications from master node to different slave processors can not be overlapped.

2.2 Definitions

To simplify the presentation, we first define notations and terminologies used in this paper.

<u>*Definition 1*</u>: In a master slave system, master processor is denoted by M and the n slaves are represented by $P_1, P_2, \ldots, P_n$, where n is the number of slave processors.

<u>*Definition 2*</u>: We use T_i to represent the time of a slave processor P_i to complete one task. In this paper, we assume the computation speed of the n processors is sorted and $T_1 \leq T_2 \leq \ldots \leq T_n$.

<u>*Definition 3*</u>: T_{comm} is the time of a slave processor to receive one task.

<u>*Definition 4:*</u> A Basic Scheduling Cycle (*BSC*) is defined as $BSC = lcm(T_1 + T_{comm}, T_2 + T_{comm}, \ldots, T_m + T_{comm})$, where m is the maximum number of processors that joins task scheduling.

<u>*Definition 5:*</u> The number of tasks a processor P_i must receive in a scheduling cycle is defined as

$$task(P_i) = \frac{BSC}{T_i + T_{comm}}.$$

Definition 6: The communication cost of processor P_i in *BSC* is defined as $comm(P_i) = T_{comm} \times task(P_i)$

Definition 7: The computation time of processor P_i in *BSC* is defined as $comp(P_i) = T_i \times task(P_i)$

Definition 8: The *performance factor* of processor P_i is defined as $\frac{T_{comm}}{T_i + T_{comm}}$. The computation capacity of a master slave system is defined as $\delta = \sum_{i=1}^{m} \frac{T_{comm}}{T_i + T_{comm}}$, where *m* is the maximum number of processors that joins task scheduling.

3 Master Slave Task Scheduling with Shortest Communication Time First (SCTF) Algorithm

In this section, we discuss the problem of task scheduling on master slave system in two cases depending on the value of system computation capacity (δ).

The *MJF* scheduling algorithm distributes tasks to slave processor according to processors' speed [1, 2]. Faster processor receives tasks first. This is obviously an efficient approach if the communication contention between master and slave processors is not considered. We present the Shortest Communication Time First (*SCTF*) algorithm.

3.1 $\delta \leq 1$ Scheduling Without Processor Idle

We consider again the example in Figure 2 for examining master-slave scheduling with $\delta \leq 1$. In the *SCTF* implementation, tasks are prior allocated to slave processor that with shortest communication costs. Therefore, P_4 first receives 2 tasks and then P_3 receives 3 tasks, P_2 receives 3 tasks; finally, P_1 receives 4 tasks in the first *BSC*. Consequently, the *SCTF* minimizes the average turnaround time.

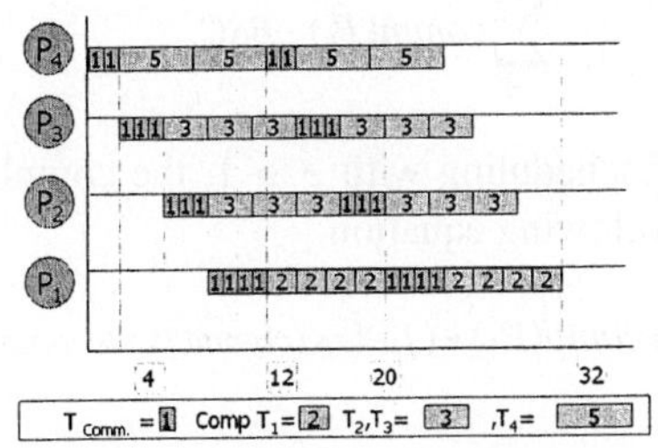

Fig. 2. Shortest Communication Time First (*SCTF*) tasking when $\delta \leq 1$

Lemma 1: Given a *SCTF* scheduling with $\delta \leq 1$, the completion time of the jth *BSC* can be calculated by the following equation.

$$T(BSC_j) = BSC + comp(P_1) + (j-1)\times(comm(P_1)+comp(P_1)) \quad (1)$$

Proof: Due to page limitation, we omit the proof in this version.

3.2 $\delta > 1$ Scheduling with Processor Dispersed Idle

We use the same example in Figure 3 to demonstrate the scheduling method with dispersive idle when $\delta > 1$. According to definition 5, we have $task(P_1)$=20, $task(P_2)$=15, $task(P_3)$=15. Applying the *SCTF* concept illustrated in section 3.1, P4 first receives 12 tasks and then P_3 receives 15 tasks, P_2 receives 15 tasks; finally, P_1 receives 20 tasks in the first *BSC* as shown in Figure 3. It becomes available and can receive more tasks for computing. However, the master processor is sending tasks to P_1. When t=62, master processor sends tasks to P_4 again. Moreover, we observe that the *MJF* algorithm finishes 60 tasks in 100 units of time. The throughput is 0.6. While in *SCTF*, there are 62 tasks completed during 102 time units. The throughput of *SCTF* is 62/102 (≈0.61) > 0.6. Consequently, the *SCTF* algorithm delivers higher system throughput. On the other hand, the average turnaround time of the *SCTF* algorithm for the first two *BSC*s is 164/124 (≈1.32) which is less than the *MJF*'s average turnaround time 160/120 (≈1.33).

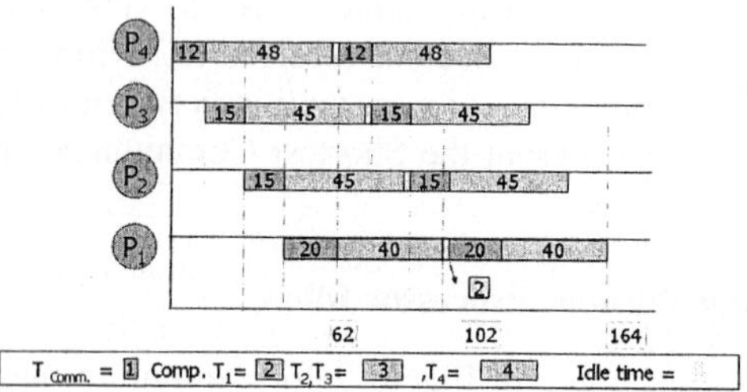

Fig. 3. Shortest Communication Time First (*SCTF*) tasking when $\delta > 1$

Corollary 1: Given an *SCTF* scheduling with $\delta > 1$, T_{idle}^{SCTF} is the idle time of each slave processor and $T_{idle}^{SCTF} = \sum_{i=1}^{\max+1} comm(P_i) - BSC$.

Lemma 2: Given a *SCTF* scheduling with $\delta > 1$, the completion time of the jth *BSC* can be calculated by the following equation.

$$T(BSC_j) = \sum_{i=1}^{\max+1} comm(P_i) + comp(P_1) + (j-1)\times(comm(P_1)+comp(P_1)+T_{idle}^{SCTF}) . \quad (2)$$

4 Performance Evaluation

To evaluate the performance of the proposed method, we have implemented the *SCTF* and *MJF* algorithms. We compare some criteria in two scenarios; section 4.1 and 4.2 studies the simulation results for slight heterogeneous processors. Sections 4.3 present the performance of the algorithm upon different processor number for computation.

4.1 The Variation of Processor Speed Is Small

In this subsection, we discussed the variation of processor speed is large than the example of section 4.1. Test in this subsection is based ±10 processor speed variation. The computation speed of slave processors are T_1=3, T_2=3, T_3=5, T_4=7 and T_5=13. Figure 4 shows the simulation results for 5 processors with ±10 speed variation when $\delta \leq 1$. We measured the average task turnaround time. The *SCTF* algorithm performs better than the *MJF* method.

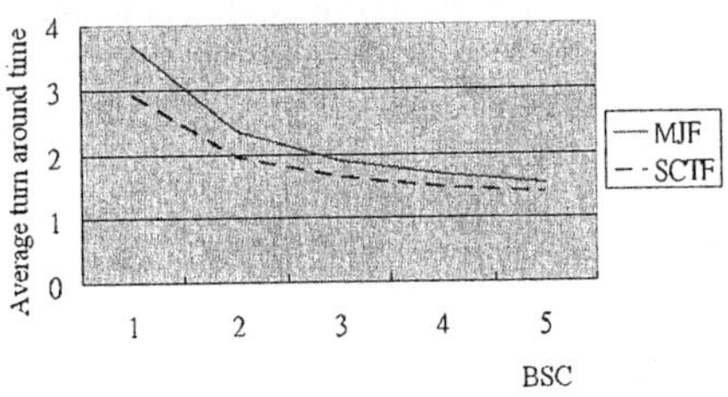

Fig. 4. Average task turnaround time of simulation results for 5 processors with ±10 speed variation when $\delta \leq 1$

4.2 The Variation of Processor Speed Is Large

In this section, Figure 5 shows the simulation results for 5 processors with ±9 speed variation when $\delta > 1$. The computation speed of processors are T_1=2, T_2=3, T_3=4, T_4=4 and T_5=11. We also calculate processor idle time in this test. Figure 5 gives average turnaround time during different number of *BSC* time period. The *SCTF* algorithm performs better than the *MJF* method.

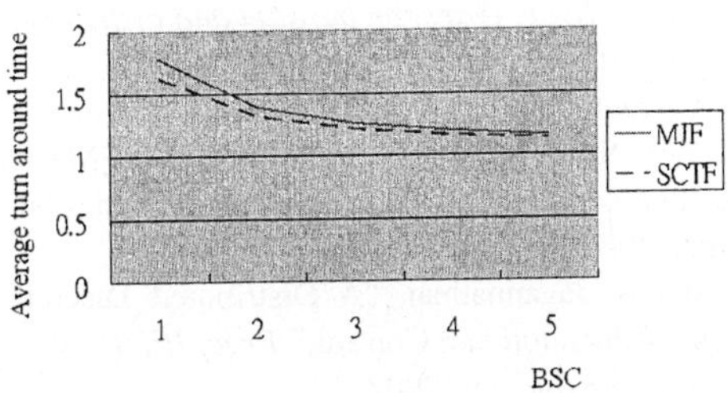

Fig. 5. Average task turnaround time of simulation results for 5 processors with ±9 speed variation when $\delta > 1$

4.3 Simulation with Different Number of Processors

Another simulation for evaluating average turnaround time is made upon different number of processors and shown in Figure6. The computation speed of those slave processors is set as T_1=3, T_2=3, T_3=5, T_4=7, T_5=11, T_6=13, and T_7=15. For the cases when processor number is 1, 2,..., 6, we have $\delta \leq 1$. When processor number

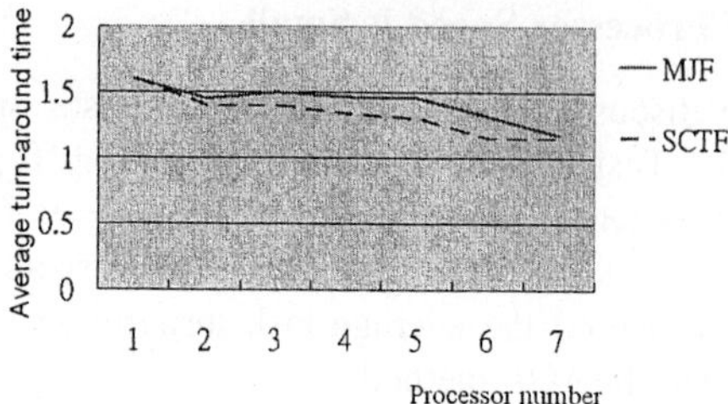

Fig. 6. Task average turnaround time on different number of processors

increases to 7, we obtain $\delta > 1$. In either case, the *SCTF* algorithm conduces better average turnaround time.

5 Conclusion

The master-slave task scheduling is a typical problem in computational grid system. In this paper, we have presented an efficient algorithm, *SCTF* for heterogeneous processors tasking. One significant improvement of the *SCTF* algorithm is that average turnaround time can be minimized. The second advantage of the proposed approach is that system throughput can be increased by dispersing processor idle time. Our preliminary analysis and simulation results indicate that the *SCTF* algorithm outperforms Beaumont's method in terms of lower average turnaround time, higher average throughput, less processor idle time and higher processors' utilization.

References

1. Oliver Beaumont, Arnaud Legrand and Yves Robert, "The Master-Slave Paradigm with Heterogeneous Processors," *IEEE Trans. on parallel and distributed systems*, Vol. 14, No.9, pp. 897-908, September 2003.
2. Cyril Banino, Olivier Beaumont, Larry Carter, Fellow, Jeanne Ferrante, Senior Member, Arnaud Legrand and Yves Robert, "Scheduling Strategies for Master-Slave Tasking on Heterogeneous Processor Platforms," *IEEE Trans. on parallel and distributed systems*, Vol. 15, No.4, pp.319-330, April 2004.
3. A.T. Chronopoulos and S. Jagannathan, "A Distributed Discrete-Time Neural Network Architecture for Pattern Allocation and Control," *Proc. IPDPS Workshop Bioinspired Solutions to Parallel Processing Problems*, 2002.
4. S. Charcranoon, T.G. Robertazzi and S. Luryi, "Optimizing Computing Costs Using Divisible Load Analysis," *IEEE Trans. Computers*, Vol. 49, No. 9, pp. 987-991, Sept. 2000.
5. Thyagaraj Thanalapati and Sivarama Dandamudi, "An Efficient Adaptive Scheduling Scheme for Distributed Memory Multicomputers," *IEEE Trans. on parallel and distributed systems*, Vol. 12, No. 7, pp.758-767, July 2001.
6. O. Beaumont, V. Boudet, A. Petitet, F. Rastello and Y. Robert, "A Proposal for a Heterogeneous Cluster ScaLAPACK (Dense Linear Solvers)," *IEEE Trans. Computers*, Vol. 50, No. 10, pp. 1052-1070, Oct. 2001.
7. O. Beaumont, V. Boudet, F. Rastello and Y. Robert, "Matrix-Matrix Multiplication on Heterogeneous Platforms," *Proc. Int'l Conf. Parallel Processing*, 2000.

Optimizing Large File Transfer on Data Grid

Teng Ma and Junzhou Luo

Dept. of Computer Science and Engineering, Southeast University,
210096, Nanjing, P.R. China
{mateng, jluo}@seu.edu.cn

Abstract. AMS02 science activities collaborated by Southeast university and CERN led by Samuel C.C. Ting are generating the unprecedented volume of data. The existing FTP has caused user to discomfort by delay and data loss according to network status. Therefore, it is necessary to efficiently raise transfer performance and minimize data loss. In this paper, we will introduce a new large file transfer tool based on QoS and multi-stream technology- BBFTP which is used in the AMS02 experiment. Through Monte Carol simulation data transfer experiments between SEU-SOC and ShanDong University node in ChinaGrid, we found the optimal parameters which help to promote BBFTP throughput performance. This paper focuses on related works about performance enhancement of large file transfer, which is critical to the performance of SOC (Science Operation Center).

1 Introduction

AMS02 science activities are generating large amount of data including Monte Carol simulation. This kind of High Energy and Nuclear Physics E-science drives the development of ultra-scale networking, whose explorations at high energy frontier are breaking our understanding of the fundamental interactions, structure and symmetries that govern the nature of matter and space-time in our universe. The HENP project like AMS02 encompasses thousands of physicists from hundreds of universities and laboratories in more than 20 countries. Collaboration on this global scale would not have been attempted if the physicists could not count on excellent network performance. Rapid and reliable data transport, at speeds of 1 to 10 Gbps in the future, is a key enabler of the global collaborations in physics. This network characteristic of grid environment is not the same as the traditional serial line of dial-up modems. The "bandwidth*delay product" is larger than traditional network. TCP performance depends not upon the transfer rate itself, but rather upon the product of the transfer rate and the round-trip delay. This "bandwidth*delay product" measures the amount of data that would fill the pipe; it is the buffer space required at sender and receiver to obtain maximum throughput on the TCP connection over the path, the amount of unacknowledged data that TCP must handle in order to keep the pipeline full. TCP performance problems arise when the "bandwidth*delay product" is large. We refer to an Internet path operating in this region as a "long fat pipe", and a network containing this path as an "LFN". In this paper, we will test BBFTP- a bulk data transfer tool- in this "LFN" environment and meanwhile find out optimal parameters for Monte Carol simulation dataset transferring.[5][7] [9]

H. Zhuge and G.C. Fox (Eds.): GCC 2005, LNCS 3795, pp. 455–460, 2005.

In the remainder of the paper, we first introduce some theories and tools related with large file transfer in high performance computing. In the third section, we give out the performance optimization way. Through large file transfer experiments by BBFTP in section 4, we conclude that the bandwidth among ChinaGrid nodes meets the AMS need by using BBFTP.

2 Related Works

To improve the performance in high bandwidth-delay product networks, congestion control keeping efficient, fair, scalable, and stable plays a key role. The easiest way to improve the performance is to open multiple TCP connections in parallel, while this approach leaves the parameter of the number of connections to be determined by the user, which may result in heavy congestion with too many connection numbers. There are several researches addressing this issue such as FAST TCP [8] [10], HighSpeed TCP [11] and BBFTP [1] [2] [3] [6].

FAST TCP [8] [10] is a new TCP congestion control algorithm for high-speed long-latency networks. The authors highlight the approach taken by FAST TCP to address the four difficulties, at both packet and flow levels, which the current TCP implementation has at large windows. They describe the architecture and characterize the equilibrium and stability properties of FAST TCP and meanwhile present experimental results comparing their Linux prototype with TCP Reno, HSTCP, and STCP in terms of throughput, fairness, stability, and responsiveness. FAST TCP aims to rapidly stabilize high-speed long-latency networks into steady, efficient and fair operating points, in dynamic sharing environments, and the preliminary results are promising.

HighSpeed TCP [11] is an attempt to improve congestion control of TCP for large congestion windows with better flexibility, better scaling, better slow-start behavior, and competing more fairly with current TCP, keeping backward compatibility and incremental deployment. It modifies the TCP response function only for large congestion windows to reach high bandwidth reasonably quickly when in slow-start, and to reach high bandwidth without overly long delays when recovering from multiple retransmit timeouts, or when ramping-up from a period with small congestion windows.

BBFTP [1] [2] [3] [6] is a file transfer system, developed by the High-Energy Physics community. BBFTP is a non-interactive FTP-like system that supports parallel TCP streams for data transfers, allowing it to achieve bandwidths that are greater than normal FTP. BBFTP first splits the file in several parts, and creates a parallel process for each part. Each process will send the data using its own socket. It implements its own transfer protocol, which is optimized for large files (larger than 2GB) and secure as it does not read the password in a file and encrypts the connection information.

3 Optimizing Way of Large File Transfer

From the existed theories and tools, we found the main factors associated with the performance of large file transfer can be classified into three types: parallel stream number、 TCP Window size and compression algorithm.

The easiest way to improve the performance of large file transfer is to open multiple TCP connections in parallel. While increasing parallel numbers may result in two problems: heavy congestion and CPU overload with too many connection numbers. Therefore there is a best value of parallel stream number for every environment.

TCP window is the amount of outstanding (unacknowledged by the recipient) data a sender can send on a particular connection before it gets an acknowledgment back from the receiver that it has gotten some of it. Traditionally, TCP only has a 16-bit field for window size, which can specify 64kB at most. 64KB by default in most OS, is too little for high bandwidth E-Science computing environment. The window scale extension expands the definition of the TCP window to 32 bits and then uses a scale factor to carry this 32-bit value in the 16-bit Window field of the TCP header. TCP extensions for High Performance allow large windows outstanding packets for long-delay, high-bandwidth paths, by using a window scaling option and timestamps. By the extension, a window-scaling factor (0 to 14 bits) can be negotiated at connection setup of end points, with which window sizes of 1 Gigabytes can be represented.

Compression algorithm is the same important for large file transfer such as Monte Carol dataset. In our transfer experiment, we used "on-the-fly" compression technology to zip the Monte Carol dataset during transfer. In following section , we will give out the experiment result by modifying the parameters associated with TCP Window、parallel stream number and compression algorithm.

4 Data Transfer Experiment

The transfer test is carried out between SDU HPC and SEU-SOC. The host "grid5.seu.edu.cn" is configured with Redhat Linux Enterprise 3、Intel Pentium 4 CPU、RAM 768 MB、60 G Disk and 100M network control. The host "lcg.seu.edu.cn" in Shan Dong HPC is configured with Redhat Linux 7.3、Intel Xeon 2.8 GHz、1G RAM、60 G Disk and 1000M infineband. Both client and server of BBFTP 3.2.0 are installed in machines in SEU and SDU including Iperf (bandwidth test tool), Traceroute and Ping network measure tools.

4.1 TCP Window

We transfer 20M Monte Carol dataset from grid5.seu.edu.cn to lcg.seu.edu.cn at each of the following TCP window sizes 128KB、256KB、512KB、1MB、2MB、3MB and 4MB. For each window size we used same number of parallel data streams to comprise each transfer. All the parallel stream numbers are 10. The gzip option is on. Each throughput is shown as Figure 1.

4.2 Multi-stream Transfer

Whereas the normal FTP protocol implements one data connection only, BBFTP opens multiple data connections depending on the number of streams required (client option -p and server option -m). The server listens on ephemeral ports which are sent

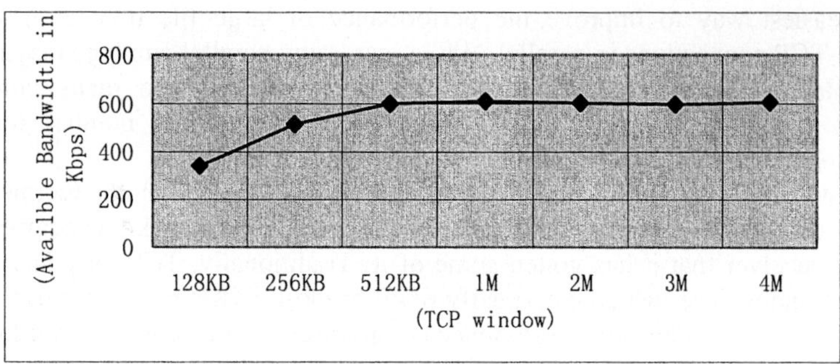

Fig. 1. Transfer throughput VS TCP window

to the client. These ports can be chosen in a range defined at compile-time or at run-time. The server initiates the data connection after the client has sent him its private IP address and the listening port. This port is ephemeral ports (>1023). (It is possible to define a range of ports when starting the client using the -D option) The server can then establish the connections to the specified ports from its port std-1 (i.e. 5020 by default).

We transfer 20M Monte Carol dataset from grid5.seu.edu.cn to lcg.seu.edu.cn. Each time we change number of parallel streams. In the experiment, the window sizes of sender and receiver are both 64KB and the parallel stream number is from 1 to 13.

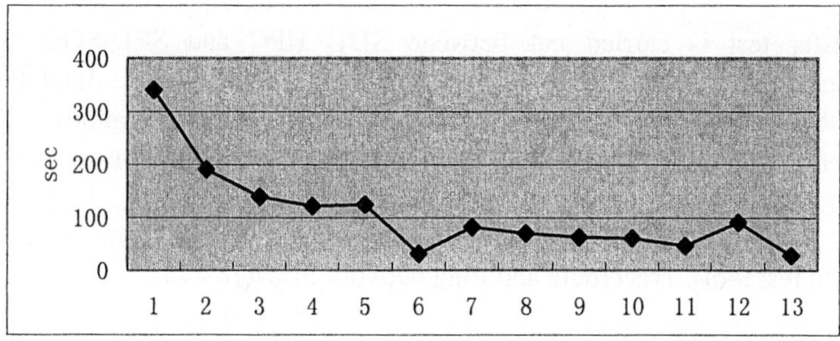

Fig. 2. Transferring time VS Parallel stream number

Figure 2 shows the situation of transferring 20M Monte Carol dataset from grid5.seu.edu.cn to lcg.seu.edu.cn. From the Figure 2, with the increasing of parallel stream number, the transfer rate is linearly increased. But after the number reach 6 and 11, because of limit of system resource, the trend of variation has changed. It is proved that transfer rate can be advanced by promoting parallel stream number.

4.3 "On-the-fly" Compression

BBFTP uses a technology "on–the-fly" data compression to zip the transferring data. This kind of compression is very suitable for Monte Carol dataset transferring.

We transfer 20M Monte Carol dataset from grid5.seu.edu.cn to lcg.seu.edu.cn with and without compressing data. In the experiment, the window sizes of send and receive are both 64KB, and the parallel stream number is from 1 to 13.

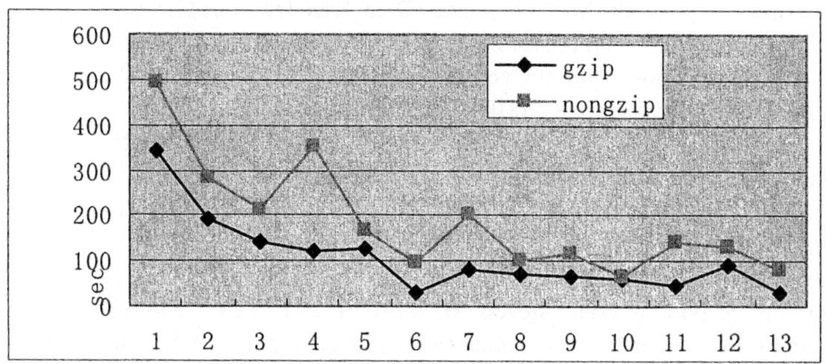

Fig. 3. Transferring with GZIP and without GZIP

Figure 3 shows the transferring 20M data with GZIP option and without GZIP. Y axis represents the parallel stream number. X axis represents the transfer time. "On the flight" packet compression during transfer has better performance than without GZIP. Then, we did a static compression experiment by RAR and GZIP compression tools. We found out that 20.9 MB Monte Carol dataset was compressed to 20.7MB size. It seems the static compression is not suitable for these datasets as a whole. "On the fly" compression during transfer after splitting into several parts sounds perfect. It greatly reduces the bandwidth consumption of Monte Carol dataset transferring.

5 Conclusions

We presented the actual environment, performance and test results of Transferring Monte Carol dataset from SEU-SOC to SDU HPC by BBFTP. Concerning BBFTP testing, three things are worth to note by Monte Carol dataset transfer. First, because of the character of Monte Carol dataset, "on-the-fly" compression is very efficient and worthy of reducing the bandwidth consumption for AMS dataset transfer.

Secondly, with parallel stream number increasing, transfer rate advances greatly. But there is a best parallel number for balance between transfer rate and CPU overload. This number varies with experiment environment and network status.

According to the BBFTP test, the average bandwidth between SEU-SOC and SDU HPC is 3.43MB/sec for large files, so that the network performance reaches AMS need for collaboration by ChinaGrid nodes. Utilizing the unused computing resource on ChinaGrid is very important for E-Science collaboration.

Acknowledgement. This work is supported by National Natural Science Foundation of China under the Special Program "Network based Science Activity Environment" (90412014).

References

1. A.Elin, A.Klimentov. Data transmission program for the AMS-02 ISS Mission, AMS Note 2001-11-02, Aug.14, 2002
2. M. Boschini , A. Favalli, M. Levtchenko. Data Transfer from Central Production Facility to Italian Ground Segment. A prototype.AMSnote-2003_10_01
3. A. Elin, A. Klimentov. Data transmission programs for the AMS-02 ISS Mission, AMS Note 2001-11-02 November 8, 2001
4. P.Fisher, A.Klimentov, A.Mujunen, J.Ritakari. AMS Ground Support Computers for ISS mission, AMS Note 2002-03-01, March 12, 2002.
5. Matthews, Cottrell. Achieving High Data Throughput in Research Networks. CHEP2001.
6. http://doc.in2p3.fr/bbftp/
7. http://www-iepm.slac.stanford.edu/monitoring/bulk/
8. Cheng Jin, David X.Wei, Steven H. Low. FAST TCP: Motivation, Architecture, Algorithms, Performance. http://netlab.caltech.edu/pub/papers/FAST-infocom20 04.pdf
9. Sylvain Ravot. TCP transfers over high latency/bandwidth network &Grid TCP. http://netlab.caltech.edu/FAST/meetings/2002july/GridTCP.ppt
10. Harvey B Newman. HENP Grids and Networks Global Virtual Organizations. http://netlab.caltech.edu/FAST/meetings/2002july/HENPGridsNets_FAST070202.ppt
11. S.Floyd, in Internet draft, draft-floyd-tcp-highspeed-02.txt (2003), http://www.icir.org/floyd/hstcp.html.

A Parallel Collaborative Algorithm Based on Partial Duality in Interconnected Power Grids

Ke-yan Liu[1], Wan-xing Sheng[2], and Yun-hua Li[1]

[1] Beijing University of Aeronautics and Astronautics,
100083 Beijing, China
liukeyan@asee.buaa.edu.cn, yunhua.l@263.net
[2] China Electric Power Research Institute,
100085 Beijing, China
wxsheng@263.net

Abstract. This paper investigated a collaborative optimal computation method in large-scale interconnected power grids. A decomposition of collaborative model based on partial duality is analyzed, and a parallel algorithm based on DC optimal power flow is presented in decomposition of interconnected power grids. The globe OPF computation of large power grid is decomposed into computations of multi regions subproblems, which are quadratic programming problem. The information of interchanging among regions is export price and boundary nodal bus phase angle. The IEEE RTS-96 with two and three interconnected regions is studied to illustrate the effect of the proposed algorithm. The total computation time is decreased and the complex system is easier to analyze.

1 Introduction

The optimization literature has been interested in studying and developing procedures that solve optimization problem with some special structure [1]. Optimization performance can be improved by taking the advantage of this structure, for example, integer and continuous variables, variable dependencies, coupling constraints, etc. A solution of very large problem can be decomposed and solved using distributed computation resources. With the increasing availability of hardware and software, distributed computation has been used in various fields.

The basic idea to solve optimization of the big system is to decompose the overall problem into a series of subproblems, and to simplify the problem by solving optimization of every subproblem. The decomposition method is to dispose large-scale system optimization with the basic idea to decompose the original problem to several independent subproblems to reduce step number that the problem solves, and to obtain the overall optimal solution. The common methods to decomposition can be categorized as: the Benders decomposition, the Dantzig-Wolfe decomposition and Lagrange relaxation decomposition. In this paper, based on the partial duality [2], the overall OPF solution problem is decomposed into online coordination optimization solutions of many regions.

In the present paper, the proposed method is a procedure to obtain the optimal solution from decomposed systems of quadratic programming, which the object is

H. Zhuge and G.C. Fox (Eds.): GCC 2005, LNCS 3795, pp. 461 – 466, 2005.

quadratic and the constraints are linear. Decomposition collaborative model based on partial duality for quadratic programming is presented and analyzed.

2 Basic Mathematical Model and Equations

Regarding the multi-regions interconnection power grid, region A and the adjacent region B are taken as an example. The mathematical model of OPF problem for the multi-regions interconnection power grid may be expressed as follows:

$$\min .F(X_A, X_B) = f(X_A, X_B) \tag{1}$$

$$h_A(X_A, X_B) = 0 \tag{2}$$

$$h_B(X_A, X_B) = 0 \tag{3}$$

$$g_A(X_A) \leq 0 \tag{4}$$

$$g_B(X_B) \leq 0 \tag{5}$$

Where F, the optimal object, represents total of the subproblem A and B, X_A and X_B are the variants of subproblem A and B. Adding multipliers λ_1 , λ_2 , μ_1 , μ_2 for constraints (2)-(5), the Lagrangian function is formed and written as follows:

$$\begin{aligned} L(y) = f(X_A, X_B) - \lambda_1^T h_A(X_A, X_B) - \lambda_2^T h_B(X_A, X_B) \\ -\mu_1^T g_A(X_A, X_B) - \mu_2^T g_B(X_A, X_B) \end{aligned} \tag{6}$$

where $\lambda_1 \in R^{p1}, \lambda_2 \in R^{p2}, \mu_1 \in R^{m1}, \mu_2 \in R^{m2}$ $y = (X_A, X_B, \lambda_1, \lambda_2, \mu_1, \mu_2)^T$.

3 Decomposition Coordinated Model

The basic idea of decomposition in interconnected power grids is to decompose a big system into independent subsystem through processing the boundary nodes. The coordination is achieved by exchanging boundary nodal data to achieve optimization. In order to elaborate the decomposition algorithm, we take two regions to explain it.

Area A and B are connected through the tie-line ij. The tie-lie is "cut" by adding two new variable T_{ij} and T_{ji} to ij, $i \in A, j \in B$. Therefore, the equality constraint for region coupling can be added in the primitive problem and need not add hypothesized generator or the hypothesized load in the boundary bus. When the subproblem of region A is to solve, tie-line ij^A is reserved, and when the region B subproblem is to solve, tie-line i^Bj is reserved, as shown in Fig. 1.

According to the coordination model P3 and P4, for tie-line ij^A, the subproblem for region A satisfies $(\theta_i^A - \theta_j^A)/x_{ij} - T_{ij}^A = 0$. The region B satisfies $(\theta_i^B - \theta_j^B)/x_{ij} - T_{ji}^B = 0$, for tie-line i^Bj. The coupling equality constraints for region A

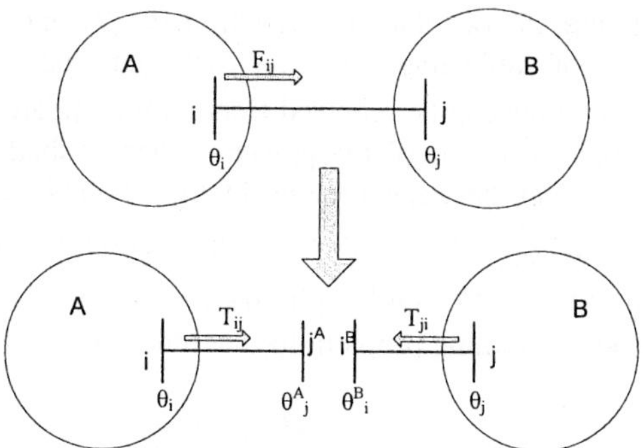

Fig. 1. DC-OPF Area decomposition

and B are $\theta_j^A = \theta_j^B$ and $\theta_i^A = \theta_i^B$. Through substituting the region coupling equality constraint in the balance equation, (17) and (20) can be obtained for corresponding coupling constraint. After the decomposition, mathematical model for region A and B can be formed as follows:

$$\min.F(x_A)=f_A(x_A)-\hat{\lambda}_{ji}^B \cdot h_B(x_A,\hat{x}_B) \tag{7}$$

$$\text{s.t.} \qquad g_A(X_A)\le 0 \tag{8}$$

$$h_A(X_A,\hat{X}_B)=(\theta_i^A-\hat{\theta}_j^B)/x_{ij}-T_{ij}^A=0 \tag{9}$$

$$\min.F(x_B)=f_B(x_B)-\lambda_{ij}^A \cdot h_A(\hat{x}_A,x_B) \tag{10}$$

$$\text{s.t.} \qquad g_B(X_B)\le 0 \tag{11}$$

$$h_B(\hat{X}_B,X_B)=(\theta_j^B-\hat{\theta}_i^A)/x_{ij}-T_{ji}^B=0 \tag{12}$$

4 Proposed Real-Time Parallel Collaborative Algorithm

According to the power grid DC-OPF model above, these subproblems can be solved in parallel or in serial after the decomposition of the overall system. The papers [4, 5] pointed out that each region has its own slack bus. In each iteration, the angle of slack bus is chosen to make mean value of boundary bus angle change for region *A* be equal to region B. The only slack bus is used in interconnected power grid in paper [6], in which the tie-line can be removed through the boundary bus nodal power interjection and a soft grounding admittance. The need for synchronization of the reference bus voltage phase angles of different areas is avoided. The disposal of slack bus that we take is similar to the paper [6].

Since the second part in the objective function of (7) and (10) are linear, the original convergence of objective function will not be changed. Parameter coordination between regions can be renewed through the update of multiplier λ with the economical significance to reveal the power exchange shadow price among the regions. Exchange variables between regions include boundary nodal phase angle $\hat{\theta}_i^A$ ($\hat{\theta}_j^B$) and export price $\hat{\lambda}_{ij}^A$ ($\hat{\lambda}_{ji}^B$). After the introduction of equality constraint and the inequality constraint, the DC OPF optimization problem of region A may be obtained: a quadratic programming problem for the unknown vectors P , T_{ij} and θ .

$$\min.F(x_A) = f_A(x_A) - \hat{\lambda}_{ji}^B \cdot h_B(x_A, \hat{x}_B) \tag{13}$$

$$S.t. \qquad B \cdot \theta_A + R_A \cdot T_A = P_A - D_A \tag{14}$$

$$\theta_{ref} = 0 \tag{15}$$

$$P_i^{\min} \le P_i \le P_i^{\max} \tag{16}$$

$$\left|(\theta_i - \theta_j)/x_{ij}\right| \le F_{ij}^{\max} \tag{17}$$

$$(\theta_i^A - \hat{\theta}_j^B)/x_{ij} - T_{ij}^A = 0 \tag{18}$$

$$|T_{ij}^A| \le T_{ij}^{\max} \tag{19}$$

The OPF solution of single area is divided into two stages. At the first stage, the branch constraint is not considered. An active power dispatch can be obtained according to classical economic dispatch solution. At the second stage, branch constraints (17) are verified. If the branch active power constraint is violated, then solve (13)-(17) again with only the violated constraints that marked before. Since the number of constraint (17) is large, a punishment-revision method is used in the value of branch in order to fasten the iteration, i.e. $F_{ij-Eff}^{\max} = \delta * F_{ij}^{\max}$, where δ is a constant in [0.9, 1].

The determination of nodal price and export price: as to (13)-(19), using optimization theory of Kuhn-Tucker first-order condition, we got that:

$$\lambda_{ij} = \lambda_i^A + \gamma_{ij}^A \tag{20}$$

λ_i^A is the boundary bus nodal price of area A. The price of exporting electricity through tie-line ij, λ_{ij} , is equal to the boundary bus i nodal price λ_i^A plus the tie-line ij transmission rent γ_{ij}^A , only in the case that the tie-line is congested. The algorithm proposed by this article is a distributional parallel algorithm shown in Fig. 2.

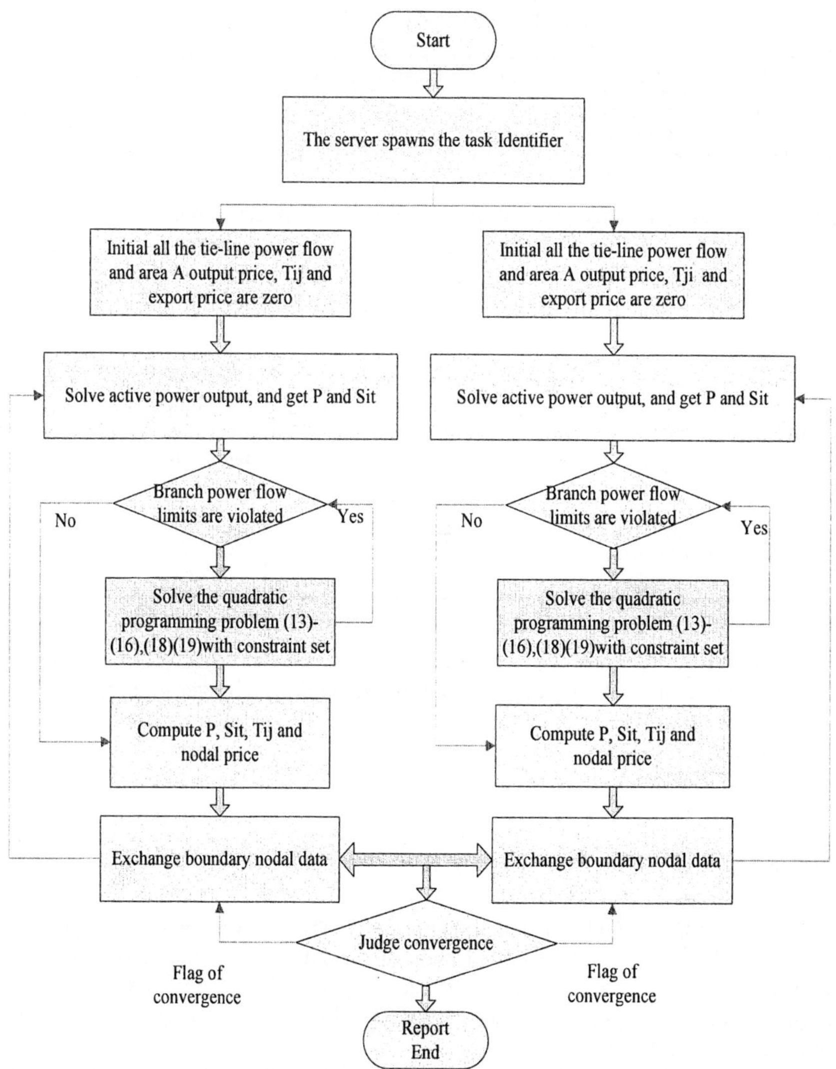

Fig. 2. Algorithm frame of distributed computation

5 Calculation and Conclusions

The proposed algorithm is evaluated using the IEEE RTS-96 2 regions and 3 regions. In this paper, we adopt the VC++6.0 programming, assisting IMSL the C 5.5 standard library functions[7] and PVM (Parallel Virtual Machine) software[8] to build the parallel computation environment and solve DC OPF problem of the interconnection power grid. PVM uses the existing PC machine hardware resources and the network resource to run the distributional simulation parallel machine, which has obtained the higher computation speed by a lower price. We select the RTS-96 test system to test. There are 2 experimental systems to be selected, and the system data is showed in Tab. 1.

Table 1. Characteristics of test systems

No	Test Name	Buses	Tie-line	Boundary Bus	Internal Lines
1	RTS96-2	48	3	6	96
2	RTS96-3	73	5	10	114

The same bus has many generators in the RTS-96 system. We use the equivalent generator theory [3] of the economical assignment significance. The output of identical bus generators is summed to the identical bus. In order to compare algorithm result, we carry on the comparison with following several algorithms as Tab. 2 shows:

Table 2. Comparison of different algorithm: A. Serial algorithm: a serial computation of the proposed algorithm in this paper. B. Parallel algorithm: a parallel computation of proposed algorithm in this paper C. Parallel algorithm: a parallel algorithm [2] proposed by Pandelis Biskas. D. Parallel algorithm: parallel algorithm [4] proposed by Baldick R.

Algorithm	A	B	C	D
Computation model	DC-OPF	DC-OPF	DC-OPF	AC-OPF
Computation time	0.183s	0.081s	0.094s	3.3s

An algorithm for the decentralized solution of DC-OPF problem has been presented and implemented on a network of workstations. Regarding a bigger system, the parallel algorithm uses multi processors to carry on the coordination optimization, and the style of distributional parallel processing also is consistent with the situation of many regions power grid networking. In a word, the proposed algorithm has a good prospect.

References

1. Y. Censor and S. A. Zenios. Parallel Optimization: Theory ,Algorithm, and Applications. Numerical Mathematics and Scientific Computation. Oxford University Press,1997.
2. Shmuel S. Oren, Andrew M. Ross. Economic Congestion Relief Across Multiple Regions Requires Tradable Physical Flow-gate Rights[J], IEEE Trans. Power Systems, vol. 17, pp.159-165, Feb.2002.
3. Li Wen Yuan. Model and Methods—Economical dispatch safely in power system[M], ChongQing University Press, 1989.(in Chinese)
4. Kim B H, Baldick R. Coarse-grained distributed optimal power flow[J]. IEEE Trans on Power Systems, 1997, 12(2): 932-939.
5. Wang X, Song Y H, Lu Q. Lagrangian Relaxation Based Multi-region Transmission on Congestion Management[J], Automation of Electric Power Systems. vol.26, no13, pp.8-13.
6. P. N. Biskas, A. G. Bakirtzis, A Decentralized Implementation of DC Optimal Power Flow on a Network of Computers[J], IEEE Transactions on Power Systems, 2002,26(13):8~13
7. IMSL C Math Library. Available on-line at http://www.vni.com.
8. PVM-Parallel Virtual Machine software. http://www.epm.ornl.gov/pvm/pvm_home.html.

Monitoring MPI Running Nodes Status for Load Balance

Qianni Deng, Xugang Wang, and Dehua Zang

Department of Computer Science, Grid Computing Center,
Shanghai Jiao Tong University, China 200030
shakspeare119@sjtu.edu.cn
deng-qn@cs.sjtu.edu.cn

Abstract. This paper presents an improvement on XMPI which is a MPI debugging tool based on LAM/MPI platform. The improvement is to monitor the involving physical nodes timely, gather the status information and display the status snapshots of the physical nodes. This function is an effective debugging method, which makes developers find their program bugs and load balance problems more effectively and efficiently. Especially after releasing of MPI-2 spec which allows developers to add and delete nodes dynamically during the MPI program running, it makes more significant in monitoring the physical nodes status.

1 Introduction

XMPI [1] is a MPI program executing, debugging and visualizing tool which is based on LAM/MPI [2] and X/Motif GUI [3], but not on MPICH [4]. It is an open source MPI debugging tool. The main subjects which XMPI faces to are communications among processes, replaying the messages delivering among all the involving processes. We can observe the startup and end time of communication messages from the original XMPI. But in a cluster Environment, the tasks may be arranged to the cluster nodes automatically and manually by programming. There must be some load balance problems, because of the different computing capability of cluster nodes. If there are lots of tasks which are arranged to a poor computing capability node among the cluster, in the meanwhile, only a few or no tasks are arranged to a high computing capability node, this situation must affect the computing efficiency. We enhance the XMPI with the improvement of monitoring running status of all physical nodes, dynamically gathering and displaying the node status information. It will help programmers to find out which node is loaded too many tasks and which node is loaded few or no tasks. With its help, programmers can fix the bugs on their program and run the program rightly and more efficiently. In section2, we present the related works. Section 3 gives a detail introduction of the architecture design. Section 4 gives the test result about our improvements and how to find load balance problems by our improved function.

2 Manuscript Preparation

Currently, there are also some debugging tools focusing on MPI and PVM programming. For example, Total View 4.0 Multi-process Debugger [5] is the most famous

H. Zhuge and G.C. Fox (Eds.): GCC 2005, LNCS 3795, pp. 467–473, 2005.

debugging tool in the field of parallel super computing, which is no matter debugging functions and generalization is the best. Vampir [6] focuses on parallel program executing result analysis and performance analysis, which is also an excellent debugging tool. But the above two tools is source code right protected, not an open source software. ParaGraph [7] is software tool that provides a detailed, dynamic, graphical animation of the behavior of message passing parallel programs and graphical summaries of their performance. Paradyn [8] is a performance measurement tool of parallel and distributed program. However Paradyn can only support PVM platform and measure isomorphic programs. All above tools always focus on different debugging platform. We are lack of an integrated, portable, general debugging tool which is also including load balance analysis functions. That is the main reason why we make these improvements on XMPI. LAM/MPI is an open source implementation of MPI specification, which is developed by Indiana University. LAM/MPI not only implements the MPI standard interfaces, but also constructs a records capturing mechanism [9]. The records capturing mechanism can record all the processes communication messages, process running status, communication startup time and end time etc of all the processes. No matter the communication succeed or fail, the communication parameter is right or wrong, all the records will be stored in the local nodes for the future debugging. LAM/MPI record capturing mechanism records the real time information in the local record chain and sends the local record information chain to the centralized debugging node.

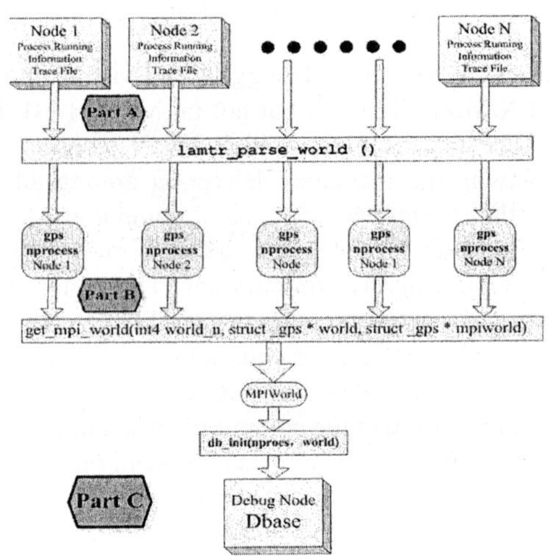

Fig. 1. Data Flow of LAM/MPI Debugging Information Collecting

Figure 1 shows the data flow of debugging information collecting in LAM/MPI. Generally it only needs one node for displaying the debugging result. The centralized debugging node shown in the part C of figure 1 collects the record information which is stored in trace files of the involving physical nodes. The debugging node coordinates the collecting information and displays the debugging results. LAM/MPI has implemented the information collecting using the functions listed in Figure 1. The part A of figure 1 shows that each node stores the record information chain into a local temporary trace file which will be collected to the debugging node in part C. LAM/MPI uses function- `lamtr_parse_world()` to capture the all the involving processes running information which is stored into structure `gps` [10] located in different nodes in Figure 1 Part B. LAM/MPI uses functions-`get_mpi_world(..)` to collect these `gps` to the debugging node and transfer these `gps` to another structure `MPIworld`. At last using function-`db_init(nproes, world)` to transfer information to the structure "`Dbase`"[10] which is a global variable in the debugging node shown in Figure 1, Part C. So "`Dbase`" has stored all the processes running information, and it is the base of XMPI and our works.

3 Monitoring Running Status of Physical Nodes

XMPI main function is monitoring the messages delivery among processes. So XMPI just focuses on the communication among processes and didn't care the physical nodes status. But the status of all the involving nodes is an important factor for programmers to find load balance problems in their programs. In most situations, nodes in a cluster environment have different computing capability, or even if, nodes have the same computing capability, they still have different available computing capability because of other tasks running on it. So if the status of the nodes can be monitored, programmers can add more tasks to nodes which have more computing capability and reduce the tasks from nodes which are overweight loaded. At last they can balance the tasks loading more rightly and reasonably. The following part presents how to get these nodes running status from the original debugging information which is stored in "`Dbase`".

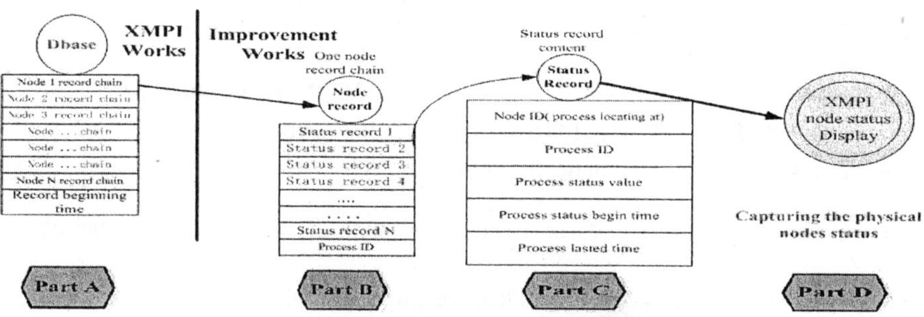

Fig. 2. Physical Nodes Status and Data Structure

Part A of figure 2 shows data structure of the global value Dbase, the information of the processes running on each nodes are collected into Dbase. Each node record (shown in part B) stores information of the processes running on that node. This information (shown in part C) includes process ID, node ID, processes running status, lasting time of processes. From the information XMPI can display and analysis the snapshot of any process, but cannot display the status of a physical node of whether it is busy in computing or waiting for message passing. So we need to calculate the physical nodes status from the processes status information. For any time, there are three kinds of situation:

- There is only one process running on the node.
- There are many processes running on the node.
- There is no process to be arranged onto local physical node.

So if there is a process remains computing status, the nodes remains computing status. If there is no process remains computing status, and if at least one process remains system overhead status. Totally we divide the nodes status into four priorities which can be shown in XPMI in different colors. P0 with green color means 'computing' status which is the highest priority. P1 (yellow color) means 'system overhead' status which is in second priority. P2 (red color) means 'communication waiting' status which is in third priority and P3 (white color) means 'no task running' status which is in forth priority. The priority is P0 >P1 >P2> P3.

We design a structure 'Node State' to store the processes status which are Physical node ID, Processes ID, Status changing starting time, Status lasted time, Processes status. Firstly we check each node's trace to get all the processes ID, then take the time from the min time till to the max time during MPI program running, we use time stamp as a parameter to check all the trace information for finding all the processes status in different physical node. Depending on the priority of processes status, we finally make a decision of nodes running status. For example, assume that:

- There are totally number of H processes in a program
- There are totally number of N nodes which are involved in the computing process.
- There are number of M_n processes in node “n”.
- T_{MIN} is the startup time of the MPI program executing.
- T_{MAX} is the end time of MPI program executing.
- $P(r,n,t)$ is the status of process “r” in node “n” at the time “t”. $P(r,n,t) \in \{P0,P1,P2,P3\}$, $TMIN<t<TMAX$, $r \in \{1, 2, 3 \cdots\ldots Mn\}$, $n \in \{1, 2, 3 \cdots\cdots N\}$
- $S(n,t)$ is the status of node “n” at the time “t”.

Now we want to get the $S(n,t)$ at the node “n” with the time “t”. From the above assumption, we know $H = \sum_{n=1}^{N} Mn$. Then the calculating algorithm is:

$$
\begin{aligned}
&\texttt{if} && (\exists r: P(r,n,t) == P_0)\ \texttt{then} && S(n,t) = P_0 \\
&\texttt{else if} && (\exists r: P(r,n,t) == P_1)\ \texttt{then} && S(n,t) = P_1 \\
&\texttt{else if} && (\exists r: P(r,n,t) == P_2)\ \texttt{then} && S(n,t) = P_2 \\
&\texttt{else if} && (\exists r: P(r,n,t) == P_3)\ \texttt{then} && S(n,t) = P_3
\end{aligned}
$$

From the above algorithm, we can calculate each node's status. Then we use graphic lib X/Motif to make the visualization of physical nodes running status. Finally we also make a status statistic of each node and calculate how much time of each kind of status used in every node during the program running. Depending on these statistics, developers can tune their program to shift more tasks from poor computing capability nodes to better computing capability nodes for enhancing the executing performance.

4 Experiment Test

4.1 Testing Platform

Table 1 shows the experiment environment. 'grid.cs.sjtu.edu.cn' has different computing capability from 'may.cs. sjtu.edu.cn'. Considering that this test focuses on function test instead of a performance test, we only use two physical nodes for showing clearly how this function can find load imbalance problems of the program.

Table 1. Hardware and Software preparation

Network	"grid",192.168.42.210, "may",192.168.42.211
Debug node	grid.cs.sjtu.edu.cn
CPU	Two P4-1.8G may,Single P3-1G grid.
MEMORY	512M for hpc, may 256M for "grid"
DISK	80G for each node
OS	Fedora－2.4.22 version
LAM/MPI	7. 0. 4 Version
XMPI	XMPI-2.2.3b8 Version
TestProgram	`alltoall.c`
Processes No	N=5

As Figure 3 shows after the program `alltoall.c` runs over, XMPI (has already been added the function of physical node status capturing and visualization), as we see the module which has been painted by pink color line: five processes running on the two physical nodes. The processes number #0、#2、#4 have been arranged to the N0-grid.cs.sjtu.edu.cn, and the processes number #1, #3 have been arranged to the N1-may.cs.sjtu.edu.cn. From the Figure 3, we can obtain that the program running begins at the time 0.000040s, ends at the time 0.002547s. When at the time of 0.000624s, which the wide white line is pointing to, the node0-grid.cs.sjtu.edu.cn shows green color which means node 'running' status, and the node1-may.cs.sjtu.edu.cn shows red color which means node 'waiting communication' status.

Table 2 shows the debugging result and analysis of the test. Depending on the requirement, we can move the white line shown in the Figure 3 and observe the two nodes running status by time. After all the processes running over, we find out that, node "grid.cs.sjtu.edu.cn" always remains computing status and waiting communication, in the meanwhile, the other node "may" always stays in system overhead and no task status. So programmer can put more tasks to node "may" and reduce the

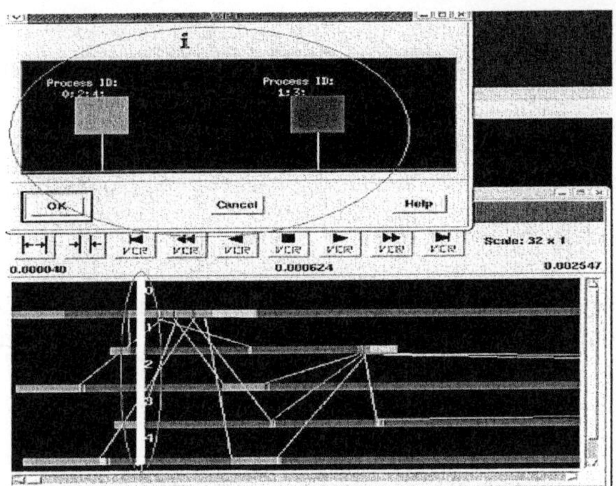

Fig. 3. Physical nodes status showing in XMPI

Table 2 Function test result and analysis

Running starting time	0. 000040s
Running ending time	0. 002547s
Capturing time	0.000624s
Processes No in 1	#0, #2, #4
Processes No in 2	#1, #3
Node 1 status	Computing status
Node 2 status	Waiting communication

overweight loaded on node "gird". After adjusting the program, the whole executing time reduces to almost 1/2 of the original executing time. So this improvement function contributes a great performance enhancement to the program executing.

5 Summary

The function of capturing and visualizing physical nodes status which is based on LAM/MPI platform is an enhancement of debugging tool XMPI. After adding this function, we have more ways to debug a parallel MPI program, finally fix the program bugs and optimize the load imbalance problems. Especially in MPI-2 [11] releasing, there are some standard functions focusing on dynamically adding and delete physical nodes during program executing. If we can monitor the nodes status dynamically, it will be more useful for developers to find problems in their programs. Even more, the improvement just enhances XMPI without modifying the LAM/MPI platform lib, so it's more portable and general for developers to use it. The source code and more technical reports of the enhanced XMPI refer to http://grid.sjtu.edu.cn/resource2.jsp.

References

1. Mark L, Green and Russ Miller. Grid Computing in Buffalo New York, Page 3, In: AS 2003. XMPI http://www.lam-mpi.org/software/xmpi/
2. Greg Burns, Raja Daoud, James Vaigl. LAM: An Open Cluster Environment for MPI, Ohio Supercomputer Center Columbus, Ohio, 1994. In: Proceedings of Supercomputing Symposium page 379—386 http://www.lam-mpi.org
3. Antony Fountain, Jeremy Huxtable, Paula Ferguson and Dan Heller. Motif Programming Manual, Open Source Edition by December 2001.
4. William Gropp and Ewing Lusk, Installation guide for MPICH, a portable implementation of MPI. Technical Report ANL-96/5, Argonne National Laboratory, 1994.
5. Rich Zwankenberg. Total View: Debugging Parallel Codes. Lawrence Livermore National Laboratory. June 23, 1998.
6. Werner Krotz-Vogel, Pallas. Linux tools for debugging and profiling MPI codes. Pallas GmbH, MRCCS.
7. Paragraph http://www.netlib.org/paragraph/
8. Barton P. Miller, Mark D. Callaghan, Jonathan M. Cargille, Jeffrey K. Hollingsworth, R. Bruce Irvin, etc. The Paradyn Parallel Performance Measurement Tool. IEEE Computer 28, 11
9. LAM/MPI Version 7.0.4 source code in the Pervasive Technology Lab of Indiana University. In: lamtrace.c, frecv.c, krecv.c, clientio.c, mrw.c.
10. XMPI-2.2.3b8 version source code in the Trustees of Indiana University http://www.lam-mpi.org/beta/ ：In: xmpi_dbase.cc
11. Message Passing Interface Forum. MPI2: Extensions to the Message Passing Interface Standard.http://www.mpi-forum.org/docs/mpi-20.ps,1997

Scheduling and Executing Heterogeneous Task Graph in Grid Computing Environment*

Weiguang Qiao, Guosun Zeng, An Hua, and Fei Zhang

Department of Computer Science and Technology, Tongji University, 200092, China
Tongji Branch, National Engineering & Technology Center of High Performance Computer, Shanghai 200092, China

Abstract. In this paper, we propose a directed hypergraph with parameters to describe general, heterogeneous, distributed and dynamic grid task requests. With the design of GHDL (Grid Heterogeneous task graph Definition Language), grid task requests are uniformly encapsulated and recognized by heterogeneous computers. Furthermore, we provide an effective solution for scheduling parallel tasks with priority constraints and data dependency. With self-adaptive scheduling strategy library, different types of tasks can be executed and optimized. We deal with the heterogeneity of grid environment and tasks by matching client with hosting machine. The dynamic resource problem is solved by runtime monitoring and task migration. A simulation experiment of tree growth in grid environment shows very promising results.

1 Introduction

Task scheduling is a key issue of parallel and distributed computing [1]. Grid resources are complex, heterogeneous, dynamic and self-autonomic in nature, it is critical to design an effective scheduling approach to gain high performance. Earlier work mainly focused on meta-tasks[2] or batch tasks[3]□which represent only particular situations in parallel computing. As for DAG (Directly Acyclic Graph), a slightly general notation, it lacks necessary scheduling information such as resource requirement and QoS (quality of service), thus can only be used in homogeneous environment. Currently, there is no widely accepted, general model for grid task description. In this paper, we propose an approach to model grid heterogeneous task with directed hypergraph, and design a grid heterogeneous task graph definition language. Then, we discuss in detail how to efficiently schedule heterogeneous task graph in grid environments.

The rest of this paper is structured as follows: Section 2 presents the definitions of directed hypergraph, and discusses how to model grid heterogeneous task. Section 3 introduces grid scheduling system for heterogeneous task graph. Experiment results are illustrated in section 4. Section 5 concludes the paper.

---

* Supported by the 863 High-Tech Project under grant of 2004AA104340, the National Natural Science Foundation of China under grant of 60173026 and SEC E-Institute: Shanghai High Institutions Grid under grant of 200301-1.

H. Zhuge and G.C. Fox (Eds.): GCC 2005, LNCS 3795, pp. 474–479, 2005.

2 Notation of Heterogeneous Task Graph

2.1 Modeling Heterogeneous Task Graph with Directed Hypergraph

The first issue of task scheduling is task description, which includes:

(1) Identification information: task id, service name and method name, and so on;
(2) Inherent information of task: input/output data, computation and communication;
(3) Priority constraints among subtasks: parent chain, and so on;
(4) Heterogeneous resource request: hardware and software request;
(5) QoS request: execution time limitation, fault tolerant level, and so on.

Next, we employ directed hypergraph to describe grid tasks. Hypergraph theory studies multi-relationship among variables in finite sets. We define hypergraph as follows:

Def. 2.1. A directed hypergraph $H=\langle V, E\rangle$ is defined as a set of vertices V and a set of hyperedges E. Each hyperedge represents a structure (X, i) , $X \subset V$, $X \neq \Phi$, $i \in V$. Parameter D_r associated denotes the correlation among vertices.

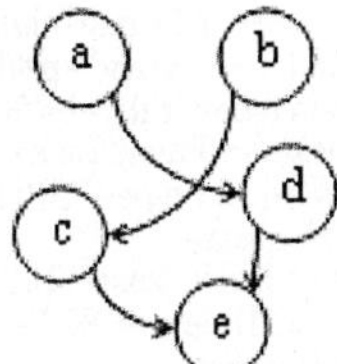

Fig.1. Basic directed hypergraph

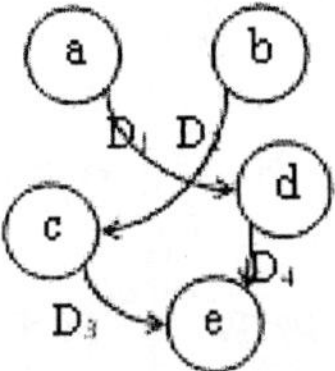

Fig. 2. Directed hypergraph with parameters

N denotes the sum of vertices; m is the number of hyperedges; s is the number of source sets, which represents distinct subsets in the left of hyperedges; and o is the number of vertices in the left set of hyperedge. As shown in Fig. 1, $H=\langle\{a, b, c, d, e\},\{(\{a\},d),(\{b\},c),(\{c, d\},e)\}\rangle$, n=5; m=3; s=3, that is {a}, {b} and {c, d}. Each subtask is mapped to a vertex with heterogeneous resource and Qos request. Each hyperedge denotes the priority constraints among subtasks. For example, ({c, d}, e) means that subtask e can not be executed until subtask c and d have been completed. D_r represents the data dependency. We add task graph structure for strategy selection.

Def. 2.2. A heterogeneous task graph is defined as a directed hypergraph with parameters. $GHTG=\langle V, E, R_V, Q_V, t\rangle$, where $V=\{ v_1, v_2 ,..., v_n \}$ is the set of subtasks, $R_V=\{r_{v1}, r_{v2} ,..., r_{vn}\}$ is the set of resource requests from subtasks , $Q_V=\{q_{v1}, q_{v2} ,..., q_{vn}\}$ is the set of QoS requests from subtasks. E is the set of directed hyperedges, which expresses priority constraints and data dependency among subtask nodes. Each hyperedge represents a structure (X, D, i), where $X \subset V$, $X \neq \Phi$, $i \in V$, and D denotes the data parameters on hyperedges. t is the structure type of a task graph. $t \in$ {Work Pool, Master-Slave, Pipeline, Phase-Synchronized, Divide-Conquer, Other}.

2.2 Grid Heterogeneous Task Graph Description Language

Besides modeling heterogeneous task with directed hypergraph, we designed a XML based Grid Heterogeneous Task Graph Description Language (GHDL). Here we choose tree simulation as an example, as shown in Fig. 3(a). Suppose T_0 is a line of length L_0, branch T_1 and T_2 are generated by stretching lines with length $L_0/2$ and $L_0/3$ at midpoint and trisection point of T_0 respectively. Such process proceeds until the last branch T_n created, where n is the simulation precision.

The task graph of tree simulation is shown in Fig. 3(b). Subtask A do some pre-processing and prepare input data for its successive subtasks B1~B5. Then B1~B5 make all corresponding branches and forward data to the successive subtask C, which build the whole tree. The GHTG expression is shown in Fig. 3(c), where "*" means the task will be executed more than once. Fig. 3(d) depicts the task script in GHDL, where "TaskTimes" represents the execution times of the subtask.

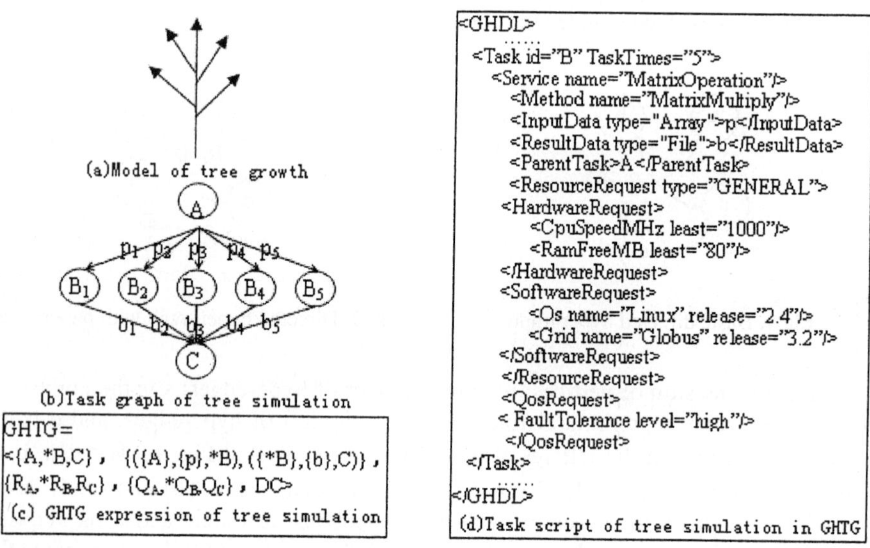

Fig. 3. GHTG example of tree simulation

3 The Grid Scheduling System for Heterogeneous Task Graph

3.1 Scheduling System Architecture

On the basis of heterogeneous task graph description, we developed a general grid scheduling system for heterogeneous task graph. It consists of task graph submission interface, task graph scheduling engine and grid information library. Grid resources are provided by heterogeneous hosts with Globus, MPI, or NetSolve installed. The system provides special containers for grid resources and services management. Java

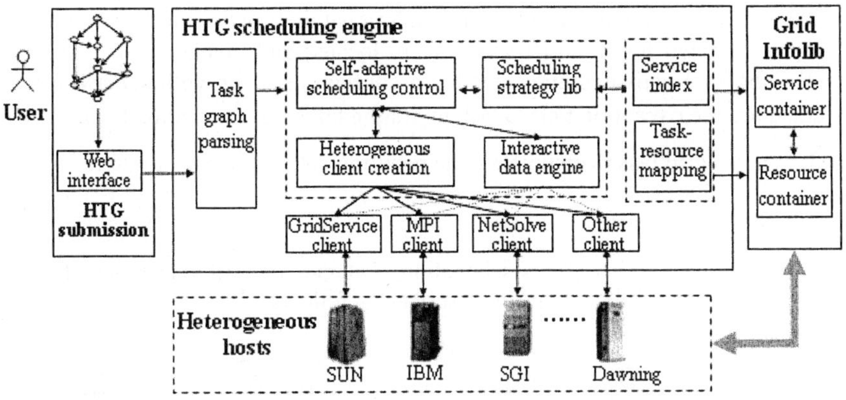

Fig. 4. Scheduling system architecture

RTTI mechanism is used to automatically create heterogeneous clients, which activate the hosts based on recognizing heterogeneous hosts and grid software. Grid information library provides abstract resource parameters by monitoring, and combines with task migration to solve the dynamic problem of resources. With resource heterogeneity hidden, different computing nodes can interoperate with each other.

The scheduling engine parses the heterogeneous task graph to get input data, service types, service handlers, resource request information, etc. Using these parameters, host-specific clients can be automatically created. For service-oriented hosts, such as WebService and GridService, the clients can be created through java reflection mechanism, and then call target services. For non-service ones, such as MPI, the clients construct configuration files for execution, and activate processes on remote hosts. Data engine exchanges data between subtasks with necessary type information in GHDL. For large data files, GridFTP is used to transfer them swiftly and reliably.

3.2 General Scheduling Algorithm

Step 1: User submits task requests and input data through Web interface. Web server extracts parameters, creates standard GHDL script, and sends it to scheduling engine.
Step 2: Heterogeneous Task Graph Scheduling Engine takes the following operations:

① Parse and convert GHDL script into particular data structure.
② Retrieve available service list from service container according to task parameters.
③ Select appropriate scheduling strategy for different types of task graphs, retrieve hosts information from grid information library, and map tasks onto heterogeneous resources which satisfy task resource and QoS requirement.
④ Identify hosts types and automatically create host-specific heterogeneous clients.

⑤ Clients execute subtasks of the task graph in parallel , with selected strategy. For service-oriented hosts, target services are located and invoked. For non-service ones, they are activated after creating a configuration file with subtask parameters. Once the execution fails, a task migration tag is set, then jump to ③.

Step 3: When a grid task is completed, the resulting data is returned to users.

3.3 Scheduling Strategy

Scheduling strategy library stores scheduling strategies for different types of heterogeneous task graph, which are briefly described as follows.

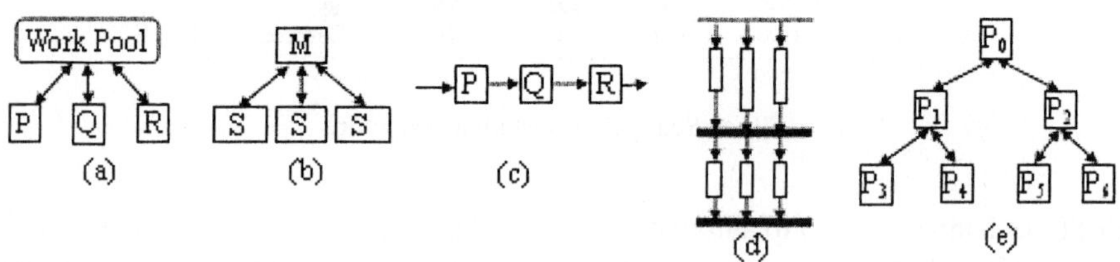

(a) Work Pool (b) Master-Slave (c) Pipeline (d) Phase-Synchronized (e) Divide-Conquer

Fig. 5. Scheduling modes

① **Work Pool scheduling.** At the beginning, work pool contains only the initial task of heterogeneous task graph. During the execution, new tasks are added into work pool, and old tasks are deleted. This process continues until the pool is empty[4].
② **Master-Slave scheduling.** The engine selects a master node according to task requirement. The master node assigns work load to slave nodes, which execute subtasks simultaneously and return their results.
③ **Pipeline scheduling.** In this mode, task graph can be treated as a series of sequential heterogeneous subtasks, each destined for a specific host type. Since different phases in pipeline can be overlapped, the makespan may be shortened.
④ **Phase-Synchronized scheduling.** Task graph is made up of super-steps[4]. In each super-step, subtasks are mutually independent. During the global communication phase, data is exchanged between nodes by the interactive data engine.
⑤ **Divide-Conquer scheduling.** Task is recursively divided into subtasks and executed.

4 Experiment Results

We test our grid scheduling system in grid environment, composing of a Dawning3000(16 Power3-II 375MHz CPU, 16GB Memory, AIX4.3.3), a Dell PowerEdge 2600 server(2 Intel Xeon 1.8GHz CPU, 1GB Memory, RedHat Linux 9.0), 16 PCs(Intel P4 2.0GHz CPU, 512 MB Memory, RedHat Linux 9.0), and Globus Toolkit, NetSolve and MPICH are installed. Fig 6 depicts tree simulation result. Fig 7

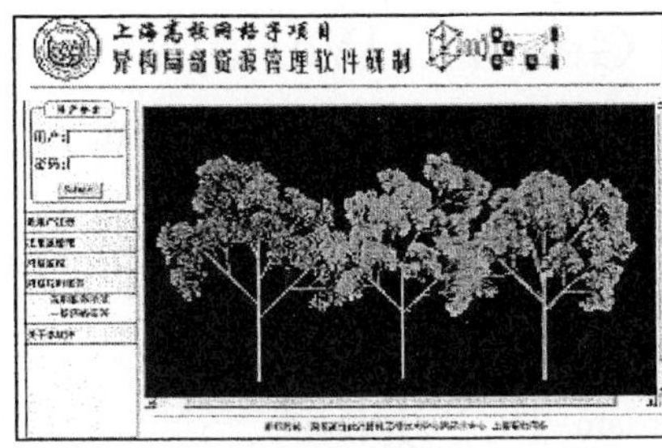
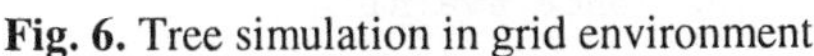

Fig. 6. Tree simulation in grid environment

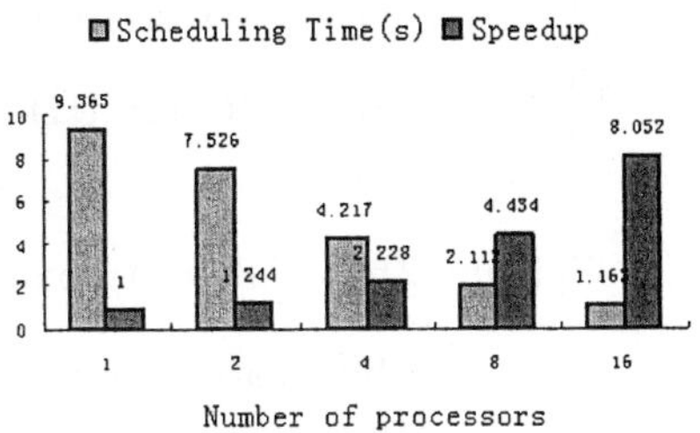

Fig. 7. Comparison of scheduling effects

shows the execution effects with different processor size. We can see that the scheduling system effectively exploits the computing power of grid platform.

5 Conclusions

In this paper, we model grid heterogeneous task with directed hypergraph, and propose a Grid Heterogeneous task graph Definition Language, which uniformly encapsulates the heterogeneous task graph including its heterogeneous resource and Qos request. In our grid scheduling system, we solve the distributed, heterogeneous and dynamic problems by scheduling strategy library construction, heterogeneous host identification and activation, real time resource status monitoring, etc. If a subtask encounters an error during execution, the scheduling system can move and re-execute it to other available nodes. In the experiment of tree simulation, we achieve satisfying speedup even in prototype system. Our future work is to further improve the grid scheduling system, and study general grid programming model.

References

1. H. El-Rewini, T. G. Lewis, H. H. Ali, Task Scheduling in Parallel and Distributed Systems, PTR Prentice Hall, New Jersey, 1994.
2. S. Vadhiyar, J. Dongarra, A Metascheduler For The Grid, Proceedings of the 11th IEEE International Symposium on High Performance Distributed Computing (HPDC 2002), IEEE Computer Society, Edinburgh, Scotland, pp343-351.
3. B. Faycal, G. Jean-Patrick, L. Laurent, et al., Designing and Evaluating An Active Grid Architecture, Advanced Grid Technologies, 2005,21(2):315-330.
4. R. F. Freund, H. J. Siegel, Heterogeneous processing, Computer, June 1993, 26(6):18-27.

Agent Technology and Generic Workflow Management in an e-Science Environment

Zhiming Zhao, Adam Belloum, Peter Sloot, and Bob Hertzberger

Informatics Institute, University of Amsterdam,
Kruislaan 403, 1098SJ, Amsterdam, The Netherlands
{zhiming, adam, sloot, bob}@science.uva.nl

Abstract. In e-Science environments, the support for scientific workflows emerges as a key service for managing experiment data and activities, for prototyping computing systems and for orchestrating the runtime system behaviour. Supporting domain specific applications via a common e-Science infrastructure enables knowledge sharing among different applications, and thus can broaden the range of the application and multiply the impact of scientific research. However, most of the existing workflow management systems are driven by the domain specific applications; the applicability to different domains is limited. In this paper, we discuss possible solutions to this problem and present our research in an ongoing project: Virtual Laboratory for e-Science (VL-e). Agent technologies are used to encapsulate the intelligence for problem solving strategies and for workflow orchestration.

1 Introduction

In e-Science environments, Scientific Workflow Management Systems (SWMS) emerge as the fibre to glue different levels of issues: experiment planning, resources deployments and the runtime execution control of the experiment. By automating the management of experiment routines, a SWMS hides the underlying details of the Grid infrastructure and allows a scientist to focus on the high level domain specific aspects of the experiments [1,2]. In the past decade, SWMSs have been realised in different application domains, e.g., in bio informatics [3,4], in high energy physics [5], and in astronomical observations [6].

Reusing the successful and stable results of SWMSs can not only improve the efficiency for developing advanced high-level application specific functionality, but also reduce cost and risks for utilising an e-Science infrastructure in a new problem domain. More importantly, supporting domain specific applications via a common infrastructure enables knowledge sharing among different applications and thus can broaden the range of the application and multiply the impact of scientific research [7]. This issue has been highlighted in a number of ongoing e-Science projects; three research efforts can be enumerated. The first one is from the resource perspective. A standard interface for coupling SWMS resources is essential to improve the reusability of a SWMS. In Taverna, an

H. Zhuge and G.C. Fox (Eds.): GCC 2005, LNCS 3795, pp. 480–485, 2005.

open world assumption is adopted [8]; Grid service is used as the basic architecture to interconnect resources, therefore the services developed by the other SWMSs can also be deployed. Using a knowledge backbone, e.g., an Ontology based mechanism, to enhance a SWMS enables the semantic level sharing and querying of various SWMS resources as in [9,10]. The second effort is to distinguish the reusable services from a SWMS and to encapsulate them as generic components in an e-Science environment, such as generic scheduling strategies in Pegasus [11]. The last one is to reuse different SWMS by providing different levels of interoperability mechanisms among them [12]. Most of the recent discussion is at the resource level, which aims to invoke software resources of another SWMS by wrapping the components. In this paper, we present our research along the third effort in the context of a Dutch e-Science project: Virtual Laboratory for e-Science (VL-e) [13].

The VL-e project aims to realise a generic e-Science framework where scientists from different domains can share their knowledge and resources, and perform domain specific research. VLAM-G (Virtual Laboratory Amsterdam for Grid) environment [14], a Grid enabled e-Science framework developed in a previous project[1], is currently used as the first prototype. The VLAM-G environment provides a user friendly interface for managing software components and for composing reusable experiment templates, but only limited support for scientific workflows. In this paper, we discuss the feasibility and challenges in including scientific workflow support as part of generic e-Science services, and propose an agent based solution.

This paper is organised as follows. First, we analyse the basic issues in realising a SWMS and briefly describe the research context of the Dutch Vl-e project. After that, we discuss the shortcomings of current implementation of the generic VL-e framework, and propose an agent based solution to improve it. The differences between our solution and the other related work are also discussed.

2 Generic Scientific Workflow Management in an e-Science Framework

In [15,16], we distinguished three main functional components from a SWMS: a workflow model, an engine and user support. Due to the diversity of the science disciplines, workflow models are often domain specific, e.g., data streams between experiment instruments and the analysis tools are modelled as a workflow in high energy physics applications [17], while human involved adaptation in predefined imaging processing are highlighted in medical imaging applications [18].

In principle, a generic e-Science SWMS can be derived from domain specific SWMSs using two basic approaches.

An *abstraction* approach abstracts the common characteristics from different SWMS implementations, including the workflow model, the engine, and the user support. Generic solutions to these abstracted issues are then encapsulated as reusable workflow services in the e-Science framework. This approach is

[1] Virtual Laboratory II.

pretty much like deriving classes from objects in an Object Orient methodology. The domain specific features will stay at application level, and all the generic workflow support will be provided by the e-Science framework.

Ideally, this approach will contribute a generic SWMS which can serve different domain specific applications. It is based on the condition that the existing SWMSs have fully captured the dynamics of the domain specific scientific experiments, and a generic workflow model can be possibly abstracted from these domain specific workflows models. However, in practice, this condition is far away from the reality. Having mature domain specific workflow models for different domains is not going to be truth in a short period of time. Domain scientists may have continuously changing requirements on the workflow model when they have new ambitions on exploring his domain problems which makes a workflow model take very long time to evolve as a *mature* one. A more practical approach, called an *aggregation* approach, can be used.

An *aggregation* approach starts from a success model of domain specific workflows and extends it to support other domains by including workflow engines for that domain into the system. Compared to the abstraction approach, this one reuses the intelligence of existing SWMSs as a whole, and avoids the reimplementation of the same workflow model.

Different levels of interoperability between a slave SWMS and the host SWMS is essential to implement this approach. It requires detailed knowledge of both SWMS implementations, in particular when the underlying middleware of SWMSs differ.

Theoretically, both approaches are applicable in realising an e-Science environment. However, from the state of the art of the domain specific SWMSs, the aggregation approach is more practically feasible. We will discuss how we apply this approach in the VL-e project in the next Section.

In the next section, an agent based solution is proposed.

3 VL-e Workflow Conductor (VLWF-Conductor)

In this section, we propose an architecture called VL-e workflow Conductor (VLWF-Conductor), which provides solutions to the missions mentioned above from three aspects: providing an enhanced workflow model, an agent based flow execution engine, and necessary user support.

3.1 A Petri Net Based Model

In our early work, we have implemented a place transition (PT) graph based mechanism called *scenario net* [19] to model the interaction constraints between components in an interactive simulation system. In a scenario net, transitions are used to model the activities that an actor (also called a role) in a flow will perform, and places and the relation links between places and transitions are used to model dependencies among activities. In a scenario net, places and the relation links from places to transitions can also associate with guard expressions. In [20], we have demonstrated the application of scenario nets in modelling scenarios in interactive simulation systems.

In VLWF-Conductor, scenario net is used as the basic mechanism to model the workflow.

3.2 An Agent Based Workflow Engine

To execute a workflow, an engine necessarily deals with different levels of issues: locating computing resources, scheduling tasks, orchestrating the activities, passing data, adapting the execution, and managing runtime information. Decentralised these control and realising them as autonomous components can encapsulate the intelligence and hide the complexity from different levels.

Agent technologies provide a suitable approach to include control intelligence in the behaviour of a set of operations; therefore, we use them to encapsulate the control intelligence and to carry out the flow control. We group the support for these phases into two parts: one is for the pre-processing and post-processing of a workflow, and one is for managing computing tasks of the workflow. The control intelligences in these parts are encapsulated as two agents: a *Study Manager* and a *Scenario Conductor*.

A *Study manager* (SM) is an agent for managing the lifecycle of an experiment. A SM is instantiated for each workflow instance; it manages different types of experiment data and schedules the execution of a workflow by applying domain specific strategies. When a SM receives a workflow description, it first does necessary pre-processing of the workflow, e.g., checking if involved resources for the workflow can be located, if similar experiments have already been executed, and if the mata data for different experiment processes available. After that, it makes plan for scheduling computing parts of the workflow.

A *Scenario Conductor* is instantiated by a SM for executing a sub-workflow with computing tasks. A SC realises the functionality for discovering resources, mapping workflow onto the resources, interpreting workflow and orchestrating the runtime activities of the resources. A SC also acts as a wrapper to a foreign workflow engine when it is employed in the workflow execution. A SC realises the engine level interoperability among different sub-workflows. When a foreign engine is included a specific sub-workflow, the execution intelligence of that engine is interfaced to the SC via top-level workflow as a whole. The SM and SC handle the coordination issues.

At runtime, agents collaboratively manage the information of an experiment and orchestrate the computing tasks.

4 Discussion and Conclusions

As we have distinguished in the introduction section that there are three efforts for deriving generic services from domain specific SWMSs. The discussion in this paper belongs to the third one: reusing existing workflow systems in an e-Science environment by enabling the interoperability among them via a generic framework.

We have not fully implemented VLWF-Conductor, yet we did test the feasibility for integrating the VLAM-G framework with the other workflow systems, e.g., Nimrod [21]. From the discussion, we can at least conclude follows:

1. Generic workflow management services are essential to realise a common e-Science framework for transferring and sharing knowledge among domains.
2. Aggregating the state of art SWMSs in an e-Science environment is a feasible approach to realise a reusable framework for domain specific applications.
3. Agent technologies are a suitable approach to implement the control intelligence for flow control.

5 Future Work

We are currently surveying a list of SWMSs. The implementation details of these SWMSs are analysed from the perspective of application characteristics. Using the survey results, we will then implement the first prototype of VLWF-Conductor and develop the interface for other workflow engines.

Acknowledgement. This work was carried out in the context of the Virtual Laboratory for e-Science project (www.vl-e.nl). Part of this project is supported by a BSIK grant from the Dutch Ministry of Education, Culture and Science (OC&W) and is part of the ICT innovation program of the Ministry of Economic Affairs (EZ). The authors of this paper would like to thank all the members in the VL-e SP2.5 sub program.

References

1. Jr. George Chin, L. Ruby Leung, Karen Schuchardt, and Debbie Gracio. New paradigms in problem solving environments for scientific computing. In *Proceedings of the international conference of Intelligent User Interface*, San Francisco, 2002.
2. R. McClatchey and G. Vossen. Workshop on workflow management in scientific and engineering applications report. *SIGMOD Rec.*, 26(4):49–53, 1997.
3. Mark Ellisman, Michael Brady, David Hart, Fang-Pang Lin, Matthias Muller, and Larry Smarr. The emerging role of biogrids. *Commun. ACM*, 47(11):52–57, 2004.
4. Robert D. Stevens, Alan J. Robinson, and Carole A. Goble. mygrid: personalised bioinformatics on the information grid. In *ISMB (Supplement of Bioinformatics)*, pages 302–304, 2003.
5. I. Augustin, F. Carminati, J. Closier, E. van Herwijnen, J. J. Blaising, D. Boutigny, and et al. Hep applications evaluation of the edg testbed and middleware. *CoRR*, cs.DC/0306027, 2003.
6. The astrogrid project homepage. In *http://www.astrogrid.org/*, 2005.
7. Jim Blythe Carl Kesselman Hongsuda Tangmunarunkit Yolanda Gil, Ewa Deelman. Artificial intelligence and grids: Workflow planning and beyond. *IEEE Intelligent Systems*, pages 26–33, January 2004.
8. Tom Oinn, Matthew Addis, Justin Ferris, Darren Marvin, Martin Senger, Mark Greenwood, Tim Carver, Kevin Glover, Matthew R. Pocock, Anil Wipat, and Peter Li. Taverna: A tool for the composition and enactment of bioinformatics workflows. *Bioinformatics Journal.*, online, June 16, 2004.

9. Carole Goble and David De Roure. The grid: an application of the semantic web. *ACM SIGMOD Record*, 31(4):65–70, 2002.
10. Srini Narayanan and Sheila A. McIlraith. Simulation, verification and automated composition of web services. In *Proceedings of the eleventh international conference on World Wide Web*, pages 77–88. ACM Press, 2002.
11. Ewa Deelman, James Blythe, Yolanda Gil, Carl Kesselman, Gaurang Mehta, Sonal Patil, Mei-Hui Su, Karan Vahi, and Miron Livny. Pegasus: Mapping scientific workflows onto the grid. In *European Across Grids Conference*, pages 11–20, 2004.
12. MyGrid. Link-up project - e-science sisters programme. In *http://www.mygrid.org.uk/linkup/*, 2005.
13. VL-e. Virtual laboratory for e-science. In *http://www.vl-e.nl/*, 2005.
14. H. Afsarmanesh, R.G. Belleman, A.S.Z. Belloum, A. Benabdelkader, J.F.J. van den Brand, and et al. VLAM-G: A Grid-based Virtual Laboratory. *Scientific Programming: Special Issue on Grid Computing*, 10(2):173–181, 2002.
15. Zhiming Zhao, Adam Belloum, Hakan Yakali, Peter Sloot, and Bob Hertzberger. Dynamic workflow in a grid enabled problem solving environment. In *Proceedings of the 5th International Conference on Computer and Information Technology (CIT2005)*, page accepted, Shanghai, China, September 2005. IEEE Computer Society Press.
16. Zhiming Zhao, Adam Belloum, Adianto Wibisono, Frank Terpstra, Piter T. de Boer, Peter Sloot, and Bob Hertzberger. Scientific workflow management: between generality and applicability. In *Proceedings of the International Workshop on Grid and Peer-to-Peer based Workflows in conjunction with the 5th International Conference on Quality Software*, page accepted, Melbourne, Australia, September 19th-21st 2005. IEEE Computer Society Press.
17. Henri Casanova. Distributed computing research issues in grid computing. *ACM SIGACT News*, 33(3):50–70, 2002.
18. Lewis Hassell and John Holmes. Modeling the workflow of prescription writing. In *SAC '03: Proceedings of the 2003 ACM symposium on Applied computing*, pages 235–239, New York, NY, USA, 2003. ACM Press.
19. Zhiming Zhao, G. D. van Albada, and P. M. A. Sloot. Agent-based flow control for hla components. *International journal of simulation transaction, special issue Agent Directed Simulation*, 81(7):in press, 2005.
20. Z. Zhao. *An agent based architecture for constructing interactive simulation systems*. PhD thesis, University van Amsterdam, Amsterdam, The Netherlands, (Promoter: Prof. Dr. P. M. A. Sloot), 2004.
21. Tom Peachey, David Abramson, Andrew Lewis, Donny Kurniawan, and Rhys Jones. Optimization using nimrod/o and its application to robust mechanical design. In *PPAM*, pages 730–737, 2003.

Query Optimization in Database Grid

Xiaoqing Zheng, Huajun Chen, Zhaohui Wu, and Yuxin Mao

Grid Computing Lab, College of Computer Science, Zhejiang University, Hangzhou, 310027, China
{zxqingcn, huajunsir, wzh, maoyx}@zju.edu.cn

Abstract. DarGrid II is an implemented database gird system whose goal is to provide a semantic solution for integrating database resources on the web. Although many algorithms have been proposed for optimizing query-processing in order to minimize costs and/or response time, associated with obtaining the answer to query in a distributed database system, database grid query optimization problem is fundamentally different from distributed query optimization. These differences are shown to be the consequences of autonomy and heterogeneity of databases in database grid. Therefore, more challenges have arisen for query optimization in database grid than traditional distributed database. Following this observation, we present the design of a query optimizer in DartGrid II , and a heuristic, dynamic, and parallel query optimization approach for processing query in database grid is proposed.

1 Introduction

In presence of web, one critical challenge is how to globally publish, seamlessly integrate and transparently locate geographically distributed database resources with such "open" settings. DartGrid II proposes a semantic-based approach supporting the global sharing of database resources using grid as platform and dynamically integrates information from autonomous local databases managed by heterogeneous database management systems in the web environment.

We use ontologies to define conceptual model or standard terminology and relations between them in certain domain. Databases are semantically registered to the web service called Semantic Registry Service by mapping from relation attributes to the properties of ontology (standard terminology in given domain). End-user browses the ontology to generate a visual conceptual query by Semantic Browser developed for DartGrid II, and then Semantic Query Service translates a semantically enriched query into a distributed query plan by mapping from shared ontology to local database schemas. Query results will be returned to user as semantically wrapped format and presented in Semantic Brower.

For a query involving more than one database, global query optimization should be performed to achieve good overall system performance. Because there are some fundamental differences between traditional distributed Database Management System (DBMS) and Database Gird System (DBGS) which stem from autonomy and heterogeneity of database nodes participating in DBGS, query optimization techniques in distributed DBMS can not nontrivially and directly be applied to DBGS. Site autonomy in DBGS refers to the situation whereby each database node retains

H. Zhuge and G.C. Fox (Eds.): GCC 2005, LNCS 3795, pp. 486 – 497, 2005.

complete control over local data and processing. This has a number of implications for query optimization in DBGS. [Veijalainen and Popescu-Zeletin, 1988] classify site autonomy into three types: design, communication, and execution.

Design autonomy implies that database nodes are responsible for optimizing local access paths and query processing methods. Consequently, reliable statistical information which is needed for effective global query optimization is not readily available and may not remain accurate as database nodes change over time. Communication autonomy in DBGS means that a database node independently determines what information it will share with the global system, when it participates in the database grid, and also when it will stop participating. This adds to the complexity of query processing and optimization since any database node system may terminate its services without any advance notice. Execution autonomy results in the situation whereby the global system interfaces with database nodes at their external user interfaces, and hence is not able to influence how query processing is being carried out in the database nodes. This means that there is no opportunity for low-level cooperation across systems and hence primitive query processing techniques proposed for distributed database system may no longer be applicable. For example, the semijoin and pipeline operation may hard to implement in efficient way for lack of facilities provided by low-level and underlying system environment.

In query optimization for distributed DBMS it is assumed that component sites are equal in terms of their processing capability. This assumption no longer seems reasonable in the context of DBGS since database nodes may vary drastically in terms of their availability and processing costs. Furthermore, the same real world object may be represented in more than one database node, but these representatives are not always structurally compatible in DBGS. By the way, database grid system is also different from multidatabse system since DBGS supports and allows database nodes dynamically participate in or quit from the system and sets target for facing more "open" settings of web environment. However, the query processing problem is much more difficult in database grid environment than in centralized, distributed, and multi database. But it is very important for the success of system. We present the design of a query optimizer in DartGrid II, and a heuristic, dynamic, and parallel optimization approach for processing query in database gird. In the following discussion, the global data modal is assumed to be relational for convenient discussion.

The remainder of this paper is organized as follows. Section 2 presents a brief overview of query optimization in traditional distributed database. In Section 3, the architecture of a database grid query optimizer is proposed. Section 4 describes the algorithms for query optimization in database grid, and some experimental results have been discussed. The conclusions and future work are summarized in Section 5.

2 Related Work

Because it is a critical performance issue, query processing has received (and is still receiving) considerable attention in both centralized and distributed DBMS. A large number of different algorithms have already been developed for query optimization in database systems. The numerous algorithms employed in various applications have already been proposed for query optimization which can roughly be divided into three categories or are combination of such basic algorithms: exhaustive search, heuristics and randomized algorithms [Kossmann and Strocker, 2000].

Typical exhaustive search algorithm is dynamic programming [Selinger et al., 1979], and [Ono and Lohman, 1990] is its improvement. All proposed algorithms of this class have exponential time and space complexity and are sure to find the best plan according to the specific cost model. Other transformation-based techniques with top-down dynamic programming are EXODUS [Graefe and DeWitt, 1987] and Volcano [Graefe and McKenna, 1993]. [Kossmann and Storcker, 2000] presents a new class of query optimization algorithms that are based Iterative Dynamic Programming (IDP) and declares that IDP algorithm can produce the best plan of all known algorithms in the situation in which dynamic programming is not viable because of its high complexity.

Heuristics algorithms have polynomial time and space complexity, but they produce plans are often more expensive than those of exhaustive search algorithms. The most outstanding representatives of this class based on "minimum selectivity" and "greedy principle" are in [Palermo, 1974], [Swami, 1989], [Shekita et al., 1993], and [Steinbrunn et al., 1997].

To avoid the high cost of exhaustive search, randomized strategies, such as Simulated Annealing [Ioannidis and Wong, 1987] and Genetic Algorithms [Jiunn-Chin et al., 1996] have been proposed. They try to find a good solution, not necessarily the best one, but avoid the high cost of optimization. The best known randomized algorithm is called 2PO which is a combination of iterative improvement and simulated annealing [Ioannidis and Kang 1990]. Other representative of this class are in [Lanzelotte et al., 1993] and [Galindo-Legaria et al., 1994].

Other important approaches of query optimization should be given appropriate attention. SDD-1 [Bernstein et al., 1981] is derived from an earlier method called the "hill-climbing" algorithm, which has the distinction of being the first distributed query processing algorithm. The main problem of SDD-1 is that the algorithm may get stuck at a local minimum cost solution and fail to reach the global minimum. R* [Selinger and Adiba, 1980] is a substantial extension of the techniques developed for system R's optimizer. Therefore, it uses a compilation approach where an exhaustive search of all alternative strategies is performed in order to choose the one with the least cost. The Parallel Nested Loop algorithm [Bitton et al., 1983] is the simplest one and the most general. The algorithm of Parallel Hash Join for specific multiprocessor architecture is given in [Valduriez and Gardarin, 1984].

3 Design of Database Grid Query Optimizer

The role of a query processor in DartGrid II is to map a high-level semantic query on ontologies into a sequence of database operations on relevant database nodes. The semantic mapping between ontologies and relational database is shown in Figure 1. We refer to database grid query optimization as generation a query execution plan for a given query defined over the collection of database nodes. The goal of a database grid optimizer (GOQ) may be summarized as follows: given a semantic query on a database grid, find a corresponding execution strategy that minimizes a system cost function that includes I/O, CPU, and communication costs. After translating an ontology-based semantic query to global relational calculus, an execution strategy is specified in terms of relational operations and communication primitives (send/receive) applied to the database nodes. Therefore, the complexity of relational operations that affect the performance of query execution is of major importance in the design of a query optimizer. Figure 2 shows the architecture of a database grid query optimizer.

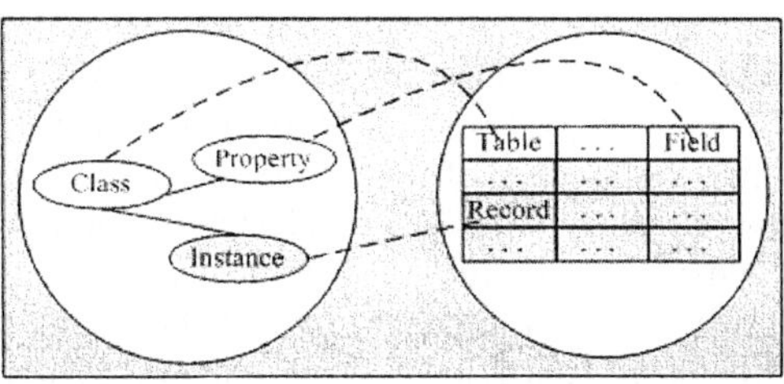

Fig. 1. The semantic mapping between ontologies and relational database

When GOQ receives a semantic query from end-user, Semantic Parser checks the syntax and semantics of the query using the schema information provided by Global Catalogue, and then, rewrites from the original query to the equivalent global relational query (see [Zhaohui Wu et al., 2004] for more details). Query Decomposer module eliminates redundant predicates in the query and decomposes it into simple relation execution at local database nodes. Some simple heuristic rules, such as applying unary operations (select/project) as soon as possible, can be used in this phase to improve performance. Subsequently, Plan Generator chooses the best point in the solution space of all possible execution strategies using database statistics and run-time system parameters (system and network workload) in terms of the cost model that typically refers to weighted combination of I/O, CPU and

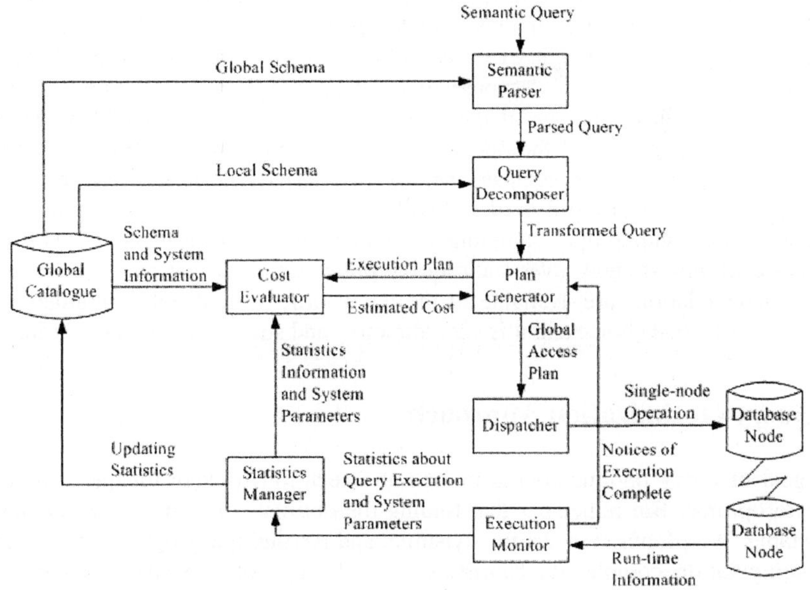

Fig. 2. Architecture of database grid query optimizer

communication costs. An immediate method for producing the sequence of operation is to search the solution space, exhaustively predict the cost of each strategy, and select the strategy with minimum cost. Although this method is effective in selecting the best strategy, it may incur a significant processing cost for the optimization itself, since the solution space can be very large.

The most powerful search strategy used by query optimizers is dynamic programming, which start from base relations, joining one more relation at each step until complete plans are obtained. Dynamic programming is almost exhaustive and assures that the "best" of all plans is found. It incurs an acceptable optimization cost when the number of relation in the query is small. However, this approach becomes too expensive when the number of relations is greater than 5 or 6. The worse is that the dynamic programming dramatically dependent on accurate statistics information. But in the environment of the database grid with numerous database nodes that will dynamically participate or quit the gird system, it is impossible and highly expensive to maintaining accurate and complete database statistics or errors in these estimates can lead to bed performance, therefore, dynamic programming and its variances are not suitable to database grid situation.

We choose another popular way of heuristics to reduce the cost of exhaustive search, whose effect is to restrict the solution space so that only a few strategies are considered. A common heuristic is to minimize the size of intermediate relations and we use this search strategy in dynamic way. Firstly, Plan generator sends Dispatcher to perform unary operations at each relevant database node. Execution Monitor will collect results of operations executed and run-time system parameters, send this information to Statistics Manager for updating Global Catalogue to reflect the effect of change, and synchronously notify Plan Generator for the end of execution. Then, Plan Generator determines the next join operation with the most selective which will produce the minimum size of intermediate results by assistant of Cost Evaluator. System runs step by step as above way and execute join operation in parallelism as can as possible to minimize response time (more discussion in Section 4). At any point of execution, the choice of the best next operation can be based on accurate knowledge of the results of the operations executed previously. Therefore, database statistics are not needed to estimate the size of intermediate results. However, little statistic information may still need and will update periodically by issuing queries to database nodes with proper sampling technique during off-peak hours. The main advantage of this strategy over static query optimization is that the actual sizes of intermediate relations are available to the query processor, thereby minimizing the probability of a bad choice and it is very attractive and suitable for database grid.

4 Query Optimization Approach

The goal of query optimization is to find an execution strategy for query which is close to optimal. But remember that finding the optimal solution is computationally intractable. We propose a heuristic, dynamic, and parallel query optimization to meet this computation complexity, heuristics for reducing solution space, dynamic for generating better execution sequences, and parallelism for minimizing response time.

4.1 Cost Model

An optimizer's cost model includes cost functions to evaluate the cost of operators, statistics and formulas to predict the sizes of intermediate results. Two common objectives are minimum total cost and minimum response time. Total cost is the sum of all times incurred in processing the operations of query at various database nodes and in transferring intermediate results among participating database nodes. Response time of query is the time elapsed for executing query. We adopt the objective of minimum total cost in our query optimization with making the best use of parallelism if possible to reduce response time.

A general formula for determining the total time of transferring x tuples from node i to node j and processing x tuples with y tuples (which are already at node j) at node j can be specified as follows:

$$Total\_time_{ij}(x, y) = Init + Ship_{ij}(x) + Process_j(x, y) \quad (1)$$

Where *Init* is the cost for generating nest query operation, startup of transmission, and control of security; The $Ship_{ij}$ is the cost function of transferring x tuples from node i to node j, which depends on channel bandwidth, error rate, distance, and other line characteristics; The $Process_j$ is the cost function of local processing by the database nodes j (typically refers to times of disk I/Os and CPU instruction).

Remember that above formula does not consider some factors like network and other dynamic characteristics of database nodes. In grid environment, we can not ignore these factors and should modify above formula to reflect the effect of dynamic changes about system and network. We use SL_j to represent the factor of workload at node j (20% for example), and let the result of $Process_j(x, y)$ divided by $(1-SL_j)$ $(Process_j(x, y)/(1-SL_j))$ to evaluate the cost of local processing at node j instead of original $Process_j(x, y)$. Adjustment in communication cost is similar to above discussion. Consider that NL_{ij} represent the factor of network load from node i to node j, and we substitute $(Ship_{ij}(x)/(1-NL_{ij}))$ for above $Ship_{ij}(x)$.

Join selectivity factors for some pairs of relations are required in order to predict the size of intermediate result which is the proportion of tuples participating in the join. The join selectivity factor, denoted SF_J, of relation R and S is a real value between 0 and 1:

$$SF_J(R, S) = card(R \bowtie S) \ / \ card(R) * card(S) \quad (2)$$

$card(R)$ represents the number of tuples of the relation R, and $\bowtie$ denotes the natural join. We say that a join has better selectivity if it has a smaller join selectivity factor. When the join selectivity factor between relation R and S is not available in Global Catalogue during the run-time, we use upper bound $(card(R \times S) = card(R) * card(S))$ divided by a constant to reflect the fact that the join result is smaller than that of the Cartesian product. The sampling method should be used to obtain information about the system, such as, startup time, transmission rate, join selectivity factor and process overhead. Such statistic information is stored in Global Catalogue and maintained by Statistics Manger. Database grid query optimizer retrieves that information when a cost needs to be evaluated for a global access plan.

4.2 Algorithm Description

As mentioned in the introduction section, the same real world object may be represented in more than one node in a database grid system (see Figure 3). The top of the Figure 3 is a semantic view of ontologies and the bottom is four different database nodes. The attributes of relation register to ontology properties according to their semantic meaning. Node 1 and 2 have medicine as well as therapy relation, whereas node 3 only possesses medicine relation, and node 4 only has therapy relation. Medicine relation keeps track of medicine names and their ingredients. Diseases and their available medicine are stored in therapy relation. In distributed database, if a relation R is horizontally decompose into fragments R_1, R_2, … , R_n and data item d_i is in R_j, it is not in any other fragment R_k ($k \neq j$). This criterion ensures that the horizontal fragments are disjoint, but this rule is not followed when refer to database gird. Therefore, the union of two relations (we call it subrelation) which materialize same relational schema at different nodes is not always equal to empty. Let us illustrate the idea of our algorithm using the following query:

Example 1. "Retrieve all diseases and their available medicine as well as its ingredient". The following are two feasible access plans to execute it:

Access Plan 1: Send all relations to node 1; perform $\cup_{(nodes = 1,2,3)} R_{medicine}$ and $\cup_{(nodes = 1,2,4)} R_{therapy}$ there ($\cup$ denotes union operation); and execute $R_{medicine} \bowtie R_{therapy}$ at node 1.

Access Plan 2: Send $R_{therapy\ (node = 1\ and\ 2\ and\ 4)}$ to each node of 1, 2, and 3; At each node i (i =1, 2, and 3), execute $\cup_{(nodes = 1,2,4)} R_{therapy}$ and $R_{medicine\ (node = i)} \bowtie R_{therapy}$ respectively. Send the results of former execution at node 2, 3 to node 1; perform union of all results at node 1.

However, above two access plan have an expensive cost obviously. But this scenario often happens in database grid, we propose *DG-PHJ* algorithm (see Algorithm 1) by extending the parallel hash join algorithm [Özsu and Valduriez, 1991] to meet this difficulty. The basic idea of *DG-PHJ* algorithm is to partition

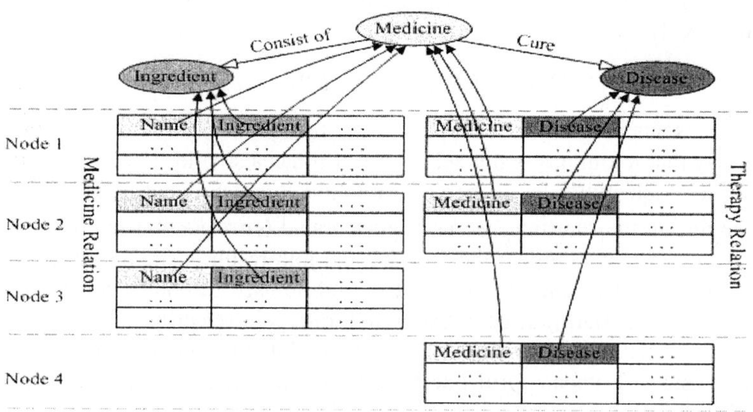

Fig. 3. Materialization of scheme relation schema at different nodes in database gird

relation R and S into the same number p of mutually exclusion sets $R_1, R_2, \ldots, R_p$, and $S_1, S_2, \ldots, S_p$ by employing hash function on the join attribute, such that

$$R \bowtie S = \cup_{(i=1\ to\ p)} (R_i \bowtie S_i) \quad (3)$$

Algorithm 1. *DG-PHJ*

```
input: R1, R2, ... , Rm: subrelations of relation R;
       S1, S2, ... , Sn: subrelations of relation S;
       JP: join predicate.
output: T1, T2, ..., Tp: result subrelations.
  begin: {JP is R.A = R.B and h is a hash function
          that returns an integer number in [1, p]}
    for i = 1 to m do in parallel {hash R on the join attribute}
    begin
      Rij ← apply h(A) to Ri (j = 1, ..., p)
      for j = 1 to p do
        send Rij to node j
      end-for
    end-for
    for i = 1 to n do in parallel {hash S on the join attribute}
    begin
      Sij ← apply h(B) to Si (j = 1, ..., p)
      for j = 1 to p do
        send Rij to node j
      end-for
    end-for
    for j = 1 to p do in parallel {perform the join at each p-node}
    begin
      Rj ← ∪ (i=1 to m) Rij                {receive from R-nodes}
      Sj ← ∪ (i=1 to n) Sij                {receive from S-nodes}
      Tj ← JOIN(Rj, Sj, JP)
    end-for
  end. {DG-PHJ}
```

the same hash function is applied to join attribute to partition R and S. Each individual join ($R_i \bowtie S_i$) is executed in parallel, and the join results are produced at p nodes. These p nodes actually are selected at run time based on the load of the system and network. Since operations can be executed in parallel at different nodes, the response time of query will be significantly less than its total cost. Figure 4 shows the application of *DG-PHJ* algorithm with Example 1. We assumed that the results are produced at nodes 1, 2, and 3. An arrow in the Figure 4 indicates a data transfer. However, *DG-PHJ* algorithm only can be applied when join predicate is equijoin that happens most frequently. The execution strategy of access plan 2 in Example 1 can be used in the situation of arbitrarily complex join, and we call this *DG-PNL* algorithm which follows the idea of parallel nested loop algorithm [Özsu and Valduriez, 1991].

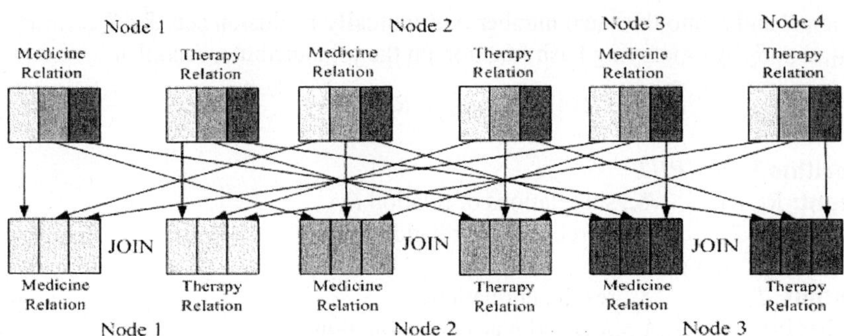

Fig. 4. Example of *DG-PHJ* Algorithm

After discussion of the cost model, *DG-PHJ* and *DG-PNL* algorithm, we now can propose the global algorithm for query optimization in database grid. As shown in Algorithm 2. The algorithm of *DG-QOA* works as follows. Firstly, each the best local

Algorithm 2. *DG-QOA*

input: query q on relations $R_1, R_2, \ldots, R_n$;
each R_i have m_i subrelations $R_{i1}, R_{i2}, \ldots, R_{i\,m_i}$;
database statistics, system characteristics, and networks load information.
output: result of the query.
Begin
for $i = 1$ **to** n **do**
for $j = 1$ **to** m_i **do**
optionPlan($\{R_{ij}\}$) = accessPlan(R_{ij}) {generate all possible local access plan}
optimalPlan(R_{ij}) = prunePlans(optionPlan($\{R_{ij}\}$)) {choose the best local access plan}
run(optimalPlan(R_{ij})) {run all one-subrelation queries}
end-for
end-for
$S = \{R_1, R_2, \ldots, R_n\}$ {S is a set of relations that need to execute join operation}
While $|S| < 1$ **do**
{choose the join pair that will produce the minimum size of intermediate results}
chooseJoinPair(R_x, R_y) where $(R_x, R_y) \subset \{R_1, R_2, \ldots, R_n\}$
if R_x and R_y all just have one subrelation **then**
R_z = join(R_x, R_y) {perform join operation in common way}
else if the join predicate on R_x and R_y is equijoin **then**
R_z = *DG-PHJ*(R_x, R_y)
else
R_z = *DG-PNJ*(R_x, R_y)
end-if
end-if
$S = (S \setminus R_x, R_y) \cup (R_z)$
end-while
assemble query results and send to the final node
end. {*DG-QOA*}

access plan of unary operations (select/projection) at relevant database nodes is generated and executed, and then, the *DG-QOA* algorithm determines first join pair (R_x, R_y) which will produce the minimum size of intermediate results with the smallest selectivity. In this phase, if both R_x and R_y have no more than one subrelation, join between R_x and R_y will performed in the common way that just likes traditional distributed database, We consider using index information and semijoin technique to minimize total cost in this situation that each operator of 2-way join just has one subrelation. Otherwise, we check the join predicate. If it is arbitrarily complex other than equijoin, the *DG-PNJ* algorithm should be applied, and if not, the algorithm *DG-PHJ* will be used. We delete R_x and R_y relations from the set *S*, and insert new relation R_z which produced by $R_x \bowtie R_y$ to the set *S*. After that, the *DG-QOA* algorithm chooses the next join pair which will produce the minimum size of intermediate relations according to accurate information about the outcomes of foregoing execution, and dynamic system characteristics and networks load. System does this loop until no join operation should be performed. Finally, the query results are assembled and sent to the final node that produces this query.

4.3 Experimental Analysis

Since the original motivation of designing and developing DartGrid II is to provide a platform for Tradition Chinese Medicine (TCM) grid. We carry out performance experiment on TCM grid that includes 17 database nodes. However, no such work for database gird has been reported, we analyze experimental results by comparing to DartGrid I without using the query optimization approach proposed by this paper (see Figure 5).

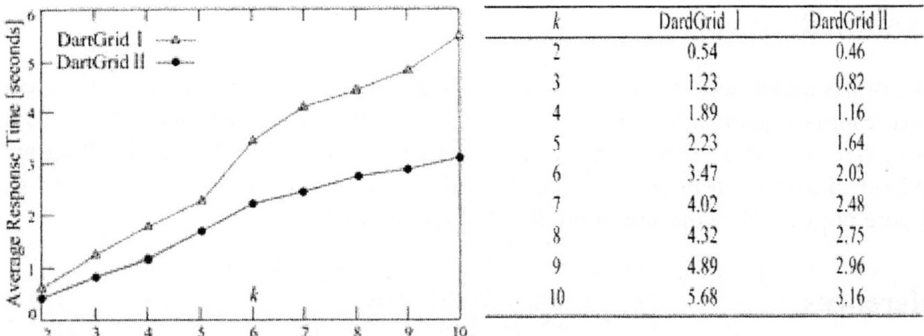

k	DardGrid I	DardGrid II
2	0.54	0.46
3	1.23	0.82
4	1.89	1.16
5	2.23	1.64
6	3.47	2.03
7	4.02	2.48
8	4.32	2.75
9	4.89	2.96
10	5.68	3.16

Fig. 5. Average Response Time of DartGrid I and DartGrid II, vary *k*, 10-way chain query

As shown in Figure 5, we can see that the average response time of DartGrid I and DartGrid II increase with *k* that denotes the numbers of relations need to join together. Obviously, DartGrid II with *DG-QOA* algorithm is more efficient than DartGrid I. Furthermore, the average response time of DartGrid I dramatically goes up after 5-way query, otherwise, that of DartGrid II increases comparatively smoothly.

5 Conclusion and Future Work

Different types of autonomy and heterogeneity which stem from design, communication, and execution aspects make query optimization in database grid fundamentally different from that in traditional DBMS. These challenges include translating ontology-based global semantic query to local access plan, lack of information about participating database nodes, dynamic and unpredictable system and network parameters, different local capabilities, and more constraints during query optimization in database grid. The existing query processing and optimization technologies must therefore be re-examined in the light of these observation.

After simply overview some major query processing approach, we present the architectural design of a database gird query optimizer which incorporates the query optimization techniques suggested in this paper. And then, the cost model used in database grid has been discussed. finally, we propose the query optimization algorithms (*DG-QOA*, *DG-PHJ*, and *DG-PNJ*) with heuristic, dynamic, and parallel characteristics, heuristics for reducing solution space, dynamic for generating better execution sequences, and parallelism for minimizing response time. The results of preliminary experiment show that our approach is not only efficient but also effective.

For the future, some modules of DartGrid II should be modified for compatible objective with query optimization, and then, more experiment can be made on a large scale to improve algorithm proposed by this paper. Though optimization problem is *NP*-hard, heuristic algorithms are deemed to be justified, another promising randomized and exhaustive research approach, especially Genetic Algorithm and Iterative Dynamic Programming, should be investigated deeply to determine whether these approaches can be integrated into DartGrid II for performance purpose.

Acknowledgement

The work is supported by China 973 fundamental research and development project: The research on application of semantic grid on the knowledge sharing and service of Traditional Chinese Medicine; Intel/University Sponsored Research Program: DartGrid: Building an information Grid for Traditional Chinese Medicine; and China 211 core project: Network based Intelligence and Graphics.

References

1. Donnald Kossmann, Konrad Storcker. Iterative Dynamic Programming: A New Class of Query Optimization Algorithms. ACM Transactions on Database Systems, March 2000, 25(1): 43–82.
2. D. Bitton, H. Boral, D. J. DeWitt, W. K. Wilkinson. Parallel Algorithms for the Execution of Relational Database Operations. ACM Trans. Database Syst, Sept. 1983, 8(3): 324-353.
3. Galindo-Legaria, C., Pellenkoft, A., Kersten, M. Fast, randomized join-order selection-why use transformations?. In Proceedings of the 20th International Conference on Very Large Data Bases, September 1994, 85-95.
4. Graefe, G. DeWitt, D. The EXODUS optimizer generator. In Proceedings of the ACM-SIGMOD Conference on Management of Data, May 1987, 160-172.

5. Graefe, G. Mckenna, W. J. The volcano optimizer generator: Extensibility and efficient search. In Proceedings of the 9th International Conference on Data Engineering, April 1993, 209-218.
6. Hongjun Lu, Beng-Chin Ooi, Cheng-Hian Goh. Multidatabase query optimization: issues and solutions. Research Issues in Data Engineering, April 1993, 137-143.
7. H. Zhuge, J. Liu, L. Feng, X. Sun and C. He. Query Routing in a Peer-to-Peer Semantic Link Network. Computational Intelligence, 2005, 21(2): 197-216.
8. Ioannidis, Y. E. Kang, Y. C. Randomized algorithms for optimizing large join queries. In Proceedings of the 1990 ACM SIGMOD International Conference on Management of Data, May 1990, 312-321.
9. Jiunn-Chin Wang, Jorng-Tzong Horng, Yi-Ming Hsu. A genetic algorithm for set query optimization in distributed database systems. IEEE International Conference on Systems, Man, and Cybernetics, October 1996, 3: 14-17.
10. J. Veijalainen, Popescu-Zeletin. Multidatabase systems in ISO/OSI environment. Standards in Information Technology and Industrial Control, 1988, 83-97.
11. Lanzelotte, R., Valduries, P., Zait, M. On the effectiveness of optimization search strategies for parallel execution spaces. In Proceedings of the Conference on Very Large Data Bases, Auguest 1993, 493-504.
12. M. Tamer Özsu, Patrick Valduriez. Principles of Distributed Database Systems. Prentice Hall, Inc., 1999.
13. Ono, K., Lohman, G. Measuring the complexity of join enumeration in query optimization. In Proceedings of the 16th International Conference on Very Large Data Bases, August 1990, 314-325.
14. Palermo, F. P. 1974. A data base search problem. In Information Systems COINS IV, 1974, 67-101.
15. P. A. Bernstein, N. Goodman, et al., Query Processing in a System for Distributed Database (SDD-1). ACM trans. Database Syst, December 1981, 6(4): 602-625.
16. P. Valduriez, G. Gardarin. Join and Semi-join Algorithms for a Multi Processor Database Machine. ACM Trans. Databases Syst, March 1984, 9(1): 133-161.
17. Qiang Zhu. Query Optimization in Multidatabase Systems. Proc. the Centre for Advanced Studies Conf. on Collaborative research, Nov. 1992, 111-127.
18. Selinger, P. G., Astrahan, M. M., Lorie, R. A., Price, T. G. Access path selection in a relational database management system. In Proceedings of the ACM SIGMOD International Conference on Management of Data, May-June 1979, 23-34.
19. Selinger, P. G., M. Adiba. Access Path Seletion in Distributed Data Base Management Systems. In Proc. First Int. Conf. on Data Bases, 1980, 204-215.
20. Shekita, E., Young, H., Tan, K. -L. 1993. Multi-join optimization for symmetric multiprocessors. In Proc. Conf. on Very Large Data Bases, Auguest 1993, 479-492.
21. Steinbrunn, M., Moerkotte, G., Kemper, A. Heuristic and randomized optimization for the join ordering problem. Auguest 1997, 191-208.
22. Swami, A. Optimization of large join queries: Combining heuristics and combinational techniques. In Proceedings of the ACM Conference on Management of Data, May 1989, 367-376.
23. Y. E. Ioannidis, E. Wong. Query optimization by simulated annealing. In proc. ACM SIGMOD Int. Conf. on Management of Data, June 1987, 9-22.
24. Zhaohui Wu, Huajun Chen, Changhuang, Guozhou Zheng, Jiefeng Xu. DartGrid: Semantic-Based Database Grid. ICCS 2004, 59-66.

Pushing Scientific Documents by Discovering Interest in Information Flow Within E-Science Knowledge Grid*

Lianhong Ding[1,2], Xiang Li[1,2], and Yunpeng Xing[1,2,3]

[1] Key Lab of Intelligent Information Processing, Institute of Computing Technology, Chinese Academy of Sciences, Beijing, China
[2] Graduate School of Chinese Academy of Sciences, 100080 Beijing, China
{lhding, xiangli, Ypxing}@kg.ict.ac.cn
[3] Hunan Knowledge Grid Lab, Hunan University of Science and Technology, Hunan, China

Abstract. The Knowledge Grid is an intelligent and sustainable Internet application environment that enables people and roles to effectively capture, publish, share and manage explicit knowledge resources. As an important function of the e-Science Knowledge Grid, this paper proposes an approach to effectively push scientific documents within research teams by detecting the social characteristics in self-organized network, discovering interest in information flow, and capturing dynamic changes of interests over time. The proposed approach can be used in any cooperative organizations.

1 Introduction

Keeping with up-to-date documents becomes increasingly important in scientific research [17, 20, 24]. Team members often search for the same documents. This leads to low efficiency of teamwork. An efficient and effective document sharing method can improve the efficiency and competitiveness of organizations.

The first step is to discover the common interest communities in large social network by graph analysis [11]. Corresponding to vertex "betweenness" proposed by Freeman [7], Girvan and Newman put forward the conception of edge betweenness and partition a graph into discrete communities of nodes based on the idea of edge betweenness centrality. The betweenness of an edge is defined as the number of shortest paths that run along it. Communities are discovered by repeatedly identifying and removing the edges of highest betweenness because the edges that connect highly clustered communities have higher edge betweenness [8].

Two rules that direct the partition process to stop or go on are proposed and applied to find communities of related genes and communities within an organization automatically [11, 13]. The first is: the component that is composed of no more than 5 vertices should not be partitioned. The second is: the partition process should stop when the highest betweenness is N–1, where N is the number of vertices. The second

* This work was supported by the National Basic Research Program of China (973 project No.2003CB317000) and the National Science Foundation of China (Grants 60273020 and 70271007).

H. Zhuge and G.C. Fox (Eds.): GCC 2005, LNCS 3795, pp. 498 – 510, 2005.

rule ends the algorithm before the isolated vertex appears. They will be called minimum component rule and N–1 betweenness rule respectively in the following.

Zhuge's Knowledge Grid is an intelligent and sustainable Internet application environment that enables people and roles to effectively capture, publish, share and manage explicit knowledge resources [18, 23, 25]. A scientific document sharing approach supported by the Knowledge Grid is introduced in this paper. It can actively push scientific documents to members by discovering their interests from information flow within e-Science Knowledge Grid [17, 19, 20, 24, 26, 28].

2 General Architecture

The general architecture of the proposed method consists of the following core modules as shown in Fig. 1.

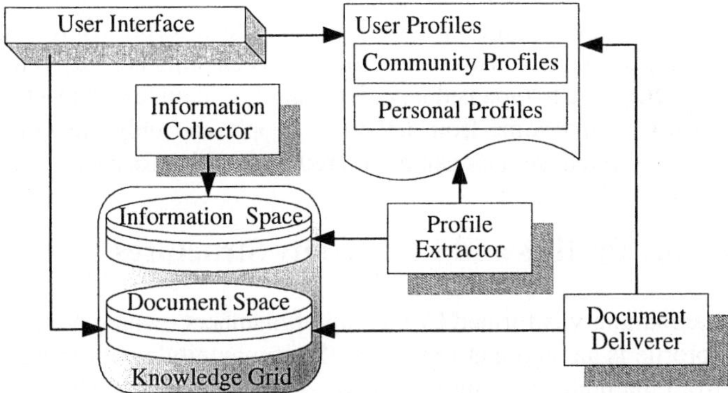

Fig. 1. General architecture of the proposed approach

Knowledge Grid manages distributed heterogeneous resources in a uniform way [23, 25]. It comprises information space and document space storing relevant contents of information flow and documents respectively [21, 22]. Document space has an *area-to-topic* structure, where each area is divided into many smaller and disjoint topics. An area review is stored in the area involved; a document emphasizing particularly on concrete issues is stored at the corresponding topic within certain area.

User profiles give *general-to-specific* description of member interests and provide supports for document deliverer. Community profile is an area covering the whole community interests. Personal profile is one or several concrete topics in the area, which exhibits difference between community members. Community profiles correspond to the area level of document space, while personal profiles correspond to the topic level.

Information collector gathers information flow in the organization and stores the useful contents into information space.

Profile extractor extracts user interests from information flow: discover community profiles by community detecting and learn personal profiles by mining.

User interface, by which members can tune their own profiles or upload scientific documents to the document space at anytime.

Document deliverer is responsible for pushing relevant documents to organization members actively by referring to user profiles [24].

3 Information Collection

There are many kinds of information flows in organizations, including email flow, flow of short message, flow in message board and flow in blog [19]. They are uniformly called messages if no special explanation.

Message like email is more than free-form text. It has additional features in the structured header in addition to the unstructured body. At regular intervals, information collector first parses each message into following six parts: *from*, *to*, *date*, *subject*, *body* and *attachment* (if any), uniforms the name of the senders and recipients and deletes quotations of other messages and signatures from message body, then stores them to information space, with each message as a record. Here, external messages and messages sent to a list of more than 10 recipients are neglected. Only the first attachment that the file type is doc, pdf, ps, html or plain text is reserved.

Junk messages mainly come from unknown people and only messages within an organization are collected, so they can be filtered out in this process.

4 Community Profiles and Community Structures

In practice, a community is formed by a group of members owning common interests. Community profile is an area that represents the community's common preference. It can be got from the understanding of anyone in the community. Here, it is approximately specified as the area that covers most of the member's interest points.

4.1 Social Network Construction

A social network is a map of the relationships between individuals where we can observe their social activities. Traditional generation of social network is time consuming and requires a large degree of cooperation from the subjects being studied.

Information flow in e-Science Knowledge Grid provides a cheaper, easier, and quicker way for social network data collection. Here, the social network for an organization is automatically constructed from information flow: vertices represent people; edges are added between pairs of correspondences that appear in the same message header. Different values can be assigned to the threshold that specifies the minimum number of messages passed between any two vertices.

4.2 Community Detecting

Our community detecting algorithm extends the idea of edge betweenness centrality to find social networks with different threshold values.

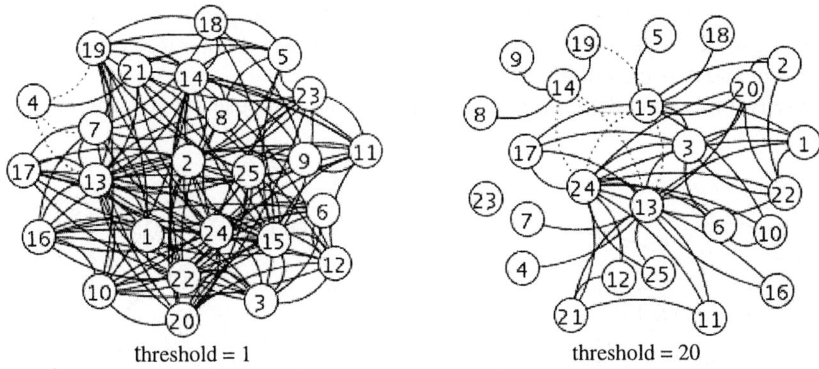

Fig. 2. Partition results following the *N*–1 betweenness rule

First, the partition algorithm follows the minimum component rule and *N*–1 betweenness rule. Fig. 2 illustrates the partition results, where dotted lines are the edges that have been removed by the algorithm. When the threshold=1, the algorithm stops with three edges removed for the *N*–1 betweenness rule. When threshold=20, it ends with six edges removed for the same reason, where node 23 is an isolated vertex in the social network itself. From above examples, we can see *N*-1 betweenness rule makes the partition process stop too early.

Then, the partition results of the algorithm discarding the *N*-1 betweenness rule are illustrated in Fig. 3. We can see the discarding of the *N*-1 betweenness rule leads to too many isolated vertices. So the rules proposed previously need modification, at least for the small-scale networks like ours.

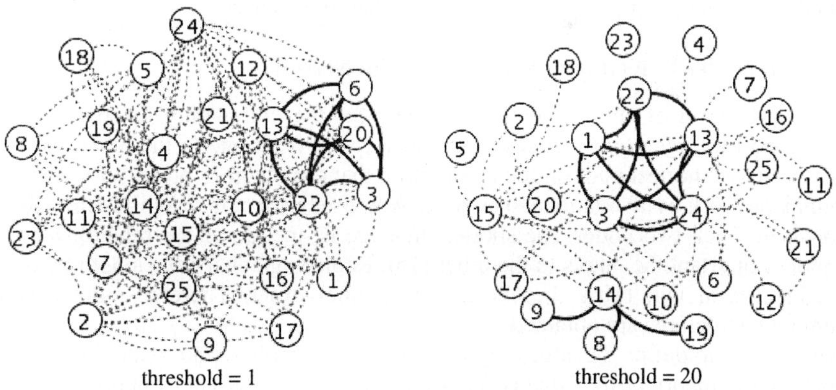

Fig. 3. Partition results discarding the *N*–1 betweenness rule

First, we replace the *N*-1 betweenness rule by the following rule: remove the edge with second highest betweenness, if the highest betweenness is *N*-1 and the component is still big enough. The number of the vertices in a component can be used to judge if the component is still big enough. It may be different for different scales and different aims.

Then, another rule that a complete graph should not be partitioned further is proposed. It can be judged if $E=N(N-1)/2$ holds, where E is the number of edges in the component and N is the number of vertices.

These two rules and the minimum community rule compose the new rules together.

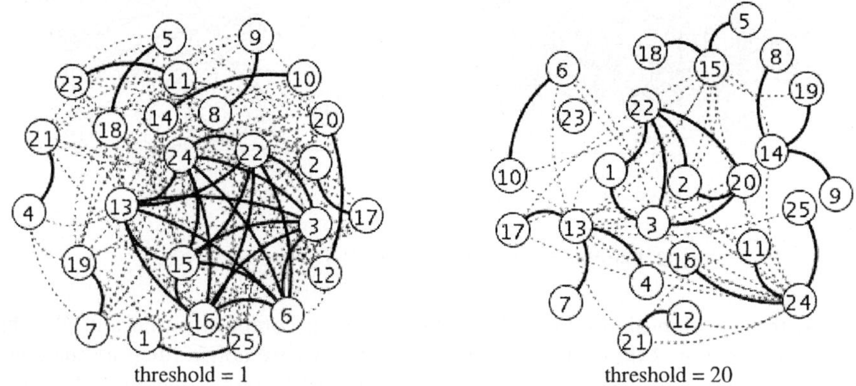

Fig. 4. Partition results following new rules

The partition results following the new rules are given in Fig. 4. Using threshold 1 as an example: after the three edges linking 4 and 13, 4 and 7, 4 and 19 are removed in order, the edge linking 4 and 21 becomes the one with the highest betweenness. Because the deletion of it will make 4 isolated, according to the new rules, the edge linking 13 and 21 is removed instead, which makes the algorithm continue. The complete graph rule newly introduced makes the community consisting of 3, 6, 13, 15, 16, 22 and 24 is reserved although there are more than five vertices.

4.3 Community Detecting of Weighted Social Network

The identification of shortest path is the key for the community discovering. The shortest path between two vertices is the fastest way from one to the other. Previous works find the shortest path on the assumption that each edge is equally long. In fact, a social network is a relational network, where edge length can illustrate the tie strength between two nodes: the shorter the edge is, the closer the relationship is or the more important the one is to the other [16]. Replacing equal edge length by different edge length will bring the shortest path more exact. Thereby, more accurate community structures are obtained.

One way is to define the edge length according to absolute importance of the edge, namely, how important the edge is for the whole network. Higher importance means shorter length. The length $Length_{ij}$ of the edge between vertex i and j is calculated as following.

$$Length_{ij} = \frac{t}{Num_{ij}} \tag{1}$$

where t is the threshold used to construct the social network from information flow and Num_{ij} is the number of messages that have been passed between i and j.

Another way is based on relative importance of the edge, that is, how important the edge is for the two vertices linked up by it.

$$Length_{ij} = \frac{Num_{i-all} \times Num_{j-all}}{Num_{i-j} \times Num_{j-i}} \tag{2}$$

where $Num_{i\text{-}all}$ is the number of messages that i has sent to others, $Num_{j\text{-}all}$ is the number of messages that j has sent to others; $Num_{i\text{-}j}$ is the number of messages that i has sent to j, and $Num_{j\text{-}i}$ is the number of messages that j has sent to i.

Table 1. Comparison between three methods. 1 means equal edge length, 2 means absolute improtance-based edge length and 3 means relative importance-based edge length.

Method	t = 1	t = 10	t = 20	t = 30	t = 40
1	24%	72%	60%	72%	56%
2	44%	88%	92%	88%	80%
3	60%	72%	92%	84%	76%

Table 1 lists the partition precision when the three methods are adopted to calculate the edge length respectively. For each method medium thresholds bring higher precision. When the threshold is equal to 10, 20, 30 and 40, the absolute importance-based edge length method brings best partition results, then the relative importance-based edge length method, and then the equal edge length method. When the threshold is equal to 1, the relative importance-based method brings highest precious. In all, different edge length methods produce better results than the equal edge length method.

4.4 Network Generator and Community Detector

To automatically get community structures in an organization, we have developed network generator and community detector. The former takes messages collected as input, and related social network data stored in a Pajek .net file as output [1]. The threshold and specific method to calculate the length of edge can be chosen. Community detector inputs the Pajek .net file and displays the social network of the organization as an undirected graph. Community structures are given in the following form: the vertices of a community are linked up by solid edges and different communities in the organization are linked up by dotted edges. Location of each vertex can be changed to view the network and communities clearly.

5 Personal Profiles and Message Mining

Like user navigational data, messages that a member has read or written also implicate his or her preference. So members' personal profiles can be got by tracing their daily using of all kinds of messages. As the Fig. 5 illustrates, it consists of unusable-message filtering, usable-message classification and personal profile computing.

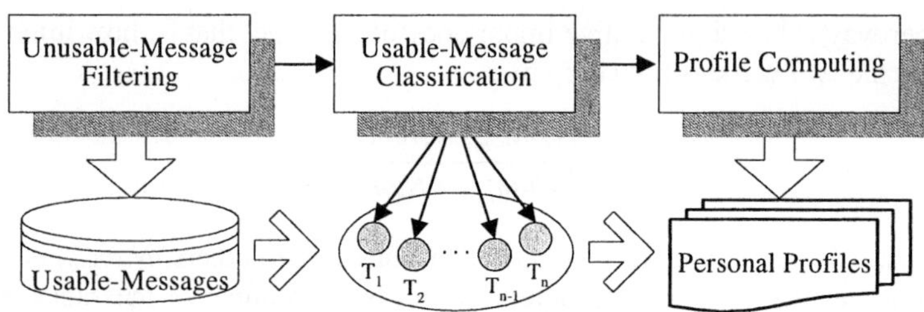

Fig. 5. Discovery of personal profiles

First, all messages stored are divided into usable-messages and unusable-messages. The former are the messages containing research information. Second, each usable-message is assigned to a specific topic by usable-message classification. The topic of a usable-message represents its main meaning. And at last, profile computing component determines personal profiles by a statistical evaluation of the results of usable-message classification. The principle directing this statistical algorithm is that the more usable-messages a member writes or reads about a topic, the more attention he or she pays to the topic.

Besides providing support to document deliverer, user profile can also benefit a research team by the following way: keeping track of what everyone is doing and has done by browsing current user profiles and history user profiles; and tuning one's own profile to make interests-describing and document-delivering more accurately.

5.1 Message Representation

Each message m is represented as a weighed term vector $\vec{m} = (m^{(1)}, m^{(2)}, ...)$ by the standard TFIDF function.

$$m^{(i)} = TF(w_i, m) \cdot \log(\frac{|D|}{DF(w_i)}) \tag{3}$$

where the term frequency $TF(w_i, m)$ is the number of times word w_i occurs in message m, $|D|$ denotes the total number of messages in the training set and the $DF(w_i)$ is the number of messages containing the word w_i at least one time.

Message is more than free-form text. The text in *subject* filed and *body* field of email is treated separately and identically in [14]: a word's one time appearance in the *subject* and in the *body* is equal. Here, we also consider the text in *subject* field and *body* field of message separately but discriminatively.

Usually, *subject* is the outline of *body* contents, so words in *subject* filed are more descriptive and discriminative in contrast to the words in *body* field. That is, they are more important for the classification. Here, words in *subject* filed are assigned larger weights. When calculating the weight of word w_i, there is no change for $DF(w_i)$. For $TF(w_i, m)$, one time appearance in *subject* field equals to t times appearances in *body* field. The enhancement of $TF(w_i, m)$ strengthens the importance of w_i, while no change for $DF(w_i)$ ensures the tuning up of w_i will not be weakened. The Increasement of words' weight reinforces their discriminative ability in turn [15].

Because message such as email is typically short and message *body*, *subject* and *attachment* normally express a common theme the text attachment reserved is treated as a part of message *body*.

5.2 Unusable-Message Filtering

All messages stored are divided into usable-messages and unusable-messages in this step. Usable-messages are messages whose contents are related to research information. Jokes or weekly meeting notices are typically unusable-messages. It can be regarded as a message classification where only usable-messages and unusable-messages exist.

Models of usable-messages and unusable-messages are represented as prototype vector $\vec{m}_1$ and prototype vector $\vec{m}_2$ respectively. For each model not only the positive examples but also the negative ones are taken into account.

$$\vec{m}_1 = \alpha \frac{1}{|M_1|} \sum_{\vec{m} \in M_1} \frac{\vec{m}}{|\vec{m}|} - \beta \frac{1}{|M_2|} \sum_{\vec{m} \in M_2} \frac{\vec{m}}{|\vec{m}|} \tag{4}$$

$$\vec{m}_2 = \alpha \frac{1}{|M_2|} \sum_{\vec{m} \in M_2} \frac{\vec{m}}{|\vec{m}|} - \beta \frac{1}{|M_1|} \sum_{\vec{m} \in M_1} \frac{\vec{m}}{|\vec{m}|} \tag{5}$$

α and β are parameters that adjust the relative impact of positive and negative examples. As recommended in [4], α and β are set to 16 and 4. M_1 and M_2 are the training messages of usable-messages and unusable-messages respectively; $|M_1|$ and $|M_2|$ are the number of messages in M_1 and M_2. $\vec{m}$ is the vector representation of message m and $|\vec{m}|$ denotes the Euclidean length of $\vec{m}$. Here, M_1 is positive examples for usable-messages and negative examples for unusable-messages. M_2 is positive examples for unusable-messages and negative examples for usable-messages. When transforming a training message into a feature vector, the words that occur with similar proportion of times in both M_1 and M_2 are deleted. Messages m is usable if cosine similarity between $\vec{m}$ and $\vec{m}_1$ is higher than that between $\vec{m}$ and $\vec{m}_2$, otherwise, it is unusable.

5.3 Usable-Message Classification and Profile Computing

The usable-message classification specifies a topic for each usable-message by general document classification. First, a prototype vector for each topic in the document space is built. Documents stored in the topic level are utilized as training documents for corresponding topics. Then, for each usable-message within certain community, a prototype vector that gives the largest cosine of the message vector and the prototype vector itself is found. This topic is a good representation for the usable-message. Here, only the prototype vectors for the topics that belong to the area corresponding to the community profile are considered.

The extent that a member has paid attention to a topic can be reflected by how many usable-messages he or she has read or written about that topic. The more usable-messages a member reads or writes about a topic, the more the member is interested in the topic. Personal profile of user U_j takes the form as a finite set of <*topic*$_i$,

$energy_{ij}$>, where $energy_{ij}$ denotes the importance degree of $topic_i$ in the personal profile of U_j which can be obtained in the following way:

$$energy_{ij} = \frac{\alpha \sum_{(m \in from_j) \cap (m \in T_i)} 2^{-\frac{age(m)}{hl}} Sim(m,t) + \beta \sum_{(m \in to_j) \cap (m \in T_i)} 2^{-\frac{age(m)}{hl}} Sim(m,t)}{\alpha \sum_{(m \in from_j)} 2^{-\frac{age(m)}{hl}} Sim(m,t) + \beta \sum_{(m \in to_j)} 2^{-\frac{age(m)}{hl}} Sim(m,t)} \quad (6)$$

where $from_j$ is the usable-messages U_j has sent to others in the community and to_j is the usable-messages U_j has received from others in the community. T_i denotes the set of usable-messages associated with $topic_i$ and $Sim(m, t)$ is the cosine similarity between m and the topic to which it belongs. α and β are parameters that adjust the relative impact of usable-messages flowing from and to U_j separately. Stronger impact is specified to the usable-messages flowing from a member by a bigger α and a smaller β.

Since user interests often change, it is important to adjust the user profile incrementally [5]. A time factor $2^{-\frac{age(m)}{hl}}$ is introduced to adjust the contribution of usable-message for personal profile according to its age $age(m)$, which makes the descriptive ability of usable-message decay with time. $age(m)$ is the algebraic difference between the current date and the date when m was sent. The half-life span hl is set to 30 on the assumption that the effect of usable-messages on a topic reduces by 1/2 in one month [10]. Personal profile adapts to changes in member's interests with the accumulation of messages and the decay of time. No techniques such as relevance feedback, user's register and user's ratings are employed.

6 Push Documents According to User Profiles

For each document, an owner list is maintained, which records all persons having owned the document. Each member can upload documents to the document space by user interface. One can only upload the document he or she owns, so the upload behavior itself shows that this document needn't be pushed to him or her. Persons who try to upload a document are added to corresponding owner list, so are the members who have received that document. No record of a person in the owner list of a document is a necessary precondition for pushing a document for that person. A review in the area level of the document space is pushed to all members in the community whose community profile is in accord with its area. A document in certain topic is pushed to the persons whose personal profile includes this topic and corresponding energy value exceeds some threshold: first we find the community whose community profile is the area to which the topic belongs, and then choose right members in this community.

Each document in the document space is sent to members as email attachment by document deliverer regularly. Email is a "push" delivery mechanism in contrast to a "pull" mechanism, such as a web page searching. So group members do see the documents without any separate action, which makes our approach very low cost for organizations to adopt. If a member wants to share a document with others the only thing he or she needs to do is to upload that document into the document space.

7 Experimental Study and Findings

To verify the design concept and evaluate the performance of our approach, we carry out a study of our method and its effect. We present the survey results of the use of 'profile extractor' over a year and 'document deliverer' over six months working in our laboratory. The evaluation focuses on both the benefits and the costs.

Table 2. Median responses to selected questions from the survey. 1 means strongly disagree, 2 means disagree, 3 means neutral, 4 means agree and 5 means strongly agree.

	Questions	Response
Benefits	1. User profile helps me stay aware of what others are doing.	4.1
	2. User profile is useful when I want to find a person to discuss with.	4.3
	3. It is a good way to get useful documents.	4.2
	4. It's worth receiving documents to get valuable information.	4.2
	5. I would like to receive documents continuously.	3.9
	6. It is a good way to share documents with others.	4.4
	7. It is worth uploading documents to share them with others.	4.1
	8. I will upload documents continuously.	3.9
Concerns	9. Before user profiles, it was easy for me to keep track of what everyone else was doing.	2.1
	10. Receiving documents disturbs my daily routine.	2.1
	11. User profile extractor threats my privacy.	1.3
	12. Uploading documents annoys me.	2.3
	13. Before that I can share documents with others easily.	1.1

Overall, we received a positive response. All members in our lab felt that we should continue to share documents by this way. Table 2 shows that using 'profile extractor' and 'document deliverer' results in group awareness and documents sharing at low cost.

Group awareness: Survey responses suggest that user profiles make them stay aware of what others are doing and it is useful when they want to find an appropriate person to discuss with (Question 1 and 2). Before that people did not find it was easy to know what others were doing (Question 9). Organization members did not have significant privacy concerns with user profile extractor (Question 11), because most of them didn't mind opening their research interests to others.

Documents sharing: Survey responses demonstrate that it is an easy way to get valuable documents and an effective method to share documents with others (Question 3, 6 and 7). Before that it was not easy to share documents with others (Question 13). The benefits of (selectively) reading documents received outweigh the cost of receiving and uploading documents (Question 4, 5 and 8). Members are also willing to upload more documents to receive documents (Question 8) and it doesn't disturb their routine work extensively (Question 10 and 12).

8 Comparison and Discussion

Learning and constructing user profiles without any intervention of human is an important property of our method. No techniques, such as relevance feedback, user's register and user's ratings are employed. A recommending system proposed in [12] asks users to evaluate a set of documents. Then a vector of keywords is extracted from these documents according to the evaluation results. The keywords vector is used to identify users. A study about document logistics in [24] has the descriptions supplied by users about their own interests as the core of user profiles initially. Then, a learning process is conducted to complement and tune user profiles until a steady state is reached.

Most recommending systems learn interests of users via relevance feedback and keep track of them daily using a search engine. It may satisfy a user's immediate information interests but usually is not sufficient for persistent interests because users are relatively poor at using them [9]. Today email has become one of the most popular communication fashions. Information flows such as email flow, short message flow and flow in message board supply a rich and persistent data resource for the learning of user profiles.

Usually, recommendations are given in the form of listing out the pages or documents when a user begins a new session of using for a system [2, 5, 9]. These occur only when a user chooses to use the system. It is an occasional and customizing behavior, not a persistent behavior. Our method pushes relevant documents by email for users at regular intervals, which ensures that users can get relevant documents in time and persistently. Users do see the documents without any separate action because email is a "push" delivery mechanism in contrast to the "pull" mechanism such as a web searching. It also makes our method very low cost for organizations to adopt.

Awareness means "understanding of the activities of others, which provides a context for your own activity" [6]. In [3] each group member has to write a 'today' message at the end of the day explaining what he or she did that day for the awareness of group. This type of awareness is immediate and short term (one day). The awareness in our work is long term. Through user profiles users can know what others have done, are doing and will do in a longer period. Members can quickly and accurately locate themselves in the whole organization by browsing community structures or user profiles. User profiles also tell us what we can learn from whom in which community.

9 Conclusion

The proposed approach has the following characteristics: (1) Introduce the community detection of social network into the interest discovering process. (2) Information flow is a rich and persistent data resource. Learning interest from information flow makes the description of user interests more accurate. (3) A time factor that weakens the impact of information flow on the user profiles with time elapsing is introduced, which makes user profiles adapt to changes in interests incrementally. (4) Actively push documents for members by email at regular intervals, which ensures that users can get valuable documents in time and persistently without any separate action. (5) Team members can know each others by observing community structures and user profiles. The approach will play a role in Zhuge's ideal of the future interconnection environment [27].

References

1. Batagelj, V., Mrvar, A.: Pajek - Analysis and Visualization of Large Networks. In: Jünger, M., Mutzel, P., (eds.): Graph Drawing Software, Springer-Verlag, Berlin (2003) 77-103
2. Bollacker, K.D., Lawrence, S., Giles, C.L.: A system for automatic personalized tracking of scientific literature on the Web. Proceedings of the Fourth ACM Conference on Digital Libraries. Berkeley, CA, USA (1999) 105-113
3. Bernheim, A.J.B., Borning, A.: 'Today' Messages: Lightweight Support for Small Group Awareness via Email. Proceedings of the 38th Annual Hawaii International Conference on System Sciences, Vol. 1. Waikoloa, Hawaii (2005)
4. Buckley,C., Salton, G., Allan, J.: The Effect of Adding Relevance Information in a Relevance Feedback Environment. Proceedings of the 17th Annual International ACM SIGIR Conference on Research and Development in Information Retrieval, Springer-Verlag, Dublin, Ireland (1994) 292–300
5. Chen, C.C., Chen, M.C., Sun, Y.: A Web Document Personalization User Model and System. User Modeling, Information Retrieval and User Modeling, Sonthofen, German (2001)
6. Dourish, P., Bellotti, V.: Awareness and Coordination in Shared Workspaces. Proceedings of the ACM Conference on Computer Supported Cooperative Work, Toronto, Canada (1992) 107-114
7. Freeman, L.: A set of measures of centrality based upon betweeness. *Sociometry*, 40(1) (1977) 35-41
8. Girvan, M., Newman, M.: Community structure in social and biological networks. Proceedings of the National Academy of Sciences of the United States of America, Vol. 99. USA (2002) 7821-7826
9. Somlo, G., Howe, A.: QueryTracker: An Agent for Tracking Persistent Information Needs. The Third International Joint Conference on Autonomous Agents and Mutli-Agent Systems, New York, USA (2004) 488-495
10. Sugiyama, K., Hatano, K. Yoshikawa, M.: Adaptive web search based on user profile constructed without any effort from users. Proceedings of 13th conference on World Wide Web, New York, USA (2004) 675-684
11. Tyler, J.R., Wilkinson, D.M., Huberman, B.A: Email as Spectroscopy: Automated Discovery of Community Structure within Organizations. Proceedings of the First International Conference on Communities and Technologies, Amsterdam, Netherlands (2003) 81-96
12. Vel, O., Nesbitt, S.: A Collaborative Filtering Agent System for Dynamic Virtual Communities on the Web. Proceedings of Conference on Automated Learning and Discovery, Pittsburgh, PA (1998)
13. Wilkinson, D.M., Huberman, B.A.: A method for finding communities of related genes. Proceedings of the National Academy of Sciences of the United States of America, Vol. 101. USA (2004) 5241–5248
14. Yang, J., Park, S.: Email Categorization Using Fast Machine Learning Algorithms. Proceedings of the 5th International Conference on Discovery Science, Lecture Notes in Computer Science, Vol. 2534. Springer-Verlag (2002) 316-323
15. Ye, Y. Ma, F. Rong, H. Huang, J.Z.: Enhanced Email Classification Based on Feature Space Enriching. 9th International Conference on Applications of Natural Languages to Information Systems, Lecture Notes in Computer Science, Vol. 3136. Salford, UK (2004)
16. Yee, J., Mills, R.F., Peterson, G.L., Bartczak, S.E.: Automatic Generation of Social Network Data from Electronic-Mail Communications. 10th ICCRTS, Track 1. Virginia (2005)

17. Zhuge, H.: Clustering Soft-Devices in Semantic Grid. *IEEE Computing in Science and Engineering*, 4 (6) (2002) 60-62
18. Zhuge, H.: A Knowledge Grid Model and Platform for Global Knowledge Sharing. *Expert Systems with Applications*, 22 (4) (2002) 313-320
19. Zhuge, H.: A Knowledge Flow Model for Peer-to-Peer Team Knowledge sharing and Management. *Expert Systems with Applications*, 23 (1) (2002) 23-30
20. Zhuge, H.: Active e-Document Framework ADF: Model and Platform. *Information and Management*, 41(1) (2003) 87-97
21. Zhuge, H.: Resource Space Grid: Model, Method and Platform. *Concurrency and Computation: Practice and Experience*, 16 (14) (2004) 1385-1413
22. Zhuge, H.: Fuzzy Resource Management in Semantic Grid: Model and Platform. *Journal of Systems and Software*, 73 (3) (2004) 389-396
23. Zhuge, H.: China's E-Science Knowledge Grid Environment. *IEEE Intelligent Systems*, 19(1) (2004) 13-17
24. Zhuge, H., .Li, Y.: Semantic Profile-based Document Logistics for Cooperative Research. *Future Generation Computer Systems*, 20(1) (2004) 47-60
25. Zhuge, H.: The Knowledge Grid. World Scientific, Singapore (2004)
26. Zhuge, H.: Exploring Epidemic and e-Epidemic with e-Science Environment. *Communications of the ACM*, 48(9) (2005)109-114
27. Zhuge, H.: The Future Interconnection Environment. *IEEE Computer*, 38 (4) (2005) 27-33
28. Zhuge, H.: Semantic Grid: Scientific Issues, Infrastructure, and Methodology. *Communications of the ACM*, 48 (4) (2005)117-119

Schema Adaptation Under Multi-relation Dependencies

MingHong Zhou, HuaMing Liao, and Feng Li

Institute of computing technology, Chinese Academy of Science
zmh@software.ict.ac.cn, {lhm, lifeng}@ict.ac.cn

Abstract. In information grid, data sources not only change their data, but also change their schema. On schema changing, the mapping may be left inconsistency. Thus, it is an essential issue to detect and update the inconsistency. We present a novel approach for adapting mappings as schema evolves. We propose a new kind of dependencies, called multi-relation dependencies. Multi-relation dependencies specify the dependent relationship between attributes across relations under a join condition. By the soundness and completeness of reasoning rules of multi-relation dependencies, our approach detects the minimal part of mapping which are inconsistent. And the algorithm adapts mappings on both local schema and global schema changing. Most current approaches do not distinguish the removal of key attributes from non-key attributes. Our study shows that removal of these two kinds of attributes results in different adaptations.

1 Introduction

One of the goals of information grid is to achieve inter-operability in heterogeneous data sources. It provides to users a global schema in which the relations are populated by local sources. And mappings specify how to populate global relations by local data. However, their consistency depends on both global and local schema. On schema changing, the mappings must be updated according to the new schema. To preserve mapping consistency is thus an essential issue.

It is a challenge to find the minimal part of affected mappings, especially in dynamic environments. The applications should not be stopped during adaptation. And the adaptation should preserve some semantics after adaptation.

Our approach could detect the minimal part of affected mappings. It is mainly because of multi-relation dependencies. They express the functional dependencies in global schema in terms of local schema. On schema changing, the attributes, which are not determined by the key of new schema, should be removed from mappings to preserve consistency.

1.1 LNCS Online

One of the goals of information grid is to achieve inter-operability in heterogeneous data sources. It provides to users a global schema in which the relations are populated by local sources. And mappings specify how to populate global relations by local data. However, their consistency depends on both global and local schema. On schema changing, the mappings must be updated according to the new schema. To preserve mapping consistency is thus an essential issue.

H. Zhuge and G.C. Fox (Eds.): GCC 2005, LNCS 3795, pp. 511–516, 2005.

It is a challenge to find the minimal part of affected mappings, especially in dynamic environments. The applications should not be stopped during adaptation. And the adaptation should preserve some semantics after adaptation.

Our approach could detect the minimal part of affected mappings. It is mainly because of multi-relation dependencies. They express the functional dependencies in global schema in terms of local schema. On schema changing, the attributes, which are not determined by the key of new schema, should be removed from mappings to preserve consistency.

2 Related Work

The mapping system can be formulated in terms of a triple <*L*, *G*, *M*> [2,6,7], in which *L* is the local schema, *G* is the global schema, and *M* is the mapping between *L* and *G*, constituted by a set of assertions of the forms $g \rightarrow q_L^g$, where g is a relation in *G* and q_L^g is a query of the same arity with *g* over local schema.

In [4], authors proposed algorithms about mapping adaptation. The algorithm dealing with constraint modification is based on Chasing. Our work differs from it in several aspects. Key constraints are in our consideration. And we do not distinguish logical association between user associations, because foreign keys are not necessarily to be a part of join condition.

You Ganmei proposed a new approach to manage schema evolution, such as foreign key and key constraints changes, and attributes modification in [1]. This work is very close to ours. However, this approach depends on an assumption, where all the key attributes of local schema should be mapped as key attributes of global schema. This restriction requires global schema designer should be familiar with local schema, and breaks the loosely coupling principle of information grid.

McBrien and Poulovassilis combine schema evolution and schema integration in one unified framework [3]. By using a series of primitive schema transformations, one can map a local schema to a global schema. However, the sequence of transformations should be manually defined by users. Furthermore, the supported changes are restricted to only deletion and renaming. Changes such as key constraints changes are not considered.

3 Multi-relation Dependency

Multi-relation dependencies (MRDs) are extended from functional dependencies. However, the attributes in a MRD may reside in different relations and a join condition is a new component in MRDs. In this work, we restrict the join condition to be a conjunction of equations and non-equations, which covers the counterpart in conjunctive query. It represents the *where clause* in mapping.

3.1 Definition of Multi-relation Dependency

A sequence $A_1, A_2 \ldots, A_n$ is denoted by $\overline{A}_i$, and index sets are denoted by I.

Definition 1. For a given set of relations $\{R_i\}_{i\in I}$, the Multi-relation dependency $\overline{A_i} \xrightarrow[JC]{} \overline{B_j}$ is hold if and only if functional dependency $\overline{A_i} \rightarrow \overline{B_j}$ is hold for $\sigma_{JC}(R_1 \times ... \times R_n)$, denoted by $\{R_i\}_{i\in I} \models \overline{A_i} \xrightarrow[JC]{} \overline{B_j}$, where $\sigma_{JC}(R_1 \times ... \times R_n)$ means a selection on the products of $\{R_i\}_{i\in I}$ over *JC*.

A set of reasoning rules has been proposed in our previous work in [5], and we have proven that our reasoning rules are sound and complete, That is, for a given set of relations $\{R_i\}_{i\in I}$, $\{R_i\}_{i\in I} \vdash f$ if and only if $\{R_i\}_{i\in I} \models f$, where $\{R_i\}_{i\in I} \vdash f$ means *f* can be derived by reasoning rules.

4 Mapping Adaptation Algorithms

In our work, mapping is expressed in terms of SQL query.

Definition 2. A *mapping* for a global relation is a triple <*S*, *F*, *W*>, where

- *S* is a set of attributes pairs, in form of < global-attribute, local-attribute>, its counterpart in sql is a "*as*" clause in "*select*" clause.
- *F* is a set of local relation names, and represents "*from*" clause,
- *W* is a join condition, and represents "*where*" clause.

A pair is denoted by *p*, the global and local attribute in *p* are denoted by *p.g* and *p.l* respectively. For a pair <*A*, *B*>, *B* is denote by *lmap*(*A*) and A is denoted by *gmap*(*B*). *S*, *F* and *W* in mapping *m* are denoted by *m.S*, *m.F*, and *m.W* respectively.

4.1 Attributes Closure Under Multi-relation Dependencies

Our work deals with constraints modification and schema pruning and expansion. In the following of this paper, suppose the adaptation occurs in mapping system *I*=<*G*, *L*, *M*>. Before the algorithms, we introduce how to compute the closure of attributes under multi-relation dependencies. In algorithm 1, *g* is a global relation, *m* is the mapping referring to *g*. Key(*g*) denotes the key attributes of relation *g*.

Algorithm 1. compute closure of attributes
Closure(*g*, *m*, *I*)

1. Let *X* be a set of attributes that eventually will become the closure. First we initialize *X* to be Key(*g*).
2. Repeatedly search for some MRD: $\overline{A_i} \xrightarrow[m.W]{} B$, such that all of A_i, *gmap*(A_i) are in *X*, but *gmap*(*B*) is not. Then add *B* to *X*.
3. Repeat step 2 until no more attributes can be added to *X*.
4. return *X* after no more attributes can be added to it is the closure

The soundness and completeness of algorithm 1 are followed by the soundness and completeness of multi-relation dependencies.

4.2 Constraint Modification

It is obvious to see that when we add key property to a global attribute or remove key property from a local attribute, the existing mappings remain consistent with the new schema. However, Removal of key property from global attribute may lead inconsistency in mapping system. Because the new key may not determine some attributes which are determined by the old keys. In algorithm 2, we removal key property from a global attribute, and the involved attribute is denoted by *A*, which resides in *g*. And m is the mapping referred to g. And adding key property in local schema also leads to inconsistency. Algorithm 3 shows how to adapt when adding key property from local attribute *A*, and the relation containing *A* is *r*.

Algorithm 2. removal key property from global attribute	**Algorithm 3. adding key property to local attribute**
RemKey(*g*, *A*, *m*, *I*) Let *g'* be the new global relation. X=Clousre(*g'*, *m*, *L*) Construct a new mapping *m'*=<Φ , *m.F*, *m.W*> For each *p* in *m.S* If *p.g* in *X*, then add *p* into *m'.S* Replace *m* by *m'* in *M* End.	AddKey(*r*, *A*, *I*) Let *L'* be the new global schema *M'*= Φ , For each *m* in *M* If *r* is used in *m* Let *g* be the global relation referred by *m* X=Closure(*g*, *m*, *L'*) Construct a new mapping *m'*=< Φ , *m.F*, *m.W*> For each *p* in *m.S* If *p.g* in *X*, then add *p* into *m'.S* Replace *m* by *m'* in *M* End if End.

Algorithm 4 shows how to adapt mapping, when the join condition in $m \in M$ is changed to be *JC*.

Algorithm 4. changes on join condition

```
ChangeJC(m, JC, I)

   Let g be the global relation referred by m
   M1 = <m.S, m.F, JC>
   X=closure(g, m1, L)
   Construct a new mapping m2=<Φ , m.F, JC>
   For each p in m.S
      If p.g in X, then add p into m'.S
           Replace m by m2 in M
End.
```

4.3 Schema Pruning or Expanding

When we add an attribute to schemas, the existing mappings are still consistent with new schemas. For example, when add a new attribute to global schema, under the existing mapping m, the column for the new attribute is null, for there is no local attributes correspondent to it. And all the constraints of global schema are still hold in the retrieved data.

It is a more complex case, when we delete an attribute from schemas, since the deleted attribute may be used in mappings. Algorithm 5 and 6 show how to delete an attribute *A* in global relation g or local relation *r* respectively, and the affected mapping is denoted by *m*.

Algorithm 5. deletion of global attribute

```
DelAttrG(g, A, m, I)
  Suppose after delete attribute A, relation g becomes
g'
  If A∈ Key(g) then
     X=Closure(g', m, L)
     Construct a new mapping m'=<Φ , m.F, m.W>
     For each p in m.S
        If p.g∈ X and p.g≠ A, then
           add p into m'.S
           Replace m by m' in M
        Else
     Construct a new mapping m'=<Φ , m.F, m.W>
     For each p in m.S
        If p.g≠A, then add p into m'.S
  End if
End.
```

Algorithm 6. deletion of local attribute

```
DelAttrL(r, A, I)
  If A∈ Key(r) then RemKeyL(r, A, I)
  Suppose after deleting, the new local schema is L'
  For each m∈ M
     If r is used in m, then
         Suppose the global relation referred by m is g
         If A is used in m.W , then
              Remove all atoms used A,
              the new join condition is denoted by JC
              ChangeJC(m, JC, I)
         Endif
         Remove the pair p∈ m.S , such that p.g=A
      Endif
   Endfor
 End.
```

If the deleted attribute is a key attribute, then we should remove the key property first and then deleted it.

For the size of the paper, the analyses and validations of algorithms are omitted.

5 Conclusions

We have introduced a novel approach for mapping adaptation. Our algorithm is based on multi-relation dependencies. By multi-relation dependencies, key constraint of global schema is expressed in terms of local schema. Thus after mapping adaptation, the retrieved data conform the key constraint of global schema. Furthermore, the completeness of multi-relation dependencies guarantees that our approach changes the minimal part of mappings to preserve mapping consistent with schemas.

References

1. You Ganmei, Liao Huaming, Sun Yuzhong. Mapping Publishing and Mapping Adaptation in the Middleware of Railway Information Grid System IFIP international conference. NPC2004. Springer.
2. Maurizio Lenzerini. Data Integration: A Theoretical Perspective. In Proc. of the twenty-first ACM SIGMOD-SIGACT-SIGART symposium on Principles of database systems, June 03-05, 2002, Madison, Wisconsin
3. McBrien P, Poulovassilis A (2002) Schema evolution in heterogeneous database architectures, a schema transformation approach. In: CAiSE, pp 484–499
4. Yannis Velegrakis, J. Miller, Lucian Popa. Preserving mapping consistency under schema changes. The VLDB Journal Volume 13, Issue 3 (September 2004) Pages: 274 - 293. Year of Publication: 2004. ISSN:1066-8888
5. Zhou MingHong, Liao HuaMing, Li Feng, Zhiwei Xu, Key Constraint Aware Schema Mapping in Data Integration. ICDM 2005 submitted.
6. A. Y. Halevy. Answering queries using views: A survey. Very Large Database J., 10(4):270–294, 2001.
7. J. D. Ullman. Information integration using logical views. In Proc. of the 6th Int. Conf. on Database Theory (ICDT'97), volume 1186 of Lecture Notes in Computer Science, pages 19–40. Springer, 1997.

Dart-Dataflow: Towards Communicating Data Semantics in Sensor Grid

Zhiyong Ye, Huajun Chen, and Zhaohui Wu

College of Computer Science, Zhejiang University,
Hangzhou, China
{yezhy, huajunsir, wzh}@zju.edu.cn

Abstract. We present the design of Dart-Dataflow, a middleware for semantic-based, publish-subscribe data fusion and data dissemination in sensor grid. In our system, data published by sensors are represented as RDF graphs based on a shared ontology, and subscriptions are represented as RDF graph patterns. The system provides a RDF Graph Filter to filter the RDF graph to meet subscriptions. And also, we design an intelligent data dissemination framework which implements multiple transport protocols to support different cases of data dissemination. Our system is suitable for fusing and disseminating heterogeneous data from multiple sensor nods in sensor networks; it can be deployed for various applications, ranging from military applications to civilian applications.

1 Introduction

There is a growing excitement about the potential application of large-scale sensor networks in diverse applications such as geophysics and environment monitoring, remote health care, and security. However, plenty of sensor nodes in the sensor network generate rapid, continuous and large volumes of stream data. The big challenge now is to develop effective methods for the automatic fusion and interpretation of the data generated by large-scale sensor networks [1]. A solution for this issue is for each sensor to publish data schema based upon a shared ontology using Semantic Web technology. Therefore, when a sensor node publishes data, users that receive these data will be able to interpret the contents without ambiguity. Semantic Web [2] is an exciting evolution of current Web. It is aimed at providing a common framework that allows data to be shared and reused across application, enterprise, and community boundaries. It is based on Resource Description Framework (RDF), which is a language for representing web information in a minimally constraining, flexible, but meaningful way. RDF integrates XML for syntax and is intended for situations in which web data needs to be exchanged and integrated without loss of semantics and meaning.

Nowadays, Grid has moved from the obscurely academic to highly popular. Grid technologies support sharing diverse resources in dynamic VOs—that is, thc creation, from geographically and organizationally distributed components, of virtual computing systems that are sufficiently integrated to deliver desired QoS. The sharing that we are concerned with is not primarily file exchange but rather direct access to computers, software, data, and other resources, as is required by a range of collaborative problem solving and resource-brokering strategies emerging in industry, science, and

H. Zhuge and G.C. Fox (Eds.): GCC 2005, LNCS 3795, pp. 517 – 522, 2005.

engineering. This sharing is, necessarily, highly controlled, with resource providers and consumers defining clearly and carefully just what is shared, who is allowed to share, and the conditions under which sharing occurs[3].

In this paper, we integrate Semantic Web and Grid technology to publish/subscribe paradigm and introduce a RDF-based system named Dart-Dataflow (DDF) for data fusion and data dissemination in sensor grid. Publish/subscribe (pub/sub) [1, 4] is a loosely coupled communication paradigm for distributed computing environments. And in DDF system, publishers and subscribers share a RDF-based ontology [2]. This releases the constraints on value-based publish/subscribe systems that publishers and subscribers must share the same data schemas. Different from relational pub/sub systems, the data correlation in our system is transparent to subscribers.

2 Architecture

In sensor grid, data published by heterogeneous sensors differ greatly in formats and semantics. If the pub/sub system is used as a general infrastructure for sensor grid and support different applications, it should have strong expressiveness. Here, we introduce Semantic Web technologies into pub/sub paradigm and propose a Semantic-based Publish/Subscribe middleware named Dart-Dataflow (DDF) for manage sensor data. It is mainly settle for some function requirements such as real-time data processing, data disseminating synchronistically, data subscribing asynchronistically, etc. It's architecture is as Figure 1 shown.

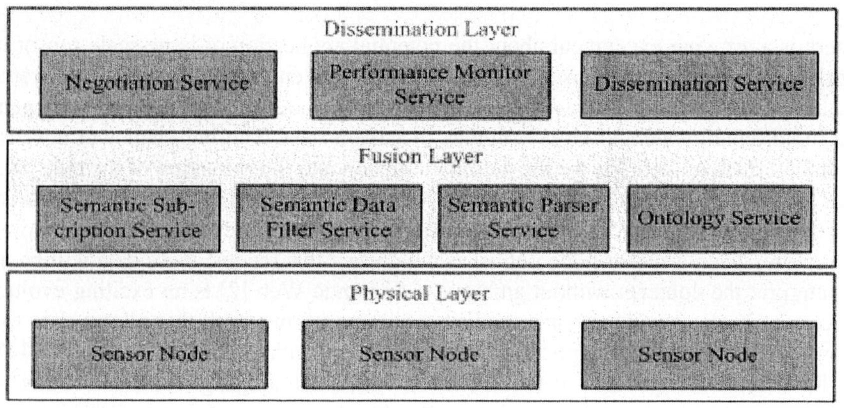

Fig. 1. Architecture of DDF

Physical layer is composed of sensor nodes deployed in sensor grid. These sensor nodes collect dynamic and real-time traffic data, weather data, geography data, road surface data and so on. This layer also provides an interface to disseminate these original data into upper layer.

Fusion layer mainly supports to fuse data from heterogeneous sensors and filter data to meet the subscriber. It includes Ontology Service, Semantic Parser Service,

Semantic Subscription Service and Semantic Data Filter Service. Services in this layer are provided for sinking data from sensor nodes, querying data schema based on the global ontology and parsing it into RDF-based data and then filtering data to meet the subscribers interesting.

Dissemination layer provides an intelligent and flexible mechanism to disseminating data to the subscriber. It includes Negotiation Service, Performance Monitor Service and Dissemination Service. In this layer, data dissemination is multiple protocols implementation, migration support, easy extensibility.

3 Fusion Layer in DDF

In DDF, data published by sensors and subscription scripts are both represented as RDF graphs, which is a kind of directed labeled graph and system filter data with subscriptions both semantically and syntactically. When data is published, it is firstly converted into a RDF graph using Semantic Parser Service based on ontology before further processing. And the same, subscriptions are specified by subscriber and are also represented as RDF graph patterns in Semantic Subscription Service. Then Data Filter Service filters data to meet the subscriber.

In DDF system, data are all represented as RDF graphs; subscriptions are in fact graph patterns which specify the shape of the graph as well as the constraints on some nodes and arcs in the graph. So we must define a semantic subscription language to support semantic subscription. Here we define a subscription language based on a number of query languages such as SPARQL [5], RDQL [6].

```
Subscribe  ?city
Where  (?city zjuns:belongto China)
       (?weather zjuns:weather cloudy)
       (?temperature zjuns:temperature ?value)
And    ?value<25
Using  zjuns for <http:.//zju.edu.cn/dart/dataflow>
```

?City
zjuns=http://zju.edu.cn/dart/dataflow#
zjuns:belong to
zjuns:temperature
zjuns:weather
China
cloudy
?value
rdf:valye
<25 °C

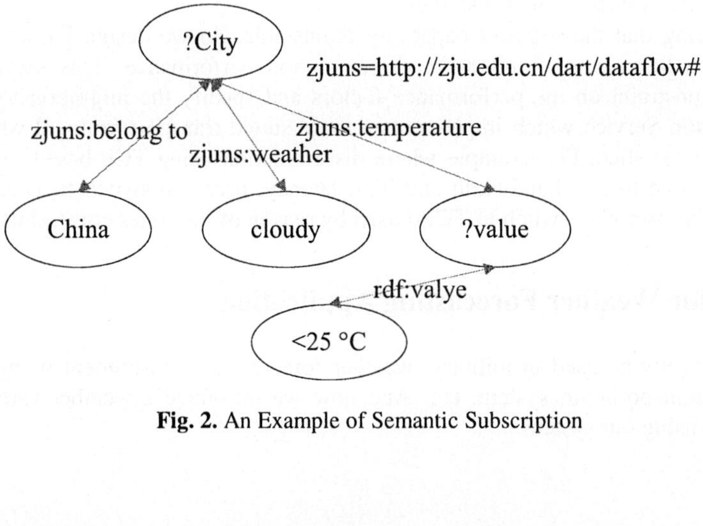

Fig. 2. An Example of Semantic Subscription

Our semantic subscription language is provided for accessing RDF graphs. A subscription mainly consists of two parts, the Subscribe clause and the Where clause. The Subscribe clause names the variable of interest to the subscriber; and the Where clause has one or more triple patterns which are composed of a subject, predicate and object delimited by parentheses, and for confining the value of object, the Where clause always defines some filter expressions.

For example, in Weather Forecasting system, if someone wants to know all cities which are in China with the temperature is below 25 centigrade thermometer and the weather is cloudy, the subscription and the corresponding RDF graph pattern can be expressed as Figure 2.

Furthermore, we must filter the incoming data to meet the subscription .We design a RDF-based Semantic Filter to support this task. Subscriptions and data are all represented as graphs in our system, and if every node and arc in a data graph can be mapped to a corresponding node and arc in the subscription graph, this data is said to meet the subscription, otherwise this data can not meet the subscription. Therefore, the filtering problem is a specific kind of graph isomorphism problem.

4 Dissemination Layer in DDF

In DDF system, Dissemination Layer is used to disseminate the RDF-base filtered data to the corresponding subscriber effectively. Here we design an intelligent framework to disseminate data more effectively based on NaradaBrokering[7], DBIS[8]. Following we introduce the design of the Dissemination Layer in detail.

As we all know, different transport protocols are suitable for different cases. For example, TCP works best where reliable delivery is at a premium, but if subscriber can sustain losses in delivery and more concentrate on the latencies, UDP is a better choice. And also, data dissemination in network is influenced by different condition and different network. So in Dissemination Layer, we design more than one Dissemination Services and each service implements a transport protocol.

DDF system provides a Negotiation Service to negotiate the best transport protocol for data dissemination. If negotiate is successful, the system specify the corresponding Dissemination Service to the subscriber.

Considering that the network capability is unstable. So we design Dissemination Performance Service to monitor the dissemination performance. This service can specify a constraint on the performance factors and specify the migration to anther Dissemination Service which implements a more suited transport protocol when this constraint is satisfied. For example where dissemination using TCP-based service is not feasible due to low bandwidth and high latency, user can switch to UDP-based and similarly, user may switch to TCP-based by reason of loss rates constraints.

5 DDF for Weather Forecasting Application

DDF can mainly be used in military, weather forecasting, environment monitor and intelligent transportation system, etc. And now we introduce a weather forecasting application using our system.

First data generated by sensors that are deployed in plenty of cities all over China are sent into DDF, and then data are disseminated to user continually through system. In our system we provide a semantic-based sink client for users, because data disseminated in DDF are semantic-based, our client is more conveniently for users to sink data.

One day Weather Satellite observes that strong cold front is emerged in Siberia and disseminates the information to DDF instantly. Users in DDF can sink the information in real time and want to follow up this information more meticulously; here, we provide a semantic-base subscription client in DDF. Users can view the global ontology about weather using this client to invoke Ontology Service and then subscribe the individual data schema they interesting. The semantic-base subscribe client is indeed the visualization of Ontology Service and Semantic Subscription Service.

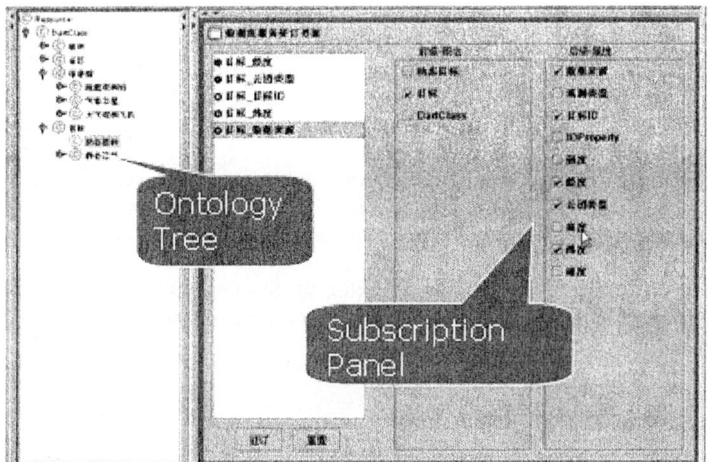

Fig. 3. Semantic-based Subscribe Client

After a while, Atmosphere Observation Plane also observes the strong cold front and users sink this information. And the same time, Ground Observation Stations deploy all over China disseminate the weather information in local area. Then users judge that this strong cold front will seriously affect the climate of south of China with integrating these data from multiple sensors and at once notify Weather Bureau the pre-alarm of strong cold front.

Through DDF for Weather Forecasting Application, we can see it effectively eliminates the influence of hazardous climate using DDF to sink data from sensor grids, fuse and disseminate RDF-based data, subscribe data that users interesting in real time.

6 Conclusion

In this paper, we propose Dart-Dataflow, a semantic-base publish/subscribe system for managing sense data in sensor networks. The data and subscriptions are all represents as RDF graphs in our system. This system can be deployed for various applications, ranging from military applications to civilian applications.

We will optimize data filtering arithmetic based on RDF graph to support numerous subscriptions more effectively in future.

References

1. Bass.T: The federation of critical infrastructure information via publish-subscribe enabled multisensor data fusion. Information Fusion, 2002. Proceedings of the Fifth International Conference on Volume 2, 8-11 July 2002 ,pp.1076 - 1083
2. T. Berners-Lee, J. Hendler, and O. Lassila. The semantic web. Scientific American, 284(5): 34-43. May 2001
3. Ian Foster and Carl Kesselman, and Heffrey Nick and Steven Tuecke. The Physiology of the Grid: An Open Grid Services Architecture for Distributed Systems Integration. Open Grid Service Infrastructure WG, Global Grid Forum, June 22, 2002.
4. P. Eugster, P. Felber, R. Guerraoui, and A. Kermarrec, "The Many Faces of Publish/Subscribe," ACM Computing Surveys, vol. 35, no. 2, Jun. 2003, pp. 114-131
5. SPARQL: Query Language for RDF: http://www.w3.org/TR/2004/WD-rdf-sparql-query-20041012/
6. RDQL: RDF Data Query Language. http://www.hpl.hp.com/semweb/rdql.htm
7. Shrideep Pallickara, Geoffrey Fox, John Yin, Gurhan Gunduz, Hongbin Liu, Ahmet Uyar, Mustafa Varank: A Transport Framework for Distributed Brokering Systems. PDPTA 2003: 772-778
8. M. Altinel, D. Aksoy, T. Baby, M. J. Franklin, W. Shapiro,and S. B. Zdonik. Dbis-toolkit: Adaptable middleware for large scale data delivery. Proc. of the ACM SIGMOD Conf.,pp. 544–546, 1999.

Data Distribution Management Modeling and Implementation on Computational Grid*

Jong Sik Lee

School of Computer Science and Engineering, Inha University,
#253, YongHyun-Dong, Nam-Ku, Incheon 402-751, South Korea
jslee@inha.ac.kr

Abstract. This paper presents a design and development of a data distribution management modeling in computational grid. The modeling focuses on system performance improvement of a satellite cluster management system which uses an inter-federation communication in HLA (High Level Architecture)-compliant grid system. The inter-federation communication allows to execute a complex large-scale cluster management system with distributed satellites and share the dispersed data assets among satellite components collaboratively. In addition, this paper discusses the data distribution management modeling with centralized and decentralized approaches to improve system performance and scalability of satellite cluster management. The analytical and empirical results on the heterogeneous OS-based computational grid show usefulness of data distribution management and inter-federation communication in the satellite cluster management system.

1 Introduction

Computational grid has been applied to a growing variety of systems including business processing modeling, process control and manufacturing, military command and control, transportation management, and so on. Computational grid is characterized by numerous interactive data exchanges among multiple distributed entities over a network. Thus, in order to provide a reliable answer in reasonable time with limited communication and computation resources, methodologies [1], [2] for reducing the interactive data exchanges are required. In Recent, there has been increasing demand to use constellations of autonomous spacecrafts which are collaboratively working on computational grid. Many mission-related organizations, including NASA, have progressed research to accomplish this mission objective. The main objective of constellations provides autonomous control over data collection and autonomously carries out scientific analysis of large datasets such as radar images, returning both those data with the highest scientific value as well as selected scientific analyses of the data, thus negating the need to return the entire dataset. For effective execution of this constellations system, a cluster paradigm [3], [4] has been noticed. This paper

* This research was supported by the MIC(Ministry of Information and Communication), Korea, under the ITRC(Information Technology Research Center) support program supervised by the IITA(Institute of Information Technology Assessment).

H. Zhuge and G.C. Fox (Eds.): GCC 2005, LNCS 3795, pp. 523–528, 2005.

proposes the high performance modeling for this autonomous constellations system with on computational grid construction and execution concepts. Especially, the bridge-based inter-federation communication in HLA (High Level Architecture)-compliant [5] computational grid supports the flexible and high performance modeling for not only communication among satellites inside cluster but also communication between two clusters and between cluster and ground system. This paper focuses an inter-federation communication system design when a cluster manager is assigned in a bridge federate [6]. In addition, this paper proposes a data distribution management method with centralized and decentralized approaches to improve the satellite cluster management system performance. The method is extended from existing data distribution management [7] methods to execute a complex and large-scale computational grid with reasonable computation and communication resources. This paper makes the method provide a functionality balancing for each satellite inside cluster and satellite intelligence.

This paper is organized as follows: Section 2 introduces the data distribution management for a satellite cluster management. Section 3 describes a design of satellite cluster management and analyzes performance effectiveness. Section 4 evaluates empirical performance of centralized and decentralized data distribution management. The conclusion is in Section 5.

2 Data Distribution Management for Satellite Cluster

In this section, this paper discusses scalability issues of a satellite cluster management system and introduces a ground system operation as a case study to discuss centralized and decentralized approaches and evaluate each performance. A ground system commands and controls a cluster of spacecrafts. Basically, a ground system requires operations to monitor the cluster, makes a decision, and sends proper command strings. For a small cluster, a centralized approach is cost effective and accepted to command and control spacecrafts individually. As Fig. 1-(a) illustrates, a ground system sends the command strings to each spacecraft. The command strings include a command to "observe a specified region, take a picture, and send the image data." The command should contain the region location. Each spacecraft receives different region location from the ground station. To optimize the ground operation cost, a decentralized approach of ground operations is proposed in this paper. The decentralized approach indicates that it separates ground functions and distributes a set of functions to spacecrafts. Performing a set of functions requires intelligence of spacecraft. A ground station separates four regions to be observed, makes four different command strings, and sends them to a cluster manager. The cluster manager parses the command strings and forwards them to each proper spacecraft. Fig. 1-(b) illustrates a decentralized approach in satellite cluster management operation. Here, this paper discusses a degree of decentrality. The definition of decentrality is a distribution of functions or operation loads to each distributed component. This paper expresses two degrees of decentrality: low and high. This paper assigns the parsing and forwarding of a ground station to a cluster manager, and this distribution is considered as a low decentrality. The parsing and forwarding classifies a lower intelligence of a cluster manager. In a high decentrality, a ground station does not separate four regions to be

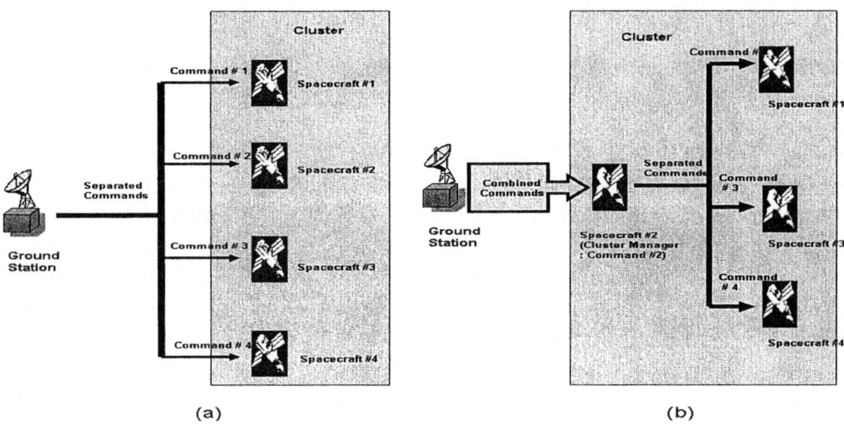

Fig. 1. (a) centralized approach; (b) decentralized approach

observed and sends a total region to a cluster manager. The cluster manager should include the intelligence for division of region to be observed. The division intelligence should understand the technology including region division, image capturing, image visualization, image data transmission, and so on.

3 Design and Performance of Satellite Cluster Management

This paper discusses an inter-federation communication architecture on a multi-federation platform and applies an inter-federation communication to a data distribution management of a satellite cluster management system. To execute the inter-federation communication, this paper uses a HLA bridge federate which is physically located in each federation and play a role of HLA message passing between federations. This paper develops two federations: cluster and ground. The cluster federation includes four federates. Each federate is assign in each spacecraft. Ground federation includes two federates: cluster manager and ground station. Both federations include the cluster manager federate which is assigned in a HLA bridge federate for the inter-federation communication.

The inside-federation communication works on a cluster/ground federation. The federation includes varying numbers of spacecraft federates, including a cluster manager, and one ground station federate. The HLA message passing for cluster data distribution management depends on the inside-federation communication. In the platform setting, this paper develops a heterogeneous OS-based computational grid system which includes various operating systems including SGI Unix, Linux, Sun Unix, and Windows. Many federates are allocated to several machines, respectively, and they are connected via a 10 Base T Ethernet network. For inter-federation communication with a bridge federate, this paper develops two federations: cluster and ground. The cluster federation includes many spacecraft federates, including a cluster manager, and the ground federation includes two federates: cluster manager and ground station. Both federations have the cluster manager federate which is called bridge federate. The HLA bridge implementation supports the bridge federate functionality for the inter-federation HLA message passing, thus it makes the inter-federation communication executable.

Performance Analysis

This paper assumes the conditions as following: 1) there exist multiple clusters; 2) a cluster includes the fixed number of spacecrafts (N); 3) the region is square-shaped and there are 4 points ((x_1, y_1), (x_2, y_2), (x_3, y_3), (x_4, y_4)); 4) the two of 32 double precision bits (e.g. 64 bits) are needed to represent a point (x_1, y_1); 5) the analysis is based on one cycle transmission. As Table 1 shows, the decentralized approach significantly reduces the number of required-communicated messages and the number of required-communicated bits. Basically, there occurs overhead bits (H) needed for satellite communication when a ground station sends a command string. The centralized approach causes an amount of overhead messages and bits since it makes a ground station to send spacecrafts messages individually. Compared the two degrees of decentrality in the decentralized approach, the high decentrality significantly reduce the required-communicated data bits since it transmits the one big region location information irrelevant to the number of spacecrafts (N) in a cluster.

Table 1. Analysis of Communication-required Data Reduction (Note: N: Number of spacecrafts in a Cluster; M: Number of Clusters; H: Number of overhead bits in satellite communication (160 bits assumed), R: Number of regions at one spacecraft on one transmission (40 bits assumed))

<table>
<tr><th colspan="2">Approach</th><th>Number of required-communicated messages</th><th>Number of required-communicated messages bits</th><th>Coefficient of N as N-> ∞</th><th>Coefficient of N & M as N-> ∞ & M-> ∞</th></tr>
<tr><td colspan="2">Centralized</td><td>R*N*M</td><td>(H + 4*64) *R*N*M</td><td>(H+4*64)*R* M</td><td>(H+4*64)* R</td></tr>
<tr><td rowspan="2">Decen-tralized (Decen-trality)</td><td>Low</td><td>M</td><td>(H + 4*64*R*N) *M</td><td>(4*64*R)*M</td><td>(4*64*R)</td></tr>
<tr><td>High</td><td>M</td><td>(H + 4*64) *M</td><td>None</td><td>None</td></tr>
</table>

4 Performance Evaluation

Evaluation is achieved with variation of number of satellites in a cluster. The centralized approach is executed on only one federation which provides inside-federation communication. The decentralized approach is executed on two federations: cluster and ground. The execution on the two federations provides inter-federation communication. As Fig. 2-(a) illustrates, the decentralized approach apparently reduces the data bits transmitted. This paper classifies a degree of decentrality and present two decentrality degrees: high and low. Especially, the use of decentralized approach with high decentrality greatly reduces the data bits transmitted. The decentralized approach with high decentrality is able to allow an execution with a small amount of transmission data bits regardless to the number of satellites. The other evaluation measure of system execution performance is system execution time. The system execution time considers both of communication and computation performance. The centralized approach requires a large amount of communication data bits. Fig. 2-(b) compares system execution time in two approaches: centralized and decentralized. The system execution time of Fig. 2-(b) is provided from the execution on only one federation with inside-federation communication. The decentralized approach apparently reduces system execution time. The system execution time reduction indicates that time reduction from communication is greater than time expense from local computation time. Fig. 2-(c) illustrates the system execution time with inter-federation communication on the two federations. The centralized approach is not existed since the approach cannot be operated with inter-federation communication. The high decentrality performs the lower execution time in the lower task load. As the task load increases, the low decentrality increases its execution time slowly, thus its execution time becomes closed to that of high decentrality.

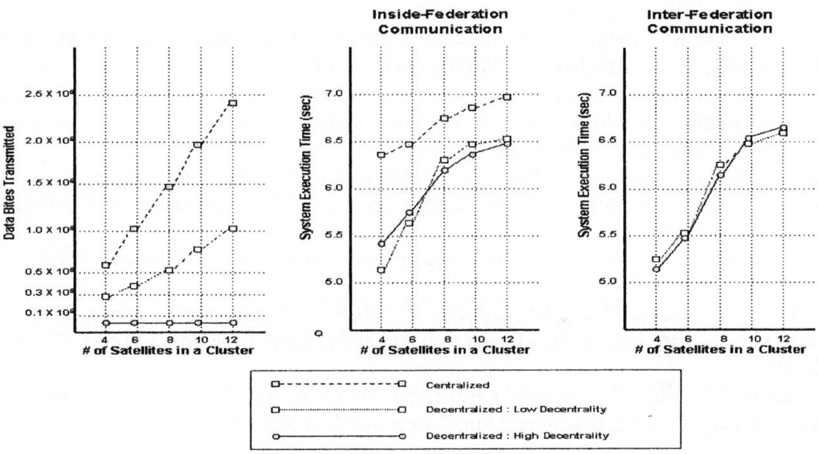

Fig. 2. (a) Data bits transmitted in centralized and decentralized approaches; (b) System execution time with inside-federation communication; (c) System execution time with inter-federation communication

5 Conclusion

For practical construction and execution of an autonomous constellations system, this paper considers computational grid construction concepts, including data distribution management, HLA-compliant inter-federation communication, functionality balancing, system modeling flexibility, scalability, and maintainability and provides a high performance modeling for the cluster paradigm with a cluster manager. The bridge-based inter-federation communication in HLA-compliant computational grid system improved the modeling flexibility and scalability by allowing multiple connections not only among satellites inside cluster but also among clusters and between cluster and ground systems. The modeling flexibility allows that we could model topologies of a variety of autonomous constellations systems, and thus analyze a complex large-scale space mission system and get empirical results.

The data distribution management with centralized and decentralized configurations focuses on a functionality balancing to each satellite and various degrees of functionality decentrality in each satellite including cluster manager. The functionality decentrality indicates function distribution to each satellite from centralized functions of a conventional ground system. The analytical and empirical results show favorable reduction of communication data and overall execution time and proved usefulness of the satellite cluster management system in scalable computational grid system.

References

1. Bassiouni, M.A., et al.: Performance and Reliability Analysis of Relevance Filtering for Scalable Distributed Interactive Simulation. ACM Trans. on Model. and Comp. Sim. (TOMACS) (1997) 293-331
2. Hall, S.B. and B.P. Zeigler: Joint Measure: Distributed Simulation Issues in a Mission Effectiveness Analytic Simulation SIW, Orlando FL (1999)
3. P. Zetocha: Intelligent Agent Architecture for Onboard Executive Satellite Control. Intelligent Automation and Control, Vol. 9. TSI Press Series on Intelligent Automation and Soft Computing, Albuquerque NM (2000) 27–32
4. D.M. Surka, M.C. Brito, C.G. Harvey: Development of the Real-Time Object-Agent Flight Software Architecture for Distributed Satellite Systems. IEEE Aerospace Conf. IEEE Press, Piscataway NJ (2001)
5. High Level Architecture Run-Time Infrastructure Programmer's Guide 1.3 Version 3. DMSO (1998)
6. J. Dingel, D. Garlan, C. Damon: Bridging the HLA: Problems and Solutions. Sixth IEEE International Workshop on Distributed Simulation and Real Time Applications, DS-RT '02 (2002)
7. Boukerche, A. Roy: A Dynamic Grid-Based Multicast Algorithm for Data Distribution Management. 4th IEEE Distributed Simulation and Real Time Application (2000)

Differentiated Application Independent Data Aggregation in Wireless Sensor Networks*

Jianlin Qiu, Ye Tao, and Sanglu Lu

State Key Laboratory for Novel Software Technology,
Department of Computer Science and Technology,
Nanjing University,
P.R. China 210093
{qjl, taoye, sanglu}@dislab.nju.edu.cn

Abstract. Wireless sensor network is now becoming a burgeoning distributed computing paradigm which resembles traditional wireless ad hoc network in some aspects such as network organization. However, wireless sensor network differs greatly from traditional wireless ad hoc network in that the nodes are highly resource limited. This paper solves the problem of delivering data with different real-time constraints and proposes a protocol called Differentiated Application Independent Data Aggregation (DAIDA) to aggregate network units according to their priorities. Simulation results show that our DAIDA protocol reduces the end-to-end delay of real-time traffics and improves energy efficiency of the wireless sensor networks.

1 Introduction

Wireless sensor network has emerged as a new paradigm for distributed computing these years. Unlike the traditional nodes in wired networks, most sensor nodes are strictly resource-limited. Due to the large number of sensors and their comparatively small sizes, the batteries of the nodes are in most cases not rechargeable. To reduce the power consumption, the processor of the sensor node runs at a much lower frequency comparing to our PCs, the memory available is often less than 1 megabyte and the wireless channel is restricted to a relatively low bandwidth.

Data aggregation is an approach to improve the energy efficiency in wireless sensor networks by reducing the wireless traffic. Much of the literature on data aggregation in sensor networks focuses on shrinking wireless traffic by local or in-network processing, thus reducing power consumptions of sensors. In this paper we deal with the aggregation of data flows with different real-time constraints in the same wireless sensor network. To ensure the on-time delivery of data with high real-time constraints, we control the degree of MAC layer data aggregation according to the priority of each data flow. The simulation results show that our solution shortens the end-to-end delay and prolongs the lifetime of the network comparing to the scheme without aggregation or aggregation unaware of data priorities.

* This work is supported by the National Natural Science Foundation of China under Grant No.60402027.

H. Zhuge and G.C. Fox (Eds.): GCC 2005, LNCS 3795, pp. 529 – 534, 2005.

2 System Architecture

Our solution is a data aggregation model which works between the MAC layer and network layer of sensor network's protocol stack. The aggregation component takes in multiple packets and converts them into a single packet. The number of packets to be aggregated at a time is affected by both the priority of the packets and the traffic conditions.

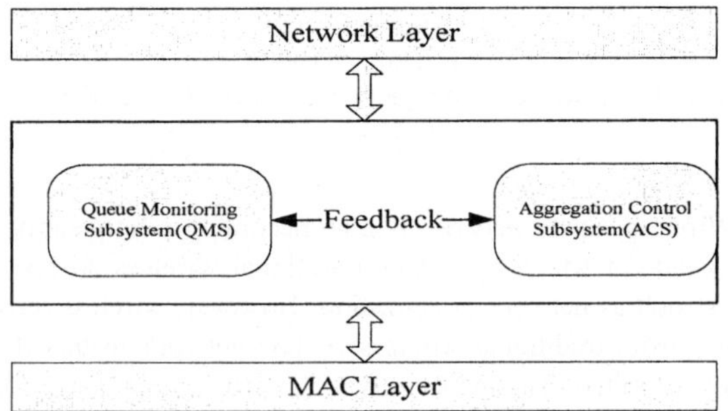

Fig. 1. DAIDA Architecture

The architecture of DAIDA model is shown in Figure 1. The DAIDA component can be divided into two parts: The Queue Management Subsystem (QMS) and the Aggregation Control Subsystem (ACS). The QMS maintains several message queues of different priorities, putting incoming message into the proper queue, performs aggregation when required by ACS, and pipes message out of its queue for further transmission. The ACS monitors the traffic out of the sensor node, controls the degree of aggregation for each different priority message queue.

3 DAIDA Design

3.1 Differentiated Sensor Queuing Model

The incoming message queues of DAIDA are tagged with its *Message Priority (MP)*, $MP \in \{0,1,2,\ldots,MP_{\max}\}$. The message with *MP* value 0 has the highest real-time constraint and thus must be delivered as soon as possible.

We abstract the input message queues as the M/D/1 queuing model, assuming the mean message arrival rate as λ_{in}.. We assume constant incoming queue length, thus the message leaving rate λ_{agg} is equal to$\lambda_{in.}$ And the outgoing queue is viewed as a FCFS queue with message arrival rate λ_{trans} and leaving rate λ_{out}.

3.2 Aggregation Buffer Management

The aggregation buffer is controlled by the aggregation control subsystem. Given a total buffer capacity of M messages, we divide it into MP_{max}+1 aggregation buffers, with each buffer the same size M/ (MP_{max}+1). Besides, each aggregation buffer is marked with a priority number P_i, ($i \in \{0,1,\ldots, MP_{max}\}$). The incoming message is appended to one of the aggregation buffers according to the priority information set in the MAC header by the original source of the message.

Each aggregation queue is initially assigned an integer aggregation factor a_i ($i \in \{0,1,\ldots, MP_{max}\}$) which can be adjusted by the ACS. Meanwhile, every aggregation buffer is associated with a *Interval Time(IT)* value IT_i ($i \in \{0,1,\ldots, MP_{max}\}$). The QMS performs aggregation on each aggregation buffer every IT_i seconds, concatenating at most a_i messages into one network unit. If there are less than a_i messages in the aggregation buffer, then all messages in that buffer will be concatenated into a single network unit.

On finishing aggregation, QMS pumps the messages into the outgoing message queue with each aggregated message marked with their original priority number.

3.3 Aggregation Control Subsystem Design

3.3.1 Double Threshold Feedback Scheme

Aggregation Control Subsystem adopts a Double Threshold Feedback (DTF) scheme to modify the aggregation degree of each aggregation queue. The outgoing queue is associated with a pair of threshold values TH_{min} and TH_{max} ($0 < TH_{min} < TH_{max} < 1$). At the beginning of each IT_0 (The meaning of IT_i is mentioned above), the ACS checks the state of the outgoing queue. If the usage percentage of the queue exceeds TH_{max}, then the aggregation factors and interval times will be double increased. On the contrary, when the usage percentage falls below TH_{min}, ACS double decreases the aggregation factor and interval time of each aggregation buffer.

3.3.2 Initial Aggregation Parameters Selection

To appropriately select the initial aggregation parameter including a_i and IT_i for each of the aggregation buffer, we first associate an *Interval Percentage(IP)* value with each priority queue, and we assume the hop-to-hop delay required by priority i lower than TD_i , ($i \in \{0,1,\ldots, MP_{max}\}$, and i ranges all the same if mentioned below),we calculate IP_i as below:

$$IP_i = TD_i \,/ \sum_{i=0}^{MP_{max}} TD_i \tag{1}$$

According to the queue model proposed in section 3.1, the arrival rate of incoming message isλ_{in}. Assuming the same arrival rate for messages of all priorities, we have the message arrival rate λ_i of priority i:

$$\lambda_i = \lambda_{in} \,/\, (MP_{max} + 1) \tag{2}$$

To fill up an empty aggregation queue, we need the time of FT_i, where

$$FT_i = [M/\,(MP_{max} + 1)] \,/\lambda_i \tag{3}$$

Combining formulary (2) and (3) we have $FT_i = M/\lambda_{in}$. We set IT_i in the manner that for higher priorities, the IT_i is smaller:

$$IT_i = FT_i * IP_i \tag{4}$$

Combining (1), (4), We get IT_i:

$$IT_i = M(TD_i)/[(\sum_{i=0}^{MP_{max}} TD_i)\lambda_{in}] \tag{5}$$

Given the IT_i set according to (5), then within this interval time, a total number of a_i packets is accumulated in each aggregation buffer , where

$$a_i = \lambda_i * IT_i = M(TD_i)/[(\sum_{i=0}^{MP_{max}} TD_i)*(MP_{max}+1)]. \tag{6}$$

4 Performance Evaluations

We compare the scheme without any data aggregation (NOAGG), the scheme of simple application independent data aggregation without any traffic differentiation (SAIDA), and DAIDA. Table 1 describes the detailed parameters for our simulation. In our simulation, we analyze the following two metrics: end-to-end delay and energy consumption.

In our simulation, we investigate the case where there is only one sink node in the entire wireless sensor network. There may be 3 types of messages marked with priority number 0 to 2 denoting hop-to-hop delay upper bound of 20ms, 40ms and 60ms

Table 1. Simulation Parameters

Routing	GF
MAC Layer	802.11 DCF
Radio Layer	Radio-ACCNOISE
Propagation Model	Two-Ray
Bandwidth	40-200kbps
Terrain	200m*200m
Number of nodes	100
Node Placement	Uniform
Payload size	32 Bytes
Radio Range	40m

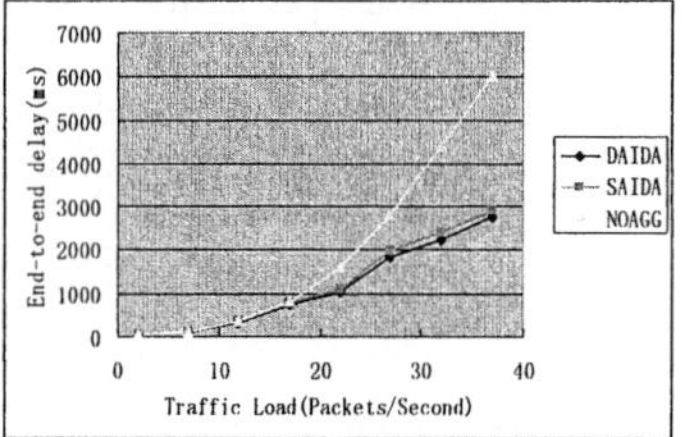

Fig. 2. End-to-end Delay under Different Schemes

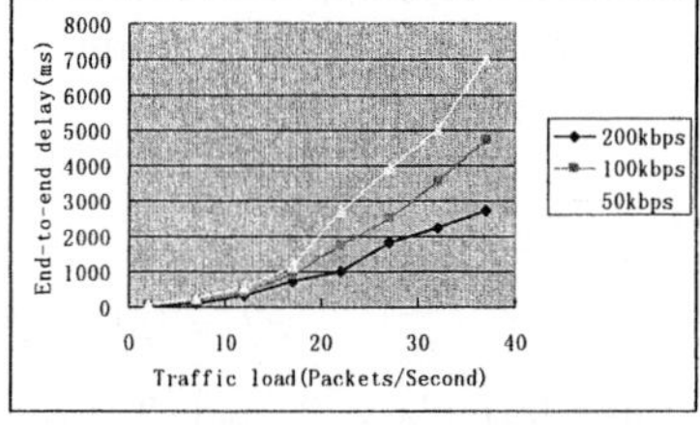

Fig. 3. End-to-end Delay under Different Bandwidths in DAIDA

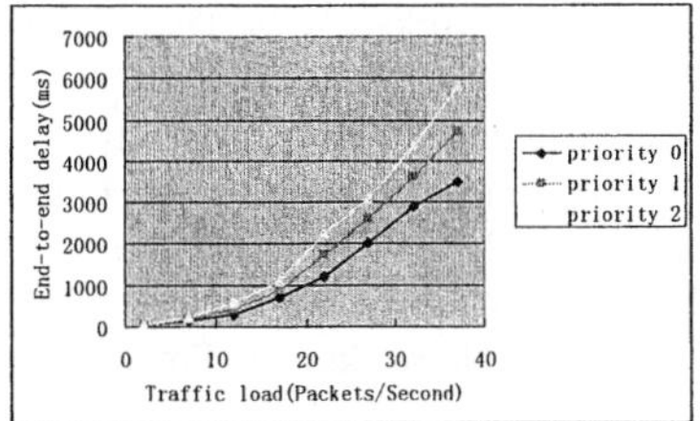

Fig. 4. End-to-end Delay of Different Priorities in DAIDA

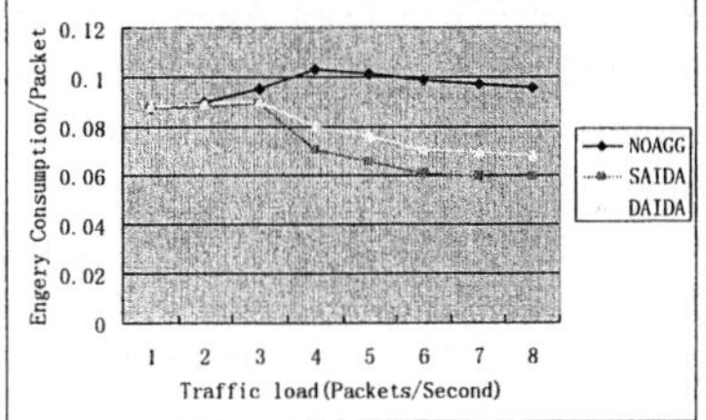

Fig. 5. Energy Consumption of Different Aggregation Protocols

respectively. Nodes are set to send CBR flows. Besides, in the simulation of DAIDA, we set TH_{min} to 0.2, and TH_{max} to 0.8.

We can see from the simulation results shown by figure 2, figure 3, figure 4 and figure 5 that our DAIDA protocol decreases the end-to-end delay in wireless sensor networks and prolong the network lifetime.

5 Related Works

Our inspiration of DAIDA derives from two aspects: the previous research works on data aggregation in wireless sensor network, and the research on differentiated services in wireless ad hoc networks and sensor networks.

For the application dependent data aggregation, [1] introduces a data aggregation scheme of performing in-network processing to reduce the amount of application data to be transmitted. And for the application independent data aggregation, work in [2] is representative, with feedback-based aggregation control which makes the aggregation more adaptive. Examples of the application of data aggregation are shown in [3] and [4].

Works on differentiated services in wireless ad hoc networks is unveiled in [5] and [6], and research on real-time capacity in wireless sensor networks is shown in [7].

6 Conclusions

In this paper we propose DAIDA, an adaptive application independent data aggregation scheme which takes the real-time constraint of hop-to-hop delay into account. DAIDA works between the MAC layer and network layer by concatenating multiple network units. By adjusting the degree of aggregation and the aggregation intervals, smaller end-to-end delay can be achieved while reducing per-packet energy consumption in the wireless sensor networks.

References

1. Intanagonwiwat, C., Estrin, D., Govindan, R., and Heidemann, J.: Impact of Network Desity on Data Aggregation in Wireless Sensor Networks. In Proceedings of the 22nd International Conference on Distributed Computing Systems, 2002.

2. Tian He, Brian M. Blum, John A. Stankovic, Tarek Abdelzaher.: AIDA: Adaptive Application Independent Data Aggregation in Wireless Sensor Networks. ACM Transactions on Embedded Computing Systems, Volume 3, Issue 2, pp. 426-457, 2002.
3. Samuel Madden, Michael J. Franklin, Joseph M. Hellerstein and Wei Hong.: TAG: a Tiny AGgregation Service for Ad-Hoc Sensor Networks. 5th Annual Symposium on Operating Systems Design and Implementation (OSDI).December, 2002.
4. 4. Samuel Madden, Michael J. Franklin, Joseph M. Hellerstein and Wei Hong.: The Design of an Acquisitional Query Processor for Sensor Networks. In Proceedings of SIGMOD, 2003.
5. Wei Liu, Xiang Chen, Yuguang Fang, John M. Shea.: Courtesy Piggybacking: Supporting Differentiated Services in Multihop Mobile Ad Hoc Networks. IEEE Transactions on Mobile Computing, vol. 03, no. 4, pp. 380-393, October 2004.
6. Y. Xiao, Y. Pan.: Differentiation, QoS Guarantee, and Optimization for Real-Time Traffic over One-hop Ad Hoc Networks, IEEE Transactions on Parallel and Distributed Systems, pp. 538-549, June 2005.
7. Tarek F. Abdelzaher, Shashi Prabh, Raghu Kiran.: In Proceedings of the 25th IEEE International Real-time System Symposium, 2004.

Dynamic Models of Knowledge in Virtual Organizations

Yan Ren and Xueshan Luo

School of Information Systems and Management,
National University of Defense Technology, Changsha 410073, P.R. China
yanzi916_78@hotmail.com

Abstract. The dynamics of knowledge is important for virtual organizations (VOs) knowledge management (KM) to improve the fast response capabilities and flexible problem solving capabilities of VOs in complex environments. This paper proposes a method of modeling knowledge dynamics in VOs, which is composed of three models: knowledge flow model, knowledge conversion model and knowledge sharing space model. The models depict the dynamics of knowledge and design the operation mechanisms of knowledge in VOs from the perspectives of flow attributes, evolution and innovation features, and sharing and cooperation of knowledge.

1 Introduction

The real and specific problem that underlies the Grid concept is coordinated resource sharing and problem solving in dynamic, multi-institutional virtual organizations[1]. Virtual Organizations(VOs) are dynamic collections of a number of semi-independent autonomous entities each of which has a range of problem solving capabilities and resources[1][2]. These entities coexist and share resources in VOs in a controlled fashion, so that they may collaborate to achieve a common goal.

Over the past few years, research efforts within the Grid community have produced a lot of protocols, services and tools that address the challenges in seeking to build scalable VOs. Nevertheless, careful study of underlying requirements leads us to identify a broad set of common concerns and requirements[1]. For example, the need for highly flexible sharing relationships and collaborative processes is fundamental to many diverse disciplines and activities. Knowledge Management(KM) plays an important role in promoting the efficient sharing and collaboration, and innovation and productivity in a cooperative team such as VO[3]. By knowledge sharing and reuse, the entities in VOs may enlarge their knowledge storage, so that they can make rapid and accurate estimation about their surroundings and problems, which produces better decisions. Furthermore, highly cooperative problem solving capabilities can be acquired by efficient knowledge sharing and collaboration throughout the whole VO, so that the efficiency and scientificalness of organization decisions can be improved.

Traditionally, it is necessary for KM to be able to capture and represent their knowledge assets, to share and reuse their knowledge for different applications and different users, and to create a culture that encourages knowledge sharing and reuse[4]. Therefore, former KM research is mainly focused on knowledge representation and dissemination, and the knowledge modeling is mainly static based on ontology[5]. But the characteristics of VOs demand more capabilities of KM such as more flexible and

H. Zhuge and G.C. Fox (Eds.): GCC 2005, LNCS 3795, pp. 535–540, 2005.

controllable knowledge sharing capabilities, and collaboration capabilities of the entities in VOs. Thus, KM in VOs needs also dynamic models of the flow attributes, evolution, sharing and collaboration relationships of knowledge in VOs, so that the operation mechanisms of knowledge in VOs can be comprehended, represented and designed more explicitly and adequately, which will improve the problem solving capabilities of VOs. Therefore, we propose three models which are suitable for depicting knowledge dynamics in VOs: knowledge flow model, knowledge conversion model and knowledge sharing space model.

2 Related Work

CommonKADS methodology has become the de facto standard for knowledge modeling which proposes six models from the perspectives of organization, task, agent, communication, knowledge and design[5]. The knowledge model is divided into models of domain concepts and relationships, a model of the required inferences, and a model of the control required on the inferences[4]. Multi-perspective modeling[4] enables a number of techniques to be used together, each technique being the most appropriate for modeling that particular aspect of knowledge. Multi-perspective modeling is important because organizational knowledge is very complex and heterogeneous, and there is no single method that can model all these accurately and appropriately[5]. This method uses a collection of knowledge models to describe knowledge in organizations from six perspectives of what, how, when, who, where and why.

Another research effort of dynamic knowledge modeling in large scale knowledge sharing and collaboration in VOs is the research work of China Knowledge Grid Research Group[6]. They proposed a multidimensional knowledge space model, a knowledge operation language, and a knowledge flow model for realizing effective knowledge sharing in VOs. And they are making progress on knowledge grid applications in cooperative research and education.

3 Knowledge Flow Model

One of the most important distinctions between knowledge flows and data flows or information flows is that there are multi-dimensional flow attributes in knowledge flows. For example, in time dimension, knowledge is successively discovered, mastered, evolved and updated; in form dimension, knowledge changes from hiding in people's heads to being able to be expressed in words, finally to being accumulated as people's experience and intuition.

Here we adopt the dynamic knowledge flow model proposed by Nissen[7], which is the integration of the spiral model and the life cycle model. The spiral model[8] employs the two dimensions of epistemological and ontological to describe a knowledge flow, which is characterized by a "spiral" dynamic through four organization processes: socialization, externalization, combination and internalization. The life cycle model includes six discrete phases of knowledge as it flows through the organizations: creation, organization, formalization, dissemination, application and evolution[7]. The two models are integrated and extended to construct a four-dimensional model of knowledge flow dynamics. The four dimensions are: life cycle, time, explicitness (epistemological) and reach (ontological). To illustrate the model using three variable pictures, we fix time at some time period as a constant and then the model is shown in Fig.1. The vector sequence K-S-E-C-I-V corresponds to the processes of knowledge creation, socialization, externalization, combination, internalization and refinement. The KMLC arcs represent knowledge management life cycle, and P&P are policies and procedures.

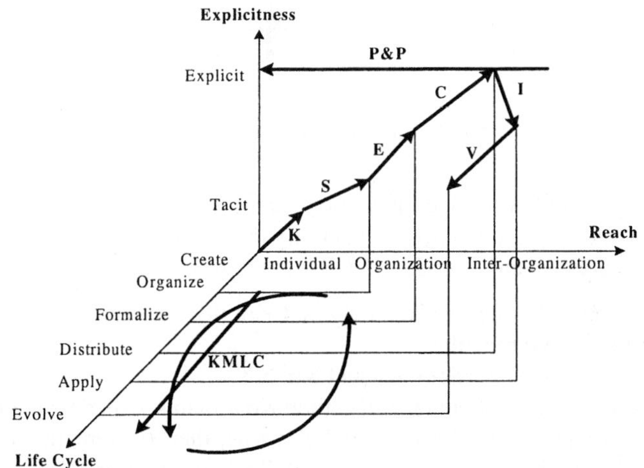

Fig. 1. Knowledge flow model (time as constant) (adapted from[7])

The model is very useful in depicting and visualizing knowledge flows. If the three-dimensional representation of knowledge flow space in which life cycle is fixed as a constant is divided into octants by making binary distinctions along each of the three axes, the three coordination approaches termed standardization, planning and mutual adjustment drawing from the organizational design and coordination theory can be mapped into several regions of the divided space. Then we can use the manifest knowledge flow pattern to determine which coordination approach is likely to be most effective in a given context[7].

4 Knowledge Conversion Model

The complexity of KM lies in the innovation feature of knowledge. Knowledge is attached to human beings so that it can be created, updated, deducted, induced and applied. We call this process Knowledge Conversion Process(KCP). If this process goes along for the problem solving goal and finally gets the useful knowledge, then the process is required. The entities in VOs share their knowledge and collaborate for a common goal so as to find satisfying knowledge conversion processes.

We classify the knowledge sources of VO entities into two classes: one is the knowledge storage of an entity (denoted as E), denoted as Ko, which on the whole behaves as the existing knowledge base distribution; the other one is the knowledge that an entity E acquires from other entities, denoted as Kg, which on the whole behaves as knowledge passing and sharing[9]. Kn represents the new knowledge that an entity E gains from the knowledge conversion process. A single process is called Knowledge Conversion Unit, denoted as CU. Along with the progress of CUs, Kn is enlarged and updated. The changes of Kg embody the interactions and collaborations between VO entities. We use a Petri-like form to illustrate the CU as Fig. 2.

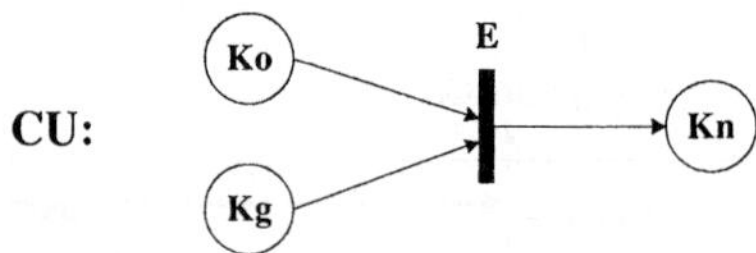

Fig. 2. Knowledge conversion unit

Apparently, not all knowledge interactions can produce KCP. According to the relationships between Kg and Ko, we may classify the interactions and the corresponding entity activities which cannot produce KCP into the following classes:

(1) If there is no relevancy between Kg and Ko, then the entities cannot make any conversion, so Ko remains;
(2) If there is relevancy between Kg and Ko, but
  - Ko is the same as or contains Kg, then Ko remains, called Containing Pattern;
  - Ko contradicts with Kg, then: if Ko is true, then Ko remains; if Ko is false, then Ko can be abandoned despite of Kg being true or false, called Contradiction Pattern;
(3) If Kg contains some rules that require the entities to decompose Ko into the knowledge with smaller granularity, then the process cannot be considered as KCP, because the process cannot produce new knowledge.

KCP appears in the following cases when there is relevancy between Kg and Ko:

(1) Complementarity Pattern, i.e. Ko and Kg are complementary so that they can be combined into new knowledge through synthesis activities of entities;
(2) Induction Pattern, i.e. the contents of Ko and Kg can be induced and generalized to new knowledge such as principles and experience;
(3) Deduction Pattern, i.e. the entities can deduce new knowledge from Ko through the preconditions or rules provided by Kg;
(4) Enlightening Pattern, i.e. the contents of Kg enlighten the entities on Ko, which results in the association of ideas and the creative activities of the entities.

5 Knowledge Sharing Space

Different entities in VOs have different objects and benefits. They hold and control their own private resources, and have relatively dependent problem solving capabilities and operation mechanisms. They come together dynamically for common tasks and goals, but their own benefits are still existent. Moreover, they expect that by sharing resources and collaborations, their own benefits can be maximized while they achieve the common goal. Therefore, this sharing must be controllable and limited. We propose the conception of Knowledge Sharing Space(KSS) which includes four related but different space concepts:

(1) Common Space: In the common space, the entities can communicate with each other and share their knowledge assets without restriction. All the knowledge resources are authorized and open completely.

(2) Private Space: In the private space, the entities manage and utilize their private knowledge assets, and keep the direct protection and absolute control power on them.

(3) Organizational Shared Space: This is the interface between common space and private space. In this space, the entities can share their knowledge and keep the control of them at the same time, and they will protect the resources from illegal intrusion and malice destruction.

(4) Accessory Space: This is used to support the knowledge requirements from non-VO entities. It can be connected to the common space through an authorized interface and the entities in the accessory space can use parts of the knowledge resources in the common space.

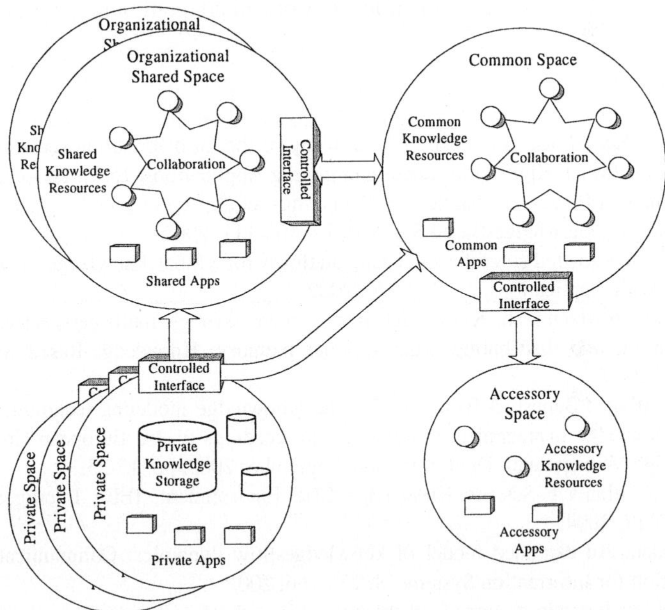

Fig. 3. Knowledge sharing space conceptual model

The KSS conceptual model is shown in Fig. 3. VOs may define their own abilities, standards and interfaces required. The entities in VOs can hold, operate and manage their private space according to their organization strategies and procedures which are consistent with the general policies. Using the KSS, the entities can share knowledge and applications and collaborate with each other while keeping security controls. According to different task requirements, the entities may adjust the usage of the shared knowledge resources and applications and integrate new knowledge resources and applications. Thus, the KSS not only ensures the flexible and controllable sharing and collaborations in VOs, but also has some extensibility, which enables VOs to meet the needs in critical moments and to adapt to rapid and continuous changes.

6 Conclusion

The paper proposes three dynamic models of knowledge in VOs from multi-perspective modeling point of view. The three models reflect the flow attributes, evolution and innovation features, sharing and collaboration relationships of knowledge in VOs. The paper only brings forward the profile of the modeling idea. The models will be refined and new models such as cooperative relationship model will be added if needed in the future.

The structures of modern large-scale VOs are becoming flat, the management and decision links are shortening, and the horizontal contacts and collaborations are being enhanced. Self-management, self-decision and active collaboration will be new patterns of organization operations. We believe KM will be more and more important as a technique of organizational coordination, control and adaptation in the future.

References

1. I.Foster, C.Kesselman, S.Tuecke, The anatomy of the Grid: Enabling scalable virtual organizations, Int'l J. High-Performance Computing Applications, 15(3): 200-222, 2001.
2. T.J.Norman, A.Preece, S.Chalmers, N.R.Jennings, et al., Agent-based formation of virtual organizations, Knowledge-Based Systems, 17: 103-111, 2004.
3. H.Zhuge, A knowledge grid model and platform for global knowledge sharing, Expert Systems with Applications, 22: 313-320, 2002.
4. J.Kingston, A.Macintosh, Knowledge management through multi-perspective modeling: Representing and distributing organizational memory, Knowledge-Based Systems, 13: 121-131, 2000.
5. M.S.Abdullah, I.Benest, A.Evans, C.Kimble, Knowledge modeling techniques for developing knowledge management systems, In: Proceedings of 3rd European Conference on Knowledge Management, Dublin, Ireland, September 2002, pp. 15-25.
6. H.Zhuge, China's E-Science Knowledge Grid Environment, IEEE Intelligent Systems, 19(1): 13-17, 2004.
7. M.E.Nissen, An extended model of knowledge-flow dynamics, Communications of the Association for Information Systems, 8: 251-266, 2002.
8. I.Nonaka, A dynamic theory of organizational knowledge creation, Organization Science 5(1): 14-37, 1994.
9. W.Dou, F.Su, S.Cai, F.Zhang, Modeling and supervision of a workflow system oriented toward the knowledge-based application and interaction, Journal of Computer Research and Development (in Chinese), 40(2): 342-350, 2003.
10. H.Zhuge, A knowledge flow model for peer-to-peer team knowledge sharing and management, Expert Systems with Applications, 23: 23-30, 2002.
11. A.Mowshowitz, Virtual organization, Communications of the ACM, 40(9):30-37, 1997.
12. D.E.O'Leary, D.Kuokka, R.Plant, Artificial intelligence and virtual organizations, Communications of the ACM, 40(1): 52-59, 1997.

Scientific Data Management Architecture for Grid Computing Environments*

Jaechun No[1], Nguyen Tien Cuong[1], and Sung Soon Park[2]

[1] Dept. of Computer Software,
College of Electronics and Information Engineering,
Sejong University, Seoul, Korea
[2] Dept. of Computer Science & Engineering,
College of Science and Engineering,
Anyang University, Anyang, Korea

Abstract. Many large-scale scientific experiments and simulations generate very large amounts of data (on the order of terabytes to petabytes), spanning thousands of files and data sets. We have developed a software system, called Grid Environment-based Data Management System (GEDAS), that provides a high-level, user-friendly interface, while maintaining the consistent data replicas among the grid communities. We describe the design and implementation of GEDAS and present performance results on Linux cluster.

1 Introduction

Many large-scale scientific experiments and simulations generate very large amounts of data [1](on the order of terabytes to petabytes), spanning thousands of files and data sets. Moreover, many data-intensive, high-performance computing applications require the efficient data management and transfer of those data generated in wide-area, distributed environments to share them between geographically distributed researchers for data analysis, data visualization, and so forth. In such environments, the replication technique for the fast data sharing between the community of researchers, and the high-performance I/O for the storage and efficient data accesses on heterogeneous resources present an extremely challenging task. Several data replication techniques, including Globus toolkit [2], have been developed to support high-performance data accesses to the remotely produced scientific data.

However, most of those data replication techniques were implemented under the assumption that the data being replicated is read-only so that once it has been generated would it not be modified in any grid site. Furthermore, those techniques mainly focus on measuring up the network performance, but ignoring the I/O overhead incurred during the data generation and replication on the heterogeneous storages.

* This work was supported in part by KOSEF award R05-2004-000-12543-0.

H. Zhuge and G.C. Fox (Eds.): GCC 2005, LNCS 3795, pp. 541–546, 2005.

We have developed a software system, called Grid Environment-based Data Management System (GEDAS), that provides a high-level, user-friendly interface to share the remotely produced data among the grid communities. GEDAS interacts with database to store application-related and system-related metadata to support the integrated data replicas and high-performance I/O on the distributed resources, while taking advantage of various I/O optimizations available in MPI-IO, such as collective I/O and noncontiguous requests, in a manner that is transparent to the user.

The rest of this paper is organized as follows. In Section 2, we discuss our goals in developing GEDAS. In Section 3, we present the design and implementation of GEDAS. Performance results on the Linux cluster located at Sejong University are presented in Section 4. We conclude in Section 5.

2 Design Motivation

Our main objectives in developing GEDAS were to maintain consistent data replication among the geographically distributed sites, to provide high-performance parallel I/O, to provide a high-level application programming interface (API), and to support a convenient data-retrieval capability.

- **Consistent Data Replication.** In order to maintain the consistently integrated data replicas among the distributed resources, GEDAS uses the version checking method that is much similar to the locking mechanism of distributed file systems [3].
- **High-Performance I/O.** To achieve high-performance I/O, GEDAS uses MPI-IO to access real data. MPI-IO is specifically designed to enable the optimizations that are critical for high-performance parallel I/O. Examples of these optimizations include collective I/O, the ability to access noncontiguous data sets, and the ability to pass hints to the implementation about access patterns, file-striping parameters, and so forth.
- **Convenient Data-Retrieval Capability.** GEDAS allows the user to specify names and other attributes to be associated with a data set. GEDAS internally selects a file name into which the data will be stored; the mapping between data sets and file names is stored in the database.

3 Implementation Details

3.1 GEDAS Metadata Structure

GEDAS provides a high-level API and stores application-related metadata and system-related metadata in a database. For regular applications where the data access pattern can be predicted before runtime, GEDAS creates five database tables: *application_registry_table*, *data_registry_table*, *file_registry_table*, *performance_registry_table*, and *system_registry_table*(see Figure 1). These database tables are made for each application to provide a high-level remote data access abstraction, while supporting a transparent, user-friendly user interface.

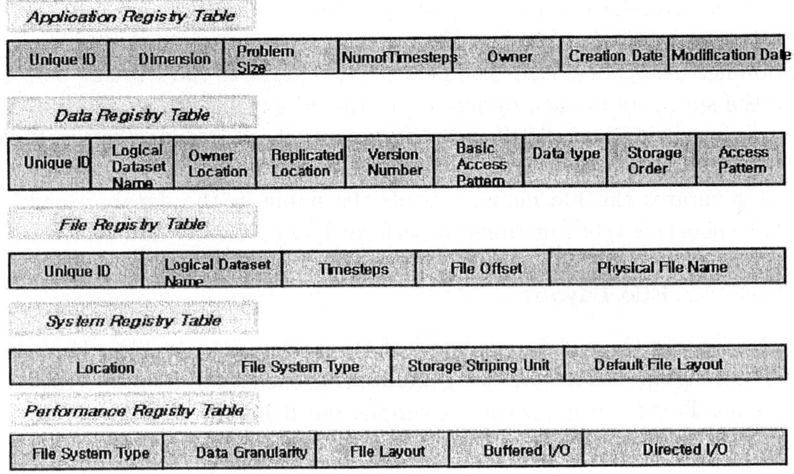

Fig. 1. Metadata Tables of GEDAS

Each time an application writes data sets, GEDAS enters the problem size, dimension, current date, data owner, and a unique identification number to the application_registry_table.

The data_registry_tabe includes the properties of each data set, such as data type, storage order, data access pattern, and global size. Also, it contains data replication-related metadata, such as the owner ip, replication location ip, and version number to be used in checking the replica consistency.

The file_registry_table stores a globally determined file offset denoting the starting offset of the file of each data set and the system_registry_table contains the system-related metadata, including filesystem type and striping unit size where the real data is stored.

The performance_registry_table includes the performance values evaluated using buffered I/O and directed I/O on each filesystem type registered in the system_registry_table.

3.2 GEDAS API

In GEDAS, users can specify groups of data sets by assigning properties to the first data set in a group and by propagating them to the other data sets belonging to the same group. The main reason for making groups of data sets is that GEDAS can then use different ways of organizing data in files, with different performance implications. For example, each data set can be written in a separate file, or the data sets of a group can be written to a single file. The properties assigned to each data set are stored in the database by invoking GEDAS_set_attributes. In case of read operation, data from a specific run can be retrieved by specifying attributes of the data, such as the date of the run. Also, the properties of the data sets need not be specified because GEDAS retrieves this information from the database.

The main GEDAS functions for writing and reading data are GEDAS_write and GEDAS_read. Before calling these functions, the user must provide the information necessary for GEDAS to perform I/O, such as the starting points and sizes of the subarray in each dimension in the case of block distribution, or the size of process grids and distribution arguments in each dimension in the case of cyclic distribution. Note that the user does not need to provide file names. GEDAS generates the file name, records the name in the database, and calls MPI-IO's collective I/O functions to perform I/O efficiently and parallel.

3.3 GEDAS File Layout

GEDAS supports three different ways of organizing data in files. In the independent file layout, each data set generated at each time step is written to a separate file. This file organization is simple, but it incurs the cost of a file open and close at each time step, which on some file systems can be quite high. For a large number of data sets and time steps, this method can be expensive because of the large number of file opens.

In the intermediate file layout, each data set (within a group) is written to a separate file, but different iterations of the same data set are appended to the same file. This method results in a smaller number of files and smaller file-open costs. The offset in the file where data is appended is stored in the file_registry_table.

In the long-length file layout, all iterations of all data sets belonging to a group are stored in a single file. As in the intermediate file layout, the file offset for each data set is stored in the file_registry_table in the GEDAS_write function. If a file system has high open and close costs, GEDAS can generate a very small number of files by choosing the long-length file layout. On the other hand, if an application produces a large number of data sets of large size, the long-length file layout would result in very large files, which may affect performance.

4 Performance Evaluation

In order to measure the performance, we used two Linux clusters located at Sejong university. Each cluster consists of four nodes having Pentium3 866MHz CPU, 256 MB of RAM, and 100Mbps of Fast Ethernet each. The operating system installed on those machines was RedHat 9.0 with Linux kernel 2.4.20-8. Each cluster uses its own PostgreSQL to store the metadata.

The performance results were obtained using the template implemented based on the three-dimensional astrophysics application, developed at the University of Chicago. The application stores block-distributed data in each dimension. In the template, we tested GEDAS library for the cyclic-distributed data as well.

On one of the clusters, the template has generated six floating-point arrays for data analysis, another six floating-point arrays for restart, and seven character arrays for visualization. The total data size generated was around 320MBytes.

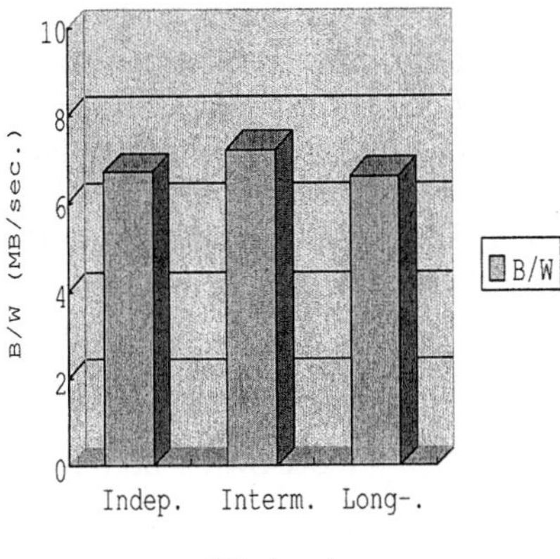

Fig. 2. Bandwidth to access the data from the remote owner in the block distribution. The accessed data is stored on the remote owner in three file layouts: independent file layout (Indep.), intermediate file layout (Interm.), and long-length file layout (Long-.).

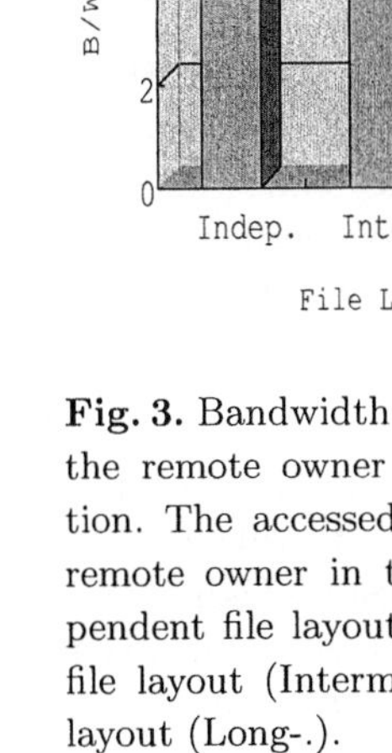

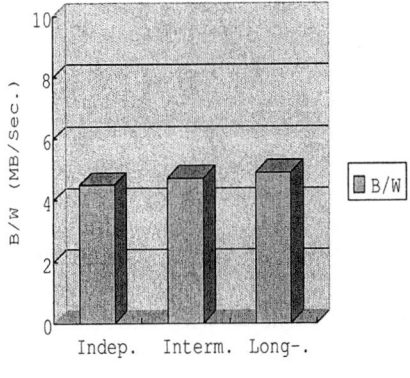

Fig. 3. Bandwidth to access the data from the remote owner in the cyclic distribution. The accessed data is stored on the remote owner in three file layouts: independent file layout (Indep.), intermediate file layout (Interm.), and long-length file layout (Long-.).

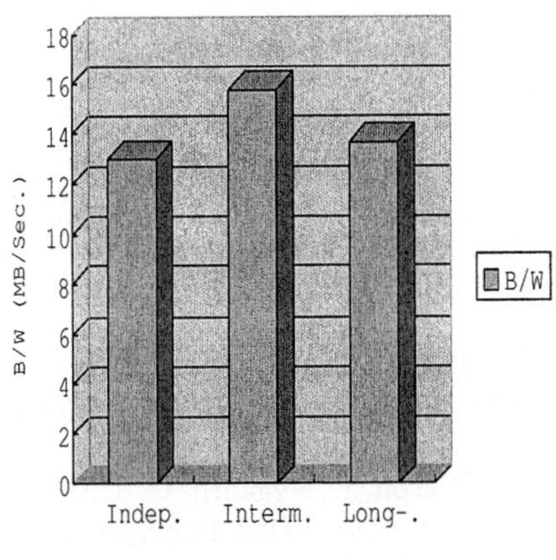

Fig. 4. Bandwidth to access the data replica in the block distribution, on top of three file layouts: independent file layout (Indep.), intermediate file layout (Interm.), and long-length file layout (Long-.)

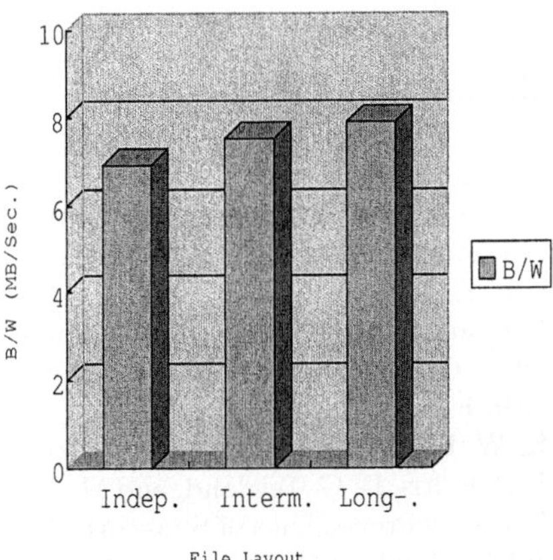

Fig. 5. Bandwidth to access the data replica in the cyclic distribution, on top of three file layouts: independent file layout (Indep.), intermediate file layout (Interm.), and long-length file layout (Long-.)

Figures 2 and 3 describe the performance results when the data sets are accessed on one cluster, while the requested data sets are stored on the other cluster in three different ways of file layout. The data access patterns tested are block distribution in Figure 2 and cyclic distribution in Figure 3. The performance values include the database overhead to access the associated metadata. As can be seen, the bandwidth measured in the block-distributed data access pattern is higher than that measured in the cyclic data access pattern due to the smaller communication overhead incurred in the MPI-IO's collective operation.

Figures 4 and 5 demonstrate the performance results obtained to access the replica of the desired data sets in the block distribution and cyclic distribution, respectively. When compared to Figures 2 and 3, accessing the data replica shows almost as much as twice bandwidth accessing from the remote owner because of the less communication overhead.

5 Conclusion

We have presented the design and implementation of a toolkit, called GEDAS, for high-performance scientific data management in data grid environments. GEDAS provides a simple, high-level interface and performs all necessary I/O optimizations to access and replicate the remote data transparently to the user. We also experimented with different ways of organizing data in files, called independent file layout, intermediate file layout, and long-length file layout. In the future, we plan to use GEDAS with more applications and evaluate both the usability and performance.

References

1. B. Allcock, I. Foster, V. Nefedova, A. Chervenak, E. Deelman, C. Kesselman, J. Leigh, A. Sim, A. Shoshani, B. Drach, and D. Williams. High-Performance Remote Access to Climate Simulation Data: A Challenge Problem for Data Grid Technologies. SC2001, November 2001
2. I. Foster, C. Kesselman, J. Nick, and S. Tuecke. The Physiology of the Grid: An Open Grid Services Architecture for Distributed Systems Integration WG, Global Grid Forum, June 22, 2002
3. K. W. Preslan, A. P. Barry, J. E. Brassow, G. M. Erickson, E. Nygaard, C. J. Sabol, S. R. Soltis, D. C. Teigland, and M. T. O'Keefe. A 64-bit Shared Disk File System for Linux. In Proceedings of Sixteenth IEEE Mass Storage Systems Symposium Seventh NASA Goddard Conference on Mass Storage Systems & Technologies, March 15-18, 1999

Efficient Join Algorithms for Integrating XML Data in Grid Environment

Hongzhi Wang, Jianzhong Li, and Shuguang Xiong

Harbin Institute of Technology, Harbin, China
wangzh@hit.edu.cn, lijz@mail.banner.com.cn, n2xiong@126.com

Abstract. For its self-description feature, XML can be used to represent information in grid environment. Querying XML data distributed in grid environment brings new challenges. In this paper, we focus on join algorithms in result merge step of query processing. In order to transmit results efficiently, we present strategies of data compacting, as well as 4 join operator models. Based on the compacted data structure, we design efficient algorithms of these join operators. Extensive experimental results shows that our data compact strategy is effective; our join algorithms outperform XJoin significantly and have good scalability.

1 Introduction

Grid is a promising computing environment. One of the important application running on gird is information processing. Information processing in gird can not only gain more computation power to process very large data but also integrate information from various data sources.

XML is an important format of information integration. One of its features making XML popular is that XML document has tags representing semantic of data. In grid environment [4], with heterogeneity among nodes, representing data by XML can make information processing in grid environment flexible.

With effective query processing techniques, queries to grid can retrieve data from all data sources in data grid like from single data source. One of the important step of query processing of grid is result merge, which is to merge intermediate results returned from data sources. Among the operators in result merge, join operation is a difficult one.

Challenges brought by Join operation in grid environment include:

- The bandwidth has limit. Strategy should be presented to save the bandwidth without affecting the query evaluation efficiency.
- The data from data sources may arrive in instable style. Even though existing algorithm for data in relation form can solve part of the problem, the join operation of XML data may be much more complex. The problem will be more interesting when the join operation is performed on the XML data compacted for transmission.

H. Zhuge and G.C. Fox (Eds.): GCC 2005, LNCS 3795, pp. 547–553, 2005.

Based on the feature of semi-structured data, we focus on efficient evaluation of join operations for XML data in the merge step of query processing in grid environment. The contributions of this paper includes:

- To save bandwidth, we design data transmission strategy for intermediate results of XQuery. This strategy supports efficient join evaluation in result merge step.
- Based on this transmission format, we present models for join operations in result merge step.
- For each join model, we give an efficient algorithm for implementation of the join operation.
- Our extensive experimental results demonstrate that our transmission strategy can save lots of bandwidth and accelerate the transmission. It also significantly outperforms XJoin in the evaluation of join over intermediate results.

The rest of the paper is organized as follows: Section 2 presents the strategy of compacting data for transmission of intermediate results. Section 3 discusses join models and their implementations. We present our experimental results and analyses in Section 4. Section 5 concludes the paper.

2 Prepare Data for Transmission

In this section, we discuss the strategy of compacting data for transmission. We have two strategies.

Tree Structure Keeping. This strategy is to keep the parent-child or ancestor-descent relationship of XML nodes. The benefit of this strategy is that it will avoid information redundancy.

Large Element Latency. When the query selectivity is small, lots of objects will not exist in the result of join. If the candidate of join is large element with complex structure but only a small part of them will be in the final result, since these objects should also be transmitted, the bandwidth is wasted. To address this problem, our strategy is that only the id of large element is transmitted with the elements to perform join operation on. In the final step of generation of final result, selected large elements are obtained from data source with their ids. We will also illustrate the benefit with an example.

3 Join Algorithms

In this section, we will present algorithms to process join of XML in grid environment.

3.1 Models of Join Operations

Based on different types of queries, we can define four join models. Both model can be represented as "$L\Box R$", where $\Box$ is a join operator. Tuples corresponding to L are called *left candidates* and tuples corresponding to r are called *right candidates.*

Natural Join. For two sets of XML fragment, nature join is to connect the fragment together with the join attributes existing once in join results. Considering XML feature, the result of the natural join is corresponding attributes with the intersection of join sets.

Combined Join. For two sets of XML fragment, combined join is the same as natural join but the result has no the intersection of join sets. Note two tuples can be combined joined only when the intersection of join sets is not empty.

Semi-join. For two sets of XML fragment, semiJoin is to filter left set with the join set of right candidates. The tuple is filtered when the intersection of join sets is not empty. The result contains the intersection of join sets.

Half Join. For two sets of XML fragment, half join is to filter left set with the join set of right candidates. The result does not contain the intersection of join sets. The tuple is filtered when the intersection of join sets is not empty.

3.2 Implementations of Join Operators

Join Algorithm for Half Join Model For implementation operation half join, basic data structure is a hash set to store all elements of join sets of right candidates. When a tuple t as left candidate comes, find each item in its corresponding set, if any item is found in the hash set, corresponding value of t is output and the processing of tuple t is finished. The algorithm is shown in Algorithm 1, where H is a hash set containing all elements of join sets in right candidate of join. Symbol *end* identifies the end of the candidates.

Algorithm 1. HalfJoin()

```
while left candidate is not end do
  if A tuple t of left candidate comes then
    for each element e in t.S do
      if e can be found in H then
        output t − t.S
  if A tuple t of right candidate comes then
    for each element e in t.S do
      insert e into t.S
```

Join Algorithm for SemiJoin Model. The implementation of SemiJoin is similar as that of half join. But For each tuple t of A, each value in $t.S$ that can be find in the hash set is outputted with $t.left$. The algorithm is shown in Algorithm 2.

Join Algorithm for Combined Join Model. The basic idea of the implementation of combined join model is to attach a signature to each tuple to represent the context of the join set, so that whether two join sets are intersected can be joined by the two signature. Since the value range of a node can not be determined, accurate signature is too long. We choose bloom filter [1] as the signature. To each tuple as left or right candidate, a bloom filter is assigned. Tuples as left or right candidates with the same bloom filter are compacted together, respectively. Two global bloom filters are maintained as the union of all bloom filters

Algorithm 2. semiJoin()

```
while left candidate is not end do
  if A tuple t of left candidate comes then
    for each element e in t.S do
      if e can not be found in H then
        delete e from t.S
    if t.S is not empty then
      output t
  if A tuple t of right candidate comes then
    for each element e in t.S do
      insert e into t.S
```

of left and right candidates, respectively. Since bloom has positive false, when a new tuple t as left candidate comes, its bloom filter b_t is computed. It is intersected with the global bloom filter of right candidates. If the result is not 0, it is intersected with each bloom filter f_r of right candidates, and it will be judged whether the intersection of $t.S$ and the candidate set of each tuple t_r as right candidate with bloom filter f_r is empty. If the answer is no, then the tuple with $t-t.S$ and $t_r - t_r.S$ is outputted. In order to accelerate the judgement, we insert all elements into a hash set H and check whether $t_r.S$ has any element in H. We perform similar steps on a tuple as right candidate but it will be compared with tuples as left candidates. The algorithm is shown in Algorithm 3, where S_l and S_r are sets of bloom filters of left candidates and right candidates, respectively; $filter_l$ and $filter_r$ are global filters of left candidates and right candidates, respectively. In this algorithm, we only give the process steps when a tuple of left candidate comes. Because of symmetry, a tuple of right candidate is processed in similar method.

Algorithm 3. Combined Join()

```
while left candidate is not end and right candidate is not end do
  if A tuple t of left candidate comes then
    b_t=bloom_filter(t)
    b_t.tuple = t
    add b_t to S_l
    filter_l = Union(filter_l, b_t)
    insert all elements of t.S into H
    if intersect(filter_r, b_t) ≠ 0 then
      for each element f_r in S_r do
        if intersection(f_r, b_t) ≠ 0 then
          for each element e in f_r.tuple.S do
            if e is in H then
              output (t − T.s, f_r.tuple − f_r.tuple.S)
```

Join Algorithm for Natural Join Model. The implementation of natural Join model can be considered as the combination of Combined Join algorithm and Xjoin[3] algorithm. That is, when a tuple t as left candidate comes, at first its bloom filter is intersected with global filter of right candidates. If the result is not 0, the tuple is joined with right candidates by XJoin algorithm. In order to perform XJoin, the join set should be split. Each tuple is converted to a set of tuples, each of which has one element in join set with all other attributes. The element from join set is *join attribute.* Two hash tables are associated to left and right candidates, respectively. Each converted tuple is inserted into corresponding bucket in the hash table based on the hash value of join attribute. Each converted tuple is also joined with the tuples in corresponding bucket of opposite hash table.

4 Experimental Results

In this section, we present results and analyses of part of our extensive experiments of data transmission strategy and join algorithms.

4.1 Experimental Setup

All of our experiments were performed on a PC with Pentium 1GMHz, 512M memory and 40G IDE hard disk. The OS is Windows 2000 Professional. We implemented our system using Microsoft Visual C++ 6.0. We implemented our data transmission strategy and half join, semiJoin, combined join and natural join algorithms. For comparison, we also implementation XJoin algorithm.

We choose XMark as test data[2]. XMark document. In the result we only give count the run time of join algorithms.

We designed a set of queries that has different characteristics. We consider comparison feature of left and right candidates: one-to-one(oo for brief) and one-to-multiple(om for brief). Queries are shown in Table 1.

Table 1. Query Set and Comparison of Data Transmission

Query	left candidate	right candidate	OEM	SEM	OQM	SQM
Q1	person/id	bidder//person	84758	84758	11047764	1972700
Q2	person//category	item//category	119804	76269	36380718	1815120
Q3	open_auction//person	person/id	108758	73129	22943812	2012104
Q4	open_auction/id	person//open_auction	62828	43019	22943812	2012104

4.2 Data Transmission Strategy

In order to evaluate our data transmission strategy, we compare the size of original data to transmit with the size of data applied our strategy to transmit. Results of data transmission strategy is shown in Table . To test "Tree Structure Keeping" strategy, we compare the number of elements to be transmitted in original XML document(OEM for brief) and in our strategy (SEM for brief). To test "Large Element Latency" strategy, we compare the quantity of data (in byte) to be transmitted for SemiJoin algorithm of all these 4 queries. The quantity of original data should be transmitted is called OQM for brief and the quantity of data compacted by our strategy is called SQM for brief. The results are shown in Table 1. From the results, in most instances, our strategy can compact data to transmit significantly. One special is Q1, OEM equals to SEM. It is because each person element only has one id and each bidder element only has one person attribute.

4.3 Results

Comparisons. In this subsection, we present comparison results with XJoin, which is a efficient join algorithm for relational model in information integration system. Since XJoin performs the 4 kinds of join operation in the same method, we compare all our join algorithms with XJoin. We fixed the number of buckets of hash 32 and the filter length 32 bits. The results of comparison are shown in Figure 1(a). From the result, our algorithms performs to XJoin significantly.

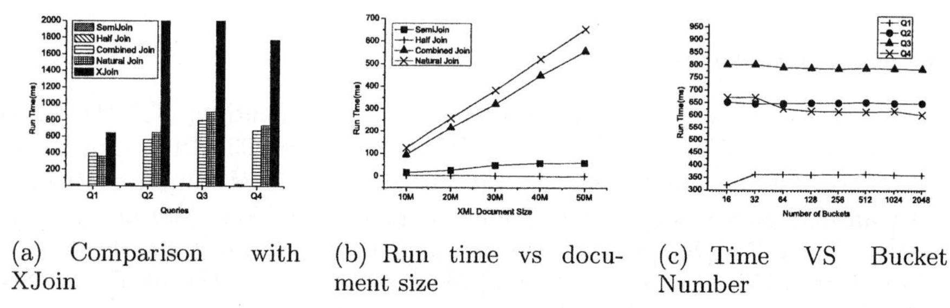

(a) Comparison with XJoin (b) Run time vs document size (c) Time VS Bucket Number

Fig. 1. Experimental Results

Scalability. We vary the size of document from 10M to 50M. The results are shown in Figure 1(b). From the result, the run time nearly linearly increases with document size. Our algorithms have good scalability.

Changing the Number of Buckets. In order to test the affect of number of buckets to the efficiency of Natural Join algorithm, we fix the length of filter 32 bits and vary the number of buckets from 16 to 2048. Results are shown in Figure 1(c). From the result, the number of buckets does not affect the efficiently remarkably. It is because that the number the selectivity of the join operation is not very large and the bloom filter filtered most of useless results.

5 Conclusions

In this paper, we focus on efficient join algorithms for information integration in grid environment based on XML. We address this problem in two aspects. One is to save bandwidth by compacting data for transmission. The other is to design efficient algorithm based on compacted structure adaptive to transmission. Our extensive experiments shows that data compacting strategies are effective and our join algorithms are efficient with good scalability. Further work includes estimating of intermediate results in grid environment and designing query optimization strategies for join operations in grid environment.

References

1. B. Bloom. Space/time trade-offs in hash coding with allowable errors. *Communications of ACM*, 13(7):422–426, 1970.
2. A. Schmidt, F. Waas, M. L. Kersten, M. J. Carey, I. Manolescu, and R. Busse. XMark: A benchmark for XML data management. In *Proceedings of 28th International Conference on Very Large Data Bases (VLDB 2002)*, pages 974–985, 2002.
3. T. Urhan and M. J. Franklin. Xjoin: A reactively-scheduled pipelined join operator. *IEEE Data Eng. Bull.*, 23(2):27–33, 2000.
4. H. Zhuge. China's e-science knowledge grid environment. *IEEE Intelligent Systems*, 19(1):13–17, 2004.

Integrated *k*-NN Query Processing Based on Geospatial Data Services

Guifen Tang, Luo Chen, Yunxiang Liu, Shulei Liu, and Ning Jing

College of Electronic Science and Engineering,
National University of Defense Technology,
ChangSha, HuNan, P.R. China
gftang0401@yahoo.com.cn

Abstract. Geospatial data service (GDS) is a type of web service that provides access to collections of geospatial data. User can search remote spatial data through the interface provided by service. This paper focuses on integrated *k*-NN query processing based on GDS. We first present the processing framework and the system architecture for integrated *k*-NN query based on GDS. We propose a filter algorithm to filter the services which can't affect the query result. As GDS is a type of data source with restricted query capability, we rewrite the *k*-NN query with BBOX spatial operator to efficiently extract objects from the services near the search point. The experiment results show that it performs well with respect to both data transmission volume and response time.

1 Introduction

Geospatial data service (GDS) is a type of web service which provides access to collections of geospatial data. User can access remote spatial data through the interface provided GDS.

The following is an application scenario of integrated *k*-NN (k Nearest Neighbor) query based on GDS (IQ4GDS). A user wants to find out k nearest gas stations for a given point. Different gas stations belong to different petroleum companies, while the spatial information belonging to one company may be de-clustered in several GDS and deployed on different servers. So the query may involve several GDS in our scenario. To get an integrated query result, we need a middle process layer, so that user can submit his query request with the uniform mode to it and get the integrated result from it. This is a typical processing of integrated *k*-NN query based on GDS. So, we can define the processing of IQ4GDS formally as following:

Def.1, P is the given search point, k is the number of the neighbors, d is the distance function and S is the set of GDS. The result of integrated *k*-NN query based on S for P denoted by $IQ4GDS(P,k,S)$ can be expressed as:

$$IQ4GDS(P,k,S)=\{(o_1,o_2,...o_k)\mid d(q,o_i)\le d(q,o'),\\ where\ 1\le i\le k, o_i\in\bigcup_{i=0}^{n}S_i, \forall o'\in\bigcup_{i=0}^{n}S_i-\{o_1,o_2,...o_k\}, S=\{S_1,S_2,...S_n\}\} \tag{1}$$

There are few researches on k-NN query based on geospatial data services. T. Schwarz et al [1] realize k-NN query based on numerous loosely coupled, autonomous

H. Zhuge and G.C. Fox (Eds.): GCC 2005, LNCS 3795, pp. 554–559, 2005.

data sources. It presents a method of iteratively enlarging and shrinking the set of relevant data sources. As not using any index, the algorithm must traverse all the data sources and query candidate services in each iterative. It is ineffective. Dan-Zhou Liu et al [2] study how to use window query to realize the k-NN query for remote spatial database. It is only suit for single GDS and the integrated k-NN query based on multiple GDS is much more complex.

The remainder is organized as follows. In section 2 we describe implement method of IQ4GDS. Experiment is given in section 3. At last, we conclude the paper.

2 Integrated k-NN Query Based on GDS

2.1 The Processing Framework of the IQ4GDS

To realize IQ4GDS, we must resolve three problems. The first one is efficient selection of GDS. The second one is searching candidate objects from the candidate services. At last, we need combine candidate objects and return final result to the user. Thus we can describe the processing framework of IQ4GDS as three steps — filter, query and combine. Now, we can design the system architecture for the IQ4GDS which shows in fig1.

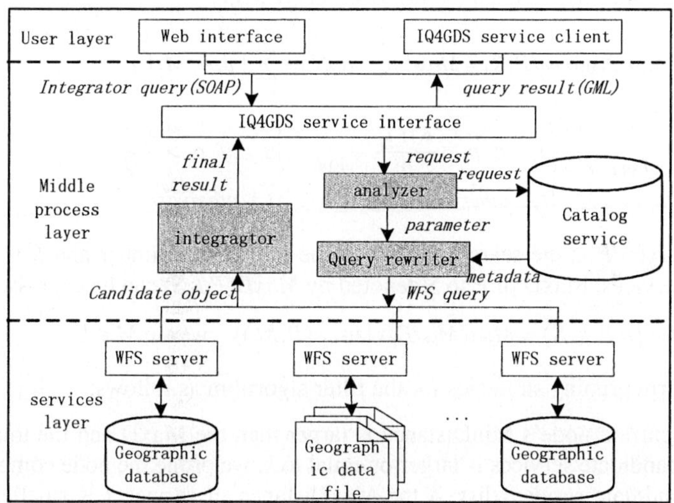

Fig. 1. System Architecture of IQ4GDS

The system is mainly composed of three layers: a user layer, a middle process layer and standard services layer. The main components of middle process layer can be described as following. Analyzer receives a request from user, analyzes the request and extracts query parameters. The filter queries catalog service to get metadata about GDS. It also applies the filter algorithm to selecting candidate GDS. Query rewriter is response to rewrite the query request for each candidate GDS. The integrator is in charge of combining all candidate objects and returning the final result to the user.

2.2 Filter Algorithm for GDS

The experiment result of [4] shows that the modification of the inner data in service has very slight influence on service's MBR, so we can build R-tree index [3] for GDS to improve the filter process.

The index includes two types of node. One is tree type, whose data structure is <*MBR*, *Child-Pointer*>, where *MBR* is the tree node's MBR; *Child-Pointer* is the pointer which points to the sub-tree node. The other one is leaf type, whose data structure can be described as <*MBR*, *NUM*, *Metadata-Pointer*>, where the *MBR* is the geospatial data service's MBR; *NUM* is the total number of objects in the service. The *Metadata-Pointer* is recorder number of the service's metadata in catalog service.

We provide two metrics to order the services in IQ4GDS. The first one is based on the minimum distance (**MinDistance**) of the service's MBR from the search point. The second metric is based on the maximum distance (**MaxD**) from the candidate services list to the search point. **MinDistance** and **MaxD** offer a lower and an upper bound on the actual distance of candidate services from the search point.

Def. 2 [3], $\|(P,o)\|$ is the minimum distance from search point *P* to spatial object o.

Def. 3, MinDistance, *P* is the given search point, the MBR of the GDS is R, MinDistance of *P* to *R* denoted by *MinDintance(P,R)*, is same as MINDIST in [3].

Def. 4, MaxDistance, *P* is the given search point, the MBR of the GDS is R, MaxDistance of *P* to *R* denoted by *MaxDintance(P,R)*,is

$$MaxDistance(P,R) = Max(|p_k - rm_k|^2 + \sum_{\substack{i \neq k \\ 1 \leq i \leq n}}^{n} |p_i - rM_i|^2),$$

$$where\ r_i = \begin{cases} s_k & if\ p_k < \frac{s_k + t_k}{2} \\ t_k & otherwise \end{cases} \quad rM_i = \begin{cases} s_i & if\ p_k > \frac{s_k + t_k}{2} \\ t_i & otherwise \end{cases} \tag{2}$$

Def. 5, MaxD, *P* is the search point, k is the neighbors number and *S* is the set of candidate services, MaxD of *P* to *S* denoted by *MaxD(P,k,S)* can be expressed by:

$$MaxD(P,k,S) = Max(MaxDistance(P,M)) \quad where\ M \in S \tag{3}$$

We confirm pruning strategies for the filter algorithm as follows:

1. When current node's MinDistance is larger than the MaxD and the total number of all candidate services is larger or equal to *k*, we prune the node completely.
2. For candidate services list, if the MaxDistance of service *I* is smaller than the MinDistance of the service *S* which is within the list between the new one and the last one, and the total number of objects of the all services before *I* is larger or equal to *k*, we can remove the *S* from the candidate services list.

The algorithm presented here implements an ordered depth first traversal. We traverse R-tree index root node and proceeds down the tree. Originally, our guess for the MaxD is infinity. During the descending phase, at each newly visited non-leaf node, the algorithm computes the ordering metric bounds for its MBR, and sorts them into a temporary list. We then apply strategy 1 to pruning the unnecessary branches and the algorithm iterates on the temporary list until the list empty. If a service inserts into candidate services list, we use pruning strategy 2 to remove the unnecessary services from the candidate services list. The algorithm is described with pseudo-code in algorithm 1.

Algorithm 1: Geospatial Data Services Filter Algorithm (FilterGDS).
INPUT: Node is current node; Point is search point; k is neighbor number; Total-Num is the total Number of the candidate GDS list; MaxD.
OUTPUT: ListDS is candidate GDS list

```
FilterGDS(Node, Point , k, ListDS, TotalNum,MaxD)
IF Node.type=LEAF   //process the leaf node
   IF PruneBranchList1 (Point, k, Node, ListDS) = FALSE
//using strategy 1 to prune
      Sort(ListDS); Reset( MaxD,TotalNum) ;
      FOR (each n between Node and the last in ListDS)
          PruneBranchList2 (Point, k, n, ListDS)
//using strategy 2 to prune
      END FOR
   END IF
 END IF
 ELSE
   IF PruneBranchList1 (Point, k, Node, ListDS) =FALSE
      Temp [] ←Node.child; Sort (Temp []);
      FOR (each n∈ Temp []) DO
        FilterGDS (n, Point,k, ListDS, TotalNum, MaxD) ;
//iterative call the FilterGDS algorithm
      END FOR
   END IF
 END ELSE
```

From the definitions 2, 3, 4 and 5 we can proof easily that the algorithm can ensure the completeness for the query result.

2.3 Query Rewrite and Combine for IQ4GDS

WFS complying with recent standard WFS implement specification [6] can't provide *k*-NN query interface. We can't submit *k*-NN query request directly to the WFS. BBOX operator is a standard spatial operator, which fetches all the objects within the region of interest. So we can rewrite *k*-NN query with BBOX spatial operator. Now the left problem is to confirm the size of the region. We use the range estimation algorithm based on density proposed in [2] to estimating the range of the region and using iterative BBOX operator until getting satisfy result.

The number of candidate objects may be larger than k, we use the existing algorithm proposed in [3] to combine them and return the final result to the user.

3 Experiment

We use synthetic spatial data (SSSD) and real world spatial data (SRSD) to test algorithm's performance. The characteristics of GDS are in table 1:

Table 1. Characteristics of GDS

	Feature type	Minimum number	Maximum number	Feature number	GDS volume (k)	Feature volume (b)
SSSD	Point	15	1 500	100	800	8
SRSD	Polygon	10	890	560	4 540	4 889

Experiment 1: We execute experiment with SSSD. The result in table 2 shows the GDS called increase with k and iteration decrease with k.

Table 2. Average Number of GDS called and Iteration of BBOX Operation in SSSD

K	1	5	10	15	20	50	100	500	1000
Called GDS	37	39	36	40	57	84	132	203	345
Iteration	4.3	3.7	3.3	3.2	3.1	2.9	1.6	1.2	1

Experiment 2: We review three type methods to implement IQ4GDS. Firstly, we use both FilterGDS algorithm and BBOX operator—B4NN; secondly, we only use FilterGDS algorithm—F4NN; lastly we download all the objects in all GDS—F4NN;

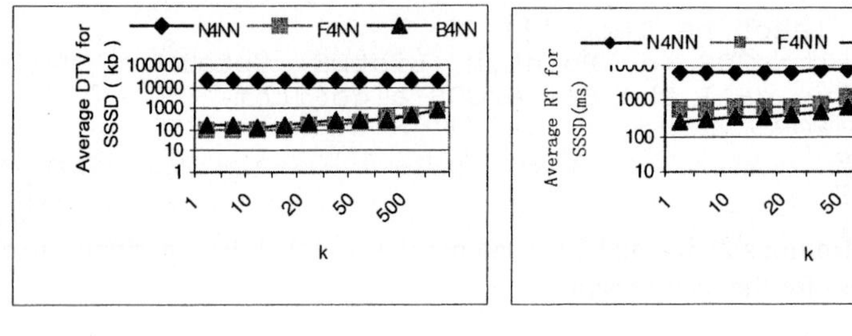

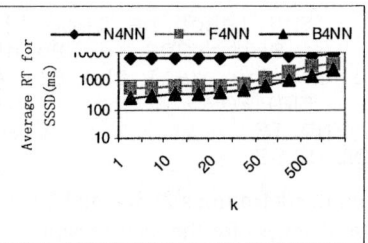

(a) Average DTV (b) Average RT

Fig. 2. Compare the Query Performance for SSSD

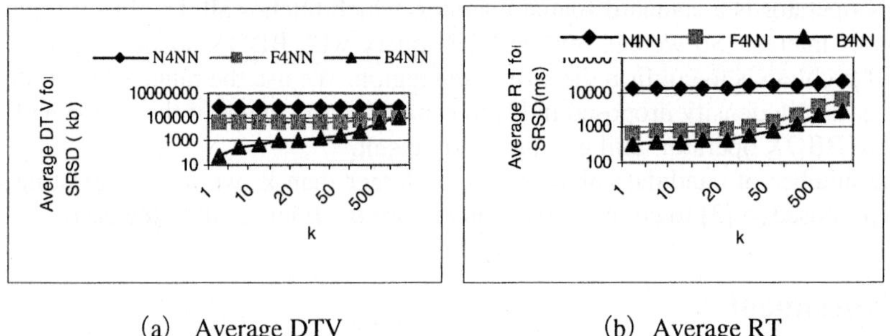

(a) Average DTV (b) Average RT

Fig. 3. Compare the Query Performance for SRSD

We use data transmission volume (DTV) and response time (RT) to evaluate the performance of the algorithm. The result shows in fig 2 and 3 from which we can know that IQ4GDS algorithm can perform well on both data transmission volume and response time.

In SSSD the data type is point. When k is small, the actual data has small proportion in the SOAP messages, thus the efficiency is not evident. However the data type in SRSD is polygon, each object has larger data. Even when k is small, the actual data has large proportion in the SOAP message. The efficient is very high. Comparing the fig 2 and 3, we can know that the larger the data is the more efficient is. As FilterGDS algorithm and efficient query rewritten method reduce the number of the candidate objects, the data transmission volume is reduced while the local k-NN query processing is quickened.

4 Conclusion

In this paper, we focus on integrated *k*-NN query based on multiple GDS. Our main contributions are:

- We propose a processing framework and design the system architecture for integrated *k*-NN query processing based on GDS, the architecture complies with SOA (Service oriented architecture).
- We realize the integrated *k*-NN query processing based on multiple GDS.
- We present an algorithm to filter GDS which can't affect the query result and discuss an efficient query rewritten method to obtain *k*-NN for GDS.
- We conduct experiments to test performance of the proposed algorithm. The results show that the algorithm performs well with respect to both data transmission volume and response time.

References

1. T. Schwarz, M. Iofcea, M. Grossmann, N. Hönle, D. Nicklas, B. Mitschang (University of Stuttgart): On Efficiently Processing Nearest Neighbor Queries in a Loosely Coupled Set of Data Source, ACM GIS'04, 2004, Washington, DC, USA, pp.184-193.
2. Dan-Zhou Liu, Ee-Peng Lim, Wee-Keong Ng: Efficient k Nearest Neighbor Queries on Remote Spatial Databases Using Range Estimation, Proc. of the 14th Intl. Conf. on Scientific and Statistical Database Management (SSDBM'02), Edinburgh, Scotland, July 2002, pp. 121-130
3. Nick Roussopoulos, Stephen Kelley, and Fr´ed´eric Vincent: Nearest neighbor queries, In Proceedings of the ACM SIGMOD, pages 71-79, 1995.
4. Roger Zimmermann, Wei-Shinn Ku, and Wei-Cheng Chu: Efficient Query Routing in Distributed Spatial Databases, ACM GIS '04, Washington,DC,USA pp.176-183.
5. A.Guttman: R-trees: a dynamic index structure for spatial searching, In Proceedings of ACM/SIGMOD Annual Conference on Management of Data, 1984,pp.47-57.
6. Open GIS Consortium: Web Feature Service Implementation Specification Document. Version: 1.1.0 3-May-2005, http://www.opengis.org/

SGII: Towards Semantic Grid-Based Enterprise Information Integration*

Jingtao Zhou, Shusheng Zhang, Han Zhao, and Mingwei Wang

National Specialty Laboratory of CAD/CAM, Northwestern Polytechnical University, Xi'an, China, 710072
zhoujt@mail.nwpu.edu.cn, {zssnet, Wangmv}@nwpu.edu.cn, zhaohanboy@hotmail.com

Abstract. To fully leverage the information from different data sources and applications, an enterprise needs a generic, interoperable and flexible infrastructure to integrate and coordinate information across back-end data sources on semantic level. Through undertaking research at the intersection of the Semantic Web and Grid, the Semantic Grid expects to establish a semantic interconnection environment to effectively organize, share, cluster, fuse, and manage globally distributed versatile resources. In this context, we introduce SGII, an EII (Enterprise Information Integration) infrastructure based on Semantic Grid vision to achieve adaptive and intelligence information sharing. A survey of existent solutions is made to provide evidence of the benefits from Semantic Grid in the context of integration and interoperation of enterprise information. A primary architecture for SGII is introduced based on the analysis of realizing the vision of an infrastructure for semantic information integration on grid.

1 Introduction

In spite of extensive R&D and successful pilots, current enterprise information infrastructure is poorly suited for dealing with the continuing, rapid explosion in enterprise data. One underlying problem has remained unsolved: data resides in thousands of incompatible formats and cannot be systematically managed, integrated, unified or cleansed [1]. On the other hand, because semantic inconsistency has become an even great problem on the explicit information or knowledge sharing among users or applications, access level data integration has never given enterprise a competitive edge. Only by semantic, or knowledge level integration can enterprise gain insight into its workflow and business process.

Meanwhile, grid is expected to be the solution to the "islands of computation" problem [2], but it could also be the solution to the "islands of information" problem when it is extended to Semantic Grid, which wants to create an internetcentered interconnection environment on the grid to effectively organize, share, cluster, fuse, and manage globally distributed versatile resources based on the interconnection semantics [3]. In the context of enterprise information integration and sharing, Semantic

* Funding for this work is supported by Chinese 863/CIMS and Chinese National Research Foundation for Doctoral Program of Higher Education through The National Key Laboratory of CAD/CAM in NWPU Contract No. (2002AA414210) and (20030699032) respectively.

H. Zhuge and G.C. Fox (Eds.): GCC 2005, LNCS 3795, pp. 560–565, 2005.

Grid could provide a competently basic infrastructure for ensuring the information interoperation and collaboration both on system and semantic level.

2 Survey

2.1 Enterprise Information Integration

Enterprises have long recognized the value of data integration. Efforts can be roughly classified into two categories: application centric integration (ACI) and data centric integration (DCI).

ACI, such as point to point integration and enterprise application integration (EAI), integrates relative data by linking applications through custom-coding or integration broker that acts as a hub to route messages between connected applications. Tight-coupling of technology and systems, N^2 problem at data layer, multiple vendors for multiple systems, lack of common protocols make these solutions difficultly suitable to an open, dynamic environment of businesses and operations in or across enterprises.

DCI can be implemented by creating either a centralized repository for data access and analysis, such as data warehouses, or a data integrating layer over a set of distinct and autonomous data sources, such as federated information systems. Although some researches on DCI follow a semantic integration approach, they are hard to implement interoperability across corporate boundaries or between them and other information systems because of the using of proprietary metadata, representation.

2.2 Data Integration on Grid

In the context of information sharing, Grid technologies distinguish current technologies in enterprise as discussed above by providing not a generic approach but also an open and standard-based infrastructure.

The current efforts of the Data Grid community concentrate on providing a global, uniform access methodology for all database resources. Meanwhile, information grid projects shift the emphasis on information integration and mediation. Moreover, the emerging of Semantic Grid is beginning to take this further, from information to semantic or knowledge. Some projects, such as COG [4] and Dart-Grid [5] explore this trend in the context of information integration.

The COG project aims to integrate disparate data sources on semantic level by using a central Information Model (i.e. ontology). However, although COG means "Corporate Ontology Grid", it does not seem to intend to use general Grid technologies. In essence, it is a solution following an ontology-based information integration approach [6]. Compared to COG, Dart-Grid is an OGSA-based Database Grid originally motivated by the application of web-based data sharing and database integration for Traditional Chinese Medicine. In particular, data sources integrated by Dart-Grid are mainly databases, other data sources such as documents, and data sources that stream data in real or pseudo-real time from applications are not supported by current Dart-Grid. Furthermore, details of some crucial issues concerned by enterprise, such as security, authorization, transaction, etc., are not addressed.

Furthermore, semantic interoperation based on single ontology such as in COG and Dart-Grid may fall short where one information source has a different view on a domain, or information sources are on changing [6]. Accordingly, in this way, it is difficult to achieve semantic interoperability across department and corporate boundaries, realize inter-domain information sharing.

Based on the review of the survey, we observe that common infrastructure and generic approach in the context of semantic information integration for enterprise business and daily operation have to date not been addressed in semantic gird community. This is a key contribution of our project.

3 Vision

SGII, described in this paper, is a generic, interoperable, pervasive, open and flexible Semantic-Grid-based infrastructure for EII in a generic way, while creating a semantic interconnection environment for enterprise information sources. The vision of SGII focuses on four aspects:

1) For infrastructure, SGII wants to provide an open platform that enables distributed information sources to be shared, managed, coordinated, and controlled both on system and semantic level.
2) For enterprise data sources, SGII aims at making them machine understandable and interoperable by enriching them using semantics and wrapping them using services.
3) For applications in enterprise, SGII expects to provide understandable and operable information and services for individual and common application domains.
4) For users in enterprise, SGII can provide a global, real time, and 360-degree view of enterprise information on semantic level.

4 Elementary Architecture

To enable the vision of SGII, we propose the elementary architecture of SGII based on the Open Grid Service Architecture [7], which makes SGII a generic infrastructure for semantic integration of enterprise information. Every function in SGII is independently realized as a grid service on top of the Open Grid Service Infrastructure and translated into semantic grid service through semantic enrichment. In essence, SGII is semantic grid service oriented architecture.

As shown in figure 1, the architecture consists of four spaces or layers: *Data Sources Space*, *Support Service Space*, *Mediation Service Space* and *Application Support Service Space*. Except Data Sources Space, the services of low-space provide more common functionality than the services of upper-space, and help reducing complexity of upper-space services.

Data Sources Space is a collection of data sources which can be classified into two categorizes: *Grid-Enabled Information Repositories* and data sources that *Stream Data from Applications*. Note that we regard stream data from applications as data

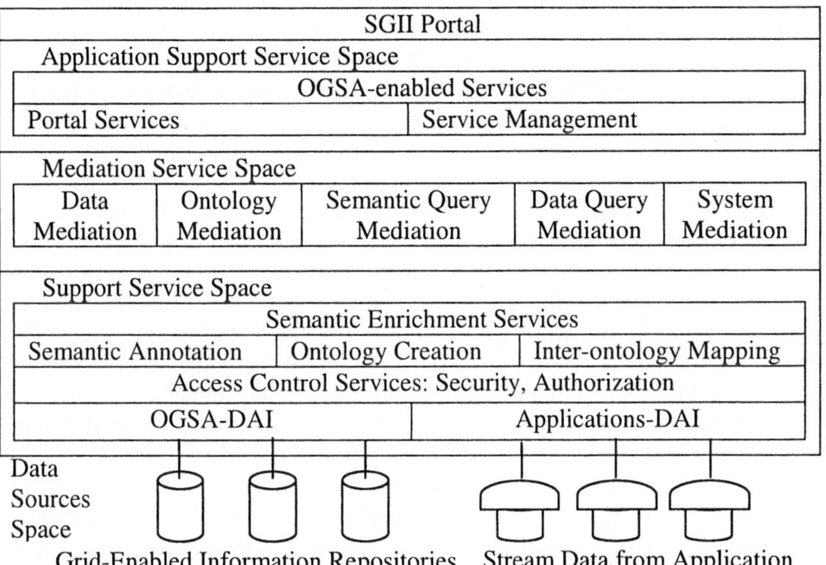

Fig. 1. Elementary Architecture of SGII

sources because there are growing needs to integrate results from applications. In particular, we may also integrate data through application when the direct access of data source is forbidden. This is the common occasion in an enterprise. The Grid-Enabled Information Repositories generally refer to the storage of all information relevant to enterprise businesses and daily operations, including data and metadata. Moreover, the information produced by SGII (including management information, operational information, and metadata for data sources and services, etc.) is also stored into grid-enabled information repositories.

Support Service Space constructs common and basic services for SGII by providing *Access Control Services* and *Semantic Enrichment Services*.

The Access Control Services are responsible for the guarantee of flexible information access control with the support of *OGSA-DAI* [8] and *Applications-DAI*. Based on OGSA, the Data Access and Integration (OGSA-DAI) infrastructure can model heterogeneous data sources as grid services and integrate them into SGII architecture. Analogy with OGSA-DAI, Applications-DAI (Data Access and Integration of application data) is responsible for wrapping data sources that stream data from applications as OGSA-compatible grid services and integrate them into SGII architecture. Furthermore, OGSA-DAI and Applications-DAI provide basic data access capability to SGII.

Semantic Enrichment Services deal with relative topics of semantic enriching, which include *Semantic Annotation*, *Ontology Creation*, and *Inter-ontology Mapping* services. Semantic Annotation service is used to enrich data and service content based on pre-defined ontologies by using automatic or semi-automatic semantic annotation tools. Ontology Creation service wraps a semi-automatic approach as OGSA-compatible grid service to create ontologies on the basis of a process of semantic discovering, explanation and user modeling. These ontologies constitute the conceptual backbone for information-level and semantic-level interoperability, which is the basis of semantic enrichment. To achieve pervasive interoperability among (extra-) enterprise information sources, SGII requires the support of multi-ontology. Accordingly, Inter-ontology Mapping service makes this to be reality by creating interconnection semantics based on semantic mapping between ontologies.

Mediation Service Space provides services to mediate conflicting processes, semantics, and information without custom written programs for the purposes of information sharing by operationalizing system, ontology and data sources. It includes five categories of services: *Data Mediation*, *Ontology Mediation*, *Semantic Query Mediation*, *Data Query Mediation* and *System Mediation*. Data Mediation is an approach to simplify the work with multiple, federated, and usually geographically distributed data sources. Built on top of OGSA-DAI, it is capable of mediating any grid enabled information repositories by mediation data models or ontologies, of which data source schemas are defined as the views. Ontology Mediation, together with Inter-ontology Mapping service in Support Service Space, is used to facilitate creating and maintaining consistency semantic interconnections between ontologies. It uses semantic relationships as semantic mediation model rather than a global ontology. Semantic Query Mediation performs semantic query following a mediation centric approach based on ontology mediation mechanism. This service decomposes semantic queries into sub-semantic-queries on corresponding ontologies. Finally, each sub-semantic-query is translated into sub-data-queries on corresponding data sources according to the semantic relations between ontologies and data sources. System Mediation Service is used to monitor, tune, and manage system transactions and resolve conflicts between transactions, such as synchronal happening of cross-data query and update on the same data sources. Furthermore, it is also in charge of dynamic clustering process of data and services for specific information integration and sharing task.

Application Support Service Space provides services called *Portal Services* for front end enterprise applications (e.g., e-commerce, B-to-B, CRM, ERP, EIP, etc.). In order to ensure that relative services in SGII can get in enterprise business and operation environment, SGII uses Portal Services on top of OGSA as delegations or broker services, which enables enterprise applications to use these services in a standard and easy way as long as they observe compatible specifications of OGSA. *Service Management* service in this space is responsible for the management of each portal service.

5 Conclusions

The application based on Semantic Grid concept for provision of effective information resource sharing in and across industrial enterprises is promising. However, it needs more industrial case studies to be carried out in order to evaluate finally the utility of information and semantic interoperability based on SGII. Many relevant aspects of a complete SGII integration environment are not addressed in this paper so far. We will show more details in our further work.

References

1. Schreiber Z.: Semantic Information Management (SIM): Solving the Enterprise Data Problem by Managing Data based On Its Business Meaning. Unicorn Executive White Paper (2003)
2. Hannus, M., Penttilä H., Silén P.: Islands of Automation. http://cic.vtt.fi/hannus/islands.html (1987 - updated by Hannus, M. 2002)
3. Hai Z.G.: Semantic Grid: Scientific Issues, Infrastructure, and Methodology. Communications of the ACM, Vol. 48, No. 4 (2005): 117–119
4. Bruijn J.: Semantic Information Integration in the COG project. Technical report by IFI (2004)
5. Zhaohui W., Huajun C., Shuiguang D., Yuxing M.: DartGrid: RDF-Mediated Database Integration and Process Coordination Using Grid as the Platform. Lecture Notes in Computer Science, Vol. 3399. Springer-Verlag, Berlin Heidelberg New York (2005) 351–363
6. Wache, H., Voegele, T., Visser U., Stuckenschmidt. H., Schuster, G., Neumann, H., Huebner, S.: Ontology-based integration of information - a survey of existing approaches. In: Proceedings of IJCAI workshop on Ontologies and Information Sharing (2001):108–117
7. Foster, I., Kesselman, C., Nick, J., Tuecke, S.: The physiology of the grid: An open grid services architecture for distributed systems integration. In: Open Grid Service Infrastructure WG, Global Grid Forum (2002)
8. Atkinson, M., et al.: Data access, integration, and management in The Grid. Blueprint for a New Computing Infrastructure. San Mateo, CA: Morgan Kaufmann (2004)

The Architecture of SIG Computing Environment and Its Application to Image Processing

Chunhui Yang[1], Deke Guo[1], Yan Ren[1], Xueshan Luo[1], and Jinfeng Men[2]

[1] School of Information Systems and Management,
National University of Defense Technology,
Changsha, China, 410073
[2] Key Lab of CFC, National University of Defense Technology
ych_ld@sina.com, aeronautic@126.com,
yanzi916_78@hotmail.com

Abstract. Spatial Information Grid (SIG) is a project of applying grid technology to share and integrate spatial data resources, information processing resources, equipment resources, and knowledge resources. SIG computing environment aims to apply the concept of SIG to share hybrid computing resources for processing remote sensing (RS) images. RS image processing is a data-intensive computing problem, and it adapts to be processed according data parallel computing model. In this paper, we discuss the architecture of SIG computing environment, which can provide a powerful computing infrastructure used to process RS image cooperatively. In order to achieve high performance, we propose a model of the image division. From the relation among the processing time, the communication latency, and the transferring ratio, we can achieve some useful conclusions to determine the strategy of the image division. Furthermore, we can discover two optimal division strategies through comparing the experimental results with those useful conclusions.

1 Introduction

With the rapid development of RS technology and the increasing complexity of computation, more and more RS images make the processing of them in a single PC almost impossible [1]. Now we can utilize the idle resources in the Internet by grid computing technology to finish many tasks which are data intensive or computing intensive. Till now, there have been some successful cases, such as EU dataGrid [2], SETI@home [3], ChinaGrid [4], VEGA [5], and so on.

The task of processing the RS image just has the properties of data intensive and computing intensive, and then it adapts to parallel processing. Dividing a computing task into smaller computing tasks and assigning them to different processors for parallel execution are the two key steps in the design of parallel algorithms [6]. In this paper, we focus on the RS image division, which is the key step of decomposing the computing task. In the division model, we discuss the situations respectively whether the idle time between communication and computing on a host exists or not. Furthermore, we get two optimal division strategies according to the trend of the processing time with the image size and the relation among processing time, communication latency, and transferring time.

H. Zhuge and G.C. Fox (Eds.): GCC 2005, LNCS 3795, pp. 566–572, 2005.

The remainder of the paper is organized as follows. The next section introduces the architecture of SIG computing environment. Section 3 focuses on the computing model of dividing image. And we validate the conclusions by the experimental results. Finally, we draw the conclusion and give out the future work in section 4.

2 The Architecture of SIG Computing Environment

SIG computing environment is mainly composed of GT [7], OpenPBS, and Condor/Condor-G [8]. OpenPBS and Condor are the local resources schedulers, each of which is responsible for managing a cluster. And the cluster's worknodes are the foundation of SIG computing environment, whose responsibilities are providing computing power. Condor-G is the upper level. Users directly contact Condor-G to submit the jobs and monitor the status of jobs. GT establishes a bridge between batch systems and Condor-G. It supplies many essential services and protocols for grid computing, such as data management, resource allocation and management, security service, and information services [9][10]. The architecture of SIG computing environment is shown in Fig.1 [11][12].

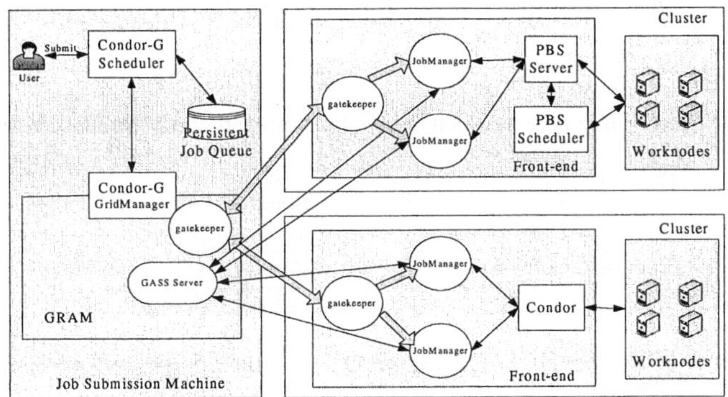

Fig. 1. The grid environment architecture

3 The Strategy of the Image Division

It is critical that scheduling the tasks of processing the small image pieces in SIG computing environment for achieving high performance. In our scenario, we pre-determine the size of each image piece. Then the parallel tasks are fixed-sized tasks. At the same time, there are no task synchronizations and no inter-task communications. Therefore, the scheduling problem is challenging due to the communication and transferring time involved when starting tasks [13].

From [14], we know that in any optimal solution all worknodes should participate in the computation. In SIG computing environment, the number of worknodes is pre-determined. Therefore, we should divide the image into pieces which are the multiple of the number of worknodes. Now the question is how many rounds we should make each worknode executing the tasks.

3.1 The Division Model and Some Conclusions

In the model, we suppose there are N worknodes, which are homogeneous platforms. At the same time, all of them are identical. Hence, the execution time of job is the same, independent of which worknode the job is place on [15]. For communications, the one-port model is used: the master can only communicate with a single worknode at a given time-step. At the same time, we fix the communication latency to simplify the model. Before submitting a job to worknode, the master needs communication with worknodes and transfers the input data into a worknode. Moreover, the communication and computing can not be overhead, i.e. each node can be assigned a new job only after it has finished the previous job.

According to whether the idle time between communication and computing on a host exists or not, we can divide the division strategy into two situations.

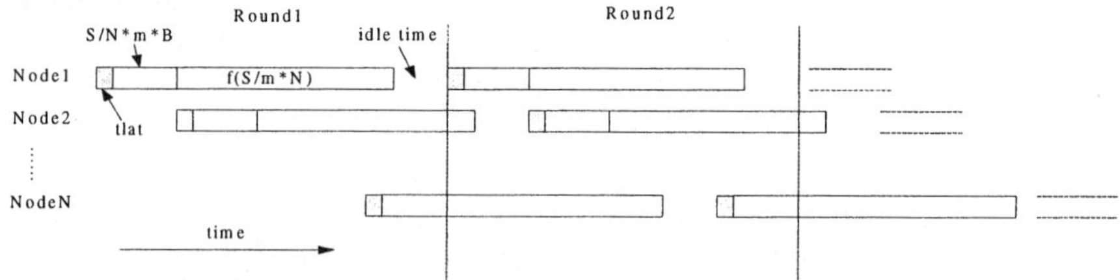

Fig. 2. There is idle time between communication and computing in situation A

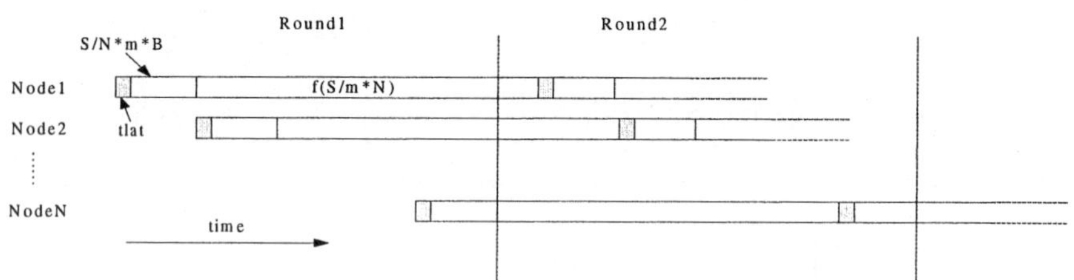

Fig. 3. There is no idle time between communication and computing in situation B

Situation A: As shown in Fig.2, there is idle time between communication and computing, that is:

$$f\left(\frac{S}{m \cdot N}\right) < \left(tLat + \frac{S}{m \cdot N \cdot B}\right) \cdot (N - 1) \tag{1}$$

Where S is the size of input data; m is the number of round, and it is a natural number; N is the number of worknodes; $tLat$ is a fixed overhead for starting a job, incurred by the master to initiate a job to a worknode [14]; B is the data transfer rate to worknode; and $f\left(\frac{S}{m \cdot N}\right)$ is the time of processing each image piece, which is the function of the image size.

In this situation, the whole processing time is:

$$T_{wm}^{(1)} = (tLat + \frac{S}{m \cdot N \cdot B}) \cdot m \cdot N + f(\frac{S}{m \cdot N}) \tag{2}$$

In this situation, there is no idle time between two communications, then the whole time is the sum of the time of all communication and transferring adding the computing time of a piece.

So, in situation A, the best division strategy is:

$$\min T_{wm}^{(1)} = (tLat + \frac{S}{m \cdot N \cdot B}) \cdot m \cdot N + f(\frac{S}{m \cdot N}) \tag{3}$$

Where m is a natural number. And equation (3) is subject to equation (1).

Situation B: As show in Fig.3, the processing time of each piece should be equal to or longer than the time of all other worknodes receiving the input data in a round. That is:

$$f(\frac{S}{m \cdot N}) \geq (tLat + \frac{S}{m \cdot N \cdot B}) \cdot (N - 1) \tag{4}$$

In this situation, the whole processing time is:

$$T_{wm}^{(2)} = (tLat + \frac{S}{m \cdot N \cdot B}) \cdot (N + m - 1) + m \cdot f(\frac{S}{m \cdot N}) \tag{5}$$

In this situation, there are no idle time between communication and computing. Therefore, the whole processing time is equal to the whole working time of worknode N add the communication and transferring time of other (N-1) worknodes in round 1.

In this situation, the best division strategy will make $T_{wm}^{(2)}$ into the minimum, i.e.

$$\min T_{wm}^{(2)} = (tLat + \frac{S}{m \cdot N \cdot B}) \cdot (N + m - 1) + m \cdot f(\frac{S}{m \cdot N}) \tag{6}$$

Where m is a natural number. And equation (6) is subject to equation (4).

Therefore, the final division strategy is the smaller one of $\min T_{wm}^{(1)}$ and $\min T_{wm}^{(2)}$. Then the image will be divided into $m \cdot N$ pieces.

We can get the best division strategy by calculating according to the above equations. But after analyzing the model, we can get some simple conclusions.

At first, we suppose the three trends of processing time with the image size are case A, B and C, each means that $m \cdot f(\frac{S}{m \cdot N})$ is greater than, equal to, and less than $(m+1) \cdot f(\frac{S}{(m+1) \cdot N})$.

In situation A, it is easy to decide the value of m, we define the $\Delta T_{wm}^{(1)}$:

$$\Delta T_{wm}^{(1)} = T_{wm}^{(1)} - T_{w(m+1)}^{(1)} = -N \cdot tLat + m \cdot f(\frac{S}{m \cdot N}) - (m+1) \cdot f(\frac{S}{(m+1) \cdot N}) \tag{7}$$

If $\Delta T_{wm}^{(1)} \geq 0$, the image should be divided unceasingly. Thus, if the function of processing time belongs to the case B or C, we should not continue dividing the image. Or else, we should continue dividing the image.

In situation B, we define the $\Delta T_{wm}^{(2)}$:

$$\Delta T_{wm}^{(2)} = T_{wm}^{(2)} - T_{w(m+1)}^{(2)} = \frac{1}{m\cdot(m+1)} \cdot \frac{(N-1)\cdot S}{N\cdot B} - tLat + m\cdot f(\frac{S}{m\cdot N}) - (m+1)\cdot f(\frac{S}{(m+1)\cdot N}) \qquad (8)$$

Where $tLat$ is usually small and the first item is always positive. Therefore, in equation (8), if $f(x)$ belongs to the case A or B, we should continue dividing the image until it is restricted by the condition of equation (6). When $f(x)$ belongs to the case C, it is difficult to make decision of division. We can only get the decision by calculation.

In our application, the time of division and makeup is the function of image size and not changing with the number of pieces, and the reduction of the whole time is only connected with the function of edge detecting.

3.2 Experimental Results

As for our application, the whole system is a mode of master and worknode. In our experiment, we apply the PBS client as the worknode and there are 4 worknodes. The parameters are as follows: $N=4$; $tLat=3.0$s; $B=10.25$Mb/s; $S=467.0$Mb.

Suppose $F(m) = f(\frac{S}{m\cdot N})$, $T_{comm} = (tLat + \frac{S}{m\cdot N\cdot B})\cdot(N-1)$, the relation of them in our application can be contracted as Fig.4. As shown in Fig.4, when $m \le 2$, $F(m) > T_{comm}$, it belongs to situation B. At the same time, $m\cdot f(\frac{S}{m\cdot N}) > (m+1)\cdot f(\frac{S}{(m+1)\cdot N})$, it accords with the condition of case A. Therefore, according to the above conclusion, $m=2$ is the best strategy in situation B. When $m \ge 3$, $F(m) < T_{comm}$, it belongs to situation A, and it also belongs to case C. Thus, $m=3$ can get the shortest executing time in situation A.

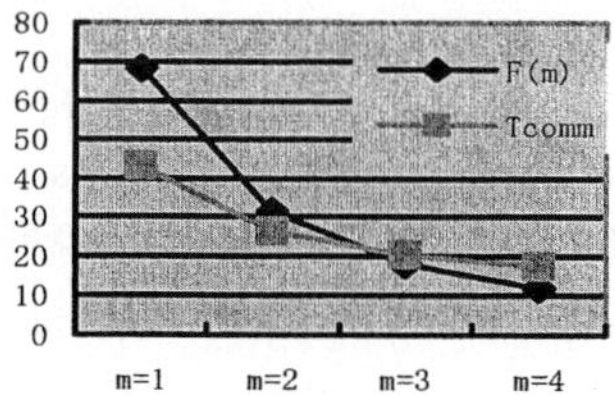

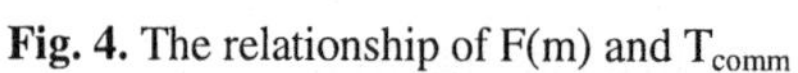
Fig. 4. The relationship of F(m) and T_{comm}

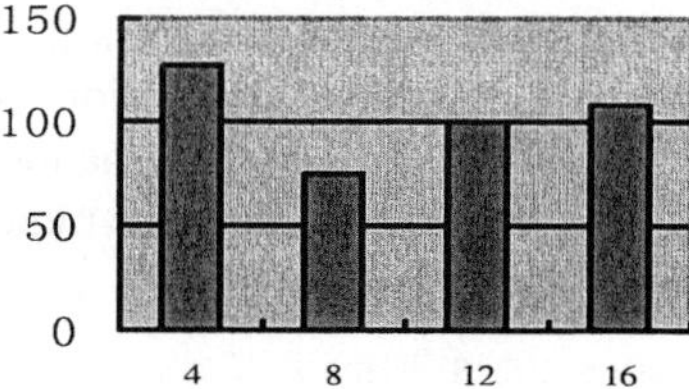

Fig. 5. Different divisions lead to different processing time

As shown in Fig.5, when the image is divided into 8 pieces, it is the best division strategy of situation B. And 12 pieces is best for situation A. Therefore, the final strategy is dividing the image into 8 pieces. The experimental results show that the division strategy is optimal.

4 Conclusion and Future Work

This paper presents SIG computing environment, which is based on the grid middleware Globus Toolkit and utilizes the computing resources with hybrid structure. We apply the SIG environment to the processing of RS image. We propose the model of the image division, which can compute the most appropriate image pieces and make the processing time short. And experimental results show that the model and the conclusions are logical.

In the future, we will develop the web portal by using the API of Condor-G and enclose the whole workflow of image processing into a service, which makes it more easily to apply. On the other hand, the study of load balance is an important part of future work.

Acknowledgement

This work is supported by the National High Technology Research and Development Program of China under grant No.2002AA104220, 2002AA131010, and 2002AA134010.

References

1. H. Zhou, X. Yang, and Y. Tang et al, Research and Implementation of Grid-Enabled Parallel Algorithm of Geometric Correction in ChinaGrid, The 3rd International workshop on Grid and Cooperative Computing (GCC2004), Wuhan, 2004, pp. 704-711.
2. http://eu-datagrid.web.cern.ch/eu-datagrid.
3. http://setiathome.ssl.berkeley.edu.
4. http://www.chinagrid.edu.cn.
5. Z. Xu and W. Li, Research on VEGA Grid Architecture, Journal of Computing Research and Development, Vol.39, No.8, 2002, pp. 923-929.
6. A. Grama, A. Gupta, and G. Karypis et al, Introduction to Parallel Computing, Second Edition, Addison Wesley, 2003.
7. http://www.globus.org.
8. http://www.cs.wisc.edu/condor.
9. I. Foster and C. Kesselman, The Grid2: Blueprint for a New Computing Infrastructure, Morgan Kaufmann Publishers, 2004.
10. S. Chen, W. Zhang, and F. Ma et al, The Design of a Grid Computing System for Drug Discovery and Design, The 3rd International workshop on Grid and Cooperative Computing (GCC2004), Wuhan, 2004, pp. 799-802.
11. J. Frey, T. Tannenbaum, and I. Foster et al, Condor-G: A Computation Management Agent for Multi-Institutional Grids, Proceedings of the Tenth IEEE Symposium on High Performance Distributed Computing (HPDC10) San Francisco, California, 2001, pp.55-64.
12. A. Waananen, M. Ellert, and A. Konstantinov et al, An overview of an Architecture Proposal for a High Energy Physics Grid, Proc. Applied Parallel Computing (PARA 2002), LNCS 2367, Springer-Verlag, 2002, pp. 76-86.

13. O. Beaumount, H. Casanova , and A. Legrand et al, Scheduling Divisible Loads on Star and Tree Networks: Results and Open Problems, IEEE Transactions on Parallel and Distributed Systems, Vol.16, No.3, 2005, pp. 207-218.
14. Y. Yang, H. Casanova, Multi-round algorithm for scheduling divisible workload applications: analysis and experimental evaluation, Tech. Rep. CS2002-0721, Department of Computer Science and Engineering, University of California, San Diego, 2002.
15. T. Hsu, J. C. Lee, and D. R. Lopez et al, Task Allocation on a Network of Processors, IEEE Transactions on Computers, Vol.49, No.12, 2000, pp. 1339-1353.

The Computation of Semantic Data Cube

Yubao Liu and Jian Yin

Department of Computer Science of Sun Yat-Sen University,
510275, Guangzhou, P.R. China
{liuyubao, issjyin}@zsu.edu.cn

Abstract. The multidimensional analysis based on data cube has been growing interest. However existing data cube model usually does not have the semantics of attributes and hence the analysis usually provides results with raw numbers and ignores the real meanings of these numbers. An example result is that the total sales of PC in this year are above 2000. The semantics of sale performance, high or low, is not clear and that is not easy to be understood for decision makers. The semantic data cube model with linguistic semantics is presented in this paper. The semantic data cube uses fuzzy set to represent the linguistic semantics of the dimensions and measures of data cube. The computation of semantic data cube is studied and the serial and parallel computation algorithms are presented. The experiments on the synthetic datasets show that the algorithms are scalable and efficient.

1 Introduction

Recently, there have been growing interests in multidimensional analysis of data warehouses [1]. Most of such analyses involve data cube [2] based summary analysis. However existing data cube model usually does not have the semantics and hence the analysis usually provides results with raw numbers and ignores the real meaning of these numbers. An example result is that the total sales of PC in this year are above 2000. The semantics of sale performance, high or low, is not clear and that is not easy to be understood for the decision makers. Fuzzy technology provides a useful method for describing the interface between human conceptual categories and data. In this paper, the semantic data cube model with such linguistic semantics is presented. It uses fuzzy set to represent the linguistic semantics of dimensions and measures of data cube. The computation of semantic data cube is studied and the serial computation algorithm sCRT and parallel psCRT (short for parallel semantic cube computation from relation table) are presented to compute the semantic data cube from relation table. The performance of the computation algorithms is tested on the synthetic (i.e. algorithmically generated) datasets and the results show that the algorithms are scalable and efficient.

There are some related works regarding our problem. In qc-trees [3], the structural semantics of data cube, such as, the roll up and drill down operations of data cube are studied. Those structural semantics are different from our linguistic semantics.

H. Zhuge and G.C. Fox (Eds.): GCC 2005, LNCS 3795, pp. 573–578, 2005.

In explanatory semantics model [4], the fuzzy technology is also used to construct fuzzy data cube model and it is the closest to the semantic data cube in this paper. However, the explanatory semantics model mainly focuses on the semantics of measure attributes. The semantics of dimension attributes are not considered. In semantic data cube, the linguistic semantics of measures and dimensions are both represented. In addition, the computation of cube model is not given in [4]. The existing cube computation algorithm [5] mainly studied the computation of general data cube from relation table. The semantics are not included in the computation algorithm. The semantic cube model is also different from the RSM model included in the knowledge grid platform [6], in the foundation, the managed objects, the normalization basis, the operation feature, and the interchange basis aspects.

2 Preliminaries

2.1 Fuzzy Set

The concept of a fuzzy set extends the notion of a regular crisp set in order to express classes with ill-defined boundaries, corresponding in particular to linguistic values such as "tall", "young", "important" etc. Within this framework, there is a gradual rather than sharp transition between non-membership and full membership. A degree of membership is associated with every element x of the universal set X. It takes its value in the interval [0,1] instead of the pair {0,1}. Such a membership assigning function $\mu_A: X \rightarrow [0,1]$ is called a membership function and the set defined by it is a fuzzy set. The concept of "α-cut" of a fuzzy set means a subset made of those elements whose membership is over or equal to α: $(A_\alpha=\{x \in X | \mu_A(x) \geq \alpha \})$. A fuzzy predicate expresses the degree to which the arguments satisfy the predicate.

2.2 Data Cube Model

The CUBE BY operator [2] is a multidimensional extension of relational GROUP BY operator and is used to compute a data cube from a relation table. While the semantics of the CUBE BY operator is to partition a relation into groups based on the values of the attributes specified in the CUBE BY operator and then apply aggregations functions to each of such groups, the CUBE BY operator computes GROUP BY corresponding to all possible combinations of attributes in the CUBE BY operator. In general, a CUBE BY operator on n attributes computes 2^n GROUP BYs, or cuboids. The grouping attributes are called dimensions and the aggregated attributes are called measures. A tuple with dimension attributes and measure attributes in a data cube is called a cell.

In this paper, we call such cuboid that is partitioned on j dimensions size-j cuboid. For example, cuboid A is a size-1 cuboid and cuboid AB, that is partitioned on dimensions A and B, is a size-2 cuboid. Especially, the cuboid ALL is called size-0 cuboid.

3 Semantic Data Cube Model

Table.1 shows a semantic data cube with historical sales data. There are three cells in the data cube. The dimensions attributes are 'product', 'year' and 'location' and the measure attribute is 'sales amount'.

Table 1. An example of a semantic data cube

Product	Year semantics	Location	Sales semantics
PC	Recent/1	Guangzhou	High/1
TV	Recent/1	Shanghai	Ordinary/0.8
Camera	Old/0.6	Beijing	Low/1

In table.1, the 'year' dimension includes the semantic information, 'recent/1' and 'old/0.6', and the 'sales amount' measure also includes the similar semantics that describe the sales performance such as 'high/1', 'ordinary/0.8' and 'low/1'. As shown in the table, the semantics of dimensions and measures attributes of data cube are included in the semantic data cube. The semantics of attributes includes the linguistic semantics such as 'recent' and the corresponding degrees of membership function such as '1' in 'recent/1'. In general, the field experts assign the membership functions according to the fact requirements.

Based on the semantic data cube model, the multidimensional analyses with the semantics can be directly supported. For example, find out the products that have high sales in the recent years based on the semantic data cube in table 1. The answer may be the product of PC and the degree is 1.

4 The Computation Algorithms

4.1 The SCRT Algorithm

The sCRT algorithm is an extension of the existing cube computation algorithm BUC [5]. Similar to the BUC algorithm, the framework of sCRT is a recursive processing and computes semantic data cube from the bottom of cuboids-tree to the up and has the same partition procedure. The difference from BUC algorithm is that sCRT is used to compute completely semantic data cube but traditional and partial data cube (i.e. iceberg cube). The description of sCRT algorithm is given in table 2. In the description, the cardinality of one attribute is the number of different attribute values. The membership function of measures and dimensions are the input arguments. In the computation process, these functions are used to compute the semantics of measures and dimensions.

Table 2. The description of sCRT algorithm

PROCEDURE sCRT

Inputs: input: the relation to aggregate. dim: the starting dimension for this iteration. memberFunction[i]: the membership function associated with the dimensions and measures.

Globals: Constant numDims: the total number of dimensions. Constant numMeas: the total number of measures. Constant cardinality[numDims]: the cardinality of each dimension. outputRec: the current output record. dataCount[numDims]: stores the size of each partition. dataCount[i] is a list of integers of size cardinality[i].

Outputs: Recursively output one record of semantic data cube.

Method:

```
Aggregate (input); {place results in outputRec }
for j=numDims; j< numDims+numMeas; j++ do
  if memberFunction[j] then {check the membership function list}
   outputRec.dim[j]= f_m(outputRec.aggr); {compute the semantics of measures }
   end if
write outputRec;
for d=dim; d< numDims; d++ do
   let C=cardinality[d]
   Partition (input, d, C, dataCount[d]);
   let k=0;
   for i=0; i<C; i++ do {For each partition}
      let c=dataCount[d][i]
      if c>=1 then {The sCRT stop here}
        if memberFunction[i] then
           outputRec.dim[d]=f_m(input[k].dim[d]); {compute dimension semantics}
           sCRT (input[k..k+c], d+1);
        end if
      end if
      k+=c;
   end for
outputRec.dim[d]=ALL;
end for
```

4.2 The PSCRT Algorithm

The size of a complete data cube is huge and the cost of cube computation is expensive. In order to enhance the computing efficiency, the parallel algorithm psCRT is designed. The algorithm assumes a shared-nothing architecture where each of n processors p_i ($1 \le i \le n$) has a private memory and the processors are connected by a communication network and can communicate by passing messages. The synchronization of processors is controlled by a processor p_1.

In psCRT, the processor-cuboid map represents the relation between a processor and the cuboids handled by the processor. For example, suppose that the processors are p_1, p_2 and p_3. The dimensions are A, B, C and D. For balancing the number of cells handled by each processor, size-1 cuboid is assigned to p_1, size-2 cuboid is assigned to p_2, and size-0, size-3 and size-4cuboid are assigned to p_3. In general, suppose that Numcuboid (i) denotes the number of cells in size-i cuboid. From the description of data cube model, it is easy to know that Numcuboid (i)≥ Numcuboid (j) where 0<i<j. The local cuboids in psCRT are computed by sCRT. The combination procedure in psCRT algorithm searches each cell of the local cuboids and inserts the cells with computed semantics into the semantic data cube D.

Table.3 The description of psCRT algorithm

PROCEDURE psCRT
Inputs: R is the given relation table, n is the number of processor, and the processor-cuboid map is a list that represents the relation between cuboids and processors. memberFunction: The membership function associated with the dimensions and measures.
Outputs: D is the semantic data cube
Method:
1. The given relation table R is evenly divided n partitions R_i ($1 \le i \le n$). The processor-cuboid map is sent to the other processors.
2. The processor p_i ($1 \le i \le n$) computes the corresponding data cube on R_i in parallel and sent the local cuboids to the corresponding processors according to the processor-cuboid map.
3. The processor p_i ($1 \le i \le n$) in parallel combines the different cuboids into a locally data cube D_i.
4. The local data cube D_i ($1 \le i \le n$) is sent to the processor p_1, and p_1 combines D_i into a complete data cube D.

5 The Performance Tests

In this section, we present our experiments on the performance of sCRT and psCRT. All experiments are performed using synthetic datasets. The dataset tuples follow the uniform distribution. The number of dimension is set to 5. The cardinality of all attributes is set to 1000. The size of datasets (i.e. the number of tuples) is varied from 10,000 to 30,000 with an interval 10,000. The aggregate function used in the cube computation algorithm is SUM function. In all tests, one dimension (the first dimension) and one measure are chosen as the semantic attributes and associated with the membership function. All experiments are conducted on PC platform and two processors are used. The first processor p_1 is with an Intel Pentium 1.5GHz CPU, 256M RAM, and the second processor p_2 is with an Intel Pentium 500M CPU, 256M RAM. The tests of sCRT are based on the first processor. The processor-cuboid map is shown as following: size-1 cuboid, size-5 cuboid, size-3 cuboid are assigned to p_1. size-2 cuboid, size-4 cuboid and size-0 cuboid (i.e. ALL) are assigned to p_2. Just as shown in table 4, both algorithms are scalable with the size of dataset. However psCRT outperforms sCRT. The key factor that affects the efficiency of the psCRT algorithm is the spending of communication between processors.

Table 4. The performance test results

Size of datasets	Runtime of sCRT (ms)	Runtime of psCRT (ms)
10,000	2433	1735
20,000	4716	3841
30,000	5758	4720

6 Conclusions

In this paper, the semantic data cube model with linguistic semantics is presented. The semantic data cube uses fuzzy set to represent the linguistic semantics of dimensions and measures of data cube. The computation algorithms for the semantic data cube are presented. The test results show that the algorithms are effective and scalable. The parallel data analysis based on the semantic cube is our future work.

Acknowledgements

The paper is supported by National Natural Science Foundation of China (No.60205007), Natural Science Foundation of Guangdong Province (No.031558, No.04300462), Research Foundation of National Science and Technology Plan Project (No.2004BA721A02), Research Foundation of Science, Technology Plan Project in Guangdong Province (No.2003C50118), Research Foundation of Science, Technology Plan Project in Guangzhou City(No.2002Z3-E0017) and Youth Research Foundation of School of Information Science & Technology at Sun Yat-sen University (No.350416).

References

1. Palpanas, T.:Knowledge Discovery in Data Warehouses. SIGMOD Record. 3 (2000) 88-100
2. Gray, J., Bosworth, A., Layman, A., Pirahesh, H.: Data cube: A relational aggregation operator generalizing group-by, cross-tab, and sub-total. In: Stanley Y.W.Su (ed.): Proceedings of Int. Conf. on Data Engineering. IEEE Computer Society Press (1996) 152-159
3. Lakshmanan, L.V.S., Pei, J., Zhao, Y.: QC-Trees: an efficient Summary Structure for semantic OLAP. In: Alon Y.Halevy, Zachary G.Ives, Doan, A. (eds.): Proceedings of ACM SIGMOD Int. Conf. on Management of Data. ACM Press (2003) 64-75
4. Feng, L., Dillon, T. S.: Using Fuzzy Linguistic Representations to Provide Explanatory Semantics for Data Warehouses. IEEE Transactions on Knowledge and Data Engineering. 1 (2003) 86-102
5. Beyer, K., Ramakrishnan, R.: Bottom-up computation of sparse and Iceberg CUBE. In: Delis, A., Faloutsos, C., Ghandeharizadeh, S. (eds.): Proceedings of ACM SIGMOD Int. Conf. on Management of Data. ACM Press (1999) 359-370
6. Zhuge, H.: Resource Space Grid: Model, Method and Platform. Concurrency and Computation: Practice and Experience. 14 (2004) 1385-1413

Knowledge Acquisition Based on the Global Concept of Fuzzy Cognitive Maps*

Xiang-Feng Luo

Grid Research Lab., Department of Computer Science and Engineering,
ShangHai University, ShangHai, China, 200072
e-Institute of ShangHai High Education Grid, ShangHai, China, 200072
luoxiangfeng@163.com

Abstract. Combination of prior knowledge and implicit knowledge hidden in the data of system can enhance the quality of information services in Knowledge Grid. Fuzzy Cognitive Maps (FCMs) are constructed by experts using prior knowledge and do not acquire the implicit knowledge from the data of systems directly, which may distort the dynamical behaviour of information services systems in which knowledge representation and reasoning are based on FCMs. We propose a global concept of FCMs method to acquire implicit knowledge and modify the false knowledge maybe done by experts from the data of system. Experiments show that this method can acquire the implicit knowledge from the data of system and modify the false knowledge hidden in FCMs, which makes the learned FCMs that acquire knowledge from the data of system more natural than the FCMs constructed by experts to emulate intelligent information services behaviors in Knowledge Grid.

1 Introduction

The Knowledge Grid is an intelligent, sustainable Internet application environment that enables people or virtual roles to effectively capture, publish, share, and manage explicit knowledge resources [1]. So, how to capture knowledge is an essential question in Knowledge Grid. To enhance the quality of information services in Knowledge Grid, we need combination of the prior knowledge of systems, objects or virtual roles, and the implicit knowledge hidden in the data of system. Fuzzy Cognitive Maps (FCMs) are aimed to mimic human causal knowledge reasoning and store the prior knowledge of experts [2]. FCMs have been widely used in economy, fault analysis, information system [3], tacit knowledge management [4], industry control [5] and virtual world [6] and so on.

Usually FCMs are constructed by experts and do not acquire the implicit knowledge from the data of system, which may distort the behaviour of system whose knowledge representation and reasoning are based on FCMs. In the other hand, implicit knowledge of systems hidden in the data of systems; the implicit knowledge is hard to

* Research work was supported by the National Science Foundation of China (Grants 60402016) and the National Grand Fundamental Research 973 Program of China (2003CB316901).

H. Zhuge and G.C. Fox (Eds.): GCC 2005, LNCS 3795, pp. 579–584, 2005.

be acquired using the weight between two concepts. The implicit knowledge in the data is about system instead of two concepts. We can acquire the weight between two concepts by hebb rule [6], but how to acquire the weights among multi-concepts. (Weight reflects the knowledge and its relations' degree between two concepts.) In FCMs, using hebb rule to acquire weight between two concepts can be regard as the local view, and the process of weights acquiring among multi-concepts needs a global concept to control.

In the reasoning process of FCMs, the enabled concepts are synchronously and equally. There is no global concept in FCMs, which leads FCMs lack the capability of weights acquiring from the data of systems. It is necessary to find a method using global view to control the weights acquiring process among multi-concepts of FCMs.

2 Knowledge Acquisition Based on Global Concept of FCMs

The dynamical behaviors of FCMs are composed by the set of concepts $\vec{C}$, the state values set $\vec{V_C}$, the set of relations $\vec{R}$ and the weights set $\vec{W}$. The influences on FCMs of the state values of causal concepts, the weights between concepts, the effect concepts at time t and $t+1$ can be synthetically reflected by the set of $\vec{V_C}$. All the state values and the weights of FCMs interaction produce the simulation of the real world or systems. In the following, we define the error of the concept's state value.

Definition 1. (The error of the concept Cj 's state value, δ_j)

$$\delta_j = \left|T(V_{Cj}(t)) - O(V_{Cj}(t))\right|,$$

where $O(V_{Cj}(t))$ is the output of C_j; $T(V_{Cj}(t))$ is the plan output of C_j. δ_j can be regard as a measure degree between C_j and information system.

We acquire the weights of FCMs according to the principle of Linsker's maximal information holding. Concretely, we should hold the minimal sum of the adjusted values of weights. So we define the adjusted value of weight as follows:

Definition 2. (The adjusted value of weights, Δw_{ij})

$$\Delta w_{ij} = \eta w_{ij}\delta_j + \delta_j \varepsilon,$$

where η is a constant; ε is a stochastic number.

After the definitions of δ_j and Δw_{ij}, we definite a global concept of fuzzy cognitive maps as follows:

Definition 3. (The global concept of fuzzy cognitive maps, h)

$$h = \eta \sum\sum \delta_j^2 \Delta w_{ij} + \sum\sum \delta_j \Delta w_{ij} \varepsilon_{ij},$$

where η is a constant; ε_{ij} is the stochastic number.

The global concept h is a measure degree between FCM and the real world, which accord with the principle of Linsker's maximal information holding. The smaller h shows that the distance between the reasoning values of FCMs and the real values of system is more close , the adjusting process of the weights needs more fine, and vice versa. The global concept h of FCM can control the weights acquiring process of FCMs from the data of system.

The arithmetic of knowledge acquisition with the global concept of FCMs as follows:

Initialization;
while (step<200)&(h>10e-8)
 $V(t+1)=V(t)\cdot W(t)$; According to $V(t+1)$, calculate $\delta_j(t+1)$;
For i=1 to n
Calculate $\Delta w_{ij}(i)$ and $h(i)$;
End
 Find the minimal h(i); Modify the adjacency matrix $W(t+1)=W(t)+\Delta W$;
End

3 Experiments

We construct a fuzzy cognitive map (denoted as FCM1) shown in Figure 1 according to the file of the leader group of the science and technology of AnHui province [WanKe.NO. (1999) 01]. FCM1 reflects which factors influence on the progress of the science and technology, which has 43 concepts and there are complex relations among these concepts shown in Figure 1. In this paper, we use global concept h to acquire the implicit knowledge and modify the false knowledge hidden in FCM1.

Figure 2 to Figure 4 are the knowledge acquisition results of FCM1 from the data of the HeFei's progress of science and technology in 1998. From Figure 2, we know there are conspicuous differences between the real values of 1998 and the first step reasoning values of FCM1 because the constructed FCM1 only consider the experts' knowledge. We know from Figure 3, there is little difference between the learned FCM1 and the real values of 1998 because the implicit knowledge is partially acquired by FCM1 from the data of system. Figure 4 shows the final results between the learned FCM1 and the real values of 1998. From this figure, we know there is inconspicuous difference between FCM1 and the real values of 1998 because the implicit knowledge and the false knowledge are been acquired and modified from the data of 1998 by the method of global concept of FCMs.

FCM1 can acquire the knowledge from the data of the HeFei's progress of science and technology in 1998 using the global concept of FCMs. So, the learned FCM1 that acquires knowledge from the data of system should have more knowledge about the progress of the science and technology. Here, we use the data of 1997 to verify the learned FCM1 that has more correct knowledge than the constructed FCM1 by experts.

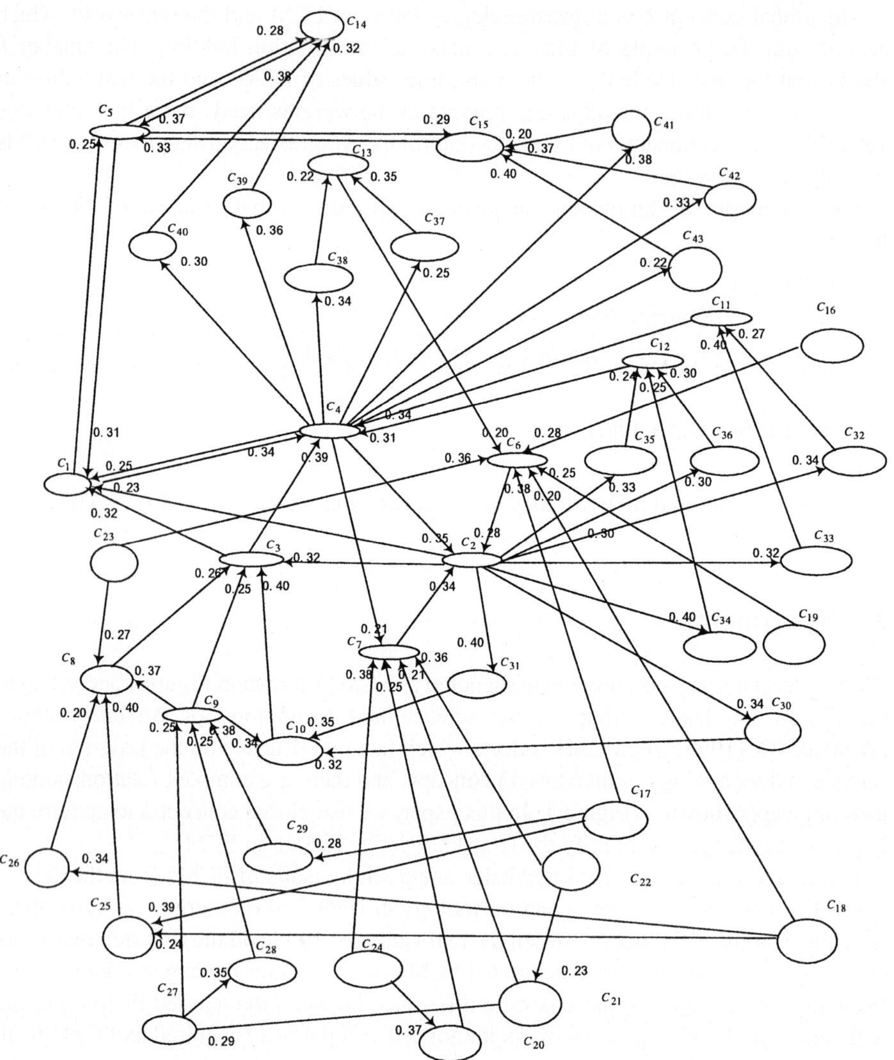

Fig.1. The fuzzy cognitive map is constructed according to the file of the science and technology leader group of AnHui province [WanKe. NO. (1999) 01]

Figure 2 shows the difference between the first step reasoning values of FCM1 constructed by experts and the real values of 1998. Figure 5 shows the difference between the first step reasoning values of the learned FCM1 and the real values of HeFei's progress of science and technology in 1997. Figure 5 compared with Figure 2, we know that there is more correct knowledge hidden in the learned FCM1 than the FCM1 constructed by experts. The global concept can acquire and learn knowledge from the data of system effectively.

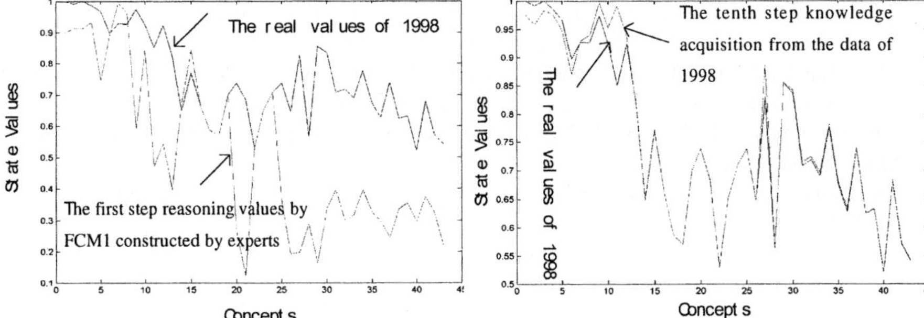

Fig. 2. The difference between the first step reasoning values of FCM1 and the real values of 1998

Fig. 3. The difference between the tenth step knowledge acquisition from the data and the real values of 1998

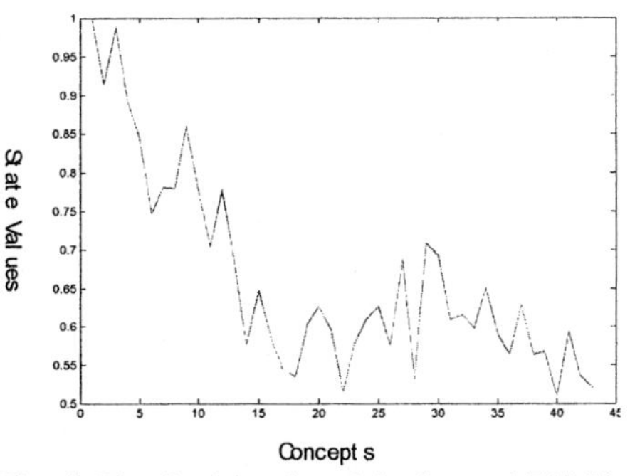

Fig. 4. The final results of the learned FCM1 and the real values of 1998

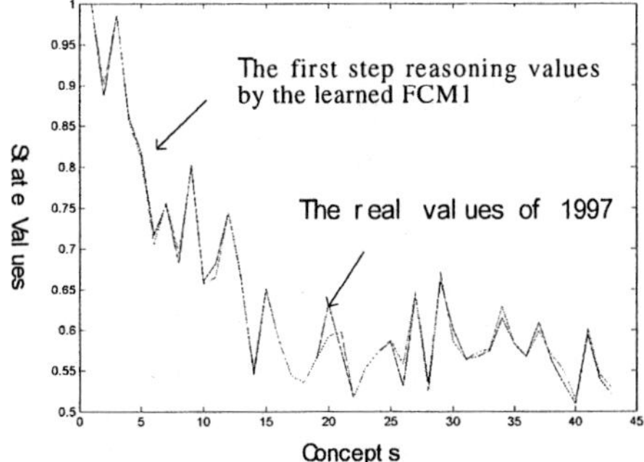

Fig. 5. The results between the first step reasoning values of the learned FCM1 and the real values of 1997

4 Conclusions

FCMs have no global concept; they are hard to acquire the implicit knowledge from the data of information systems. A global concept is proposed to acquire and learn the implicit knowledge and modify FCM's false knowledge that maybe done by experts. Compared with the reasoning results of the FCM1 constructed by experts, we know that the learned FCM1 has the capability of acquiring implicit knowledge and modifying the false knowledge of FCM from the data of systems effectively.

References

1. H.Zhuge, China's E-Science Knowledge Grid Environment, IEEE Intelligent Systems, 19(1) (2004) 13-17.
2. H.Zhuge, X.F. Luo. Knowledge Map: Mathematic Model and Dynamical behaviour. Journal of Computer Science and Technology, 2005, 20(3), pp.289-295.

3. Z.Q.Liu, .R.Satur Contextual Fuzzy Cognitive Maps for Decision Support in Geographic Information Systems. IEEE Transactions on Fuzzy Systems, 7(10), 1999, pp, 495-502.
4. J.B.Noha, K.C. Lee. A Case-based Reasoning Approach to Cognitive Maps-driven Tacit Knowledge Management. Expert Systems with Applications, 19, 2000, pp, 249-259.
5. P.P. Groumpos, C.D.Stylios. Modeling Supervisory Control Systems Using Fuzzy Cognitive Maps. Chaos Solitons and Fractals, 11, 2000, pp, 329-336.
6. J.A. Dickerson, B.Kosko. Virtual Worlds as Fuzzy Dynamical Systems. Spring, 3(2), 1994, pp, 173-189.

The Architecture and Implementation of Resource Space Model System*

Peng Shi[1,2], Yunpeng Xing[1,2], Erlin Yao[1,2,3], Zhen Wang[1,2], Kehua Yuan[1,2,3], Junsheng Zhang[1,2,3], Jianzeng Wang[1,2], and Fei Guo[1,2]

[1] China Knowledge Grid Research Group, Key Lab of Intelligent Information Processing, Institute of Computing Technology, Chinese Academy of Sciences, Beijing, China
[2] Graduate School of the Chinese Academy of Sciences, Beijing, China
{pengshi, ypxing, alin.yao, wangzhen, kehua, junsheng, wjz, guofei}@kg.ict.ac.cn
[3] Hunan Knowledge Grid Lab, Hunan University of Science and Technology, Hunan, China

Abstract. Resource Space Model (RSM) is a semantic model to manage and share heterogeneous resources on the Internet. This paper focuses on the general architecture, physical implementation and application of RSM. The RSM system adopts Client/Server mode for users to utilize resource spaces through the Internet. The resource spaces are designed based on domain knowledge and stored as XML files in the server. The tool 3DBrowser provides a friendly interface with three-dimensional scene to display resource spaces, locate and operate on resources. Based on the architecture and tools, a Dunhuang RSM system has been developed as a collaboration platform to organize and share the resources of Dunhuang Culture Grid. The system provides an efficient resource locating way based on the classification of resources and improves the efficiency of research.

1 Introduction

The Internet is an open platform for data exchange and provides varied modes for users to share their information conveniently. Traditional information management methods are inefficient for the multifarious and disorderly resources on the Internet. Researchers have established several theories and prototypes to improve data organization on the Internet. Semantic Web focuses on representing information in a machine-understandable way by using markup languages and ontology-relevant mechanisms [1]. Computing grid tries to combine the computing abilities from the Internet into a universal platform with great power [2]. It involves the large scale and high-performance computing technology, but not the semantic issues. To manage resources effectively, discovering the rules that govern the future interconnection environment is a major challenge [12]. Semantic grid creates a new environment incorporating the

* This work was supported by the National Basic Research Program of China (973 project No.2003CB317000) and the National Science Foundation of China (Grants 60273020 and 70271007).

H. Zhuge and G.C. Fox (Eds.): GCC 2005, LNCS 3795, pp. 585 – 590, 2005.

Internet, sensor networks, mobile devices, and the interconnection semantics [3, 11]. Knowledge grid is an e-Science environment to support complex demands on knowledge mining and reasoning [4, 5, 8]. It includes three key problems: normal organization, semantic interconnection and intelligent clustering of resources.

Zhuge's Resource Space Model RSM is a semantic model to uniformly specify and organize resources on the Internet [6, 7]. The RSM aims at mapping versatile resources including information, knowledge and services into a uniform semantic space called resource space. A resource space uses a series of independent axes and coordinates to represent the classification of resources. A resource or a set of similar resources in a resource space is specified by a tuple of coordinates. The design of resource space is based on domain knowledge and consists of four main steps: resource analysis, top-down resource partition, design of two-dimensional resource space and join between resource spaces [7]. Users can locate resources in a resource space through their coordinates and operate on them. There are several normal forms and integrity theory to restrict and regulate resource spaces [9, 10]. They ensure the legal operations, classification semantics and concurrency of resource spaces.

This paper focuses on the key problems of implementation of RSM and its application in Dunhuang Culture Grid. It first describes the general architecture and the storage of resource spaces in XML files. The 3DBrowser is a tool with three-dimensional scene to browse resource space, locate and operate on resources. A RSM system has been developed to organize and share resources in Dunhuang Culture Grid.

2 General Architecture and Storage

2.1 General Architecture of the RSM System

An RSM system is an interaction and collaboration platform for users to normally organize and share resources based on RSM theory. The system adopts Client/Server mode consisting of a server and many clients connected through networks. The server, called RS server, stores resource spaces and provides portal and interface for users' access. The clients maintain resources and provide them for resource spaces. The users of RSM system are divided into three types: administrator, owner and customer. The administrators create, maintain and update resource spaces and operate the server. The owners, who provide resources for the system, manage their resources and usually operate the clients. The resources can be modified by their owners. If the modifications influence the resource spaces, the system updates them automatically. The customers are read-only users and can access the system through networks.

2.2 Storage of Resource Space and Representation of Resource

A resource space consists of the classified resources and n independent axes, where n is the space's dimension number. The storage of resource space should contain two parts: axes and resources. For uniform and convenient data exchange, XML file is chosen to store resource spaces. The XML file can also represent the hierarchy of classification conveniently because it owns a tree like structure. A uniform schema is adopted to store resource space. There are a couple of tags named <RS_name> to define the name of resource spaces. The axes and resources are stored in the child nodes named <AXES> and <RESOURCES>, respectively.

Fig. 1 (a) shows an example resource space with two axes named FORMAT and CONTENT. CONTENT-axis owns two coordinates: *painting* and *statue*. *Video* and *graph* are the coordinates on FORMAT-axis. R_1 and R_2 are the identifiers of two resources in the space. Resource R_1 has a location as (*statue*, *graph*). That means R_1 is the resource whose format is graph and content is statue. The coordinates of resource R_2 is (*painting*, *video*). Fig. 1 (b) is the storage structure of the example in XML file. Every child node of <AXES> indicates one same name axis. The only element of axis node is a string combined with its coordinates, connected and separated by comma. The child nodes between the tags <RESOURCE> indicate the resources and are listed according to their coordinates. Its name is a combination of the coordinates connected one by one through underscores. The resources with the same coordinates are listed as child nodes named by their identifiers. The underscore and comma are the preserved characters in this schema. This schema can bring better access efficiency when locating resources according to their coordinates. The description of resource is omitted in Fig. 1 (b) and will be described in detail below.

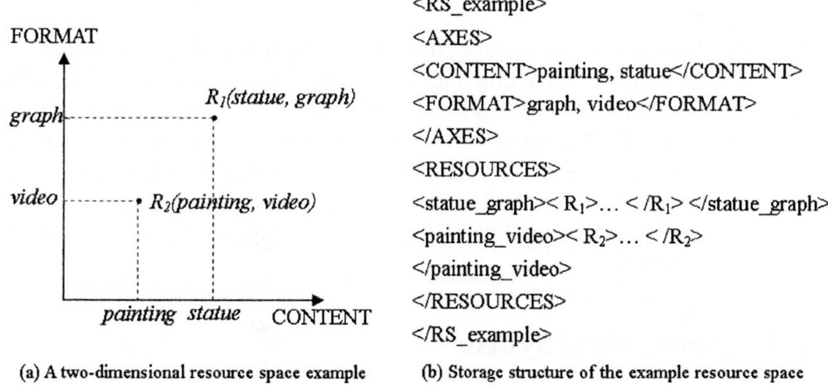

(a) A two-dimensional resource space example

(b) Storage structure of the example resource space

Fig. 1. An example of resource space and its storage structure in XML file

A uniform structure is needed to represent heterogeneous resources. In this paper, a resource is represented by a tuple of attributes as: {*identifier, location, abstract, physical-address, interface, author, owner, version, privilege, effective-duration, related-material, particular*}. The *identifier* is the unique name to distinguish one resource from others. The *location* accurately locates the resource through its coordinates in a specific resource space. Since resources are distributed on the Internet, the *physical-address* is necessary for users' access. It's unavailable for users but available for the system to guarantee the system's security. The *abstract* shortly describes the basic characteristics of a resource such as its content and functions. It helps the user to determine if this resource satisfies his/her demand. The *interface* shows the method to use the resource correctly. The *author* and *owner* show the person or organization that created the resource and provided it for the resource space, respectively. The *version* indicates the different editions of a resource for user to choose. The *privilege* includes the permitted users and their available operations on a resource. The *effective-duration* is the period when a resource keeps effective. The *relate-material* is a list of materials relative to the resource such as other resources, web pages or files. The item *particular* holds the characteristic or original information of a resource. The details of resource R_1, which are omitted in the example Fig. 1 (b), are shown as follows.


```
<R1>
<ABSTRACT> a graph that describes statue </ABSTRACT>
<PHYSICAL-ADDRESS>192.168.168.5/graph/r1.jpg</PHYSICAL-ADDRESS>
<INTERFACE> graph file </INTERFACE>
<AUTHOR> Academy </AUTHOR>
<OWNER> KG-ICT </OWNER>
<VERSION> 1.0 </VERSION>
<PRIVILEGE> all, read </PRIVILEGE>
<EFFECTIVE-DURATION> permanent </EFFECTIVE-DURATION>
<RELATED-MATERIAL>http://www.culturegrid.net</RELATED-MATERIAL>
<PARTICULAR><resolution>1024*768</resolution></PARTICULAR>
</R1>
```


The schema above shows the storage structure of a resource space and resources in XML files. It may cause low parsing and access efficiency to use one XML file to store resource space and resources together when there are large numbers of resources in the resource space. An alternative method is to maintain a smaller file to store the axes only. The resources with the same coordinates are stored in another independent file. This strategy can decrease the burden of parsing large XML file. However, it brings additional tasks to manage lots of files. Which strategy should be chosen depends on practical situations.

3 The Dunhuang RSM System

3.1 Dunhuang Resource Spaces

Dunhuang Culture includes the materials originally located in the caves near Dunhuang town and relative research area. All the digital files, web services and other relative materials are resources of Dunhuang Culture Grid. The classification criteria of Dunhuang resources include *format, content, dynasty* and *cave-number*. The format indicates the type of resources including graph, document, video, audio and service. The content includes four main types: architecture, wall-painting, statue and artifact. The dynasty indicates when the artifacts were created originally. The cave-number is a unique number to distinguish one cave from others. All the classification above combines the resource spaces of Dunhuang Culture Grid.

3.2 The 3DBrowser and the System Application

The 3DBrowser is a three-dimensional browser for users to browse resource spaces, locate and operate on resources. The interface is divided into two sub-windows vertically, shown in Fig. 2. The right window lists located resources for user to operate. The left window shows a perspective of coordinates with three orthogonal axes. Every small transparent cube, composed of line frame, indicates the resources with same coordinates.

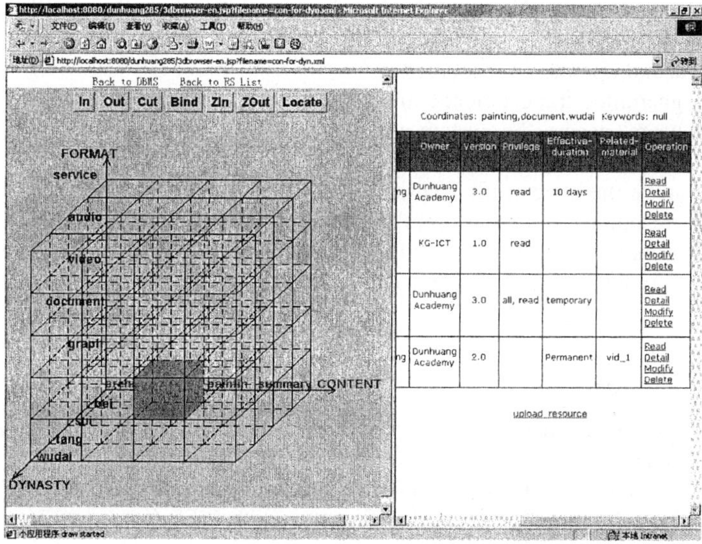

Fig. 2. The interface and appearance of locating resource in 3DBrowser

There is a gray cube called *focus cube* to show the current operable cube. The focus cube is changed along with mouse moving on the surface parallel to the screen. Two buttons named "In" and "Out" are to move the focus cube in the direction vertical to the screen. "Locate" button allows user to input coordinates to locate resources directly. During the locating procedure, user can click the right mouse button to observe current coordinates of focus cube through a popup window. There are also several functions and buttons to assist the users to browse resource spaces. User can click the "Cut" button to remove the top level cubes and observe the cubes behind, and the reverse operation is realized through "Bind" button. "ZIn" and "ZOut" buttons can zoom in and zoom out the space to get a whole and detailed scene, respectively. User can also move the whole scene through mouse drag. When the user reaches the target cube, he can double click the left mouse button to select it. Then the resources denoted by the cube are listed in the right window. User can observe the details of resources and operate on them. A simple query function based on keywords is also added into the system to get specific resources from located resources.

4 Conclusion, Problems and Ongoing Work

Based on Zhuge's RSM theory, a semantic model to normally organize and efficiently share resources based on their classification, this paper discusses the key problems about the implementation of RSM. The general architecture of system and the storage structure of resource space are proposed. A system based on them has been applied to manage and share heterogeneous resources of Dunhuang Culture Grid (http://www.culturegrid.net). The resource spaces have been created to represent the classification of resources. The resources are well organized and uniformly located in the resource spaces. By this classification, users can locate resources efficiently. In the system, the 3DBrowser provides a friendly interface for users to browse resource space, locate and operate on resources.

How to guarantee the efficiency and robustness is still unsolved here when large amount of users' access the system simultaneously. Some effort is focusing on the problem to extend the system for more users on the Internet. This system uses a lock strategy to solve the concurrent access. When a user accesses a resource, the strategy protects the resource from other users' operations. This guarantees the consistency of resources. A more suitable and flexible strategy will be studied to realize Zhuge's ideal: the future interconnection environment [3, 11, 12].

References

1. Berners-Lee, T., Hendler, J., Lassila, O.: The Semantic Web. *Scientific American*, 284(5) (2001) 34-43
2. Foster, I.: Internet Computing and the Emerging Grid. *Nature*, 408 (6815) (2000)
3. Zhuge, H.: Clustering Soft-Devices in Semantic Grid, *IEEE Computing in Science and Engineering*, 4 (6) (2002) 60-62
4. Zhuge, H.: A Knowledge Grid Model and Platform for Global Knowledge Sharing, *Expert Systems with Applications*, 22 (4) (2002) 313-320
5. Zhuge, H.: China's E-Science Knowledge Grid Environment, *IEEE Intelligent Systems*, 19(1) (2004) 13-17
6. Zhuge, H.: Resource Space Grid: Model, Method and Platform, *Concurrency and Computation: Practice and Experience*, 16 (14) (2004) 1385-1413
7. Zhuge, H.: Resource Space Model, Its Design Method and Applications, *Journal of Systems and Software*, 72 (1) (2004) 71-81
8. Zhuge, H.: The Knowledge Grid, World Scientific, Singapore (2004)
9. Zhuge, H., Yao, E., Xing, Y., Liu, J.: Extended Normal Form Theory of Resource Space Model, *Future Generation Computer Systems*, 21 (1) (2005) 189-198
10. Zhuge, H., Xing, Y.: Integrity Theory for Resource Space Model and Its Application, Keynote, *WAIM2005*, LNCS 3739, (2005) 8-24
11. Zhuge, H.: Semantic Grid: Scientific Issues, Infrastructure, and Methodology, *Communications of the ACM*. 48 (4) (2005) 117-119
12. Zhuge, H.: The Future Interconnection Environment, *IEEE Computer*, 38 (4) (2005) 27-33

Using Fuzzy Cognitive Map to Effectively Classify E-Documents and Application*

Jianzeng Wang[1,3], Yunpeng Xing[1,3], Peng Shi[1,3], Fei Guo[1,3], Zhen Wang[1,3], Erlin Yao[1,2,3], Kehua Yuan[1,2,3], and Junsheng Zhang[1,2,3]

[1] Key Lab of Intelligent Information Processing, Institute of Computing Technology, Chinese Academy of Sciences, Beijing, 100080, China
{wjz, ypxing, pengshi, guofei, wangzhen, alin.yao, kehua, junsheng}@kg.ict.ac.cn
[2] Hunan Knowledge Grid Lab, Hunan University of Science and Technology, Hunan, China
[3] Graduate School of the Chinese Academy of Sciences, Beijing, China

Abstract. In the current Web, e-document has been the most common vehicle for delivering and exchanging information. As the amount of e-documents has grown enormously, effective classification facilities are urgently needed to classify and query e-documents users want. In this paper, we propose a method to classify e-documents into a set of predefined categories based on Fuzzy Cognitive Map (FCM). The e-documents are collected from Internet by a meta-search engine. FCM has been employed to capture the semantic relationships between keywords of e-documents. Experiments with a set of local e-documents have proved that this approach has high performance and can help users getting the e-documents efficiently and effectively. The proposed method has been implemented and integrated into the Dunhuang Feitian System to manage and classify e-documents.

1 Introduction

The World Wide Web provides us with a large-scale and universal information space. E-document has been the most common vehicle for delivering and exchanging information in the current Web. However, the enormous amount of e-documents makes it difficult to search, access, present, and maintain the information. Searching for specific information or discovering useful information from the large amount of information in the Web has been becoming a difficult, time-consuming and challenging task. So effective classification and search facilities are urgently needed to efficiently classify and query e-documents users want in the open and dynamic World Wide Web environment.

Document classification, as originally used to improve the precision, especially top-level precision, of information retrieval systems, is the process of assigning a

* This work was supported by the National Basic Research Program of China (973 project no.2003CB317000) and the National Science Foundation of China (Grants 70271007, 60273020, 60402016).

H. Zhuge and G.C. Fox (Eds.): GCC 2005, LNCS 3795, pp. 591 – 596, 2005.

document to one of the predefined categories based on the document content [1]. In the classification process, traditional document classification methods such as *vector space model*, only consider the appearance frequency of keywords. But it has been well acknowledged in such fields as traditional database management system and information retrieval that the more semantics about data are understood and considered by a system, the more precise queries and searches can be achieved [2, 6].

In this paper, a method to effectively classify e-documents into a set of predefined categories based on FCM is proposed. FCMs capture the relationships between the keywords to improve the classification accuracy. The proposed method has been implemented and integrated into the Dunhuang Feitian System to manage and classify e-documents. One of the important aspects about such classification is that it could provide semantics (similarity at the conceptual level between documents) without requiring the classification process to use any extra semantics. And the classification process is adaptive.

2 Effective E-Document Classification Based on FCM

2.1 Fuzzy Cognitive Map

Fuzzy Cognitive Map is a directed and weighted graph of concepts and relationships between the concepts [3]. FCM is derived from Cognitive Map. Based on the CM structure, FCM was proposed by Kosko [4, 5]. As a great improvement compared to CM, FCM introduces fuzzy quantitative relationship between concepts to describe the weight of the causal relationship. FCM has iterative characteristic. In FCM, the arcs are not only directed to show the direction of causal relations, but also accompanied by a quantitative weight within the interval [0, 1].

The formulation for calculating the state value of concepts is proposed as follows:

$$A_i^t = f(k_1 \sum_{\substack{j=1 \\ j \neq i}}^{n} A_j^{t-1} W_{ji} + k_2 A_i^{t-1}) \tag{1}$$

A_i^t is the state value of C_i at step t; A_j^{t-1} is the state value of the interrelated causal concept C_j at step t-1; A_i^{t-1} is the state value of C_i at step t-1; W_{ji} is the interrelation's weight from concept C_j to C_i and f is a threshold function, here $f(x) = \tanh(x)$. In this paper, it is assumed that $k_1 = k_2 = 1$. The coefficient k_2 represents the contributive proportion of the previous value to the new state value.

2.2 Construction of Basic Category FCM (BC-FCM)

In order to effectively classify documents into a set of predefined categories, it is necessary to construct a BC-FCM to represent a category first. BC-FCM plays an important part in the process of classification. It may greatly affect the performance of document classification systems, because its broadness and granularity influence the coverage and specificity of classification categories.

Based on the representative documents whose categories have been predetermined, the BC-FCM for each category is constructed as the following steps:

First, keywords should be extracted as BC-FCMs' concepts from the representative documents. Using the statistical characteristic of the keywords, we pick out those keywords that can represent each category best. Intuitively, the best way to represent each a category is to select only the exclusive keywords [1]. But in BC-FCMs, the quantitative weight of each causal relation in different BC-FCMs may be different, so the proposed method also considers those overlapped keywords.

Then the concept state value should be determined. In the paper, the concept state value V_{ci} is calculated by Eq. (2):

$$V_{ci} = 1 / 1 + e^{-cy} \tag{2}$$

where c is a constant, herein $c = 0.6$ and it can be manually adjusted by user according to the experiment result. $y = f\,(location, frequency)$, $V_{ci} \in [0, 1]$. In the proposed classification system, we only consider the appearance frequency of keywords.

2.3 Effective E-Documents Classification Based on FCM

In this subsection, the classification method based on FCM is described in detail. The proposed method has been implemented and integrated into the Dunhuang Feitian System, and it is named as SRCC component, representing Search Results Clustering and Classification. The architecture of the SRCC component is given in fig. 1.

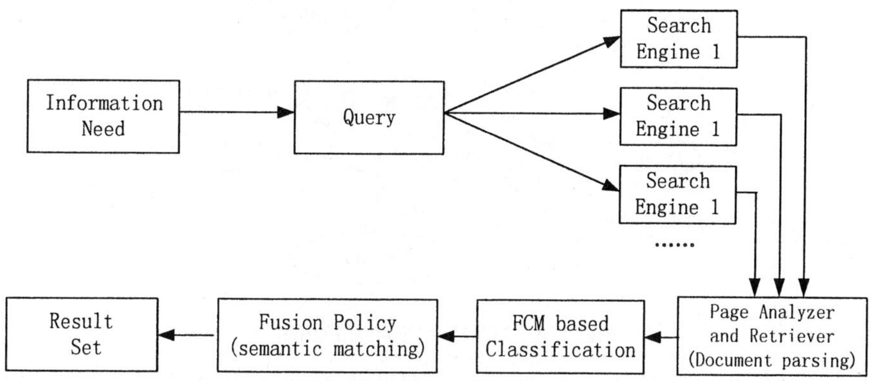

Fig. 1. The architecture of the SRCC component

As a whole, collecting e-documents from Internet by the meta-search engine firstly, and the search results are stored in a database. Then the FCM based classification method is used to classify the search results into predefined subclasses for helping users to access the web pages effectively and efficiently.

After choosing out keywords from an e-document, we match these keywords with concepts included in each BC-FCM; then we get the matching keywords' state values, and put them into Eq. (3) to calculate the matching degree (*md*). The matching degrees are used to determine which category the document belongs to.

$$md = \frac{1}{1 + e^{-c \times \sum_{1}^{n} V_{ci}}} \quad (3)$$

where c is a constant, herein $c = 0.6$ and it can be manually adjusted; V_{ci} is calculated by Eq. (2) and n is the total number of concepts in a BC-FCM.

A document D_i is classified into the category C_j where the matching degree (*md*) is the maximum among all the categories and also it is bigger than the threshold. The threshold is an adjustable variable in the system, and usually it is 0.75.

3 Implementation in the Dunhuang Feitian System

The proposed method is implemented and integrated into the Dunhuang Feitian System, a part of Dunhuang Culture Knowledge Grid [7-14]. Feitian is a typical representative of the ancient Dunhuang art. Because of the cultural relic conservation and geographical restrictions, she hasn't been familiar to most people in the world. Under such circumstances, the Dunhuang Feitian System is undertaken to help people enjoying this humankind's ancient culture more conveniently. The SRCC component is integrated into the Dunhuang Feitian System for providing useful knowledge of Dunhuang Feitian art to visitors and researchers.

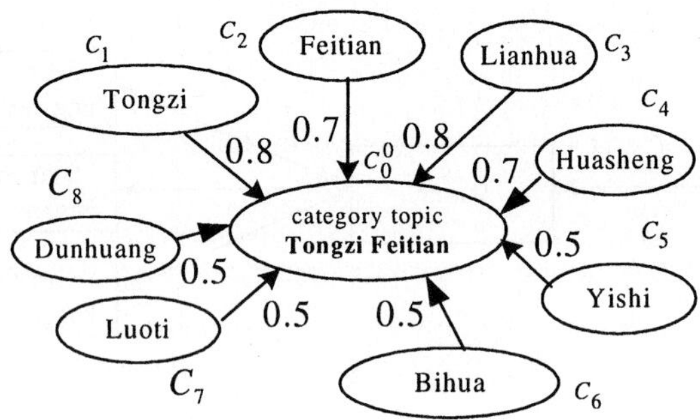

Fig. 2. BC-FCM for "Tongzi Feitian"

In the implementing process, it is also necessary to construct BC-FCMs for each subclass of Dunhuang Feitian. Under the domain background knowledge of Dunhuang Culture as well as referring to some professional dictionaries, the BC-FCMs for subclasses of "Dunhuang Feitian", such as "Tongzi Feitian", are constructed. Fig. 2 is the BC-FCM for "Tongzi Feitian".

3.1 Major User Interface and Results Analysis

We use the software *Macromedia Flash* to organize the pictures and generate the whole animation of the Feitian System. The SRCC component is used to search and access the corresponding on-line e-documents.

Users can input query keyword(s) in the search box, and then click the "Go" button. Query keyword(s) is (are) transmitted to Web search engines. Search results are returned by the meta-search engine and classified by the proposed classification method.

The scenario of the search results corresponding to subclass "Tongzi Feitian" is shown in fig. 3. When user selects a subclass, the corresponding e-document list is shown to the user, with query words highlighted. This e-document list could be in the original order, or be re-ranked according to some ranking algorithms.

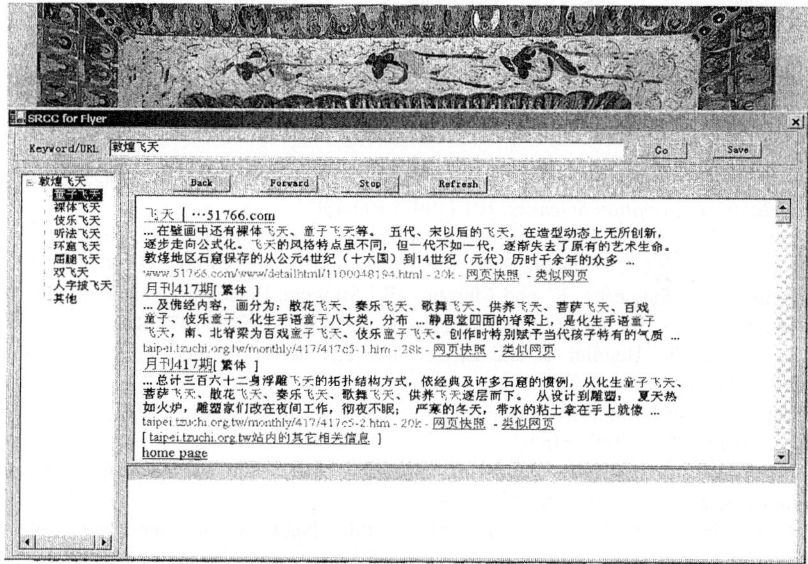

Fig. 3. The scenario of the search results corresponding to "Tongzi Feitian"

In the meta-search engine, if a user inputs "Dunhuang Feitian" as the query keywords, there are nearly 30,000 search results returned by included search engines. Among these search results, using the proposed classification method, there are about 6430 search results belonging to "Tongzi Feitian"; 8160 search results belonging to "Luoti Feitian"; 826 search results belonging to "Jiyue Feitian"; 454 search result belonging to "Shuang Feitian" and 709 search results belonging to "Qutui Feitian" etc.

4 Conclusions

An approach of using FCM to effectively classify e-documents returned by a meta-search engine into a set of predefined categories is proposed. FCM has been employed to capture the semantic relationships between keywords extracted from an e-document. The classification process is adaptive: if some documents don't belong to any of the predefined categories, they will not be wrongly assigned to any existing categories. Experiments with a set of local e-documents have proved that this approach has high performance and can help users getting the e-documents. This method has been implemented to help users know culture effectively, and can help implement the future interconnection environment [15]. Zhuge's Resource Space Model [10-12] is used to store and effectively manage documents. Ongoing work is to incorporate the FCM with the SLN [7-9] to form more powerful semantic representation approach for the Semantic Grid [7, 14].

References

1. Haruechaiyasak, C., Shyu, M. and Chen, S.: Web Document Classification Based on Fuzzy Association. In: Proceedings of the 26th Annual International Computer Software and Applications Conference (COMPSAC'02), Oxford, England, 2002.
2. Lee, J., Lee, K. and Kim, W.: Preparations for Semantics-Based XML Mining. In: Proceedings of the 2001 IEEE International Conference on Data Mining, California, USA, 2001.
3. Tsadiras, A. and Margaritis, K.: Cognitive Mapping and Certainty Neuron Fuzzy Cognitive Maps. *Information Sciences*, 101 (1997) 109-130.
4. Hart, J.: Comparative Cognition: Politics of International Control of Oceans. In: Axelrod, R. (ed.): Structure of Decision. Princeton: Princeton University Press, (1976) 180-217.
5. Tsadiras, A., Margaritis, K. and Mertzios, B.: Strategic Planning Using Extended Fuzzy Cognitive Maps. *Studies in Informatics and Control*, 4(3) (1995) 237-245.
6. Berners-Lee, T., Hendler, J. and Lassila, O.: The Semantic Web. *Scientific American*, 284(5) (2001) 34-43.
7. Zhuge, H.: Clustering Soft-device in the Semantic Grid. *IEEE Computing in Science and Engineering*, 4(6) (2002) 60–62.
8. Zhuge, H.: Active e-Document Framework ADF: Model and Platform. *Information and Management*. 41(1) (2003) 87-97.
9. Zhuge, H. and Jia, R.: Semantic Link Network Builder and Intelligent Browser. *Concurrency and Computation: Practice and Experience*, 16(14) (2004) 1453 –1476.
10. Zhuge, H.: The Knowledge Grid. World Scientific, 2004.
11. Zhuge, H.: Resource Space Grid: Model, Method and Platform. *Concurrency and Computation: Practice and Experience*, 16(14) (2004) 1385–1413.
12. Zhuge, H.: Resource Space Model, Its Design Method and Applications. *Journal of Systems and Software*, 72(1) (2004) 71-81.
13. Zhuge, H.: China's E-Science Knowledge Grid Environment. *IEEE Intelligent Systems*, 19(1) (2004) 13-17.
14. Zhuge, H.: Semantic Grid: Scientific Issues, Infrastructure, and Methodology. *Communications of the ACM*. 48(4) (2005) 117-119.
15. Zhuge, H.: The Future Interconnection Environment. *IEEE Computer*, 38(4) (2005) 27-33.

A Scalable Resource Locating Service in Vega Grid

Hai Mo[1,2], Zha Li[2], and Liu Haozhi[2]

[1] Graduate School of the Chinese Academy of Sciences,
Beijing 100039

[2] Software Division, Institute of Computing Technology, Chinese Academy of Sciences,
Beijing 100080, P.R. China

{haimo, char, liuhaozhi}@software.ict.ac.cn

Abstract. With the dynamic and heterogeneous characteristics of resources in grid environment, efficient resource locating becomes a challenging issue. We propose an approach to the grid resource locating issue based on globally unique and location-independent virtual name. We implement a distributed locating service-router service, which hides the heterogeneity and dynamism of underlying resources, provides single system imaged interfaces of location-transparent global resource locating. Routers can be interconnected to arbitrary topology. The routing table of all routers maintains global router information. Changes in router information are propagated dynamically to all routers by using an incremental propagation mechanism which decreases communication traffic. The process of resource locating will not exceed three hops according to our two-segmented virtual naming scheme. Caching and replication technology is adopted to increase the efficiency and reliability of resource locating. Performance evaluation shows that, compared to existing locating mechanisms, our approach achieves a better locating efficiency, scalability and adaptability.

1 Introduction

The Grid computing model offers an effective way to build high-performance computing system and allows users to efficiently access and integrate geographically distributed computers, data, and applications. In traditional single computer system and cluster system, the distribution of resources is very centralized, so resources can be easily located and the influence of resource locating to computational performance is very small. While in grid environment, with the distributed and heterogeneous characteristics of resources, locating needed resource efficiently becomes very important for the performance of grid computing. This paper presents an approach to the grid resource locating issue.

In order to adapt to the dynamic and heterogeneous characteristics of resources in grid, we abstract physical resources to virtual resources by creating a location-independent virtual name for each physical resource, and we propose an approach to resource locating based on globally unique virtual name. We implement a distributed naming and locating service–router service, which not only functions as naming and locating resources, but also implements full life cycle management of resources. Each router service has a virtual name which is created automatically the first time it start-ups. Different from [1], the routing table records the mapping between the name and

H. Zhuge and G.C. Fox (Eds.): GCC 2005, LNCS 3795, pp. 597 – 608, 2005.

address of each router and has a lower space complexity. How to keep the routing table of all routers consistent is a key issue for our resource locating mechanism. We introduce an incremental propagation policy, which solves this problem and decreases communication traffic.

Our infrastructure for resource locating has three features: simplicity, efficiency and scalability. It is simple because it only maintains a binding between permanent name and current address of each local resource, and its routing table only stores the mapping between the name and address of each router. Furthermore, it takes at most three hops to locate a resource assuming the routing table is accurate and no router fails, so it is efficient. Previous work on resource locating lacks a good scalability because the routing hops increases with the increasing of the number of nodes. In contrast, our locating mechanism finishes each locating by at most three hops, which bears no relation with the number of nodes.

This paper is organized as follows: Section 2 gives related work on the resource locating. Section 3 introduces our approach to resource locating in detail. Section 4 gives experiments and evaluation. In Section 5 we conclude and discuss future work.

2 Related Work

Much work is relevant for our study. In the early years of Grid computing, resource discovery was achieved via centralized services that contained all stored information. An example is the Condor matchmaker [2], While efficient for a local-area network, this system breaks down for large VOs as it is both a performance bottleneck and a single point of failure. UDDI [3] also implements centralized management of resources, which includes the description, registry and search of resources. It lacks good scalability and can't tolerate failure of a single point. Similarly, the Globus Toolkit's Monitoring and Discovery Service (MDS) [4] was initially designed as a centralized way to obtain grid information, which inevitably limits scalability and reliability. Later designs in MDS-2 [4] have moved to a decentralized approach where Grid information is stored and indexed by index servers that communicate via a registration protocol. However, the well defined hierarchical naming structure requires that prior arrangements on name space structure should be established between participants, which proves problematic in practice. The research of [5] combines peer-to-peer technology with grid and applies them to resource discovery. The P2P architecture is fully distributed and all the nodes are equivalent. But all request forwarding algorithms they have proposed cannot make up for that every node has little knowledge about the distribution of resources and their status. So they are not effective.

P2P systems identify resources through their names and use a variety of strategies to locate a specified resource, including flooding(Gnutella[6]), centralized index servers(Napster[7]], and intelligent positioning of data into search-optimized, reliable, and flexible structures for efficient and scalable name-based retrieval, such as in CAN[8],Chord[9], Pastry[10] and Tapestry[11]. Gnutella[6] adopts a kind of flooding mechanism. Requests for resources are propagated the same way: they flood the network until their time to live expires. It has a good search performance but causes too much unnecessary network traffic. Napster[7] uses a centralized approach: a file index is maintained at a central location. To provide files to the Napster community, a node registers the filenames and their location with the central index. A user queries the central index for a specific file and retrieves a set of locations. It lacks good scalability and can not tolerate failure of a single point. CAN[8] Chord[9], Pastry[10] and Tapestry[11] build search-efficient indexing structures that provide good scalability and search performance. However, because they are all structured, to update the routing table of all nodes when a node joins or leaves is more complicated than router service.

DNS[12] provides a host name to IP address mapping. Compared to DNS, router service has more advantages. First, DNS relies on a set of special root servers while router service requires no special root servers and each router is equivalent; Second, DNS uses a predefined hierarchical naming scheme but we adopt a non-hierarchical naming scheme; Last, DNS servers are rigid tree structure while router service can be interconnected to arbitrary topology.

3 Resource Locating Mechanism

3.1 Overview

A computer system approach[13] is adopted in the Vega Grid projects at the Institute of Computing Technology, Chinese Academy of Sciences. The main feature is to view grid as a computer system platform at the hardware and operating system level. Vega GOS, the grid operation system layer of Vega Grid, adopts a hierarchical software architecture of loosely coupled and service oriented. It implements the EVP address space model[14] but with some modification. Physical address space consists of web services called physical resource. The web service's endpoint called physical address is registered into the router service, and the interconnected router service forms a global virtual address space with single system image. Each registered physical resource will get a globally unique virtual address from its registering router service. The virtual address will be put into agora[13] manually, and will be assigned a readable name called effective address. An effective resource is described as a group of customized access control and authorization policies which can be indexed by an effective address in a certain agora. All resources in all agoras build up the effective address space. The transition from effective to virtual address of a resource is done by agora; while the transition from virtual to physical address of a resource is done by router service. The main function of router service is to provide interfaces on physical resource engaging and global resource locating. It also provides global views on virtual resources and gives a path for each locating request. The architecture of router service is shown in Figure 1. R denotes a router service, and p denotes a physical resource. Each router maintains information of global routers and local resources which register to it. And each router is connected with a set of routers called neighbors of this router. A connection between two neighbors is a logical state that enables them to directly exchange updated global router information at intervals. When the client sends a locating request to one router service, the router will process that request internally or forward the request to another router.

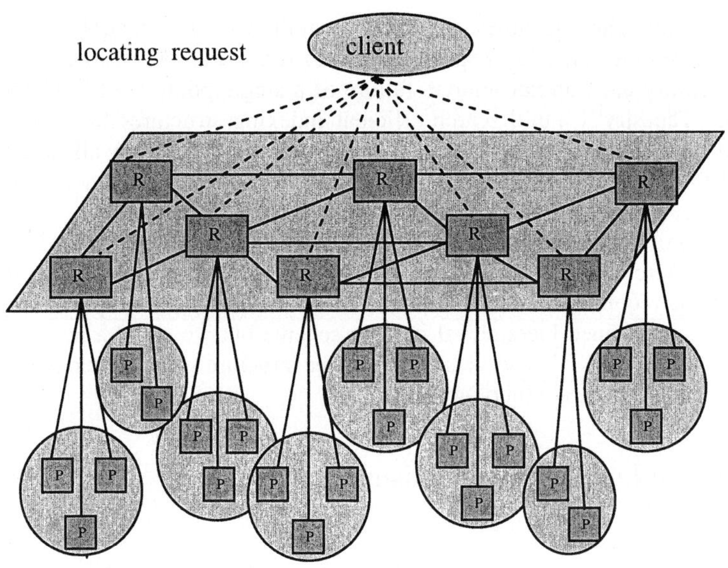

Fig. 1. Architecture of router service

3.2 Resource Naming

To locate a resource in grid, it's very important to how to globally name resources. Unfortunately, location-dependent name makes it hard to handle resource location migration. Each time a physical resource changes an access point, or an access point is reassigned to a different resource, the application that binds to this resource must be rewritten to adapt to this change. Therefore, location-independent name for a resource is necessary in grid environment.

In our router service, we propose a two-segmented naming scheme which is location-independent and scalable. Once a physical resource has registered to a router, it will create a globally unique and location-independent virtual name for this resource. No two resources ever have the same virtual name, even if generated 100 years apart in distant countries. The virtual name is two-segmented. The first segment deals with router name spaces, and the name of each router is created automatically the first time it startups. The second segment deals with resource name spaces, which are independent of router name and keep track of each resource's physical address. Hence, physical resources registered in the same router will have the same former segment but different latter segment on its virtual name. The two parts cooperate to locate a resource. Both router name and resource name are all *Global Unique Identifier*. The virtual name can scale to very large numbers of grid resources distributed across a wide area network.

An important property of our virtual name is its stability: Once it is created by router and assigned to a resource, it will remain the same during that resource's lifetime, no matter where the resource moves. We allow a resource to regularly change its location, that is, to regularly change the binding between its virtual name and physical address. The advantage of our naming scheme is that it allows a grid resource to be migrated both spatially and temporally while preserving the virtual name of the resource.

The syntax of our naming scheme in BNF is as follows:

```
<virtual_name>::= <prefix><router_name><separator><res_name>
<prefix>::=”vres://”|”VRES://”
<router_name>::=<guid>
<separator>::=”:”
<res_name>::=<guid>
<guid>::=<string>
```

3.3 Incremental Propagation Mechanism

Our locating service is based on the idea that each router stores the global router information, which maintains the mapping between router name and router address. A router would fail and recover, or join and leave while other routers are still running, so the global router information dynamically changes. Once the global router information in one router changes, the updated router information will propagate to other routers in the grid. The key issue is how to keep global router information in all routers consistent. What we adopt is a kind of incremental propagation policy which saves bandwidth utilization.

Each router keeps an update queue which records the updated global router information. It learns updated router information from its neighbors by invoking their update interface periodically. Upon receiving the updated information, the router will accordingly update its global router information. A router may fail or recover, so we set a status for each router. And each router will periodically invoke the ping interface of its neighbors to verify whether they are alive. When it finds its neighbor fails, it will set this neighbor's status as dead. And once the neighbor recovers, it will set this neighbor's status as alive. On the other hand, the topology changes dynamically, a neighbor of one router may be added or deleted, which also causes the change of global router information. How the changes propagate to other routers in the grid so that the global router information in all routers attains consistency? Each router requests its living neighbors for the updated router information at intervals. We set a timestamp for each neighbor of every router. Let's take a router router1 as an example and see how it works. Initially the timestamp for its each neighbor is set to zero. It periodically sends a request of invoking the update interface together with a timestamp to its living neighbors. When one of its living neighbors router2 receives the request, it will first check whether the timestamp in the request is zero. If it is zero, router2 will return the global router information to router1. Otherwise it will select the router information updated after the timestamp from its update queue and return it to router1. For the clock in each router is not synchronized, we return router2's current timestamp to router1 together with the updated router information. And then router1 updates router2's timestamp using the new timestamp. Next time router1 sends an invocation request to router2 with the new timestamp. Once router1 has received the updated router information from all its neighbors, it will update its global router information accordingly and add the updated router information to its update queue. Each router works like that. Global router information of all routers will be consistent in finite time.

To avoid ring problems, we introduce source router name and priority in the updated router information. There exists a router originating each propagation, which we call the initiator. At the initiator, the priority is set to 1 which is the highest. When the changed router information goes through a router, the priority is increased by 1. A piece of changed router information propagates from the initiator through all the other routers in the grid. For the same initiator, if the changed router name is equal, the router will not learn from its neighbor with a lower priority, which means that router1 will not learn a piece of updated router information from its neighbor router2 which first learns from router1 the information.

3.4 Scalable Resource Locating

In order to increase efficiency, fault tolerance and adaptability of resource locating, we adopt the caching and replication techniques. Each router maintains a cache of the mapping between virtual name and physical address of each resource it recently accesses. Before forwarding a resource locating request towards another router, a router first checks whether the requested resource is in its own cache and if so, can itself satisfy the request without forwarding it any further. The number of caches from which a locating request can be served grows in direct proportion to its popularity and the act of locating a resource makes it more widely available. When a resource is registered to a connected router, the router will store replicas of resource information in some of its neighbors. The adequate replication of resource information can withstand the failure of some router.

When a physical resource is registered to a connected router, the router will create a globally unique virtual name for this resource. At the same time the status of the resource is set to be local. Once a physical resource has been registered to a router, it can also change its registering location to another router. The source router will record the address of destination router called link router and set the resource's status as remote. Thus the resource changes the registering location but remains the original virtual name.

If a user sends a locating request to a router, this router will first check the router name of the resource's virtual name, if it is local router, it will query its local resources information and return the physical address of this resource to the user. Otherwise, it will search the resource in its cache. If the resource cannot be found in the cache, it will get the router address mapping the router name from the routing table, and forward this request to the remote router. If the remote router is alive and this resource's status is local, it will return the physical address of this resource to the local router. And if the remote router is alive and the resource's status is remote, it will forward the locating request to the link router. But if this remote router crashes, the local router will forward the locating request to one of the living neighbors of this remote router. Upon receiving the response from this remote router, the local router will record the mapping from virtual name to physical address of this resource in the cache and return the physical address to the user.

The combined effect of two-segment virtual name is an extremely short search path. In the worst case, it takes three routing hops to finish a resource locating assuming accurate routing tables and no recent router failures, which is a considerable improvement over existing approaches and shows a good scalability. Figure 2 illustrates the course of resource locating in the worst case.

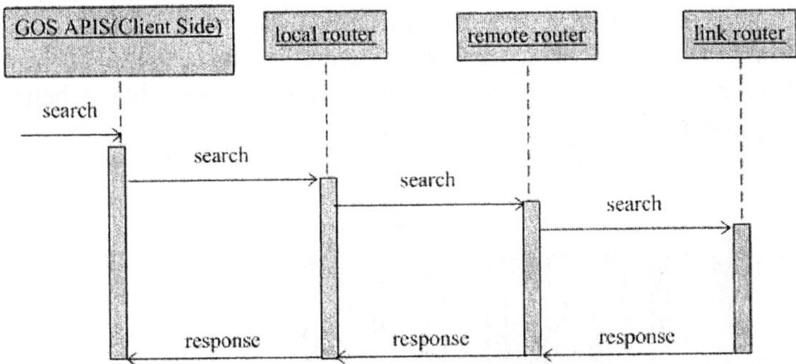

Fig. 2. Resource Locating sequence diagram

4 Experiments and Evaluation

Router service is a key component in Vega GOS, which implements the binding from the virtual name to the access point of a resource. We evaluate it from performance, scalability and adaptability.

4.1 Performance

To get an insight into the resource locating performance of router service, we do experiments in wide area network. And we deploy router service on ten physical sites. Two metrics are considered to evaluate the locating performance. They include:

Success rate. A resource locating request is successful if the physical address of this resource is found. We define the success rate as the ratio of successful to total resource locating requests.

Communication traffic. Communication traffic refers to the traffic caused by the exchange of information between neighbor routers.

The input parameters of our experiments include:

Topology. All experiments are done on a fixed tree topology.

Routing table update period. A router will invoke the update interface of its neighbors to learn the lately updated router information each routing table update period.

Router status change period. A router join and leave or fail and recover each router status change period;

Request distribution. Request distribution refers to the pattern of users' requests for resources. In our experiments, user request follows Poisson process and the requested resource is randomly selected.

Resource distribution. In our experiments, resources are distributed evenly in routers. Each router has the same number of resources.

Figure 3 compares the average success rate of router service and old version Vega resource router [15] under different ratio of routing table update period to router status change period. We observe that the average success rate of router service is higher than [15] under the same ratio, which shows router service has a better locating performance than [15].

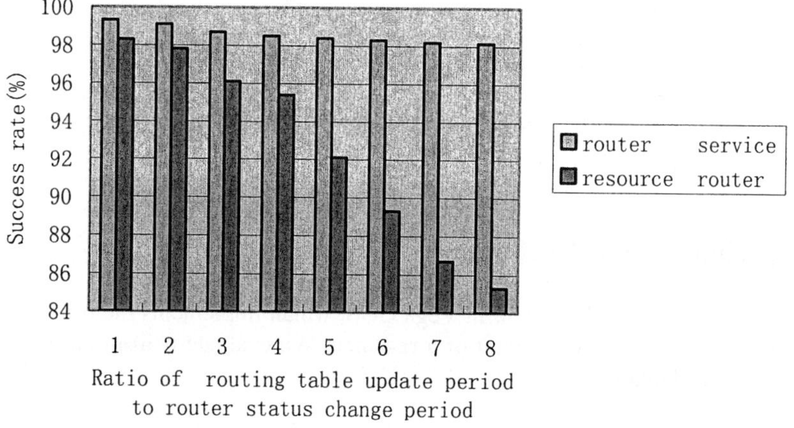

Fig. 3. Success rate of router service and resource router under different ratio of routing table update period to router status change period

Next we analyze the communication traffic of each router. Table 1 gives the symbols and definitions. There are two types of communication in our system:

Keep-alive messages. Each router will periodically invoke the ping interface of its neighbors to verify whether they are alive. Since keep-alive messages are sent every routing table update period and these messages contain no message body, the size of this message and the acknowledgement are therefore $\frac{v \cdot \overline{d}}{t}$.

Update messages. Each router will learn the updated router information from its neighbors by invoking its neighbors' update interface every routing table update period. This message only contains one neighbor's timestamp, and the acknowledgement contains the updated router information. So the size of this message is $\frac{(v+8) \cdot \overline{d}}{t}$, and the size of the acknowledgement is $r \cdot N \cdot m \cdot \overline{d} + \frac{v \cdot \overline{d}}{t}$.

Table 1. Symbols and Definitions

Symbol	Definition
N	The number of nodes in the overlay network
E	The number of edges in the overlay network
$\overline{d}$	The average outdegree of the nodes of the backbone network: $\overline{d} = \frac{2 \cdot E}{N}$.
v	The number of bytes of per-message protocol overhead
m	The number of bytes of a piece of updated router information
t	Routing table update period
r	The ratio of routers which join and leave or fail and recover per second to total routers

Therefore the bandwidth utilization on each router (both upstream and downstream) is $\frac{4 \cdot v \cdot \overline{d}}{t} + \frac{8 \cdot \overline{d}}{t} + r \cdot N \cdot m \cdot \overline{d}$. According to Lemma 2 in [16], the number of edges of a graph E can be estimated as a function of the number of nodes, N, and the rank exponent, $\Re$:

$$\mathrm{E} = \frac{1}{2 \cdot (\Re+1)} \cdot \left(1 - \frac{1}{N^{\Re+1}}\right) \cdot N \ . \tag{1}$$

Substituting equation 1 into $\overline{d} = \frac{2 \cdot E}{N}$, it goes into

$$\overline{d} = \frac{1}{\Re+1}\left(1 - \frac{1}{N^{\Re+1}}\right) . \tag{2}$$

Thus we can compute the communication traffic on each router. In this computations we use v=4000 bytes, m=132 bytes, r=0.0002, t=40 seconds and $\Re$ =-0.7. In a system with 5000 nodes, the load on a router is 1.71KB/s. Given these values and the formula 2, we can plot the communication traffic per router in a system of various sizes. The results of this calculation are shown in Figure 4. Note that the traffic increases only linearly with the size of the system. The communication traffic is not larger than 2.14 KB/s even in a system of 10000 nodes, which proves very bandwidth-efficient.

4.2 Scalability

With the number of resources in grid increases continuously, the space consumption of the routing table in router service doesn't increase accordingly, for the routing table only records information of routers, which has no relation with the number of resources. The space complexity of router service is $O(N^2)$, N is the number of routers; while the space complexity of [15] is O(RN), R is the number of resources. The number of routers is so small compared with the number of resources so the space consumption of router service is less than [15] which shows a good scalability of of router service. The routing hops to locate a resource of router service is not larger than 3 which is not relevant with the number of nodes and topology; while in [15] the routing hops is $O(W_{max})$ in the worst case, W_{max} is the length of the longest path in the topology. Compared to DNS[12], router service requires no special root servers and imposes no naming structure. Furthermore, each router can be interconnected to arbitrary topology which also shows a good scalability of router service.

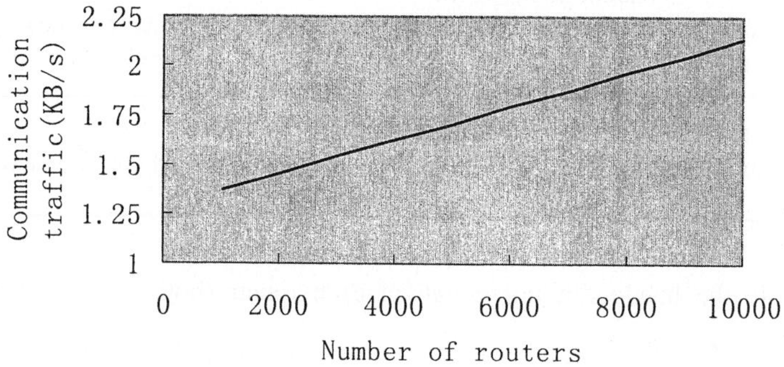

Fig. 4. Communication traffic under different number of routers

In table 2 we compare the routing hops and the number of messages to finish a resource locating of different locating mechanisms. N is the number of nodes which use IDs of base b, d is the dimensions of Cartesian coordinate space which is partitioned into n equal zones, Wmax is the length of the longest path in the topology. We can see that router service outperforms other locating mechanisms in routing hops and the number of messages generated by per request, which shows a good scalability.

Table 2. Comparison of routing hops and messages per request of different locating mechanisms

Locating mechanism	Routing hops	Messages per request
CAN	$O(dn^{1/d})$	$O(dn^{1/d})$
Chord	O(logN)	O(logN)
Pastry	O(logN)	O(logN)
Tapestry	$O(\log_b N)$	$O(\log_b N)$
Resource router	$O(W_{max})$	$O(W_{max})$
Router service	O(1)	O(1)

4.3 Adaptability

Because our infrastructure for resource locating adopts a decentralized architecture, it tolerates failure of a single router well. Any router can join or leave freely, without influencing the running of other routers. As we adopt caching and replication technology, the influence of any router's failure to the success rate and routing hops is minor which shows router service has a good adaptability in the face of failure of any router.

Figure 5 compares the average success rate of router service and old version Vega resource router [15] under different router fail rate. Here we set the routing table update period as 40 seconds. We observe that the average success rate of router service is higher than [15] under the same router fail rate, and the router fail rate has a less great influence on the success rate of router service than it could have on the resource router, which shows router service has a better adaptability than [15].

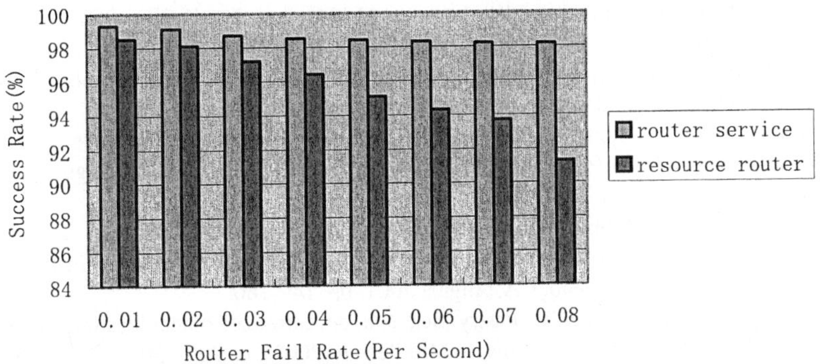

Fig. 5. Success rate of router service and resource router under different router fail rate

5 Conclusion and Future Work

In this paper, we propose an approach to the grid resource locating based on globally unique virtual name. We implement a distributed naming and locating service-router service, which not only functions as naming and locating resources, but also implements full life cycle management of resources. All routers maintain global router information. And how to keep it consistent is a key issue for our resource locating performance. We introduce the incremental propagation mechanism, which solves this problem and decreases communication traffic. The combined effect of two-segment virtual name we adopt is an extremely short search path. In at most three hops it is possible to locate a resource. This is a considerable improvement over existing approaches. Furthermore, caching and replication technology is adopted to increase the efficiency of resource locating and adaptability in the face of failure of any router.

In the future, we plan to extend our router service, implement searching a resource by attributes and optimize the incremental propagation algorithm in order for all routers to converge in a shorter time. We are in the process of benchmarking the current system so that we can measure the improvement in locating performance as we develop more effective router service.

References

1. W. Li, Z. Xu, F. Dong and J. Zhang , Grid resource discovery based on a routing-transferring model , In Proceedings of the 3rd International Workshop on Grid Computing, pp.145-156, Baltimore, MD, 2002.

2. Raman, R., Ljvny, M., and Solomon, M. , MatchMaking: Distributed Resource Management for High Throughput Computing , In 7th IEEE International Symposium on High Performance Distributed Computing , 1998.
3. UDDI.org, 2000. http://www.uddi.org.
4. Czajkowski, K., Fitzgerald, S., Foster, I., Kesselman,C., Grid Information Services for Distributed Resource Sharing, Proc.10th IEEE International Symposium on High Performance Distributed Computing (HPDC-10), IEEE Press, August, 2001, pp.181-194.
5. Ianmitchi, A., Foster, I., On Fully Decentralized Resource Discovery in Grid Environments, In Proc. the international Workshop on Grid Computing, Denver, 2001, pp. 51-62.
6. Gnutella Protocol Specification, http://www.gnutella.com/
7. C-NET NEWS. Napster among fastest-growing Net technologies. 2000. http://new.com.com/2100-1023-246648.html
8. S. Ratnasamy, P. Francis, M. Handley, R. Karp, and S. Shenker., A Scalable Content Addressable Network, In Proc. ACM SIGCOMM 2001, San Diego, CA, August 2001, pp. 161-172
9. Ion Stoica, Robert Morris, David Karger, M. Frans Kaashoek, and Hari Balakrishnan, Chord: A Scalable Peer-to-peer Lookup Service for Internet Applications, In Proc. ACM SIGCOMM 2001, San Diego, CA, August 2001, pp. 149-160.
10. Rowstron, A., and Druschel, P., Pastry: Scalable, decentralized object location, and routing for large-scale peer-to-peer systems, In Middleware(2001), pp.329-350.
11. Zhao, B. Y., Kubiatowicz, John., and Joseph, A. D., Tapestry: An infrastructure for fault-tolerant wide-area location and routing, Tech. Rep. CSD-01-1141, Berkeley, 2001.
12. Mockapetris, P.V., and Dunlap, K. J., Development of the Domain Name System, In Proc. ACM SIGCOMM (Stanford, CA,1988), pp. 123–133.
13. Z. Xu, W. Li, Vega Grid: A Computer Systems Approach to Grid Research, in Grid and Cooperative Computing, 2nd International Workshop, December 2003, pp. 480-486
14. W. Li, Z. Xu, A Model of Grid Address Space with Applications, Journal of Computer Research and Development, 2003, 40(12), pp. 1756-1762.
15. E. Tan., L. Zha, Application and Improvement of Vega Grid Router, Journal of Computer Research and Development, 2004, 40(12), pp. 2164-2169.
16. Michalis Faloutsos, Petros Faloutsos, and Christos Faloutsos, On power-law relationships of the internet topology, In SIGCOMM, pp. 251-262, 1999.

rBundle: An Iterative Combinatorial Auction-Based Approach to Supporting Advance Reservation

Zhixing Huang and Yuhui Qiu

Computer and Information Science Faculty,
Southwest China Normal University
{huangzx, yhqiu}@swnu.edu.cn

Abstract. Advance Reservation for global grids becomes an important research area as it allows users to gain concurrent access for their applications to be executed in parallel, and guarantees the availability of resources at specified future times. In this paper, we propose a market-based framework for advance resource reservation through iterative combinatorial auction, and we also introduce three variant price updating methods and compare the revenue of the service providers, the duration of the auction, and the satisfaction of the users when all users use best-response bidding strategy.

1 Introduction

Grid Computing has emerged as a new paradigm for next-generation computing. It supports the creation of virtual organizations and enterprizes that enable the sharing, exchange, selection, and aggregation of geographically distributed heterogenous resources for solving large-scale problems in science, engineering, and commerce. In spite of a number of advantages in Grid computing, resource management and scheduling in such environments continues to be a challenging and complex undertaking. In recent years, distributed computational economy has been recognized as an effective metaphor [1] for the management of Grid resource, as it: (1) enables the regulation of supply and demand for resource, (2) provides economic incentive for grid service providers, and (3) motivates the grid service consumers to trade-off between deadline, budget, and the required level of quality-of-service.

Moreover, the Grid is a highly dynamic environment with servers coming on-line, going off-line, and with continuously varying demands from the clients[2]. In most Grid scheduling systems, submitted jobs are initially placed into a queue if there are no available resources. Therefore, there is no guarantee as to when these jobs will be executed. This causes problems in parallel applications, where most of them have dependencies among each other. And grid resources are not storable, thus that capacity not used today can be put aside for future use. So, the advance reservation of these resources are needed for users to request resources from multiple scheduling systems at a specific time and thus gain simultaneous access to enough resources for their application[3]. As is defined in [4], an

H. Zhuge and G.C. Fox (Eds.): GCC 2005, LNCS 3795, pp. 609–620, 2005.

Advance Reservation is a possibly limited or restricted delegation of a particular resource capability over a demand time interval, obtained by the requestor from the resource owner through a negotiation process [2]. Example resource capabilities: number of processors, amount of memory, disk space, software licences, network bandwidth, etc. Moreover, the works of advance reservations, started within the GGF (Global Grid Forum) to support advance reservations, are currently being added to some test-bed of grid toolkit, such as Nimrod-G [1], Portable Batch System (PBS), Maui scheduler etc.

In this paper, we investigate a market-based approach to automatic resource reservation through software agents participating a combinatorial auction. The remainder of this paper is structured as follows. In Section 2, we give a brief review of the related works about our research.In Section 3, the definition and the states of advance reservation used in this paper are given, and the model of advance reservation by combinatorial auction is discussed. In Section 4, we demonstrate the empirical evaluation of the three different price update methods, the revenue of the service providers, the duration of the auction, and the satisfaction of the user agents has been compared in the experiments. Finally, in Section 5 we present the conclusions and future work.

2 Related Work

Auctions provide useful mechanisms for resource allocation problems with automates and self-interested agents[17]. Typical applications include task assignment and distributed scheduling problems, and are characterized with distributed information about agents' local problems and multiple conflicting goals. Auctions can minimize communication within a system, and generate optimal (or near-optimal) solutions that maximize the sum value over all agents. In traditional auctions, the resources are auctioned sequentially. We have investigated the advance reservation method through agents participating in multi-overlapping ascending auctions[6]. In this case, if an agent wants to obtain a combination of the auctioned resources, it has to estimate which other resource it will receive in other auctions, which is heavily relied on how other agents will bid[15]. Such an estimation or look-ahead is uncertainty due to incomplete information about other bidders. This leads to inefficient allocations of resources[8].

Combinatorial auctions can be used to overcome these deficiencies[9]. In a combinatorial auction, bidders may submit bids on combinations of resources. This allows the bidders to express complementarities between resources instead of speculating the valuation of a resource with the impact of possibly getting other complementary resource[10]. Due to above advantages, the combinatorial auctions can be applied to the task allocation, planning and time scheduling in multi-agent systems where the items to be allocated are complementary or substitutable. *i*Bundle[11] is the first ascending-price bundle auction that guaranteed to compute optimal bundle allocations with a best-response agent bidding strategy. Other researchers also proposed some efficient algorithms to solve this problem and discuss related issues about the combinatorial auctions. However, in these studies the items are restricted to being discrete (Single-unit or Multi-unit), their methods cannot be directly used in continuous objects, such as the service time. Wellman [16] proposed an (single) auction-based method for a factory-scheduling problem, in which agents compete for periods of time on shared machine. His work is based on single service provider. It's quite different from the reality of grid environment.

In the following section, we will extend our previous work and propose a framework based on combinatorial auction for supporting resource advance reservations.

3 Problem Statement

Suppose there are $M = \{1, 2, \cdots, m\}$ service providers willing to provide computation service, there are $N = \{1, 2, \cdots n\}$ user agents, each agent with one task to fulfill. Each agent has its own financial budget, deadline, task size and requests for the services, etc.

Table 1. Problem 1

Task	Budget	Size	Deadline	Server
A	284	29	140	[0 1]
B	106	53	111	[1 1]
C	282	29	162	[0 1]

Table 1 demonstrates an example that we will refer back to later in the paper. As is shown in Table 1, A, B, C are three different users' tasks. Each task's budget, deadline and task size are listed in the table. Note that the last column in the Table 1 indicates the user agent requested services, we simply call them service 1 and service 2. For example, task A and C only need the service 2, however task B needs both services simultaneously. As we mentioned above, the resources are owned by different owners and the user want to use the resource simultaneously, the efficient way of the reservation of the resources is through a centralized iterative combinatorial auction. In this section, we propose a iterative combinatorial auctions framework to support resource advance reservation.

The iterative combinatorial auction is proceeded by **rounds**, in which the user can submit a bid in each round, and after receiving all the bids the auctioneer then decide on the winner of current round and adjust the price of the service of each server. Based on the feedback information from the auction, the user decides whether or not to bid in the next round. If there is no bidder submits bid or no valid bid arrives, the auctioneer announces the termination of current turn and updates the price and service information for the next **turn** auction. The winners in the current turn will book the services, and the loser can continue to bid in the next turn. The details of the iterative auction are discussed below.

3.1 States of Advance Reservation

As is noted in Global Grid Forum (GGF) draft [4], Transitions between the states are defined by the operations that a user performs on the reservation. For simplicity, we only consider the following states, which means the booked that reservation can not be altered and cancelled.

- Requested: Initial State of the reservation, when a user has requested a set of resources for a reservation. If the reservation accepted, it goes to being booked. Otherwise, it becomes declined.
- Accepted: A request for a new reservation has been approved.
- Declined: The reservation is not successfully allocated for some reason.
- Booked: A reservation has been made, and will be honored by the scheduler. From here, the reservation can become active.

3.2 Timing Issues

Iterative auctions may be *asynchronous*(or continuous), with the state of the auction continuously updated as bids are received; or *synchronous* (based on rounds), with the state of the auction updated only after a period of time that provides all bidders with the opportunity to revise their bids.

3.3 Bidding Language

In combinatorial auctions, we are mainly concerned with bidding and allocation strategies. While bidding each bidder can bid on any subset of items. Since an exponential number of such subsets are possible, we need a language which helps us express the bids efficiently. The bidding language should be such that only is it easy to express any vector of bids but is should also simple to manipulate the bids. And in combinatorial auctions, a bid can be a complex and expressed in terms of logical connectives. One popular bidding language is exclusive-or(XOR), in which bid $(S_1, p_1) xor (S_2, p_2) xor \cdots xor (S_k, p_k)$ has semantics "I will buy at most one of these bundles" at the stated bid price. Another popular language is additive-or(OR) bidding languages in which bid $(S_1, p_1) or (S_2, p_2) or \cdots or (S_k, p_k)$ has semantics "I will buy one or more of these bundles" at stated bid price. Others bidding languages include: Atomic bids, OR-of-XOR bids, XOR-of-OR bids, OR bids with phantom items, etc. Issues of bidding language are discussed in detail by Nissan and Sandholm [8]. In this paper, for simplicity and also for avoiding computational complexity of winner determination, we propose the variant of *Atomic bids* Language as the following:

The user agents submit a set of bids, $\mathbf{B} = \{B_1, B_2, \cdots, B_n\}$. A bid is a tuple $B_i =< S_i, c_i, T_i >$, $i \in N$, where $S_i \subseteq M$ is a nonempty set of items (the identifier of the service providers) and c_i is the cost of the user i who offers for this set. And T_i is the time span of the user i's task. And we assume that $T_i = (s_i, e_i)$, where s_i is the starting time of the task and e_i is the ending time, $0 \leq s_i < e_i \leq T_{max}$. And we define that $T_i \bigcap T_j = \emptyset$, for any $i, j \in N$, if $s_i \geq e_j$ or $e_i \leq s_j$, which means there will be no conflict between their task execution.

3.4 Service Provider

Suppose the services of the providers are heterogenous. The service of provider j, $j \in M$, can be started at time s_j. Each service provider has its lowest price r_j for providing service (also call reserve price) and the minimal increase of the price λ_j in the auction. In each round of auction, the next probable starting time of each server is also announced by the auctioneer. Those information can be known by all the user agents. We also call the service provider server later on.

3.5 User Agent

Suppose each agent has one task to fulfill. The execution of the agent i's task will take t_i on specified server set S_i. Moreover, the task should be accomplished within a budget m_i and before the deadline d_i. The information of other agents' task execution time, deadline and budget are private information, and the distributions of these information are all unknown to the agent. Suppose the current price of the service j is p_j, and the requested server set is S_i, the cost to user agent i is c_i. The expenses depends on the auction variation. One of the methods to calculate the cost can be the following equation:

$$c_i = t_i * \sum_{j \in S_i} p_j. \tag{1}$$

And we will discuss later the others . Moreover, if the server j in agent i requests set S_i start at s_j in current turn, the expected end time of agent i's task is

$$e_i = \max_{j \in S_i}\{s_j\} + t_i. \tag{2}$$

The utility of agent is decided by the expenses of fulfilling the task and the task's ending time. In this paper, we use a constant elasticity of substitution (CES) function to present user agent's utility u_i. If $d_i < e_i$ or $m_i < c_i$ then $u_i = 0$, otherwise

$$u_i = A_i(\delta_{i1}(d_i - e_i)^{\rho_i} + \delta_{i2}(m_i - c_i)^{\rho_i})^{1/\rho_i} \tag{3}$$

The satisfaction of the user agent is defined as what follows:

$$\theta_i = \frac{u_i}{A_i(\delta_{i1}{d_i}^{\rho} + \delta_{i2}{m_i}^{\rho})^{1/\rho}} \tag{4}$$

The agents may make trade-offs between the task finishing time and the cost of the execution. The bidding strategy is *myopic best-response* to the current state of the auction (prices and allocation). We do not consider agents with information about other agents. The strategy is not optimal in a game-theoretic sense, and deviations could increase an agent's utility in some auction scenarios. In this paper, we suppose that all the agents use a best-response bidding strategy.

3.6 The Winner Determination

In each round, the auctioneer determine problem of the advance reservation is to label the bids as winning $x_i = 1$ or losing $x_i = 0$ so as to maximize the auctioneer's revenue under the constraint that each service can be allocated to at most one bidder, and the :

$$\max \sum_{i=1}^{N} x_i c_i$$
$$s.t. \sum_{j|i \in S_j} x_i \leq 1, \forall j = 1, 2, \ldots, m,$$
$$x_i \in \{0, 1\}, \ \forall i = 1, 2, \cdots, n. \tag{5}$$

This problem is a well-known NP complete problem. It is equivalent to weighted set packing. However, in recent study, Sandholm and their colleagues [8][9][10] proposed that a series of Algorithms can optimally solve large CAs in practice. In this paper, we adopt the algorithm Bob which has been proposed in [8] for the winner determination. After the execution of Bob in a round, we can call the winning agent *active*,and the active agent need not to bid in the next round. The agent losing in current round is called *inactive*, they should update their bids based on price updating rules.

3.7 Termination

The auction terminates when one of the two simple rules holds, designed to detect quiescence. The auctioneer then implements the resource reservation, and the user agents pay the prices that they bid. The auction terminates when either:

T1) All user agents that have booked the resource, or
T2) No agent is willing to bid in the successive rounds.

Condition T1 implies that quiescence for all the agents have booked the resource which they requested to. Condition T2 is little stronger, and implies some agents miss the opportunity for booking resources, such as the resources have been booked by other agents, so the deadline condition of these agents cannot be satisfied any more.

3.8 Price Update

Finally, when the auction does not terminate, the auctioneer updates prices. The price-update rule depends on the auction variation.

***r*Bundle(1).** Prices in *r*Bundle(1) are anonymous. The ask price of the service is increased when two or more user agents request the same service with a time conflict. The ask price of the service p_j^{t+1} is computed as: $p_j^{t+1} = p_j^t + \lambda_j$. So the new bid of agent i for servers S_i should be:

$$c_i^{t+1} = t_i * \sum_{j \in S_i} p_j^{t+1} \tag{6}$$

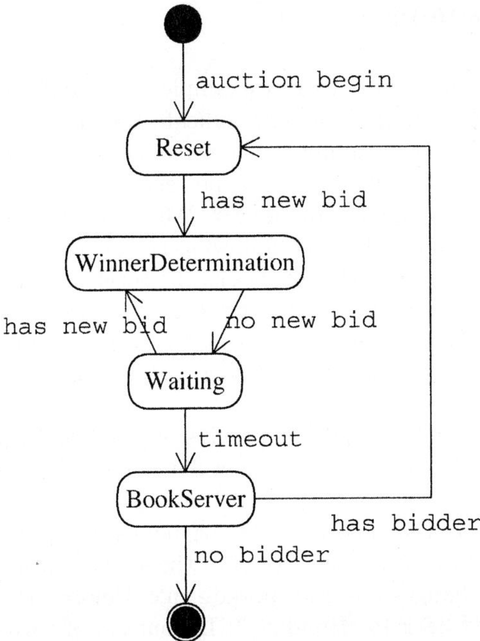

Fig. 1. The States of the Auctioneer

***r*Bundle(2).** Prices in *r*Bundle(2) are discriminatory, and there is a set of ask prices for every agent. Price increases to each agent are only based on the bids received from that agent. Prices only increase when an agent's request is declined, and then only when the agent bid at within ϵ of the current ask price. We denote $h_i^t = max\{c_j^t\}$,for $j \neq i$ and $S_i \bigcap S_j \neq \emptyset$. The new ask price to agent i is updated as the following:

$$c_i^{t+1} = max\{c_i^t, h_i^t + \epsilon\} \tag{7}$$

However, the initial bid price is based on Bundle(1). In other words, the initial bid of user agent i is calculated as $c_i^1 = t_i * \sum_{j \in S_i} r_j$.

***r*Bundle(d).** Prices in *r*Bundle(d) are initially anonymous, but can become discriminatory during the auction. The auction maintains a set $anon(t)$ of agents that receives anonymous prices in round t, initially containing all agents. The price update rule for the anonymous prices is the same as for *r*Bundle(1). The prices update rule for the agents that receive discriminatory prices is the same as for *r*Bundle(2).

Once an agent starts to receive discriminatory prices it does in all future rounds. A simple test determines whether to start charging an agent discriminatory prices. The auctioneer tests whether the revenue of auction dose not increase and no agent submits a valid bid in the last rounds. The inactive agent is removed from the set $anon(t + 1)$, and its prices are initialized to the current anonymous prices before they are updated.

4 Worked Example

In this section we present a worked example of *r*Bundle(1), *r*Bundle(2) and *r*Bundle(3). The 1st and 2nd columns indicate the turn and the round of the auction. The 3rd, 4th, 5th columns in the table indicate the bidding price of the user, the 6th indicates the unit price of the service, and the last column of the table shows the revenue of the auctioneer. We suppose the $\epsilon = 1$ and $\lambda_j = 1$. The process is demonstrated in the following tables. Note that in these tables, $(-)$ indicates that the agent already books the service, so it needn't bid in the next turn, and $(\underline{n})$ means the explicit price of the service is not announced to users. In other words, it takes the function to restrict the lowest bound of the user' bid price. Moreover the star mark $(*)$ indicates which agent is the winner in each round.

Table 2 demonstrates the bidding process of problem 1 using *r*Bundle(d). In turn1, from round 1 to round 9 the price update rule is based on the *r*Bundle(1), in round 10 it changed to adopt *r*Bundle(2) and in round 31. At the end of turn 1, A wins the auction with a cost of 262 and books service 2 from time 0 to 29. Note after round 10 in turn 1, the prices of the services just indicate the prices before the auction changes the price update rule. Before turn 2 begin, the price update rule changed back to *r*Bundle(1). In round 4 of turn 2, user C win the

Table 2. *r*Bundle(d)

Turn	Round	A	B	C	Price	Revenue
1	1	29	106*	29	[1 1]	106
1	2	58	106*	58	[1 2]	106
1	4	116*	106	116	[1 4]	116
1	5	116	0	145*	[1 6]	174
1	9	223	0	261*	[1 9]	261
1	10	262*	0	261	[1 9]	262
1	31	283*	0	282	[$\underline{1}$ $\underline{9}$]	283
2	1	-	106*	29	[1 6]	389
2	4	-	0	116*	[1 4]	399
3	1	-	106*	-	[1 1]	505

Table 3. *r*Bundle(2)

Turn	Round	A	B	C	Price	Revenue
1	1	29	106*	29	[1 1]	106
1	2	107	106*	107	[$\underline{1}$ $\underline{1}$]	106
1	178	283*	0	282	[$\underline{1}$ $\underline{1}$]	283
2	1	-	106*	29	[1 1]	389
2	2	-	0	107*	[$\underline{1}$ $\underline{1}$]	390
3	1	-	106*	-	[1 1]	496

Table 4. *r*Bundle(1)

Turn	Round	A	B	C	Price	Revenue
1	1	29	106*	29	[1 1]	106
1	2	107	106*	107	[1 2]	106
1	9	223	0	261*	[1 9]	261
2	1	-	106*	29	[1 6]	367
2	4	-	0	116*	[1 4]	377
3	1	-	106*	-	[1 1]	483

auction with cost 116 and booked service 2 for time 29 to 58. Finally in the turn 3, user B books the service 1 and 2 with cost 106 from time 58 to 111.

Table 3 and Table 4 show the bidding process of problem 1 using *r*Bundle(2) and *r*Bundle(1) individually. The differences between the two methods are that *r*Bundle(2) takes total 181 rounds when the *r*Bundle(1) only takes 15 rounds, moreover the revenue of *r*Bundle(2) is 496 more than *r*Bundle(1)'s 483, whereas the reserve time of the service is the same for all the service. In the next section we present the results of simulations of our model while considering a variety of parameters.

5 Experiment Analysis

5.1 Experimental Setup

In this section, we assume that the agent's task size is normally distributed between $[10, 60]$, the deadline is normally distributed between [30,180], and the budget is normally distributed between $[100, 300]$. A service will be requested by a user at the rate of 25%. And each user requests at least one service. In each case, at least 100 simulations of advance resource reservation are played among agents. we present the results of simulations of our model while considering a variety of the number of bids and the number of the service providers.

5.2 Results

Revenue. As is shown in figure 3, we can see when the number of bids increases, the revenue of the auctioneer will also increase, but *r*Bundle(d) outperforms the other two price updating methods.

Satisfaction. In this comparison, all the agents are of the same type, that is, in each simulation each agent uses the same bidding strategies. We assume that $\delta_{i1} = \delta_{i2} = 1$, $A_i = 1$, ρ_i=2. As is shown in figure 4, we can see when the number of bids increases, the average satisfaction of the agent will also decrease, *r*Bundled and *r*Bundle(1) outperform *r*Bundle(2). .In this case, *r*Bundle(1) outperforms the other two price updating methods when the number of agents is less than 30, however *r*Bundled gains a similarity result with *r*Bundle(1) when the number of agents is more than 30.

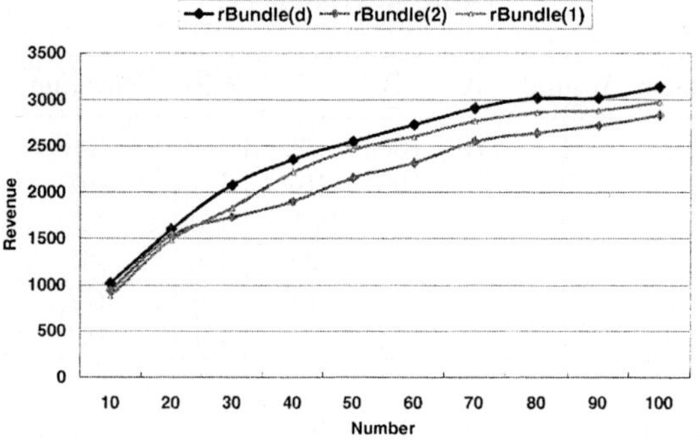

Fig. 2. Comparison of the revenue when bids increase

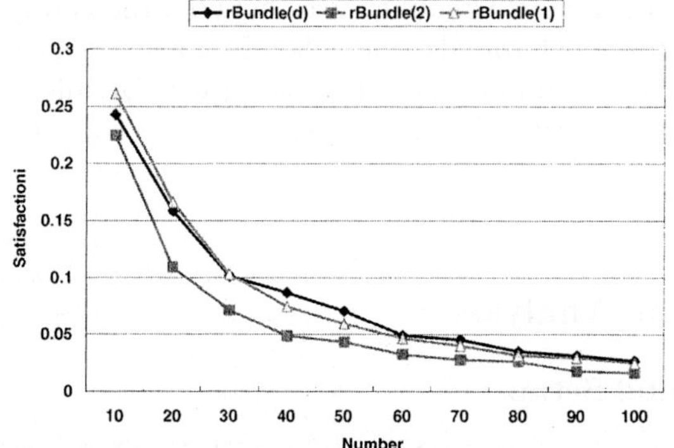

Fig. 3. Comparison of the sum of user's satisfaction

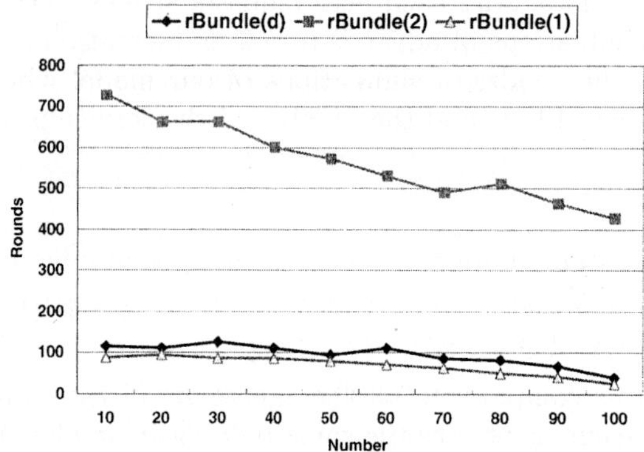

Fig. 4. Comparison of the calculation time

Performance. As is shown in figure 4, we can see when the number of bids increases, the average rounds of the auction will increase, *r*Bundle(1) outperforms the other two price updating methods.

From above comparisons, we can see that in rBundle(d) the auctioneer can get more profit than other two methods, and auction requires relatively less completion time, and the user also can obtain the resources with a relatively high satisfaction.

6 Conclusion and Future Work

In this paper, we propose a market-based framework for advance resource reservation through iterative combinatorial auction, and we also introduce three variant price updating methods and compare the revenue of the service providers, the duration of the auction, and the satisfaction of the users when all users use best-response bidding strategy.

In current work, we assume that our agents have little prior information about the system, and since the auctions don't close simultaneously, it is difficult to predict the remaining active agents in the system except the next turn, so their bidding strategies are quite myopic. We believe that a more effective decision mechanism needs to use the explicit probability distribution over possible agent's task size, agent's budget, and the predication of each auction's closing time. And the different price predication functions and bidding strategies also need to be investigated.

References

1. Rajkumar Buyya, David Abramson, Jonathan Giddy and Heinz Stockinger: Economic models for resource management and scheduling in Grid computing, *The Journal of Concurrency and Computation*, Volume 14, Issue 13-15, Wiley Press, USA, 2002.
2. W. Smith, I. Froster, V. Taylor: Scheduling with Advanced Reservations, *Proc. of the IPDPS Conference*, May, 2000.
3. G. Cheloitis, C.Kneyon and R. Buyya: 10 Lessons from Finance for Commercial Sharing of IT Resources, *Peer-to-Peer Computing: The Evolution of a Disruptive Technology*, IRM Press, Hershey, PA, USA, 2004.
4. Advance Reservation State of the Art: Grid Resource Allocation Agreement Protocol Working Group, *URL http://www.fz-juelich.de/zam/RD/coop/ggf/graap/graap-wg.html.*
5. R. Min and M. Maheswaran: Scheduling Advance Reservation with Priorities in Grid Computing Systems. *Thirteenth IASTED International Conference on Parallel and Distributed Computing Systems(PDCS'01)*, Pages 172-176, Aug, 2000.
6. Zhixing Huang, Yuhui Qiu. A Comparison of Advance Resource Reservation Bidding Strategies in Sequential Ascending Auctions. 7th Asia-Pacific Web Conference, LNCS 3399, Shanghai, China.
7. Aram Galstyan, Karl Czajkowski, and Kristina Lerman: Resource Allocation in the Grid Using Reinforcement Learning. *Proc. of the International Conference on Autonomous Agents and Multi-Agent Systems AAMAS-03*, New York, NY. 2003.
8. T. Sandholm, S. Suri. BOB:Improved winner determination in combinatrial auctions and generalization. Artifical Intelligence 145 papes 33-58. 2003.

9. T. Sandholm. An Algorithm for Optimal Winner Determination in Combinatorial Auctions. Artificial Intelligence, 135, 2002, 1-54.
10. T. Sandholm, S. Suri, A. Gilpin, and D. Levine, CABOB: A Fast Optimal Algorithm for Winner Determination in Combinatorial Auctions. Management Science, Special issue on Electronic Markets. Earlier version in Proceedings of the International Joint Conference on Artificial Intelligence (IJCAI-01), Seattle, WA
11. David C. Parkes. iBundle: An Efficient Ascending Price Bundle Auction
12. P. Anthony, N. R. Jennings: Developing a Bidding Agent for Multiple Heterogeneous Auctions, *ACM Trans on Internet Technology* 3 (3) 185-217. 2003.
13. M. He, N. R. Jennings and A. Prugel-Bennett: An adaptive bidding agent for multiple English auctions: A neuro-fuzzy approach. *Proc. IEEE Conf. on Fuzzy Systems*, Budapest, Hungary. 2004.
14. M. He, N. R. Jennings, and H. F. Leung: On agent-mediated electronic commerce. IEEE Transaction on Kowledge and Data Engineering, 2003.
15. P. Vytelingum, R. K. Dash, E. David and N. R. Jennings: A risk-based bidding strategy for continuous double auctions", *Proc. 16th European Conference on Artificial Intelligence*, Valencia, Spain. 2004.
16. Michal P. Wellman, William E. Walsh, Peter R. Wurman and Jeffrey K. Mackie-Mason: Auction protocols for decentralized scheduling. *Game and Economic Behavior.* 2001.
17. A. Byde: A comparison among bidding algorihms for multiple auctions. Technical report, HP Research Labs. 2001.
18. A. Byde, C. Preist, and N.R.Jennings: Decision Procedures for Multiple Auctions. *Proc. of the first International Joint Conference on Autonomous Agents and Multi-Agents System*, Pages 613-620, 2002.

Decentralized Grid Resource Locating Protocol Based on Grid Resource Space Model

Deke Guo[1], Honghui Chen[1], Chenggang Xie[2], Hongtao Lei[1], Tao Chen[1], and Xueshan Luo[1]

[1] Key Laboratory of C[4]ISR Technology, National University of Defense Technology, Changsha, 410073, P.R. China
aeronautic@126.com, chh0808@sohu.com

[2] Business School of Central South University, Changsha, 410073, P.R. China
Chenggangxie@sohu.com

Abstract. This paper focuses on how to model grid resource and locate grid resource using efficient and scaleable protocol under a grid environment. A mathematic model of grid physical resource space and logical resource space is built based concept of virtual organization. Then, a mathematical method based the binary equivalent relation is presented to divide grid physical resource space. Then, this paper proposes the concept of grid resource domain, and introduce a fully decentralized grid resource locating protocol based it from aspects of the overlay network of grid resource domains and query routing protocol among different grid resource domains. On the other hand, in order to propagate query among information nodes within given grid resource domain, this paper presents informed search protocol based bloom filters. Our resource locating protocol can enhance the query success rate and recall rate, and avoid too much unnecessary query messages.

1 Introduction

As an important information technology solving distributed complex problem cooperatively, grid aims to congregate, share and integrate large-scale, heterogeneous, distributed resources across dynamic resource organization and management domain. In the small-scale and tight-coupled environment, resource space model may be not necessary. But if we hope to deploy grid application successfully under the environment in which resources is widely distributed and heterogeneous, the issues that how to model and organize resources will become more significant. Moreover, successful large–scale grid applications always need efficient and scaleable grid resource locating mechanism without centralized management and control.

Research institutes and enterprises have done lots of work on grid resource model and grid resource space model. The representative achievements of grid resource model include Web service, Service Domain, OGSA, WS-Resource and so on. The research work about grid resource space model in homeland is developed from aspects of service grid, information grid and knowledge grid by the researcher group coming from institution of computing technology, Chinese academy of science. The EVP grid resource space model [1] and resource space grid [2] are two kinds of

H. Zhuge and G.C. Fox (Eds.): GCC 2005, LNCS 3795, pp. 621 – 632, 2005.

representative production. On the other hands, researchers have proposed many solutions for resource locating problem in the fields of web services and grid, but the foundation or basic idea of those solutions can derive from related research result of peer-to-peer network.

The available decentralized resource locating and sharing protocol can be classified as unstructured, loosely structured, and highly structured peer-to-peer network according the control mechanism over data location and overlay topology [3]. In an unstructured p2p network such as Gnutella [4], no rule exists which defines where data is stored and the overlay topology is arbitrary. In a loosely structured network such as Freenet[5], both the overlay structure and the data location are not precisely determined. In a highly structured P2P network such as CAN [6] and Chord [7], both the overlay topology and the data placement are precisely specified. Searching in unstructured P2P network covers both blind search schemes and informed search schemes. Blind searches include iterative deepening [8], k-walker random walk [9] and so on. Informed searches include local indices [10], adaptive probabilistic search [11] and so on.

This paper doesn't research concrete grid resource model, it should be the work of related standardization organization, such as W3C, GGF and so on. The major contribution of this paper includes:

1. Proposes a mathematical model of grid physical resource space and logical resource space.
2. Presents the mathematical method used to partition grid physical resource space based on the binary equivalent relation, and the method used to partition grid logical resource space based on the concept of content similarity.
3. Defines the concept of grid resource domain, and design the grid resource locating protocol based on grid resource space division from aspects of overlay topology, bootstrap system, and query routing protocol among grid resource domains.
4. Presents one informed search protocol based bloom filters, and use it to forward query within the same grid resource domain.

The rest of this paper is organized as follows. Section 2 proposes grid resource space model. Section 3 presents grid resource locating protocol based on grid resource domain from aspects of overlay topology, bootstrap system and query routing mechanism among different grid resources domains. Section 4 presents one informed search protocol based bloom filters used to route query within a grid resource domain. Section 5 concludes this paper.

2 Grid Resource Space Model

Grid can utilize idle or dedicated large-scale, heterogeneous, distributed resources delivered by different persons or organizations to realize goal of resource sharing and problem solving cooperatively across different manage domains. Grid also is viewed as an infrastructure which provides necessary resources and services with high QOS for certain applications and users. Grid systems and applications are often associated with the concept of virtual organization (VO). Each independent resource organization would like to contribute its idle or dedicated kernel resources and services to one or several virtual organizations according to common goal. In fact, virtual organization is one kinds of basic conceptual model of grid system and application. In this section, we try to establish the grid resources space model based the concept of virtual organization.

2.1 Physical Resource Space Model

Definition 1. A network can be denoted as (O,E) satisfying $E \subseteq [O]^2$; thus the elements of E are 2-element subsets of O. The elements of O are all kinds of resource organization providing resources; the elements of E are the links among elements of O. The resource organization is a pair $o=(r,lacl)$ of sets. The elements of r are local physical resource; the elements of $lacl$ are corresponding resource access control rules for r.

Definition 2. Virtual organization is consisted of the resources provided by each resource organization for the identical global goal. For virtual organization vo_j, it can be denoted as $VO_j = \bigcup_{k=1}^{|O|} (w_{kj} \times o_k)$.

Each resource organization need provide a resource sharing vector to indicate their contribution degree and access control method of owned resources for given virtual organization. Let l denote the number of resources owned by resource organization O_k, resource sharing vector provided by O_k for virtual organization vo_j can be denoted as $w_{kj}=\{w_{kj1},f_{kj1},w_{kj2},f_{kj2},\ldots,w_{kjl},f_{kjl}\}$. w_{kjl} is denote the quality and quantity of resource r_{kl} delivered to vo_j. f_{kjl} is used to denote the mapping relation between access control of resource r_{kl} for local application and that for virtual organization vo_j.

Definition 3. Let vo denotes a concept model of given grid system or application G. The physical resource space of G is the projection of resource space of all resource organization based on *goal* of corresponding vo_j, and also is identical with the physical resource space of corresponding virtual organization.

2.2 Logical Resource Space Model

The kernel resources and services provided to corresponding *vo* by each resource organization display similarity on the type and function. There are at least two reasons for these phenomena. First, the type of all resources which can be accessed through Internet is limited and confirmable for each application filed, and this can results in many similar resource instances hosting in the same grid physical resource space. Second, the interface of web service trend to become uniform and standard in many application fields, and there are many similar services instances deployed in the same grid physical resource space.

In reference [1], authors proposed the "homogeneous" binary relation on the grid physical resource space and divide it into the no-overlapping subsets. But they didn't present a rigorous and explicit definition for the conception of the "homogeneous physical resource". In this section, we will design the binary "equivalent" relation on the grid physical resource from the point of service function characteristic, and uses this binary equivalent relation to divide the grid physical resource space.

Definition 4. Let assume R is a binary relation on the grid physical resource space R_{grid}, and there is a corresponding elementary set called the base of binary relation R. R can be defined as following statement: $\forall x, y \in R_{grid}, (x, y) \in R, \ \exists z \in Base$, and the resource type, metadata model and derived functions of x and y are both the same z.

Definition 5. S is a division of a grid physical resource space R_{grid}. Only if it satisfies those three conditions, we call S a division about binary equivalence R on R_{grid}, and there is a one by one mapping *f: Base—>S*.

(1) $|S| = |Base|$; (2) If $\forall x, y \in T_1, T_1 \in S$, then $(x, y) \in R$;

(3) If $\forall x \in T_1, T_1 \in S$ and $y \in T_2, T_2 \in S$, then can't deduce that $(x, y) \in R$.

Definition 5 proposes the method used to divide grid physical resource space R_{grid} based on the binary equivalent relation R. At the same time, it also can be used to judge whether a division of a grid physical space satisfies the binary equivalent relation R. The elementary work before applying definition 5 is to identify the base of the binary equivalent relation R.

Definition 6. The grid logical resource space R_{vgrid} is the base of binary equivalent relation R on the grid physical resource space R_{grid}. Each grid logical resource is one element of *Base*, and $|R_{vgrid}| = |Base|$. There is a scheduling function g between each grid logical resource and the most suitable physical resource, which use to discover, select and invoke most suitable physical resource according to given logical resource.

Grid applications are established on open and dynamic environment, this leads to the uncertainty of the reliability and usability of resources or services instance involved by application at the running phase. Therefore, grid application should be established on logical resource rather than concrete physical resource. Grid application realizes the initialization of various logical resources at the compiling phase, and dynamically instead logical resource with most suitable resource instance at the running phase, and guarantee application possess excellent fault-tolerant and loading balance capability.

2.3 Division of Grid Logical Resource Space

As mentioned above, grid application should be established on logical resource instead of physical resource instance directly. Thus it is need to pay more attention to the organization and management methods of grid logical resource. We will study the division methods used to cluster elements of grid logical resource space.

Definition 7. Let M denote the size of R_{vgrid}, R_{vgrid} is organized as a tree called grid logical resource tree (GLRT), and the depth of GLRT is denoted as N. For any x and y belonged to R_{vgrid}, the degree of similarity between them is denoted as *Similarity(x, y)*. $leaf_x$ and $leaf_y$ are the corresponding leaf node of that GLRT. If $Similarity(x, y) = \infty$, we can say that x and y are not accessible each other; otherwise, they are accessible.

The similarity between any two grid logical resources can be computed according following steps: (1) $Similarity(x, x) = 1$;(2) Find the corresponding path from $leaf_x$ and $leaf_y$ to the root node of GLRT, and denoted as $route_x$ and $route_y$;(3) If the length of

$route_x$ and $route_y$ are one, *Similarity(x, y) =1*.Otherwise, it is need to compute the first overlap node of $route_x$ and $route_y$; (4) If the first overlap node is the root node of GLRT, *then Similarity(x, y) =*∞. Otherwise, compute the length $length_x$, $length_y$ from $leaf_x$, $leaf_y$ to the first overlap node, and *Similarity(x, y) =Max (*$length_x$, $length_y$*)*.

The algorithm based content similarity to divide grid logical resource space is embodied by algorithm1. The parameter Q has influence on the granularity of division result for same grid logical resource space. This paper does not focus on this problem.

Algorithm 1. DivideLogicalGridResourceSpace (Rvgrid Base, Similarity *Q*)

```
1. Let the size of Base be M. Let the element of Base be base1,
base2,…,baseM , sorted by the order of leaf when traversing the tree
from left to right.
2. Let Grd denote the result after dividing up the Base, the initial-
ized value is null.
3. For i=1 to M do
4.    If basei has been in Grd then continue Else
5.        Create Set named answer, initialized value of answer is null
6.        For j=i to M do
7.           If basej has been in Grd then continue
8.           Else If Similarity (basei, basej) is less than Q then
9.              answer= answer Union {basei , basej }
10.          End if
11.       End for
12.       Add answer to Grd
13.    End if
14. End for
15. Return Grd
```

We will give an example to embody this algorithm. We assume parameter *Q* is one, *Base= {K, L, F, G, M, I, J}*, and the corresponding grid logical resource tree is illustrated by figure1, the set of leaf node of this GLRT equals to R_{vgrid}. According to this configuration, algorithem1 can response such a division result *Grd*={{R,S}, {N,O}, {F,G},{H,I},{T,V},{Q},{K,L}}.

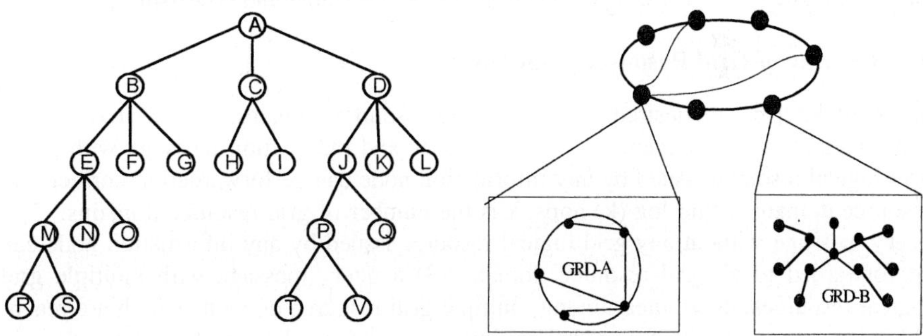

Fig. 1. A grid logical resource space tree

Fig. 2. The overlay of grid resource domain

3 Resource Locating Protocol Based Resource Space Model

Definition 8. Grid Resource Domain *(GRD)* is comprised of its resource entity and inner overlay network, and is denoted as *(T, G).T* is an element of one division result G*rd* of given grid logical resource space. The inner overlay network of given grid resource domain is modeled as a graph $G= (N, E)$, and N is the information node set of this GRD, E is the edge set among the nodes. The responsibility of each information node is limited by T. They only are willing to store information of grid physical resources which corresponding grid logical resources belong to T. For any two different grid resource domains GRD_x and GRD_y, x is a random element of $GRD_x.T$, and y is a random element of $GRD_y.T$, if $Similarity(x, y) =\infty$, GRD_x and GRD_y are not accessible each other, otherwise they are accessible.

We will present a new grid resource locating protocol based grid resource domain. At its heart, it can be viewed as a two-tier structure as shown in figure 2. The top tier structure means the overlay network of grid resource domains, and second tier means the inner overlay network of each grid resource domain. Note that the interconnection of domains shown in the figure2 is only conceptual, and is actually realized as part of the interconnecting information nodes.

3.1 Bootstrap System

To join this peer-to-peer system, a new information node with responsibility of given grid logical resource must look up some or all information nodes within corresponding grid resource domain in order to set its intra-domain links, at the same time it also need discovery some or all information nodes within other grid resource domains in order to build its inter-domain links. Thus, there should be a bootstrap system to store and maintain grid logical resource tree, division result of grid logical resource space and all grid resource domains of given grid application. Whether this system is centralized or decentralized, it must provide standard and open interface to deliver those information to new information node, grid resource provider, and resource consumer. On the other hand, it allows these kinds of user to pull or cache information on-demand. We don't focus detail about this bootstrap system and assume it has been deployed successfully, but prefer structured peer-to-peer protocol to other protocols, and it will better if nodes within bootstrap system are stable and powerful.

3.2 Overlay of Grid Resource Domains

We now describe the desired overlay of grid resource domains. The desired overlay can guarantee these characteristics: (1) a query and publication message with given grid logical resource issued by any information node can be forwarded to correct grid resource domain within log (k) hops, k is the number of grid resource domains; (2) a query message without any grid logical resource issued by any information node can be forwarded to all grid resource domains;(3) a query message with multiple grid logical resources, distributed among multiple grid resource domains which are reachable each other, can be forwarded to any one corresponding grid resource domain within (k) hops, and then forward to other grid resources domain within one hop.

In order to guarantee those characteristics mentioned above and avoid the disadvantage of centralized system, we will use the Chord-like structure [7] as a conceptual interconnection network of grid resource domains, other structured p2p structure maybe also suitable. First, a conceptual link between any two grid resource domains means, for any information node n1 belonged to one domain, there exists some node n2 belonged to another domain, such that node n1 links to node n2. Second, each grid resource domain need make sure it's identifier in order to define inter-domain structure. The identifier can be a hashing code of the uniform name of each grid resource domain, and can also be a bloom filters of the set consisted of all grid logical resource name within each grid resource domain. Third, grid resources domains are then arranged in a circular space using their domain identifier, and are interconnected obeyed Chord protocol. Finally, grid resources domains which are reachable each others are interconnected each other. Each link from one grid resource domain to another is implemented by a set of inter-node links, as described above. The neighbor relationship among domains should be defined once the whole grid logical resource was divided according method mentioned at section 2, and should be stored by bootstrap system. Of course, once a new grid logical resource appears, the neighbor relationship should be redefined, and then update related information stored by bootstrap system.

After outline the desired overlay of grid resource domains, we present solutions to information node arrival and grid resource registration problem. New information node arrival operation can be processed by following steps: (1)A new information node publishes its grid logical resource and its description information to the bootstrap system, and that information would be appended to the entry for its hosting grid resource domain in bootstrap system; (2)The new information node retrieves some or all candidate nodes within its hosting grid resource domain, then sets link to those nodes obeyed to the protocol used by this grid resource domain;(3)The new information node retrieves one information nodes for every neighbor grid resource domains of its hosting grid resource domain by accessing the bootstrap system, and then sets link to those nodes obeyed to the protocol mentioned above.

We assume that grid resource provider can identify the name of logical resource which corresponding physical resource will be published to the peer-to-peer registration system, and has knowledge about one information node within system. The registration message can be first submitted to that information node and enter one grid resource domain, the information node will retrieve the identifier of desired grid resource domain from bootstrap system. If current grid resource domain is not the desired one, the message will be forwarded to the desired grid resource domain within log (k) hops according to local routing table (include routing entries obeyed chord protocol and the obeyed the reachable rule of grid resource domains). Furthermore, the message will be redistribution among the desired domain according to related load balance protocol.

3.3 Inter-GRD Search Protocol

After discussing the overlay network of grid resource domains and two major problems (information node arrival and grid resource registration), it is time to focus on grid resource discover problem at the level of grid resource domains, the same problem within one grid resource domain will be discussed at following section.

For a query without payload about grid logical resource information, it will be submitted to any information node within any grid resource domain, and then the information node first finds all answers to the query within its own grid resource domain. If the number of answers proves insufficient, it attempt to find answers from one additional grid resource domain. While the number of answers still insufficient, it will propagate the query to more grid resource domain until either a sufficient number of answers are discovered, or all the grid resource domains have been searched. Detail about query broadcast algorithms can be found from literature [12].

On the other hand, we assumed that the grid resource consumer has knowledge about the desired logical resource used as part of query payload. For this kind of query, it will be submitted to any information node within any grid resource domain, and then the information node obtain the desired grid resource domains through the bootstrap system using the desired grid logical resource as input parameter. If its own domain is the only desired domain, then it just need find all answers to the query among its own domain according the query protocol used by this domain. Otherwise, it will forward the query to the only desired grid resource domain or other desired grid resource domains. In fact, the forward decision is first made by taking care of the local routing entries defined according the reachable rule of grid resource domains, then made according the local routing entries obeyed chord protocol.

After the deployment of grid resource domains network, if grid resource consumer appends desired grid logical resource in the query message, resource locating protocol mentioned above can enhance the query success rate and recall rate, at the same time it can avoid too much unnecessary query messages.

4 Intra-GRD Informed Search Protocol Based Bloom Filters

In this section, we focus on how to route query among different information nodes within the same grid resource domain. The overlay and search protocol for given grid resource domain should not be imposed. The candidate overlay can be classified as three categories: unstructured, loosely structured, and highly structured based on the control mechanism over data location and network topology. In this section, we will introduce a new informed search protocol based bloom filters for unstructured peer-to-peer, and make use it to forward query among the same grid resource domain.

4.1 Preliminary Introduction of Bloom Filters

A bloom filter is a compact data structures for probabilistic representation of a set in order to support membership queries. A bloom filter for representing a set $S=\{s_1, s_2, ..., s_n\}$ of n elements is described by an vector of m bits, initially all bits are set to 0. A bloom filter uses k independent hash functions $h_1, h_2, \ldots, h_k$ with range $\{1, ..., m\}$. These hash functions map each item in the universe to a random number uniform over the range $\{1, ..., m\}$. For each element *x* of *S*, the bits $h_i(x)$ are set to 1 for $1 \leq i \leq k$.To check whether an element *x* belongs to *S*, one just need to check whether all the *hi(x)* bits of the vector are set to 1. If not, then *x* is not a member of *S*. Otherwise, we assume that *x* is a member of *S*, although we are wrong with some probability. Hence a bloom filter may yield a *false positive*, for which it suggests that an element *x* is in *S* even though it is not. Each false positive is due to a filter collision, in which all bits indexed were set to 1 by other elements previously [13].

4.2 Informed Search Protocol Based Bloom Filters

In nature, informed search protocol is one kind of forward-based routing protocol. It has two major components, the construction and maintenance mechanism of routing table, and a query forward mechanism using the routing table. In our informed protocol, the routing table is a set of bloom filters, each corresponding to a link. When a peer needs to forward a query, bloom filters corresponding to each link will be scanned and desired links will be filtered out as the forwarding directions.

In order to construct a routing table, A. Kumar has presented an interesting method in [14]. Each peer must construct local bloom filter and send a routing advertisement (in the form of bloom filter) to the neighbor at a connection setup. Then the neighbor can construct a routing entry for the link from itself to the new peer. The initial advertisement is created by taking the decay union of all advertisements received from neighbors other than the target neighbors, allowing this combined advertisement to decay by the decay factor d. We believe that it should adopt gossiping protocol [15] to exchange advertisement between sources and sink peer instead of push or pull. The experiment according to algorithem2 shows that the convergent speed of gossiping protocol is faster than in a single push protocol.

Only this kind of mechanism is not enough to make sure that each routing entry contains whole summary information of the reachable data along the corresponding link direction. In fact, the majority of early arriving peers have little information about the later peers, although the later peers have enough information about the early peers. Thus, we should pay more attention to routing table update and maintenance mechanism. A. Kumar has presented a push protocol in which each peer constructs and pushes the update advertisement for each neighbor in a given interval. In our experiment, we found that it is not necessary to update for all link directions. We also adopt asynchronous gossiping update protocol, and each peer creates an update advertisement for a random link direction at each gossiping round, and exchanges update advertisements in that direction. Please refer algorithem2 for details.

```
Algorithm 2. Gossip (node i)
Obtain local bloom filters for node i and its neighbors;
Select a node j from neighbors of node i randomly
Create Update (node i, node j);
Create Update (node j, node i);
Create Update (node i, node j)
Obtain local bloom filters A_i of node i;
U_j=A_i;
While (x belongs to neighbors of node i)
For r=1 to m
   If A_x[r] ==1
      U_j[r] =1;
   End if
End for
End while
Node i send U_j to node j;
Node j constructs routing entry for link j-->i with U_j.
```

The query forward mechanism is tightly associated with the bloom filters corresponding to each link. It is easy to know that queries about data hosted at given peers may be issued at any time from any peer, before the corresponding bloom filters of one given peer propagate over whole p2p network without any information loss. In fact, the protocol may be design to make the information of given source peer decay during the propagate process in order to save bandwidth and make protocol become more scalable, such as [14]. In order to overcome these kinds of information uncertainty, we combine informed forward based bloom filters with random walker. First, current peer make forward decision according to route table. If it works well, it is not need any more compensation. Others, it needs random walker protocol as the assistant forward mechanism. Please refer algorithm3 for detail.

```
Algorithm 3. Forward Query (node i, query y):
For cach neighbor j of node i
    obtain the routing entry A_j for link i-->j;
    If all hash_l[y] bits of A_j equals one,for 0<l<=k
        Deliver Query(Y, i);
End for
If there isn't any neighbor satisfied above condition
    Deliver Query(Y, random neighbor i);
```

4.3 Simulation of Intra-GRD Search Protocol

We use the PeerSim p2p simulator to design and implement our experiments. Peersim was delievered by BISON project[16], and is an open source, Java based, P2P simulation framework aimed to develop and test any kind of P2P algorithm in a dynamic environment.

In this section, we will simulate Gnutella0.4, Random walk, and informed search protocol based bloom filters under random overlay with 5000 nodes. There are multiple instances of the same object at different locations. The model we use for replication of content is based on the zipf distribution, frequently used to model the replication of objects on the web. The ith most popular elementary object of a space will has $1/i^a$ times as many replicas as the most replicated object. In our experiment, the whole the size object space is 50000, the size of elementary object space is 5000, and the parameter *a* used by zipf law is set to be 0.5. The whole queries is 10000, and the distribution of query's payload is also obeyed the zipf law, and the parameter *a* is set to be 0.5. In order to model the data and query distribution among all peers, we use zipf law to model this and embody the popularity distribution of peer.

Performance issues in real p2p systems are extremely complicated. In addition to issues such as load on the network, load on network participants, decay and success rate of query, there are a host of other criteria. In our experiment, we focus on efficiency aspects of algorithms, and use the following simple metrics.

Pr (success): the probability of finding the queried object before the search terminates. Different algorithms have different criteria for terminating the search; it depends on the search semantics. Recall: the ratio between numbers of relevant documents presented to the user to total number of relevant documents in the p2p network. Nodes visited: the number of p2p network participants that a query's search messages travel through. This is an indirect measure of the impact that a query generates on the whole network.

The simulation result of search for all copy (get all the copies of given elementary object) under protocol Gnutella0.4 and our informed search based on bloom filters is illustrated by figure 3. For any query, informed search protocol can obtain high recall without visit large portion of whole peers in order to process the query, while Gnutella-like protocol can obtain relative lower recall with cost of visit large portion of whole p2p network. It is show that informed search based bloom filters can avoid bring huge message copies and blind forward.

The simulation result of search for one copy (get at least one copy of given elementary object) under protocol random walker (the number of walker can be lager upon the degree of peer issued the query) and our informed search based on bloom filters is illustrated by figure 4. For any query, informed search protocol can obtain high Pr (success) compare to random walker with the same ration of visited peers to whole network. When there are multiple instances distributed randomly among whole

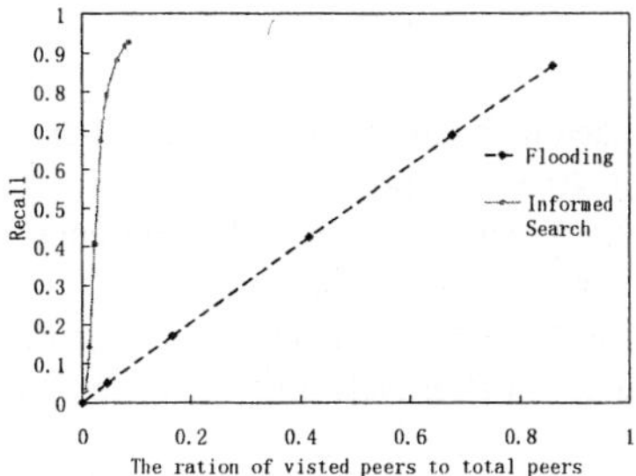

Fig. 3. The ration of visted peers for one query to total peers vs. recall

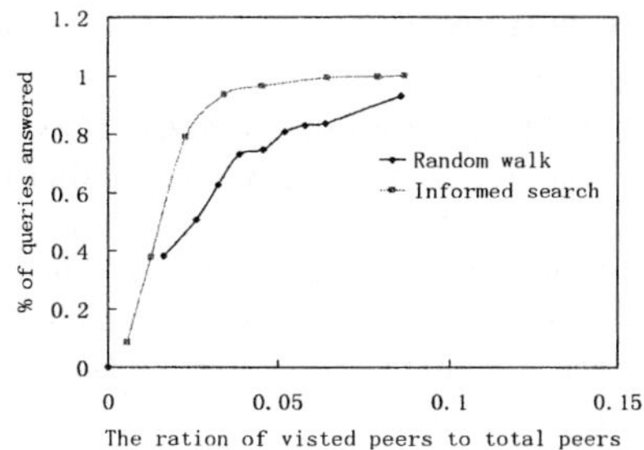

Fig. 4. The ration of visted peers to total peers vs. % of queries

peers for any elementary object, the Pr (success) of both kinds of protocol cans almost 1 after visiting peer less than 10% of whole network. It is also explained that informed search based bloom filters possesses advantage than blind search.

The overhead of our informed search protocol is the need to exchange information between peers at given gossiping rate. This operation can merge with the stabilize operation of neighbor ship. Furthermore, the transmit size can become small by adopting bloom filters and compressed bloom filters.

5 Conclusion

During the research process of the grid resource space model, we find that it is difficult to keep the availability of the grid physical resources during the running phase, and grid application should build on the logical resources other than the physical resources. The grid resource space model presented in this paper can deal with that problem mentioned above, and can be used to realized the service virtualization model. The basic idea of our resource locating protocol, which based on the grid resource space division and grid resource domain, is to control the topology of the grid resource locating system and the distribution of resources registration information. Our protocol try to instruct any query messages with information about grid logical resource to be forwarded to corresponding grid resource domain without unnecessary message, and also present a informed search protocol based bloom filters used to locate grid resources within any grid resource domain. The grid resource locating mechanism possesses good expansibility and robustness. If it is companied with proper guide for the action of resource registration, it can respond the query message using grid logical resource as part of payload more quickly. The information service of Spatial Information Grid (SIG) [17] adopts the resource locating protocol based on the grid resource space model. The information service has been applied and popularized in National Geography Grid (NGG) project [18].

Acknowledgements

This work was supported by the national high technology research and development program of China under grant No. 2003AA135110 and 2002AA131010.

References

1. Wei Li, Zhiwei Xu, "A Model of Grid Address Space with Applications", Journal of Computer Research and Development (in Chinese), vol. 40, no.12, pp.756-1762, 2003.
2. H.Zhuge, "Resource Space Grid: Model, Method and Platform". Concurrency and Computation: Practice and Experience, vol.16, no.14, pp.1385-1413, 2004.
3. X. Li, J. Wu,"Searching Techniques in Peer-to-Peer Networks", Handbook of Theoretical and Algorithmic Aspects of Ad Hoc, Sensor, and Peer-to-Peer Networks, J. Wu (ed.), CRC Press, 2005.
4. Matei Ripeanu, Adriana Iamnitchi, and I. Foster, "Mapping the gnutella network", IEEE Internet Computing, vol. 6, no.1, pp: 50–57. 2002.
5. I. Clarke, O. Sandberg, B. Wiley, T. W. Hong, "Freenet: A distributed anonymous information storage and retrieval system", in: Proc. of ICSI Workshop on Design Issues in Anonymity and Unobservability, 2000.
6. S. Ratnasamy, P. Francis, M. Handley, and R.M. Karp, "A scalable content-addressable network", in: Proc. ACM SIGCOMM 2001.
7. I. Stoica, R. Morris, D. Karger, M. F. Kaashoek, and H. Balakrishnam, "Chord: A scalable peer-to-peer lookup service for internet applications", in: Proc. ACM SIGCOMM 2001.
8. B. Yang, H. Garcia-Molina, "Improving search in peer-to-peer networks", in: Proc. of the 22nd IEEE International Conference on Distributed Computing, 2002, pp.5-14.
9. Q. Lv, P. Cao, E. Cohen, K. Li, and S. Shenker, "Search and replication in unstructured peer-to-peer networks", in: Proc. of the 16th ACM International Conference on Supercomputing, 2002, pp.84-95.
10. Q. Lv, P. Cao, E. Cohen, K. Li, and S. Shenker, "Search and replication in unstructured peer-to-peer networks", in: Proc. of the 16th ACM International Conference on Supercomputing, 2002, pp.84-95.
11. A. Crespo, H. Garcia-Molina, "Routing indices for peer-to-peer systems", in: Proc. of the 22nd International Conference on Distributed Computing, 2002, pp.23-32.
12. Q. Sun, P. Ganesan, and H. Garcia-Molina, "The InfoMatrix: Distributed Indexing in a P2P Environment". http://wwwdb.stanford.edu/~qsun/research/infomat.pdf.
13. B. Bloom, "Space/time tradeoffs in hash coding with allowable errors," Commun. ACM, vol. 13, no. 7, pp. 422–426, July 1970.
14. A. Kumar, J. Xu, E.W. Zegura, "Effcient and Scalable Query Routing for Unstructured Peer-to-Peer Networks", in: Proc. of Proceedings of Conference on Computer Communications (IEEE INFOCOM), 2005.
15. S. Boyd, A. Ghosh, B.Prabhakar, D.Shah, "Gossip Algorithms: Design, Analysis and Applications", in: Proc. of Proceedings of Conference on Computer Communications (IEEE INFOCOM), 2005.
16. G.D. Caro, F. Ducatelle, P. Heegaard, M. Jelasity, R. Montemanni, A. Montresor, "Evaluation of basic services in AHN,P2P and Grid networks", http://www.cs.unibo.it/ bison /deliverables/D07.pdf.
17. Deke Guo, Honghui Chen, Xueshan Luo, "Resource information management of spatial information grid", Lecture Notes in Computer Science, Vol. 3032, Springer, 2003, 240-243.
18. Tang Yu, He kaitao, Xiao nong et al, "Study on System Framework and Key Issues of National Geological Application Grid", Journal of Computer Research and Development (in Chinese), vol.40, no.12, pp. 1682-1688, 2003.

A Constellation Resource Discovery Model Based on Scalable Multi-tape Universal Turing Machine*

Yinfeng Wang, Xiaoshe Dong, Hua Guo,
Xiuqiang He, and GuoRong Liu

School of Electronics and Information Engineerin, Xi'an Jiaotong University,
Xi'an, 710049, China
xsdong@mail.xjtu.edu.cn
{wangyf, guohua}@mailst.xjtu.edu.cn

Abstract. Constellation resource discovery model is a novel model for discovering the dynamic resources in Grid. In constellation model, we propose a new Scalable Multi-tape Universal Turing machine (SMUTM) to present the processes of simultaneous discovery tasks on the constellation nodes, and formally describe the usability of the Grid resource based on the SMUTM. In this research, we design an algorithm used in the constellation resource discovery, which guarantees overlaying all the nodes in Grid and optimizes the network cost. Preliminary simulation shows that this algorithm complexity is linear; the average response time can be reduced by 12%. Constellation model ensures the QoS of the resource discovery in the scalable and dynamic Grid environment.

1 Introduction

A basic service in Grid is resource discovery: given a description of resources desired, a resource discovery mechanism returns a set of resources that matches the description [1]. MDS [2] is the typical centralized resource discovery mechanism. MDS organizes the resources into a layered tree structure. As Grid sizes increase, some of centralized or hierarchical functions should be decentralized to avoid the bottlenecks and guarantee scalability.

Peer-to-Peer (P2P) model can be adopted to overcome the deficiency of the centralized or hierarchical mechanisms. In order to solve the flooding-based search mechanism and topology mismatch problem, location-aware topology matching (LTM) was proposed [3]. But other problems still exist. In P2P, each peer acts as client and server to implement resource discovery. Although peers have different performance and different network connections, they have to do the same computation tasks and maintain the same size record of overlay connections, which unnecessarily consume Grid resources and increase the response time.

Super-Peer network [4] is growing popularity, which combines the efficiency of autonomy, load balancing and robustness of distributed search. However, in Grid,

* This research is supported by 863 project of China (Grant No.2002AA104550) and China Education and Research Grid (Grant No.CG2003-CG008).

H. Zhuge and G.C. Fox (Eds.): GCC 2005, LNCS 3795, pp. 633–644, 2005.

service node is organized by Virtual Organizations and future interconnection environment will be a large-scale human-machine environment [5]. Using P2P system, the management and organization of nodes become difficult with the enlarging of the scale of Grid, and security of Grid is also difficult to be guaranteed. Because the nodes join and leave Grid frequently, the overlay network built on them is unsteady, and need to rebuild at a regular intervals, so the number of hops required covering all the nodes and the quality of service (QoS) of services in Grid is uncertain.

In this paper, we adopt the constellation model [6] for the resource discovery to resolve the problems mentioned above. Just like the constellation in the sky can guide the voyage, the constellation in Grid can navigate resource discovery.

A Scalable Multi-tape Universal Turing Machine (SMUTM) is proposed in this paper. SMUTM is used to denote the behavior of the concurrent tasks and their relations in dynamic Grid environment, and to describe the Grid resources' properties for the constellation model. We design a new discovery algorithm to reduce the response time of resource discovery, and it provides benefits such as anonymity and using less bandwidth.

The rest of the paper is organized as follows. Section 2 introduces the constellation model. Section 3 gives a formal description of resource discovery and the properties of the Grid resources. Section 4 discusses a new discovery algorithm and its optimization solutions. Section 5 analyzes the results of the simulation on a prototype. Section 6 draws a conclusion.

2 Architecture of Constellation Model

Reference [6] proposes a Constellation model for Grid resource management, which addresses the criterions for node selection and redundancy. The nodes in Grid constitute multiple constellations according to geographically dispersed or application policy. Nodes in a constellation can be divided into fixed star, planet and meteor nodes. Each planet and meteor node must connect to at least one fixed star node, and the fixed star nodes constitute a steady formwork of the constellation. Resources are published on the constellation. Constellations are connected together to form a virtual galaxy overlay network.

The architecture of the resource discovery based on constellation model is shown in figure1. The constellation layer is the core layer. Galaxy overlay network can be built on constellation layer in various ways. Nodes in the service provider layer could choose any constellation to publish its services. Based on some policies such as the load balancing, the services will be finally published on a chosen fixed star or planet node. User can submit requests via some portal or other job-entry interface. The portal shown in the figure could then transfer the request to an appropriate local constellation according to the location of the user.

Various communication protocols and security policies can be used inside the constellation. A constellation could be a little laboratory or large-scale industry. It can extend to multiple organizations or multiple physical locations.

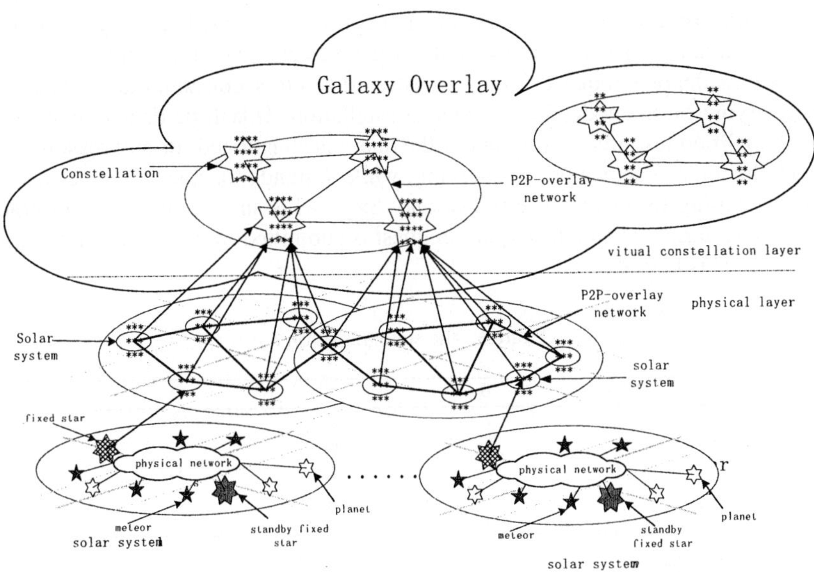

Fig. 1. The Architecture of Constellation Model

3 Formalization Descriptions

3.1 The States Transition of Discovery Process

Automata is a model of computation that can record the states at any given time and identify the input of system. It can be used to describe the process of resource discovery in Grid, discovery events and transitions of the states as a result of an action.

Definition 1: Automata of resource discovery is based on the constellation model $M=\{\{s_0,s_1,s_2,s_3,s_4\},\{0,1,2\}, \delta,\{s_0\},\{s_0,s_4\}\}$ where $K=\{s_0,s_1,s_2,s_3,s_4\}$, K is a finite set of states; $\Sigma=\{0,1,2\}$, Σ is an input alphabet; δ is a transition function from $K\times\Sigma$ to K; $s_0\in K$ is the initial state. $F=\{s_0,s_4\}$, F is the set of final states, $F\subseteq K$.

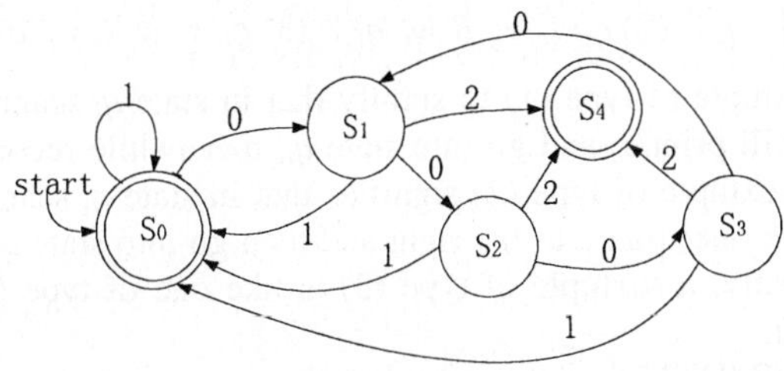

Fig. 2. States diagram represent the transition of states in M

If the value returned by the query function is true, it means that resource discovery is successful, and *M* is driven to s0. State s1 denotes choosing the neighbor constellation. State s2 denotes request's being transferred to other constellations. State s3 denotes querying on the nodes in the same constellation. *M* will be driven to state s4 if none of qualified resources are found or the query is abandoned for any reasons.

In *M*, the letter *0* shows doing querying, while *1* stands for query is successful and *2* denotes exiting for errors. The transitionδ: S$\times\Sigma\rightarrow$S is shown in table 1. In practice *M* must be restarted when a new query request is submitted to the system, no matter at which state *M* is before.

Table 1. The state transition δ

δ :S$\times\Sigma\rightarrow$S	0	1	2
s_0	s_1	s_0	/
s_1	s_2	s_0	s_4
s_2	s_3	s_0	s_4
s_3	s_1	s_0	s_4
s_4	/	/	/

3.2 Scalable Multi-tape Universal Turing Machine

Universal Turing machine U is suitable to analyzing single algorithm or program. Intuitively, U takes two arguments, a description of a machine "*M*", and a description of an input string "*w*". We want U to have the following property: U halts on input "*M*", "*w*" if and only if *M* halts on input *w*. It is U("*M*","*w*")="*M*(*w*)" [7]. But resource discovery in Grid includes many concurrent tasks and actions, and various query policy could be used in the constellations.

The Turing machine is not durable. The history computation cannot be utilized, so we need to modify U in order to describe the behavior of the concurrent tasks and their relations. We added work-tapes to U for recording the previous output. Multiple input and output tapes are added so that there will be a durable work-tape for each output one. The output of the computation will be recorded as part of the input for the next computation.

Definition 2: SMUTM is a finite set of sextuples. A sextuple is an expression of one of the following forms consisting of six symbols:

(1) $q_i\ s_j\ w_j\ s_k\ w_i\ q_l$； (2) $q_i\ s_j\ w_j\ R\ w_i\ q_l$； (3) $q_i\ s_j\ w_j\ L\ w_i\ q_l$；

We intend a sextuple of type (1) to signify that in state q_i scanning symbol s_j and w_j, the device *M* will print s_k and go into state q_l, meanwhile record w_i on the work-tape. Similarly, a sextuple of type (2) signifies that in state q_i scanning s_j and w_j, the device *M* will move one square to the right and then go into state q_l, and record w_i on the work-tape. Finally, a sextuple of type (3) is like one of type (2) except that the motion is to the left.

We can use the SMUTM model to simulate the process of resource discovery. The leftmost end of the tape is always marked by a special symbol denoted by $\triangleright$. Computations of resource discovery take place in all k tapes of the SMUTM. Resource

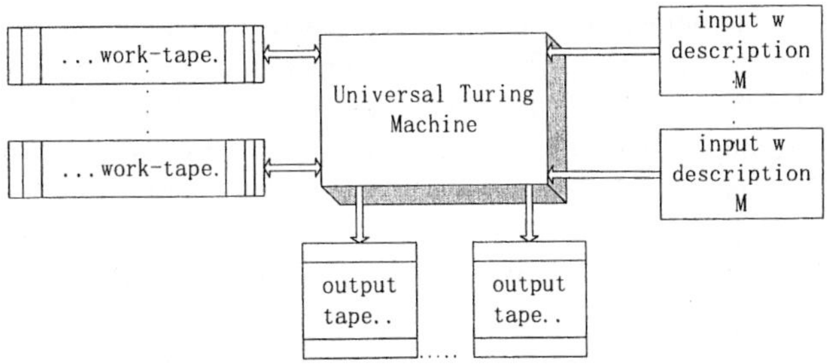

Fig. 3. SMUTM model

discovery automata M in definition 4 could simulate the working process of each tape head. A configuration of such a machine must identify the state, the tape contents, and the head position in each of the k tapes. A configuration is a member of $K \times (\triangleright \Sigma^* \times (\Sigma^*(\Sigma - \{B\}) \cup \{e\}))^k \times (\Sigma^* \times (\Sigma^*(\Sigma - \{B\}) \cup \{e\}))^k$. B denotes blank symbols. The symbol e denotes ending.

SMUTM reads string Mw as its input. If the last required resource could be found in the next computation, the information on the work-tape will be copied to the output tape and regarded as the output of this discovery task.

Computations can be performed concurrently when new requests come. The discovery process should return all the resources that match a requirement description

3.3 Formal Definition of Resource's Property

In the OGSA framework each resource is represented as a Grid Service [8], thus the Grid can be regarded as a scalable set of Grid services. In order to research the characteristics of resources in Grid, we will give a formal definition of them and introduce some theorems and their proofs.

Definition 3: A pair R denotes available resource (M, W). M is a SMUTM; W is a nonempty finite services set. *Available* means resources can accept requests from users and return the acceptable results.

SMUTM reads the request $\omega$and writeω' on the tape, If$\omega' \in W$, which indicates that a result can be returned to the user after the service is invoked. If ω is a request for a certain resource, when SMUTM reads it, the result will appear on output tape. If $\omega' \notin W$, then SMUTM will reject the request and the service become available.

Theorem 1: An available resource has the following 4 characteristics: service is stateful within a lifecycle; service can halt even when exceptions happen; service is self-reproducing; and service has standard interfaces.

Proof: We say SMUTM computes lifetime function f. $f:(\Sigma-\{\triangleright,B\})^* \mapsto (\Sigma-\{\triangleright,B\})^*$, if the following two conditions hold for all $w \in (\Sigma-\{\triangleright,B\})^*$

a) $\exists N$, depending on SMUTM andω,such that there is no configuration C satisfying $(s, \triangleright \underline{B}\,\omega) \vdash_M^N C$

b) $(s, \triangleright \underline{B}\,\omega) \vdash_M^* (h, u\underline{a}v)$ if only if $ua = \triangleright B$, and $v = f(w)$

We say SMUTM compute f; N is an "upper bound" depending on the machine and the input (condition (a) above). There is no computation continuing after N steps. It demonstrates that SMUTM for all resource discover and f halt. Use Step-Counter Theorem [9]. Adding a step counter, which limits the maximum resources that requestor occupies, such as CPU time, disk space etc. One simply "runs" program number y for up to t steps.

Use the Recursion Theorem corollary $\exists e, for\ \forall x, \phi_e(x) = e$ [9]

This result means the program with number e consumes its "environment" and outputs a copy of it. When users release the resource, the service will be self-reproducing.

Use the Fixed Point Theorem [6].

Let $f(z)$ is a computable function. $\exists e, \forall x, \phi_{f(e)}(x) = \phi_e(x)$.

This means all the resources must provide a standard interface (GridService [8]).

Corollary 1: A P2P network can be represented by an undirected graph [10]. Resources discovery issue is how to cover all the nodes in the Grid. Services can be published on some nodes; if we can find all the nodes in Grid, all exist services will be discovered. Moreover we can discover the resources using minimum nodes set and reduce the consuming of Grid resources. But the *VERTEX-COVER* [9] is NP-complete problem. APPROX-VERTEX-COVER algorithm returns a vertex-cover that is almost twice the size of an optimal cover.

3.4 Formal Describe the Constellation Model Discovery

Resources in constellation model can be denoted by the formal definition in Section 3.3. A node in constellation can be treated as a SMUTM according to definition 3. The services will be available during the using of the requestor, which conform to Theorem 1.The fix-star and planet nodes in a constellation can be organized into various models, such as C/S or P2P. If only any fixed star node accepts a request, the whole constellation could deal with it ultimately.

- The discovery execution time T (n) is presented in the following expression

$$T(n) = \begin{cases} \Theta(1), & if\ n=1 \\ Max(T(n/m)) + \Theta(n), & if\ n>1 \end{cases} \tag{1}$$

Where n denotes that a request has n items; $\Theta(1)$ is the execution time of an undivided request. If a request can be divided into several sub-requests, each sub-request will have $\lfloor n/m \rfloor$ items. $\Theta(n)$ stands for the merging result time that is only relative to n. The execution time of a resource discovery is determined by the last task, which can avoid one task blocking the following.

- The architecture of constellation model can be expressed as

$$\Phi = \{SMUTM,\ Network,\ QoS\text{-}Radius\}. \tag{2}$$

Φ means the set of all performance features of constellation model, for each element $\phi_i \in \Phi$ quantitatively describe the tolerable variation in ϕ_i. From the point of view of Operating System, Grid Service typically consists of one or more processes; so let *SMTUM* represent the service and data of a constellation. *Network* denotes the overlay network connecting the constellations together according to different optimizations. The values of all of the system and environment parameters may impact the QoS performance features called perturbation parameters [11]. *QoS-Radius* is a two-element perturbation vector $<a_i^{min}, a_i^{max}>$. gives the bounds of the tolerable variation in ϕ_i. Take response time as an example, the acceptable variation is up to 50 percent of the estimated discovery time. ϕ_i is the time required to finish the assigned discovery task by the *i*th constellation, and its corresponding$<a_i^{min}, a_i^{max}>$could be <0, 1.5×*(estimated response time)*>.

4 Discovery Algorithms and Optimization

In the traditional P2P system such as Gnutella, the query response is forwarded back along the reverse path that carried the incoming query message, which can guarantees the anonymity of query source and avoids the bombard temporary direct connection requests. While this method has the following shortages:

- Firstly, if the status of nodes is dynamic or the network is unsteady, the discovery response could not return for the failure of the nodes or network.
- Secondly, it will take a long time for the responder's return when the path is very long. Because the response results should be stored in each node in the path and then sent to the next node, a lot of unwanted operations are performed, which probably make the response time unacceptable;
- Thirdly, the path that incoming query message follows is the same as query response message, which will likely to cause network congestion. While the other paths are free.

Apply constellation model to resource discovery, the query source such as from planet can take the fixed star as proxy, therefore keep its anonymity. The fixed star can support more direct connection that reduces the aggregate bandwidth. Hence, using equation 1 and 2 we bring forward new algorithms in that the response messages are sent back to the user directly.

4.1 Non-Original-Trace Return (NOTR) Algorithm

The resource discovery is represented as a service. Users create an instance of the resource query service with a randomly created name *RandomGSH*. The instance has a service data named *ServicesFound* recording the query result, and a method named *RecordServices* to record the query result in ServicesFound.

A request is firstly submitted to a constellation called the **beginning constellation**, and then transferred to other constellations called the **midst constellations**. This algorithm includes operations performed on the two separate parts.

1. Procedures on the beginning constellation:

```
Beginning constellation: ( Do local querying, and then judge the result of the local query)
If (no qualified services are found )
{
    Add RandomGSH into the query request message;
    Update the request message;
    Send the message to filtered neighbors of this constellation;
    While (the time to stop querying is not reached )
    {
        If (ServicesFound is updated )
        { Notify the query result to the user application; }
    }
    Destroy the RandomGSH instance;
    Stop listening ;
    Stop resource querying;
}//end if;
Else
{
    return the query result to requestor;
    stop resource querying;
}
```

2. Procedures on the midst constellations:

```
Midst constellations: ( Do local querying, and then judge the result of the local query)
If (no qualified services are found)
{
   Update the query request message;
   Send the message to the filtered neighbors of this midst constellation;
   Exit;
}
Else
{
   Invoke the method RecordServices of the instance RandomGSH to update the ServicesFound
   Exit;
}//end
```

RandomGSH is sent to neighbor constellations as part of the request. When some qualified services are found in any constellation, the method *RecordServices* of the *RandomGSH* instance will be invoked to modify *ServicesFound* directly, thus the response is returned to the beginning constellation without passing along other constellations. Then the Notification-mechanism in GT3 will notify the result to requestor immediately. Therefore, the response time of the resource discovery could be decreased.

4.2 Constellation Response Time Optimizations

In [12], messages that will be delivered to the same node are buffered and sent in a single packet at regular time intervals, while messages with the same header are merged into a single message with a cumulative body. This protocol efficiently reduces the number of Grid services operations. In order to further reduce the response time, some optimization solutions are proposed as follows:

- All the constellations in the path that incoming request followed must be recorded, and this information will be sent to neighbors within the request. If some neighbors have been present in the experienced path, the request will not be sent to them.
- A request will carry the name of its beginning node and the serial number of itself in the beginning node as its mark. If a constellation had handled with the same request, it will simply discard the request without doing anything. Otherwise it will cache the mark of the request before processing in local.

5 Prototype Simulations

The prototype system of constellation model is implemented in the National High-performance Computing Environment of Xi'an Jiaotong University. Overlay network simulator on the constellation layer adopts the 3-CCC (3-node cycle cube-connected cycles) [13] connected-network model.

5.1 NOTR Algorithm

The query request messages are produced randomly. We will examine the response time of the prototype, which adopts the (NOTR) algorithm and the follows the route of original trace return algorithm respectively. Moreover the average time of all the query results is also calculated. The result is shown in figure 4.

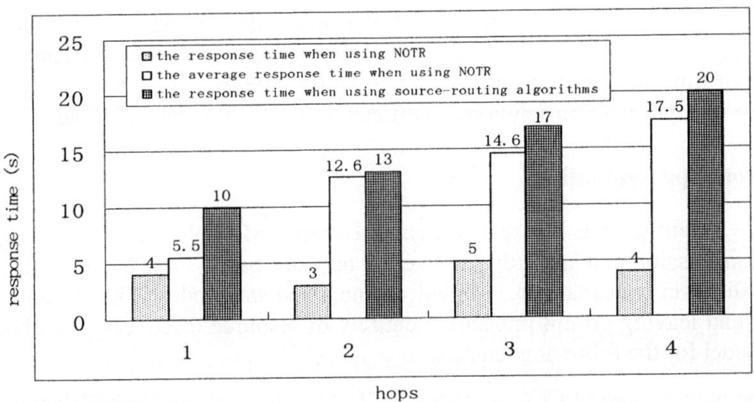

Fig. 4. The comparison response time while adopting the NOTR algorithm and others

The response time only depends on the location of the qualified service firstly found in NOTR. But the response time is linear with the biggest hops when adopting the traditional algorithm. The NOTR algorithm reduced the response time greatly. The average time of query results is also reduced nearly by 12%.

5.2 Constellation Network Load Optimization Solution

The scale of the constellation layer is as much as 80 constellations. We send to the prototype with an unfruitful query request message, to which no services will be matched. This unfruitful request is transmitted among the nodes in the constellation layer. We measure the network load of the constellation layer using the times of the request's being transmitted. Figure 5 shows the times of transmitting when using simple flooding algorithm and when using our optimization solutions.

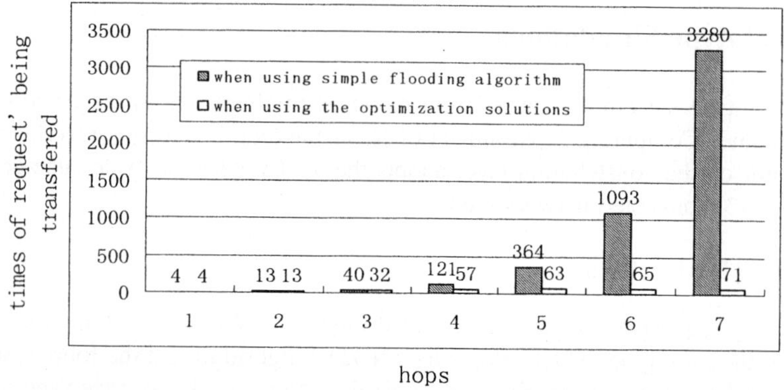

Fig. 5. Transmitting times comparison

The times increase exponentially with the increasing of constellation scale when only simple flooding algorithm is used. But optimization solutions can limit the amount of times to a limitary range, which will not exceed the number of constellations. So the optimization solution can efficiently reduce the network load.

5.3 Prototype Evaluation

With the advent such as Dense Wavelength Division Multiplexing (DWDM) in fiber-optic transmission and so forth, the overlay network based on it is also reliable. Resource discovery mechanism is based on the fixed-star nodes. The dynamic nodes joining and leaving do not impact the entirety of resource discovery. We choose the CCC model for the following reasons:

- The node degree of CCC is always 3. "From crawls of the Gnutella network performed in June 2001, we found the average outdegree of the network to be 3.1" [4]. So the adoption of the CCC model can represent the characteristics of network, and overlay network will be easy to construct.
- The CCC model is characterized by its good scalability.

Table 2. The CCC model attributes[13]

Model	Degree	Diameter	Scale
CCC	3	2k–1+[k/2]	N = k×2k

The letter k denotes the dimension of the CCC model. N is the number of nodes in the constellation layer. Given N=100; 1000; 10,000; 100,000; then k=5; 8; 10; 13. The diameters are 11; 19; 24; 31 correspondingly. The number of hops required to cover all the nodes in the constellation layer equals the diameter adding 1.

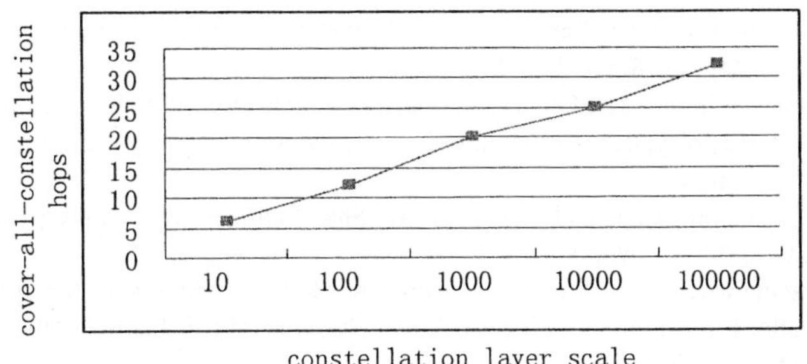

Fig. 6. The least number of hops with the scale of the constellation layer

In terms of the sharp increasing of the scale of the constellation layer, the minimal number of hops can be acceptable. The complexity of the resource discovery can be limited in an acceptable range for a relatively reliable environment as shown in figure 6. Only the QoS of resource discovery service can be guaranteed if there are qualified services in Grid could be found.

6 Conclusions

We have presented the constellation model for the Grid resource discovery. This model has the following advantages: it could avoid the network congestion resulted by flooding, cancel the limit of discovery hops; it has good scalability; resources can join dynamically; the optimized path could be found after the galaxy overlay network is built. We propose a scalable multi-tape universal Turing machine model, and use the SMUTM model to formally describe the process of resource discovery and properties of resources. To investigate issues in QoS in the constellation model is among our further research goals.

References

1. Adriana Iamnitchi, I.Foster: On Fully Decentralized Resource Discovery in Grid Environments. Second International Workshop on Grid Computing, 2001
2. The Globus Toolkit 3 Programmer's Tutorial3.
3. Yunhao Liu,Li Xiao,Xiaomei Liu,Lionel M. Ni ,Xiaodong Zhang: Location Awareness in Unstructured Peer-to-Peer Systems. Parallel and Distributed Systems, IEEE Transactions on Feb. 2005, Volume: 16, Issue: 2, pp. 163- 174
4. Beverly Yang, B. Garcia-Molina, H: Designing a super-peer network. Proceedings. 19th International Conference on Data Engineering, March 2003, pp 49 - 60

5. H.Zhuge, The Future Interconnection Environment, IEEE Computer, 38 (4), 2005, pp. 27-33
6. Yinfeng Wang, Xiaoshe Dong, Xiuqiang He, Hua Guo,Fang Zheng and Zhongsheng Qin: A Constellation Model for Grid Resource Management. The Sixth International Workshop on Advanced Parallel Processing Technologies (APPT 2005), LNCS 3756, pp 263-272, 2005
7. Harry R.Lewis, Christor H.Papadimitrion：Elements of the theory of computation 2nd Ed. Prentice-Hall, Inc, 1998, pp. 247-250
8. I.Foster, H. Kishimoto: The Open Grid Services Architecture, Version 1.0 June 7, 2004
9. M.D Davis, E.J Weyuker: Computability, Complexity and Languages. Academic Press, 1986, pp.59-60,66-67
10. Bin Xiao, Jiannong Cao, and Edwin H.-M. Sha: Maintaining Comprehensive Resource Availability in P2P Networks, GCC 2004, LNCS 3251, pp. 543-550
11. Ali,S. Maciejewski, A.A. Siegel, H.J. Jong-Kook Kim: Measuring the robustness of a resource allocation. Parallel and Distributed Systems, IEEE Transactions on July 2004, Volume: 15, Issue: 7, pp. 630- 641
12. Domenico Talia and Paolo Trunfio：Web Services for Peer-to-Peer Resource Discovery on the Grid. DELOS Workshop: Digital Library Architectures 2004: pp.73-84
13. F.P.Preparata and J.Vuillemin: the cube-connected cycles: A versatile network for parallel computation, Comm, ACM, Vol.24, No.5, 1981. pp.300-309

Replica Placement in Data Grid: A Multi-objective Approach

Rashedur M. Rahman, Ken Barker, and Reda Alhajj

Department of Computer Science, University of Calgary,
2500 University Drive, N.W. Calgary, AB T2N 1N4
{rahmanm, barker, alhajj}@cpsc.ucalgary.ca

Abstract. One of the challenges in data replication is to select the candidate sites to place replicas. We use the *p*-median and *p*-center models to address the replica placement problem. In our problem, the *p*-median model finds the locations of *p* candidate sites to place a replica to optimize the total (or average) response time. The *p*-center model hosts replicas to *p* candidate sites by minimizing the maximum response time among sites. A Grid environment is highly dynamic so placing a replica by considering one objective, *i.e.*, optimize average response time or optimize maximum response time, may not be always a good choice. We propose a multi-objective model that considers the objectives of *p*-median and *p*-center simultaneously to select the candidate sites that will host replicas. Simulation results demonstrate that the multi-objective model outperforms single objective models in dynamic environments such as Data Grids.

1 Introduction

Science today is more collaborative and multi-institutional [11] so it needs access to computing resources and special classes of scientific devices or instruments located around the globe. A large number of scientific and engineering applications require a huge amount of computing time to carry out their experiments using simulation [3]. Research driven by this has promoted the exploration of a new architecture known as "The Grid" for high performance distributed applications and systems.

Grid computing can coordinate resource sharing and problem solving across dynamic multi-institutional environments [5]. Large scientific initiatives such as global climate change, high energy physics, and computational genomics require large data collections and these are beginning to emerge in their communities. These large data stores must be shared by researchers around the world. High performance Data Grid architectures facilitate these requirements by applying various technologies in a coordinated fashion to support data intensive petabyte scale applications. Data Grid technology has been developed to permit data sharing across many organizations in geographically disperse locations so data replication is becoming critical to ensure data is cached close to users [14]. For example, the data grid envisioned by GriPhyN [12] is hierarchical in nature. It consists of multiple tiers with all data generated at Tier 0; Tier 1 consists of national centers; and regional centers below these. Each tier has its own storage capacity which varies from tier to tier. Replicas can then be placed

H. Zhuge and G.C. Fox (Eds.): GCC 2005, LNCS 3795, pp. 645–656, 2005.

at each tier to increase the data availability among different sites. Thus, replication stores copies of data in different locations so that it can be easily recovered if one copy at one location is lost or is unavailable.

Transferring a file from a server to a client consumes a substantial bandwidth. One possible way to reduce the access latency and bandwidth consumption is to replicate data across different sites. Replication also facilitates load balancing and improves reliability by creating multiple data copies. However, the files in the Grid are large (*i.e.*, 500MB-1GB) so replication to every site is infeasible. One challenge is to locate the candidate sites where we can host the replicas. We use two models: the *p*-median and *p*-center models [13], for selecting the candidate sites to host replicas. The *p*-median model places replica at sites that optimize the request-weighted average response time. Response time is the time required to transfer a file from the nearest replication site. The response time is effectively zero if a local copy exists. Request–weighted response time is calculated by multiplying the number of requests at site *i* by the response time for site *i*. The average is calculated by averaging the request-weighted response time for all sites. The *p*-center model selects the candidate sites to host replicas by minimizing the maximum response time. A Grid environment is highly dynamic so predicting user requests and network load *a priori* is difficult. Therefore, when only considering a single objective; variations in user requests and network load will have larger impacts on system performance. Thus, we consider a multi-objective approach that combines the *p*-center and *p*-median objectives to decide where to place replica. The multi-objective model minimizes the median objective while ensuring requesting sites are always near replication sites.

The balance of the paper is organized as follows. Section 2 presents related work and the evaluated replica placement strategies are presented in Section 3. The simulation model is described in Section 4. Section 5 evaluates and compares the replication strategies. Section 6 concludes and indicates possible future research directions.

2 Related Work

Decision problems arise in wide range of public and private sector environments. Different models such as the set covering model [20], *p*-center, and *p*-median models address such problems. The general problem is to locate objects (or facilities) to optimize some objective. Distance, or some measure more or less functionally related to distance (e.g., travel time or cost, demand satisfaction), is fundamental to those problems. The set covering and *p*-center models are based on maximum distance, whereas the *p*-median model is based on the total (or average) distance. The set covering model locates the minimum number of facilities required to cover all the demand nodes. The *p*-median model finds *p* locations to minimize the total traverse distance that customers must travel to reach the closest facility [9]. The *p*-center model addresses the problem of minimizing the maximum distance to the closest facility. Applications for these models include locating bus stops, licensing bureaus, airports, blood bank, emergency medical services, *etc* [8, 9].

Kavitha *et al.* [15] propose a strategy for creating replicas automatically in a generic decentralized peer-to-peer network. The model's goal is to maintain replica availability with some probability. Although the approach may be applicable on

DataGrids, it is hampered because each peer only utilizes partial information (the part they retain); so a more global approach should achieve better results.

Ranganathan and Foster [14] discuss various replication strategies for a hierarchical DataGrid architecture. They test six different replication strategies: 1) No Replication: only the root node holds replicas; 2) Best Client: replica is created for the client who accesses the file the most; 3) Cascading: a replica is created on the path to the best client; 4) Plain Caching: a local copy is stored upon initial request; 5) Caching plus Cascading: combines plain caching and cascading; 6) Fast Spread: file copies are stored at each node on the path to the best client. These algorithms assume that popular files at one site are popular at others. The client site counts hops for each site that holds replicas, and the model selects the one with the least number of hops from the requesting client. It does not consider current network bandwidth. Our model lifts this constrained so we capture both Grid file transfer and other network traffic over the same link. Our model also considers heterogeneous link capacities and is more general than hierarchical.

Kavitha *et al.* [16] develop a family of job scheduling and replication algorithms that they simulate to evaluate. Three different replica placement algorithms are considered: 1) no active replication; 2) a replica is created at a random site based on a threshold; and 3) a replica is created at the site with the smallest number of waiting jobs based on a threshold. These three replication strategies are combined with four scheduling strategies: 1) jobs are scheduled to a random site; 2) jobs go to the site with fewest waiting jobs; 3) jobs are scheduled to the site containing the required data and with the fewest waiting jobs; or 4) jobs are always run locally. The work shows that when there is no replication, simple local scheduling performs best. However, when replication is used, scheduling jobs to sites containing the required data is better. The key result is that dynamic replication reduces hotspots created by popular data and enables load sharing.

OptorSim [2] is the simulator used here. It was developed as a part of European DataGrid project to carry out different replication and scheduling algorithms. The simulator models a Grid consisting of sites where each can have zero or more computing elements, and/or zero or more storage elements. The computing element facilitates job execution while the storage site serves as data repository. The simulator also supports routers which forward requests to other sites and do not have any processing power or storage capacity. A resource broker acts as a meta-scheduler that controls the scheduling of jobs to different computing elements. The simulator uses an economic model in which sites buy and sell files using an auction mechanism.

Finally, there is other work on replica management including Chervenak *et al.* [5] who provide an architectural framework and define the each component's role. Allcock *et al.* [1] develop a replica management service using the Globus Toolkit. Zhao *et al.* [21] develop a grid replica selection service using the Open Grid Service Architecture (OGSA) which facilitates the discovery and incorporation of the service by other Grid components. Cai *et al.* [4] propose a fault tolerant and scalable Peer-to-Peer Replica Location Service (P-RLS) that might be applicable to a Data Grid.

In several research efforts [2, 14, 16] user requests are the only parameter considered for replica placement so network latencies are ignored. However, network bandwidth plays a vital role in transferring files. We can save substantial transfer time if we place a replica of a file at a site that is connected to its neighbors with limited bandwidth and if its request for that file is above average. In our earlier work [18], we show that considering both the current network state and file requests produces better results than file requests times alone. We start our replication algorithms by placing the master files at one site. We then calculate the expected utility or risk index for each site that does not currently hold a replica and then place one on the site that optimizes the expected utility or risk. The algorithms proposed based on *utility* selects a candidate site to host a replica by assuming that future requests and current load will follow current loads and user requests. Conversely, algorithms using a *risk* index expose sites far from all other sites and assume a worst case whereby future requests will primarily originate from that distant site. One major drawback of these strategies is that the algorithms select only one site per iteration and places a replica there. The Grid environment is highly dynamic and there might be a sudden burst of requests such that we need to place a replica at multiple sites simultaneously to quickly satisfy the large spike of requests. In this research, we extend our earlier work by selecting p candidate sites to host replicas. The objectives that we consider are a p-median, p-center combined in a multi-objective model.

3 Replica Placement Algorithms

Before discussing the multi-objective replica placement algorithm we discuss the Set Covering Problem, the p-center problem, and the p-median problem.

3.1 Set Covering Problem

In this model, the objective is to locate the minimum number of sites to place a replica so as to cover all the requesting sites. The candidate sites that host replicas will be at least some covering time/distance away from the requesting sites. Mathematically we can formulate the Set Covering Problem (SCP) as follows:

$$\text{Minimize} \quad \sum_{j=1}^{n} x_j \tag{1}$$

$$\text{Subject to} \quad \sum_{j=1}^{n} a_{ij} x_j \geq 1, \quad i = 1,\ldots\ldots, n \tag{2}$$

$$x_j \in (0,1), \quad j = 1,\ldots\ldots, n \tag{3}$$

where

$$a_{ij} = \begin{cases} 1 \text{ if replication site } j \text{ covers the requesting site } i \\ 0 \text{ if not} \end{cases} \text{ and } \quad x_j = \begin{cases} 1 \text{ if site } j \text{ is chosen to host a replica} \\ 0 \text{ if not} \end{cases}$$

The constraint (1) minimizes the number of sites selected. The objective function (2) ensures that each requesting site must be covered by at least one replication site. The last constraint (3) satisfies the integrality constraint which determines if the site will be selected as the replica placement location. For example, if the covering time/distance is 19 seconds, the $n \times n$ zero-one matrix a_{ij} is shown in Fig 1 for the corresponding adjacent network. One of the popular solutions to SCP is Lagrangian relaxation [10]. The basic idea is to relax some constraints of the original model and

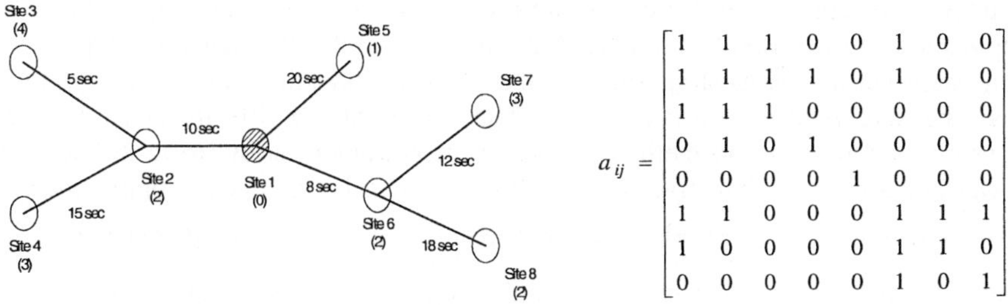

Fig. 1. A small network and corresponding 0-1 covering matrix

add those constraints, multiplied by Lagrange multiplier to the objective function. We then try to solve the relaxed problem optimally. For example, we relax constraints (2) in SCP and add this into objective function (1) by multiplying by the Lagrange Multipliers and solve it optimally (see [19]).

3.2 P-Center Problem

The *p*-center problem addresses the problem of minimizing the maximum response time using a given number of *p* replication sites that host a replica. The *p*-center problem can be formulated as:

$$\text{Minimize} \quad W \tag{4}$$

$$\text{Subject to} \quad \sum_{j=1}^{n} x_j = p; \tag{5}$$

$$\sum_{j=1}^{n} y_{ij} = 1, \ i = 1,\ldots\ldots,n \tag{6}$$

$$y_{ij} - x_j \le 0, \ \ i = 1,\ldots\ldots,n \ \ j = 1,\ldots\ldots,n \tag{7}$$

$$W \ge \sum_{j=1}^{n} d_{ij} y_{ij}; \ i = 1,\ldots\ldots,n \tag{8}$$

$$x_j \in (0,1), \ \ j = 1,\ldots\ldots,n \tag{9}$$

$$y_{ij} \in (0,1), \ j = 1,\ldots\ldots,n; \ i = 1,\ldots\ldots,n \tag{10}$$

where

W = the maximum response time between a requesting site and the replication site to which it has been assigned

$$x_j = \begin{cases} 1 \text{ if site } j \text{ is chosen to host replica} \\ 0 \text{ if not} \end{cases}$$

$$y_{ij} = \begin{cases} 1 \text{ if the requesting site } i \text{ is assigned to a candidate replication site } j \\ 0 \text{ if not} \end{cases}$$

The objective function (4) minimizes the maximum response time between a requesting site and the closest site from which it can retrieve the replica. Constraint (5) states that exactly *p* sites are to be located to place the replica. Constraint (6) states that each requesting site should be allocated exactly one replication site from which it can fetch the replica. Constraint (7) states that requests at site i can only be assigned at replication site j if a replica is placed at site j. Constraint (8) states that the response time between any requesting site and the nearest replication site should be smaller than the maximum response time (W). The constraints (9, 10) are general integrity constraints. One solution method of the p-center problem is by using the upper and lower bounds of the objective function. Let U and L be the current upper and lower bounds of the p-center problem. We calculate the covering time distance $C = \left\lfloor \frac{U+L}{2} \right\rfloor$ and solve the set covering problem for the current covering response time C. If the number of sites found by SCP is equal to p, we stop the algorithm; otherwise we modify the upper and lower bound and solve the SCP problem again (detail provided by Daskin [8]).

3.3 P-Median Problem

The P-median model finds the p replica placement sites to minimize the total response time between the requesting sites and the replication sites to which they are assigned. This model is formulated as:

$$\text{Minimize} \sum_{i=1}^{n}\sum_{j=1}^{n} h_i d_{ij} y_{ij} \tag{11}$$

$$\text{Subject to} \sum_{j=1}^{n} x_j = p \tag{12}$$

$$\sum_{j=1}^{n} y_{ij} = 1, \; i = 1,\ldots\ldots,n \tag{13}$$

$$y_{ij} - x_j \le 0, \;\; i = 1,\ldots\ldots,n \;\; j = 1,\ldots\ldots,n \tag{14}$$

$$x_j \in (0,1), \;\; j = 1,\ldots\ldots,n \tag{15}$$

$$y_{ij} \in (0,1), \; j = 1,\ldots\ldots,n\,;\; i = 1,\ldots\ldots,n \tag{16}$$

The objective function (11) minimizes the request-weighted total (or average) response time between each requesting site and the nearest replication site. Constraints (12-14) and (15-16) are similar to constraints (5-7) and (9-10) of the p-center problem, respectively. Here h_i represents the requests at site i. The Lagrange relaxation technique is used to find the solution of this problem.

3.4 Multi-objective Approach

Our multi-objective strategy combines the p-center and the p-median objectives to place a replica. The purpose is to minimize the median objective without having any requesting site too far from a candidate replication site. Therefore, the problem is to minimize the p-median objective subject to the restriction that the value of the p-center objective does not exceed a certain level. We use the constrained method [13] to solve the multi-objective problem. The steps of the constrained method are:

1. Set a value of p at the beginning of the algorithm. Solve the p-median and the p-center problems individually. Let W_M and W_C be the values of the objective functions found by the p-median and the p-center problems, respectively.
2. Choose the number of different values of L_k that will be used to generate *noninferior* solutions. *Noninferior* solutions are defined as feasible solutions if there is no other feasible solution that will yield an improvement in one objective without causing degradation in at least one other objective [7]. The number of values is r.
3. Solve the constrained problem for every combination of values of L_k

$$L_k = W_c + \left[\frac{t}{r-1}\right](W_m - W_c),\ t = 0,1,......,r-1 \tag{17}$$

Finally, the multi-objective problem is defined as:

$$\text{Minimize } \sum_{i=1}^{n}\sum_{j=1}^{n} h_i d_{ij} y_{ij} \tag{18}$$

$$\text{Subject to } \sum_{j=1}^{n} x_j = p \tag{19}$$

$$\sum_{j=1}^{n} y_{ij} = 1,\ i = 1,.....,n \tag{20}$$

$$L_k \geq \sum_{j=1}^{n} d_{ij} y_{ij}\ ;\ i = 1,.....,n \tag{21}$$

$$y_{ij} - x_j \leq 0,\ i = 1,.....,n \quad j = 1,.....,n \tag{22}$$

$$x_j \in (0,1),\ j = 1,.....,n \tag{23}$$

$$y_{ij} \in (0,1),\ j = 1,.....,n\ ;\ i = 1,.....,n \tag{24}$$

This problem can be solved in the same way as the p-median problem.

4 Simulation

Replica placement algorithms must be tested thoroughly before deploying them in real Data Grid environments. One way to achieve a realistic evaluation of the various strategies is through simulation that carefully reflects real Data Grids. On a Data Grid different jobs are submitted from various sites. Mean job execution time is a good measure of effectiveness of the replication strategies. Jobs in the Data Grid request a number of files. If the file is at a local site, response time is effectively zero; otherwise the file must be transported from the nearest replication site. Thus, job execution time incorporates the response time required to transport a file. The best replication strategy minimizes the mean job execution time and should also minimize the average response time. We validate our replica placement algorithms with average response times. We will validate our placement algorithms with mean job execution time in the future. Our replica placement algorithms are evaluated with a simulator written in Java. The simulation generates random background traffic and grid data requests.

4.1 Grid Configuration

The study of our replica placement algorithms is carried out using a model of the EU Data Grid Testbed 1 sites and their associated network geometry [2]. Site 0 is the CERN (European Organization for Nuclear Research) location. Initially all master files are distributed to CERN. A master file contains the original copy of some data samples and cannot be deleted. Each circle in Fig 2 represents a testbed site and a star represents a router. Each link between two sites shows the available network bandwidth. The network bandwidth is expressed in Mbits/sec (M) or Gbits/sec (G). We include the storage capacity at each router, *i.e.*, intermediate nodes. The intermediate nodes have higher storage capacity than the testbed sites but smaller capacity than CERN. Placing data at intermediate nodes moves it closer and makes it more accessible to testbed sites. File requests are generated from the testbed sites only.

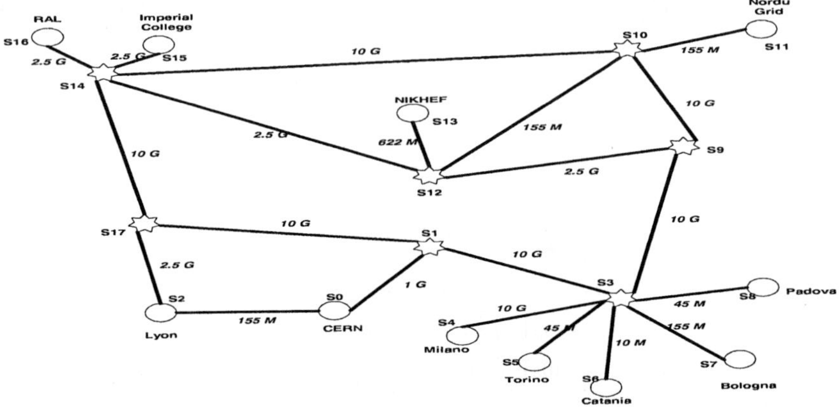

Fig. 2. The EU Data Grid Testbed 1 Sites and the Approximate Network Geometry

4.2 Simulation Input

The simulation's input is from two configuration files. One file describes the network topology, *i.e.,* the link between different sites, the available network bandwidth between sites, and the size of disk storage of each site. The second file contains information about the number of requests generated by each testbed site and the current network load. The network load is varied to test the impact on our replication algorithm. We consider low, medium, or heavy traffic. File requests may either follow uniform or normal distribution. We set three maximum values for uniform file requests where each testbed site can generate requests that are uniformly distributed with a maximum of 10, 30, or 50. We also consider ten random normally distributed requests with different means and variances. The testbed site that generates each random request is chosen arbitrarily. We consider uniform and normal requests with diverse variances to analyze how well the replication algorithms performs when there is no co-relation among previous requests, that is., the requests are totally random.

5 Simulation Results

Each site records the time taken for each file requested to be transported to it. This time record forms the basis to compare various replication strategies. We compare our replication algorithm with respect to average response time. Response time is the time that elapses from a request for a file until it receives the complete file. The average of all response times for the length of the simulation is calculated. The best replication strategy will have lowest response time. Each file is 100 MB in size. After some initial runs, we place a replica to the sites that will optimize either one of the objectives, *i.e.*, the *p*-median, the *p*-center, or the multi-objective strategy. We test our algorithm for two different values of *p*, i.e., *p*=5 or *p*=7. The maximum response time, request-weighted average response time, and the candidate sites chosen by those algorithms are shown in Tables 1 and 2. The trade-off is illustrated by the curve for the maximum response time and the request-weighted average response time for different algorithms as depicted in Fig 3. We calculate the average response time for future requests in

Table 1. The objective function values for different models and candidate set for *p=5*

Model	Maximum Response Time	Request-Weighted Average Response Time	Candidate Sites
P-median	18010	73450	S0, S5, S6, S11, S14
Multi-obj1	5400	128800	S0, S5, S6, S8, S14
P-center	5240	135680	S0, S5, S6, S8, S9

Table 2. The objective function values for different models and candidate set for *p=7*

Model	Maximum Response	Request-Weighted Average Response Time	Candidate Sites
P-Median	5400	39440	S0,S5,S6, S8, S11, S13, S14
Multi-obj1	1280	65440	S0, S5, S6, S7, S8, S11, S13
Multi-obj2	1600	46640	S0, S5, S6, S7, S8, S11, S13
P-Center	1280	100960	S0, S5, S6, S7, S8, S11, S14

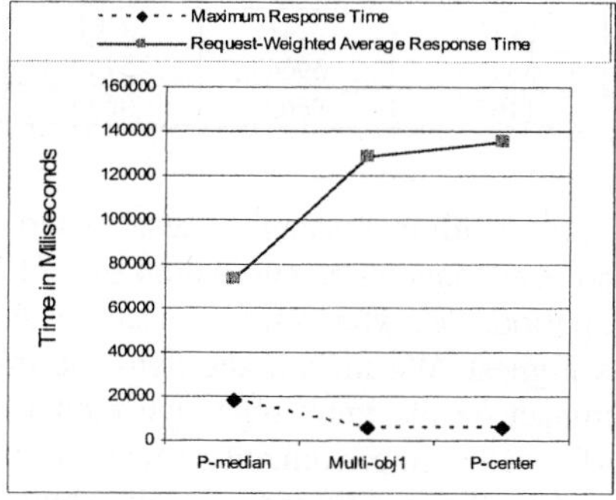

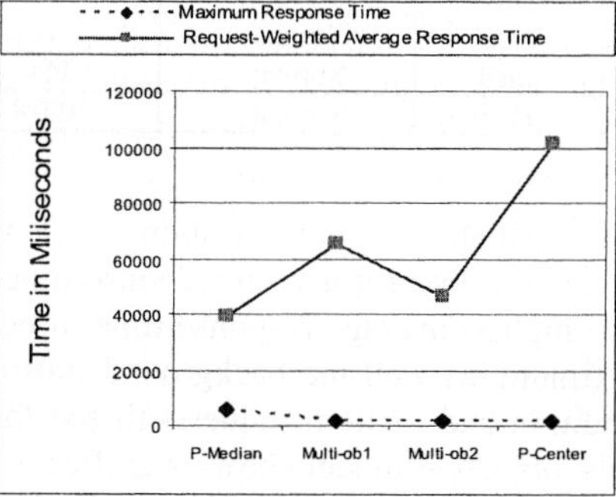

Fig. 3. The objective values for different replication models for left) *p=5* and right) *p=7*

Table 3. Average response time for different models, network loads, user requests when p=5

Traffic	Request	P-median	P-center	Multi-obj1
Low	Uniform (10)	1150	1043	1028
Med	Uniform (10)	3738	3230	3207
High	Uniform (10)	3415	3257	3192
Low	Uniform (30)	2444	2128	2096
Med	Uniform (30)	7256	5896	5779
High	Uniform (30)	17133	9166	8956
Low	Uniform (50)	4290	3532	3498
Med	Uniform (50)	15742	13834	13698
High	Uniform (50)	23511	19822	19717
Low	Normal	9718	9136	8972
Med	Normal	30799	26456	25835
High	Normal	37317	36046	35600

different network load by asuming the replicas are now at the candidate sites. We solve the multi-objective algorithm for 6 different L_k values (r=6). For, p=5, we get one *noninferior* solution, and for p=7 we get two inferior solutions, which are labeled as Multi-obj1 and Multi-obj2.

We accumulate the average response time for the next sixty runs to analyze the performance of the replica placement algorithms. We also vary the network load with other background traffic to see its impact on the replication algorithm. The results of accumulated average response time (in seconds) are shown in Tables 3 and 4.

Table 4. Average response time for different models, network loads, user requests when p=7

Traffic	Request	P-median	P-Center	Multi-obj1	Multi-obj
Low	Uniform	199	226	194	189
Med	Uniform	630	685	622	585
High	Uniform (10	1056	822	827	703
Low	Uniform	741	861	797	661
Med	Uniform	2455	2136	1728	1821
High	Uniform	2597	2671	2100	2239
Low	Uniform	1357	1292	1099	1084
Med	Uniform	3231	4307	3214	3521
High	Uniform	4298	5323	4005	4120
Low	Normal	2371	2731	2241	2162
Med	Normal	5744	6350	5964	5152
High	Normal	10028	11671	9662	9645

Table 4 shows that the response time increases with increasing requests. There is a strong correlation between response time and user requests as one would expect. We have highest average response time in peak period, *i.e.*, when user requests reach the maximum, as well the background traffic is highest. We include the dynamic traffic condition and random requests to see the impact on the multi-objective model. The multi-objective model shows significant performance improvement compared to single objective models in different background traffic conditions as well when user requests vary randomly, that is, no relation with previous requests (uniform random), or the future requests are normally distributed and centered on previous requests.

The proposed mathematical models require little computational time to reach the solution by p-median, p-center, and multi-objective. The simulation was carried out on a Pentium 4 processor 2GHz with 512 MB RAM. With current network size, the computational time is only 10 seconds on average to reach a solution using p-median, p-center, or multi-objective model.

6 Conclusions

We propose a multi-objective approach for replica placement and analyze the performance of the algorithm on future requests in different network loads. We observe that considering a multi-objective approach is better than considering a single objective one. The results obtained are very promising. The replication strategies have significant benefits. They are based on distributed and decentralized models; and they are dynamic in that they can adapt to changes to both network and user behavior while improving the performance of the overall system. We plan to implement the placement algorithms in OptorSim Data Grid simulator to analyze performance with respect to job time, response time, and different replica replacement algorithms such as LRU, LFU, and economic based strategies supported by OptorSim.

References

1. Allcock, B., J. Bester, J. Bresnahan, A. Chervenak, I. Foster, C. Kesselman, S. Meder, V. Nefedova, D. Quesnel, S. Tuecke, Secure, Efficient Data Transport and Replica Management for High Performance Data-Intensive Computing. *Proc. of IEEE Mass Storage Conference*, 2001.
2. Bell, W., D.G. Cameron, L. Capozza, P. Millar, K. Stockinger, and F. Zini, OptorSim - A Grid Simulator for Studying Dynamic Data Replication Strategies. *International Journal of High Performance Computing Applications*, 17(4), 2003.
3. Buyya, R., D. Abramson, and J. Giddy, G. Nimrod, An Architecture of a Resource Management and Scheduling System in a Global Computational Grid, *Proc. of HPC Asia 2000*, pp 283-289, Beijing, China.
4. Cai, M., A. Chervenak, M. Frank, A Peer-to-Peer Replica Location Service Based on a Distributed Hash Table, *Proc. of the SC2004 Conference*, Nov. 2004.
5. Chervenak, A., I. Foster, C. Kesselman, C. Salisbury, and S. Tuecke. The Data Grid: Towards and Architecture for the Distributed Management and Analysis of Large Scientific Data Sets. *Journal of Network and Computer Applications*, 23(3):187-200, 2000.
6. Chervenak, A., E. Deelman, I. Foster, L. Guy, W. Hoschek, A. Iamnitchi, C. Kesselman, P. Kunszt, M. Ripeanu, B. Schwartzkopf, H. Stockinger, K. Stockinger and B. Tierney, Giggle: A Framework for Constructing Scalable Replica Location Services. *Proceedings of the Supercomputing Conference*, 2002.
7. Cohon, J.L., Multiobjective Programming and Planning, Academic Press, New York, 1978.
8. Daskin., M.S., Network and Discrete Location Models: Algorithms and Applications, John Wiley & Sons, 1995.
9. Drezner, Z., and H. W. Hamacher, Facility Location Applications and Theory, Springer Verlag, Berlin, Germany, 2002.

10. Fisher, M.L., The Lagrangian relaxation method for solving integer programming problems, *Management Sciences*, 27, 1-18.
11. Foster, I., Internet Computing and the Emerging Grid, Nature Web Matters, 2000.
12. The GriPhyN Project, http://www.griphyn.org
13. Hakami, S., Optimum location of switching centers and the absolute centers and medians of a graph, *Operations Research*, 12, 450-459.
14. Kavitha, R. and I. Foster, Design and Evaluation of Replication Strategies for a High Performance Data Grid, *Computing and High Energy and Nuclear Physics*, 2001.
15. Kavitha, R., A. Iamnitchi, and I. Foster, Improving Data Availability through Dynamic Model Driven Replication in Large Peer-to-Peer Communities. *Proc. of Global and Peer-to-Peer Computing on Large Scale Distributed Systems Workshop*, Berlin, May 2002.
16. Kavitha, R., and I. Foster, Decoupling Computation and Data Scheduling in Distributed Data-Intensive Applications. *Proc. of IEEE International Symposium on High Performance Distributed Computing*, Edinburgh, July 2002.
17. Marglin, S., Public Investment Criteria, 103 pp. MIT Press, Cambridge, Massachusetts.
18. Rahman, R. M., K. Barker and R. Alhajj, Replica Placement on Data Grid: Considering Utility and Risk. *Proc. of IEEE International Conference on Coding and Computing*, April 2005.
19. Revees, C.R, *Editor*. Modern Heuristic Techniques for Combinatorial Problems, Oxford Blackwell Scientific Publication, 1993
20. Toregas, C., R. Swain, C. Revelle and L. Bergman, The location of emergency service facile ties, *Operations Research*, 19, 1363-1373.
21. Zhao, Y., and Y. Hu, Gress - a Grid Replica Selection Service. *Proc. of ICSA Parallel and Distributed Computing Systems*, 2003.

Grid Resource Discovery Using Semantic Communities

Juan Li and Son Vuong

Computer Science Department, University of British Columbia,
2366 Main Mall, Vancouver, B.C. Canada
{juanli, vuong}@cs.ubc.ca

Abstract. Grid technologies enable the sharing and collaborating of a wide variety of resources. To fully utilize these resources, effective resource discovery mechanisms are necessities. However, the complicated and dynamic characteristics of the grid resources make sharing and discovering them a challenging issue. In this paper, we propose a semantic community approach to assisting the efficient resource discovery and query in grids. Semantic community is a natural arrangement of distributed systems. It prunes the searching space and reduces the cost of searching. Moreover, it exhibits many desirable properties, including being fully decentralized and supporting complex queries. Our simulation results show how searching the girds can take advantage of semantic communities to reduce the searching cost and improve the quality of search results.

1 Introduction

Information service is one of the key services of grids, which provides information of resources and services to users and their tools. To make the information available to users in a timely and reliable manner, an effective and efficient resource discovery mechanism is crucial. However, grid resources can potentially have a very large number and varieties of types. Moreover, individual resources are not under central control and they can enter and leave the grid systems at any time. For all the above reasons, resource discovery in a large-scale grid environment can be very challenging.

Traditionally, resource discovery in grids is based mainly on centralized or hierarchical models. For example, in the Globus Toolkit [6], users can get a node's resource information by directly querying a server application running on that node, or querying dedicated information servers that publish and retrieve the organization's resource information. Although interactions between these information servers are supported, the general-purpose decentralized service discovery mechanism is still absent. As the size of grids used for complex applications increases from tens to thousands of nodes, it is necessary to decentralize their services to avoid bottlenecks and ensure scalability.

In this paper, we propose a community-based peer-to-peer (P2P) model to discover resources in more dynamic, large-scale, and distributed grid environments. By utilizing the P2P structure, the system is fully distributed. There are no servers or central meeting points in the system, thus it avoids the single point of failure and improves the scalability. The system proposes the concept of semantic community. Communities are implicitly formed based on common semantic attributes and can overlap. They are reflections of the activities and interests of grid nodes. Communities help prune the searching space and disseminate information only to related participating nodes,

H. Zhuge and G.C. Fox (Eds.): GCC 2005, LNCS 3795, pp. 657–667, 2005.

thus reducing unnecessary communication within the network and further improving the scalability and efficiency. The community construction and maintenance are fully decentralized and self-organizing. As we show in this paper, the system exhibits many plausible characteristics, such as rich query support, fast response, low bandwidth, and robust behavior.

The remainder of this paper is organized as follows. Related work is discussed in Section 2. Section 3 describes the construction, maintenance and routing of the community overlay networks. Section 4 gives the experimental results. Section 5 concludes the paper.

2 Related Work

In grids, resource discovery is usually managed with centralized or hierarchical mechanisms. In the Globus Toolkit 2, Monitoring and Discovery Service (MDS) [4] is an LDAP based network directory. Its two components (GIIS and GRIS [4]) use a hierarchical mechanism similar to DNS to share resource information. In GT3 [6], all services are described in a standardized XML schema, called SDES [6]. Index Services provide high-level API functionalities to register, aggregate, and query SDES. Condor's Matchmaker [7] uses a centralized mechanism to locate desirable resources. Each node in the Condor system advertises its resources and reports resource status to a central manager. The central manager then matches the advertisements between resource requesters and resource providers.

To discover resources in more dynamic, large-scale, and distributed environments, P2P techniques have been used in grids. For example, [30] organizes information nodes into a flat unstructured P2P network and random-walk based methods are used for query forwarding. Random-walks are not efficient in response time for a very large system. [12] proposes a hierarchical structure to organize information nodes to reduce redundant messages. However, a well-defined hierarchy does not always exist, and the global hierarchy is hard to maintain in a dynamic environment. DHT-based multi-attribute resource discovery approaches are studied in [22] and [23]. However, they may incur either high traffic load for result intersection, or large overhead for multiple publication and update.

Many recent P2P based searching techniques are related to our research. Flooding is the predominant search method in unstructured P2P networks. This method, though simple, does not scale well in terms of message overhead. There have been numerous attempts [1–3] to enhance its scalability. Random Walks [14, 20] are an alternative to flooding for unstructured searches. They can reduce the amount of network traffic, but it is at the cost of query latency. Recently, hierarchical super-peer systems [13] have been proposed to improve searching efficiency. DHTs [16–19] have received a lot of attention in the last few years. These systems have been shown to be scalable and efficient. However, a missing feature is the inherent support for complex queries. Another hurdle to DHT deployment is its tight control of both data placement and network topology, which makes it more sensitive to failures and difficult to keep the content and path locality [9]. More recently, a few studies [10, 21, 22] extend the DHT scheme to support keywords or multi-attribute queries. The basic idea is to map each keyword to a key. A query with multiple keywords then uses the DHT to lookup each keyword and returns the intersection. In order to do that, large amounts of data must be transferred from one peer to another, and the traffic load may be high [24]. Systems like [23] avoid this multiple lookup and intersection by storing a complete keyword list of an object on each node, but this may incur more overhead on publishing and storing the keywords.

Semantic Web [5] attempts to define the metadata information model for the World Wide Web to aid in information retrieval and aggregation. Currently, many P2P applications [8, 27, 28] have leveraged semantic web technologies to add semantics to P2P systems. It improves the effectiveness of resource and query representation, and the efficiency of searching.

3 Semantic Communities

This section gives a detailed explanation of the system architecture and illustrates how to provide efficient formation, discovery and management techniques to constantly changing community structures.

3.1 Communities and Policies

The motivation behind the grid community strategy is the observation that grid network is analogous to human social network. In fact, many existing solution for efficient searching in distributed networks were motivated by the observations of similar solutions in social networks [11, 15]. Both grid communities and human communities consist of members that are actively engaged in the sharing, communication and promotion of common interests. In a human society, people naturally form all kinds of communities by occupation, by interest, by location, etc. People always utilize these communities to gain knowledge or share information. For example, if one has a medical question, one would like to ask a friend who is a doctor. Even if the doctor friend doesn't know the answer, he or she would probably know other doctors (an implicit doctor community) who may have the answer. In a human social network, to search information in a particular domain, an efficient way is to first find a person who is familiar with this domain, then let this person propagate the question in his/her community. In this way, the query can get more and accurate responses. Similarly, the computing grids can create communities in scientific domains, such as physics, biomedical research, neuroscience, mathematics, and computer science. Communication and collaboration can operate on top of the communities. With communities, grid users can conveniently work in groups, although they may not always be located in geographical proximity. They can easily share resources and knowledge within the community. For example, members of a science group can easily query and access related data to perform analyses or simulations, and their work may result in new data that will be of interest to other scientists in the group.

To create grid communities, we need a clustering policy to cluster nodes. Since a peer's interests can be represented by its local data possession, data ontology properties can be used to classify peers. Ontology is defined as "a formal, explicit specification of a shared conceptualization" [32], which can refer to the shared understanding of some domains of interests. The criteria of ontology classification can be very flexible; for example, it can be a global taxonomy like interest groups very flexible; for example, it can be a global taxonomy like interest groups defined in Yahoo [31], Google [26], and DMOZ [25], or general ontology formalizing notions such as processes and events, time and space, physical objects, and so on. We can assume taxonomy is defined in the data ontology and each data item can be classified into one type. We assume queries can be classified with the same policy as well.

3.2 System Architecture

After clustering policies have been determined, the system can cluster nodes according to the policies and create communities. Fig. 1 shows the system architecture. There are two layers in the figure. The bottom is the physical node layer. Edges in this layer represent physical connections. Directly connected nodes are neighbors. Nodes in this layer form a simple unstructured Gnutella-style network. Communities of different categories are sitting on top of the unstructured network. Each community captures a category defined in content ontology. Message propagation is limited to related communities, therefore, process overhead is reduced. A node may join several communities at the same time, therefore communities may overlap. For example, node n_1 in the bottom layer registers in both cluster c_1 and c_3.

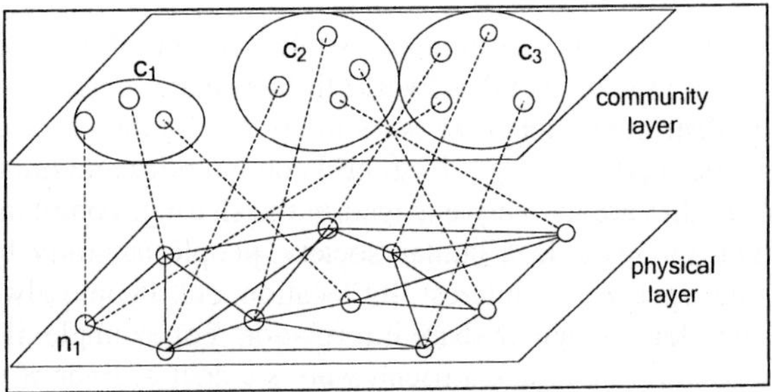

Fig. 1. System architecture

3.3 Community Construction

Communities are built in a decentralized adaptive manner. They allow users with similar interests to learn of each other without relying on a central meeting point. Each node keeps a community routing table as shown in Table. 1. A node's routing table collects this node's knowledge of the communities in the network. A routing table includes three columns: (1) the domain name, (2) the community charges that domain, (3) representative nodes to contact to, which are also called neighbors of the owner of the routing table, because the owner node connects with them directly. Neighbors in the local community are called local neighbors, and neighbors in other communities are called remote neighbors. The first row represents the node's local community, which includes its local interested domain name, local community id, and neighbors in the local community. The rest of the rows record other communities this node knows of. Since each domain corresponds to one community, it seems that we do not need to use two separate fields – "domain name" and "community id" – to represent the same thing. The reason of using two fields is explained in the next section.

Table 1. Example of a community routing table

domain name	community id	contact list (neighbors)
d_1	c_1	*a, b, c*
d_2	c_2	*m, n*
d_3	c_3	*t*

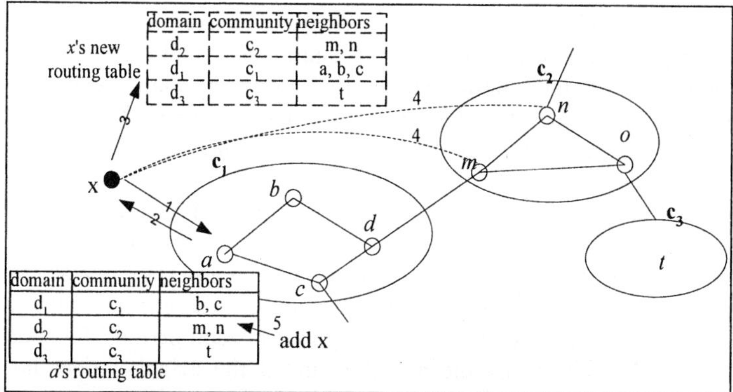

Fig. 2. Community construction

When a node joins the network, it connects to an existing node in the network and downloads the routing table of the existing node. Then the joining node tries to find its interested communities from the downloaded community routing table. If it finds the interested community, it joins the community by connecting the community's contact nodes. To keep a good connectivity, the new node also connects with some representative nodes in other communities. If the joining node cannot find its interested community, it will create such a community by adding a row in its routing table, and propagate this community information to all neighbors. Fig. 2 illustrates the node joining process. A new node *x*, whose interest domain is d_2, joins the network by connecting an existing node *a*. There are 5 steps for the joining process.

1. *x* sends a *join* request to *a*.
2. If *a*'s degree is less than *max degree*, it agrees to the *join* request. *a* sends its routing table to *x*.
3. *x* creates its new routing table by copying *a*'s routing table.
4. *x* finds its interested community c_2 (with domain d_2). *x* joins c_2 by connecting the contacting nodes: *m* and *n*. After *x* joins community c_2, *x* may know more nodes in this community, and it may add more local neighbors to its routing table.
5. *x* contacts nodes in other communities, and they may add *x* in their contact list.

Now let's see why we need both community id and domain id in the routing table. We use gossip to exchange community routing information. It takes time for nodes to know the up-to-date community information. Therefore, it is possible that one domain is separated into two (or more) communities. For example, *x* joins the system by contacting a. If a does not know the existence of a community with interest d_2, i.e., c_2 is not in a's routing table. Then x will create a new community, setting the domain id as d_2 and randomly generate a community id. Later, when communities with the same domain name find each other, they will unify the community id and merge to one community.

3.4 Community Maintenance

It is necessary to maintain the community overlays to ensure that they remain working as nodes update, join and leave the network. The main task of maintenance is to keep the community routing table up-to-date, so that nodes can locate relevant communities correctly. From a node's point of view, there are two kinds of communities: local community and other communities. We explain the maintenance of these two types of communities in this section.

Nodes in the same community form an unstructured P2P overlay network. The basic Gnutella Ping/Pong protocol is used to update nodes' neighbor lists. In addition, nodes need to detect failures and repair faulty neighbors. They periodically send a hello message to every node in its neighbor list. Since its neighbors do the same, each node should receive a message from each neighbor in each period. If a node does not receive this message, it probes the neighbor and if the neighbor does not reply, it marks this neighbor faulty.

A node should also update its knowledge about all other communities. It periodically probes remote neighbors from other communities, and only keeps the active neighbors in its routing table. Neighbors use gossip to exchange the routing information. Gossip-based protocols have been used extensively for creating and maintaining group membership in dynamic networks. Each node in the network knows a partial, possibly inaccurate set of community entry nodes. When a node has information to share, it sends the information to some constant number of randomly chosen neighbors. A node that receives new information processes it. For example, it may add some new neighbors learned from the received information. Then this node gossips further to some random neighbors. Eventually, with high probability, all nodes will learn about all. To control the overhead, the gossip period can be adaptively adjusted.

Another task of community maintenance is to merge communities sharing same interest. When a node finds two communities sharing the same domain name, it will inform nodes from both of the two communities and let them connect with each other and unify their community id. Then nodes in the merged community gossip this change to other nodes in the network.

3.5 Query Routing

Searching in the network takes advantage of the semantic community by forwarding queries only to related communities and avoiding flooding of the whole network. Any node that needs to search a resource in the network constructs a query with a list of meta-information that describes the resource. Meta-information should first specify the domain/category of the resource. Then the query is forwarded to the community charging that domain and propagated in that community. Various strategies can be used for request forwarding inside the community overlay. For example, if controlled flooding such as the Gnutella searching protocol is used, the query is forwarded to neighbors until the time-to-live (TTL) value reaches zero. We do not focus on how queries are routed within a community overlay, since it has been well studied in many literatures.

It is possible, though infrequent, that a node may not find the community related to the query from its routing table. This may happen for some reasons: (1) The community exists, but the node does not know it. (2) The community does not exist at all. When this happens, the query will be forwarded to some random neighbors until the TTL expires. The community is likely to be located within several hops if it exists. To alleviate the lookup overhead, a node will first check its own local host cache to see whether it has cached query. Moreover, the node can also query neighboring nodes on their local caches.

4 Experiment

We performed extensive simulations to evaluate the performance of the community-based routing scheme. In this section, we first describe our simulation methodology, and then present results for different simulation scenarios.

The topology of the network defines the number of nodes and how they are connected. In our model, we used BRITE [29], a well-known topology generator to create two kinds of network topologies: the random graph and the power-law graph. The network was created by adding nodes one by one. The performance test started after all nodes have joined the network. The resource set included 50,000 resources, and falling in 500 categories. We modeled the location of these resources using two distributions: the uniform distribution and a 70/30 biased distribution. Requesters were randomly chosen from the network. The following dynamic network behaviors were simulated: In every unit simulation time, an active node had a 20 percent possibility to create a query, 2 percent to gossip the routing information, 1 percent possibility to update its resources, and 1 percent possibility to leave the system. Also, the same number of offline nodes joined the system, and started functioning without any prior knowledge. Our evaluation metrics were: (1) the recall rate which was defined as the number of results returned divided by the number of results actually available in the network; (2) the number of messages to forward queries; (3) the number of hops to resolve a query.

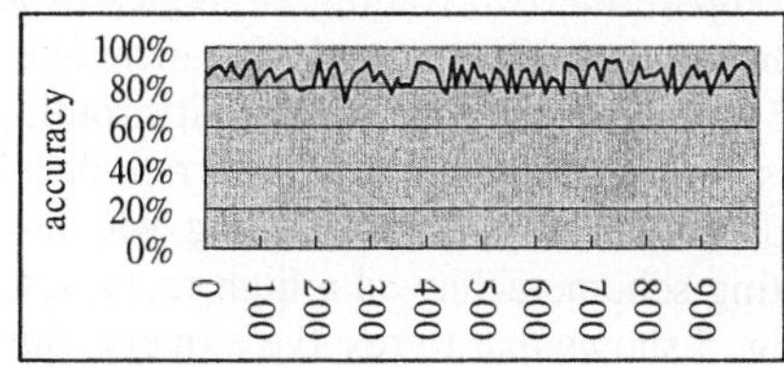

Fig. 3. Routing table accuracy versus simulation time

Fig.3 shows the average accuracy of nodes' community routing table. We defined the accuracy of a community routing table as the ratio of correct community mappings to the total mappings. From the result, we can see that the accuracy was retained at about 80~90%, which means that every node had reasonable accurate knowledge of the network.

In the following experiments, we used Gnutella protocol as our intra-community searching protocol. We present evaluation results of the performance of our community routing compared to basic Gnutella routing.

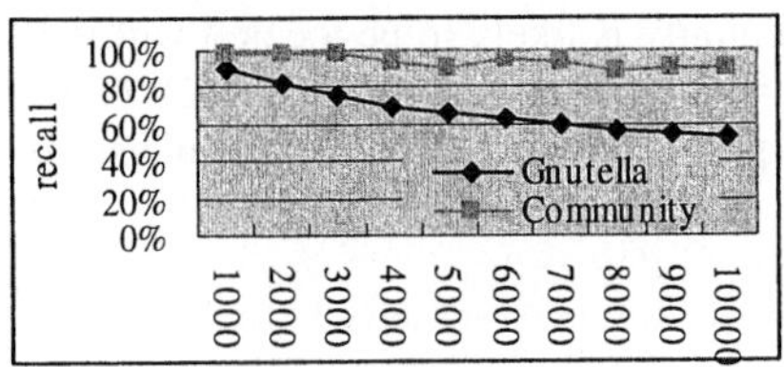

Fig. 4. Recall rate versus network size

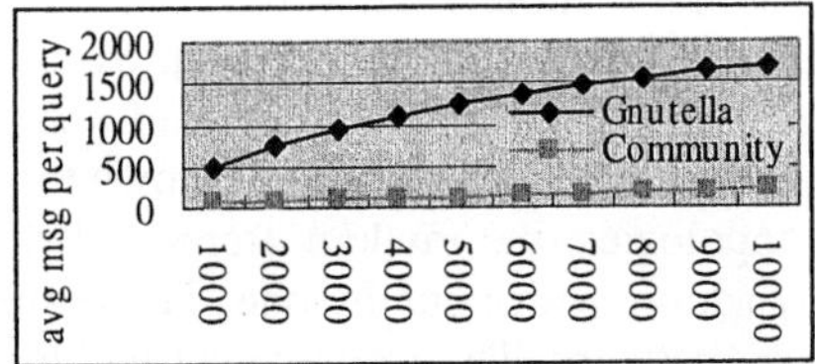

Fig. 5. Message overhead versus network size

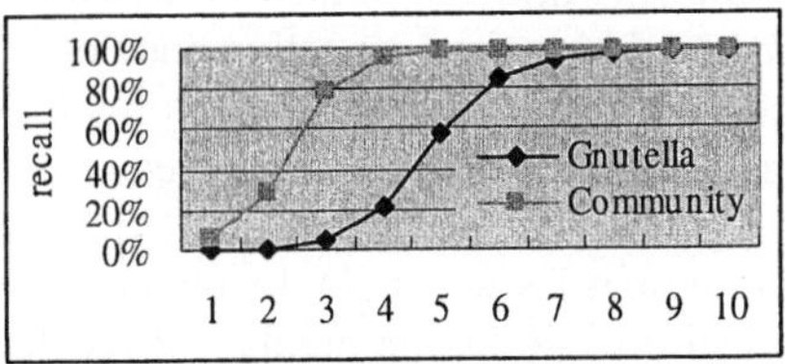

Fig. 6. Recall rate versus TTL

Fig. 4 and Fig. 5 compare the two routing strategies in terms of query recall rate and query message consumption. The network size increases from 1000 to 10000 and the TTL value is set 5. As expected, our community routing outperformed Gnutella routing on both metrics. In Fig. 4, Gnutella's recall rate decreased substantially as the network size increased, but our community routing was not directly affected by the network size. Our routing scheme achieved a high recall rate even when the network size was very large. Fig. 5 shows that to resolve a query, our community routing sent significantly fewer messages than Gnutella did, i.e., our system accrued lower costs. This is because our community routing can select a small number of overlay networks whose nodes have a higher number of hits for a query. Nodes that have few results for this query will not receive it, thus avoiding wasting resources on the request.

Figure 6 illustrates the relationship of the query recall rate with the query TTL. The network size was 8000 in this experiment. Under the same TTL value, our community routing could achieve higher recall rate compared to Gnutella. With our community routing, a recall rate near 100 percent can be achieved with a very small TTL value.

5 Conclusion

Grid technology is receiving an increasing attention both from the research community and from industries and governments. As more and more resources appear in grids, there is an increasing need to find an effective and efficient way to discover and query these resources. In this paper, we've presented an ontology-based community routing architecture to optimize searching in grids. This architecture adopts a decentralized technique for identifying groups of nodes with common interests and building overlays that mirror shared interests. The community-based overlay network achieves higher search efficiency and scalability than a pure flooding-based or history-based search scheme. At the same time, the system also retains many desirable features of unstructured overlays. For example, it is robust, self-organizing, and it inherently supports for rich descriptions of both resources and queries. Simulation experiments show that the proposed routing schemes are both efficient and scalable.

References

1. Chawathe, Y., Ratnasam, S., Breslau, L. Lanhan, N. Shenker, S. "Making Gnutella-like P2P Systems Scalable", In Proceedings of ACM SIGCOMM'03.
2. B.Yang, H.Garcia-Molina, "Efficient search in peer-to-peer networks", Proc. of CDCS'02, Vienna, Austria, July 2002
3. Banaei-Kashani, F. and C. Shahabi. "Criticality-based analysis and design of unstructured peer-to-peer networks as complex systems". Proceedings of the 3rd IEEE/ACM International Symposium on Cluster Computing and the Grid, pp. 351-358.
4. K. Globus Czajkowski, S. Fitzgerald, I. Foster, and C. Kesselman, "Grid information services for distributed resource sharing". Proc. of 10th IEEE symposium on High Performance Distributed Computing (2001).
5. T Berners-Lee, J Hendler, O Lassila, "The semantic web". Scientific American, 2001, 284(5):34–43.
6. Globus Toolkit: http://www.globus.org/toolkit/
7. R. Raman, M. Livny, M. Solomon: Matchmaking: Distributed Resource Management for High Throughput Computing. Proc. of IEEE Intel. Symp. On High Performance Distributed Computing, Chicago, USA (1998).
8. M. Schlosser, M. Sintek, S. Decker and W. Nejdl. "A Scalable and Ontology-Based P2P Infrastructure for Semantic Web Services". Second International Conference on Peer-to-Peer Computing (P2P'02) September 05-07, Linkoping, Sweden 2002.
9. N. J.A. Harvey, M.B. Jones, S. Saroiu, M. Theimer, and A. Wolman. "SkipNet:A Scalable Overlay Network with Practical Locality Properties". In Proceedings of the Fourth USENIX Symposium on Internet Technologies and Systems (USITS '03), Mar. 2003.

10. S. Shi, Y. Guanwen, D. Wang, J. Yu, S. Qu and M. Chen "Making Peer-to-Peer Keyword Searching Feasible Using Multi-level Partitioning". Proc. Of the 3rd International Workshop on Peer-to-Peer Systems, San Diego, CA, USA, February.
11. A. Iamnitchi, M. Ripeanu, and I. T. Foster. Locating data in (small-world?) peer-to-peer scientific collaborations. In Proceedings of International Workshop on Peer-to-Peer Systems(IPTPS), pages 232–241, March 2002.
12. H. Lican, W. Zhaohui, and P. Yunhe. "A scalable and effective architecture for Grid Services discovery". In Proceedings of the First Workshop on Semantics in Peer-to-Peer and Grid Computing, in conjunction with the Twelfth International World Wide Web Conference, 2003.
13. B.Yang and H.Garcia-Molina, "Designing a Super-Peer Ntrwork", Proc. 19th Int'l Conf. Data Engineering, Los Alamitos, CA, March 2003
14. Lv, C., Cao, P., Cohen, E., Li, K., Shenker, S. "Search and replication in unstructured peer-to-peer networks". In: ACM, SIGMETRICS 2002.
15. M. Khambatti, K. Ryu and P. Dasgupta, "Structuring Peer-to-Peer Networks using Interest-Based Communities", Int'l Work. On Databases, Information Systems and Peer-to-Peer Computing,Berlin, Germany, September 2003.
16. B. Y. Zhao, J. D. Kubiatowicz, and A. D. Joseph. "Tapestry: An Infrastructure for Fault-Tolerant Wide-Area Location and Routing," Technical Report, UCB/CSD-01-1141, April 2000.
17. A. Rowstron and P. Druschel. "Pastry: Scalable, Distributed Object Location and Routing for Large-Scale Peer-to-Peer Systems," Proceedings of the IFIP/ACM International Conference on Distributed Systems Platforms, Middleware, November 2001.
18. I. Stoica, R. Morris, D. Karger, M. F. Kaashoek, and H.Balakrishnan. "Chord: A Scalable Peer-to-Peer Lookup Service for Internet Applications," ACM SIGCOMM, 2001
19. S. Ratnasamy, P.Francis, M.Handley, R.Karp, and S. Shenker. "A Scalable Content-Addressable Network," ACM SIGCOMM, August 2001
20. Adamic, L., Huberman, B., Lukose, R., Puniyani, A.: "Search in power law networks". Physical Review (2001)
21. P.Reynolds and A. Vahdat. "Efficient Peer-to-Peer Keyword Searching". In Proceedings of ACM/IFIP/USENIX Middleware, June 2003
22. M. Cai, M. Frank, J. Chen and P. Szekely, " MAAN: A Multi-Attribute Addressable Network for Grid Information Services"The 4th International Workshop on Grid Computing, 2003.
23. C.Tang and S.Dwarkadas. "Hybrid Gloablal-Local Indexing for Efficient Peer-to-Peer Information Retrieval". In Proceedings of USENIX NSDI, March 2004.
24. LI, J., LOO, B. T., HELLERSTEIN, J., KAASHOEK, F., KARGER, D. R., AND MORRIS, R. "On the Feasibility of Peer-to-Peer Web Indexing and Search". *In Proceedings of the 2nd International Workshop on Peer-to-Peer Systems*, (IPTPS '03). (Berkeley, CA, Feb. 2003).
25. DMOZ website. http://www.dmoz.org
26. Google website. http://www.google.com/
27. W. Nejdl, M. Wolpers, W. Siberski, A. Loser, I. Bruckhorst, M. Schlosser, and C. Schmitz. "Super-Peer-Based Routing and Clustering Strategies for RDF-Based Peer-To-Peer Networks." In Proceedings of the Twelfth International World Wide Web Conference (WWW2003), Budapest, Hungary, May 2003.
28. A. Halevy, Z. Ives, I. Tatarinov, and P. Mork. Piazza: Data management infrastructure for semantic web applications. In Proc. of the Int. WWW Conf., 2003.

29. A.Medina, A. Lakhina, I.Matta, and J. Byers, "BRITE: An Approach to Universal Topology Generation," Proc. The International Workshop on Modeling, Analysis and Simulation of Computer and Telecommunications Systems- MASCOTS, Cincinnati, Ohio, August 2001.
30. Iamnitchi A, Foster I, "On Fully Decentralized Resource Discovery in Grid Environments", Proc. The 2nd IEEE/ACM International Workshop on Grid Computing 2001, Denver, November 2001.
31. Yahoo website. http://www.yahoo.com
32. T. R. Gruber, "Toward principles for the design of ontologies used for knowledge sharing," in Formal Ontology in Conceptual Analysis and Knowledge Representation, N. Guarino and R. Poli, Eds., March 1993.

Dynamic Multi-stage Resource Selection with Preference Factors in Grid Economy*

Yu Hua and Chanle Wu

School of Computer, Wuhan University, Wuhan, P.R. China
yhuastar@hotmail.com

Abstract. It is well known that grid technology has the ability to realize the resources shared and tasks scheduled coordinately. However, the problem of resource management and scheduling has always been one of main challenges. Recently, the theory of grid economy, which is analogous to the real market-based economy, can become a good candidate for solving the problem efficiently. But, in grid economy, the decision problem of resources selection with portfolio optimization has been paid little attention to. In this paper, the portfolio model and algorithm for dynamic multi-stage resource selection with preference factors were provided, analyzed and explained based on the grid economy in detail. The results of the experiments proved that corresponding methods were feasible and efficient in dynamic and distributed environments.

1 Introduction

Generally speaking, grid technology aims to coordinately use distributed and heterogeneous resources and efficiently make resource management in dynamic and multi-institutional virtual organizations. In order to complete a certain task, the grid system need select and aggregate all kinds of geographically distributed resources and utilize the methods of self-adaptation and self-management for resource management and scheduling. Most of main research challenges based on grid infrastructure are how to schedule tasks (dependent or independent) over multiple distributed and heterogeneous resources with cost and deadline limitations in order to realize the time or cost optimization [1],[9]. Recently, the theory of grid economy, which is analogous to the real market-based economy, can be a good candidate for solving the problem efficiently. In grid economy, the allocation of resources and scheduling of tasks are according to different prices and auction models. As for grid economy, Buyya [1] has presented the framework, components and function of grid resource broker, together with optimized algorithms based on the time and cost constraints. His works provided an economy-driven resource management system in grid environments, and could provide agent-based architecture to aggregate all kinds of middleware tools and software components for realizing the resource management efficiently. Other pricing and auction models can be found in Rajkumar Buyya [1], [10] and Chris Kenyon and Giorgos Cheliotis [8], [7].

* The works were supported by Nation High Technology 863 Development Plan (Grant No 2003AA001032), Open Fund from National Key Laboratory in Software Engineering (SKLSE03-14), Key Technologies R&D Program of Hubei Province (Grant No.211130757).

H. Zhuge and G.C. Fox (Eds.): GCC 2005, LNCS 3795, pp. 668 – 677, 2005.

However, for each application or task, decision of resources selection in commercial context is necessary and important. The grid system need timely allocate and schedule all kinds of sub-tasks based on the information of distributed and heterogeneous resources, which have different time intervals available. As a result of the cost and time constraints, the adjustment between time periods was necessary, but couldn't be at random and should be based on the rule of maximized returns and minimized risks. Generally speaking, the situation of decision in grid is often similar to the portfolio problem based on the asset-liability models. The application of correlated economic theory also absorbed some researchers. In grid scheduling, the fundamental problem is to find an optimized schedule based on specified performance model and requirements. Classical equilibrium theory is such a micro-economy theory that can be used to solve scheduling optimization problem in grid environment scope. Chris Kenyon and Giorgos Cheliotis in [8] and [7] introduced the basic framework, definition, components and policy of grid resource commercialization.

2 Portfolio Optimization in Classical Economic Theory

In nature, market is also a decentralized dynamic system with the transaction of competitive resources [12]. The basic dynamic portfolio optimization problem consists of an individual investor's decisions for allocating wealth among various expenditures and investment opportunities over time, typically the investor's expected lifetime. Markowitz's mean-variance (M-V) portfolio selection model [4] in a single period aims to maximize the final wealth with the mean time to minimize the risk. The criterion of the risk was the variance in order to enable investors to seek the highest return with the acceptable risk level. In addition, transaction cost has been also considered and become the important factor in decision making. Other concrete theory and methods are beyond the scope of this paper and may be found in Edwin J. Elton's publications [6]. Generally, the classical portfolio model is to maximize:

$$(1-w)\times\sum_{i=1}^{n} R_i x_i - w\times\sum_{i=1}^{n}\sum_{j=1}^{n}\delta_{ij} x_i x_j \tag{1}$$

where n is the number of securities, x_i is the proportion of investment in security i, R_i is the expected returns in security i, δ_{ij} is the co-variance of expected returns between security i and j, w is used to describe the aversion degree to risks, $0 \le w \le 1$. When $w=1$, the investor is conservative extremely and he only focuses on the risk, not the returns. On the contrary, when $w=0$, the investor pursues the returns regardless of the risks.

3 Portfolio Optimization in Grid Economy

In grid environments, the problem of portfolio optimization also exists and is rather important to realize the resource management and scheduling efficiently. However, little attention has been paid to the problem and in this paper, the problem of portfolio optimization is solved in grid environments. Although some researchers have begin to consider the infrastructure of grid economy and resource commercialization in [1] and [7], as for the portfolio selection, to the best of our knowledge, this may be the first paper to deeply discuss the decision support based on portfolio optimization in grid environments. Real market and grid environments have similar characters in dynamic resource management and real-time task scheduling. The basic components in a market are producer, consumer, and commodities, analogous to resource owner, resource user (application), and various virtual resources in grid environment. Certain micro-economy theories, such as the classical equilibrium theory, can be applied to solve some optimization problems in grid scheduling based on certain restrictions and assumptions. Portfolio optimization aims to realize the resource selection efficiently and task scheduling dynamically.

The main purpose of this paper focuses on the essence of decision support based on portfolio selection in grid resource commercialization. The ability of resource varies with time series and is a random variable. Thus, the return and corresponding risk can be the mean of resource ability and covariance between resources' abilities. Concretely speaking, the return of resource i at time t is $E(r_{i,t})$. The covariance between resource i and j at time t can be presented as $\delta_{i,j,t}$. In dynamic environments, adjustment and re-scheduling often take place among different agents. However, the costs are rather high and sometimes affect the system performance on the whole. Therefore, the operation of adjustment is necessary, but corresponding cost need be also considered carefully and comprehensively. Random and casual adjustments are not welcome and should be limited. At the same time, transaction cost in classical economy may be modeled as the adjustment cost in grid economy. Like the definition in classical economy [4], grid environments could be a market with friction. The transaction charge ratio is defined in each unit at time t for resource i, $k_{i,t}$. Here, the resource portfolio at time t is assumed to be already known, $x_t = (x_{1,t}, x_{2,t}, \cdots, x_{n,t})$ and $\sum_{i=1}^{n} x_{i,t} = 1$. At the same time, adjustment and re-scheduling are assumed to happen at time $t+1$. Furthermore, we assume that the transaction cost at time $t+1$ is function of V type (i.e., it is the difference between known portfolio at time t and new one at time $t+1$). Then, transaction cost for resource i at time $t+1$ may be $k_{i,t+1}\left|x_{i,t+1} - x_{i,t}\right|$. The total transaction cost at time $t+1$ is $\sum_{i=1}^{n} k_{i,t+1}\left|x_{i,t+1} - x_{i,t}\right|$. Therefore, the portfolio model in grid economy is to maximize:

$$(1-w)\times\left[\sum_{i=1}^{n} E(r_{i,t})x_{i,t} - \sum_{i=1}^{n} k_{i,t+1}\left|x_{i,t+1} - x_{i,t}\right|\right] - w\times\sum_{i=1}^{n}\sum_{j=1}^{n}\delta_{i,j,t}x_{i,t}x_{j,t} \tag{2}$$

Thus, by the methods of portfolio optimization, the resource selection can be implemented in the way of optimization and coordination. Due to the constraints of resource availability and costs for specified task, the task wouldn't be allocated only on resources with prefect performance because better performance means higher cost and stronger competition. Thus, the selection and allocation of grid resources would become more reasonable and feasible.

4 Dynamic Multi-stage Resource Selection

4.1 Problem Modeling

Generally speaking, in order to complete certain tasks, several constraints, including the time, cost and risk factors, should be considered in the dynamic management environments. In particular, requests from some tasks need the multi-stage solution in order to achieve not only final maximum value but also the fastest increasing rate. Thus, both the absolute and relative increase methods should be considered comprehensively. In addition, in each stage, although cost, risk and time are the basic constraints, there is the preference difference among three factors. Thus, the decision vector $D_m = \{risk, cost, time\}$, $m = 1,2,\cdots,p$ during p stages can be defined to present the most important factor in current stage. Furthermore, several kinds of assumption are explained here.

Assumption 1. Here, the partition of multiple stages is based on the tasks, not time. Concretely speaking, the judgment on whether a stage is over would depend on whether all tasks assigned to current stage have been completed efficiently.

Assumption 2. In grid economy, the measurement of utilization cost may be based on the grid currency, like methods in [1]. When task request enters the grid environments, initial wealth is Z_0 at time 0.

Assumption 3. In order to explicitly describe the approach, we assume that in each stage there exist lots of independent sub-tasks executed and dependent tasks can be implemented among the stages. Thus, dependent tasks that are realized lasting for several stages can be divided into sub-tasks, which may be executed in each stage.

Thus, enlightened by the ideas and methods in [2], [3], [11], and [13], considering the non-storage and strong time-related characters of grid resources, the paper provides both the largest and fastest wealth methods for decision support with transaction cost. In brief, the service request may achieve the fastest increasing wealth according to the first method and this is based on the *relative* viewpoint. At the same time, if the service request needs the solution by which the largest wealth can be achieved, the *absolute* method can be utilized.

4.2 The Fastest Increasing Method

We define the price ratio of the beginning value to the end value of current stage. There are n resources at stage m. Their returns are the vector $r_m = \left(r_m^1, r_m^2, \cdots, r_m^n\right)'$, which could be random variable according to the independent and identical distribution. Their mean and co-variance are $E(r_m)$ and $\mathrm{cov}(r_m)$. Furthermore, x_m^i ($i = 1,2,\cdots,n$, $m = 1,2,\cdots,p$) is the percentage of resource i selected at stage m

and then, the related vector is $x_m = \left(x_m^1, x_m^2, \cdots, x_m^n\right)'$. In addition, c_m is the transaction cost at stage *m*. Thus, the problem can be solved based on the dynamic programming method.

Here, L_m is the price ratio of the beginning value to the end value of current stage. The function was $L_{m+1} = L_m (r_m' x_m - c_m)$ and $L_1 = 1$ .As for certain tasks, the grid system needs provide the decision support in order to make the feasible balance between the mean and variance of $L_{p+1} = \prod_{m=1}^{p} (r_m' x_m - c_m)$ and give the selection policy $\{x_1, x_2, \cdots, x_p\}$ with time, cost and risk constraints. With the conditions, $L_{m+1} = L_m (r_m' x_m - c_m)$ and $L_1 = 1$, the final wealth can be maximized:

$$Z = \max\left[(1-\omega)E\left(L_{p+1}\right) - \omega Var\left(L_{p+1}\right)\right] \tag{3}$$

The requirement threshold of constraints is the vector $require_m^1 = \left(cost_m, risk_m, time_m\right)'$, which is the basic conditions for completing certain tasks. Dynamic programming method for finding the results can use the auxiliary function:

$$f_m\left(L_m\right) = \max_{x_m} E\left[f_{m+1}\left(L_{m+1}\right)\right] = \max_{x_m} E\left[f_{m+1} L_m (r_m' x_m - c_m)\right] \tag{4}$$

After computing, $x_m = \left(\dfrac{1-\omega}{2L_m\omega} + c_m\right) E^{-1}\left(r_m r_m'\right) E\left(r_m\right)$ is the optimal solution.

4.3 The Solution for Largest Value

Here, let Q_m be the difference value between the beginning value and the end value of current stage. Then, $Q_{m+1} = Q_m + r_m' x_m - c_m$ and $Q_1 = 0$. Thus, the optimal policy $\{x_1, x_2, \cdots, x_p\}'$ is needed in order to make the good balance between the mean and variance of $L_{p+1} = \sum_{m=1}^{p} (r_m' x_m - c_m)$.

With the conditions, $Q_{m+1} = Q_m + r_m' x_m - c_m$ and $Q_1 = 0$, the final wealth can be:

$$Z = \max\left[(1-\omega)E\left(L_{p+1}\right) - \omega Var\left(L_{p+1}\right)\right] \tag{5}$$

Similarly, the dynamic programming method can use the auxiliary function:

$$f_m\left(Q_m\right) = \max_{x_m} E\left[f_{m+1}\left(Q_{m+1}\right)\right] = \max_{x_m} E\left[f_{m+1}(Q_m + r_m' x_m - c_m)\right] \tag{6}$$

After computing, $x_m = \left(\frac{1-\omega}{2\omega} - Q_m + c_m\right) E^{-1}\left(r_m r_m^{'}\right) E\left(r_m\right)$ is the optimal result.

In addition, the results are different from those in [2]. Firstly, transaction cost was considered as an important factor in grid scheduling and the factor would affect related decisions for grid economy. Secondly, due to the non-storage and strong time-related characters of grid resources, there isn't the return from no-risk resource and therefore the factor was ignored here. Thirdly, the returns were connected with the risks by the parameters of the aversion degree to risks. Thus, returns and risks were analyzed and considered together.

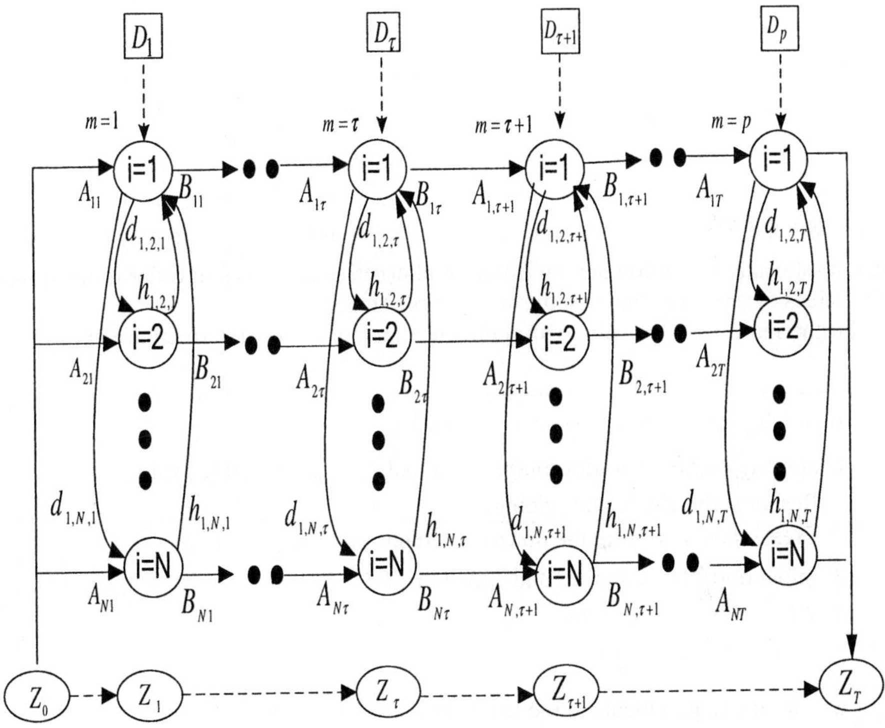

Fig. 1. The flowchart of multi-stage resource selection with preference factors

Generally speaking, the process of portfolio selection is based on the dynamic and multi-period conditions, especially in grid environments. As for the resource management and scheduling, dynamic re-scheduling and re-allocation with time series would be rather necessary and important. Because the heterogeneous and distributed resources are with dynamic characters and uncertainty, the grid system need often adjust the allocation policy and the percentage of the grid resources after certain time periods in order to achieve better performance with cost and time constraints according to the dynamic and updated information of resources. The purpose of portfolio selection is to optimally allocate and schedule divided sub-tasks to candidate resources, which are available for certain time periods. Concretely, the process of dynamic multi-period portfolio selection can be described in fig.1. The whole stage-based time period $[1,2,\cdots,T]$ may be divided into two sub-intervals $[1,2,\cdots,\tau]$ and $[\tau,\tau+1,\cdots,T]$. The current time period τ is faced with decision making of portfolio selection.

Let A_{it} be the amount of independent tasks selected for resource i completion in period t before adjustment, B_{it} be the amount of independent tasks selected for resource i completion in period t after adjustment, $d_{i,j,t}$ be the amount of independent tasks transferred away from resource i into resource j during adjustment period t, $h_{i,j,t}$ be the amount of independent tasks transferred into resource i from resource j during adjustment period t, $r_{i,t}$ be the average yield of resource i between t and $t+1$, and Z_t be the intermediate value of the total return at period t. The whole scenario could be understood explicitly from the description in fig.1 with the preference vector $D_m = \{risk, \cos t, time\}$. The system may re-schedule and re-allocate proportion among different alternative resources in order to maximize the values of objective function during multiple stages.

Furthermore, the algorithm with preference factors can be described in Fig.2.

```
Input: D_m, ω, L_m or Q_m, (risk, cos t, time)';
Output: x_m (relative or absolute) for optimal f_m(L_m) or f_m(Q_m) value;
1: Resource discovery and pricing;
2: Create the list to store the portfolio temporarily, SL_m = null;
3: Initial portfolio is created and added to SL_m;
4: While { SL_m ≠ null } do
5:   Searching the SL_m;
6:   If{ the requirements in the list ≥ (risk, cos t, time)' }
7:        Then delete corresponding portfolio from SL_m;
8:   End If;
9: End While;
10: According to D_m value, select the portfolio;
11:
```

$$x_{relative}=\left(\frac{1-\omega}{2L_m\omega}+c_m\right)E^{-1}\left(r_m r_m'\right)E(r_m) \text{ or } x_{absolute}=\left(\frac{1-\omega}{2\omega}-Q_m+c_m\right)E^{-1}\left(r_m r_m'\right)E(r_m)$$

Fig. 2. The algorithm of dynamic multi-stage resource selection

5 Performance Study

The grid environments consist of three domains with cost and risk constraints: HPrx2600server (2000, 86%), HP cluster (1700, 90%) and 50 PC (1300, 75%); Two storage domains: HP DS2300 (1600, 92%) and 50 PC (1100, 70%). The average cost and risk in network resources were set to 350 and 75%. The transaction cost was 100. The upper limits of time, cost and risk were 200min, 400000 and 0.24. In order to compare the results, SPMD (Single Program Multiple Data) was considered as the task model with $M = 3$ and $N = 100$. The whole process can be divided into three stages and each stage should consider the preference factors: cost, risk, and time, respectively. The basic amounts of tasks in three stages were 70, 115, and 25. Two results from *relative* and *absolute* methods were considered together with DBC (Deadline and Budget Constrained, [1]).

The situations could be shown in fig.3 and fig.4. The number of tasks completed versus time was provided and *Relative* was 311, *Absolute* was 280, and *DBC* was 225. From the results above, *Relative* and *Absolute* had better results because they could disperse the risks and made adaptation according to the situations.

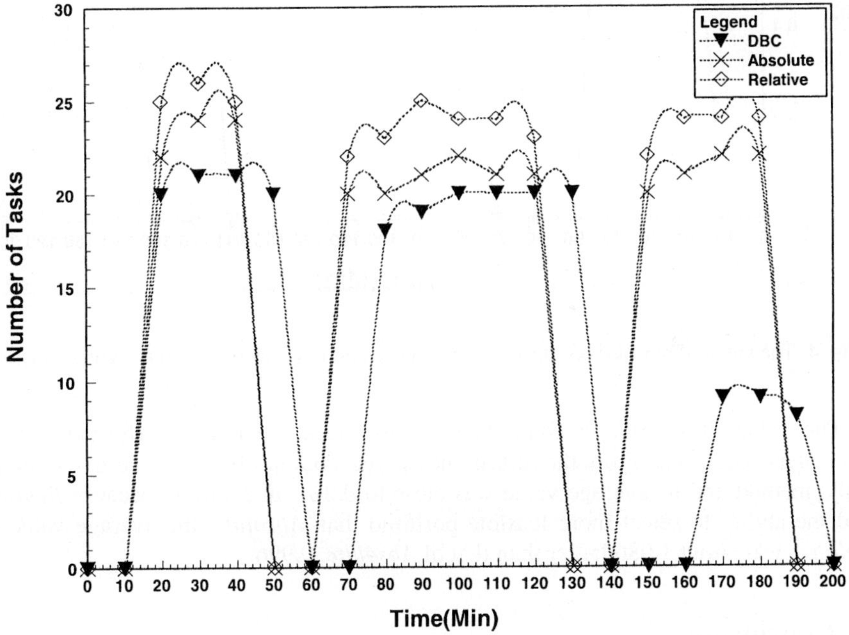

Fig. 3. The number of tasks during multi-stage resources selection with preference factors

At the same time, according to the results of comparison, the performance of *Relative* was better than that of *Absolute* because of finding increasing approach more easily. At the same time, due to the time preference in the first stage, the whole execution time was rather short, but the cost and risk would increase together. In particular, in the first stage, DBC spent one more time segment than other two methods. Furthermore, the cost was the preference factor in the second stage and cheaper resources had been selected for completing corresponding tasks. Owing to the accumulation of risks, resources with better performance should be selected so as to avoid risks efficiently.

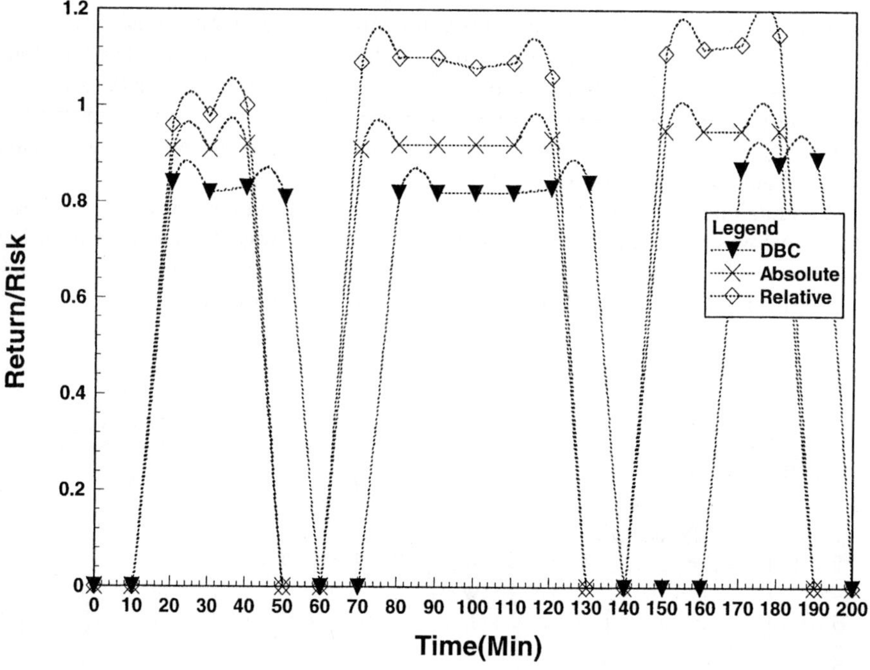

Fig. 4. The value of return/risks during multi-stage resources selection with preference factors

The value of return/risk could be used to check the return performance with equivalent risk levels. From the results shown, risk couldn't be dispersed based on the DBC method and its average value was close to 0.824. In addition, because *Relative* had the ability to select more feasible portfolio than *Absolute*, the average value of *Relative* was about 1.086 larger than that of *Absolute*, 0.996.

6 Conclusion

The resources selection with portfolio optimization was important in order to efficiently manage heterogeneous and distributed resources. This paper introduced the definition, model and possible solutions of portfolio optimization and compares the difference and relationship between classical economy theory and grid economy. Because grid environments were dynamic and full of random factors, multi-stage scheduling and management could be rather pivotal to realize the optimal selection and allocation of resources. In order to solve the resource management in dynamic and multi-stages environments, we provided the prototype of dynamic multi-stage resource selection methods with preference factors in grid environments. Results of simulation showed the advantages of dynamic resources management.

References

1. Rajkumar, Buyya., David, Abramson., Srikumar, Venugopal.: The Grid Economy. Proceedings of the IEEE. 3 (2005) 698-714
2. Zhongfei, Li., Shouyang, Wang.: Portfolio Optimization and No-Arbitrage Analysis. Science Publisher. 5 (2001)
3. Hiroshi, Konno., Annista, Wija.: Portfolio Optimization Problem under Concave Transaction Costs and Minimal Transaction Unit Constraints. Math. Program. 9 (2001) 233- 250
4. H, Markowitz.: Portfolio Selection Efficient Diversification of Investment. Wiley New York (1959)
5. Wlodzimierz, Ogryczak.: Multiple Criteria Linear Programming Model for Portfolio Selection. Annual of Operations Research. (2000) 143-162
6. Edwin, J. Elton., Martin, J. Gruber., Jeffrey, A. Busse.: Are Investors Rational Choices Among Index Funds, Journal of Finance, Vol. 59. 2(2004)
7. Chris, Kenyon., Giorgos, Cheliotis.: Grid Resource Commercialization Economic Engineering and Delivery Scenarios. Grid Resource Management: State of the Art and Research Issues. Kluwer (2003)
8. Chris, Kenyon., Giorgos, Cheliotis.: Architecture Requirements for Commercializing Grid Resources. Proceedings of the 11th IEEE International Symposium on High Performance Distributed Computing. 7(2002) 215-224
9. Yu, Hua., Chanle, Wu., Jianbing, Xing.: Grid QoS Infrastructure: Advance Resource Reservation in Optical Burst Switching Networks. Proceedings of the Third International Conference on Grid and Cooperative Computing (GCC2004). 10 (2004) 979-982
10. R, Buyya., D, Abramson., J, Giddy.: A Case for Economy Grid Architecture for Service-Oriented Grid Computing. Proceedings of the 15th International Conference on Parallel and Distributed Processing Symposium. 4 (2001) 776-790
11. Yoshimoto A. The Mean-Variance Approach to Portfolio Optimization Subject to Transaction Costs. Journal of the Operations Research Society of Japan. (1996) 99 -117
12. Y, Simaan.: Estimation Risk in Portfolio Selection The Mean Variance Model Versus The Mean Absolute Deviation Model. Management Science (1997) 1437–1446
13. Yanglan, Zhang., Yu, Hua.: Portfolio Optimization for Multi-stage Capital Investment with Neural Networks. Proceedings of International Symposium on Neural Networks (ISNN2004). 8(2004) 982-987

On-Demand Resource Allocation for Service Level Guarantee in Grid Environment

Hailan Yang, Gongyi Wu, and Jianzhong Zhang

Department of Computer Science,
College of Information, NanKai University,
300071, Tianjin, China
yanghailan@mail.nankai.edu.cn

Abstract. With the evolution of Grid technology, the quality of service assurance includes service level agreement and attainment is becoming more and more important. There is strong correlation between the resource allocation and the service level guarantee in the grid environment. And the large traffic variations of grid service complex the resource allocation. In this paper, we formally define and analyze these relationships and present a constrained mathematical model for resource allocation. Moreover, we show how to integrate this model into the online system of on-demand resource allocation which can guarantee the service level to compensate environmental changes. The simulation results show that our model and solution are practical and efficient.

1 Introduction

Recently, the quality of grid service assurance has been brought forward by OGSA[1], Grid service providers need to supply services with some quality demands to service customers based on Service Level Agreements (SLA) [2][3]. To achieve and maintain reliable quality of a certain service level, appropriate resources should be allocated.

Advance reservation [4] is a typical method. When using reservations, applications usually specify quality of service (QoS) requirements and do not change them subsequently [5][6]. But Grid application services usually experience very large traffic variations [7]. Some of these variations can be predicted and some cannot. During these sudden peaks, the current resource allocation which is based on some agreed SLA and reservation will not be able to cope with this new traffic. Service customers increasingly require support for peak loads. On the other hand, fixed-capability reservations may waste resource in some occasions. Hence a dynamic resource allocation according to both the Service Level demand and the request rate variation is necessary.

In this paper, we describe a mechanism with on-demand resource allocation to address the issues just noted. The main contributions of this approach by which service level can be guaranteed are:

- A mathematic model that describes a theoretical relationship among SLA requirement, requests arrival rate and resource requirement;

H. Zhuge and G.C. Fox (Eds.): GCC 2005, LNCS 3795, pp. 678 – 689, 2005.

- An On-demand control mechanism which allows service provider to adjust resource allocation dynamically to attain the service level;
- Decision procedures that support a rich set of resource management policies.

The paper is organized as follows: Some related works are reviewed in Section 2; Section 3 provides a mathematical analysis of on-demand resource allocation; Section 4 presents the preparative work of resource allocation; Section 5 describes the architecture of the on-demand resource allocation framework; Experiment and evaluation are presented in Section 6, and we conclude in Section 7.

2 Related Work

Various dynamic allocation mechanisms have been explored in the area of distributed systems and internet data center.

The Oc´eano [8] project has designed and developed a pilot prototype of a scalable, manageable infrastructure for a large scale computing utility power plant. A group of servers can be automated to handle the IT needs of many users, including on-the-fly changes in the load requirements. In Oc´eano, preparing another hosting environment for overloaded services takes relatively long time, due to the restarting and the reconfiguration of the server in order to meet the requirements of the new services. Thus, adjusting the size of a service domain has to be made carefully.

SODA [9] is another kind of the service platform which supports dynamic service deployment. HUPs(Hosting Utility Platform) are installed in the physical hosts which runs one or more virtual service nodes. With HUP, SODA can support mechanism for adjusting the amount of virtual service nodes according to the service request rate. The level of adaptation of SODA is similar to our proposal. However, SODA is based on the virtual machine to provide hosting environment for a service while our work is focused on the general grid resource allocation.

Eole project's [10] goal was to build an online optimization framework dedicated to telecom applications. The framework can consider environmental events, temporal constraints and resource constraints. This work was able to enhance the Quality of Services of network providers, by increasing their overall flexibility. The Eole project is building a system with many similarities to our framework. But we address the problem for grid service providers not only for network providers.

In [11], a resource assignment of multi-tier e-commerce applications has been presents. Authors use mathematical integer programming (MIP) mixed with dedicated heuristics to solve this hard problem. Our approach also supplies a mathematical model and is much more versatile and adaptive since we perform successive reallocations through monitoring.

DistAnt project [12] provides a mechanism for deploying user's application on remote resource. However, DistAnt only focuses on deploying and instantiating custom applications, and does not consider the resource allocation for service provider.

3 Resource Allocation Model

In order to get the relationship among the QoS requirements of Service Level, request arrival rate and resource requirement, a mathematic model is built to modify and calculate the relationship in this Section. Before describe the model, two QoS metrics are proposed and the concept of Resource Entity is introduced which help to build the model.

3.1 QoS Metrics

Many kinds of Grid service QoS metrics have been proposed [13][14]. In this paper, we focus on the attributes which are tightly related to the performance of the services, and these attributes are impacted more by resource allocation than others. Two metrics, Service Response Time and Guarantee Service Rate, are used here, and this method can easily be extended with other QoS metrics.

- **Service Response Time (SRT).** This performance related attribute denotes maximum time (measured in seconds) that elapses from the moment that a grid service receives a legitimate request until it produces the corresponding success reply.
- **Guarantee Service Rate (Gsr).** This attribute denotes the probability of a grid service being capable to produce a successful reply in response to a legitimate request within the maximum SRT.

The SRT attribute is indicative of how fast or how slow a grid service responds to requests, and it is valuable as a basis of comparison between different services. Referring to the Service Level definition in the area of network, we use the second metric to cooperate as a dimension of comparing different services level and differentiating their QoS. In the light hours, SRT can be assured to customers for each service level. But in the peak hours, higher service level customers can still get the SRT within the range with higher probability than the lower service level customers. The differences between higher level and lower level can be indicated by the Gsr metric.

3.2 Resource Entity

Before the description of the mathematical model, a concept Resource Entity will be introduced first. Resource here is the concept of virtual resource [15][16] on which a Grid service instance can be performed. It can be a resource or a set of resources supplied by the resource providers. Many resource broker systems [17][18][19][20] can discover and select resources which satisfy the requirement of service providers in the Grid environment. The resource handles which enable the accessing and using of the resources can be gotten by those resource brokers [1].

Resource entity is the unit of the resource in capacity with the search constraint to the resource of the service instance execution rate.

For example, the search constraint of execution rate is 1000, it means that the resource can perform the specify application service in the rate of 1000 jobs per second. An IBM p570 server has been found that can finish 1000 jobs per second averagely. An IBM p595 server also has been found, and it can finish 2000 jobs per second averagely. Then the former is regarded as one Resource Entity, and the later is regarded as two Resource Entities.

With this conversation, we get a uniform policy to model the resource allocation.

3.3 Resource Allocation Mathematic Model

A mathematical model for the Resource Allocation is proposed to facilitate the understanding of the different variables at play. The two QoS metrics are presented in 3.1. While the QoS metrics are not constrained to those two, it is much easier to construct a tractable model for other SLA attributes in the grid environment. Table1 defines the variables used in this model. The model is based on the following assumptions.

1. Appropriate resource entities, which ensure the execution rate of service instances, can be found by a Resource Broker and be employed to perform service instances with the same probability by a Load Balance Deplorer.
2. The execution rates of service instances in every resource entity are independent and identically distributed (i.i.d.) random variables, with the same negative exponential distribution with the mean execution rate μ.
3. The arrival of the service requests are Poisson distribution random variable with the parameter λ.
4. The arrival requests of same service level have been severed in FIFS (first in, first be served) order.
5. The queue is unlimited, that means the request doesn't be rejected.

Note that the request admission policy is not relevant to this model; the analysis provided here should serve as input to such an admission control policy, thus enabling optimal decision.

Table 1. Variables in the Resource Allocation Model

λ	the mean arrival rate of service request
μ	the execution rate of service instances in a resource entity
c	the amount of resource entities
Pi	the probability that there are i requests in the service system
Ln	the queue length in the service system
Wq	the waiting time of a request
Ws	the staying time of a request, include waiting time and execution time

For a stable queue system (the values of λ, μ and c are known), the probability that there are i requests in the system are:

$$p0 = \left[\sum_{n=0}^{c-1} \frac{r^n}{n!} + \frac{c \cdot r^c}{c!(c-r)} \right]^{-1}$$

$$pi = \frac{r^i}{i!} p0 \text{ , } i <= c \qquad \text{or} \qquad pi = \frac{r^i}{c^{i-c} c!} p0 \text{ , } i > c \tag{1}$$

When a request arrives, if there are i requests in the service system, we get the queue length as:

$$Ln = 0 \ , \ i <= c \quad \text{or} \quad Ln = n - c \ , \ i > c$$

For it's a stable queue system, so the waiting time of this request is:

$$Wq(i) = Ln / \lambda$$

Hence the total staying time, which is the actual service time, of the request is:

$$Ws(i) = Wq + 1/\mu$$

$$\therefore Ws(i) = \frac{1}{\mu} \ , \ i <= c \qquad \text{or} \qquad Ws(i) = \frac{i-c}{\lambda} + \frac{1}{\mu} \ , \ i > c \tag{2}$$

It can be found that the number of the request determines the request staying time in the service system. So in order to ensure the maximum of request staying time, we should ensure the request number probability.

For an appointed value of Gsr, we can get the least N to satisfy the following formula:

$$\begin{aligned} \exists N, \ P(Ws(i) < Ws(N)) &= P(i < N) \\ &= \sum_{i=0}^{N} pi > Gsr \end{aligned} \tag{3}$$

From (1), (2) and (3), we can get the SRT with N:

$$SRT = Ws(N) \tag{4}$$

From the above formulas, we can calculate the theoretical relationship among QoS metrics in SLA, request arrival rate and resource requirement.

The mathematic model helps to build a repository called RASDB (Resource Allocation Statistic Database). RASDB store the relationships and the required resource entity number can be queried by given condition. The building process and the query interface of RASDB are described in Section 4.

4 Resource Allocation Statistic Database Building

In order to implement on-demand resource allocation, RASDB must be built first.

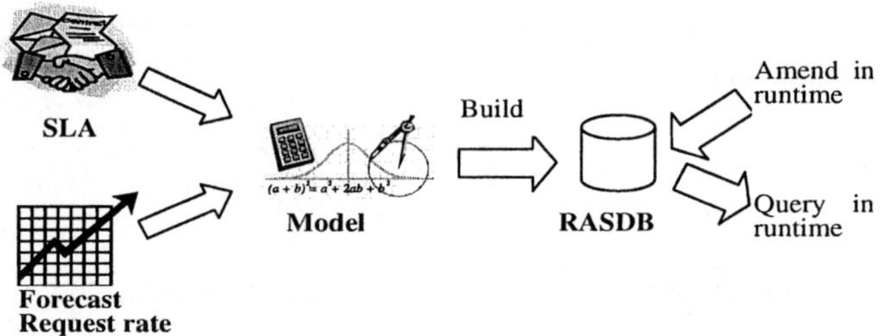

Fig. 1. Building the RASDB

To the service provider, Service Level classifier and detail parameters must be defined and calculated before SLA negotiation with service customer. Here we describe the associate steps of on-demand resource allocation preparative works in the Service Level establishment and SLA negotiation process.

1) Constitute the Service Level Claim.
2) First, according to the application-specific knowledge and the resource technical parameters, get the technical parameters of the application service, such as execution rate with corresponding resource demand. Then according to the resource cost and other costs to employ the application, get the service price range. At last, according to the policies of sale, constitute the Service Level Claim. The Service Level claim has following format:

   Service Level 1= { |Q[attribute, constrain]|, price}

   Service Level 2= { |Q[attribute, constrain]|, price}

   Q[attribute, constrain] describes the QoS metric and the value. Such as Q[Service Response Time, T<0.01s], Q[Guarantee Service Rate, Gsr>90%]. There must be one or more Q[attribute, constrain] elements in the Service Level Claim.

   Price describes the service cost. It can be different forms, such as price per request or price per month with an undertaken-whole service.
3) Build RSADB.

   According to the Service Level Claim and the entire forecast of possible customer request rate, calculate the resources allocation statistic data by the mathematic model described in Section3. The calculation process gets the relationship among SRT, Gsr, Resource entity number, λ(request arrival rate) and μ(execution rate). The statistic results are stored in the RASDB (Resource-Allocation statistic database). RASDB supply a unique query interface:

   Resource entity number = queryResourceAllocation (A1[attribute, value], A2[attribute, value]...)

   A[attribute, value] describe the input value of SRT, Gsr, λ and μ.

   While service running, a heuristic algorithm in the on-demand resource allocation framework will amend the theoretical data and modify the RASDB according to the monitor result. It will be described in Section 5. With other QoS metric and extension model, the RASDB can be scalable extended by add new data calculated by new model.
4) Publish the Service with the Service Level Claim to UDDI.
5) Customer who is interested in the service [4] contacts with service provider to negotiate SLA, and strikes a service contract with the SLA. The SLA can has follow elements:

   SLA={|Q[specify, constrain]|, Price, Service ID, Customer ID, Service Duration(start time and end time), Violation policy, ...}

   The meaning of first five elements is obviously. "Violation policy" defines the rules when irresistible station occurs, such as "reject request when the service can't perform the request on QoS" or "continues in best-effort manner when the service can't perform the request on QoS". Other SLA elements can also be added. Then add the haggled SLA to SLADB.
6) According to the SLADB, add new data to RASDB if needed.
7) Trigger the resource initiation allocation with appropriate resources when the "Service Duration" starts by Schedule module described in Section 5.

5 On-Demand Resource Allocation Framework

5.1 Architecture

The architecture of the On-demand Resource Allocation framework is showed in Figure2. It also presents a scenario of the resource allocation when customers, who belong to two different Service Levels (service level 1 and service level 2), access the "service1" which is supplied by the service1 provider. The Admission Control makes decisions according to the security, authority and capacity policy. To assure the QoS respectively, the Service Level Classifier divides the requests into two queues according to their service levels. Load Balance Deployer manages the requests queues, creates service instances for them, and deploys them to the resource entities. The resource entities handles are gotten by the On-demand Resource Allocator from the Resource Broker.

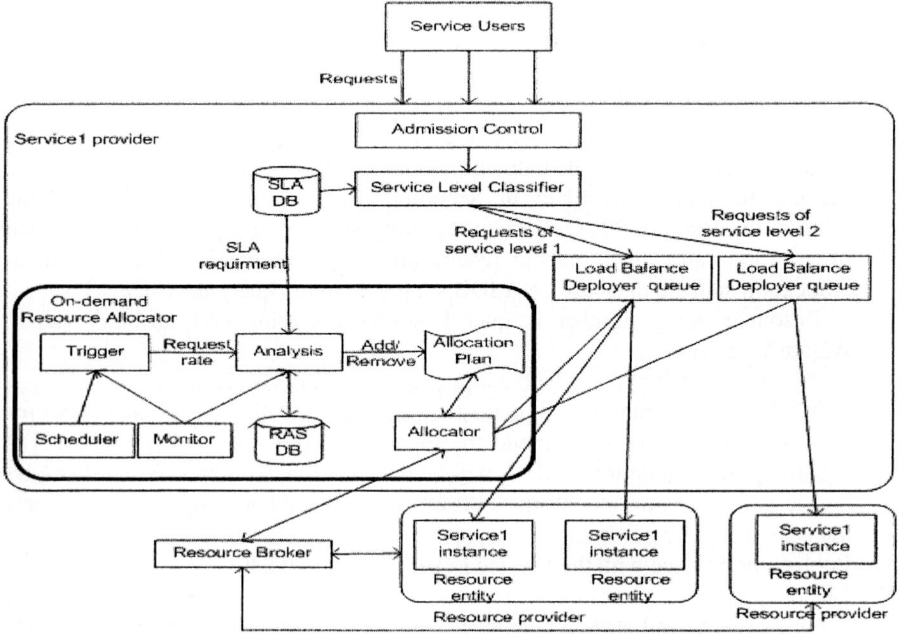

Fig. 2. Architecture of the On-demand Resource Allocation

5.2 Resource Allocation Mechanism

The main component of this framework is the On-demand Resource Allocator. Its main function is making the decision when and how many resources should be allocated, and executing the decision.

Two conditions will trigger the resource allocation process: the predictable request arrival rate variation and the unpredictable request arrival rate variation. Predictable request arrival rate variation includes the start of 'Service Duration' in SLA and the forecast of request arrival rate from some forecast module. The Scheduler module indicates this kind of request arrival rate change and triggers the allocation process. Following values are observed by Monitor: λc (current average request arrival rate), Gsr_c (Current Gsr, it's be calculated by the statistic of service response time) and resource utility rate. Unpredictable request arrival rate change will be indicated by Monitor.

As an amender to the possible distortion of theoretical values, the violation of Gsr which be monitored will trigger the allocation too. In this condition, a heuristic function will also be triggered to add a modified relationship into RASDB.

The resource utility rate is used to help determining whether to trigger the resource remove function. Note that the remove policy should consider the impaction on the performance in case the request arrival rate frequently changes in a short time.

5.3 Workflow of Resource Allocation

The process steps are described here:

1) With the dedicated parameters of Gsr, SRT in SLA, initiate the C0 (resource entity number) for each service level by querying RASDB;
2) Use C0 and the resource constraint μ to get Resource entity handles from Resource Broker;
3) Pass these handles to Load Balance Deployer;
4) Query the Scheduler;
5) If request arrival rate increasing will occur soon, trigger the Add function;
6) If request arrival rate decreasing will occur soon and the resource utility rate is less than the policy defined, trigger the Remove function;
7) Query the Monitor result;
8) When λc increases, trigger the Add function;
9) When λc decreases and the resource utility rate is less than the policy defined, trigger the Remove function;
10) When Gsr_c is less than Gsr, trigger the Add function and the Heuristic function;
11) Go to 4).

Add function:

1) Query corresponding resource entity number Ct from RASDB with request rate, Gsr and SRT;
2) Cp=max(1,Ct-C), while C is the current resource entity number. The operation 'max' used here is because: When the request rate doesn't increase, the factor bring on the SLA violation may be other reasons, so at least one resource entity should be added even the request rate is not increasing;
3) Get Resource entity handles from Resource Broker with Cp and constraint μ. If success, go to 4), otherwise go to 5);
4) Pass these handles to Load Balance Deployer and return;
5) Ignore and return if the Violation Policy is "best-effort"; Report to Admission Control if the Violation Policy is "reject".

Remove function:

1) Query corresponding resource entity number Ct from RASDB with request rate, Gsr and SRT;
2) If C>Ct, Cp= C-Ct; if C<=Ct, Cp=0, while C is the current resource entity number;
3) Release Cp resource entities.

Heuristic function:

1) Record the λc from monitor and SRT from SLA;
2) Get the Gsr_c from monitor after Add function, record the resource entity number C only when the Gsr_c is satisfied;
3) Add the new relationship into RASDB.

6 Evaluation

In order to evaluate the model and the framework of this paper, we did some experiments and simulations.

The theoretical relationships calculated by resource allocation model described in section 3 are shown in the Figure3.

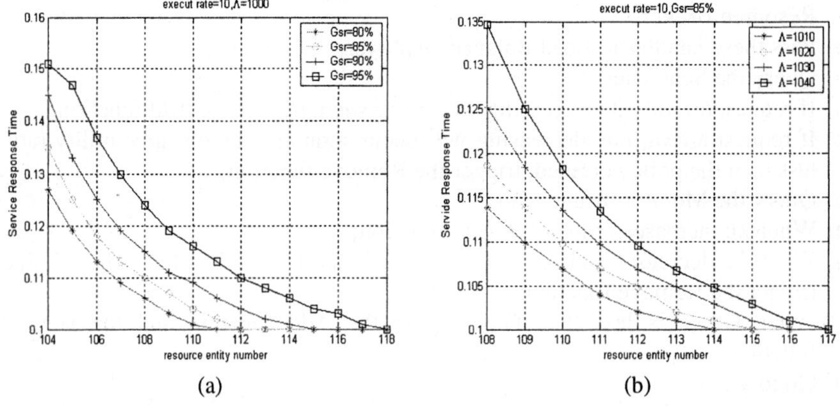

Fig. 3. Service Response Time to resource entity number in different Gsr and request arrival rate

Figure3.(a) shows the Service Response Time in some certain Guarantee Service Rate for different values of resource entities according to Formula (4) . For example, with the same SRT, 0.11, when there are different Gsr(80% and 95%), services need different resource entities numbers, which are 107 and 112 respectively. Then we can determine the amount of resource entities that should be allocated to guarantee the SLA with QoS metric SRT and Gsr.

Figure3.(b) shows the SRT to the resource entities, in a certain Gsr, for different values of request arrival rate. During the service running period, when the request arrival rate changes unpredictable, especially increase quickly, the service provider must adjust the resource entities to ensure the SRT and Gsr in SLA.

Then we present simulation experiment results that provide insights into the performance of the on-demand resource allocation framework. The SLA attributes are: Gsr = 95%, SRT = 0.2(second). We did the simulation with two kinds of request arrival rate: Poisson distribution and Random distribution. The experiment includes 4 phases with different mean values of request arrival rate.

Table 2. On-demand resource allocation result

		Phase1	Phase2	Phase3	Phase4
Poisson Distribution	λ	100	200	170	140
	Resource entity number	11	22	18	15
Random Distribution	Mean rate	100	200	170	140
	Resource entity number	[11,16]	[22,24]	[18,23]	[15,19]

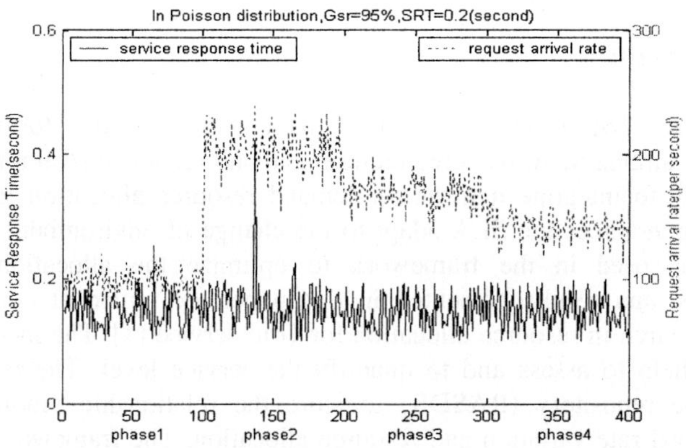

Fig. 4. Experiment result with Request arrival rate in Poisson distribution

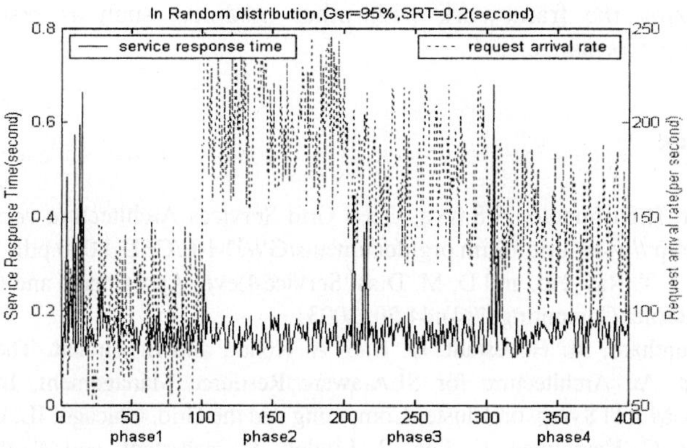

Fig. 5. Experiment result with Request arrival rate in Random distribution

The result of allocated resource entity number is showed in Table 2. It can be seen that, in the case of Random distribution, the resource entity number will reach a larger value than in the case of Poisson distribution by the heuristic function. The results of Service Response Time are showed in Figure4 and Figure5. It can be seen from Figure4 that while the request arrival rate change all the time, the system behaves well with Gsr_c=99%. Figure5 shows that although the request arrival rate variety is much larger than expected, the result is still acceptable with Gsr_c=95%.

From the experiment results, we can see that our framework is proved to be efficient with the Poisson distribution of request arrival rate. If the arrival rate distribution is far from the Poisson, the model can't exactly calculate the probability of arrival rate. By the using of heuristic algorithm, the QoS can still be reached, but in a slower manner. When such thing occurs, the model can easily be extended by adding the new arrival rate distribution into the model to calculate the probability of the request number in the service system and keeping the other steps.

7 Conclusion

In this paper, we have presented a mathematical model formally define the relationship among SLA, resource requirement and request arrival rate. Moreover, we showed how to integrate it in an on-demand resource allocation framework which efficiently guarantees the SLA adapt to the change of environment. And a heuristic algorithm is used in the framework to optimize the allocation. The analysis, experiments, and results presented in this paper are aimed at complementing the ongoing research in resource allocation for Grid service [1]. The metrics presented in this paper help to assess and to quantify the service level. The model is used for building the repository (RASDB) to store the relationship among QoS metrics, request arrival rate variation and resource allocation. The framework, which directly makes use of the repository, is independent of the model. When the condition is not coincident with the constraints in this paper, new model can easily be extended to add new relationship into the repository. The future work includes extending the model and optimizing the framework with other modules, such as resource broker, to increase the performance.

References

1. I. Foster, H.Kishimoto, A.Savva, Open Grid Services Architecture *version 1.0,* See Web site at: http://www.gridforum.org/documents/GWD-I-E/GFD-I.030.pdf, 2005.1
2. A. Leff, J. T. Ray_eld, and D. M. Dias. Service-Level Agreements and Commercial Grids. IEEE Internet Computing, 7(4):44.50, 2003.
3. L.-O. Burchard, M. Hovestadt, O. Kao, A. Keller, and B. Linnert. The Virtual Resource Manager: An Architecture for SLA-aware Resource Management. In Proc. of the 4th IEEE/ACM Int'l Symp. on Cluster Computing and the Grid, Chicago, IL, USA, April 2004.
4. I. Foster, C. Kesselman, C. Lee, B. Lindell, K. Nahrstedt, and A. Roy. A Distributed Resource Management Architecture that Supports Advance Reservations and Co-Allocation. In Proceedings of the 7th International Workshop on Quality of Service, London, UK, June 1999.

5. Rashid J. Al-Ali, G-QoSM: Grid service discovery using OoS properties. Computing and Information Journal, Special Issue on Grid Computing, 21(4):363-382, 2002
6. Thomas R¨oblit, Alexander Reinefeld , Co-Reservation with the Concept of Virtual Resources. IEEE CCGrid 2005.
7. Youssef Hamadi, Continuous Resources Allocation in Internet Data Centers. IEEE CCGrid 2005.
8. K. Appleby, S. Fakhouri, L. Fong, G. Goldszmidt, M. Kalantar, S. Krishnakumar, D. P. Pazel, J. Pershing, and B. Rochwerger, "Oc´eano–SLA Based Management of a Computing Utility," Proceedings of the IFIP/IEEE International Symposium on Integrated Network Management, 2001.
9. X. Jiang, D. Xu, "SODA: a Service-On-Demand Architecture for Application Service Hosting Utility Platforms," Proceedings of the IEEE International Symposium on High Performance Distributed Computing, 2003.
10. S. Givry, Y. Hamadi, J. Mattioli, P. G´erard, M. Lema^ıtre, G. Verfaillie, A. Aggoun, I. Gouachi, T. Benoist, E. Bourreau, F. Laburthe, P. David, S. Loudni, and S. Bourgault. Towards an on-line optimisation framework. In CP-2001 Workshop on On-Line combinatorial problem solving and ConstraintProgramming (OLCP'01), pages 45–61, Paphos, Cyprus, December 1 2001.
11. X. Zhu and S. Singhal. Optimal resource assignment in internet data centers. In Ninth International Symposium in Modeling, Analysis and Simulation of Computer and Telecommunication Systems MASCOTS'01, pages 61–69, August 2001.
12. W. Goscinski and D. Abramson, "Distributed Ant: A System to Support Application Deployment in the Grid," IEEE/ACM International Workshop on Grid Computing, 2004.
13. Dimitris Gouscos, "An Approach to Modeling Web Service QoS and Provision Price", IEEE WISEW'03
14. A. Dan, D. Davis, R. Kearney, A. Keller, R. King, D. Kuebler, H. Ludwig, M. Polan, M. Spreitzer, and A. Youssef. Web services on demand: WSLA-driven automated management. IBM Systems Journal, 43(1):136.158, 2004.
15. K. Czajkowski, I. Foster, N. Karonis, C. Kesselman, S. Martin, W. Smith, and S. Tuecke. A Resource Management Architecture for Metacomputing Systems. Proc. of the 4th Int'l Workshop on Job Scheduling Strategies for Parallel Processing, Orlando, FL, USA, LNCS(1459):62.82, 1998.
16. C. Liu, L. Yang, I. Foster, and D. Angulo, "Design and Evaluation of a Resource Selection Framework for Grid Applications," Proceedings of the IEEE International Symposium on High-Performance Distributed Computing, 2002.
17. W. Lee, S. McGough, S. Newhouse, and J. Darlington, "Load-balancing EU-DataGrid Resource Brokers," UK e-Science All Hands Meeting, 2003.
18. D. Thain, T. Tannenbaum, and M. Livny, "Condor and the Grid," Grid Computing: Making The Global Infrastructure a Reality, John Wiley, 2003.
19. R. Buyya, D. Abramson, and J. Giddy, "Nimrod/G: An Architecture for a Resource Management and Scheduling System in a Global Computational Grid," Proceedings of the IEEE International Conference on High Performance Computing and Grid in Asia Pacific Region, 2000.
20. Y.-S. Kim, J.-L. Yu, J.-G. Hahm, J.-S. Kim, and J.-W. Lee, "Design and Implementation of an OGSI Compliant Grid Broker Service," Proceedings of the IEEE International Symposium on Cluster Computing and the Grid, 2004.

A Prediction-Based Parallel Replication Algorithm in Distributed Storage System*

Yijie Wang and Xiaoming Zhang

National Laboratory for Parallel and Distributed Processing, Institute of Computer, National University of Defense Technology, Changsha, China, 410073
wwyyjj1971@vip.sina.com

Abstract. Data replication can be used to reduce bandwidth consumption and access latency in the distributed system where users require remote access to large data objects. In this paper, according to the intrinsic characteristic of distributed storage system, the prediction-based parallel replication algorithm PPR is proposed. In the PPR, according to the characteristic of spatial data, the data that will be accessed is predicted, then the data is prefetched; during replication, according to the network state, several replicas of a data object are selected, which are of the least access cost; the different parts of the data object are transferred from these replicas, and they are used to make a new replica. The results of performance evaluation show that the PPR can utilize the network bandwidth efficiently, provide high data replication efficiency and substantially better access efficiency, and can avoid the interference between different replications efficiently.

1 Introduction

There is a growing demand for the automatic, online archiving of data resources. For decades, industry and other users have relied on tape to back up their critical data, but this scheme requires a human administrator to maintain the tape drivers, file drivers, and the tapes themselves. As the amount of data resources in the world explodes, this maintenance will become too costly to be feasible. At present, how to aggregate the geographically distributed heterogeneous storage resources to form the virtual storage space and provide secure efficient data storage service is becoming a challenging research topic in the worldwide.

The replication scheme of distributed storage system determines how many replicas of each data object are created, and to which nodes these replicas are allocated. This scheme critically affects the performance of distributed storage system, since reading a data object locally is less costly than reading it from a remote node, especially for large data objects. There are two major motivations for replication–increasing availability and increasing system performance. Replication creates redundant information in the network, which allows the system to remain

* This work is supported by the National Grand Fundamental Research 973 Program of China (No.2002CB312105), A Foundation for the Author of National Excellent Doctoral Dissertation of PR China (No.200141), and the National Natural Science Foundation of China (No.69903011, No.69933030).

H. Zhuge and G.C. Fox (Eds.): GCC 2005, LNCS 3795, pp. 690 – 700, 2005.

operational in spite of node and link failures and thus increase reliability. Also, if data is replicated near the node where it is accessed, communication cost is greatly reduced. Due to the dynamic of network, sometimes the network bandwidth is relatively very low. That leads to a focus on reducing network transmission cost, on utilizing the redundant network bandwidth sufficiently, and hence on the performance issue.

Peer-to-peer distributed storage systems are positioned to take advantage of gains in network bandwidth, storage capacity, and computational resources to provide longterm durable storage infrastructures. Systems such as Farsite([1]), Intermemory([2]), Freenet([3]), CFS([4]), PAST([5]), and OceanStore([6]) seek to capitalize on the rapid growth of resources to provide inexpensive, highly-available storage without centralized servers. The designers of these systems propose to achieve high availability and long-term durability, in the face of individual component failures, through replication techniques.

Optimising the use of Grid resources is critical for users to effectively exploit a Data Grid. Data replication is considered a major technique for reducing data access cost to Grid jobs([7],[8],[9]). Replication involves the creation of identical copies of data files and their distribution over various Grid sites. This can reduce data access latency and increase the robustness of Grid applications.

In the most research projects on peer-to-peer distributed storage system and Data Grid, the traditional replication technology is utilized to achieve the high availability and durability. In the traditional replication technology, if a new replica R' of data object DO is to be made on node A, the best replica R of data object DO should be found, then make a copy of R and transfer it to node A, that is replica R'. If the network bandwidth is relatively low and the data object need to be replicated is very large, the efficiency of replication will be low, thus the availability and system performance will be reduced.

In this paper, according to the intrinsic characteristic of mass spatial data, the prediction-based parallel replication algorithm PPR is proposed. Section 2 describes the prediction-based parallel replication algorithm PPR. Section 3 presents the results of performance evaluation. Section 4 provides a summary of our research work.

2 Prediction-Based Parallel Replication Algorithm PPR

In the prediction-based parallel replication algorithm PPR, firstly, according to the characteristic of spatial data, the data that will be accessed is predicted, then the data is prefetched; secondly, according to the network state, NUM replicas of data object DO are selected, which are of the least access cost; thirdly, different parts of data object DO are transferred from different replicas, then these parts are combined to make the new replica of data object DO. Compared with the traditional replication technology, the PPR predicts the data access, thus the hit rate of data access is increased; the PPR utilizes several network links to transfer a copy of data object, thus the availability of network bandwidth is improved, and the efficiency of data replication is improved, so the efficiency of data access is improved efficiently.

The PPR includes two algorithms: the access prediction algorithm and parallel replication algorithm.

2.1 The Access Prediction Algorithm

In general, spatial data is accessed regularly. In the access prediction algorithm, in order to match the regular of spatial data access, utilizing the interpolation, the equation of spatial physical motion is built, which is used to predict the data access in the future.

Assuming that the time series of data requirements are $t_0, t_1 \cdots t_n$, the coordinates of required spatial data are $A_0, A_1 \cdots A_n$, utilizing the Lagrange interpolation, we can get the following formulas.

$$A = \sum_{k=0}^{n} \left(\prod_{\substack{i=0 \\ i \neq k}}^{n} \frac{t - t_i}{t_k - t_i} \right) A_k \tag{1}$$

$$t = \sum_{k=0}^{n} \left(\prod_{\substack{i=0 \\ i \neq k}}^{n} \frac{A - A_i}{A_k - A_i} \right) t_k \tag{2}$$

If the current time is t_n, then the coordinates of spatial data accessed on time t_{n+1} can be predicted by $A_0, A_1 \cdots A_n$.

2.2 The Parallel Replication Algorithm

The parallel replication algorithm includes two strategies: the replica selection strategy and data quantity assignment strategy.

2.2.1 The Replica Selection Strategy

The replica selection strategy decides which replicas are used to make the new replica. Firstly, the access cost of each replica should be evaluated; secondly, the number of replicas to be selected should be decided; lastly, the replicas with the least access cost are selected.

The access cost of replica lies on the network bandwidth and the distance between the two nodes. In figure 1, a new replica of data object DO will be made on node A, and there is a replica R of data object DO on node B, and the number of hops between node A and node B is k+1, the available bandwidth of each link between any two nodes is bw_1, bw_2, bw_3, ……,bw_k, bw_{k+1}, thus the access cost of replica is $\sum_{i=1}^{k+1} \left(size(R) / bw_i \right)$.

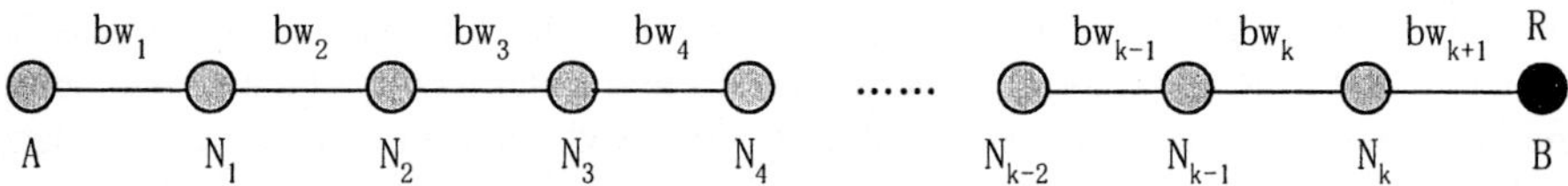

Fig. 1. The access cost of replica

In fact, it is not true that more replicas selected will get more profit. If more than one replica will be transferred through the same link, then the available bandwidth of each replica will be relatively low. On the other hand, if one replication occupies too many links, the other replications will be affected badly. In view of the system performance, the number of replicas selected will be decided according to the degree of node A.

The basic idea of the replica selection strategy is as follows:

1. Calculate the access cost of each replica R, which is $\sum_{i=1}^{k+1}\left({size(R)}/{bw_i} \right)$.
2. Select the replicas used to make the new replica of data object DO. The selection conditions include:
   a) The replicas selected are of the least access cost;
   b) The replicas selected do not share the same links;
   c) The number of replicas selected is not more than the degree of node A.

2.2.2 The Data Quantity Assignment Strategy

The efficiency of replication is decided by not only the replicas selected, but also the data quantity transferred from each replica. There are two fundamental principles of data quantity assignment: 1) the access cost of replica is less, the data quantity transferred from it is larger; 2) the data transfer of all replicas finish simultaneously.

The basic idea of the data quantity assignment strategy is as follows:

1. Calculate the transfer rate of each replica selected by the replica selection strategy. In figure 1, the access cost of replica R is $Cost_R = \sum_{i=1}^{k+1}\left({size(R)}/{bw_i} \right)$, the transfer rate of replica R is $TR_R = {1}/{Cost_R}$.
2. Calculate the sum of transfer rate of selected replicas. Assume the number of selected replicas is NUM, the selected replicas are R_1, R_2, …, R_{NUM}, and the transfer rate of them are TR_1, TR_2, …, TR_{NUM}, so the sum of transfer rate of selected replicas is $SUM\_TR = \sum_{j=1}^{NUM} TR_j$.
3. According to the transfer rate of each selected replica, assign the data quantity of each replica. The data quantity of replica R_k is assigned to $size(DO)\dfrac{TR_k}{SUM\_TR}$, $size(DO)$ is the size of data object DO.

In the traditional replication algorithm, a replica of the least access cost is selected, so the time of replication is ${size(DO)}/{\max(TR_1, TR_2, ..., TR_{NUM})}$.

In the PPR, the NUM replicas are selected, which are of the least access cost. The different parts of data object DO are transferred from the different replicas, so the time of replication is $size(DO)/SUM\_TR$.

It is clear that the PPR utilizes the network bandwidth more efficiently than the traditional replication algorithm, and can improve the efficiency of replication evidently.

2.2.3 Algorithm Description

The description of the parallel replication algorithm is as follows.

BEGIN

Step_1: Get the degree of node A on which a new replica of data object DO will be made, let DG denote the degree of node A.

Step_2: Get the replica set of data object DO from metadata catalog, let Set_R denote the replica set of DO, let Num_Set_R denote the number of replicas in Set_R.

Step_3: Evaluate the access cost of each replica in Set_R. Let $Cost_R$ denote the access cost of replica R, $Cost_R = \sum_{i=1}^{k+1} \left(size(R) / bw_i \right)$.

Step_4: Initialization: i = 0, Set_Selection = ∅.

Step_5: Num_Selection = min(Num_Set_R, DG).

Step_6: DO

{

Select the replica R_Selection from Set_R, the access cost of which is the least in Set_R, $Cost_{R\_Selection} = \min(Cost_R, R \in Set\_R)$;

$Set\_Selection = Set\_Selection + R\_Selection$;

i = i +1;

$Set\_R = Set\_R - R\_Selection$;

FOR each R'∈ Set_R

{

IF R_Selection and R' share the same links

THEN $Set\_R = Set\_R - R'$;

}

}WHILE (i< Num_Selection AND Set_R ≠ ∅)

Step_7: Calculate the transfer rate of each selected replicas.

$$TR_R = 1 / Cost_R \ , \ R \in Set\_Selection \ ,$$

TR_R denotes the transfer rate of replica R.

Step_8: Calculate the sum of transfer rate of selected replicas.

$$SUM\_TR = \sum_{R \in Set\_Selection} TR_R \ .$$

Step_9: Assign the data quantity of each replica R in Set_Selection to $size(DO)\dfrac{TR_R}{SUM\_TR}$.

END

3 Performance Evaluations

OptorSim([10],[11],[12]) is a simulator used to evaluate the replication strategies. In our simulation, the system topology (see Figure 2) comprises 11 nodes. Each SE of node has a capacity of 150 GB. Each data object has size of 1 GB and the total size of the data object set is 120 GB.

We assume that initially each data object has only one physical instance referred to as master copy, and the number of replicas of each data object is a random number between 0 and 2. The initial data object distribution is that all master copies and replicas are randomly distributed among all nodes. If the access frequency of a data object from one node reaches the threshold, then a new replica of data object should be made on the node.

Access pattern determines the order in which a job requests data objects. The following two access patterns are considered in our simulation:

1. Gaussian random walk access pattern: successive data objects are selected from a Gaussian distribution centred on the previous data objects;
2. turbulent straight-line motion access pattern: the coordinates of data objects accessed are approximately straight-line, with some turbulence.

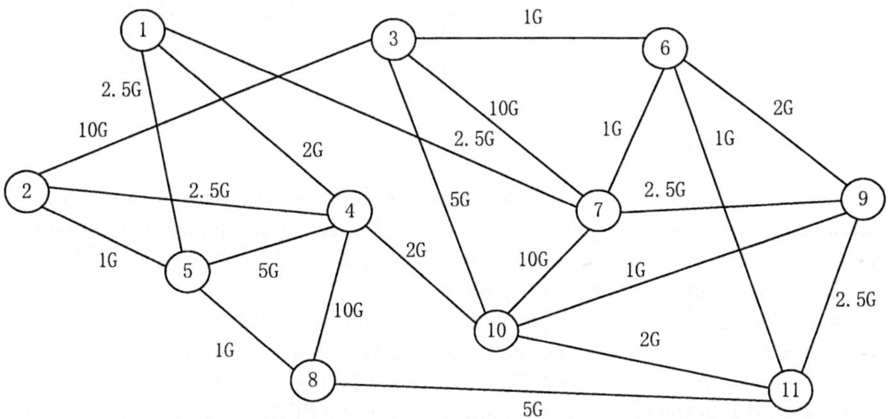

Fig. 2. System topology for simulation

The economy-based replication algorithm ([9],[13]) is proposed for Data Grid, it optimises both the selection of replicas for running jobs and the dynamic creation of replicas in the nodes. In this strategy, optimization agents are located on nodes and use an auction protocol for selecting the optimal replica of a data object and a prediction function to make informed decisions about local data replication. Data objects are "purchased" by CEs for running jobs and by SEs to make an investment that will improve their expected future revenue. These data objects are sold by SEs to either CEs or other SEs. CEs try to minimize the data object purchase cost, while SEs attempt to maximise their profits. CEs and SEs interact with intelligent optimization agents which perform the reasoning required in the strategy.

The performance comparison between the economy-based replication algorithm and the PPR includes three aspects:

1. Relation between the access patterns and the system performance;
2. Relation between the number of the different data objects accessed by jobs and the system performance;
3. Relation between the size of replication space and the system performance.

There are 6 job types in our simulation. The difference between job types is the data quantity accessed by jobs. The data quantity and probability distribution of each job type is shown in Table 1. Jobs were submitted at five seconds intervals. The estimated time taken to complete a job was calculated as the execution time on the node, not including the time waiting in the queue at the node.

Table 1. Job types

Job Type	Data Quantity (GB)	Probability
1	1	17%
2	5	17%
3	10	16%
4	25	17%
5	30	16%
6	50	17%

3.1 Access Patterns

The results comparing the two algorithms for each access pattern are shown in Figures 3 and 4. The total job time is averaged over 10 simulation runs. Figure 3 shows results for Gaussian random walk access pattern, Figure 4 shows results for turbulent straight-line motion access pattern.

The results show that the PPR provides substantially better throughput for jobs that have a Gaussian random walk access pattern and turbulent straight-line motion access pattern, this also means that the PPR can provide higher data access efficiency. The main reason is that the replication is parallelized in the PPR, and that it can utilize the network bandwidth more efficiently.

The results also show that both the economy-based replication algorithm and the PPR are not sensitive to the access patterns.

3.2 Number of Data Objects

The results comparing the two algorithms for the number of the different data objects accessed by jobs are shown in Figure 5 and 6, 1000 jobs are executed. The access patterns of jobs are Gaussian random walk access pattern and turbulent straight-line motion access pattern. The number of the different data objects accessed by jobs is changed from 50 to 120. The total job time is averaged over 10 simulation runs.

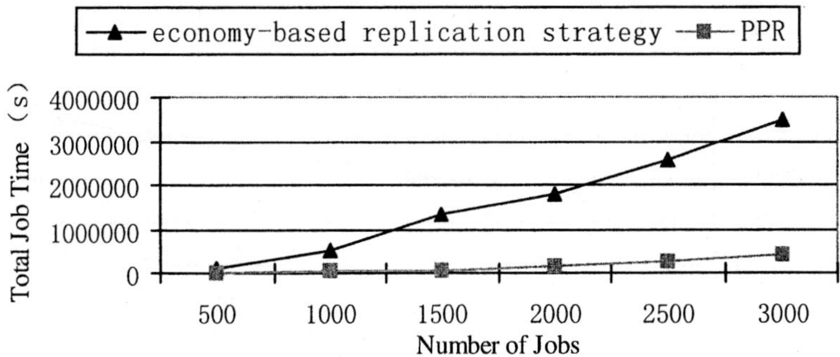

Fig. 3. Total job times for Gaussian random walk access pattern

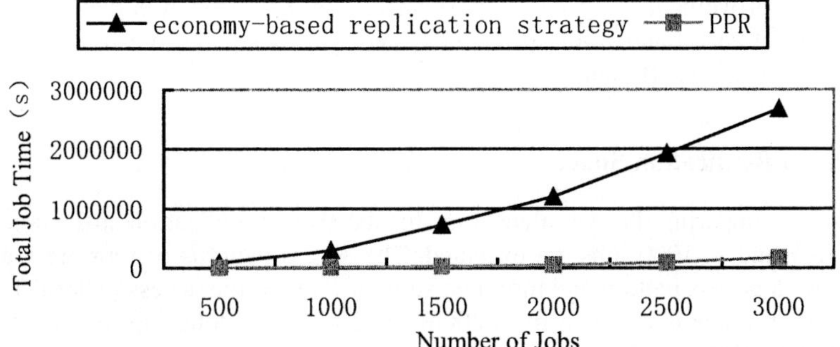

Fig. 4. Total job times for turbulent straight-line motion access pattern

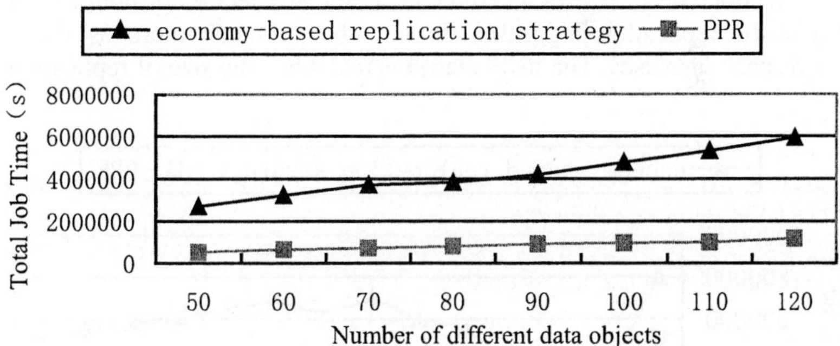

Fig. 5. Relation between the number of different data objects and total job times for Gaussian random walk access pattern

The results show that the difference between the PPR and the economy-based replication algorithm is increased as the number of the different data objects accessed by jobs increases. In the PPR, if there are more different data objects to be replicated, the interference between different replications will be more serious, but it will not

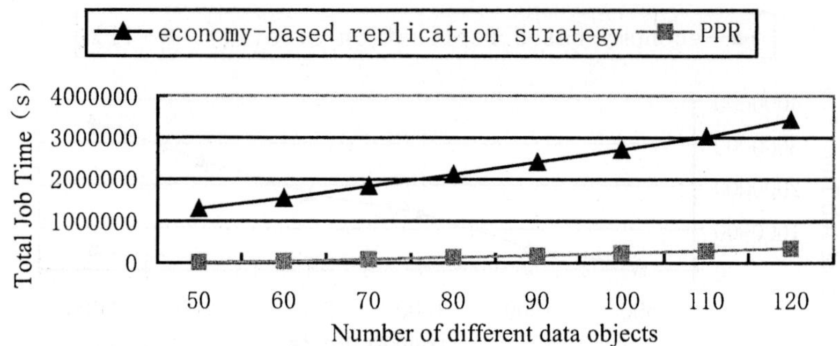

Fig. 6. Relation between the number of different data objects and total job times for turbulent straight-line motion access pattern

affect the improvement of system performance. The main reason is that the PPR can utilize the network bandwidth sufficiently, and can avoid the interference between different replications efficiently.

3.3 Size of Replication Space

The results comparing the two algorithms for the size of replication space are shown in Figure 7 and 8, 1000 jobs are executed. The access patterns of jobs are Gaussian random walk access pattern and turbulent straight-line motion access pattern. The size of replication space is changed from 20GB to 150GB. The total job time is averaged over 10 simulation runs.

The results show that the PPR provides higher data access efficiency than the economy-based replication algorithm with the same size of replication space. If the size of replication space reaches a certain value, the efficiencies of both PPR and the economy-based replication algorithm do not change much more as the size of replication space increases. The main reason is that when the size of replication space

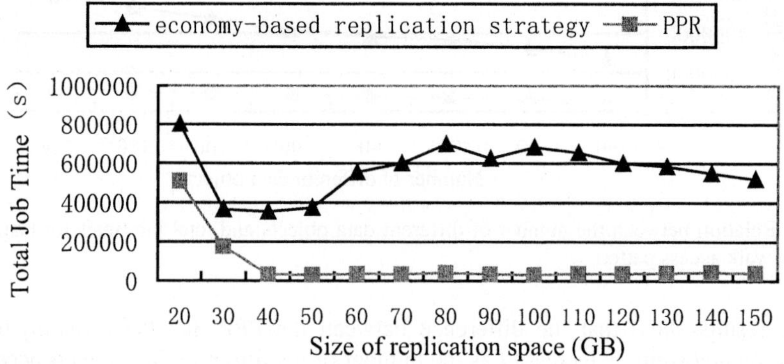

Fig. 7. Relation between the size of replication space and total job times for Gaussian random walk access pattern

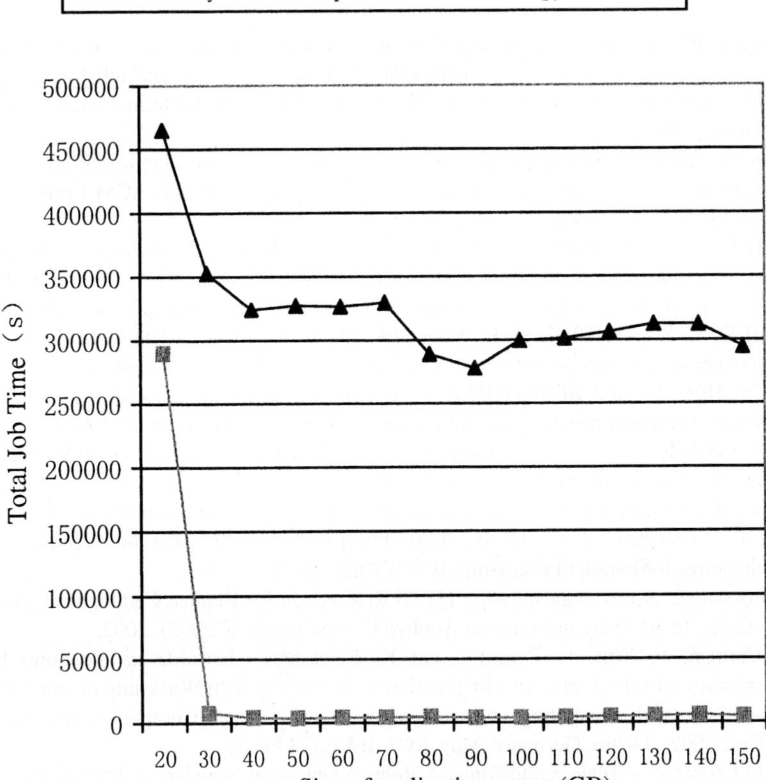

Fig. 8. Relation between the size of replication space and total job times for turbulent straight-line motion access pattern

reaches a certain value, the data objects in the replication space will not replaced frequently, so the efficiency of replication will not be affected badly.

4 Conclusions

In the prediction-based parallel replication algorithm PPR, in order to utilize the network bandwidth efficiently, firstly, the data access is predicted, and the data object is prefetched; secondly, the replication is parallelized, the different parts of a data object are transferred from different replicas, which are used to make the new replica of the data object. Compared with the economy-based replication algorithm, the PPR utilizes the network bandwidth more efficiently, provides higher data replication efficiency and substantially better access efficiency. The PPR is not sensitive to the access patterns, and can avoid the interference between different replications efficiently. If the size of replication space reaches a certain value, the efficiency of PPR will not change much more as the size of replication space increases.

References

1. A. Adya, W. Bolosky, M. Castro, G. Cermak, R. Chaiken, J. Douceur, J. Howell, J. Lorch, M. Theimer, and R. Wattenhofer. FARSITE: Federated available and reliable storage for incompletely trusted environments. In 5th Symp on Operating Systems Design and Impl., December 2002.
2. Chen, Y., Edler, J., Goldberg, A., Gottlieb, A., Sobti, S., and Yianilos, P. A prototype implementation of archival intermemory. In Proceedings of the 4th ACM Conference on Digital libraries (Berkeley, CA, Aug. 1999), pp. 28--37.
3. CLARK, I., SANDBERG, O., WILEY, B., AND HONG, T. Freenet: A distributed anonymous information storage and retrieval system. In *Proc. of the Workshop on Design Issues in Anonymity and Unobservability* (Berkeley, CA, July 2000), pp. 311–320.
4. DABEK, F., KAASHOEK, M. F., KARGER, D., MORRIS, R., AND STOICA, I. Wide-area cooperative storage with CFS. In *Proc. of ACM SOSP* (October 2001).
5. DRUSCHEL, P., and ROWSTRON, A. Storage management and caching in PAST, a largescale, persistent peer-to-peer storage utility. In *Proc. of ACM SOSP* (2001).
6. KUBIATOWICZ, J., ET AL. Oceanstore: An architecture for global-scale persistent storage. In *Proc. of ASPLOS* (Nov. 2000), ACM.
7. H. Lamehamedi, B. Szymanski, Z. shentu, and E. Deelman, "Data Replication Strategies in Grid Environments," Proc. Of the Fifth International Conference on Algorithms and Architectures for Parallel Processing (ICA3PP'02), 2002.
8. H. Stockinger and A. Hanushevsky. HTTP Redirection for Replica Catalogue Lookups in Data Grids. In ACM Symposium on Applied Computing (SAC2002), 2002.
9. M. Carman, F. Zini, L. Serafini, and K. Stockinger. Towards an Economy-Based Optimisation of File Access and Replication on a Data Grid. In Workshop on Agent based Cluster and Grid Computing at Int. Symposium on Cluster Computing and the Grid (CCGrid 2002), Berlin, Germany, May 2002. IEEE-CS Press.
10. WP2 Optimisation Team. OptorSim - A Replica Optimiser Simulation. http://cern.ch/edg-wp2/optimization /optorsim.html/.
11. W. H. Bell, D. G. Cameron, L. Capozza, P. Millar, K. Stockinger, and F. Zini. Optorsim - a grid simulator for studying dynamic data replication strategies. International Journal of High Performance Computing Applications, 17(4), 2003.
12. W. H. Bell, D. G. Cameron, L. Capozza, P. Millar, K. Stockinger,and F. Zini. Design of a Replica Optimisation Framework. TechnicalReport DataGrid-02-TED- 021215, CERN, Geneva, Switzerland, December 2002.
13. W. H. Bell, D. G. Cameron, R. Carvajal-Schiaffino, A. P. Millar, K. Stockinger, and F. Zini. Evaluation of an Economy-Based File Replication Strategy for a Data Grid. In Proceedings of 3nd IEEE Int. Symposium on Cluster Computing and the Grid (CCGrid'2003).

Reliability-Latency Tradeoffs for Data Gathering in Random-Access Wireless Sensor Networks

Haibo Zhang, Hong Shen, and Haibin Kan

Graduate School of Information Science,
Japan Advanced Institute of Science and Technology,
1-1, Asahidai, Nomi, Ishikawa 923-1292 Japan
{haibo, shen}@jaist.ac.jp

Abstract. Gathering sensor data at high reliability and low latency is one of the key design challenges for wireless sensor networks(WSNs). In this paper, we explore the reliability-latency tradeoffs for data gathering in random-access multi-hop wireless sensor networks. We introduce a model considering both packet delivery reliability and latency for the objective to construct an optimal data gathering tree, which can minimize the packet delivery latency for each node while providing guaranteed per-link packet successful delivery probability. We formulate this problem as an optimization problem and propose a sink targeted shortest path algorithm(STSPA). The solution for calculating optimal channel access parameters is also presented. We evaluate the performance of our model by extensive simulations, and results show that our model can provide good tradeoffs between reliability and latency. Furthermore, our model is robust to environmental interference.

1 Introduction

Wireless sensor networks are expected to be used in a wide range of applications, such as habitat sensing, healthcare monitoring, target tracking, etc.. In most applications, data gathering is a critical operation needed for collecting useful information from the sensor nodes to the base station(sink) to perform further analysis. This leads to the demand of constructing an efficient topology for data gathering which can provide high reliability and low latency for packet delivery.

Reliable data transportation is a key concern in wireless sensor networks. Since most WSNs are composed of low cost sensor nodes with low power RF transceivers, the channels are error prone and packets must be delivered in multi-hop fashion. Furthermore, collisions will occur when multiple nodes simultaneously transmit packets to the same node, so the data loss rate in WSNs is very serious [1]. In many applications, such as fire or gas leak detection and healthcare monitoring, the demand for reliable data gathering is high, otherwise, wrong decisions may be made due to the insufficient information collected by the sink. So it is critical to design high reliable data delivery strategies for WSNs.

To improve the data delivery reliability in WSNs, many strategies based on retransmission have been proposed[2,6]. However, link-layer retransmission is

H. Zhuge and G.C. Fox (Eds.): GCC 2005, LNCS 3795, pp. 701–712, 2005.

unable to reduce the variability of data loss[1]. Furthermore, it will lead to more undesired overhead and the data delivery latency may also be prolonged. In some applications, such as fire or gas leak detection, low packet delivery latency is also important besides reliability.

In this paper, we explore the tradeoffs between reliability and latency for data gathering in random-access multi-hop WSNs. We consider a real-time scenario where raw data generated by the sensor node must be periodically reported to the sink. In our model, we use a random access communication model; we also believe that sensors will not need elaborate multiple access or transport protocols since typical packets will be small and RTS-CTS may be too much of an overhead [3]. In random access communication model, the nodes must access the channel through contention with its neighbors, which will cause packets collision and lead to severe data loss. In our model, we deem that packets collision is the main factor that results in data loss in random access WSNs and we will not consider nodes failure which can be solved by failure detection techniques. We will show that our model is robust to the environmental interference which also is an important factor that causes data loss in WSNs. Our model is suitable for many applications that require either high reliability and low latency. The user can easily acquire a trade-off between reliability and latency by adjusting the per-link packet successful delivery probability.

The rest of this paper is organized as follows. Section 2 reviews some related work. Section 3 gives the network model and formulates the problem as an optimization problem. In section 4, we describe the approaches for optimal data gathering tree construction and optimal channel access parameters calculation. Section 5 provides the simulation results and analysis. Concluding remarks are given in the last section.

2 Related Work

Previous work on reliable data transportation in WSNs has largely focused on protocol design, which takes advantage of either multi-path packet delivery or packet retransmission. For example, an ASCENT algorithm for data gathering in densely distributed sensor networks was proposed in[4]. It exploited nodes redundancy to construct multi-path for data transportation. In this algorithm, a parameter called loss threshold(LT) was introduced which could react when links experience high packet loss. In[5], a family of protocols based on multi-path broadcast was presented. The protocols were based on random backoff and could significantly reduce the number of collisions and increase the rate of successful packet delivery by trading off the average propagation delay. In [6], a protocol for data collection based on packet retransmission was designed.

Data delivery latency is also an important factor for WSN, and much work has been done on latency reduction. In[7], the authors explored the the energy-latency tradeoffs in wireless communication. They proposed algorithms to minimize the overall energy dissipation of the sensor nodes in the aggregation tree subject to the latency constraint. In[8], a protocol named DMAC was designed to solve the interruption problem and allowed continuous packet forwarding by giving the sleep schedule of a node an offset that depends upon its depth on the tree. It can provides significant energy savings and latency reduction.

To the best of our knowledge, this is the first paper that addresses the problem of exploring reliability and latency tradeoffs for data gathering in a random-access multi-hop wireless sensor network. Since different applications of WSNs may have different requirements for data delivery reliability and latency, it is desired to propose a model in which reliability and latency tradeoffs can be tuned by the user. In our model, the per-link packet successful delivery probability can be specified by the user. Compared with other models, our model is more practical and suitable for practical applications.

3 Problem Formulation

A wireless sensor network can be envisioned as a distributed system consisting of a large number of sensor nodes. In our model, we assume that there is only one sink, and without loss of generality, the sink is placed in the center of the region to reduce the average hops. All the information collected by the sensor nodes should be reported to the sink periodically through multi-hop paths with high reliability and low latency.

Different applications may have different requirements for the sensors and the network. In our model, a wireless sensor network has the following features.

- All sensor nodes are homogeneous, and they all transmit/receive on a common carrier frequency using omni-directional antennas. Compared with the sensor nodes, the sink is more powerful, and can perform complex tasks.
- Random channel access model is used for data communication. All the nodes are roughly synchronized to each other. Time is slotted and each time slot is designed to accommodate the the transmission of some fixed packets.
- All colliding packets will be lost. Although it is possible that the receiver may correctly decode the packet from the transmitter if the signal to interference ratio(SIR)exceeds a given threshold, in our model, we assume that all colliding packets will be lost.
- At each time slot, each node can be in one of the following three states: transmit, receive or sleep. By using random method, the probabilities that each node randomly selects to go into these three states are P_T,P_R and P_S respectively. Clearly, $P_T + P_R + P_S = 1$. In order to simplify the construction and maintenance of the optimal data gathering tree, we assume that all nodes have the same channel access parameters P_T,P_R and P_S.

We model the network as a directed graph $G = (V, E)$, where $V = (v_1, v_2, ..., v_n)$ is the set of sensor nodes, and E is the set of network links. The network is composed of n sensor nodes and v_1 represents the sink node. Given a node v_i, we define its neighbors, denoted by N_i, as the set of nodes that fall into its transmission range, and n_i corresponds to the cardinality of N_i. In our model, $Link(i, j)$ is treated differently from $Link(j, i)$. $Link(i, j)$ represents the link that node v_i is the transmitter and node v_j is the receiver, while $Link(j,i)$ denotes the link that node v_j is the transmitter and node v_i is the receiver.

To address the problem in more detail, we first give some definitions.

Definition 1: At a given time slot t, $P_L(i,j)$ is defined as the function for calculating the probability that time slot t is collision-free for $Link(i,j)$.

$$P_L(i,j) = P_T P_R (1 - P_T)^{n_j - 1} \tag{1}$$

It is easy to see that time slot t is collision-free for $Link(i,j)$ if and only if node v_i is in transmit state, and node v_j is in receive state, while all other neighbors of node v_j are in non-transmit states at this time slot.

Let $S_{i,j}$ denote the number of time slots that should be consumed to guarantee that node v_j can successfully receives the packet from its neighbor node v_i with specified packet successful delivery probability. $C_{i,j}$ denotes the total number of collision-free time slots among $S_{i,j}$ time slots. Since the states at different time slots are independent, $C_{i,j}$ can be modeled as a binomial random variable:

$$C_{i,j} \sim Binomial(S_{i,j}, P_L(i,j)) \tag{2}$$

Definition 2: $P_L(i,j,S_{i,j})$ is the function for computing the probability that at least one time slot is collision-free in the $S_{i,j}$ time slots.

$$\begin{aligned} P_L(i,j,S_{i,j}) &= P(C_{i,j} \geq 1) = 1 - P(C_{i,j} = 0) \\ &= 1 - [1 - P_T P_R (1 - P_T)^{n_j - 1}]^{S_{i,j}} \end{aligned} \tag{3}$$

$P_L(i,j,S_{i,j})$ is called the *per-link packet successful delivery probability* (PPSDP) in our model. Given a threshold T for $P_L(i,j,S_{i,j})$, $S_{i,j}$ can be calculated using the following equation.

$$S_{i,j} = \left\lceil \frac{\log(1-T)}{\log(1 - P_T P_R (1 - P_T)^{n_j - 1})} \right\rceil \tag{4}$$

Definition 3: Let $P(i)$ denote the path from node v_i to the sink, and $E(i)$ be the set of links on $P(i)$. $L(v_i)$ is defined as the latency for delivering a packet from node v_i to the sink on the condition that each link in $E(i)$ has the same per-link packet successful delivery probability T.

$$L(v_i) = \sum_{(k,j) \in E(i)} S_{k,j} \tag{5}$$

In fact, $L(v_i)$ is the maximum latency for delivering a packet for node v_i to the sink because our model is based on random channel access.

In our model, each $Link(i,j)$ is assigned with the same per-link packet successful delivery probability. Our primary goal is to construct an optimal data gathering tree for any given graph G, which can minimize packet delivery latency for each node while providing guaranteed per-link packet successful delivery probability. We call this problem as *Optimal data gathering tree construction problem*(ODGTCP), which can be generalized as an optimization problem as follows:

$$\begin{aligned} \min_{(v_1, v_2 \ldots, v_n)} \quad & L(v_i) \\ s.t. \quad & P_L(k,j,S_{k,j}) \geq T \qquad (k,j) \in E(i) \end{aligned} \tag{6}$$

Where T is the user specified threshold for $P_L(k,j,S_{k,j})$.

4 Solution

4.1 Optimal Data Gathering Tree Construction

All our algorithms are centralized and performed at the sink node. We assume that the sink node knows the whole topology of the network. In practical applications, a neighbor discovery process should be firstly performed, and the neighbor information for each node should be delivered to the sink.

We propose a sink targeted shortest path algorithm(STSPA) for constructing the optimal data gathering tree. In our algorithm, each node maintains a distance label, which is the upper bound on the shortest path length from this node to the sink node, and we define the distance label as $L(v_i)$. The algorithm designates a set of nodes, say S, as permanently labeled and the remaining set of nodes, say $\bar{S}$, as temporarily labeled. At each iteration, the algorithm designates a node v_i with the minimum temporary delivery latency as permanent node, and then examines each incoming $Link(j,i)$ and modifies the latency of node v_j to $min\{L(v_j), L(v_i) + S_{j,i}\}$.

Proposition 1. Given any node $v_i \in V$, $\forall v_j \in N_i$, $\forall v_k \in N_i$, $S_{j,i} = S_{k,i}$.

Proof. In our model, all the nodes have the same P_T,P_R and P_S. According to Def(1), $\forall v_j \in N_i$, and $\forall v_k \in N_i$, $P_L(j,i) = P_L(k,i)$, which are all determined by the number of neighbors n_i of node v_i. Since each link of the network is assigned with the same successful packet delivery probability T, then according to Eq.(4), $S_{j,i} = S_{k,i}$.

It is clear from Proposition 1 that for any node v_i, all its neighbors need the same number of time slots to ensure that their packets can be successfully delivered to node v_i with specified per-link packet successful delivery probability T. Thus, there may be multiple nodes in $\bar{S}$ that have the same minimum temporary latency. A best node should be selected among these nodes if this case occurs. For each node v_i, let *hop*(v_i) denote the minimum number of hops that a packet issued by this node to the sink must travel, then the maximum successful delivery probability of node v_i is $T^{hop(v_i)}, 0 < T \leq 1$. To maximize the successful delivery probability, the optimal node should be the node with minimum hops.

Now we present the optimal data gathering tree construction algorithm STSPA.

Algorithm. STSPA(G,P_T,P_R,T)

Initialize P_T,P_R and T;
for each $Link(i,j)$ in G calculate $S_{i,j}$;
S={v_1}; $\bar{S} = V - \{v_1\}$;
$L(v_1) = 0$ and $pred(v_1) = 0$;
for each node v_i
  if $v_i \in N(1)$;
    $L(v_i) = S_{i,1}$, $hop(v_i) = 1$;
  else $L(v_i) = \infty$, $hop(v_i) = \infty$;
while $|S| < n$
  C=min{L(j); $j \in \bar{S}$};
  if $|C| > 1$
  let $v_j \in$ C that $hop(v) = min\{hop(j)|j \in C\}$;
  else v_j is the unique node in C;
  $S = S + v_j$; $\bar{S} = \bar{S} - v_j$
  for each $v_i \in \bar{S}$;
  if $L(v_i) > L(v_j + S_{i,j})$;
    $L(v_i) = L(v_j + S_{i,j})$
    $pred(v_i) = j$; $hop(v_i) = hop(v_j) + 1$;

It is easy to see that the running time of this algorithm is $O(n^2)$, where n is the number of nodes of WSN.

4.2 Optimal P_T, P_R Selection

Give fixed P_T, P_R and expected per-link packet successful delivery probability T, the optimal data gathering tree can be constructed using STSPA algorithm. However, all the nodes have the same P_T,P_R and P_S in our model. Therefore, the selection of optimal channel access parameters is very important, otherwise, the delivery latency for each node may not be minimized.

It can be easily seen from Eq.(4) that given any $T > 0.25$, $S_{i,j} \geq 1$. In this subsection, we first give the lower bound of $S_{i,j}$ for each link, and then simplify the optimal channel access parameters calculation problem as one-dimensional global minimization problem and use a recursive random search algorithm(RRS) to obtain the near-optimal solution.

Theorem 1. Given the guaranteed per-link successful packet delivery probability T , the minimum number of time slots $S_{i,j}$ for $Link(i,j)$ is $\lceil \frac{\log(1-T)}{\log(1-\alpha)} \rceil$ where $\alpha = \frac{1}{n_j+1}(\frac{n_j}{n_j+1})^{n_j}$, only when $P_T = \frac{1}{n_j+1}$ and $P_R = 1 - \frac{1}{n_j+1}$.

Proof. Given the expected per-link packet successful delivery probability T, $S_{i,j}$ is determined by P_T, P_R and n_j. Thus, the problem of finding the minimum for $S_{i,j}$ can be generalized as the follow optimization problem.

$$
\begin{array}{lll}
\min_{(i,j)\in E} & S_{i,j} = \lceil \frac{\log(1-T)}{\log(1-P_T P_R (1-P_T)^{n_j-1})} \rceil & \\
& s.t. \quad 0 < P_T < 1 & \\
& \quad 0 < P_R < 1 & \\
& \quad 0 < P_T + P_R \leq 1 &
\end{array} \tag{7}
$$

Note that $0 < 1 - P_T P_R (1 - P_T)^{n_j - 1} < 1$ and $0 < 1 - T < 1$, Problem 6 is equivalent to the following problem.

$$
\begin{array}{ll}
\max_{v_j \in V} & f(P_T, P_R) = P_T P_R (1 - P_T)^{n_j - 1} \\
& s.t. \quad 0 < P_T < 1 \\
& \quad 0 < P_R < 1 \\
& \quad 0 < P_T + P_R \leq 1
\end{array} \tag{8}
$$

Because $f(P_T, P_R)$ is continuous when $0 < P_T < 1$, $0 < P_R < 1$ and $0 < P_T + P_R \leq 1$, there must be a maximum value for $f(P_T, P_R)$ by Weierstrass Theorem. The maximum will be obtained either at the edge point or at the point satisfying the following equations set.

$$
\begin{cases}
\frac{\partial f(P_T, P_R)}{\partial P_R} = P_T (1 - P_T)^{n_i - 1} = 0 \\
\frac{\partial f(P_T, P_R)}{\partial P_R} = P_R (1 - P_T)^{n_i - 1} \\
\qquad\qquad -(n_i - 1) P_T P_R (1 - P_T)^{n_i - 2} = 0
\end{cases} \tag{9}
$$

It is easy to see that equations set (8) has no solution, thus $f(P_T, P_R)$ will get the maximum when $P_T + P_R = 1$. Then $f(P_T, P_R) = P_T (1 - P_T)^{n_j}$, and the maximum is obtained if and only if $P_T = \frac{1}{n_j+1}$ and $P_R = 1 - \frac{1}{n_j+1}$.

Let $\alpha = \frac{1}{n_j+1} (\frac{n_j}{n_j+1})^{n_j}$. Therefore, the minimal $S_{i,j}$ for $Link(i, j)$ is $\lceil \frac{\log(1-T)}{\log(1-\alpha)} \rceil$.

From Theorem 1, we can see that the minimum $S_{i,j}$ is only dependent on the number of neighbors of node v_j, so our model is more scalable, but $S_{i,j}$ is sensitive to n_j. In many applications, the packet is very small. For example, beep-like packet only contains several bytes besides the header, and the time slot can be less than 10ms. Therefore, even a node has 20 neighbors, the lower bound for $S_{i,j}$ is no larger than 2sec when T=0.9.

However, Theorem 1 just gives the lower bound for each $S_{i,j}$. Let $S^*_{i,j}$ denote the lower bound for $S_{i,j}$ and let $L^*(v_i)$ be the packet delivery latency for node v_i when each $Link(i, j)$ is assigned with $S^*_{i,j}$ time slots. Obviously, $L^*(v_i)$ is also the lower bound for $L(v_i)$. Note that no feasible P_T and P_R can ensure that each $L(v_i)$ gets the lower bound if different node has different number of neighbors, but $L^*(v_i)$ can be used as a benchmark for computing the optimal P_T and P_R.

Clearly, the closer of each $L(v_i)$ to $L^*(v_i)$, P_T and P_R would be more suitable for the network. Therefore, the optimal P_T and P_R calculation problem can be be generalized as the following optimization problem:

$$
\begin{aligned}
Minimize \quad J(P_T, P_R) &= \sum_{i=1}^{n} [L(v(i)) - L^*(v(i))] \\
&= \sum_{i=1}^{n} [\sum_{(k,j)\in P(i)} S_{k,j} - \sum_{(l,n)\in P^*(i)} S^*_{l,n}]
\end{aligned} \tag{10}
$$

where $P(i)$ denotes the path form node v_i to the sink in the tree constructed with P_T and P_R, while $P^*(i)$ represents the path form node v_i to the sink in the tree constructed when each $Link(i, j)$ is assigned with $S^*_{i,j}$ time slots.

Proposition 2. $J(P_T, P_R)$ can be minimized only when $P_S = 0$.

Proof. *Let $S_{i,j}(\alpha, \beta)$ be the minimum time slots allotted to $Link(i, j)$ and $L(v_i, \alpha, \beta)$ be the minimum latency for node v_i when $P_T = \alpha$ and $P_R = \beta$. Suppose that $J(P_T, P_R)$ is minimized when $P_T = \gamma$ and $P_R = \delta < 1 - \gamma$. For any $Link(i, j)$ in E, $S_{i,j}(\gamma, \delta) > S_{i,j}(\gamma, 1 - \gamma)$, which can be easily seen from Eq.(4). Therefore, for any node v_i in V, $L(v_i, \gamma, \delta) > L(v_i, \gamma, 1 - \gamma)$. Clearly, $J(\gamma, \delta) > J(\gamma, 1 - \gamma)$, which is contrary to the assumption.*

Proposition 3. Let P^* be the optimal value for P_T, $n_{max} = \max\{n_i, i \in [1..n]\}$, $n_{min} = \min\{n_i, i \in [1..n]\}$, then $P^* \in [\frac{1}{n_{max}+1}, \frac{1}{n_{min}+1}]$.

Proof. $\forall\, p \in (0, \frac{1}{n_{max}+1})$, let $S_{i,j}(p)$ denote the number of time slots required for $Link(i, j)$ and $L(v_i, p)$ be the latency for node v_i when $P_T = p$ and $P_R = 1 - p$. According to Theorem 1, for any $Link(i, j)$, we can get $S_{i,j}(p) > S_{i,j}(\frac{1}{n_{max}+1})$, and it can also be easily seen from Fig.1. Thus, $L(v_i, p) > L(v_i, \frac{1}{n_{max}+1})$, then we get $J(p, 1 - p) > J(\frac{1}{n_{max}+1}, 1 - \frac{1}{n_{max}+1})$. For any $p \in (\frac{1}{n_{min}+1}, 1)$, the proof is the same. Therefore, $P^* \in [\frac{1}{n_{max}+1}, \frac{1}{n_{min}+1}]$.

Based on Proposition 2 and 3, Problem 10 can be simplified as the following one dimensional minimization problem.

$$\begin{aligned} & Minimize \quad J(P) = \sum_{i=1}^{n} [L(v(i)) - L^*(v(i))] \\ & s.t. \quad \tfrac{1}{n_{max}+1} \le P \le \tfrac{1}{n_{min}+1} \end{aligned} \tag{11}$$

In this problem, the objective function $J(P)$ is non-linear, non-differentiable and even may be multi-model. This type of problems are also called "black-box" optimization problems where the objective function is modeled as black box. Most of black-box optimization problems are NP-hard and can only be solved for near-optimal solutions with heuristic search algorithms.

Many heuristic search algorithms have been proposed and demonstrated to be very successful in practice, such as, multi-start hill-climbing, genetic algorithm and simulated annealing. Because the black-box optimization problem is not the core of this paper, we directly use the recursive random search(RRS) algorithm proposed in [10] to compute the near-optimal value for P_T. RRS is able to provide a strong probabilistic convergence guarantee. Furthermore, it overcomes the drawbacks of random search and is very suitable for our problem. Due to the limited space, we omit the description of RRS algorithm in this paper.

5 Simulation and Performance Evaluation

In this section, we evaluate the performance of our model through extensive simulation experiments. A simulator was developed using the QualNet[11] software, and three metrics were employed in our experiments: average packets delivery ratio and average packets delivery latency and robustness to environmental interference.

5.1 Simulation Setup

In our simulation experiments, we randomly deploy 88 sensor nodes in a 10×10 $unit^2$ region, with the sink being placed in the center. we model the spatial distribution of these sensors as a two-dimensional Poisson point process with intensity λ per $unit^2$. However, our model is applicable to any deployment of sensors. Each node has the same transmission range R, and we control the number of neighbors for the nodes by adjusting parameter R. Consider the scenario in practical applications, the distance between any two nodes should not be too close, and we use a parameter T_{md}(threshold for the minimum distance between two nodes) to ensure this when deploying nodes. Fig.1 (a) gives the node deployment and connectivity graph and Fig.1(b) shows the optimal data gathering tree constructed.

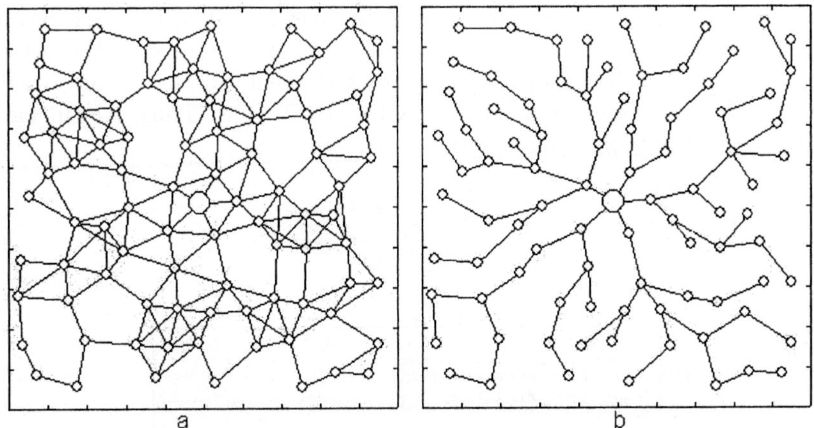

Fig. 1. (a)Connectivity graph generated by 88 sensors nodes with $\lambda = 0.7$ per $unit^2$ and R=1.3unit, T_{md}=0.2unit, $n_{max} = 7$,$n_{min} = 2$.(b)Optimal data gathering tree constructed by STSPA for the network showed in Fig.1 (a) with $P_T = 0.15, P_R = 0.85$.

5.2 Reliability and Latency Tradeoffs

We first evaluate the reliability of our model for data gathering by tuning the expected per-link packet successful delivery probability. In our simulation model,

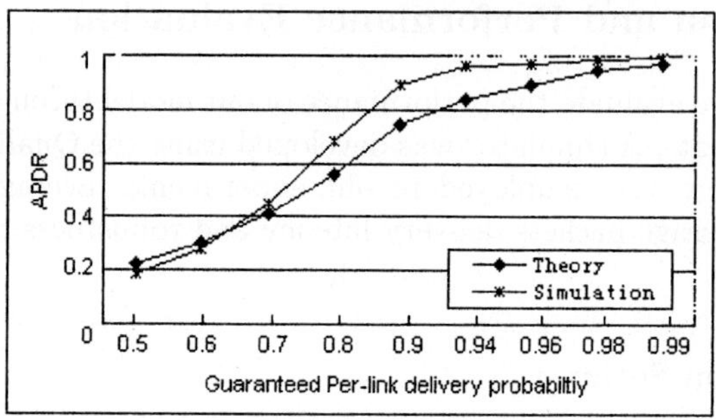

Fig. 2. Average packet delivery ratio(APDR) with different guaranteed per-link packet delivery probability

all the nodes report their reading to the sink periodically. Let τ denote the data gathering interval for the network, and τ can be fixed by the application. In our simulation, we define τ as the max latency $L(v_i)$ among the nodes. In WSNs, data fusion and aggregation have been proved to be an effective way to enhance packet delivery ratio. In our simulation, each node can fuse its reading into the packet that it receives from its child node and then forwards the packet to its parent node.

We measure the reliability of data gathering using the average packet delivery ratio metric, and we define the average packet delivery ratio(APDR) as the number of nodes(n_{succ}) that can successfully send packet to the sink in a data gathering interval to the number of nodes (n) that composed of the network. Since our model is based on random-access channel, all the results obtained in our experiments are averaged over N (N=1000) runs. Thus, APDR can be calculated used the following equation.

$$APDR = \frac{1}{N} \sum_{i=1}^{N} \frac{n_{succ}}{n} \tag{12}$$

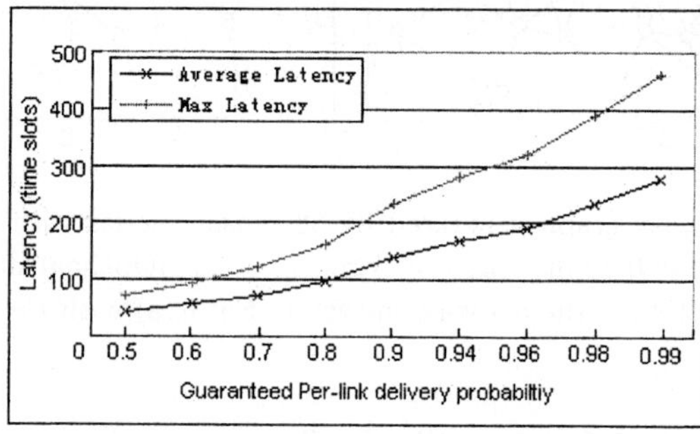

Fig. 3. Average and max data delivery latency with different per-link packet successful delivery probability

Fig.2 shows the simulation results with different PPSDP. We compare the results with the theoretical results. It is easy to see that the simulation results are very close to the theoretical results when PPSDP is relative small, for instance, when $PSPDP < 0.7$. However, when PPSDP increases, the APDR obtained from simulation becomes higher than the theoretical results. The reason for this case is obvious. Because each immediate node can fuse its reading in the packet it receives, the probability that an immediate node's reading being delivered to sink by packet issued by its descendants becomes higher with the increase of PPSDP. Thus, APDR will be greatly improved.

Fig.3 depicts the average and max latency with different PPSDP. By analyzing Fig.3 together with Fig.2, the tradeoff between reliability and latency is clear, and different applications can select different tradeoff between them. For example, the improvement of APDR is only 3.7% when we change PPSDP from 0.94 to 0.99, but the average latency and max latency have been prolonged by 102 and 182 time slots respectively.

5.3 Robustness to Environmental Interference

In our model, we assume that packets collision is the key factor for data loss in random access wireless sensor networks. However, in real-time applications, the links are error-prone due to the environmental interference. To investigate the robustness of our model to the environmental noise, we model the number of error links at a give time slot as a one-dimensional Poisson distributed with parameter λ. Fig.4 illustrates the changes of APDR with the increase of λ. When $\lambda = 20$, the external interference is very serious, but APDR drops only 4.7% compared with the case that there is no external interference.

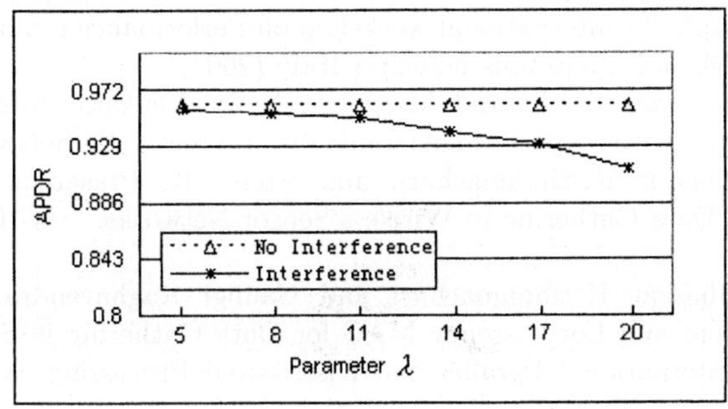

Fig. 4. Average packet delivery ratio for different external interference

6 Conclusion

Data delivery reliability and latency are two important problems in wireless sensor networks. Different applications may have different requirements for this two factors. In this paper, we explore the reliability and latency tradeoffs for data gathering in random-access multi-hop wireless sensor networks. A model considering both packet delivery reliability and latency is proposed and solutions for optimal data gathering tree construction and optimal channel access parameters calculation are presented. Extensive simulation experiments have been performed to evaluate the performance of our model, and results show that our model has a good tradeoff between reliability and latency for data gathering in wireless sensor network. Further, it is worth noting that our model is robust to environmental interference and suitable for practical applications.

Acknowledgement

This work is supported by the 21st Century Center of Excellence Program in JAIST on "Verifiable and Evolvable e-Society".

References

1. Jerry Zhao and Ramesh Govindan.: Understanding Packet Delivery Performance In Dense Wireless Sensor Networks. Sensys03, Los Angeles, CA, USA (2003)
2. E. Biagioni, S. Chen.: A Reliability Layer for Ad-Hoc Wireless Sensor Network Routing. The 37th Hawaii International Conference on System Sciences (2004)
3. Aditya Karnik, Anurag Kumar:Distributed Optimal Self-Organisation in a Class of Wireless Sensor Networks. in IEEE INFOCOM (2004)
4. Alberto Cerpa and Deborah Estrin.: ASCENT: Adaptive Self-Configuring sEnsor Networks Topologies. In the IEEE Transactions on Mobile Computing Special Issue on Mission-Oriented Sensor Networks, Volume 3, Number 3, (2004) 272-285
5. Ioannis Chatzigiannakis,Athanassios Kinalis,Sotiris Nikoletseas: Wireless sensor networks protocols for efficient collision avoidance in multi-path data propagation. The 1st ACM international workshop on Performance evaluation of wireless ad hoc, sensor, and ubiquitous networks,Italy (2004)
6. Qi Han, Iosif Lazaridis, Sharad Mehrotra, Nalini Venkatasubramanian.: Sensor Data Collection with Expected Reliability Guarantees. PerSeNS (2005)
7. Yang Yu, Bhaskar Krishnamachari, and Viktor K. Prasanna.:Energy-Latency Tradeoffs for Data Gathering in Wireless Sensor Networks. in IEEE INFOCOM (2004)
8. Gang Lu, Bhaskar Krishnamachari and Cauligi Raghavendra.: An Adaptive Energy-Efficient and Low-Latency MAC for Data Gathering in Sensor Networks. IEEE 18th International Parallel and Distributed Processing Symposium, April (2004)
9. Abtin Keshavarzian, Elif Uysal-Biyikoglu.: Energy-efficient Link Assessment in Wireless Sensor Networks. INFOCOM (2004)
10. Tao Ye, Shivkumar Kalyanaraman.: A recursive random search algorithm for large-scale network parameter configuration. ACM SIGMETRICS international conference on Measurement and modeling of computer systems (2003)
11. http://www.scalable-networks.com/

An Optimistic Replication Algorithm to Improve Consistency for Massive Data*

Jing Zhou, Yijie Wang, and Sikun Li

School of Computer Science, National University of Defense Technology, China
jingle77@126.com

Abstract. Data replication introduces well-known consistency issues. For massive data, how to improve update propagation and how to minimizing space overhead effectually are important. An optimistic replication algorithm is proposed. In our algorithm, home replica is used to resolve updates conflict and pair-wise communication supports the reconciliation of any two replicas. A new anti-entropy partner selection method based on the distribution of updates and the information of local write-log is presented. The algorithm uses write-log truncation appropriately during updates propagation to remove out-of-date updates in time. The simulation results show that the partner selection mechanism can achieve good scalability and adaptability, the average number of updates in write-log does not exceed the number of replicas, and the variety for running different numbers of updates is not obvious.

1 Introduction

Data grid [1, 2] and peer-to-peer distributed storage [3, 4] are effective approaches to manage massive datasets, which are terabytes or petabytes of information in wide-area, distributed, data-intensive, high-performance computing environments. As for massive datasets, not only the data gross amount is huge, but also single data object is enormous. Hence, it is often desirable to make copies or replicas of the data to minimize access time and network load.

Data replication is a fundamental technique for improving the performance, availability, and persistence of large-scale distributed systems. Because no replication system can have perfect performance properties or perfect availability and consistency, systems designed for different environments make different trade-offs among these factors by implementing different consistency policies.

We describe an optimistic replication algorithm to improve consistency and to offer effective write-log management (CWLM) for massive datasets, which is based on three principles: *log-transfer*, update conflict reconciliation using *home replica* [5] method, and update propagation by *pair-wise communication*.

* This work is supported by the National Grand Fundamental Research 973 Program of China (No.2002CB312105), A Foundation for the Author of National Excellent Doctoral Dissertation of PR China (No.200141), and the National Natural Science Foundation of China (No.69903011).

H. Zhuge and G.C. Fox (Eds.): GCC 2005, LNCS 3795, pp. 713–718, 2005.

The remainder of this paper is organized as follows. We describe our algorithm in detail in Section 2, and discuss two extensions that arise in practice in Section 3. Section 4 evaluates the design experimentally and Section 5 highlights our conclusions.

2 The Optimistic Replication Algorithm

We make some assumptions about the environment for CWLM: Any replica may be read or written at any time. Replicas exchange updates in a peer-to-peer fashion. There are replica additions, removals, failures and network partitioning. The replicas have loosely synchronized clocks. The home replica has strong process ability and reliable performance so that there is not bottleneck during system running.

In CWLM, the Update record represents an update to the object, which consists of five fields. Its *NodeID* field indicates on which replica is this update firstly received from external applications. *Clock* field records the wall-clock time when the update is received on *NodeID* replica. As the home commits an update, it assigns a monotonically increasing commit sequence number (*CSN*) to the update. *DoneR* field specifies the set of replicas that have acknowledged the update. *UpdateBody* field describes the body of the update.

For every replica, there is a *write-log* to record the following data structures: Committed update vector (*CUV*) records all the committed update that this replica has received. Tentative update vector (*TUV*) records updates received by this replica but have not been committed. *TargetR* is a set of replicas and the member of *TargetR* is the replica that should receive the update. *R.DCSN* is a utility statistic information we deduce from *CUV* and *TUV*, which is the *CSN* of the committed update that was just been removed from R.

Home replica is used to resolve update conflict because which commits updates with much less communication potentially. There is an additional data structure for home replica. Committing vector (*CV*) is maintained to hold the information of sites and clock in turn where and when the committed update has been received firstly.

2.1 Partner Selection of Update Propagation

Pair-wise anti-entropy communication supports the peer-to-peer reconciliation of any two replicas independently of the variety of possibly changing communication topologies. One replica brings another one up-to-date by propagating missing updates to the receiving replica. Optimal policies for choosing anti-entropy partners depend on a number of complex factors such as available bandwidth and cost of communication.

In CWLM, we choose partners based on the order of committing update and the information of local write-log, as is shown in Figure 1. During partner selection, an update occurrence factor (*uof*) as shown formula (1) in Figure 1 is introduced for the motive to dynamically self-adaptive the random of update arising and to avoid depressing performance for too frequent sessions on some one replica, which takes the number and distribution of updates into account synthetically. In the formula, it is to assume that the latest update information has been added into *CV*.

```
SelectPartner(R)
  //For home replica
    if   R has sent request of committing update w to home replica recently   then
      if (L = 1)   then R.AEP = φ       // L is the size of CV
        else if (CV(L−1).NodeID = CV(L−2).NodeID = R)     then R.AEP = φ
```

$$\text{else} \quad uof = \sum_{i=1}^{L-1} \frac{(CV(L-1).Clock - CV(0).Clock)}{(CV(i).Clock - CV(0).Clock)} \qquad (1)$$

Where $(CV(i).NodeID = CV(L-1).NodeID)$ for the members in CV

```
          if (uof < Δf)     then R.AEP = φ
            else  R.AEP = CV(L−2).NodeID
      return R.AEP      // R.AEP is returned by home replica with committed update
  //For replica R
    Initializing partner: R.AEP = φ
    if    R.AEP ≠ φ     then
      anti-entropy is initiated between R and R.AEP
      else if  some replicas have not communicated with others for Δt  then
               // Making the choice of partners based on CUVs in their local write-logs.
               TempSet = TargetR − {u.NodeID | u ∈ R.CUV}
               if    TempSet ≠ φ     then
                  Choosing some one of TempSet as R.AEP randomly
                  else  R.AEP = u.NodeID    Where u ∈ R.CUV and
                        u.CSN = max{u'.CSN | u' ∈ R.CUV ∧ u'.NodeID ≠ R}
```

Fig. 1. Partner selection. *R.AEP* is the partner of incoming anti-entropy of replica R.

2.2 Sending and Receiving Updates

Our algorithm in reconciliation based on Bayou [6] improves on information comparison and truncating write-log. For two replicas in communicating, it distinguishes sender replica from receiver. Updates flow only from the sender to the receiver. At the beginning of one session, the sender acquires the update control information from the receiver. Then, comparisons are done at the sender and updates are sent to the receiver. Finally, the receiver deals with the update according to the information.

The comparisons done at the sender process on three levels: Firstly, a full data object transfer will be carried out in case that the sender has truncated any updates that the receiver has missed, which occurs usually after failure nodes recover. Secondly, because updates may be propagated along two completely different paths, so for the same updates, the *DoneR*s of sender and receiver are united. It can accelerate the *DoneR* to the *TragetR*. Lastly, the sender checks if there are updates that have not been received by receiver.

As we have known that *DoneR* is introduced to record what replicas have received the update, the comparison during the above process is processed according to different issuers, which can enhance the accuracy of comparison. Whereas write-log truncations impenetrate into the processes of sending and receiving, the size of every parameter is control to be small that will not increase the cost of communication.

2.3 Write-Log Management

Once the *DoneR* vector of the update in local write-log is same to the *TargetR* vector and the replica has received all the updates of small *CSN*, this update is taken as being valid to the local replica, which should be executed and removed from local write-log.

CWLM introduces *WaitRemoveList* to record updates that meet the former condition but miss the latter. It is caused mostly of indeterminate network delay. When new removing occurs, we will check if updates in the list can meet the removed condition.

Additionally, updates for some replica may not meet the removed condition, but the status of other replicas is removed, which is brought also from network delay. We introduce *R.DCSN* to enhance truncating. The process is described in Figure 2.

TruncateLog(R, w)

if $w.DoneR = w.TargetR$ **then**

  if $w.CSN = \min\{u.CSN \mid u \in R.CUV\}$ **then**

    Execute w to the local replica, Remove w from local write-log and $R.DCSN = w.CSN$

    while $\left(WaitRemoveList \neq \phi \wedge WaitRemoveList.head{=}min\{u.CSN \mid u \in R.CUV\}\right)$ **do**

      Execute $u \mid (u \in R.CUV \wedge u.CSN = WaitRemoveList.head)$ to the local replica, Remove u from local write-log, Remove $u.CSN$ from $WaitRemoveList$ and $R.DCSN = u.CSN$

TruncateLog(R,w,S.DCSN)

if $S.DCSN \geq 0$ **then** $TS = \{u \mid u \in R.CUV \wedge u.CSN \leq S.DCSN\}$

  if $TS \neq \phi$ **then for** *each* $u \in TS$

    Execute u to the local replica, Remove u from local write-log and $R.DCSN = u.CSN$

Fig. 2. Write-log truncation. R is the replica where is to truncate and S is the session partner.

It is obvious that update propagation is rapider; the course to fill the gap between *DoneR* and *TargetR* is shorter. But there are often node and link node failures or sudden node retirements. Such replicas create an unbounded amount of backlog of updates that eventually fill up the disks on other replicas. We will present solution next.

3 Extensions

In the real world, there are often crash or never recover for computers and network connections failures. Our algorithm handles such a situation by setting up *BlackList*. When a replica finds that the difference between *DoneR* and *TargetR* of some one update is very little, it tries to communicate with replicas not in *DoneR*. If it cannot receive feedback for several times from session partner, the partner replica is added to *BlackList* and which is propagated in system with updates. When a replica has been in *BlackList* for a predefined period, the replica is thought to be long-term failure and cannot recover again. Then, the replica will be removed from *TargetR*.

The system for creating additional replicas is run when a user tries to access a data object not present in its local node. A replica is removed because the node has run out of disk space or the cost of keeping the replica outweighs its benefits. To create a replica X, it is always to forward the replicate request to a nearby existing replica X′. This request is met and X′ integrates the new replica X into *TargetR* so that X can propagate updates and receive updates from other replicas. Similarly, to remove a replica R, R sends notices to a nearby existing replica R′ before it is removed really. Thus R′ removes R from *TargetR* set and the new set is propagated in replicas.

4 Simulation

OptorSim [7, 8] was developed to study the complex nature of a typical Data Grid and to evaluate the effectiveness of replica optimization algorithms.

In our simulation, parameters are set as followings: The size of each data object is 1GB and each update is 100MB. The time required to send a message from one replica to another was assumed to be negligible compared to the time between anti-entropy sessions. Time is measured as the mean interval from initiating an anti-entropy event to the session end. Δt is two time units and Δf is 0.6.

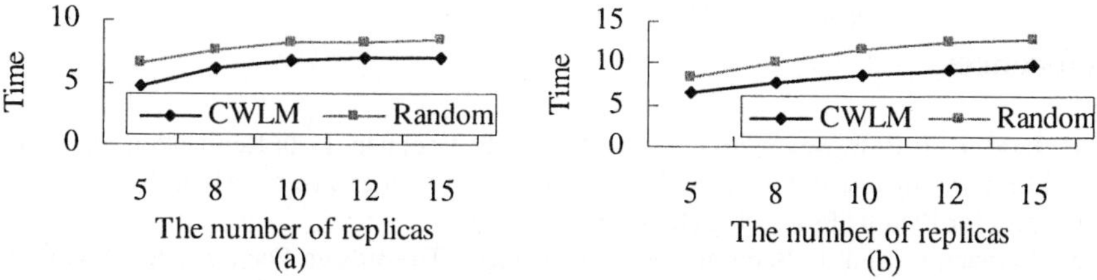

Fig. 3. (a) The time that an update has been received by all replicas for varying numbers of replicas. (b) The latency required from the time when an update is issued to the time when acknowledgments are received by every replica. The outcomes show that our method is superior.

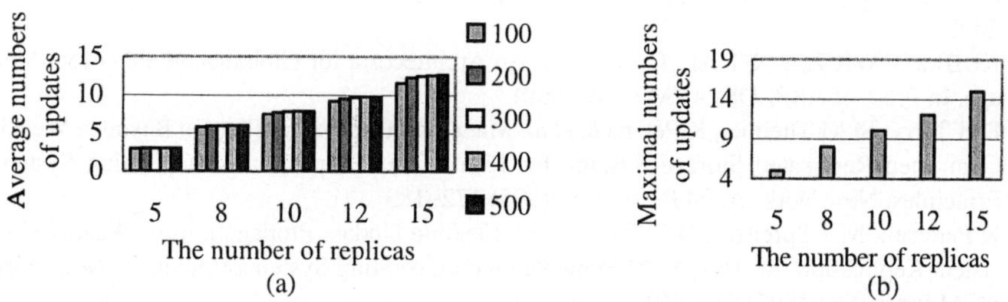

Fig. 4. (a) Average number of updates in write-log. (b) Maximal number of updates in write-log. The outcomes show that the average number of updates does not exceed the number of replicas, and the variety for running different numbers of updates is not obvious. The maximal number of updates is equal to the number of replicas. That is to prove that CWLM can offer lesser space overhead.

We test our algorithm from two aspects. The first one is shown in Figure 3. The simulator was run until 500 updates had been processed. Likewise, we simulate *random* partner selection and compare its outcomes with our method. The second test is to observe the space overhead in write-log, as is shown in Figure 4. The simulator was run until 100, 200, 300, 400 and 500 updates had been processed respectively.

5 Conclusions and Future Work

CWLM is an optimistic consistency algorithm to provide effective write-log space overhead designed for massive data in peer-to-peer system.

We take distribution of updates into account and avoid maintaining a great deal of management information or measuring the state of other replicas. The partner selection mechanism is topology independence and it can achieve good scalability, adaptability and ease of implementation. Truncating write-log in time is based on propagating updates rapidly. We analyze the occasion that updates would be removed and import truncating timing, so the outdated updates cannot possess write-log space.

As to future work, we plan to expand the scale of simulations, and study the setting about key parameters. In addition, we want to discard home replica and investigate data consistency in a fully peer-to-peer environment.

References

1. H. Lamehamedi, B. Szymanski, Z. shentu, and E. Deelman. Data Replication Strategies in Grid Environments. Proc. Of the Fifth International Conference on Algorithms and Architectures for Parallel Processing (ICA3PP'02), 2002.
2. M. Carman, F. Zini, L. Serafini, and K. Stockinger. Towards an Economy-Based Optimisation of File Access and Replication on a Data Grid. In Workshop on Agent based Cluster and Grid Computing at Int. Symposium on Cluster Computing and the Grid (CCGrid 2002), Berlin, Germany, May 2002. IEEE-CS Press.
3. A. Adya, W. Bolosky, M. Castro, G. Cermak, R. Chaiken, J. Douceur, J. Howell, J. Lorch, M. Theimer, and R. Wattenhofer. FARSITE: Federated Available and Reliable Storage for Incompletely Trusted Environments. In 5th Symp on Operating Systems Design and Impl. (Dec 2002)
4. KUBIATOWICZ, J., ET AL. Oceanstore: An Architecture for Global-scale Persistent Storage. In Proc. of ASPLOS, ACM (Nov 2000)
5. D B Terry, M M Theimer, K Petersen, *et al.* Managing Update Conflicts in Bayou, a Weakly Connected Replicated Storage System. In: 15th ACM Symposium on Operating Systems Principles. New York: ACM Press (Dec 1995) 172~183
6. K Petersen, M J Spreitzer, D B Terry, *et al.* Flexible Update Propagation for Weakly Consistent Replication. In: 16th ACM Symposium on Operating Systems Principles. New York: ACM Press (Oct 1997) 288~301
7. W. H. Bell, D. G. Cameron, L. Capozza, P. Millar, K. Stockinger, and F. Zini. Optorsim - a Grid Simulator for Studying Dynamic Data Replication Strategies. International Journal of High Performance Computing Applications, Vol. 17(4). (2003)
8. W. H. Bell, D. G. Cameron, L. Capozza, P. Millar, K. Stockinger,and F. Zini. Design of a Replica Optimisation Framework. TechnicalReport DataGrid-02-TED- 021215, CERN, Geneva, Switzerland (Dec 2002)

A SLA-Based Resource Donation Mechanism for Service Hosting Utility Center*

Yufeng Wang, Huaimin Wang, Yan Jia, Dianxi Shi, and Bixin Liu

National University of Defense Technology, ChangSha 410073, China
yfwang@nudt.edu.cn, whm_w@163.com, yanjia@nudt.edu.cn, dxshi@nudt.edu.cn, bxliu@nudt.edu.cn

Abstract. The increasing cost of owning and managing IT systems is leading to outsourcing commercial online services to service hosting utility centers by means of service level agreements (SLAs). Low resource utilization and partial service overload are two main issues in utility centers operation. The paper describes a SLA-based fine-grained resource donation mechanism to encourage applications to share under-utilized server resources. Donated resources can be dynamically borrowed by overloaded applications to relieve transient workload surge. Two donation strategies are presented to compensate the "donors" based on their quantified contribution. Compared with resource stealing, the proposed mechanism has advantages in two-fold. First, it's an incentive-compatible one in that both donor applications and utility centers can benefit from resource donation. Secondly, the donors can manifestly specify donation constraints in SLAs to reflect both QoS requirements and resource consumption patterns, which can help improve reliability of resource sharing.

1 Introduction

Increasing cost of owning dedicated computer systems has been encouraging more and more service providers to run their applications on service hosting centers under the utility computing paradigm. These service hosting centers usually employ cluster of application servers with layered architecture to deploy multiple application under certain SLAs. Service level agreement guarantee has been the basic concern in the design and operation of these utility centers, especially under dynamic Internet workload conditions. However, the unpredictability of clients' scope and visiting patterns makes burstiness a fundamental property of computing systems workload, and be observed across all time scales [1]. Dynamically surging workload is becoming the main cause of service degradation and server overload. On the other hand, statistical observations show that most servers are underutilized in hosting data center environment. For example, the utilization of nearly 80% of thousands of servers of HP Data Center is below 30% [2], which further manifests the inconsistency between overload handling requirements and resource underutilization.

* This research was partially supported by the National Basic Research 973 Program of China (No.2005CB321804), the National Natural Science Foundation of China (No.90412011), the National High Technology Research and Development 863 Program of China (No.2004aa112020).

H. Zhuge and G.C. Fox (Eds.): GCC 2005, LNCS 3795, pp. 719–724, 2005.

To address this inconsistency, several techniques have been proposed for utility computing environment, such as dynamic server allocation [3,8], CPU cycles stealing [4]. Dynamic server allocation scheme reacts to changing workloads by reallocating servers to overloaded applications from free serve pools or under-utilized hosted applications. Although this technique is widely used, server-granularity resource management cannot fully utilize the hosting center resources compared with fine-grained resource sharing [5].CPU cycles stealing, as a well-known technique in grid computing, advocates utilizing fine-grained resources, such as idle CPU cycles, of other applications in a covert way. Because the resource stealer has no ideas of the resource usage pattern of the stolen one, stolen applications will inevitably experience performance disturbance or even SLA violation during stealing process. When commercial services providers pay for the utility server resources under some SLAs, these in-the-dark resource reallocation or stealing mechanisms seem improper. In this paper, we design a SLA-based open resource donation mechanism for component application hosting center with the goal of fully utilizing fine-grained idle server resources to relieve overloaded application. The mechanism encourages hosted applications to donate unused server resources on their own initiative through SLA declaration, and has the donors compensated for their quantified resource contribution in two ways: price refund or higher priority of borrowing donated resources.

The proposed mechanism can complement existing utility center resource management techniques in two aspects. First, it's an incentive-compatible one in that both donor applications and utility centers can benefit from resource donation. Secondly, the donors can manifestly specify resource donation constraints in SLAs to reflect quality of service requirements and resource consumption patterns, which can help improve resource utilization.

To fairly share server resources between underutilized and overloaded applications, several questions must be answered, of which we try to attack the following ones:

- How to reward the donors, based on their actual quantified resource donation?
- How to design resource donation terms in SLAs to reflect donation constraints such as quality of service requirement, privacy and resource usage patterns?
- How to keep the "rascals" from free-riding the donated resources?

This paper describes our initial work on the resource management for overload handling through controlled resource donation and borrowing. The paper is organized as follows. Section 2 gives the background of component application hosting utility centers. Section 3 presents the SLA-based resource donation mechanism and our answers to above three questions. Finally section 4 concludes the paper.

2 Background

Application server technologies such as J2EE greatly simplify the development and deployment of component-based applications, which attracts us to emphasize on component-based application hosting environments. Although component applications are always presented in multi-tier architecture, this paper focuses on resource donation in business logic layer, which is built on application server cluster. Throughout the paper, we refer to the component applications hosting infrastructure simply as *utility center*, which is composed of cluster of application servers and a utility management node which provides workload distribution, SLA monitoring and application reconfiguration. We refer to the component application deployed under certain SLAs as *cluster application*. While the resource of the utility center could be multiplexed by more than one application, each cluster application may behave to its clients as if the whole utility center were exclusively occupied by itself. We refer to the application who donates the under-utilized nodes as *donor application*, and the one who borrows donated nodes as *borrower application*. Figure 1 sketches the relations between utility center and cluster applications and figure 1-(c) shows the case where application R borrows the donated node N3 from the donor application T.

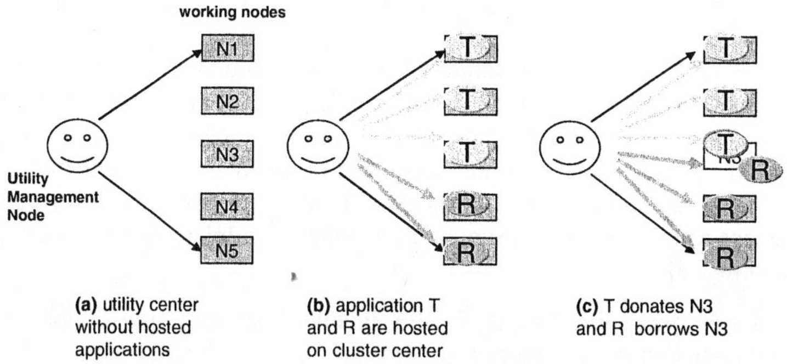

Fig. 1. Utility center and hosted cluster applications

Typically, a cluster application pays the utility center for leasing cluster servers to fulfill their own commercial profits by providing add-value services. Rights and obligations of both sides are often manifestly specified in the service level agreements, including how many server nodes are leased for what price per day, what quality of service should be guaranteed, and what is the penalty for SLA violation [6]. For simplicity of discussion, we only consider average response time as quality of service criterion, and CPU as the resource to be shared.

3 SLA-Based Resource Donation Mechanism

3.1 Incentive Strategies for Donor Applications

Application-unaware dynamic resource provisioning, such as CPU stealing, is an effective method to utilize resource to improve performance under grid environment for scientific computing. However as commercial applications pay for the use of the utility resources under SLAs, we believe it improper to keep application unaware of resources transfer. On the contrary, we advocate an open SLA-based resource donation to aboveboard utilize idle resources in an incentive-compatible way. To encourage cluster applications to share idle resources, incentive measures should be designed so that the donors can see benefits from resource sharing after balancing potential performance disturbance. In our mechanism, we provide two kinds of benefits: price refund or priority of borrowing resources. The main idea behind the mechanism is the more an application shares its resources through donation, the more benefits he can gain.

Price refund. In this incentive strategy, the donor will get price refund when its donated resources are used to partake of the overloaded applications requests. The amount of refund is determined by the amount of gains of utility center through serving these excess requests. For the utility center will incur penalty for SLA violation when turning down workloads, it has the incentive to utilize donated server resources to avoid loss. Price refund for the donor p is computed as follows.

$$\text{refund}_p = d \cdot \lambda \cdot t \cdot c \tag{1}$$

c denotes the gain of serving per request from overloaded application X, λ denotes the average request rates from X on the donated nodes, t denotes time interval for donated nodes being borrowed, and d denotes the *discount rate*, 100% of which means utility center refund all gains to the donor. Discount rate can be specified in SLA by the donor to express the degree of willingness of donation. And the utility center will prefer the donors with lower discount rate, when candidate donors have the same spare capability.

Priority of resources borrowing. In this incentive strategy, the donor who makes more actual contribution (i.e. more resources are borrowed) will obtain higher priority of borrowing resources from others to handle its own overload in the future. Just like insurance business, applications have incentive to donate unused resources for its own performance good in case of overload occurrence. The contribution of the donor p in once resource sharing can be computed according to its actual amount of donated resource as follows.

$$\text{contribution}_p = \lambda \cdot t \cdot s \tag{2}$$

s denotes the average service demand from overloaded application X, λ denotes the average request rates from X on the donated nodes, t denotes time interval for donated nodes being borrowed. In our mechanism, when more than one application needs borrowing resources to handle their overload, the donor who makes the most accumulated contributions will have the highest priority to do so. After an overloaded applications utilize the borrowed notes from the donor p, its contribution will be subtracted by the amount of resource borrowed (i.e. contribution_p). On the other hand, the utility center will choose the donors with the least contribution for resource borrowing to balance the fairness of the whole system.

3.2 SLA-Based Resource Donation

With the proposed incentive measures, both cluster applications and utility center have the incentives to donate and utilize idle server resources. This sections, we describe how SLAs are used to specify donation preconditions and constraints. In our mechanism, hosted cluster applications make SLA-based declarations to specify:

- whether applications are willing to donate resources, and to what degree;
- what preconditions for resource donation, including what time of day to donate resource, to whom the donated resource can be borrowed;
- what constraints to be met during resource sharing.

These declarations are supported through following SLA clauses (see Table 1).

Table 1. SLA-based declarations for resource donation

claus syntax	meaning
SUPPORT *(NO)SHARING* with discount-rate *k%*	"SUPPORT NOSHARING" means application won't donate nodes; otherwise it permits donation with *k%* discount rate.
IF *a*<time<*b* , *resource* utilization< *u%* and borrowed by *A*	The nodes can be donated, only if the borrower comes from set *A*, current time is within [*a*, *b*] range, and *resource* utilization is below *u%*.
CONSTRAINTS *resource* utilization< *v%* and response< *r*	The *resource* utilization should be kept below *v%*, and request response time should be guaranteed less than *r* during resource being borrowed.

For example, the following SLA segment says that an application supports nodes donation only if the time is between 06:00 and 20:00 and CPU utilization is less than 20%, while during resource sharing the CPU utilization should kept below 90% and response time should be less then 150 ms.

> ***SUPPORT*** *SHARING,* ***IF*** *06:00<time<20:00 and CPU utilization < 20%, with* ***CONSTRAINS*** *CPU utilization < 90% and response time < 150ms.*

Note that donor applications can employ donation preconditions in SLAs to specify its own resource usage patterns and privacy considerations. The SLA-based resource donation mechanism can make full use of this heuristic information to evade applications' rush hour to improve resource sharing.

Service level agreements, such as donation constraints, must be well guaranteed during resource borrowing and overload handling. Techniques have been proposed to address this issue in literature [7]. Detailed SLA guarantee mechanisms are beyond the scope of this paper.

3.3 Avoidance of Free-Rider

Although the proposed incentive strategies can well encourage applications to donate idle resources, the mechanism still potentially suffers free-rider [9] from the "rascal" applications, which intentionally lease less server resource than their workload requirements and tap the donors to process their normal "overload". In "priority of resources borrowing" strategy, these rascal applications may utilize donated servers more often than honest applications because of their higher probability of overload occurrence. And in the price refund mode, free-rider harms the benefits of utility centers. To avoid free-rider, our mechanism is enhanced in two aspects. First, the lowest resource contributions threshold is setup, the applications with accumulated contributions below which will be forbidden to borrow resources. Secondly, utility center will punish the hosted applications if their claimed throughput is abnormally lower the actual workload. The concrete definition of "contribution threshold" and "abnormal workload" will be a tricky and application-specific task, which will be further addressed in future work.

4 Conclusions

In this paper, we present an incentive-compatible SLA-based resource donation mechanism to encourage applications to donate under-utilized server resources. Two donation strategies are designed to reward the donors based on their quantified contribution. Compared with covert resource stealing mechanism, active resource donation is more suitable in service hosting utility center environment. Future work will focus on mechanism enhancement to efficiently prevent resource free riding.

References

1. W. Leland, M.S. Taqqu, W. Willinger, and D.V. Wilson. On the Self-Similar Nature of Ethernet Traffic. IEEE/ACM Transactions on Network v2, February 1994.
2. A. Andrzejak, M. Arlitt, and J. Rolia. Bounding the Resource Savings of Utility Computing Models. Technical Report HPL-2002-339, HP Labs, Dec. 2002.
3. Bhuvan Urgaonkar, Prashant Shenoy, Abhishek Chandra, and Pawan Goyal, Agile, Dynamic Capacity Provisioning for Multi-tier Internet Applications, the 2nd IEEE International Conference on Autonomic Computing (ICAC 2005).
4. Ryu, K.D., Hollingsworth, J.K., Resource policing to support fine-grain cycle stealing in networks of workstations, IEEE Transactions on Parallel and Distributed Systems, Volume 15, Issue 10, (2004) 878- 892
5. Abhishek Chandra, Pawan Goyal and Prashant Shenoy□Quantifying the Benefits of Resource Multiplexing in On-Demand Data Centers, Proceedings of the First ACM Workshop on Algorithms and Architectures for Self-Managing Systems (Self-Manage 2003), San Diego, CA, June 2003.
6. A. Hiles, The Complete IT Guide to Service Level Agreements—Matching Service Quality to Business Needs, Rothstein Associates Inc., Brookfield, CT (1999/2000).
7. G. Goldszmidt, K. Appleby, S. Fakhouri, L. Fong, M. Kalantar, S. Krishnakumar, D. Pazel, J. Pershing, and B. Rochwerger. Océano- SLA based management of a computing utility. In 7th IFIP/IEEE International Symposium on Integrated Network Management (IM), May 2001.
8. James Norris, Keith Coleman, Armando Fox, George Candea, OnCall: Defeating Spikes with a Free-Market Application Cluster. ICAC 2004, 198-205.
9. Sujay Sanghavi, Bruce Hajek, A new mechanism for the free-rider problem, Proceeding of the 2005 ACM SIGCOMM workshop on Economics of peer-to-peer systems, Philadelphia, USA, (2005) 122-127.

Credit in the Grid Resource Management*

Manfu Ma, Jian Wu, Shuyu Li, Dingjian Chen,
and Zhengguo Hu

Computer school, Northwestern Polytechnical University,
Xi'an, Shaanxi, 710072, China
mamanff@sohu.com

Abstract. Grid computing systems that have been the focus of much research activities in the past years for controlled sharing of resources across institutional boundaries. Trust is one major concern in grid resource management that enables remote scheduling and execution. Reputation mechanism can be used for providing trust in Grid systems, but the additional overhead caused by it negate the performance advantages gained by Grid computing. Besides, Reputation mechanism is not suitable for large-scale resource sharing. In this paper, we present a credit model for Grid resource management that is based on computational economy and show how the model can be used to incorporate the trust implications into scheduling algorithms. Simulations are performed to evaluate the performance.

1 Introduction

In grid resource management, various approaches [1] have been used in different projects. Among these, the management model based on computation economy [2] has been widely recognized because of its improvement of the efficiency of management and simplification of the complexity of resource scheduling. In the area of computation economic models, lots of research has been investigated, which covers from economic models, security to grid bank. But few works are focused on the credit problem of grid resource. To facilitate resource evaluation, the concept of credit is proposed in this paper. Credit reflects the essence of the resource, that is, whether the resource can be treated as the reliable object. The credit for the Commodity Market Model [1] is investigated in the rest of this paper.

There are a number of parts to the paper. Section 2 provides the concept of credit and relative constituent components. Section 3 describes the credit computation. A credit-based resource scheduling algorithm is proposed in Section 4. Section 5 derives the simulation and analysis for validating the improvement of the credit approach compared with other approaches. In section 6, related work is discussed. We conclude and point our future work in section 7.

* This paper is supported by key project (No. 2GS047-A52-002-04) of Gansu province of China.

H. Zhuge and G.C. Fox (Eds.): GCC 2005, LNCS 3795, pp. 725–731, 2005.

2 Credit Model

2.1 Definition of Trust, Reputation and Credit

The notion of trust, reputation and credit are complex subject relating to a firm belief in attributes such as reliability, honesty, and competence of the trusted entity. There is a lack of consensus in the definition of them. The definition of trust and reputation that we will use in this paper is adopted from Farag Azzedin[3].

Trust is the firm belief in the competence of an entity to act as expected such that this firm belief is not a fixed value associated with the entity but rather it is subject to the entity's behavior and applies only within a specific context at a given time.

The reputation of an entity is an expectation of its behavior based on other entities' observations or information about the entity's past behavior at a given time.

The definition of credit that we will use in this paper is as follows:

The credit of an entity is an expectation of its behavior based on a third party organization's observations or information about the entity's past behavior at a given time.

Like trust and reputation, the credit is a dynamic value and spans over a set of values ranging from very trustworthy state to very untrustworthy state. The credit's level is built on past experience by a third party organization's observations and given for a specific context. When making credit-based decisions, entities can rely on the third party organization for information pertaining to a specific entity. Credit is a unique and public value in the grid administration domain. While reputation is a private value between any two entities and varies with different entities.

2.2 Credit and Constituent Components

Suppose x is a resource identifier that is defined by RUR(Resource Usage Record[4]), then the resource credit $R_c(x)$ can be defined as follows:

$$R_c(x) = \alpha \cdot R_{c,old}(x) + \beta \cdot R_{c,new}(x) \tag{1}$$

$$R_{c,new}(x) = \chi \cdot \frac{\sum_i (b_{io} - b_i)}{\sum_i b_{io}} + \delta \cdot \frac{\sum_i (t_{io} - t_i)}{\sum_i t_{io}} \qquad i=1,2,3,\dots \tag{2}$$

In the equations above, $\alpha, \beta \geq 0, \alpha + \beta = 1. \chi, \delta \geq 0, \chi + \delta = 1$, $b_{io} \geq b_i, t_{io} \geq t_i$, $R_{c,old}(x)$ means the current value of resource credit, that is, the result of latest evaluation. $R_{c,new}(x)$ is the result of current evaluation which including two factors: time and cost. And b_{io} is the budget value of each record and b_i is the actual cost. Similarly, t_{io} is the estimative time and t_i is the actual cost. χ、δ means the contribution rate of the cost and time to the credit respectively. $0 \leq R_c(x) \leq 1$, $R_c(x) = 1$ means the best credit and $R_c(x) = 0$ means the worst credit.

In the equation about $R_{c,new}(x)$, the actual cost will surpass the budget if $b_{io} < b_i$ in certain resource usage. Similarly, the time expended will surpass the budget if $t_{io} < t_i$. Both of these two cases belong to break of contract. After having broken a contract, the update method of resource credit is defined as follows:

$$R_c(x) = (1 - \varepsilon)R_{c,old}(x) \qquad 0 \le \varepsilon \le 1 \tag{3}$$

Credit is a function that varies with time. In certain period T (greater than the evaluation period), if certain resource doesn't produce the new usage record, then its credit function is as follows:

$$R_c(x) = (1 - \phi)R_{c,old}(x) \qquad 0 \le \phi \le 1 \tag{4}$$

Obviously, if resource doesn't provide service for the grid, its credit decreases as time elapses.

3 The Credit Computation

3.1 Credit Coefficient, Initial Value and Update

The coefficient value embodies the corresponding weight. To reflect the more important contribution of the new-arriving scheduling to the credit, the value of β should not be small. The system concerns more about the scheduling cost if $\chi > \delta$, otherwise the system concerns more about the actual finish time of the resource.

The choice of initial credit value closely relates to the resource's behavior in the grid. If a resource finds its credit value is smaller than initial value because of breach of contract, it may choose to register again after having logged out. Setting "0" as the initial credit value may solve this problem, but on the other hand, this may greatly depress the new-coming users and resources. The approach that we have adopted is to delete a record of breach of contract after having dealt with it, which has no effects on the next evaluation. Besides, the credit value will unconditionally smaller than the initial credit value.

There are two approaches that can be used in the update of credit: the event-driven approach and the time-driven approach. Since the credit evaluation is not sensitive to the features of performance and real-time, we believe that the time-driven approach is a more suitable one. The deleting strategy we have adopted is as follows: Deleting its record if a resource has not logged in during a period (three months, for example); deleting the record of the resource provider means deletes all the records of the resources it owns.

3.2 Algorithm Implementation

Suppose τ is the latest evaluating time, $\Delta\tau$ is the inter-evaluating time, $R_{ini}(r_i)$ is the initial value of the resource r_i, then the pseudo-code of the evaluation algorithm is as follows:

```
while ( current time = τ+Δτ)
  collect RUR, price and cost data into CEM database
 for all r_i do
  NewCredit := CE(r_i, τ+Δτ)
  if NewCredit = -1 then
     R_c(r_i) :=max [(1-φ)R_c,old(r_i), R_ini(r_i)];
    if new ≥1 then
       for i:=1 to NewCredit do
        R_c(r_i) := (1-ε)R_c,old(r_i);
      R_c(r_i) :=max [R_c(r_i), R_ini(r_i)]
    else R_c(r_i) := α·R_c,old(r_i) + β· NewCredit
 enddo
  τ:=current time;  R_c,old(r_i)=R_c(r_i)
  results release
 endwhile
```

Suppose TimeofDecrease is the period in which the credit value of certain resource decreases because this resource has not been scheduled; Suppose TimeofFree means the total time counting during which certain resource has not been scheduled; Suppose that count is the counter for the records of breach of contract. Based on those, the credit evaluation function is defined as follows:

```
function CE(r_i, τ+Δτ)
{count :=0
 S := r_i usage record between time τ and τ+Δτ
 if S := Ø then
      if  TimeofFree +Δτ ≥TimeofDecrease  then
             TimeofFree :=0
             return -1;
      else for all record in S
       If  (b_io ≥ b_i) and (t_io ≥ t_i) then
```

$$\text{return } \chi\cdot\frac{\sum_i (b_{io}-b_i)}{\sum_i b_{io}}+\delta\cdot\frac{\sum_i (t_{io}-t_i)}{\sum_i t_{io}}$$

```
  for all record in S
    if  (b_io ≤ b_i) or (t_io ≤ t_i)  then
     count :=count+1
     return count
 }
```

4 Credit-Based Resource Scheduling Algorithm

To satisfying the goal of minimizing the cost and time, we have designed a credit-based resource scheduling algorithm that can be expressed as follows:

a. Sorting the resources that meet the task requirement according to the credit value firstly, then selecting m resources from the sorted sequence;
b. For the candidate sequence (*m* in length) gotten by step a, sorting it by increasing cost and then selecting n resources as the candidate resource set;
c. For each resource in candidate resource set (*n* in length), calculate the next completion time for an assigned job, taking into account previously assigned jobs.
d. Sorting resources by next completion time.
e. Assign one job to the first resource for which the cost per job is less than or equal to the remaining budget per job.
f. Repeat all steps until all jobs are assigned.

5 Simulation Experiment and Result Analysis

To facilitate the comparison between our credit-based algorithm, time-minimization algorithm [5] and cost-minimization algorithm, we select Nimrod/G as the platform of simulation experiment.

The system is composed of 100 nodes and each node provides a CPU resource in either 2.0GHz or 2.5GHz. Besides, each node is not only a resource provider but also a task host. The agent residing in the node administers the resource and performs the model strategy. Every task in the system owns running time of 100s by estimate and a budget of 2800G$. To acquire precise initial credit value, we adopt random tasks scheduling strategy and control the running time greater than 50 evaluation periods so that the credit evaluation has been performed at least 50 times. In the simulation experiment, we mainly focus on the following aspects: throughput per time-unit, Turnover, rate of resource utilization and average finish time of task. The price of resources is classified by credit ranking and price of 10, 12, 14, 16, 18, 20, 22, 24, 26,

Table1. Scheduling times per time-unit

Algorithm name	1	2	3	4
Credit	3240	3318	3260	3325
Cost Minimization	3105	3050	3139	3087
Time Minimization	3232	3280	3308	3256

Table 2. Transaction volume in different periods (G$)

Algorithm	1	2	3	4
Credit	8100	8246	7928	8340
Cost Minimization	7238	7430	7142	7608
Time Minimization	8610	8360	8250	8490

Table 3. Average task cost (G$)

Algorithm	1	2	3	4
Credit	2500	2485	2432	2508
Cost Minimization	2331	2436	2275	2464
Time Minimization	2525	2549	2494	2607

Table 4. Resource utilization, completed rate and average finish time

Algorithm	Utilization (%)	Completed (%)	Finish time(s)
Credit	87.35	98	83.5
Cost Minimization	84.27	92	92.4
Time Minimization	85.2	97	82.3

28G$/s corresponds to credit level (0, 0.1), [0.1, 0.2)... [0.9,1) respectively. In the credit-based scheduling algorithm, parameters m and n are assigned as 5 and 3 respectively. Our experiment results are achieved during 4 periods (/hour), the result is depicted in Table 1 to table 4.

As shown in Table 1, compared with the cost-minimization algorithm and the time-minimization algorithm, using the credit-based algorithm, the system throughput has 5.5% enhancement and 1.8% enhancement respectively. In Table 2, time-minimization one gains the maximal transaction volume and credit-based one decreases a little, while the cost-minimization one decreases greatly. In Table 3, the cost-minimization one, the credit-based one and the time-minimization one achieve the cost of 2376 G$, 2481 G$, 2543 G$ on average respectively. As shown in Table 4, the credit-based one is the best in terms of both resource utilization and rate of completed tasks, and its average finish time is close to the time-minimization one.

According to the results above, the credit-based algorithm is the best one in aspects of throughput, rate of resource utilization and rate of completed tasks. While in the aspects of turnover, average task finish time and average task cost, the credit-based one is a tradeoff between the time-minimization one and the cost-minimization one.

6 Related Work

Currently, the research of trust model are mainly focused on the area of electronic business, most products, such as ONSALE Exchange [6], eBay [7], Sporas and Histos [8], perform comprehensive evaluation according to the history data of the bargainers that are judged and formed by the satisfaction degree of users. The results of this approach are local to the bargainers and vary with different bargainers. In the area of grid resource management, researchers try to solve the trust problem [9, 10] in the similar way and have achieved some results [8, 11]. But those works basically migrate the evaluation methods from the area of electronic business to the area of grid or P2P computing; currently no practical models have been found.

7 Conclusion

The results of simulation experiments above validate the efficiency of the credit evaluation. It is feasible to establish credit architecture for the resources and their service partners in the grid. In this way, we could not only constrain the behavior of GSPs and GSCs but also enhance the QoS(Quality of Services) of the grid. In future, we plan to extend our credit architecture to the multiple grids and take up more resources, such as credit for the Gridbank, into our evaluation architecture. And we also want to integrate the evaluation mechanisms in real life with our evaluation model, which will help the grid computation economics become more practical.

References

1. K. Krauter, R. Buyya, M. Maheswaran.: A Taxonomy and Survey of Grid Resource Management Systems, Software—Practice & Experience, Volume 32, Issue 2 (February 2002) 135 - 164
2. K. Czajkowski, I. Foster et al.: A Resource Management Architecture for Metacomputing Systems, Proc. IPPS/SPDP '98 Workshop, on Job Scheduling Strategies for Parallel Processing, (1998)62-82
3. F. Azzedin, M. Maheswaran.: Towards trust-aware resource management in Grid computing systems, 2nd IEEE/ACM International Symposium (CGRID2002)419 -424
4. Global Grid Forum.: RUR - Resource Usage Record, Working Group, http://www.gridforum.org/
5. R. Buyya, J. Giddy, D. Abramson.: An Evaluation of Economy-based Resource Trading and Scheduling on Computational Power Grids for Parameter Sweep Applications, Proceedings of the 2nd International Workshop on Active Middleware Services, 221-230
6. OnSale Exchange.: http://www.onsale.com/exchange.htm
7. eBay.: http://www.ebay.com
8. G. Zacharia, P. Maes.: Trust management through reputation mechanisms, Applied Artificial Intelligence Journal, Vol. 14 (9)881-908
9. F. Azzedin, M. Maheswaran.: Evolving and Managing Trust in Grid Computing Systems, IEEE Canadian Conference on Electrical & Computer Engineering (CCECE '02), (2002) 1424-1429.
10. P. Munindar, Singh.: Trustworthy Service Composition: Challenges and Research Questions, Proceedings of the Autonomous Agents and Multi-Agent Systems Workshop on Deception, Fraud and Trust in Agent Societies, Springer-Verlag, 2002.
11. F. Azzedin, M. Maheswaran.: Integrating Trust into Grid Resource Management Systems. In Proceedings of International Conference on Parallel Processing (2002)

Grid Resource Trade Network: Effective Resource Management Model in Grid Computing*

Sung Ho Jang, Da Hye Park, and Jong Sik Lee

School of Computer Science and Engineering, Inha University,
Incheon 402-751, South Korea
ho7809@hanmail.net, parkdh@inhaian.net,
jslee@inha.ac.kr

Abstract. Grid computing is the next generation platform that maximizes computing performance of system as using numerous computing resources on computer networks. Grid computing not only shares computing resources but also efficiently utilizes available computing resources. Therefore, grid computing needs resource management policies that handle and manage grid computing resources. This paper reviews existing resource management models based on economic principles such as auction model and commodity market model. This paper proposes an efficient resource management model, which is called the grid resource trade network model, and presents its bidding algorithms for grid users and grid providers. The proposed model reduces idle resources, improves resource utilization, and provides effective resource distribution. Empirical results show usefulness and efficiency of the grid resource trade network model.

1 Introduction

Today, grid computing has been recognized as an efficient solution to manage large-scale data and execute complex applications in distributed network environments. As problems that aren't resolved by existing systems such as super-computer and cluster system are appeared gradually, demands for grid computing are increased and necessity of resource management is also increased. Grid computing is a new concept architecture which maximizes the value of computing resources and integrates heterogeneous systems by standardization in computer networks [1]. Recently, grid computing has been used to various fields of science, engineering and commerce and has been developed by enterprises and organizations due to advantages of maximizing the value of resources and aggregating resources and convenience of managing resources.

Processing components in grid environments are connected with computer networks to share entire computing resources. We have to know that it is very important to maximize resource utilization and user satisfaction by control of supply and demand for resources. Therefore, we need resource management policies that allocate resources to proper processing components because the number of processing

* This research was supported by the MIC(Ministry of Information and Communication), Korea, under the ITRC(Information Technology Research Center) support program supervised by the IITA(Institute of Information Technology Assessment).

H. Zhuge and G.C. Fox (Eds.): GCC 2005, LNCS 3795, pp. 732 – 737, 2005.

components is infinite and computing resources in grid environments are geographically and methodically dispersed. But, grid resource management is very difficult and complex due to dynamical system environments of grid computing.

In this paper, we propose the grid resource trade network model for efficient management of grid computing resources. The grid resource trade network model controls demands for grid computing sources and provides resource allocation suitable for processors. The grid resource trade network model creates resource transactions that can be satisfied with both customers and providers by application to market principles and reduces idle resources by revitalization of grid resource market. This paper executes the grid resource trade network model on the DEVS modeling and simulation [2] to evaluate its usefulness and efficiency.

This paper is organized as follows. Section 2 presents existing resource management models such as tender/contract-net model, auction model and etc. Section 3 proposes the grid resource trade network model and the bidding algorithm. Section 4 demonstrates efficiency of our model with experiment results. The conclusion of this paper is in Section 5.

2 Related Works

Many models based on economic principles applicable for grid computing are widely utilizing for resource allocation and management in grid computing environments [3]. Typical models are commodity market model, bargaining model, tender/contract - net model, and auction model.

In commodity market model [4], customers don't participate in pricing and resource prices is defined and flexed in advance. The bargaining model [5] restricts resource prices because they are controlled by customer's requirements. The tender/contract-net model [6] connects a customer to a resource provider suitable for conditions of a customer by resource provider's bidding. The auction model [7] is one of the most used models for resource management in grid computing environments and supports negotiation between a resource provider and many customers.

The grid resource trade network model is based on the auction model and the tender/contract-net model and provides a double auction mechanism that can be satisfied with both customers and resource providers and introduces a distribution method by market principles. Besides, contrary to the general double auction model, the grid resource trade network model supports N: N relation between numerous providers and customers with regard to grid computing environments including large-scale resources and focuses on the improvement of resource utilization.

3 Grid Resource Trade Network Model

This paper proposes the grid resource trade network model to allocate grid resources to grid users and to manage grid resources. The grid resource trade network model aims to reduce idle resources and improves resource utilization and satisfaction of grid users and grid resource providers by the double auction mechanism [8] and bidding algorithms. The grid resource trade network model consists of three types of components as Fig. 1: provider (grid service provider), customer (grid user) and mediator (grid broker).

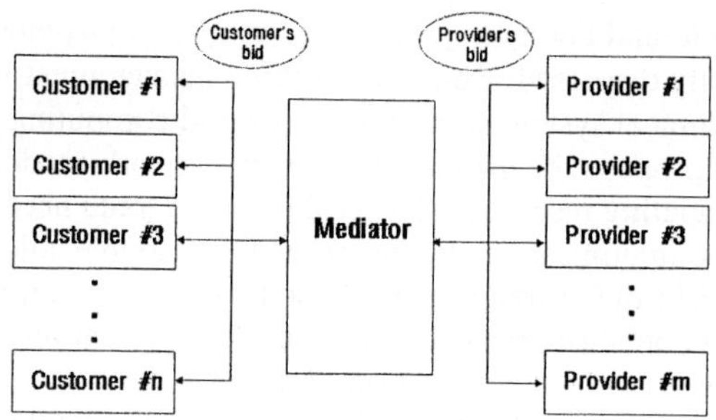

Fig. 1. Composition of the grid resource trade network model

A mediator accomplishes resource transactions and arbitrates between providers and customers. All interactions between providers and customers are progressed through a mediator that is similar to an auctioneer of the auction model. The grid resource trade network model provides the double auction mechanism that identifies whether prices of both customers and providers by continuous bidding are matched or not. A mediator provides transaction prices and resource information and proposes a price that can be simultaneously satisfied with both customers and providers by the double auction mechanism. A mediator also searches for resources which are suitable to customer's conditions and executes resource selection and resource transaction. Customers request grid resources for service execution and make a bid according to a transaction price and customer's bidding strategy. Providers also make a bid according to a transaction price and provider's bidding strategy to sell resources. In the grid resource trade network model, customers propose low prices for minimizing of prices to purchase resources and providers propose high prices for maximizing of sale profits. Therefore, a mediator gives priority to the highest bidding price of providers when providers make a bid while it gives priority to the lowest bidding price of customers when customers make a bid. And a mediator decides transaction prices through control of bids between customers and providers. The grid resource trade network model provides transparency and fairness of grid resource market because a mediator announces transaction prices to grid participants.

We resolve problems of resource allocation as applying market principles to the grid resource trade network model. Low price promotes customer's demand for resources and restrains provider's resource supply while high price restrains customer's demand for resources and promotes provider's resource supply. That is to say that the grid resource trade network model guarantees efficient resource allocation as the model provides characteristics of market called by the name of invisible hand. The grid resource trade network model has to determine transaction prices according to opinions of grid participants because it is competitive market model such as general trade market model. Therefore, providers can't confer on the bidding and monopolize grid resources because they are geographically dispersed and have individual marketing plans. Customers also can't control demands for grid resource and transaction prices at their pleasure. Providers can supply more resources to customer with bidding prices lower than transaction prices to maximize sale profits because sale profits of providers are related to transaction prices.

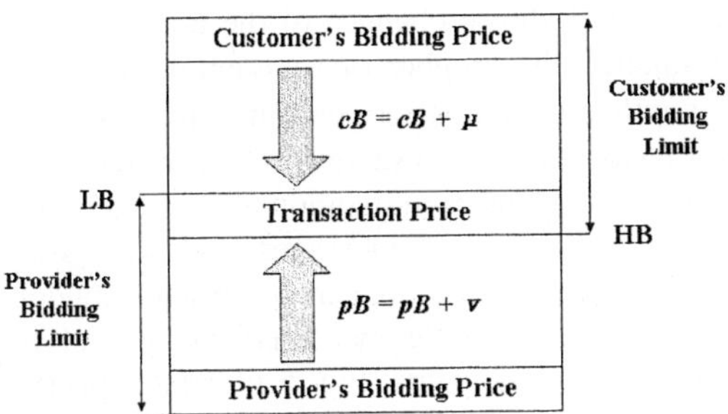

Fig. 2. Transaction Price Formation (LB indicates the lowest affordable bid of provider, HB indicates the highest affordable bid of customer, cB indicates customer's bid, μ indicates price elasticity of customer, pB indicates provider's bid and v indicates price elasticity of provider)

The first bidding price of customer is different from the first bidding price of provider. But it finally builds up a same price such as Fig. 2 through price negotiation. A customer has HB (Highest Bid: the maximum bid limit of customers) and a provider has LB (Lowest Bid: the minimum bid limit of providers). If HB is higher than a transaction price, customer's demands for grid resource are increased. And if LB is lower than a transaction price, competition among providers becomes intense and sale prices of providers are decreased. That is to say that HB and LB are parameters which indicate demand curve and supply curve of the market economic theory. Customers and providers can bid as using the bidding algorithm. The bidding algorithm can be separated to two algorithms: the customer bidding algorithm and the provider bidding algorithm.

The customer bidding price function is $P_{customer}(s) = cB + \mu * \Delta s$ where cB indicates customer's bid and μ indicates price elasticity of customer and s is time parameter and Δs indicates the elapse of time. If customers can't succeed in buying necessary resources as time elapse, proposed bidding prices of customers to purchase resources rise gradually. That is, the customer bidding price function indicates that customer's bid is directly proportional to time units. Customers begin to bid with minimum limit of affordable prices. And they can't bid a price higher than HB to reduce prices for purchasing resources. The provider bidding price function is $P_{provider}(s) = pB - v * \Delta s$ where pB indicates provider's bid and v indicates price elasticity of providers. If providers can't succeed in selling resources as time elapse, proposed bidding prices of providers to sell resources are fallen gradually. Namely, the provider bidding price function indicates that provider's bid is inversely proportional to time units. Providers begin to bid with maximum limit of affordable prices. And they can't bid a price higher than LB to increase sale profits.

4 Experiments and Results

We implemented the grid resource trade network model on the DEVSJAVA modeling and simulation environment and conducted two experiments to evaluate its efficiency. The first experiment is to observe interaction between transactions and price elasticity of bidding algorithms. Fig. 3 shows changes of the number of transactions per time units. As V become smaller, the number of transactions is decreased. Fig. 4 shows that changes of the number of messages per time unit. As V becomes smaller, the number of messages is increased. These results show that high price elasticity is advantageous to improve grid resource utilization as increasing the number of transactions and to reduce transmission of messages and idle providers. The second experiment is to test that the grid resource trade network model effectively reflects principles of supply and demand. We measured changes of transaction prices as diversifying the ratio of grid participants. Fig. 5 illustrates price variations when the number of providers is larger than the number of customers. As the number of providers is increased, transaction prices are decreased. Fig. 6 illustrates price variations when the number of customers is larger than the number of providers. As the number of customers is increased, transaction prices are increased. These results demonstrate that our model guarantees effective resource distribution as it provides principles of supply and demand.

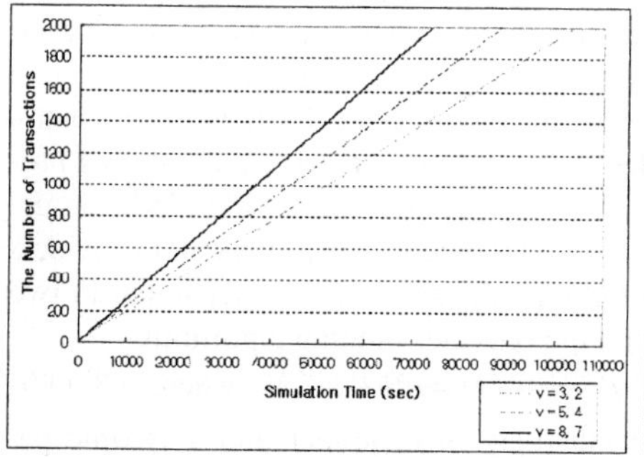

Fig. 3. Number of Transaction (V : price elasticity of providers)

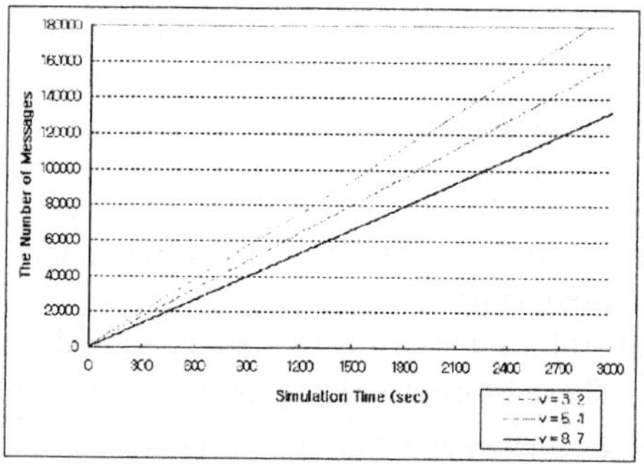

Fig. 4. Number of Message (V : price elasticity of providers)

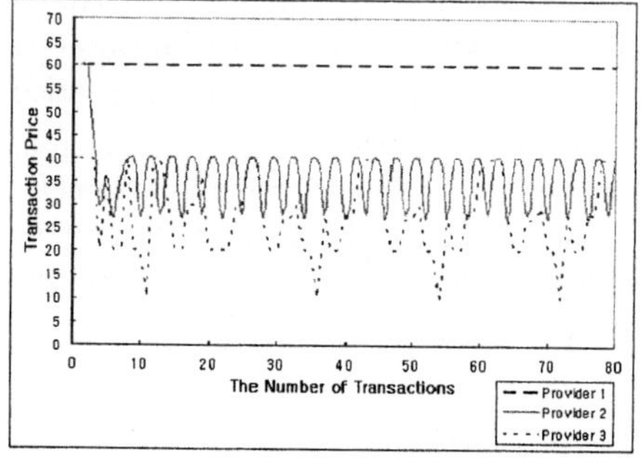

Fig. 5. Transaction Price on various Providers

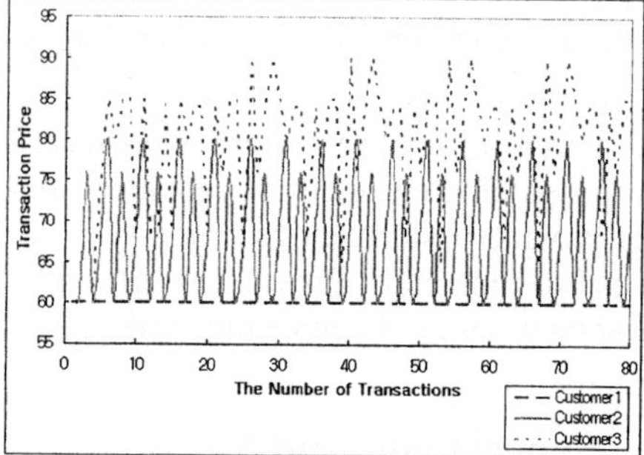

Fig. 6. Transaction Price on various Customers

5 Conclusion

This paper proposes the grid resource trade network model to manage grid computing resources in grid computing environment. We introduce bidding algorithms and apply market principles for solving problems of grid resource management and allocation. The grid resource trade network model controls transaction prices and checks idle grid resources through continuous double auction and bidding algorithms and provides efficient mechanism that reflects every participant's opinion. As the grid resource trade network model supports N: N relation contrary to existing economic models such as general double auction model, we can connect customers with all providers on grid through computer network. In grid resource trade network model, providers represent grid service providers that supply grid services and customers represent grid users that use grid services. Grid users and grid service providers can make a contract and use information about grid resource market through a mediator. As the grid resource trade network model reduces idle resources on grid and increases the number of resource transactions, we improve grid resource utilization and efficacy and provide appropriate resource distribution. Satisfaction of grid participants is also improved because transaction prices can be satisfied with both customers and providers by maximizing provider's profits and minimizing user's expenses. Experiment results demonstrate that the grid resource trade network model is an effective solution to distribute, utilize, and manage resources on grid computing environments.

References

1. F. Berman, G. Fox and T. Hey: Grid computing: making the global infrastructure a reality. J. Wiley, New York (2003)
2. Zeigler, B.P., et al.: The DEVS Environment for High-Performance Modeling and Simulation. IEEE C S & E, Vol. 4, No.3 (1997) 61-71
3. R. Wolski, J. Plank, J. Brevik, and T. Bryan: Analyzing Market-based Resource Allocation Strategies for the Computational Grid. International Journal of High performance Computing Applications, Sage Publications, Vol.15, No.3 (2001) 258-281
4. M. Litzkow, M. Livny, and M. Mutka: Condor - A Hunter of Idle Workstations. Proceedings of the 8th International Conference of Distributed Computing Systems (ICDCS 1988), IEEE CS Press, USA (January 1988)
5. R. Buyya: Economic-based Distributed Resource Management and Scheduling for Grid Computing. Available at http://www.buyya.com/thesis/ (April 2002)
6. M. Stonebraker, R. Devine, M. Kornacker, W. Litwin, A. Pfeffer, A. Sah, and C. Staelin: An Economic Paradigm for Query Processing and Data Migration in Mariposa. Proceedings of 3rd International Conference on Parallel and Distributed Information Systems, IEEE Com-puter Society Press, USA (1994) 28-30
7. N. Nisan, S. London, O. Regev, and N. Camiel: Globally Distributed computation over the Internet: The POPCORN project. International Conference on Distributed Computing Systems (ICDCS'98) (May 1998)
8. R. Das, J. Hanson, J. Kephart, and G. Tesauro: Agent-Human Interactions in the Continuous Double Auction. In Proceedings of the International Joint Conferences on Artificial Intelligence (IJCAI) (August 2001)

Survivability Analysis of Grid Resource Management System Topology*

Yang Qu[1], Chuang Lin[1], Yajuan Li[1], and Zhiguang Shan[2]

[1] Department of Computer Science and Technology, Tsinghua University, Beijing 100084, P.R. China
{quyang, clin, yjli}@csnet1.cs.tsinghua.edu.cn
[2] Department of Informatization Research, State Information Center, Sanlihe road 58, XiCheng District, Beijing 100045, China
shanzg@mx.cei.gov.cn

Abstract. The resource management system is one of the essential components of Grids. A resource management system may be made up of one or many resource management nodes. The organization manner of the resource management nodes, i.e. the topology of a resource management system, is a key factor that should be considered carefully during the architecture design of resource management systems with respect to some specified requirements (e.g., performance, survivability). In this paper, a new survivability definition is proposed and the survivability of three typical Grid resource management system topologies (centralized, hierarchical, and peer-to-peer) is analyzed.

1 Introduction

A Grid is a very large-scale distributed network computing system that can scale to Internet size environments [1]. The term "resources" denotes any capability that may be shared and exploited in a networked environment. This definition includes both traditional resources (e.g., a computer, storage system, network) and virtualized ones (e.g., database, data transfer, simulation) [2]. Resource management system (RMS) is in charge of controlling how capabilities provided by Grid resources are made available to users.

A resource management system may be made up of one or multiple resource management nodes which are called resource managers (RM). If there is only one RM in a resource management system, this node manages all Grid resources in centralized manner. Otherwise, multiple RMs work cooperatively to manage the Grid resources in decentralized manner, such as hierarchical manner and peer-to-peer manner.

The organization manner of the RMs, i.e. the topology of a RMS, is a key factor that should be considered carefully during the architecture design of resource management systems. Our work aims at evaluating the survivability of different Grid RMS topologies. As we know, this is the first work on evaluating survivability of RMS from the topological point of view. The contributions are as follows:

* This work is partly supported by the National Natural Science Foundation of China (No. 90412012 and No. 60373013).

H. Zhuge and G.C. Fox (Eds.): GCC 2005, LNCS 3795, pp. 738 – 743, 2005.

- A new survivability definition is proposed, which distinguishes and combines the affect of faults and attacks in survivability analysis.
- The survivability of three typical Grid RMS topologies (centralized, hierarchical, and peer-to-peer) is analy
- zed.

The organization of this paper is as follows. In Section 2, a new survivability definition is proposed. In Section 3, survivability of three typical Grid RMS topologies is analyzed. Finally, conclusions are made in Section 4.

2 Survivability Definition

Survivability is an important property in both the dependability domain and the security domain [6]. As described in [7], survivability is the capability of a system to fulfill its mission, in a timely manner, in the presence of attacks, failures, or accidents.

By now, various mathematical definitions of survivability have been proposed in different disciplines [3, 4, 5]. However, these definitions don't distinguish failures caused by faults and those caused by attacks. Although both faults and attacks may cause system failures, their affects differ from each other if all parts of a system are not in peer positions. While faults may occur randomly in each part of a distributed system, attacks often aim at the most important part of it. Therefore, the affects of faults and attacks should be distinguished and survivability should be regarded as a composite measure of the fault-tolerance ability and the attack-tolerance ability. We proposed a new survivability definition as follows to capture this composite measure.

Definition 1. A survivability specification is a seven-tuple, $\{F, A, C, C_F, C_A, O, S\}$ where

- F is a statement of the assumed fault environment for the system, which includes details of the various faults to which the system might be exposed together with all of the corresponding parameters. In this paper, it is assumed that every RM suffers from failures caused by faults with the same probability. And the probability that there are i RMs suffering from failures caused by faults is denoted by P_i^F .
- A is a statement of the assumed attack environment for the system, which includes details of the various attacks to which the system might be exposed together with all of the corresponding parameters. In this paper, it is assumed that different RM suffers from failures caused by attacks with different probability. Crucial RM such as the root RM in hierarchical topology is more likely to be attacked. It is supposed in this work that attacks always aim at the RM whose failure will bring the most loss to capability of the RMS. And the probability that there are i RMs suffering from failures caused by attacks is denoted by P_i^A .
- C is a specification of quantifying the capability of the system to fulfill its mission. E.g., the capability of a system may be specified as its throughput, the maximum of users it can accommodate, and so on. In this paper, the capability of a resource manager RM_i to meet users request is decided to a great extent by the number of resources whose information can be acquired by this RM. Therefore, the capability of an RMS herein is specified as the sum of the number of acquired resources of every RM in the RMS.

- C_F is the ratio of the capability of the system in the presence of faults stated by F to the capability of the system without failures. C_F is a measure of fault-tolerance ability.
- C_A is the ratio of the capability of the system in the presence of attacks stated by A to the capability of the system without failures. C_A is a measure of attack-tolerance ability.
- O is an operation which combines C_F and C_A to express the survivability.
- S is a measure denoting the survivability of a system, which can be expressed by $S=O(C_F, C_A)$.

3 Survivability Analysis of RMS Topology

In the following analysis, it is assumed that a Grid RMS has m RMs and manages r resources. When some failure occurs in a RM caused by faults or attacks, this RM is removed from the topology of the RMS. C_F and C_A quantify the capability of the system in the presence of faults and attacks respectively.

As mentioned in Section 2, survivability measure S is the composition of C_F and C_A through the operation O. In this paper, O is defined as the "vectorization" of C_F and C_A. That is S is a 2-dimensional vector

$$S = (C_F, C_A) \tag{1}$$

3.1 Centralized Topology

Because there is only one RM in centralized RMS topology and it manages all resources, the information of all resources can be acquired by the unique RM. So, the capability of the RMS is r if there is no failure. When the unique RM suffers from some failure, its function will be lost and the capability of the RMS will be 0. Faults and attacks have the same affect in this case. Thus we have,

$$C_F = \frac{0 \cdot P^F{}_1 + r \cdot (1 - P_1^F)}{r} = (1 - P_1^F) \tag{2}$$

$$C_A = \frac{0 \cdot P_1^A + r \cdot (1 - P_1^A)}{r} = (1 - P_1^A) \tag{3}$$

Using (1), (2) and (3), the survivability measure of the centralized topology is that

$$S = (1 - P_1^F, 1 - P_1^A) \tag{4}$$

3.2 Hierarchical Topology

It is assumed that an RMS with hierarchical topology has a root node and h hierarchies. Every RM except those in the lowest hierarchy has d son RMs. So there are d^{l-1} RMs in the lth hierarchy (l = 1, 2, …, h) and $m = \frac{d^h - 1}{d - 1}$ RMs totally. It is also assumed that every RM in the lowest hierarchy manages s resources. Therefore, an RM in the lth hierarchy (l = 1, 2, …, h) manages $d^{h-l}s$ resources, and $d^{h-1}s = r$.

For an RM in the lth hierarchy, the number of resources whose information can be acquired by it is $d^{h-l}s$. And the capability of the RMS without any failure can be calculated by $\sum_{j=1}^{h} d^{l-1}d^{h-l}s = hd^{h-1}s = hr$.

Let C_i^F (C_i^A) denotes the capability of the system when there are i (i = 1, 2, …, N) RMs suffering from failures caused by faults (attacks), thus we have,

$$C_F = \frac{\sum_{i=0}^{N} P_i^F C_i^F}{hr} \text{ and } C_A = \frac{\sum_{i=0}^{N} P_i^A C_i^A}{hr}.$$

For the sake of avoiding the tedious calculation, C_i^F ($i > 0$) are educed approximately as follows. The lth hierarchy has d^{l-1} RMs, so there is $\frac{i}{m}d^{l-1}$ failed RMs in the lth hierarchy on average. A working resource manager RM$_i$ in the lth hierarchy manages d^{h-j} resources. If RM$_i$ is failed, then it and all the RMs on the path from it to the root RM will lose the capability to acquire information of $d^{h-j}s$ resources. So C_i^F can be calculated approximately by

$$C_i^F \approx hr - \sum_{l=1}^{h} l\frac{i}{m}d^{l-1}d^{h-l}s = hr(1 - \frac{i}{m}\frac{h+1}{2}), \quad i > 0 \tag{5}$$

For $P_0^F = 1 - \sum_{i=1}^{N} P_i^F$ and $C_0^F = hr$, we have

$$C_F = 1 - \sum_{i=1}^{N} P_i^F \frac{i}{m}\frac{h+1}{2} \tag{6}$$

Because i attacks always occur in the i most important RMs, i.e., the root RM as well as the i-1 RMs in the second hierarchy, C_i^A can be calculated by

$$C_i^A = (h-1)r - (i-1)d^{h-2}s = (h-1)r - (i-1)\frac{r}{d}, \quad i > 0 \tag{7}$$

For $P_0^A = 1 - \sum_{i=1}^{N} P_i^A$ and $C_0^A = hr$, we have

$$C_A = 1 - \sum_{i=1}^{N} P_i^A \frac{1}{h}(1 + \frac{i-1}{d}) \tag{8}$$

Using (1), (6) and (8), the survivability measure of hierarchical topology is that

$$S = (1 - \sum_{i=1}^{N} P_i^F \frac{i}{m}\frac{h+1}{2}, 1 - \sum_{i=1}^{N} P_i^A \frac{1}{h}(1 + \frac{i-1}{d})) \tag{9}$$

3.3 Peer-to-Peer Topology

It is assumed that a RMS with peer-to-peer topology comprises m RMs and every RM manages s resources. Thus $ms = r$.

When there is no failure in the RMS, every RM can acquire the information of all the resources from its peers. Therefore, the capability of the RMS without any failure is $mr = m^2 s$. When some RM suffers from failures, it loses its functions, and the information of the resources it manages can not be acquired by the other RMs any more. The failed RM will be removed from the topology, and all the other working RMs will reorganize in peer-to-peer way.

Because all the RMs in a peer-to-peer topology are in peer positions, the affects of faults and attacks are the same. Therefore, we have,

$$C_F = \frac{\sum_{i=0}^{N} P_i^F C_i^F}{m^2 s} \text{ and } C_A = \frac{\sum_{i=0}^{N} P_i^A C_i^A}{mr}.$$

For $P_0^F = 1 - \sum_{i=1}^{N} P_i^F$, $C_0^F = m^2 s$ and $C_i^F = (m-i)^2 s$, we have

$$C_F = 1 - \sum_{i=1}^{N} P_i^F \frac{i}{m}(2 - \frac{i}{m}) \tag{10}$$

For $P_0^A = 1 - \sum_{i=1}^{N} P_i^A$, $C_0^A = mr$ and $C_i^A = (m-i)^2 s$, we have

$$C_A = 1 - \sum_{i=1}^{N} P_i^A \frac{i}{m}(2 - \frac{i}{m}) \tag{11}$$

Using (1), (10) and (11), the survivability measure of peer-to-peer topology is that

$$S = (1 - \sum_{i=1}^{N} P_i^F \frac{i}{m}(2 - \frac{i}{m}), 1 - \sum_{i=1}^{N} P_i^A \frac{i}{m}(2 - \frac{i}{m})) \tag{12}$$

4 Conclusions

In this work, a new survivability definition is proposed, which distinguishes and combines the affect of faults and attacks on system survivability. Based on the new survivability definition, the survivability of three typical Grid RMS topologies (centralized, hierarchical, and peer-to-peer) is analyzed.

In the future work, the survivability of some hybrid topologies (e.g. that combining hierarchical topology with peer-to-peer topology) will be studied.

References

1. Krauter K., Buyya R., Maheswaran M. A Taxonomy and Survey of Grid Resource Management Systems for Distributed Computing. Software: Practice and Experience. 2002, 32(2): 135-164.
2. Foster I., Kesselman C. (eds.). The Grid: Blueprint for a New Computing Infrastructure. Morgan Kaufmann, San Francisco, CA, 2004.
3. Knight J., Sullivan K. On the definition of survivability. Technical Report CS-00-33, Department of Computer Science, University of Virginia, December 2000.
4. Liew S.C., Lu K.W. A framework for characterizing disaster-based network survivability. IEEE Journal on Selected Areas in Communications. 1994, 12(1):52–58.
5. T1A1.2 Working Group on Network Survivability Performance. Technical report on enhanced network survivability performance. Technical report, February 2001.
6. Nicol D.M., Sanders W.H., Trivedi K.S. Model-Based Evaluation: From Dependability to Security. IEEE Transaction on Dependable and Secure Computing. 2004, 1(1): 48-65.
7. Ellison R.J., Fisher D.A., Linger R.C., Lipson H.F., Longstaff T., Mead N.R. Survivable Network Systems: An Emerging Discipline. Technical Report CMU/SEI-97-TR-013, CMU Software Engineering Institute, Nov. 1997.

SATOR: A Scalable Resource Registration Mechanism Enabling Virtual Organizations of Enterprise Applications

Chen Liu[1,2], Fanke Cheng[1,2], and Yanbo Han[1]

[1] Software Division, Institute of Computing Technology, Chinese Academy of Sciences, Beijing 100080
[2] Graduate University of the Chinese Academy of Sciences, Beijing 100080
{Liuchen, chengfanke, yhan}@software.ict.ac.cn

Abstract. Virtual organization of enterprise applications is an indispensable means to realize spontaneous resources sharing and business collaboration among enterprises in an open and dynamic environment. The underlying, often standalone information systems need to be dynamically integrated. However, independent enterprise resources are difficult to be naturally integrated due to their incompatibleness in semantics. To shield semantic incompatibleness and facilitate resource discovery and utilization in the virtual organization, this paper defines a scalable resource registration mechanism called SATOR, which is semantics-based and supports the dynamic integration of heterogeneous enterprise resources. The mechanism has been validated in a real-world project dealing with dynamic supply chains of a large-scale electronic manufacturing enterprise.

Keywords: Application integration, scalable resource registration, semantic-level interoperation.

1 Introduction

New collaboration patterns such as virtual organization (VO) focus more on flexible and efficient resource sharing in an open, networked environment. However, today's information islands plague the daily operation of enterprises, and disable spontaneous resources sharing and business collaboration among enterprises in particular. The AmGrid (Advanced Manufacture Grid) platform is developed correspondingly for managing dynamic supply chains in a large-scale electronic manufacturing enterprise [1].

According to their usage, we classify enterprise resources into 3 categories: service resources, information resources and actor resources. Service resources encapsulate functions provided by information systems and can be invoked. Information resources represent business data to be transferred among enterprises such as bills and product information. Actor resources indicate involved people who are authorized to use or manipulate resources. A resource to be registered is composed of two parts: the first part is the semantics of the resource, which can be regarded as the metadata used to describe a resource. The second part is instances of the resource, which represent the real data stored in a registry center.

H. Zhuge and G.C. Fox (Eds.): GCC 2005, LNCS 3795, pp. 744 – 749, 2005.

Today, UDDI [2] provides a standardized method for registering web services. However, considering enabling virtual organization, these semantically heterogeneous and multipurpose enterprise resources pose many new challenges for resource registration, making UDDI insufficient. In AmGrid, VO is established on an open and networked environment [1]. Therefore, we cannot presume which enterprise will join the VO, which means the resources to be registered also cannot be confirmed in advance. Therefore, resources supported by the registration mechanism must be scalable. Owing to the uncertainty of VO partners, we also cannot predefine a static global ontology library to satisfy all requirements just as many traditional integration projects did [3-7]. Therefore, the registration mechanism should be established on a scalable semantic environment, in which the semantics of resources should be subject to changes. In addition, considering the diversity of resources and the uncertainty of availability in the sharing, we cannot provide the searching approach merely based on keywords. The searching approach based on semantics is absolutely necessary. This demands the classification and description of resources should be consistent with metadata defined in the semantic environment. As stated above, the resources semantics are subject to changes, therefore the registry information also should be scalable.

Apparently, UDDI is not able to directly solve these problems. Therefore, we present a scalable mechanism called SATOR (ScAlable enTerprise resOurce Registration) for massive and heterogeneous enterprise resources registration in an open environment. This paper is organized as follows: In section 2, we introduce the virtual organization of enterprise applications and relations between it and SATOR. In section 3, we propose the mechanism of SATOR and its working theories. In section 4, we introduce how the SATOR is applied in the AmGrid project. The conclusion is given in section 5.

2 Virtual Organizations of Enterprise Applications

In AmGrid, the established VO is represented as business process. In the running of process, VO will snatch needed resources from available partners dynamically. As figure1 shows, resource registry centers are the foundation of virtual organization.

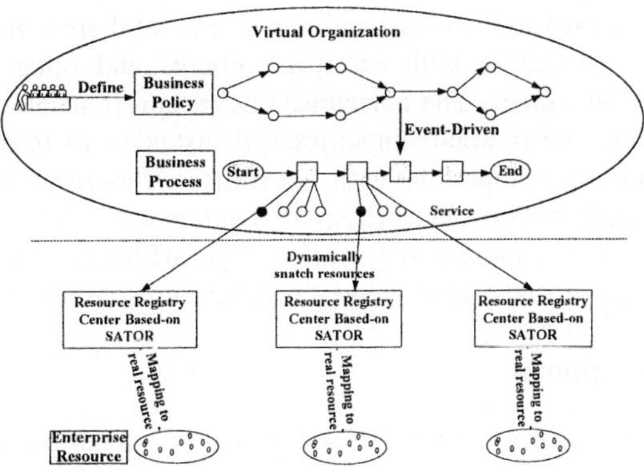

Fig. 1. The Rationale of Virtual Organization

Providers, dealers, manufacturers and logistic companies will register resources into the SATOR registry center. Registry centers are geographically distributed. The resources needed in the running of VO may come from different registry centers. However, each enterprise has its own norm of semantics. To sum up, SATOR will support the VO to access resources and shield the semantic incompatibleness problem.

3 Rationales of the SATOR Mechanism

3.1 The Architecture of SATOR

The architecture of SATOR is illustrated in figure2:

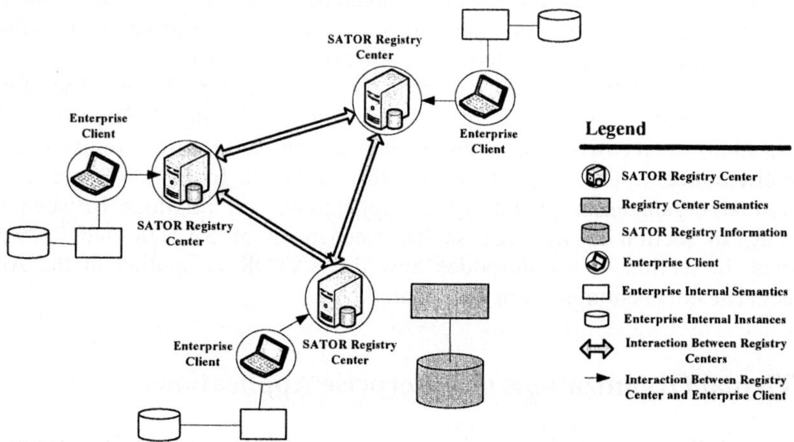

Fig. 2. The Architecture of SATOR

The SATOR Registry Center represents a real network node. Its main responsibility is to maintain the registered resources and their semantics. Besides, it is also in charge of interacting with enterprise clients and other registry centers to provide the needed resources. The enterprise client represents an enterprise resources provider. It maintains its internal semantics and instances of resources. The internal semantics may not be compatible with semantics of registry center. In addition, registry center should not be isolated. Registry centers may affiliate together to satisfy the need of large-scale resources registration. The affiliation will provide resources providers and users a virtual global view of registered resources.

3.2 Registration Patterns

Whether to reuse the enterprise internal semantics is a focal point when considering resource registration. Taking this point into account, two different registration patterns are supported in SATOR, namely, the newborn pattern and reuse pattern.

- **Newborn pattern:** In this registration pattern, when an enterprise registered a resource, it will not simultaneously provide the internal semantics of this resource. Being the resource provider, it will redefine the semantics of this resource on the basis of the semantics in the registry center. In this pattern, the mappings of enterprise internal semantics and redefined semantics should be maintained manually by the enterprise itself.
- **Reuse pattern:** In this registration pattern, when an enterprise registered a resource, it will also provide the internal semantics about this resource. The registry center will reuse this semantics to the greatest extent. However, restricted by the today's semantic technologies, not all semantics provided by the enterprise can be reused and integrated into the registry center seamlessly. In regard to those failure situations, registry center will go back to the first registration pattern automatically.

3.3 Registration Process

There are three tightly related steps for an enterprise to register its resources:

- **Identify the Semantic Relationships:** Registry center will first identify what semantic relationships existed between resources to be registered with those already registered. For example, if we plan to registry a resource named "Notebook", but there is an already registered resource named "Laptop". These two resources may represent the same kind of product and have strong semantic relationships.

  Semantic matching techniques aim at identifying these semantic relationships. In SATOR, borrowing ideas from [12], we divided these relationships into three levels based on the following matching features: names, attributes and relations. Corresponding to those features, these three matching levels are named lexical matching, structural matching and contextual matching. Distinguished from [12], we don't adopt affinity coefficients to assess the degree of matching two resources because there is no good for us to design the following adjustment algorithm. In the contrast, we develop sub-relations for every matching level to denote the relationships that we can identify and handle. For example, we develop subsume sub-relation to denote that two similar resources that the set of attributes of one is subsumed by the other.
- **Define the Semantics:** According to the relationships identified in the previous step, the registry center will recommend related resources semantics to assist and facilitate enterprise to define the semantics. Enterprises can choose their needed semantics from those recommended ones and enlarge these semantics if needed. However, they are not allowed to delete or modify already existed semantics. There exists a special situation when we register resources in SATOR. For example, if enterprise A will registry a resource named "Notebook", but there is an already registered resource named "Notebook". As stated in the above, the semantics of already registered "Notebook" will be recommended. However, if recommended semantics will not satisfy the need of enterprise A, then it will enlarge the recommended semantics. This will result in the inconsistency between new defined semantics about "Notebook" with already existed registry

information. Therefore, registry center should also adjust its registry information to keep the consistence with newly defined semantics.

The adjustment algorithm has two parts: the first part is an extensible set of adjusters. Each adjuster is implementing a corresponding adjustment policy and to cope with one sub- relation defined above. The other part is a fixed-point algorithm to invoke the needed adjusters repeatedly according to the matching result. The fixed-point algorithm will invoke the needed adjusters one by one until all identified relationships are adjusted. Besides, all the adjusters must conform to the monotonic principle, which means adjusters don't retract any adjustments that have already been established.

- **Register the Instances:** This step is to register the instances of resource according to the semantics established in the prior step. Registry center organizes and stores resources information in the pattern of business unit. A business unit is a container for one enterprise resources, in which resources will be described, classified, organized and saved.

4 Application of SATOR Mechanism

AmGrid[1] is a grid application platform aimed at realizing the dynamic and cross-organizational resource sharing. To reach this goal, SATOR mechanism is applied in AmGrid to enable resource registration and utilization in the open environment. According to SATOR two core components are implemented, which are enterprise specifications management tools and enterprise resources management tool illustrated in Figure 3. Enterprise specifications management tool mainly performs the definition and maintenance of the registry center semantics. They compose of ontology management tool, semantic matching tool and semantic mapping tool. Enterprise resources management tools are used to create and maintain the registry information.

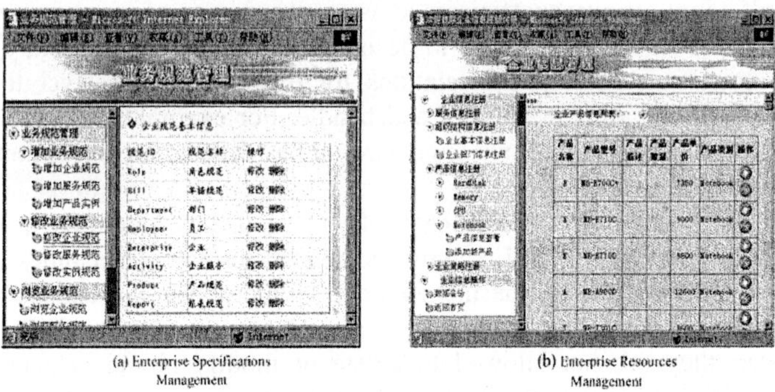
(a) Enterprise Specifications Management (b) Enterprise Resources Management

Fig. 3. The Application of SATOR

5 Conclusion

In this paper we have presented a set of challenges that the resources registration encountered when enabling VO of enterprise applications. To cope with these challenges, we put forward a scalable resources registration mechanism named SATOR which can be used in the open environment to enable the construction and running of VO. To validate our mechanism, we develop a prototype system based on the scenario of notebook manufacturing for a large-scale electronic manufacturing enterprise. In the prototype system, we implemented a suite of tools in the foundation of SATOR core technologies to solve the above-mentioned problems. These tools are independent from specific applications and can be used in other similar scenarios to support the dynamic resource integration in the open environment.

References

1. Liang, Y., Hu, S., Han, Y.: Study on the Architecture and Key Technologies of Grid Application Platform in Network Manufacture. Journal of Computer Research and Development. Vol. 41(12) (2004) 2060~2065 (In Chinese)
2. Bellwood, T., Clément, L., Ehnebuske, D., et al: UDDI Version 3.0. UDDI Spec Technical Committee Specification (2002)
3. Arens, Y., Hsu, C., Knoblock, C.A.: Query processing in the sims information mediator. In Advanced Planning Technology. AAAI Press, California, USA (1996)
4. Mena, E., Kashyap, V., Sheth, A., Illarramendi, A.: Observer: An approach for query processing in global information systems based on interoperability between pre-existing ontologies. In Proceedings 1st IFCIS International Conference on Cooperative Information Systems (CoopIS '96), Brussels (1996)
5. Goh, C.H.: Representing and Reasoning about Semantic Conflicts in Heterogeneous Information Sources. Phd, MIT (1997)
6. Wache, H., Scholz, T.H., Stieghahn, H., K¨onig-Ries, B.: An integration method for the specification of rule–oriented mediators. Proceedings of the International Symposium on Database Applications in Non-Traditional Environments (DANTE'99). Kyoto, Japan (1999) 109–112
7. Stuckenschmidt, H., Wache, H., V¨ogele, T., Visser, U.: Enabling technologies for interoperability. Workshop on the 14th International Symposium of Computer Science for Environmental Protection. Bonn, Germany, TZI, University of Bremen (2000) 35–46
8. W3C Web Services Activity, http://www.w3.org/2002/ws/
9. Noy, N.F., Musen, M.A.: Ontology Versioning in an Ontology Management Framework. Intelligent Systems, IEEE. Vol.19, Issue.4, July-Aug (2004) 6 – 13
10. Gruber, T.: A translation approach to portable ontology specifications. Knowledge Acquisition. Vol.5 (2) (1993) 199–220
11. Wache, H., Vögele, T., Visser, U., Stuckenschmidt, H., Schuster, G., Neumann, H., Hübner, S.:Ontology-Based Integration of Information-A Survey of Existing Approaches. In Proceedings of the 17th International Joint Conference on Artificial Intelligence (IJCAI-01). Workshop: Ontologies and Information Sharing. Seattle, USA (2001)
12. Castano, S., Ferrara, A., Montanelli, S., Zucchelli, D.: HELIOS: a general framework for ontology-based knowledge sharing and evolution in P2P systems. In Proc. of DEXA'03 2nd Web Semantics Workshop. Prague, Czech Republic, September (2003)
13. Miller, A.G.: WordNet: A lexical database for English. Communications of the ACM. Vol.38 (11) (1995) 39–41

Collaborating Semantic Link Network with Resource Space Model*

Yunpeng Xing[1,2,3], Jie Liu[1,2], Xiaoping Sun[1,2,3], and Erlin Yao[1,2,3]

[1] China Knowledge Grid Research Group, Key Lab of Intelligent Information Processing, Institute of Computing Technology, Chinese Academy of Sciences, Beijing 100080, China
http://kg.ict.ac.cn

[2] Graduate School of Chinese Academy of Sciences, Beijing, China
{ypxing, lj}@kg.ict.ac.cn

[3] Hunan Knowledge Grid Lab, Hunan University of Science and Technology, Hunan, China

Abstract. The Semantic Link Network model SLN and Resource Space Model RSM are semantic models proposed separately for effectively specifying and managing versatile resources across the Internet. Collaborating the relational semantics of SLN with the classification semantics of the RSM can support richer semantic modeling in applications. This paper introduces the Resource Class Hierarchies into the SLN and investigates to cooperatively model with the RSM. The proposed approach can be used as a normalized semantic overlay of the Knowledge Grid environment.

1 Introduction

The relational data model is the milestone of data management [1, 2]. Different from the hierarchical and network models, it separates the logical data representation from physical implementation. Object-oriented databases and object-relational databases extend the application scope of the relational databases [5, 8, 10]. Several graph-based semantic models built on the traditional hierarchical and network data models have been proposed [4, 6, 7, 9, 11]. But, these data models are incapable of effectively managing heterogeneous, distributed and ocean resources in an open and dynamic Internet environment.

The Resource Space Model RSM is a semantic data model for uniformly, normally and effectively specifying and managing resources. Its theory basis is the normal forms based on orthogonal classification semantics and relevant resource operations [13, 14, 15, 18]. The Semantic Link Network model SLN is a semantic model for semantically interconnecting resources [15]. The SLN has the advantages of enabling rich semantic representation, reasoning, execution, referential search, and normalization.

To facilitate the cooperation between RSM and SLN, this paper extends the SLN by introducing a structure called Resource Class Hierarchy, which can be derived

* This work was supported by the National Basic Research Program of China (973 project No.2003CB317000) and the National Science Foundation of China (Grants 60273020 and 70271007).

H. Zhuge and G.C. Fox (Eds.): GCC 2005, LNCS 3795, pp. 750–755, 2005.

from the RSM. The combination of the classification semantics of RSM and the relational semantics of SLN can support richer semantic modeling and applications in the open and dynamic Internet environment [16, 19].

2 Resource Space Model and Semantic Link Network Model

A resource space is an n-dimensional space, denoted as $\boldsymbol{RS}(\boldsymbol{X}_1, \boldsymbol{X}_2, \ldots, \boldsymbol{X}_n)$ or just by name $\boldsymbol{RS}$ in simple [13]. Axis is defined by a set of coordinates denoted as $\boldsymbol{X}_i = \{\boldsymbol{C}_{i1}, \boldsymbol{C}_{i2}, \ldots, \boldsymbol{C}_{im}\}$. A point $\boldsymbol{p}(\boldsymbol{C}_{1,j1}, \boldsymbol{C}_{2,j2}, \ldots, \boldsymbol{C}_{n,jn})$ is determined by the coordinate values at all axes. Every point in the space can uniquely determine a resource set, where each element is called a resource entry. Point and resource entry are two fundamental operation units of RSM.

A Semantic Link Network (SLN) is a network consisting of nodes and semantic links between nodes. A node can be either a resource defined in the name space or an SLN. The Semantic Link Network can be formally represented as a directed graph *SLN=<Resources, SemanticLinks>*, where *Resources* and *SemanticLinks* represent the sets of nodes and semantic links respectively. The operations, normal form theory, characteristics, criteria and integrity constraints have been proposed in [15]. A set of semantic relationships such as *Cause-effect*, *Implication*, *Inclusion*, *Similar-to*, *Instance*, *Membership*, *Sequential* and *Reference* has been introduced in [12]. More types of semantic links can be imported according to application requirements. The SLN theory has been applied to the peer-to-peer environment to achieve efficient query routing [17].

3 The Extended Semantic Link Network

Fig.1 illustrates a part of an extended semantic link network representing a simple teaching system. The dotted circles represent *resource class hierarchies*, each of which corresponds to a resource space. The rectangles in dotted circles denote the *resource classes* corresponding to classes of resources in a resource space. The edges in the dotted circles represent the *inclusion relationships* between resource classes. The formal definitions of resource class hierarchy, resource class and inclusion relationship will be introduced in section 4. And other nodes and edges are from the generic concepts defined in the original SLN.

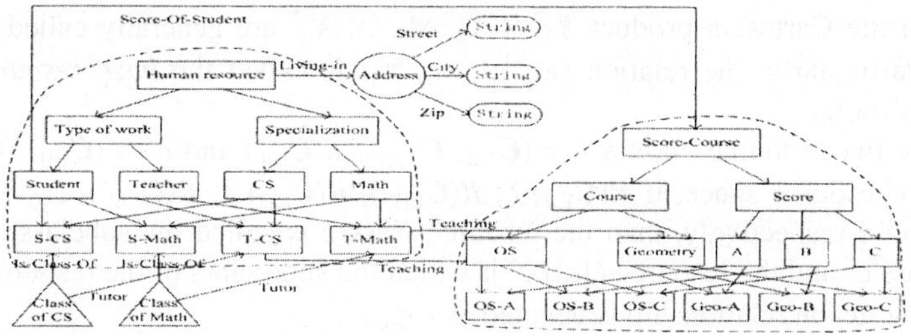

Fig. 1. A Semantic Link Network with resource class hierarchies

Definition 1. The extended Semantic Link Network is a triple $S = (VE, RE, RCH)$, where VE is a finite set of nodes in the extended Semantic Link Network which could include resources, generic classes and resource classes; RE is a finite set of triple $<v_1, v_2, re>$, where re represents the relationship between nodes v_1 and v_2 coming from VE; and, RCH is a finite set of resource class hierarchies, each of which corresponds to a resource space in the RSM.

Through incorporating the RSM and the SLN, the extended SLN has the following three advantages.

(1) The extended SLN provides an efficient mapping mechanism from RSM to SLN. The extended SLN has increased the mapping granularity from RSM to SLN. In contrast with the original SLN, a point, an axis and even a resource space in the RSM can be mapped to a node in the extended SLN. Secondly, the extended SLN provides not only resource mappings but also operation mappings from the RSM to the SLN.
(2) The extended SLN makes use of the RSM to facilitate the SLN modeling. Since quick and easy modeling is one of the salient features of the RSM, the *resource class hierarchies* in the extended SLN make the SLN modeling easier without conflict with other approaches such as Entity-Relationship model [3].
(3) The extended SLN can enhance the interoperability between SLNs. Most of the operations of the original SLN are mainly based on the structure information. The extended SLN has introduced some new RSM-based operations, which emphasize on not only structure but also semantic information of SLNs.

4 Resource Class Hierarchy

Let δ be a resource space, an axis, a point or a coordinate of the RSM, and $\boldsymbol{R}(\delta)$ be the resources that δ can contain in the RSM. Let $\boldsymbol{RS}(\boldsymbol{X}_1, \boldsymbol{X}_2, \ldots, \boldsymbol{X}_n)$ be a resource space. Its axis $\boldsymbol{X}_i = \{\boldsymbol{C}_{i1}, \boldsymbol{C}_{i2}, \ldots, \boldsymbol{C}_{im}\}$ can be extended to $\boldsymbol{X}_i^* = \{\boldsymbol{C}_{i1}, \boldsymbol{C}_{i2}, \ldots, \boldsymbol{C}_{im}, \pi_i\}$, $1 \le i \le n$. A point taking the coordinate value π_i on the axis $\boldsymbol{X}_i$ means that the axis $\boldsymbol{X}_i$ has no restriction on the point. Meanwhile, we introduce a constant γ_i at each axis $\boldsymbol{X}_i$ such that $\boldsymbol{R}(\gamma_i) = \boldsymbol{R}(\boldsymbol{C}_{i1}) \cup \boldsymbol{R}(\boldsymbol{C}_{i2}) \cup \ldots \cup \boldsymbol{R}(\boldsymbol{C}_{im})$.

Definition 2. Let $\boldsymbol{RS}(\boldsymbol{X}_1, \boldsymbol{X}_2, \ldots, \boldsymbol{X}_n)$ be a resource space and $\boldsymbol{X}_i^*$, $1 \le i \le n$, be its extended axes. The set of resources represented by $(\pi_1, \ldots, \pi_{i-1}, \gamma_i, \pi_{i+1}, \ldots, \pi_n)$ is defined as the *axis resource class* of axis $\boldsymbol{X}_i$, denoted as ac_i. Axis resource class and each relation in the Cartesian product $\boldsymbol{X}_1^* \times \boldsymbol{X}_2^* \times \ldots \times \boldsymbol{X}_n^*$ are generally called *resource classes*. Particularly, the relation $(\pi_1, \pi_2, \ldots, \pi_n)$ is called the *base resource class*, denoted as root_{RS}.

For any two resource classes $c = (\boldsymbol{C}_{1,j1}, \boldsymbol{C}_{2,j2}, \ldots, \boldsymbol{C}_{n,jn})$ and $c' = (\boldsymbol{C}_{1,j1}', \boldsymbol{C}_{2,j2}', \ldots, \boldsymbol{C}_{n,jn}')$ in a resource space, if $\boldsymbol{R}(\boldsymbol{C}_{1,j1}) \subseteq \boldsymbol{R}(\boldsymbol{C}_{1,j1}')$, $\boldsymbol{R}(\boldsymbol{C}_{2,j2}) \subseteq \boldsymbol{R}(\boldsymbol{C}_{2,j2}')$, ..., $\boldsymbol{R}(\boldsymbol{C}_{n,jn}) \subseteq \boldsymbol{R}(\boldsymbol{C}_{n,jn}')$ hold respectively, then the resource class c is called the subclass of the resource class c' and the resource class c' is called the superclass of the resource class c. And this inclusion relationship is denoted as $c \subseteq_c c'$.

Definition 3. Let $\boldsymbol{RS}(\boldsymbol{X}_1, \boldsymbol{X}_2, \ldots, \boldsymbol{X}_n)$ be a resource space. The *resource class hierarchy* of $\boldsymbol{RS}$ is defined as the directed graph $\boldsymbol{RSG}(CS, E)$ where

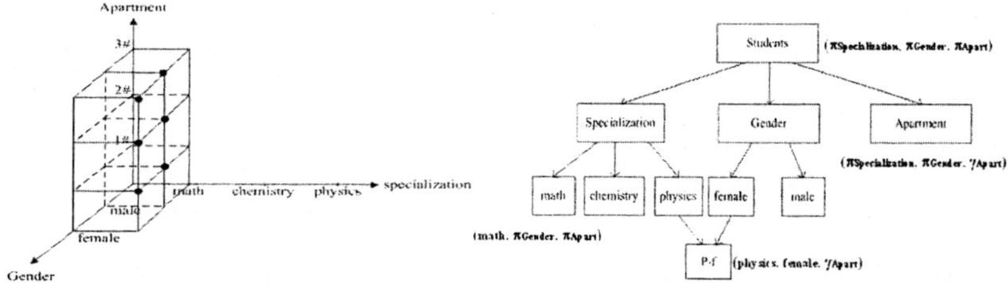

Fig. 2. A resource space and a part of its resource class hierarchy

(1) $CS = X_1^* \times X_2^* \times \ldots \times X_n^* \cup \{(\pi_1, \ldots, \pi_{i-1}, \gamma_i, \pi_{i+1}, \ldots, \pi_n) \mid 1 \leq i \leq n\}$;
(2) For any resource classes $c_1, c_2 \in CS$, if $<c_1, c_2> \in E$, then $c_2 \sqsubseteq_c c_1$ holds;
(3) For any resource classes $c_1, c_2 \in CS$, if $c_2 \sqsubseteq_c c_1$ holds, then there exists at least one path $\Gamma(c_1, c_{j1}, c_{j2}, \ldots, c_{jm}, c_2)$.

The resource class hierarchy of a given resource space can be viewed as a directed graph consisting of resource classes and the inclusion relationships. $\Gamma(v_1, v_2, \ldots, v_n)$ is used to denote one path from v_1 to v_n in a directed graph. Fig. 2 is the illustration of a resource space and a part of its resource class hierarchy.

5 Operations in the Extended Semantic Link Network

The extended SLN not only maps resource spaces to resource class hierarchies but also inherits all operations of the RSM. There exist four types of operations in the RSM: Join, Disjoin, Merge and Split [13]. The following is the formal definitions of these four operations on resource class hierarchies of the extended SLN.

Theorem 1. (Rsm-Join) Let $\boldsymbol{RS}_1(X_1, \ldots, X_t, X_{t+1}, \ldots, X_m)$ and $\boldsymbol{RS}_2(X_{t+1}, \ldots, X_m, X_{m+1}, \ldots, X_n)$ be two resource spaces that can be joined together to form the resource space $\boldsymbol{RS}(X_1, \ldots, X_t, X_{t+1}, \ldots, X_m, X_{m+1}, \ldots, X_n)$. Assume that $\boldsymbol{RSG}_1(CS_1, E_1)$ and $\boldsymbol{RSG}_2(CS_2, E_2)$ are the resource class hierarchies of $\boldsymbol{RS}_1$ and $\boldsymbol{RS}_2$ respectively. The Rsm-Join operation on $\boldsymbol{RSG}_1(CS_1, E_1)$ and $\boldsymbol{RSG}_2(CS_2, E_2)$ is defined as the directed graph $\boldsymbol{RSG}(CS, E)$ such that:

(1) $CS = X_1^* \times X_2^* \times \ldots \times X_n^* \cup \{(\pi_1, \ldots, \pi_{i-1}, \gamma_i, \pi_{i+1}, \ldots, \pi_n) \mid 1 \leq i \leq n\}$;
(2) For any two classes $c = (C_1, \ldots, C_t, C_{t+1}, \ldots, C_m, C_{m+1}, \ldots, C_n)$ and $c' = (C_1', \ldots, C_t', C_{t+1}', \ldots, C_m', C_{m+1}', \ldots, C_n')$ in CS, $<c, c'> \in E$ holds if and only if both $<(C_1, \ldots, C_t, C_{t+1}, \ldots, C_m), (C_1', \ldots, C_t', C_{t+1}', \ldots, C_m')> \in E_1$ and $<(C_{t+1}, \ldots, C_m, C_{m+1}, \ldots, C_n), (C_{t+1}', \ldots, C_m', C_{m+1}', \ldots, C_n')> \in E_2$ hold.

Then, $\boldsymbol{RSG}(CS, E)$ is the resource class hierarchy of resource space $\boldsymbol{RS}$.

Theorem 2. (Rsm-Disjoin) Let $\boldsymbol{RS}_1(X_1, \ldots, X_t, X_{t+1}, \ldots, X_m)$ and $\boldsymbol{RS}_2(X_{t+1}, \ldots, X_m, X_{m+1}, \ldots, X_n)$ be two resource spaces which derive from the Disjoin operation on the resource space $\boldsymbol{RS}(X_1, \ldots, X_t, X_{t+1}, \ldots, X_m, X_{m+1}, \ldots, X_n)$. Assume that $\boldsymbol{RSG}(CS, E)$ is the resource class hierarchy of $\boldsymbol{RS}$. The Rsm-Disjoin operation on $\boldsymbol{RSG}(CS, E)$ is defined as $\boldsymbol{RSG}_1(CS_1, E_1)$ and $\boldsymbol{RSG}_2(CS_2, E_2)$ (similar to $\boldsymbol{RSG}_1(CS_1, E_1)$) such that:

(1) $CS_1 = X_1^* \times X_2^* \times \ldots \times X_m^* \cup \{(\pi_1, \ldots, \pi_{i-1}, \gamma_i, \pi_{i+1}, \ldots, \pi_m) \mid 1 \le i \le m\}$;

(2) For any two resource classes $c = (C_1, \ldots, C_t, C_{t+1}, \ldots, C_m)$ and $c' = (C_1', \ldots, C_t', C_{t+1}', \ldots, C_m')$ in CS_1, $<c, c'> \in E_1$ holds if and only if there exists at least a pair of resource classes $(C_1, \ldots, C_t, C_{t+1}, \ldots, C_m, C_{m+1}, \ldots, C_n)$ and $(C_1', \ldots, C_t', C_{t+1}', \ldots, C_m', C_{m+1}', \ldots, C_n')$ in $RSG(CS, E)$ such that $<(C_1, \ldots, C_t, C_{t+1}, \ldots, C_m, C_{m+1}, \ldots, C_n), (C_1', \ldots, C_t', C_{t+1}', \ldots, C_m', C_{m+1}', \ldots, C_n')> \in E$ holds.

Then, $RSG_1(CS_1, E_1)$ is the resource class hierarchy of resource space RS_1.

Theorem 3. (Rsm-Merge) Let RS_1 and RS_2 be two resource spaces that can be merged into the resource space RS by merging X' and X'' into X. Assume that $RSG_1(CS_1, E_1)$ and $RSG_2(CS_2, E_2)$ are the resource class hierarchies of RS_1 and RS_2 respectively and that ac, ac' and ac'' are the axis resource classes corresponding to axes X, X' and X'' respectively. The Rsm-Merge operation on $RSG_1(CS_1, E_1)$ and $RSG_2(CS_2, E_2)$ is defined as the directed graph $RSG(CS, E)$ such that:

(1) $CS = CS_1 \cup CS_2 \cup \{ac\} - \{ac', ac''\}$;

(2) $E = E_1 \cup E_2 \cup \{<ac, c> \mid <ac', c> \in E_1 \text{ or } <ac'', c> \in E_2\} \cup \{<c, ac> \mid <c, ac'> \in E_1 \text{ or } <c, ac''> \in E_2\} - \{<ac', c> \mid <ac', c> \in E_1\} - \{<ac'', c> \mid <ac', c> \in E_2\}$.

If RS is in 2NF, then $RSG(CS, E)$ is the resource class hierarchy of resource space RS.

Theorem 4. (Rsm-Split) Let $RS_1(X_1, X_2, \ldots, X_m, X')$ and $RS_2(X_1, X_2, \ldots, X_m, X'')$ be two resource spaces deriving from the Split operation on the resource space $RS(X_1, X_2, \ldots, X_m, X)$ in 2NF. Assume that $RSG(CS, E)$ is the resource class hierarchy of RS and that ac, ac' and ac'' are the axis resource classes of axes X, X' and X'' respectively. The Rsm-Split operation on $RSG(CS, E)$ is defined as $RSG_1(CS_1, E_1)$ and $RSG_2(CS_2, E_2)$ (similar to $RSG_1(CS_1, E_1)$) such that:

(1) $CS_1 = X_1^* \times X_2^* \times \ldots \times X_m^* \times X'^* \cup \{(\pi_1, \ldots, \pi_{i-1}, \gamma_i, \pi_{i+1}, \ldots, \pi_m, \pi) \mid 1 \le i \le m\} \cup ac'$;

(2) $E_1 = \{<c, c'> \mid c \in CS_1 \wedge c' \in CS_1 \wedge <c, c'> \in E\} \cup \{<ac', c> \mid c \in CS_1 \wedge <ac, c> \in E\} \cup \{<c, ac'> \mid c \in CS_1 \wedge <c, ac> \in E\}$.

Then, $RSG_1(CS_1, E_1)$ is the resource class hierarchy of resource space RS_1.

Theorem 5. All of the RSM-based operations on the extended SLN (Rsm-Join, Rsm-Disjoin, Rsm-Merge and Rsm-Split) keep 1NF, 2NF and 3NF of the Semantic Link Network.

6 Conclusion

The collaboration between the Semantic Link Network and the Resource Space Model is realized by extending the Semantic Link Network and defining the resource class hierarchy and the RSM-based operations on the extended SLN. The extended SLN provides an efficient mapping mechanism for the cooperation between RSM and SLN, facilitates modeling with RSM and SLN, and enhances the interoperability between SLNs by defining semantic-rich operations.

Ongoing work is to design an efficient algorithm for automatically transforming resource spaces to resource class hierarchies, to propose more operations on the extended SLN, to propose its theory on integrity constraint, and to develop tools for assisting integrity and normalization checking in future environment.

References

1. Abiteboul, S., Hull, R. and Vianu, V.: Foundations of Databases. Addison-Wesley, Reading, MA (1995).
2. Codd, E.F.: A Relational Model of Data for Large Shared Data Banks. *Communications of the ACM*, 13(6) (1970) 377-387.
3. Chen, P.: The Entity-Relationship Model□Toward a Unified View of Data. *ACM Transactions on Database Systems*, 1(1) (1976) 9-36.
4. Gyssens, M., Paredaens, J., Bussche, J. and Gucht, D.: A Graph-Oriented Object Database Model. *IEEE Transactions on Knowledge and Data Engineering*, 6(4) (1994) 572-586.
5. Kim, W.: Introduction to Object-oriented Databases. MIT Press, Cambridge, 1990.
6. Levene, M. and Loizou, G.: A Graph-based Data Model and Its Ramifications. *IEEE Transactions on Knowledge and Data Engineering*, 7(5) (1995) 809-823.
7. Levene, M. and Poulovassilis, A.: The Hypernode Model and Its Associated Query Language. In: Proceedings of Jerusalem Conference on Information Technology, Jerusalem, 520-530 1990.
8. Mok, W.Y.: A Comparative Study of Various Nested Normal Forms. *IEEE Transactions on Knowledge and Data Engineering*, 14(2) (2002) 369-385.
9. Poulovassilis, A. and Levene, M.: A Nested-graph Model for the Representation and Manipulation of Complex Objects. *ACM Transactions on Information Systems*, 12(1) (1994) 35-68.
10. Rumbaugh, J., Blaha, M., Premerlani, W., Eddy, F. and Lorensen, W.: Object-Oriented Modeling and Design. Prentice-Hall, 1991.
11. Ullman, J.D.: Principles of Database and Knowledge-Base Systems, vol. I. Computer Science Press, 1988.
12. Zhuge, H.: Active e-Document Framework ADF: Model and Platform. *Information and Management*, 41(1) (2003) 87-97.
13. Zhuge, H.: Resource Space Model, Its Design Method and Applications. *Journal of Systems and Software*, 72(1) (2004) 71-81.
14. Zhuge, H.: Resource Space Grid: Model, Method and Platform, *Concurrency and Computation: Practice and Experience*, 16(14) (2004) 1385 – 1413.
15. Zhuge, H.: The Knowledge Grid. World Scientific Publishing Co., Singapore, 2004.
16. Zhuge, H.: China's E-Science Knowledge Grid Environment, *IEEE Intelligent Systems*, 19(1) (2004) 13-17.
17. Zhuge, H., Liu, J., Feng, L., Sun, X. and He, C.: Query Routing in a Peer-to-Peer Semantic Link Network. *Computational Intelligence*, 21(2) (2005)197-216.
18. Zhuge, H. and Xing, Y.: Integrity Theory for Resource Space Model and Its Application, Keynote at WAIM2005, *Springer LNCS* 3739, pp.8-24, 2005.
19. Zhuge, H.: Semantic Grid: Scientific Issues, Infrastructure, and Methodology, *Communications of the ACM*. 48(4) (2005)117-119.

RSM and SLN: Transformation, Normalization and Cooperation*

Erlin Yao[1,2], Yunpeng Xing[1,2,3], Jie Liu[1,2], and Xiaoping Sun[1,2]

[1] Institute of Computing Technology, Chinese Academy of Sciences, Beijing, China
alin.yao@kg.ict.ac.cn
[2] Graduate School of Chinese Academy of Sciences, Beijing, China
[3] Hunan Knowledge Grid Lab, Hunan University of Science and Technology, Hunan, China

Abstract. The Resource Space Model RSM and Semantic Link Network SLN are models of future interconnection environment, and the combination of them forms a rich semantic layer for the next-generation web. This paper investigates the combination between RSM and SLN. The methods of the transformation between RSM and SLN are proposed. From the perspective of transformation, the correlations between the normal forms of RSM and SLN are investigated. The investigations show that although RSM and SLN are independently proposed, they are well-cooperated models for the future Semantic Web and Knowledge Web.

1 Introduction

The current web is based on the HTTP and HTML protocols as well as the client/server infrastructure. It enables people to share web information to some extent in form of using browsers to retrieve web pages. It could not meet the needs of the rapid expansion of the Internet applications like e-business. There also exist issues like accuracy and efficiency from the viewpoint of information retrieval. To overcome the shortcomings of the current web, people have made efforts towards the next-generation web. The Semantic Web, the Web Service and the Grid are three new areas, where many leading research institutes and companies have been involved in.

The Resource Space Model RSM is a semantic data model for uniformly, normally and effectively specifying and managing resources. RSM is to organize versatile Web resources according to semantic normal forms [6, 8, 14]. Given a set of coordinates of the space can uniquely determine one or a set of resources. The model includes normal forms based on the orthogonal classification semantics and relevant criteria and methods.

The motivation of Semantic Web is obviously right, however, easy-to-use and easy-to-build are two important criteria that determine the success or failure of new

* This work was supported by the National Basic Research Program of China (973 project no.2003CB317000) and the National Science Foundation of China (Grants 60273020 and 70271007).

H. Zhuge and G.C. Fox (Eds.): GCC 2005, LNCS 3795, pp. 756 – 760, 2005.

techniques. We have proposed the Semantic Link Network SLN as a model to facilitate the Semantic Web [5, 7]. The links among resources (documents, images, and concepts etc) are not simply hyperlinks but semantic links, which support certain semantic reasoning. The semantic link network is the semantic "map" of distributed versatile resources to enable people to publish, manage and browse resources according to the map.

The combination of RSM and SLN forms a rich semantic layer for the next generation Web [9, 11, 12, 15]. Users make and use the orthogonal semantic space and the semantic link network according to their cognitive spaces. The orthogonal semantic space can help users focus their operation destination. The SLN reflects the semantic relationships between versatile resources [13, 16].

In this paper, the integration of RSM and SLN are discussed. First given a semantic link network, the corresponding high-level resource space is constructed, and the correlations between their normal forms are discussed. Then on the contrary, we give a method to construct a semantic link network that is semantically equivalent to a given resource space. In this perspective, the corresponding relationships between the normal forms of RSM and SLN are discussed.

2 The Transformation from SLN to RSM and the Correlations

Each resource defined in the RSM has a mapping image in the SLN. In this section, given a semantic link network, the corresponding high-level resource space is constructed. And the correlations between their normal forms are discussed.

The semantic similar nodes in *SLN* (*N*, *SL*) can be looked as a point in the high-level resource space, so we can get the corresponding high-level resource space from a semantic link network as follows:

For a semantic link network *SLN* (*N*, *SL*), let $SLN = \{C_1, C_2, \ldots, C_m\}$, where C_i is a strong connected component of *SLN* and $C_i \cap C_j = \Phi$, $1 \leq i, j \leq m$. Then $N(SLN) = \cup N(C_i)$, where $N(C_i)$ denotes the nodes of C_i. Suppose we can describe *SLN* from such aspects in semantics as $X_1, X_2, \ldots, X_n$, then all C_i can be represented as $C_i(x_1, x_2, \ldots, x_n)$, where x_k is the value of C_k in the semantic of X_k. If we view every $C_i(x_1, x_2, \ldots, x_n)$ as a point pi(x1, x2, …, xn) in a resource space, then we get the high-level resource space RS(X1, X2, …, Xn).

Well normalized data makes programming (relatively) easy, and works very well in multi-platform, enterprise wide environments [1, 2]. The normal forms are to guarantee the correctness and effectiveness of operations [3, 4].

Then the correlations between the normal forms of the semantic link network and the resource space will be discussed.

Corollary 1 (1NF): The first-normal-form of a semantic link network *SLN* is also the first-normal-form of the corresponding resource space *RS*.

Proof: If *SLN* is 1NF, then there does not exist semantic-equivalent nodes in it. From the definition of strong connected component, there can't exist the same strong component in *SLN*. Suppose *RS* is the high-level resource space, then there can not be the same points in it. So we can get that there does not exist name duplication between coordinates at any axis in *RS*. Then *RS* is also the first-normal-form.

Corollary 2 (2NF): The second-normal-form of a semantic link network *SLN* is also the second-normal-form of the corresponding resource space *RS*.

Proof: If SLN is 2NF, then there does not exist inconsistent semantic links and duplicate semantic links between the same pair of nodes, this guarantees that the strong components of *SLN* are got correctly in semantics. Suppose $\{C_1, C_2, \ldots, C_m\}$ is the set of strong components of *SLN* and *RS* is the high-level resource space, then $RS=\{p_1, p_2, \ldots, p_m\}$, where p_i is corresponding to C_i, $1\leq i \leq m$. If *RS* is not the second-normal-form, then there exist some points p_i and p_j are not independent from each other, i.e., $R(C_i)\cap R(C_j)\neq \Phi$, which means $C_i\cap C_j\neq \Phi$. This is not consistent with that C_i and C_j are different strong components in *SLN*, so the *RS* is also the second-normal-form.

Corollary 3 (3NF): The third-normal-form of a semantic link network *SLN* is also the third-normal-form of the corresponding resource space *RS*.

Proof: If *SLN* is 3NF, then there does not exist isolated nodes (accessible from each other), therefore all the strong components of *SLN* are accessible from each other. Suppose *RS* is the high-level resource space, we can get that any of its point are reachable from the others, then every axis X_i can represent all the resources in *RS*, which is equivalent to that any two axes of *RS* are orthogonal with each other [10], so *RS* is also the third-normal-form.

The above three corollaries tell that although we have defined the normal forms of the RSM and SLN respectively, they have the common properties in solving the redundancy and inconsistency, are the same in some sense.

3 The Transformation from RSM to SLN and the Correlations

In the above section, given a semantic link network, the high-level resource space is constructed and the correlations between them are discussed. But much semantics is lost in the procedure of from SLN to RSM. Then on the contrary, we will compare the RSM with the SLN in the perspective of constructing a semantic link network that is semantically equivalent to a given resource space.

Given a resource space *RS* (*P*, *E*), we can construct a *SLN* (*N*, *SL*) that is semantically equivalent to it as follows:

First let *N* (*SLN*)=*P* (*RS*), then for any two nodes n_1 and n_2 in the *SLN*, we can refer them as $p_1(x_1, x_2, \ldots, x_n)$ and $p_2(y_1, y_2, \ldots, y_n)$ in *RS* respectively. Then we define $SL(n_1, n_2)=\{ SL(x_i, y_i) \mid 1\leq i\leq n\}$, where

$$SL(x_i, y_i) = \begin{cases} \mathrm{Im}\, p_i, & \text{if } < x_i, y_i >\in E(RS) \text{ or } x_i = y_i; \\ \Phi, & \text{otherwise.} \end{cases}$$

In the resource space *RS* (*P*, *E*), if $<x_i, y_i>\in E(RS)$ or $x_i= y_i$, then $R(x_i)\supseteq R(y_i)$, i.e., x_i implies y_i. So here we can look every Imp_i as an instance of the '*Implication link*' [5], $1\leq i\leq n$. Then we can get *SL* (*SLN*) from $SL(SLN)= \cup_{n1,n2\in N} SL(n_1, n_2)$.

Because the semantic links are directed, $SL(x_i, y_i) \neq SL(y_i, x_i)$ in most cases. If $x_i= y_i$, then $SL(x_i, y_i) =SL(y_i, x_i)= Imp_i$. And on the contrary, if $SL(x_i, y_i) = Imp_i$ and

$SL(y_i, x_i)= Imp_i$, then $x_i = y_i$. It is obvious that the link Imp_i is transitive. Note that for any node $n(x_1, x_2, \ldots, x_n)$ in the resulting SLN (N, SL), $R(x_i)=\cup\{R(y_i)|SL(x_i, y_i) = Imp_i\}$. Then from the steps of constructing, it is clear that the resulting *SLN* (*N*, *SL*) is semantically equivalent to the resource space *RS* (*P*, *E*).

In a resource space *RS*, an axis with hierarchical coordinates can be transformed into an axis with flat coordinates if only the leaf nodes of each hierarchy are considered. So we focus on the flat cases in this section.

The corresponding semantic link network *SLN* of *RS* becomes more regular when *RS* is in the flat case. In this case, for any two points $p_1(x_1, x_2, \ldots, x_n)$ and $p_2(y_1, y_2, \ldots, y_n)$ in *RS*, we have $x_i = y_i$ or $R(x_i)\cap R(y_i)=\Phi$, $1\leq i\leq n$, i.e., both x_i implies y_i and y_i implies x_i hold or neither hold. Correspondingly, for any two nodes $n_1(x_1, x_2, \ldots, x_n)$ and $n_2(y_1, y_2, \ldots, y_n)$ in the *SLN*, $SL(x_i, y_i) =SL(y_i, x_i)= Imp_i$ or $SL(x_i, y_i) =SL(y_i, x_i)= \Phi$, i.e., there are no semantic links between x_i and y_i.

Given a resource space *RS*, there is a *SLN* that is semantically equivalent to it, so we can compare the normal forms of *RS* and the corresponding *SLN* to study the correlations between the normal forms of RSM and SLN.

Corollary 4 (1NF): The first-normal-form of a resource space *RS* is also the first-normal-form of the corresponding *SLN*.

Proof: If *RS* is 1NF, then there does not exist name duplication between coordinates at any axis, so there can't be the same points in *RS*. Suppose *SLN* is the corresponding semantic link network of *RS*, from *N* (*SLN*)=*P* (*RS*), we can get that there does not exist semantic-equivalent nodes in *SLN*, so *SLN* is also the first normal form.

Corollary 5 (2NF): The second-normal-form of a resource space *RS* is also the second-normal-form of the corresponding *SLN*.

Proof: If *RS* is 2NF, then for any axis, any two coordinates are independent from each other. Suppose *SLN* is the corresponding semantic link network of *RS*, then there does not exist semantic-equivalent nodes in *SLN*. And for any pair of nodes $n_1(x_1, x_2, \ldots, x_n)$ and $n_2(y_1, y_2, \ldots, y_n)$ in the *SLN*, the semantic links between them fall into the two cases: $SL(x_i, y_i) =SL(y_i, x_i)= Imp_i$ or $SL(x_i, y_i) =SL(y_i, x_i)= \Phi$, so there does not exist inconsistent semantic links and duplicate semantic links between n_1 and n_2, then we say that the *SLN* is the second normal form.

Corollary 6 (3NF): The third-normal-form of a resource space *RS* is also the third-normal-form of the corresponding *SLN*.

Proof: If *RS* is 3NF, then any two axes of it are orthogonal with each other, which is equivalent to $R(X_1)=R(X_2)=\ldots=R(X_n)$, i.e., every axis X_i can represent all the resources in *RS* [10], this guarantees that any points in the form of $\{ p(x_1, x_2, \ldots, x_n)| x_i \in X_i\}$ are meaningful. Suppose *SLN* is the corresponding semantic link network of *RS*, from *N* (*SLN*)=*P* (*RS*), we can get that any nodes in *SLN* in the form of $\{ n(x_1, x_2, \ldots, x_n)| x_i \in X_i\}$ are also meaningful. Then for any two nodes $n_1(x_1, x_2, \ldots, x_n)$ and $n_2(y_1, y_2, \ldots, y_n)$ in the *SLN*, if there exists some i, $1\leq i\leq n$, such that $x_i=y_i$, then $SL(x_i, y_i) =SL(y_i, x_i)= Imp_i$, then n_1 and n_2 can be accessed from each other. Else if $x_i\neq y_i$, for $1\leq i\leq n$ hold, let $n_3= n_3(x_1, x_2, \ldots, x_{n-1}, y_n)$, from $x_1\neq y_1$ and $x_n\neq y_n$, we can get $n_3\neq n_1$ and $n_3\neq n_2$. Then there exists semantic links $n_1\text{–}Imp_1\rightarrow n_3$, and $n_3\text{–}Imp_n\rightarrow n_2$, so n_1 and n_2 can also be accessed from each other by the chain n_1–Imp_1→ n_3–Imp_n→n_2. So any two nodes in the *SLN* are accessible from each other, i.e., the *SLN* is the third-normal-form.

The above three corollaries indicate that although we have defined the normal forms of the RSM and SLN independently, they have the common properties in solving the redundancy and inconsistency, and are the same in some sense.

4 Conclusion

The investigation of the relationship between RSM and SLN indicates that although RSM and SLN are proposed respectively, they are well-cooperated models for the future semantic and knowledge networking environment [15, 16]. Based on the theory of the RSM [6, 8, 10, 14] and SLN [5, 13], this paper proposes a method of constructing the corresponding high-level resource space from a semantic link network, investigates the correlations between the normal forms of the SLN and RSM, and provides a method of constructing a *SLN* that is semantically equivalent to a given resource space.

References

1. Codd, E. F.: A Relational Model of Data for Large Shared Data Banks, *Communications of the ACM*, 13 (6) (1970) 377-387
2. Codd, E. F.: Normalized Database Structure: A Brief Tutorial, *ACM SIG-FIDET Workshop on Data Description, Access, and Control*, San Diego, California, Nov., 1971
3. Mok, W. Y.: A Comparative Study of Various Nested Normal Forms, *IEEE Transactions on Knowledge and Data Engineering*, 14 (2) (2002) 369-385
4. William, K.: A Simple Guide to Five Normal Forms in Relational Database Theory, *Communications of the ACM*, 26 (2) (1983) 120-125
5. Zhuge, H.: Active e-Document Framework ADF: Model and Platform, *Information and Management*, 41 (1) (2003) 87-97
6. Zhuge, H.: Resource Space Model, Its Design Method and Applications, *Journal of Systems and Software*, 72 (1) (2004) 71-81
7. Zhuge, H.: The Knowledge Grid, World Scientific, 2004
8. Zhuge, H.: Resource Space Grid: Model, Method and Platform, *Concurrency and Computation: Practice and Experience*, 16 (14) (2004) 1385-1413
9. Zhuge, H.: China's E-Science Knowledge Grid Environment, *IEEE Intelligent Systems*, 19 (1) (2004) 13-17
10. Zhuge, H., Yao, E., Xing, Y. and Liu, J.: Extended Normal Form Theory of Resource Space Model, *Future Generation Computer Systems*, 21 (2005) 189-198
11. Zhuge, H.: Semantic Grid: Scientific Issues, Infrastructure, and Methodology, *Communications of the ACM*, 48 (4) (2005)117-119
12. Zhuge, H.: The Future Interconnection Environment, *IEEE Computer*, 38 (4) (2005) 27-33
13. Zhuge, H., Liu, J., Feng, L., Sun, X. and He, C.: Query Routing in a Peer-to-Peer Semantic Link Network, *Computational Intelligence*, 21 (2) (2005) 197-216
14. Zhuge, H. and Xing, Y.: Integrity Theory for Resource Space Model and Its Application, *Keynote at WAIM2005, LNCS 3739*, pp.8-24, 2005
15. Zhuge, H. and Shi, X.: Toward the Eco-Grid: A Harmoniously Evolved Interconnection Environment, *Communications of the ACM*, 47 (9) (2004) 79-83
16. Zhuge, H.: Exploring an Epidemic in an E-Science Environment, *Communications of the ACM*, 48 (9) (2005) 109-114

Contingent Pricing for Resource Advance Reservation Under Capacity Constraints

Zhixing Huang and Yuhui Qiu

Faculty of Computer and Information Science,
Southwest China Normal University
{huangzx, yhqiu}@swnu.edu.cn

Abstract. In this paper, we develop a novel framework for resource advance reservation which is based on contingent pricing mechanism. We study the special case where each consumer has a computational demand, but at the time of request for capacity the consumer is uncertain whether or not this demand will occur. We proposed an incentive compatible mechanism where consumers have the incentive to reveal this private information.

1 Introduction

Grid Computing has emerged as a new paradigm for next-generation computing. It supports the creation of virtual organizations and enterprizes that enable the sharing, exchange, selection, and aggregation of geographically distributed heterogenous resources for solving large-scale problems in science, engineering, and commerce. In spite of a number of advantages in Grid computing, resource management and scheduling in such environments continues to be a challenging and complex undertaking. In recent years, distributed computational economy has been recognized as an effective metaphor [2] for the management of Grid resources, as it: (1) enables the regulation of supply and demand for resources, (2) provides economic incentive for grid service providers, and (3) motivates the grid service consumers to trade off between deadline, budget, and the required level of quality-of-service.

Moreover, the Grid is a highly dynamic environment with servers coming on-line, going off-line, and with continuously varying demands from the clients[3]. In most Grid scheduling systems, submitted jobs are initially placed into a queue if there are no available resources. Therefore, there is no guarantee as to when these jobs will be executed. This causes problems in parallel applications, where most of them have dependencies among each other. And grid resources are not storable, thus that capacity not used today can be put aside for future use. So, the advance reservation of these resources are needed for users to request resources from multiple scheduling systems at a specific time and thus gain simultaneous access to enough resources for their application[4]. The works of advance reservations, started within the GGF (Global Grid Forum) to support advance reservations, are currently being added to some test-bed of grid toolkit, such as Nimrod-G [2] etc.

H. Zhuge and G.C. Fox (Eds.): GCC 2005, LNCS 3795, pp. 761–766, 2005.

The remainder of this paper is structured as follows. In Section 2, the definition and the states of advance reservation used in this paper are given, and the model of advance reservation and dynamic programming analysis is discussed. In Section 3, we propose the incentive compatible contingent pricing mechanism. In section 4, the parameters of our model are evaluated through experiments. Finally, in Section 5 we present the conclusions and future work.

2 Problem Statement

2.1 States of Advance Reservation

As be noted in GRAAP-WG [5], the state of advance reservation has nine different states. For the sake of simplicity, in this paper we only consider the following four most important states: Requested, Declined, Booked and Cancelled. That is, the booked reservation can be cancelled but can not be altered.

2.2 The Model

The analysis in this paper assumes that time is discrete and indexed by $t = 1, 2, \cdots, T, T+1$. Potential consumers are allowed to book during the periods $t = 1, 2, \cdots, T$. Then, the contracted service is delivered in period $T+1$ when no further bookings can be made. Each potential consumer has a task to fulfill, the length of the consumer i's task is $l_i \in \{1, 2, \cdots, L\}$, L is the maximum possible job length of the consumer. The potential consumer population with job length l is a fraction denoted by π_l, $0 \leq \pi_l \leq 1$. Moreover, we define $\pi_0 = 1 - \sum_{l=1}^{L} \pi_l$ as the fraction of the population who never books the service. We denote by K the amount of service capacity, which equals the maximum possible total capacity of bookings that can be made. Hence, by the end of period T, the total capacity of bookings cannot have exceeded to K, and $K < LT$.

The analysis in each period t is divided into two parts:

Booking decision: In each booking period t, we determine a decision rule $d_t(l_t) \in \{0, 1\}$ which indicates whether to reject or accept a booking request for the length associated with the price $P(l_t)$. The period t decision rule is determined by maximizing the sum of current profit associated with the requested p_t, and all future value of remaining capacity k_{t+1}.

Expected value of capacity: Given the optimal period t decision rule $d_t(l_t)$, we compute the expected value of period t available capacity which we denote by $EV(k_t)$.

The profit-maximizing decision rule in each booking period $t \leq T$ is

$$d_t(l_t) = \begin{cases} 1 & \text{if } P(l_t) \geq EV_{t+1}(k_t) - EV_{t+1}(k_t - l_t) \text{ and } k_t \geq l_t > 0 \\ 0 & \text{otherwise} \end{cases} \quad (1)$$

The booking decisions associated with the accepted booking classes given in equation (1) imply that the resulting expected period t value of capacity is given by

$$EV_t(k_t) = \sum_{l_t=1}^{L} \pi_l \Big\{ d_t(l_t) \big[EV_{t+1}(k_t - l_t) + P(l_t) \big] + \big[1 - d_t(l_t) \big] EV_{t+1}(k_t) \Big\} \quad (2)$$

3 Contingent Pricing

Let m represent the reverse refund rate[1], $0 \leq m \leq 1$, which is announced by the service provider before the reservation. Each potential consumer has a probability θ_i, and he will in fact need this capacity at time $T+1$, this probability is his private information. Whether or not the capacity is needed at time $T+1$ is unobservable to the service provider. In the general case, the consumer's uncertainty may be in the quantity of computational resources needed at run time, and such uncertainty is quite common for many applications such as optimization programs, complex multi-join queries, financial analysis, sorting algorithms, etc.

In our contingent pricing mechanism, consumer i needs pay $\theta_i P(l_i)$ if his request has been booked and has been completed, but the consumer pay $m\theta_i P(l_i)$ if the booked request has been cancelled by himself, and need not pay if the request has been declined. We assume that the utility of the consumer is following:

$$u_i = \begin{cases} (1-\theta_i)P(l_i) & \text{Completed} \\ -m\theta_i P(l_i) & \text{Cancelled} \\ 0 & \text{Declined} \end{cases}$$

The revenue of the service provider is $\theta_i P(l_i)$ if the consumer i's request is accepted and the booked reservation is completed, and it gains $m\theta_i l_i$ if consumer i cancels the booked reservation, otherwise the revenue is 0.

We denote $\phi(\theta) = \theta + m(1-\theta)\theta$. In each period t, the service provider

$$d_t(l_t) = \begin{cases} 1 & \text{if } \phi(\theta)P(l_t) \geq EV_{t+1}(k_t) - EV_{t+1}(k_t - l_t),\ k_t \geq l_t > 0 \\ 0 & \text{otherwise} \end{cases} \quad (3)$$

Based on the distribution of consumers' θ_i, the service provider should decide the optimal threshold value of β and calculate the serial values $EV_t(k_t)$ for maximizing the profit, and the value of β and $EV_t(k_t)$ are private information of the service provider. The booking decisions associated with the accepted booking classes given in equation (3) imply that the resulting expected value of capacity in period t is given by

$$EV_t(k_t) = \sum_{l_t=1}^{L} \pi_l \Big\{ d_t(l_t) \big[EV_{t+1}(k_t - l_t) + \phi(\beta)P(l_t) \big] + \big[1 - d_t(l_t) \big] EV_{t+1}(k_t) \Big\} \quad (4)$$

[1] In general, $1-m$ represent the refund rate.

Proposition. The dominant strategy of the consumer under this mechanism is truthfully reporting their private information θ_i.

Now, we will prove this mechanism is incentive compatible. For simplicity, we omit the subscription i and the task price $P(l_i)$. Suppose the consumer reports a higher value of θ than the real one, that is $\theta' > \theta$, and we denote $\theta' = \theta + \varepsilon$, $0 \le \varepsilon \le 1$, thus $EU - EU' = \varepsilon\theta + m\varepsilon(1-\theta) > 0$, that means if consumer reports θ' higher than the real probability θ, his expected utility will decrease. On the other hand, because the values of $\phi(\theta)$ increase monotonically when $m \in [0,1]$, $\theta \in [0,1]$, and the information of the value *beta* and $EV_t(k_t)$ is not known by the consumer, if consumer reports $\theta' < \theta$, he will face the risk that his request will be declined by the service provider due to the lower profit.

4 Experiment Analysis

4.1 Experiment Setup

In this section we present the results of simulations of our model while considering a variety of parameters. To minimize the variance in the outcomes and to help us study the factors of interest, for each correlation value, we repeat the experiment with the same 1000 trails. In each scenario, we assume that the capacity of the service is 10, the maximum task length is 3, the distribution of the task length is $\pi = 0.25$, $i \in \{0,1,2,3\}$, the price of the task is $P(l_i) = l_i * 10$, and the probability of the consumers' willingness is uniformly distributed in [0,1], and the value of the reverse refund rate m and β vary between [0,1] with an interval of 0.05.

4.2 The Influences of m and β

In this scenario, to study the influences of the reverse refund rate m and the acceptance threshold β, we assume that the total number of booking periods is fixed, $T = 30$. The revenues of service provider achieved under various value of the reverse refund rate m and the threshold β are illustrated on the left of Figure 1, and the sum of the consumer's utilities is on the right of Figure 1.

It can be easily seen that when the value of the acceptance threshold β is fixed, the revenue of the service provider monotonically increases with the increase of the reverse refund rate m. It means that the relation between the provider's revenue and the reverse refund rate is positively correlated. However, if the value of the reverse refund rate m is fixed, the revenue gradually increases when the threshold β increases in the beginning, and decreases later on.

The effects of the reverse refund rate m and the acceptance threshold β on the sum of the consumer's utilities are illustrated on the right of Figure 1. The sum of the consumer's utilities reaches higher value when either the reverse refund rate or the acceptance threshold becomes smaller, or both. Conversely, the sum of the consumer's utilities reaches lower value when m or β becomes larger. That means the sum of the consumer's utilities is negatively correlated with the reserve refund rate m and the acceptance threshold β.

4.3 The Influence of T

In this scenario, to study the influence of the total number of the booking periods on the providers' revenue, and the variance of the value of optimal acceptance threshold β where the welfare reaches its highest, we assume that the reverse refund rate is fixed, $m = 0.5$, and the total booking period T is selected from $[10, 100]$ with an interval of 10. In each trial of different total booking period number, the optimal β value and maximum value of the revenue and the average value of the revenue with the variant acceptance threshold β are recorded. In Figure 2, the left part demonstrates the relation between the social welfare and the total booking period number, and the right part demonstrates how the β very with the change of the total booking period number.

It is clear that in the beginning the revenue of the service provider increases quickly with the increase of the total booking period number T, however, the maximum value and the average value of revenue under the variance of T keeps to being a constant later on due to the constraint of the capacity of the service and the price of the task. And the increase of the booking period implies that the higher acceptance threshold should be adopted to the profit-maximizing. The optimal value of β depends on the distribution of the task length, the price of the task, and the total booking period number. We obtain the value through the simulation. It should be noted that when the value of the acceptance threshold β reaches relatively high value, the increase of the value of β will dramatically decrease the revenue of the provider. A straightforward reason is the probability of the requests which satisfies the standard decrease dramatically. In this case, for the probability θ is uniformed distributed in $[0, 1]$, when $\beta \geq 0.9$ the revenue will reaches its lowest level as is shown in Figure 1.

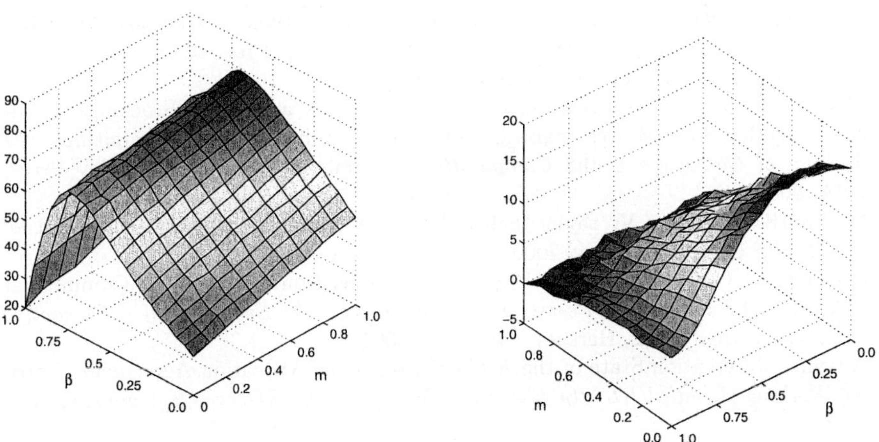

Fig. 1. a) The revenue of the service provider b) the sum of the consumers' utility under the various value of the reverse refund rate m and threshold β

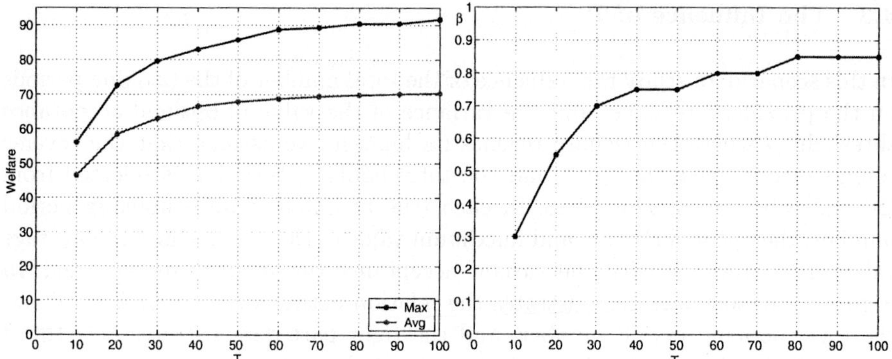

Fig. 2. a) The social welfare b) the value of the optimal acceptance threshold β under the variance of the total booking period number

5 Conclusion and Future Work

In current work, we assume that the request can only be cancelled by the consumers. However, sometimes the service provider also faces the trouble that he can not provide the service on time due to that the requested resources are unavailable, or there exists more profitable requests, thus the mechanism which functions as compensation to the consumers are needed. And, it is a necessary that we should analytically calculate the optimal acceptance threshold if we are to know the related parameters. We will extend our work in the future.

References

1. Hemant K. Bhargava, Shanker Sundaresan: Contigent Bids in Auctions: Availability, Commitment and Pricing of Computing as Utitily. Proc. of the 37th Hawaii International Conference on System Sciences. 2004.
2. Rajkumar Buyya, David Abramson, Jonathan Giddy and Heinz Stockinger: Economic models for resource management and scheduling in Grid computing, *The Journal of Concurrency and Computation*, Volume 14, Issue 13-15, Wiley Press, USA, 2002.
3. W. Smith, I. Froster, V. Taylor: Scheduling with Advanced Reservations, *Proc. of the IPDPS Conference*, May, 2000.
4. G.Cheloitis, C.Kneyon and R. Buyya: 10 Lessons from Finance for Commercial Sharing of IT Resources, *Peer-to-Peer Computing: The Evolution of a Disruptive Technology*, IRM Press, Hershey, PA, USA, 2004.
5. Advance Reservation State of the Art: Grid Resource Allocation Agreement Protocol Working Group, *URL http://www.fz-juelich.de/zam/RD/coop/ggf/graap/graap-wg.html.*
6. Michal P. Wellman, William E. Walsh, Peter R. Wurman and Jeffrey K. Mackie-Mason: Auction protocols for decentralized scheduling. *Game and Economic Behavior.* 2001.

Anonymous Communication Systems in P2P Network with Random Agent Nodes

Byung Ryong Kim[1] and Ki Chang Kim[2]

[1] Department of Computer Science and Engineering, Inha Univ.,
253, YongHyun-Dong, Nam-Ku, Incheon, 402-751, Korea
doolyn@super.inha.ac.kr
http://super.inha.ac.kr

[2] Department of Information and Communication Engineering, Inha Univ.,
253, YongHyun-Dong, Nam-Ku, Incheon, 402-751, Korea
kchang@inha.ac.kr

Abstract. P2P networks provide a basic form of anonymity. The anonymity, however, breaks down at download/upload time because the IP address of the host from which the data is downloaded (or to which it is uploaded) can be known to the outside. We propose a technique to provide anonymity for both the client and the server node. A random node along the path between the client and the server node is selected as an agent node and works as a proxy: the client will see it as the server and the server looks at it as the client, hence protecting the identity of the client and the server from each other.

1 Introduction

Peer-to-Peer(P2P) is characterized by resource sharing among computing machines that participate in the network. In Server/Client environment, the user sends query messages to the server, and a popular server suffers a heavy load resulting degraded service. P2P network alleviates this problem by distributing the server data among the participating nodes and providing a mechanism to locate the data dynamically. This way copies of data are scattered around in the network, and the load concentration problem can be handled; however, it became harder and more expensive to find out which nodes have the data.

Currently locating data is done via Flooding techniques as in FreeNet[1] or Gnutella[2] or Distributed Hash Table techniques as in Tapestry[3,4], Can[5], or Chord[6]. Flooding model involves a repeated broadcasting of a query and inevitably causes a heavy traffic. Distributed Hash Table reduces query traffic considerably but still has the problem of keeping the table fresh. Both, however, do not provide anonymity for server locations and could expose servers to DoS or storage flooding attack[7,8].

In this paper, we propose a technique to provide anonymity both for the client and the server node. An intermediate node is selected as the agent who goes between the client and the server. This agent will pose itself as the server to the client and creates this illusion by replacing the true server IP with its own one in the query hit message packets. It also relays the client's content request to the true server and relays the data back to the client pretending as the true server.

H. Zhuge and G.C. Fox (Eds.): GCC 2005, LNCS 3795, pp. 767 – 775, 2005.

The rest of the paper is as follows. Section 2 summarizes previous researches on providing anonymity in P2P network. Section 3 looks at the probabilistic characteristics in P2P packets which will be used in our algorithm that is explained in Section 4. Section 5 shows the experimental results, and Section 6 concludes the paper.

2 Related Researches

Anonymity problem in P2P networks is studied in MUTE[9], Onion Routing[11,12], Crowds[13], and Mantis[10] as shown in Fig. 1. MUTE forces all intermediate nodes along the path between the client and the server node to work as proxies to protect the identities of the client and the server. Every node in the path including the client and the server thinks its previous node is the client and its next one the server. Therefore the data from the true server will be relayed node by node along the path causing a heavy traffic, especially for large multimedia files.

Onion routing hides routing header to guarantee anonymous connection and uses encryption to avoid statistical attack on the routing path. Client selects a route and sends a connection packet to a proxy that will help the encryption process. Once reached the proxy, the packet will be transferred between Onion routers. Each router peels off each level of encryption to know the next router, and this process continues until the packet reaches the final destination. The response path follows the same pattern: only this time the encryption layers will be added at each router. This scheme provides a strong anonymity protection but with the high encryption cost.

Crowds technique was developed to protect the client's privacy while he/she is web-browsing. The client in Crowds network does not communicate directly with the server that has the needed contents: it does not know where the server is. Instead the client asks one of participating node in Crowds, and this helping node sets up the link with the server. The server, therefore, has no way of telling who was the original requester for its information. This technique requires a central Crowds server to maintain the list of helping nodes. Mantis is similar to Crowds in that there are helping nodes to propagate the request to the candidate servers anonymously. Since Mantis preserves the anonymity of the server only, the server knows where is the client. The server sends the requested data to the client directly but in UDP hiding its IP. UDP is convenient to hide the server's identity but due to the packet loss inevitable in UDP Mantis needs additional packet retransmission mechanism.

Our technique is similar to Onion routing in that it uses a proxy node to hide the identity of the client and the server. But it differs from it in that the proxy node is selected dynamically for each session and not fixed as in Onion routing. The fixed proxy might be convenient to use and is useful when loaded with additional features such as encryption as in Onion routing. However it is a sort of compromise from P2P point of view: we are introducing something similar to a control center that could become a bottleneck in the network. Temporary proxy doesn't have this problem: it is used once and discarded, and later another node is selected as the proxy. However using temporary proxy has a different problem: it is hard to find the right proxy. It should be in a particular path set up between the client and the server, and it should be in some position where the proxying service can be most efficiently performed. In this paper, we show a technique to find such proxy, explain the rationale behind the decision, and prove its effectiveness through experimentation.

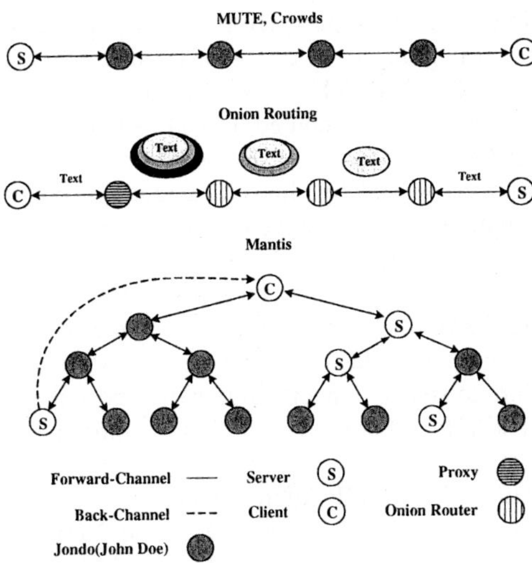

Fig. 1. Techniques for providing anonymity

3 Providing Anonymity Via Random Agent Nodes

To hide the client and the server from each other, our algorithm selects a limited number of random agent nodes and let them relay the actual data between the server the client. The agents are selected dynamically per each session, hence it is hard to trace the location of the server or the client via the agent nodes. Also our algorithm makes sure the number of selected agents is very limited, in most cases one or two, so that the relay overhead can be minimized. The algorithm each node performs as it receives a packet is given in Fig. 2. We explain the algorithm in following sections.

```
If Received_Pakcet is QueryHit
  random_hop = random number between [0, path lenght between client & server]
  if Received_Packet->hops == random_hop
    Replace IPAddress and Port of the Received_Packet with MY IPAddress and Port
    Remember this connection in SessionTable
    Send out the packet
  else
   Pass the packet
else if Received_Packet is HTTP GET
  if HTTP_GET_Request->ServantSessionUUID != MY->global.sessionGUID
    // This means I should work as a proxy for this request.
    for each SessionRecord at SessionTable
      if found Session Record with HTTP_GET_Request->ServantSessionUUID
        Make a PUSH packet to send to the sever node remembered in it.
              Send out the packet through SessionRecord->Connection
      endif
    endfor
  endif
................
endif
```

Fig. 2. Packet processing at each node

When the incoming packet is a QueryHit packet, each node performs an algorithm to determine whether it is going to be an agent for this query. It generates a random number in [0..PATH_LEN-1]. PATH_LEN is the length of the communication path this query belongs to and can be computed by TTL + Hops - 1 in the received packet. When added, TTL and Hops in the QueryHit packet represents the length of the path between the client and the server; by choosing a random number in [0..PATH_LEN-1], we hope approximately one node in the communication path will establish itself as an agent node. If the random number is 0, it becomes an agent. There is a chance no node in the path will pick 0; in this case there will be no agent node. There is also a chance that multiple nodes pick 0's; then we have multiple agent nodes. Multiple agent nodes will increase the relay-overhead but will strengthen the degree of anonymity as well. Failure to select an agent node will expose the client and the server to each other; but both still don't know for sure that the other part is the actual server or client.

The agent node will replace the IP Address and Port in the QueryHit packet with its own ones. The ServantSessionUUID remains the same. Now this packet will have the IP Address and Port of the agent instead of the original server, but it still has the ServerSessionUUID of the original server. The client, after receiving this packet, will contact the specified IP Address with a wrong UUID, and this discrepancy will be detected by our agent node allowing it to act as a proxy between the client and the server. For this purpose, the information about the original server is saved in the SessionTable of the agent node as shown in the algorithm. The same algorithm is repeated at following agent nodes when there are more than one agent. For the second agent, the first agent will be treated as the original server, and it will establish itself as a proxy between the client and the first agent node. This argument goes on for the third and fourth agent nodes as they are added in the path. Note we are not adding all intermediate nodes between the client and the server as agent nodes as in MUTE; we are selecting only those who picks 0.

Fig. 3 shows a typical flow of a Query and QueryHit packet. Node 1 broadcasts a Query packet for which Node 7 has the requested data. Node 7 sends a QueryHit packet back to Node 1 via the same path that the Query packet followed. Without anonymity mechanism, the client can contact Node 7 directly since the QueryHit packet contains the IP Adress and Port of Node 7. Node 7, on the other hand, also contacts node 1 directly to answer the request; hence both are exposed to one another.

In our scheme, some agent nodes will be elected as the QueryHit packet traces back to Node 1. Suppose Node 6 and Node 3 are such agent nodes. Upon deciding to become an agent, Node 6 starts to modify the packet header: the IP Address and Port

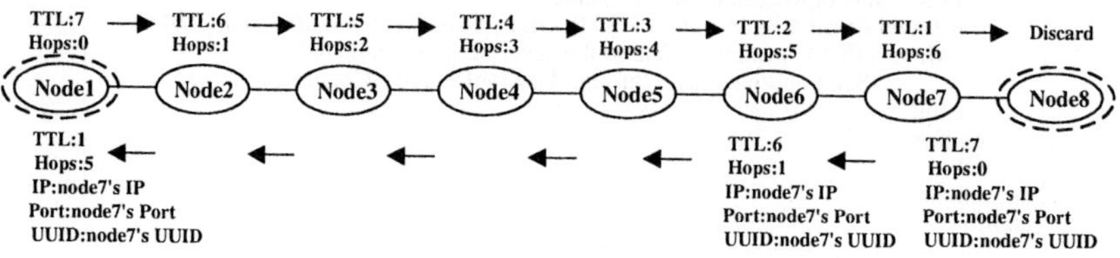

Fig. 3. Flow of Query and Query Hit packets

of Node 7 are replaced with those of Node 6. And the related information is saved in the SessionTable. Node 6 now acts as if it is the server who has sent the QueryHit packet. Node 3 also processes the packet similarly, but in this case, it thinks Node 6 is the server and sends the modified packet to Node 1 as a proxy for Node 6.

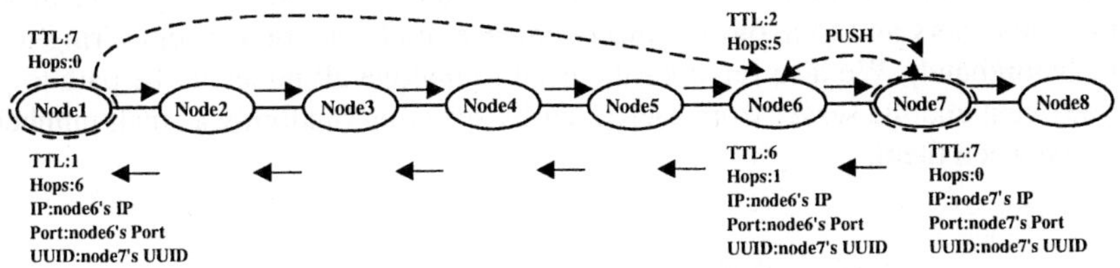

Fig. 4. Selection of agent nodes and flow of requested data through them

Node 1, upon receiving QueryHit packet, contacts Node 3, the first agent, and sends HTTP header to it requesting data. The UUID included in the packet, however, is that of Node 6. Node 3 knows that this packet should be delivered to Node 6 by noticing this mis-matching between UUID and the destination IP address. It builds a PUSH packet to request the indicated data from Node 6. Now Node 3 works as an agent between Node 1 and Node 6. The response from Node 6 will be relayed to Node 1 via Node 3. Similar events happen in Node 6 because it is another agent between Node 3 and the final server. Two agents, Node 3 and Node 6, will relay the data from the actual server to the client hiding the identities of both ends successfully.

4 Experimentation

Onion Routing sets up an Onion Proxy to separate the client and the server from each other. Onion Proxy prepares an anonymous path between the client and the server consisting of Onion Routers. The data itself is encrypted and decrypted at each router until it reaches the final destination. MUTE utilizes all nodes in the path between the client and the server to provide a strong anonymity. For a large file, the transmission

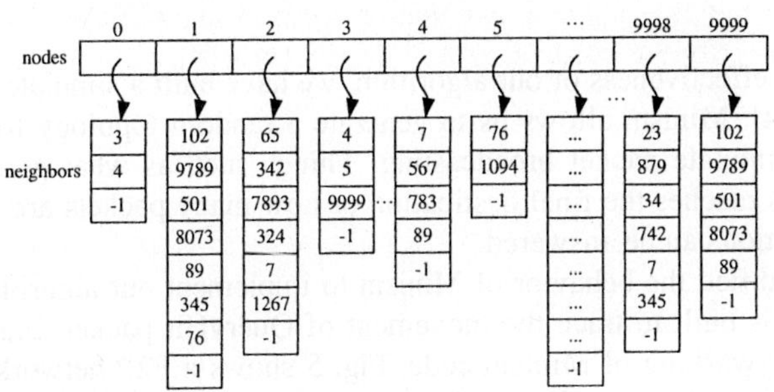

Fig. 5. A P2P network generated by Minism

speed is severely affected because of this. Mantis, on the other hand, tries to solve this problem by employing UDP protocol. With UDP, the client doesn't have to set up a connection with the server: the server can send directly to the client when the request from the client reaches it through the intermediate nodes. But to compensate the instability of the protocol, it generates additional control packets. Our technique excludes the use of a static proxy as in Onion Routing to avoid the exposure of such proxy to attackers and to avoid the inconvenience at client side (of registering to the proxy beforehand). We also removes the need to invlove all nodes in the path to protect the client and the server from each other by selecting randomly a small number of agents between them.

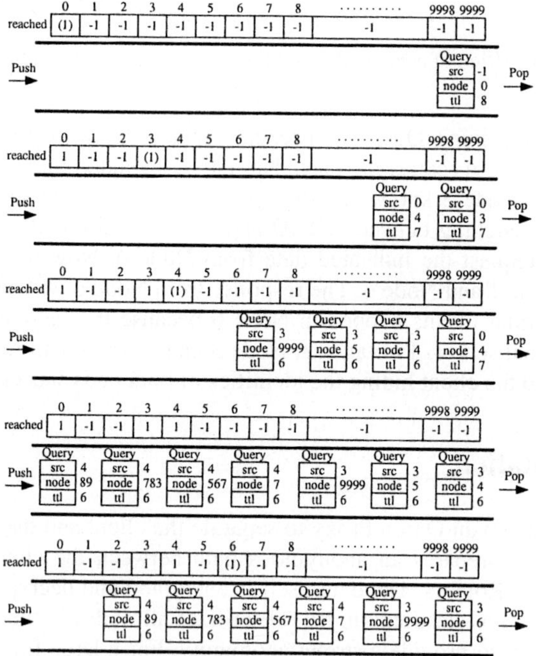

Fig. 6. The propagation of a Query packet

To prove the effectiveness of our algorithm, we have built a simulated P2P network with Minism[14]. Minism allows us to generate a random topology for a number of nodes and to simulate packet broadcasting. Things such as what percentage of the original packets reaches the final destination or how many packets are discarded during the propagation can be answered.

We have modified the behavior of Minism to implement our algorithm. Especially a routing table is built to trace the movement of QueryHit packet. Fig. 5 and Fig. 6 shows the inner-working of Minism code. Fig. 5 shows a P2P network generated by Minism. The figure shows each node is assigned a number of neighbor nodes: node 0 has neighbors of node 3 and 4; node 1 has neighbors of node 102, 9789, etc. Fig. 6

shows the propagation of Query packet. The "reached" array shows the nodes the Query packet reached at each stage. In "reached" array, nodes with -1 are ones that are not reached yet; nodes with 1 are those that are visited already; finally a node with (1) is one we are going to visit next. Below "reached" array, we can see the state of the stack that contains the Query packet. To simulate the propagation of a packet, the stack shows at each stage which path each duplicated Query packet should follow (from which node to which node). For example, at stage 1, all nodes are marked with -1 except node 0 since we haven't visited any node yet, and the starting node is node 0. The stack contains the path we should relay the packet: from -1 (no where) to 0 (the starting node). At stage 1, we can see node 0 is already visited (at stage 1); the next node we should visit is node 3 because node 0 has two neighbors - node 3 and 4 - and node 3 is selected as the next one. The stack shows the two path segments we should take (from 0 to 3 and from 0 to 4) for the Query packet. The segment at the top of the stack (from 0 to 3) will be chosen.

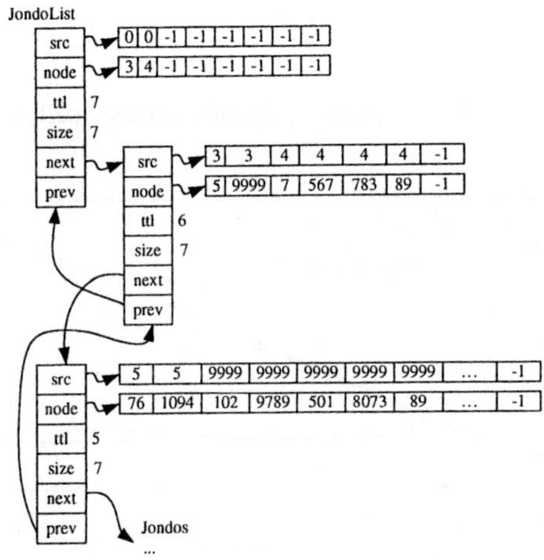

Fig. 7. A routing history table

To implement our algorithm, we have included routing tables that show at each stage which path the Query packet has followed. Fig. 7 shows such tables. At stage 1, the first table shows route(0,3) and rout(0,4) has been taken. At stage 2, it shows that route(3,5), route(3,9999), route(4,7), etc. has been taken. With these tables, we can backtrack the paths starting from the destination all the way back to the original client.

The result is shown in Fig. 8 and 9. Fig. 8 shows the number of packets generated for our simulation. Path length between the client and the server is chosen to vary from 2 to 11. Fig. 9 shows the performance of our algorithm compared to that of MUTE. As expected MUTE increases the traffic linearly as the path length gets longer, while ours stays almost the same. In most cases only one node chooses to be an agent. Since we do not allow any additional controlling packet to relay the information about this selection process, there is a chance that no node will decide to become the agent or all nodes become the agents. The latter case will make our algorithm to mimic that of MUTE, the former to that of no anonymity case. It could be a problem if there are no node selected as an agent: the client and the server is not hidden from each other. But as explained in the previous section, with our scheme the client or the server never knows that it is dealing with the other side directly. The chance is very small and each side cannot attack the other with such a small percent of certainty.

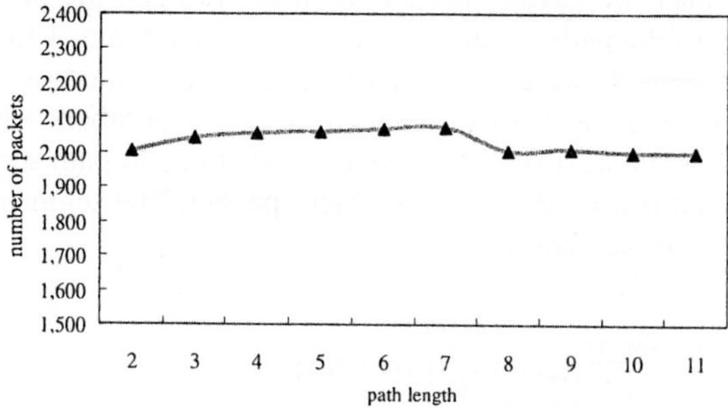

Fig. 8. Number of packets generated for each path length

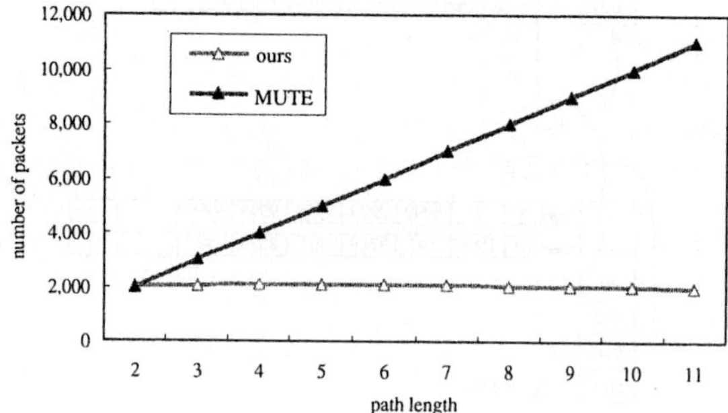

Fig. 9. Comparison between MUTE and our technique in terms of generated traffic to deliver the contents

5 Conclusions

Currently, many techniques are suggested to provide anonymity for both the client and the server. Some of them guarantee anonymity by setting up a static proxy and forcing all communication to go through it. The clients, however, should know the presence of the proxy beforehand. Other techniques provide anonymity by allowing all intermediate nodes to participate in the data transmission. The data delivery time suffers delay inevitably. We proposed a technique that stood about in the middle of these two approaches. We employed the idea of a proxy but not static one. The proxy is selected dynamically during the traverse of the QueryHit packet. Since the selection process is truly distributed, no one knows exactly how many proxies, or agents, are selected and where they are located. The agents are linked together only by neighbors:

each agent knows only its previous and the succeeding one. We have designed the process such that only very limited number of agents are selected. Since these agents are used only for the current session (and will be replace by others in the next session), it is hard to attack them or to predict the location of the client or the server by analyzing their packets. We explained how it works and showed that its performance improved substantially over previous techniques through experimentation.

Acknowledgements

This work has been supported by INHA UNIVERSITY Research Grant.

References

1. The Freenet Project, http://freenet.sourceforge.net/
2. The Gnutella Protocol Specification v0.41 Document Revision 1.2., http://rfc.gnutella.sourceforge.net/developer/stable/index.html/
3. Kirsten Hildrum, John Kubiatowicz, Satish Rao and Ben Y. Zhao., Distributed Object Location in a Dynamic Network, Theory of Computing Systems (2004)
4. Ben Y. Zhao, Ling Huang, Jeremy Stribling, Sean C. Rhea, Anthony D. Joseph, and John Kubiatowicz., Tapestry: A Resilient Global-scale Overlay for Service Deployment, IEEE Journal on Selected Areas in Communications (2004)
5. Sylvia Ratnasamy, Paul Francis, Mark Handley, Richard Karp, Scott Schenker, A scalable content-addressable network, Proceedings of the 2001 conference on Applications, technologies, architectures, and protocols for computer communications table of contents
6. Ion Stoica, Robert Morris, David Liben-Nowell, David R. Karger, M. Frans Kaashoek, Frank Dabek, Hari Balakrishnan., Chord: a scalable peer-to-peer lookup protocol for internet applications, IEEE/ACM Transactions on Networking (2003)
7. Neil Daswani, Hector Garcia-Molina., Query-flood DoS attacks in gnutella, Proceedings of the t e 9th ACM conference on Computer and communications security table of contents (2002)
8. P. Krishna Gummadi, Stefan Saroiu, Steven D. Gribble., A measurement study of Napster and Gnutella as examples of peer-to-peer file sharing systems, ACM SIGCOMM Computer Communication Review (2002)
9. MUTE: Simple, Anonymous File Sharing, http://mute-net.sourceforge.net/
10. Stephen C. Bono, Christopher A. Soghoian, Fabian Monrose., Mantis: A Lightweight, Server-Anonymity Preserving, Searchable P2P, Information Security Institute of The Johns Hopkins University, Technical Report TR-2004-01-B-ISI-JHU (2004)
11. Michael G. Reed and Paul F. Syverson., Onion Routing, Proceeding of AIPA '99 (1999)
12. Roger Dingledine, Nick Mathewson, Paul Syverson., Tor: The Second-Generation Onion Router, Proceedings of the 13th USENIX Security Symposium (2004)
13. Michael K. Reiter, Aviel D. Rubin., Crowds: anonymity for Web transactions, ACM Transactions on Information and System Security (TISSEC) (1998)
14. Gnutella Developer Forum, http://groups.yahoo.com/group/the_gdf/

An Efficient Cluster-Hierarchy Architecture Model ECHP2P for P2P Networks

Guangxue Yue[1,2], Renfa Li[1,3], Zude Zhou[3], and Ronghui Wu[1]

[1] College of computer and communication, Hunan University, Changsha, Hunan 410082, P.R. China
guangxueyue@yahoo.com.cn
[2] The Department of Computer Science, Huaihua Institute, Huaihua, Hunan. 418000, P.R. China
[3] Wuhan University of Technology, Wuhan, Hubei. 430070, P.R. China

Abstract. P2P systems have emerged as a popular way to share huge volumes of data. It offers many attractive features, such as autonomy, load balancing, availability and anonymity. However, it also faces some serious challenges, such as poor scalability and low efficiency. This paper propose a new distributed P2P network model of ECHP2P with hierarchical structure based on cluster, with ECHP2P, peers are grouped into clusters according to proximity, and super peers are selected from regular peers to act as cluster leaders. These leaders are connected to each other, forming a backbone overlay network. To manage the routing and to limit duplicate messages on it, we propose an application level route strategy: Optimized-Flooding. Simulation results about ECHP2P system show that it could effectively solve the above problems, and larger the network size is, more efficient its comprehensive performance is, so the model is reasonable and effective.

1 Introduction

In very large P2P networks, it is not always easy to find desired resources. For any given system, the efficiency of any search technique depends on the needs of the application. Currently, there are two types of P2P lookup services widely used for decentralized P2P system[1]: structured searching mechanism and unstructured searching mechanism.

Structured systems such as CAN[2], Pastry[3], Chord[4] and Tapestry[5] are designed for applications running on well-organized networks, where availability and persistence can be guaranteed. In such systems, queries follow well-defined paths from a querying node to a destination node that holds the index entries pertaining to the query. These systems are scalable and efficient, and they guarantee that content can be located within a bounded number of hops. To achieve this performance level, the systems have to control data placement and topology tightly within their networks[6]. However, this results in several limitations[7]: first, they require stringent care in data placement and the deployment of network topology, and second, these systems can only support search-by-identifiers and lack the flexibility of keyword searching, a useful operation for finding content without knowing the exact name of

H. Zhuge and G.C. Fox (Eds.): GCC 2005, LNCS 3795, pp. 776–786, 2005.

the object sought. Third, these systems offer only file level sharing, and do not share particular data from within the files.

Unstructured systems like Gnutella[8] and Freent[9] are designed more specifically for the heterogeneous Internet environment, where the nodes' persistence and availability are not guaranteed. Under these conditions, it is impossible to control data placement and to maintain strict constraints on network topology, as structured applications require[6,7]. Currently, these systems are widely deployed in real life. Which support many desirable properties such as simplicity, robustness, low requirement for network topology and supporting keyword searching. Unstructured systems operate under a different set of constraints than those faced by techniques developed for structured systems. In unstructured systems, a query is answered by flooding the entire network and searching every node. Flooding on every request is clearly not scalable, and it has to be curtailed at some point, therefore it may fail to find content that is actually in the system. Furthermore, a network that uses flooding might be bombarded with excess messages and activity, and at certain points it might fail. To overcome these problems, we propose a hierarchical structure and an efficient routing strategy: Optimized-Flooding.

2 Hierarchies Architecture

In P2P networks, participating peers exhibit considerable heterogeneity in terms of storage capacity, processing power, bandwidth and online availability. For the best design, we should take advantage of this heterogeneity and assign greater responsibility to the peers that are capable of handling it. ECHP2P utilizes these differences in a hierarchical P2P design, in which peers with different capabilities take different roles. Specifically, peers in the system act as client peers and super-peers(we call the cluster leaders) in different hierarchies[10,11]. Figure 1 illustrates the hierarchical structure, in which peers are grouped together if they are topologically close, and it forms the cluster. Autonomous systems (AS) can be regarded as a form of existing clusters. These clusters define their invariants as those destinations recognized by the routers as having the same BGP(Border Gateway Protocol)[12] gateways into the cluster, generally based on the subnet masks of the IP address. Each AS has a globally unique number, an autonomous system number, associated with it, this number is used in both the exchange of exterior routing information (between neighboring autonomous systems), and as an identifier of the AS itself. Cluster leaders are selected from regular peers according to their computing resources and bandwidth capabilities, the volume of files they store, and the behavior of being seldom offline. Cluster leaders act as local search hubs, building indices of the content files shared by each peer connected to them, and proxying search requests on behalf of these peers. Cluster leaders are connected with each other and organized amongst themselves into a backbone overlay network on the super-peer tier[7,10,11]. The hierarchical structure of this system combines advantages of both centralized and pure P2P systems. Because of the introduction of a new level of hierarchy in the system increases the scale and speed of query lookup and forwarding processes, so it is more stable. Finally, cluster leader overlay routing protocol Optimized-Flooding reduces the workload of cluster leaders significantly by avoiding many flooding duplications.

Figure 2 illustrates the ECHP2P logical structure. The ECHP2P protocol arranges the set of peers into a hierarchy, the basic operation of the protocol is to create and maintain the hierarchy. The member hierarchy is crucial for scalability, since most members are in the bottom of the hierarchy and only maintain state about a constant number of other members. The members at the very top of the hierarchy maintain state about *O(logN)* other members[13]. Logically, each member keeps detailed state about other members that are near in the hierarchy, and only has limited knowledge about other members in the group.

In this paper, we use peer-to-peer latency as the distance metric between hosts. While constructing the ECHP2P hierarchy, members that are "close" with respect to the distance metric are mapped to the same part of the hierarchy.

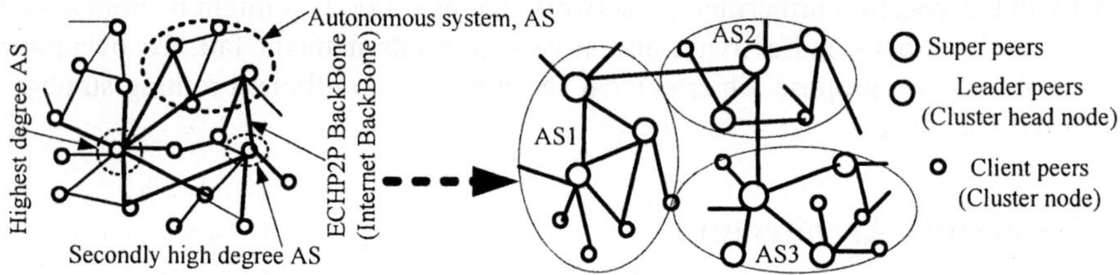

Fig. 1. ECHP2P system architecture

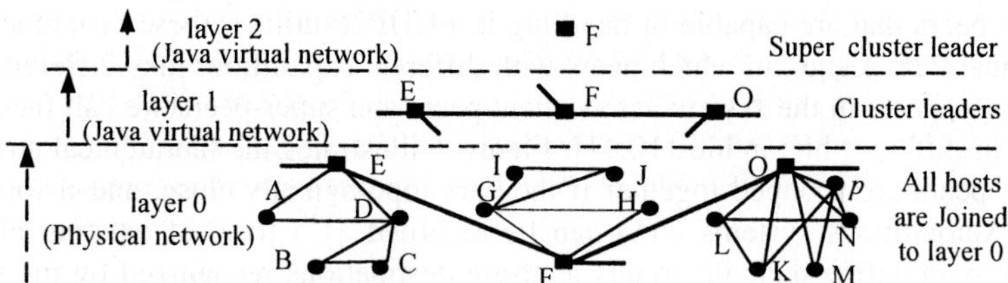

Fig. 2. ECHP2P system architecture

2.1 Hierarchical Arrangement of Members

The ECHP2P hierarchy is created by assigning members to different layers as illustrated in Figure 2. Layers are numbered sequentially with the lowest layer of the hierarchy being layer zero (denoted by L_0). Hosts in each layer are partitioned into a set of clusters. Each cluster is of size between K and $3K-1$, where K is a constant, and consists of a set of hosts that are close to each other[13]. Further, each cluster has a cluster leader. The protocol distributedly chooses the (graph-theoretic) center of the cluster to be its leader. This choice of the cluster leader is important in guaranteeing that a new joining member is quickly able to find its appropriate position in the hierarchy using a very small number of queries to other members.

Hosts are mapped to layers using the following scheme: All hosts are part of the lowest layer, L_0 . The clustering protocol at L_0 partitions these hosts into a set of clusters. The cluster leaders of all the clusters in layer L_i join layer L_{i+1}.

2.2 Cluster Membership

The functions a cluster must support with respect to membership fall into two categories, super peers and client peers.

Super peers act as cluster leaders and service providers for a subset of client peers, providing four basic services to the clients: join, update, leave and query. Super peers are connected with each other to form an application-level overlay network. Which are not only cluster leaders for their client peers, but also members of the super peer overlay network. Therefore they supply interfaces to both client peers and to adjacent neighbor super peers.

Client peers act as both clients and servers, yet. They send requests to cluster leaders like clients, and receive other peers' file download requests like servers. While providing this functionality, client peers can offer easy-to-use interfaces, through which users can connect to the system, discover resources in the network and finally obtain the required content. Client peer locates content through cluster leaders; it opens a connection and downloads directly from the node where the content is located.

2.3 Analysis

Each cluster in the hierarchy has between K and $3K-1$ members. Then for the control topology, a host that belongs only to layer L_0 peers with $O(K)$ other hosts for exchange of control messages. In general, a host that belongs to layer L_i and no other higher layer, peers with $O(K)$ other hosts in each of the layers $L_0 \ldots\ldots L_i$. Therefore, the control overhead for this member is $O(K,i)$. Hence, the cluster leader of the highest layer cluster, peers with a total of $O(K\log N)$ neighbors. This is the worst case control overhead at a member.

It follows using amortized cost analysis that the control overhead at an average member is a constant. The number of members that occur in layer L_i and no other higher layer is bounded by $O(\log N)$. Therefore, the amortized control overhead at an average member is[13]:

$$C \leq 1/N \sum_{i=0}^{\log N} iNK/K^i = O(K) + O(\log N/N) + O(1/N) \Rightarrow O(K) \quad (1)$$

with asymptotically increasing N. Thus, the control overhead is $O(K)$ for the average member, and $O(K\log N)$ in the worst case.

3 Protocol Descriptions

We assume that the super peer is always the leader of the single cluster in the highest layer of the hierarchy. The ECHP2P protocol itself has three main components: initial cluster assignment as a new host joins, periodic cluster maintenance and refinement, and recovery from leader failures.

3.1 New Host Joins

When a new host joins the cluster, it must be mapped to some cluster in layer L_0. We illustrate the join procedure in Figure3[13]. Assume that host *h* wants to join the network. First, it contacts the super peer with its join query. The super peer responds with the hosts that are present in the highest layer of the hierarchy. The joining host then contacts all members in the highest layer to identify the member closest to itself. In the example, the highest layer L_2 has just one member, *F*, which by default is the closest member to *h* amongst layer L_2 members. Host *F* informs *h* of the three other members (*M*, *E* and *O*) in its L_1 cluster. *h* then contacts each of these members with the join query to identify the closest member among them, and iteratively uses this procedure to find its L_0 cluster.

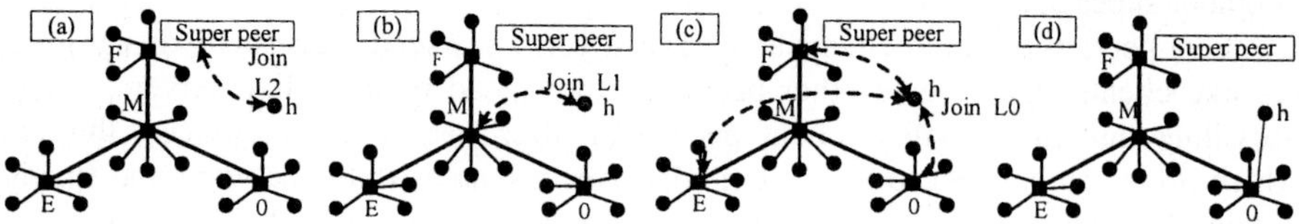

Fig. 3. Host h joins the ECHP2P

The joining process involves a message overhead of *O(KlogN)* query-response pairs. The join-latency depends on the delays incurred in this exchanges, which is typically about *O(logN)* round-trip times[14]. To reduce the delay between a member joining the cluster, and its receipt of the first data packet on the overlay, we allow joining members to temporarily peer, on the data path, with the leader of the cluster of the current layer it is querying. For example, in Figure 3, when *h* is querying the hosts *M*, *E* and *O* for the closest point of attachment, it temporarily peers with *F* (leader of the layer L_1 cluster) on the data path. This allows the joining host to start receiving multicast data on the group within a single round-trip latency of its join.

3.2 Cluster Maintenance and refinement

Each member *h* of a cluster *F*, sends a *HeartBeat* message every *x* seconds to each of its cluster peers. The message contains the distance estimate of *h* to each other member of *F*.

The cluster leader includes the complete updated cluster membership in its *HeartBeat* messages to all other members. All of the cluster member state is sent via unreliable messages and is kept by each cluster member as soft-state, refreshed by the periodic *HeartBeat* messages. A member *h* is declared no longer part of a cluster independently by all other members in the cluster if they do not receive a message from *h* for a configurable number of *HeartBeat* message intervals.

All of the cluster leader periodically checks the size of its cluster, and appropriately splits or merges the cluster when it detects a size bound violation. A cluster that just exceeds the cluster size upper bound, *3K-1* is split into two equal-sized clusters.

Similar, when it violate the cluster size lower bound and require a cluster merge operation to be performed.

When a host *h* leaves the cluster, it sends a remove message to all clusters to which it is joined. This is a graceful-leave. However, if *h* fails without being able to send out this message all cluster peers of *h* detects this departure through non-receipt of the periodic *HeartBeat* message from *h*. If *h* was a leader of a cluster, this triggers a new leader selection in the cluster. Selection a peer from remaining regular peers acts as the new cluster leader, and establishes connection with other cluster leaders through exchange of regular *HeartBeat* message, and updates the cluster leader's index table.

The introduction of one more level of hierarchy makes the system more efficient, but the cluster leader becomes a potential area of single-point failure for its cluster. When the cluster leader fails or leaves the system, the entire cluster content index information is lost. To increase the reliability of the system, in backbone network, we introduce a backup peer as redundancy for the cluster leader. Thus, every cluster has a super peer acting as a cluster leader and a backup leader acting as a redundancy server. The backup leaders are selected from the client peers too. They copy the cluster leader's index table periodically, and when a cluster leader fails or leaves the network, its backup leader replaces it and the cluster selects a new backup leader for redundancy. The possibility of both a cluster leader and its backup leader failing simultaneously is much smaller than failure of the cluster leader alone, and thus the introduction of a backup leader greatly improves a system's robustness. Furthermore, a backup leader is dynamically selected from client peers in the cluster, so there is no extra burden for the redundancy.

4 Backbone Overlay Routing: Optimized-Flooding

Our algorithm aims at suppressing flooding by reducing the number of duplicated query messages. There are many approaches to eliminating flooding, the most popular of which uses tree-based broadcasting. However, all tree-based approaches require huge messaging overhead. In most P2P systems, participant nodes are typically PCs at homes or offices with their own tasks, and thus they cannot afford many resources for P2P applications. In addition, they can be very dynamic, so messages updating tree structures overwhelm the network[7]. In light of these considerations, our objective is to use limited topology information and simple computing to decrease the duplication queries created by flooding.

In a well-connected network, several different paths may exist to connect two particular nodes, which is the reason that extensive duplications may be created by flooding. If node *x* can anticipate that one of its neighbor *y*, receives query messages from another path, however, then *x* does not forward the query to *y*. To achieve this type of anticipating, we use a rule directing the nodes that duplicate and forward messages while we keep track of topology information to compute the forwarding set.

The following definitions are used in the Optimized-Flooding algorithm. The algorithm describes the routing process for the current node, *x*, when it receives a query from its neighbor, *y*.

```
(1)Neighbor: set of neighbour of node n;
(2)Connection: already it know have connect node of re-
lation to (x,y) set;
(3)Receive: set of identification(ID)of the search mes-
sages that has already been received;
(4)Temp: have already received the node index set which
has searched for message.
(5)if i∈Temp, then node b_i has already received mes-
sage.
(6)When node n receives one m of message from node a,
operate followingly:
(7)If(ID(m)∈Receive) ignore;/*It's time to search for
message to already receive, neglect this message.*/
(8)else{for(to every neighbour node b_i of node
n∈Neighbor)
(9){if(a= b_i){b_i ⇒Temp; node b_i of identification has
already received message m;}
(10)else{if((a,b_i)∈Connection) b_i ⇒Temp; node b_i of
identification has already received message m;}/*node b_i
and a are adjoint directly, b_i will receive the search
message that a will be transmitted, does not need
transmitting through n.*/}}
(11)for(to every neighbour node b_i of node n∈Neighbor)
(12){for(to every neighbour node b_j of node b_i, and
(b_i,b_j)∈Connection)
(13)if(j∈ Temp){two routes can transmit message m to
node b_i; one is transmitted by node b_j, anotherone is
transmitted by node n; scheme:
(14)if(address of node b_j <address of node n){node b_j
transmitting; b_i ⇒ Temp;node b_i of identification has
already received message m;}
(15)else{node n transmitting; b_i ⇒Temp; node b_i of
identification has already received message m;}
node n sends out the inquires information of heartbeat
to b_j;
(16)if(node b_j does not exist) {node n transmitting; b_i
⇒ Temp; node b_i of identification has already received
messages m;}}}
(17)for(to every neighbour node b_i of node n∈Neighbor)
(18){if(b_i∉Temp){transimt search message m to node b_i;}}
    end.
```

Assuming the network is connected, the protocol described above guarantees a query message be forwarded to all nodes in the network. For an arbitrary node v, which receives forwarding query from its neighbor node u, the entry (u,v) in the routing table of v decides which neighbors the query would be forwarded. And the entries in the routing table is computed with the following principle: If v's neighbor $x \in Temp(u, v)$(where $Temp(u,v)$ is the forward reaching set of u for the current node v), then v need not forward the query to x, because v knows x has been reached by u. If $x \notin Temp(u)$, but x's neighbor $y \in Temp(u)$, we compare the *id* of y and v, if v's id is smaller, then v forward the query to u, otherwise, v leave the query for y that has a smaller *id* to forward the query. Therefore, for an arbitrary neighbor of v, it would be reached either by v or by other nodes in u's reaching set, whose *id* is smaller than v's. Consequently, all nodes in the network will be reached by the forwarding protocol. The algorithm time overhead is $O((n/m)^2)$ and algorithm's route chain length upper bound is $O(\log\sqrt{n/m})^{1+\varepsilon}$ [14,15].

In optimized-flooding algorithm, combine its advantages both the flooding distributed forward search and spanning tree algorithm. In cluster leaders search adopts optimized-flooding and in clusters search adopts simple flooding, keeps the robust and validity searched for of the networks with certain redundant messages, and makes the workload of locating service and all the network host-count of range query bring down to that of clusters, so as to effectively control the request flood produced by network.

5 Simulation Experiments

5.1 Experiment Environment

The experiment environment is made up of 16 PCs : CPU Intel P4 2. 4 GHz, RAM 256M, HDD 80G*IDE, router: HUAWEI Quidway R2501E, data switching exchange: Fast Ethernet ES-3124RLO 24-port 10/100Mbps, and all the PCs are running the systems software Red Hat Linux 9/Windows2000 operating system, JAXT2.0[10] A computer be used in the protocol and flowing anaysis. There are a total of 100 different files in the system. Every peer maintains 50 files and each of the files is around 10KB. The 15 PCs are grouped into three super clusters, and each PC simulates 200 peers, i.e. the cluster size 200 peers. To evaluate the system performance, we compare ECHP2P with a Gnutella system. The topology of Gnutella is randomly generated with an average degree of 3~5. In both systems, to generate the network traffic peers send queries every two seconds. Because the experiments are conducted on a LAN, the transmission time between two nodes is too short to reflect the real Internet environment; therefore we add 1 second delay for every transition between two nodes.

5.2 Performance Test

Figure 4 compare the system overhead when using Optimized-Flooding with the overhead when using simple flooding. In the simulation, we set the TTL = 7s. For each topology, we vary the network size and repeat the tests five times, then compute the average results. The results reveal that Optimized-Flooding greatly reduces network overhead for Gnutella, compared with flooding. For any time period, our system creates less traffic than Gnutella does. Therefore, our system accrues lower costs than Gnutella.

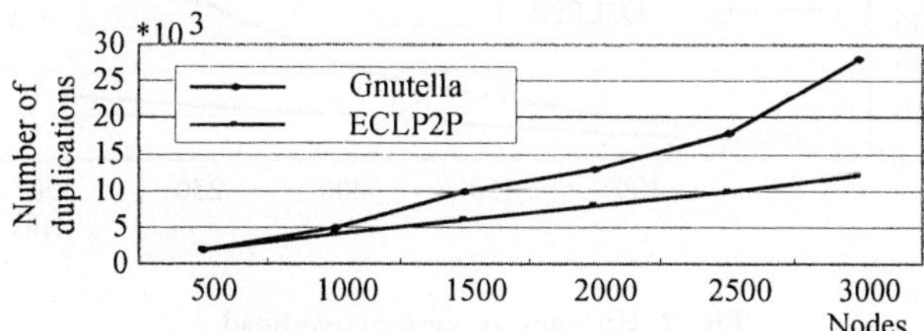

Fig. 4. Average system overhead

Figure5 depicts the relationship of network duplication ratios and network average degrees. The experiment is performed on a random topology network with 3000 nodes. The network duplications increase with the network average degree in the flooding situation. For Optimized-Flooding, when network average degree grows to some extent, the duplication ratio begins to decrease with the increase of average node degrees.

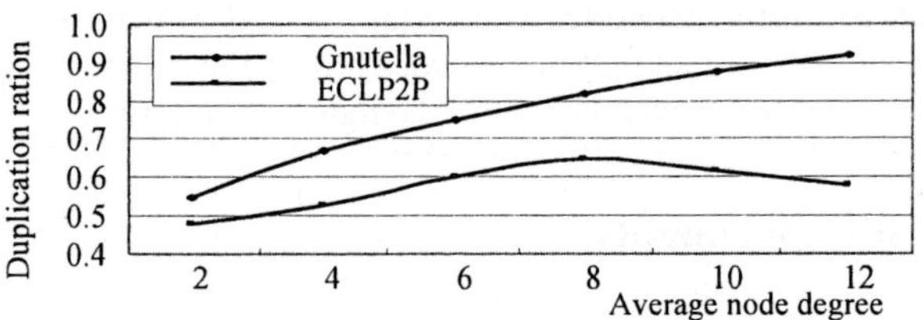

Fig. 5. Degree vs. duplication

Figure 6 is performed on the random topology with 3000 nodes and an average degree of 5. The content is replicated at 10% of the randomly selected nodes in the network. The relationship of query success probability to the number of messages produced in the system. Figure 6 shows the query hits and number of messages needed. To attain the same number of successful query hits, ECHP2P sends significantly fewer messages than Gnutella does.

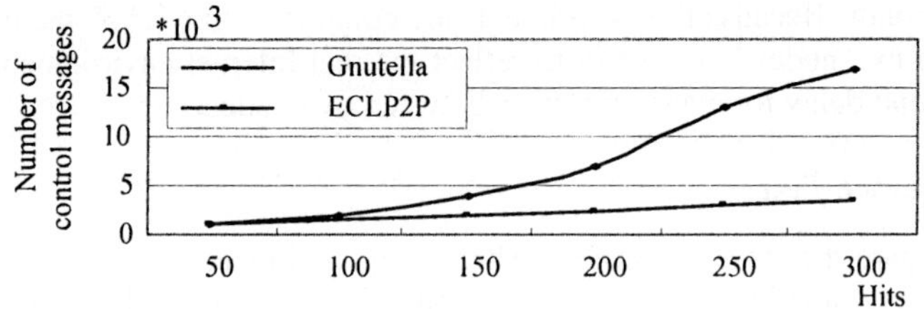

Fig. 6. Hit rates vs. system overhead

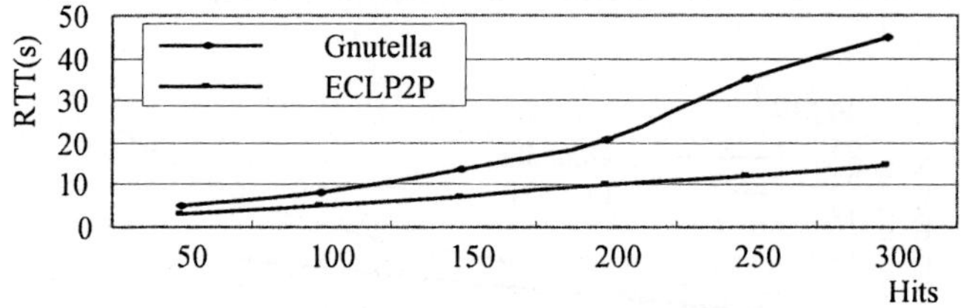

Fig. 7. Hit rates vs. system overhead

Figure 7 compare ECHP2P and Gnutella in terms of query hits and completion time. The simulation result shows, ECHP2P system uses much less time to finish the same amount of queries, with the same time limit, it can finish more queries.

In Figure 8, we show the byte-overheads for control traffic at the access links of the hosts. Each dot in the plot represents the sum of the control traffic (in Kbps) sent or received by each member in the cluster, and averaged over 10 second intervals. Thus for each 10 second time slot, there are two dots in the plot for each (remaining) host in the multicast group corresponding to the control overheads for Gnutella and ECHP2P. The curves in the plot are the average control overhead for each protocol. As can be expected, for cluster of size 200, ECHP2P has an order of magnitude lower average overhead, e.g. at simulation time 2000 seconds, the average control overhead for ECHP2P is 4.6 Kbps versus 7.3 Kbps for Gnutella. Note that the ECHP2P control traffic includes all protocol messages, includes messages for cluster formation, cluster splits, merges, layer promotions, and leader elections.

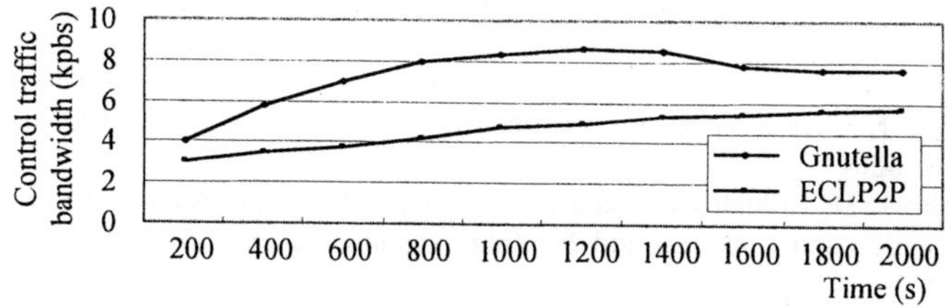

Fig. 8. Control bandwidth required at host access link

All experiments performed on different network environments demonstrate that compared with Gnutella (simple flooding), ECHP2P reduces many overheads of individual nodes as well as the loads of the whole network. It achieves better performance and scalability than flooding does, especially when the network is well connected or the network size is large.

6 Conclusions

In this paper, we investigate P2P systems currently in use, primarily on decentralized, unstructured systems. Two major deficiencies of unstructured P2P networks are addressed: scalability and efficient search mechanisms. To overcome these problems, we combine advantages of centralized and pure P2P systems, propose a new distributed P2P network model of ECHP2P with hierarchical structure based on cluster, and its prototype system is implemented in this paper. With ECHP2P, peers are grouped into clusters according to their topological proximity, and super-peers are selected from regular peers to act as cluster leaders and service providers. These cluster leaders are also connected to each other, forming a backbone overlay network. In this paper, combine its advantages both the flooding distributed forward search and spanning tree algorithm, we propose an application level broadcasting route strategy: Optimized-Flooding. In the cluster leader search adopts optimized-flooding and in the cluster search adopts simple flooding, keeps the robust and validity searched for of the networks with certain redundant messages, and makes the workload of locating service and all the network host-count of range query bring down to that of clusters, which is much more efficient and scalable than flooding. Simulation results about ECHP2P system show that it could effectively solve the above problems, and the larger the network size is, the more obvious the superiority of its comprehensive performance is, so the model is reasonable and effective.

References

1. Parameswaran M, Susarla A, Whinston AB. P2P networking: An information-sharing alternative. Computing Practices, 2001,34(7):31-38
2. S. Ratnasamy, P. Francis, M. Handley, R. Kasuper peer, and S. Shenker. A Scalable Content-Addressable Network:, In ACM SIGCOMM, pages161-172, August 2001
3. A. Rowstron and P. Druschel. Pastry: Scalable, Distributed Object Location and Routing for Large-Scale Peer-to-Peer Systems. Proceedings of the IFIP/ACM International Conference on Distributed Systems Platforms (Middleware 2001), November
4. I. Stoica, R. Morris, D. Karger, M. F. Kaashoek, and H.Balakrishnan. Chord: A Scalable Peer-to-Peer Lookup Service for Internet Applications. In ACM SIGCOMM, pages 149-160,August 2001
5. B. Y. Zhao, J. D. Kubiatowicz, and A. D. Joseph. Tapestry: An Infrastructure for Fault-Tolerant Wide-Area Location and Routing. Technical Report UCB/CSD-01-1141, April 2000
6. Beverly Yang, Hector Garcia-Molina. Efficient Search in Peer-to-Peer Networks. http://www.cs.utexas.edu/users/browne/CS395Tf2002/Papers/GarciaMolina-showDoc.pdf/2004-12-10
7. Juan Li, Son Vuong. An Efficient Clustered Architecture for P2P Networks. Proceedings of the 18th International Conference on Advanced Informatin networking and Application(AINA'04)
8. Gnutella website. http://gnutella.wego.com/2004-12-10
9. Clarke I, Sandberg O, Wiley B, Hong TW. Freenet: A distributed anonymous information storage and retrieval system. http://www.doc.ic.ac.uk/~twh1/academic/papers/icsi-revised.pdf/2004-12-10
10. Bernard Traversat, Ahkil Arora, Mohamed Abdelaziz,Mike Duigou, Carl Haywood, Jean-Christophe Hugly, Eric Pouyoul, Bill Yeager. Project JXTA 2.0 Super-Peer Virtual Network. http://www.jxta.org/project/www/docs/JXTA2.0protocols1.pdf/2004-12-10
11. Super-Peer Architectures for Distributed Computing. http://www.fiorano.com/whitepapers/supesuper peereer.pdf/2004-12-10
12. Y. Rekhter, T. Li. A Border Gateway Protocol 4 (BGP-4). RFC 1654, Internet Engineering Task Force, July. 1994
13. Suman Banerjee, Bobby Bhattacharje, Christopher Kommareddy. Scalable Application Layer Multicast. http://www.cs.unc.edu/Courses/comp249-s05/ readings/nice-appmulti.pdf/2004-12-10
14. J Kleinberg. The Small-World phenomenon: An algorithmic perspective. ACM Symp on Theory of Computing, 2000
15. D Kempe, J Kleinberg, A Demers. Spatial gossip and resource location protocols. In: Proc of the 33rd ACM Symp on Theory of computing, Crete, Greece, 2001

Building Efficient Super-Peer Overlay Network for DHT Systems*

Yin Li, Xinli Huang, Fanyuan Ma, and Futai Zou

The Department of Computer Science and Engineering, Shanghai Jiaotong University, Shanghai, China, 200030
{li-yin, huang-xl, fyma, zoufutai}@sjtu.edu.cn

Abstract. DHT technique has been widely applied in P2P systems because it provides reliable services. However, large overheads are inevitable for maintaining the topology of DHT overlay, which limits its application especially in highly dynamic network environments. This paper proposes a DHT based super-peer overlay network called SPChord in which peer nodes are clustered according to the session time and physical network locality. With an evolving process, SPChord gradually makes DHT overlay stable and reliable. Therefore the high maintaining overheads for DHT overlay are effectively controlled. Experimental results show that the DHT overlay maintaining overheads are reduced dramatically while the overlay stability and the data availability are also greatly improved.

1 Introduction

Peer-to-peer (P2P) systems are gaining popularity quickly due to their scalability, fault-tolerance, and self-organizing nature. Progress in P2P has been made in applications such as storage[1][2], DNS, media streaming[3], collaborative Web server[4], and distributed content-based search[5]. To all these P2P applications, the efficiency of the underlying overlay network is of great importance.

Distributed hash table (DHT)-based systems such as Chord[6], and Pastry[7] present applications with a homogeneously structured application-level overlay network. These systems improve over unstructured P2P systems like Gnutella by providing high scalability for large number of participating nodes as well as deterministic and efficient O(log$N$) lookup and routing. This is a big improvement over flooding techniques used in traditional unstructured techniques, greatly reducing latency, node and link stress in the network.

However, apart from research projects, Few DHT systems have been deployed successfully in the Internet with a large number of users. On the contrary, some unstructured P2P systems based on Gnutella protocol, such as Morpheus and Limewire etc., have millions of Internet users. From the point of overlay topology, we think there are two main reasons:

(1) There are too high maintaining overheads in DHT overlay.
(2) DHT ignores the heterogeneity of the peer node.

* Supported by The Science & Technology Committee of Shanghai Municipality Key Project Grant 03dz15027 and 03dz15028.

H. Zhuge and G.C. Fox (Eds.): GCC 2005, LNCS 3795, pp. 787 – 798, 2005.

This paper studies the session heterogeneity between nodes in the dynamic P2P network, and proposes a novel super-peer overlay based on Chord system which is called SPChord. SPChord not only cluster nodes that are physically close in network distance by exploiting physical network locality; but also constructs DHT overlay with higher stable nodes by means of session heterogeneity, which effectively increases the stability of DHT systems. As a result, SPChord resolves the problems of high maintenance overhead and limited scalability under dynamic environment. The experimental results show that SPChord can effectively cut down the maintenance overheads of DHT overlay, enhance the stability, and improve the data availability. Though we take Chord as an DHT example to construct super-peer overlay, SPChord can he directly applied to all the P2P systems based on DHT model such as Chord, Pastry, CAN and Tapestry, etc.

2 Session Heterogeneity in P2P Network

Stefan Saroiu et al[8] have experimentally traced the session distribution of Napster and Gnutella showed as Fig.1. From Fig.1, we can clearly observe that there are 50% nodes whose session time are over 10 hours, which presents the great heterogeneity existing in the overlay nodes. According to the experiments in[8], P2P systems show high dynamic, but P2P systems can still keep the normal work due to a few specific nodes as the core. These nodes have enough long session time to keep stability and burden the routing repaired and topology maintenance. The radical principle is rooted on the small world model[9]. For clear statement, we give the definition as follows:

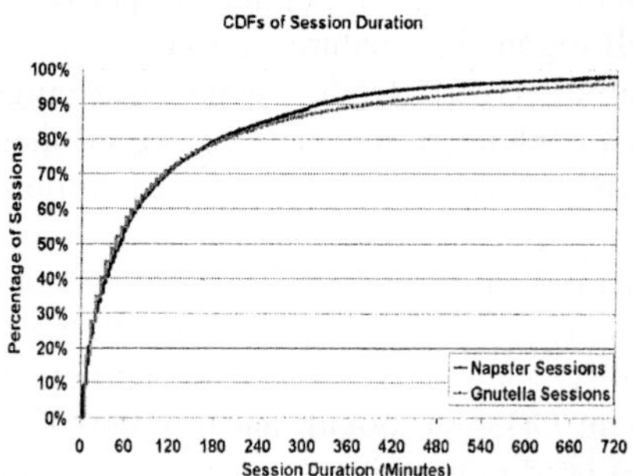

Fig. 1. The Session CDF of Napster/Gnutella

Definition 1: Let *X* be the probability of session time which is less than or equal to x. Then the CDF (Cumulative distribution function) of session time of the node, namely C, is : $X \to Y, \forall y \in Y, 0 \le y \le 1$.

Definition 2: If *X* is the event that the fault on x session time, then the fault rate function G is defined by : $X \to Y, \forall y \in Y, 0 \le y \le 1$.

As the node session time is x, then the fault rate of the node on x is: the fault probability of the node as it lies in the area $[x, x+\Delta x]$, where $\Delta x \to 0$. From Fig.1, it can be presented as to the fraction of the probability of the node ranging from area $[x, x+\Delta x]$ to area $[x, \infty)$, thus the fault rate of the node on x is defined by:

$$G(x) = \lim_{\Delta x \to 0} \frac{C(x+\Delta x) - C(x)}{\Delta x(1 - C(x))} \tag{1}$$

Fig.2(a) is the session PDF (Probability Density Function) curve corresponding with the session CDF curve showed in Fig.1. Fig.2(b) shows the curve of the fault rate G(X) computed by formula (1). From the curves shown in Fig.2, it can be clearly observed that:

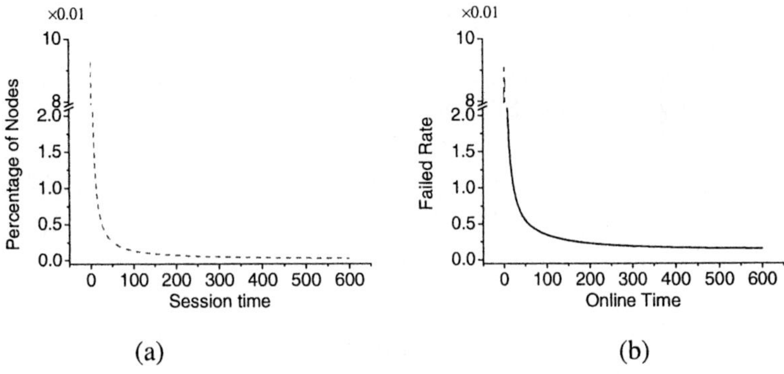

Fig. 2. (a) The session PDF. (b) The fault rate.

(1) There is great heterogeneity of session time.
(2) There is an uneven distribution of session time among nodes. While many nodes' session time is very short, only a few nodes' session time is long.

This observation can explain why structured P2P systems have huge maintaining overheads. Many nodes whose session time is short would join and then leave the P2P network so frequently as to disturb the construction of network topology, rapidly increasing the maintaining overheads of structured P2P topology. Considering this fact, the intuitive idea is to exclude these nodes from joining the normal DHT topology. Therefore, we utilize the great heterogeneity of session time to construct the super-peer overlay where stable nodes act as super-peers for unstable peers. The stable nodes would construct the DHT circle (We generalize the topology which is constructed by DHT technique such as Chord, Pastry, CAN and Tapestry as a ring space structure, called DHT circle), the other dynamic unstable nodes are clustered to the outside of the DHT circle so as to reduce the dynamic changes of the DHT circle. With these stable nodes on the DHT circle, the maintaining overhead for DHT circle can be reduced greatly and thus the total maintaining overheads can be reduced a lot. In this paper, the stability of the node is evaluated by the online session time. The node whose session time is the longest in the cluster would be selected as the super-peer onto the DHT circle. Maybe more arguments such as CPU power, bandwidth etc. can be tradeoff when selecting the node onto the DHT circle; however, the session time is still the dominating one among factors which affect the maintaining overheads. We do not discuss the tradeoff in this paper because of the limitation of space.

3 Super-Peer Overlay Construction

3.1 Super-Peer Overlay Topology

According to the analysis of section 2, we propose a super-peer overlay based on Chord which is called SPChord(Super-Peer based Chord). SPChord distinguishes two kinds of nodes on constructing the overlay topology of P2P network. The node whose fault rate is low would acts as a super-peer and joins to the DHT circle which is organized by Chord protocol in SPChord, while the node whose fault rate is high would join to the super-peer and acts as a member in the super-peer cluster. The super-peer overlay topology of SPChord is shown in Fig.3.

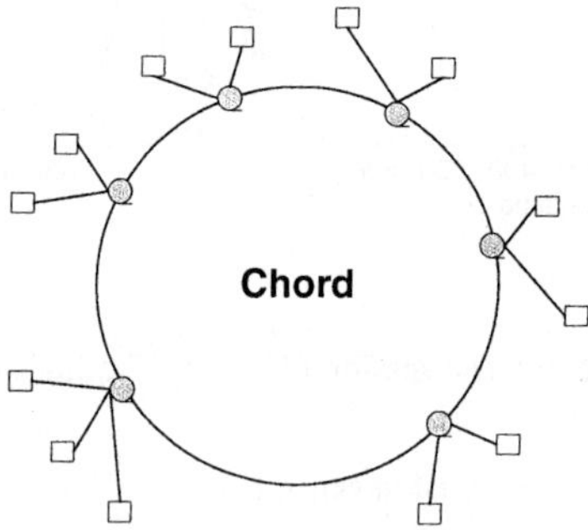

Fig. 3. The Super-Peer overlay topology of SPChord

The super-peer nodes on the DHT circle are called father nodes, while the others out of the circle but around a parent node are called son nodes. One father node and its son nodes are called a cluster. Father is only one and son may be many around the father in a cluster. For a network with *n* nodes, we limit the number of sons for each father node by *m*. The expectation is that with a reasonable size *m*, a highly stable node can be found to become the father node so as to form a stable DHT circle.

Therefore, the topology of super-peer overlay is composed of the cluster set $S=\{C_1,C_2,C_3,\ldots,C_i,\ldots\}$, where C_i is a cluster and $i\in[1,n]$. For$\forall C_i\in S$, $C_i=\{f, s_1,s_2,s_3,\ldots,s_i,\ldots\}$, where f is the father node, and s_i is the son node of f. All father nodes constitute a DHT circle, that is, $D=\{f_1,f_2,f_3,\ldots,f_i,\ldots\}$ and $i\in[1,n]$. The core of SPChord is to select stable nodes as father nodes onto the DHT circle. So each father node would maintain the son node list *L*, which includes the registered information (nodeID, IP, session time) on all son nodes. Father is selected from *L* and it gradually forms a stable DHT circle with an evolving approach. To reduce the communication costs in a cluster, SPChord tries to organize the nodes physically nearby in network distance in the same cluster by exploiting network locality.

3.2 Node ID Assignment

A two-step approach is used to generate ID for each node in SPChord. In the first step, we model the internet as a geometric space and compute the coordinates of nodes in a d-dimensional Cartesian space, using GNP[10] or other techniques [11][12]. Then in the second step, the ID of each node is generated by mapping from its coordinates to a circular ID space. Id-mapping can be performed using space-filling curves. Xu et al. [13] demonstrated to use space-filling curves to map points in the domain R^d into R^l such that the closeness relationship among the points is preserved. As a result, the nodes physically nearby in network distance have close ID number either.

3.3 Node Join

The process for an arbitrary node *a* to join the P2P overlay network is described as follows:

(1)Node *a* first computes its ID number, say NID_a, by the approach described in section 4.2. Then node *a* contacts a known introducer node *b*, and *b* will use NID_a as a key to do the lookup process to find the super-peer node *f* in DHT circle which is responsible for key NID_a by Chord routing algorithm. According to Chord algorithm, we know that NID_a is close to the ID number of super-peer node *f*. Thus, according to the node ID generation approach based on network locality described in section 4.2, node *a* and super-peer node *f* are physically nearby in network distance.

(2)Node *a* sends the join request to super-peer *f* to add itself into the cluster of *f*, say *C*.

(3)If the size of the cluster *C* is large than *m*, then cluster *C* is split into two clusters.

a) Select node β whose session time is the longest from all son nodes of cluster *C*, and add node β into the DHT circle and then create new cluster called *C'*. Node β is the father node of the cluster *C'*.

b) Migrating $\lfloor m/2 \rfloor$ son nodes from cluster *C* to cluster *C'*.

If all the nodes in SPChord obey the join process described above, the nodes in the same cluster are physically nearby in network distance, and therefore the communication costs within a cluster can be reduced.

3.4 Node Left

In SPChord, we have different ways to deal with the left of the different types of nodes. When a son node leaves, a notification of updating son node list is sent to its father node. When a father node leaves, the stable node is selected from its son node list as the new father node, and then the new father node is added to the DHT circle. The dynamic maintenance of son node list and the process of father selection will be described in section 3.5.

3.5 Stabilize Super-Peer Overlay with Evolving Approach

Though the join and left of nodes are very simple, it can form the stable DHT circle with an evolving approach. Here we say that an evolving process means that the topology is gradually changed towards the desirable topology. The father node is selected from the cluster in two cases: (1) the size of the cluster is over *m*. (2) the fault events of the father node happen (e.g. node leaves or power off). Hence it ensures that the father is the most stable node in the cluster. The selection is very critical for a stable DHT circle. To form a stable DHT circle, there are still two questions:

(1) How to keep a feasible and reliable selection?
(2) Whether these father nodes can make DHT circle reach the desirable state?

First, we deal with the question (1) through maintaining the son node list. For a cluster, father node keeps the son node list which is an ordered list of father node candidates: the longer a node remains, the better a father node candidate it becomes. Furthermore, to deal with some exceptional failure conditions such as power off, broken network etc., this list is sent periodically to each son node of the cluster. Because adopted SPChord exploits network locality of the nodes, the cost on son node list dissemination will not be high. When a father node fails or disconnects, the node in the list whose session time is the longest becomes father node and joins into the DHT circle. Through this approach, the selection would be feasible and reliable.

Second, let us consider the question (2). A desirable stable state of DHT circle is defined as follows:

Definition 3: Let *node.session* be the session time of the node. Let *U* be the set of all son nodes. For a network with *n* nodes and cluster size *m*, if it satisfies the two conditions:

(1) $D=\{f_1, f_2,\dots, f_v\}, v=\lceil n/(m+1)\rceil$ where $f_i(i=1,2,..,v)$ is father node.
(2) $\forall f \in D, \forall u \in U, f.session > u.session$ then it is the stable state of the DHT circle.

The clustering technique would finally leave *v* father nodes on the DHT circle. Thus it satisfies the condition (1). Let *F* be the father node set, where $F=D=\{f_1,f_2,\dots,f_v\}$ and let the responding cluster set be *C*, where $C=\{C_1,C_2,\dots,C_v\}$.

For $\forall f_i \in F$, $f_i.session$ is the maximum of cluster C_i based on the selection strategy. However, it may be less than the maximal session of son nodes set in other clusters. Thus, we use a random algorithm to adjust it. Fig.4 shows the pseudo code of the algorithm. The function adjust(C_i) would adjust the DHT circle to satisfy the condition (2), where $C_i \in C$. Line 1~3 define if there exists a random selected cluster whose father's session is less than the maximal session of son node set in C_i. If it is true, then line 4~5 would update the father of the random selected cluster.

By the random adjustment algorithm, $f_i.session$ ($\forall f_i \in F$) would be the maximum not only in its own cluster but also in any other clusters. Therefore, by Definition 3, the desirable stable DHT circle is formed. Due to the extremely heterogeneous distribution of session time, stable nodes can be selected rapidly so a stable DHT circle is rapidly formed. It can be observed from our experimental results.

```
Adjust(C_i)
1.  Randomly select a cluster c, where c∈C ∩ c≠C_i.
2.  Select node t whose session is the maximum of the son nodes set in C_i
3.  If (t.session > c.f.session)
4.  C_i = C_i - {t} + {c.f} // adjusts Cluster C_i
5.  c.f = t       // updates the father of cluster c with t.
```

Fig. 4. The random adjustment algorithm

4 Experimental Results

4.1 Experimental Setup

We designed and implemented a simulator prototype where nodes follow the steps outlined in previous section to form clusters and perform search. In particular, the construction of the DHT circle is based on Chord protocol and has the same stabilizing mechanism as Chord does (30 seconds as stabilizing interval time). Here we call it SPChord.

We setup two simulating experiment environments. The first simulating experiment is to observe the effects of the cluster size *m*. We add 2000 nodes into P2P network with the rate of one node per 5 seconds. The distribution of session time follows up the CDF as Fig.1 describes. The stabilizing time is 5 minutes and the search is performed by 5 times per minute on average. During constructing the overlay, the cluster size *m* is changed from 1 to 40 so as to observe the relationship between the stability, maintenance overheads, lookup failure rate of SPChord and the cluster size *m*. Section 4.2, 4.3, 4.4 show these experimental results.

The second simulating experiment is different from the first as follows: there are 20000 nodes to join the network, and the cluster size *m* is fixed by 10. The experiment runs 24 hours, and snapshots the system performance every 10 minutes. The aim of this experiment is to observe how the stability, lookup failure rate and maintenance overheads are changed as the time goes in an extremely dynamic network, and comparing it with Chord. Section 4.5 shows this experimental result.

4.2 Stability

Fig.5 shows the relationship between the stability of SPChord and the cluster size *m*. The stability is evaluated by the in/out rate per minute in the DHT circle. With *m* increasing, the in/out rate in DHT circle would be dramatically decreased. After *m* is larger than 10, the change tends to be smooth. The reason is that the cluster technique can prevent the highly dynamic nodes from frequently joining and leaving the DHT overlay so that the stability of the DHT circle can be improved. Due to the uneven distribution of session time, the small size (e.g., 10 in the experiment) would provide a good effect. After *m* is over 10, the nodes in DHT circle would be stable enough, and therefore the change of in/out rate in DHT circle is smooth. The result is consistent with the fault rate curve shown in Fig.2.

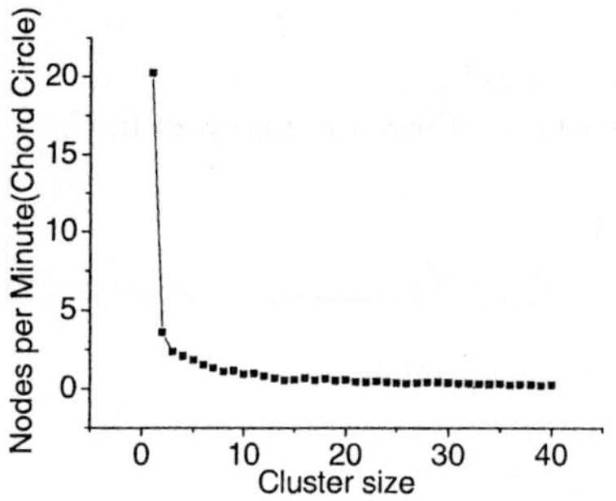

Fig. 5. The relationship between the stability and the cluster size m

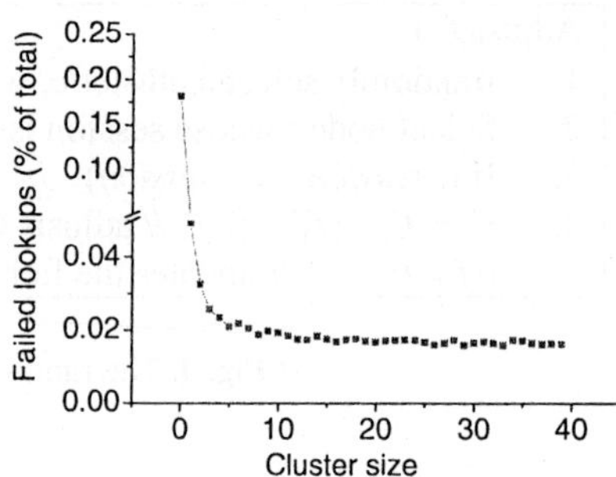

Fig. 6. The relationship between the lookup failure rate and the cluster size m

4.3 Lookup Failure Rate

Fig.6 shows the relationship between the lookup failure rate of SPChord and the cluster size *m*. The experimental result indicates that the lookup failure rate gradually decreases as the cluster size *m* increases. The reason is that the stability of the node would be increased with increasing *m* as described in section 4.2, what will result in the decrease of look failure rate. The result of Fig.6 is consistent with the result of Fig.5. Similarly, we observe that the improvement of the lookup failure rate tends to be smooth after *m* is over 10.

4.4 Maintenance Overheads

Fig.7 shows the relationship between the maintenance overheads of SPChord and the cluster size *m*. Maintenance overheads are computed by messages per minute. Compared with pure DHT overlay, SPChord decreases the maintenance overheads of DHT circle, while it increasing the maintenance overheads in the cluster. The first curve in Fig.9 shows the maintenance overheads of DHT circle reduce quickly as *m* increases. From the second curve in Fig.7, the maintenance overheads of the cluster smoothly increase as *m* increases. In a word, the whole overheads are greatly decreased because the decreased messages are evidently more than the increased messages. We think there are two reasons: (1)The maintenance overheads for the node in DHT circle are $O(\log^2 N)$ messages, but for the son nodes in the cluster are just $O(1)$ messages. (2) The in/out rate of DHT circle is lower than that of outer of the DHT circle. Because the node of DHT circle is more stable, the ratio of the in/out rate for inner and outer of DHT circle would even lower than 1:m, where m is the cluster size. The experiment reveals that SPChord can effectively reduce the maintenance overheads of DHT systems.

We also observe that the improvement of maintenance overheads is trivial after *m* is over 10. While the threshold to join DHT circle quickly goes high as *m* reaches to 10, the nodes in DHT circle are so stable that the in/our rate of DHT circle is almost smooth, which results in a trivial decrease on maintenance overheads.

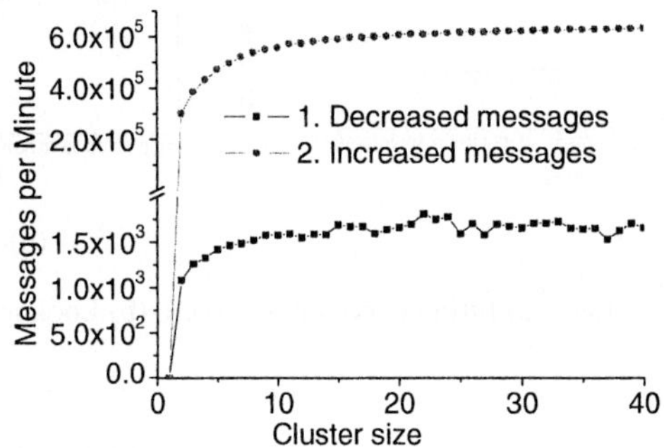

Fig. 7. The relation between the maintenance overheads and the cluster size m

4.5 Performance Comparison with Chord

Fig.8 shows the stability curve of SPChord and Chord during 24 hours. Each unit of X axis represents 10 minutes, and each unit of Y axis represents the number of in/out nodes per a minute. The result shows that SPChord has a remarkable stability, an order of magnitude better than Chord.

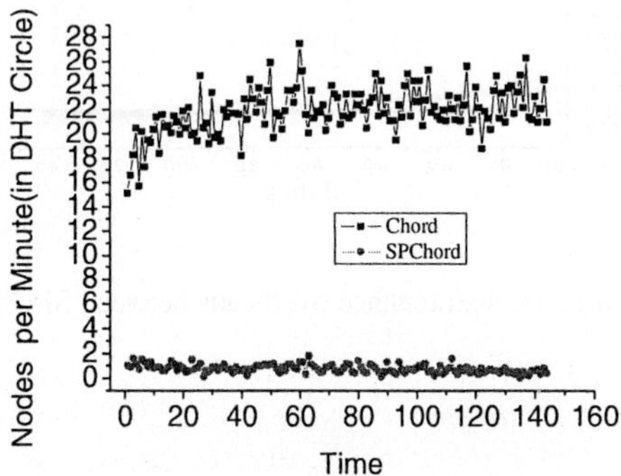

Fig. 8. The stability of SPChord and Chord

Fig.9 shows the lookup failure rate and fitting curve by SPChord and Chord respectively, in which the dotted line is fitting curve. From the fitting curve, the lookup failure rate is 0.005 by SPChord and 0.04 by Chord. The rate by SPChord has an order of magnitude less than by Chord. Otherwise, it can be observed that the rate fluctuates as the time goes, which is in consistent with the fluctuation of the query executed in the extremely dynamic network.

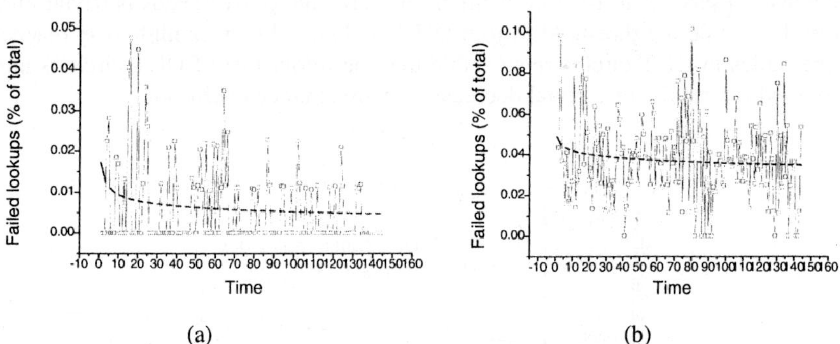

Fig. 9. (a) Lookup failure rate and fitting curve on SPChord. (b) Lookup failure rate and fitting curve on Chord.

In Fig.10, we see that the maintenance overheads in SPChord are about 0.2 million messages, but that of Chord need 2 million messages during 24 hours simulating time. There are an order of magnitude difference between SPChord and Chord. The reason is that the low adjusting overheads of topology change lead to the more stable DHT circle by cluster technique.

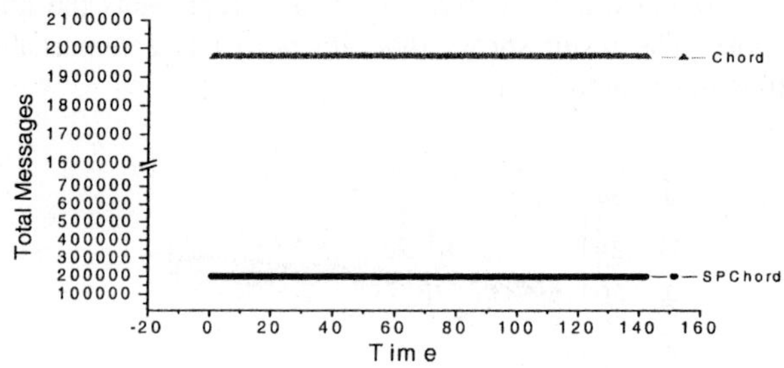

Fig. 10. Comparing the maintenance overheads between SPChord and Chord

5 Related Work

The high dynamic and heterogeneous characteristics of P2P network were confirmed by the experimental observation in recent researches[8][14]. Since Ratnasamy et al.[15] proposed the question if the performance of P2P network could be improved by exploiting the heterogeneity, some ongoing researches yielded good results by using the different heterogeneity characteristics of bandwidth[10], host[17], and geography [12][18]. This paper suggests using the session heterogeneity to build efficient super-peer overlay network.

Liben-Nowell et al.[19] analyzed the dynamic characteristics of P2P network and researched the maintaining process of the topology when nodes join and leave.

Mahajan et al.[20] proposed a model for controlling and reducing maintaining overheads of DHT. The key idea was to adjust the maintenance measures so as to smooth the dynamic change of P2P network. In essence, it is an inactive method and maintaining overheads in highly dynamic environment may be unnecessarily excessive because too much unstable nodes have to be dealt with. On the contrary, SPChord can actively control the dynamic effect through filtering out the unstable nodes. Thus SPChord can build a stable DHT circle so as to efficiently control the cost of topology maintenance.

Super-Peer based overlay architecture has been widely studied in unstructured P2P research area. B. Yang et al.[17] gives suggestions on the designing parameters for the super-peer network. Examples of super-peer networks are JXTA, Edutella or Morpheus. In these systems, super-peers have extra capabilities and cache metadata for client peers. They have the duties to answer the queries on behalf of the client peers. There are other super-peer systems clustering peers based on the information the client providing[21]. Unlike these systems, The purpose of SPChord is to reduce DHT overlay maintenance overheads, and the super-peers are only responsible for efficiently maintaining DHT topology, not caching the metadata or semantic information for the client peers.

6 Conclusions

This paper takes the excessive overheads of DHT model into account and proposes a new super-peer based overlay topology which clusters peer nodes based on the session time and physical network locality to achieve a nice performance in the large dynamic network environment.

Although the overlay construction is based on Chord in this paper, it can be easily applied to any others DHT systems such as Pastry, Tapestry, and so on. Furthermore, by exploiting the session heterogeneity, it can not only adapt DHT model to dynamic network, but also easily apply to the topology construction of non-DHT systems such as Morpheus, Limewire etc.

References

1. J. Kubiatowicz, D. Bindel, Y. Chen, P. Eaton, D. Geels, R. Gummadi, S. Rhea, H. Weatherspoon, W. Weimer, C. Wells, and B. Zhao, "Oceanstore: An architecture for global-scale persistent storage," in 17th ACM Symposium on Operating Systems Principles (SOSP '00), November 2000, pp. 190–201.
2. F. Dabek, M. F. Kaashoek, D. Karger, R. Morris, and I. Stoica, "Widearea cooperative storage with CFS," in 18th ACM Symposium on Operating Systems Principles (SOSP '01), October 2001, pp. 202–215.
3. V. N. Padmanabhan, H. J. Wang, P. A. Chou, and K. Sripanidkulchai, "Distributing streaming media content using cooperative networking," in 12th International Workshop on Network and Operating Systems Support for Digital Audio and Video, May 2002.
4. V. N. Padmanabhan and K. Sripanidkulchai, "The case for cooperative networking," in 1st International Workshop on Peer-to-Peer Systems (IPTPS), March 2002.
5. C. Tang, Z. Xu, and M. Mahalingam, "pSearch: Information retrieval in structured overlays," in 1st Workshop on Hot Topics on Networks (HotNets-I), October 2002.

6. I. Stoica, R. Morris, D. Karger, F. Kaashoek, and H. Balakrishnan, "Chord: A scalable Peer-To-Peer lookup service for internet applications," in 2001 ACM SIGCOMM Conference, 2001, pp. 149–160.
7. A. Rowstron and P. Druschel, "Pastry: Scalable, decentralized object location, and routing for large-scale peer-to-peer systems," in IFIP/ACM International Conference on Distributed Systems Platforms (Middleware), November 2001, pp. 329–350.
8. SAROIU, S., GUMMADI, K., AND GRIBBLE, S. A measurement study of peer-to-peer file sharing systems. In Proceedings of Multimedia Conferencing and Networking (San Jose, Jan. 2002).
9. Jonathan Ledlie, Jacob M. Taylor, Laura Serban, Margo Seltzer, Self-Organization in Peer-to-Peer Systems, SIGOPS'02
10. S. Eugene Ng and Hui Zhang. Predicting Internet Network Distance with Coordinates-Based Approaches. In IEEE INFOCOM'02, 2002.
11. Marcelo Pias, Jon Crowcroft, Steve Wilbur, Tim Harris, and Saleem Bhatti. Lighthouse for Scalable Distributed Location. IPTPS 2003.
12. Zhichen Xu, Chunqiang Tang, Zheng Zhang. Building Topology-Aware Overlays Using Global Soft-State. ICDCS 2003
13. Zhichen Xu, Mallik Mahalingam and Magnus Karlsson. Turning Heterogeneity into an Advantage in Overlay Routing. Infocom'03, 2003.
14. Evangelos P. Markatos, Tracing a large-scale Peer to Peer System: an hour in the life of Gnutella, 2nd IEEE/ACM International Symposium on Cluster Computing and the Grid, 2002
15. Sylvia Ratoasamy, Scon Shenker, Ion Stoica. Routing Algorithms for DHTs: Some Open Questions. Proceedings for the 1st International Workshop on Peer-to-Peer Systems (IPTF'S '02), 7-8 March 2002, Cambridge, MA, USA.
16. Hazel, S.,Wiley, B.,2002. Achord: A variant of the chord lookup service for use in censorship resistant peer-to-peer publishing systems. In Proceedings of the 1st International Workshop on Peer-to-Peer Systems (IPTPS '02), MIT Faculty Club, Cambridge, MA, USA.
17. B. Yang and H. Garcia-Molina. Designing a super-peer network. In Proccedings of the ICCDE, March 2003.
18. Wu, Z. D., Ma, F. Y., Rao, W. X. , Super-proximity routing in Structured P2P Networks. Journal of Zhejiang University SCIENCE, 2004, 5(1): 16-21.
19. Liben-Nowell, D., Balakrishnan, H., Karger, D., Analysis of the evolution of peer-to-peer systems. In: Proceedings of the Twenty-First Annual Symposium on Principles of Distributed Computing, 2002, ACM Press, p. 233–242.
20. Mahajan, R.,Castro,M., Rowstron, A., Controlling the Cost of Reliability in Peer-to-Peer Overlays. In: the 2nd International Workshop on Peer-to-peer systems, 2003, Berkeley, CA, USA
21. Alexander Loser, Felix Naumann, Wolf Siberski, Wolfgang Nejdl, and Uwe Thaden. Semantic overlay clusters within super-peer networks. In Proceedings of the International Workshop on Databases, Information Systems and Peer-to-Peer Computing in Conjunction with the VLDB 2003.

Exploiting the Heterogeneity in Structured Peer-to-Peer Systems

Tongqing Qiu and Guihai Chen

State Key Laboratory of Novel Software Technology, Nanjing University, China
qtq@dislab.nju.edu.cn, gchen@nju.edu.cn

Abstract. The structured peer-to-peer system, which is based on the distributed hash table, offers an administration-free and fault-tolerant application-level overlay network. However, a randomly structured overlay can not reflect the heterogeneity of a peer-to-peer system. In this paper, we propose a two-phase approach to exploit the heterogeneity in structured peer-to-peer systems. First, by exploiting the effects of both connections and nodes, we adjust the structure of overlay to reduce the lookup latency. And then a novel load balancing scheme based on lottery scheduling is proposed to balance not only the load but also the movement cost of the load. Our simulation results show that the performance, including query quality from the users' view and load balance from the system's view, can be greatly improved in a heterogeneous environment.

1 Introduction

The last few years have witnessed the emergence and the development of a class of structured peer-to-peer (P2P) systems ([1], [2], [3], etc.). They are all based on a scalable, fault-tolerant distributed hash table (DHT). However, in order to simplify the management of a large-scale distributed system, the structured P2P systems construct an overlay which hides many heterogeneous factors. We classify the factors into two categories: *network heterogeneity* and *node heterogeneity*. First, in a large-scale area like the Internet, the connections between any two nodes may vary in transmission delay and bandwidth. Things become more complicated in an overlay network as a logical connection of an overlay is composed by several physical connections. Second, different nodes have various capacities, including process speed, available bandwidth, and storage. Without discovering the heterogeneity of the network, "bad" connection may be chosen to construct the routing table. As a result, the query delay may be too large to be acceptable. In addition, because all nodes are responsible for the similar scale of data items, the nodes with poor capacities and heavy loads become the bottleneck of the whole system.

In order to exploit the heterogeneity, researchers have done some work in two different aspects. On the one hand, there are several contributions about the overlay structure. The basic idea is that the structure should reflect the heterogeneity of the system. Z. Xu et al construct an auxiliary expressway network to take advantage of heterogeneity [4]. However, they just speed up routing, without solving the other problem - bottleneck of the system. SmartBoa

H. Zhuge and G.C. Fox (Eds.): GCC 2005, LNCS 3795, pp. 799–810, 2005.

[5] constructs a totally different P2P overlay network. It categorizes the nodes into different levels according to their capacities. The heterogeneous information can be broadcasted in this tree-like structure. But there is not any experiment results in this paper. Furthermore, the authors didn't explain the scalability, fault-tolerance and other important characteristics which a peer-to-peer system should have. On the other hand, other researchers just keep the original structure invariable. Instead, they change the load of each node to solve the load balancing problem that node heterogeneity brings. Most of load balancing methods are based on the conception of virtual servers [2]. B. Godfrey et al propose two load balancing algorithms in structured P2P systems [6] [7]. The first one [6] achieves the goal of making its algorithm effective in a dynamic environment. As each node has many virtual servers, the number of links each node should maintain will increase. So the second one [7] is proposed to reduce this kind of overhead. Nevertheless, to our knowledge, there is no work to take notice of the unbalance of load movement. We will discuss this problem in section 3. Different from other work, our contributions are as follows.

- A novel structure-adjustment algorithm is proposed. It can be developed easily in any structured P2P systems without destroying the original topology of the overlay. Both network and node heterogeneities are considered during the adjustment. After the adjustment, the lookup latencies are significantly reduced. In addition, if more queries are directed to the powerful node, the performance can be much better.
- We propose a novel load balancing algorithm which is based on lottery scheduling. The heterogeneity of nodes can be naturally quantified by the number of lottery tickets. To the best of our knowledge, this approach is the first one which achieves not only the balance of load but also the balance of load movement.
- We exploit the heterogeneity in two relative phases. The first phase can inherently reduce the overhead of load movement in the second one.

The remainder of the paper is organized as follows. Section 2 describes the method of overlay adjustment. Section 3 introduces our load balancing algorithm. In section 4, we evaluate our approach using simulation. Section 5 provides other related work and section 6 concludes the paper.

2 Phase One: Overlay Adjustment

In this section, we introduce a generic method to make structured P2P systems heterogeneity-aware. The original algorithm we proposed in [8] just makes the systems topology-aware. Here, we extend it into a multi-factor area. In our current discussion, the factors include both the latency and the process speed. The basic idea is that the overlay can be optimized by a series of swap operations. Table 1 gives several useful notations for our expression. We assume there is a potential swap between node A and B. t_0 and t_1 represent time before and after a swap respectively. We view the overlay as an undirected graph, so the

Table 1. The notation table

Notation	Meaning
t_0	the time before nodes A and B swap
t_1	the time after nodes A and B swap
$R(A)$	the routing table of node A
$N_{t_i}(A)$	the neighbor set of node A at time t_i
d_{ij}	latency between node i and node j
p_i	processing delay of node i
$H(A)$	heterogeneous information of node A

neighbor set of node A is defined as $N(A) = \{i | i \in R(A) \vee A \in R(i)\}$. In order to simplify the neighbors' processing, we extend the routing table by recording not only successor nodes but also predecessor ones[1]. The size of extended routing table is about twice as large as the size of the original one. In some symmetrical systems like CAN [1], there is even no increase. The heterogeneous information is measured by the transmit delay d plus the processing one p. For example, $H_{t_0}(A)$ can be expressed in equation 1. k represents the importance of the node heterogeneity related to the network one.

$$H_{t0}(A) = \sum_{i \in N_{t_0}(A)} (d_{Ai} + k \cdot p_i) \tag{1}$$

At the beginning of adjustment, each node A gets its neighbor list $N_{t_0}(A)$ and the initialized heterogeneous information $H_{t_0}(A)$. After the initialization, the node A will periodically contacts a random node B in a fixed time interval T. Node B is h hops away from node A[2]. Then nodes A and B exchange their initialized heterogeneous information, address lists and process delays of their neighbors. Both of them calculate the heterogeneous information $H_{t_1}(A)$ and $H_{t_1}(B)$ if the potential swap operation occurs. Then nodes A and B exchange their local heterogeneous information and calculate the variable $Diff$ independently.

$$Diff = H_{t_0}(A) + H_{t_0}(B) - H_{t_1}(A) - H_{t_1}(B) \tag{2}$$

If $Diff \leq 0$, it means that a swap can not gain any benefit. So no operation is performed. If $Diff > 0$, nodes A and B will do swap operation. They exchange their identifiers and routing tables respectively. Besides, both of them will notify their predecessors to change the routing tables and recalculate the initialized sums. As the routing table is extended, the notification can be realized directly. Even if there is no extension of the routing table, exchange of two nodes can be realized using a series of *leave()* and *join()* procedures. However, because each *leave()* and *join()* procedure leads to complicated reconstruction operations, it is not practical to use this method.

[1] As a matter of fact, most structured P2P systems selectively record several predecessor nodes in order to improve the ability of fault resilience.

[2] After a series of experiments, we found that $h = 2$ is a reasonable choice. So in section 4, we just set $h = 2$.

There are several characteristics of our adjustment. First, as we just exchange the node IDs, the original structure of overlay will not change. The structured P2P protocols can still be effective without any modification. As a result, our adjustment is *protocol-independent*, which can be developed on any structured P2P systems. Second, because we use both latency and process delay as the criterion of swap, the overlay after adjustment will reflect both network and node heterogeneity. The experiments in section 4 will show the effectiveness of node swap. Due to the limitation of the paper size, the reason why our method works and the detailed algorithms about overhead control will not be introduced. Readers may refer [8] to get more information.

3 Phase Two: Load Balancing

The adjustment of the structure tries to avoid inefficient routing in a heterogeneous environment. It can not solve the bottleneck problem we mentioned in section 1. So it is necessary to balance the load of different nodes. In this section, we propose a novel load balancing algorithm based on lottery scheduling. This method can achieve not only load balance but also load movement balance.

3.1 Background

Virtual Server. The concept of virtual servers was first proposed in Chord [2] to improve load balance. Like a physical peer node, a virtual server is responsible for a contiguous portion of the DHT's identifier space. A physical peer node can host multiple virtual servers and, therefore, can own multiple noncontiguous portions of the DHT's identifier space. From the perspective of load balancing, a virtual server represents certain amount of load (e.g., the load generated by serving the requests of the data items whose IDs fall into its responsible region). When a node becomes overloaded, it may move part of its loads to some lightly loaded nodes. Here the basic unit of load movement is one virtual server. Hence, load balance can be achieved by moving virtual servers from heavy nodes to light nodes. In our work we address the load-balancing issue by taking advantage of virtual servers. But we also utilize the heterogeneity to guide load balancing. As a result, the reassignments of virtual server can reflect the capacities of nodes. Furthermore, as we adjust the structure in the first phase, the cost of transferring virtual servers can be reduced.

Lottery Scheduling. Lottery scheduling [9] is a randomized resource allocation mechanism. Resource rights are represented by lottery tickets. Each allocation is determined by holding a *lottery*. The resource is granted to the client with the winning ticket. This effectively allocates resources to competing clients in proportion to the number of tickets that they hold. Besides, any dynamic changes are immediately reflected in the next allocation decision, and no special actions are required. Lottery scheduling is widely used in operating system area. Taking the advantage of lottery scheduling, we make each load reallocation by holding a lottery. Each node (client) holds some tickets. The number is determined by the node's available capacity. In a P2P system, the available capacity of each node may change from time to time. The dynamic characteristic of lottery scheduling ensures that the change can be reflected immediately.

The Balance of Load Movement. In order to achieve the load balance, the load from heavy nodes will move to light nodes. The movement cost of the load is a main performance factor of the whole load balance process. If some powerful, light nodes receive too heavy load in a short interval, they may become the bottleneck of the system. We assume that m_i is the movement cost of load whose target is node i. The capacity of node i is c_i. In order to balance the load movement, m_i needs to be proportional to c_i. In other words, the movement target should be selected carefully.

3.2 Load Balancing Algorithm

The basic idea of our algorithm is trivial. A number of *rendezvous nodes* are responsible to periodically schedule reassignments of virtual servers to achieve better balance. The node IDs of rendezvous nodes are well-known. When one node i joins into the system, it will randomly choose one rendezvous node as its *master*. Then node i will report its capacity information c_i. and the loads $l_{i1}, l_{i2}, \ldots, l_{im}$ of the m virtual servers for which it is responsible. In each time interval t, each rendezvous will computes a schedule of virtual server transmissions based on information of its slave nodes. Each entry of the schedule list L is (v, j). The element v represents a virtual server which needs to be transmitted, and j represents the destination node of the transmission. After completing a set of transmissions scheduled, the relative nodes will choose other random rendezvous to repeat this procedure. More precisely, each normal node runs the following algorithm 1, and each rendezvous node runs the following algorithm 2. Each rendezvous node collects the load information from its slave nodes. In each time interval t, it computes the utilization u_i[3] of each slave node. If the u_i is larger than a threshold, the according node will move one of its random virtual servers into the load pool P. Then the rendezvous node reassigns these virtual servers using lottery scheduling algorithm. Algorithm 3 describes the function of lottery scheduling. The *ticket* of each node equals to its available capacity. The *winning token* is generated randomly from zero to the sum of all tickets. Then the node which owns the winning token is selected. It is worth to notice that other load balancing algorithms always move the virtual servers from heavy node to light node in a *deterministic* way. For example, it will move the virtual server to the node which has the least load [10]. Or it will move the virtual server to the node to achieve the minimal utilization of that node [6]. The disadvantage of these methods is that similar nodes have no similar chance to get loads. Our approach is a *probabilistic* way to make the load movement fair. In section 4, the balance of load movement will be shown.

[3] $u_i = \sum_{j=1}^{m} l_{ij}/c_i$

Algorithm 1. The periodical operation of node i

for Each time interval t **do**
  $MasterNode \leftarrow RamdomRendezvou()$
  Send information $Cap(c_i), Load(l_{i1}, l_{i2}, \ldots, l_{im})$ to $MasterNode$
  Waitfor the scheduled list L from $MasterNode$
  while $L.hasNextEntry()$ **do**
    $(v, j) \leftarrow GetNextEntry()$
    $Transmit(v, j)$
  end while
end for

Algorithm 2. The periodical operation of rendezvous node

Receive information of node i $INFO_i \leftarrow Cap(c_i), Load(l_{i1}, l_{i2}, \ldots, l_{im})$
The whole information $INFO \leftarrow INFO \bigcup INFO_i$
for Each time interval t **do**
  Set the unallocated load pool $P = \{\}$
  for each node i **do**
    if $u_i > threshold$ **then**
      Remove a random virtual server from node i
      Move it into load pool P
    end if
  end for
  for each virtual server $v \in P$ from heaviest to lightest **do**
    Node $n \leftarrow SelectNodeByLottery()$
    Add List entry (v,n) into list L_i
    Send the scheduled list Li to node i
  end for
end for

Algorithm 3. The function $SelectNodeByLottery()$

for each slave node i the rendezvous node has **do**
  $ticket_i \leftarrow c_i - (l_{i1} + l_{i2} + \ldots + l_{im})$
  $ticketSum \leftarrow ticketSum + ticket_i$
end for
Generate the random number $winning\ token \in [0, ticketSum]$
$LastSum \leftarrow NextSum \leftarrow 0$
for each slave node i the rendezvous node has **do**
  $LastSum \leftarrow NextSum$
  $NextSum \leftarrow NextSum + ticket_i$
  if $winning\ token \in [LastSum, NextSum]$ **then**
    return node i
  end if
end for

3.3 The Choice of Parameters

The threshold th is the criterion to define the overloaded node. It is based on the average utilization $\overline{\mu}$ of the slave nodes. We set that $th = (1 + \overline{\mu})/2$. The number of rendezvous nodes is another important parameter. We believe that it is relative to the scale of the system. If the number of rendezvous nodes is too large, each rendezvous node will just cover the small fraction of the whole system. Oppositely, if the number is too small, these rendezvous may burden too much cost of load balancing. In our experiments, we set the number 16, which is justified practically in [6]. Time interval t determines the frequency of load balancing. It controls the tradeoff between low load movement and low quality of balance. Intuitively, smaller value of t provides a better balance at the expense of greater load movement. As the choice the interval t depends on the dynamics of P2P systems which is relative to the specific application, we will not show the effect of t's changing in our experiments.

4 Experimental Evaluation

4.1 Simulation Methodology

Network Heterogeneity. We use the GT-ITM topology generator [11] to generate transit-stub models of the physical network. "Ts-large" topology is chosen to represent a situation in which the overlay consists of nodes scattered in the entire the Internet and only very few nodes from the same edge network join the overlay. It has 70 transit domains, 5 transit nodes per transit domain, 3 stub domains attached to each transit node and 2 nodes in each stub domain. We also assign latencies of 5, 20 and 100ms to stub-stub, stub-transit and transit-transit links respectively. We choose 1000 nodes from this physical network. Chord [2] is chosen as the platform of our simulation. But the approach can be used on any DHT based P2P systems.

Node Heterogeneity. There are many resource factors of node heterogeneity, including process speed, storage and bandwidth. As our approach considers the processing delay in step one and abstracts the nodes' capacity in a unique factor in step two. To simulate the processing delay, we use two different distributions: *bimodal* and *Gnutella-like* distributions. For *bimodal* distribution, we assume that there are two kinds of nodes - fast and slow. The processing delay of fast nodes is 10ms, while the delay of slow ones is 100ms. The fraction of fast nods varies from 5% to 25% [12]. For *Gnutella-like* distribution, the maximum processing delay is α second, so the processing delay of nodes is assigned as α, $\alpha/10$, $\alpha/100$, $\alpha/10^3$ and $\alpha/10^4$ with probability of 20%, 45%, 30%, 4.9%, and 0.1% respectively. To account for heterogeneity of node capacity in step two, we used two capacity profiles. For *Gnutella-like* profile, We assign capacity of 1, 10, 10^2, 10^3 and 10^4 to Chord nodes with probability of 20%, 45%, 30%, 4.9%, and 0.1% respectively [10]. For the *Zipf-like* one, when sorted, the ith Chord node has capacity of $1000 * i^{-\beta}$ (where β is 1.2) The assignment of these two profiles are both based on nodeID. The node with smaller identifier owns less capacity.

Load Distribution. The load of a virtual server is generated using a *Pareto distribution* with the shape parameter 1.5 and the scale $0.5^{1.5}$. Due to the heavy-tailed nature of this distribution, it presents a particularly bad case for load balancing [13]. We change the factor of the Pareto function to achieve the utilization of the system equals to 0.6.

4.2 Overlay Adjustment

Fig.1 and Fig. 2 show the effect of the overlay adjustment under two different processing-delay distributions. "random" means the original state without any adjustment. "dist" means the state after swapping operations which are only based on the transferring delay. The factor k in equation 1 is 0. "dist+cap" represents the state after swapping operations which are based on both transferring and processing delay. The factor k is 1. The average lookup latency is calculated by 10^6 random lookup operations. It is not the real lookup latency which is measured by millisecond, but the relative value which is the real one divides the average latency of the network. The common characteristic of these two figures is that "dist+cap" is better than the other two. It shows that consideration of the heterogeneity of both networks and nodes can achieve better performance. In Fig. 2, when the maximum processing delay is getting larger, the difference between "dist" and "dist+cap" becomes more obvious. The reason is that when α increases, the effect of node heterogeneity is getting more important than the network heterogeneity. The same effect can be achieved by varying the factor k.

Fig. 3 illustrates another important feature of our approach. In real P2P systems, powerful nodes provide much more services than poor ones. Accordingly, the destination of more lookup operations is powerful nodes. We simulate this phenomenon by increasing the faction of lookups whose destination is fast node

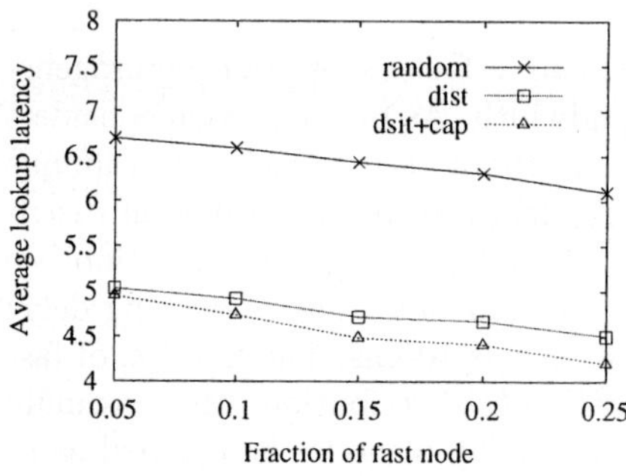

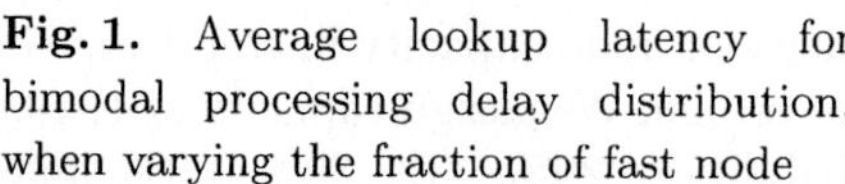
Fig. 1. Average lookup latency for bimodal processing delay distribution, when varying the fraction of fast node

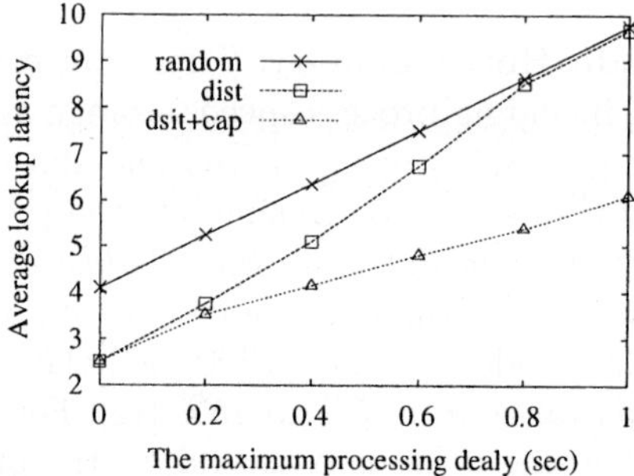

Fig. 2. Average lookup latency for Gnutella-like processing delay distribution, when varying the maximum processing delay

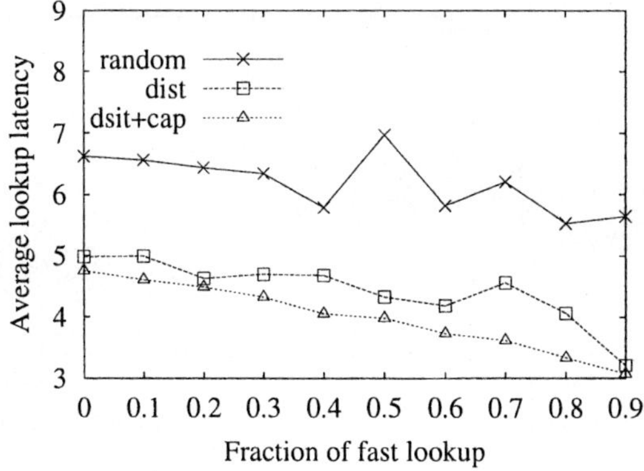

Fig. 3. Average lookup latency for bimodal processing delay distribution, when varying the fraction of fast node lookup

in the *bimodal distribution* environment. The lookup latencies of both "random" and "dist" fluctuate when the faction increases. Only the latency of "dist+cap" keeps decreasing. In other words, only "dsit+cap" approach can be efficient in this phenomenon. We will explain it in two aspects. On the one hand, given that the physical network we construct is "Internet-like", only very few nodes from the same edge network join the overlay. So the query with largest latency is usually from a slow node to another slow one in different areas. As a result, the latency of a query to slow node trends to be larger than the one to fast node with a high probability. On the other hand, our approach judges the processing delay as one factor to make swapping operation. The fast nodes with low processing delay own a higher prior to be adjusted. So with a high probability, fast nodes may move to a better position where the average lookup latencies are reduced.

4.3 Load Balancing

Fig. 4 and Fig. 5 show the scatter plot of loads each node has with *Zipf-like* and *Gnutella-like* capacity profiles respectively. It is obvious that after load balancing, the loads of most nodes are less than 1.0.[4] In section 3, we explain the characteristics of our load balancing algorithm based on lottery scheduling. Fig. 6 illustrates the balance of movement. We use *Gnutella-like* capacity profile, so the nodes with node ID from 950 to 995 have capacity 1000.

The reason we just show the movement of these nodes is that most of movement operations occur in this range. We compare two methods: the *normal* way and the *lottery* way. The normal way is to move the virtual servers to one node so that it can achieve the minimal utilization of that node. Apparently, several nodes in the normal way burden too much load to move. Oppositely, the load balancing algorithm based on lottery scheduling can achieve the balance of load movement.

[4] Actually, it is below 0.7. It can not be discovered from the figures.

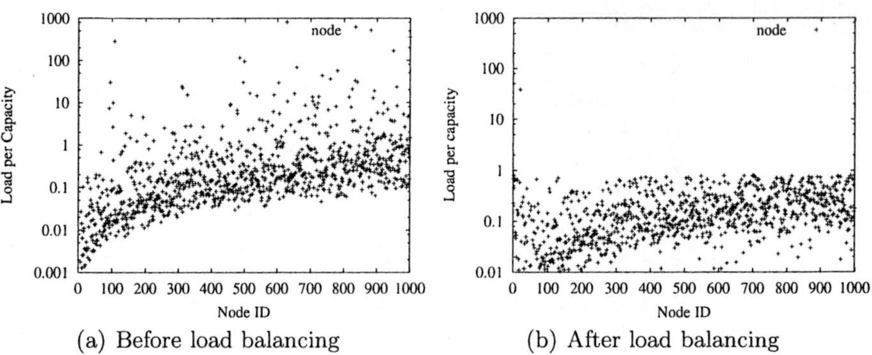

(a) Before load balancing (b) After load balancing

Fig. 4. Results for the Zipf-like capacity profile

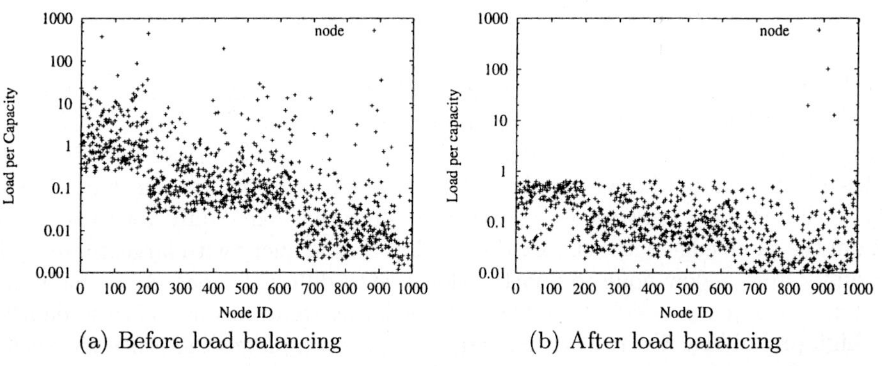

(a) Before load balancing (b) After load balancing

Fig. 5. Results for to the Gnutella-like capacity profile

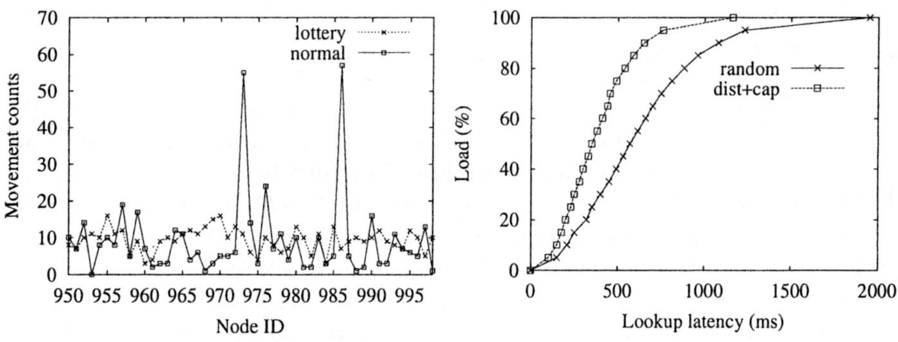

Fig. 6. Balance of load movement

Fig. 7. CDF of the average delay of load movement

There are many relations between phase 1 and 2. The adjustment in phase 1 uses one of the capacity factors - processing delay as the criterion to make swapping operation. In addition, phase 1 constructs a better overlay for load balancing. The movement cost of load reassignment can be greatly reduced. Fig. 7 shows this kind of improvement. In order to move 80% of all loads, the average delay without the adjustment is twice as large as the one after adjustment.

5 Related Work

There are several methods that try to solve the heterogeneity problem. Most of them are introduced in section 1. There are two researches that are the most related to our work. Chun et al. study the impact with a generalized cost model for overlay construction that takes into consideration different types of heterogeneity, such as node capacity and network proximity [12]. But their study is limited in the neighbor selection area for Pastry-like systems. There is no consideration about the relationship between overlay and load balance. In addition, they did not discover the phenomenon we explained in section 4 and showed in Fig. 3. Y. Zhu et al use proximity information in load balancing [10]. However, in order to balance the load and utilize the proximity information, they construct *k-ary* tree structure on top of a DHT, which brings the complexity and overhead of system maintenance. Besides, the *k-ary* tree is just an auxiliary structure of load balancing. It can not affect the lookup latency of the P2P system.

6 Conclusions

This paper proposes a two-phase approach to exploit the heterogeneity of the structured P2P system. In phase 1, by exploiting the heterogeneity of both networks and nodes, we adjust the structure of overlay to reduce the lookup latency. In phase 2, a novel load balancing scheme based on lottery scheduling is used to balance not only the load but also the movement cost of nodes. With the help of phase 1, the cost of load movement can be greatly reduced. Our simulation results show that the performance, including query quality from the users' view and load balance from the system's view, can be improved considerably in a heterogeneous environment.

Acknowledgement. This work is supported by the China NSF grant, the China Jiangsu Provincial NSF grant (BK2005208), the China 973 project (2002CB312002) and TRAPOYT award of China Ministry of Education.

References

1. Ratnasamy, S., Francis, P., Handley, M., Karp, R., Shenker, S.: A scalable content-addressable network. In: Proceedings of the ACM SIGCOMM. (2001)
2. Stoica, I., Morris, R., Karger, D., Kaashoek, M.F., Balakrishnan, H.: Chord: A scalable peer-to-peer lookup service for Internet applications. In: Proceedings of the ACM SIGCOMM. (2001)

3. Rowstron, A., Druschel, P.: Pastry: Scalable, distributed object location and routing for large-scale peer-to-peer systems. In: IFIP/ACM International Conference on Distributed Systems Platforms (Middleware). (2001)
4. Xu, Z., Mahalingam, M., Karlsson, M.: Turning heterogeneity into an advantage in overlay routing. In: Proceedings of IEEE INFOCOM. (2003)
5. Hu, J., Li, M., Zheng, W., Wang, D., Ning, N., Dong, H.: Smartboa: Constructing P2P overlay network in the heterogeneous Internet using irregular routing tables. In: 3rd International workshop on P2P Systems(IPTPS04). (2004)
6. Godfrey, B., Lakshminarayanan, K., Surana, S., Karp, R., Stoica, I.: Load balancing in dynamic structured P2P systems. In: Proceedings of IEEE INFOCOM. (2004)
7. Godfrey, P.B., Stoica, I.: Heterogeneity and load balance in distributed hash tables. In: Proceedings of IEEE INFOCOM. (2005)
8. Qiu, T., Wu, F., Chen, G.: A generic approach to make structured P2P systems topology-aware. In: Third International Symposium on Parallel and Distributed Processing and Applications (ISPA'2005). (2005)
9. C.A.Waldspurger: Lottery and Stride Scheduling: Flexible Proportional-Share Resource Management. PhD thesis, Massachusetts Inst. Technol. (1995)
10. Zhu, Y., Hu, Y.: Towards efficient load balancing in structured P2P systems. In: Proceedings of the 18th International Parallel and Distributed Processing Symposium (IPDPS04). (2004)
11. Zegura, E.W., Calvert, K.L., Bhattacharjee., S.: How to model an internetwork. In: Proceedings of INFOCOM. (1996)
12. Chun, S.G., Zhao, B.Y., Kubiatowicz, J.D.: Impact of neighbor selection on performance and resilience of structured P2P networks. In: International workshop on P2P Systems(IPTPS05). (2005)
13. Rao, A., Lakshminarayanan, K., Surana, S., Karp, R., Stoica, I.: Load balancing in structured P2P systems. In: 2nd International workshop on P2P Systems(IPTPS03). (2003)

Dynamic Scheduling Mechanism for Result Certification in Peer to Peer Grid Computing*

SungJin Choi[1], MaengSoon Baik[1], JoonMin Gil[2], ChanYeol Park[2], SoonYoung Jung[3], and ChongSun Hwang[1]

[1] Dept. of Computer Science & Engineering, Korea University
{lotieye, msbak, hwang}@disys.korea.ac.kr
[2] Korea Institute of Science and Technology Information (KISTI)
{jmgil, chan}@kisti.re.kr
[3] Dept. of Computer Science Education, Korea University
jsy@comedu.korea.ac.kr

Abstract. In a peer to peer grid computing environment, volunteers have heterogeneous properties and dynamically join and leave during execution. Therefore, it is essential to adapt to an unstable and widely distributed environment. However, existing scheduling and result certification mechanisms do not adapt to such a dynamic environment. As a result, they undergo high overhead, performance degradation, and scalability problems.

To solve the problems, we propose a new scheduling mechanism for result certification. The proposed mechanism applies different scheduling and result certification algorithms to different volunteer groups that are classified on the basis of their properties such as volunteering service time, availability, and credibility. It also exploits mobile agents in a distributed way in order to adapt to a dynamic peer to peer grid computing environment.

1 Introduction

A grid computing system is a platform that provides access to various computing resources owned by institutions by making virtual organization [4,5]. On the other hand, a peer to peer grid computing system is a platform that achieves a high throughput computing by harvesting a number of idle desktop computers owned by individuals (called volunteers) at the edge of the Internet using peer to peer computing technologies [1,2,3,4,5,6,7,8,9,10,11,12,13,14]. The peer to peer grid computing systems usually support embarrassingly parallel applications that consist of a lot of instances of the same computation with each own data. The applications are usually involved with scientific problems that need large amounts of processing capacity over long periods of time. Recently, there has been a rapidly growing interest in peer to peer grid computing systems because of the success of the most popular examples such as SETI@Home [1] and distributed.net [2].

* This work was supported by the Korea Institute of Science and Technology Information.

H. Zhuge and G.C. Fox (Eds.): GCC 2005, LNCS 3795, pp. 811–824, 2005.

In a peer to peer grid computing environment, any nodes can participate as volunteers (i.e., resource providers). That is, some malicious volunteers tamper with the computation and return corrupted results. Therefore, the peer to peer grid computing systems must detect and tolerate the erroneous result in order to guarantee reliable execution in such an untrusted environment. To this end, exiting peer to peer grid systems exploited result certification mechanisms such as majority voting and spot-checking [6,7,10]. The result certification is tightly related with scheduling in the sense that both the special task for spot-checking and the redundant tasks for voting are allocated to volunteers in a scheduling procedure. Existing peer to peer grid systems mainly used the eager scheduling mechanism [6,8,11,12,13]. However, when the existing eager scheduling mechanism performs the result certification, it causes serious problems because it does not adapt to a dynamic peer to peer grid computing environment.

First, existing scheduling and result certification mechanisms do not adapt to unstable environment. In a peer to peer grid computing environment, volunteers at the edge of the Internet are exposed to link and crash failures. In addition, they can dynamically join and leave in the middle of the execution without any constraints. Thus, *public execution* (i.e., the execution of a task as a volunteer) is stopped arbitrarily. Moreover, volunteers are not totally dedicated only to a peer to peer grid computing, so public executions get temporarily suspended by *private execution* (i.e., the execution of a private job as a personal user). In this paper, we regard the unstable situations as *volunteer autonomy failures* because they lead to the delay and blocking of the execution of tasks and even partial or entire loss of the executions. The volunteer autonomy failures occur more frequently than in a grid computing environment because a peer to peer grid computing system is based on dynamic desktop computers. The volunteer autonomy failures make it difficult for a volunteer server to schedule tasks and to manage the allocated tasks. Moreover, they delay and even prevent finishing the result certification. Existing mechanisms, however, do not reflect the volunteer autonomy failures in scheduling and result certification phases.

Second, existing scheduling and result certification mechanisms do not consider various properties of volunteers such as *availability*, *volunteering service time*, and *volunteer autonomy failures.* The same scheduling, result certification, and fault tolerant algorithms are applied to all volunteers without considering their various properties. In addition, existing mechanisms are performed only by a volunteer server in a centralized way in a widely distributed environment. As a result, they cause high overhead, performance degradation, and scalability problems.

To solve these problems, we propose a new scheduling mechanism for result certification that adapts to a dynamic peer to peer grid computing environment. The scheduling mechanism dynamically performs result certification according to the properties of volunteers such as location, service time, availability, and credibility. To this purpose, our mechanism is based on the volunteer groups that are classified on the basis of properties of volunteers. To apply appropriate scheduling and result certification algorithms to each volunteer group, we make use of mobile agent technology in a distributed way. Therefore, the dynamic scheduling mechanism for result certification reduces the overhead and latency while guaranteeing reliable results. In addition, it solves the scalability problem by using mobile agents. Finally, it tolerates various failures (especially, volunteer autonomy failures) frequently occurred in a peer to peer grid computing environment.

2 Background and Motivation

In a peer to peer grid computing environment, the result certification approaches are categorized into majority voting and spot-checking mechanisms [6,7,10].

In a majority voting approach, the same task is performed at different volunteers as much as the number of redundancy. Redundancy allows us to identify the correct result against erroneous one if there are sufficiently more good volunteers than bad ones. There are two ways to construct a voting group: parallel voting group and sequential voting group like Fig 1. Suppose that a voting group is composed of V_0, V_1, and V_2. In the parallel voting approach, the same task (i.e., T_i) is distributed to all members at the same time like dotted lines in Fig. 1(a), and then it is executed simultaneously. Therefore, the voting procedure for each task is completed step by step. On the other hand, in the sequential voting group, the same task (i.e., T_{i+2}) is distributed and executed sequentially like dotted lines in Fig. 1(b).

In a spot-checking approach, the special task whose result is already known is performed at randomly selected volunteers. If a volunteer returns an erroneous result, it is regarded as malicious one. Majority voting approach is apparently more costly than spot-checking, because it requires a redundancy of at least two per task.

In addition, the peer to peer grid computing systems mainly used the eager scheduling algorithm [6,8,11,12,13]. In this algorithm, the tasks are continuously allocated to faster volunteers, and therefore they execute more tasks than slow volunteers.

A few studies have been made on scheduling and result certification in a peer to peer grid computing environment. Bayanihan [6,7] proposed majority voting and spot-checking based on eager scheduling algorithm. Especially, it also proposed credibility-enhanced eager scheduling algorithm. In this algorithm, the more a volunteer passes the spot-checking, the higher its credibility becomes. The

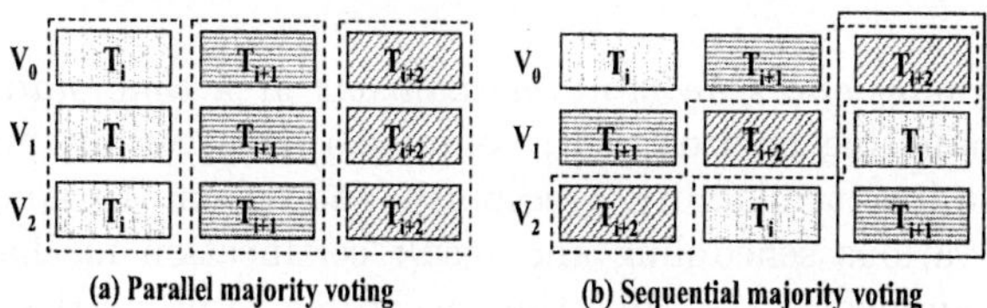

Fig. 1. Construction of voting group

more volunteers within voting group agree on a result, the higher its credibility becomes. Volunteers continue to compute the task and perform spot-checking until the credibility threshold is satisfied. When the desired credibility threshold is reached, the result is accepted as a final. In these algorithms, the voting group for majority voting is not built before tasks are distributed to volunteers. Instead, the voting group is built on the fly. That is, whenever a faster volunteer is allocated to a task, it is added to the voting group for the task. As a result, the members in the voting group have different credibility. Javelin [11,12] proposed the advanced eager scheduling algorithm based on tree. It provides the scalability and fault tolerance. XtremWeb [8,9,10] proposed a spot-checking mechanism on the basis of property testing. It reduces the sample size for spot checking by using property testing.

However, there are some problems in existing scheduling and result certification mechanisms.

1) *They do not adapt to dynamic peer to peer grid computing environment.* Existing scheduling and result certification mechanisms do not take into account volunteer autonomy failures in scheduling and result certification procedures. As a result, they require more redundancy to achieve result certification as well as more overhead. Sometimes, they cannot complete result certification because of the delay and blocking of the execution.

2) *There is no dynamic scheduling mechanisms for result certification.* Result certification is tightly related with scheduling in the sense that both the special task for spot-checking and redundant tasks for voting are allocated to volunteers in a scheduling procedure. In addition, in the presence of failure, the failed tasks are reallocated to new volunteers in a fault tolerant scheduling procedure. However, existing peer to peer grid computing systems simply use eager scheduling mechanism, which is not appropriate for result certification. In Bayanihan [6,7], a voting group is built on the fly. That is, when a volunteer is allocated to a task, it is added to the voting group for the task. At this time, eager scheduling simply selects the fastest volunteer as a member of voting group for the task without considering the credibility of the volunteer. As a result, the credibility of voting group fluctuates. In other words, although a volunteer with high credibility makes the credibility of voting group higher, another volunteer with low credibility makes the credibility lower. As a result, it is difficult to agree on same result. That is, more volunteers are needed to reach the agreement. Consequently, delay and overhead problems arise. In the case of failures, when the failed volunteer are replaced with a new volunteer, the same problems also arise.

3) *They use only one scheduling mechanisms at a time statically.* In peer to peer grid computing environment, volunteers have various properties such as capacity, location, availability, credibility, and so on. To adapt to various properties, the various scheduling and result certification mechanisms should be dynamically applied at the same time according to properties of volunteers. However, existing mechanisms use only one mechanism at a time statically. That is, the same scheduling, result certification, and fault tolerant algorithms are

applied to all volunteers without considering their various properties. Moreover, the scheduling mechanism is performed only by a volunteer server in a centralized way. As a result, they undergo high overhead and scalability problems.

3 Dynamic Scheduling Mechanism for Result Certification

Our mechanism dynamically performs different scheduling and result certification algorithms suitable for volunteer groups that are classified on the basis of the properties of volunteers such as *volunteer availability*, *volunteering service time*, and *volunteer credibility*. It also exploits mobile agent to adapt to dynamic peer to peer grid computing environment in a distributed way. In this section, we firstly illustrate how to construct volunteer group according to properties of volunteers. Then, we introduce how to apply scheduling and result certification algorithms to volunteer groups by means of mobile agents.

3.1 Constructing Volunteer Group

To apply different scheduling and result certification algorithm suitable for volunteers in a scheduling phase, volunteers are required to first be formed into homogeneous groups. Our mechanism classifies volunteers into four volunteer groups on the basis of *volunteer availability* α_v, *volunteering service time* Θ, and *volunteer credibility* C_v, that is, A', B', C', and D' volunteer group.In the A' volunteer group, all features are high. In the B' volunteer group, both α_v and C_v are high. In the C' volunteer group, only Θ is high. Finally, in the D' volunteer group, all features are low.

Classifying Volunteers. When volunteers are classified, their CPU and memory capacities are important factors. The most important factors, however, are volunteering time, availability, and credibility because a peer to peer grid computing systems are based on dynamic desktop computers. In a peer to peer grid computing environment, the capacities of desktop computers are similar, while the volunteering time, availability, and credibility are very various [15,16,18,22]. Therefore, the computation time is more affected by the latter factors. In this paper, we classify the volunteers according to volunteer availability and volunteering service time. The volunteering time, volunteer availability, and volunteering service time are defined as follows.

Definition 1 (Volunteering time). *Volunteering time (Υ) is the period when a volunteer is supposed to donates its resources.*

$$\Upsilon = \Upsilon_R + \Upsilon_S$$

Here, the *reserved volunteering time* (Υ_R) is reserved time when a volunteer provides its computing resources. Volunteers mostly perform public execution during Υ_R, rarely private execution. On the other hand, the *selfish volunteering time* (Υ_S) is unexpected volunteering time. Thus, volunteers usually perform private execution during the Υ_S, sometimes public execution.

Definition 2 (Volunteer availability). *Volunteer availability (α_v) is the probability that a volunteer will be operational correctly and be able to deliver the volunteer services during volunteering time Υ*

$$\alpha_v = \frac{MTTVAF}{MTTVAF + MTTR}$$

Here, the $MTTVAF$ means "mean time to volunteer autonomy failures", and the $MTTR$ means "mean time to rejoin". The MTTVAF means the average time before the volunteer autonomy failures happen, and the MTTR means the mean duration of volunteer autonomy failures. The α_v reflects the degree of volunteer autonomy failures, whereas the traditional availability in distributed systems is mainly related with the crash failure.

Volunteer service time is defined as follows.

Definition 3 (Volunteering service time). *Volunteering service time (Θ) is the expected service time when a volunteer participates in public execution during Υ*

$$\Theta = \Upsilon \times \alpha_v$$

In scheduling procedure, Θ is more appropriate than Υ because Θ represents the time when a volunteer actually executes each task in the presence of volunteer autonomy failures.

Volunteers are categorized into four classes (i.e., A, B, C, D classes) according to α_v and Θ like Fig. 2 (a).

Classifying and Making Volunteer Groups. A volunteer server selects volunteers as volunteer group members according to the properties of volunteers such as volunteering service time and volunteer credibility.

Volunteer credibility is defined as follows.

Definition 4 (Volunteer credibility). *Volunteer credibility C_v is the probability that represents correctness of results which a volunteer will produce.*

$$C_v = \frac{CR}{ER + CR + IR}$$

Here, ER means the number of erroneous results, CR means the number of correct results, and IR means the number of incomplete results. $ER + CR + IR$ means the total number of tasks that a volunteer executes. The IR occurs when

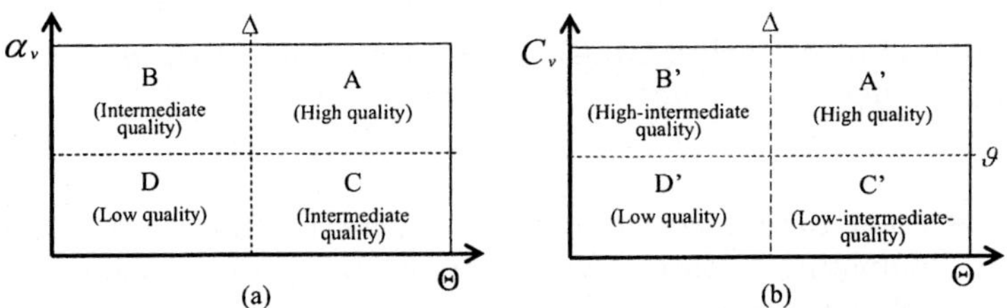

Fig. 2. The classification of volunteers and volunteer groups

```
// V_A : A class, V_B: B class, V_C : C class, V_D: D class
// VG_A' : A' class, VG_B': B' class, VG_C' : C' class, VG_D': D' class
// To classify the registered volunteers into A, B, C, D classes, respectively
ClassifyVolunteers(V);
// To construct volunteer groups
if (V_i ∈ V_A) then  // V_i : one of the classified volunteers
   if (V_i.C_v ≥ ϑ) then
      V_i → VG_A';  // → : assign
   else
      V_i → VG_C';
   fi;
else if (V_i ∈ V_B) then
   if (V_i.C_v ≥ ϑ) then
      V_i → VG_B';
   else
      V_i → VG_D';
   fi;
else if (V_i ∈ V_C) then
   V_i → VG_C';
else
   V_i → VG_D';
fi;
```

Fig. 3. Algorithm of volunteer group construction

a volunteer does not complete spot-checking or majority voting on account of crash failure and volunteer autonomy failures. If a volunteer passes the spot-checking, the credibility becomes higher. If volunteers within voting group reach the agreement for majority voting, their credibility also becomes higher.

When both Θ and C_v are considered in grouping volunteers, volunteer groups are categorized into four classes like Fig. 2 (b). Here, Δ is the expected computation time of a task. ϑ is the desired credibility threshold which a task achieves.

Fig. 3 shows the algorithm of volunteer group construction. The registered volunteers are classified into A, B, C, and D classes according to volunteering service time and volunteer availability. Then, each volunteer group is constructed according to volunteer credibility and volunteering service time.

3.2 Applying Scheduling and Result Certification to Volunteer Group

In order to dynamically apply scheduling and result certification to volunteer groups, scheduling agents are used. Each scheduling agent has own scheduling, result certification, and fault tolerant algorithms in order to control its volunteer group according to the properties of volunteer group, respectively.

Result Certification for Volunteer Group. Result certification is dynamically applied to each volunteer group. Each scheduling agent of volunteer groups provides the following result certification strategies.

The A' volunteer group has high C_v, high Θ, and high α_v enough to execute tasks reliably. There is high possibility that produce correct results in the A' volunteer group. If voting is used for result certification, the sequential voting group approach is more appropriate than the parallel one because the former can perform more tasks. In Fig. 1 (b), in case of the T_{i+2} task, if first two results generated at V_1 and V_0 are same, there is no need to execute the T_{i+2} task at V_2 because majority (i.e., 2 out of 3) is already achieved. Therefore, since other tasks can be executed instead of the executions that the solid line in Fig. 1(b) includes, the sequential voting group can perform more tasks.

The B' volunteer group has high C_v and high α_v, but low Θ. It has a high possibility that produce correct results. However, it cannot complete their tasks because of lack of the computation time. In addition, volunteer autonomy failures occur frequently in the middle of execution. Therefore, the manager of B' volunteer group must provide not only task migration in order to execute the tasks continuously, but also fault tolerant algorithms to tolerate volunteer autonomy failures. During task migration, a previous volunteer affects the result of the volunteer to which a task is migrated. In other words, if the latter volunteer (i.e., migrated volunteer) is selected wrongly, it can ruin the correct result that the former volunteer generated. Therefore, the migrated volunteer must be chosen among the B' or A' volunteer groups, not C' or D' volunteer groups. In addition, spot-checking is additionally performed at the former volunteer as well as the migrated volunteer to check their correctness again. In addition, the sequential voting group is more appropriate than the parallel voting group like the A' volunteer group.

The C' volunteer group has high Θ, but low C_v and low α_v. It has a time enough to execute tasks. However, its results might be incorrect. Therefore, in order to strength the credibility, the C' volunteer group requires more spot-checking and redundancy than the A' or B' volunteer group. The parallel voting group is more appropriate than the sequential voting group. If a scheduling agent adopts sequential voting group, the voting procedure is delayed frequently because each volunteer suffers from volunteer autonomy failures owing to low α_v. It also takes a long time and high overhead for scheduling agents to complete result certification. In the case of parallel voting group, however, the overhead and the completion time are relatively small because voting procedure for each task is completed within a step like Fig. 1 (a).

The D' volunteer group has low C_v, low Θ, and low α_v. It has insufficient time to execute tasks. In addition, there is little possibility to produce correct results. Moreover, volunteer autonomy failures occur frequently in the middle of execution. Therefore, tasks are not allocated to the D' volunteer group not only because management cost is too expensive, but also because results are incorrect.

Scheduling for Result Certification. Each scheduling agent has its own scheduling algorithm for result certification according to the above strategies. In general, the tasks are scheduled in the following order, that is, A', C', and B' volunteer groups sequentially because A' and C' volunteer groups have enough times to execute tasks. The scheduling algorithms for each volunteer group are as follows.

The A' scheduling agent performs scheduling for result certification as follows. 1) Order A' volunteer group by α_v and then by Θ. 2) Evaluate the number of redundancy or spot-checking rate. 3) Construct a sequential voting group, or choose some volunteers for spot-checking on the basis of Θ. 4) Distribute tasks in a way of sequential voting group, or allocate special tasks for spot-checking. 5) Check the collected results. Here, a task is distributed as the form of a task agent which consists of parallel code and data.

The B' scheduling agent performs scheduling for result certification as follows. 1) Order A' volunteer group by Θ and then by α_v. 2) Same to A' volunteer group. 3) Construct a sequential voting group, or choose some volunteers for spot-checking on the basis of Θ. 4)~5) Same to A' volunteer group. Especially, B' scheduling agent must perform additional spot-checking during task migration because of lack of volunteering service time.

The C' scheduling agent performs scheduling for result certification as follows. 1) Order C' volunteer group by C_v and then α_v. 2) Evaluate the number of redundancy or spot-checking rate. 3) Construct a parallel voting group, or choose some volunteers for spot-checking on the basis of C_v. 4)~5) Same to A' volunteer group. C' scheduling agent should handle the volunteer autonomy failures.

In the above 2) phases, the number of redundancy for majority voting and the number of spot-checking are differently applied to each volunteer group. In the case of redundancy for majority voting, the C' volunteer group has the greater number of redundancy than the A' and B' volunteer groups because of low credibility. Similarly, the number of spot-checking is ordered as C', B', and A'. Especially, the B' volunteer group has more the number of spot-checking than the A' volunteer group on account of task migration.

The number of redundancy for majority voting is dynamically regulated by each scheduling agent through the following Eq. 1. The number of redundancy r for majority voting is dynamically calculated through Eq. 2. Here, $r = 2k + 1$. The final error rate of majority voting is evaluated as follows [21].

$$\varepsilon(C'_v, r) = \sum_{i=k+1}^{2k+1} \binom{2k+1}{i} (1 - C'_v)^i (C'_v)^{(2k+1-i)} \tag{1}$$

which is bounded by $\frac{[4C'_v(1-C'_v)]^{k+1}}{2(2C'_v-1)\sqrt{\pi k}}$.

Here, the parameter C'_v means the probability that volunteers within each volunteer group generate correct results.

Suppose that a desired credibility threshold is ϑ. Our mechanism calculates the number of redundancy for each volunteer group if $(1 - \vartheta) \geq \varepsilon(C'_v, r)$. Consequently, the A' and B' volunteer groups have a small r, so it can reduce the overhead of majority voting and execute more tasks. In contrast, the C' volunteer group has a large r. The large r makes the credibility high.

The rate of spot-checking q is also regulated by each scheduling agent. The final error rate of spot-checking is evaluated as follows [7].

$$\varepsilon(q, n, C'_v, s) = \frac{sC'_v(1 - qs)^n}{(1 - C'_v) + C'_v(1 - qs)^n} \tag{2}$$

where, n is the saboteur's share in the total work. s is the sabotage rate of a saboteur.

```
// DVS : deputy volunteer set
// CDVS : candidate deputy volunteer set
// TDVS : temporal deputy volunteer set
// CDVS ⊂ VG_A'
TDVS = OrderedBy(CDVS.α_v);
// HC : harddisk capacity, NB : network bandwidth
DVS = OrderedBy(TDVS.(Θ + HC + NB));
DVS = OrderedBy(DVS.C_v);
// Pop the best deputy volunteer from DVS
DV = PopBestDV(DVS)
```

Fig. 4. Algorithm of deputy volunteers selection

In a similar way of majority voting, if n and s are given, the spot-checking rate q of each volunteer group is calculated by Eq. 2. Our mechanism calculates the rate of spot-checking for each volunteer group if $(1 - \vartheta) \geq \varepsilon(q, n, C'_v, s)$. The rate of spot-checking for the A' and B' volunteer groups are smaller than that of the C' volunteer group. Therefore, the A' and B' volunteer groups can reduce the overhead, and therefore execute more tasks. The C' volunteer group can increase its credibility.

The scheduling agent is executed at a deputy volunteer. The deputy volunteer is selected by the algorithm like Fig. 4. The deputy volunteers are ordered by volunteer availability, volunteering service time, and volunteer credibility, and also by hard disk capacity and network bandwidth. The deputy volunteers for each volunteer groups are selected among the best ones in A' volunteer group. Each scheduling agent is sent to the selected deputy volunteers.

4 Implementation and Evaluation

We evaluate our dynamic scheduling mechanism for result certification on the basis of the Korea@Home [22,23,24]. Now, Korea@Home has 6,712 Volunteers, and its performance is 364.47 Gflops at maximum and 290.53 Gflops on average for last 24 hours. Korea@Home contains applications such as global risk man-

Table 1. Simulation Environment

Case		A'	B'	C'	D'	Total
Case1	P.	84 (42%)	26 (13%)	70 (35%)	20 (10%)	200
	α_v	0.84	0.88	0.81	0.83	0.84
	Θ	41	17	39	16	35 min.
	C_v	0.98	0.98	0.88	0.86	0.93
Case2	P.	71 (35.5%)	31 (15.5%)	76 (38%)	22 (11%)	200
	α_v	0.87	0.89	0.80	0.82	0.84
	Θ	41	17	39	16	34 min.
	C_v	0.98	0.98	0.84	0.85	0.91
Case3	P.	76 (38%)	27 (13.5%)	80 (40%)	17 (8.5%)	200
	α_v	0.86	0.82	0.77	0.71	0.81
	Θ	35	17	33	16	30 min.
	C_v	0.98	0.98	0.82	0.85	0.91
Case4	P.	42 (21%)	59 (29.5%)	30 (15%)	69 (34.5%)	200
	α_v	0.80	0.78	0.70	0.69	0.73
	Θ	28	12	25	13	24 min.
	C_v	0.98	0.98	0.89	0.89	0.94

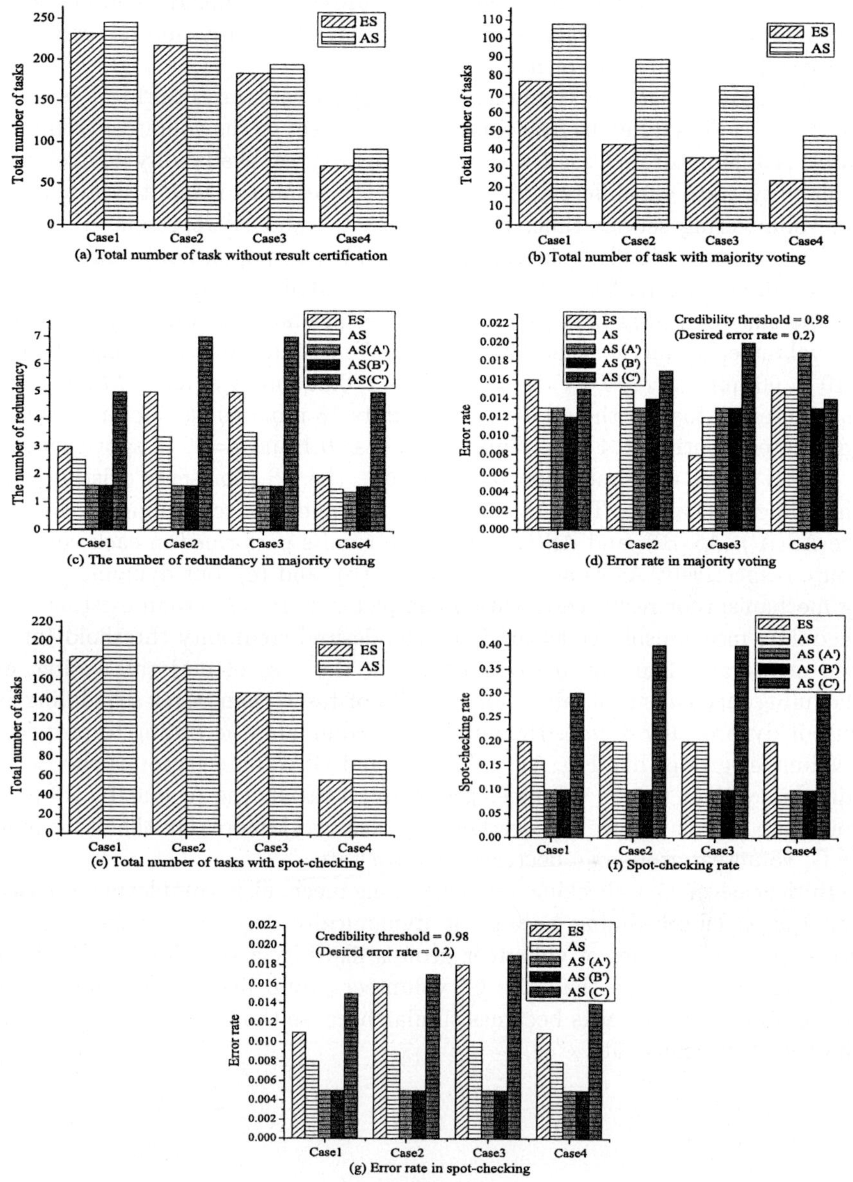

Fig. 5. Simulation results

agement, new drug candidate discovery, and climate prediction. In addition, the scheduling and task agents are based on ODDUGI mobile agent system [25,26].

We compare our scheduling mechanism with eager scheduling. Even though there are a lot of scheduling heuristics such as min-min, max-min, sufferage, and so on in a grid computing environment [16,17,18], we adopt eager scheduling because it is mainly used in a peer to peer grid computing environment

[6,8,11,12,13]. In addition, this simulation focuses on how much we obtain performance improvement, depending on whether the volunteer groups are considered in a scheduling procedure or not.

We evaluated the 200 volunteers with respect to 4 cases during 1 hour like Table 1. Case 1 is different from Case 2 with respect to the volunteer credibility. Case 3 is different from Case 1 with regard to volunteer availability and volunteer availability. Case 4 is different form Case 1 with respect to volunteer availability and volunteering service time. Here, A', B', C', and D' represent A', B', C', and D' volunteer groups, respectively. Here, *P.* (i.e., population) represents the number of volunteers. Each simulation was repeated 10 times per each case.

The 200 volunteers have various volunteer availability, volunteer credibility, and volunteering service time like Table 1. We assume that the range of MVT is 10 $\sim$ 60 minutes, $MTTVAF = 1/0.2 \sim 1/0.05$ minutes, and $MTTR$ is 3 $\sim$ 10 minutes. A task in the application exhibits 18 minutes of execution time on a dedicated Pentium 1.4 GHz. Suppose that s=0.1 and n=10 in spot-checking.

Fig. 5 shows the simulation results. Here, the ES represents existing eager scheduling mechanism. The AS represents our dynamic scheduling mechanism. The AS(A'), AS(B'), and AS(C') mean the results performed in each volunteer group, respectively. As shown in Fig. 5 (a), (b), and (e), our dynamic scheduling mechanism for result certification completes more tasks than existing eager scheduling mechanism, while satisfying the desired credibility threshold (or desired error rate) like Fig. 5 (d) and (g). In the case of majority voting, our scheduling mechanism obtains more results of tasks than eager scheduling because it dynamically decides the number of redundancy according to properties of volunteer groups like Fig. 5 (c). The A' and B' volunteer groups choose less redundancy than the C' volunteer group. As a result, the A' and B' volunteer groups are able to reduce the overhead, so they work more. On the other hand, the C' volunteer group can decrease its error rate.

In the case of spot-checking, our scheduling mechanism completes more tasks than the eager scheduling because it dynamically decides spot-checking rate according to properties of volunteer groups like Fig. 5 (f). However, if the A' volunteer group is less than the C' volunteer group like Cases 2 and 3, the number of completed tasks becomes similar because the C' volunteer group has a high spot-checking rate.

5 Conclusion

In this paper, we proposed a new scheduling mechanism for result certification that adapts to a dynamic peer to peer grid computing environment. The proposed mechanism applies different scheduling, result certification, and fault tolerant algorithms to volunteer groups according to their properties by using mobile agent in a decentralized way. We found that our dynamic scheduling mechanism for result certification completes more tasks than existing eager scheduling mechanism, while satisfying the desired credibility threshold. In addition, it solves the scalability problem by using mobile agents.

References

1. SETI@home, "http://setiathome.ssl.berkeley.edu"
2. Distributed.net, "http://distributed.net"
3. D. S. Milojicic, V. Kalogeraki, R. Lukose, K. Nagaraja, J. Pruyne, B. Richard, S. Rollins, and Z. Xu, "Peer-to-Peer Computing", HP Laboratories Palo Alto HPL-2002-57, March 2002.
4. Ian Foster and Adriana Iamnitchi, "On Death, Taxes, and the Convergence of Peer-to-Peer and Grid Computing", IPTPS'03, February 2003.
5. F. Berman, G. C. Fox, and A. J. G. Hey, "Grid Computing : Making the Global Infrastructure a Reality", Wiley, 2003
6. L. F. G. Sarmenta, S. Hirano. "Bayanihan: Building and Studying Volunteer Computing Systems Using Java", Future Generation Computer Systems, Vol. 15, No. 5/6., 1999.
7. L. F. G. Sarmenta, "Sabotage-Tolerance Mechanisms for Volunteer Computing Systems", Future Generation Computer Systems, 18(4), 2002.
8. G. Fedak, C. Germain, V. Neri, and F. Cappello, "XtremWeb: A Generic Global Computing System", CCGrid'01 workshop on Global Computing on Personal Devices, pp. 582-587, May 2001.
9. O. Lodygensky, G. Fedak, F. Cappello, V. Neri, M. Livny, D. Thain, "XtremWeb & Condor : sharing resources between Internet connected Condor pool", CCGrid'03 workshop on Global and Peer-to-Peer Computing on Large Scale Distributed Systems, pp. 382-389, May 2003.
10. C. G. Renaud, N. Playez, "Result Checking in Global Computing Systems", ICS'03, pp. 226-233, June 2003.
11. M. O. Neary, S. P. Brydon, P. Kmiec, S. Rollins, and P. Cappello, "Javelin++: Scalability Issues in Global Computing", Concurrency: Parctice and Experience, pp. 727-735, December 2000.
12. M. O. Neary, P. Cappello, "Advanced eager scheduling for Java-based adaptive parallel computing", Concurrency and Computation: Practice and Experience, Volume 17, Issue 7-8, pp. 797-819, 2005
13. A. Baratloo, M. Karaul, Z. Kedem, and P. Wyckoff, "Charlotte: Metacomputing on the Web", The 9th ICPDCS, 1996.
14. D. P. Anderson, "BOINC: A System for Public-Resource Computing and Storage", GRID'04, pp. 4-10, November 2004
15. D. Kondo, M. Taufer, J. Karanicolas, C. L. Brooks, H. Casanova and A. Chien, "Characterizing and Evaluating Desktop Grids: An Empirical Study", IPDPS'04, pp. 26-35, April 2004.
16. D. Kondo, H. Casanova, E. Wing, F. Berman, "Models and scheduling mechanisms for global computing applications", IPDPS'02, pp.79-86, April 2002.
17. M. Maheswaran, S. Ali, H. J. Siegel, D. Hensgen, and R. F. Freund, "Dynamic Matching and Scheduling of a Class of Independent Tasks onto Heterogeneous Computing Systems, HCW'99, pp. 30-44, April 1999.
18. D. Thain, T. Tannenbaum, and M. Livny, "Distributed Computing in Practice : The Condor Experience", Concurrency and Computation: Practice and Experience, Volume 17, Issue 2-4, pp. 323-356, 2005.
19. P. Jalote, "Fault Tolerance in Distributed Systems", Prentice-Hall, 1994
20. A. S. Tanenbaum and M. V. Steen, "Distributed Systems: Principles and Paradigms", Prentice Hall, 2002.

21. Yu. A. Zuev, "On the Estimation of Efficiency of Voting Procedures", Volume 42, Number 1, pp. 73-81, Theory of Probability & Its Applications, 1998.
22. Korea@Home, http://www.koreaathome.org/eng/
23. M. Baik, S. Choi, C. Hwang, J. Gil, H. Yu, "Adaptive Group Computation Approach in the Peer-to-peer Grid Computing Systems", AGridM 2004, Semtember 2004.
24. S. Choi, M. Baik, C. Hwang, J. Gil, and H. Yu, "Volunteer Availability based Fault Tolerant Scheduling Mechanism in Desktop Grid Computing Environment," NCA-AGC2004, pp.476-483, August, 2004.
25. ODDUGI mobile agent system, http://oddugi.korea.ac.kr/
26. S. Choi, M. Baik, and C. Hwang, "Location Management & Message Delivery Protocol in Multi-region Mobile Agent Computing Environment," ICDCS 2004, pp. 476-483, March, 2004.

A Hybrid Peer-to-Peer Media Streaming

Sunghoon Son

Division of Computer Software, Sangmyung University,
Seoul 110-743, Korea
shson@smu.ac.kr

Abstract. In this paper, we present a media streaming service architecture over peer-to-peer network for large scale media streaming service. The proposed architecture is hybrid in that it combines both pure peer-to-peer streaming model and centralized server model in order to take advantages of them. We first describe overall streaming operation based on the hybrid architecture. Then, we deal with streaming load allocation problem under the proposed scheme. Extensive performance study based on simulation is carried out. The results show that the performance of the proposed system is much better than that of existing streaming system in numerous streaming performance metrics.

1 Introduction

Currently most legacy multimedia streaming services are based on the client-server architecture. However it has been proved that the traditional client-server architecture is an obstacle to providing scalable multimedia streaming service. Although centralized server attached to high-bandwidth backbone network is easy to deploy, it has a lot of defects in terms of scalability, reliability, high cost, and load on backbone networks. In order to cope with these difficulties, architectures such as content distribution network (CDN) [1,8] or proxy cache [7,10] are introduced. These architectures utilize intermediary servers like proxy servers (in proxy cache) or edge servers (in CDN) to replicate some of multimedia contents to geographically closer nodes to clients. However, they still suffer from the same problems as the client-server case, since they are fundamentally based on client-server paradigm from the viewpoint of proxy server or edge server.

Recently, peer-to-peer network gradually has been gaining a lot of attention as an alternative platform to existing media streaming service platforms. Compared with existing one, peer-to-peer network-based media streaming system is much more scalable in terms of the number of concurrent clients and provides much larger streaming capacity in a cost-effective manner. However, in real world, *pure* peer-to-peer network-based media streaming service is next to impossible due to the following facts. Firstly, peers are usually autonomous entities; even in the middle of the streaming operation, they join and leave the system whenever they want to. They do not worry about overall system's serviceability or availability. Secondly, it is very difficult to service unpopular contents by pure peer-to-peer network-based system only, since most peers have similar tendency to access and store popular contents only. Finally, peers are very unreliable; they may suffer from performance degradation due to network congestion, etc. Therefore, in order to deploy peer-to-peer paradigm in media

H. Zhuge and G.C. Fox (Eds.): GCC 2005, LNCS 3795, pp. 825–835, 2005.

streaming service in real world, there must be a scheme to overcome such difficulties in the pure peer-to-peer network based media streaming system.

There have been a lot of researches on pure peer-to-peer network-based media streaming systems [2,4,5,6,9,12]. Especially, some multi-source on-demand media streaming systems have been proposed. [14] deals with the media data assignment problem in non-parallel fashion and fast system capacity amplification method for multi-source media streaming. Similar to our work, a hybrid system which combines pure peer-to-peer system with CDN is proposed in [13]. Different from our work, peers are regarded as reliable entities. The authors assume that a peer is always up, have no bandwidth degradation, and never stop streaming anyway. Moreover, once a media file is dispersed throughout the system, subsequent streaming requests for that media file are served by peers without intervention of centralized server. They call it handoff and try to optimal handoff time for a given media file. After handoff time, the hybrid system is regressed to pure peer-to-peer system. Even in the middle of hybrid period, a media streaming session is serviced either by CDN server only or by peers only.

Generally, modeling of peers in previous literatures is too ideal. As mentioned above, peers are in no way reliable in real world, and it is not reasonable to guarantee deterministic service with unreliable peers. In this paper, we propose a hybrid peer-to-peer network-based media streaming architecture for large scale media streaming service. The proposed architecture combines peer-to-peer system and centralized server to exploit advantages of the both models. In the proposed scheme, several peers who want to play the same media file form a streaming peer group. Each peer in the group performs two operations, caching and streaming. Once joining a group, a peer receives and plays a part of media file from source peers outside the group. At the same time, it caches the media data in local disk. In addition to caching, a peer also performs streaming of media file to other peers in the group. On receiving a streaming service request from other peers in the group, the peer send the cached data to requesting peer. The scheme guarantees that the media data for streaming is always in the cache of other peers in the group.

In this paper, we also present a solution to the problem of streaming load allocation based on the proposed architecture. Given centralized servers and a set of peers with heterogeneous bandwidth capacities, we suggest a policy to select subset of available centralized servers and supplying peers for streaming a media file. Especially we take account of the unreliable property of peers.

Our contribution can be divided into two parts. First, we integrate pure peer-to-peer network-based media streaming architecture with centralized client-server based streaming service architecture. Second, we solve a streaming load allocation problem under the proposed architecture to cope with unreliable peers while maximizing the number of concurrent users. We carry out comprehensive performance evaluation on the proposed scheme. Our results show that the proposed scheme, compared with legacy streaming server with similar capacity, significantly increases the number of concurrent clients. The proposed scheme outperforms existing streaming system in other various streaming performance metrics too.

The rest of this paper is organized as follows. In Section 2, we propose a hybrid peer-to-peer network-based streaming service architecture and explain the system operations under the proposed architecture. In Section 3, we formulate a problem of streaming load allocation under the proposed scheme and propose a load allocation strategy and its admission control algorithm which continues streaming service against peer failure or degradation. We describe the simulation setup and discuss the results of performance evaluation in Section 4. Finally, we present our conclusions in Section 5.

2 Architecture of Hybrid Media Streaming System

In this section, we present a hybrid peer-to-peer media streaming architecture. We first describe overall system operations of the architecture. Then we explain creation of peer group, peer join/leave procedure, etc.

2.1 System Operation

In this section, we present a hybrid peer-to-peer media streaming architecture and explain overall system operations based on the architecture.

The hybrid streaming system consists of a few streaming servers, an index server, and a set of ordinary peers. The major role of a centralized streaming server in our architecture a legacy streaming server that participates in hybrid streaming session as a server, (2) source of all media files in the system, i.e. a seed peer in the peer-to-peer network. Hereafter we call them *source peers* in the sense of "source of all media files." Compared with ordinary peer, source peer is a true server in the meaning that they are always up and in operation. The number of source peers in the system is dependent on the scale of the network and client population. An *index server* of peer-to-peer network knows all the information about which peer is dead or alive, which peer owns which parts of each media file, which peers are joining which streaming sessions, and so on. Each *peer* is either a supplying peer or a requesting peer depending on the role of the peer in the streaming session. A peer may be both supplying peer and requesting peer at the same time. Before receiving any streaming service, the client is a requesting peer. After finishing streaming service, the requesting peer caches parts of the media file in its local disk and it becomes a supplying peer of the media file. A supplying peer may participate in several streaming session as a server at the same time. The heterogeneity of supplying peers is modeled by its maximum number of out-bound sessions, upper limit on the aggregate out-bound bandwidth, and the degree of reliability. We assume that each peer has enough disk storage to contain several video files.

The peer-to-peer media streaming in the proposed architecture operates as follows. In the proposed scheme, several peers who wish to stream the same media file form a *streaming peer group*. Each peer in the group performs two kinds of operation: caching and streaming. Once joining a group, a peer receives a portion of media file from source peers outside the group and caches the media data in local disk. The cached media data will be used by other peers who join the group later. In addition to caching, a peer also performs streaming of media file. On receiving a streaming request from other peers in the group, the peer send the cached data to requesting peer for playback. The scheme guarantees that the media data for streaming is always in the cache of other peers in the group.

A new peer group is created by a peer who makes an initial request of the media file. After a peer group is created, the initial peer begins receiving media file from some source peers outside the group for caching and playback. The peer continues caching of the media file until another peer requests the media file. When a new peer arrives, the initial peer stop caching and the new peer succeed caching from the point where the initial peer stopped. The initial peer, who just ceases to cache media data from external source peers, continues streaming the media file from the second peer who just joined the group and started caching. This can be possible because the second peer begins caching as soon as it joins the group. The second peer has already been caching media data needed by the initial peer in its local disk.

This caching procedure is repeated whenever a new peer joins the group. New peer begins caching from the point where the previous one stopped caching. It continues caching until the next peer arrives.

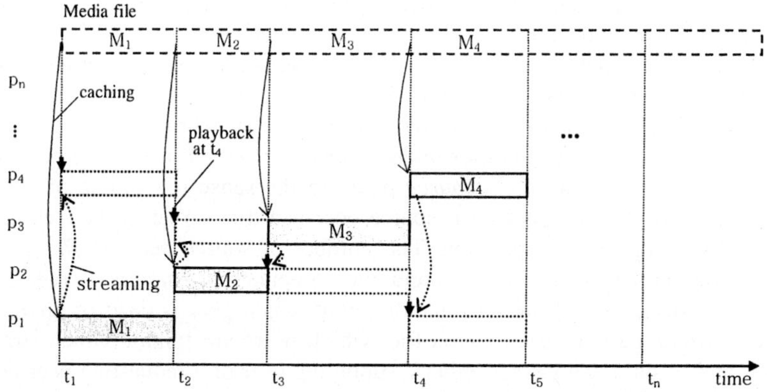

Fig. 1. A hybrid peer-to-peer streaming

Fig 1 shows a streaming peer group of n peers who request the same media file. In this figure, the group is created at time t_1 by peer p_1 who initially requests the media file. P_1 receives and playback the media data from some source peers. At the same time it caches the media data M_1 in its local disk in order to stream it to other peers later. When a request arrives by p_2 at t_2, p_2 first become a member of the streaming peer group and receives (and playbacks) the initial parts of media file from p_1. At the same time, p_2 receives parts of media file M_2 from source peers outside the group and caches it in local disk. This procedure is repeated whenever a new peer arrives in the system. As a result, the whole media file is divided into several media data according to peers' arrival time. Since media data needed by a peer for playback has already been cached by preceding peers, the real streaming is processed within the group (Especially Fig. 1 shows the state of caching and streaming of peer p_1, p_2, p_3, and p_4 at time t_4).

The main feature of the proposed scheme is the fact that the source of streaming changes as the streaming proceeds since the whole media file is divided by several peers. Different from the previous works which form a tree or chain according to peer's arrival time, the scheme form a streaming peer group for a media file, and peers exchange media data at appropriate time.

A caching session from external source peers (not streaming session within a group) involves at least one source server and several supplying peers. In order to guarantee continuous playback of media file, the sum of their out-bound bandwidth contribution is at least the same as the media playback rate. On receipt of media playback request, the index server first determines source peers in the neighborhood of the requesting peer. It also checks if there are active supplying peers who own the media file such that (1) they have an available out-bound slot and (2) the sum of their out-bound bandwidth, including source peers, is greater than or equal to the playback rate of the media. If so, the request will be served by the selected supplying peers and source peers servers; otherwise, the request will be served by the source peers only.

For a given media file and possible candidate supplying peers (including source peers), there may exist many possible ways to select a subset of candidate supplying peers who will participate in streaming session of the media file. There are certain criteria in designing peer selection policy. These include (1) guaranteeing continuous playback, (2) to minimize initial buffering delay, (3) to be resilient from (sending) peer degradation or failure, (4) to maximize the remaining streaming capacity of the system, (5) to minimize load on network, (5) to disseminate the media file as fast as possible. The principal objective of the streaming service is to guarantee continuous playback. In legacy client-server paradigm, continuous playback is guaranteed by reliable centralized server. However, in peer-to-peer paradigm, peers acting as a server are not reliable at all. They may go down, suffer from degradation or failure. Moreover, one cannot predict theses failures in advance. Therefore, the unreliable property of peers makes it difficult to guarantee continuous playback. In what follows, we propose a peer selection policy considering unreliable property of peers.

2.2 Peer Group Creation and Peer Join

In the proposed scheme, the size of media cache depends on the arrival time of next peer. Large inter-arrival time between two peers requires big cache size for the preceding one. In this section, we present a solution to the problem of large cache request.

Fig. 2 shows a streaming peer group of three peers. Peers p_1, p_2, and p_3 join the group at t_1, t_2, and t_3, respectively, and caches parts of the media file. If a request does not arrive for a long time since p_3 begins caching at t_3, the cache size of p_3 becomes too large. If there were no new request since t_3, p_1 and p_2 should receive media data from p_3 until the end of streaming. To prevent this problem, the proposed scheme limits the inter-arrival time between the consecutive requests. That is, if a new request does not arrive during a threshold time $T_{threshold}$, the state of the group is changed to 'closed', which means that no more peers can join this group. Therefore, if a new request arrives since t_4, it creates a new streaming peer group instead of joining the existing group, even if the new peer requests the same media file.

Once the state of group becomes closed, caches of previous peers can be reclaimed to reuse it for caching other parts of the stream. That is, once the group becomes closed at t_4 in the figure, caches of p_1 and p_2 can be reclaimed to cache other parts of the media file at t_4 and t_5.

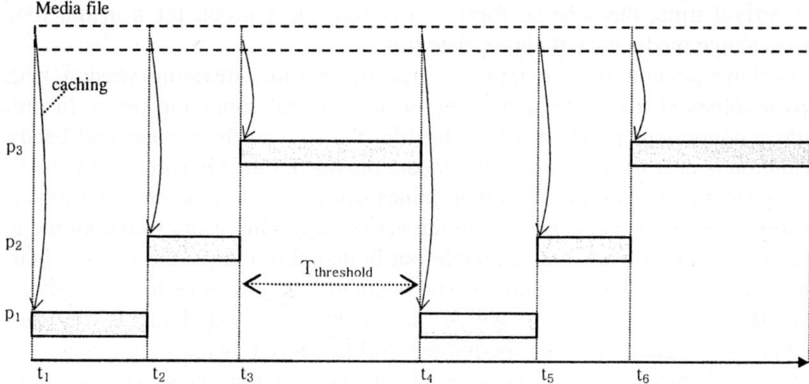

Fig. 2. Creation of new peer group

3 Streaming Load Allocation

In this section, we try to answer the following question; *how to distribute a streaming load among source peers and ordinary supplying peers?* We first define clearly the streaming load allocation problem, and then we suggest a streaming load allocation policy in consideration of peer's reliability. We also propose a failure resilience scheme dealing with degradation of peers in the middle of streaming session.

Before discussing the streaming load allocation, we first model the heterogeneity of peers as follows. Each peer has two attributes concerning heterogeneity; the degree of reliability and out-bound bandwidth limit. Let the *degree of reliability* of each supplying peer i be specified as a percentage p_i of the total amount of media data that is supposed to arrive on time. That is, in worst case, a requesting peer receives only p_i of the data the supplying peer i tries to send. If a peer is a source peer, p_i is always 1; otherwise, for ordinary supplying peers, it is less than 1 (p_i is even zero when peer i is down). Let the *out-bound bandwidth limit* of peer i be specified as f_i^{max}. Namely, peer i limits its out-bound bandwidth contribution by f_i^{max}.

Now consider a media streaming session of m possible candidate peers (including source peers). We assume that supplying peers can service the requesting peer by proceeding in periodic rounds, retrieving and sending a fixed amount of media data for each round. Let $f_1, f_2, \ldots, f_n$ denote the amount of media data sent in each round. The problem of streaming load allocation is to find n ($n \le m$) and f_i ($i = 1, \ldots, n$), which satisfy the following inequality:

$$p_1 * f_1 + p_2 * f_2 + \cdots + p_n * f_n \geq q * F$$

$$\text{subject to} \quad \begin{cases} 0 \leq p_i \leq 1 \\ 0 < f_i \leq f_i^{\max} \\ \sum_{i=1}^{n} f_i^{\max} \geq F \end{cases}$$

where F is the total amount of data needed by requesting peer during a round for best-quality playback and q is the streaming quality requirement provided by requesting peer. The left hand side of the equation represents the lower bound on the expected amount of media data received during a round in worst case. The right hand side means the amount of media data that is needed by client while satisfying the client-supplied QoS parameter[1].

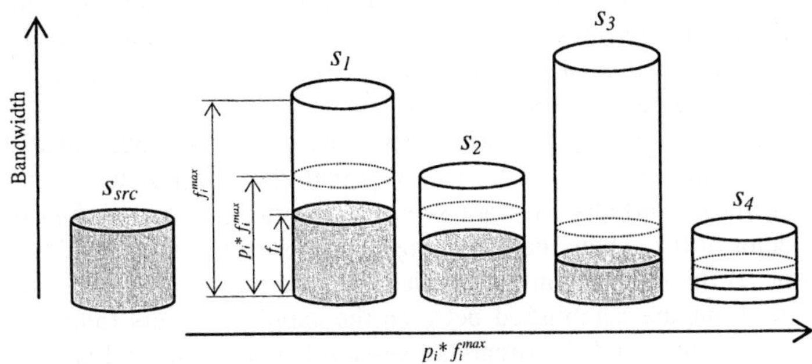

Fig. 3. Streaming load allocation for four supplying peers

This problem can be solved using the following algorithm. First of all, we should include one or more source peers, if available, in order to guarantee minimum quality of streaming. Then, given m candidate peers, we sort the supplying peers according to their values of p_i* f_i^{max} in decreasing order. We start with the largest value peers and assign its f_i to be α*p_i*f_i^{max}, where α is a appropriate constant less than 1. We then continue to assign to each supplying peer this value, beginning with the ones with larger values and moving to the ones with smaller values, until the above equation is satisfied. As an example, Fig. 3 shows the streaming load allocation for four supplying peers with the value of p_i* f_i^{max} decreasing from left to right. The height of each cylinder shows the available bandwidth, f_i^{max}, for that supplying peer. As shown in the figure, since supplying peer p_4 has the smallest value of p_i* f_i^{max} and since sum of bandwidth from peer p_{src}, p_1, p_2 and p_3 is large enough to accommodate the request, it is unnecessary to assign load to p_4.

Now we discuss the failure resiliency feature of the proposed scheme. By failure resiliency, we mean a recovery from the situation where peer's degree of reliability is changing due to some reasons such as network congestion on links between supplying peer and receiving peer, abrupt overload on supplying peers, etc.

Consider a simple case involving two supplying peers. For supplying peer s_1, p_1 is 1.0 and f_1 is 10 and, for supplying peer s_2, p_2 = 0.6 and f_2 is 10. Then, the amount of media data received by requesting peer per each round is 1*10 + 0.6 * 10 = 16. After a while, the degree of reliability of s_1 changes to 0.9, which may results in the decrease of streaming quality in the near future. We can avoid the situation by simply changing the values f_i of other supplying peers who shows stable degree of reliability. In our example, we increase the value of f_2 by 2, we can easily maintain the streaming quality such as 0.9 * 10 + 0.6 * 12 $\geq$16.

[1] The equation can be used as an admission control criteria by index server when admitting a new requesting peer.

4 Experiments

We evaluate the performance of the proposed architecture through extensive simulation experiments. We present the simulation setup and the results in this section.

We use the Network Simulator ns-2 [11] in the experiments. We use large Internet-like network topology generated by GT-ITM topology generator [3], add peers via DSL or LAN to the routers in the topology. We use 112 media files of 30-minute durations each recorded at a rate of 192Kb/s. Each peer has 128Kb/s out-bound bandwidth of 2~6 concurrent streaming sessions.

We simulate the following scenario. First source peers introduce media files into the network. According to the uniform arrival pattern, a peer joins the network and requests a media file. Media files are selected according to the zipfian distribution with skew factor of 0.7. Then, the streaming steps described in section 2 and 3 are put into operation. If the request can be satisfied, i.e., there is a sufficient capacity in the system, connections are established between the supplying peers (and source peers) and the requesting peer and the streaming session begins. The send and receive over UDP and carries CBR traffic. When the streaming session is over, the requesting peer caches the whole media file.

First we show the performance of the proposed hybrid streaming scheme compared with the legacy CDN-based streaming service. In this experiment, 600 clients make 4,100 requests during 270-minute simulated interval. For legacy streaming service, we use 10 streaming servers and, for hybrid peer-to-peer service, we use 3 source peers.

Fig. 4 compares the number of concurrent clients between the hybrid system and the legacy system. As shown in Fig. 4, the proposed scheme accepts much lager number of client's requests. More specifically, the number of concurrent clients increases by 67.2% on average.

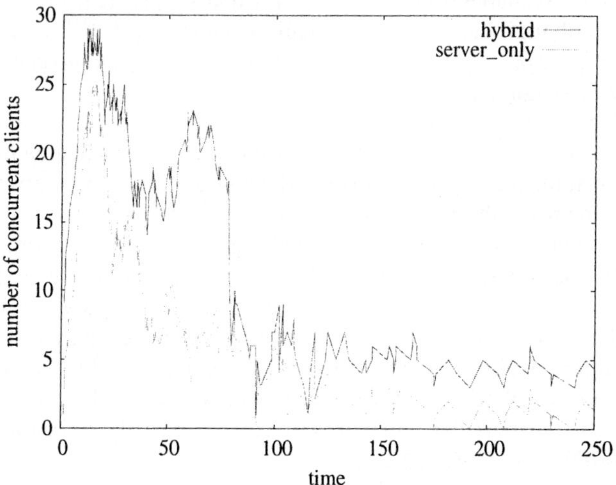

Fig. 4. Comparison of number of concurrent users

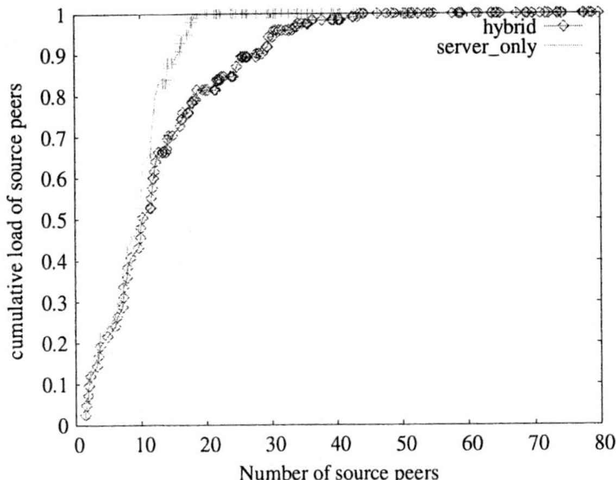

Fig. 5. Comparison of cumulative load of source peers

In order to find the optimal number of source peers in the hybrid system streaming service, we measure the effects of the number of source peers on the reject ratio of client's request with various source peer capacities. As shown in Fig. 6, when the number of source peers is relatively small, the reject ratio decrease drastically as the number of source peers increases. However, more source peers does not affect greatly when the number of source peers are large.

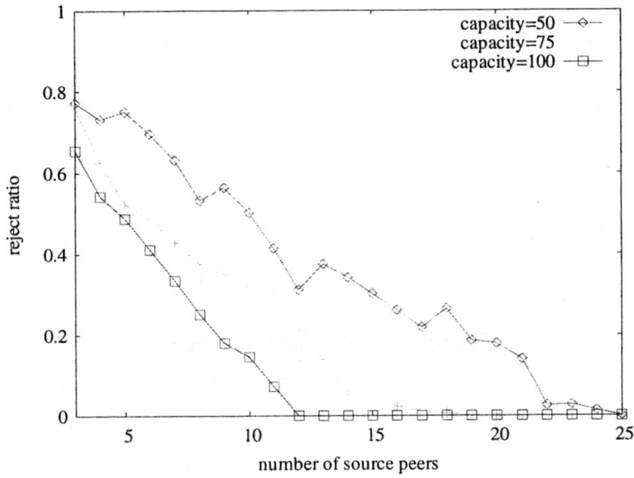

Fig. 6. Effects of number of source peers on reject ratio

Fig. 7 shows the effects of buffer size on server load. Two lines in the figure represent the cases when the average inter-arrival time is 5 sec and 10 sec, respectively. As shown in the figure, the streaming load on server decreases as the buffer size increase. Especially, the load is small when the inter-arrival time is small.

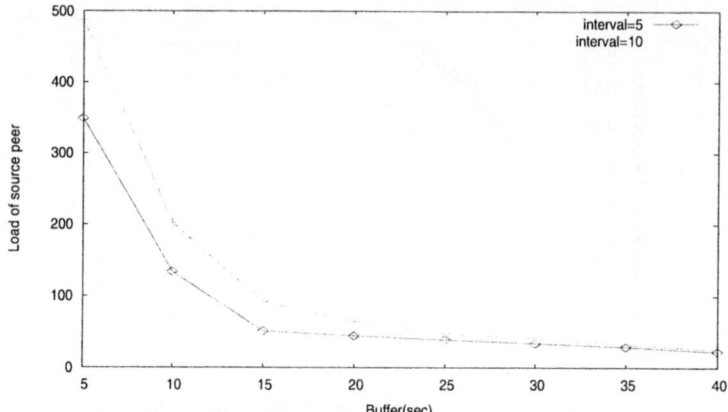

Fig. 7. Effects of buffer size on server load

Fig. 8 compares the server load as a function of threshold value on inter-arrival time. As shown in the figure, it is helpful to reduce the server load by determining a proper threshold value which leads to the creation of a new group.

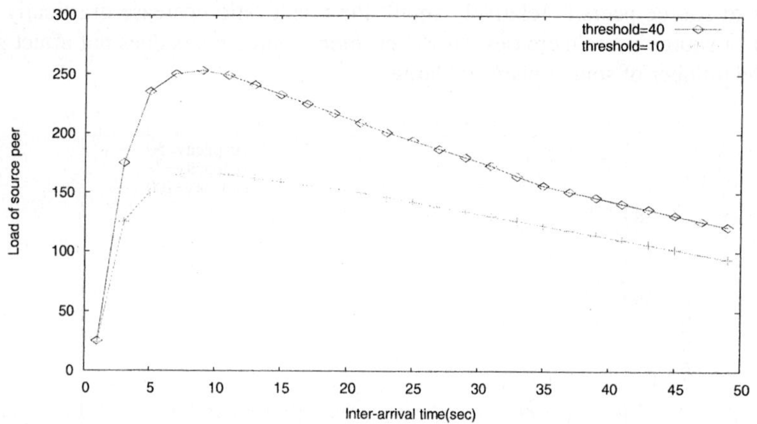

Fig. 8. Effects of threshold on server load

5 Conclusion

In this paper, we propose a hybrid peer-to-peer media streaming architecture which integrates pure peer-to-peer media streaming architecture with legacy client-server architecture. We also present a solution of the streaming load allocation problem under the proposed scheme in order to maximize the number of concurrent users for a given set of peers. The proposed hybrid architecture with the load allocation scheme has many desirable features such as (1) the scheme takes advantage of both client-server streaming and pure peer-to-peer streaming, (2) at least one source peer is involved with each streaming session, which provides more stable streaming quality, (3) by considering the degree of reliability of peers in streaming load allocation, the scheme can be easily applicable to real-world service, (4) the allocation scheme easily adapts itself to peer's failure or network congestion. We carry out extensive performance evaluation on the proposed scheme. Our results show that the proposed scheme outperforms existing streaming systems in various streaming performance metrics.

References

1. Akamai. http://www.akamai.com.
2. C-star. http://www.centerspan.com.
3. Calvert, K., Doar, M., and Zegura, E. Modeling Internet Topology. IEEE Transactions on Communications, pages 160--163, December (1997)
4. Castro, M., Druschel, P., Kermarrec, A., Nandi, A., Rowstron, A., and Singh, A.: SplitStream: High-bandwidth Content Distribution in a Cooperative Environment. In Proceedings of International Workshop on Peer-to-Peer Systems (2003)
5. Deshpande, D., Bawa, M., and Garcia-Molina, H.: Streaming Live Media over a Peer-to-Peer Network. Stanford Database Group Technical Report 2001-20 (2001)
6. Gummadi, K.P., Dunn, R.J., Saroiu, D., Gribble, D., Levy, H.M., and Zahorjan, J.: Measurement, Modeling, and Analysis of a Peer-to-Peer File-Sharing Workload. In Proceedings of ACM Symposium on Operating Systems Principles (2003)
7. Jin, S., Bestavros, A., and Iyengar, A.: Accelerating Internet streaming media delivery using network-aware partial caching. In Proceedings of IEEE ICDCS 02, Vienna, Austria, July (2002)
8. Nguyen, T. and Zakhor, A.: Distributed Video Streaming over Internet. In Proceedings of SPIE/ACM MMCN (2003)
9. Padmanabhan, V.N., Wang, H.J., Chou, P.A., and Sripanijkulchai, K.: Distributing Streaming Media Content Using Cooperative Networking. In Proceedings of NOSSDAV (2002)
10. Sen, S., Rexford, J., and Towsley, D. Proxy prefix caching for multimedia streams. In Proceedings of IEEE INFOCOM 99, New york, USA, (1999)
11. The Network Simulator – ns2. http://www.isi.edu/nsnam/ns
12. Tran, D.A., Hua, K.A., and Do, T.T.: A Peer-to-Peer Architecture for Media Streaming. IEEE Journal on Selected Areas in Communications, Vol. 22. Issue 1. (2004)
13. Xu, D., Chai, H., and Kulkarni, S. Analysis of a Hybrid Architecture for Cost-Effective Media Distribution. In Proceedings of SPIE/ACM Conference on Multimedia Computing and Networking , Santa Clara, CA (2003)
14. Xu, D., Hefeeda, M., Hambrusch, S., and Bhargava, B.: On Peer-to-Peer Media Streaming. In Proceedings of ICDCS (2002)

Trust Model Based on Similarity Measure of Vectors in P2P Networks*

Leitao Guo, Shoubao Yang, Jing Wang, and Jinyang Zhou

Department of Computer Science, University of Science and Technology of China, Hefei, 230026, P.R. China
ltguo@mail.ustc.edu.cn, syang@ustc.edu.cn, {joycew, jjyyzhou}@mail.ustc.edu.cn

Abstract. For the rationality and selfishness of peers, the traditional security schemes can hardly solve the fake services providing and free-ridings in P2P networks. The trust model based on reputation can restrain the malicious behaviors, and avoid malicious peers abusing of resources. However, it suffers much from dishonest feedbacks and strategically altering behaviors of malicious peers. Recurring to the trust model of society network, a trust model based on similarity measure of vectors and a distributed implementation scheme based on R-Chain are proposed. In this model, "time-sensitive factor" has improved the sensitiveness of detecting peers' behaviors, "service-type factor" and recommendation trust based on similarity measure of vectors have prevented collusion and bad-mouthing among peers. Consequently, theoretic analysis and simulation show that this model is effective and has favorable feasibility of implementation.

1 Introduction

P2P (Peer-to-Peer) technology has been widely used in file-sharing applications, distributed computing, e-market and information management [1], but some malicious behaviors and unreliable services providing have held back the development of these systems. In P2P networks, the peers share resources voluntarily. They may arbitrarily terminate services, and some peers may provide fake services, so the QoS of services are not reliable [2]. Moreover, peers in P2P networks are self-interest and rationality. Some peers always abuse resources but seldom contribute their own resources, which induces the free-riding in P2P networks [2]. Consequently, it is necessary to build an effective trust model, which can ensure the high availability and improve the development of P2P networks.

In traditional networks, the trust relationships are always built up by an independent trusty third part, such as Certification Authorization. But this centralized trust model is not suitable for the P2P networks [3]. In research [3,4,5][10], the reputation-based trust model is brought forward to prevent peers abusing of network resources and restrain the malicious behaviors of peers. But there are some vulnerabilities of a

* This paper is supported by the National Natural Science Foundation of China (Contract No.60273041) and the National '863' High-Tech Program of China (Contract No. 2002AA104560).

H. Zhuge and G.C. Fox (Eds.): GCC 2005, LNCS 3795, pp. 836 – 847, 2005.

reputation-based trust model. One of the detrimental vulnerabilities is that a malicious node may strategically alter its behavior in a way that benefits itself such as starting to behave maliciously after it attains a high reputation. Another widely recognized vulnerability is the shilling attack [14], where malicious peers submit dishonest feedback and collude with each other to boost their own ratings or bad-mouth non-malicious peers. Last but not the least, malicious nodes can flood numerous fake feedbacks through fake transactions in transaction-based feedback system [6][7].

Recurring to the trust model of society network [3], a trust model based on similarity measure of vectors [8] and a distributed implementation scheme based on R-Chain [9] are proposed. In this model, "time-sensitive factor" has improved the sensitiveness of detecting peers' behaviors. "Service-type factor" and the evaluation of the recommendation credibility based on similarity measure of vectors have prevented collusion and bad-mouthing attacks among peers. Consequently, theoretic analysis and simulation show that this model is effective and has favorable feasibility of implementation.

In the second section, the related works are introduced; the trust model based on similarity measure of vectors will be illuminated in the third section; in fourth section a distributed implementation scheme based on R-Chain is proposed, and in the fifth section, a simulation about this model is laid out. Conclusions and future works are in the end.

2 Related Works

The related research on trust model in P2P networks can be classified into three categories:

(1) Trust model based on PKI (Public Key Infrastructure)**.** In these systems, some center nodes monitor the network, and publish illegal nodes periodically. This kind of systems, such as eBay [10], is always center node dependent, which has bad scalability and the single point of failure problem.

(2) Global reputation-based trust model. In these systems, every participant in the distributed applications has a global reputation, which is calculated by iterating the mutual satisfaction degree among neighbors. Eigentrust[5] and research [3] are all global reputation-based trust model. But, the global reputation-based trust model does not differentiate between the direct trust and indirect trust [11]. Moreover, for lacking of differentiation of different trust classes, the global reputation-based trust model is restrained and not suitable for complex environments.

(3) Local reputation-based trust model. Different from global reputation-based trust model, many researchers consider that trust is subjective. In P2P networks, different participants may take different measures to evaluate a node's trust value. Therefore, the trust value of a node is different for different observers. Peertrust [4] is a trust model based on local reputation. In this model, a peer's reputation is evaluated by collecting the feedback information of its history transactions. A distributed implementation scheme and a trust data management scheme are also proposed based on the structured P2P networks [15]. However, the overhead of the trust data management over the structured P2P networks is very high. Furthermore, the evaluation of recommendation credibility in Peertrust is depending on the common set of peers that have interacted with requestor and the recommendatory peers. As the increase of peers' quantity, the common set is always very small [12][16]. This evaluation algorithm of .recommendation credibility is not reliable.

This paper proposed a distributed trust model based on similarity measure of vectors, which is effective even when the common set of two peers is very small.

3 Trust Model Based on Similarity Measure of Vectors

3.1 Trust Evaluation Algorithm

There are two kinds of trust relationships among peers, namely, direct trust and indirect trust [11]. The direct trust of A to B can be evaluated from the direct transaction feedback information between A and B. The indirect trust of A to B can be computed according to the transaction feedback information of peers who have interacted with B.

Let U denote the service requestor in P2P networks, the service provider is denoted by S, and *sclass* denotes the type of the requested service. The trust value of U to S's service is denoted by $T_{U \to S, sclass}$, which is defined in formula (1).

$$T_{U \to S, sclass} = \lambda * D_{U \to S} + (1 - \lambda) * R_{U \to S} . \quad (1)$$

Where $D_{U \to S}$ denotes the direct trust value of U to S, and $R_{U \to S}$ denotes the indirect trust value. The "self-confidence factor" is denoted by λ, which means that how a peer is confident to its evaluation of direct trust value.

Let $Eval_{U \to S}$ denote the feedback evaluation from U to S, where real number $Eval_{U \to S} \in [-1, 1]$. The direct trust value from U to S is defined in formula (2).

$$D_{U \to S} = \frac{1}{n} * \sum (Eval_{U \to S} * Factor_{sclass}) . \quad (2)$$

Where n is the number of transactions between U and S. $Factor_{sclass}$ denotes the "service-type factor", namely the services' similarity degree to the *sclass* service.

Let *RSet* denote the set of recommendation peers, namely, the peers interacted with S directly except peer U. $\forall R \in RSet$ is a recommendation peer. Peer R's recommendation credibility is denoted by $C_{U \to R}$. So the indirect trust value from U to S is defined in formula (3), where m is the number of transactions between peer R and S.

$$R_{U \to S} = \frac{1}{|RSet|} * \sum_{\forall R \in RSet} [C_{U \to R} * \frac{1}{m} * \sum (Eval_{R \to S} * Factor_{sclass})] . \quad (3)$$

From formula (2) and (3), we redefine $T_{U \to S, sclass}$ in formula (4).

$$\begin{aligned} T_{U \to S, sclass} &= \lambda * \frac{1}{n} * \sum (Eval_{U \to S} * Factor_{sclass}) + \\ &(1 - \lambda) * \frac{1}{|RSet|} * \sum_{\forall R \in RSet} [C_{U \to R} * \frac{1}{m} * \sum (Eval_{R \to S} * Factor_{sclass})] \end{aligned} . \quad (4)$$

3.2 Sensitiveness Enhanced Trust Evaluation Algorithm

The trust evaluation algorithm based on formula (4) treats all the transaction feedback information equally, and does not consider the time of the transactions. So, some peers in the P2P network may loose their incentive for providing good services after accumulate some reputations. At the same time, some peers may attempt to "hide" behind their cumulative reputation in order to discriminate on the quality of service they provide to different buyers [6]. Therefore, the trust evaluation algorithm must consider the time of the transactions, and it must represent the current states of peers.

Let $T_{U\to S,sclass,\Delta t}$ denote the trust evaluation algorithm considering the time factor. Δt denotes the time segment from a threshold time to current time, and $\Delta t'$ denotes the time segment from the beginning to the threshold time. The trust evaluation algorithm with the time factor is defined in formula (5).

$$T_{U\to S,sclass} = \delta * T_{U\to S,sclass,\Delta t} + (1-\delta) * T_{U\to S,sclass,\Delta t'} \,. \tag{5}$$

δ denotes the "time-sensitive factor". It is the weight of trust evaluation based on the transaction feedback information in Δt. The bigger the "time-sensitive factor" is, the more sensitive of the trust evaluation algorithm to the peers' current states.

3.3 Evaluation of the Service-Type Factor

Let $TC = \{TC_1, TC_2, ..., TC_n\}$ denote the set of service types peers provided. $T = \{t_1, t_2, ..., t_m\}$ denotes the set of characteristic items of a certain of service type. Consequently, the service type TC_i can be defined by the vector of the characteristic items, namely $W_i = \{W_{i1}, W_{i2}, ..., W_{im}\}$, where W_{ij} denotes the weight of t_j in TC_i. According to the vector space model [8], the similarity of TC_i and TC_j can be defined by the cosine of the angle between their corresponding vectors, that is the cosine of the angle between W_i and W_j. The smaller of the two vectors' angle, the more similar of the two types of service. The "service-type factor" is defined in formula (6).

$$Factor_{sclass} = \cos(W_i, W_{\mathtt{sclass}}) = \frac{W_i \bullet W_{\mathtt{sclass}}}{|W_i| \times |W_{\mathtt{sclass}}|} \,. \tag{6}$$

3.4 Evaluation of the Recommendation Credibility

For the open and self-determination of the P2P networks, the peers may take collusion and bad-mouthing attacks to the reputation-based trust model to maximize their own benefits [6]. For example, a peer may collude with a group of peers in order to be given unfairly high ratings by them. This will have the effect of inflating this peer's reputation, therefore allowing this peer to receive more orders from other peers and at a higher price than it deserves. Moreover, a peer may collude with some peers in order to "bad-mouth" other peers that it want to drive out of the market. In such a situation, the conspiring peers provide unfairly negative ratings to the targeted peers, thus lowering their reputation.

These two kinds of collusive behaviors mainly attack the indirect trust evaluation of the reputation-based trust model. According to the statistic in [10], 89.0% of all seller-buyer pairs conducted just one transaction during the time period, and 98.9% conducted no more than four. So, the trust evaluation is mainly depended on the indirect trust. In this paper, the credibility of recommendation is evaluated based on similarity measure of peers' feedback information vectors.

Let $ComSet_{UR} = \{C_1, C_2, C_3, ..., C_n\}$ denote the common set of peers that have interacted with both peer U and the recommendation peer R. The transaction feedback evaluation from peer U to each peer C_i in $ComSet_{UR}$ have formed the vector $\overrightarrow{UComSet} = [\overline{V}_{U1}, \overline{V}_{U2}, \overline{V}_{U3}, ..., \overline{V}_{Un}]$, where $\overline{V}_{ij}$ denotes the average evaluation from peer i to peer j. Similarly, the vector $\overrightarrow{RComSet} = [\overline{V}_{R1}, \overline{V}_{R2}, V_{R3}, ..., \overline{V}_{Rn}]$ is formed by the transaction feedback evaluation from R to C_i. The recommendation credibility of peer R can be measured by the similarity of feedback evaluation information between peer U and peer R. According to the vector space model [8], the similarity of feedback evaluation information can be measured by the cosine of the angle between the vector $\overrightarrow{UComSet}$ and the vector $\overrightarrow{RComSet}$. If the cosine of the angle is greater than some threshold value, the two vectors are considered to be similar. The recommendation credibility of peer R is denoted in formula (7), where $0^\circ \le \theta \le 180^\circ$.

$$C_{U \to R} = \cos(\theta) = \overrightarrow{UComSet} \bullet \overrightarrow{RComSet} = \frac{\sum_{\forall C_i \in ComSet_{UR}} \left(\overline{V}_{UC_i} * \overline{V}_{RC_i}\right)}{\sqrt{\sum_{\forall C_i \in ComSet_{UR}} \left(\overline{V}_{UC_i}\right)^2} * \sqrt{\sum_{\forall C_i \in ComSet_{UR}} \left(\overline{V}_{RC_i}\right)^2}} . \tag{7}$$

3.5 Veracity Enhanced Recommendation Credibility Evaluation

The veracity of the recommendation credibility evaluation in formula (7) depends on the common set of peers that have interacted with both peer U and peer R. But with the development of P2P networks, the magnitudes of peers and the provided services grow rapidly. This has resulted in the extreme sparsity of peers' feedback evaluation information. In this situation, the similarity measure methods work poor [12][16]. Considering the extreme sparsity of peers' feedback evaluation information and a small quantity of common set of peers interacted with both peer U and peer R, the algorithm of estimating the trust value of unknown peers is put forward. This algorithm is based on the well known statistical estimation technique – maximum likelihood estimation.

Given the quality of service provided by a peer is distributed according to a normal distribution, thus the feedback evaluation information to this peer's service is also distributed according to a normal distribution [13]. Therefore, the quality of service provided by this peer can be estimated based on the feedback evaluation information to its service [13]. Let I_U denote the set of peers that have interacted with peer U. I_R denotes the set of peers that have interacted with peer R. Each peer I_{R_i} in the set

$I_R - ComSet_{UR}$ has never interacted with peer U, but its quality of service can be estimated based on the feedback evaluation information to it.

Assuming the quality of service provided by peer I_{R_i} is distributed according to the normal distribution $N(\mu, \sigma^2)$, and the set of feedback evaluation information to peer I_{R_i} is denoted by $X = \{x_{i1}, x_{i2}, \ldots, x_{in}\}$. The peer U can estimate the parameters μ and σ^2 through the method of maximum likelihood estimation on the set X.

First, select a subset with m elements from the set X randomly, and sort these m elements in ascending or descending order. Secondly, select $x_{i,ma+1}, x_{i,ma+2}, \ldots, x_{i,m-ma}$ from this subset as the random selected samples, where $a \in (0, 0.5)$. If ma is not an integer, then adopt $\lceil ma \rceil$. Therefore, the likelihood function is denoted in formula (8).

$$L(x_{ma+1}, x_{ma+2}, \ldots, x_{m-ma}; \mu, \sigma^2) = \prod_{i=ma+1}^{m-ma} \frac{1}{\sigma\sqrt{2\pi}} e^{-\frac{(x_i-\mu)^2}{2\sigma^2}} = \left(\frac{1}{2\pi\sigma^2}\right)^{\frac{m-2ma}{2}} \exp\left[\frac{-1}{2\sigma^2} \sum_{i=ma+1}^{m-ma} (x_i - \mu)^2\right] \cdot \tag{8}$$

Using the logarithmic operation on formula (8), calculating the partial derivative operation on the above equation about μ and σ^2, and solving the equation group, we get the maximum likelihood estimation values of μ and σ^2. The estimated feedback evaluation from peer U to peer I_{R_i} can be denoted by $\hat{\mu}$ in formula (9).

$$\hat{\mu} = \frac{1}{m - 2am} \sum_{i=ma+1}^{m-ma} x_i \,, \quad \hat{\sigma}^2 = \frac{1}{m - 2am} \sum_{i=ma+1}^{m-ma} (x_i - \mu)^2 \,. \tag{9}$$

Through this method, peer U can estimate feedback evaluation to each peer in $I_R - ComSet_{UR}$, and the peer R also can estimate feedback evaluation to each peer in $I_U - ComSet_{UR}$. In this situation, the common set of peers that interacted with both peer U and peer R can be defined by $I_U \cup I_R$, namely $ComSet_{UR} = I_U \cup I_R$.

The algorithm of estimating the trust value of unknown peers has enhanced the veracity of the recommendation credibility in the situation of small common set of peers.

4 Distributed Implementation Scheme

The state-of-the-art trust models construct the trustworthy relationships among peers according to the feedback evaluation information of peers' transactions. In this paper, we adopt R-Chain [9] to manage the feedback information. Every peer in this P2P networks maintain a data structure shown in Fig. 1(a). TR denotes a peer's transaction record. Each TR includes the previous transaction ID, so the peer's feedback evaluation information is organized into a single linked chain, namely R-Chain. With all TRs organized in a linked chain, the owner peer cannot remove or change any elements in the middle, but it can still discard TRs from the end. To prevent this attack, before every transaction, the randomly selected witness peer should verify the last TR in the R-Chain really represents the last transaction the peer has participated in.

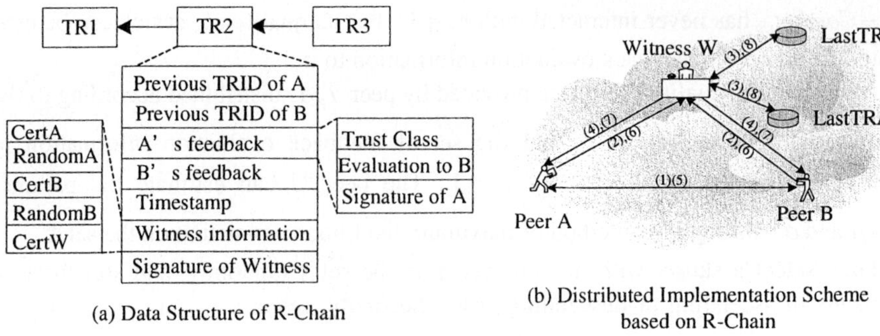

(a) Data Structure of R-Chain

(b) Distributed Implementation Scheme based on R-Chain

Fig. 1. Distributed Implementation Scheme

The trust model based on similarity measure of vectors can be deployed on R-Chain compatible structured P2P networks. Fig. 1(b) shows a distributed implementation scheme based on R-Chain.

(1). Peer A and peer B exchange their R-Chains, and randomly select a witness to judge the transaction; Witness W can be selected by the formula (10);

$$ID_W = Hash(Cert_A, Cert_B, Random_A, Random_B, Timestamp). \tag{10}$$

(2). A and B send each other's last TR to W;
(3). W contacts the previous transaction witnesses of A and B for verification;
(4). W ask A and B to process;
(5). A and B calculate the trust evaluation to each other based on similarity measure of vectors, and decide whether to process;
(6). After the transaction, each participated peer send W the feedback information;
(7). W builds a TR and saves a copy locally, and also sends the TR to A and B;
(8). W notifies the previous transaction witness to remove their saved TRs.

The R-Chain based feedback information management and the distributed implementation scheme have guaranteed the integrity of the feedback information. At the same time, this scheme has reduced the management cost of feedback information. Moreover, every peer calculates trust value to other peers locally. This has improved the robustness of the reputation-based trust model in P2P networks.

5 Experimental Evaluation

5.1 Simulation Parameters

In this simulation we analyze the trust models' convergence, effectiveness, sensitiveness and the immunity to collusion and bad-mouthing attacks. The parameters of the simulation are as follows:

(1). Given that there are 100 peers in the file-sharing P2P network, every peer is both requesters and service providers. Every peer initiates 5 sharing files. The peers randomly request a certain file every few seconds.

(2). Given that peers can search all the peers owning needed files. Without trust mechanism, peers can randomly choose candidate peers to download files. While in trust mechanism, peers can calculate every candidate peer's trust value and download the file from the peer of the maximum trust value with the possibility of p%, and download files from the other candidate peers with the possibility of (1-p) %. We take p=95 in this simulation.

(3). The quality of peers' file-sharing services are classified into 4 levels, that is QoS={3,2,1,0}, and the corresponding feedback evaluation is {1,0.5,-0.5,-1}. The services with the QoS<2 denote fake services. As shown in table 1, peers are classified into 5 categories according to the rate of all kinds of service they provided. At the same time, best peer and good peer are denoted honest peers, while, bad peer and worst peer denote malicious peers.

(4). Table 2 shows 7 simulation scenarios, where the percentage of malicious peers is gradually increase.

(5). The computed trust value is between -1 and 1, and the initial trust value is 0.0.

Table 1. Classification of Peers

Type of Peers		QoS=3	QoS=2	QoS=1	QoS=0
Honest peers	best peer	90%	5%	3%	2%
	good peer	10%	80%	5%	5%
Malicious peers	bad peer	5%	10%	80%	5%
	worst peer	2%	3%	5%	90%
Uncertain peer		35%	15%	15%	35%

Table 2. Simulation Scenarios

Scenarios	Best Peers	Good Peers	Bad Peers	Worst Peers	Uncertain Peers
SCE1	50%	50%	0%	0%	0%
SCE 2	40%	45%	5%	5%	5%
SCE 3	35%	40%	10%	10%	5%
SCE 4	20%	30%	25%	20%	5%
SCE 5	15%	20%	30%	30%	5%
SCE 6	5%	10%	40%	40%	5%
SCE 7	0%	5%	40%	50%	5%

5.2 Evaluation and Comparison

- **Convergence of the Trust Model**

This simulation evaluates the convergence of the trust model based on similarity measure of vectors. Given that there are 100 peers distributed under the scenario SCE3, and each peer randomly downloads 400 files. We calculate the rate of fake services a peer encountered. Fig. 2(a) shows the rate of fake services with respect to the number of transactions in the trust mechanism and non-trust mechanism. From the figure we can conclude that, in the non-trust mechanism, the rate of fake services reduces gradually with respect to the number of transactions, but the extent is not obvious. While in the trust mechanism, every peer downloads files from the peer of the maximum trust value with the possibility of 95%, and the rate of fake services reduces rapidly with respect to the number of transactions. After every peer finishes 400 transactions with trust mechanism, the trust relationship among peers has steadily built up, and the rate of fake services is 9.4%, while rate of fake services is 20.6% when peers only download 50 files. This shows that the trust model based on similarity measure of vectors can quickly build up the trust relationships among peers, and effectively reduced the rate of fake services in the P2P networks.

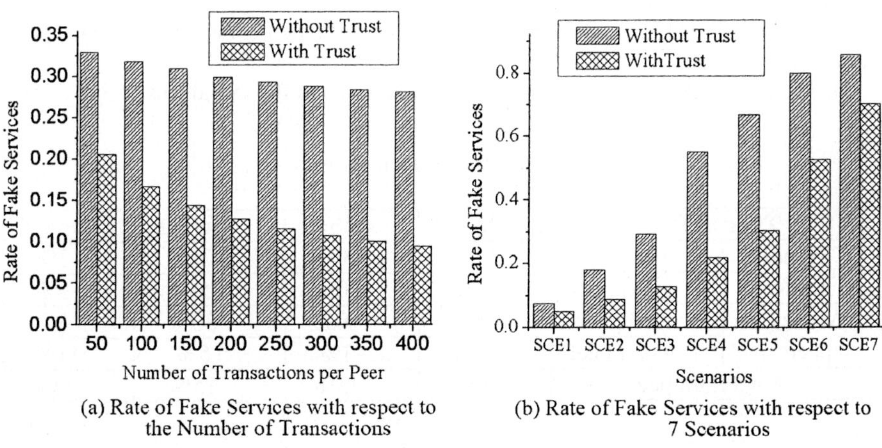

(a) Rate of Fake Services with respect to the Number of Transactions

(b) Rate of Fake Services with respect to 7 Scenarios

Fig. 2. Convergence and Effectiveness of the Trust Model

- **Effectiveness with respect to Percentage of Malicious Peers**

In this simulation, we evaluate the effectiveness of the trust model based on similarity measure of vectors with respect to 7 scenarios. We calculate the rate of fake services a peer encountered when it download 200 files in trust mechanism and non-trust mechanism. Fig. 2(b) shows the rate of fake services with respect to 7 scenarios. In SCE1, there are no malicious peers, so the gap of the rate of fake services between trust mechanism and non-trust mechanism is not obvious. For the trust relationships have steadily built up after each peer downloads 200 files, the rate of fake services reduced greatly comparing with non-trust mechanism in the scenarios SCE4, SCE5 and SCE6. This shows that the trust model based on similarity measure of vectors is effective even when the percentage of malicious peers is very high (90% in SCE7).

- **Sensitiveness to Strategically Alter Behaviors of Peers**

This simulation evaluates the sensitiveness of the trust model based on similarity measure of vectors to peers' strategically alter behaviors. The peers' trust values are computed periodically from an honest peer. Fig. 3(a) shows the computed trust values of five kinds of peers shown in table 1.

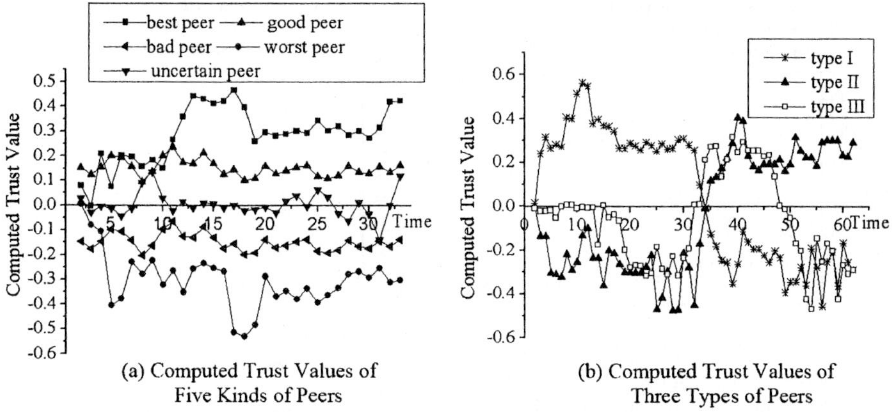

(a) Computed Trust Values of Five Kinds of Peers

(b) Computed Trust Values of Three Types of Peers

Fig. 3. Sensitiveness of the Trust Model to Strategically Alter Behaviors of Peers

Fig. 3(b) shows the computed trust value of three types of peers shown in table 3. These peers strategically alter behaviors in different time. From fig. 3, we conclude that the trust model can distinguish different kinds of peers and it is very sensitive to peers' strategically alter behaviors.

Table 3. Three Types of Peers

Types of Peers	Characteristic
type I	Best peer in time [1, 30]; Worst peer in time (30, 60].
type II	Worst peer in time [1, 30]; Best peer in time (30, 60].
type III	Uncertain peer in time [1, 20]; Worst peer in time (20, 30]; Best peer in time (30, 45]; Worst peer in time (45, 60].

- **Immunity to Collusion and Bad-mouthing Attacks**

This simulation evaluates the immunity of the trust model to the collusion and bad-mouthing attacks. Assuming that there are 100 peers distributed under the scenario SCE3, and we calculate the rate of fake services a peer encountered.

Fig. 4(a) shows the rate of fake services with respect to the number of transactions in collusive and non-collusive setting. In the non-collusive setting, every peer provides transaction feedback information practically, so the rate of fake services of honest peers and malicious peers is gradually reduced. While in the collusive setting, malicious peers' collusive behaviors hardly disturb honest peers' judgment. However, the collusive behaviors of malicious peers have greatly influence on the malicious.

Fig. 4(b) shows the comparison of the immunity to the collusive behaviors between PeerTrust and trust model based on similarity measure of vectors. From the figure, we conclude that the algorithm based on the maximum likelihood estimation has

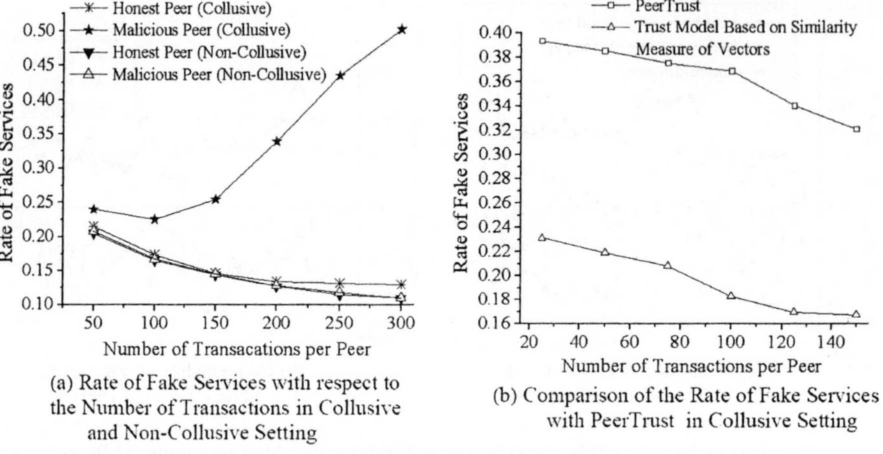

(a) Rate of Fake Services with respect to the Number of Transactions in Collusive and Non-Collusive Setting

(b) Comparison of the Rate of Fake Services with PeerTrust in Collusive Setting

Fig. 4. Immunity to Collusion and Bad-mouthing Attacks

enhanced the veracity of the recommendation credibility in the situation of small common set of peers. The Trust model based on similarity measure of vectors has reduced the rate of fake services when peers' feedback information is not plenty, and it works better than PeerTrust in collusive setting.

6 Conclusions and Future Works

We propose in this paper a trust model based on similarity measure of vectors and its implementation scheme based on R-Chain. In this model, "time-sensitive factor" has improved the sensitiveness of detecting peers' strategically alter behaviors, "service-type factor" and recommendation trust based on similarity measure of vectors has prevented collusion and bad-mouthing among peers. Theoretic analysis and simulation show that this model can quickly build up the trust relationships among peer, and effectively reduce the fake services in P2P networks. It is also sensitive to peers' strategically alter behaviors, and immunizing to malicious collusive behaviors.

In the future works, we will enhance this trust model with the mechanism for providing the incentives for reporting truthful feedback. We will also implement this model in a file-sharing P2P network.

References

1. Andy Oram: Peer to Peer: Harnessing the power of disruptive technologies. ISBN 0-596-00110-X, 2001
2. Eytan Adar and Bernardo Huberman: Free Riding on Gnutella. First Monday, 5(10), October 2000.
3. DOU Wen, WANG Huai-Min, JIA Yan, ZOU Peng: A Recommendation-Based Peer-to-Peer Trust Model. 2004 Vol.15 No.04 Journal of Software

4. L. Xiong and L. Liu: A reputation-based trust model for peer-to-peer ecommerce communities. In IEEE Conference on E-Commerce (CEC'03), 2003
5. S. Kamvar, M. Schlosser, and H. Garcia-Molina: Eigentrust: Reputation management in p2p networks. In Proceedings of the 12th WWW Conference, 2003
6. C. Dellarocas: Immunizing Online Reputation Reporting Systems Against Unfair Ratings and Discriminatory Behavior. In ACM Conference on Electronic Commerce, pages 150–157, 2000
7. Mudhakar Srivatsa, Li Xiong, Ling Liu: TrustGuard: countering vulnerabilities in reputation management for decentralized overlay networks. WWW 2005: 422-431
8. SALTON, G., WONG, A., AND YANG: A vector space model for automatic indexing. Communications of the ACM 18, 11, 613--620.
9. Lintao Liu, Shu Zhang, Kyung Dong Ryu, and Partha Dasgupta: R-Chain: A Self-Maintained Reputation Management System in P2P Networks. 17th International Conference on Parallel and Distributed Computing Systems (PDCS-2004), September 2004, San Francisco, CA, USA, pages 131-136
10. P. Resnick, R. Zeckhauser: Trust Among Strangers in Internet Transactions: Empirical Analysis of eBay's Reputation System. Working Paper for the NBER workshop on empirical studies of electronic commerce, Jan 2001
11. Thomas Beth, Malte Borcherding, Birgit Klein: Valuation of Trust in Open Networks,Proc. 3rd European Symposium on Research in Computer Security -- ESORICS '94
12. Zhou Jun Feng, Tang Xian, Guo Jing Feng: An Optimized Collaborative Filtering Recommendation Algorithm. Journal of Computer Research and Development (in Chinese), 2004, Vol.41, No.10
13. Z. Despotovic, K. Aberer: A Probabilistic Approach to Predict Peers' Performance in P2P Networks. Eighth International Workshop on Cooperative Information Agents, CIA 2004, September 27 - 29, 2004, Erfurt, Germany
14. S. K. Lam and J. Riedl: Shilling recommender systems for fun and profit. In Proceedings of the 13th World Wide Web Conference, 2004
15. Androutsellis-Theotokis S, Spinellis D.: A survey of peer-to-peer content distribution technologies. ACM Comput. Surv., Vol. 36, No. 4. (December 2004), pp. 335-371
16. Zhao Liang, Hu Naijing, Zhang Shouzhi: Algorithm design for personalization recommendation system. Journal of Computer Research and Development (in Chinese), 2002, 39(8): 986~991

A Large Scale Distributed Platform for High Performance Computing

Nabil Abdennadher and Régis Boesch

University of Applied Sciences, Western Switzerland,
4 rue Prairie, 1202 Geneva, Switzerland
{abdennad, rboesch}@eig.unige.ch

Abstract. This paper describes a Global Computing (GC) environment, called XtremWeb-CH (XWCH). XWCH is an improved version of a GC tool called XtremWeb (XW). XWCH tries to enrich XW in order to match P2P concepts: distributed scheduling, distributed communication, development of symmetrical models. Two versions of XWCH were developed. The first, called XWCH-sMs, manages inter-task communications in a centralized way. The second version, called XWCH-p2p, allows a direct communication between "workers". XWCH is evaluated in the case of a real high performance genetic application.

1 Introduction

High Performance Computing (HPC) landscape has radically changed since the end of the last decade. Based initially on the use of parallel and vectorial computers equipped with specific development environments, computing power consumers are adopting a new approach which takes advantage of the Internet development. The idea consists on deploying High Performance applications on anonymous connected computers by using their available resources. Indeed, the challenge today is to extract, at low cost, a reasonable computing power from a widely distributed platform (by executing interactive applications) rather than extracting the maximum power from a local supercomputer (by executing batch applications). In another words, the majority of the world's computing power is no longer in supercomputer centers and institutional machine rooms. Instead, it is now distributed in a hundred of millions of personal computers all over the world. This concept is known as Global Computing (GC).

The majority of GC projects adopted a centralized structure based on a Master/Slave Architecture: SETI@home [1], Entropia [2], United Devices [3], Parabon [4], XtremWeb [5], etc. A natural extension of the GC consists on distributing the "decisional degree" of the master in order to avoid any form of centralization. Thus, architectures such as Clients/Servers and Master/Slaves would be withdrawn. This concept, known as Peer-To-Peer (P2P), was successfully used to share and exchange files between computers connected to Internet. The most known projects are Gnutella [6] and Freenet [7]. Indeed, file sharing is well adapted to this model. However, the use of P2P in the field of HPC raises several theoretical and practical problems. Dynamic scheduling algorithms for parallel/distributed applications can not be easily distributed. P2P Computing also goes against the policies and safety techniques largely used nowadays on Internet: Firewalls, NAT addresses, etc. The objective of

H. Zhuge and G.C. Fox (Eds.): GCC 2005, LNCS 3795, pp. 848 – 859, 2005.

these techniques is to protect resources connected to Internet from any voluntary or involuntary abusive use. Internet is then partitioned in several protected zones which are unable to cooperate mutually. Problems related to the development of a true P2P environment for HPC needs remain open.

This document describes a GC environment, called XtremWeb-CH (XWCH), which converges towards a P2P system. XWCH is an improved version of a GC tool called XtremWeb (XW). XWCH tries to enrich XW in order to match P2P concept: distributed scheduling, distributed communication, development of symmetrical models, etc. In P2P systems, nodes are assumed to be customers and servers at the same time. Although it is utopian, this idea was retained as guide line in the XWCH project.

This document is organized as follows: paragraph 2 presents the features that should be satisfied by a GC platform in order to be considered as a real P2P system. Paragraph 3 introduces the XW tool in its original version. Paragraph 4 details the new concepts XWCH introduces compared to XW. Paragraph 5 presents the experiments carried out in order to evaluate XWCH. Lastly, the paragraph 6 gives some perspectives of this research.

2 What Is a Real Peer-To-Peer System?

A true P2P environment should satisfy four criteria:

- *Natural scalability*: A P2P system should be scalable by itself and not by "doping". For that purpose, the performance of the system should be provided by its distributed structure: distributed algorithms, distributed warehouses, distributed scheduling algorithms, etc. This structure should allow open access and search procedures. The search engine should take into account the dynamic nature of the network. The system should be based on a demand-driven computation model: users' queries are only processed when needed and prior results are stored in warehouses, where they can be accessed later on.
- *Symmetric view*: a node belonging to a P2P platform should be server and client at the same time.
- *Platform heterogeneity*: The system should support heterogeneous architectures (hardware) and platforms (software and operating systems). Since these resources are anonymous, the system should take into account all administration policies implemented by local administrators.
- *Multi-service*: The system should be able to serve any kind of request: HPC, file sharing, etc. We believe that we cannot design a system that can satisfy every user's needs. However, the system should be able to supply users with adequate tools that allow the implementation of specific services not initially foreseen.
- Systems like *Gnutella* and *Freenet* satisfy the three first criteria, but these systems are mono-service since they only target file sharing needs. *XtremWeb*, *Seti@home*, *Entropia* and other GC environments do not satisfy any of these criteria. They are based on a non symmetric view (Master/Slaves) and exclusively HPC oriented. They are not scalable since the master is overloaded when the number of slaves increases. The only tool which seems to satisfy all these constraints is WOS (Web Operating System) [8]. Unfortunately, this tool remained in a purely conceptual state and no prototype was born.

3 XtremWeb

XW is a GC research project carried out at Université d'Orsay (France). Like other Large Scale Distributed Systems (LSDS), *XW* platform uses remote resources (pocket computers, PCs, workstations, servers) connected to Internet to execute a specific application (client). The aim of *XW* is to investigate how a LSDS can be turned into a High Performance Parallel Computer. *XW* belongs to the more general context of Grid research and follows the standardisation effort towards Grid Services [9]. *XW* satisfies the three main constraints imposed by any Large Scale Distributed Environment: volatility, heterogeneity and security.

Security is particularly difficult in the context of LSDS because it's impossible to trust hundreds of thousands resources. Three main security problems are linked to GC and P2P systems:

- Data integrity/privacy: This problem could be resolved by applying the well known solutions of encryption, public/private keys, etc.
- Protection of participating resources: No aggressive application should be able to corrupt data or system of any participating resource. Sandboxing is the well known technique to resolve this problem. The idea consists on filtering the system calls which appear to be the main security holes of recent operating systems. [10] explains how does *XW* use the sandboxing to resolve the resource protection problem.
- Result certification procedure: This problem is linked to the lack of trust regarding the result provided by the remote resource. Indeed, there is no way to control precisely what happens on a participating resource. Faulty and malicious behaviour must be detected.

A typical *XW* platform is composed of one coordinator and several workers (remote resources). The coordinator is a three-tier layer allowing connection between clients and workers through a coordination service. This layer is designed so as it allows the mobility of clients and the volatility of workers.

3.1 The Coordinator

The coordinator is a three-tier architecture which adds a middle tier between client and workers. There is no task direct submission/result transfer between clients and workers. The coordinator accepts task requests coming from several clients, distributes the tasks to the workers according to a scheduling policy, transfers application code to workers if necessary, supervises task execution on workers, detect worker crash/disconnection, re-launches crashed tasks on any other available worker, collects and store task results to client upon request.

The coordinator is composed of three services: the repository, the scheduler and the result server. The repository is an advertisement services. It publishes services (client applications) to make them available through standard communication ports (Java RMI, XML-RPC). These applications/services are first read from a database and inserted into the task set. The scheduler is the service factory. It instantiates applications and manages their life cycle. It starts them on workers (a task is an instantiation of service or application), stops them as expected and corrects faults (if any) by finding available workers to re-launch them. Finally the result server collects results as they are provided by workers.

3.2 Workers

The worker architecture includes four components: the task pool, the execution thread, the communication manager and the activity monitor. The activity monitor controls whether some computations could take place in the hosting machine regarding some parameters determined by the worker configuration (% CPU idle, mouse/keyboard activity, etc.). The tasks pool (worker central point) is managed by a producer/consumer protocol between the communication manager and the execution thread. Each task should be in one of the three states: *ready* to be computed, *running* or *saving*. The first state concerns downloaded tasks, correctly inserted into the pool. The second state is for tasks being computed. The last state corresponds to tasks which need to upload result file to the result server. The communication manager ensures communication with the coordinator; it downloads task files (binaries and input data) and upload results, if any. When download completes, the task is inserted into the task pool. The execution thread extracts the first available task from the pool, recreates the task environment as provided by the client (binary code, input data, directories structure, etc.), writes on disk the task status, starts computation and waits for the task to complete. When the task completes, it creates the results file which includes standard output and updates task status on disk. The execution thread finally marks the task state as completed, allowing the communication manager to send results. It then expects notification from the result server to send again in case the upload went wrong or definitively remove the task.

In its original version, *XW* applications are standalone modules. The system does not support any interaction between different modules. However, developers can use asynchronous Remote Process Call called *XWRPC* in order to distribute (parallelize) their applications [11].

4 XtremWeb-CH

XtremWeb-CH (*XWCH*) is an upgraded version of *XW*. The aim of *XWCH* is to build an effective Peer-To-Peer LSDS which satisfies the four criteria detailed in paragraph 2. *XWCH* adds four functionalities to *XW*:

1. Automatic execution of Parallel and Distributed Applications (PDA)
2. Automatic detection of the smallest granularity that can be implemented according to the number of available workers.
3. Support of direct communication between workers.
4. *XWCH* provides a set of monitoring tools allowing users to visualize the execution of their applications.

4.1 Automatic Execution of Parallel and Distributed Applications (PDA)

In *XW*, jobs submitted to the system are standalone. In case of PDA, communicating modules are executed as separate jobs (tasks). It's the user responsibility to link manually output and input data of two communicating tasks. Contrary to this approach, *XWCH* supports the execution of a whole PDA. A PDA is a set of communicating modules that can be represented by a data flow graph where nodes are modules and edges are communications inter-modules (Fig. 1). According to the semantics of the PDA, modules can have the same or different codes. In Fig. 1, modules having the same shape have the same code.

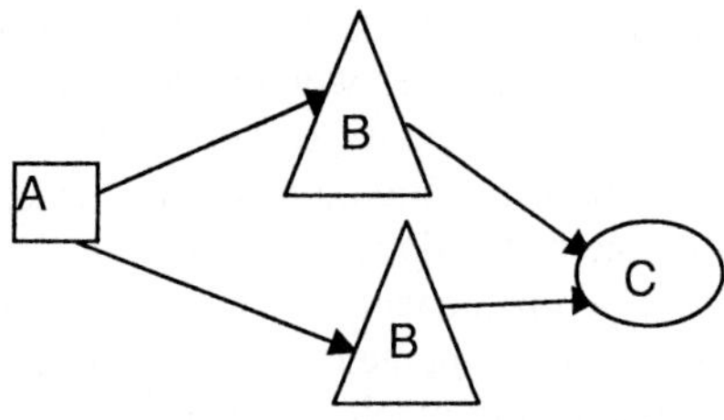

Fig. 1. Data flow graph representing a PDA application

The data flow graph is represented by an XML file whose syntax is detailed in Fig. 2.

An application is composed of several modules (*Module* element in Fig. 2). A module is represented by a source code and can have several binary versions (*Binary* element in Fig. 2). A task is an instantiation of one module. Thus, several tasks can correspond to the same module. The maximum number of tasks for a given module is fixed by the *Restriction* element. This element fixes the smallest granularity of the application during its execution. It can be extracted from the "state" of the platform just before the execution time (see paragraph 4.2 for details). It represents the maximum number of workers that can be used to execute the corresponding module.

Precedence rules between tasks are described by *Task* elements. A task can have several inputs (*Input* element in Fig. 2) but only one output (*Output* element in Fig. 2). The element *cmdLine* indicates arguments/parameters used by the task. This field is optional.

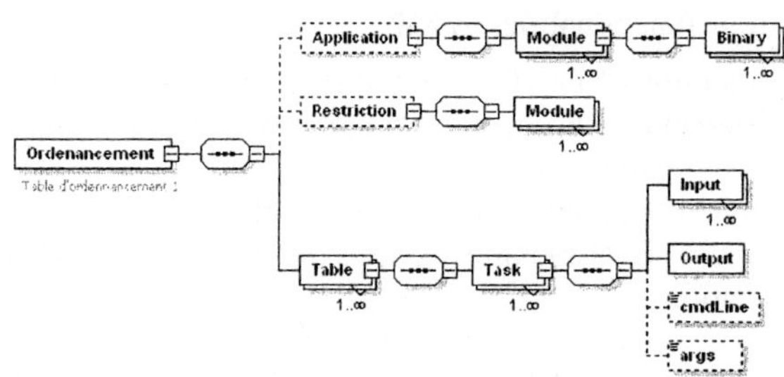

Fig. 2. XML syntax of a PDA application

A PDA is thus, represented by:

- its XML file representing its data flow graph,
- the binary codes of its modules. Let's recall that one module can have several binary codes,
- its input data.

These files are compressed into one file.

XWCH can be perceived as a layer on *XW* that takes into account the communications between tasks belonging to the same PDA. In this context, a task belonging to a given PDA is considered by *XW* as a standalone application.

A client can submit his PDA to *XWCH* by uploading its corresponding compressed file. In addition to the three states *ready*, *running* and *saving*, *XWCH* adds a fourth state: *blocked*. Tasks of a given PDA are initially *blocked* and cannot be assigned to any worker, since their input data are not available. Only tasks whose input data are given by the user are in *ready* state and can be allocated to workers. When they are assigned to a worker, they move from *ready* to *running* state. Input data needed by *blocked* tasks are progressively provided by *running* tasks which finish their processing. *XWCH* detects the *blocked* tasks which can pass to ready state and can, thus, be assigned by the scheduler to a worker.

4.2 Granularity of the PDA

In parallel computing, the selected size of the grain (granularity) depends on the application and the number of processors in the target parallel machine. This number is generally known and fixed during the execution. Thus, the granularity is fixed during the development of the application. In our context, the computer is the network, workers are free to join and/or leave the GC platform whenever they want. The exact number of available workers is known just before the execution and could be varied during the execution. As a consequence, the granularity should be fixed only at execution time. The client indicates, in the XML file describing his PDA (*Restriction* element), the number of workers each module of the PDA can use during its execution (*max_workers*). This number depends on the semantic of the application and should be provided by the client. To deploy an application on *XWCH*, three steps are required:

1. Discovery step: Search for a set of available workers to execute the PDA. The number of workers should be less or equal to *max_workers*.
2. XML generation step: this step consists on generating the XML file of the application to be deployed according to the number of available workers. In general, it's the user responsibility to generate this file. However, for a specific family of applications, this file can be automatically generated according to the *XWCH* platform status: number of available workers, network status, etc. Thus, the number of tasks is fixed just before the execution. In another words, granularity of the parallelization is dynamically fixed according to the number of available workers and the state of the targeted P2P platform.
3. Execution step: the application is launched on the *XWCH* platform.

4.3 Direct Communication

Two versions of *XWCH* were developed. The first, called *XWCH-sMs*, manages inter-tasks communications in a centralized way. The second version, called *XWCH-p2p*, allows a direct communication between workers without passing by the coordinator

In the *XWCH-sMs* (slave-Master-slave) version, workers cannot directly communicate, they cannot "see" each other. Any communications between tasks take place through the coordinator. This architecture overloads the coordinator and could affect the application performances.

In order to cure the gaps of the *XWCH-sMs* version, it is necessary to have direct worker-to-worker communications. In other term, the worker executing module *A* (called *worker A* in Fig. 3) must be able to directly send its results to *workers B* and *C*.

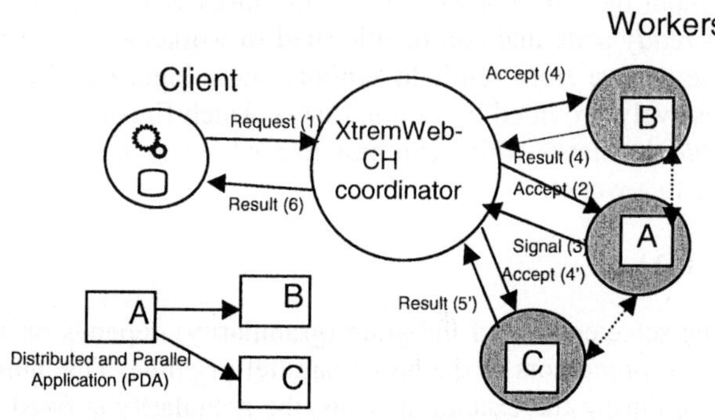

Fig. 3. Execution of a PDA on a XWCH-p2p platform

The *XWCH* coordinator can, thus, allocate tasks *B* and *C* to two available workers. Every worker receives the binary code of the module it will execute and the necessary information relating to its input file (IP address, path and name of the input file). Data transfer between workers *A* and *B* (*resp.* C) can thus take place on the initiative of the receiver. This version called *XWCH-p2p* has two main advantages:

1. it discharges the coordinator from data routing and,
2. it avoids the duplication of communications.

In this context, the coordinator keeps only the task scheduling management. *XWCH-p2p* tends towards the Peer-To-Peer concept which one of its principles is to avoid any centralized control.

Direct communication can only take place when the workers can "see" each other. Otherwise (one of the two workers is protected by a firewall or by a NAT address), direct communication is impossible. In this case, it is necessary to pass by an intermediary (*XWCH* coordinator for example). This scenario is similar to *XWCH-sMs* version. However, to avoid overloading the coordinator, one possible solution consists on installing a relay machine, called "data collector" which acts as an intermediary. This machine is used by worker *A* (in our example) to store its results and by workers

B and *C* to seek their data. "Data collector" machine is chosen by the user when launching the application. This machine must be reachable by all workers contributing to the execution of the concerned application.

4.4 Monitoring Tools

XWCH proposes a package of tools allowing the user to debug and/or visualize the progress of his PDA execution:

- Tasks allocation: The user can "spy" the execution of his PDA. He can follow the allocation of tasks (which worker is executing which task)
- Progress of tasks execution: When executing, every task can send progress report to its worker informing it about its state. Currently, this progress report is expressed in term of percentage of execution. 60% means that the task has finished 60% of its execution.
- Step by step execution: It's a debugging mode. When activated, every task sends messages to the worker. These messages are inserted in the source code by the developer.

5 Experimental Measures

The purpose of this section is to assess the performances of *XWCH* in a real case of a CPU time consuming application. *XWCH* was evaluated in the case of a phylogenetic application. Phylogenetic is the science which deals with the relationships that could exist between living organisms, it reconstructs the pattern of events that have led to "the distribution and diversity of life". These relationships are extracted from the Desoxyribo Nucleic Acid (DNA) sequences of species. A phylogenetic tree, also called life tree, is then built to show relationship among species. This tree shows the chronological succession of new species (and/or new characters) appearances.

In a medical context, the generation of a life tree for a family of microbes is particularly useful to trace the changes accumulated in their genomes. These changes are due, inter-alia, to the "reaction" of the virus to the treatments (antibiotic for example).

A multitude of applications aiming at building phylogenetic trees are used by the scientific community. These applications are known to be CPU time consuming, their complexity is exponential (*NP-difficult* problem). Approximate and heuristic methods do not solve the problem since their complexity remains polynomial with an order greater than 5: $O(n^m)$ with $m > 5$. Parallelisation of these methods could be useful in order to reduce the response time of these applications.

The *Tree Puzzle* method [12] [13] is one of the heuristic techniques used for the generation of phylogenetic trees. [14] and [15] propose a parallel implementation of the Tree Puzzle method written in C and using Message Passing Interface (MPI) communication routines. This implementation, particularly optimized for a cluster of computers, was adapted to our *XWCH* platform. MPI routines were replaced by file transfers. However, no code optimization was done. Our goal is not to develop an optimized version of the *Tree Puzzle* algorithm for an *XWCH* platform, but to validate choices retained within the framework of the *XWCH* project.

The input data of *Tree Puzzle* algorithm is represented by the DNA sequences of the species to be classified. A DNA sequence is modeled by a chain of few hundreds of characters. The algorithm generates a structure representing the phylogenetic tree of the species given in the entry. The *Tree Puzzle* algorithm is not detailed in this document. However, its structure, expressed in term of tasks (data flow graph) is given in Fig. 4. This structure is common to several families of PDA. An XML file generator was developed. The goal is to automatically generate this file according to the number of available workers and structure of exchanged data between tasks.

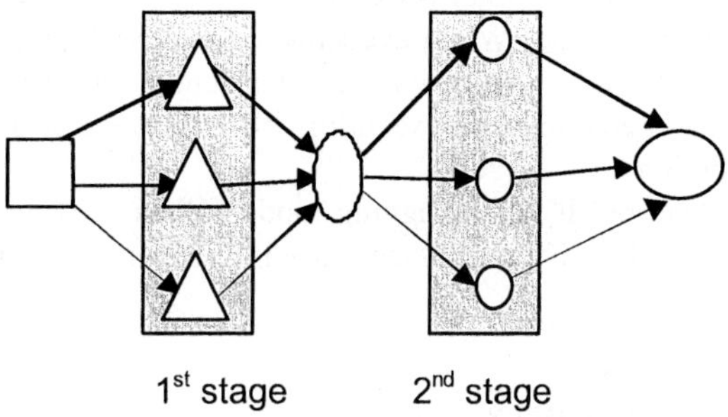

Fig. 4. Structure of the Tree Puzzle algorithm

Tasks belonging to the 1st stage (*resp.* 2nd stage) have the same code, their number is equal to *N – 3* where *N* is the number of DNA sequences. The number of tasks belonging to the 2nd stage is variable and can be chosen by the programmer, but can never exceed *N*.

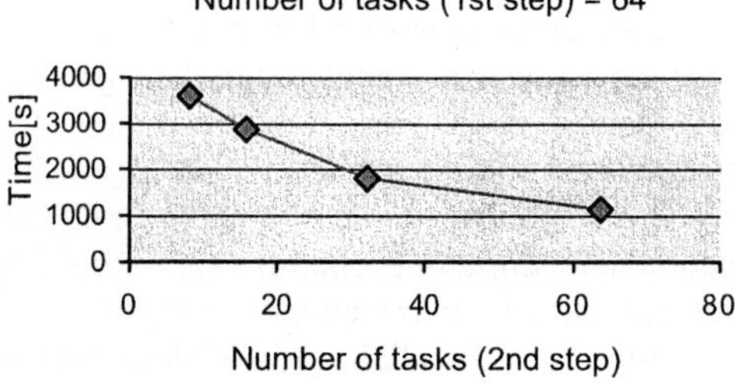

Fig. 5. Execution time of *tree puzzle* algorithm. Number of sequences = 64.

Tree Puzzle application was executed on *XWCH* (*XWCH-p2p* and *XWCH-sMs* versions) with two jets of input data: 64 (128 tasks) and 128 sequences of DNA (256 tasks). *XWCH* was installed on more than 100 heterogeneous PC (Pentium 2, 3, 4) with Windows and Linux operating systems distributed between two sites: University of Applied Sciences (Geneva-Switzerland) and Polytechnic School of Lille (France).

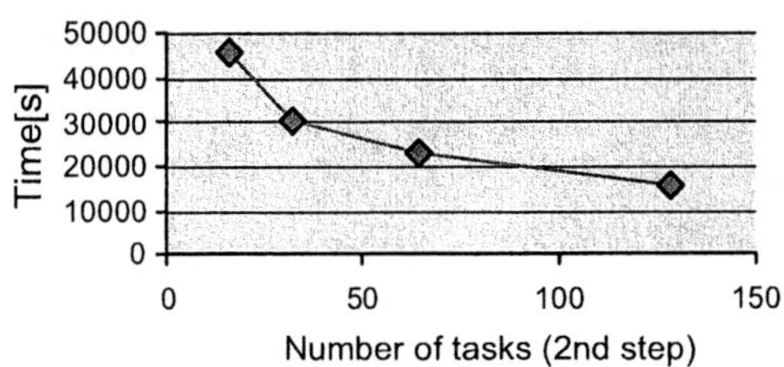

Fig. 6. Execution time of *tree puzzle* algorithm. Number of sequences = 128.

The 2nd stage of the application consumes 70% of the processing time. For this reason, tests focused on varying the number of tasks at this stage. In Fig. 5 (*resp.* 6), *Tree Puzzle* application was executed by varying the number of tasks of the 2nd stage: 8, 16, 32 and 64 (*resp.* 32, 64 and 128). When the number of DNA sequences is equal to 128 (Fig. 6), and with a number of sequences equal to 8 (*resp.* 16), the execution time is estimated to 7 days (*resp.* 3 days).

During the execution, some of the available workers were not "exploited" by the application. Indeed, the number of tasks in the 2nd stage never exceeds that of workers. On the other hand, during the execution of the 1st stage, task allocation process is faster than the execution itself. Consequently, the scheduler assigns 1st stage tasks to workers having already executed the same code (workers already having the binary code).

The objective of these measurements was to validate our approach. In this context, no optimization was brought to the parallel *Tree Puzzle* algorithm. However, several improvements could be carried out in order to adapt the algorithm to the targeted platform. Indeed, a specific parallelization of the *Tree Puzzle* algorithm adapted to *XWCH* platform could decrease the response time of the application.

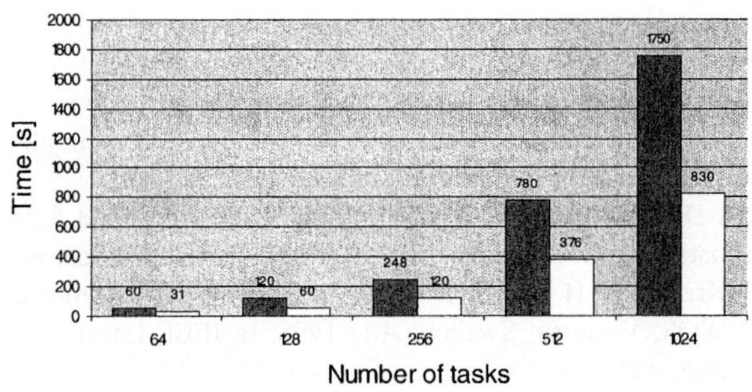

□ XWCH-p2p

■ XWCH-sMs

Fig. 7. XWCH-sMs vs. XWCH-p2p

Fig. 7 shows execution times of another parallel/distributed application (parallel *mergesort* algorithm) when executed on *XWCH-sMs* and *XWCH-p2p versions*. Indeed, communication costs of this application are more important than those generated by the Tree Puzzle algorithm.

These Measurements (Fig. 7) are foreseeable: *XWCH-sMs* version consumes twice more communications than the *XWCH-p2p* version.

6 Conclusion

This paper presents a new GC environment (*XtremWeb-CH*), used for the execution of high performance applications on a highly heterogeneous distributed environment. *XWCH* can support direct communications between workers, without passing by the coordinator. The execution of a testbed application (generation of phylogenetic trees) has demonstrated the feasibility of our solution. Other experiments are in progress to evaluate *XWCH* in other High Performance applications cases.

One of the ideas that could constitute the perspectives of this work is to extend the *XWCH-p2p* version in order to converge towards a true P2P system which one of its principles is to eliminate any centralized control. The current version of XWCH allows the decentralization of communications between workers. The next step consists on designing a distributed scheduler, executed by workers. This scheduler should avoid allocating communicating tasks to workers that can not reach each other. Although not specifically discussed, this approach offers a strong basis onto which we could develop distributed and dynamic scheduler and should confirm and reinforce the tendency detailed in section 2.

References

1. http://setiathome.berkeley.edu/
2. http://www.entropia.com/
3. http://www.ud.com/home.htm
4. http://www.parabon.com/
5. Gilles Fedak et al. XtremWeb : A Generic Global Computing System. CCGRID2001, workshop on Global Computing on Personal Devices. Brisbane, Australia. May 2001.
6. KAN G., Peer-to-Peer: harnessing the power of disruptive technologies, Chapter Gnutella, O'Reilly, Mars 2001.
7. Ian Clarke. A Distributed Decentralised Information Storage and Retrieval System. Division of Informatics. Univ. of Edinburgh. 1999. http://freenet.sourceforge.net/
8. Babin, G; P. Kropf; and H. Unger. A two-level communication protocol for a Web Operating System: WOS. Vasteras, Sweden, Aug 1998. In IEEE Euromicro Workshop on Network Computing, 939–944.
9. I. Foster, C. Kesselman, J. Nick, and S. Tuecke. Grid Services for Distributed System Integration. IEEE Computer, pages 37-46, June 2002.
10. Franck Cappello et al. Computing on Large Scale Distributed Systems: XtremWeb Architecture, Programming Models, Security, Tests and Convergence with Grid. In Future Generation Computer Science (FGCS), 2004.

11. Samir Djilali. P2P-RPC: Programming Scientific Applications on Peer-to-Peer Systems with Remote Procedure Call. GP2PC2003. Tokyo Japan, May 2003.
12. http://biowulf.nih.gov/apps/puzzle/tree-puzzle-doc.html
13. http://www.tree-puzzle.de/
14. http://www.dkfz.de/tbi/tree-puzzle/
15. Heiko A. Schmidt, Phylogenetic Trees from Large Datasets, 'Ph.D.' in Computer Science, Düsseldorf, Germany, 2003.

An Adaptive Service Strategy Based on User Rating in P2P*

Jianming Fu[1,2], Lei Zhang[1], Weinan Li[1], and Huanguo Zhang[1]

[1] School of Computer, Wuhan University,Wuhan 430072,China
[2] State Key Laboratory of Software Engineering, Wuhan University, Wuhan 430072, China
fujms@public.wh.hb.cn

Abstract. In order to deal with free riding in P2P system, incentive mechanism or rating system is presented, and each user rating is computed by itself, which causes that some users exaggerate their ratings. In this paper, three aspects are developed for free riding and for improving service performance in P2P. First of all, it is useful to keep away fake rating that each user rating is calculated by the responders. Secondly, three kinds of user ratings including single user rating and two group ratings are exploited to get better service performance. The last aspect is to provide a service strategy that is adaptive to the responder workload. Finally, the experimental results demonstrate that this strategy can effectively handle the problem of free riding, and especially, group ratings can greatly boost response rate of the whole P2P system.

1 Introduction

Peer-to-Peer (P2P) technology can mask the implementation of low layer in computing system, and provide open and shared computing environment. Hence this technology has been widely applied and studied [1,2,3]. P2P systems are generally designed on the assumption that all peers will be altruists voluntarily contributing the resources to a global pool. However, the behavior of peers is quite different, some peers might provide services benevolently, while other peers might be malicious or stingy and might not provide services. The behavior of participants consuming many resources while contributing little is regarded as free riding and such participants are called free-riders. P2P system may gradually degrade into a model of client/server due to the free riding. The studies [1] have showed that most participants engage in freeloading: almost 70% of Gnutella peers share little or no files and top 1% hosts provide about 50% of all services. Therefore, incentive mechanism is introduced to ensure that some hosts with high contribution get high quality of service, while other hosts with little contribution have to get low quality of service, even are rejected.

* Supported by the National Natural Science Foundations of China under Grant No.90104005 and No.66973034, and by the Hubei Natural Science Foundations of China under Grant No.2005AA101C44

H. Zhuge and G.C. Fox (Eds.): GCC 2005, LNCS 3795, pp. 860–870, 2005.

In fact, a query message in Gnutella carries the information about sharing the disk space and uptime of the client peer, according to which the server peer provides different services. In addition, Gnutella can limit the search scope according to the client's contribution. The more contribution it has, the larger its TTL is. User rating in KaZaA [2] is defined as the ratio of uploads to downloads. However, these ratings are calculated by the requestors, hosts with little contribution may juggle their contributions in order to get better service. If there is a centralized directory service for storing and searching the user rating, juggling the contribution could be avoided. However, it is unfeasible due to the bottleneck and single-point failure of directory server. Hence, how to design a distributed rating system is open issue.

We state our motivations as follows. Firstly, user ratings are computed by service providers to avoid fake ones. Secondly, three kinds of user ratings are exploited to enhance the response rate of whole system. Finally, the service capacity of service providers should be considered, and whether the requests could be satisfied not only depends on the requestor's rating but also the service capacity of service providers. That is, the provider's serving is sensitive to its workload. On the basis of these motivations, an adaptive service strategy based on user rating is presented to deal with free riding in unstructured P2P.

The rest of this paper is organized as follows. Section 2 reviews some related work in a brief. Section 3 states our strategy besides some definitions. We evaluate our strategy in section 4, and give conclusion in section 5.

2 Related Work

Vivek Vishnumurthy[4] provides an economic framework using Karma. Karma represents the user rating, and it increases when uploading files, while decreases when downloading. Any peer can't download any file until its Karma achieves a certain value. The Karma of each user is stored at a Bank-set, which also take part in the dealing. Chiranjeeb Buragohain[5] studies a game theoretic framework for incentives, and each peer is rational and politic to pursue its maximum utility, which is based on its rating, so that the Nash equilibrium point can be obtained. Debojyoti Dutta[6] provides two verification schemes for checking the requestor' rating. Qixiang Sun[7] proposes SLIC mechanism based on link, which calculates a peer's rating by the neighbor's history records. There are many researches on peer trust and reputation[8,9,10], and each user is assigned a reputation by system that reflects its contribution and its participation in the system. In addition, XU FEI designs a P2P system based on peer group[11], which is useful to group peers, and Hai Zhuge presents query routing mechanism using semantic links among neighbors[12] to speed up queries and the future interconnection environment including P2P[13].

Three kinds of ratings are used in our strategy, and are different from SLIC, in which only the single user rating between neighbors is used.

3 Adaptive Service Strategy

In P2P system, there are two roles for each peer: Service Providers (SP) which providing others with service and Service Requestors (SR). Although each peer has two roles, we just pay attention to one role when we state our strategy. Before a SP makes a decision for a query, it must calculate the rating of the query requestor. There are three key points in our strategy: how to collect information for rating, how to rate a requestor, and how to provide service on the ratings. We will discuss these issues as below.

3.1 Definition

Each peer will rate other peers based on the service it receives from them and will store its own rating. This service includes factors like the number of successful requests it makes, response delay, download speed of file transferring transaction, or length of downloaded file, etc. Here, three tables are used to store basic information and logs: MI, GT and ST.

The all peers in P2P are divided into different groups. Each peer has an identifier PID, and it must belong to a group. At the same time, each group has an identifier GID. In order to compute ratings, each peer keeps the following. MI=$\{PID, TimeStamp\}$, records all members of a group, here $TimeStamp$ indicates the time when a member join this group. GT= $\{PID, GID, FID, FS, TimeStamp\}$, records logs describing a peer's getting service from the system, here PID is an identifier of a SP, GID is a group identifier of the SP, FID is an identifier of file to be downloaded, FS is the length of this file, and $TimeStamp$ indicates the time when this file is downloaded. ST=$\{PID, GID, FID, FS, TimeStamp\}$, records logs containing a peer's providing files, here PID is an identifier of a SR, GID is a group identifier of the SR, and FID, FS, $TimeStamp$ is the same as the one of GT respectively.

The records in GT and ST come from transactions in the past. After a peer N_{sr} downloads a file with FID from a peer N_{sp}, N_{sr} will insert a record $\{N_{sp}.PID, N_{sp}.GID, FID, FS, T1\}$ into its GT, meanwhile N_{sp} will insert a record $\{N_{sr}.PID, N_{sr}.GID, FID, FS, T1\}$ into its ST, where $T1$ is a timestamp.

In traditional rating system, a service provider decides its service based on the rating which the requestor claims. The rating R_i of user u_i is defined by the set of all users it served within some sliding window, so it reflects all contribution of u_i to the P2P system within some sliding window. However, it is easy to fake this rating, because this rating is computed by the requestor. Hence, this rating system requires some verification scheme to check the rating[6].

In our strategy, the rating R_i of user u_i on user u_j is defined by u_j whom u_i served within some sliding window, and it is computed by u_j without any verification schemes. This rating is also called single user rating defined as $Definition 1$. Nevertheless, this rating reflects partial contribution of u_i to the P2P system, even has very small value that reduces the response rate of whole P2P system. In order to improve the response rate, two group ratings are introduced in $Definition2$ and $Definition3$. One group rating R_i of user u_i on user u_j is defined by u_j's group whom u_i served. The other group rating R_i of user u_i on user u_j is defined by u_j's group whom u_i's group served. And two group ratings are calculated by the group of u_j without any verification schemes.

When N_{sp} receives a query from N_{sr}, N_{sp} must choose its strategy for service, and N_{sp} decides how to rate N_{sr}. And three kinds of rating of N_{sr} vs. N_{sp} are defined as below.

$Definition1$: Rating of Peer vs. Peer (RPP) is defined as:

$$RPP(N_{sr}, N_{sp}) = \frac{\sum_{i \in N_{sp}.GT and i.PID = N_{sr}.PID} i.FS}{\sum_{i \in N_{sp}.ST and i.PID = N_{sr}.PID} i.FS) + \delta} \tag{1}$$

RPP is a ratio of the service level to the consumption level of N_{sr} vs. N_{sp}.

$Definition2$: Rating of Peer vs. peer's Group (RGP) is defined as:

$$RGP(N_{sr}, N_{sp}) = \frac{\sum_{j \in N_{sp}.MI} \sum_{i \in j.GT and i.PID = N_{sr}.PID} i.FS}{\sum_{j \in N_{sp}.MI} (\sum_{i \in j.ST and i.PID = N_{sr}.PID} i.FS) + \delta} \tag{2}$$

RGP is a ratio of the service level to the consumption level of N_{sr} vs. N_{sp}'group.

$Definition3$: Rating of peer'Group vs. peer's Group (RGG) is defined as:

$$RGP(N_{sr}, N_{sp}) = \frac{\sum_{j \in N_{sp}.MI} \sum_{i \in j.GT and i.GID = N_{sr}.GID} i.FS}{\sum_{j \in N_{sp}.MI} (\sum_{i \in j.ST and i.GID = N_{sr}.GID} i.FS) + \delta} \tag{3}$$

RGG is a ratio of the service level to the consumption level of N_{sr}'group vs. N_{sp}'group.

δ is the constant bias, which is useful when the consumption level is zero in above equations. RGP and RGG are group ratings, and are introduced to improve performance of P2P system, because many queries may be rejected thanks to low RPPs that are used to decide the service level by providers.

Without loss of generality, the size of ST and GT is limited, so each record in any tables must expire after the interval of T_Period, which is time constant. In other words, when a period of T_Period elapses after a record is inserted, this record ought to be deleted. In addition, we will introduce sliding windows as weights reflecting impacts of timestamps on user rating, which motivates users to contribute to the community continuously. During a period of valid time, the more recent the activity happens, the larger the weight is. Assume current time is $Current\_time$, $i.FS$ of the definitions above should be modified as the following.

$$i.FS = i.FS * \frac{i.Timestamp - Current\_time + T\_Period}{T\_Period} \tag{4}$$

The logs of all members in a group are needed to compute *RGP* and *RGG*. In order to decrease the number of communications and network traffic, N_{sp} may choose q members randomly from its group for computing group ratings, here $q <| N_{sp}.MI |$.

3.2 Service Strategy

After a query is reached from N_{sr}, N_{sp} must handle this query by certain strategy such as responding at once, responding with delay, or rejecting. There are two kinds of relationship between N_{sp} and N_{sr}. One is $N_{sp}.GID = N_{sr}.GID$, which indicates that the query comes from the same group, and let the proposition *ingroup* (N_{sp}, N_{sr}) be true(denoted *ingroup*). The other is $N_{sp}.GID \neq N_{sr}.GID$, which indicates that the query comes from other group, so *RPP*, *RGP* and *RGG* need to be computed on demand.

Besides ratings, our strategy is adaptive to the workload of *SP*, so assume the service capacity of N_{sp} is $N_{sp}.C$ per time unit, and current workload is $(N_{sp}.RN+ N_{sp}.SN)$. Here, $N_{sp}.RN$ is the number of queries per time unit originated by N_{sp}, and $N_{sp}.SN$ is the number of responses per time unit for N_{sp}. For simplicity, we should unify the workload, as $N_{sp}.LD = (N_{sp}.RN + N_{sp}.SN)/N_{sp}.C$. For convenience of service decision, we import the thresholds of workload μ_1, μ_2, μ_3 and μ_4, which follow an order $\mu_1 < \mu_2 < \mu_3 < \mu_4$. These thresholds may influence the service quality. At the same time, we introduce rating thresholds α_1, β_1 and γ_1, where α_1 is a threshold of *RPP*, β_1 is a threshold of *RGP*, and γ_1 is a threshold of *RGG*. All thresholds will be subject to our strategy.

Suppose $\alpha = RPP(N_{sr}, N_{sp}), \beta = RGP(N_{sr}, N_{sp}), \gamma = RGG(N_{sr}, N_{sp})$, then the decision of *SP* is shown as follows according to our adaptive service strategy.

(1) if $N_{sp}.LD < \mu_1$ then if *ingroup* or $\alpha > \alpha_1$ or $\beta > \beta_1$ or $\gamma > \gamma_1$ then responds at once. else responds with probability ρ as well as delay of $DELAY\_CONST$.

(2) else if $N_{sp}.LD < \mu_2$ then if *ingroup* or $\alpha > \alpha_1$ or $\beta > \beta_1$ then responds at once. else if $\gamma > \gamma_1$ then responds with delay of $DELAY\_CONST$. else refuses this query.

(3) else if $N_{sp}.LD < \mu_3$ then if *ingroup* or $\alpha > \alpha_1$ then responds at once. else if $\beta > \beta_1$ then responds with delay of $DELAY\_CONST$. else refuses this query.

(4) else if $N_{sp}.LD < \mu_4$, then refuses this query.

Here, $DELAY\_CONST$ is time constant. Our strategy includes 4 parts:

- When the workload of *SP* is very light ($N_{sp}.LD < \mu_1$), *SP* immediately serves *SR* who shares the same *GID*, or has certain ratings about α, β, γ. Or else *SP* provides service with ρ besides delay. That is, *SP* refuses this query with 1-ρ.

- When the workload of *SP* is lighter ($\mu_1 \leq N_{sp}.LD < \mu_2$), *SP* immediately serves *SR* who shares the same *GID*, or has certain ratings about α, β. Or else

SP provides service with delay while SR has certain rating of γ. For other cases, SP refuses this query.

- When the workload of SP is heavier ($\mu_2 \leq N_{sp}.LD < \mu_3$), SP immediately serves SR who shares the same GID, or has certain rating of α. Or else SP provides service with delay while SR has certain rating of β. For other cases, SP refuses this query.
- When the workload of SP is the heaviest ($\mu_3 \leq N_{sp}.LD < \mu_4$), SP refuses this query.

For above strategy, what is the first considered is RPP, then is RGP, and the last is RGG. In order to shorten response time, SP firstly computes its workload, and determines where the query come from, then decides whether it is necessary to compute RGP and RGG.

4 Performance Analysis

For evaluating the efficiency of our strategy, we will introduce the experiment preparation, methodology and the experimental results.

4.1 Preparation

Our experimental network is similar to that of Gnutella except for file searching. There are 300 peers and 3000 files (objects) in an unstructured P2P system.

There are many ways to construct groups [14], among which we introduce a simple one. First we should fix the number of groups as 15. Then, we randomly choose 15 peers as seed peers representing 15 groups, and each peer of the rest joins the corresponding group in a certain probability in term of its distances to groups.

All ratings are related to file sizes, so it is necessary to choose size for each file. The main file type in Gnutella which people have interests in is multimedia, which takes 95% of all the files. Among all audio is 35%, video is 59% and others are 6%[15]. And the results [15] also show that the distribution of the file lengths is 10% of 0.01MB-2MB, 75% of 2MB-9MB, 10% of 9MB-100MB and 5% of 100MB-600MB. We assume that the distribution of file lengths is uniform within each interval, and the distribution of all file lengths in our experiment follows that in Gnutella.

In order to minimize the search cost and encourage sharing, users should share the files after they get them, and there are many replication strategies [16]. In Gnutella, files are shared immediately when they have been downloaded. Hence the copy of the files will increase, and eventually the copies of files will obey Zipf-like distribution. For simplicity, our experiment does not use any replication strategy.

4.2 Methodology

Generally speaking, let $\alpha_1 = \beta_1 = \gamma_1 = 1$, which means if the client peer contributes more than it consumes, that is, the client's user rating for the server

Table 1. Definition and values of symbols

Parameter	Value	Description
$\alpha_1, \beta_1, \gamma_1$	1	rating thresholds
C	2.5	service capacity
λ	5	mean number of queries per round for a peer
ρ	0.5	service probability
$\mu_1, \mu_2, \mu_3, \mu_4$	0.5, 0.7, 0.8, 0.9	workload thresholds
δ	100	rating bias

is more than 1, this peer may get better services. The service probability for low rating's requestors is decided by ρ, let ρ=0.5, so that the rejection of query and delayed service have the same prob-ability. We may enlarge its value to improve the response rate of whole system.

In order to get statistic performance of our model, assume that a round consisting of 100 time units is regarded as a period, and each performance is computed per round. The time window T_Period has important influences on the calculation for user rating, and let it be 1000 time units. And a delay factor of $DELAY\_CONST$ is 10 time units.

In each round, 12.5% of the whole peers are chosen randomly to send queries. Without loss of generality, the number of requests sent by each peer per round follows the Possion distribution with λ, which is mean number of requests. And the requested files obey Zipf-like distribution. The various files in Gnutella system have different popularities. Therefore, the more popular the file is, the more frequently it is requested. And the research has proved that the requests in Gnutella, Napster and Web follow Zipf-like distribution[17], that is and q_i is the popularity of the ith file, and α =1.2[16]. In order to obtain RGP and RGG, several members should be asked for the information, and let q=5 to get more information. The bigger q is, the more precise these ratings are. Finally, our experiment runs 80 rounds, and other parameters are listed in $Table1$.

The service capacity in $Table1$ is assigned 2.5, which depends on average workload of whole system. Because we don't know this workload, we use estimated workload as 1.25. The workload per peer is not uniform, since the distribution of requested files is subject to zipf-like that. Therefore, C is assigned 2.5, two times of 1.25.

4.3 Results

We evaluate the efficiency of our strategy in two metrics. One is Successful Request Rate (SRR) indicating that how many peers receive the answers after queries submission, and the other is Mean Latency (ML) indicating the average delay of all responses. In addition, the reason of query failure is either lower rating of service requestors or overload of service providers, so we will give exact reason while a query fails. The whole experiment consists of 4 parts. Part A evaluates the impacts of rating thresholds on ML and SRR. Part B evaluates the impacts of service capacity on ML and SRR. Part C evaluates the impacts

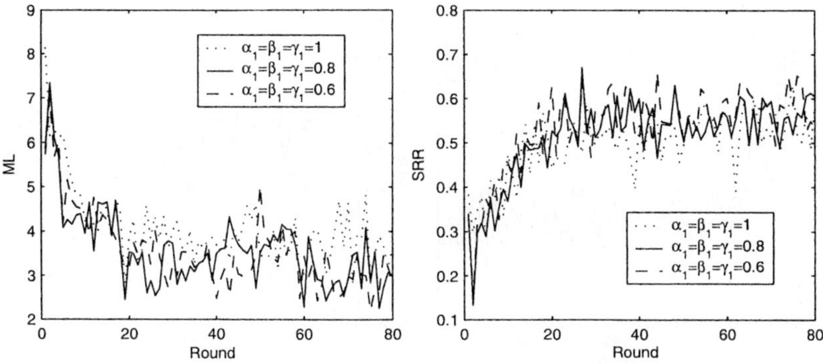

Fig. 1. ML and SRR for various rating thresholds

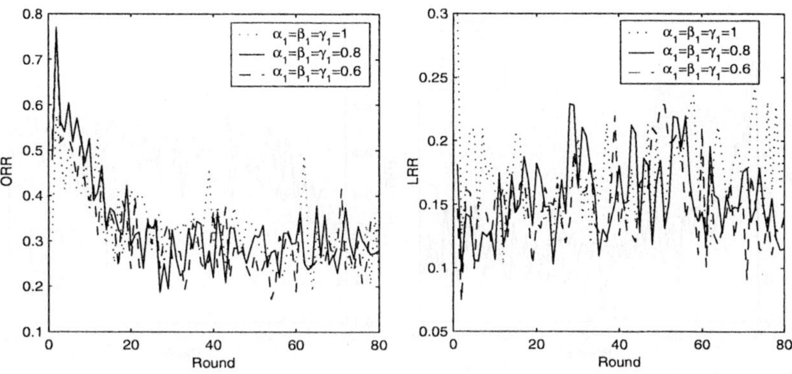

Fig. 2. The left denotes Refusal Rate for Overload(ORR)and the right is Refusal Rate for Low-rating(LRR)

of query loads on ML and SRR. Part D evaluates the impacts of three ratings on ML and SRR. The parameters are assigned the same as that in $Table1$ except for the variational parameter annotated in the figures.

In Fig.5, the symbol of 'α' represents that only RPP is employed in our strategy, the symbol of '$\alpha + \beta$' indicates both RPP and RGP are employed, and the symbol of '$\alpha + \beta + \gamma$' means three ratings are used. From all figures, we obtain some observations as follows:

- For whole system, we can improve response rate and reduce average latency via a way of reducing the rating thresholds of α_1, β_1 and γ_1. Moreover, the rate of query failure due to overload is close to two times of that owing to lower rating. The lower the rating thresholds are, the lower two rates (ORR and LRR) are.
- For whole system, we can improve response rate and reduce average latency via a way of enlarging the service capacities of service providers.

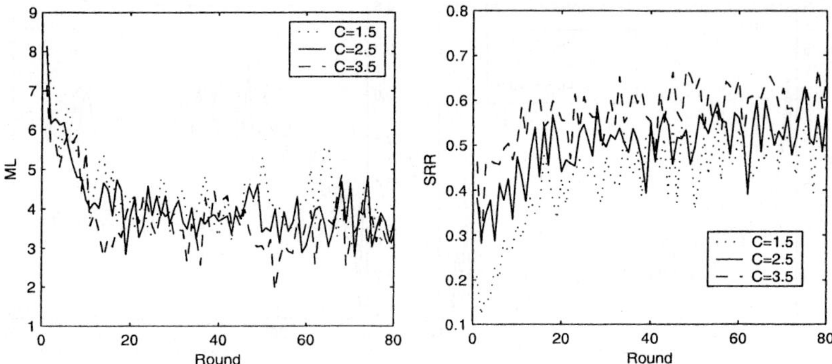

Fig. 3. ML and SRR for various service capacities

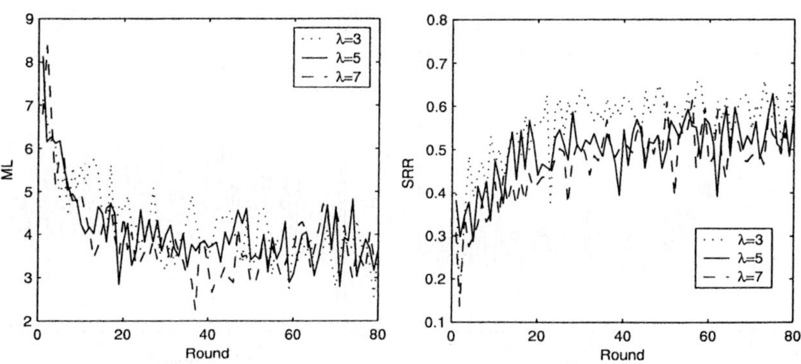

Fig. 4. ML and SRR for various query loads

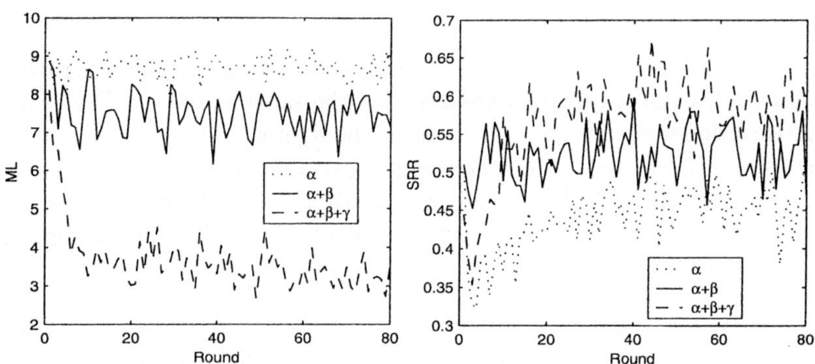

Fig. 5. ML and SRR for various rating

- If the mean number of queries is larger, then the latency is smaller, and response rate is smaller. This is because large queries may result in overload of SP.

- In terms of implementation of our strategy, the more the ratings employed are, the smaller the latency is and the larger the response rate is. Specially, RGP and RGG can greatly improve response rate compared with only RPP.

5 Conclusion

This paper presents an adaptive service strategy based on user ratings to deal with free riding in unstructured P2P. The user ratings include single user rating and two group ratings, and are computed by the service providers in light of the historical logs to avoid masquerading ratings. This rating mechanism does not need any verification schemes, and is collusion free in nature. Moreover, the strategy is adaptive to the workload of service providers, and provides the different services according to these ratings. So the host with little contribution can hardly get services from others. Finally, the experimental results demonstrate that this strategy can effectively handle the problem of free riding, and the group ratings can improve the response rate of whole P2P system. Although our strategy can make the free-rider get bad service or no service, how to identify and eliminate a greedy peer is our future research.

References

1. E. Adar and B. A. Huberman. Free riding in Gnutella, Xerox PARC report, Oct 2000, avail-able at www.parc.xerox.com/istl/groups/iea/papers/gnutella.
2. KaZaA, "http:// www.kazaa.com".
3. Aoying Zhou, Bo Ling, Zhiguo Lu et al. E.cient Semantic Search in Peer-to-Peer Systems. WAIM 2003, LNCS 2762, pp. 278-289, 2003.
4. Vivek Vishnumurthy, Sangeeth Chandrakumar, and Emin Gun Sirer. KARMA: A Secure Economic Framework for P2P Resource Sharing. In Proceedings of the Workshop on the Economics of Peer-to-Peer Systems, Berkeley,California, June 2003.
5. Chiranjeeb Buragohain, Divyakant Agrawal, Subhash Suri. A Game Theoretic Framework for Incentives in P2P Systems. Proc. of the Third International Conference on P2P Computing (P2P2003), Linkoping Sweden, 2003.
6. D. Dutta, A. Goel, R. Govindan, and H. Zhang. The Design of A Distributed Rating Scheme for Peer-to-peer Systems. In Workshop on Economics of Peer-to-Peer Systems, 2003.
7. Qixiang Sun, Hector Garcia-Molina. SLIC: A Selfish Link-Based Incentive Mechanism for Unstructured Peer-to-Peer Networks. 24th International Conference on Distributed Computing Systems (ICDCS'04), March, 2004. Hachioji, Tokyo, Japan.
8. Dou W, Wang HM, Jia Y, Zou P. A recommendation-based peer-to-peer trust model. Journal of Software, 2004,15(4): 571 583.
9. Seungjoon Lee, Rob Sherwood, Bobby Bhattacharjee. Cooperative Peer Groups in NICE. IEEE Infocom, April 2003.

10. Yao Wang, Julita Vassileva, Bayesian Network Trust Model in Peer-to-Peer Networks. The Second International Workshop on Agents and Peer-to-Peer Computing (P2PC 2003).
11. XU Fei, YANG Guang-Wen, JU Da-Peng. Design of Distributed Storage System on Peer-to-Peer Structure. Journal of Software, 2004, 15(2): 2-9.
12. H. Zhuge, J. Liu, L. Feng, X. Sun and C. He. Query Routing in a Peer-to-Peer Semantic Link Network. Computational Intelligence,21(2)(2005)197-216.
13. H.Zhuge, The Future Interconnection Environment, IEEE Computer, 38 (4)(2005) 27-33.
14. S. Ratnaswamy, M. Handley, K. Karp, and S. Shenker. Topologically-aware overlay con-struction and server selection. In Proceedings of INFOCOM,June 2002.
15. Stefan Saroiu, Krishna P. Gummadi, Richard J. Dunn, Steven D. Gribble, and HeNsry M. Levy, An Analysis of Internet Content Delivery Systems. Proceedings of the 5th Symposium on Operating Systems Design and Implementation Boston, MA, December 9-11, 2002.
16. Qin Lv Pei Cao Edith Cohen Kai Li Scott Shenker, Search and Replication in Unstructured Peer-to-Peer Networks. Proceedings of the 16th international conference on Supercomput-ing, June, 2002, New York, USA.
17. Kunwadee Sripanidkulchai. The popularity of gnutella queries and its implications on scalability. In O'Reilly'swww.openp2p.com, February 2001.

P2PGrid: Integrating P2P Networks into the Grid Environment

Jiannong Cao and Fred B. Liu

Internet and Mobile Computing Lab,
Department of Computing Hong Kong Polytechnic University,
Hung Hom, Kowloon Hong Kong
csjcao@comp.polyu.edu.hk, 01900270d@comp.polyu.edu.hk

Abstract. The current Grid architecture suffers from high complexity, inefficiency in leveraging common PC capabilities, and the single point of failure problem originated from Grid's Client-Server mode of interaction. We propose an approach to solve the problems by incorporating P2P networks with the Grid environment. A two-layer integration model is proposed, which consists of a Grid layer and an underlying P2P layer that can be accessed from but not limited to the Grid layer. A prototype implementation of the model, called P2PGrid, has been developed and experimented with example applications built on the platform. The results show that the complexity for common PCs to participate the Grid can be greatly reduced, the resource aggregation efficiency has been increased, and the single point of failure problem can be solved by using P2P mode of communication in the Grid environment.

1 Introduction

Grid Computing has emerged as an important new field in distributed computing area. It focuses on large-scale resource sharing, innovative applications, and, in some cases, high-performance computing, all of which make it distinguished from conventional distributed computing technologies [3]. Peer-to-Peer (P2P) computing is another hot topic in distributed computing field. Because of the similar purposes and complementary features of Grid and P2P computing, there is a common belief that these two technologies will finally converge. In this paper, we study the issues of combining the two technologies in order to take their advantages while overcoming the problems encountered in each field.

Despite that Grid and P2P computing technologies have been more and more popular in recent years, neither of them is yet mature and has limitations or bottlenecks in different aspects. For the Grid, first, current Grid middleware are designed with strong capability of integrating heterogeneous systems for supporting large institution / organization oriented applications, thus most of the resources involved in the Grid are from computing or scientific facilities that have above average capabilities or for special purposes. Second, the complexity of setting up, configuring, and using the Grid is too high for commodity use, because the current Grid middleware is designed for

H. Zhuge and G.C. Fox (Eds.): GCC 2005, LNCS 3795, pp. 871 – 883, 2005.

implementing / integrating sophisticated "high end" distributed systems. Third, for current OGSA [1] Grid middleware, the system communication, in essence, is still in client/server mode. For example, in Globus, there are architectural distinctions between service provider and consumer. Therefore, despite the sophisticated service integration and load balancing mechanisms that Grid middleware provides, current Grid systems are still not immune to problems of the traditional client/server mode systems, especially as the scale of the Grid increases.

P2P systems have similar purposes as the Grid (coordinated resource sharing), but with complimentary features. P2P systems are well known for making use of the resources on the edge of Internet, mainly from millions of desktops [7]. The tasks handled by most P2P systems, however, are comparatively simple (file sharing, e.g.), and most popular P2P applications are implemented vertically. Despite the fact that the capability of a single peer is limited, the capability of the P2P network as a whole (in the form of storage or computational capability, for instance) is appealing. In addition, P2P systems also have other attractive features such as high decentralization, high scalability, fault tolerance, etc.

In the past several years, efforts have been made on applying P2P computing technologies to overcome difficulties encountered in the Grid [10] [11] [13] [19]. One trend of Grid development is to employ P2P substrate for underlying message routing or resource discovering and coordinating but use Grid as upper layer middleware providing service semantics. However, the detailed ways of implementation is still unclear. In the light of the problems and development trends of the Grid technology, the objective of our research reported in this is to integrate P2P networks into the Grid environment so that the Grid can benefit the P2P mode of communication and thus providing solutions of the existing problems. A two-layer model for the integration of the Grid and P2P networks is proposed. In the platform, called P2PGrid, that implements this model, a P2P layer can be formed, which can be accessed from, but not limited to the Grid layer, while all the Grid Services in the Grid layer work in the standard Grid manner. In the P2P layer, the Grid Services and ordinary PCs willing to participate in Grid activities can be identified as a peer with the ability to provide or consume resources provided in the Grid. By making use of this P2P layer, on the other hand, we can enable the Grid to use the vast resources on the edge of Internet in a scalable way, and at the same time, let this layer serve as a P2P routing substrate for the upper layer Grid entities. In other words, with the help of the P2P layer, ordinary PC participants can form peer groups and provide aggregated resources as Grid Service to others, meanwhile, ordinary Grid Services can use this P2P layer to communicate or coordinate with each other in a P2P manner.

The main contribution of this paper is to provide an effective and efficient model for integrating P2P networks into the Grid environment. A platform prototype, called P2PGrid, was implemented, and a sample application was developed to show the efficiency and effectiveness of the platform. Technically, Globus's OGSA/OGSI framework is chosen as the infrastructure for Grid Computing; for P2P Computing, Sun Microsystem's JXTA [2] is chosen as the primary developing platform.

The rest of the paper is organized as follows. We will firstly present works related to our paper in Section 2. Then the two-layer integration model is described in details in Section 3. Section 4 presents the system design of the P2PGrid platform, which implements the two-layer integration model. In Section 5, an example application making built on the P2PGrid platform is used to conduct experimental evaluation of the proposed framework. Finally, the conclusion section summarizes the achievements and contributions of this paper.

2 Related Works

Over the past years, work has been done on applying P2P technologies in the Grid environment to build scalable, efficient, and reliable distributed systems. Naradabrokering is a distributed middleware framework and architecture for enabling durable Peer-to-Peer Grids [12]. It aims at providing a flexible brokering system that is able to integrate grid, P2P systems, web services and other message oriented systems. It basically consists of multiple brokers, which can run either on separate machines or on clients. These brokers are interconnected in a P2P manner, forming a dynamic P2P broker cloud, through which messages can be sent and received by service publisher and subscriber. For Grid Services, by making using of Naradabrokering system, the message routing between service provider and consumer can enjoy the benefits of P2P mode of communication. However, it is more suitable to consider Naradabrokering as a P2P messaging framework for integrating different systems, rather than a system specifically designed for applying P2P techniques in the Grid environment.

In [13], a P2P style of task scheduling mechanism for Grid Computing is presented. In this mechanism, the task scheduling process is decentralized and distributed to each node on the Grid, rather than performed by a centralized scheduler node as in the traditional Grid systems. In this way, the efficiency and scalability of the Grid can be improved. One tradeoff, however, is that all the Grid entities using this scheduling mechanism will have interoperability problems with other normal Grid entities.

Since in OGSI, Grid Service is a specialized kind of Web Service, it also worth studying papers aiming at enabling interaction between Web Services with P2P applications. [24] presents a paper for enabling Web Service access for a JXTA based P2P application. This aim is achieved by implementing both the JXTA and Web Service modules on some proxies in the system, so that one form of requests can be translated correspondingly to the other form. Some issues and difficulties encountered in the paper are well discussed, most of which are originated from different level of incompatibilities between the two protocol sets (JXTA and Web Services).

Although the papers described above are different either in their purpose, methodologies, or final results, they are common in the way that they apply P2P techniques / integrate P2P applications with the Grid / Web Services. All of these papers are trying to solve their problems on a single layer, or in the other word, they are all using a horizontal way of integration. As we will discuss in the next section, this one-layer model for integration has several shortcomings.

3 Two-Layer Model for Integrating P2P Networks into the Grid

We can make use of the one-layer model as used in existing works for the horizontally integration of P2P networks with the Grid. As we choose JXTA as the P2P platform and OGSA/OGSI as the Grid infrastructure, using the one-layer model implies that we have to do the translation between the JXTA Protocols and Grid Service Protocols (mainly SOAP), and each Grid entity has to implements two modules to understand both set of protocols. Upon receiving a request in one form, a node can either choose to finish the request by itself or translate the request to another form and/or resend it to other Grid entities.

Although this type of design can be viewed as a "pure integration solution" as it integrates the two platforms at the protocol level, it would face several obstacles and problems similar to those discussed in [24] (incompatible entity identification and searching systems, different transport and messaging protocols for the communications, different security implementation models, and decreased system efficiency and increased system complexity). Maintaining current Grid systems on common PCs is already difficult to achieve, adding additional components for translating Grid and JXTA protocols will only make it further impossible to push Grid technology for commodity use.

In order to overcome the problems in the one-layer model, we propose a Tow-Layer-Model of integration. There are two layers in the system: the Grid layer and the P2P layer. In [7] a similar model is roughly mentioned as a prediction for the trend of the convergence of the Grid and P2P technologies. But neither actual implementation nor further elaboration is provided. The remaining part of this section describes this model in details. Figure 1. shows the two-layer model. In the Grid Layer, all entities work in the traditional way as specified by the current Grid standards. In particular, in our system, this layer is a Globus Layer where all the services are Grid Services defined in OGSI. In the P2P layer, all participants are peers that have the same type of identity, and can communicate in a P2P manner, self-organizing into peer groups for specific purpose. As we use JXTA as the underlying P2P platform, peers at this P2P layer are standard JXTA peers with all JXTA provided P2P functionalities like searching, discovering peers and peer groups, communicating through pipes etc.

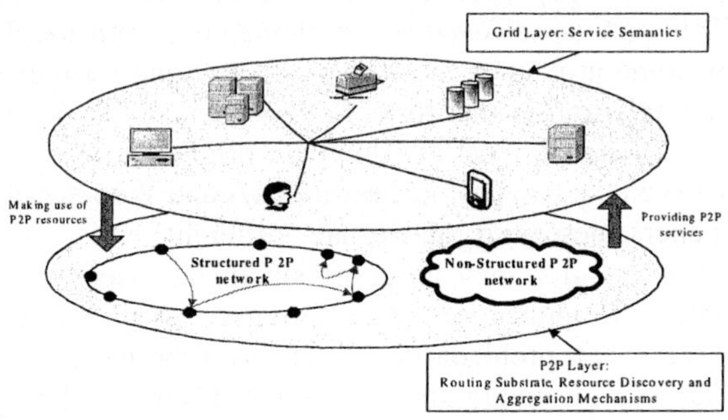

Fig. 1. Two-Layer Model of Integrating P2P Networks into the Grid

The integration of the two layers can be considered as virtualization of P2P computing resources as Grid resources. As specified conceptually in the OGSA and technically in the OGSI, in essence, the Grid Service only defines the services' "appearance", rather than the underlying implementation. Thus the Grid Service can be designed as a wrapper of the underlying P2P resources or a portal for common Grid clients to access the underlying P2P networks. For example, on the P2P layer there are many PCs forming a P2P network, sharing a set of data; this P2P group itself can actually be viewed as a single storage. This single storage can then be exposed to Grid Service clients, being wrapped as a Grid Service. In this case, at the Grid Layer, a service representing the storage is implemented by the underlying P2P resources. Grid Services on the Grid Layer can not only use the resources gained from the underlying P2P networks, but also make use of functionalities provided by the P2P layer such as P2P mode of service discovery, searching etc. In general, the Grid Layer in the two layer model is responsible for providing service semantics while the P2P layer serves as a resource pool and a routing substrate providing P2P mode of resource discovery and aggregation.

The two-layer model is preferred over the one-layer model due to several reasons. Firstly, in each layer, all the original communication mechanisms are preserved without modifications, so there would be no need of any kind of protocol translation which may pose problems as in the One Layer Model. Secondly, since the P2P layer of service implementation is separated from the Grid Layer, the more efficient way of P2P manner of communication will only be happening in the P2P layer, thus will not affect the efficiency of the upper Grid Layer. In addition, JXTA by itself is quite simple (as compared with Globus), so that for resources on the edge of Internet, it is much easier for them to donate their power to the Grid Layer through the JXTA P2P layer. In this way, we can say that the complexity for common resources for joining the Grid environment is decreased

4 The P2PGrid Platform

We have developed a prototype platform, called P2PGrid, to implement the proposed two-layer integration model. In the light of the maturity of OGSA/OGSI and GT3, we decided to choose GT3 for implementing our Grid Services. For the P2P layer, we choose to use JXTA because it is an extensible general purpose P2P development platform and is simple, efficient and interoperable.

4.1 P2PGrid System Architecture

Figure 2 shows the system architecture of the P2PGrid platform. There are mainly three parts. The round corner rectangle at the top represents the Grid Layer in the two-layer model, containing different Grid entities (Grid Service (GS), client (GSC), Grid Service Proxy (GSP), and ordinary Grid Service (oGS)). All these Grid entities communicate with each other in a standard Grid manner. GS is the Grid service that can access the underlying P2P layer. It contains a component called JXTAAgent, which enables it to create a peer, representing the existence of the Grid Service in the underlying P2P network. GSP is a kind of proxy that can help Grid Services that don't have JXTAAgent to create corresponding peers in the P2P layer.

The dotted ellipse (P2PGrid Layer) in the middle represents the P2P layer. All the entities in this layer are peers that can provide and consume resources. The only

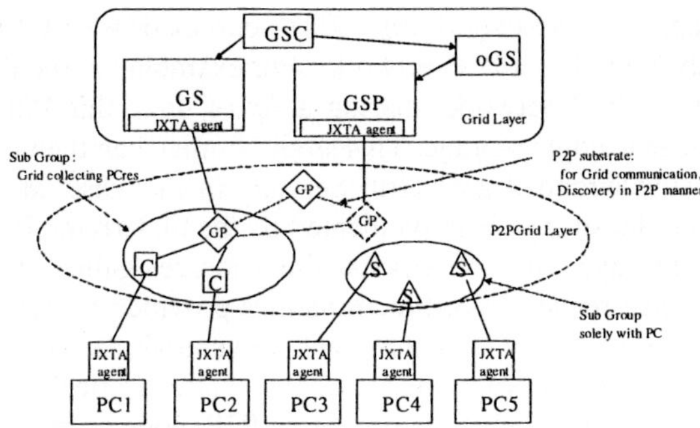

Fig. 2. P2PGrid Platform Running Architecture

difference among these peers is that some of them are created by JXTAAgent from a Grid Service (diamonds labeled "GP" for Grid Peer),and some are created by JXTAAgent from common PCs without any Grid System (Globus) installed (the "C" and "S" peers). All these peers can form peer groups and cooperate with each other in a P2P manner for certain tasks no matter where they are created (from Grid Service or common PCs). This P2P layer is implemented on the JXTA virtual network.

The array of boxes at the bottom represents PCs with ordinary capacity, i.e. resources on the edge of Internet. Each PC has to have a JXTAAgent to be able to create a peer to access the P2P Layer. JXTAAgents create peers on the P2PGrid layer, representing the existence of the corresponding PCs. Since these peers are able to communicate with Grid Peers (GPs) and can donate resources to, or use resources from the GPs, we can say that, in this way, the common PCs can provide or consume Grid resources without the hassles of maintaining Grid middleware packages (Globus).

The main component of the P2PGrid system is the JXTAAgent, which is essentially a wrapper of main JXTA functionalities. It provides the Grid Service and the PCs the ability of creating the peer, accessing the P2P network, creating, joining and leaving peer groups, communicating with pipes etc.

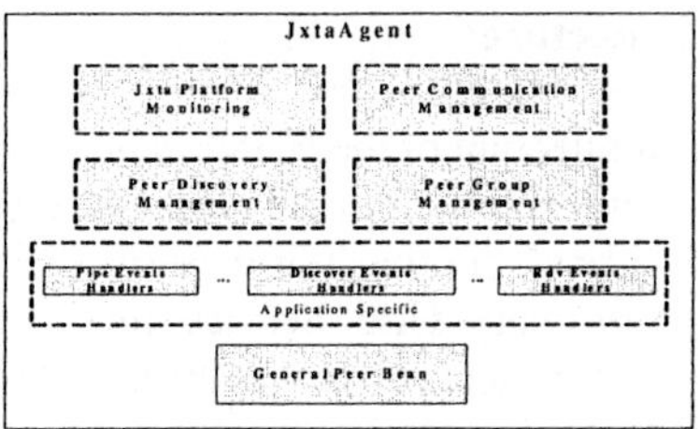

Fig. 3. General Structure of JXTAAgent

The structure of JXTAAgent is sillustrated in Figure 3. There are three main parts: General Peer Bean, event handlers, and wrappers of JXTA functionalities. General Peer Bean contains the general information of the Peer including the Peer ID, Group ID, etc.

Event Handlers contain application specific logic provided either by a Grid Service or a common PC application. In order to fulfill as many P2P applications' need as possible, the basic JXTA communication is designed to be connectionless, and unidirectional. Therefore, some discovery mechanisms are event driven. How to respond to each type of event is highly application specific, thus, intuitively, most of the application logic is implemented in different event handlers. Therefore, JXTAAgent serves as a holder of those event handlers. The wrapper modules of the functionalities provided by JXTA to build P2P applications simplify some procedures like initialization of the platform, and hide some low level details like management of communication pipes etc.

4.2 Services in P2PGrid

By making use of the P2PGrid platform, Grid services can have access to the potentially large pool of resources in the underlying P2P layer. Since peers created for the Grid Services can now communicate with each other in a P2P manner, it is possible for them to cooperate in a way that is originally impossible or difficult to achieve in the Grid Layer. P2PGrid Platform can provide many of these services. In this section, we describe three such services, namely distributed computing, enhanced P2P mode of Grid service discovery, and shared distributed storage.

Distributed Computing is one of the main motivations for enabling Grid services to access the resource on the P2P network. SETI@home [29] is a classic example showing the vast computational power that can be collected from idle PCs on the Internet. Using current Grid systems, it is difficult to implement SETI@home type of applications mainly because every participant that shares their CPU power would have to maintain Globus, which is too complicated for a common PC user. However, by making use of the P2PGrid platform, the computational resources can be collected from the P2P layer, so that there's no need for maintaining the Grid middleware. After the resources are collected, they can be shown as a standard Grid Service to be invoked by any Grid client.

Another type of important services that could be provided by the P2PGrid platform is Service Discovery. At the lowest level, the current resource discovery mechanism in the Grid (Globus in particular) is, to a large extent, centralized: Grid clients have to get the Grid Service's handle - GSH (Grid Service Handle) to be able to invoke it. Normally these GSHs of different Grid Services are stored in a special Grid Service: Registry, which plays the role of a server for providing Grid Service information to Grid clients. Therefore it is possible that upon massive client requests, the Registry may get overloaded and finally collapse, which is an inevitable flaw of systems using C/S mode of communication. Although this problem can be partially solved by making use some higher level grid services like MDS [1], it would be beneficial to solve this problem by decentralizing the Registry Service at the bottom level by putting the GSH discovery functionalities down to the P2P layer. Using the P2PGrid platform, GSHs can be distributed among multiple peers rather in a single service entity, and some efficient P2P mode of service discovery can be applied in the Grid environment for retrieving the GSHs.

Specifically the GSHs of all the Grid Services are published in the P2P layer, potentially held by many peers, or shared among a group. The Grid entity that would like to find a GSH of a Grid Service, can create a peer in the underlying P2P layer, and search the GSH on the P2P network. The search mechanisms on this P2P layer falls into the two categories: Searching on unstructured P2P networks and Searching on structured P2P networks.

For service discovery on unstructured P2P networks, Peers containing the GSHs are not organized in a structured manner. Message flooding is the basic mechanism for searching the GSH; i.e. the peer that is searching for the GSH will issue search requests to peers that it knows, if those peers don't have the GSH, they forward the search request to other peers that they know; this process continues until the GSH is found. Some message loop-back prevention mechanism is needed. Particularly in JXTA, rendezvous peers can be used to increase the efficiency of this type of search.

For searching on structured P2P networks, the Peers that have the GSHs are organized into a regular manner so as to increase the efficiency of the search. Currently the structured P2P substrate is almost a synonym of Dynamic Hash Table [7] Particularly a GSH can be assigned a unique hash number or a key. The requestor that would like to find the GSH can randomly choose one node which is a part of the DHT to start the search. Before the maximum number of jumps is reached, the GSH should be able to be found; otherwise it means the GSH is not known in the key space of the DHT.

Another possible application of our P2PGrid platform is to implement a *Shared Distributed Storage System*. Intuitively this kind of service can be implemented by letting common peers to open a local storage space, and the Grid Peer will be responsible for collecting these storages and exposing the integrated storage as a whole at the Grid Layer, providing Grid Storage services to others. A directory mechanism is needed to be implemented in the Grid Peer; also, similar to Distributed Computing services, auditing mechanisms are needed to ensure there is not data lost or corruption.

5 Experiments with P2PGrid

We have built an example application on P2PGrid to experiment with the platform and evaluate the effectiveness and performance. In this section, we describe the application, its implementation issues, and performance evaluation results.

5.1 Example Application

The application is to render a fractal pattern as a colorful picture (Mandelbrot Set) - implementing the Mandelbrot Algorithm to render an image with a fractal pattern, and visualizing the Mandelbrot set in the Complex Number Space [26]. It is parallel in nature - the whole image is cut into multiple slides, and each slide is given to a worker node to calculate the color of each pixel in that slide according to the Mandelbrot algorithm. Figure 4 shows an example image generated by our application.

The application is designed to show some services provided by the P2PGrid system. We applied two services supported by the P2PGrid platform in this example application: Distributed Computing and the P2P mode of Service Discovery. The functionality of rendering the picture is exposed as a Grid Service, but the underlying implementation (calculating the color of different parts of the picture) is done by peers on the P2P layer. This is the sample application of the Distributed Computing Service.

In addition, the Grid client that invokes the Mandelbrot Service adopts the P2P mode of service discovery to get the GSH of the Mandelbrot Service. For simplicity, the discovery mechanism is based on the unstructured P2P way of resource discovery.

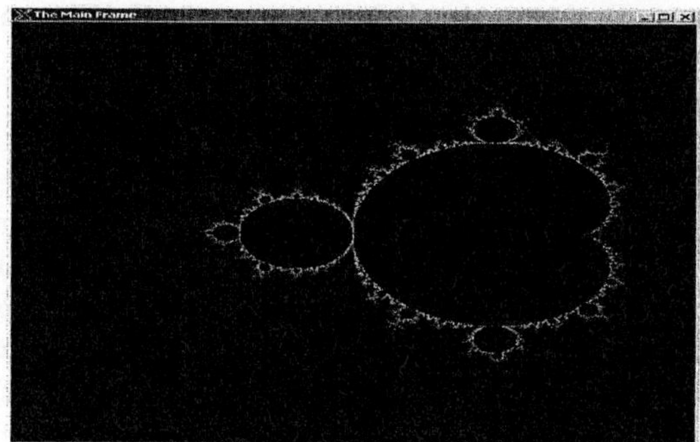

Fig. 4. Fractal Pattern Visualization of Mandelbrot Set

The whole system is deployed into seven cluster nodes: Ostrich021 is the one exposing Mandelbrot Grid Service providing the function of rendering a Mandelbrot Set image. Ostrich028 serves as the Mandelbrot Grid Service Client which will trigger the calculation of the Mandelbrot set on ostrich021. Ostrich027 is the peer that contains the GSH of the Mandelbrot Service for ostrich028 to use to invoke the Mandelbrot Grid Service. Ostrich022 to ostrich025 are worker peers that will donate their computational powers to the ostrich021 to calculate the Mandelbrot set. Figure 5 shows the application workflow. There are two phases in the entire workflow: P2P Service Discovery (step 0 to step 3), and Distributed Computing (step 4 to step7). Figure 8 shows the details of the application workflow.

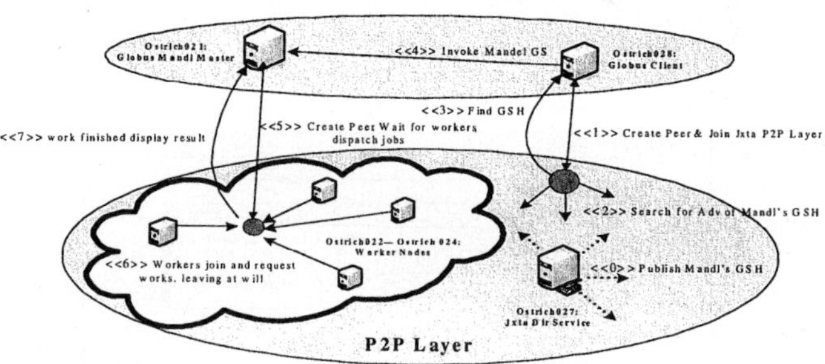

Fig. 5. Application Workflow

5.2 Performance Evaluation

The performance metrics used are execution time and speed-up. Suppose m is the number of jobs in the task, t is the average amount of time for processing each job, and n is the number of workers. The total amount of time for completing the whole task is given by $T = (m / n) \times t = m \times t \times (1 / n)$. Thus, we have $T = C / n$, where $C = m \times t$. This function describes the ideal relationship of the total time used for calculating the entire Mandelbrot Set at a specific resolution. As the value of C is not certain, we decided to take the total amount of time needed for n = 1 as C. The speed-up for parallel computing is defined as:

Speedup = (Completion time for 1 node) / (Completion time for N nodes)

We did the experiments of generating 300*300 Mandelbrot Set Image. The number of worker nodes ranges from 1 to 6 (in order to get more experimental results, when doing the experiment, we also include ostrich027 and ostrich028 in as worker peers). The worker nodes can join in the work at any time, and can leave even when the work is not finished yet. The computational pool is add-hoc rather than pre-structured. This is one of the main motivations for Integrating P2P networks into the Grid Environment. In the experiment, to simulate the unreliable and add-hoc nature of the P2P network, we intentionally stopped some of the worker nodes when it has not yet finished its job got from the Master node. Finally, the master's auditing mechanism ensures all the jobs has been dispatched and received, with no case of failure in collecting enough and correct results.

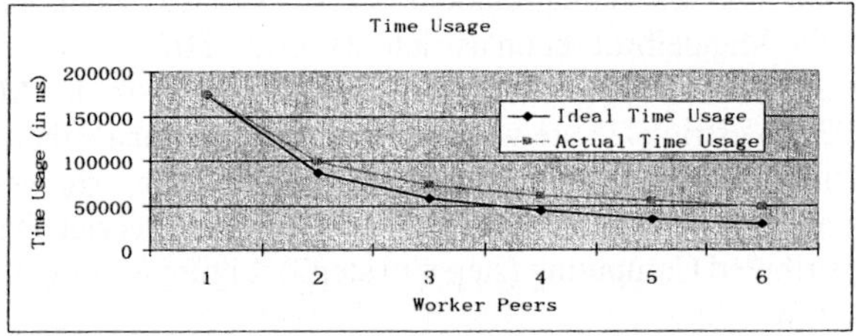

Fig. 6. Experimental Result: Time Usage

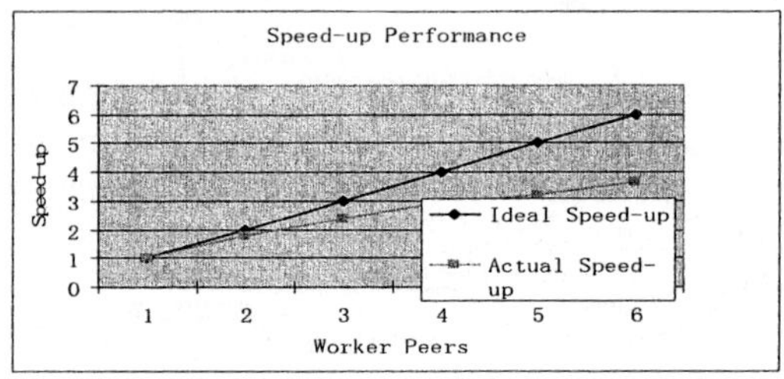

Fig. 7. Experimental Result: Speed-up

Due to the unreliable nature of the P2P networks (especially the flooding way of resource discovery), for each case of *n* number of nodes, we did 5 experiments, and the mean value of the total amount of time used is taken as the total amount of time needed for completely calculating the 300*300 Mandelbrot set. Since at $n = 1$, the tested total amount of time is 173597ms The C value is taken as 173597. Figure 6 shows the experimental result of the time usage when the number of peer worker increases and its difference between the ideal case. As we can see from the figure, as the number of nodes increases the system will use more times than the idea case. This reflects the system overheard over the communication.

Figure 7 shows the speed-up of the system. We can see that, basically, the systems achieve the desirable speedup, but the system also has overhead. The overheard is mainly from the communication cost between worker nodes and the master nodes. As a loosely coupled distributed parallel application, the overhead of inter-node communication is more significant than those highly coupled distributed systems. On the other hand, the more time each node needs to complete a job, the better the speed-up performance would be. This is has been proved by our experience: at the beginning, we implemented the application in the way that each worker peer will calculate a pixel of the image each time, rather than a part of the image. In that case, the time spent on the actual work calculation is too short compared with the communication overhead, so that the speed up is too bad to accept.

On average, Globus platform initialization time is 42s, whereas JXTA platform initialization time is around 5.6s (mean value calculated from all experimental results). This is a clear indication showing the fact that Globus is relatively heavy-weighted, regardless of the extra installation, maintenance and development complexity.

In addition, installing Globus and deploying services is not an easy task as using JXTA, it needs understandings of many related technologies. On the other hand, deploying a pure JXTA based component (as in our P2PGrid environment), is fairly easy (in principle, you just need to make sure that all 5 JXTA library jar files exist on your classpath, the P2PGrid will work). Therefore, without our system, if someone would like to implement a similar service using pure Globus, all worker nodes would require Globus installed, in which case the installing, deploying and maintenance overhead would be much higher than in the two layer model P2PGrid platform.

6 Conclusion

In this paper, we considered the benefits of integrating the two popular computing paradigms of Grid and Peer-to-Peer computing. Grid computing and P2P computing have many similar features and thus have the trend to converge. This paper shows a possible solution for integrating the P2P networks into the Grid environment: by making use of a Two-Layer Model. Each entity on the Grid Layer has a corresponding peer in the underlying P2P network layer. The underlying P2P layer on the other hand is also accessible by peers created by machines that do not have Grid middleware installed. All the peers communicate and coordinate in the P2P layer in a P2P manner, while the Grid entities on the Grid Layer still work with each other in a standard Grid manner.

We have developed the P2PGrid platform that implements the two layer model and developed an example application to show the performance of the system. From the application example, we can see that by making use of the P2PGrid platform, the Grid can benefit from: (a) P2P mode of communiction, providing decentralization to prevent single point of failure, add-hoc resource utilization, higher scalibility of the system, and efficient message routing and service discovery mechanisms; (b) reduced development and maintenance complexity of Grid Systems; (c) increased efficiency for the Grid to leverage the resources on the edge of Internet, which means P2PGrid can help common PC users to participate Grid activities without the harness of maintaining complicated Grid middleware.

Acknowledgement

This work is partially supported by Hong Kong University Grant Council under the CERG grant B-Q822 (PolyU 5183/04E).

References

1. Globus: www.globus.org
2. JXTA: www.JXTA.org
3. Foster, I., Kesselman, C. and Tuecke, S. The Anatomy of the Grid: Enabling Scalable Virtual Organizations. International Journal of High Performance Computing applications,15 (3). 200-222. 2001 www.globus.org/research/papers/anatomy.pdf
4. Foster, I., Kesselman, C. Nick, J. and Tuecke, S. The physiology of the grid: An open grid services architecture for distributed systems integration. http://www.globus.org/research/papers/ogsa.pdf , 2002
5. Traversat, B., Abdelaziz, M., Duigu, M. Hugly, J. Pouyoul, E. and Yeager, B. Paper JXTA Virtual Network, Sun Microsystem, Inc
6. Asadzadeh, P. Buyya, R. Chun, L.K., Nayar, D., and Venugopal, S. Global Grids and Software Tookits: A Study of Four Grid Middleware Technologies, Software-Practice and Experience, 2002
7. Foster, I., Kesselman, C. The Grid 2: Blueprint for a New Computing Infrastructure. Morgan Kaufmann Press, 2004, ISBN: 1-55860-933-4
8. Flenner, R., Abbott, M., Boubez, T., Cohen, F., Krishnan, N., Moffet, A., Ramamurti, R., Siddiqui, B., and Sommers, F. Java P2P UNLEASHED with JXTA, Web Services, XML, Jini, JavaSpaces, and J2EE, Press SAMS, 2002, ISBN: 0-672-32399-0
9. Brookshier, D., Govoni, D., and Krishnan, N. JXTA: Java P2P Programming. Press SAMS, 2002 ISBN: 0672323664
10. Ledlie,J. Shneidman, Seltzer, J. and Huth, J. Scooped, Again iptps03.cs.berkeley.edu/final-papers/ scooped.pdf
11. Talia, D., and Trunfio, P. Toward a Synergy Between P2P and Grids IEEE Internet Computing IEEE Computer Society 1089-7801/03/ 2003 IEEE
12. Shrideep Pallickara and Geoffrey Fox, NaradaBrokering: A Distributed Middleware Framework and Architecture for Enabling Durable Peer-to-Peer Grids in Proceedings of ACM/IFIP/USENIX International Middleware Conference Middleware-2003, Rio Janeiro, Brazil June 2003
13. Cao, J. Kwong, O. M.K., Wang, X. and Cai, W. A Peer-to-Peer Approach to Task Scheduling in Computation Grid, Grid and Cooperative Computing: Second International Workshop, GCC 2003, Shanhai, China, December 7-10, 2003, Revised Papers, Part I

14. Beiriger, J. Jhnson, W., Bivens, H., Humphreys, S.and Rhea, R., Constructing the ASCI Grid. In Proc. 9th IEEE Symposium on High Performance Distributed Computing, 2000 IEEE Press
15. Brunett, S., Czajkowski, K., Fitzgerald, S., Foster, I, Johonson, A., Kesselman, C., Leigh, J. and Tuecke, S., Appication Experiences with the Gloubus Toolkit. In Proc. 7th IEEE Symp. On High Performance Distributed Computing, 1998, IEEE Press, 81, 89.
16. Johonson, W.E., Gannon, D. and Nitzberg, B., Grids as Production Computing Environments: The Engineering Aspects of NASA's Information Power Grid. In Proc. 8th IEEE Symposium on High Performance Distributed Computing, 1999, IEEE Press.
17. Grimshaw, A. and Wulf, W., Legion - A View from 50,000 Feet. In Proc. 5th IEEE Symposium on High Performance Distributed Computing, 1996, IEEE Press,89-99
18. Open Grid Service Infrastructure Working Group: https://forge.gridforum.org/papers/ogsi-wg
19. Edited by Nabrzyski,J, Schopf, J.M., and Weglarz, J. Grid Resource Management: State of the Art and Future Trends. P413-415, Kluwer Academic Publishers. 2004 ISBN 1-4020-7575-8
20. Stefan Saroiu, Krishna P. Gummadi, Steven D. Gribble, Measuring and analyzing the characteristics of Napster and Gnutella hosts Multimedia Systems, Springer-Verlag New York, Inc. Secaucus, NJ, USA, 2003
21. Josh Cates, Robust and Efficient Data Management for a Distributed Hash Table, Master'sThesis, Massachusetts Institute of Technology, May, 2003
22. AIT Rowstron, P Druschel; Pastry: Scalable, decentralized object location and, Middleware, 2001 - springerlink.com
23. I Stoica, R Morris, D Karger, MF Kaashoek, Chord: A Scalable Peertopeer Lookup Service for Internet Applications, SIGCOMM, 2001 - portal.acm.org
24. Changtao Qu, Wolfgang Nejdl, Interacting the Edutella/JXTA Peer-to-Peer Network with Web Services, Applications and the Internet, 2004. Proceedings.
25. J Verbeke, N Nadgir, G Ruetsch, I Sharapov, Framework for Peer-to-Peer Distributed Computing in a Heterogeneous, Decentralized Environment, GRID, 2002 - springerlink.com
26. Mandelbrot and Julia Set Overview: http://www.gpf-omics.com/dl/mandel/java/docs/mandel.html
27. Gnutella, www.gnutella.wego.com
28. Napster: http://www.napster.com
29. SETI@home: http://setiathome.ssl.berkeley.edu

An Efficient Content-Based Notification Service Routed over P2P Network

Xixiang Hu[1,3], Yuexuan Wang[2], and Yunhe Pan[1]

[1] College of Computer Science & Technology, Zhejiang University, Hangzhou 310027, China
huxx@zjip.com

[2] National CIMS Engineering Research Center, Department of Automation, Tsinghua University, Beijing 100084, China
wangyuexuan@tsinghua.edu.cn

[3] College of Computer and Software, Hangzhou Dianzi University, Hangzhou 310018, China
huxx@hziee.edu.cn

Abstract. Event-based, Publish/Subscribe, systems are receiving increasingly greater attention as a prevalent approach to decouple various large-scale distributed applications such as Internet wide systems. However, their efficiency is closely tied to the architecture of the underlying notification service, which conveys the event notifications from publishers to subscribers. Peer-to-Peer network topology can offer inherently bounded delivery depth, load sharing and self-organization. In this paper, we present a content-based notification service system over peer-to-peer network topology, and couple it with an efficient filter model and routing algorithms. We also study the performance of our approaches, comparing them with corresponding works. The result shows that our approaches greatly reduce network bandwidth for subscription or filter update propagation, and storage requirement for keeping filter routing information.

1 Introduction

Publish/subscribe system has become a new paradigm for building large-scale distributed systems. It has the advantages of loosely coupling communication partners and providing a simple applications programming model. In publish/subscribe systems, both producers and consumers of messages (called subscriptions or event notifications), are clients of an underlying notification service. Event notifications are sent to the notification service system via a *publish()* interface rather than being published to specific receivers. The notification service observes the occurrence of event notifications publishing from any producers/publishers, and conveys the published event notifications to all interested consumers/subscribers with a matching subscription set. Publishers, who are completely unaware of the existence of the consumers, deliver event notifications through notification service system by specifying the values of a set of defined attributes. The consumers are expressing their interest through appropriate subscriptions and wait until they are informed about a matching to their interest events.

H. Zhuge and G.C. Fox (Eds.): GCC 2005, LNCS 3795, pp. 884 – 893, 2005.

The underlying notification service infrastructure of publish/subscribe systems, relies on a network of event brokers, which forward notifications according to filter-based routing table. The topology of the event brokers network affects the performance of the overall system significantly, and it is often chosen to be a single tree in order to simplify the routing algorithms. However, the single tree is a bottleneck of the system, because each node is a single point of failure and the central nodes are likely to carry the major part of the load. In order to provide more reliable and scalable topology for notification routing, the paper presents a publish/subscribe notification service routed over a peer-to-peer network. The peer-to-peer network can offer inherently bounded delivery depth, load sharing and self-organization. Moreover, an efficient filter model was presented based on subscription mergence and routing algorithms for notification or filter update propagation. Finally, we evaluate the performances of our approaches, against a baseline approach where all brokers broadcast their subscriptions to all, and against the well-known SIENA subsumption-based algorithm [12]. Compared to other methods, our approaches performed well on reducing network traffic for subscription or filter update propagation, and storage requirement for keeping subscriptions or filter routing information.

2 Related Works

Many publish/subscribe system exist that implement different variants of the publish/subscribe model. A major distinction is how event subscriptions express the interest of event subscribers. Generally speaking, three are three forms of publish/subscribe model with respect to subscription mechanism. The first is called channel-based or topic-based system. The topic-based systems [1,2] are similar the newsgroups, which categorize events into predefined groups. Users subscribe to the groups of interest and receive all events/notifications for these groups. The others are called subject-based systems. In subject-based systems [8,9], each event notification contains a well-known tag describing it subject, which give users the ability to express their interests about event subjects flexibly by using string patterns. By extending the domain of filters to whole content of notifications we obtain another class of subscriptions called content-based, conceptually very similar to subject-based system. However, They allow subscribers to declare their interests with respect to contents of the events by more expressive and readable filters and enable some consistency checking.

Normally, the large-scale publish/subscribe applications are realized as distributed content-based notification service systems, avoiding the lack of scalability and tolerance of centralized approaches. However, most distributed content-based notification service based on structured network use routing tree to disseminate the events to interested users based on multicast techniques [4,5,7]. Some other attempts use the notion of rendezvous nodes, which ensure that events and subscriptions meet in the system [3].

Above works efficiently implement a simple form of publish/subscribe. However, these systems just propagate notifications or subscriptions in a simple routing model, broadcasting subscriptions or filter among neighbor nodes. Each network node keeps a very large routing table to keep incoming subscriptions or filter information.

Obviously, the routing table size grows linearly with the number of subscriptions as active filters are simply added to the routing table in a simple routing mode. This will not only result in expensive routing filter entries covering, but also increasing network traffic heavily.

When we present a content-based notification service system routed over Chord [6], a representative DHT scheme, and couple it with an efficient filter model and routing algorithms. It not only takes advantage of the features of the scalability and fault tolerance of a P2P system, but also provides a performance improvement for network bandwidth and storage requirement of whole system.

3 Design Philosophy

Chord is a fairly simple structured peer-to-peer network based on Distributed Hash Tables (DHTs). DHTs have been widely adopted to create peer-to-peer data networks, such as CAN [10], Pastry [11]. All of these systems were built to allow efficient key lookup. In steady state with a N-node system, each node maintains information about only O(log N) other nodes, and resolves all lookups via O(log N) messages to other nodes. The concept from DHT is applied to the notification and subscription propagation in our notification service.

We assume that we have an efficient and robust DHT available as the underlying infrastructure. The goal is to build an efficient and robust notification propagation path for our notification service. In our notification service system, the nodes of topology graph are special broker machines which publish/subscribe on behalf of themselves and possibly loosely connected client machines. They maintain connections to several peer broker nodes in order to route notifications and subscriptions. Each directed edge in our topology graph is a network link joining two brokers. On each edge there associates exactly one content-based filter, which determines if an event notification should be forwarded to the associated peer broker. The filter may update as new subscriptions received.

It is known that a more general graph than a tree is required in most cases. However, there is no purpose in sending a given notification or filter update to the same node many times. Therefore, to ensure that a given notification or filter update is forwarded to a broker node only once, every broker node use a different spanning subtree of entire graph to propagate notifications or subscriptions. That means each broker node is at the root of its own distinct tree to use for delivering a published notification. On the other hand, the subscriptions from any of the nodes in that tree must propagate up that tree to make the routing of whole topology graph behave correctly. For example, let the path $u \rightarrow v$ denote the route taken in the tree rooted at u to publish a notification to v. Then the subscription tree rooted at v must follow $u \rightarrow v$ in reverse to reach u. Otherwise, it may happen that a notification will be dropped early.

Every edge in the spanning trees associates with a filter, which determines if an event notification will be forwarded to the peer node. A filter consists of a set of subscriptions. A given set of filters can be merged into a new filter if there is no cover among them. Perfectly merged filters only accept notifications that are accepted by at least one of the base filter. We also should ensure the filters on a route of the trees keep partial descending order to make globally correct filter decision locally at each node. In next section we will discuss them in more detail.

4 Implementation

4.1 Notation Definition

Definition 1. We define our topology graph of the notification service infrastructure as $G=(G_V, G_E)$ for the sets of vertices and edges respectively. Where, G_V represents the set of all brokers. G_E represents the set of all publishable event notification. $N=|G_V|$ is the number of broker nodes in the graph.

Definition 2. $(u, v) \in G_E$ denotes the directed edge from $u \in G_V$ to $v \in G_V$. In text,$(u \to v)$ is used to denote (u, v) for readability. Whenever edges are indicated such as $v \to w$, the edge is always interpreted with direction with respect to publishing.

Definition 3. Those edges leaving a node u, call its publishing edges and denote the set of target nodes with $p(u \in G_V)=\{ v \in G_V \mid (u, v) \in G_E \} \cup \{ u \}$.The loopback edge, $u \to u$, is used by u to express its and its clients' subscriptions.

Definition 4. Those edges entering a node u, call its subscription edges and denote the peer nodes with $s(v \in G_V)=\{u \in G_V \mid (u, v) \in G_E \} \cup \{ v \}$ .The loopback edge, $v \to v$, is used by v to publish notifications on its own behalf.

Definition 5. Define $f((u \to v) \in G_E) \to A \subseteq G_E$ as a filter function mapping an edge to the set A of event notifications which the corresponding filter accepts.

Definition 6. A Responsibility Function, $r_{u \in G_V}(v \in G_V) \to R \subseteq K$, is a function returning the subset R of the Key space which node u holds and v responsible for forwarding publishing notification to those keys' nodes directly.

Definition 7. Define $p_{\frac{1}{2^k}}(u \in G_V)$ denotes a peer node $w \in p(u)$ such that w is at the least $1/2^k$ clockwise around the circle from u.

4.2 Construction of Spanning Tree

An efficient and robust tree structure is built and maintained to propagate notifications and subscriptions. We assume that an efficient DHT with a circular and continuous namespace. Each node u has a location on the circle and a function, $key(u \in G_V) \to k \in K$, maps node u to its key value k. The spanning tree for a node constructs as follows:

Step 1. For $k=1,...m$ (*ex*, m=160), a node u selects an edge to the first node which is clockwise by a distance of $1/2^k$ or more along the circle. That is,

$$p(u)=\{ p_{\frac{1}{2^k}}(u \in G_V), k=1...m \} \quad (1)$$

Step 2. Node u takes all of the nodes got from (1) and draws them in their appropriate locations on the circle.

Step 3. Node u assigns responsibility $r_u(v)$ to each $v \in p(u)$ by taking the section of the circle clockwise of node v up to the next node. Therefore, the entire key space is partitioned. when the network contains $N=2^4$ nodes, for node u, the entire key space is partitioned for five segments by $u, v_1, v_2, v_3, v_4 \in p(u)$. The notifications follows the path indicated in figure 1. Pulling this routing out of the circle, we get the spanning tree of node u.

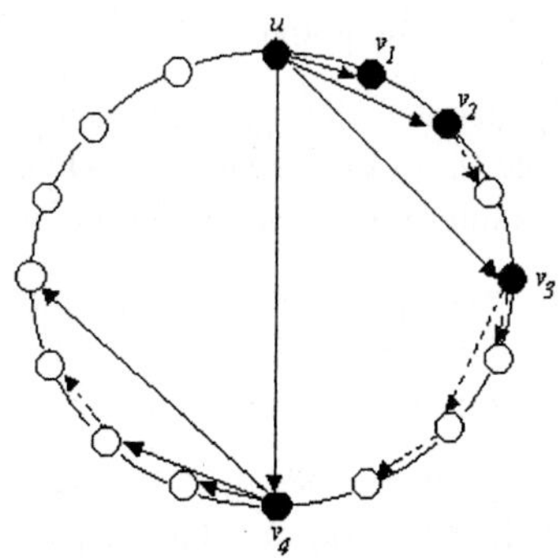

Fig. 1. Node u connects with $v_1, v_2, v_3, v_4 \in p(u)$ directly and then each of them takes the responsibility to deliver notifications to others nodes in $r_u(v_i)$

In P2P environment, the nodes often join and leave dynamically, so we need to maintain the tree carefully. Upon a new node w joining, the node publishes a special node-join notification message including *key(w)*. All nodes u subscribe for a node-join notification in range, $[Key(u)+|K|/2^k, Key(p_{\frac{1}{2^k}}(u)))$. Thus, when a w joins inside this range, u can update its $p_{\frac{1}{2^k}}(u)$ peer to be w and node w set u as one of its subscription peer, adding u *to* $s(w)$. At same time, w also publishes another special node-location notification to find $p_{\frac{1}{2^k}}(w)$ nodes as $p(w)$.

In some cases, a node v or edge $u \to v$ fails, the peer node u need to seek a new neighbor peer and reestablished associated edges. And the new peer takes in hand the responsibility of $r_u(v)$ for the failed node v.

4.3 Processing Subscriptions

If a notification is distributed through one tree, a subscription from any of the nodes in that tree must propagate up that tree. When $u \to v$ denotes the route taken in the tree rooted at u to publish a notification to v, then the subscription tree rooted at v must follow in reverse to reach u. This is necessary to ensure published notification to follow a path on which the filters are always subset so that no early filter will reject a notification which would have been accepted later. i.e., for a path $u \rightarrow v \rightarrow w$, the follow equation must always be kept true.

$$\forall u \in G_V \forall v \in p(u) \forall w \in p(v) : r_u(v) \cap r_v(w) \neq 0 = f(u - v) \supseteq f(v - w) \quad (2)$$

A subscription may lead to loopback filter update on the originating node. Only when the filter updates, the originating node propagates a filter update message up that tree. As a node u receives a filter update message from a peer v with a filter g, it checks if the filter $f(u \rightarrow v)$already covers g. If $f(u \rightarrow v)$ does cover g, u stops processing. Otherwise, u must merge $f(u \rightarrow v)$ *and* g, *set* $f = f(u \rightarrow v) \cup g$.

In order to maintain the invariant (2) correct, every node should have an algorithm to correctly calculate the filter and propagate it to subscription edges' peer nodes. Considering a node v, it calculates the filter as following algorithm.

for $\forall x \in p(v)$ and $\forall u \in s(v)$ do

if $r_u(v) \cap r_v(x) \neq 0$ then

$$f(u - v) = f(u - v) \cup f(v - x)$$

When node v receives a filter update message from its publishing peer nodes $p(v)$, v propagates the filter set f to the peer node $s(v)$. This algorithm will terminate with the edge which crosses 1/2 key space.

4.4 Processing Notification

We simply supposed that messages which carry an event notification include a range field, $r \in k$. The range field indicates that the receiving node is responsible for delivering the notification to all interested nodes whose keys are in the range $[key(v), r)$. Before sending a notification message, the publishing node first sets the initial range to the entire key space of the circle. Assumed that a node u receives a notification e for range $[key(u), r)$ via loopback edge, u processes the notification e according to the following algorithm.

Set $R_u = [key(u), r)$

for $\forall v \in p(u)$ do

set $R_v' = R_u \cap r_u(v)$

if $R_v' \neq 0$ and $e \in f(u \bullet v)$ then

route e down edge $u \bullet v$,

update e with new range, R_v'

The algorithm matching *e* against the filter $f(u \rightarrow v)$ is discussed in following section. The above algorithm ensured that a notification would not be delivered to a node out of the range of R_v' and at most once to nodes in the range of R_v'. It means,, let *u* be a publisher of notification *e* and *v* a subscriber for event notification *F* with $e \in F$. If no edges on the delivery path fail during delivery of *e*, we guarantee that *v* receives *e*.

5 Filter Model

As previously noted that each edge associates with a filter. The filter determines whether a notification is forwarded to a peer broker. In previous studies such as SIENA[12], the filter bases on subsumption relations among subscriptions, which is called subscription-centric. However, our contribution is based on subscription merging. The schema of subscription consists of a fix set of attributes, such as a finite sequence $V=\{v_1, v_2,..., v_n\}$. Each attributes v_i has a type $type(v_i) \in \{INTEGER, DOUBLE, STRING\}$, and a corresponding domain $D_{type(vi)}$ of constants. Usually, a subscription message simply is a partial assignment to the attributes, i.e., a mapping m: $V \rightarrow \bigcup_{v \in V} D_{type(v)} \cup \{NULL\}$, which can also be denoted a pattern expression, for example, *7.0<price<8.4*, *symbol=*T**. A pattern actually is a constraint on a range of the attribute value.

Our filter is defined as a set of attribute and patterns tuple, illustrated as follows.

$$F=\{<v_i, pattern_1, pattern_2,....pattern_n>\},\ v_i, \in V,\ \bigcap_j pattern_j = 0 \tag{3}$$

Each incoming subscription is dissolved into *<attribute, pattern>* pairs, which are in turn merged into the filter data structure (3). Only when the incoming subscription updates the set of associated filter F, it need to propagate the filter update message to related peer broker. Otherwise it is unnecessary to propagate every subscription among brokers. This will ensure performance benefits with respect to 1) the network bandwidth required to propagate subscription among brokers and 2) the storage overhead to maintain them. The algorithm for matching an incoming message *e* against the filter *F* associated with an edge is as follows:

```
Set K=sizeof(V)
Set R=2^K-1, //R is a binary of K bits
for each v_i∈V of notification e do
  if value(v_i) ∈ ⋃_j F.v_i.pattern_j then R=R &2^i
if R & 2^(K-1) =2^(K-1) then
      e∈F   // F accept e
else
      F filter out e              //F reject e
```

The proposed filter paradigm not only result in faster filtering and matching of incoming notifications, but also greatly reducing the communication among brokers since there is no need to propagate every incoming subscriptions.

6 Analysis of Performance

From Chord, the DHT infrastructure provides an efficient way to maintain the topology graph shaped via O(log N) message. In this section, our method is compared with a baseline approach where all brokers broadcast their subscriptions to all, and being compared to the SIENA's subsumption-based algorithm. In our simulation, the network has total 50 peer brokers.

1) The network bandwidth performance for subscription or filter update propagation
We measured the network bandwidth performance as the cost for all brokers to propagate their subscriptions or filter update messages in a period. Figure 2 presents the total bandwidth measured in message number.

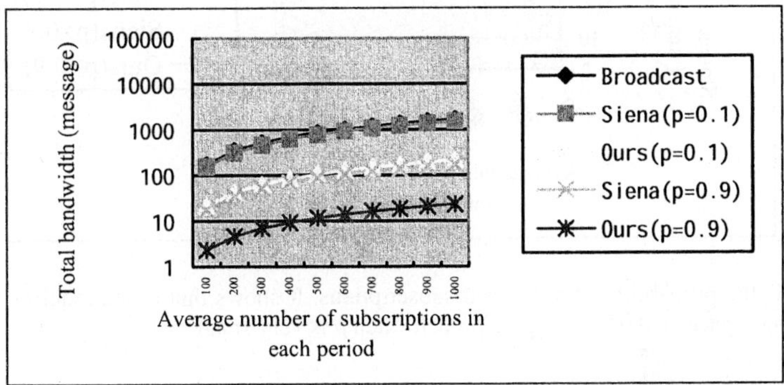

Fig. 2. The y-axis is logarithmic. p is the probability of subsumed subscriptions. It is obviously stated that our approach is better than the others with respect to network bandwidth requirement.

2) Hops performance for notification propagation
We measure the number of hops needed for a notification to be routed to all matched brokers. In our approach the filter associated with each edge determines the routing path of notifications. In SIENA, the routing paths for events are set by subscriptions received. We study both methods for varying event popularities. Figure 3 shows the mean number of hops required to process 100 events or notifications for each broker.

3) Storage Requirement for Subscription or Filter
Figure 4 shows the total storage requirement across all brokers, where each broker receives and propagates a varying number of subscriptions or filter update in each period. It is shown that our approach cost less storage requirement for storing filter

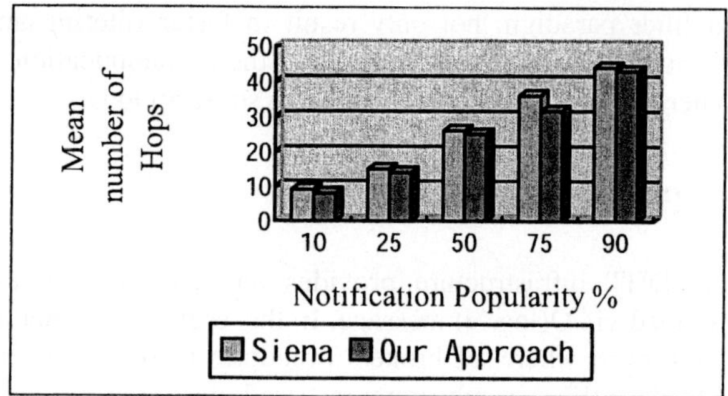

Fig. 3. Our approach is shown to be a little better than the Siena's when notification popularity varies from 10% to 90%

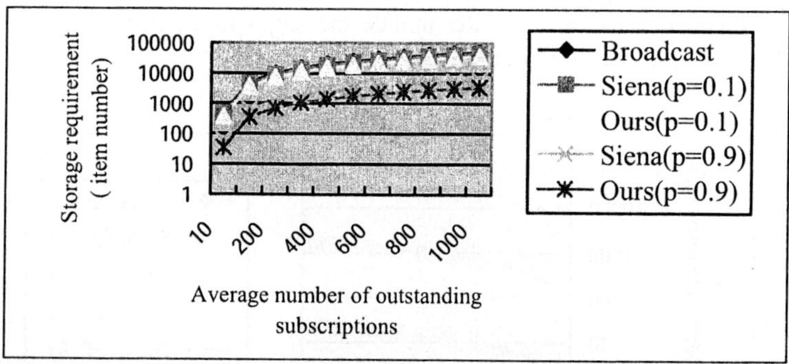

Fig. 4. p is the probability of subsumed subscriptions. It shows that Siena requires almost the same storage space as the broadcast approach when p is very small.

information than Siena's. The reason for this improvement lies in the generalization per attribute achieved by our filter patterns.

7 Conclusion

A new paradigm for publish/subscribe notification service systems is built on top of a P2P network. It distributes load equally by maintaining independent delivery tree for each node. Details of algorithm of notification and filter update propagation are provided and proven correct. These algorithms ensured that a notification is forwarded to a broker node only once. Moreover, we present a filter model based on the generalization of subscriptions and the corresponding algorithm for routing notifications. Our results show that it can achieve a big improvement based on the bandwidth requirements, hop count to propagate subscriptions, and storage requirement for subscription or filter information. The main advantage of our system is the unique combination of efficient content-based filter and the scalability and fault tolerance of a P2P system.

References

1. M. Castro, P. Druschel, A. Kermarrec, and A. Rowstron.: Scribe: A large-scale and decentralized application-level multicast infrastructure. IEEE Journal on Selected Areas in Communication, Vol. 20. IEEE Press, New York (2002)
2. S. Q. Zhuang, B. Y. Zhao, A. D. Joseph, R. H. Katz, and J. D. Kubiatowicz.: Bayeux: An architecture for scalable and fault-tolerant wide-area data dissemination. 11th ACM NOSSDAV. ACM Press, New York (2001) 11-20
3. P. R. Pietzuch and J. Bacon.: Peer-to-Peer Overlay Broker Networks in an Event-Based Middleware, in Proceedings of the DEBS'03 conference. ACM Digital Library (2003)
4. G. Banavar, T. Chandra, B. Mukherjee, J. Nagarajarao, R. E. Strom, and D. C. Sturman.: An efficient multicast protocol for content-based publish-subscribe systems. In Proceedings of the 19th ICDCS. IEEE Press, New York (1999) 262–272
5. A. Carzaniga, D. S. Rosenblum, and A. L. Wolf.: Design and evaluation of a wide-area event notification service. ACM Transactions on Computer Systems, Vol. 19. ACM Press, New York (2001) 332–383
6. I. Stoica, R. Morris, D. Karger, F. Kaashoek, and H. Balakrishnan.: Chord: A scalable Peer-To-Peer lookup service for internet applications. In Proceedings of the 2001 ACM SIGCOMM Conference, ACM Press, New York (2001) 149-160
7. P. Triantafillou, A. Economides.: Subscription Summarization: A New Paradigm for Efficient Publish/Subscribe Systems, In proceedings of the ICDCS'04. IEEE Press, New York (2004)
8. G. Cugola, E. D. Nitto, and A. Fuggetta.: The JEDI event-based infrastructure and its application to the development of OPSS WFMS. IEEE Transactions on Software Engineering, Vol. 27. IEEE Press, New York (2001)
9. B. Oki, M. Pfluegl, and A. Siegel.: The Information Bus – an architecture for extensible distributed systems. Operating Systems Review, Vol. 27. ACM Press (1993) 58–68
10. S. Ratnasamy, P. Francis, M. Handley, R. Karp, and S. Schenker.: A scalable Content-Addressable network. In Proceedings of the 2001 Conference on Applications, Technologies, Architectures, and Protocols for Computer Communications (SIGCOMM), San Diego, California, United States, ACM Press (2001) 61-172
11. A. Rowstron and P. Druschel.: Pastry: scalable, decentralized object location and routing for large-scale peer-to-peer systems. In Proceedings of the 18th IFIP/ACM International Conference on Distributed Systems Platforms (Middleware), volume 2218 of LNCS. Springer-Verlag, Heidelberg Germany (2001) 329-350
12. Antonio Carzaniga.: Architectures for an Event Notification Service Scalable to Wide-Area Networks. PhD thesis. Politecnico di Milano, Milano, Italy, December (1998)

Distribution of Mobile Agents in Vulnerable Networks

Wenyu Qu[1], Hong Shen[1], and Yingwei Jin[2]

[1] Graduate School of Information Science,
Japan Advanced Institute of Science and Technology,
1-1 Asahidai, Tatsunokuchi, Ishikawa, 923-1292, Japan
[2] Dalian University of Technology Press,
Dalian University of Technology,
No 2, Linggong Road, Ganjinzi District, Dalian, 116024, China

Abstract. This paper focuses on behavior analysis on mobile agents used in network routing. We describe a general agent-based routing model and classify it into two cases based on the reaction of mobile agents to a system failure, namely MWRC (mobile agents with weak reaction capability) and MSRC (mobile agents with strong reaction capability). For each case, we analyze the population distribution (the number of mobile agents) of mobile agents which as an important measure for monitoring the computational resource consumption and network performance. Our analysis reveal theoretical insights into the statistical behaviors of mobile agents and provide useful tools for effectively managing mobile agents in large networks.

Keywords: Mobile agents, vulnerable networks, population distribution.

1 Introduction

Mobile agent, a relatively new paradigm for network software development, has become an accessible technology in recent years. The potential benefits of this technology, including the reduction of network bandwidth consumption and latency, have drawn a great deal of attention in both academia and industry [3, 11, 19, 20, 24]. A mobile agent is a program that acts on behalf of a user to perform intelligent decision-making tasks. It is capable of migrating autonomously from node to node in an information network.

In recent years, many intelligent mobile agent-based network management techniques have been proposed and implemented [1, 6, 10, 14]. When a mobile agent is encapsulated with a task, it can be dispatched to a remote node. Once the agent has completed its tasks, the summary report for its trip is sent back to the source node. Since there are very few communications between the agent and the source node during the process of searching, the network traffic generated by mobile agents is very light. So mobile agent is an effective way for improving network performance.

H. Zhuge and G.C. Fox (Eds.): GCC 2005, LNCS 3795, pp. 894–905, 2005.

Network routing is an important issue for network performance. Advanced research in mobile agent has brought in some new methods for network routing [5, 15]. Ant routing algorithm is a recently proposed routing algorithm for use in large dynamic networks [7, 13, 17, 21]. The idea is similar to the shortest path searching process of ants. For an agent-based network, agents can be generated from every node in the network, and each node in the network provides to mobile agents an execution environment. A node which generates mobile agents is called the server of these agents. Once a request for sending a packet is received from a server, the server will generate a number of mobile agents. These agents will then move out from the server to search for the destination. Once a mobile agent finds the destination, the information will be sent back to the server along the same path. When all (or some of) the mobile agents come back, the server will determine the optimal path and send the packet to the destination along the optimal path. At the same time, the server will update its routing table.

Since mobile agents will be generated frequently in the network, there will be many agents running in the network. If there are too many mobile agents running in the network, they will consume too much computational resource, which will affect the network performance due to the limited network resource and ultimately block the entire network. Therefore, analysis on the distribution of mobile agents is necessary and important for network management. Unfortunately, few work has been done on this aspect.

In [18], an ant routing model was proposed . and the number of mobile agents was estimated under the assumption that nodes in the network will not fail. Thus, it can be viewed as a special case of the model in this paper. In [16], a smaller upper bound of the number of mobile agents was provided based on the same model in [18]. In this paper, we describe a general mobile agent-based routing model and classify it into two cases based on the reaction capability of mobile agents to a system failure. For each case, we analyze the population distribution of mobile agents. Our contributions are summarized as follows:

- A general agent-based routing model is described and is classified into two cases based on the reaction of mobile agents to a system failure: MWRC and MSRC.
- Analysis on population distribution of mobile agents is presented for both cases, providing a useful tool to reduce the computational resource consumption by adjusting the number of agents to be generated at individual nodes and the life-span of these mobile agents.

The rest of this paper is organized as follows. Section 2 discusses related work. Section 3 describes our model. Section 4 introduces the notations used in this paper and presents the analytical results for mobile agents. Section 5 concludes the paper.

2 Related Work

A mobile agent is an autonomous object that possesses the ability for migrating autonomously from node to node in a computer network. Usually, the main task of a mobile agent is determined by specified applications of users, which can range from E-shopping and distributed computation to real-time device control. In recent years, a number of research institutions and industrial entities have been engaged in the development of elaborating supporting systems for this technology [11, 23]. In [11], several merits for mobile agents are described, including network load and latency reduction, protocol encapsulation, adaption, heterogeneity, robustness and fault-tolerance. Successful examples using mobile agents can be found in [10, 12].

Network routing is a problem in network management. Ant routing is a recently proposed mobile agent based network routing algorithm for use in these environments [21,22]. The continuing investigation and research of naturally occurring social systems offer the prospect of creating artificial systems that are controlled by emergent behavior and promise to generate engineering solutions to distributed systems management problems such as those in communication networks [5, 17].

Real ants are able to find the shortest path from a food source to the nest without using visual cues. Also, they can adapt to changes in the environment, for example finding a new shortest path once the old one is no longer feasible due to a new obstacle [2,9]. In the ant routing algorithm described in [7,18], artificial ants are agents which concurrently explore the network from node to node and exchange collected information when they meet each other. They irrespectively choose the node to move by using a probabilistic function which was proposed here to be a function of the connecting situation of each node. Artificial ants probabilistically prefer nodes that are connected immediately. Initially, a number of artificial ants are placed on randomly selected nodes. At each time step they move to new nodes and select useful information. When an ant has completed it's task, it will send a message back to the server.

In [4], Brewington et al formulated a method of mobile agent planning, which is analogous to the travelling salesman problem [8] to decide the sequence of nodes to be visited by minimizing the total execution time until the destination is found. In the preliminary work of this paper [16], the population distribution of mobile agents is analyzed. The model can be seen as a special case of the one in this paper.

3 Mobile Agent-Based Routing Model

Once a request is received by a server, the server generates a number of mobile agents. These agents will then move out from the server searching for the destination. Once an agent finds the destination, it will traverse back to the server following the searched path and leave marks on the nodes along the path. When a certain number of agents have come back (others may have dead, or are still in the searching process), the server will evaluate the costs of those collected paths and pick up the optimal one. The main idea of our algorithm is as follows:

1. In a network with n nodes, agents can be generated from every node in the network. Each node in the network provides mobile agents an execution environment.
2. Initially, there are a pile of requests for sending packets in the network. Then, a number of mobile agents are generated for each request.
3. At any time t, the expected number of requests received from one node is m. Once a request arrives, k agents are created and dispatched into the network.
4. Those agents traverse the network from the server to search for the destination. Once an agent reaches a node, it will check whether the node is its destination or not. If so, the agent will turn back to the server with information of the searched path. Otherwise, it will select a neighboring node to move on.
5. The server will compare all the path collected and pick up the optimal path. Then, the packet is sent out to the destination along the optimal path. At the same time, the server updates its routing table.
6. To avoid the user from waiting for a too long time, an agent will die if it cannot find its destination within a given time bound, which is called the agent's life-span limit in this paper.

4 Mathematical Analysis

Since any component of the network (machine, link, or agent) may fail at any time, we classify mobile agents into two kinds based on their reaction to a failure: weak and strong. A mobile agent with weak reaction capacity (MWRC) will die if it subjects to a failure, while one with strong reaction capacity (MSRC) will go back to the previous node, reselect another node, and go on its trip. In this section, we analyze the population distribution for each case, respectively.

Suppose that the network topology we used in this paper is a connected graph so that there is at least one path (directly or indirectly) between any two nodes. Matrix $\Phi = (\varphi_{ij})_{n\times n}$ is the connectivity matrix which describes the connectivity of the graph, i.e., if there is a direct link between node i and node j, then $\varphi_{ij} = \varphi_{ji} = 1$; otherwise, $\varphi_{ij} = 0$. Specially, $\varphi_{ii} = 0$ for any i. Let φ_j be the j-th column vector of matrix Φ. That is, $\Phi = (\varphi_1, \varphi_2, \cdots, \varphi_n)$. Furthermore, $c_j = \|\varphi_j\|_1 = \sum_{i=1}^{n} |\varphi_{ij}|$, $\sigma_1 = \max_{1\leq j\leq n} c_j$, and $\sigma_n = \min_{1\leq j\leq n} c_j$. Obviously, $C =$

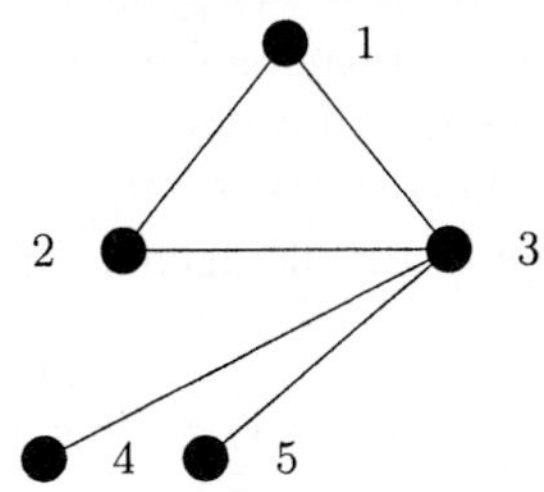

Fig. 1. An example of a small network

$diag(c_1, c_2, \cdots, c_n)$ is a diagonal matrix that indicates the connectivity degree of the network topology. It is easy to see that c_j is the number of neighboring nodes of the j-th node including itself, and $\|\Phi\|_1 = \max_{1\le j\le n} \|\varphi_j\|_1 = \sigma_1$. For example, suppose that the graphical structure of a small network is shown in Figure 1.

Accordingly, we have $n = 5$, $\sigma_1 = 4$, $\sigma_5 = 1$. Matrix Φ and matrix C can be given as follows:

$$\Phi = \begin{pmatrix} 0\,1\,1\,0\,0 \\ 1\,0\,1\,0\,0 \\ 1\,1\,0\,1\,1 \\ 0\,0\,1\,0\,0 \\ 0\,0\,1\,0\,0 \end{pmatrix}, \quad C = \begin{pmatrix} 2\,0\,0\,0\,0 \\ 0\,2\,0\,0\,0 \\ 0\,0\,4\,0\,0 \\ 0\,0\,0\,1\,0 \\ 0\,0\,0\,0\,1 \end{pmatrix}.$$

4.1 The Population Distribution of Mobile Agents for MWRC

First, we consider the situation that the agents run in the network with infinite life-span. Assume that at time $t-1$, there are $p_i(t-1)$ agents in the i-th node, these agents search for the destination locally, and the expected number of agents that cannot find the destination is equal to $\left(1-\frac{1}{n}\right)p_i(t-1)$, and the expected number of mobile agents that move from the i-th node to the j-th node is equal to $\left(1-\frac{1}{n}\right)\frac{1-p}{c_i}p_i(t-1)$. The total number of agents that move to the j-th node at time t is $\sum_{i\in NB(j)}\left(1-\frac{1}{n}\right)\frac{1-p}{c_i}p_i(t-1)$, where $NB(j)$ denotes the set of the neighboring nodes of the j-th node. Consider the new generated agents in the j-th node at time t, we have the following equation:

$$p_j(t) = km - \Omega_j(t) + \sum_{i\in NB(j)} \left(1-\frac{1}{n}\right)\frac{1-p}{c_i}p_i(t-1),$$

where m is the average number of requests initiated at time t at a node, k is the number of agents generated per request, and $\Omega_j(t)$ indicates the number of mobile agents on the j-th node at time t that are generated at time $t-d$. We eliminate the number of these agents from $p_j(t)$ because these agents will die at time t. Let $A = (1-p)(1-\frac{1}{n})(\Phi - I)C^{-1} = (a_1, a_2, \cdots, a_n)$ be an $n \times n$ matrix, where a_j is the j-th column vector of A. Obviously, we have $\|a_j\|_1 = (1-p)(1-\frac{1}{n})\frac{c_j-1}{c_j}$. Let $\overrightarrow{p}(t) = (p_1(t), p_2(t), \cdots, p_n(t))^T$, and $\overrightarrow{e} = (1, \cdots, 1)^T$. At any time, the distribution of newly generated mobile agents is $km\overrightarrow{e}$ based on the assumption that the average number of requests received by a node is m. After searching d nodes, the distribution of survival agents among these agents is $A^d km\overrightarrow{e}$. Therefore, we have $\overrightarrow{\Omega}(t) = (\Omega_1(t), \cdots, \Omega_n(t))^T = A^d km\overrightarrow{e}$. Thus, the population distribution of mobile agents can be expressed in vector-matrix format as follows:

$$\overrightarrow{p}(t) = A\overrightarrow{p}(t-1) + km\overrightarrow{e} - A^d km\overrightarrow{e} \tag{1}$$

Regarding to the population distribution of mobile agents with limited life-span, we have the following theorem based on the above analysis.

Theorem 1. *The distribution of mobile agents can be expressed as follows:*

$$\vec{p}(t) = \begin{cases} 0 & t = 0; \\ \sum_{i=0}^{t-1} A^{i-1} km\vec{e} & 0 < t \le d; \\ \sum_{i=0}^{d-1} A^{i-1} km\vec{e} & t > d. \end{cases} \tag{2}$$

Proof. If the distribution of mobile agents generated at time 0 is $\vec{p}(0)$, then after time t, the distribution of the agents is $A^d\vec{p}(0)$. Thus, according to the assumption that an agent will die if it cannot find the destination in d steps, we have
(1) When $t \le d$,

$$\begin{aligned}\vec{p}(t) &= km\vec{e} + A\vec{p}(t-1) \\ &= km\vec{e} + A\left[km\vec{e} + A\vec{p}(t-2)\right] \\ &= (I + A)km\vec{e} + A^2\vec{p}(t-2) \\ &= \cdots \\ &= \sum_{i=0}^{t-1} A^i km\vec{e} + A^t\vec{p}(0).\end{aligned}$$

Since the initial population of mobile agents $\vec{p}(0) = 0$, the result for $t \le d$ is proven.
(2) When $t > d$, then at time t, all the survival agents generated at time $t-d$ will die, so the distribution of agents under this case can be illustrated as

$$\begin{aligned}\vec{p}(t) &= km\vec{e} + A\vec{p}(t-1) - A^d km\vec{e} \\ &= \sum_{i=0}^{t-d-1} A^i km\vec{e} + A^{t-d}\vec{p}(d) - A^d \cdot \sum_{i=0}^{t-d-1} A^i km\vec{e} \\ &= \sum_{i=0}^{t-d-1} A^i km\vec{e} + A^{t-d} \cdot \left[\sum_{i=0}^{d-1} km\vec{e} + A^d\vec{p}(0)\right] - A^d \cdot \sum_{i=0}^{t-d-1} A^i km\vec{e} \\ &= \sum_{i=0}^{d-1} A^i km\vec{e}.\end{aligned}$$

Hence the theorem is proven.

From the theorem above, we can easily see that the distribution of mobile agents will not exceed $(I + A + \cdots + A^{d-1})km\vec{e}$, that is, the number of mobile agents in our model will not increase infinitely.

Since mobile agents are generated frequently and dispatched to the network, it is important to estimate the maximum number of mobile agents running in the network and in each node. When there are too many agents in the network, they will introduce too much computational overhead to node machines, which will eventually become very busy and indirectly block the network traffic.

Regarding to the number of agents running in the network, we have the following theorem.

Theorem 2. *The number of agents running in the network can be estimated as follows:*

$$\sum_{j=1}^{n} p_j(t) \leq \frac{n^2\sigma_1 km}{n+\sigma_1-1}. \tag{3}$$

Proof. By the definition of matrix 1−norm,we have

$$\begin{aligned}\sum_{j=1}^{n} p_j(t) &= \|\vec{p}(t)\|_1 \\ &\leq \|km\vec{e}\|_1 \cdot \|\sum_{i=0}^{d-1} A^i\|_1 \\ &\leq nkm \cdot \sum_{i=0}^{d-1}(\|A\|_1)^i \\ &\leq \frac{nkm}{1-\|A\|_1}.\end{aligned}$$

Due to $\|A\|_1 = (1-p)\left(1-\frac{1}{n}\right)\frac{\sigma_1-1}{\sigma_1}$, it is easy to prove that

$$\begin{aligned}\|\vec{p}(t)\|_1 &\leq \frac{nkm}{1-(1-p)\left(1-\frac{1}{n}\right)\left(1-\frac{1}{\sigma_1}\right)} \\ &= \frac{n^2\sigma_1 km}{pn\sigma_1+(1-p)(n+\sigma_1-1)}.\end{aligned}$$

Since $n\sigma_1 \geq n+\sigma_1-1$, the theorem is proven.

Regarding to the number of agents running in a node, we have the following theorem.

Theorem 3. *The number of agents running in the j-th node can be estimated as follows:*

$$p_j(t) \leq km + \frac{nc_j km}{(np+1-p)\sigma_n}(1-\alpha^t) \leq km + \frac{nc_j km}{(np+1-p)\sigma_n},$$

where $\alpha = (1-\frac{1}{n})(1-p)$.

Proof. The theorem can be proved by induction. First, for $t=0$, it is easy to see that the theorem is hold. Assume that for any t, the theorem is hold, that is,

$$p_j(t) \leq km + \frac{nc_j km}{(np+1-p)\sigma_n}(1-\alpha^t)$$
$$= km + \frac{c_j km}{\sigma_n} km \sum_{l=1}^{t-1} \alpha^l,$$

then for $t+1$, we have

$$\begin{aligned}
p_j(t+1) &= km + \sum_{i \in NB(j)} \left(1 - \frac{1}{n}\right) \frac{1-p}{c_i} p_i(t-1) \\
&= km + \alpha \sum_{i \in NB(j)} \frac{p_i(t-1)}{c_i} \\
&\leq km + \alpha \cdot \sum_{i \in NB(j)} \left(\frac{km}{c_i} + \frac{km}{\sigma_n} \sum_{l=1}^{t-1} \alpha^l \right) \\
&\leq km + \frac{c_j km}{\sigma_n} \sum_{l=1}^{t} \alpha^l \\
&\leq km + \frac{nc_j km}{(np+1-p)\sigma_n}(1-\alpha^{t+1}) \\
&\leq km + \frac{nc_j km}{(np+1-p)\sigma_n}.
\end{aligned}$$

Hence, the theorem is proven.

From the above analytical results, we can claim that both the number of mobile agents in the network and the number of mobile agents on each node will not increase infinitely over time t. The upper bound of these two numbers can be controlled by tuning the number of mobile agents generated per request.

4.2 The Population Distribution of Mobile Agents for MSRC

For MSRC, a mobile agent will not die when it moves to a failing node. It will return back to the previous node and reselect another neighboring node to move. Thus, similar to the analysis for MWRC, the population distribution of mobile agents can be expressed as follows.

$$\vec{p}(t) = \begin{cases} 0 & t = 0; \\ km\vec{e} & t = 1; \\ A\vec{p}(t-1) + p \cdot \vec{p}(t-2) + km\vec{e} & 2 \leq t \leq d; \\ A\vec{p}(t-1) + p \cdot \vec{p}(t-2) + km\vec{e} - A^d km\vec{e} & t \geq d. \end{cases} \quad (4)$$

From Eq. (4), we can estimate the number of mobile agents running in the network as follows:

Theorem 4. *The total number of mobile agents running in the network is no more than* $\frac{n^2\sigma_1 km}{(n+\sigma_1-1)(1-p)}$.

Proof. By the definition of vector norm, the total number of mobile agents running in the network can be expressed as $\sum_{j=1}^{n} p_j(t) = \|\overrightarrow{p}(t)\|_1$. Therefore, from Eq. (4), it is easy to see that

$$\|\overrightarrow{p}(t)\|_1 \leq \|A\|_1 \|\overrightarrow{p}(t-1)\|_1 + p\|\overrightarrow{p}(t-2)\|_1 + \|km\overrightarrow{e}\|_1,$$

since all the parameters a_{ji}, k, m are positive. For $t=0$ and $t=1$, we have

$$\|\overrightarrow{p}(0)\|_1 = 0 \leq \frac{n^2\sigma_1 km}{(n+\sigma_1-1)(1-p)}$$

and

$$\|\overrightarrow{p}(1)\|_1 = nkm \leq \frac{n^2\sigma_1 km}{(n+\sigma_1-1)(1-p)}.$$

If the theorem is hold for $t-1$ and $t-2$, then for t, we have

$$\begin{aligned}\|\overrightarrow{p}(t)\|_1 &\leq \left[(1-p)\left(1-\frac{1}{n}\right)\left(1-\frac{1}{\sigma_1}\right)+p\right] \cdot \frac{n^2\sigma_1 km}{(n+\sigma_1-1)(1-p)} + nkm \\ &= \frac{n^2\sigma_1 km}{(n+\sigma_1-1)(1-p)},\end{aligned}$$

where $\|A\|_1 = (1-p)\left(1-\frac{1}{n}\right)\frac{\sigma_1-1}{\sigma_1}$. Hence, the theorem is proven.

Regarding to the maximum number of mobile agents running on a node, we have the following theorem.

Theorem 5. *The number of mobile agents running on a node is no more than* $\frac{nc_j km}{(1-p)\sigma_n}$.

Proof. From Eq. 4, we know that when $t \leq d$,

$$p_j(t) = km + p \cdot p_j(t-2) + \sum_{i \in NB(j)} \left(1-\frac{1}{n}\right)\frac{1-p}{c_i} p_i(t-1).$$

Define $f_j(t) = (1-\frac{1}{n})\frac{1-p}{c_j} p_j(t)$ and substitute it in the above function, we have

$$f_j(t) = \left(1-\frac{1}{n}\right)\frac{1-p}{c_j} km + p \cdot f_j(t-2) + \left(1-\frac{1}{n}\right)\frac{1-p}{c_j} \sum_{i \in NB(j)} f_i(t-1).$$

By induction, we can prove that

$$f_j(t) \leq \frac{n-1}{\sigma_n} km.$$

Therefore, it can be easily prove that for all $0 \leq t \leq d$,

$$p_j \leq \frac{\frac{n-1}{\sigma_n} km}{\left(1-\frac{1}{n}\right)\frac{1-p}{c_j}} = \frac{nc_j km}{\sigma_n(1-p)}.$$

When $t \geq d$, since

$$\overrightarrow{p}(t) = A\overrightarrow{p}(t-1) + p \cdot \overrightarrow{p}(t-2) + km\overrightarrow{e} - A^d km\overrightarrow{e},$$

we have

$$p_j(t) \leq km + p \cdot p_j(t-2) + \sum_{i \in NB(j)} \left(1 - \frac{1}{n}\right) \frac{1-p}{c_i} p_i(t-1).$$

Similar to the analysis for $0 \leq t \leq d$, the upper bound $p_j(t) \leq \frac{nc_j km}{\sigma_n(1-p)}$ is also hold. Hence, the theorem is proven.

It is easy to see that both the total number of mobile agents running in the network and the number of mobile agents running on a node are greater than that for MWRC. The reason is because mobile agents in MWRC case have a higher death rate than in MSRC case. It also can be seen that the number of mobile agents can be justified by tuning the number of mobile agents generated per request.

5 Concluding Remarks

In this paper, we addressed the problem of network routing and management by deploying mobile agents. We analyzed the population growth of mobile agents under our agent-based routing model. For mobile agents with weak reaction capability (MWRC), we obtained the following analytical results: (1) The total number of agents running in the network is less than $\frac{n^2\sigma_1 km}{n+\sigma_1-1}$, where $\sigma_1 = \max_{1\leq j\leq n} c_j$, and m is the average number of requests keyed in one node once. (2) The number of mobile agents running in each node, $p_j(t)$, is less then $km + \frac{nc_j km}{(np+1-p)\sigma_n}$. For mobile agents with strong reaction capability (MSRC), we obtained the following analytical results: (1) $\sum_{j=1}^{n} p_j(t) \leq \frac{n^2\sigma_1 km}{(n+\sigma_1-1)(1-p)}$, where $\sigma_1 = \max_{1\leq j\leq n} c_j$. (2) $p_j(t) \leq \frac{nc_j km}{(1-p)\sigma_n}$, where $\sigma_n = \min_{1\leq j\leq n} c_j$.

We can see that the number of agents is a monotonically increasing function on k, n, d and a monotonically decreasing function on p. We can see that for the same k and p, the number of agents for MWRC are less than those for MSRC. Based on these results, we can dispatch a small number of mobile agents and achieve a good network performance by selecting an optimal number of mobile agents generated per request and giving them an optimal life-span limit.

Acknowledgements

This research is conducted as a program for the "21st Century COE Program" by Ministry of Education, Culture, Sports, Science and Technology.

References

1. F. Abbattista, A. Paradiso, G. Semeraro, and F. Zambetta. *An Agent that Learns to Support Users of a Web Site.* Applied Soft Computing, Vol. 4, No. 1, pp. 1-12, 2004.
2. R. Beckers, J. L. Deneubourg, and S. Goss. *Trails and U-turns in the selection of the shortest path by the ant Lasius niger.* Jorunal of Theoretical Biology, Vol. 159, pp. 397-415,1992.
3. F. M. T. Brazier, B. J. Overeinder, M. Steen, and N. J. E. Wijngaards. *Agent Factory: Generative migration of Mobile Agents in Heterogeneous Environments.* Proc. of the ACM Symp. on Applied Computing (SAC02), pp. 101-106, 2002.
4. B. Brewington, R. Gray, K. Moizumi, D. Kotz, G. Cybenko, and D. Rus. *Mobile Agents in Distributed Information Retrieval.* Intelligent Information Agents: Agents-Based Information Discovery and Management on the Internet, M. Klusch, ed., Springer-Verlag, Berlin, chapter 15, pp. 355-395, 1999.
5. G. D. Caro G. and M. Dorigo. AntNet: A Mobile Agents Approach to Adaptive Routing. Tech. Rep. IRIDIa/97-12, Universite Libre de Bruxelles, Belgium, 1997.
6. J. Claessens, B. Preneel, and J. Vandewalle. *(How) Can Mobile Agents Do Secure Electronic Transactions on Untrusted Hosts? A Survey of the Security Issues and the Current Solutions.* ACM Trans. on Internet Technology, Vol. 3, No. 1, pp. 28-48, 2003.
7. M. Dorigo and L. M. Gambardella. *Ant Colonies for the Traveling Salesman Problem.* BioSystems, Vol. 43, pp. 73-81, 1997.
8. M. Garey and D. Johnson. *Computers and Intractability: A Guide to the Theorey of NP-Completeness.* Freeman, 1979.
9. S. Goss, S. Aron, J. L. Deneubourg, and J. M. Pasteels. *Self-Organized Shortcuts in the Argentine Ant.* Naturwissenschaften, Vol. 76, pp. 579-581, 1989.
10. G. Karjoth D. Lange, and M. Oshima. *A Security Model for Aglets.* IEEE Internet Computing, Vol. 1, No. 4, pp. 68-77, 1997.
11. D. Lange and M. Oshima. *Seven Good Reasons for Mobile Agents.* Communications of the ACM, Vol. 42, pp. 88-89, 1999.
12. D. Lange and M. Oshima. *Programming and Developing Java Mobile Agents with Aglets.* Addison Wesley, 1998.
13. Z. J. Lee, C. Y. Lee, and S. F. Su. *An Immunity-Based Ant Colony Optimization Algorithm for Solving Weapon-Target Assignment Problem.* Applied Soft Computing, Vol. 2, No. 1, pp. 39-47, 2002.
14. T. Li and K. Lam. *An Optimal Location Update and Searching Algorithm for Tracking Mobile Agent.* AAMAS'02, pp. 15-19 Bologna, Italy, July, 2002.
15. J. H. Moore, L. W. Hahn, M. D. Ritchie, T. A. Thornton, and B. C. White. *Routine discovery of complex genetic models using genetic algorithms.* Applied Soft Computing, Vol. 4, No. 1, pp. 79-86, 2004.
16. W. Qu, H. Shen, and J. Sum. *New Analysis on Mobile Agents Based Network Routing.* Proc. of the 3rd Int'l Conf. on Hybrid Intelligence Systems (HIS'03), pp. 769-778, 2003 (Best Student Paper Award).
17. R. Schoonderwoerd, O. Holland, and J. Bruten. Ant-like Agents for Load Balancing in Telecommunications Networks. Proc. of Agents'97, Marina del Rey, CA, ACM Press pp. 209-216, 1997.
18. J. Sum, H. Shen, C. S. Leung, and G. Young. *Analysis on Mobile-Agent Based Algorithm for Network Routing and Management.* IEEE Tran. on Paralell and Distributed Systems, Vol. 14, No. 3, pp. 193-2002, 2003.

19. L. Tang and B. Pagurek. *A Comparative Evaluation of Mobile Agent Performance for Network Management.* Proc. of the 9th Annual IEEE Int'l Conf. and Wksp. on the Engineering of Computer-Based Systems(ECBS'02), pp. 258 - 267, 2002.
20. Y. Wang *Dispatching Multiple Mobile Agents in Parallel for Visiting E-Shops.* Proc. of the 3rd Int'l Conf. on Mobile Data Management(MDM'02), pp. 61-68, 2002.
21. T. White, B. Pagurek, and F. Oppacher. *ASGA: Improving the Ant System by Integration with Genetic Algorithms.* Proc. of the 3rd Conf. on Genetic Programming (GP/SGA'98), pp. 610-617, 1998.
22. T. White, B. Pagurek, and F. Oppacher. *Connection Management Using Adaptive Agents.* Proc. of the Int'l Conf. on Parallel and Distributed Processing Techniques and Applications (PDPTA'98), pp. 802-809, 1998.
23. D. Wong, N. Paciorek, and D. Moore. *Java-Based Mobile Agents.* Communications of the ACM, Vol. 42, pp.92-102, 1999.
24. H. Zhuge, J. Liu, L. Feng, X. Sun and C. He. *Query Routing in a Peer-to-Peer Semantic Link Network.* Computational Intelligence, Vol. 21, NO. 2, pp. 197-216, 2005.

A Mathematical Foundation for Topology Awareness of P2P Overlay Networks

Habib Rostami and Jafar Habibi

Computer Engineering Department,
Sharif University of Technology, Tehran, Iran
{Habib, Habibi}@sharif.ir

Abstract. In peer-to-peer (P2P) overlay networks, the mechanism of a peer randomly joining and leaving a network, causes a topology mismatch between the overlay and the underlying physical topology. This causes a large volume of redundant traffic in the underlying physical network as well as an extra delay in message delivery in the overlay network. Topology mismatch occurs because overlay networks are not aware of their underlying physical networks. In this paper we present a mathematical model for topology awareness of overlay networks (degree of matching between an overlay and its underlying physical network) and the efficiency of message delivery on them. We also after determining the computational complexity of the model, propose an optimization heuristic algorithm to increase topology awareness of P2P overlay networks. Then we present the results of running the algorithm on different kinds of random graphs and show, how we can implement the algorithm over P2P networks.

1 Introduction

A peer-to-peer (P2P) overlay is a logical network on top of a physical network. This means that an overlay organizes the computers in a network in a logical way so that each node (computer) connects to the overlay network just through it's neighbors.

In many existing P2P overlays like HyperCup [1], Chord [2], CAN [3], KazaA [4], Gnutella [5], Pastry [6] and P2PSLN [7] when a node joins the network, it is not optimally positioned in the overlay in respect of the underlying network such as IP network, however some of them like Coral [8], CAN [3] and Pastry [6] consider the topology that they ride. Not caring about network topology, in addition to losing performance, increases the network link stress and causes a large amount of unnecessary traffic over the physical links. Studies in [9] and [10] show that P2P traffic contributes the largest portion of the Internet traffic on some popular P2P systems such as Gnutella [5]. There are some reasons for this problem. The most important is the mechanism of a peer randomly choosing overlay neighbors without any knowledge about the underlying physical network, which causes topology mismatch between the overlay and the underlying physical network. Because of this problem, the same message may traverse the same physical underlying link multiple times, causing redundant traffic and extra delay.

For example, assume that nodes A, B, C and D are connect through a physical network shown in Fig. 1. If these nodes participate in an overlay network according

H. Zhuge and G.C. Fox (Eds.): GCC 2005, LNCS 3795, pp. 906–918, 2005.

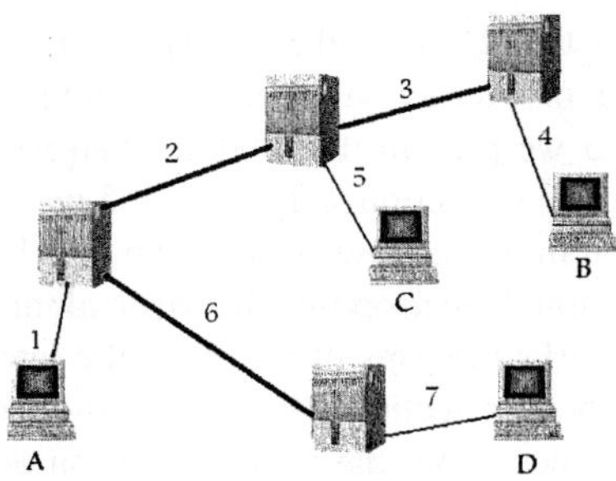

Fig. 1. Physical network which connects peers A, B, C and D

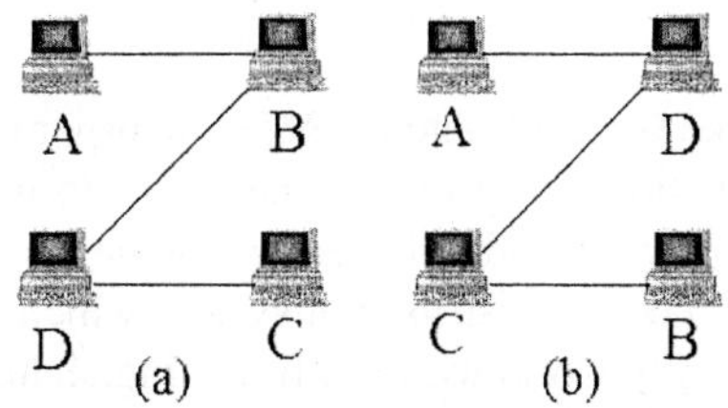

Fig. 2. Position of peers in the overlay network

to one of the two positions presented in Fig. 2(a) and 2(b) then we will have different performances.

In the overlay of Fig. 2(a), node A sends messages to D through node B. In this way, a message will pass across the following sequence of physical links (Fig. 1) to reach node D from node A: $1 \rightarrow 2 \rightarrow 3 \rightarrow 4 \rightarrow 4 \rightarrow 3 \rightarrow 2 \rightarrow 6 \rightarrow 7$. In the overlay of Fig. 2(b), node A sends messages to C through node D. In this way, a message will pass across the following sequence of physical links (Fig. 1): $1 \rightarrow 6 \rightarrow 7 \rightarrow 7 \rightarrow 6 \rightarrow 2 \rightarrow 5$.

If we assume that delay of sending a fixed size message over each physical link is t milliseconds, then in the overlay of Fig. 2(a), the transfer cost of edge AB is $4t$ milliseconds, the cost of BD is $5t$, the cost of DC is $4t$ milliseconds and the cost of the overlay (sum of the costs of all edges of the overlay) is $13t$ milliseconds. With the same assumptions, the cost of overlay 2(b) is $10t$. Therefore the overlay 2(b) is more congruent with the underlying physical network than overlay 2(a).

Many existing overlay networks are not congruent with their underlying physical network topology. Thus, a fundamental challenge in using large-scale overlay networks is to incorporate underlying topological information in the construction of the overlay to improve message delivery performance [11].

Some examples of overlay networks which introduce topology awareness are Coral [8], TOPLUS [12], SkipNet [13], Pastry [6] and CAN [3]. They use topological information to reduce the latency of sending messages in the overlays.

The contribution of this paper is the presentation of a mathematical model for topology awareness of overlay networks (degree of matching between overlay networks and their underlying physical networks) as well as a heuristic optimization algorithm to increase topology awareness of overlay networks. In the next section we review some related works. In section 3 we present the model. Then we show the computational complexity class of the model in section 4. In section 5 we represent some definitions and results about the model. In section 6 we study the model based on a distance prediction mechanism and in section 7 we propose a heuristic algorithm to improve topology awareness of overlay networks in terms of reducing the latency of message delivery in the overlay networks. Then, in section 8 we show results of running the algorithm. In section 9, we present issues about the implementation of the algorithm over P2P networks and finally in section 10 we conclude this study.

2 Related Work

Some overlay networks like Coral [8] and CAN [3] incorporate underlying topological information in the construction of the overlay networks to improve message delivery performance. In this section we provide an overview of the mentioned overlay networks.

Coral is a peer-to-peer content distribution system which is based on a distributed sloppy hash table (DSHT) [8]. Coral uses the following technique to enable distance-optimized object lookup and retrieval. In order to restrict queries to nearby machines, Coral gathers nodes in groups called clusters. The diameter of a cluster is the maximum desired round-trip time (RTT) between any two nodes it contains. Therefore Coral uses round-trip time as distance metric obtained from the underlying topology to gain better performance [8].

Content Addressable Network (CAN) is a peer-to-peer overlay network which can be described as a distributed, Internet-scale hash table. To enable distance-optimized communication between nodes, CAN assumes the existence of a well known set of machines (for example, DNS root name servers) that act as landmarks on the Internet. It achieves a form of "distributed binning" of CAN nodes based on their relative distances from this set of landmarks. Every CAN node measures its round-trip time to each of these landmarks and orders the landmarks in order of increasing RTT. According to these distances, topologically close nodes are likely to have the same ordering and hence neighbors in the overlay are likely to be topologically close on the Internet [3].

In [14] a method is presented to enhance topology awareness of unstructured peer-to-peer systems. And [15] proposed a method to enhance topology awareness of structured peer-to-peer systems.

We saw that the mentioned overlays use underlying topological information to improve their communication performance. In other words these overlays are aware of their underlying network and use this awareness to improve their performance. Also [14] and [15] presented some techniques to enhance topology awareness of some kinds of overlay networks. But can we compare the degree of awareness of these overlays? or can we say which overlay network is more congruent with its physical underlying network? or can we increase awareness of an overlay to increase its performance?

In this paper we are going to answer these questions by modelling the topology awareness of overlay networks. Therefore our model provides a metric for comparison of overlay networks in terms of topology awareness.

3 Topology Awareness Model

In this section we define a mathematical model which models the topology awareness of overlay networks.

As we mentioned before, topology mismatch between an overlay network and its underlying physical topology, causes redundant traffic in the physical topology and extra latency in the delivery of messages in the overlay network. So the topology mismatch problem can be studied based on both redundant traffic and extra latency. We will study the problem based on extra latency in message transferring. Although there is a positive correlation between these factors. To have a sense about this correlation, roughly assume that all physical links have the same properties in terms of propagation delay and bandwidth. And assume that when a message passes across a link, causes f volume of traffic and consumes t units of time. So if a message that is sent in the overlay network, passes across n physical links, then it causes $n \times f$ volume of traffic in the physical network and consumes $n \times t$ units of time. So the volumes of traffic and latency have positive correlation.

Hereafter, we study the degree of matching between an overlay network and its underlying physical network (topology awareness of the overlay network) based on extra latency in message delivery and build our model based on it.

We define $L(IP_u, IP_v)$ as the communication cost of sending a message between two neighboring nodes u and v in terms of latency ($L(IP_u, IP_v)$ approximates the distance of nodes u and v in a physical topology in terms of delivery time). We assume that $L(.)$ is symmetric[1]. This means that $L(IP_u, IP_v) = L(IP_v, IP_u)$. Also the value of $L(IP_u, IP_v)$ is not constant and may change by time. So we assume that $L(IP_u, IP_v)$ is the average communication cost of sending a message between two neighboring nodes u and v. We call $L(IP_u, IP_v)$ the weight of the edge which connects u and v. Also $\sum_{uv \in E(overlay)} L(IP_u, IP_v)$ is the sum of weights of all the edges.

There are several metrics to estimate the distance between two internet hosts in terms of latency. For example IP path length, autonomous system path length, actual geographic distance and previously measured round trip times (RTT) [16]. Several efforts to obtain various sorts of distance information and other Internet characteristics were done in [17], [18], [19], [20], [21] and [22]. We can compute $L(IP_u, IP_v)$ using any of the mentioned metrics. So we will not go through the computation of $L(IP_u, IP_v)$ more. Instead we assume that the function is given and we build our model based on it. Although in section 6 we will verify our model based on computing $L(.)$ according to the GNP [21] mechanism. In the rest of this paper we assume that the range of $L(.)$ is positive integers (including zero). This assumption is correct because in the real world we can use smaller units like nanoseconds instead of milliseconds to free from decimal values.

Definition 1. *If $G = (E, V)$ is the representative graph of an overlay, we define layout function ϕ as follows: $\phi : V \rightarrow \{IP_1, \ldots, IP_{|V|}\}$, $IP_i \geq 0$, $if\ i \neq j \rightarrow IP_i \neq IP_j$.*

Definition 2. *If $G = (E, V)$ is the representative graph of an overlay with layout ϕ, we define the overlay cost as follow: $cost(G, \phi) = \sum_{uv \in E} L(\phi(u), \phi(v))$.*

[1] If we assume that $L(.)$ is not symmetric then we can model an overlay using a directed graph.

The goal is to find a layout ϕ that minimizes $cost(G, \phi)$. It means that nodes are positioned in the overlay in such a way that the latency of a message delivery becomes minimum in average. We define $opt(G) = min_{\forall\phi} cost(G, \phi)$. In fact we model the topology awareness of an overlay network with representative graph G, by $cost(G, \phi)$ where the function ϕ shows positions of nodes in the overlay.

When $opt(G) = cost(G, \phi(v))$, it is expected that messages deliver over paths in optimal way in terms of latency. It is clear that in the case of $opt(G) = cost(G, \phi(v))$, according to definition of $opt(G)$, messages are transferred over edges optimally in average. It means that if we send a message over all edges of the graph, then the sum of costs (latencies) is minimized.

On the other side, if we consider all paths with $n > 2$ nodes (probably with common edges) and send a message over each of them, then the total cost is $\sum_{uv \in E(G)} \alpha_i L(u, v)$. In the optimum case, we have $\sum_{uv \in E(G)} \alpha_i L(u, v) = \alpha opt(G) + \sum_{uv \in E(G)} \beta_i L(u, v)$ where $\beta_i = \alpha_i - \alpha$ and $\beta_i \geq 0$. For graphs that all edges participate equally in paths with a given size [2], $\sum_{uv \in E(G)} \beta_i L(u, v)$ becomes zero. Therefore the sum of transfer costs over paths with $n > 2$ nodes is minimized. For graphs that all edges don't participate equally in paths with a given size, the value of $\sum_{uv \in E(G)} \beta_i L(u, v)$ is not zero. Therefore for these kinds of graphs we will not reach the exact minimum values for some paths with a given size, but yet we have a reasonably accurate model for these special paths. Because the cost of each edge of the graph is optimal in average, according to definition of $opt(G)$.

Hereafter we call the problem of finding $opt(G)$, IP labelling. If we define the distance of u and v as $L(\phi(u), \phi(v)) = |\phi(u) - \phi(v)|$, it can be seen that IP labelling is a generalization of the Minimum Linear Arrangement problem [23]. The Minimum Linear Arrangement (MINLA) problem was stated in 1964 by Harper [23]. Harper's aim was to design error-correcting codes with minimal average absolute errors on certain classes of graphs.

To provide a metric for topology awareness of overlay networks we define $\alpha(G, \phi)$, which shows topology awareness of an overlay with representative graph G and layout ϕ.

Definition 3. *Topology awareness of overlay G with layout ϕ is $\alpha(G, \phi)$ where*

$$\alpha(G, \phi) = \begin{cases} 1, & cost(G, \phi) = 0 \\ \frac{opt(G)}{cost(G, \phi)}, & otherwise \end{cases} .$$

According to definition 3 and the definitions of $cost(G, \phi)$ and $opt(G)$, we can see that $\alpha(G, \phi) \in (0, 1]$ (greater values exhibit more topology awareness). Our metric has at least three applications: comparison of different overlay networks in terms of matching with their underlying physical network, evaluation of algorithms and techniques that enhance matching between an overlay and its underlying physical network ([14] and [15] presented some algorithms and we also offer such an algorithm in section 7) and using it as a guideline to construct topology aware overlay networks.

[2] Many overlays have this property.

4 Computational Complexity of the Problem

In respect to the point that MINLA optimization is a NP hard problem, it is natural that IP labelling is NP hard also. The following theorem shows this fact.

Theorem 1. *IP labelling optimization problem is NP hard.*

Proof. We give a reduction from MINLA to IP labelling. In graph $G = (V, E)$, if $p \in MINLA$ we define $p^{'} \in IP\ labelling$ such that $\phi : V \rightarrow \{IP_1, \ldots, IP_{|V|}\}$, $IP_i = i$ and $L(\phi(u), \phi(v)) = |\phi(u) - \phi(v)|$. By this statement the reduction is complete and we have the proof.

We showed that IP labelling is a NP hard problem so in general cases we should not expect to have an efficient algorithm to solve the problem. Therefore we should seek approximation or heuristic algorithms or solve the problem for particular cases.

5 Preliminary Definitions and Results

In this section we present a lower bound and an upper bound for $cost(G, \phi)$. Before presenting these bounds, we define some concepts formally.

Definition 4. *Given a graph $G = (V, E)$ and $u \in V$ and $\phi : V \rightarrow \{IP_1, \ldots, IP_{|V|}\}$, $IP_i \geq 0$, $if\ i \neq j \rightarrow IP_i \neq IP_j$, then $cost(u, \phi) = \sum_{uv \in E} L(\phi(u), \phi(v))$.*

It is clear that $cost(G, \phi) = \frac{1}{2} \sum_{u \in V} cost(u, \phi)$.

Definition 5. *Given a graph $G = (V, E)$ and $\phi : V \rightarrow \{IP_1, \ldots, IP_{|V|}\}$, $IP_i \geq 0$, $if\ i \neq j \rightarrow IP_i \neq IP_j$, then $L_{min} = min_{u,v \in V} L(\phi(u), \phi(v))$ and $L_{max} = max_{u,v \in V} L(\phi(u), \phi(v))$.*

Proposition 1. *If $G = (V, E)$ is a graph then $|E| L_{min} \leq cost(G, \phi) \leq |E| L_{max}$.*

Proof. The graph has $|E|$ edges, the weight of each edge is at least L_{min} and at most L_{max}, so the cost of G is at least $|E| L_{min}$ and at most $|E| L_{max}$.

Proposition 1 shows that the lower bound of $cost(G, \phi)$ is proportional to the number of the graph edges and the communication latency between nearest nodes. Also the upper bound denotes that if the nodes of the overlay are near in terms of latency, the communication becomes faster even for badly formed overlays. This conclusion is natural and makes sense.

6 Topology Awareness Model Based on GNP Distance Mechanism

Global network positioning (GNP) is based on absolute coordinates from modelling the Internet as a d-dimensional geometric space [21]. It is an architecture for network distance prediction that is based on peer-to-peer computing. In this mechanism, each node is assigned an absolute d-dimensional coordinate and each node maintains its own coordinates. Since nodes maintain their own coordinates, these approaches allow nodes to compute their distance from other nodes as soon as they discover each other [21].

In this section, we study the computation of $opt(G)$ if we compute $L(.)$ according to the d-dimensional GNP geometric space. We study the problem for $d = 1$ in subsection 6.1 and then in subsection 6.2 we discuss the problem for arbitrary d.

6.1 IP Labelling Based on One Dimensional GNP

In the case of a one dimensional geometric space, computing *opt*(G) (IP Labelling), becomes a version of MINLA [23] which instead of assigning numbers $1 \ldots n$ to vertices, we assign n positive integers to the vertices. Therefore

$$\begin{gathered} opt(G) = min_{\forall\phi} \textstyle\sum_{uv \in E(G)} |c(\phi(u)) - c(\phi(v))| \text{ where} \\ \phi : V(G) \rightarrow \{IP_1, \ldots, IP_n\}, IP_i \geq 0, if\ i \neq j \rightarrow IP_i \neq IP_j, \\ c : \{IP_1, \ldots, IP_n\} \rightarrow \{k_1, \ldots, k_n\}, k_i \geq 0 \text{ and } L(u,v) = |c(\phi(u)) - c(\phi(v))|. \end{gathered}$$

In the rest of this subsection we show that how we can compute the exact value of *opt*(G), when G is a hypercube based overlay network.

Harper has considered the problem of assigning the integers $1, \ldots, 2^n$ to the vertices of an n-cube so as to minimize $\sum \Delta_{ij}$, where the sum runs over all neighboring pairs of vertices and Δ_{ij} is the absolute value of difference of the numbers assigned to the vertices. He showed that the following polynomial time algorithm produces all such assignments: having assigned $1, \ldots, l$, assign $l + 1$ to an unnumbered vertex (not necessarily unique) which has the most numbered nearest neighbors [23].

Steiglitz and Bernstein proved that Harper's algorithm is correct even when we use 2^n positive integers ($k_1 \leq \ldots \leq k_{2^n}$) instead of $\{1, \ldots, 2^n\}$ [24]. They also showed that the minimum value is

$$\sum \Delta_{ij} = (2r_1 - n)(k_1 - k_{2^n}) + \sum_{i=2}^{2^{n-1}} (2r_i - n)(k_i - k_{2^n - i + 1}) \tag{1}$$

where r_i is the number of ones in the binary expansion of $i - 1$.

It is clear that the problem that was solved by Steiglitz and Bernstein is IP Labelling problem based on one dimensional GNP. So we can compute the exact value of *opt*(G) based on one dimensional GNP for overlay networks like HyperCup [1] which use hypercube as their overlay topology.

Corollary 1. *If G is a n-dimensional hypercube based overlay and we compute $L(.)$ according to one dimensional GNP mechanism so that $k_1 \leq \ldots \leq k_{2^n}$ are coordinates of nodes then we have* $opt(G) = (2r_1 - n)(k_1 - k_{2^n}) + \sum_{i=2}^{2^{n-1}} (2r_i - n)(k_i - k_{2^n - i + 1})$.

Therefore to compute $\alpha(G, \phi)$ for a hypercube based overlay G, we only need to compute $cost(G, \phi)$ in steady state, which can be done using simulation techniques.

6.2 IP Labelling Based on d-Dimensional GNP

In the case of d-dimensional geometric space, computing *opt*(G) (IP Labelling), becomes a version of MINLA [23] which instead of assigning numbers $1 \ldots n$ to vertices, we assign n d-tuples of positive integers (d-dimensional vectors) to vertices. Therefore

$$\begin{gathered} opt(G) = min_{\forall\phi} \textstyle\sum_{uv \in E(G)} |\overrightarrow{c}(\phi(u)) - \overrightarrow{c}(\phi(v))| \text{ where } \phi : V \rightarrow \{IP_1, \ldots, IP_n\}, \\ IP_i \geq 0, if\ i \neq j \rightarrow IP_i \neq IP_j, c : \{IP_1, \ldots, IP_n\} \rightarrow \{\overrightarrow{k_1}, \ldots, \overrightarrow{k_n}\}, \overrightarrow{k_i} \in \mathbb{Z}^{+d} \text{ and} \\ L(u,v) = |\overrightarrow{c}(\phi(u)) - \overrightarrow{c}(\phi(v))|. \end{gathered}$$

In the following we present a lower bound for $opt(G)$, so we can have a lower bound for $\alpha(G, \phi)$.

Lemma 1. *If* $P = v_1v_2\ldots v_n$ *is a path,* $\phi : V(P) \rightarrow \{IP_1, \ldots, IP_n\}$ *and* $c : \{IP_1, \ldots, IP_n\} \rightarrow \{\overrightarrow{k_1}, \ldots, \overrightarrow{k_n}\}$ *and* $opt(G) = cost(G, \phi)$*then* $opt(P) \geq |\overrightarrow{c}(\phi(v_n)) - \overrightarrow{c}(\phi(v_1))|$.

Proof. $opt(P) = cost(P, \phi) = \sum_{i=1}^{n-1} |\overrightarrow{c}(\phi(v_i)) - \overrightarrow{c}(\phi(v_{i+1}))| \geq |\sum_{i=1}^{n-1} \overrightarrow{c}(\phi(v_i)) - \overrightarrow{c}(\phi(v_{i+1}))| = |\overrightarrow{c}\phi((v_n)) - \overrightarrow{c}(\phi(v_1))|$.

Theorem 2. *If* $G = (V, E)$ *is a k-connected graph,* $\phi : V \rightarrow \{IP_1, \ldots, IP_{|V|}\}$ *and* $c : \{IP_1, \ldots, IP_{|V|}\} \rightarrow \{\overrightarrow{k_1}, \ldots, \overrightarrow{k_{|V|}}\}$ *and* $\overrightarrow{k_1} \leq \ldots \leq \overrightarrow{k_{|V|}}$ *then*

$$opt(G) \geq k \times |\overrightarrow{k_{|V|}} - \overrightarrow{k_1}|.$$

Proof. In a k-connected graph, there are k disjoint paths between each two nodes [25]. Now consider two nodes u and v such that $\overrightarrow{c}(\phi(u)) = \overrightarrow{k_1}$ and $\overrightarrow{c}(\phi(v)) = \overrightarrow{k_{|V|}}$ (ϕ is a layout that $opt(G) = cost(G, \phi)$). Therefore there are k disjoint paths between u and v. According to lemma 1, weight of each path is greater than $|\overrightarrow{k_{|V|}} - \overrightarrow{k_1}|$ so the weight of the k paths is at least $k \times |\overrightarrow{k_{|V|}} - \overrightarrow{k_1}|$.

Corollary 2. *If G is a hypercube based overlay network (n-dimensional) then because a n-dimensional hypercube is n-connected, based on GNP mechanism we have:*

$$opt(G) \geq n \times |\overrightarrow{k_{2^n}} - \overrightarrow{k_1}|, \text{ where } |\overrightarrow{k_1}| \leq \ldots \leq |\overrightarrow{k_{2^n}}|.$$

7 Optimization Algorithm

In this section we present a heuristic optimization algorithm to increase $\alpha(G, \phi)$ by reducing $cost(G, \phi)$ in graph G. Given that the function *cost* is a model for latency of message delivery, the algorithm reduces message delivery latency in an overlay network. Also according to definition 3, our algorithm increases topology awareness of overlay networks. The following algorithm uses a local optimization to reduce the total cost of its input graph. According to the algorithm, each node tries to stand in a position in such a way that the communication cost of the overlay becomes minimum. Therefore each node checks whether swapping its node with a neighbor reduces the cost function. Also according to the algorithm, the overlay topology remains fix and only nodes swap their positions.

Algorithm 1 is highly scalable because each node only needs to know about its neighbors and IP of neighbors of neighbors, which receives from its neighbors.

Algorithm 1. `Input. G=(V,E).`
```
repeat
 cond = false
 for all edges uv of G do
  if (cost(u,phi) + cost(v,phi) >
    cost(u,phi') + cost(v,phi')) then
```

```
        swap positions of u and v
        cond = true
    while(cond = true)
```

In algorithm 1, alpha' and phi' stand for α and ϕ functions if we swap positions of u and v. The following theorem reveals the correctness of the mentioned algorithm.

Theorem 3. *In the algorithm 1, $cost(G, \phi)$ is reduced by each swap.*

Proof. After swap of u and v we name the mapping function, ϕ' . So

$$cost(G, \phi') = cost(G, \phi) \underbrace{-cost(u, \phi) - cost(v, \phi) + cost(u, \phi') + cost(v, \phi')}_{<0}.$$

Therefore $cost(G, \phi') < cost(G, \phi)$ and the proof is complete.

Proposition 2. *Algorithm 1 on graph G, terminates with at most $|E|(L_{max} - L_{min})$ node swaps.*

Proof. According to proposition 1, the difference between the worst case and the best case is $|E|(L_{max} - L_{min})$. If each swap reduces the cost only by one unit ($L(.)$ and $cost(G, \phi)$ are integers), then after at most $|E|(L_{max} - L_{min})$ swaps, we will reach the minimum value and the algorithm terminates.

8 Experimental Results

In this section we describe the methodology and results of running the algorithm 1 on some different random graphs. In this simulation we use one dimensional GNP mechanism [21] to compute the distances of nodes. So we assign a random positive integer to each node as its coordination in GNP space. And therefore $L(\phi(u), \phi(v))$ equals to the absolute difference of the assigned numbers to the nodes. For example if 1000 is assigned to u and 300 is assigned to v then $L(\phi(u), \phi(v))$ is 700. During the simulation the graph is static. It means that there is no dynamic node arrival and departure during the simulation. We aim to compute the percent of optimization in topology awareness of the tested graphs by running the algorithm 1 on them. We use the following formula to compute optimization rate:

$$optimization\ rate = 100 \times \frac{\alpha(G,\phi') - \alpha(G,\phi)}{\alpha(G,\phi')} = 100 \times \frac{cost(G,\phi) - cost(G,\phi')}{cost(G,\phi)}.$$

Where ϕ is the layout of nodes in graph G before running the algorithm and ϕ' is the layout of nodes after running the algorithm.

We use the JUNG [26] library to write a java program for execution of alorithm 1. We generate simple random[3], Kleinberg small world with clustering exponent 2 [27], Eppstin power law [28] and Watts beta small world with $\beta = 0$ [4][29] graphs with 1000

[3] Simple graphs where $|V|$ vertices are generated and $|E|$ random edges are chosen pairwise uniformly.

[4] β is the probability of an edge being rewired randomly.

nodes and run the algorithm on them[5]. Then we run the algorithm on the same kinds of graphs with 1500 nodes and then 2000 nodes and . . . 8000 nodes. In these graphs the number of edges is 10 times the number of nodes ($\frac{|E|}{|V|} = 10$). Then we generate the same kinds of graphs with the same number of nodes but this time the number of edges is 15 times the number of nodes. We Also repeat the process by graphs with $\frac{|E|}{|V|} = 20$. Also we run the algorithm on Kleinberg graphs with parameter zero. Fig. 3 shows the results of running the algorithm on mentioned graphs.

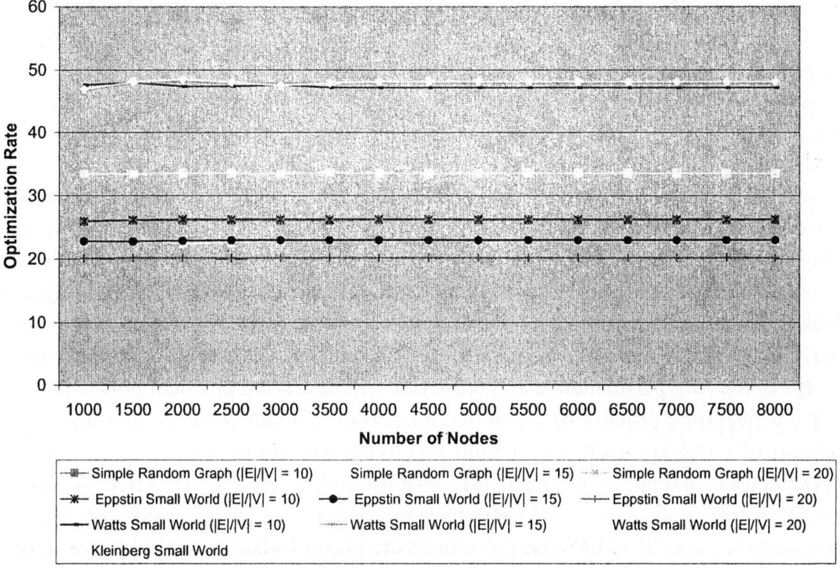

Fig. 3. The results of running the algorithm on the graphs

As it can be seen, in the tested graphs, increasing the number of nodes will not change the performance of the algorithm in terms of improvement of topology awareness. So the algorithm is highly scalable. Also the optimization rate is different for the different kinds of graphs. For example, the improvement of topology awareness in the Watts small world graphs with $\beta = 0$ is about 48 percent while this improvement for Eppstin power law graphs is about 22 percent. Therefore the optimization rate is dependent to the structure of the input graphs. On the other side when we increase ratio of edges to nodes, In the simple random graphs and the Eppstin power law graphs, the performance of the algorithm decreases while this performance increases for Watts beta small world graphs with $\beta = 0$. So the performance of the algorithm to increase topology awareness, in addition to the type of graphs, is dependent to density of graphs.

[5] We generate each kind of graph with a fixed size 15 times and run the algorithm on them. Then the average of the results was represented as the result of running the algorithm on that kind with the given size.

9 Implementation over P2P Networks

To support algorithm 1, each node, keeps a list of its neighbors' IP as well as a boolean flag against each neighbor. The flag indicates that whether the node should check the swapping condition or the neighbor does it. It means that if u and v are neighboring nodes in the overlay network then if $u.flag_v = false$ and $v.flag_u = true$, then v should check the swapping condition (we say that v is an active node and u is a passive node). It is important that the two sides of a connection should not have the same flag, so we set that for a connection uv, the flag of the node with the greater IP (each IP can be assumed as a 32 bit positive integer) will be true and the flag of other node for the connection is false. Active nodes periodically (each t seconds) check the swapping condition. An active node v which connect to node u, sends its neighbors' IP to u, and waits for the response of u. Node u sends back its neighbors' IP as well as its distance to its neighbors and the neighbors of v (Node u can compute its distance to the neighbors of v using any of the mentioned methods in section 3, but the most straight forward method is using round-trip time (RTT) by pinging target nodes). After that, v has enough information to check the swap condition. If the swap condition is true then v informs u to start the swapping process. The algorithm 1, may never converge in a real P2P system because of the continuous joining and departure of nodes. But the algorithm causes a continuous improvement in the P2P network in terms of matching with its underlying physical network. And therefore we will have continuous improvement in message delivering performance and reduction of underlying physical network traffic.

In the swapping process between two neighboring nodes u and v, u connects to all neighbors of v (except itself) and v connects to the neighbors of u. Then they put their old connections (except uv connection) into a to-cut list (see Fig. 4). After this process, a peer will not send or forward messages to connections in its to-cut list, but these connections are kept alive because these links are needed when receiving previous query responses that have to be forwarded according to their inverse search path. A connection in a to-cut list will be cut after a certain time period. We can find the optimal value of the period using simulation techniques.

In some peer-to-peer networks, when two nodes swap, they should update some information and tables. We update by building temporary tables and information as we do for connections. In addition to the mentioned guidelines for peer swapping that we pointed out in this section, we should note that swapping process is a network dependent operation and should be designed independently for each overlay network.

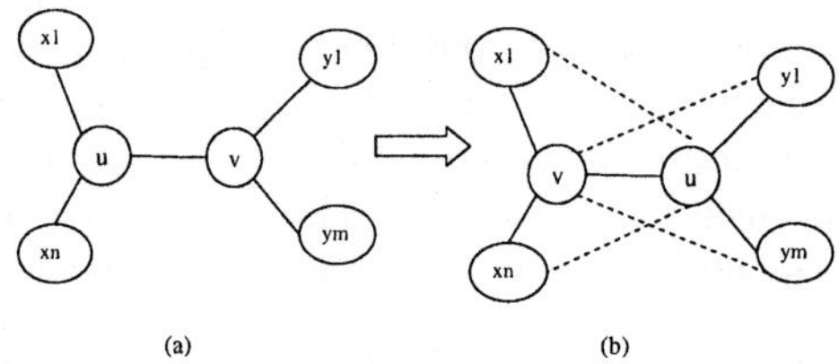

Fig. 4. Swapping process. In (b), the dashed lines show to-cut connections.

Node v before checking the swap condition with node u, should compute its distance with its neighbors and neighbors of u. Also u should know its distance with its neighbors and the neighbors of v. We assume that $L(.)$ is dynamic. So node x have to communicate with node y to find its distance to it.

If we assume that in average, each node has σ neighbors then in the worst case, $O(\sigma)$ messages are needed to check the swapping condition and doing the swapping process. If the frequency of checking the swapping condition by nodes is f, then the extra messages that are caused by the algorithm is $O(n\sigma f)$, where n is the number of nodes in the network. Because f is a constant, the order of extra messages created by the algorithm in one minute (unit of time) is $O(n\sigma)$. As observed in [30], each peer issues 0.3 queries per minute in average. Thus, the traffic incurred by an unstructured P2P network with n peers which uses broadcast to search objects is $O(n^2)$ and the traffic caused by a structured P2P network which causes $log(n)$ message per search is $O(nlog(n))$. Studies in [10] show that σ is very smaller than the number of nodes in the network (in some structured overlays like HyperCup [1] and Chord [2], σ is equal to $log(n)$). Therefore in both cases, the algorithm will not increase the order of traffic of the network. As we saw before, the algorithm will decrease traffic by increasing topology awareness.

10 Conclusion

We introduced a mathematical metric for the degree of topology matching between an overlay network and its underlying physical network. We constructed the model based on an optimization problem that we called it IP labelling. Also we have shown that IP labelling optimization is a NP hard problem. Then we showed that this NP hard problem is solvable in polynomial time for some particular inputs. Also we proposed an optimization heuristic algorithm to solve the problem for general cases. Then we ran the algorithm on different kinds of random graphs and we presented the results. We also noted how the algorithm can be implemented on P2P networks.

References

1. Schlosser, M., Sintek, M., Decker, S., Nejdl, W.: Hypercup - hypercubes, ontologies and efficient search on p2p networks. In: International Workshop on Agents and Peer-to-Peer Computing, Bologna, Italy (2002)
2. Stoica, I., Morris, R., Karger, D., Kaashoek, M.F., Balakrishnan, H.: Chord: A scalable p2p lookup service for internet applications. In: Proc. ACM SIGCOMM'01. (2001)
3. Ratnasamy, S., Francis, P., Handley, M., Karp, R., Shenker, S.: Scalable content-addressable networks. In: Proc. ACM SIGCOMM'01. (2001)
4. : Kazaa. http://www.kazaa.com (2003)
5. : Gnutella. http://gnutella.wego.com (2003)
6. Rowstron, A., Druschel, P.: Pastry: Scalable, decentralized object location, and routing for large-scale peer-to-peer systems. In: International conference on Distributed Systems platforms (Middleware). (2001) 329–350
7. Zhuge, H., Liu, J., Feng, L., Sun, X., He, C.: Query routing in a peer-to-peer semantic link network. Computational Intelligence **21** (2005) 197–216

8. Freedman, M., Mazieres, D.: Sloppy hashing and self-organizing clusters. In: Proc. 2nd International Workshop on Peer-to-Peer Systems (IPTPS03). (2003)
9. Saroui, S., Gummadi, K.P., Dunn, R.J., Gribble, S.D., Levy, H.M.: An analysis of intener content delivery systems. In: Proc. IEEE Fifth Symp. Operating Systems Design and Implementation. (2002)
10. Sen, S., Wang, J.: Analyzing peer-to-peer traffic across large networks. In: Proc. ACM SIGCOMM Internet Measurement Workshop. (2002)
11. Ratnasamy, S., Handley, M., Karp, R., Shenker, S.: Topologically-aware overlay construction and server selection. In: Proc. IEEE INFOCOM'02. (2002)
12. Garces-Erice, L., Ross, K., Biersack, E., Felber, P., Urvoy-Keller, G.: Topology-centric lookup service. In: Proc. The 5th International Workshop on Networked Group Communications (NGC'03). (2003)
13. Harvey, N.J.A., Jones, M.B., Saroiu, S., Theimer, M., Wolman, A.: Skipnet: A scalable overlay network with practical locality properties. In: Proc. The Fourth USENIX Symposium on Internet Technologies and Systems (USITS03). (2003)
14. Liu, Y., Xiao, L., Liu, X., Ni, L.M., Zhang, X.: Location awareness in unstructured peer-to-peer systems. IEEE Transactions on Parallel and Distributed Systems **16** (2005) 163–174
15. Ferreira, R.A., Jagannathan, S., Grama, A.: Enhancing locality in structured peer-to-peer networks. In: Proc. ICPADS04 Tenth International Conference on Parallel and Distributed Systems. (2004)
16. Huffaker, B., Fomenkov, M., Plummer, D., Moore, D., Claffy, K.: Distance metrics in the internet. In: IEEE International Telecommunications Symposium (ITS). (2002)
17. P. Francis, S. Jamin, V.P.L.Z.D.F.G.Y.J.: An architecture for a global internet host distance estimation service. In: Proc. IEEE INFOCOM'99. (1999)
18. Guyton, J.D., Schwartz, M.F.: Locating nearby copies of replicated internet servers. In: Proc. ACM SIGCOMM'95. (1995)
19. Savage, S., Collins, A., Homan., E.: The end-to-end effects of internet path selection. In: Proc. ACM SIGCOMM'99. (1999)
20. Paxson, V.: End-to-end routing behavior in the internet. In: Proc. ACM SIGCOMM'96. (1996) 25–38
21. Ng, T.E., Zhang, H.: Predicting internet network distance with coordinates-based approaches. In: Proc. IEEE INFOCOM'02. (2002)
22. Chen, Y., Katz, R.: On the placement of network monitoring sites. http://www.cs.berkeley.edu/yanchen/vnms/ (2001)
23. Harper, L.: Optimal assignments of numbers to vertices. J. Soc. Industrial Appl. Math. **12** (1964) 131–135
24. Steiglitz, K., Bernstein, A.J.: Optimal binary coding of ordered numbers. J. Soc. Industrial Appl. Math. **13** (1965) 441–443
25. West, D.B.: Introduction to Graph Theory. second edn. Prentice Hall (2001)
26. White, S., OMadadhain, J., Fisher, D., Boey, Y.B.: Jung-java universal network/graph framework. http://jung.sourceforge.net/index.html (2004)
27. Kleinberg, J.: The small-world phenomenon: An algorithmic perspective. In: Proc. 32nd ACM Symposium on Theory of Computing. (2000)
28. Eppstein, D., Wang, J.: A steady state model for graph power laws. ACM Computing Research Repository (2002)
29. Watts, D.: Small world: The dynamics of networks between order and randomness. Princeton Univ. Press (1999)
30. Sripanidkulchai, K.: The popularity of gnutella queries and its implications on scalability. http://www2.cs.cmu.edu/knunwadee/research/p2p/gnutella.html (2001)

SChord: Handling Churn in Chord by Exploiting Node Session Time*

Feng Hong, Minglu Li, and Jiadi Yu

Department of Computer Science & Engineering,
Shanghai Jiao Tong University, China
{hongfeng, li-ml, jdyu}@cs.sjtu.edu.cn

Abstract. Peer-to-peer systems are distinguished from traditional distributed systems in that nodes join and leave the p2p system at high rates, called *churn* problem. SChord, a p2p system, is illustrated in this paper, which is constructed on Chord system and aims to handle churn. We analyze the past experimental studies on churn of p2p systems and do some theoretical analysis on the probability distribution of node session time. SChord is based on such analysis which can distinguish nodes of long session time from other p2p nodes and exploit these long session nodes with its special routing algorithm. The simulation shows that SChord has achieved better performance of churn handling than Chord.

1 Introduction

The popularity of widely-deployed file-sharing services has recently motivated considerable research into peer-to-peer(P2P) systems. Compared to a traditional client/server approach, decentralized peer-to-peer systems have the advantage to be more reliable, available and efficient. The p2p systems are often based on common desktop machines called *peers* or *nodes*, distributed over a large-scale network such as the Internet. These nodes share data (as well as the management of the data) that is conventionally stored on a central server. The lack of a central server means that individuals can cooperate to form a p2p network without any investment in additional high-performance hardware to coordinate it. Furthermore, p2p networks suggest a way to aggregate and make use of the tremendous computation and storage resources that remain unused on idle individual computers. Finally, the decentralized, distributed nature of p2p systems makes them robust against certain kinds of faults, making them potentially well-suited for long-term storage or lengthy computations.

Usually, nodes are under control of individual users who turn their machines on or off at any time. Such nodes join and leave the p2p system at high rates called *churn*, a problem that is not existent in orthodox distributed systems. In

* This research is supported by National Natural Science Foundation of China(grant No.60433040), National Basic Research Program of China(grant No.2002CB312002), ChinaGrid Program of MOE of China and Grand Project of the Science and Technology Commission of Shanghai Municipality(grant No.03dz15027).

H. Zhuge and G.C. Fox (Eds.): GCC 2005, LNCS 3795, pp. 919–929, 2005.

other words, a p2p system consists of unreliable components only. This makes challenging several issues which are trivial in a system with a fixed membership, which distinguishes p2p systems from traditional distributed systems. Nevertheless, p2p systems should provide a reliable and efficient service.

Recently, p2p research has focused on the design of better p2p algorithms, especially in the area of structured p2p systems based on distributed hash tables, such as Tapestry [1], Pastry [2], Content-Addressable Networks(CAN) [3] and Chord [4]. These systems provide a mapping of keys in some key space to nodes in the network and a lookup protocol to allow any searcher to find the particular node responsible for any key on the one hand. On the other hand, these systems present the maintenance algorithms to handle churn by updating control information and routing tables of the concerning nodes in the overlay to ensure that the overlay remains globally connected and supports efficient lookups.

Meanwhile, some research on p2p systems has focused on observing deployed networks [5], [6] and [7]). An important result of this research is that such networks are characterized by a high degree of churn. One important measure of churn is node session time: the time between when a node joins the network until the next time it leaves. Median session time as short as a few minutes has been observed in deployed networks. However, there are some nodes with the session time longer than several hours, which shows the great difference in node session time in the deployed p2p systems.

If these nodes with long session time can be found out and made use of, they will help the nodes in p2p system to correct their control and routing information efficiently while churn happening. On the basis of analysis of the probability distribution of node session time in p2p system, this paper presents SChord system which is directly born from the above idea. SChord is an improved p2p system built on Chord, which aims to achieve better performance in churn handling by exploiting the nodes with long session time, which is why we name it SChord. The design of SChord can be summarized as two major problems: how to find the nodes with long session time in p2p system and how to make use of these nodes. Though we realize our idea on the basis of Chord in this paper, we believe that our idea can easily be extended to other structured p2p systems.

The rest of this paper is organized as follows. The past experimental studies on churn of p2p systems and the probability distribution of node session time are analyzed in Section 2, which aims to deal with how to find the nodes with long session time. The core design of SChord is described in Section 3 which illustrates how we exploit the nodes with long session time. The simulation is given out in Section 4, which shows the performance of SChord to handle churn, comparing to Chord protocol. Conclusion is discussed in Section 5.

2 Analysis of Node Session Time

2.1 Observations of Node Session Time

Experimental studies have shown the observations of node session time in p2p systems. Saroiu, Gummadi, and Gribble [5] presented the earliest study we have found of session time in p2p systems. Using active probing, they found the median session time in both Napster and Gnutella to be around 60 minutes and there are about 10% nodes in the p2p system whose session time is longer than 6 hours.

Another active study of Napster and Gnutella by Chu, Labonte, and Levine [6] found that 31% of observed sessions were shorter than 10 minutes, and less than 5% were longer than 60 minutes. On the other hand, they observed a small fraction of sessions (less than 0.01%) lasting thousands of minutes at a time.

A study of Kazaa recently published by Gummadi et al. [7] used passive measurement techniques to estimate session time as the length of continuous periods during which a node was actively retrieving files. They found a median session length of only 2.4 minutes, and a 90th percentile session length of 28.25 minutes.

Table 1. Observed session times in various p2p systems

First Author	Systems Observed	Session Time
Saroiu [5]	Gnutella, Napster	50%≤60 min, 10%>360 min
Chu [6]	Gnutella, Napster	31%≤10 min, 5%>60 min
Gummadi [7]	Kazza	50%≤2.4 min, 10%>28.25 min

The session times observed in the works referenced above are summarized in Table 1. It can be concluded that there has been great difference between nodes' session time. 5-10% nodes' session time is more than 6 times of average session time. Above 3 experimental studies have also shown that the probability distribution of node session time is like exponential distribution, which gives us a way to do theoretical analysis on node session time.

2.2 Model of Node Session Time

In order to give the quantitative analysis on the probability distribution of node session time in p2p system, a cumulative distribution function, exponential distribution with parameter μ,

$$F(t) = 1 - e^{-\mu t} \tag{1}$$

is introduced to model the distribution of session time as same as [8]. $F(t)$ means the probability of the event that the node session time is no more than t. And $1 - F(t)$ means the probability of the event that the session time of the node is longer than t.

As the probability distribution of node session time is modelled, the failure rate of the node at the time t, can be defined as following:

Definition 1. *$R(t)$, failure rate at time t, is defined as the probability of the event that the node fails at exactly time t.*

The failure rate at time t can be calculated as the probability that the node session time is t, i.e.

$$R(t) = \lim_{\Delta t \to 0} \frac{F(t + \Delta t) - F(t)}{\Delta t(1 - F(t))} = \mu \tag{2}$$

Equation.2 shows that the failure rate at t is an constant independent of time t, which illustrates that the time at which the node fails doesn't concern with the time that the node has been in the p2p system.

Then we compare the probability of the event that the node has been alive for x time in p2p system and will be alive not more than y time to the probability of the event that the node's session time is no longer than y. To illustrate this two event clearly, we give out Definition.2.

Definition 2. *$P(x, y)$, the probability of the event that the node has been alive for* x *time in p2p system and will be alive not more than* y *time more.*

Therefore,the probability of the event that the node's session time is no longer than y can be calculated as P(0,y).

Theorem 1. *P(x,y)=P(0,y)*

Proof. *P(x,y)* can be explained as the probability of the event that the node session time is more than x and less than $x + y$. The probability of the event that the node session time is more than x and more than $x + y$ is $\frac{1-F(x+y)}{1-F(x)}$,

therefore, $P(x, y) = 1 - \frac{1-F(x+y)}{1-F(x)} = 1 - \frac{1-(1-e^{-\mu(x+y)})}{1-(1-e^{-\mu x})} = 1 - e^{-\mu y}$
because, $P(0, y) = F(y) = 1 - e^{-\mu y}$
therefore, $P(x, y) = P(0, y) \diamond$

Theorem.1 illustrates that the node have been alive in p2p system for some time x, and the probability of the event that the node will still be in p2p system for any time more doesn't concern with the past time x that the node has been alive.

Lemma 1. *The node has been in the system for* t *time, then the probability of the event that the node will still be in p2p system for* t *time more is the same as the probability of the event that the node session time passes* t.

Proof. From Theorem.1, $P(t, t) = P(0, t) = F(t) \diamond$

Lemma.1 illustrates that if the node has been in p2p system for t time, it will still be in the system for t time more with the same probability.

2.3 Distinguishing Nodes of Long Session Time

After analyzing the experimental studies and theoretical model of node session time, we can design our way to distinguish nodes of long session time from other nodes. For the remainder of the readers, this section only concerns on how to distinguish the nodes with long session time and how to exploit them is illustrated in section 3.

First, we limit the nodes with long session time to the set of nodes which is 10% nodes of the longest session time in the p2p system and we call this set of nodes as *target set*. From Equation.1,

$$F(t_{target}) = 1 - e^{-\mu t} = 90\% \tag{3}$$

the target time t_{target} can be calculated as

$t_{target} = \frac{1}{\mu} log 10 = 2.3026 \frac{1}{\mu}$.

As the average session time of the node is $\frac{1}{\mu}$, these 10% nodes' session time is more than 2 times of average session time. We can get this conclusion from Lemma.1 that if a node has been alive for $\frac{1}{2}t_{target}$, it will live $\frac{1}{2}t_{target}$ more with the same probability. Therefore, we make the time $t_{point} = \frac{1}{2}t_{target}$ as the distinguished point for the long session node, which means the node in the *target set* will begin to take more function in the p2p system's routing and maintenance protocol for at least t_{point} time, which is bigger than $\frac{1}{\mu}$ time.

As not all the nodes which session time has passed t_{point} can be in the *target set*, we must let the nodes gradually increase their functions in the p2p system's routing and maintenance protocol. To illustrate the word "gradually", we use another time segment $t_{gradual}$.

Let $F(t_{gradual}) = 10\%$, so $t_{gradual} = \frac{1}{\mu} log \frac{10}{9} = 0.1054 \frac{1}{\mu}$.

According to Equation.1 and Theorem.1, $t_{gradual}$ can be explained as that the node can be still alive after the next time segment of $t_{gradual}$ with 90% probability.

Therefore, the whole method to distinguish *target set* from other nodes can be summarized as: when a node has been alive for more than t_{point} in the p2p system, it begins to play extra roles in the whole system's routing and maintenance protocols. As long as the node is still alive, it will play more and more role in the whole system's routing and maintenance protocols when each segment of $t_{gradual}$ passes. The next section will explain what extra function such a node will play when its alive time increases. And in the section of simulation, the whole design of our idea will be described in details of each above parameters.

3 Core Design of SChord

3.1 Virtual Nodes

If the nodes of long session time can contribute more to routing and maintenance procedure, the whole p2p system will correct its control and routing information better to handle churn, as we believe. We expand the usage of virtual nodes [9] to let the nodes of long session time to play more role. The notion of virtual nodes is used to show that a real node can act as multiple virtual nodes and the Chord protocol operates at the virtual node level. In [9], virtual node is used to do some load balancing work on the whole Chord ring. Here we let the nodes of long session time hold multiple virtual nodes according to some virtual nodes expanding rule. And the node with longer session time will have more virtual nodes. As the Chord protocol operate at the virtual node level, the node with multiple virtual nodes will take more part in routing and maintenance procedure of the p2p system. As all the multiple virtual nodes of one real node won't fail until the real node fails, this mechanism will build the comparatively stable part of the Chord ring. Meanwhile, one real node holds multiple virtual nodes, which means that this real node has all the control and routing information of all virtual nodes on its own. As a virtual node only has its own routing information which is limited comparing to the real node which it belongs, the virtual node should ask help from the real node in its routing and maintenance procedure. Therefore there should be some change in the common Chord protocol to fully make use of the idea of virtual node and real node of SChord. We first illustrate the expanding rule of virtual nodes in section 3.2 and describe the main modification of SChord to Chord in section 3.3.

3.2 Expanding Rule of Virtual Nodes

As mention above, the real node with long session time will take more part in the routing and maintenance procedures of the whole system when its alive time passes every segment of $t_{gradual}$. This increasing function of the real node is completed by this real node holding more virtual nodes. Because every additional virtual node will take part in the whole p2p system, the number of nodes on the Chord ring will increase. And many important parameter is decided by the number of the nodes on the Chord ring, the increment of virtual nodes means that the overhead of the whole p2p system increases. Meanwhile, additional virtual nodes will lead to more severe churn when the real node holding them fails. Therefore, we choose the linear expanding sequence to add virtual nodes on the real node. i.e. additional virtual nodes will be added to the real node when the real node has been in the systen after each time segment of $t_{gradual}$ according to the sequence of $C, 2C, 3C, ...$(C is a constant decided by the application). The linear increment sequence is a little conservative, but it avoids the challenging of severe churn when a real node with a big number of virtual nodes fails. Hence the number of virtual nodes that a real node holds reflects the session time of the real node. And a real node has more virtual nodes will in sequence take more part in routing and maintenance procedure. So the difference of nodes' session time is described quantitatively by virtual nodes, and will be exploited by the routing and maintenance algorithms of SChord.

3.3 Main Modification of SChord to Chord

Background on Chord. Chord [4] [8] is one of the typical DHT peer-to-peer system. Chord uses a one-dimensional circular key space. The node responsible for the key is the node whose identifier most closely follows the key (numerically); that node is called the key's *successor*. Routing correctness is achieved with the pointer *successor*. Routing efficiency is achieved with the *finger list* of $O(logN)$ nodes spaced exponentially around the key space, where N is the number of

```
// ask node n to find the successor of id.
n.find_successor(id)
  if (id ∈ (n, n.successor])
    return n.successor;
  else
    n' := closest_preceding_node(id);
    return n'.find_successor(id);

// search the local table for the highest predecessor of id.
n.closest_preceding_node(id)
  return the largest node u in finger[1...m] or successor_list
         so that u ∈ (n, id) and u is alive;
```

(a) Pseudocode to handle routing

```
// join the system using information from node n'.
n.join(n')
  predecessor := nil;
  successor := n'.find_successor(n);
  build_fingers(n');

// update finger table via searches by node n'.
n.build_fingers(n')
  i0 := ⌊log(successor − n)⌋ + 1; // first non-trivial finger.
  for each i ≥ i0 index into finger[];
    finger[i] := n'.find_successor(n + 2^(i−1));
```

(b) Pseudocode for joining

```
// periodically verify n's successor s, and inform s of n.
// do not run until join() is complete.
n.idealize()
  x := successor.predecessor;
  if (x ∈ (n, successor))
    successor := x;
  successor.notify(n);

// n' thinks it might be our predecessor.
n.notify(n')
  if (predecessor = nil or n' ∈ (predecessor, n))
    predecessor := n';

// periodically refresh finger table entries.
n.fix_fingers()
  build_fingers(n);

// periodically reconcile with successor's successor list.
n.fix_successor_list()
  ⟨s1, ..., sr⟩ := successor.successor_list;
  successor_list := ⟨successor, s1, s2, ..., s(r−1)⟩;

// periodically update failed successor pointer, if necessary.
n.fix_successor()
  if (successor has failed)
    successor := smallest live node u in
                 finger[1...m] or successor_list;

// periodically flush predecessor pointer, if necessary.
n.fix_predecessor()
  if (predecessor has failed)
    predecessor := nil;
```

(c)Pseudocode of maintenance

Fig. 1. Pseudocode of Chord Overlay

nodes in Chord. Node's *predecessor* and *successor_list* is used in the maintenance algorithm. The routing and maintenance algorithm of Chord is described in Fig.1.

Routing Algorithm. Fig.1 shows that the routing procedure *n.find_successor(id)* is the key procedure of Chord, for it is not only used in the routing procedure, but also used in the node joining procedure of *n.build_fingers()* and used in the node maintenance procedure of *n.fix_fingers()*. Moreover, *n.closest_proceding_node(id)* is the key procedure used in *n.find_successor(id)*, whose function is to decide the next hop of routing by exploiting the Chord node's local routing information. As mentioned above, the real node with long session time will hold multiple virtual nodes in SChord, this real node will have more routing information to use in the routing process. Therefore the key modification of SChord to Chord is to modify the *n.closest_proceding_node(id)* to exploit these kinds of extra routing information. The routing algorithm of SChord's virtual node and real node is shown in Fig.2.

It can be got from Fig.2 that real node's *r.closest_proceding_node(id)* has made use of all the routing information of all virtual nodes it holds. If the next hop is still decided as the entry from the original virtual node's local routing information, this hop of routing process is the same as Chord's, which comes

```
//ask virtual node v to find the successor of id
v.find_successor(id){
    if(id∈(v,v.successor))
      return v.successor;
    else{
      v'=v.closest_preceding_node(id);
      return v'.find_successor(id);
    }
}

//ask virtual node v to find the closest preceding node to id
v.closest_preceding_node(id){
    //get the real node r virtual node v belongs
    r=v.get_realnode();
    //ask real node r to find the closest finger to id from all virtual nodes on it
    return r.closest_proceding_node(id);
}

//ask real node r to find the closest preceding node to id
r.closest_preceding_node(id){
    //find the closest finger to id by each virtual node v on r
    for each v∈r.virtual_node_list
      closest_preceding_list[i]=v.closest_preceding_finger(id);
    }//end for
    return the largest node u precede to id in closest_preceding_list
}

//search v's local routing information for the highest predecessor of id.
v.closest_preceding_finger(id)
    return the largest node u in finger[1..m] or successor_list so that u∈ (v,id);
}
```

Fig. 2. pseudocode of routing algorithm of SChord

along to the node with the identifier closer preceding to the target *id* than current virtual node. Otherwise, the next hop is decided as the entry from the other virtual node's local routing information. In such condition, the next hop is chosen as a hop with identifier closer to target *id*'s *successor* than common Chord's hop in key space. Therefore, it can be concluded that the next hop is chosen as local optimum for message routing from all the routing information of the real node. As a result, the whole hop number and whole message number in the routing process will be decreased. So the probability of the event that the routing path cross the failed node will be decreased, whether this procedure is used in the system's routing or maintenance procedure.

4 Simulation

We implement the simulation in a discrete-event simulator. The simulated network consists of 8,192 nodes. Nodes crash and rejoin at exponentially distributed intervals with a mean session time of one hour to model churn. This choice of mean session time is consistent with [5]. All experiments involve only key lookup, as opposed to data retrieval. Nodes issue lookups for random keys at intervals exponentially distributed with a mean of ten minutes, so the lookup rate guarantees that nodes perform several lookups per session. The experiment runs for six hours of simulated time, and nodes keep their IP address and ID for the duration of the experiment. We simulate both Chord and SChord on this simulator network to compare the result. Both Chord and SChord use the same time parameter for periodically running maintenance protocol, which is ten seconds for *successor list* maintenance interval and one minute for *finger list* maintenance interval. And the maintenance operations belongs to the virtual node in SChord.

In the simulation process, we adopt the failure-stop model for the lookup. The lookup is recorded as failure if the node *v'* fails when the node *v* does remote procedure call to *v'* in the procedure of *v'.find_successor(id)* in Fig.1. and Fig.2. In traditional p2psim, if a failed *v'* is met, *v* will run *v.closest_preceding_node(id)* again to select another node from its local routing information, until the node *v'* can be communicated. According to the failure-stop model here, the failure rate of lookup F_l, can be defined as the ratio of the number of failure lookup to the number of all lookups. F_l reflect the error rate of the control and routing information of the whole p2p system during churn happening. And the error rate of the control and routing information reflects the p2p system's ability to handle churn. Therefore, F_l directly reflects the ability of churn handling of p2p system. Meanwhile, the hop number of each success lookup is logged, which reflects the routing efficiency of the p2p system.

As we use the same exponentially distribution to model the churn of p2p system, the system will be running to the dynamically steady state with the total number of nodes is about 4096. For SChord, we can calculate the parameter for expanding rule of virtual nodes now. Let $\frac{1}{\mu} = 3600$, for the mean session time of node is one hour. Therefore, $t_{point} = 8289.4$, $t_{target} = 4144.7$ and $t_{gradual} = 379.44$ can be calculated. The expanding sequence is defined as 10,20,30.... i.e. 10 additional virtual nodes adds to the real node when its alive time passes one time segment of $t_{gradual}$. And as we only care about the failure rate of all lookups and the hop number of successful lookup, the latency between pair of nodes is adopted all the same as 76ms, which is the average latency estimated in [10].

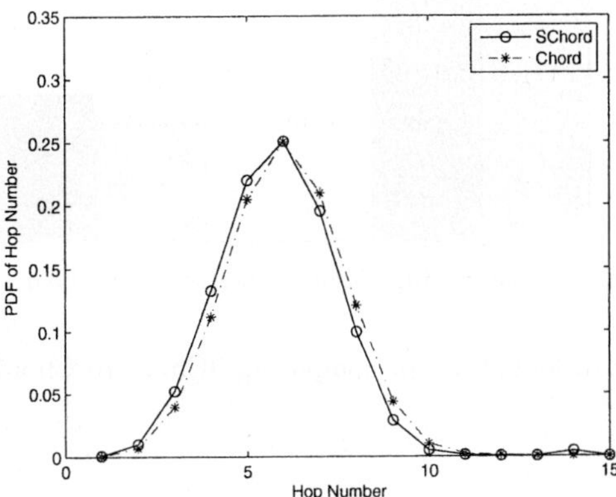

Fig. 3. comparing routing hop number per successful lookup between SChord and Chord

Table 2. Distribution of virtual nodes on real node in SChord when simulation ends

Number of virtual nodes on one real node	1	10	20	30	40	50	60	70	80
Number of real nodes	4038	3	3	3	2	1	1	1	1

Fig.3 shows probability density function(PDF) of the hop number of successful lookup in SChord comparing to Chord. The average hop number of successful lookup in SChord is 5.81, and 6.07 in Chord, which shows that SChord has only increase 4.3% routing efficiency than Chord. The decrease of hop number is not big enough here, which is because the overhead in SChord is higher than Chord. As mentioned above, the number of nodes in the system is an important metric to the overhead of p2p system. For SChord has 4038 real nodes and 4558 virtual nodes and Chord has 4044 nodes when the simulation ends. The distribution of virtual nodes of SChord is shown in Table.2. And in the simulation process the number of virtual nodes in SChord is higher than the number of nodes in Chord, too. As SChord protocol operates at the virtual node level, it can be concluded that the modification of routing algorithm of SChord helps in decreasing the hop number of lookup.

Fig.4 shows the lookup failure rate and the details of lookup in SChord and Chord. The failure rate of lookup is 34.48% on Chord and 27.59% on SChord. Therefore, it can be calculated that SChord decrease 19.98% failure rate of lookup than Chord. Because the failure rate of lookup directly reflect the correctness of the control and routing information of all nodes in the p2p system, which is the key metric that shows that SChord has better performance in churn handling than Chord as expected.

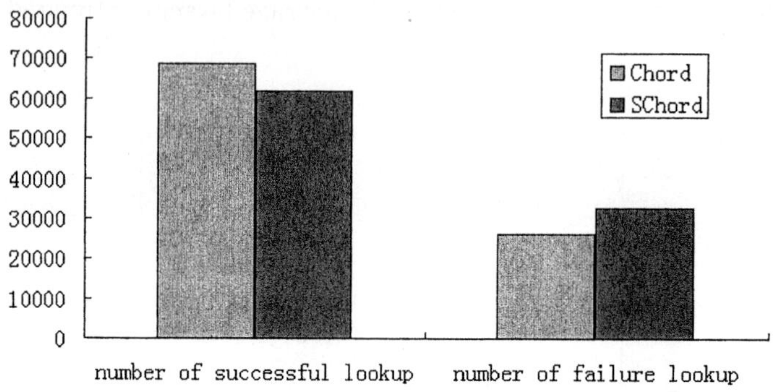

Fig. 4. lookup result comparing SChord to Chord

5 Conclusion

In this paper, we present SChord to handle the churn problem of p2p system. We analyze the past experimental studies on churn problem of p2p system and do some theoretical analysis on the model of node session time. SChord is based on such analysis which can distinguish nodes of long session time from other p2p nodes and exploit these long session nodes with its special routing algorithm. The Simulation shows that SChord has achieved better performance to handle churn than Chord as expected.

References

1. B. Y. Zhao, J. Kubiatowicz, and A. D. Joseph: Tapestry: An infrastructure for fault-tolerant wide-area location and routing. Technical report, UCB/CSD-01-1141, University of California at Berkeley, Computer Science Department(2001)
2. A. Rowstron and P. Druschel: Pastry: Scalable, decentralized object location and routing for large-scale peer-to-peer systems. In Proceedings of the 18th IFIP/ACM International Conference on Distributed Systems Platforms(2001)
3. S. Ratnasamy, P. Francis, and M. Handley: A scalable content-addressable network. In Proceedings of NGC'01(2001)
4. I. Stoica, R. Morris, D. Karger, M. F. Kaashoek, and H. Balakrishnan: Chord: A scalable peer-to-peer lookup service for internet, IEEE/ACM Transactions on Networking, Vol. 11, No. 1,17-32(2003)
5. S. Saroiu, P. K. Gummadi, and S. D. Gribble: A measurement study of peer-to-peer file sharing systems. In Proceedings of Multimedia Conferencing and Networking(2002)
6. J. Chu, K. Labonte, and B. N. Levine. Availability and locality measurements of peer-to-peer file systems. In Proc. of ITCom: Scalability and Traffic Control in IP Networks(2002)
7. K. P. Gummadi, R. J. Dunn, S. Saroiu, S. D. Gribble, H. M. Levy, and J. Zahorjan. Measurement, modeling, and analysis of a peer-to- peer file-sharing workload. In Proc. ACM SOSP(2003)
8. D. Liben-Nowell, H. Balakrishnan, and D. Karger: Analysis of the Evolution of Peer-to-Peer Systems. In ACM Conf. on Principles of Distributed Computing (PODC)(2002)
9. F. Dabek, M. F. Kaashoek, D. Karger, R. Morris, and I. Stoica:Wide-area cooperative storage with CFS. In SOSP'01(2001)
10. Krishna P. Gummadi, Stefan Saroiu, and Steven D. Gribble. King: Estimating latency between arbitrary Internet end hosts. In Proceedings of the 2002 SIGCOMM Internet Measurement Workshop(2002)

Towards Reputation-Aware Resource Discovery in Peer-to-Peer Networks[1]

Jinyang Zhou, Shoubao Yang, Leitao Guo, Jing Wang, and Ying Chen

Computer Science Department, University of Science and Technology of China, Hefei 230026, P.R. China
jjyyzhou@mail.ustc.edu.cn, syang@ustc.edu.cn, {ltguo, joycew, ychen34}@mail.ustc.edu.cn

Abstract. The resource discovery algorithms in Peer-to-Peer networks are based on the assumption that reliable resources are provided by each peer. The feather that significantly contributes to the success of many P2P applications is dynamic, anonymity and self-organization. However, they also bring about some malicious nodes to provide untrustworthy and pseudo services. To address this problem, this paper introduces a robust and flexible reputation mechanism in unstructured P2P and presents the heuristic resource discovery algorithm based on reputation-aware to ensure that resource requester can obtain reliable resources and services. This new resource discovery algorithm can effectively suppress the deceptive and fake services of P2P network, improve the reliability and security and decrease network load.

1 Introduction

P2P network is distributed application paradigm with data sharing, collaborative computing and big storage. There is no central server or control. Each peer has equal capabilities and responsibilities for providing resources, consuming resources and communicating information. Peers can communicate with each other directly, rather than through a central server. But the dynamic, self-organizing and anonymity of P2P network can't guarantee all peer nodes provide good quality services and reliable resources. Some peers provide services different from description, even imposture services which will damage requester and other peers with illegal and uncertain resources. Therefore, in P2P network with many dynamic and anonymous users, it's necessary to resolve how to avoid those fraudulent services and guarantee all peers will provide reliable resources and services. According to these requirements, this paper presents Reputation-Aware Resource Discovery Algorithm (RARDA), based on Directed-BFS （Breadth-First Traversal） algorithm [1] and reputation concept, and performs simulated experiment and analyses experiment results. Analysis shows that the new resource discovery algorithm can effectively restrain the deceptive and pseudo service of P2P network, improve reliability and security, decrease network load as well.

[1] This paper is supported by the National Natural Science Foundation of China under Grant No.60273041 and the National '863' High-Tech Program of China under Grant No. 2002AA104560.

H. Zhuge and G.C. Fox (Eds.): GCC 2005, LNCS 3795, pp. 930–940, 2005.

The rest of this paper is organized as following. Section 2 introduces resources discovery algorithms in current unstructured P2P network. Section 3 describes trust concept and how to compute reputation value in P2P network based on polling, and presents RARDA based on Directed-BFS algorithm and integrated with Reputation Factor. Simulations and results analysis are given in section 4. And conclusions and future works are in section 5.

2 Related Works

Peer-to-Peer essentially comes in three flavors: 1) centralized P2P network, such as Napster [2]. 2) distributed unstructured P2P network, such as Gnutella[3] and Freenet [4]. 3) distributed structured P2P network, such as CAN [5], Chord [6]. All P2P networks rely on peers' collaboration. P2P is mainly used in file sharing, distributed processing and instant messaging. All these usage focuses on resource discovery and resource usage. Thus, resource discovery is the primitive service in P2P system. Resource discovery means giving out detail description of expected resource and searching all resources matching with the description.

In structured P2P system, files distribution is relative with network topology compactness. Files are accurately distributed in the network according to P2P topology logic addresses. Distributed Hash Table (DHT) is used to locate resources in structured P2P network, such as CAN. This method assures that each peer can be visited under limited maximum hops which can be derived from log (n) (n is peers number in P2P network).

In unstructured P2P system, files distribution is related with network topology looseness. BFS(Breadth-First Traversal) can be used to locate resources. BFS technology makes each node forwards the received query message to all its neighbors by the means of simple flooding algorithm, and ends the query messages until meeting predefined hops number. Figure 1 shows flooding algorithm query process.

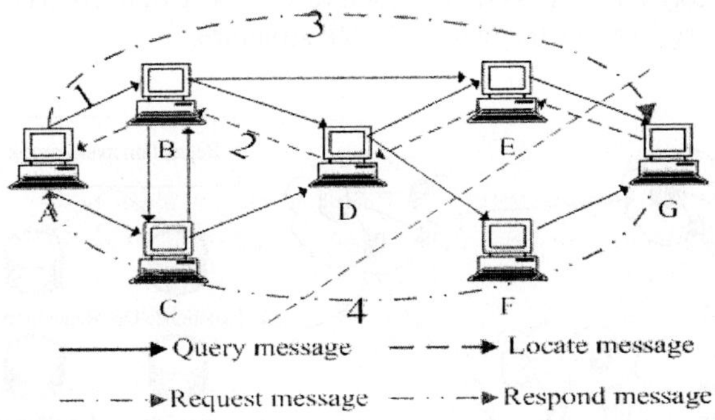

Fig. 1. Flooding Algorithm in Unstructured P2P Network

To find out a file, peer A generates a query message and broadcasts it to its neighbor peers B and C, then B and C broadcasts this message to their neighbors, respectively. The rest may be deduced by analogy. As long as one peer finds the file;

it will return the result along with original path. In case, if TTL (Time to Live) is equal to 2, the query can't access peer F and peer G. The resources locating method of flooding algorithm is only used in certain radius scope from source peer. When the query goes beyond this scope, it stops searching. So the method of flooding can't guarantee the validity of the search. But flooding is completely distributed and it can effectively avoid the problem of single failure.

BFS is ideal in theory because it can pass query message to each node as soon as possible, but data stream is increased at exponential level which wastes a lot of resource and network bandwidth, and the system has no good scalability as well. Hence, in paper [1], a compromised method without debasing the quality of query result was introduced: Directed-BFS algorithm. Directed-BFS algorithm forwards query information to a node's neighbor subset according to history experience to reduce network cost. The key of this technology is to select neighbor nodes intelligently so that it will not debase query quality. But Directed-BFS algorithm can't guarantee each response peer provides reliable and good services. Some malicious peers and pseudo peers will provide fraudulent and unreliable services [7]. To ensure P2P system reliability and provide good Quality of Service, this paper proposes Reputation-Aware Resource Discovery Algorithm (RARDA), based on Directed-BFS. RARDA evaluates reputation of each peer based on history exchanging information and considers reputation factor when selecting neighbor subset and resource providers. The purpose of algorithm is to obtain the honest service, to decrease the communication load and enhance scalability of P2P system.

3 Heuristic Resource Discovery Algorithm

P2P system has no fixed network topology structure. Its topology structure is formed spontaneously when peers join in and leave dynamically. Each peer needs to send massages to its neighbor peers when it joins in or leaves system, from which P2P system can update topology dynamically. For objective and valid evaluation reputation value, the original P2P system structure can be extended based on reputation mechanism. Figure 2 shows the extended P2P structure.

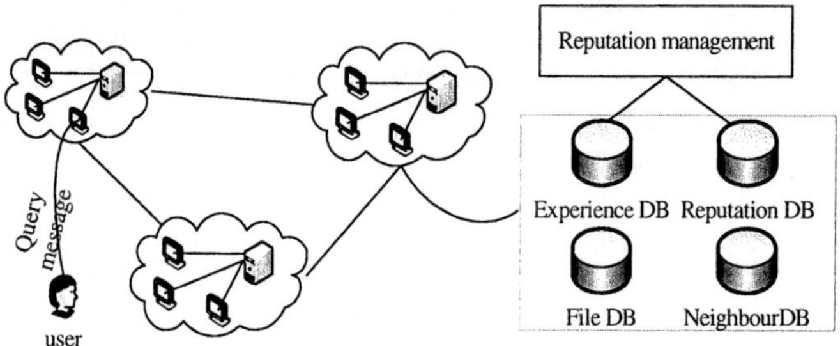

Fig. 2. The Extended P2P Structure

Each peer not only maintains file sharing information database and neighbors information database, but also extends history experience information database, in which, data is managed by the reputation management mechanism. Figure 3 shows how each peer maintains the data structure in P2P system.

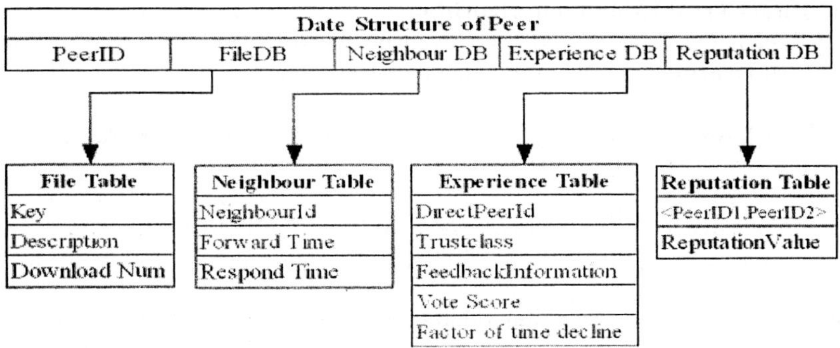

Fig. 3. Data Structure of Peer in Unstructured P2P Network

a. the file table includes the description and download number of a file, and the file keywords generated from hash function SHA-1[8].

b. the neighbor table expresses neighbor peers' identifier and history exchanging information, including message forwarding times and message responding times of neighbor peers.

c. the experience table includes the IDs of the neighbor peers which have directly interacted with current peer, the trust class, the feedback information and the factor of time decline. The reputation value will gradually decline along with the increment of time.

d. the reputation table stores the trust degree between peers according to the trust evaluation algorithms.

3.1 The Trust Evaluation Algorithm

This paper uses Diego Gambetta's trust definition [9]. There are two kinds of trust between peers: Direct trust and Recommendation Trust [10]. Direct Trust means two peers directly exchanged information; the value of reputation is based on direct experience from their exchange status. It is shown by solid line. Recommendation Trust is that two peers never exchange information directly, it is shown by dotted line, and they establish trust relationship based on recommendation from other peers, the reputation value is from other peers' evaluation.

This paper uses Trust Class and Reputation Value to describe trust relationship between each pair of peers. Trust Class is a kind of service provided by service provider. Reputation Value is trust degree of two trusted peers based on trust class. It's the quantity evaluation to trust between peers. The computing formula can be formalized as:

$$\mathrm{ReputationValue}_A^{\mathrm{TrustClass}_A^B}(B) = \lambda \times \mathrm{DRv}_A^{\mathrm{TrustClass}_A^B}(B) + (1-\lambda) \times \mathrm{RRv}_A^{\mathrm{TrustClass}_A^B}(B). \quad (1)$$

DRv is direct reputation value, RRv is recommendation reputation value, λ is trust degree of a peer for direct exchange evaluation.

3.1.1 Direct Trust Evaluation Algorithm

Direct Reputation Value of two peers evaluates history exchanging information and gets the trust capability of one peer to another peer for certain behavior.

It can be formalized as $DRv_A^{TrustClass_A^B}(B)$. The reputation value formula is:

$$DRv_A^{TrustClass_A^B}(B) = \frac{1}{n} \times \sum_n Score_A^{Trustclass_A^B}(B) . \quad (2)$$

$Score_A^{Trustclass_A^B}$ shows evaluation value of peer A to peer B in a history exchange, $Score_A^{Trustclass_A^B} \in [-1,1]$. For example, when peer A downloads file from peer B, and the file is authentic, then the evaluation value is positive; if the file is unauthentic, modified or the downloading process is interrupted, then the evaluation value is negative. n is the history exchange times between peer A and Peer B.

3.1.2 Recommendation Trust Evaluation Algorithm

Besides getting direct experience from peer's history experience, the peer will accept recommendation for target peer from other peers. This paper uses reputation value passing to get recommendation reputation. It can be formalized as $RRv_A^{TrustClass_A^B}(B)$. Figure 4 gives multi-path recommendation.

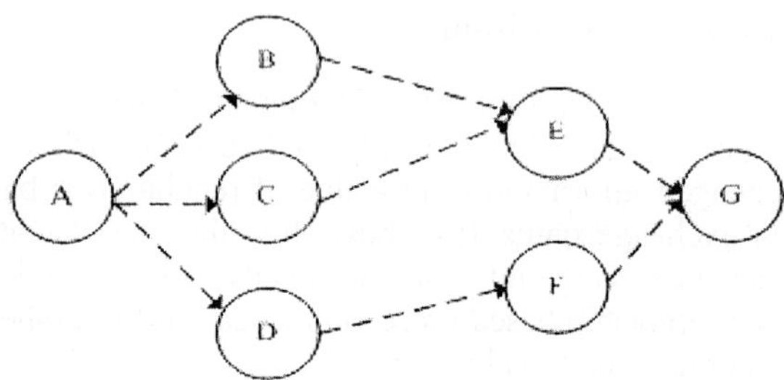

Fig. 4. Multi-path Recommendation in P2P networks

Peer A can reach Peer G through different paths. There are three assumed paths between A and G. α, β, γ is weight for each recommended path, $\alpha - \beta - \gamma = 1$. The recommendation reputation value is from following formula:

$$RRv_A^{TrustClass_A^G}(G) = \alpha * \left(RV_A^B * RV_B^E * RV_E^G\right) + \beta * \left(RV_A^C * RV_C^E * RV_E^G\right) + \gamma * \left(RV_A^D * RV_D^F * RV_F^G\right). \quad (3)$$

From above, the $\mathrm{ReputationValue}_{A}^{\mathrm{TrustClass}_{A}^{B}}(B)$ between Request Peer A and respond Peer B is

$$
\begin{aligned}
RV_{A}^{\mathrm{TrustClass}_{A}^{B}}(B) = {} & \frac{\lambda}{n} \times \sum_{n} \mathrm{Score}_{A}^{Tc_{A}^{B}}(B) + \\
& (1-\lambda) \times \left(\alpha * \left(RV_{A}^{B} * RV_{B}^{E} * RV_{E}^{G}\right) + \beta * \left(RV_{A}^{C} * RV_{C}^{E} * RV_{E}^{G}\right) + \gamma * \left(RV_{A}^{D} * RV_{D}^{F} * RV_{F}^{G}\right)\right).
\end{aligned}
\quad (4)
$$

3.2 Resource Discovery Work Flow

Comparing with flooding algorithm, Directed-BFS improves on network bandwidth consumption and processing cost. But it can't guarantee service-providing peers provide authentic services and reliable resources. Therefore, this paper presents Reputation-Aware Resource Discovery Algorithm, RARDA. Reputation concept can be used in the following aspects:

a. Select neighbor sets intelligently to transmit query message according to reputation value.

b. Select peer with higher reputation value to be service peer when more than one peer responds the request

c. If forwarding peers don't keep reputation value of neighbor peers, then update peers reputation table based on Formula (4)

Figure 5 illustrates the improved resource discovery algorithm workflow:

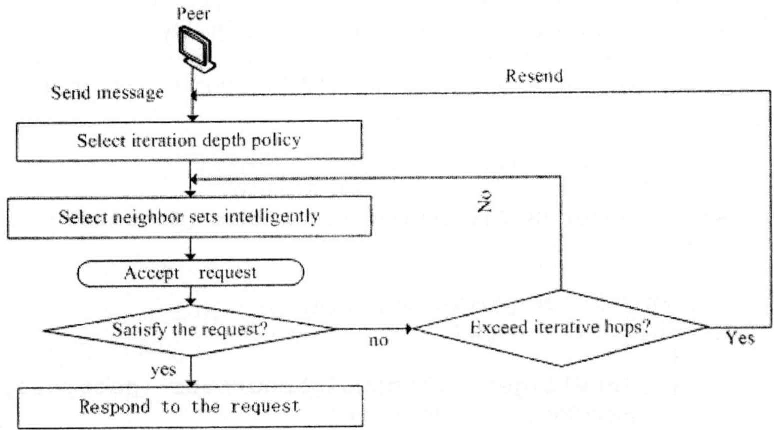

Fig. 5. Resource Discovery Algorithm Workflow

(1) Request peer sends out query message, Message={SourcePeerId, FileId, Rv_{min}}, SourcePeerId is request peer identifier, FileId is request file resource identification, Rv_{min} is minimal reputation value that request peer needs.

(2) Select iteration depth policy; if policy is Policy={Depth1,Depth2}, select Policy.Depth1 as iteration flooding hops.
(3) Update peers Reputation table based on exchanging history information in experience table and select peer whose reputation value is more than or equal to Rv_{min} message requesting peers as neighbor subset to transmit message. Then select peer with more responding times or transmitting times during message querying to be transmitting peer in neighbor subset.
(4) Make judgment if there is peer to meet searching requirement. If there are more than one peer meet the requirement, then select peer with higher reputation value to respond the request and algorithm is terminated, otherwise, jump to (5).
(5) Make judgment if iteration jump time is more than Policy.Depth1, if not, then jump to (2). Otherwise, resend message, freeze all searching peers in Policy.Depth1, jump to (1), select Policy.Depth2 as iteration flooding jump number, and repeat step (2) and (3).
(6) If response time is over or there is no peer to respond resource query when iteration depth is reached, then use flooding algorithm to search.

3.3 Pseudo Code Descriptions

This paper uses resource discovery algorithm based on reputation-aware in unstructured P2P system. Instead of changing the bottom routing algorithm during the course of locating and forwarding information, the heuristic reputation-aware algorithm adds an extra overlay on the under layer network topology. Further more, the algorithm is based on flooding algorithm. In the worst case, algorithm will perform simple flooding algorithm. Thus, this algorithm has better flexibility. This paper computes reputation value based on history exchanging information. It not only avoids malicious peers providing fraudulent or fake service to guarantee Quality of Service, but also doesn't impact percentage of hits of algorithm searching, and in the mean time, it reduces network load and increases system scalability. Pseudo code of RARDA is shown as follows:

```
Depth-policy: p= {depth1, depth2, depth3}
Message= {SourcePeerID, FileId, Rvmin}
Heuristic Resource-Discovery Algorithm (Message):
    i=0;
    Do {
        hops=SelectPolicyDepth (p);
        While (i<=hops)
        {
        (5)IntelligentSelectNeighbourSets (peersets);
           SendMessage(Message);
           if(FileId exist Peersets) return success;
           else i=i+1;
         }
         Frozen(PastForwardPeers);
         Resend(message);
         }
     until((i>=SelectPolicyDepth)or(overtime))
     Flooding(message);
```

From above, details of step 5 are given by underneath of program code, which illustrates intelligent neighbor peers selecting algorithm.

```
IntelligentSelectNeighbourSets(peersets):
  for( all NeighbourPeers)
  {
  Select and lookup ReputationTable;
  if (ReputationTable.ReputationValue>Message.Rvmin)
          return(peer∪NeighbourPeerSets)
  else {RandomSelectPeers ReputationTable.RV>num1};
  while((Respondtime>=a)and( Forwardtime>=b))
          return (select peers from NeighbourPeerSets );
  }
```

When a resource query message is sent out, resource request peer selects iteration depth policy, then seeks node's reputation table, neighbor table and experience table. If file table includes requested resource matching reputation requirement, then peer responds request message. Otherwise, peer will intelligently select neighbor peers to transmit message according to reputation value, responding times and forwarding times. If reputation table has no reputation value for those two peers, it will compute and update reputation value as Formula (4).

3.4 Algorithm Performance Analysis

To a certain extent, RARDA algorithm can guarantee that peer provides reliable and honest service. At the same time, it decreases communication load of P2P network. Here is the algorithm performance analysis.

Assume that there is an edge between any two peers A and B. S (A) is peer A and its neighbor peers set. S (B) is peer B and its neighbor peers set. If peer A is request peer and $S(A)^{translate}$ is transmit neighbor peers of peer A selected through intelligent select policy, then after one hop, searched peer number will be $S(A)^{translate} \cup S(B)$. At the worst condition, the algorithm will perform flooding. If the maximum diameter in connection graph from network is $d(n)$ (diameter of network with n peers), then its round complexity is $d(n)$.

The communication complexity of this algorithm depends on edge number in this network. $E_{num}(n)$ means initial edge number in the network with n peers. The worst case is that all peers start to search at same time and all go through the longest path $d(n)$. Then the network communication complexity is $\Omega(E_{num}(n) \times d(n))$.

4 Simulations and Results Analysis

BRITE [11] network generator is used in this paper to perform simulations, which is similar to real network structure, and accords with power laws [12]: $y = x^{\alpha}$. Simulation network topology structure uses bottom-to-top two-layer topology. The entire structure generates 1000 peers. Waxman model is used as route structure. The maximum and minimum bandwidth is 1024 and 10. This paper uses the Cooperative

Association for Internet Data Analysis (CAIDA)[13] visual tool Otter0.9 to show the topology structure.

During simulation, resource searching is simplified as searching shared files of peers. Thus, this paper designs and evaluates tests based on unstructured file sharing system Gnutella Protocol. It is assumed that there are 10,000 files distributed in those 1000 peers randomly without considering the trust class among peers. Assume that each peer is distributed 100 files with different content. Reputation value between any two peers depends on history exchanging evaluation information. Simulation performs flooding algorithm, Directed-BFS algorithm and Reputation-Aware Resource Discovery Algorithm, respectively.

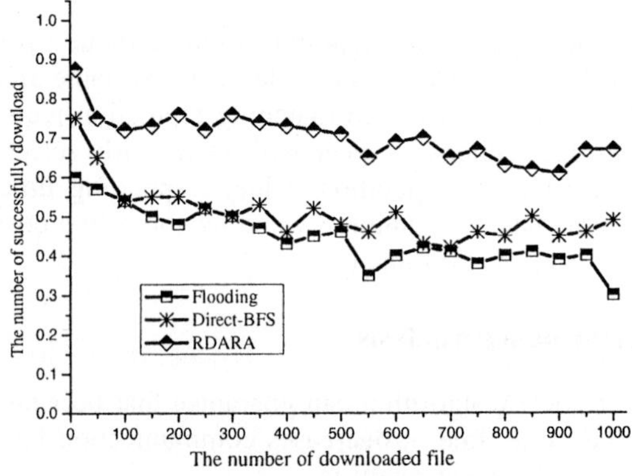

Fig. 6. The Proportion of Successfully Downloading

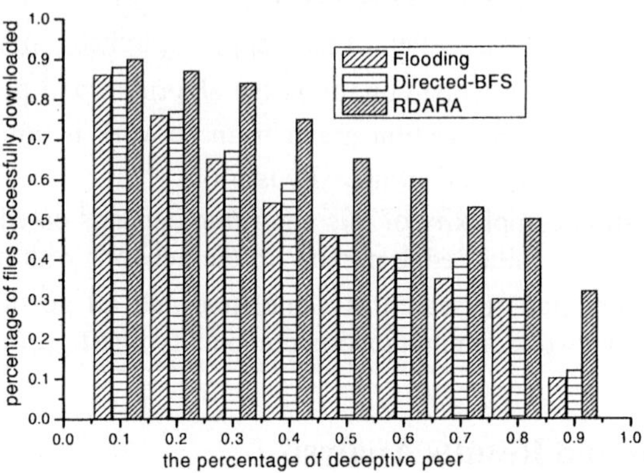

Fig. 7. The Proportion of Successfully Downloading

It is shown in figure 6 of the percentage of reputation peers over all the responding ones in the three resource searching algorithm. The three curves of Fig 6 show that the RDARA algorithm ratio of successful download file is higher. Experiment result indicates that Reputation-Aware Resource Discovery Algorithm can ensure more download resources are provided by authentic and reliable peers to insure reliable Quality of Service. It is assumed that 1000 files are downloaded in different percentage of deceptive peers. Figure 7 shows percentage of downloaded authentic files under different malicious peer percentage. This result proves authentic and reliable files can still be downloaded even when 90% peers are malicious peers.

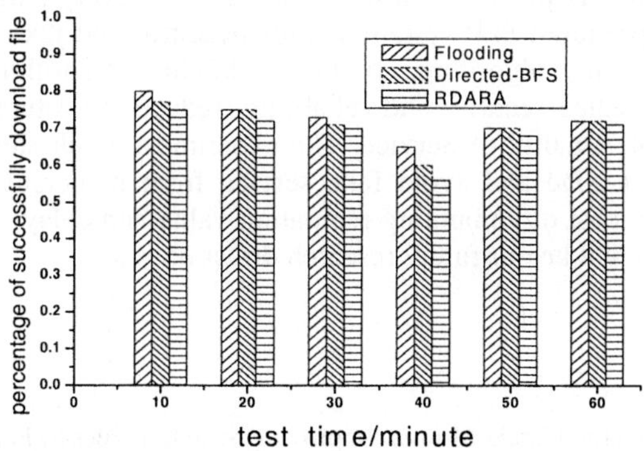

Fig. 8. Ratio of Resource Successful Discovery

Success rate is the rate of successfully query number comparing with entire query times during some period. These three algorithms have no big difference in Figure 8, which shows RARDA doesn't reduce resource searching success rate and it has better usability.

The numbers of system messages when the algorithm is running is shown in Figure 9. x coordinate shows requester peers number of p2p networks in a certain time. Y coordinate shows messages quantity. The result shows RARDA can decrease system message load obviously and improve system expansibility.

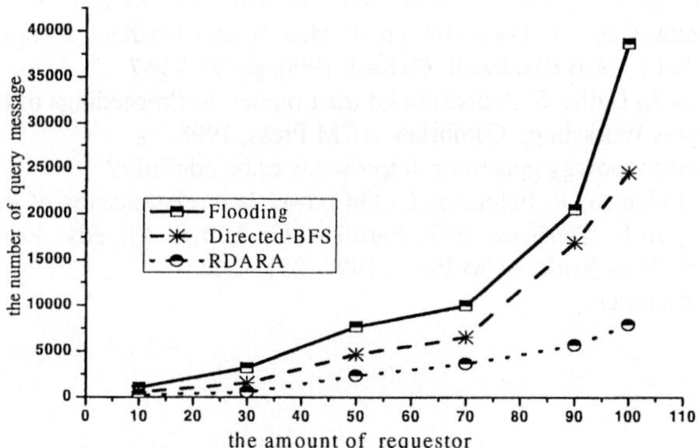

Fig. 9. System Message Load Compare

From above analysis, RARDA can discover more unauthentic and unreliable peers to a certain degree which will avoid selecting them during resource searching reduce fraud and fake service and improve system reliability and expansibility.

5 Conclusions and Future Work

This paper presents Reputation-Aware Resource Discovery Algorithm based on Reputation in unstructured P2P system against deceitful and fake service during resource searching. This algorithm combines flooding algorithm with reputation mechanism to guarantee security and reliability, reduce imposture and fake service and provide reliable Quality of Service. The experiment result shows this algorithm can reduce network load and avoid fake service from malicious peers. Algorithm efficiency analysis, cost of computing reputation value and delay, peer collusion and peer bad-mouthing will be our future research direction.

References

1. Beverly Yang Hector, Garcia-Molina: Improving Search in Peer-to-Peer Networks. In Proceedings of the 22nd International Conference on Distributed Computing Systems (ICDCS'02), 2002.
2. Napster Inc, http://www.napster.com/
3. Gnutella, http://www.gnutelliums.com/
4. Freenet documentation, http://freenet.sourceforge.net/doc/book.html
5. Sylvia Ratnasamy, Paul Francis, Mark Handley, Richard Karp, Scott Shenker: A scalable content-addressable network. In Proc. ACM SIGCOMM (San Diego, CA, August 2001),pp. 161–172.
6. Ion Stoica, Robert Morris and David Karger: Chord: a scalable peer-to-peer lookup service for Internet applications. Proceedings of ACM SIGCOMM`01, San Diego.
7. M.S. Khambatti, K.D. Ryu, P. Dasgupta: Efficient Discovery of Implicitly formed Peer-to-Peer Communities. International Journal of Parallel and Distributed Systems and Networks, Vol. 5, No. 4, 2002. pp.155-164
8. William Stallings: Cryptography and Network Security: Principles and Practice Second Edition. 2001,Publishing House of Electronics Industry, pp.223-228
9. Diego Gambetta: Can We Trust? In, Trust: Making and Breaking Cooperative Relations, Gambetta, D (ed.). Basil Blackwell. Oxford, 1990, pp. 213-237.
10. Abdul-Rahman A, Hailes S: A distributed trust model. In Proceedings of the 1997 New security Paradigms Workshop, Cambrian, ACM Press, 1998.
11. Brite: a network topology generator. http://www.cs.bu.edu/brite/
12. Faloutsos M, Faloutsos P, Faloutsos C: On power-law relationships of the Internet topology. In: Chapin L, Sterbenz JPG, Parulkar G, Turner JS, eds. Proc. of the ACM SIGCOMM'99. New York: ACM Press, 1999. 251 ~262.
13. http://www.caida.org/

Constructing Fair-Exchange P2P File Market

Min Zuo and Jianhua Li

Department of Electronic Engineering, Shanghai Jiaotong University,
Shanghai, China
{zuomin, lijh888}@sjtu.edu.cn

Abstract. P2P is a promising technology to construct the underlying supporting layer of a Grid. It is known that contribution from all the peers is vital for the sustainability of a P2P community, but peers are often selfish and unwilling to contribute. In this paper we describe how to construct a fair file-exchanging P2P community. We name this community a P2P file market. Our scheme forces peers to contribute by a micropayment-based incentive mechanism.

1 Introduction

P2P(Peer-to-Peer) networking is a promising way to construct the underlying supporting layer of a Grid[1]. Some most attracting features of P2P networks are: they are independent of servers (totally or partly); they are self-organized and robust; and, they are rich in resources (computing power, bandwidth, storage, valuable files, etc.). However, none of these features can be achieved without cooperation of the peers.

In theory, a peer in a P2P community can be both a consumer and a server. But serving others usually means sacrificing some resources of one's own interests. If peers are autonomous and self-interested, or if they are on behalf of rational individuals (as compared with *altruistic* ones), they will tend to act as pure consumers (called "free-riders" in [2]). Free-riding makes a P2P community unfair. This will eventually paralyze the whole community and lead to a "Tragedy of the Commons "[3]. To solve this problem, some kind of *incentive* mechanism is needed. In this paper, we take the file-sharing application as an example. We suggest that a P2P file-sharing community be upgraded into a "file market". In this market, every peer is allowed to share and download files, but they have to pay the provider if they want to download a file. They can earn the necessary "money" by sharing their own files in the community.

The rest of this paper goes as follows: we present some of the design considerations in section 2; then we describe the setup, file-trading, and accounting process in section 3-5; finally, we give some remarks and conclude this paper in section 6.

2 Design Considerations

There are some design considerations we'd like to mention before going into details. First is the overall architecture. There are basically three kinds of entities in the market: peers (P) who exchange files, a trusted third party (TTP) to resolve conflicts, and an accounting center (AC) acting as a central bank. We'd like to point out that, any entity trusted by the involved two parties could act as the TTP in a transaction.

H. Zhuge and G.C. Fox (Eds.): GCC 2005, LNCS 3795, pp. 941 – 946, 2005.

Then is the problem of identity and key management. We assume each peer to be identified by a unique ID and each ID bond with a pair of public and private keys. Anonymous peers may be permitted, but they can only download and provide cost-free files (usually they are deemed as less valuable than priced ones). Here are some of the notations used in this paper: $SIG_X(M)$ denotes peer X's signature with its private key on a message M; $E_X(M)$, $D_X(M)$ denote the encryption of M with peer X's public key, and the decryption with the corresponding private key; $SE_K(M)$, $SD_K(M)$ denote the encryption and decryption of M with symmetry key K; H() is a public hash function, such as MD5, to generate message digests. We suggest the adoption of *Identity-based Cryptosystem* [4] because of its easiness in key management (IDs are also the public keys). In our file market, the AC also acts as the KGC (Key Generation Center). It sets the public parameters and holds the secret master key to compute a private key for each ID.

Last is the problem of fair exchanges. One of our most important tasks is to ensure the fairness of the trading process. We borrow the ideas in [5] to design a fair exchange protocol for our system. It is an *optimistic* protocol. It guarantees fair exchange of two electronic items between two mutually distrusting parties by the mediation of a third party (TTP), but the involvement of TTP is needed only when a conflict happens. Therefore, if most of the peers are well-intentioned, the TTP is hopefully involved infrequently. With this protocol, the trading process will be able to go in a P2P fashion as much as possible.

3 System Setup

Each new peer has to register at the AC before it can participant in the file market. During each registration, AC performs the following operations: (1) choosing a unique ID for the peer; (2) computing the private key for the ID and sending this private key to the peer; (3) issuing an initial *capital certificate* to the peer; (4) adding an item for this new peer in its account database. The communication of a registration session must be performed through a safe link (eg. SSL/TSL).

A *capital certificate* (CC) is a digital certificate. It contains the subject's ID, the expiration time of this certificate (*Cash-Exp*), the upper bound of the value (*Max-Value*) and number (*Max-Num*) of valid cheques during this period, and the signature of the AC. We can compare it to a cheque-book issued by a bank. It allows the peer to issue a maximum of *Max-Num* pieces of cheques, each valued no more than *Max-Value*. And these cheques must be cashed before the time limit *Cash-Exp*.

The initial values of *Max-Value, Max-Num,* and *Cash-Exp* are set to a system default. This initial capital is necessary to make the whole market start to function at the beginning. However, malicious users could make use of the initial capitals to free-ride. For example, one could abundant an ID every time he has used up its initial capital, and register as a newcomer to get another share. This is called "white-washing" in [6]. To combat these abuses, we require that AC perform some sophisticated checking when a newcomer registers its ID. One possible method is to use e-mail confirmation, which is widely adopted in many applications on today's Internet.

4 Downloading and Paying

When a file is put on the market for sale, it is divided into several pieces as in BitTorrent. The metadata information (file ID, file name, description, size, hash values, provider ID, address, port, accepted TTP list, price, etc.) is recorded in the community's index service and made public to all. A peer makes search queries to find what it wants. A list of matching records is returned to the querier. It then checks the list to see if a file is likely to be what it wants (file name, description, size, etc), if the price is acceptable and affordable, and if there is a TTP they commonly trusted, etc.

4.1 Negotiating

After a peer has decided which file to download, there will be a negotiating phase between the downloader (peer B) and the provider (peer A) before the download starts. The message flow of this phase is illustrated in Fig. 1. CC_X is peer X's capital certificate (see section 4). The mark "||" denotes a sequence of two or more parts.

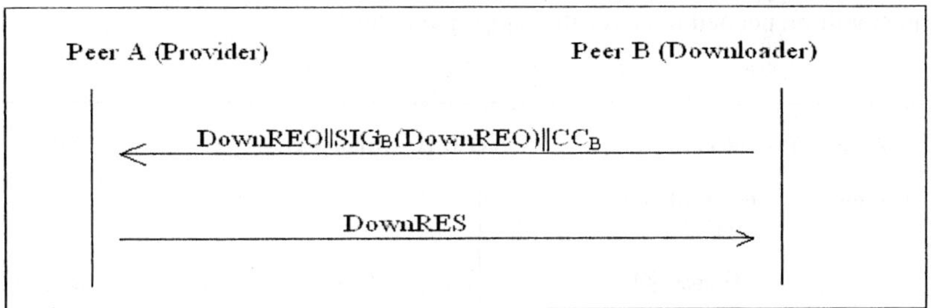

Fig. 1. Negotiating Protocol

$$\text{DownREQ} = \text{FileID}||\text{DownloaderID}||\text{ChequeSN}||\text{TS}. \tag{1}$$

Each peer maintains a personal counter. It is reset to zero each time the peer gets an updated capital certificate, and increased by one each time the peer issues a new payment cheque. "ChequeSN" is the current value of this counter. It should not be greater than *Max-Num* of this peer's current capital certificate, or the request will be rejected by other peers. "TS" is the timestamp.

When A receives the signed DownREQ and the capital certificate from B, it first verifies the signatures using B's and AC's public key respectively. Then A makes sure that ChequeSN is no greater than *Max-Num* in the certificate and there is still enough time before *Cash-Exp*. If all these succeed, A randomly chooses a piece (to be encrypted) in the file and sends its sequence number in the DownRES message. Otherwise, A sends an error message to B, or just ignores this request.

4.2 Downloading

Then begins the downloading. If there are several concurrent downloaders, the provider will redirect some of the data requests between them, so that more bandwidth can be spared to serve the rarest pieces (Due to space limitation, we won't dwell on the details here.). For each downloader there is an encrypted key piece (KP). This key piece can only be got from the original provider. When a downloader requests for the key piece, the provider will randomly choose a key K, encrypt the piece with K and send the encrypted piece to the downloader.

4.3 Paying

When the downloading finishes, downloader B gets the requested file with one of the pieces encrypted. To reconstruct the file, B has to get the decryption key (K). To get the key, B has to give the provider (A) a payment cheque as they have negotiated in section 4.1. The exchange of K and the cheque must be fair. The following protocol can make sure that B gets K *iff* (if and only if) A gets the cheque, and vice versa. The message flow is illustrated in Fig. 2. "C" denotes the payment cheque:

$$C = ID_{Payee}||ID_{Payer}||ID_{TTP}||ChequeSN||Price||TS||H(KP)||H(SE_K(KP)). \quad (2)$$

The value of "Price" shouldn't be greater than *Max-Value* in the payer's capital certificate. If the price is greater than this max value, two or more cheques (signed together) will be needed to cover the entire payment.

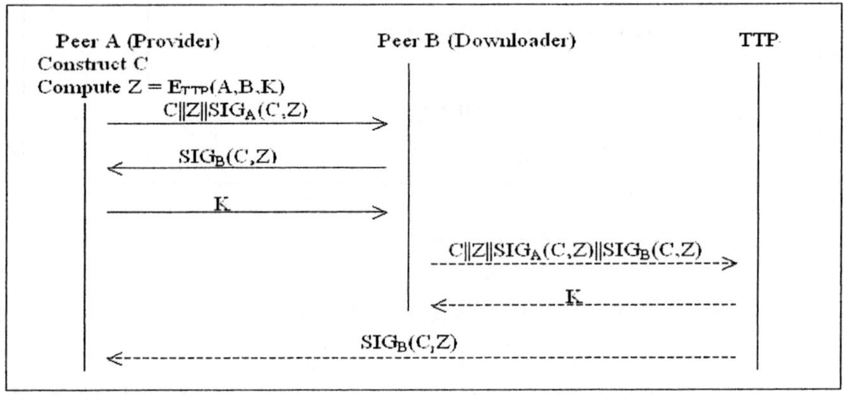

Fig. 2. Paying Protocol - a Fair Exchange Protocol

If the provider (payee) and the downloader (payer) are both honest, then the protocol only needs three message exchanges between them directly, without the interference of a third party (optimistic scenario):

A1. Peer A first constructs C and Computes $Z = E_{TTP}(A,B,K)$. Then it sends C, Z and $SIG_A(C,Z)$ to peer B.

B1. After B receives C, Z and $SIG_A(C,Z)$, it first check the contents of C and make sure that all fields of C are correct. Then B checks the validity of the signature. If all the checks succeed, B generates $SIG_B(C,Z)$ and sends it to A.

A2. If A receives properly signed $SIG_B(C,Z)$ from B, it sends K to B as plaintext.

In the case that the provider is dishonest, it may refuse to give K to the downloader (step A2) after it receives the downloader's signature on the check. In this case the downloader can contact the TTP (dotted lines in Fig. 2):

B2. B sends C, Z, $SIG_A(C,Z)$ and $SIG_B(C,Z)$ to the TTP.

TTP1. The TTP parses C to learn the ID of the provider and the downloader. Then it verifies the two signatures. If both signatures are correct, it decryptes Z with its own private key. If $D_{TTP}(Z)$ is a triplet and the first two parts are A and B, then it: (i) sends the third part (K) to B; (ii) sends $SIG_B(C,Z)$ to A.

In another case, if the downloader is dishonest and tries to directly access the TTP to learn K and bypass step B1 after it receives C, Z and $SIG_A(C,Z)$, it has to send both $SIG_A(C,Z)$ and $SIG_B(C,Z)$ to TTP. Then, if K is sent to the downloader, $SIG_B(C,Z)$ will also be sent to the provider.

When this protocol finishes, A gets the payment and B can reconstruct the file using the key. Here a fair file-exchange is completed.

5 Accounting

Accounting operations are initiated by peers periodically. To reduce the burden of AC, peers are discouraged from frequently contacting AC by a certain amount of accounting fees imposed on each accounting request.

When a peer contacts AC and request for accounting, it gives AC a package of all the payment cheques it has earned since its last accounting. Each cheque in the package should be a quadruplet in the form of (C, Z, $SIG_x(C,Z)$, K).

AC maintains an account database for all the registered peers in the community. For each peer, AC stores the information about its balance, capital certificate, credit-cheques (this peer as the payee) and debit-cheques (this peer as the payer) that have been cashed but still not expired, etc.

When AC receives the package of cheques, it first rejects the expired ones. Then it checks the IDs and sequence numbers in the cheques to detect "double-accounting" and "double-spending". If it happens, the corresponding cheque will be rejected, and a *debit* (for example 10% of this cheque's nominal value) will be imposed on the payee (double-accounting) or the payer (double-spending) as a punishment. For each remained cheque, AC further checks if the following is correct: (1)$Z = E_{TTP}(ID_{payee}, ID_{payer}, K)$; (2)$SIG_{payer}(C, Z)$ is correct. Those do not satisfy these conditions will be deemed as invalid and rejected. After all these checkings, AC begins to update the balances of the involved peers according to the "Price" in the valid cheques. An accounting fee is also subtracted from the requester's account. At last, AC sends a confirmation message back to the requester, together with a list of accepted cheques.

If the requester's current capital certificate is about to expire or it has issued *MaxNum* checks, it will also apply for a new certificate. If its balance is greater than a certain lower bound, AC will issue a new certificate to it and updates the corresponding information in the database. Otherwise, the requester will have to "sell" some more files to earn enough "money", or it can no longer download any priced files from the community after its current certificate expires.

There is another problem to be considered. Due to the debits and accounting fees, the per-peer capital of the community will decrease as time passes by. That means the whole community will become poorer and poorer until no one can afford a download. However, intuitively as more files are shared and exchanged, the per-peer capital should increase gradually. Thus we add a 0.1% per day "credit interest" for each non-negative account. These interests also serve as an additional incentive for peers to share more files and accumulate more capitals.

6 Remarks and Conclusion

In this paper we describe how to construct a fair P2P file-sharing community. We name it a P2P file market. Our scheme is a "pay-per-transfer" scheme [7], forcing peers to contribute by a micropayment-based incentive mechanism.

The most important features of our scheme include: a fair-exchange protocol ensuring the fairness of peer-to-peer trading process (to our best knowledge, most P2P micropayment schemes do not guarantee fair exchanges), a sophisticated accounting policy, and the support for multi-source parallel download (it is one of the most attracting merits of P2P technology).

In the future, we will further examine if there are other "rational attacks" [8] possibly existing in our system. Also we will try to find an efficient way to distribute the role of the accounting center onto several peers. Finally we hope to implement a prototype in a real user environment soon and observe its performance in practice.

References

1. H. Zhuge, J. Liu, L. Feng, X. Sun and C. He. "Query Routing in a Peer-to-Peer Semantic Link Network". Computational Intelligence, 21(2) pp197-216. (2005)
2. E. Adar and B. Huberman. "Free Riding on Gnutella". First Monday, 5(10), (2000)
3. G. Hardin, "The Tragedy of the Commons," Science, vol.162, pp1243–1248, (1968).
4. A. Shamir. "Identity-Based Cryptosystems and Signature Schemes". In: Proc. of Crypto'84, LNCS-196, Springer Verlag, (1985).
5. Micali S. "Simple and fast optimistic protocols for fair electronic exchange". In: Proc. of ACM PODC, (2003).
6. M. Feldman, C. Papadimitriou, J. Chuang, and I. Stoica, "Free-Riding and Whitewashing in Peer-to-Peer Systems," In: Proc. of ACM SIGCOMM'04 Workshop on Practice and Theory of Incentives in Networked Systems (PINS), (2004)
7. B. Yang and H. Garcia-Molina. "PPay: Micropayments for Peer-to-Peer Systems". In: Proc. of ACM CCS'03, (2003)
8. SJ Nielson, SA Crosby, and DS Wallach. "A Taxonomy of Rational Attacks". In: Proc. of the 4th International Workshop on Peer-To-Peer Systems, (2005)

A Novel Behavior-Based Peer-to-Peer Trust Model

Tao Wang, Xianliang Lu, and Hancong Duan

College of Computer Science and Engineering, UESTC, Chengdu, 610054
twang@uestc.edu.cn

Abstract. In P2P systems, every user can release files freely, which makes the large-scale file-sharing feasible. However, with malicious nodes increasing, lots of faked files and deceptive behaviors restrict the development of P2P application. Current P2P trust models can't guarantee the Quality of Service(QoS), and take no consideration for trust decay and cooperative cheat. To address these problems, this paper presents a novel behavior-based P2P trust model. The direct trust and reputation trust are considered, and the time decay function and reputation adjustment factor are provided in the model. Results of simulations show that compared to the current trust models, the proposed model is more efficient and scalable.

Keywords: P2P, trust, decay function, QoS.

1 Introduction

In P2P systems, every node is both client and server, and users can make use of resources freely. Open and anonymity are the characters of P2P system, so nodes can join or leave system in anytime, and what's more, nodes are not responsible for their behaviors. On one hand, lots of malicious nodes provide faked files, and spread useless or bad files, such as Trojan horse and virus. These nodes take positive response to all queries in P2P system, and then provide the decoy files. On the other hand, irresponsible clients may interrupt downloads arbitrarily. All the above situations can't guarantee the Quality of Service(QoS) in P2P file-sharing.

Marsh proposed a trust model[1], and the model was built based on the trust of society characters, which was complex and infeasible. According to local reputation, another trust model[2] used distributed poll to evaluate the provider's trust value. The advantage of this model is simple, but nodes' trust values were always local and unilateral. In Trust model EigenRep[3], when node I wants to know the trust value of node K, system compute the global trust value of node K by using local trust values of nodes which have trades with node K. In Dou model[4], to address the problems of EigenRep, authors proposed a nonlinear trust model. However, these two models have convergence problem and the huge system payload restrict them only fit to small-scale networks.

Current models take no consideration for trust decay. As we all know, if there is no direct or indirect touch between nodes in a long time, the trust relationship will decay. The factor will be considered in the following calculation of our trust model.

H. Zhuge and G.C. Fox (Eds.): GCC 2005, LNCS 3795, pp. 947–952, 2005.

The rest of paper is organized as follows. Section 2 gives a detailed analysis for trust in P2P network. Section 3 presents our trust model in P2P. Experiments and simulations are shown in section 4. Finally, in section 5, we summarize our model.

2 Trust in P2P

Trust in P2P networks can be classified into identity trust and behavior trust. Identity trust mainly takes charge of the identity authentication, user rights and etc.. By using encrpytion technique, digital signature and authentication mechanism, identity trust can be realized and there are many solutions in the field of network security, such as authentication[5] and signatures[6]. Behavior trust pays attention to trust problems with wide significance, which are more important in P2P system. Users can make use of the past behavior between partners and other users' evaluation to adjust the trust value dynamically. In this paper, we focus on behavior trust.

Behavior trust in P2P is composed of direct trust and reputation trust(indirect trust)[7].

Direct trust is based on the past behaviors of direct trades between nodes. If there is no trade history between nodes, recommendation from other nodes is the only way to take, which is called reputation trust.

3 P2P Trust Model

Definition 1. Let DT_{ij} denote the direct trust value between node i and j, which is calculated by the past direct behavior between nodes. Then, DT_{ij} is defined:

$$DT_{ij} = \frac{Sat_{ij} - Dissat_{ij}}{Sat_{ij} + Dissat_{ij}} \times \theta(\text{t-t}_{ij}) \tag{1}$$

where $Dissat_{ij}$ represents the number of dissatisfied trades between node i and j. Faked files, virus and interrupting downloads will lead to dissatisfaction. Sat_{ij} represents the number of satisfied trades. In the time decay function $\theta(\text{t-t}_{ij})$, t_{ij} represents the time of the latest trade between node i and j.

Definition 2. Let R_j denote the reputation value of node j, which is an average value. It can be evaluated from all nodes which have trades with node j. R_j is defined:

$$R_j = \frac{\sum_{k=1}^{n} DT_{kj}}{\sum_{k=1}^{n} N_{kj}} \tag{2}$$

where $N_{kj} = \begin{cases} 1 & \textit{if there is direct trust between node k and j} \\ 0 & \textit{if there is no direct trust between node k and j} \end{cases}$.

Since the time decay factor has been included in DT_{ij} (Equation 1), $\theta(\text{t-t}_{kj})$ is needless here.

- Cooperative cheat

Cooperative cheat means node i and j raise up the reputation values of partners by giving the faked positive response frequently. To address the problem, we define a reputation adjustment factor σ_{ij} , which is inverse proportion with the familiar degrees between nodes. The more frequent node i and j submit high reputation values mutually, the less σ_{ij} is. The value of σ_{ij} lies in [0,1]. Generally, we set $\sigma_{ij}=1$. When system detects that there are frequent high evaluation from the same node, the value of σ_{ij} will be dropped down reasonably. So R_j can be rewrited as:

$$R_j=\frac{\sum_{k=1}^{n}\left(\frac{Sat_{kj}-Dissat_{kj}}{Sat_{kj}+Dissat_{kj}}\right)\times\theta(\text{t-t}_{\text{kj}})\times\sigma_{\text{kj}}}{\sum_{k=1}^{n}N_{kj}} \tag{3}$$

Definition 3. Let Trust_{ij} denote the global trust value between node i and j.

$$\begin{cases}Trust_{ij}=\alpha\times DT_{ij}+\beta\times R_j\\ \alpha+\beta=1 \qquad \alpha\,,\,\beta\in[0\,,1]\end{cases} \tag{4}$$

Furtherly, we can get

$$\begin{cases}Trust_{ij}=\alpha\times\left(\frac{Sat_{ij}-Dissat_{ij}}{Sat_{ij}+Dissat_{ij}}\right)\times\theta(\text{t-t}_{\text{ij}})+\beta\times\frac{\sum_{k=1}^{n}\left(\frac{Sat_{kj}-Dissat_{kj}}{Sat_{kj}+Dissat_{kj}}\right)\times\theta(\text{t-t}_{\text{kj}})\times\sigma_{\text{kj}}}{\sum_{k=1}^{n}N_{kj}}\\ \alpha+\beta=1 \qquad \alpha\,,\,\beta\in[0\,,1]\end{cases} \tag{5}$$

4 Experiments and Analyses

In order to analyse our trust model, we conduct simulation experiments for file-sharing in P2P system. Users will query files and download them from the node with the highest trust value. According to successful downloads and authentic files, we judge whether the trade is successful. We simulate several kinds of problem nodes, such as Identity-changed nodes[8], Trust decay nodes and Cooperative cheat nodes.

We simulate a P2P network with 1000 nodes. 5000 sharing files are distributed in nodes randomly and the queries for sharing files are also random. After downloads finish, replicas of files will be stored in local nodes. Every user must complete above 50 downloads and every download will be executed from node with the highest trust value, which stores the queried file.

In simulation experiments, the final criterion is the Successful Downloads Ratio(SDR) (the sum of successful downloads /the sum of downloads) in P2P

Firstly, we compare P2P systems with and without trust model in different-scale malicious nodes. From the Figure 1, we can conclude that with the ratio of malicious nodes increasing, our trust model can maintain the successful downloads ratio in a high level, even when malicious nodes take 50% of the whole nodes, SDR is still above 85%.

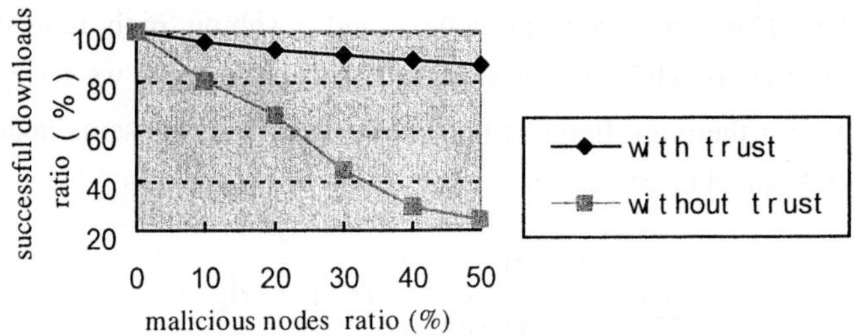

Fig. 1. SDR in P2P system with and without trust model

Secondly, we simulate three kinds of problem nodes respectively.

1. Identity-changed nodes

We simulate different initial trust values of nodes and record the different effects on our model with Identity-changed nodes. Results can be found in Figure 2.

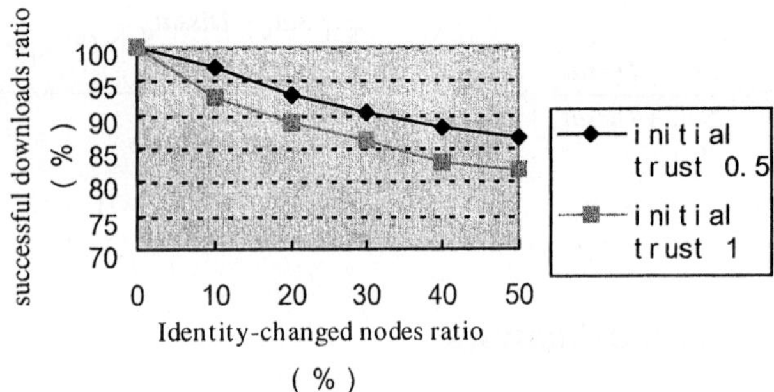

Fig. 2. SDR with different initial trust values in trust model

In Figure 2, we can find that the initial trust value of nodes makes great effects on P2P system with Identity-changed nodes. The SDR of initial value 1is lower than the SDR of initial value 0.5 markedly. This is because that a higher initial trust value may urge malicious nodes to reenter the system with a new identity, which will get an inborn high trust value. However, being a cooperative P2P system, we should encourage new nodes to join, so the initial trust value should not be lower than 0.

2. Trust decay nodes

We simulate different-scale trust decay nodes in P2P system with our trust model to detect the effects of time decay. Meanwhile, we simulate the EgienRep trust model[3] of Standford to make a compare, which take no consideration for decay.

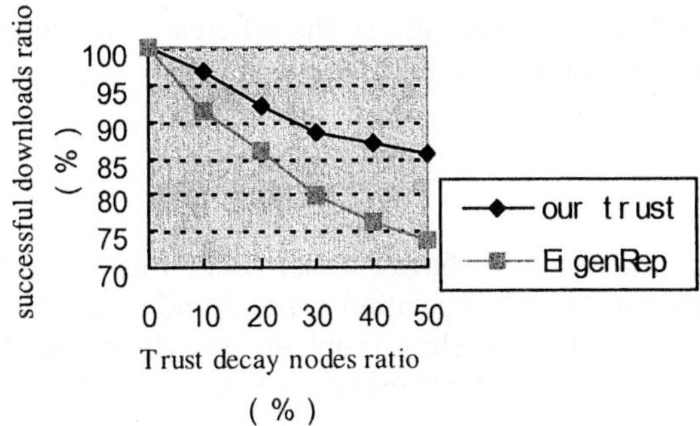

Fig. 3. SDR with trust decay nodes in two trust models

In Figure 3, Compared with the EigenRep, the decay function $\theta(t\text{-}t_{ij})$ in our trust model is effective in the trust decay situation.

3. Cooperative cheat nodes

We simulate different-scale cooperative cheat nodes in our trust model, EgienRep and Dou-trust model [4]. Results can be found in the following.

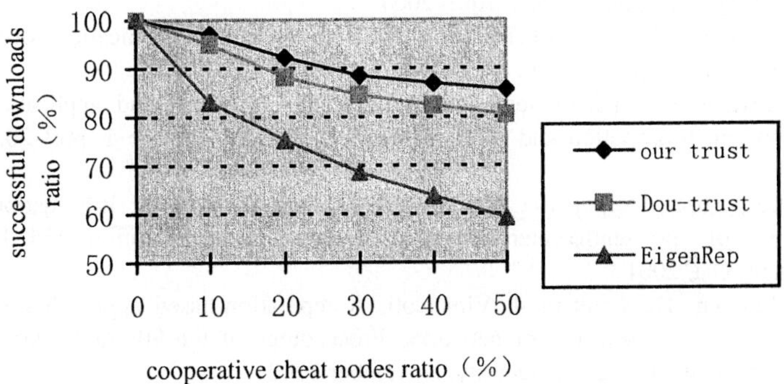

Fig. 4. SDR with different scale cooperative cheat nodes in three models

In Figure 4, our trust model and Dou-trust model do well in the cooperative cheat nodes and SDR can be maintained at about 80%~85%. However, the SDR of EgienRep will drop down markedly with the cooperative cheat nodes increasing and lower than 60% in the end.

The difference between our trust model and Dou-trust model [4] lies in the following. We make use of the reputation adjustment factor σ_{ij} to modify our model, while in Dou-trust model, in order to restrain the cooperative cheat, not only should the applicant propose an evaluation after downloads finish, but also the provider should give a confirm information. Obviously, this policy produces an extra payload in the system and needs more bandwidth, so the efficiency can not be guaranteed in Dou model, especially in a large-scale P2P system.

5 Conclusion

In this paper, we propose a behavior-based P2P trust model, which takes consideration for direct trust and reputation trust. Some solutions are provided to address trust decay and cooperative cheat problems. Results of simulation prove that our model is more effective and scalable than current trust models.

References

1. Marsh S, Formalising Trust as a Computational Concept Ph.D Thesis, University of Stirling, 1994
2. Damiani E, De Capitani di Vimercati, A reputation-based approach for choosing reliable resources in peer-to-peer networks, the 9th ACM Conference on Computer and Communications Security, Nov. 2002
3. Kamvar S D, Schlosser M, and Garcia-Molina H, Eigenrep: Reputation management in p2p networks, Proc. of the 12th International World Wide Web Conf., 2003
4. Dou W, Wang HM, and etc, A recommendation-based peer-to-peer trust model, Journal of Software, 2004, 15(4), pp.571-583, April 2004
5. Amit Basu, Steve Muylle, Authentication in e-commerce, Communications of the ACM, Volume 46, Issue 12, pp.159-166, December 2003
6. Giuseppe Ateniese, Verifiable encryption of digital signatures and applications, ACM Transactions on Information and System Security, Volume 7, Issue 1, pp.1-20, February 2004
7. Karl Aberer, Zoran Despotovic, Managing Trust in a Peer-2-Peer Information System, Proceedings of the tenth international conference on Information and knowledge management, Oct. 2001
8. Ernesto Damiani, De Capitani di Vimercati, A reputation-based approach for choosing reliable resources in peer-to-peer networks, Proceedings of the 9th ACM conference on Computer and communications security, November 2002

A Topology Adaptation Protocol for Structured Superpeer Overlay Construction

Changyong Niu, Jian Wang, and Ruimin Shen

Department of Computer Science and Technology,
Shanghai Jiaotong University,
Shanghai, China
{cyniu, jwang, rmshen}@sjtu.edu.cn

Abstract. Peer-to-peer networks can be divided into structured and unstructured based on their overlay topologies. In reality, unstructured p2p networks with superpeers have proved their capacities to support millions of users simultaneously. However, applications deployed on this kind of overlay networks, such as file-sharing, require flooding or gossip-based message routing, which puts more overhead on underlying networks and provides no guarantee on resource discovery. In this paper we propose an overlay adaptation protocol which allows structured superpeer overlay construction from unstructured p2p overlay networks with the potential to leverage the advantages of structured p2p overlay networks such as efficiency, scalability and guaranteed look-up services. The simulation result shows that our protocol can build the structured superpeer overlay with efficiency and scalability.

1 Introduction

P2P networks can be classified as being either structured or unstructured. Recent developments of structured [1,2] and unstructured [3,4] overlay networks point to a new direction for overlay research to address these major challenges such as scalability, efficiency and flexibility.

Structured P2P networks implement efficient distributed P2P lookup services by organizing the peers in structured overlay networks and determining routing messages to the peer that is responsible for a given key. These implementations of distributed lookup service are often referred to as Distributed Hash Tables (DHTs). In contract, nodes in unstructured overlay network have the flexibility to choose the number and destinations of their connections, and adapt them to network heterogeneity for improved network performance. Especially by introducing the concept of superpeer [5, 6] into unstructured overlay network, the heterogeneity of P2P networks is further explored without compromising their decentralized nature. However, unstructured overlay networks often require flooding or gossip to route messages, which limits their efficiency and puts more overhead on the underlying physical networks.

In this paper we explore the integration of structure and unstructured overlay network, in a way that superpeers are selected from operational unstructured overlay networks and further organized into structured network to tackle the challenges of scalability, efficiency and flexibility. The potential advantages of this method include:

H. Zhuge and G.C. Fox (Eds.): GCC 2005, LNCS 3795, pp. 953–958, 2005.

- Load Balance: load balance among superpeers is achieved not only on the number of object references maintained but also on the number of clients handled by superpeers.
- DHT Enhanced: By organizing superpeers into structured overlay, applications over resulting overlay networks can easily take advantages of DHTs.
- Efficiency: simulation shows that the presented protocol is efficient for superpeer overlay construction in terms of underlying network overhead.

Rest of this paper is organized as follows. Related superpeer overlay construction protocols are presented in section 2. In section 3, the proposed protocol for building structured superpeer overlay will be described in detail. In section 4, the protocol performance will be analyzed and experimental results will be illustrated.

2 Related Work

The concept of superpeer has been introduced to improve the performance of P2P overlay networks and above applications. A superpeer is expected to be more stable and powerful to operate as a server for a group of common peers, and as an equal to other superpeers. Some superpeer overlay designs have been introduced in literature. The system in [7] is based on a two-tier hierarchical overlay network. All nodes are part of the bottom tier: a Chord ring. In a Chord ring, each node keeps track of other nodes that are 1/2-ring away, 1/4-ring away, 1/8-ring away, etc. To construct the upper superpeer tier, the Chord ring is divided into a number of arcs with equal length. In each arc, some node is selected as superpeer of this arc, and all superpeers form the upper tier. Another two-tier superpeer overlay is the system in [8]. Each node belongs to exactly one group of the bottom tier and different groups form separate overlays which may or may not be the same in structure. One or more superpeer is selected from each group and all superpeers form the upper tier overlay which is a modified Chord ring. And the relationship between superpeer and group peer is many-to-many.

Other superpeer overlay networks include HONet [9]. In HONet, peers are first clustered into groups based on localities in a structured way. Then superpeers selected from each group are connected using random walk. Superpeer selection and hierarchical overlay construction protocol presented in [6] is gossip based. The resulting overlay resembles the characteristics of one-to-many relationship between superpeer and group peer; random network structure of superpeer overlay and minimized number of superpeers (also called target superpeer overlay). Same as HONet, nodes in groups are not totally separated but are connected through gossip based links. So the robustness of protocol is achieved in price of network overhead. However the total overhead of overlay construction scales sub-linearly with the size of the network, which is very efficient.

P2P overlay networks have been used in many applications, such as application-level multicast, file-sharing, media streaming, data storage and most recently semantic layer of Knowledge Grid [10].

3 Structured Superpeer Overlay Construction

We start the superpeer overlay construction from a network consisting of a large collection of nodes, in which each node having a unique identifier can potentially communicate with any other node through message exchanges. Also the network is highly dynamic with each node joining and leaving, even crashing at any time. Nodes in the network are heterogeneous with different capacities. To differentiate the nodes according to these heterogeneities, each node is associated with a value representing its capacity according to its own characteristics. Based on this information, we can select the nodes with larger capacities to act as superpeers and determine the number of clients that a superpeer may handle.

The protocol presented in this paper will gradually adapt an unstructured overlay into a structured superpeer overlay, which has a number of important advantages compared to the flat unstructured overlay networks.

- Handling heterogeneity: the upper-layer overlay is consisting of more powerful and stable superpeers.
- Transparency: client joining, leaving and crashing under some superpeer are totally transparent to other groups. And the client floating, i.e. from one superpeer to another, is also transparent from object lookup services.
- Efficiency: the structured organization of superpeers may further provide more efficient lookup services; also this efficiency may further lead to fewer network overheads.

3.1 Superpeer Selection and Structurization

Instead of building a superpeer overlay from scratch, we build the superpeer overlay as an additional overlay, superimposed over an existing connected topology. The rationale behind this is that even if all superpeers crashed simultaneously, the network would not be disconnected and the superpeer overlay may still be rebuilt from scratch.

We use tapestry as the superpeer overlay structure and implement the adaptation algorithm in Peersim. Although specific structured overlay protocol is used in this work, the overlay adaptation paradigm is general enough to adopting other DHT protocols. The construction may be divided into two stages.

The idea of the first stage superpeer selection is fairly simple. We assume each node in the existing overlay knows about its own capacity. Besides the neighbor table, each node also maintains a table of superpeers and superpeer/client table. The superpeer table of a node *A* maintains a sample of superpeers that *A* has already seen in current overlay; and superpeer/client table maintains the current clients of *A* if *A* is a superpeer or the current superpeer of *A* if it is a client. The role of superpeer and client is determined by competition. The competition strategy is illustrated in Table 1, which is similar to the superpeer selection algorithm in [6]. However, instead of generating the minimum number of superpeers, we have adapted the algorithm for load balance purposes. Each superpeer has three satisfaction levels: unsatisfied if its number of clients less than its pre-defined min-client threshold; satisfying if the number of clients is between min-client and max-client threshold; and over-satisfied if the number of clients exceeds max-client. Over-satisfied is only allowed when a superpeer can take over another superpeer and all its clients. And load balance is handled in top-layer overlay compete strategy.

Table 1. Let *p* being a local peer and *p-superpeer* being its superpeer table; L_p is *p*'s current load; C_p is the capacity of *p*; $C_{p\text{-max}}$ is the max-client threshold of *p*; $C_{p\text{-min}}$ is the min-client threshold of *p*;let *r*, *q* being temporary remote peers

S={*r*| $r \in$ *p-superpeer* && $C_r > C_p$ && $L_r < C_{r\text{-max}}$ }
Probing the load (used capacity) L_q of q that $q \in \{q \mid q$ belongs to S}
Finding q that $(C_q - L_q) > L_p$
If found *q* then *q* accommodate *p* and all its clients
Else finding *q* that $\max(L_{q\text{-max}} - L_q)$
  Transfer min $(L_{q\text{-max}} - L_q, L_p)$ clients for *p* to *q*
  if exists client $r \in q$ and $C_r > C_p$ then
    exchange the role of $_r$ and $_p$, letting *p* to be a client of *q* and *r* to be a superpeer taking over the clients of *p*

After the selection of the first stage superpeers, every superpeer in current snapshot will apply to join the upcoming superpeer overlay. Here we draw the same assumption as tapestry does, that there are well-known federation and static tapestry nodes in the overlay for bootstrap purpose.

Since the goal of the top-tier overlay is load balance, it is reasonable that the resulting overlay contains large capacity superpeers and each superpeer have some client in its domination. To achieve this goal, we design a superpeer compete strategy which is described as follows.

Table 2. p is the node querying for a superpeer; S_0 is it's accessing point to top-layer superpeer overlay; L_X is node X's current load; C_X is the capacity of X; $CMAX_X$ is the max-client threshold of X; $CMIN_X$ is the min-client threshold of X; TEMP, t, S are temporary variables

TEMP =p; S= S_0;
while (S != null){
  if (L_S > $CMAX_S$) // S is not over-satisfied
  { S accepts TEMP; break;}
  find k from S's client table which has the max capacity
  if (C_k > C_{TEMP})
  { t.superpeer=k.superpeer
    t=k; // TEMP replace k in the client table of S
    TEMP = t; }
  S pick out next hop H for S in his routing table
  if (H == null)
  { TEMP join as a supernode}
  else
  { S = H}
}

p is the node querying for a superpeer; S_0 is it's accessing point to top-layer superpeer overlay, and L_X is node X's current load with C_X being the capacity of X; $CMAX_X$ is the max-client threshold of X; $CMIN_X$ is the min-client threshold of X; The superpeer finding algorithm is described as follows and illustrated in Table 2.

1. If S_0 is not over-satisfied and has the spare capacity to accept p as a client then the finding is success.
2. If S_0 could not accommodate p, take a look in S_0's client table to find C_k, where k is the node with largest capacity in the client table, and compare it with C_p. If C_p is larger then forward the finding to the routing successor of S_0.
3. If C_k is larger, then node p becomes the client of S_0, and the client node k gracefully leaving S_0, and using S_0 as the accessing point to find himself a superpeer. (k replaces p to be the node querying for a superpeer.)
4. The adaptation process continues until p successfully finding himself a superpeer or the the routing successor of S_0 being null. In the latter case, p joins the superpeer overlay as a superpeer, and the finding process is ended.

3.2 Load Balance

We design a milder way to explore the capacity heterogeneity and with a focus on load balance and fairness. To achieve this, each selected superpeer initializes a (min-client, max-client) pair. Each superpeer aggressively maintains its number of clients between min-client and max-client. When a new superpeer joins the top-tapestry overlay, it grabs clients from its neighbors to achieving this goal. And when the number of clients of a superpeer exceeds max-client, it splits some clients to its neighbors. As long as the resulting number of clients is between the threshold, a superpeer is always willing to accept (or split) clients from (or to) other superpeers. The rationale for a client could be reassigned to another superpeer is explained as follows. In a structured superpeer overlay, information of objects is published as (key, value) pairs. A key says K_1 is derived from the keywords associated with an object says O_1, and the value coupled with K_1 is corresponding to the machine hosting O_1. All (key, value) pairs are distributed among top-tapestry nodes as object references. As long as a lookup for a key gets the reference, the "value" within the reference could direct the query to the hosting machine, no matter which superpeer the hosting machine belongs to. So the client floating is totally transparent from object lookup.

4 Analysis and Future Work

Because we focus our current work on efficient protocol design of structured superpeer overlay construction, in the following we compare the efficiency of our protocol with that of [6] in terms of network overhead and operations performed by each node to form such superpeer overlays. To compute the overall network overhead, we aggregate messages sent by all nodes for neighbor information probing and neighbor transferring which are needed for overlay construction. The aggregations are performed under different network sizes with a power law node capacity distribution and max node capacity of 500. The comparison of total network overhead is illustrated in figure 1. For simplicity, we average the total messages

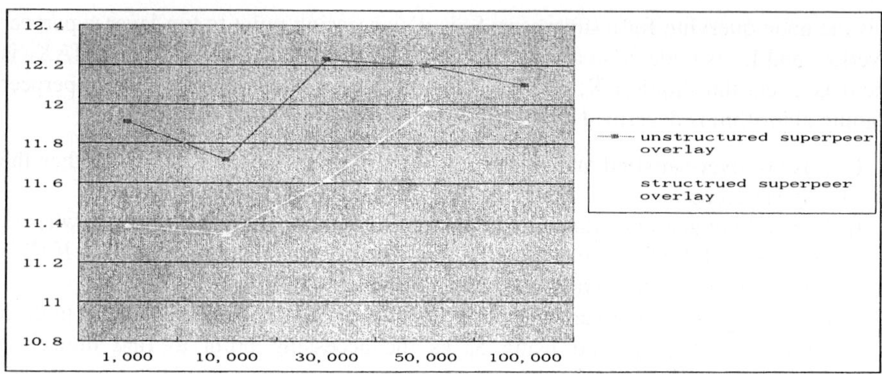

Fig. 1. Network overhead comparison between the constructions of unstructured and structured superpeer overlays: the main reason that our protocol performs better is because we focus on load balance among superpeers

among all nodes in the network. The average could be read as number of operations taken by each node for probing or transferring. As for our protocol, the operations also include messages for tapestry node join and routing table maintenance during overlay construction. And the experiment result is illustrated in Figure 1.

In this paper, we propose a topology adaptation protocol for building structured superpeer overlay. The simulation result shows that the protocol can build a structured superpeer overlay from an unstructured p2p network with efficiency and scalability. Future work includes to incorporate the model with the ability of handling locality heterogeneity and to explore the behavior of such hierarchical topology under churn.

References

1. Stoica, I., Morris, R., Kaashoek, M. and Balakrishnan, H., Chord: a scalable peer-to-peer lookup service for internet applications, Proceedings of ACM SIGCOMM 2001
2. Zhao, B.Y., Kubiatowicz, J. and Joseph, A.D., Tapestry: an infrastructure for fault-tolerant wide-area location and routing, Technical Report, University of California, Berkeley, 2001
3. "Gnutell." http://www.gnutell.com
4. Kermarrec, A.M., Massoulié, L. and Ganesh, A.J., Probabilistic reliable dissemination in large-scale systems. IEEE Transactions on Parallel and Distributed Systems, 2003
5. Yang, B. and Garcia-Molina, H. Designing a super-peer network, Proceedings of the 19th International conference on Data Engineering, 2003
6. Montresor, A., A robust protocol for building superpeer overlay topologies, Technical Report UBLCS-2004-8
7. Manku, A.T., Cheng, Y., Kumar, V., and Savage, S., Structured superpeers: leveraging heterogeneity to provide constant-time lookup proceeding of IEEE Workshop on Internet Applications, 2003
8. Garces-Eric, L., Biersack, E.W., Felber, P.A., Ross, K.W., and Urvoy-Keller, G., Hierarchical peer-to-peer systems, Proceeding of INFOCOMM'03, 2003
9. Ruixiong Tian, Yongqiang Xiong, Qian Zhang, Bo Li, Ben Y. Zhao, Xing Li, Hybrid overlay structure based on random walks, Proceeding of iptps05, 2005
10. Zhuge, H., Liu, J., Feng, L., Sun, X., He, C., Query routing in a peer-to-peer semantic link network, Computational Intelligence, Volume 21, 2005

A Routing Protocol Based on Trust for MANETs

Cuirong Wang[1,2], Xiaozong Yang[1], and Yuan Gao[2]

[1] School of Computer Science & Technology, Harbin Institute of Technology, 150001 Harbin, China
[2] Qinhuangdao School, Northeastern University, 066000 Qinhuangdao, China
wangcr@mail.neuq.edu.cn

Abstract. Ad hoc network is a peer-to-peer grid system. The combination of the Knowledge Grid and ad hoc network could have a great effect on the future interconnection environment. In the existed researches about ad hoc routing protocols, knowledge with trusted requirements is not supported. In this paper, the trust level is used as knowledge for routing. The security rather than shortest path is the primary concern of the method. The performance evaluation via simulations shows that the method is a promising trust routing algorithm for MANETs. The effects of this trust model on DSR route discovery mechanism are analyzed. Results show that our model can improve the performance of DSR route discovery.

1 Introduction

In an ad hoc network nodes cooperate in dynamically establishing wireless networks and maintaining routes through the network, forwarding packets for each other to facilitate multi-hop communication between nodes not in direct transmission range. On-demand routing protocols for mobile ad hoc networks, such as Dynamic Source Routing (DSR), generate routes for unknown destination paths on an as needs be basis. The protocols mostly employ flooding approaches to discovery routes. The flooding approach forwards a node's queries to all its neighbors, which results in traffic problems. To be effective, a query-routing strategy should forward queries only to nodes who propose certain related knowledge.

The proposed routing solutions deal only with number of hops. Connections with trust requirements are not supported. In this paper, we propose a trust-based routing algorithm for ad hoc network. Security rather than optimality is the primary concern of the algorithm. In the case of general routing algorithms, it is better to find a route very fast in order to have a good response time to the speed of topology change, than to search for the optimal route but without meaning, because the network condition is changed and this route does not exist anymore. In this paper, trust parameters of nodes are used for routing decision. To evaluate the performance of the protocol(tr-DSR), we carried out the simulations for different network conditions.

H. Zhuge and G.C. Fox (Eds.): GCC 2005, LNCS 3795, pp. 959–964, 2005.

The paper is organized as follows. In Section 2, we introduce the related work. The proposed routing algorithm tr-DSR is described in Section 3. The performance evaluation and analysis of the tr-DSR are discussed in Section 4. Finally, conclusions are given in Section 5.

2 Related Work

2.1 DSR and Secure Routing Protocol

The Dynamic Source Routing protocol[1] is a simple and efficient routing protocol designed specifically for use in multi-hop wireless ad hoc networks of mobile nodes. Using DSR, the network is completely self-organizing and self-configuring, requiring no existing network infrastructure or administration. In DSR, although it is possible to end up with route discovery failures to some extent, re-broadcasting route request packets with certain trust probability can be considered as a performance improvement technique[2].

In response to a single Route Discovery, a node may learn and cache multiple routes to any destination. This support for multiple routes allows the reaction to routing changes to be much more rapid, since a node with multiple routes to a destination can try another cached route if the one it has been using should fail. This caching of multiple routes also avoids the overhead of needing to perform a new Route Discovery each time a route in use breaks.

The trust of node is a very important constrain in wireless network. If a node or a route has very low trust value, this route will be dangerous. Moreover, this can have also a bad effect on the network data packets: there are some nodes that will be dropped. To this end, we propose a trust routing establishment mechanism and we apply it to the DSR routing protocol. The main feature of our work compared to the related works in this area is that it is simple and efficient according to the obtained performance enhancement comparing to the results obtained with the basic DSR protocol.

2.2 Trust Quantization

An ad-hoc network of wireless nodes is a temporarily formedcreated, operated and managed network by the nodes themselves. Nodes assist each other by passing data and control packets from one node to another. The execution and survival of an ad-hoc network is solely dependent upon the trusting nature of its nodes.

A number of protocols have been developed to secure ad-hoc networks using cryptographic schemes, but all rely on the presence of an omnipresent, and often omniscient, trust authority. The dependence on a central trust authority is an impractical requirement for ad-hoc networks. We present a model for trust-based communication in ad-hoc networks. In the model, a central trust authority is a superfluous requirement. The routes discovered using our model is not cryptographically secure but each one of them carries a confidence measure regarding its suitability in the current. According to Josang[3], trust and security represent two sides of the same thing. Both these terms are so highly interconnected that they cannot be evaluated independently.

The principle drawback to find route based trust is the route discovery efficiency. So, in the simulation, we predigested the computing of trust. Each node in the network stores other node's trust value. The trust value of a node is computed and updated by trust agents that reside on network nodes[8]. In our simulation, the trust values of all nodes are stored in each node in advance. We signify trust -1 to +1, representing an unremitting range from complete distrust to absolute trust.The trust value in route R by source node S is represented as $T_S(R)$ and given by the following equation.

$T_S(R)=W_S(N_i)*T_S(N_i)$, $W_S(N_i)=1$, $0<W_S(N_i)<1$ where $W_S(N_i)$ represents the weight assigned to node N_i by source node S and $T_S(N_i)$ represents the trust value in node Ni by source node S. $T_S(R)$ is a probabilistic value. To simply, in our simulation, let $T_S(R)=\min(T_S(N_i))$, i.e., $W_S(N_i)=0$, $\forall$ i $\neq$ j , $W_S(N_j)=1$, $T_S(N_j)= \min(T_S(N_i))$.

3 Routing Algorithm Based on Trust

In this paper, we extended DSR to trust-based tr-DSR. Each node maintains two routes to a destination[9]. This increases the number of different routes returned, giving the source a better choice from which to select two maximal trust probability routes from these replies. Although tr-DSR is capable of maintaining more than two routes, we only experimented with the two-path version, since the results in previous indicate that the largest improvement is achieved by going from one to two or three paths[2,4,5].

The routing protocol uses the path with the larger trust value of route and less delay of packet among multiple route options as two metrics unlike standard DSR protocol that only uses minimum hop count. The idea behind this is to maximize preemptive route creation by choosing the route that is expected to security. How well the trust of a route can be estimated plays a key role in the performance of this protocol. Routing data packets algorithm is as Fig.1.

4 Analysis of Simulation Results

To analyze the effects of the trust value of a node and a route computing on route discovery mechanism, we give the parameters used in our model as following.

N Average number of nodes per route;

R Average number of paths returned for the same route request and for the source-destination pair;

T Average trust probability.

A node re-broadcasts or returns a route reply with probability T. Thus, the probability that all of the nodes on a path with average length N will re-broadcast the route request or return the route reply from their cache is P^N.

Step 1 if (routing cache is empty) then routing discovery algorithm is run;
{ Source node *S* Broadcast RREQ message:
Intermediate node x received the RREQ massage re-broadcasts the RREQ or return a route reply with trust probability $T_S(x)$;
If source received RREP message
{ Then if number of route <2 then
{ if RREP timeout
Then discard the RREP message
else compute trust value of the route contained the RREP message;
if the trust value of the route >threshold then cache the source routes
else discard the RREP message }
else discard RREP message } }
Step 2 if routing cache is not empty
then search the routing cache for to the desired destination;
routing original data packet through the route with the less number of hops;
Step 3 if (no route is found) then (discard the packet) end if.

Fig. 1. Routing data packets algorithm

The probability of at least one of the nodes on a path with average length N will not re-broadcast the route request packet is denoted by T_0 and given as follows.

$T_0 = 1 - P^N$.

T_0 is also the probability of this path to be broken.

Since there are different R paths to the destination and the trustless nodes behave independently on deciding to re-broadcast or not, we may assume that each of the paths has a probability of T_0 of being broken. Thus, the overall probability of all of the paths being broken, route discovery failure probability PR, is given as follows.

$T_R = (1 - T)^R$.

The tr-DSR protocol algorithm is simulated in OpNet Modeler 10.0 environment. The example network consists of 50 static nodes. The routing protocol used is DSR.

Fig.2 shows that number of route replies is, on the average, four times more than the number of route requests in the standard DSR protocol.

The change of T_R with respect to T for the simulated networks described above is depicted in Fig. 3.

In our simulation, senders are randomly selected among the nodes in the system. We gradually increased the average trust probability and observed the number of route requests and route replies. Below are the simulation results of the trust-based scenarios

Trust based route reply reduced the ratio of route reply message over the number of route requests. Thus, we analyzed this ratio in our simulation.

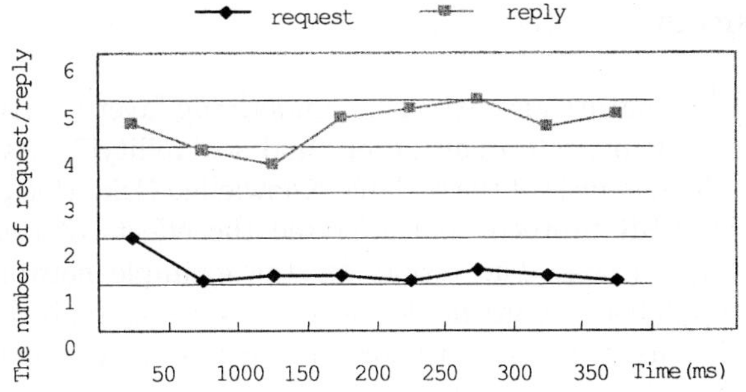

Fig. 2. The number of Request/reply ratio vs. simulation time

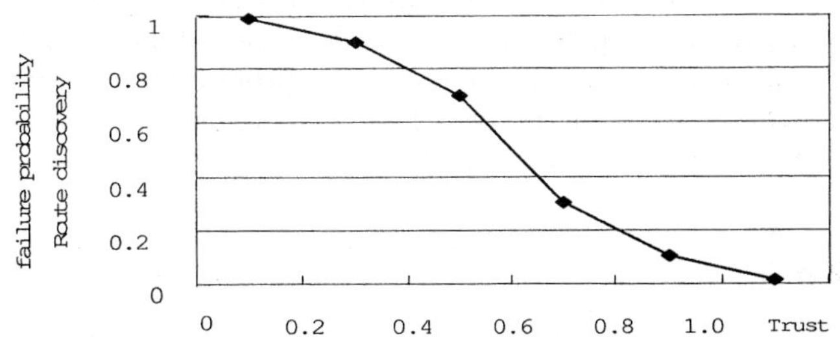

Fig. 3. Route discovery failure probability vs. trust

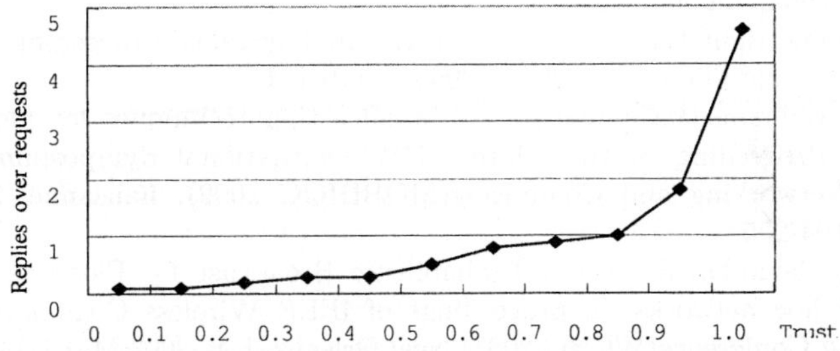

Fig. 4. Simulation results of request/reply ratio vs. trust

Fig.4 shows that even if all of the nodes are trustless, the number of route replies over number of route requests is still above the threshold value of 1 up to p=0.2. For this case, the route failure probability T_R can be calculated as 0.04.

The above analysis shows that some of route replies are redundant and an optimization may be possible on the number of route request re-broadcasts. If DSR is modified in such a way that the legitimate nodes rebroadcast the route requests with a probability of T, which should be engineered carefully, route discovery success ratio will still be acceptable and there will be a decrease in number of routing packets that are flooded to the network.

5 Conclusions

Ad hoc network is a nature and extensible underlying layer for Knowledge Grid because of its autonomy, self-organization, and scalability[7]. As a solution to routing reply at the semantic of the scalable Knowledge Grid, this paper proposes a trust model on DSR protocol and analyzed the effects of this trust model on route discovery success. The results for the example networks show that such a trust probabilistic route model decreasing route reply packets. When all the nodes are trustless in the network, route discovery is not so disrupted up to a certain trustless probability 1-T value. This is due to redundant route replies for a route request. The tr-DSR protocol performance be improved. Such a change of re-broadcast mechanism in DSR route discovery and route select phase come with some advantages. The most important advantage is the increase in network utilization by decreasing the overhead of redundant broadcasts.The tr-DSR protocol based on trust may not be cryptographically secure but they do establish relative levels of trustworthiness with them. We believe that our tr-DSR will be suited to ad hoc networks.

References

1. David, B., Johnson, D.A., Maltz, J. B.: The Dynamic Source Routing Protocol for Multi-Hop Wireless Ad Hoc Networks. Ad Hoc Networking, Addison-Wesley, 2001
2. Ozleyis, O., Burak B., Albert, l.: A Probabilistic Routing Disruption Attack on DSR and Its Analysis. Third Annual Mediterranean Ad Hoc Networking Workshop,2004,Jun:300-306
3. Josang,A.:The right type of trust for distributed systems. Proceeding of the ACM New Security paradigms workshop,1996,sep:119-131
4. Camp,T., Williams,B.:Comparison of broadcasting techniques for mobile ad hoc networks. Proceeding of the Third ACM International Symposium on Mobile Ad Hoc Networking and Computing(MOBIHOC 2002), Lausanne, Switzerland, 2002,Jun:194-205
5. Sasson,Y., Cavin,D., Schiper,A.:Probabilistic Broadcast for Flooding in Wireless Mobile ad hoc networks. In proceedings of IEEE Wireless Communications and Networking Conference(WCNC 2003),New Orleans, LA, 2003,Mar:1-14
6. Wu,K.,Harms,J.:QoS Support in Mobile Ad Hoc Networks. Crossing Boundaries-an interdisciplinary journal, 2001,1(1):92-106
7. Hai Zhuge: Query routing in a peer-to-peer semantic link network. Computation Intelligence, 2005,21(2):198-216
8. Pirzada, A.A., McDonald,C.:Establishing Trust in Pure Ad-Hoc Networks. Proceeding of 27th Australasian Computer Science Conference(ACSC'04),2004,26(1):47-54
9. Jie W.:An Extended Dynamic Source Routing Scheme in Ad Hoc Wireless Networks. Telecommunication System, a special issue on Wireless Networks and Mobile Computing,2003,22(1-4):61-75

Dynamic Zone-Balancing of Topology-Aware Peer-to-Peer Networks*

Gang Wu[1] and Jianli Liu[2]

[1] College of Computer Science Beijing University of Technology
wugang@email.bjut.edu.cn

[2] College of Computer Science Beijing University of Technology
liujianl@bjut.edu.cn

Abstract. Building a topology-aware peer-to-peer overlay network can bring many advantages, such as providing locality-aware connectivity and reducing routing path length. While its benefits on performance have been recognized, an uneven overlay zone distribution has emerged. Recent work has shown that topology-aware neighbor selection during construction can aggravate the unbalance of zone distribution while it reduces routing path length. The imbalance in zone sizes may lead to performance decrease and an unfair load distribution.

In this paper, we present an even topology-aware peer-to-peer network based on De Bruijn Graph by developing a dynamic zone-balancing approach.

1 Introduction

The representive structured peer-to-peer networks [1] [2] possess $\Theta\ log(N)$ diameter and $\Theta\ log(N)$ degree at each node (where N is the number of peers in the system). Several peer-to-peer overlay networks based on de Bruijn graph which achieve a constant degree k and $\Theta\ log_k(N)$ diameter have been proposed [3] [4].

However each overlay hop is likely to involve different multiple physical routing hops. So a topology-aware structured peer-to-peer overlay network will significantly improve overall performance. To build an efficient routing overlay, two different methods based on network proximity have been suggested in the recent researches, one is proximity-based ID selection [5] [6] [7] [8], the other is proximity-based routing selection.

However smart node ID selection for building a topology-aware peer-to-peer overlay can lead to an unbalanced overlay structure, the imbalance in zone sizes(responsible key space). To describe the unbalance of overlay structure, we define N_k to be the number of the nodes which zone size are larger than k times of average zone size of the overlay network, and define F_k to be the ratio of the N_k to the total nodes number N in the overlay network.

$$F_k \leftarrow N_k/N \tag{1}$$

* Supported by the Project from Beijing Municipal Commission of Education No.KM200510005015.

H. Zhuge and G.C. Fox (Eds.): GCC 2005, LNCS 3795, pp. 965–970, 2005.

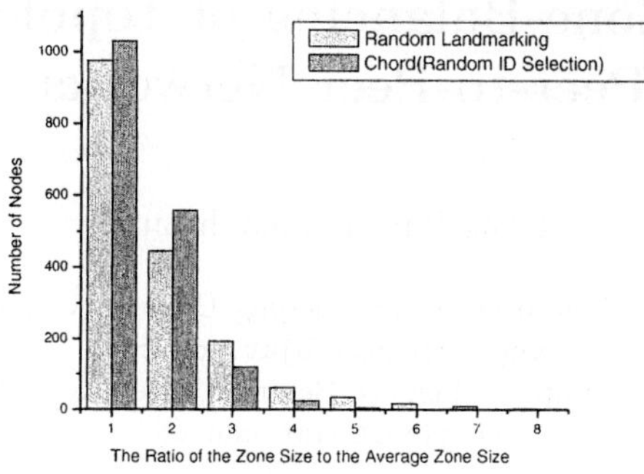

Fig. 1. Average overlay Peer zone size distribution in real-world data set(Random Landmarking [8] and Chord [2])

In the Fig 1 we illuminate the phenomenon of the unbalance overlay structure which results from a proximity-based ID selection in a Random Landmarking overlay network. There are the same total nodes number, say 1740, in both overlay networks of Fig 1. Figure 1 shows that N_2 in a Random Landmarking overlay network is 319, larger than 151 in Chord(Random ID Selection). Because the overlay uses proximity selection, some nodes in the system are more popular than others. But many performance metrics in a dynamic graph are determined by the balance of overlay ID distribution. The imbalance in zone sizes may cause increased diameter, smaller node degree, lower bisection width, and higher local congestion during routing through the graph.

In this paper, we design a new topology-aware peer-to-peer network based on de Bruijn Graph. And a novel dynamic zone balancing algorithm is proposed to handle the imbalance caused by proximity ID selection and dynamic peers join/leave.

2 Building a Topology-Aware Overlay

In the recent research it has shown that de Bruijn graphs possess both short routing distances and high fault tolerance. Several peer-to-peer overlay networks based on de Bruijn graphs have been suggested, such as koorde [4] and ODRI [3]. Our proposal based on foregoing de Bruijn graph peer-to-peer overlay.

Let 2^m be the maximum key in the system. Organize the keys space into a key circle modulo 2^m. Each existing peer holds a consecutive stretch of the key space, denoted by $[z_1, z_2]$, and $z_1, z_2 \in [0, 2^m - 1]$. Each key x in k degree de Bruijn graphs is a base-k integer H_x and its routing rules can be expressed as :

$$H_x \rightarrow (kH_x + i) \quad mod \quad 2^m, i = 0, 1, ..., k - 1, \tag{2}$$

Because a shift left by one digit is equivalent to multiplication of H_x by k.

Suppose node x that owns zone $Z_x : [z_1, z_2]$,through de Bruijn equation 2, we get the corresponding the de Bruijn zone $Z_y : [y_1, y_2]$, y_1 equal to $k * z_1 \ mod \ 2^m$ and y_2 equal to $k * z_2 \ mod \ 2^m$. And node v owned zone is Z_v, There is an edge (x,v) if and only if $Z_v \cap Z_y \neq \Phi$ and v belong to the de Bruijn graph routing table R_x

Each node has a neighborhood set M which contains the nodes that are closest (according the Key space) to the local node. The neighborhood set can be used in routing messages and maintaining resilience properties. And the size L of the neighborhood set can be customized. The neighborhood set M will help the implementation of fault resilience.

2.1 Join Policy and Proximity Node Zone Selection

In this section we describe join policy for handling the zone balancing and routing locality with respect to the proximity metric in our proposed structured peer-to-peer network. The join policy will play an important rule in the topology-aware property. And there are two different locality to build a topology-aware peer-to-peer network, routing locality and neighbor locality. Our proposed join policy consider both of the routing locality and neighbor locality.

When a new node P_{new} arrives, the new node P_{new} needs to find the nearest optimal node P_o by exploiting the climbing-hill method. And we select a node P_n which is the nearest node among the de Bruijn graph routing table node P_o from the new node P_{new}. The consecutive stretch of node P_n we found in the last step will be split to two equal parts and the left part will assign to the new node P_{new}. The routing table R and neighborhood set M of the split node P_n will share with the new joined node P_{new},when the P_{new} join the peer-to-peer network all the related nodes need adjust their related information. For example, the node P_o need add the P_{new} to its routing table, and the neighborhood set M of the node P_n need be changed according to the new joined node P_{new}.

The join procedure is shown in pseudo code form in Algorithm 1.

Algorithm 1. The Join Policy

```
P_n ⇐ 0
R_i ⇐ WellknowNodesSet
P_o ⇐ GetNearestNode(R_i)
repeat
   if P_n ≠ 0 then
      P_o ⇐ P_n
   end if
   R_i ⇐ GetRoutingTable(P_o)
   P_n ⇐ GetNearestNode(R_i)
until Distance(P_o) > Distance(P_n)
P_new insert left to the node P_n
```

3 Dynamic Zone Balancing

In distributed dynamic hash systems the imbalance in zone size has the consequences for increased diameter and higher congestion during routing through the graph. In a nutshell, uneven zone distribution results in hot-spots for object allocations and routing messages in certain parts of the graph. Proximity node zone selection and Proximity node ID selection may lead to unbalanced overlay structure.

3.1 Proximity Zone Selection and Zone Balance

In recent researches it has been shown that intelligent zone selection during construction can significantly improve the performance of peer-to-peer overlay network. But such intelligent zone selection can result in unbalanced overlay structure. Because some nodes will be more popular than others when the overlay is constructed exploited proximity zone selection scheme.

3.2 Dynamic Zone Balancing Algorithm

To resolve the performance problems brought on by intelligent zone selection, we proposed a novel dynamic zone balancing algorithm to balance the zone distribution in peer-to-peer overlay networks employing intelligent zone selection.

To make the zone distribution balance, several node join mechanisms have been proposed in the recent peer-to-peer researches, such as multi-point sampling methods. But the multi-point sampling methods [9] have no effect on the zone distribution balance in the zone selection mechanism based on proximity. We propose a novel dynamic zone balance in the algorithm 2 to solve this problem. The peers zone will be changed upon the zone size of peer and its neighbor when the algorithm 2 be invoked. Peers in this peer-to-peer system invoke algorithm 2 periodically. P:the current node.

P_{left}:the left neighbor of the P node.
P_{right}:the right neighbor of the P node.
$P.S$.the key stretch of the node P.
$P.S_{left}$:the left part of the stretch of the node P.
$P.S_{right}$:the right part of the stretch of the node P.
$P.R$:the de Bruijn graph routing table of the node P.
$P.R_{left}$:the left part of this routing table according $P.S_{left}$.
$P.R_{right}$:the right part of this routing table according $P.S_{right}$.

4 Peer-to-Peer Simulations

We simulated the dynamic zone-balancing system by exploiting p2psim [10] to examine the behavior and performance of this system. P2psim is a free, multi-threaded, discrete event simulator to evaluate, investigate, and explore peer-to-peer (p2p) protocols. We used the real-world data set in our simulations which

Algorithm 2. The simple dynamic zone balancing Policy

1: **if** $P.S \leq \frac{(P_{right}.S)}{2}$ **then**
2: $P.S \Leftarrow P.S \cup P_{right}.S_{left}$
3: $P_{right}.S \Leftarrow P_{right}.S_{right}$
4: $P.R \Leftarrow P.R \cup P_{right}.R_{left}$
5: $P_{right}.R \Leftarrow P_{right}.R_{right}$
6: **end if**

measured a distance matrix of RTTs among 1740 Internet DNS servers based on the King method [11]. The DNS servers were obtained from an Internet-scale Gnutella network trace.

We used the same network settings to evaluate the zone distribution. We compared 3 different approaches: Dynamic Zone-Balancing, Random Landmarking and Chord(Random ID Selection).

We compared the three approaches in the Fig 2. The total number of nodes is 1740 in the both overlay network of Fig 2. The number N_2 in Dynamic Zone-Balancing is 94 less than 319 in Random Landmarking and 151 in Chord (Random ID Selection). The ratio F_2 in Dynamic Zone Balancing is 0.054 less than 0.183 in Random Landmarking and 0.089 in Chord(Random ID Selection). As can be seen, Dynamic Zone Balancing in a proximity-based ID selection overlay which be proposed in this paper achieves a more even zone-size distribution than Chord(Random ID Selection) which doesn't consider the locality properties in the construction of the overlay network.

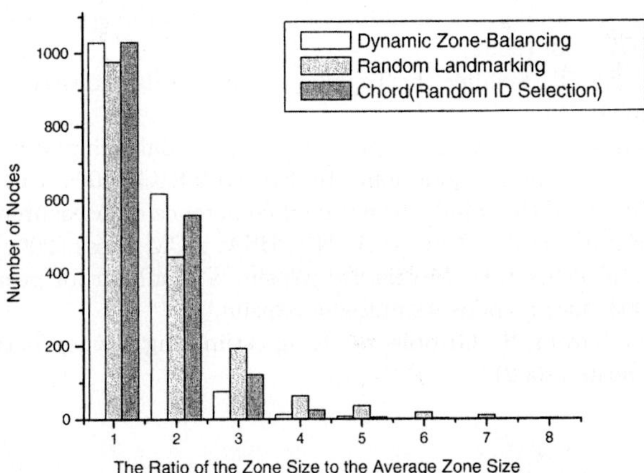

Fig. 2. Average overlay peer zone size distributions in real-world data set(Dynamic Zone-Balancing, Random Landmarking and Chord)

5 Conclusion

This paper presents an even topology-aware peer-to-peer overlay network based on de Bruijn Graph. Then proposed and evaluated a dynamic zone-balancing algorithm to build an even topology-aware peer-to-peer network. We found that the dynamic zone-balancing algorithm can build an even peer-to-peer overlay network. Future work involves mathematic analysis of the dynamic zone-balancing algorithm and more evaluations of the dynamic zone-balancing in different network topologies, parameters and settings.

References

1. Zhuge, H., Liu, J., Feng, L., Sun, X., He, C.: Query routing in a peer-to-peer semantic link network. Computational Intelligence **21**(2) (2005) 197–216
2. Stoica, I., Morris, R., Karger, D., Kaashoek, M.F., Balakrishnan, H.: Chord: A scalable peer-to-peer lookup service for internet applications. In: Proceedings of the ACM SIGCOMM '01 Conference, San Diego, California (2001)
3. Loguinov, D., Kumar, A., Rai, V., Ganesh, S.: Graph-theoretic analysis of structured peer-to-peer systems: routing distances and fault resilience. In: Proceedings of the 2003 conference on Applications, technologies, architectures, and protocols for computer communications, ACM Press (2003) 395–406
4. Kaashoek, F., Karger, D.R.: Koorde: A simple degree-optimal hash table. In: Proceedings of the 2nd International Workshop on Peer-to-Peer Systems (IPTPS03), Berkeley, CA (2003)
5. Ratnasamy, S., Handley, M., Karp, R., Shenker, S.: Topologically-aware overlay construction and server selection. In: Proceedings of IEEE INFOCOM'02. (2002)
6. Waldvogel, M., Rinaldi, R.: Efficient topology-aware overlay network. ACM Computer Communication Review **33**(1) (2003)
7. Xu, Z., Tang, C., Zhang, Z.: Building topology-aware overlays using global soft-state. In: ICDCS'03. (2002)
8. Winter, R., Zahn, T., Schiller, J.: Topology-aware overlay construction in dynamic networks. (2004)
9. Wang, X., Zhang, Y., Li, X., Loguinov, D.: On zone-balancing of peer-to-peer networks: analysis of random node join. In: SIGMETRICS 2004/PERFORMANCE 2004: Proceedings of the joint international conference on Measurement and modeling of computer systems, New York, NY, USA, ACM Press (2004) 211–222
10. Gil, T., Li, J., Kaashoek, F., Morris, R.: p2psim: a simulator for peer-to-peer (p2p) protocols (2003) http://pdos.lcs.mit.edu/p2psim/.
11. Gummadi, K., Saroiu, S., Gribble, S.: King estimating latency between arbitrary internet end hosts (2002)

A Localized Algorithm for Minimum-Energy Broadcasting Problem in MANET

Chao Peng and Hong Shen

Graduate School of Information Science,
Japan Advanced Institute of Science and Technology,
1-1 Tatsunokuchi, Ishikwa, 923-1292, Japan
p-chao@jaist.ac.jp

Abstract. In Mobile Ad Hoc Networks the energy conservation problem is a very critical issue since in most cases the nodes are battery-operated. While the energy efficiency can be achieved by routing along the path that requires the lowest total energy consumption and can be solved in polynomial time for unicast communication, it was proved to be NP-complete for the construction of a Minimum-Energy Spanning Tree if the antenna is not unidirectional. Some heuristic solutions have been proposed for this problem, in this paper we present a novel distributed algorithm which effectively exploits the wireless multicast advantage. The analysis results also show that our scheme is economic for energy consumption, and efficient for time and communication complexity.

Keywords: MANET, Broadcasting, Energy-efficient Routing.

1 Introduction

A Mobile Ad Hoc Network (MANET) is a mobile network with dynamic, sometimes rapidly-changing, random, multihop topologies which usually contains relatively bandwidth-constrained wireless links. MANET can be rapidly deployed without relying on pre-existing fixed network infrastructure and thus has potential applications in military mission, emergency disaster relief and etc[1].

Each node in a MANET has a limited energy resource and an omnidirectional antenna to transmit and receive signals. A communication session can be established either through a single-hop transmission if the communication parties are close enough or through relaying by multi-hop path otherwise.

In this paper we focus on the design of algorithms for energy-efficient broadcast communications. According to the source node distribution, the current existing protocols can be roughly classified into two families: topology control oriented protocols and broadcast oriented protocols. According to the antenna transmission angle, we can also distinguish three communication models: one-to-all model, one-to-one model and variable angular range model[7]. Here we are mainly interested in broadcast oriented protocols in one-to-all communication model in MANET by using omnidirectional antennas, in which a node can send data to many neighboring nodes via a single transmission.

H. Zhuge and G.C. Fox (Eds.): GCC 2005, LNCS 3795, pp. 971–977, 2005.

We design a new algorithm that only requires local information and extend it into a distributed protocol. In our localized protocols, each node requires only the 2-hop distance neighborhood info, i.e., the knowledge of its distance to its neighboring nodes and the neighbor-distance info of them. Here we do not need GPS service, distances can be measured mutually by using signal strength, time delay or more sophisticated techniques like microwave distance.

2 System Model

We assume throughout this paper that there is ample bandwidth, and that each node has an omnidirectional antenna and enough transceivers to accommodate all service requests. Another assumption is that the nodes are static.

In broadcasting communication, we can represent a MANET by a directed graph $G = (V, E)$ where V is the set of nodes and E is the set of edges. Since we only require that a broadcast message from the source can be transmitted to all nodes in the network, then what we need is the connectivity from source node to all other nodes and thus a spanning tree T rooted at the source is enough.

Each node has a power resource and the consumption rate of power is related to the distance to the furthest node it can and want to communicate directly. The maximum power level that a node i can use is p_i^{max} and the related distance it can reach is r_i^{max}, while the corresponding neighbor nodes of i is N_i^{max}. We assume that each node i has a set of discrete power levels P_i (or else at any power level in the range $[0, p_i^{max}]$) and a set of vicinity radius R_i, it can dynamically adjust its transmitting power according to the distance of the receiving nodes and environment for the purpose of energy conservation. Thus we have $E = \{(u,v)|u,v \in V \wedge\ dist(u,v) \leq r_u^{max}\}$, where $dist(u,v)$ is the distance between node u and node v. We adopt a commonly used wireless propagation model in which the general energy consumption formula for a node u in the final broadcasting tree T is $\mathcal{E}(u) = k \cdot max\{dist(u,v)|(u,v) \in T\}^{\alpha} + c$ and the total power $\mathcal{E}(T)$ required to maintain the tree T will be: $\mathcal{E}(T) = \sum_{u \in V} \mathcal{E}(u)$.

However, the problem of computing such a tree T that can minimize the value of $\mathcal{E}(T)$ was already proved to be NP-Complete and so there won't exist a polynomial time centralized algorithm for it until $P = NP$[2, 4].

3 A Power Efficient Protocol for Broadcasting

We start from the simple small MANETs with destinations all reachable from the source directly, and then extend our approach to larger multi-hop MANETs by means of a recursive technique. There is a crucial difference between wired and wireless networks. In wired networks, the broadcasting problem can be formulated as the well-known minimum-cost spanning tree (MST) problem, which can be solved in polynomial time [3]. This formulation is based on the existence of a cost associated with each link in the network and the total cost of the broadcast tree is simply the sum of the link costs. However, the situation in wireless networks is different because of the wireless multicast advantage property which permits all nodes within communication range to receive a transmission without additional expenditure of transmitter power. Therefore, the standard MST problem, which reflects the link-based nature of wired networks, does not capture the node-based nature of wireless ad hoc networks with omnidirectional antennas.

3.1 The Centralized Algorithm

Let us first consider the simple case where all nodes are within one hop. We use the link-based minimum energy path tree (MEPT) as the basic step for our Centralized Neighbor Forwarding Tree (CNFT) algorithm. The main reason we take MEPT is that it performs quite well even as a final solution to our problem. Let G be the graph, C denote the set of covered nodes in a network, T the set of core transmitting nodes of the broadcast tree, and U the set of uncovered nodes. Notice that the contents of the above sets change throughout the execution of the CNFT, and that the sets do not hold any information about the MEPT. Initially, $C = r$, where s is the source node.

Algorithm 1. CNFT

1 $C = \{s\}$, $T = \{s\}$, $U = G - C$;
2   *Compute the MEPT of* s;
3 **For** *each unvisited node* t *in* T *do*
4   *Let* f *be the neighbor of* t *in MEPT with maximum energy distance;*
5     $T = T \cup \{f\}$, *set* $p(t)$ *as the necessary power level to cover* f;
6   **For** *all nodes* d *in* $N_t^{p(t)} \cap U$ *do*
7         $C = C \cup \{d\}$, $U = U - \{d\}$;
8   **For** *all nodes* u *in* U *do*
9   **If** *there is no other node in* T *on the path* $u \to t$ *then*
10   *Let* v *be the nearest node covered by* t, $T = T \cup \{v\}$;
11   *Mark* t *as visited;*

For any transmitting node, the CNFT algorithm will add two kind of forwarding transmitting nodes for it. One is the uncovered neighbor node in its MEPT with maximum distance. Another is when a uncovered node find that there is no transmitting node on its shortest path to the current source node, it will request that one of the covered node in its shortest path to the source node should be set as a transmitting node. Else it will deem itself as in a safe status, which means that it will be covered later.

Proposition 1: When Algorithm CNFT is finished, $U = \emptyset$.

Proof: We will prove this proposition by proving the following loop invariant: $U \neq \emptyset \Rightarrow$ there exists unvisited node in T. This is evidently true at the initial step. For the following runs, we can check the "for" loop in line 8. Since for any uncovered node, there will be a transmitting node to make it safe. And when we come to the run when this transmitting node is deemed as a source, the algorithm should either cover that uncovered node or find another transmitting node to make it safe. So this loop invariant is always true. And when Algorithm CNFT is finished, all nodes in T will be visited and thus $U = \emptyset$.

3.2 The Distributed Algorithm

Since the above centralized algorithm only consider a small graph within one hop distance, it cannot be used in a real MANET, in which the transmitting radius of each node is limited and usually a multi-hop path is necessary for two nodes to communicate with each other. So we need to extend it to the distributed case, the following Distributed Neighbor Forwarding Tree Algorithm will be run at each transmitting node t during the broadcasting tree building session.

Algorithm 2. Algorithm DNFT

Combine the whole graph of N_t^{max} *and the 2-hop nodes to form* G' ;
Cover t *and get the uncovered node sets* U *in* G';
Compute the MEPT of t *in* G';
Let f *be the neighbor of* t *in MEPT with maximum energy distance;*
Mark f *as a* T *node, set* $p(t)$ *as the power level to cover* f;
For *all nodes* d *in* $N_t^{p(t)} \cap U$ *do*
    $C = C \cup \{d\}$, $U = U - \{d\}$;
For *all nodes* u *in* U *do*
    If *there is no other unvisited* T *node on the path* $u \rightarrow t$ *then*
        Let v *be the nearest node covered by* t, $T = T \cup \{v\}$;
Mark t *as visited;*

In the distributed case, for the first time, a source node s will initiate a broadcast session by send out a broadcast tree construction request message $< btc_{s,id} >$ to all his neighbors reachable by power level p^s_{max}. Based on Algorithm DNFT, the nodes in the MANET will cooperatively discover the set of transmitting nodes :

- The source node s:
  1. Send a broadcasting tree construction request message $< btc_{s,id} >$ to all his neighbors reachable by power level p_s^{max};
  2. Based on the ACK message from all neighbors, compute N_s^{max};
  3. Based on the N_v^{max} info of all neighbors, compute the 2-hop graph G';
  4. Run Algorithm DNFT to compute the transmitting neighbor set;
  5. Send $< btt_{s,id} >$ to all transmitting neighbors.
- On receipt of a *btc* message at node v:
  1. Send back an ACK message;
  2. Broadcast its own *btn* message;
  3. Based on the ACK message from all neighbors, compute its N_v^{max};
  4. Send back an N_v^{max} message.
- On receipt of a *btn* message: Send back an ACK message.
- On receipt of a *btt* message: Run the same procedures as a source node.

A node will discard an already received message in this session. And after it every transmitting node will have a list of neighbor transmitting nodes. Every node will know which node cover himself. Now a source node will broadcast

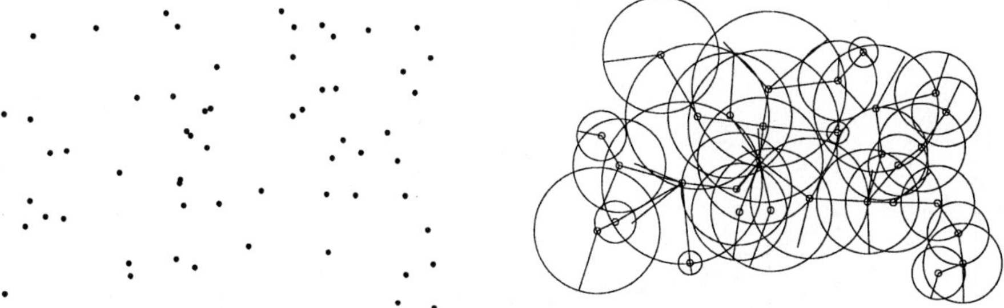

Fig. 1. L) The topology of a given MANET; R) The broadcasting relay map

the data according to the range computed in the tree construction session. And only those transmitting nodes will forward the data according their computed power rang respectively. All the duplicated message will be discarded, and all other common nodes need only to receive data from a transmitting node. The following Figure 1 shows the cover map of a 60 nodes $1km \times 1km$ MANET computed by our protocol.

4 Performance Evaluation

We evaluate our protocol and compare its performance with the RBOP protocol proposed by J. Cartigny et. al in [7], whose performance could compete with the centralized BIP protocol in [6].

The parameters are almost the same as in [7] for consistency. The number of nodes $n = 100$. The maximum communication radius $r^{max} = 5*50$ meters. Nodes are uniformly distributed in a square area whose size is adjusted to obtain a given density (from 6 nodes per communication zone to 30). For each measure, 5000 broadcasts have been run. The observed parameter is the energy consumption according to two commonly used energy models: $k = 1, \alpha = 2, c = 0$ and $k = 1, \alpha = 4, c = 10^8$[5, 8]. For each broadcast session, we calculate the total energy consumption: $\mathcal{E}(T) = \sum_{u \in V} \mathcal{E}(u)$. Usually $\mathcal{E}(T)$ is very large, so we divided it by the total energy consumption needed for blind flooding prtocol with maximal range: $\mathcal{E}_{flooding} = n \times (R^\alpha + c)$.

The percentage number of this quotient is named to be the average Expended Energy Ration (EER): $\mathcal{EER} = 100 \times \mathcal{E}(T)/\mathcal{E}_{flooding}$.

We show the comparison of DNFT with RBOP, BIP and RTCP in Figure 2, from which we can observe that our DNFT is better than RBOP when the degree is high. This is because RBOP will choose all its RNG-neighbors as transmitting nodes. But sometimes the distance from the source node to its RNG-neighbors will be far different to each other, and some short range nodes will be unnecessarily put into transmitting. So the final number of transmitting nodes in DNFT will be less than that in RBOP, and the reachability is always 100%.

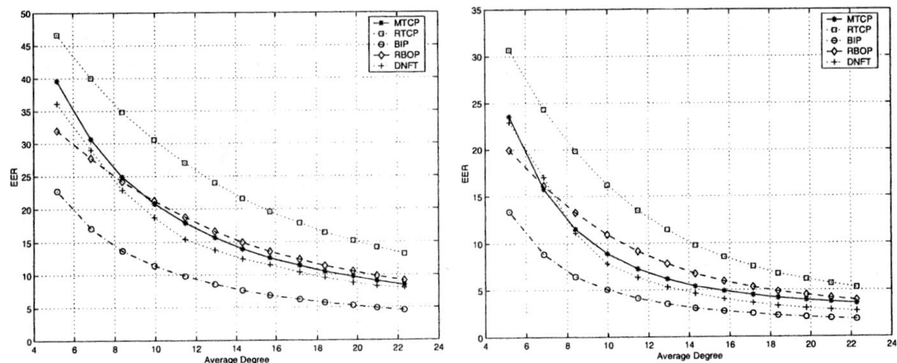

Fig. 2. L) EER when $\alpha = 2, c = 0$; R) EER when $\alpha = 4, c = 10^8$

It is not surprising to see that the best algorithm is the globalized BIP, since with the whole knowledge one can always make better choice. But when the density rises, the difference between all these protocols converge together. And the direction is certainly downward since with high density the blind flooding will choose more unnecessary nodes as transmitting nodes.

5 Conclusion

In this paper we first presented the *CNFT* Algorithm for the computation of an energy efficient broadcasting tree in a small MANET, then we extend it to the distributed case algorithm *DNFT* and proposed our protocol for the construction of an energy efficient broadcasting tree in a large MANET. We have shown by simulation that our protocol is more energy efficient than *RBOP*, and it is also very flexible and scalable.

References

1. MANET. IETF mobile Ad-hoc Network Working Group, MANET. *http://www.ietf.org/html.charters/manet-charter.html.*
2. Mario Cagalj, Jean-Pierre Hubaux and Christian Enz. Minimum-energy broadcast in all-wireless networks: NP-completeness and distribution issues. *Proceedings of ACM MobiCom 2002*, Atlanta, USA, September 2002.
3. R. G. Gallager , P. A. Humblet , P. M. Spira. A Distributed Algorithm for Minimum-Weight Spanning Trees. *ACM Transactions on Programming Languages and Systems (TOPLAS)*, v.5 n.1, p.66-77, Jan. 1983.
4. M. R. Garey , D. S. Johnson. Computers and Intractability: A Guide to the Theory of NP-Completeness. *W. H. Freeman and Company*, New York, NY, 1979.
5. V. Rodoplu and T. H. Meng. Minimum energy mobile wireless networks. *IEEE Journal on Selected Areas in Communications* , 17(8), August 1999.

6. J. Wieselthier, G. Nguyen, and A. Ephremides. On the construction of energy-efficient broadcast and multicast trees in wireless networks. *Proceeding of IEEE Infocom'2000*, Tel Aviv, Israel, 2000, pp. 585C594.
7. J. Cartigny, D. Simplot and I. Stojmenovic. Localized Minimum-Energy Broadcasting in Ad-hoc Networks. *Proceeding of IEEE Infocom'2003*, USA, 2003.
8. S. Lindsey and C. Raghavendra. Energy efficient broadcasting for situation awareness in ad hoc networks. *Proceeding of ICPP'01*, Valencia, Spain, 2001.

Multipath Traffic Allocation Based on Ant Optimization Algorithm with Reusing Abilities in MANET*

Hui-Yao An, Xi-Cheng Lu, and Wei Peng

School of Computer, National University of Defense Technology,
410073, Changsha, P.R. China
{hyan, xclu, wpeng}@nudt.edu.cn

Abstract. It is important that how to distribute traffic into multiple paths with reason and timing in Mobile Ad Hoc networks. Otherwise, it will cause the performance of these routing schemes to degrade drastically. Most of the traffic distributing schemes proposed in MANET so far don't take limited resource and frequent topology change into account. In these schemes, it doesn't reuse the distribution result, and the same size load is distributed into the various paths regardless of their qualities. It will lead to increased computing overhead. In order to circumvent these problems, a novel multipath traffic distribution method that is based on Ant Optimization Algorithm with Reusing Abilities is proposed. Experimental results indicate that, our method improves distribution efficiency about 20%, and improves the quality of multipath routing.

1 Introduction

Ad Hoc Networks1 is a peer-to-peer mobile network consisting of large number of mobile nodes. Multipath is an important scheme for Ad Hoc Networks. Main problems exist in the existing multipath scheme2-4 in Ad Hoc network is: 1). Instead of change the size of traffic allocation with various path quality, they distribute traffic with a fixed same size into multiple path; 2)every time the information updates, they distribute traffic into multiple paths again. It leads to a high redundancy; 3) in the phase of traffic allocation, they don't reuse the previous phase allocation result, it leads to a high computing overhead.

2 Model of Multi-path

Consider a simple fork topology shown in Figure 1, where a source-destination pair are connected by n disjoint paths $p_1, p_2, \ldots, p_n$. Each path p_k has a (bottleneck) capacity c_i of units of bandwidth, and is assumed to be known to the source s. Suppose flows arrive at the source s at an average rate λ, and the average flow holding time is 1/u. Throughout this section, we assume that flow arrivals are Poisson, and flow

* This research was supported by the National Grand Fundamental Research 973 Program of China under Grant No. 2003CB314802, the National Natural Science Foundation of China under Grant No. 90104001 and Higher Education and Research Program of Hunan Province.

H. Zhuge and G.C. Fox (Eds.): GCC 2005, LNCS 3795, pp. 978–983, 2005.

holding times are exponentially distributed. For simplicity, we also assume that each flow consumes 1 unit of bandwidth. In other words, path p_k can accommodate c_k flows at any time. Therefore, the question is how to route flows along these n paths so that the overall blocking probability is minimized, and throughput is maximized.

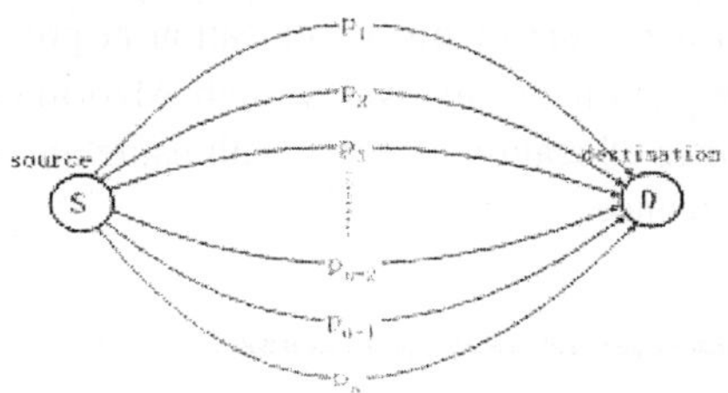

Fig. 1. A set of disjoint paths between a source and a destination

Definition 1. We define the delay time of path k between source s to destination t pair as the length of the path p_k, denoted by $l(p_k)=\frac{1}{2}\sum_{i=s}^{d} D(i,j)$.

Definition 2. If we define minimal delay time from source s to destination d as minimal length, denoted by $l_{\min(s,d)}$; then for link (i,j), if $l_{\min(j,d)} \le l_{\min(i,d)}$, we define the link (i,j) as available-link, and define the minimal length along the link (i,j) to destination node as available-link length:

$$al_{(i,j)} = l_{(i,j)} + l_{\min(j,d)} \tag{1}$$

Definition 3. Let $\overline{l_i}$ be the average length of all available paths attach to node i, then the weight value of the available link (i,j) is:

$$p_{e(i,j)} = EXP[\frac{-k * al_{(i,j)}}{\overline{l_i}}] \tag{2}$$

and the reliability value of the node i is the sum of the weight value of all the available links attach to node i:

$$p_{n(i)} = \sum_j p_{e(i,j)} \tag{3}$$

k is system parameter relative to the number of the path attach to node i, about 3.0-3.5.

Definition 4. Given any path p_k, the reliability value of the path is derived as:

$$p_{p(k)} = \prod_{i=1}^{n} p_{e(i)} * \prod_{i=s}^{d} p_{n(j)} \tag{4}$$

and traffic allocation rate of the path p_k is:

$$r_{pk} = \frac{w_{pk}}{\sum_{k=1}^{n} w_{pk}} \tag{5}$$

3 Multipath Traffic Allocation Based on Ant Optimization Algorithm with Reusing Abilities

The Multipath Traffic Allocation Scheme Based on Ant Optimization Algorithm with Reusing Abilities can be viewed to operate in two stages: 1) assign traffic initialization of every path with the value of traffic allocation at previous time, and convert these results into initial pheromone for Ant System Algorithm, 2) and then search for optimal result of traffic allocation of every path using ant algorithm with positive feedback and fast convergence.

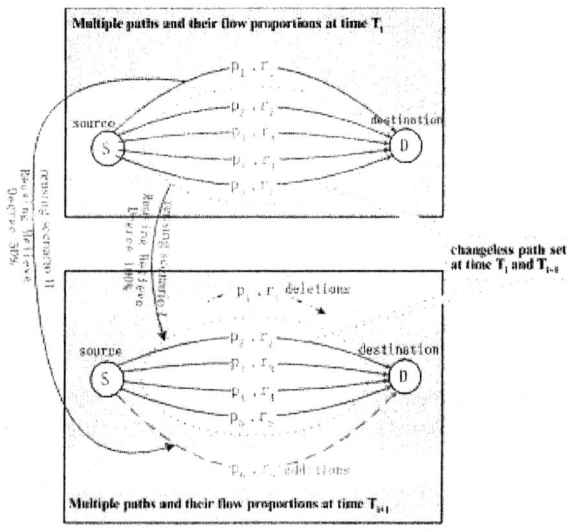

Fig. 2. Traffic Initialization of multiple paths

3.1 Assign the Initialization of Traffic

When one or certain nodes moves, the network topology will change. This will cause some paths to break and some new paths to add. The most of paths are on a changeless status. We assign an initialization of traffic allocation to these paths with the quondam value. And we switch the traffic of the broken paths to the new paths, proportions of flows along the new paths will be initialized based on the weight of those paths. The total load along the new paths equals to the total load of the broken paths. As shown Fig. 2, path p_3, p_4, p_5 have no change, their initialization of traffic at time T_{i+1} is respective r_3, r_4, r_5, is the same as the size of traffic at time T_i. The initialization of the new addition path p_6 is $r_1 + r_2$ which is the sum of the traffic of the path p_1, p_2 at time T_i.

3.2 Convert Initialization of Traffic into Initial Pheromone

In order to avoid too early convergence of Initialization of Traffic allocation searching, we adopt Max-Min Ant System introduced in5,6, and we limit the pheromone intensity Ant System Algorithm between $[\tau_{\min}, \tau_{\max}]$. Then, the process of converting Initialization of Traffic into initial pheromone is: The proportions of flows of each path at time Ti+1, and the value of initial pheromone τ_{inital}, is decided by the reuse ratio $p_{ref-reuse}$ of this path, and we make the initial pheromone τ_{inital} distributes uniformly in space $[\tau_{\min}, \tau_{\max}]$. Therefore, the probability distribution density of initial pheromone τ_{inital} at space $[\tau_{\min}, \tau_{\max}]$ is $1/(\tau_{\max} - \tau_{\min})$, and the relationship between τ_{inital} and $p_{ref-reuse}$ is:

$$p_{ref-reuse} = \int_{\tau_{\min}}^{\tau_{initial}} \frac{1}{\tau_{\max} - \tau_{\min}} dt \tag{6}$$

When we perform integral and predigestion on the right part of this equation, we have:

$$p_{ref-reuse} = \int_{\tau_{\min}}^{\tau_{initial}} \frac{1}{\tau_{\max} - \tau_{\min}} dx = \frac{x}{\tau_{\max} - \tau_{\min}} \Bigg|_{\tau_{\min}}^{\tau_{initial}} = \frac{\tau_{initial} - \tau_{\min}}{\tau_{\max} - \tau_{\min}} \tag{7}$$

From above deduction, we get the conversion equation from initial traffic assignment results into initial pheromone as following:

$$\tau_{inital} = \tau_{\min} + p_{ref-reuse} * (\tau_{\max} - \tau_{\min}) \tag{8}$$

Where, τ_{inital} is the value of initial pheromone, $\tau_{\min}$ and $\tau_{\max}$ are the maximum and minimum value of pheromone in MMAS Ant System Algorithm, and $p_{ref-reuse}$ is the reusing believe degree of proportions of flows on each path at time T_i. If we set $p_{ref-reuse} = 0$, the initial pheromone τ_{inital} is minimum value $\tau_{\min}$. If we set $p_{ref-reuse}=1$, the initial pheromone τ_{inital} is maximum value $\tau_{\max}$. With the increment of reusing believe degree $p_{ref-reuse}$ of proportions of flows, the initial pheromone increases too, so the process of traffic allocation searches toward optimal results.

4 Simulation

4.1 Performance Metrics

We study our scheme performance using CBMRP algorithm. We compare CBMRP+ (using our scheme) and CBMRP according to the following metrics:

Packet Delivery Ratio (PDR): $PDR = \frac{\text{Number of Data Received}}{\text{Number of Data Originated}}$

Control overhead: The control overhead is defined as the total number of routing control packets normalized by the total number of received data packets.

Load balancing: We use a graph $G = (V, E)$ to denote the network, where V is the node set and E is the link set. We define a state function $f : V \rightarrow I$ where I is the set of positive integers. $f(V)$ represents the number of data packets forwarded at node v. Let $CoV(f) = \frac{\text{standard variance of f}}{\text{mean of f}}$. We use $CoV(f)$ as a metric to evaluate the load balancing. The smaller the $CoV(f)$ is, the better the load balancing is.

4.2 Simulation Results

Fig.3 shows the throughput in packet delivery ratio. We can see our scheme improves the throughput. Clearly, both of them will decrease throughput when the mobile speed increases. This is because that when the mobile speed increases, the change frequency of the network topology and network overhead will increase, this leads to throughput decrease. The figures show that the throughput of CBMRP+ is larger than that of CBMRP, this is because CBMRP+ use Ant Optimization Algorithm to search for optimal results, this algorithm has positive-feedback mechanism, so it is possible to lead the traffic distribution procedure to have higher optimal results searching speed. So CBMRP+ can delivery more packets to destination node. CBMRP+ also has some packets losses.

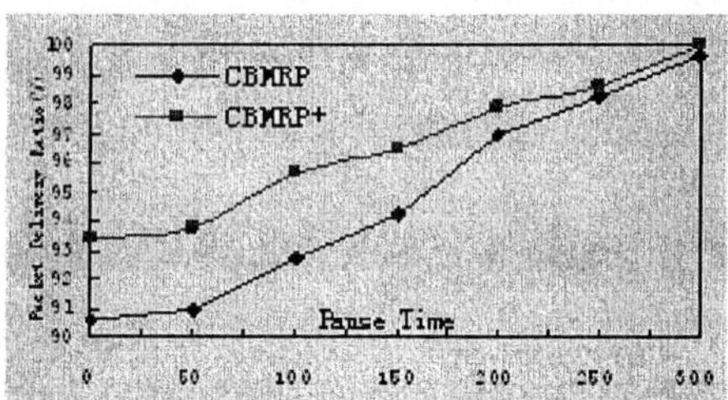

Fig. 3. Packet delivery ratio

Figure 4 studies the control overhead. When the number of session is 20, the control overhead for CBMRP is less than CBMRP+. But when the number of session is 40, the control overhead for CBMRP is slightly more than CBMRP+. However, propagation overhead will decrease after distributing traffic into diverse multiple paths in our method. Therefore, the total control overhead of CBMRP+ is lower than that of CBMRP when the session number increases large enough. The bigger the number of the session is, the lower the cost of CBMRP+ is relative to CBMRP.

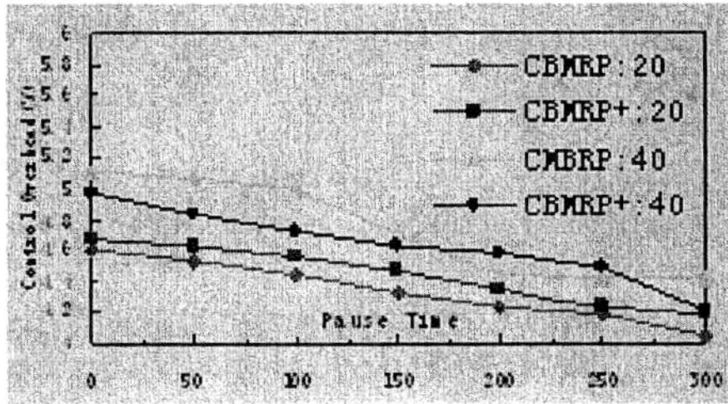

Fig. 4. Control overhead with varying speed

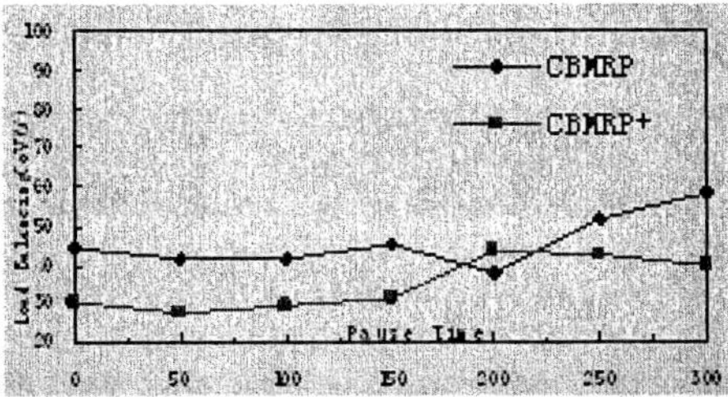

Fig. 5. CoV of the network load with varying speed

Figure 5 gives the results of load balancing. The CoV of network load for CBMRP is higher than that for CBMRP+. This is because CBMRP+ can distribute the network traffic along different paths with appropriate load. In other words, our scheme can be more fairly assign duties to every path. This can be more beneficial to load balancing. With the decrease of pause time, the CoV of network load for the unipath routes and the multipath routing also decrease. This shows that the increase in mobility could result in better load balancing of the traffic among the nodes. "Hot spots" are likely removed due to mobility.

References

1. Ephremides, J. E. Wieselthier and D. J. Baker, "A design concept for reliable mobile radio networks with frequency hopping signaling," Proc. IEEE, vol. 75, no. 1, Jan. 1987, pp. 56-73.
2. R. Krishnan, and J.A. Silvester, Choice of Allocation Granularity in Multi-path Source Routing Schemes. IEEE NFOCOM'93, vol. 1, pp.322-29.
3. I. Cidon, R. Rom, Y. Shavitt, Analysis of Multi-path Routing, IEEE/ACM Transactions on Networking, 7(6), pp. 885-896, 1999.
4. Alvin Valera, Winston K.G. Seah and SV Rao, Cooperative Packet Caching and Shortest Multipath Routing in Mobile Ad hoc Networks, IEEE INFOCOM 2003
5. M. Dorigo, V. Maniezzo, A. Colorni. Ant System: Optimization by a Colony of Cooperating Agents. IEEE Transactions on Systems, Man and Cybernetics, Part-B, 1996, 26(1): 29~41
6. T. Stutzle, H. H. Hoos. MAX-MIN Ant System. Future Generation Computer System, 2000, 16(8): 889~914

Routing Algorithm Using SkipNet and Small-World for Peer-to-Peer System*

Xiaoqin Huang, Lin Chen, Linpeng Huang, and Minglu Li

Department of Computer Science and Engineering, Shanghai Jiao Tong University,
No.1954, HuaShan Road, Shanghai, 200030
{huangxq, chenlin}@sjtu.edu.cn

Abstract. In this paper, we design a new routing algorithm using SkipNet and Small-World for peer-to-peer system. The algorithm divides the routing space into two layers, SkipNet layer and Small-World layer. In the SkipNet layer, the routing method using numeric ID is discussed. In the Small-World layer, the routing method using small-world theoretical results is discussed. We also consider the dynamic circumstance-the node's join and departure. The comparison of our algorithm with other algorithms is presented. Our algorithm supports content and path locality, it is very important for security consideration. In our algorithm, a few shortcuts to distant peers are inserted with some probabilities and the average path length is reduced. The preliminary simulation results show that our algorithm is efficient.

1 Introduction

Scalable overlay networks, such as Chord [1], CAN [2], Pastry [3], and Tapestry [4], have become the hotspot for study. They emerged as flexible infrastructure for building large peer-to-peer systems. These networks use a distributed hash table (DHT), which allows data to be uniformly diffused over all the participants in the peer-to-peer system [5]. Although DHTs provide nice load balancing properties, they have at least two disadvantages: Data may be stored far from its users and it may be stored outside the administrative domain to which it belongs [5]. Papers [5] [6] introduce SkipNet or Skip Graphs, a distributed generalization of Skip Lists [7], to meet the goals of peer-to-peer systems. The scheme supports content locality and path locality, which can provide a number of advantages for data retrieval, performance, manageability and security. Content locality can improve security by allowing one to control the administrative domain in which data resides [5]. A social network exhibits the small-world phenomenon [8]. Recent work has suggested that the phenomenon is pervasive in networks, especially in the structural evolution of the World Wide Web [9].

In this paper, we propose an algorithm which combines the SkipNet and Small-World Scheme. So our algorithm has the content and path locality properties by adopting SkipNet scheme, and the average routing length is reduced by adopting the Small-World scheme, it can perform a well-ordered search from a global view.

* This paper is supported by SEC E-Institute: Shanghai High Institutions Grid project, the 863 high Technology Program of China (No. 2004AA104340 and No. 2004AA104280).Natural Science Foundation of China (No. 60433040 and No. 60473092).

H. Zhuge and G.C. Fox (Eds.): GCC 2005, LNCS 3795, pp. 984–989, 2005.

The rest of this paper is organized as follows: Section 2 describes related work. Section 3 describes routing algorithm. Section 4 presents simulation experimental evaluation. Section 5 gives the comparisons and Section 6 concludes the paper.

2 Related Work

Skip List Data Structure. A skip list [7] is a randomized balanced tree data structure organized as a tower of increasingly sparse linked lists. Level 0 of a skip list is a linked list of all nodes in increasing order by key. In a doubly linked skip list, each node stores a predecessor pointer and a successor pointer for each list in which it appears. The lists at higher level act as "express lanes" that allow the sequence of nodes to be traversed quickly. Searching for a node with a particular key involves searching first in the highest level, and repeatedly dropping down a level whenever it becomes clear that the node is not in the current level [6].

The SkipNet Structure. First of all, we define the concept of a skip graph. As in a skip list, each node in a skip graph is a member of multiple linked lists. The level 0 list consists of all nodes in sequence. Where a skip graph is distinguished from a skip list is that there is may be many lists at level i [6]. We transform the concept of a Skip List to a distributed system setting by replacing data records with computer nodes, using the string name IDs of the nodes as the data record keys, and forming a ring instead of a list. The ring must be doubly linked to enable path locality [5]. A skip graph supports search, insert, and delete operations analogous to the corresponding operations for skip lists. For node 6 (in Fig.1), the routing table may be as in Fig.2.

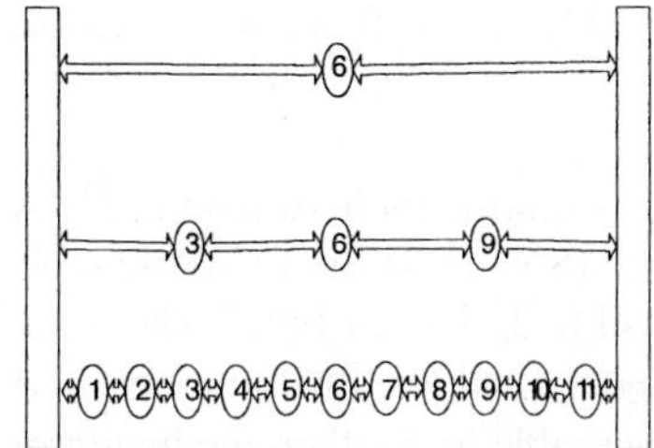

Fig.1. A Skip List

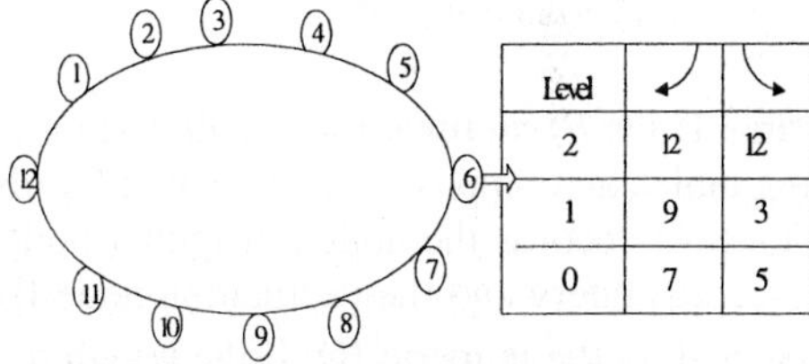

Fig.2. SkipNet nodes and routing tables of node 6

Small-World Phenomenon and Model. Duncan J. Watts and Steven H. Strogatz present a usual Small-Word model [9] [11]: N nodes are distributed in a ring, initially; each node has K links and links to the nearest K nodes. Then each node's link is adjusted in turn, the linked terminal is changed randomly in probability P, but don't link to itself. $D(i, j)$ is the shortest distance between nodes i and j, the average path distance $L=\frac{1}{n(n-1)/2}\sum_{1\le i\, j\le n} D(i,j)$. When $p \approx 0$, $L \sim \frac{n}{2k}$, the network is in regular state. When $0.001 < p < 0.01$, $L \sim \frac{\ln n}{\ln k}$, the node is not only connected to neighbor nodes but also to remote nodes. These shortcuts shorten the L the entire network is of small-world characteristic. Kleinberg [8] modeled social networks by taking a two dimensional grid and connecting each node u to q edges when edge (u, v) exists with probability proportional to $\| u - v \|^{-2}$. For simplicity, we remove the parameter q and assume that each edge (u, v) is connected with probability $\| u - v \|^{-2}$. For any dimension $d > 1$, the small world graph of dimension d has n^d nodes associated with the points of a d dimensional mesh, where edge (u, v) is occupied with probability $\| u - v \|^{-d}$ [10].

3 Routing Algorithm

Key Composing. In our algorithm, we consider the question of how to transfer a message from explorer.sjtu.edu.cn to receiver.sjtu.edu.cn, just in the range of *.sjtu.edu.cn, not passing intruder.tsinghua.edu.cn. So we can guarantee the message path locality and the message security. We employ two separate, but related address spaces: a string name ID space and a numeric ID space. Node names and content identifier strings are mapped directly into the name ID space. Each node's random choice of ring memberships can be encoded as a unique binary number, which we refer to as the node's numeric ID. We don't use the hash method as in Chord, CAN, Gnutella and Pastry et al. For example, the node explorer.sjtu.edu.cn can be mapped to its numeric ID 011.101.1001. The first three bits of the numeric ID represents the country, the second three bits represents the school and the third four bits represents the school's various users.

Routing Table Structure. Each node has to maintain a routing table of length K. A routing table can composed of two parts: SkipNet table (SNT) and Small-World table (SWT). SNT records the node's neighbor node in level 0, 1, 2 as in Fig.2. The SWT table records query and the destination node ID, the query and destination node ID is represented by the numeric ID. If the length of SkipNet table is L, then the length of the Small-World table is then $K - L$. The routing table of our algorithm is as in Table 1.

Routing Table Renewal Strategy. SWT renewal strategy is similar to paper [11]. We define the shortest distance between nodes a, b as $D(a,b)$. $D(a,b) = \min\{| a - b |, | M - a - b |\}$, Where M is the total amount of nodes in the ring. The SWT renewal of node u is as follows:

(1) Select the nearest nodes adding to node u's SWT until the SWT is full.

(2) Calculating each record's deletion probability, the key v's deletion probability $P(v) = \frac{D(u,v)^{-1}}{\sum_{w} D(u,w)^{-1}}$,where w is the random key in the SWT table [11].

Randomly select a key as the deletion record, denoted as key_{Del}.

(3) Recalculating the deletion probabilities of key_{Del} and key_{Ins} as in [11].

The deletion object is determined by the deletion probability, so the SWT table can be adjusted. Because the renewal algorithm renew the SWT table by the probability, the SWT table can introduce a little of shortcuts.

Table 1. Routing table of algorithm

Node 6			
	Key		Node ID
SWT	011.101.1001	...	011.101.1010
	LEVEL	←	→
SNT	2	12	12
	1	9	3
	0	7	5

Routing by Numeric ID. If we want to route messages to a given numeric ID for example 011.101.1010 from node A, we first route the message to the node in the level 0 whose numeric ID matches the destination numeric ID in the first digit. At this point the routing operation jumps up to this node's level 1 ring, which also contains the destination node. The routing operation then examines nodes in this level 1 ring until a node is found whose numeric ID matches the destination numeric ID in the second digit [5]. The routing operation proceeds in this way to satisfy the first six bits. These operations are conducted in the SNT table. Then we route the message in SWT table. In our algorithm, the query is the key. Because we adopt the probability algorithm in the SWT table, there are some shortcuts to the remote nodes. So the key searching length can be reduced efficiently.

Node Join and Departure. Node join and departure process is similar to paper [5]. To join a SkipNet, a newcomer must first find the top-level ring that corresponds to the newcomer's numeric ID. The newcomer then finds its neighbors in this top-level ring, using a search by name ID within this ring only. Starting from one of these neighbors, the newcomer searches for its name ID at the next lower level and thus finds its neighbors at this lower level. This process is repeated for each level until the newcomer reaches the root ring.

4 Simulation Experiment

To evaluate the routing algorithm, we do some simulation experiment. We consider the average path length as the main evaluation values [12]. Because the average path length determines the message's waiting time. We run simulations in which we compared the performance of our algorithm in two circumstances: The performance of the NoN Small-World algorithm (just using SkipNet scheme) and the performance of SkipNet and Small-World algorithm. For each graph size we run 10 executions. The routing table capacity is 100, SNT is 30 and SWT is 70. We randomly select the starting node. The experimental result is as follows: We use the ratio of average path length in SkipNet and NoN Small-World and SkipNet with Small-World. When node number is 10^3, the ratio is 1.4. The node number is 10^4, the ratio is 2.1. The node number is 10^5, the ratio is 3.5. In the initial experimental result, we can see the Small-World phenomenon effect is obvious with the node number increasing. In the future work, we will give more performance analysis, For example, the routing success rate, the relationship of the routing success rate with the routing table's capacity et al.

5 Comparisons

Our routing algorithm use the SkipNet and Small-Word scheme, so our routing algorithm has a fundamental philosophical difference from existing overlay networks, such as Chord and Pastry whose goal is to implement a DHT. The basic philosophy of systems like Chord and Pastry is to diffuse content randomly throughout an overlay in order to obtain uniform, load-balanced, peer-to-peer behavior. The basic philosophy of SkipNet is to enable systems to preserve useful content and path locality [5]. Path locality allows SkipNet to guarantee that messages between two nodes within a single administrative domain will never leave the domain. So it can prevent attacks from other administrative domain. Our algorithm also used the Small-World scheme; there are some shortcuts to the remote nodes. The shortcuts can play the role of reducing the path length. So our algorithm can reduce the average path length.

In previous peer-to-peer overlay designs [1] [2] [3] [4], node placement in the overlay topology is determined by a randomly chosen numeric ID. Nodes within a single organization are placed uniformly throughout the address space of the overlay. When a single organization fails together, it can affect the entire network. Since SkipNet name IDs tend to encode organizational membership, and nodes with common name ID prefixes are contiguous in the overlay, failures along organization boundaries do not completely fragment the overlay, but instead result in ring segment partitions [5]. When the message is routing in the organization disconnected from the Internet network, the message also can reach the destination. So our algorithm has good fault tolerance.

In our routing algorithm, we put routing table on each node instead of a distributed hash table. Most unstructured peer-to-peer systems with a distributed hash table run a blind and not global search. There is a lack of the global properties. In our scheme, it can perform a well-ordered search from a global view. The disadvantage of our algorithm is that each node has to preserve some cache space and some computation capacity.

6 Conclusion

In this paper, we design a peer-to-peer routing algorithm using SkipNet and Small-World scheme. In our routing algorithm, we put routing table on each node instead of a distributed hash table. It can perform a well-ordered search from a global view, Furthermore, our algorithm supports content and path locality and has good fault tolerance, it is very important for security consideration. Shortcuts to remote peers are inserted with some probabilities and the average path length is reduced. The performance of our algorithm is discussed. The preliminary simulation results show that our algorithm is efficient. In the future, we will give more performance analysis, for example, the routing success rate, the relationship of the routing success rate with the routing table's capacity et al.

References

1. Stoica, I., Morris, R., Karger D.et al.: Chord: A Scalable Peer-to-Peer Lookup Service for Internet Applications. In Proceedings of ACM SIGCOMM, Aug. (2001).
2. Ratnasamy, S., Francis, P., Handley, M. et al.: A Scalable Content-Addressable Network. In Proceedings of ACM SIGCOMM, Aug. (2001).
3. Rowstron, A. and Druschel, P.: Pastry: Scalable, distributed object location and routing for large-scale peer-to-peer systems. In International Conference on Distributed Systems Platforms (Middleware), Heidelberg, Germany, Nov. (2001) 329-350.
4. Zhao, B. Y., Kubiatowicz, J. D. and Joseph, A. D.: Tapestry: An Infrastructure for Fault-Resilient Wide-area Location and Routing. Technical Report UCB//CSD-01-1141, UC Berkeley, April (2001).
5. Nicholas J.A. Harvey, Michael B. Jones, Stefan Saroiu et al.: SkipNet: A Scalable Overlay Network with Practical Locality Properties. Fourth USENIX Symposium on Internet Technologies and Systems (USIT'03), Seattle, WA, March (2003).
6. J. Aspnes and G. Shah. Skip graphs. In fourteenth ACM SIAM Symposium on Discrete Algorithms (SODA), (2003) 384-393.
7. Pugh, W.: Skip Lists: A probabilistic Alternative to Balanced Trees. In Workshop on Algorithms and Data Structures, (1989).
8. Kleinberg, J.: The small-world phenomenon: an algorithmic perspective. Cornell Computer Science Technical Report, (2000) 99-1776.
9. Watts, D. and Strogatz, S.: "Collective dynamics of small-world networks". Nature 393, 440 (1998).
10. Moni Naor, Udi Wieder.: Know thy Neighbor's Neighbor: Better Routing for Skip-Graphs and Small Worlds. IPTPS 04, (2004).
11. Zhou, J., Lu H. and Li, Y. D.: Using Small-World to Devise Routing Algorithm for Unstructured Peer-to-Peer System. Journal of Software. Vol.15, No.6, (2004).
12. Yang, B., Garcia-Molina H.: Improving search in peer-to-peer networks. Proceedings of the Int'l Conference on Distributed Computing Systems. IEEE Computer Society, (2002). 5-14.

Smart Search over Desirable Topologies: Towards Scalable and Efficient P2P File Sharing

Xinli Huang, Yin Li, Wenju Zhang, and Fanyuan Ma

Department of Computer Science and Engineering, Shanghai Jiao Tong University, Shanghai, P.R. China, 200030
{huang-xl, liyin, zwj03, fyma}@sjtu.edu.cn

Abstract. Gnutella-like peer-to-peer networks exhibit strong small-world properties and power-law node degree distributions. However, the existing flooding-based query algorithms used in such overlay networks, knowing very little about these inherent natures, scale poorly with inefficient search and heavy traffic load, which is always a challenging problem to solve. In this paper, we eye our viewpoints upon the role of overlay topology in the search performance and propose a novel solution towards scalable and efficient peer-to-peer distributed file sharing, by making better use of such emergent topological properties of these networks. We first, by examining what inspirations can be taken from these properties, provide several helpful guidelines as the design rationale of our solution, and we then propose a new technique for constructing *Desirable Topologies* and a novel *Smart Search* algorithm operating on them, as two key components of our solution. To justify the performance gains of our techniques, we also conduct extensive experiments under realistic network conditions and make an all-around comparison with currently well-known systems.

1 Introduction

As the representative unstructured Peer-to-Peer (P2P) networks, Gnutella and its extensions [1] support uncoupled data placements, elaborate semantic queries and highly dynamic scenario. These properties make such systems extraordinary suitable for applications of large-scale distributed file sharing, which is still the most dominant application in use on current P2P-powered systems [2]. The main difficulty in designing search algorithms for these systems is that currently, very little is known about the nature of the network topology on which these algorithms would be operating. The end result is that even simple protocols may result in complex interactions that directly affect the overall system's performance. Based on this situation, the aim of this paper is to develop techniques to improve the search efficiency and the network utilization of Gnutella-like P2P file-sharing systems, by examining the role of overlay topologies on the performance of these systems, and by taking inspirations from the intrinsic topological properties such as: the small-world phenomena and the power-law node degree distributions. Numerous contributions have been made to achieve such a goal in recent years [3]. However, most among them concentrate their viewpoints on the measurement studies [4] or algorithmic optimizations [5] like query, data placement and replication, knowing very little about the nature of network topology as well as its impact upon the performance of the systems, with very few

H. Zhuge and G.C. Fox (Eds.): GCC 2005, LNCS 3795, pp. 990–995, 2005.

exceptions [6, 7, 8]. The authors in [6] propose *Gia*, a P2P file-sharing system extended from Gnutella, by focusing on strong guarantees of the congruence between high-capacity nodes and high-degree nodes. But they do not consider neighbors' proximity in underlying networks and assume that high-degree nodes certainly process high capacity and be more stable than the average, which is in fact not the truth in highly dynamic and transient scenario of P2P networks. In [7], the authors introduce *Acquaintances* to build interest-based communities in Gnutella through dynamically adapting the overlay topology based on query patterns and results of preceding searches. Such a design, because of no feasible measures to limit the explosive increase of node degree, could quickly become divided into several disconnected subnetworks with disjoint interests. The authors in [8], through studying the role of overlay topologies on the performance of unstructured P2P networks, develop a particular topology where every node has many close neighbors and a few random neighbors. But such a method destroys the power-law link distributions, yielding no guarantee of low diameter and large clustering.

In this paper, we eye our viewpoints upon the role of overlay topology in the search performance and propose a novel solution towards scalable and efficient P2P file sharing, by making better use of emergent topological properties of these networks. We first, by examining what inspirations can be taken from these properties, provide several helpful guidelines as the design rationale of our solution, and we then propose a new technique for constructing *Desirable Topologies* and a novel *Smart Search* algorithm operating on them. To justify the performance gains of our techniques, we also conduct extensive experiments under realistic network conditions and make an all-around comparison with other currently well-known systems.

The rest of the paper proceeds as follows: we detail the new techniques that used for constructing desirable topologies in Section 2, and propose the Smart Search algorithm in Section 3. To evaluate our solution, Section 4 describes the experimental setup and presents the simulation results. We conclude the paper in the last section.

2 Building Gnutella-Like P2P Networks with *Desirable Topologies*

Recent studies [4, 9, 10] have shown that Gnutella-like P2P networks demonstrate strong small-world properties, power-law degree distributions, and a significant mismatch between logical overlay and its projection on the underlying network, which can greatly impact the performance of algorithms such as those for routing and searching [11]. Therefore the existence of these properties in P2P networks presents an important issue to consider when designing new, more scalable application-level protocols. Inspired by these intrinsic topological properties and their key roles in system performance above, we advocate generating an overlay topology following such principles as: a) self-sustaining power-law degree distributions, b) dividing neighbors into many short ones and a few long ones, and c) creating better neighbourship via selecting *high-availability* nodes as direct neighbors. The aim of these suggestions is to build an overlay topology with *desirable* properties, adapt peers towards *better* neighbors, and direct queries to *right* next hops with as few duplicated messages as possible. Fig.1 illuminates

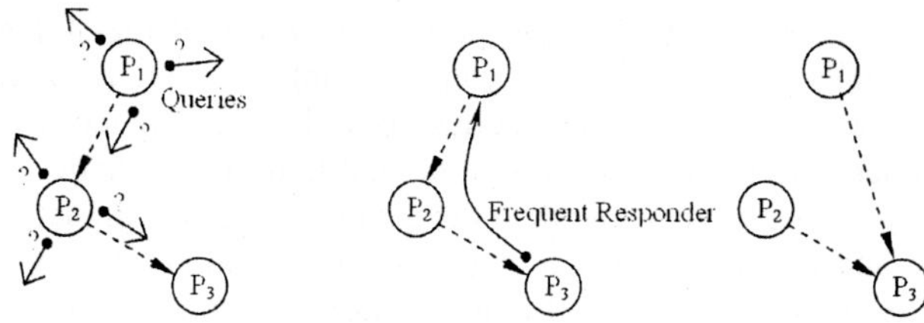

Fig. 1. How to self-sustain the out-degree of a node during adapting towards better neighbors

how to self-sustain the power-law degree distribution of a node while adapting the overlay topology towards neighbors with higher availability.

By increasing the fraction of links rewired we get the required low diameter. If the fraction of links deleted and rewired is p, then for very small p the average path length $L(p)$ comes down by orders of magnitude whereas the clustering coefficient $C(p)$ is still much large similar to that of a regular graph [13]. This is just what we desire: "small-world" properties. Below we give the pseudo code, showing how to build Gnutella-like P2P networks with these desirable topological properties:

```
Variables:
   NbrsList: Ordered list of neighbors, ordered by Я
   CandList: List of candidate neighbors, ordered by Я
   short_NbrsList, long_NbrsList: List of short/long neighbors
   Я(P): the availability of node P, measured by the number of rele-
         vant results returned successfully by P in the near past
   α: Proximity factor, the fraction of links that are short
   β: Aging factor, with value in (0,1)
   δ: closeness between two nodes in the underlying network

// Upon a successful query from the requester Pr answered by Pa
WHILE (min(Я(Pi, ∀Pi∈NbrsList)) < max(Я(Pj, ∀Pj∈CandList))) DO
   {NbrsList←cand_node_max; CandList←nbr_node_min}
age all nodes in NbrsList and CandList by a factor β;
Я(Pa) ++;
IF (Pa ∈ NbrsList)     // Pa is an existing neighbor
   do nothing; return;
IF (Я(Pa) > min(Я(Pi, ∀Pi∈NbrsList)))//Pa is a candidate or a new node
   {NbrsList←Pa; CandList←nbr_node_min; return}
ELSE
IF (Pa ∉ CandList)
   {CandList←Pa; return}

// Upon a neighbor, say Py, leaving the network
IF (CandList != ∅)
  {NbrsList←cand_node_max; return}
ELSE
initiate K peers in CandList randomly by means of existing neighbors;
enforce a neighbor randomly chosen from CandList;

// Ranking nodes in NbrsList by δ incrementally, build short_NbrsList
// and long_NbrsList by α for further utilization by Smart Search
short_NbrsList←first α·N peers of all the N nodes in NbrsList;
long_NbrsList←the remaining peers of NbrsList;
```

3 *Smart Search*: A Scalable and Efficient Search Algorithm

In this section, we propose *Smart Search*, a bi-forked and directed search algorithm: rather than forwarding incoming queries to all neighbors (the way of the Gnutella) or randomly chosen neighbors (the way of random walks), a node forwards the query to: 1) all short neighbors using scoped-flooding with a smaller *TTL*, and 2) *k* long neighbors using random walks with the mechanism of adaptive termination-checking.

As for short neighbors, although they dominate the number of a node's neighbors in our design, they are relative more local in the underlying network, and are also highly available to the requester. So we can flood queries to all of them by a much smaller *TTL* value and thus reduce the network traffic without significantly affecting the success rate. This is obtained mainly because such a consideration makes duplicated messages kept in a very local range and being alive in a small duration of time. Besides, we also incorporate the determination-checking (used in the long-neighbor case below) into this *TTL* method to create a novel adaptive termination mechanism.

As for long neighbors, these nodes are distributed across a relative global region on average. In such a random-graph case, the flooding-based search, even with only a small fraction of long neighbors, can cause explosive duplicated messages and heavy traffic load. So in *Smart Search*, we apply a *k*-walkers random walking for long neighbors: that is, a requesting node sends *k* queries to the first *k* best long neighbors at one time, and each query takes its own way. Here *k* is a pre-designed parameter much smaller than the number of long neighbors of the requester. To obtain adaptive query termination, we introduce an adaptive termination-checking mechanism: a walker periodically checks with the original requester before walking to the next step. An additional advantage that can not be benefited from [5] is: with the termination-checking, a walker can learn whether a result is hit not only from other walkers during probing long neighbors, but also from the successful response of short neighbors. This means: if only a request is responded successfully by a short-neighbor probing, all the queries during the long-neighbor probing will be terminated in time. Due to the space limitation, we omit the detail algorithmic description in the paper.

4 Experimental Setup and Results

To evaluate the performance gains of our solution, we consider a P2P network made of 4,096 nodes, which corresponds to an average-size Gnutella network [4]. We rely on the *PLOD*, a power-law out-degree algorithm, to generate an overlay topology with desired degree distribution over the P2P network simulator [12]. In the simulations, 100 unique files with varying popularity are introduced into the system. Each file has multiple copies stored at different locations chosen at random. The number of copies of a file is proportional to their popularity. The count of file copies is assumed to follow a Zipf distribution with 2,000 copies for the most popular file and 40 copies for the least popular file. The queries that search for these files are also initiated at random hosts on the overlay topology. Again the number of queries for a file is assumed to be proportional to its popularity.

We focus on the performance aspects of search efficiency and network utilization, using the following metrics: 1) the success rate of queries—*Pr*(*success*), 2) the percentage of duplicate messages—*duplicate msgs* (%), 3) the distance to search result—*D*, and 4) the variation of mean stress [9] on the underlying network—*v*. We evaluate our solution of Smart Search over Desirable Topologies (*SSDT*) by making comparisons with the following currently well-known systems of a) Flooding over Gnutella (*FG*) and b) Random Walks over Random Topologies (*RWRT*).

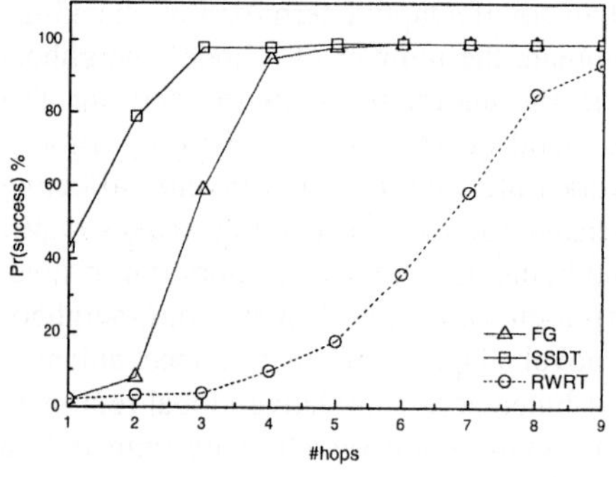

Fig.2. Success rate of queries *Pr(success)* as a function of *#hops*, the average hops number

Fig.3. The percentage of duplicate messages *duplicate msgs* (%) as a function of *#hops*

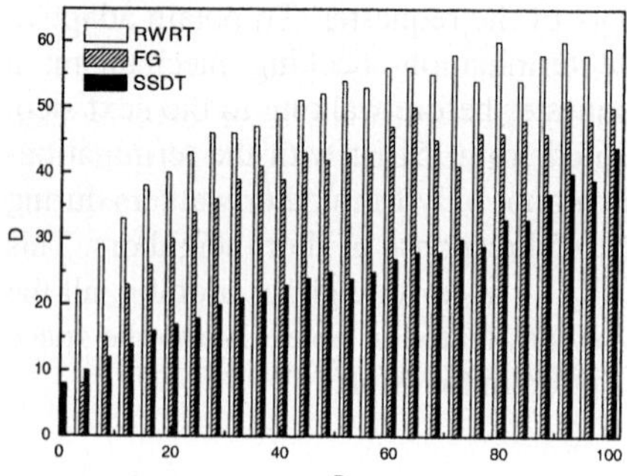

Fig.4. The distance to search result (*D*) as a function of variable file popularities (*P*)

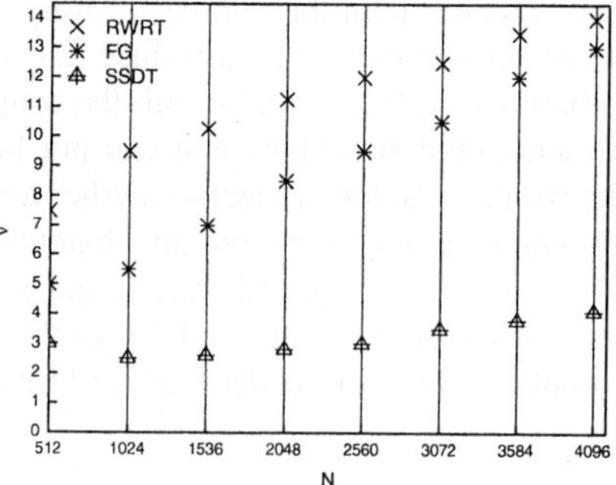

Fig.5. The variation of mean stress (*v*) as a function of increasing node population (*N*)

Fig.2 plots the success rate of queries as a function of the average number of hops needed, showing that, by using our solution, we can set TTL to a much smaller value (e.g., TTL=3) than that of the other systems without reducing the success rate much. In Fig.3, we can see that, with our solution, the percentage of duplicate messages keeps at a very low level, especially after going through several hops, which results from the deliberate design and combination of desirable topological properties and the efficient *Smart Search* strategy. As for the aspect of the network utilization, we can see from both Fig.4 and Fig.5 that our solution can make better use of the knowledge of underlying network, by dynamically optimizing the neighborhood quality to reduce the distance to search result, and by mapping more logical links to local physical links. These results verify the significant performance gains of our solution.

5 Conclusions

Driven by the emerging collective properties behind the P2P network topology and the ignorance of the topology's role on the performance of systems when in algorithm design, we propose a unique solution, named *Smart Search over Desirable Topologies*, with the aim of building more scalable and efficient peer-to-peer file-sharing systems. We achieve this goal by constructing overlay topologies with *desirable* properties, adapting peers towards *better* neighbors, and directing queries to *right* next hops with as few duplicated messages as possible. The experimental evaluation has shown that our techniques are more effective at improving search efficiency and reducing underlying network traffic load, compared with the currently well-known systems. Further work on the search algorithm and the factor considerations like the issues of large-sized file downloading [14], resources booking and reservation, are orthogonal to our techniques and could also be used to further improve the performance of our solution.

References

1. Gnutella. http://gnutella.wego.com
2. A. Oram, Ed., "Peer-to-Peer: Harnessing the Power of Disruptive Technologies", O'Reilly and Associates, March 2001
3. John Risson et al, "Survey of Research towards Robust Peer-to-Peer Networks: Search Methods", Technical Report UNSW-EE-P2P-1-1, University of New South Wales, 2004
4. Mihajlo A. Jovanovic, et al. "Scalability issues in large peer-to-peer networks - a case study of Gnutella". Technical Report, University of Cincinnati, 2001
5. C. Lv, P. Cao, E. Cohen, K. Li, "Search and replication in unstructured peer-to-peer networks", in ACM International Conference on Supercomputing (ICS), June 2002
6. Y. Chawathe, S. Ratnasamy, L. Breslau, N. Lanham, and L. Breslau, "Making Gnutella-like P2P systems scalable," in ACM SIGCOMM, Aug. 2003
7. V. Cholvi, P. Felber, E.W. Biersack, "Efficient Search in Unstructured Peer-to-Peer Networks", In European Transac-tions on Telecommunications, Special Issue on P2P Networking and P2P Services, Volume 15, Issue 6, 2004
8. Shashidhar Merugu, et al, "Adding Structure to Unstructured Peer-to-Peer Networks: The Role of Overlay Topology", NGC/ICQT, p83-94, 2003
9. M. Ripeanu, et al, "Mapping the Gnutella Network: Properties of Large Scale Peer-to-Peer Systems and Implications for System Design," IEEE J. on Internet Computing, 2002.
10. Mihajlo A. Jovanovic, Fred S. Annexstein, Kenneth A. Berman. "Modeling Peer-to-Peer Network Topologies through Small-World Models and Power Laws", in Proc. of IX Telecommunications Forum Telfor, Belgrade, November 2001
11. Kleinberg, J. "The small-world phenomenon: An algorithmic perspective", Technical Report 99-1776, Cornell University Computer Science Dept, Oct 1999
12. Christopher R. Palmer, J. Gregory Steffan, "Generating Network Topologies That Obey Powers", in Proc. of *Globecom'2000*, San Francisco, November 2000
13. Amit R Puniyani, Rajan M Lukose and Bernardo A. Huberman, "Intentional Walks on Scale Free Small Worlds", LANL archive: cond-mat/0107212, 2001
14. Saroiu S., Gummadi K. P., Dunn R. J., Gribble S. D., Levy H. M. An Analysis of Internet Content Delivery Systems. In Proc. of OSDI'2002, Boston, MA, December 2002

A Scalable Version Control Layer in P2P File System*

Xin Lin, Shanping Li, Wei Shi, and Jie Teng

College of Computer Science, Zhejiang University, Hangzhou, P.R. China, 310027
{alexlinxin, starsear}@hotmail.com,
shan@cs.zju.edu.cn, shiwei@zj139.com

Abstract. Challenges revealed in constructing a peer-to-peer (P2P) file system are due to the difficulties of version control. There have appeared no P2P systems, which can solve these problems smoothly. In this paper we show our efforts towards solving the problems by developing a new application, SVCL (a Scalable Version Control Layer in P2P file system), in which version control servers are woven into a peer-to-peer network so that the system will not crash under single node failure. As a result, users can carry out both file updating and reading operations. Experiments have demonstrated the high performance of the proposed system.

1 Introduction

Even the experienced observers may be amazed at the explosive development of peer-to-peer (P2P) systems, which are now one of the most popular Internet applications and a very important source of Internet traffic. Our work focuses on file updating in P2P file systems, which are frequently used in mobile computing storage systems. Fig. 1 shows an example scenario. By storing their regular files in a remote file service, people can access wanted files while traveling around with the help of low storage capacity devices, such as PDA, cell phone, and so on. And a group of distributed file severs collaborate to provide this file service in P2P style. These servers form a network, in which files would be pushed to the nearest server for clients to fetch them more easily. Contrast with conventional client/server overlay, P2P network has the advantages in achieving high scalability and preventing system from crashing under single points of failure.

Current P2P systems are grouped by Lv et al. [1] into three categories: (1) Centralized (e.g. Napster [2]) ;(2) Decentralized but Structured (e.g. Freenet [3] and other DHT algorithm [8,9,10]); (3) Decentralized and Unstructured (e.g. Gnutella [4]). There are many previous studies on each of them. However, strictly speaking, most of them are not real file systems because file-updating operations are not supported. We have developed a new Scalable Version Control Layer in P2P file system (SVCL), in which this problem is resolved gracefully.

The key point of SVCL is weaving file version controllers into ordinary peers instead of centralizing them in a single server or some specific ones. Each peer acts as both an access server (AS) of users and a manager server (MS) of some files (see Fig. 1). In our scheme, AS and MS can be regarded as client and server respectively. As a result, the

* This work is supported by National Natural Science Foundation of China (No. 60473052).

H. Zhuge and G.C. Fox (Eds.): GCC 2005, LNCS 3795, pp. 996 – 1001, 2005.

load of the centralized version control server is balanced into peers and single points of failure are avoided. Each file is managed by an appointed MS, which takes charge of the version control and information recording of the file. SVCL consists of two layers, version controller layer (VC layer) and distributed hash table layer (DHT layer). The VC layer stores detailed information of each file. Every updating operation on a file is logged. Whenever read/write operations on a file are initiated, VC layer of AS resorts to DHT layer to find out the corresponding MS of the requested file and retrieves its information.

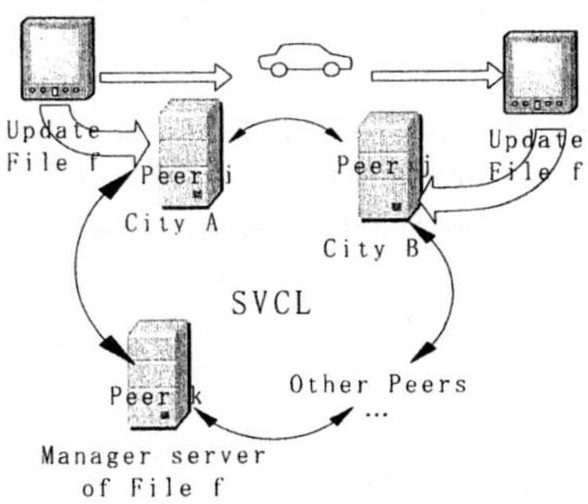

Fig. 1. An example scenario of SVCL

The rest of the paper is organized as follows. Section 2 presents the architecture of SVCL. We evaluate the performance by experiments in Section 3 and draw the conclusion in Section 4.

2 Architecture of SVCL

2.1 Overview

SVCL supports both file updating and reading operations. It consists of a collection of peers, which provide file storage services. In SVCL, users can perform similar file operations as in ordinary file systems. As shown in Fig. 2, each peer functions as both sever and client in distributed file system.

As mentioned in Introduction, the main contribution of SVCL is distributing file version controller among ordinary peers. In other words, each peer, as a little version controller, is in charge of some files' version control. In fact, each peer takes the responsibilities of locating wanted files and managing these files. SVCL consists of two layers: DHT layer and VC layer, which realize the two functions mentioned above respectively. (Shown in Fig. 2)

The main task of DHT layer is to locate the manager server (MS) of requested files. We adopt Chord algorithm [8] in DHT layer to achieve this goal. In Chord, each file and peer is assigned a unique identifier (ID). These IDs are computed by consistent hashing [5] according to some attributes of files or peers, such as file name or peer IP.

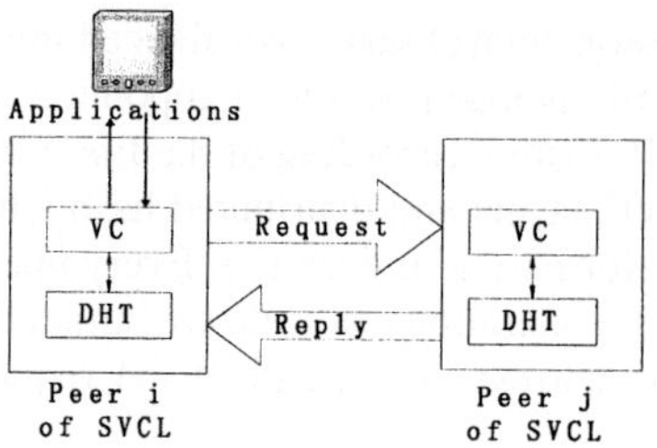

Fig. 2. The architecture of SVCL

Each file is assigned to the peer that has the most similar ID. In SVCL, this peer is defined as the MS of the files stored on it.

VC layer, which is built on top of DHT layer, encapsulates the file operations and provides similar interfaces to normal file systems, such as read, write and close. It resorts to DHT layer to look up the MS of a given file and takes charge of distribution, caching and replication of managed files. The VC layer on the MS of file *f* stores the latest content and version information of file *f* with a specified data structure. All updating operations on file *f* are logged. The detailed implementation of SVCL will be introduced in next section.

2.2 Normal File Operations

As mentioned in the previous section, VC layer encapsulates normal file operations, such as writing and reading. To avoid overloading the traffic of networks, the VC layer of each peer caches the files operated by it. Not only the content but also the version information and operating status are cached. In this paper, we focus on single-writer and multi-reader model and the multi-writer model will be discussed in future work. As a result, a lock-based mechanism is borrowed from database technique to achieve the data consistence. The compatibility of lock-based mechanism in SVCL is illustrated in Tab.1. In this table, the entry *True* denotes that the two locks are compatible. It's clear that only multiple read locks could be imposed on the same file.

Table 1. Compatibility table of lock-base protocol

	Read lock	Write lock
Read lock	*True*	*False*
Write lock	*False*	*False*

We now present the typical process of file operation in SVCL. Suppose there is some user with a PDA who want to access file *f* stored in SVCL (either read of write). The nearest SVCL peer, say *p*, is selected as the access server (AS) to conserve energy. The first job is to impose the needed access lock on *f*. Access is only allowed when the imposed lock is compatible with locks already imposed on *f*. Then the file content is downloaded from *f*'s MS and cached on *p* for user access. Note that only a incremental script, which describes the difference between old version and the latest version, is transferred when some version of f is already cached on p. Similarly, when the user issues a SAVE command, the incremental script mechanism is used to transfer changes to the MS. Finally a CLOSE operation is performed to release the locks.

Some exceptions will make these operations fail, such as failure of AS or power exhausting of users' PDA. To avoid a permanent lock on a file, a specific timeout is imposed on each lock. AS keeps sending refreshing request to MS to reset the timeout.

SVCL treats directories and files equally, which is similar to the Unix model. Listing a directory is essentially reading the content of the directory file. Creating or deleting of a file contains two steps: adding or removing the file in the corresponding MS and updating the directory file.

2.3 Peer Joining and Departure

Frequent joining and departure of peer, namely churn [6], is a remarkable feature of P2P system. After a new peer firstly joins the Chord ring, it finds out its successor and takes over the files that should be managed by it from the successor. See Fig. 3a, the MS of file 13, 15 and 25 is Peer 27. After Peer 20 joins, it becomes the MS of file 13 and 15. So Peer 20 has to take over file 13 and 15 (see Fig. 3b). The content and file information of file 13 and 15 will be transferred to Peer 20 from the former MS, Peer 27. If some files are being modified by other peers and cannot be pulled to peer 20 immediately, a pointer is set in peer 20 to redirect requests to peer 27 (e.g. File 15 in Fig.3b). Peer departure is a reverse process of joining.

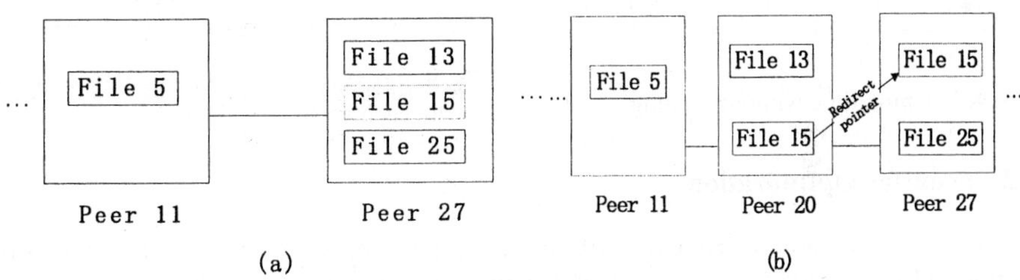

Fig. 3. The joining process in SVCL

3 Experimental Result and Discussion

We have developed the evaluating version of SVCL using C programming language on LINUX. All the experiments are performed on a 16-peers cluster. Each peer is configured with Intel(R) Xeon(TM) CPU 2.40GHz and 1 Gbytes of main memory. SVCL is run on LINUX REDHAT 9.0. All peers are connected with 100 Mbps LAN. In the DHT layer of each peer, Chord algorithm maintains a successor list and finger table with at most 4 entries respectively.

3.1 Fetching File Without Caching

As mentioned in Section 2.2, if the AS doesn't cache the requested file, it has to fetch the whole file from MS. The first experiment is performed to evaluate the cost of fetching different sizes of file in multiple peers system without caching. Fig. 4 shows the result of fetching 0.58K, 1.56K, 98.8K, 215K, 562K, 1027K and 3766K bytes of files from SVCL with 2 peers, 4 peers and 16 peers. The results indicate that in 16 peers system, the overhead is little more than that in 2 peers system. It is easily explained theoretically. The fetching time consists of lookup overhead in DHT layer and file transfer time in VC layer. It's proved in [7] that the lookup overhead in Chord algorithm is O(logN) RPCs, while N is the number of peers. The file transfer speed is invariant in the same network environment. Unobvious rising of fetching time with the increasing of the number of peers demonstrates the good scalability of SVCL. In this experiment, FTP software is also performed in the same network environment for comparison. The results show that the fetching time of SVCL is just little more than that of FTP!

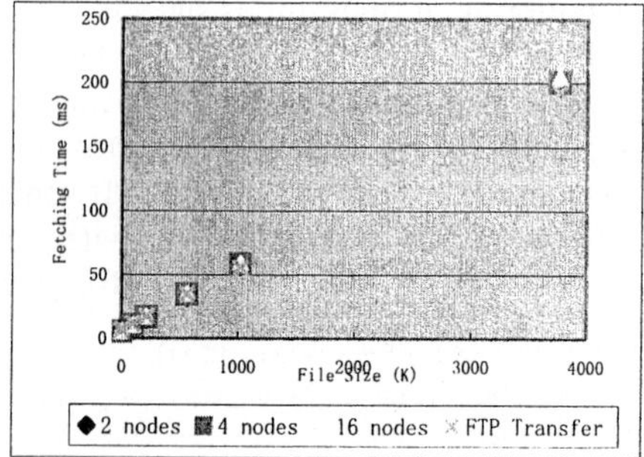

Fig. 4. Fetching time without caching

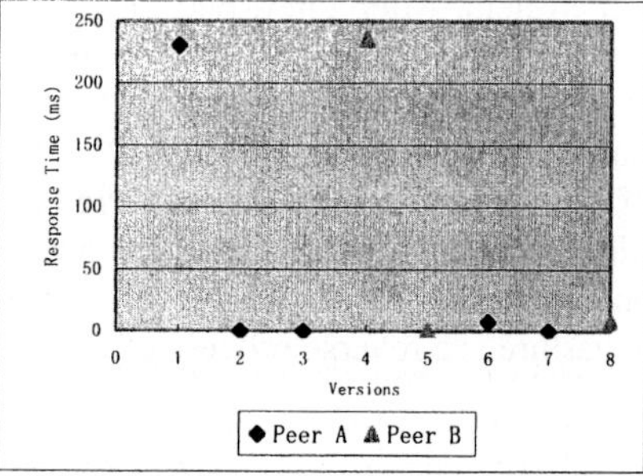

Fig. 5. Response time cost for getting ready to update each version of given file

3.2 Transfer Optimization

In SVCL, cache and incremental script are adopted to optimize file transfer, which is mentioned in Section 2.2. The second experiment is conducted to show this transfer optimization. In this experiment, the example file is 4 Mbytes initially and each updating operation produces 0.5 Kbytes of incremental script. We perform the operations in two peers, A and B, which are regarded as AS in SVCL. Version 1,2,3, 6 and 7 are produced in peer A and Version 4,5 and 8 are produced in peer B. Neither of these two peers are the MS of the example file. Fig. 5 shows the simulation results. The response time of Version 1 and 4 is much longer than that of other versions. It is because they are the first operation on each peer respectively and the whole file must be downloaded from MS. The response time of version 2, 3 and 7 is close to zero thanks to the latest version cached in peer A. Because there are old versions in peer A and B when version 6 and 8 are produced, only the incremental scripts need to be transferred from MS. This experiment demonstrates that the transfer optimization in SVCL reduces the network traffic dramatically.

4 Conclusions

We have presented the design and evaluation of SVCL, a new scalable version control layer in P2P file system, in this paper. It provides file services to users through an ordinary file system interface. SVCL employs DHT algorithm to locate the MS of requested files and the VC layer to manage the version information of files in this system. As a result of considerate mechanism of peer joining and departure, it still runs smoothly when underlying topology changes. Improvements are still needed in this system, but the current results have shown the good performance of SVCL.

References

1. Lv, Q., Cao, P., Cohen, E., Li, K., and Shenker, S.:Search and Replication in Unstructured Peer-to-Peer Networks. In Proceedings of 16th ACM International Conference on Supercomputing (ICS'02) (2002).
2. Napster website. http://www.napster.com
3. Clark, I., Sandberg, O., Wiley, B., and Hong, T. W: Freenet: A distributed anonymous information storage and retrieval system. In Proceedings of the ICSI Workshop on Design Issues in Anonymity and Unobservability (2000).
4. Gnutella website. http://gnutella.wego.com
5. FIPS 180-1: Secure Hash Standard. U.S. Department of Commerce NIST, National Technical Information Service (1995).
6. Chawathe, Y., Ratnasamy, S., Breslau, L., Lanham, N. and Shenker, S.: Making Gnutella-like P2P Systems Scalable. In Proceeding of ACM SIGCOMM (2003).
7. Dabek, F., Kaashoek, M. F., Karger, D., Morris, R., and Stoica, I.: Wide-area cooperative storage with CFS. In Proceeding of . ACM SOSP'01 (2001).
8. Storica, I., Morris, R., Karger, D., Kaashoek, F., AND BALAKRISHNAN, H.: Chord: A Scalable Peer-to-peer Lookup Service for Internet Applications. In Proceedings of ACM SIGCOMM 2001 (2001).
9. Ratnasamy, S., Francis, P., Handley, M., Karp, R., and Shenker, S.: A scalable content-addressable network. In Proc. ACM SIGCOMM (2001) 161–172.
10. Rowstron, A., and Druschel, P. :Pastry: Scalable, distributed object location and routing for large-scale peer-to-peer systems. In Proceedings of the 18th IFIP/ACM International Conference on Distributed Systems Platforms (2001).

A Framework for Transactional Mobile Agent Execution

Jin Yang[1], Jiannong Cao[1], Weigang Wu[1], and Chengzhong Xu[2]

[1] Internet and Mobile Computing Lab, Department of Computing,
Hong Kong Polytechnic University, Hung Hom, Kowloon, Hong Kong
{csyangj, csjcao, cswgwu}@comp.polyu.edu.hk

[2] Cluster and Internet Computing Lab Dept of Electrical and Computer Engg.,
Wayne State University Detroit, Michigan 48202, USA
czxu@ece.eng.wayne.edu

Abstract. This paper proposes a framework for transactional Mobile Agent (MA) execution. Mechanisms and algorithms for transactional execution of single MA and multiple MAs are developed. In addition to preserving the basic transaction semantics, the proposed framework also have three desirable features. First, the framework is designed as an additional layer on top of the underlying existing system, so it can be well integrated with the existing systems without having much interference with the existing system functionality. Second, an adaptive commitment model is proposed for transaction MA execution. Third, fault tolerance support is provided to shield MA execution from various failures, so as to increase the commitment rate. The results obtained through experiments show that our framework is effective and efficient.

1 Introduction

Mobile agent has a great potential of being used to develop networking/distributed systems and applications in various areas including telecommunications, e-commerce, information searching, mobile computing, and network management. For mobile agent to be widely deployed in these fields, especially in e-commerce and network management, the support for transactional mobile agent execution is necessary. More specifically, a transactional mobile agent execution should ensure *Atomicity*, *Consistency*, *Isolation*, and *Durability* (ACID) properties [2,3]. For example, suppose we want to build a path through 10 switches in a telecommunication network, the path can only be built when there is a free in-port and a free out-port for each of the ten switches on the path. Otherwise the path can not be built. This all-or-nothing property [1]corresponds exactly to the atomicity property of a transaction.

Transaction has been extensively studied for over a decade, and related algorithms have been proposed and wildly deployed in existing transaction support systems, such as the centralized/distributed database systems. There are some works addressing problems related to MA transactions, such as how to maintain ACID, open/close

* This work is supported in part by the University Grant Council of Hong Kong under the CERG Grant PolyU 5075/02E and China National 973 Program Grant 2002CB312002.

H. Zhuge and G.C. Fox (Eds.): GCC 2005, LNCS 3795, pp. 1002 – 1008, 2005.

transaction [2] models etc. However, very few works consider how to implement MA transactional execution in a real environment. In order to do so, the following challenging problems need to be solved: 1). Considering the mobility characteristic of MA (MA will migrate among several organizations' sites) and the long execution time that may cause the problem of long lived transaction [2], a new type of commitment model is needed. 2). The transaction mechanisms need to support both single MA and multiple MA execution modes of MA transaction. 3). If a MA or the MA platform failed during the MA's execution, the transaction must be aborted. So, fault tolerance is needed to tolerate these failures. The novel contribution of this paper is that it does not only identify these problems, but also provide solutions to them. An adaptive commitment model is proposed for MA transactions. An algorithm for the transactional execution of single MA and multiple MA is developed. MA fault tolerant mechanisms are designed for MA transactional execution so as to avoid the abortion due to mobile agent system's failures and to increase the commitment rate.

The rest of the paper is organized as follows. Section 2 summarizes previous works on MA transactions. Section 3 presents the proposed framework for MA transactional execution. We describe our performance evaluation study in section 4 and conclude this paper in section 5.

2 Related Works

The related works can be classified into two categories. The first category focuses on how to maintain the ACID properties, how to support open or close transaction model, etc. However, they did not consider these issues in realistic execution environment and context. Another category of works discuss MA transaction within existing distributed transaction models/standards.

The survey paper [6] summarizes the research in the first category. It divides existing approaches into blocking and non-blocking solutions according to the close or open commitment model respectively. In [1], a model based on open nested transaction is proposed. A single agent migrates from site to site to execute the assigned tasks. If a local sub-transaction is committed, The MA will migrate to the next site and start a new sub-transaction. Otherwise, the abortion of the sub-transaction will cause the whole MA transaction to be aborted. A similar model is adopted in [5], and a fault tolerance mechanism based on MA platform redundancy is introduced. The idea is that the MA is replicated and sent to a set of places at the same time. So the set of replicated MAs can proceed the transaction despite the failures of some MA systems. A fatal problem is that it may cause deadlock. In [8], the blocking model is relaxed by allowing parallel transactions to run over different parts of the itinerary. However, for realistic applications, it is hard to identify and execute parallel transactions.

For the second category, the solution in [7] is based on conventional transaction technology used in X/Open DTP and CORBA OTS. A similar approach has been presented in [10]. These models use DTP to ensure the exactly-once semantic and the reliable instantiation of agents at a remote node but do not add transaction semantics at the application level. In [9], the authors presented an extension of the OMG-OTS model with multiple mobile agents. This model is well suited for long running activities in dynamically changing environments. It is true that MA transactions share the same characteristics with distributed transactions. The difference is that the platforms supporting distributed transaction are usually deployed within one organization/company, while in a MA transactional execution, the MA may migrate across several organizations, and the hosts visited by the MA can host a centralized database or a distributed database that support distributed transaction model. So MA transaction can not only rely on these standard models. A new framework is needed for MA transaction.

3 MA Transactional Execution Framework

The transaction functionalities of existing transaction support systems provide the local transaction support (2PL, Logging, Shadow file etc.) and the distributed transaction support (distributed commitment and distributed locking) within one organization. Based on this fact, we model an existing transaction support system as two sub-layers (see Fig. 1). The low layer is the *Source Data* layer. Source data can be ordinary file, table, some simple database (e.g., MS Access), or other structured data, such as an MIB. Source data layer will not provide any transaction support. The upper layer is the *Source Data Server* layer. Source data server provides APIs for accessing and manipulating source data and local transaction support: local concurrency control mechanisms, local logging/Shadow file, and local commit /abort mechanisms. In the framework, the mobile agent platform acts as an added layer on the top of the existing transaction support system. From the view of the existing transaction support system, the mobile agent platform is just an application. The advantage of this system structure is that the added layer will not interferer the existing system due to the loose coupling.

Table 1. MA Platform1's locking table

Resource's ID	*Holder*	*Waiter*
MP1_R1	T_MA1	T_MA2

Table 2. MA Platform2's locking table

Resource's ID	*Holder*	*Waiter*
MP2_R1	T_MA2	T_MA1

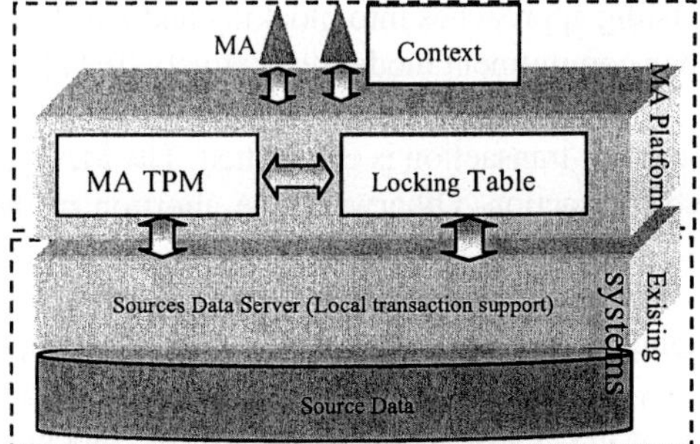

Fig. 1. MA Transaction support modules

Fig. 1 illustrates the two layered nested transaction model in our framework. Mobile agents execute the top-level transactions. Transaction Processing Monitor (TPM) and related data structures like locking table manage the top-level transactions, which includes the commitment protocol and concurrency control functionalities. The commitment protocol preserves the atomicity and duration properties. The TPM and MA's context store the information about the commitment model. Concurrency control guarantees the consistency and isolation properties. Tables 1 and 2 show a distributed deadlock happening between MA1&2 on MA platform1&2. Traditional edge chasing algorithm [2] can be used to detect and resolve the deadlock.

Source data servers manage the local transactions (sub-transactions) which are nested in the top-level transaction. Top-level transactions control the whole transaction process - the top-level commitment protocol and concurrency control mechanisms control the processing of local sub-transactions. According to top-level's commands and configuration, sub-transactions are responsible for the local concurrency control, local logging/shadow file, local commit/abort and recovery mechanisms.

3.1 Commitment Models and the Adaptive Commitment Protocol

A suitable commitment model can avoid the problems like long lived transactions. The guidelines for selecting a commitment model are based on the compensability of a transaction's operations and the scarcity of the resources needed by the transaction. According to the two attributes, either the open (commit the sub-transaction directly) or the close (commit at end of execution) commitment model can be selected [2].

The scarcity of a resource varies with different applications and even with the different execution context for the same application. Take the ticket selling service as an example: if there are plenty of tickets, the customers are allowed to book a ticket. The customer can cancel the booked ticket (abort) or pay for the booked ticket (commit) at the last moment. This situation can be modeled as a close transaction. However, if the tickets become scare and there are still many buyers, the booking service usually will be cancelled and the tickets are only sold to buyers who pay the cash immediately. This situation can be modeled as an open transaction.

As mentioned, a MA may travel many sites of different organizations. It is possible that the ticket is sold using the open commitment model at company *A*; while at company *B*, the ticket is sold using the close commitment model. So an adaptive commitment model is needed to perform open commitment model at *A* and close commitment model at *B*. We define the Resource Scarcity Valve Value (SVV) to support the adaptive commitment model. SVV is configurable for each kind of resource. If a resource's quantity is greater than its SVV, the close commitment model is a preferred choice for the resource. If a sub-transaction needs more than one kind of resource on a host, *AND* operation is needed to make the final decision. Suppose a sub-transaction needs *N* types of resources, and we use 0 to denote the close commitment model and 1 for the open commitment model. For each type of resource, we first calculate its Resource's preferred Commitment Model (*RCM*) which is either 1 or 0. We get the final result by applying AND to all RCMs: $(RCM_1 \cap \ldots \cap RCM_n)$. That is to say, if one resource's commitment model is the close commitment model, then this sub-transaction has to select the close commitment model.

The commitment model selected is stored in the MA context and TPM. When the MA decides to commit the whole transaction, it will make the respective commitment operation according to the commitment model stored in its context. If the transaction needs to be aborted (for example, the MA failed), the sub-transaction will be aborted according to the commitment model stored in TPM.

3.2 MA Transaction Execution Models

In our framework, there are two MA execution modes: SMA and MMA. With the three types of commitment models, we have six combinations, as shown in table 3.

Table 3. Combinations MA transactional execution modes

Exe mode \ Commit model	*Open model*	*Close model*	*Adaptive model*
Single MA (SMA)	SMA Open model	SMA Close model	SMA Adaptive model
Multiple MA (MMA)	MMA Open model	MMA Close model	MMA Adaptive model

For the SMA execution model, there is only one MA. The MA starts execution from the first host. The MA platform on the first host generates a transaction ID to represent this transaction. This ID will be carried by MA's context and also stored by the TPM of each visited host. TPM will log the operations for this MA transaction. Once the MA finishes the execution on a host successfully, it will perform (open model) or not perform (close model) the local commitment of this sub-transaction and migrate to the next host, until it reaches the end of its itinerary. For the open commitment model, when the MA commits the sub-transaction on the last host, it finishes its transactional execution and returns. If abort occurs, the compensation procedure will read the log to make the compensations. For the close commitment model, the MA starts the commitment procedures (2PC or 3PC) only on the last host. For the adaptive commitment model, the MA has two groups of hosts in its context: one group's sub-transactions execute the close model and another follows the open model. The MA will commit them according to the required model respectively.

For MMA, each MA first proceeds independently according to the procedures of SMA except the operation at the last host, where one MA will be elected out to execute the same commitment protocol as SMA. This MA will collect and merge all MAs' contexts and commit the whole transaction according to the merged context.

3.3 Fault Tolerance

An existing transaction support system can be considered as a robust system since they are usually equipped with fault tolerance devices such as the backup host, UPS, etc. In our proposed framework, the MA system is an added layer and running on the top of the existing transaction support system. So we need not consider the host failure. We only consider the failures caused by the MA systems. The failures of MA systems may lead to the abortion of the MA transaction. Although the ACID properties can be guaranteed through the abort operations, a higher commitment rate is what we want. So fault tolerance mechanisms for MA system are needed. We have designed several replication based MA algorithms [11] for fault tolerant MA executions.

4 Performance Evaluations

The experiments for performance evaluation are done on 5 server hosts. Each server is equipped with Pentium 4 processors, 256MB RAM and 100M Ethernet. Cisco Catalyst 3500 XL Switch provides connections. The system is implemented on the Naplet MA platform [4]. For the close commitment model, 2PL and 2PC is adopted for top-level transaction supporting.

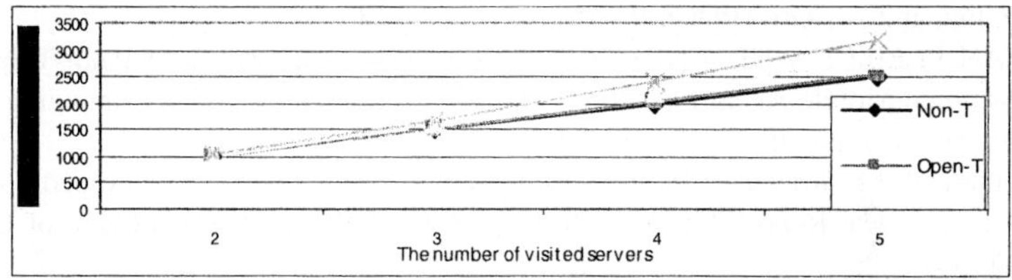

Fig. 2. The comparison of Execution time for Four MA Execution models

Since we only want to compare the execution time of the three commitment models, the deadlock problem is not considered. On each server host, we implement an air ticket booking system. We first perform the experiment ten times on 2 servers and four MAs are dispatched. One MA does not support transaction and the rest MAs support open, adaptive and close commitment models respectively. Later the same experiment is performed on 3, 4 and 5 servers. The experiment results as illustrated in Fig. 2 show that the open model is the fastest model (nearly the same with MA non-transactional execution) and its execution time increases linearly with the server increasing. The close model is the slowest one and its execution time is not linear but accelerative with the server increasing. The execution time for adaptive model is in the middle and depends on system's configuration (e.g. the SVV), so it is a flexible commitment model.

5 Conclusion

In this paper, we proposed a framework for MA transactional execution, which can be integrated with existing transaction support systems. . By our proposed adaptive commitment protocol and fault tolerant mechanisms, the problems we identified in section 1 can be solved. We have implemented the proposed framework in the Naplet MA platform. The experiment results not only show that this framework is workable, but also give the performance comparison of the execution modes in our framework. The proposed framework provides user a flexible choice of suitable execution mode based on their requirements and the application's characteristics.

References

1. ASSIS SILVA, F. AND KRAUSE, S. 1997. A distributed transaction model based on mobile agents. In Proc. of the 1st Int. Workshop on Mobile Agents (MA'97), K. Rothermel and R. Popescu-Zeletin, Eds. LNCS 1219. Springer-Verlag, 198–209.
2. GRAY, J. AND REUTER, A. 1993. Transaction Processing:Concepts and Techniques. Morgan Kaufmann, San Mateo, CA.
3. Harder, T. and Reuter, A. 1983. Principles of transaction oriented database recovery—a taxonomy. ACM Comput. Surv. 15, 4 (Dec.), 289–317
4. A flexible and reliable mobile agent system for network-centric pervasive computing. http://www.ece.eng.wayne.edu/~czxu/software/naplet.html
5. PLEISCH, S. AND SCHIPER, A. 2003a. Execution atomicity for non-blocking transactional mobile agents. In Proc. of Int. Conference on Parallel and Distributed Computing and Systems (PDCS'03) (Marina del Rey, CA).
6. STEFAN PLEISCH AND ANDR´E SCHIPER 2004. Approaches to Fault-Tolerant and Transactional Mobile Agent Execution—An Algorithmic View ACM Computing Surveys, Vol. 36, No. 3, September 2004, pp. 219–262.
7. K. Rothermel, M. Straßer: A Protocol for Preserving the Exactly-Once Property of Mobile Agents, Technical Report TR-1997-18, University of Stuttgart, Department of Computer Science, 1997
8. SHER, R., ARIDOR, Y., AND ETZION, O. 2001. Mobile transactional agents. In Proc. of 21st IEEE Int. Conference on Distributed Computing Systems (ICDCS'01) (Phoenix, AZ). 73–80.
9. Vogler, H.; Buchmann, A.; Using multiple mobile agents for distributed transactions Cooperative Information Systems, 1998. Proceedings. 3rd IFCIS International Conference on 20-22 Aug. 1998 Page(s):114 – 121
10. H. Vogler, T. Kunkelmann, M.-L. Moschgath: An Approach for Mobile Agent Security and Fault Tolerance using Distributed Transactions, 1997 Int'l Conf. on Parallel and Distributed Systems (ICPADS'97), Seoul, Korea, 1997
11. Jin Yang, Jiannong Cao, Weigang Wu, Chengzhong Xu Parallel Algorithms for Fault-Tolerant Mobile Agent Execution. 2005 Proceedings. 6th International Conference on Algorithms and Architectures (ICA3PP-2005) on Oct. 2005 246-256

Design of the Force Field Task Assignment Method and Associated Performance Evaluation for Desktop Grids

Edscott Wilson García[1,*] and Guillermo Morales-Luna[2,**]

[1] Instititutо Mexicano del Petróleo
edscott@imp.mx
[2] Computer Science, CINVESTAV-IPN
gmorales@cs.cinvestav.mx

Abstract. In the case of desktop grids, a single hardware-determined latency and constant bandwidth between processors cannot be assumed without incurring in unnecessary error. The actual network topology is determined not only by the physical hardware, but also by the instantaneous bandwidth availability for parallel processes to communicate. In this paper we present a novel task assignment scheme which takes the dynamic network topology into consideration along with the traditionally evaluated variables such as processor availability and potential. The method performs increasingly better as the grid size increases.

Keywords: task assignment, load distribution, desktop grids.

1 Introduction

The complexity of contemporary scientific applications with increased demand for computing power and access to larger datasets is setting a trend towards the increased utilisation of grids of desktop personal computers [1]. In the quest for load balance, an important consideration to maximise the utilisation of a desktop grid is the question of optimal task assignment to processors in a parallel program.

As pointed out by Zhuge [2], in the future interconnection environment, resources will flow from high to low energy nodes. The basic laws and principles governing this field require more investigation. The work presented in this paper is a step in that direction.

A promising parallel computing model suggested by Valiant [3] is the *Bulk Synchronous Parallel Computer* (BSP) which emulates the von Neumann machine with respect to simplicity. This model is characterised by dividing the parallel program into a sequential run of *super-steps*. BSP might not be the most efficient model for each and every problem to solve, but several advantages are evident: scalability, predictability, and portability are the main promises of

* Supported by the graduate studies fund of the *Instituto Mexicano del Petróleo*.
** Partially supported by the *Consejo Nacional de Ciencia y Tecnología*.

H. Zhuge and G.C. Fox (Eds.): GCC 2005, LNCS 3795, pp. 1009–1020, 2005.

the BSP model. A further characteristic, which is used in the force field task assignment method, is that upon barrier synchronisation the system reaches a known state. In the canonical BSP model, all processors are seen as equally costly to communicate with. For the force field task assignment, the BSP cost model must be extended with the considerations made by the LogP model.

The LogP model proposed by Culler *et al.* [4] is a generalisation of BSP, providing asynchronous communication, and accounting for latency and bandwidth costs of implementation. Using these cost features to extend the BSP model, but retaining barrier synchronisation, force field task assignment can be applied to the environment defined by a desktop grid.

The BSP model has great potential in its application towards desktop grids because the model provides for scalability. One of major features of desktop grids is precisely the ability to grow, and so scalability is an important issue. In 2001 Tiskin[5], developed a divide-and-conquer method under the BSP model and suggested that load balancing can be done in an efficient manner under the BSP model. With the bandwidth-aware BSP, not only this is possible, but also an error recovery algorithm can be implemented with very little extra computational overhead.

In order to harness the potential of networked computers, systems such as Globus [6] and Condor [7] distribute work tasks among a computer grid. These systems address in great detail issues such as job scheduling, access control and user/resource management. The mechanism provided by Condor [7] for sharing resources —by harnessing the idle-cycles on desktop machines—, enables high throughput using off-the-shelf components. A disadvantage arises from the organisation of the grid under the administration of a single central manager, statically configured. Details of job scheduling and migration are exclusive to the central manager. All tasks wait in a queue until the appropriate resource for execution can be located within the grid by the centralised server. Failure of this node brings down the entire Condor grid. Furthermore, there is no provision to share the workload of grid management: degraded system performance may arise with an overloaded server environment.

With respect to sharing resources amongst multiple Condor pools, recent work [8] has provided algorithms for automatising the discovery of remote Condor pools across administrative domains. In this work a p2p scheme based on a proximity-aware routing substrate [9] is used in conjunction with the Condor flocking facility. But within the Condor flock, as with most load distributing schemes, there is no mechanism for resolving the proximity-aware issue and take this factor into consideration while doing task assignment or migrations.

Empirical studies of desktop grids, such as the one done at the San Diego Supercomputing Center [10], provide the basis for elaborating theoretical evaluations for new load distribution schemes

The main contributions of the work in this paper are as follows:

– We describe an algorithm that uses proximity-aware along with cycle availability considerations for optimising task assignment on a desktop grid.

– We evaluate the proposed scheme by means of a simulator based on empirical characteristics of a desktop grid.

The rest of the paper is organised as follows. Section 2.1 gives an overview of the BSP model and task assignment problem on a desktop grid. Section 3 presents our proposed force-field scheme for task distribution on desktop grids, where the proximity-aware concept is developed. Section 4 presents an evaluation and analysis of the proposed scheme. Finally, section 5 provides concluding remarks.

2 Background

2.1 BSP Computational Model

Description. A *bulk synchronous parallel (BSP) computer* [11, 3] consists of a set of processor-memory pairs, a global communication network, and a mechanism for the efficient barrier synchronisation of the processors [12]. In the BSP model the parallel computation is divided into *super-steps*, each of which consists of a number of parallel-running threads that contain any number of operations. These threads perform only local communication until they reach a synchronisation barrier where all global communication takes place.

Task Assignment Overview. Consider the parallel application executing in the BSP machine composed of n parallel nodes, the application consists of m parallel tasks to be performed at super-step i. In order to assign task threads to processors at the beginning of a BSP super-step, a load balancing scheme should be used. Recent strategies [13] have been guided by the considerations of minimising communication costs [14, 15] and attaining load balance [16]. While this strategy will produce good results with small grids, the force field approach presented in this article will produce results which are closer to the minimum execution time as the grid size increases, as shown in section 4.

When dealing with the force field method, there are two considerations to take into account to determine the task assignment. The first —called the computational charge— is a combination of the memory cost for the task with the computational ability of the remote desktop computer. From the global desktop grid configuration, all nodes which lack the sufficient resources —mainly memory— to process the tasks will produce a net positive force, thus will repulsive and eliminated as candidates. The product of the amount of idle cycles per unit time that are available at the remote computer with the reciprocal of the cost in cycles which the memory utilisation of the task will determine the first main consideration for the force field method. This product is represented by the size of the circle in figure 1(a) and addressed in more detail in section 3.2. Note that the canonical *greedy idle-cycle* scheme will assign the first task to the machine with the most available cycles per unit time, which is *not necessarily* equivalent to largest circle in the figure since the memory cost is not taken into account in the same fashion.

The second main consideration is the cost in communications. This factor is dealt with an inverse-square formula. This takes both bandwidth availability and latency into consideration. In figure 1(a) the cost in communication is represented by the distance from the central assigning node to each of the remote computers —numbered 1 through 10. The canonical *greedy network-proximity* scheme will assign the first task to the machine with the least communication cost, *i.e.*, the closest circle.

The task assignment of the force field method is not evident from figure 1(a) because both the size and distance of the circles must be taken into account to determine the net effect. The novelty of the force field method is the way both the network-proximity and cycle-availability considerations are merged into a single force field to determine which node will receive the task. Figure 1(b) shows a three dimensional representation of the force field determined by the nodes in figure 1(a). The slope of the force field will determine in which direction the task will *roll* and reach a particular node, represented by a depression in the force field surface. The positive force indicates the node where the tasks are generated and distributed from.

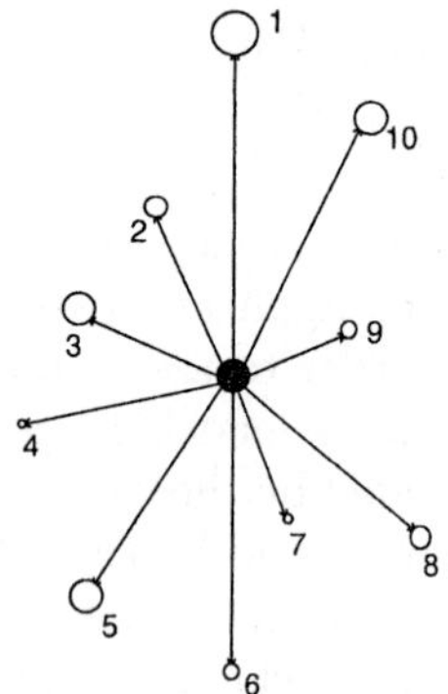

(a) Participating computer nodes

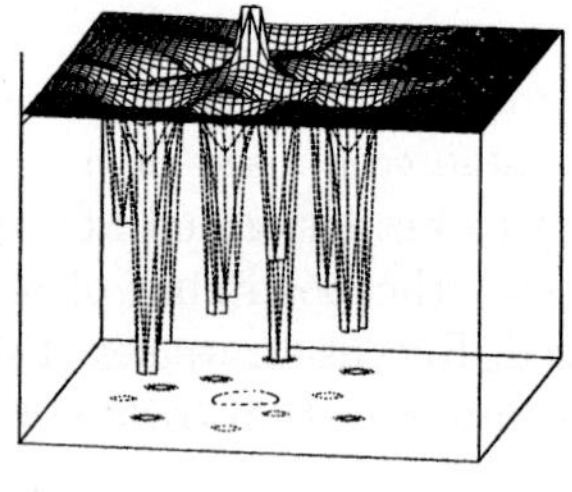

(b) Task assignment force field

Fig. 1. Task assignment considerations

The force field method for synchronisation operates as follows. Upon reaching the synchronisation barrier, each node sends a completion message to all other processors participating in the super-step. Of these, one will currently be acting as a synchronisation master or sync-master (which will be the node in charge of distributing the tasks). Summing up, the sync-master will determine the force field and assign tasks to where the force field is strongest. To calculate the forces, the sync-master needs to know the available idle cycles and available memory at each node, besides the effective communication cost. The first two parameters are readily known and used for task assignment by systems such as Condor. For the third parameter evaluation, the BSP cost model [17] is extended with the full bandwidth and latency cost considerations of the LogP [4] model.

At the barrier all communications are completed and the system reaches a known state. The resulting force field values are ordered and nodes with the most negative values (attraction) receive the tasks. Positive force field values indicate a net repulsion for the assignment of new tasks, and are generated when the available memory of the node is inferior to the net memory requirements of the task.

The ubiquitous desktop computer suggests that desktop grids will continue growing. Our results indicate that the force field method yields even better results as the size of desktop grid increases.

Design Issues. On applying the BSP computational model there is an important aspect not to be overlooked. All tasks must synchronise at the BSP barrier and all communication takes place at this point. The cost of communication relative to the cost of computation is important. As processor speed increases at a rate faster than that of communication hardware, the ratio between the two will also increase. Parallel applications such as data distribution [13] already have a greater communication cost and can readily profit from the force field task assignment method. This is due to the increasingly better performance as the communication to computation cost ratio increases and the desktop grid size grows.

2.2 Desktop Grids

Network. While the opportunity to perform large computations at low-cost is a clear motivation for using desktop resources for parallel processing, the *uncertainty* of the resources which will be available at a given moment is the challenge in designing an effective task assignment strategy. The main points which characterise a desktop grid are the real-time network topology and the individual computational capacities of each desktop resource. The real-time network topology is determined in an instantaneous manner from the latency and available bandwidth characteristics of the desktop grid. While this topology is limited by the hardware with which the grid is built, the usage pattern by applications outside the BSP context will determine the effective topology available to the BSP machine and determines the *network cost* between any two points in the desktop grid.

Network proximity. The network proximity —or latency— is the amount of computation cycles taken to establish communication between any two nodes. This parameter is determined by the communications hardware.

Network capacity. The network capacity —or bandwidth— is the amount of information that can be transmitted between hosts once communication has been established. Since the network utilisation is not uniform nor static, the network capacity between any two nodes is not necessarily uniform nor constant through time.

3 Design

An important consideration with regard to desktop grids is that the we can assume that the number of parallel tasks to be completed during a super-step is less than or equal to the number of available processors in the grid. We can make this assumption because the increasing the grid size with off-the-shelf equipment is relatively easy and cheap.

In the design of an improved task assignment scheme under the bandwidth-aware BSP computational model, we borrow from the concept of force field to elaborate our proposed algorithm. On doing so, we part from an important fact: during the last years, computational speed has been increasing geometrically, while the speed in communication has only experienced a linear increase. This indicates that the trends in future parallel computing will be defined by communications. The question is not whether this will happen, but rather *when* the turning point will be. This is besides the fact that many data intensive parallel computations are already governed by the communications.

Consider that the costs in computational cycles for each tasks in a BSP super-step need not be equal. If C_i is the cost in cycles to solve a particular task i, and ξ_j is the amount of available cycles per unit time at node j, then the time to solve the task i can be written as C_i/ξ_j.

Without considering any communications cost when dealing with a computational grid of size m, the optimum for n parallel tasks is the minimum of the combinatorial set obtained by associating tasks to processors. If the cost in communication is considered, the complexity of the problem increases dramatically. The set of all super-steps in a BSP problem then becomes similar to a DAG determination, which is an NP-hard problem.

3.1 Fundamental Laws of Motion

A successful load balancing scheme using gravitational forces can be found in Hui and Chanson [18], although in this case the gravitational forces are masked behind the theory of hydrodynamics. This effective method of load balancing has found application with the PRAM parallel machine model. A computational model which is less dependent on system architecture, such as BSP, calls for a simpler expression of the laws governing task assignment.

A drawback to the hydrodynamic load balancing's use of Newton's Law of Universal Gravitation is the absence of repulsive forces. The hydrodynamic fluid cannot flow from a lower to a higher level. Only with repulsive forces may any particular node reject tasks where requirements surpass the node's resources.

On the other hand, the BSP model allows for direct application of Newton's laws. Nonetheless, gravitational forces are only attractive. Therefore, Coulomb's law is more appealing for this work.

How does this fit into the BSP model? At the synchronisation barrier the system reaches a well defined state upon which attractive and repulsive forces associated to emerging tasks can be determined. Network workstations participating in the BSP machine which temporarily are removed from the grid need only to switch the sign on their computational capacity, with which all new tasks are repelled and sent to other available nodes on the desktop grid.

3.2 The Force Field Load Distribution

The Computational Distance. To find the physical equivalent for distance in the task assignment problem, we must calculate the cost in communications. Consider the case of performing task assignment on a BSP parallel computer composed of a network of workstations using shared communications resources. Available bandwidth between any two nodes will vary with time. What is important is not the instantaneous value at any particular moment but rather the average value during the particular time interval where the instantaneous value is located.

The Computational Charge. When dealing with the computational charges the force field method refers to two charges. The first lies within the remote computer and the second within the task to be assigned.

Remote computer charge. Represented by q_j, is the computational potential of node j, and is equivalent to the available computational cycles per unit time. This number is always positive or equal to zero. If node j sets $q_j = 0$, then neither attraction nor repulsion will exist. Whether or not the node actually receives a task depends on the force field values determined for other nodes on the grid.

Task charge. Represented by q_i, is a computational ease associated to the memory requirements of the task. Computational ease —inversely proportional to cost— is an important parameter which is often overlooked: the current bottleneck in the execution of most tasks is not in processor speed but rather the moving of data between memory storage and processor registers.

In other words, if the available memory on node j is less than that required for task i, then q_i is assigned a positive sign, ensuring a repulsive force. Otherwise the sign will be negative. If c_i is the cost in computation cycles entailed by the memory requirements of task i, then $q_i = \frac{1}{c_i}$ is the charge associated to the task[1]. Note that the memory requirements of every task has to be known to any assignment scheme, otherwise the determination of whether the remote node has the potential resources to deal with the job would be impossible. The cost in cycles that will be required for the task is not used at any time. In our simulator we use the Large Numbers Law to obtain values for this parameter and randomly assign these values to tasks.

[1] A further distinction may be made whether the available virtual memory is fully in RAM or partly distributed in disk swap. This further refinement is not considered in the results presented in this paper.

4 Performance Evaluation

For each run the absolute minimum execution time —which considers all possible combinations of task/processor assignments— is also obtained for comparison with the task assignment algorithms being tested.

In the tests conducted, mean values were obtained from 1000 simulations for each data point. Thus, figures 2(a)–(c) show the results for an increasing amount of tasks in the parallel set to be completed, and where the grid size is equal to 1000 desktop computers. Computational availability, communications cost, task memory requirements and task computational costs are all determined by Gaussian distributions and randomly assigned to different identifiers.

The purpose of the evaluation is to determine which strategy is *better* for task assignment on a desktop grid. Every process can be qualified with the following considerations:

- The amount of memory required for data storage.
- The amount of computation cycles that are required to complete all programmed operations.
- The time units consumed by the communication requirements.

Strictly speaking, the second point will depend on the hardware and can be associated among different platforms by linear proportionality. On the other hand, computation cycles can be dealt with in an abstract manner —architecture independent— such as Papadimitriou and Yannakakis [19] do in the presentation of the directed acyclic graphs model. In this paper the same approach is used.

With these qualities the merits of any particular task assignment scheme may be evaluated. The first point —memory requirements— is necessary data to determine if the remote computer has the necessary resources to complete the job. The second point —the cycles required by the task and the cycle available per unit time at the remote node— allows the execution wall clock time to be obtained. Nonetheless, the knowledge of the amount of cycles each task will require is not generally known, except for the most elemental applications. Besides, in the tabulation of a parallel job, the time associated to communication costs must also be considered.

For the optimum calculation, it is necessary to know the amount of cycles that each task will require. This will be used to evaluate the performance of the different algorithms compared (these algorithms, of course, may not use this information). An algorithm will be *better* than another if the times obtained are closer to the optimum values.

Figure 2(a) shows the results when the cost in communication is low with respect to the cost in computation. In this graph the greedy computation cost quickly becomes asymptotic with the minimum attainable value when the number of simultaneous tasks in the BSP super-step reaches 25% of the configured processors in the desktop grid. For super-steps with simultaneous tasks occupying less than 2.5% of the configured processors, the force field task assignment

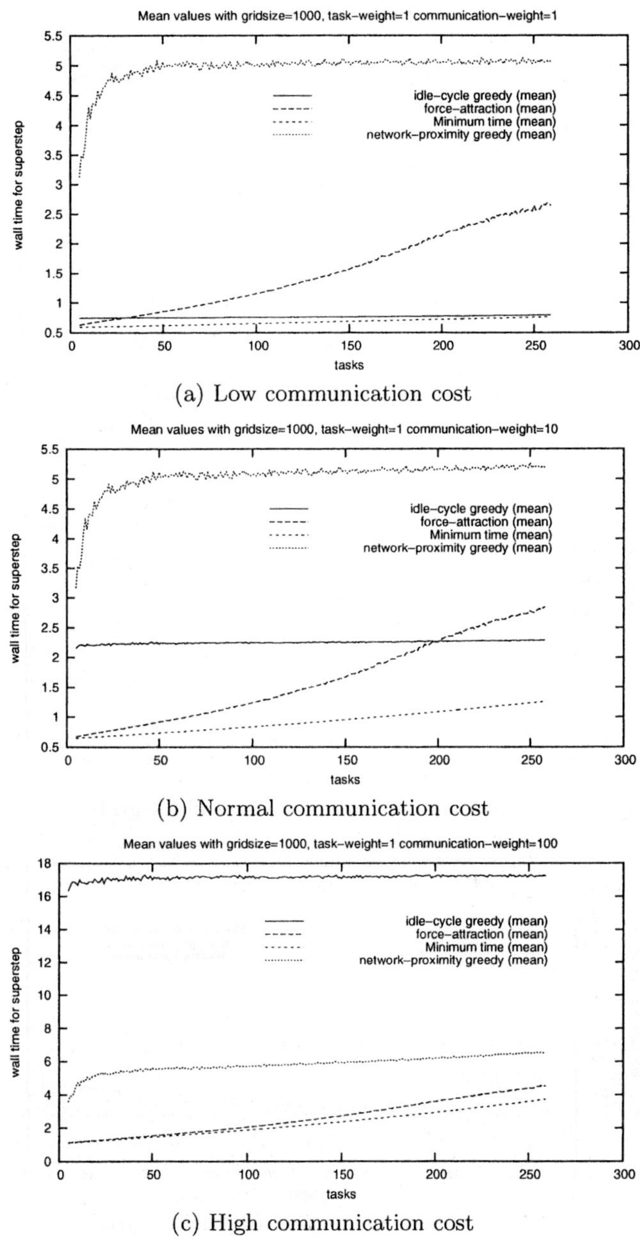

(a) Low communication cost

(b) Normal communication cost

(c) High communication cost

Fig. 2. Mean values for different communication costs

out performed the greedy computation cost scheme. When the grid size starts to increase, as seen *ut infra*, the situation changes dramatically in favour of the force field task assignment scheme.

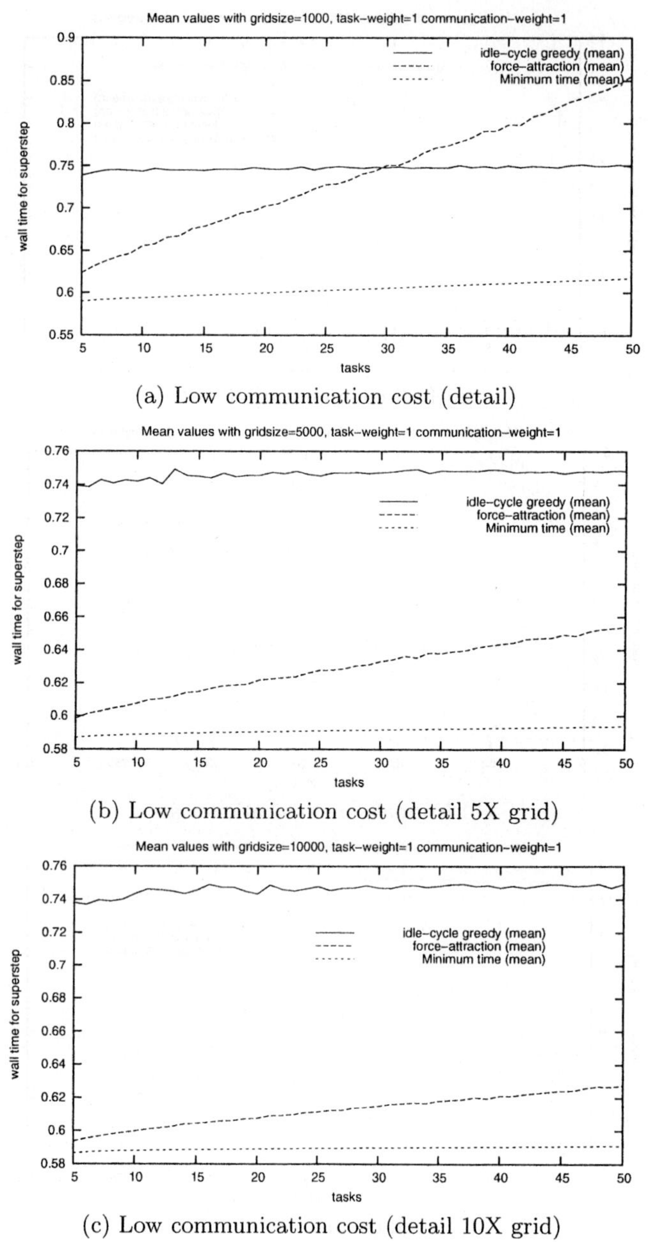

(a) Low communication cost (detail)

(b) Low communication cost (detail 5X grid)

(c) Low communication cost (detail 10X grid)

Fig. 3. Mean values for low communication cost and growing grid size

In figure 2(b), are the results for a parallel program where a computation cost still exceeds the communication cost. Many parallel applications fall into this category. In this case, we can observe that the force field assignment scheme exceeds the greedy computation cost scheme well up to the utilisation of 20% of the configured desktop grid for the simultaneous execution of a single BSP super-step.

In the third graph of the simulation results, figure 2(c), communication costs exceed computation costs. Distributed data applications fall into this category, as well as an increasing number of other parallel applications as computing speed increases geometrically while communication speed does so linearly. In this case the force field approach far exceeds both the greedy communication cost and greedy computation cost and remains quite close to the theoretical minimum performance that can be obtained.

In the foreseeable future the size of available desktop grids is bound to increase, and for this reason it is important to analyse how the force field task assignment will perform in relation to the greedy schemes as the grid grows in size. In figures 3(a)–(c) we can observe that, as the number of computers participating in the grid configuration increases, the force field task assignment outperforms the greedy schemes. As our results demonstrate, this is even with tasks involving a low communications cost. This points to the force field as an important option to consider when large desktop grids are to be used for parallel computing.

5 Conclusions

Although the physical motivation behind the force field task assignment algorithm may not be a consequence of formal computer science, in practise the analogies made with the laws of physics converge to a good strategy for task assignment in the case of a dynamic network bandwidth topology and growing grid size configurations.

The effect that communications has on the time to complete a BSP superstep is a factor which should not be disregarded when dealing with desktop grids of growing size. The effect of communications in performing parallel computation will have an increasingly greater effect on parallel programs as growth in computation speed out paces growth in communication speed.

Task assignment strategies which take both factors into consideration, such as the force field algorithm, should be preferred when there is reason to assume the performance shall be better than the respective greedy strategies.

In the development of this algorithm we have considered the force field as a scalar field. Notwithstanding, the analysis as a vector field could produce better results allowing for a more homogeneous load balancing of the entire desktop grid. More work remains to be done in this direction.

References

1. Foster(Ed.), I., (Ed.), C.K.: The GRID: Blueprint for a New Computing Infrastructure. Morgan Kauffmann Publishers (1999)
2. Zhuge, H.: The future interconnetion environment. IEEE Computer **4** (2005) 27–33

3. Valiant, L.G.: A bridging model for parallel computation. Communications of the ACM **8** (1990) 103–111
4. Culler, D., Karp, R., Patterson, D., Sahay, A., Schauser, J., Santos, E., Subramonian, R., von Eicken, T.: Logp: Towards a realistic model of parallel computation. In: Fourth ACM SIGPLAN Symposium on Principles and PRactice of PArallel Programming. (1993) 1–12
5. Tiskin, A.: A new way to divide and conquer. Parallel Processing Letters **4** (2001)
6. Foster, I., Kesselman, C.: Globus: A metacomputing infrastructure toolkit. The International Journal of Supercomputing Applications and High Performance Computing **2** (1997) 115–128
7. Litzkow, M., Livny, M., Mutka, M.: Condor - a hunter of idle workstations. In: Proceedings 8th International Conference on Distributed Computing Systems (ICDCS 1988). (1988) 104–111
8. Butt, A.R., Zhang, R., Hu, Y.C.: A self-organizing flock of condors. In: Proceedings Super Computing 2003, ACM (2003) 15–21
9. Castro, M., Druschel, P., Hu, Y.C., Rowstron, A.: Exploiting network proximity in peer-to-peer overlay networks. Technical report, Microsoft Research (2002) Technical Report MSR.TR-2002-82.
10. Kondo, D., Taufer, M., Brooks, C.L., Casanova, H., Chien, A.A.: Characterizing and evaluating desktop grids: An empirical study. Technical report, San Diego Supercomputer Center and University of California, San Diego (2004) Work supported by the National Science Foundation under Grant ACI-0305390.
11. Gibbons, A.M., Spirakis, P., eds. In: General Purpose Parallel Computing. Cambridge University Press (1993) 337–391
12. van Leeuwen, J., ed. In: Scalable Computing. Springer-Verlag (1995) 46–61
13. Sujithan, K.R.: Towards a scalable parallel object database - the bulk synchronous parallel approach. Technical report, Wadham College Oxford (1996) Technical Report PRG-TR-17-96.
14. Adler, M., Byers, J.W., Karp, R.M.: Scheduling parallel communication: The h-relation problem. Technical report, International Computer Science Institutue, Berkeley (1995) Technical Report TR-95-032.
15. Goodrich, M.T.: Communication-efficient parallel sorting. In: Proceedings of the Twenty-Eighth Annual ACM Symposium on Theory of Computing, ACM (1996) 247–256
16. Shi, H., Schaeffer, J.: Parallel sorting by regular sampling. Journal of Parallel and Distributed Computing **4** (1992) 361–372
17. Baumker, A., Dittrich, W., Heide, F.M.: Truly efficient parallel algorithms: 1-optimal multisearch for an extension of the bsp model. Theoretical Computer Science (1998)
18. Hui, C.C., Chanson, S.T.: Hydrodynamic load balancing. IEEE Trans. Parallel and Distributed Systems **10** (1999)
19. Papadimitriou, C., Yannakakis, M.: Towards an architecture-independent analysis of parallel algorithms. SIAM J. Comput. **19** (1990) 322–328

Performance Investigation of Weighted Meta-scheduling Algorithm for Scientific Grid

Jie Song[1], Chee-Kian Koh[1], Simon See[1], and Gay Kheng Leng[2]

[1] Asia Pacific Science and Technology Center, Sun Microsystems Inc.,
50 Nanyang Avenue, N3-1c-10, Singapore 639798
{Jie.Song, Chee-Kian.Koh, Simon.See}@sun.com
http://apstc.sun.com.sg

[2] Information Communication Institute of Singapore,
School of Electrical & Electronic Engineering,
Nanyang Technological University,
50 Nanyang Avenue, Singapore 639798
eklgay@ntu.edu.sg

Abstract. Scientific computing requires not only more computational resource, but also large amount of data storage. Therefore the scientific grid integrates the computational grid and data grid to provide sufficient resources for scientific applications. However, most of meta-scheduler only considers the system utilization, e.g. CPU load to optimize the resource allocation. This paper proposed a weighted meta-scheduling algorithm which takes into account of both system load and data grid workload. The experiments show the performance improvement for applications and achieve better load balance by efficient resource scheduling.

1 Introduction

Scientific applications require not only computational resources, but also large amount of data storage. Computational grid can provide distributed large size computational resource [1]. Data grid is designed to support large size of data storage [2]. Therefore the scientific grid consists of computational grid and data grid to provide sufficient resources for scientific computing.

However, most meta-scheduler is designed for computational grid. It optimizes the resource allocation only based on the system load. For example, the meta-scheduler such as Sun Grid Engine [3] will always allocate the server with lowest system load to the current job request. Some meta-scheduler uses the economic parameters to optimize resource utilization with budget constrain [4]. But for the applications has lots of data access, or request for large size of data transfer, or query from the huge amount of database, the workload of the data grid will significantly affect the application execution performance [5]. Therefore, the meta-scheduler should consider the data grid workload combined with the computational system load to optimize the application performance.

H. Zhuge and G.C. Fox (Eds.): GCC 2005, LNCS 3795, pp. 1021 – 1030, 2005.

In this paper, a weighted meta-scheduling algorithm is proposed. It takes into account of both system load and data grid workload to allocate the resources. We investigate the performance affect by different load metrics, and a set of experiments have been done to evaluate the performance improvement of the weighted meta-scheduling algorithm.

The rest of paper is organized as follows: The related works are introduced in Section 2. Section 3 presents the design of weighted meta-scheduling algorithm in details. In Section 4, we illustrate the experiments setup and analyze the performance results comparing to the least-load scheduling algorithm. The future works is discussed in Section 5. Finally, Section 6 gives the conclusion.

2 Related Work

There are many challenges in the research of Meta-scheduling algorithm. For example, the simulation for different combination of grid scheduling algorithms has been done to investigate the relationship of data scheduler and job scheduler [6]. The Genetic scheduling algorithm is implemented using agent technologies [7] or applied for data grid applications [8]. Some researchers consider parallel tasks scheduling problems [9] and distributed dynamic resource scheduling problems [10].

Our research is based on the solution proposed in [11] to integrate computational grid and data grid. The Sun Grid Engine is used as the meta-scheduler to allocate data grid resource to the job requests. The load formula is the key for resource scheduling. The idea is to revise the load formula, so that it can reflect the affect of data grid workload. In the solution, new parameters such as buffer and number of read thread are introduced to represent the data grid workload and combine with the original system load parameter. The scheduler will select the resource with smallest value calculated using the specified load formula. However, these new parameters may not easily be collected and the range of value is dynamic and differs from various systems configuration. Therefore, we investigate the possible data grid performance metrics, and proposed the new weighted meta-scheduling algorithm. The performance of the proposed algorithm is analyzed based on the experiment results.

3 Weighted Meta-scheduling Algorithm

Figure 1 shows the procedure of meta-scheduler to allocate grid resources for scientific applications. Once the meta-scheduler received an application request, it will look for the grid resources satisfied all the application requirements and generate the resource candidate list. Then it calculates the load formula using the current load values collected from each resource. Finally, it can select the resource from the candidate list with smallest or largest value according to the policy and allocate to the applications. It is obvious that the load formula is the most important key for the meta-scheduler algorithm. Different kinds of application may have different load formulas to optimize the performance for application execution.

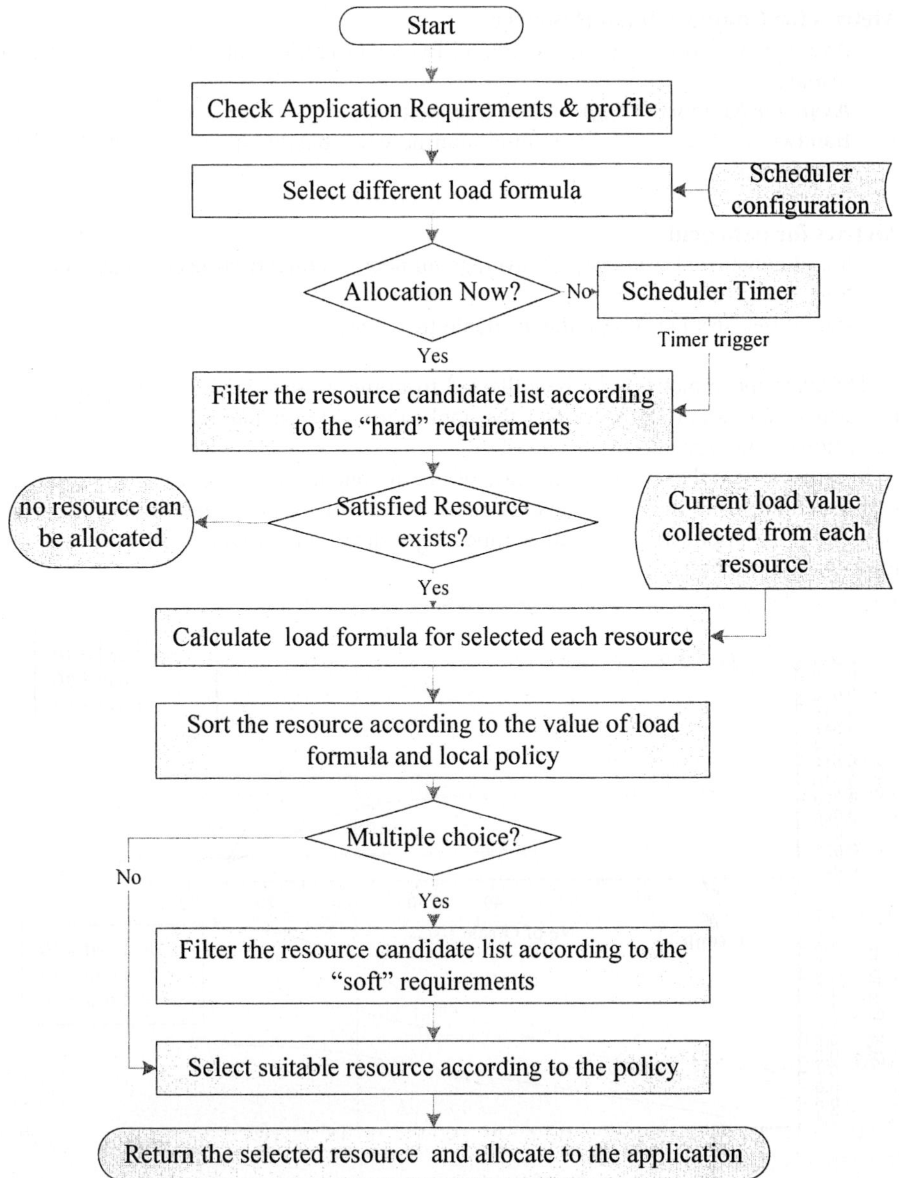

Fig. 1. Procedure of weighted meta-scheduling algorithm

3.1 Load Metrics

The load metrics are parameters that represent the current usage of grid resources. It is able to be used to configure the load formula. Considering the features of the scientific grid, we can use the two types of metrics to define the load formula.

Metrics for Computational Resource

- Average system Load (L_{avg}): average CPU load to reflect the utilization of system resource.
- Available Memory (C_{mem}): size of free memory
- Bandwidth (C_{band}): maximize/minimum network bandwidth to estimate the data transfer speed.

Metrics for data grid

- no. of concurrent users (N_{user}): average number of concurrent users to access data grid
- size of free storage (C_{disk}): the available free storage

There are more metrics can be collected from the grid resource, but only the metrics which may significantly affect the application performance will be used in the definition of load formula.

Figure 2 shows that with the increase of no. of concurrent oracle users, the application execution time increased quickly until the no. of users exceed about 60 users. After that, the application execution time keeps steadily even under different system load.

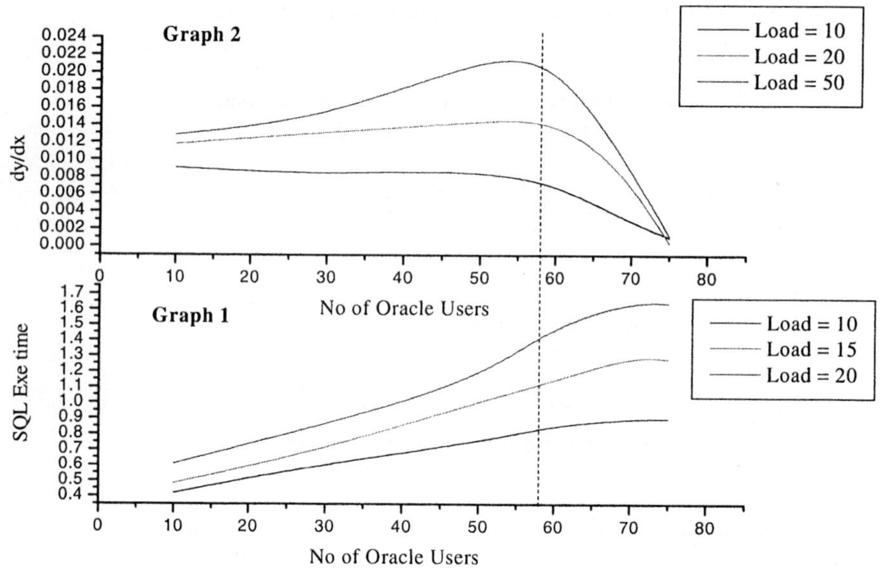

Fig. 2. Performance affect by no. of concurrent users

3.2 Performance Metrics

The following performance metrics shown in Figure 3 are used in our study to evaluate the performance of proposed meta-scheduling algorithm.

- Response time (T_r) is the amount of time between submitting the job from the client host and starting the job on the allocated host by Meta-scheduler.
- Execution Time (T_e) is the average amount of time generated by the SQL SELECT statement.
- Job Execution Time (T) is the time taken from when a job is submitted till it ends. The job is considered completed only when the entire output has been transferred to the client host.

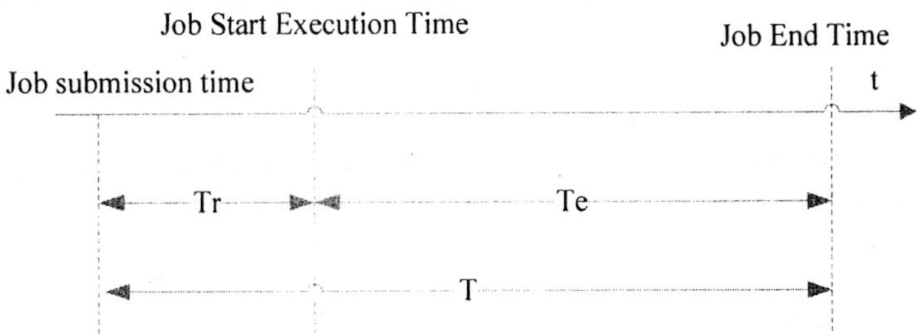

Fig. 3. Performance metrics

3.3 Weighted Load Formula

The general definition of weighted load formula is shown as Formula (1):

$$\Phi = \sum(\pm \lambda_k P_k), \ \sum \lambda_k = 1 \tag{1}$$

λ is the weight for each metrics in the load formula. k is the no. of metrics within he range of [1..N], where N is the maximum number of metrics to define the load formula. P is the metrics included in the formula. Φ is the value of load to schedule grid resource for applications.

4 Experiment Results

The experiment aims to evaluate the performance for the weighted meta-scheduling algorithm. We investigate the performance by adjusting the different system load, and also compare with the widely used least-load scheduling algorithm.

4.1 Experiment Setup

The test bed used in our experiments consists of 3 workstations running Linux OS or Solaris 9. It installed Oracle 10g to set up the data grid and uses Sun Grid Engine 5.3 to setup a computational grid.

For a j number of jobs running on node i, the load formula used in our experiments is defined as follows:

$$\Phi_{i,j} = \lambda \, N_{i,j} / Avg(N_{usr}) + L_{avgj} \tag{2}$$

Where $\Phi_{i,j}$ is the total load when there are j number of jobs on node i. λ denotes the normalizing factor necessary to balance the equation. Let $N_{i,j}$ represent the no of connections running on the node, assuming j number of jobs contributes j no of connections. The average number of Oracle Connections required to provide the homogeneity factor is $Avg(N_{usr})$ L_{avg} is the np_load_avg of the node i.

The experiments have three steps:

1) Test under different system load

2) Test performance by changing the data grid workload

3) Compare the performance with original SGE least load scheduler algorithm. The load formula is shown as below:

$$\Phi_{i,j} = L_{avgj} \tag{3}$$

In our experiments, the meta-scheduler allocates grid resources according to the value of above load formula. The experiment results are analyzed in the following sections.

4.2 Response Time

As shown in Figure 4 and Figure 5, it is noted that almost only 15% of the jobs using least load algorithm have response time greater than 10 seconds while it is a much higher 62% using the weighted scheduling algorithm.

The increase in the response time due to the increased complexity of new load formula which consider the Oracle database information. The computation of load formula is longer and the collection of data grid performance also takes more system resources. Therefore, the response time of weighted meta-scheduling algorithm is longer.

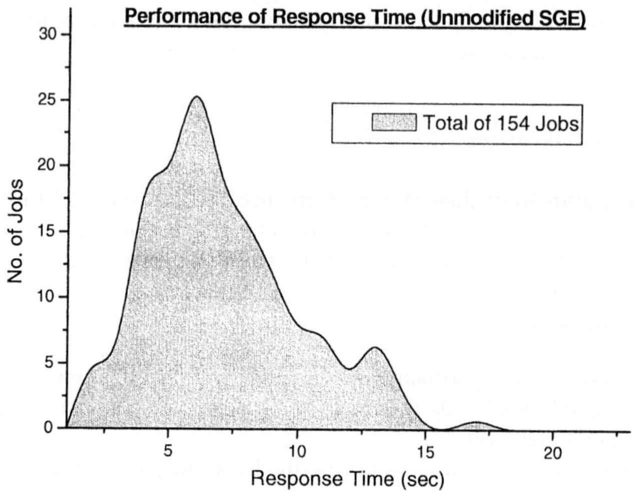

Fig. 4. Response Time for least load algorithm

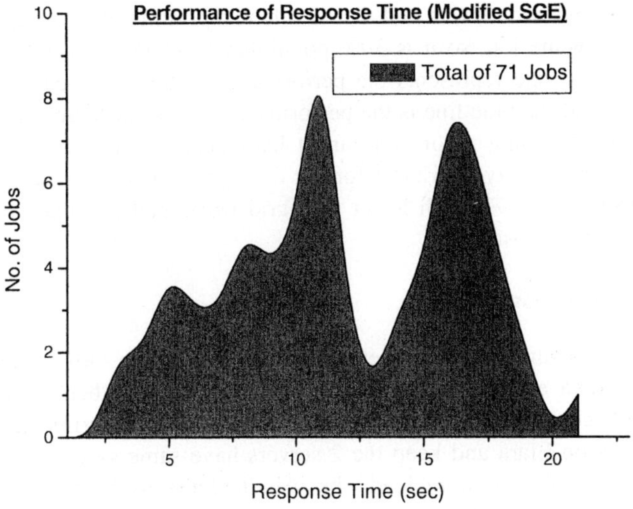

Fig. 5. Response Time for weighted meta-scheduling algorithm

4.3 Overall Performance

Figure 6 compare the overall application performance interns of execution time between the two scheduling algorithms.

We note that the performance line (green color) of the selected machine using proposed scheduling algorithm lays in between the performance lines of the two servers using the least load scheduling algorithm in SGE. Since we keep the average system

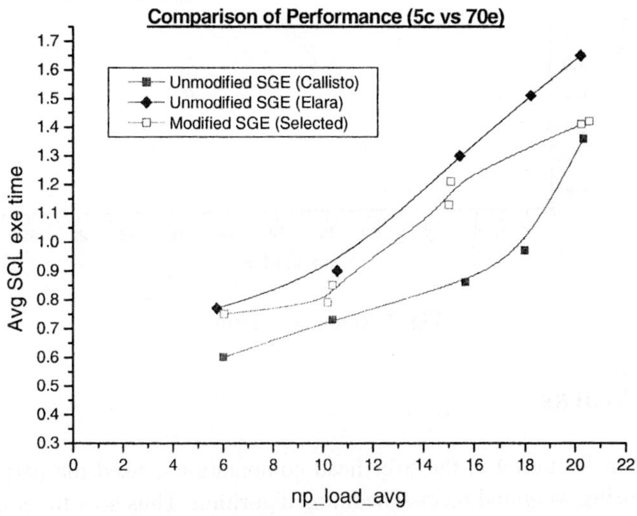

Fig. 6. Performance Comparison

load as same on the two servers and the least load algorithm always select the lowest load server to execute job, so it is 50% possibility to choose either faster or slower server. So the read line represents the performance in the worst case of using least load algorithm, and the blue line is the performance in best case. So we can say using weighted meta-scheduling algorithm can at least achieve medium performance, so that it provides the quality guarantee for the data grid applications. It is because the scheduler selects the server with lower data grid work load and makes execute data grid application much faster.

4.4 Resource Selection

Figure 7 show that the weighted meta-scheduling algorithm will always select the resource which can execute the application faster. In our testbed, server Elara has better hardware configuration than server Callisto. In this experiment, we set more concurrent users on Elara and keep the 2 servers have same system workload. With the increase of average system load, the weighted meta-scheduler always selects server Callisto to execute job, that because Callisto has less no. of concurrent users so the data grid application will be executed faster. Therefore, the proposed algorithm can select resources intelligently with considering data grid workload.

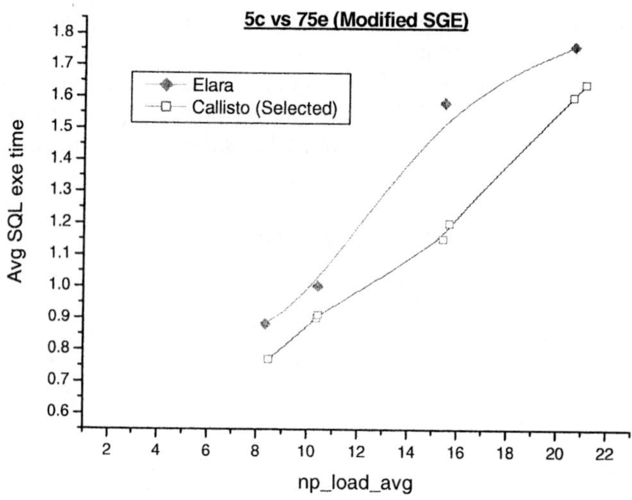

Fig. 7. Resource Selection

5 Future Works

As discussed in Section 4.2, the over head computation caused the performance decrease when using weighted meta-scheduling algorithm. Thus how to reduce the overhead mechanism is one of challenging problem.

Current investigation only test on the platform of SGE and Oracle 10g, we will do more experiments on different grid platforms to figure out the performance in scientific grid environment. And more work can be done to schedule resources for parallel applications over grid.

6 Conclusion

In this paper, we proposed the weighted meta-scheduling algorithm for the scientific grid. The key idea is to introduce the data grid workload into the load formula, which is used to determine the grid resource allocation. Several experiments have been done to investigate the performance and compared with least load scheduling algorithm in Sun Grid Engine.

Given a situation when two hosts are balanced in CPU load but having different data grid load, this proposed scheduling algorithm dynamically detects data grid load imbalance on nodes of a cluster, and effectively assigns jobs to the node with the lower data grid load. Therefore, the proposed scheduling algorithm has shown to be more intelligent in the selection of the execution hosts for jobs execution.

A tradeoff of this modification is a general slight drop in performance in terns of response time and the average SQL execution time. It is mainly caused by complex computation for load formula and more system resources are taken by the scheduler to keep updating the data grid workload dynamically.

Hence, with the integration solution of Oracle 10g resource metadata and load sensors and with the aid of an efficient load mechanism, the proposed weighted meta-scheduling algorithm indeed proves to be a smarter and more efficient system.

Acknowledgement

The authors acknowledge for the contribution from all the students involved in this project. We thank Mr. Tay Chai Yee and Miss Heng Bao Jin for the completion of experiments. We also appreciate the initial research and development work done by Mr. Sajindra Jayasena, Mr. Yee Chin Peng and Mr. Wong Wai Hong.

References

1. Chris Smith, Computational Grids meets the database, Platform Computing white papers.
2. Heinz Stockinger, Flavia Donno, Erwin Laure, Shahzad Muzaffar, Peter Kunszt, Grid Data Management in Action: Experience in Running and Supporting Data Management Services in the EU DataGrid Project, CERN
3. Sun Grid Engine Load sensor architecture, http://gridengine.sunsource.net/project/gridengine/howto/loadsensor.html
4. S. Venugopal, R. Buyya, and L. Winton, A Grid Service Broker for Scheduling Distributed Data-Oriented Applications on Global Grids, 2nd International Workshop on Middleware in Grid Computing, October 2004
5. W.H. Wong, Integration of Sun Grid Engine 5.3 with Oracle Database 10g, APSTC Internship report, 2004

6. J. Song, Z.H. Yang and C.W. See, Investigating Super Scheduling Algorithms for Grid Computing: A Simulation Approach, proceedings of the Fifth International Conference on Parallel and Distributed Computing, Applications and Technologies, LNCS 3320, December 2004, pp. 372-375
7. G. Chen, Z.H. Yang, C.W. See, J. Song and Y.Q. Jiang, Agent-mediated Genetic Superscheduling in Grid Environments, proceedings of the Fifth International Conference on Parallel and Distributed Computing, Applications and Technologies, LNCS 3320, December 2004, pp. 367-371
8. S. Kim and J.B. Weissman, A Genetic Algorithm Based Approach for Scheduling Decomposable Data Grid Applications, Proceedings of International Conference on Parallel Processing, August 2004, pp. 406-413
9. S. Zhuk, A. Chernykh, A. Avetisyan, S. Gaissaryan, D. Grushin, N. Kuzjurin, A. Pospelov and A. Shokurov, Comparison of Scheduling Heuristics for Grid Resource Broker, Proceedings of 5th International Conference in Computer Science, September 2004, pp. 388-392
10. W.Z Zhang, B.X. Fang, H. He, H.L. Zhang and M.Z. Hu, Multisite Resource Selection and Scheduling Algorithm on Computational Grid, Proceedings of 18th International Parallel and Distributed Processing Symposium, April 2004, pp. 105
11. S. Jayasena and C.P. Yee, Integrating Sun Grid Engine Computational Grid Services with Oracle Data Grid Service, APSTC Internship Report, 2004

Performance Analysis of Domain Decomposition Applications Using Unbalanced Strategies in Grid Environments

Beatriz Otero, José M. Cela, Rosa M. Badía, and Jesús Labarta

Dpt. d'Arquitectura de Computadors, Universitat Politècnica de Catalunya,
Campus Nord, C/ Jordi Girona, 1-3, Mòdul D6, 109, 08034, Barcelona-Spain
{botero, cela, rosab, jesus}@ac.upc.edu

Abstract. In this paper, we compare the performance of some mesh-based applications in a Grid environment using the domain decomposition technique and unbalanced workload strategies. We propose unbalanced distributions in order to overlap computation with remote communications. Results are presented for typical cases in car crashing simulation where finite element schemes are applied in fine mesh. The expected execution time is basically the same when two unbalanced techniques are used, but it is up 34% smaller that the one requires by the classical balanced strategy. We also analyze the influence of the communication pattern on execution times using the Dimemas simulator.

Keywords: Domain decomposition, Grid environments.

1 Introduction

Nowadays the computational solution of huge-sized problems has become feasible by using a grid computing which enhances limited computational resources of an individual company. The use of Globus allows the cooperation of many computing resources distributed in a wide area to solve and analyze macro-sized problems. Usually, such problems arise from the discretization of elliptic partial differential equations on meshes whose solution involves computational matrix algebra operations, such as vector-matrix and matrix-matrix multiplications. In this paper, we consider distributed applications that carry out matrix-vector product operations. In order to achieve good performance of these applications, the spatial domain must be divided among the available processors in an efficient manner [1], and each processor performs a numerical treatment on its assigned sub-domain. However, efficient implementations of matrix algebra operations are also required to wisely exploit the computational facility.

Mesh partitioning for homogeneous systems has been extensively studied [2], [3]; however, mesh partitioning for distributed system in Grid environments is a relatively new area of research. Previous work [4], present studies on latency, bandwidth and optimum workload to take full advantage of available resources using balanced workload. In this work, we use an unbalanced distribution where the workload could be different for each processor. Basically, this distribution assigns

H. Zhuge and G.C. Fox (Eds.): GCC 2005, LNCS 3795, pp. 1031 – 1042, 2005.

less workload to processors responsible for sending updates outside of his host. This data domain with a few loads is defined like *special domains*. For instance, in [5] we found that this strategy was more effective than the balanced technique in most of the cases considered. In this work, we proposed a new distribution pattern for the data in which the workload is different depending on the processor (many *special domains* per host). Nevertheless the scalability of this unbalanced distribution is moderate.

In this paper, we propose to assign all *special domains* to a single CPU in each host, who concurrently manages communications, from this host. We use the Dimemas tool to simulate the behavior of the distributed applications in Grid environments.

The paper is organized as follows: Section §2 present the tool used to simulate the Grid environment. Section §3 proposes the workload assignment patterns. Section §4 shows the results obtained in the environments specified for different data distribution patterns. Conclusions from this work are presented in Section §5.

2 Grid Environment

This section describes the generation trace and the configurations of the Grid environment studied. Moreover, we present Dimemas [6], [7], the tool used for simulating Grid environments. This tool is developed by CEPBA[1] for the simulating parallel environments. In DAMIEN[2] project, Dimemas is extended to work in a distributed and heterogeneous Grid environment [8], [9]. Dimemas is a performance prediction simulator for message passing applications. Dimemas is fed with a trace file and a configuration file. In order to obtain the tracefile, the parallel application is executed using an instrumented version of MPI. Therefore, the tracefile has an execution of the application on a source machine that captures the CPU bursts the communication pattern information. The configuration file contains details of the simulated architecture, such as number of nodes, latency and bandwidth between nodes. Dimemas generates an output file that contains the execution times of the simulated application for the parameters specified in the configuration file.

Dimemas simulator considers a very simple model for point to point communications. This model decomposes the communication time in five components: latency time, resource contention time, transfer time, WAN contention time and flight time. Latency time ($T_{Latency}$) is a time required to start the communication. This time is defined once per each machine. Resource contention time ($T_{Resource}$) is a time simulated by Dimemas that depends on the availability of links and buses. Transfer time (T_{Send}) is a time that depends on the message size and connection bandwidth. The WAN contention time (T_{WAN}) is a time that models the effect of the traffic on the network. It is a factor that reduces the connection bandwidth. Finally, the flight time (T_{Flight}) is a time simulated by Dimemas that model the transmission of the message to the destination. It depends on the distance between hosts [10]. The flight time is a square matrix of N_host x N_host.

---

[1] European Center for Parallelism of Barcelona, www.cepba.upc.edu.

[2] Distributed Applications and Middleware for Industrial use of European Networks.

If consider the before communication model, we suppose an infinite number of buses for the interconnection network and as many full-duplex connections as different remote communication has the host with others hosts ($T_{Resource}$ is negligible). We consider the same number of processors per host. For the WAN contention time (T_{WAN}), we use a lineal model to estimate the traffic present in the external network [11]. Thus, our communication model depends of three parameters: latency, bandwidth and flight time. To estimate these parameters, we have used the ping program. Depending on the network situation at each moment, the nominal values of the WAN parameters can vary at each moment. Afterwards, measurements of distributed executions between machines were performed to work. Moreover, we considered set values according to what is commonly found in present networks [12], [13], [14], [15]. The communications between *processors* are relatively fast, and depend of latency and bandwidth between processors inside a node. The *inter-node* communication is relatively slow and depends of latency, bandwidth and flight time between hosts. Table 1 shows the values for the internal and external host communications. The internal column defines the latency and bandwidth between processors inside a host. The external column defines the latency and bandwidth values between hosts.

Table 1. Communication parameters values

Parameters	Internal (Processors)	External (Hosts)
Latency	25 μs	10 ms and 100 ms
Bandwidth	100 Mbps	64 Kbps, 300 Kbps and 2Mbps
Flight time	-	From 1 ms to 100 ms

Our Grid environment is formed by a set of connected hosts; each of them can be a network of symmetric multi-processors (SMP) or a parallel machine. Different hosts are connected through an external WAN. The communications between different hosts are defined like the remote communications.

3 Domain Decomposition

Domain decomposition is used for efficient parallel execution of mesh-based applications, such as finite element or finite difference modelling of phenomena in engineering and sciences. Mesh-based applications use a meshing procedure to discretize the problem domain, which is partitioned into several sub-domains; each of them is assigned to individual processors in the Grid environment.

In these applications, one matrix-vector operation is performed for each iteration of the explicit method. To realize the matrix-vector operation, we use the domain decomposition strategy. The initial mesh is split in sub-domains, and each sub-domain must exchanges boundary values with all its neighbours [16]. The common boundary between sub-domains defines the size of the interchanged messages. In the previous section, we defined a host as a set of processors. When processors at the same host exchange boundary values, we said that this communication is local. In other hand, a remote communication occurs when one processor exchange data with a processor in other host. The remote communications are slower than the local communications. Therefore, we consider two unbalanced data distributions for to overlap computation with remote communications.

3.1 Unbalanced Distribution Pattern That Depends on Remote Communication (*U-Bdomains*)

In this unbalanced partition, each domain is equivalent to one parallel process assigned to one CPU. Then we have as many domains as CPUs. The partition of the data is done in a two-step partitioning. The first step splits the mesh into *host* partitions by using METIS [17], and each partition is assigned to one host. This procedure guarantees that the computational load is balanced between hosts. Now, the second step involves an unbalanced division of the data per host. We create as many *special domains* as remote communications have a host with different hosts. These *special domains* are called *Bdomains.* The *Bdomain* contains only boundary nodes, so the computational load for the processes with Bdomains is negligible. Finally, the remaining host partition is decomposed in (*nproc-Bdomains*) domains. These domains are called *Cdomains.*

3.2 Unbalanced Distribution Pattern That Do Not Depend on the Remote Communications (*U-1domains*)

In this distribution pattern, the total number of processes is equal to: $((T_{CPU} - T_{hosts}) + T_{RemComm})$, where T_{CPU} represents the total number of CPUs in the Grid, T_{hosts} is the total number of host, and $T_{RemComm}$ is the total number of remote communications with different hosts per iteration. Each remote communication is a *Bdomains*, and *Bdomains* in each host are assigned to a single CPU. Too as in the case of *U-Bdomains*, we perform the decomposition in two phases, and the first phase is basically the same. Now, in the second phase, we create as many *Bdomains* as remote communication could be in the host, but, all *Bdomains* are assigned to a single CPU inside the host. The remaining host-partition is decomposed in (*nproc-1)* domains.

Below, we show an example of these unbalanced distributions. A finite element mesh of 256 degrees of freedom (dofs) is considered, and a grid configuration of 4 hosts and 8 CPUs per host is assumed. First at all, we make an initial decomposition in four sub-graphs. Figure 1 shows this balanced partition with boundary nodes *(Bdomains)*. For every sub-graph we assign each *Bdomains* to one domain, if the unbalanced distribution is *U-Bdomains*. The remainder sub-graph is divided in five balanced *Cdomains* (figure 2). However, if the unbalanced distribution is *U-1domains*, all of the *Bdomains* are assigned to one CPU. Then, the remaining sub-graph is split in seven balanced *Cdomains* (figure 3).

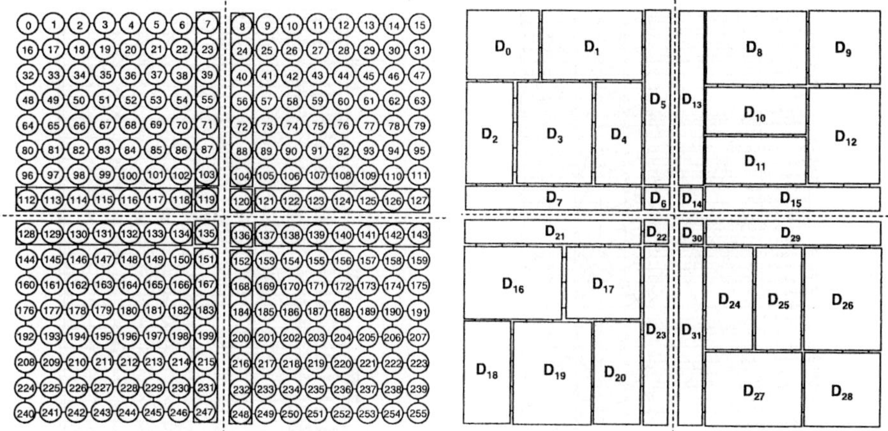

Fig. 1. Specials domains

Fig. 2. *U-Bdomains* distribution

Figure 4 shows the communication pattern and the relationship among processes-host in this example. Arrows in the diagram denote processes that interchange data. The source of an arrow identifies the sender, and the end identifies the receiver. A short arrow represents local communications inside a host, whereas a long arrow represents remote communications between hosts. In figure 4.a, each process is assigned to one processor. Notice that, 62.5% of processors inside hosts are busy, while the remaining processors are performing remote communications. In figure 4.b, processes with remote communication are assigned to the same processor. Then, 87.5% of processors have computation to do. In both cases, all remote communications are overlapped inside a host. Figure 4.b depicts a case with one local communication more and less calculation than one in figure 4.a.

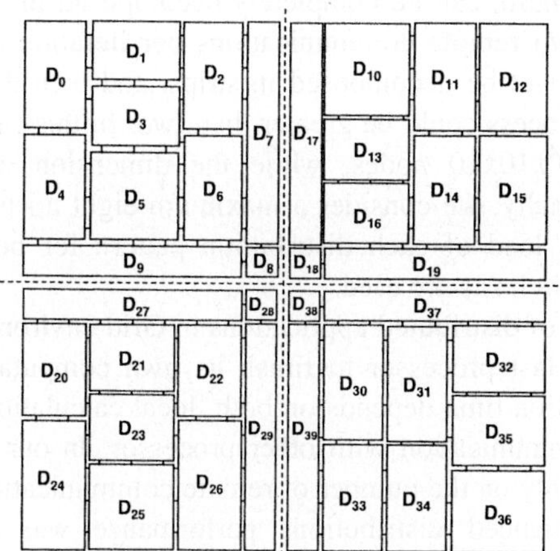

Fig. 3. *U-1domains* distribution

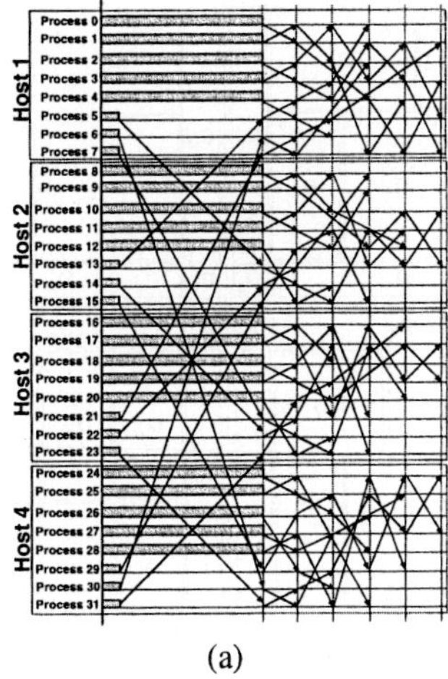

(a)

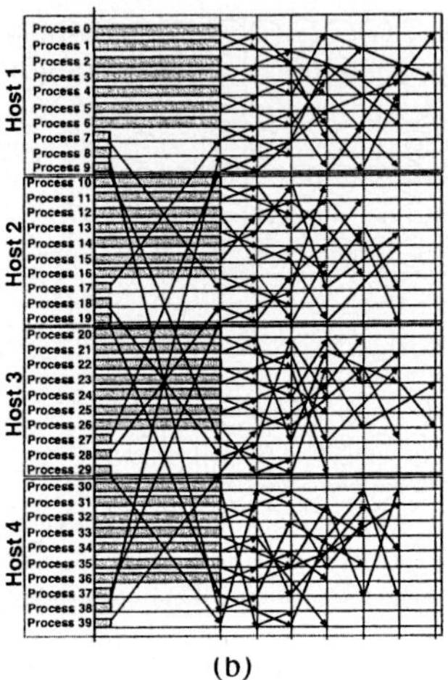

(b)

Fig. 4. Diagram of communication for one computational iteration: (a) *U-Bdomains* (b) *U-1domain*

4 Results

In this section, we evaluate the performance of distributed applications in Grid environment when data distribution is handled by *U-Bdomains* and *U-1domains* techniques. In these experiments, we have supposed a maximum number of processors equal to 128, and the data set is given by a finite element mesh (FEM) of 1,000,000 dofs. This data set was obtained from simulations of car crashing [18] and sheet stamping models [19]. However, similar data sets are common in other industrial problems. For our purposes, FEM's are classified in two different kinds. The first one, a stick mesh, can be completely decomposed in strips; therefore each parallel process has two remote communications per iteration at most. The second kind, a box mesh, can not be decomposed in strips, and then the number of remote communications per process could be greater than two. In this case, the dimension of the stick mesh is 10^4x10x10 nodes, while the dimension of the box mesh is 10^2x10^2x10^2 nodes. Finally, we consider a maximum eight hosts. Table 2 shows the average computational load of each distribution pattern for both kinds of meshes when two, four and eight hosts are used.

The execution time of distributed applications in Grid environment is given by the execution time of the last processor to finish its own computation load. It is well known, that this execution time depends on both, local calculations performed by the processor and any communication with other processor. In our case, this execution time has depended mainly on the number of remote communications. The metric used to compare our unbalanced distributions performance was the execution time reduction. Figures 5 and 6 show the time reduction percentages as a function of bandwidth for each grid environment in the case of stick mesh. These percentages allow comparing the balanced distribution with *U-1domains* and *U-Bdomains* distributions.We noticed that *U-Bdomains* distribution reduces the execution time of the balanced distribution in most cases. However, the *U-Bdomains* distribution creates as many special domains per host as external communications. Therefore, the scalability of *U-Bdomains* distribution is moderate, because of in each special domain one processor is devoted only to perform communications. Our simulations show that scalability for this distribution is between 40% and 98%, while scalability of *U-1domains* distribution is between 75% and 98%.

Table 2. Average of computational load per processor

STICK MESH						
	Processes with remote communications		***U-1domains***		***U-Bdomains***	
Hostx CPUs	**Nodes per process *Bdomains***	**Number of process *Bdomains***	**Nodes per process *Cdomains***	**Number of process *Cdomains***	**Nodes per process *Cdomains***	**Number of process *Cdomains***
2x4	101	2	166633	6	166633	6
2x8	102	2	71414	14	71414	14
2x16	101	2	33327	30	33327	30
2x32	100	2	16126	62	16126	62
2x64	100	2	7935	126	7935	126
4x4	101	6	83283	12	99940	10
4x8	102	6	35693	28	38438	26
4x16	101	6	16657	60	17231	58
4x32	100	6	8060	124	8192	122
8x8	100	14	17832	56	19972	50
8x16	102	14	8321	120	8759	114

BOX MESH						
	Processes with remote communications		***U-1domains***		***U-Bdomains***	
Hostx CPUs	**Nodes per process *Bdomains***	**Number of process *Bdomains***	**Nodes per process *Cdomains***	**Number of process *Cdomains***	**Nodes per process *Cdomains***	**Number of process *Cdomains***
2x4	10334	2	163222	6	163222	6
2x8	10329	2	69953	14	69953	14
2x16	10325	2	32645	30	32645	30
2x32	10324	2	15796	62	15796	62
2x64	10364	2	7772	126	7772	126
4x8	3486	10	34469	28	43870	22
4x16	3664	10	16056	60	17840	54
4x32	3499	10	7782	124	8178	118
8x8	1816	38	16625	56	35807	26
8x16	1814	38	7759	120	10345	90

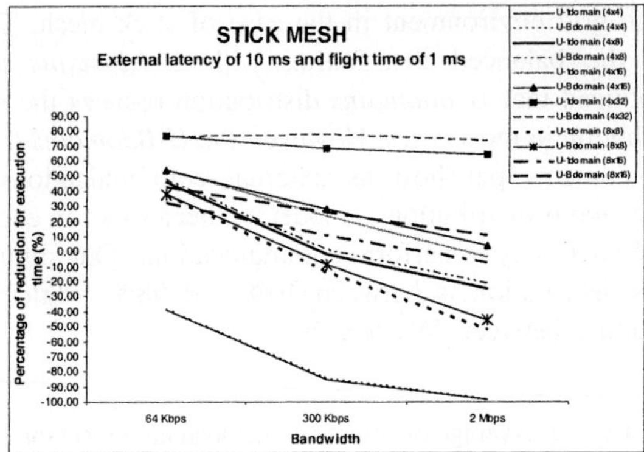

Fig. 5.a. Execution time reduction with external latency of 10 ms and flight time of 1ms

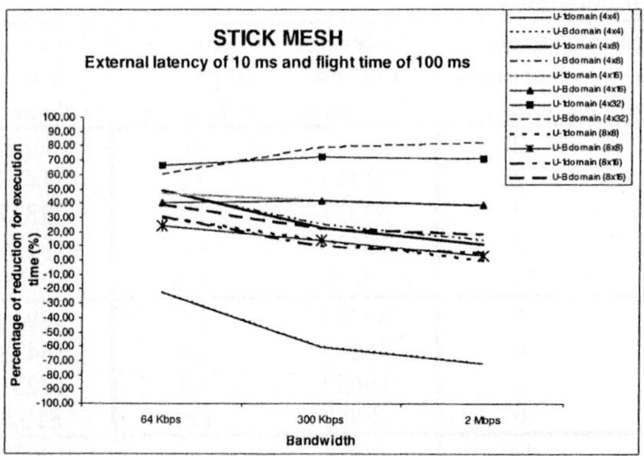

Fig. 5.b. Execution time reduction with external latency of 10 ms and flight time of 100ms

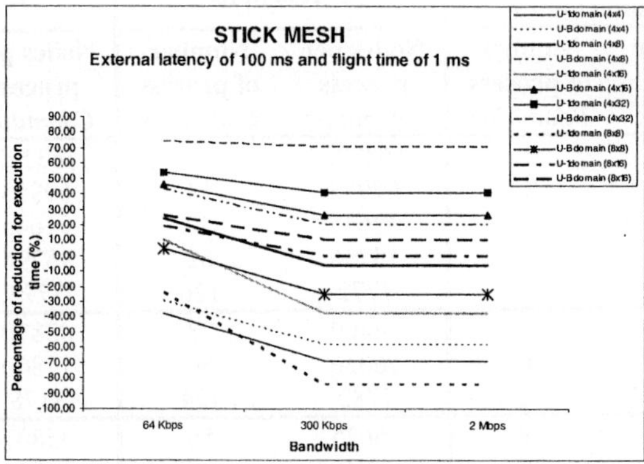

Fig. 6.a. Execution time reduction with external latency of 100 ms and flight time of 1 ms

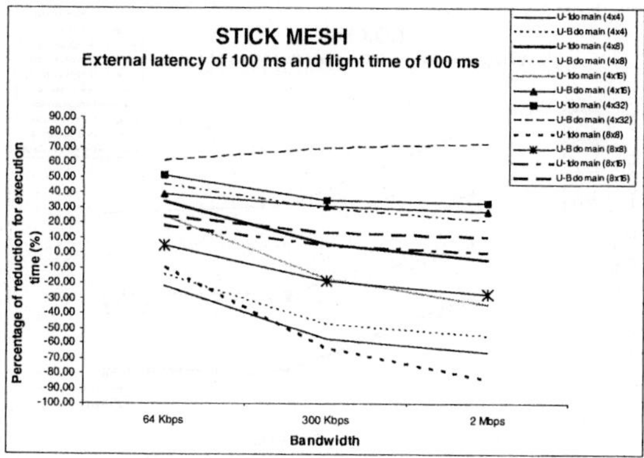

Fig. 6.b. Execution time reduction with external latency of 100 ms and flight time of 100 ms

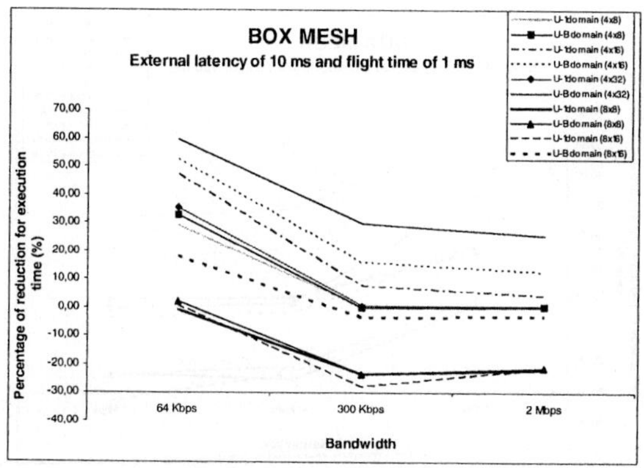

Fig. 7.a. Execution time reduction with external latency of 10 ms and flight time of 1 ms

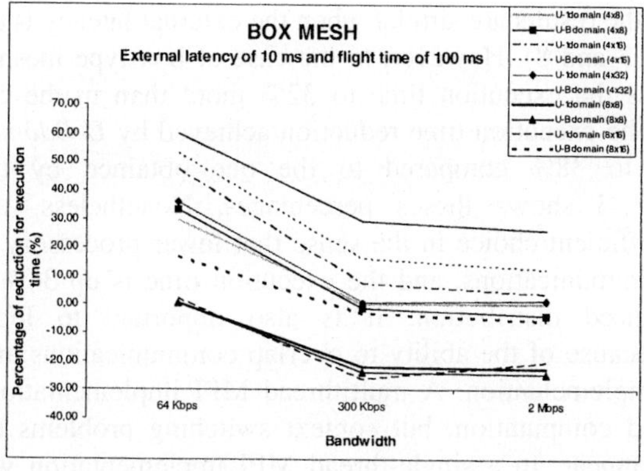

Fig. 7.b. Execution time reduction with external latency of 10 ms and flight time of 100 ms

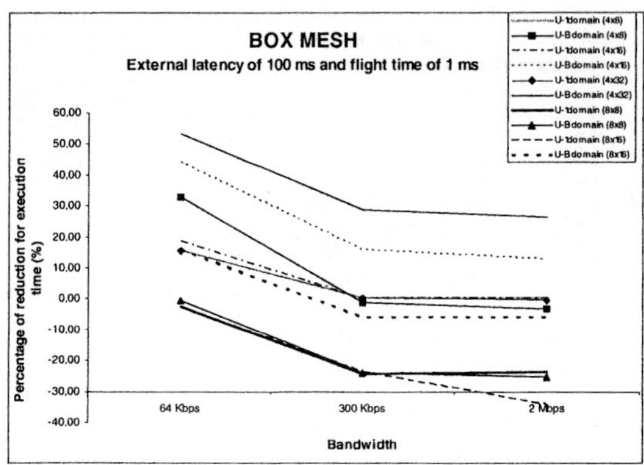

Fig. 8.a. Execution time reduction with external latency of 100 ms and flight time of 1 ms

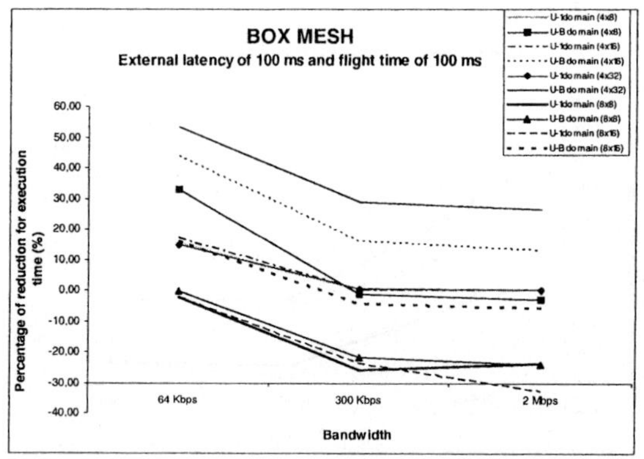

Fig. 8.b. Execution time reduction with external latency of 100 ms and flight time of 100ms

As it is shown, the results are similar when the external latency is considered equal to 100 ms (figures 7 and 8). However, in the case of box-type meshes, *U-Bdomains* distribution reduces the execution time to 32% more than in the case where stick meshes are used. The execution time reduction achieved by *U-Bdomains* distribution ranges from 1% to 38% compared to the one obtained by the *U-1domains* distribution. Table 3 shows theses percentages. Nonetheless, the *U-1domains* distribution is an efficient choice in the sense that fewer processors are dedicated to perform remote communications, and the execution time is up 34% smaller than in the case of balanced distribution. It is also important to look at the MPI implementation, because of the ability to overlap communications and computations depends on this implementation. A multithread MPI implementation could overlap communication and computation, but context switching problems between threads and interferences appear. In a single-thread MPI implementation we can use non-blocking send/receive calls with a wait_all routine, but we have observed some problems with this approach.

Table 3. Average of the additional percentage of *U-1domains* compared with *U-Bdomains*

	Process B-domains per host		Additional Percentage (External latency 10 ms)		Additional Percentage (External latency 100 ms)	
Host	**Stick Mesh**	**Box Mesh**	**Stick Mesh**	**Box Mesh**	**Stick Mesh**	**Box Mesh**
2	1	1	0 %	-4.65E-06%	0 %	-8.84E-06 %
4	1 or 2	2 or 3	-6.91 %	-18.68 %	-35.74 %	-37.74 %
8	1 or 2	3, 5 or 6	-9.04 %	-17,21 %	-23.81 %	-23,98 %

These problems are associated with the internal order of execution. In our experiment, we solved these problems by programming explicitly the proper order of the communications. However, these problems remain in the general case. We conclude that is very important to have non-blocking MPI primitives that really exploit the full duplex channel capability. In a future work, we will consider other MPI implementations that optimize the collective operations [20].

5 Conclusions

In this work the performance of some distributed applications in grid environments is studied when two different unbalanced-workload distributions, *U-Bdomains* and *U-1domains*, are utilized. By using these unbalanced distributions, the execution time is 53% better that the one spent by the traditional balanced-workload distribution. Our results show that *U-Bdomains* becomes 38% faster than *U-1domains* distribution, but it requires 25% more processors to perform remote communications. In other cases, the *U-1domains* distribution reduced the execution time until 34%. We show that these unbalanced distributions exploit more efficiently the pool of available processors to perform computation and allows a greater scalability.

Acknowledgements

This work was supported by the Ministry of Science and Technology of Spain under contract TIN2004-07739-C02-01, the HiPEAC European Network of Excellence and BSC (Barcelona Supercomputing Center).

References

1. Taylor V. E., Holmer B. K., Schwabe E. J. and Hribar M. R.: Balancing Load versus Decreasing Communication: Exploring the Tradeoffs. HICSS 1 (1996) 585-593
2. Berger M. and Bokhari S.:A partitioning strategy for non-uniform problems on multiprocessors. IEEE Transactions on Computers (1997) C-36:5
3. Simon H. D., Sohn A. and Biswas R.: Harp: A fast spectral partitioner. 9th ACM Symposium on Parallel Algorithms and Architectures, Newport, Rhode Island (1997)

4. Gropp W. D., Kaushik D. K., Keyes D. E. and Smith B. F.: Latency, Bandwidth, and Concurrent Issue Limitations in High-Performance CFD. Conference on Computational Fluid and Solid Mechanics, Cambridge, MA (2001) 839-841
5. Otero B., Cela J. M., Badia R. M. and Labarta J.: A Domain Decomposition Strategy for GRID Environments. 11th European PVM/MPI 2004, LNCS Vol. 3241, Hungary, (2004) 353-361
6. Dimemas. Internet, http://www.cepba.upc.es/tools/dimemas/ (2002)
7. Girona S., Labarta J. and Badía R. M.: Validation of Dimemas communication model for MPI collective operations. LNCS, vol. 1908, EuroPVM/MPI 2000, Hungary (2000)
8. Badia R. M., Labarta J., Giménez J. and Escale F.: DIMEMAS: Predicting MPI Applications Behavior in Grid Environments. Workshop on Grid Applications and Programming Tools (2003)
9. Badia R. M., Escale F., Gabriel E., Giménez J., Keller R., Labarta J.and Müller M. S.: Performance Prediction in a Grid Environment. 1st European across Grid Conference (2003)
10. Badía R. M., Escalé F., Giménez J. and Labarta J.: DAMIEN: D5.3/CEPBA. IST-2000-25406
11. Badía R. M., Giménez J., Labarta J., Escalé F. and Keller R.: DAMIEN:D5.2/CEPBA.IST-2000-25406
12. http://clik.to/adslvelocidad
13. http://www.bandwidthplace.com/speedtest
14. Bjørndalen J. M., Anshus O. J., Vinter B. and Larsen T.: The Impact on Latency and Bandwidth for a Distributed Shared Memory System Using a Gigabit Network Supporting the Virtual Interface Architecture. NIK 2000, Norsk Informatikk Konferanse, Bodø, Norway (2000)
15. Wolman A., Voelker G.M., Sharma N., Cardwell N., Karlin A. and Levy H. M.: On the scale and performance of cooperative Web proxy caching. Proceedings of the seventeenth ACM symposium on Operating systems principles, ACM Press New York, USA (1999) 16-31
16. Keyes D. E.: Domain Decomposition Methods in the Mainstream of Computational Science. 14th International Conference on Domain Decomposition Methods, Mexico (2003) 79-93
17. Metis, Internet, http://www.cs.umn.edu/~metis
18. Frisch N., Rose D., Sommer O., and Ertl Th.: Visualization and pre-processing of independent finite element meshes for car crash simulations. The Visual Computer 18:4 (2002) 236-249
19. Sosnowski W.: Flow approach-finite element model for stamping processes versus experiment. Computer Assisted Mechanics and Engineering Sciences, vol. 1 (1994) 49-75
20. Keller R., Gabriel E., Krammer B., Müller M. S. and Resch M. M.: Towards Efficient Execution of MPI Applications on the Grid: Porting and Optimization Issues. Journal of Grid Computing, Vol. 1, Issue 2 (2003) 133-149

Cooperative Determination on Cache Replacement Candidates for Transcoding Proxy Caching*

Keqiu Li[1], Hong Shen[1], and Di Wu[2]

[1] Graduate School of Information Science,
Japan Advanced Institute of Science and Technology,
1-1, Asahidai, Nomi, Ishikawa, 923-1292, Japan
[2] Department of Computer Science and Engineering,
Dalian University of Technology,
No 2, Linggong Road, Ganjingzi District, Dalian, 116024, China

Abstract. In this paper, the performance evaluation of an optimal Solution for coordinated cache replacement in Transcoding Proxies is present. We compare the performance over three impacts: impact of cache size, impact of object access frequency, and impact of the number of client classes. The extensive simulation results show that the coordinated cache replacement model greatly improves network performance compared to local replacement models that determine cache replacement candidates from the view of only a single node.

Keywords: Web caching, multimedia object, transcoding proxy, cache replacement, performance evaluation, Internet.

1 Introduction

As the transcoding proxy is attracting an increasing amount of attention in the environment of mobile computing, it is noted that new efficient cache replacement policies are required for these transcoding proxies. There are many cache replacement algorithms for proxy caching proposed in literature. An overview of these caching replacement algorithms can be found in [2]. However, they cannot be simply or directly applied to solve the same problem for transcoding proxy caching due to the new emerging factors in the transcoding proxy (e.g., the additional delay caused by transcoding, different sizes and reference rates for different versions of a multimedia object) and the aggregate effect of caching multiple versions of the same multimedia object. Although the authors have elaborated these issues in [7], they considered the cache replacement problem at only a single node. Cooperative caching, in which caches cooperate in serving each other's requests and making storage decisions, is a powerful paradigm to improve cache

* This work was partially supported by Japan Society for the Promotion of Science (JSPS) under its General Research Scheme B Grant No. 14380139). Corresponding author H. Shen (shen@jaist.ac.jp).

H. Zhuge and G.C. Fox (Eds.): GCC 2005, LNCS 3795, pp. 1043–1053, 2005.

effectiveness [8, 12]. Efficient coordinated object management algorithms are crucial to the performance of a cooperative caching system, which can be divided into two type of algorithms: placement and replacement algorithms. There are a number of research on finding efficient solutions for cooperative object placement [10, 16]. However, there is little work done on finding efficient solutions for cooperative object replacement.

In [11], we presented an original model which determines cache replacement candidates on all candidate nodes in a coordinated fashion with the objective of minimizing the total cost loss. However, no simulation experiments are conducted to validate the performance of the proposed model. In this paper, we present the performance evaluating results for comparing the relative performance of our model with existing models. We compare the performance over three impacts: impact of cache size, impact of object access frequency, and impact of the number of client classes. The extensive simulation results show that the coordinated cache replacement model greatly improves network performance compared to local replacement models that determine cache replacement candidates from the view of only a single node.

The rest of this paper is organized as follows: Section 2 briefly describes a cooperative cache replacement scheme for transcoding proxy caching. In Section 3, the simulation model is introduced. We present performance evaluation in Section 4. Finally, we conclude this paper in Section 5.

2 Cooperative Cache Replacement for Transcoding Proxy Caching

In this section, we briefly introduce the algorithm proposed in [11]. The problem addressed in [11] is to determine where a new or updated version O_{i_0} should be cached among nodes $\{v_1, v_2, \cdots, v_n\}$ and which version of object j should be removed at that node to make room for O_{i_0} such that the total cost loss is minimized. Suppose that $P \subseteq V$ is the set of nodes at each of which $X_{i,k_i} \in A^i$ should be removed to make room for O_{i_0}, then this problem can be formally defined as follows:

$$L(P^*) = \min_{P \subseteq V} \{L(P)\} = \sum_{v_i \in P} (l(X_{i,k_i}) - g_i(O_{i_0})) \tag{1}$$

where $L(P)$ is the total relative cost loss, $l(X_{i,k_i})$ is the cost loss of removing X_{i,k_i} from node v_i, and $g_i(O_{i_0})$ is the cost saving of caching O_{i_0} at node v_i.

Now we begin to present an optimal solution for the problem as defined in Equation 1. In the following, we call the problem a k-optimization problem if we determine cache replacement candidates from nodes $\{v_1, v_2, \cdots, v_k\}$. Thus, the original problem (Equation (1)) is an n-optimization problem. Theorem 1 shows an important property that the optimal solution for the whole problem must contain optimal solutions for some subproblems.

Theorem 1. *[11] Suppose that* $X = \{X_{i_1,k_{i_1}}, X_{i_2,k_{i_2}}, \cdots, X_{i_\alpha,k_{i_\alpha}}\}$ *is an optimal solution for the* α*-optimization problem and* $X^{'} = \left\{X_{i_1^{'},k_{i_1^{'}}}, X_{i_2^{'},k_{i_2^{'}}}, \cdots, X_{i_\beta^{'},k_{i_\beta^{'}}}\right\}$ *is an optimal solution for the* $k_{i_\alpha} - 1$*-optimization problem. Then we have* $X^* = \left\{X_{i_1^{'},k_{i_1^{'}}}, X_{i_2^{'},k_{i_2^{'}}}, \cdots, X_{i_\beta^{'},k_{i_\beta^{'}}}, X_{i_\alpha,k_{i_\alpha}}\right\}$ *is also an optimal solution for the* α*-optimization problem.*

Based on Theorem 1, an optimal solution for the n-optimization can be obtained by checking all possible removed candidates from node v_1 to node v_n in order. Therefore, it is east to get that the time complexity of this solution is $O(n^2+mn\log n)$ based on our previous result that the complexity for computing all $S(r_{i,k})$ is $O(mn\log n)$, where n is the number of nodes in the network and m is the number of versions of object j.

3 Simulation Model

We outline the system configuration in section 3.1 and introduce existing models used for the purpose of comparison in Section 3.2.

3.1 System Configuration

To the best of our knowledge, it is difficult to find true trace data in the open literature to simulate our model. Therefore, we generated the simulation model from the empirical results presented in [1, 3, 4, 5, 7, 10].

The network topology was randomly generated by the Tier program [5]. Experiments for many topologies with different parameters have been conducted and the relative performance of our model was found to be insensitive to topology changes. Here, only the experimental results for one topology was listed due to space limitations. The characteristics of this topology and the workload model are shown in Table 1, which are chosen from the open literature and are considered to be reasonable.

The WAN (Wide Area Network) is viewed as the backbone network to which no servers or clients are attached. Each MAN (Metropolitan Area Network) node is assumed to connect to a content server. Each MAN and WAN node is associated with an en-route cache. Similar to the studies in [4, 6, 9, 15], cache size is described as the total relative size of all objects available in the content server. In our experiments, the object sizes are assumed to follow a Pareto distribution and the average object size is $26KB$. We also assume that each multimedia object has five versions and that the transcoding graph is as shown in Figure 1. The transcoding delay is determined as the quotient of the object size to the transcoding rate. In our experiments, the client at each MAN node randomly generates the requests, and the average request rate of each node follow–s the distribution of $U(1, 9)$, where $U(x, y)$ represents a uniform distribution between

Table 1. Parameters Used in Simulation

Parameter	Value
Number of WAN Nodes	200
Number of MAN Nodes	200
Delay of WAN Links	Exponential Distribution $p(x) = \theta^{-1}e^{-x/\theta}$ $(\theta = 0.45\ Sec)$
Delay of MAN Links	Exponential Distribution $p(x) = \theta^{-1}e^{-x/\theta}$ $(\theta = 0.06\ Sec)$
Number of Servers	100
Number of Web Objects	1000 objects per srever
Web Object Size Distribution	Pareto Distribution $p(x) = \frac{ab^a}{a-1}$ $(a = 1.1, b = 8596)$
Web Object Access Frequency	Zipf-Like Distribution $\frac{1}{i^\alpha}$ $(i = 0.7)$
Relative Cache Size Per Node	4%
Average Request Rate Per Node	$U(1,9)$ requests per second
Transcoding Rate	$20KB/Sec$

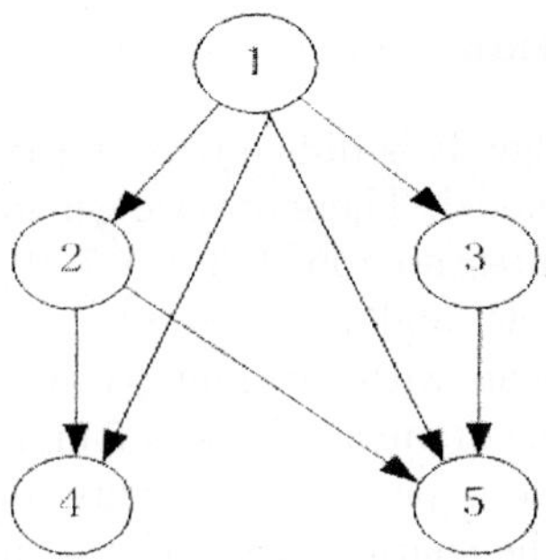

Fig. 1. Transcoding Graph for Simulation

x and y. The access frequencies of both the content servers and the objects maintained by a given server follow a Zipf-like distribution [4, 13]. Specifically, the probability of a request for object O in server S is proportional to $1/(i^\alpha \cdot j^\alpha)$, where S is the ith most popular server and O is the jth popular object in S. The delay of both MAN links and WAN links follows an exponential distribution, where the average delay for WAN links is 0.46 seconds and the average delay for WAN links is 0.06 seconds.

The cost for each link is calculated by the access delay. For simplicity, the delay caused by sending the request and the relevant response for that request is proportional to the size of the requested object. Here, we consider the average object sizes for calculating all delays, including the transmission delay, and transcoding delay. The cost function is taken to be the delay of the link, which means that the cost in our model is interpreted as the access latency in our simulation.

We apply a "sliding window" technique to estimate the access frequency to make our model less sensitive to transient workload [15]. Specifically, for each object O, $f(O,v)$ is calculated by $K/(t-t_K)$, where K is the number of accesses recorded, t is the current time, and t_K is the Kth most recently referenced time (the time of the oldest reference in the sliding window). K is set to 2 in the simulation. To reduce overhead, the access frequency is only updated when the object is referenced and at reasonably large intervals, e.g., several minutes, to reflect aging, which is also applied in [10].

3.2 Evaluation Models

- *LRU*: Least Recently Used (*LRU*) evicts the web object which is requested the least recently. The requested object is stored at each node through which the object passes. The cache purges one or more least recently requested objects to accommodate the new object if there is not enough room for it.
- *LNC − R [14]*: Least Normalized Cost Replacement ($LNC-R$) is a model that approximates the optimal cache replacement solution. It selects the least profitable documents for replacement. Similar to *LRU*, the requested object is cached by all nodes along the routing path.
- *AE [7]*: Aggregate Effect (*AE*) is a model that explores the aggregate effect of caching multiple versions of the same multimedia object in the cache. It formulates a generalized profit function to evaluate the aggregate profit from caching multiple versions of the same multimedia object. When the requested object passes through each node, the cache will determine which version of that object should be stored at that node according to the generalized profit.
- *CCR*: Cooperative Cache Replacement (*CCR*) determines cache replacement candidates on all candidate nodes in a coordinated fashion with the objective of minimizing the total cost loss.

4 Performance Evaluation

In this section, we compare the performance results of our model (described in Section 2) with those models introduced in Section 3.2 in terms of several performance metrics. The performance metrics we used in our simulation include delay-saving ratio (*DSR*), which is defined as the fraction of communication and server delays which is saved by satisfying the references from the cache instead of the server, average access latency (*ASL*), request response ratio (*RRR*), which is defined as the ratio of the access latency of the target object to its size, object hit ratio (*OHR*), which is defined as the ratio of the number of requests satisfied by the caches as a whole to the total number of requests, and highest server load (*HSL*), which is defined as the largest number of bytes served by the server per second. In the following figures, CCR ,LRU, $LNC-R$, and AE denote the results for the four models introduced in Section 3.2, Table 2 lists the abbreviations used in this section.

Table 2. Abbreviations Used in Performance Analysis

Meaning	Abbreviation	Decription
Performance Metric	DSR	Delay-Saving Ratio (%)
	ASL	Average Access Latency (Sec)
	RRR	Request Response Ratio (Sec/MB)
	OHR	Object Hit Ratio (%)
	HSL	Highest Server Load (MB/Sec)
Caching Model	CCR	Coordinated Cache Replacement
	AE	Standing for Aggregate Effect
	$LNC-R$	Least Normalized Cost Replacement
	LRU	Least Recently Used

4.1 Impact of Cache Size

In this experiment set, we compare the performance results of different models across a wide range of cache sizes, from 0.04 percent to 15.0 percent.

The first experiment investigates DSR as a function of the relative cache size per node and Figure 2 shows the simulation results. As presented in Figure 2, we can see that our model outperforms the other models since our coordinated cache replacement model determines the replacement candidates cooperatively among all the nodes on the path from the server to the client, whereas existing solutions, including LRU, $LNC-R$, and AE, consider decide cache replacement candidates locally, i.e., only from the view of a single node. Specifically, the mean improvements of DSR over AE, $LNC-R$, and LRU are 21.2 percent, 18.9 percent, and 13.0 percent, respectively. Figure 3 shows the simulation results of ASL as a function of the relative cache size at each node; we describe the results of RRR as a function of the relative cache size at each node in Figure

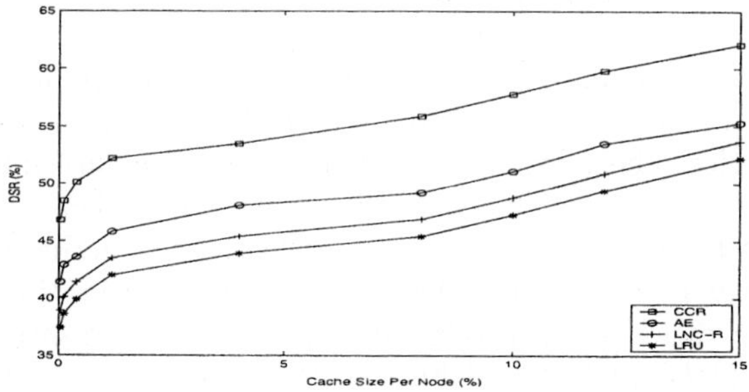

Fig. 2. Experiment on DSR

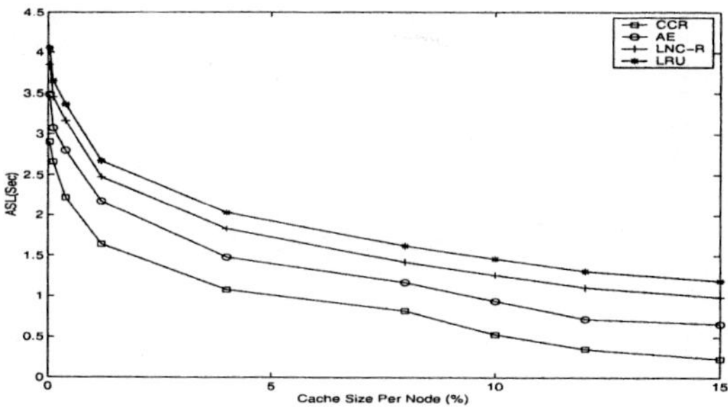

Fig. 3. Experiment on ASL

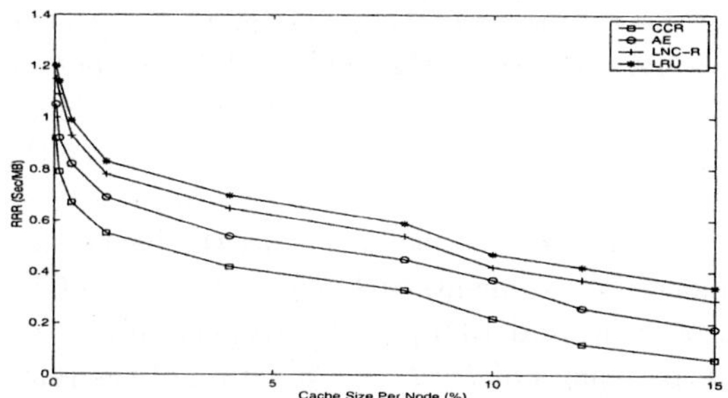

Fig. 4. Experiment on RRR

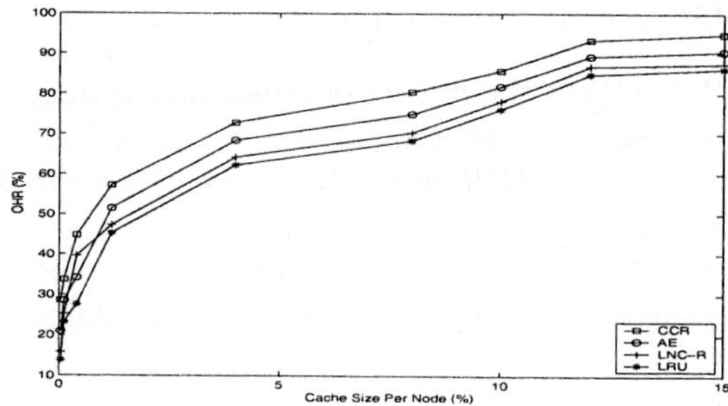

Fig. 5. Experiment for OHR

4. Clearly, the lower the ASL or the RRR, the better the performance. As we can see, all models provide steady performance improvement as the cache size increases. We can also see that CCR significantly improves both ASL and RRR compared to AE, $LNC - R$ and LRU, since our model determines the cache replacement candidates in an optimal and coordinated way, while the others decide the replacement candidates only by considering the situation of a single node. For ASL to achieve the same performance as CCR, the other models need 2 to 6 times as much cache size.

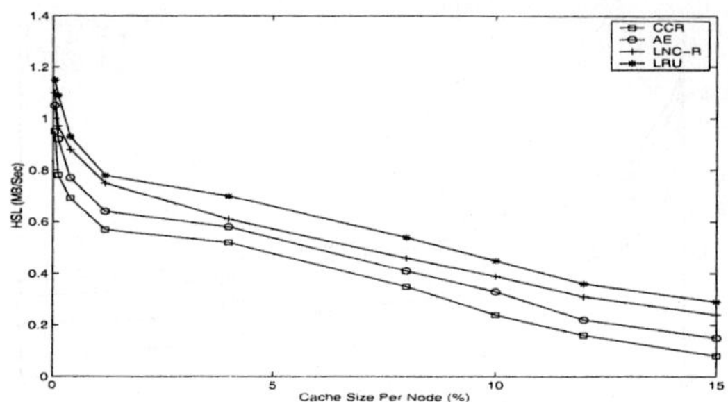

Fig. 6. Experiment for HSL

Figure 5 shows the results of OHR as a function of the relative cache size for different models. By computing the optimal replacement candidates, we can see that the results for our model can greatly outperform those of the other solutions, especially for smaller cache sizes. We can also see that OHR steadily improves as the relative cache size increases, which conforms to the fact that more requests will be satisfied by the caches as the cache size becomes larger. Particularly, the mean improvements of DSR over AE, $LNC-R$, and LRU are 27.1 percent, 22.5 percent, and 13.9 percent, respectively.

Figure 6 shows the results of HSL as a function of the relative cache size. It can be seen that HSL for our model is lower than that of the other solutions. We can also see that HSL decreases as the relative cache size increases.

4.2 Impact of Object Access Frequency

This experiment set examines the impact of object access frequency distribution on the performance results of different models. Figures 7, 8, and 9 show the performance results of DSR, RRR, and OHR respectively for the values of Zipf parameter α from 0.2 to 1.0.

We can see that CCR consistently provides the best performance over a wide range of object access frequency distributions. Specially, CCR reduces or

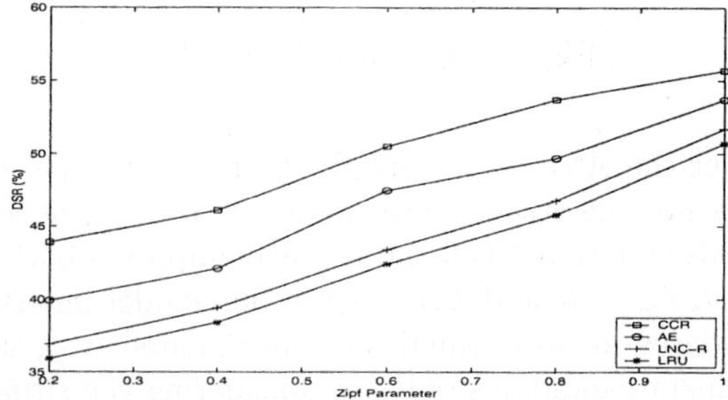

Fig. 7. Experiment for DSR

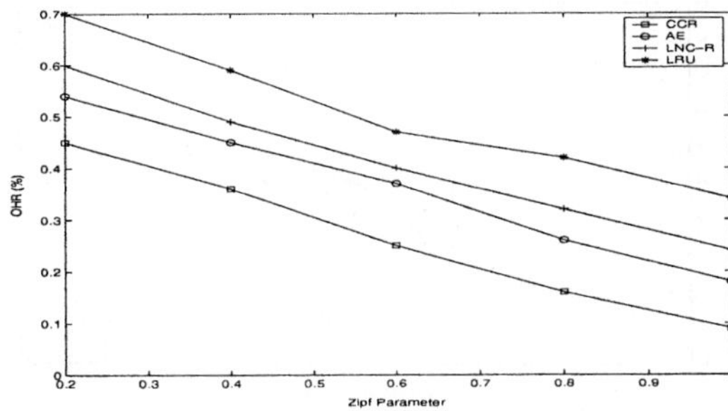

Fig. 8. Experiment on *RRR*

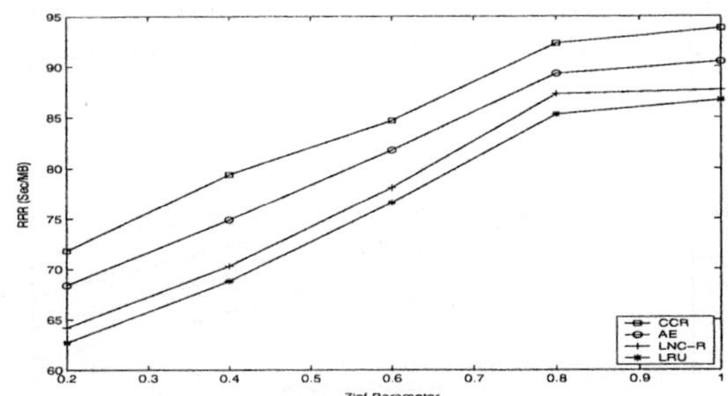

Fig. 9. Experiment for *OHR*

improves DSR by 17.7.4 percent, 15.0 percent, and 7.5 percent compared to LRU, $LNC - R$, and AE, respectively; the default cache size used here (4 percent) is fairly large in the context of en-route caching due to the large network under consideration.

4.3 Impact of the Number of Client Classes

The last experiment set examines the impact of the number of client classes on the performance results of different solutions. The number of client classes refers to the number of transcodable versions. In our experiments, the number of transcodable versions is set to be 5 and the relevant vectors are $(100\%, 0, 0, 0, 0)$, $(50\%, 0, 50\%, 0, 0)$, $(50\%, 0, 30\%, 0, 20\%)$, $(40\%, 0, 30\%, 20\%, 10\%)$, and $(20\%,$ $15\%,$
$20\%, 15\%, 30\%)$.

Figures 10 and 11 show the simulation results on DSR and RRR, respectively. We can see that DSR and RRR decrease as the number of the transcodable versions increase due to the fact that the requests from the clients will tend to disperse with increasing the number of the transcodable versions. Specifically, the mean improvements of DSR over AE, $LNC - R$, LRU are 9.5 percent, 8.2 percent, and 5.1 percent, respectively.

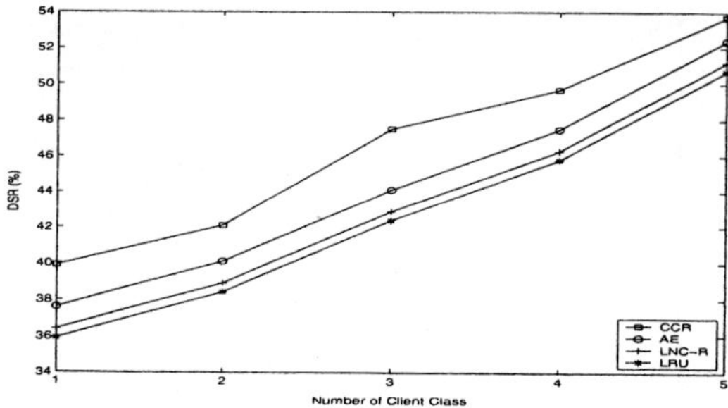

Fig. 10. Experiment for *DSR*

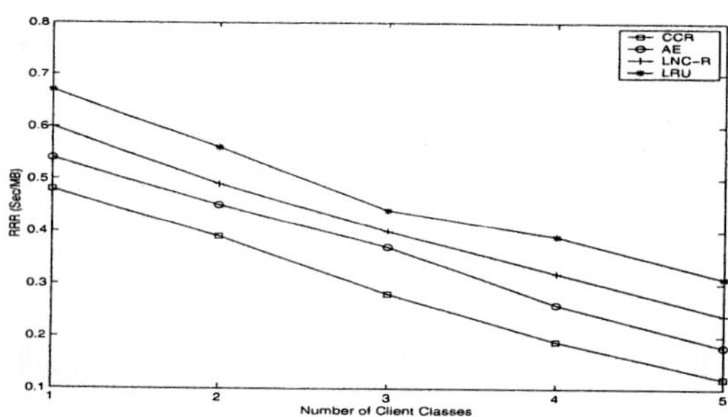

Fig. 11. Experiment on *RRR*

5 Conclusion

In this paper, we presented performance evaluation for four existing models, including our coordinated cache replacement model in transcoding proxies where multimedia object placement and replacement policies are managed in a coordinated way. Extensive simulation experiments have been performed to compare the proposed coordinated cache replacement model with several existing models. The results show that our model effectively improves delay-saving ratio, average access latency, request response ratio, object hit ratio, and highest server load. The proposed coordinated cache replacement model considerably outperforms local cache replacement models that consider cache replacement at individual nodes only.

References

1. C. Aggarwal, J. L. Wolf, and P. S. Yu. *Caching on the World Wide Web.* IEEE Trans. on Knowledge and Data Engineering, Vol 11, No. 1, pp. 94-107, 1999.
2. A. Balamash and M. Krunz. *An Overview of Web Caching Replacement Algorithms.* IEEE Communications Surveys & Tutorials, Vol. 6, No. 2, pp.44-56, 2004.

3. P. Barford and M. Crovella. *Generating Representive Web Workloads for Network and Server Performance Evaluation.* Proc. of ACM SIGMETRICS'98, pp. 151-160, 1998.
4. L. Breslau, P. Cao, L. Fan, G. Phillips, and S. Shenker. *Web Caching and Zip-like Distributions: Evidence and Implications.* Proc. of IEEE INFOCOM'99, pp. 126-134, 1999.
5. K. L. Calvert, M. B. Doar, and E. W. Zegura. *Modelling Internet Topology.* IEEE Comm. Magazine, Vol. 35, No. 6, pp. 160-163, 1997.
6. P. Cao and S. Irani. *Cost-Aware WWW Proxy Caching Algorithms.* Proc. of First USENIX Symposium on Internet Technologies and Systems (USITS), pp. 193-206, 1997.
7. C. Chang and M. Chen. *On Exploring Aggregate Effect for Efficient Cache Replacement in Transcoding Proxies.* IEEE Trans. on Parallel and Distributed Systems, Vol. 14, No. 6, pp. 611-624, June 2003.
8. M. D. Dahlin, R. Y. Wang, T. E. Anderson, and D. A. Patterson. *Cooperative Caching: Using Remote Client Memory to Improve File System Performance.* Proc. of First Symp. Operating Systems Design and Implementations, pp. 267-280, 1994.
9. S. Jin and A. Bestavros. *Greeddual* Web Caching Algorithm: Exploiting the Two Sources of Temporal Locality in Web Request Streams.* Computer Comm., Vol. 4, No. 2, pp. 174-183, 2001.
10. K. Li and H. Shen. *Coordinated En-Route Multimedia Object Caching in Transcoding Proxies for Tree Networks.* ACM Trans. on Multimedia Computing, Communications and Applications (TOMCAPP), Vol. 5, No. 3, pp. 1-26, August 2005.
11. K. Li, H. Shen, and F. Chin. *Cooperative Determination on Cache Replacement Candidates for Transcoding Proxy Caching.* Proc. of The 2005 International Conference on Computer Networks and Mobile Computing (ICCNMC 2005), pp. 178-187, 2005.
12. M. R. Korupolu and M. Dahlin. *Coordinated Placement and Replacement for Large-Scale Distributed Caches.* IEEE Trans. on Knowledge and Data Engineering, Vol. 14, No. 6, pp. 1317-1329, 2002.
13. V. N. Padmanabhan and L. Qiu. *The Content and Access Dynamics of a Busy Site: Findings and Implications.* Proc. of ACM SIGCOMM'00, pp.111-123, August 2000.
14. P. Scheuermann, J. Shim, and R. Vingralek. *A Case for Delay-Conscious Caching of Web Documents.* Computer Network and ISDN Systems, Vol 29, No. 8-13, pp. 997-1005, 1997.
15. J. Shim, P. Scheuermann, and R. Vingralek. *Proxy Cache Algorithms: Design, Implementation, and Performance.* IEEE Trans. on Knowledge and Data Engineering, Vol 11, No. 4, pp. 549-562, 1999.
16. J. Xu, B. Li, and D. L. Li. *Placement Problems for Transparent Data Replication Proxy Services.* IEEE Journal on Selected Areas in Communications, Vol. 20, No. 7, pp. 1383-1398, 2002.

Mathematics Model and Performance Evaluation of a Scalable TCP Congestion Control Protocol to LNCS/LNAI Proceedings

Li-Song Shao, He-Ying Zhang, Yan-Xin Zheng, and Wen-Hua Dou

Computer School, National University of Defence Technology,
Changsha, China
lsshao@sina.com

Abstract. So far the AIMD (Additive Increase Multiplicative Decrease) mechanism used by the conventional TCP congestion control protocol has been supported nearly by every Internet hosts. However, the conventional TCP has been designed without the theoretic foundations, so as to result in some problems in the long distance high speed network, such as the low bandwidth efficiency and the RTT (Round Trip Time) bias. Based on the flow fluid model, this paper models a scalable TCP congestion control protocol by the continuous differential equation on the RTT timescale, analyzes the condition for stability, and discusses the interrelations among stability, fairness and efficiency, which is aid to guide the design of end-to-end congestion control in the future.

1 Introduction

At all times the issue of end-to-end congestion control is a research hotspot. If the traffic load coming into network exceeds highly the capability of the network, the network performances will fall down. Routers introduce AQM (Active Queue Management) mechanism in order to prevent its output buffer from overflowing and inform hosts implicitly or explicitly about the congestion; while hosts adopt end-to-end congestion control to modify their packet sending rates according to the feedback congestion signal from the routers.

The design difficulties of end-to-end congestion control protocol are its decentralized nature [4], route complexity, and conflicts between the target performances. Each host on the edge of network can not apperceive other host's information, but its RTT and the congestion state of the links passed through by the flows from itself; Each router at the center of network can not obtain information on the congestion state of other router, even of the neighboring router, but the traffic arriving itself and the consuming state of its own resources, such as buffer and bandwidth. Routers determine the next hop for individual packet, so it is possible that the packets of the same flow experience different paths and RTTs. On the other hand, if a link passed through by a flow fails to function suddenly, the residual packets of the flow have to select a new route path. A congestion control protocol must assure primarily that the global network system is stable. Additionally the fairness and efficiency properties are important too: roughly speaking, "fairness" means that no user is penalized compared to others that share the same bottleneck links; "efficiency" means that no bandwidth is

H. Zhuge and G.C. Fox (Eds.): GCC 2005, LNCS 3795, pp. 1054 – 1065, 2005.

wasted in the sense that the throughput of any active flow is limited only by the capacity of bottleneck links on its path[25]. An ideal congestion control protocol makes trade-off among above these performances.

P.Kelly presented Primal Algorithm based on user utility, and demonstrated global stability of network without propagation delays using a Lyapunov argument [8]. R.Johar extended this result to give local stability in a general network where all flows have s single RTT, and conjectured that s similar result might hold for a general network where flows have heterogeneous RTTs [6]. Vinnicombe proved that local stability of the Primal Algorithm interconnected with a general network in which flows can have heterogeneous RTTs, and extended this result to a broader class of Congestion control protocol [3], [4]. T.Kelly putted forward STCP protocol to improve the conventional TCP performance in the long distance high speed network [9], such as the backbone network. S.Floyd offered a similar scheme, HSTCP protocol [17].

The organization of the paper is as follows. Section 2 introduces a basic mathematics model which is the foundation of our work. Section 3 analyzes the problems of the conventional TCP in the high speed network, and points out that the window-based and AIMD mechanisms become the bottleneck of the expanding Internet. Section 4 models the dynamic network system using a scalable TCP protocol on the RTT level timescale, and proves that the protocol is capable to make the network system stable around an equilibrium point, and discusses the protocol's fairness and efficiency properties. Section 5 concludes.

2 Flow Fluid Model

Given a communication network, identify J with the set of links and R with the set of all flows between the sources and the receivers; a route r, corresponding to a user, is the ordered subset of J that the flow traverses. Throughout this paper route, flow and user will be interchangeably in reference to an element $r \in R$. Let $Ajr = 1$ if $j \in r$ and $Ajr = 0$ otherwise; then the matrix $A=(Ajr; j \in J, r \in R)$ is the routing matrix. The sending rate of route r is denoted by xr. It is assumed that routing is not altered on timescales comparable with RTT. Let Cj be the capacity of link j for all $j \in J$. Suppose that congestion at a given link j is signaled to a source with probability μj, where yj is the instantaneous link load on link j. It has been assumed that μj is a static function over the timescale of interest, is determined by the packet arrival process at a link , and is independent on other links.

$$\mu_j(t) = p_j(y_j(t)) \tag{1}$$

where congestion measure function pj is an increase function of the arrival traffic yj(t). The probability that an acknowledgement, received at the source of route r at time t, signals congestion is

$$q_r(t) = 1 - \prod_{j \in J} (1 - A_{jr} \mu_j (t - T_{jr})) \tag{2}$$

where the product is over each link forming the route r. In general, congestion measure function pj is small enough to obtain high bandwidth efficiency. Then relation (2) is replaced approximately by

$$q_r(t) = \sum_{j \in J} A_{jr} \mu_j (t - T_{jr}) \tag{3}$$

The return delay from link j for the acknowledgement via the receiver of route r is denoted by Tjr, and the load at link j is given by

$$y_j(t) = \sum_{r \in R} A_{jr} x_r (t - T_{rj}) \tag{4}$$

where Trj is the forward delay from the source on route r to link j. On route r the round trip time, Tr, is given by

$$T_r = T_{jr} + T_{rj} \quad \forall j \in r \tag{5}$$

It has been assumed that queuing delay is negligible in comparison to RTT. Another assumption implicit in these relations is that a route's load is invariable from the source to the receiver. This is not the case in a network which experiences significant packet drop rates. In such a network the rate arriving at links near to the source will be closer to the sending rate xr than those near to the receiver.

Consider the vectors: Y(t)=(yj(t): j∈J), U(t)=(μj(t): j∈J), X(t)=(xr(t): r∈R), Q(t)=(qr(t): r∈R), the dynamic system (3)(4)(5) is extended to the corresponding forms in the frequency flied:

$$Y(s) = R(s)X(s) \tag{6}$$

$$Q(s) = diag(e^{-T_r s})A^T(-s)U(s) \tag{7}$$

Because sources and links of the network in Figure 1 are distributed, the corresponding controls are the diagonal matrixes. The source of route r implements end-to-end congestion control to adjust sending rate xr according to the probability qr. Link j implements AQM adjust the congestion probability μj according to the consuming state of its own resources.

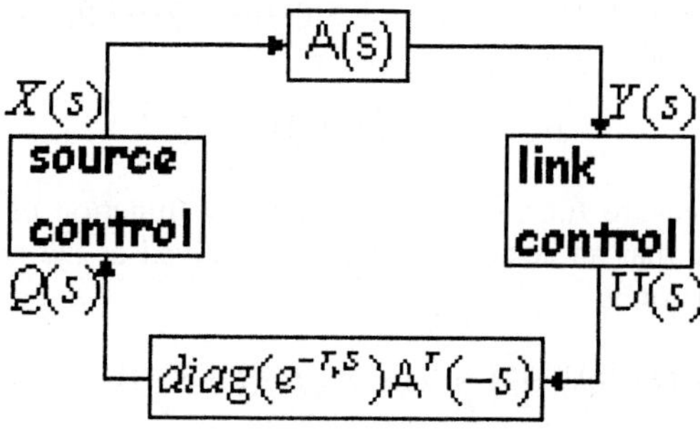

Fig. 1. The Closed loop structure of flow fluid model

3 The Conventional TCP

Slow start and Congestion avoid algorithms putted forward by V. Jacobson is the basic framework of TCP Reno protocol controlling the conventional Internet successfully. Because the design of TCP Reno is short of the theoretic guidance, its core mechanisms, window-based and AIMD, become gradually bottleneck of the expanding Internet.

When many flows share a single bottleneck link, the window-based mechanism results in RTT bandwidth allocation bias that the flow with the smaller RTT can obtain higher bandwidth. In this way, network bandwidth allocation is very unfairness to the flows traversing a long distance. For example, the TCP flows with RTT time of 10ms can obtain as twenty times bandwidth as ones with RTT time of 200 ms.

In a long distance high speed backbone link, AI of TCP Reno is too slow and MD too fast which result in low bandwidth efficiency. Additionally TCP Reno can lead to dramatic oscillations in network queues that not only cause delay jitter but can even impact bandwidth efficiency [15].

Suppose that the TCP flow sharing a single bottleneck link has a round trip time of T seconds and a packet size of L bytes. An available bandwidth of B bps allocated for the flow corresponds to the congestion window of about W=BT/(8L) packets. Based on the response curve of the TCP Reno [26]

$$W \approx \sqrt{1.5/q} \tag{8}$$

The relation between the bandwidth delay product BT and the probability q in equilibrium state is given by

$$q \propto \frac{1}{(BT)^2} \tag{9}$$

This places a serious constrain on the congestion windows that can be achieved by TCP Reno in realistic environments. For example, passing through a backbone link traversing ocean with RTT of about 100ms and bandwidth of about 1Tbps, a single TCP flow with the average packet length of 1.5KB can obtain bandwidth of 10Gbps in equilibrium state. The corresponding window is 83,333 packets and the corresponding probability q must be smaller than 2×10-10 in the sense that the links must run continuously at least 1.6 hours without any discarded or marked packet which is an unrealistic requirement for current networks.

To resolve the above questions, many new end-to-end congestion control protocols have been offered, where HSTCP and STCP are two typical protocols. The primary aim of HSTCP is that the routes with the large BT adjust the increase and decrease parameters to improve the sending rate. Its basic idea is that when congestion window exceeds a threshold value, increase and decrease parameters of AIMD are modified according to the current congestion window [17], [18]. STCP takes two questions into account: On one hand, for the sake of bandwidth efficiency, it increases the congestion window rapidly using MI instead of AI; on the other hand, it updates the increase and decrease parameters of MIMD periodically on a smaller timescale than RTT in order to correct unfairness of the conventional TCP [9], [10].

4 The Scalable TCP Protocol

The source of each TCP flow manages a congestion window which records the packets sent but not acknowledged. TCP Reno updates the value of congestion window, W, according to AIMD mechanism which increases the window by one every RTT if there is no mark in the RTT, and halves window otherwise. There are two versions of AIMD on the packet level timescale and the RTT level timescale respectively [12]. Old version called Reno-1 implements AIMD on the packet level timescale, which increases the reciprocal of W or halves W depended on whether a mark is detected or not, every time an acknowledgement packet is received. Whereas new version called Reno-2 implements AIMD on the RTT timescale, which increases one packet or halves W only once depended on whether there is mark or not in the RTT. They have slightly the different static and dynamic attributions, such as fairness property and differential equation.

Many congestion controls are suggested and analyzed based on the packet timescale, whereas this paper suggests a scalable TCP protocol on the RTT timescale that the congestion window will increases aW n if there is not any mark and decrease bW m only once otherwise in the RTT.

At time t, the route r sends W r(t) packets in a RRT. Then the probability that no packet is discarded or marked in the RTT is given by

$$1-(1-q_r(t))^{W_r(t)} \tag{10}$$

where qr(t) is so small that expression (10) is approximately qr(t)Wr(t). Then the probability that there is one or more packet discarded or marked is 1-qr(t)Wr(t). So the expected change in the congestion window Wr per RTT is approximately

$$\Delta W_r(t) = aW_r^n(t)(1-q_r(t)W_r(t)) - bW_r^m(t)q_r(t)W_r(t) \tag{11}$$

Because it has been assumed that queuing delay is negligible in comparison to RTT, the RTT of route r is close to a constant Tr. Since the time between window-updated steps is about 1/xr(t)=Tr /Wr(t), the expected change in the rate xr per unit time is approximately

$$\Delta W_r(t)x_r(t)/T_r \tag{12}$$

Motivated by (11) and (12), we model the scalable TCP protocol by the system of differential equations

$$dx_r(t)/dt = \{a(x_r(t)T_r)^n - q_r(t)[a(x_r(t)T_r)^{n+1} + b(x_r(t)T_r)^{m+1}]\}/T_r^2 \tag{13}$$

Thus we model the network traffic by a closed loop dynamic system (1)(2)(4)(5)(13), which is the foundation of the following content.

4.1 Local Stability Condition

Theorem 1. If there is a constant B in the dynamic network system (1)(2)(4)(5)(13), the AQM algorithm satisfies the condition (14) and the scalable TCP protocol satisfies the condition (15), the dynamic network system is stability around a equilibrium point.

$$y_j p_j'(y_j) \le B p_j(y_j) \quad , j \in J \tag{14}$$

$$a_r (x_r T_r)^{n-1} < \frac{\pi}{2B} \quad , r \in R \tag{15}$$

Proof: Let xr(t)=xr+δxr(t), qr(t)=qr+(1-qr)δvr(t). Then the equilibrium point (xr ,qr) of the system (1)(2)(13) has the form

$$q_r = \frac{1}{x_r T_r + \frac{b}{a}(x_r T_r)^{m-n+1}} \tag{16}$$

Linearizing the system about (xr ,qr), using the relation (2)(13)(16), we can obtain the equations

$$\frac{d\delta x_r(t)}{dt} = -\Phi_r \delta x_r(t) - \frac{a(x_r T_r)^{n-1}(1-q_r)}{q_r T_r} x_r \delta v_r(t) \tag{17}$$

$$v_r(t) = \sum_{j\in J} A_{jr} \frac{p_j'}{1-p_j} \sum_{s\in R} A_{js} \delta x_s(t - T_{sj} - T_{jr}) \tag{18}$$

where Φr is the coefficient of δxr(t) around the equilibrium point. According to the Appendix [6], the linear system (17)(18) is stable if for r∈R

$$\frac{a(x_r T_r)^{n-1}(1-q_r)}{q_r} \sum_{j\in J} A_{jr} \frac{p_j'}{1-p_j} \sum_{s\in R} A_{js} x_s < \frac{\pi}{2} \tag{19}$$

The probability that the packet on route r is marked exactly once is

$$\sum_{j\in J} A_{jr} p_j \prod_{\substack{k\in r \\ k\neq j}} (1-p_k) = \sum_{j\in J} \frac{A_{jr} p_j (1-q_r)}{1-p_j} \tag{20}$$

And the probability that the packet on route r is marked at least once is qr. Suppose that the relation (14) will hold, then

$$\frac{1-q_r}{q_r} \sum_{j\in J} A_{jr} \frac{y_j p_j'}{1-p_j} \le \frac{B}{q_r} \sum_{j\in J} A_{jr} p_j \frac{1-q_r}{1-p_j} \le B \tag{21}$$

The relation (15) is a sufficient condition of relation (19) based on the relation (21). ■

Theorem 1 shows that the stability of the linear system with the scalable TCP protocol depends only on the increase process around the equilibrium point: the increase amount of congestion window around the equilibrium point must be small enough to ensure stability of the network system.

Lemma 1. The stability of the network system with the scalable TCP protocol around the equilibrium point conflicts with the bandwidth efficiency.
The relation (14) will hold with equality if

$$p_j(y_j) = (y_j / C_j)^B \tag{22}$$

The relations (14) and (22) show that for the sake of the high bandwidth efficiency the bottleneck link expects to increase constant B; however, a large constant B will destroy the relation (15) easily and result in the instability of the network system.

4.2 Response Curve and Fairness

Response curve is used to describe the static attributes of the congestion control protocol around the equilibrium point. In a sense the static attributes involves the relation between the sending rate xr of route r and the congestion probability qr on route r, and often is used to analyze the bandwidth efficiency and fairness property among the flows. Suppose that β=b/a and θ=m-n+1, the response curve of the scalable TCP protocol is given by

$$q_r = \frac{1}{x_r T_r + \beta (x_r T_r)^\theta} \tag{23}$$

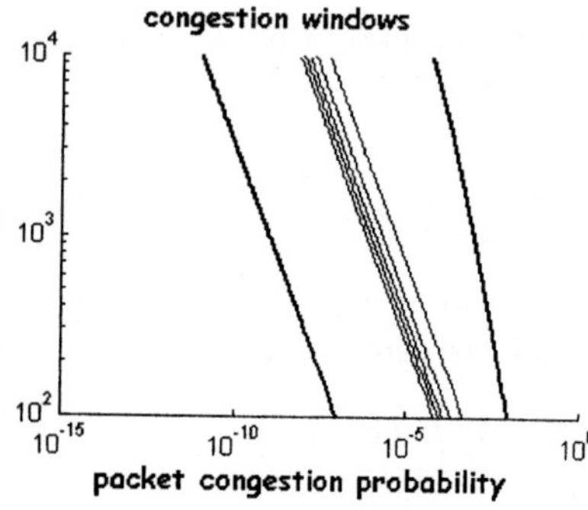

Fig. 2. Impact of β on the Response Curve

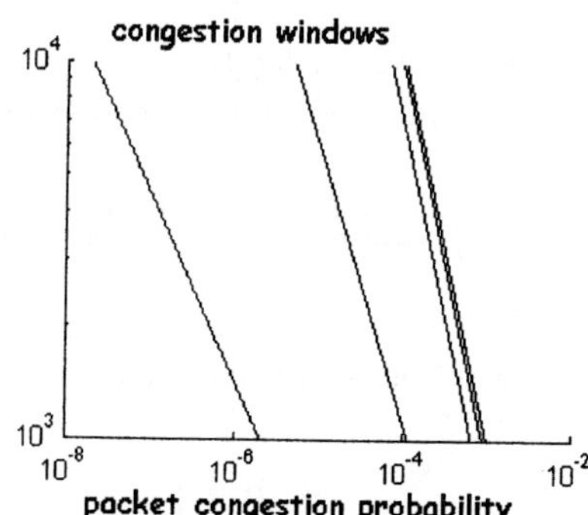

Fig. 3. Impact of θ on the Response Curve

The AIMD is the instance of the scalable TCP with β=0.5 and θ=2, and the MIMD with θ=1. Firstly we review the impact of the parameter β on the response curve with θ=2. Fig.2 shows that the corresponding response curves rightward when β is set 100,

1.5, 1.1, 0.8, 0.5, 0.2 and 0.001 respectively, and that the flow with larger β obtains a smaller window around the equilibrium point.

Secondly we review the impact of the parameter θ on the response curve with β=0.5. Fig.3 shows that the corresponding response curves rightward when θ is set 2, 1.4, 1, 0.8, 0.01 and -0.9 respectively, and that the flow with larger θ obtains a smaller window around the equilibrium point. Notice that right three curves almost overlap.

It is a reasonable hypothesis that there is a maximum value of 1/β, or else the network system is instability. The relation (23) with the large window has the approximate form (24) called demand function.

$$x_r = \begin{cases} \frac{1}{T}\frac{1}{{}_r q_r} & \theta << 1 \\ \frac{1}{T_r}\frac{1}{(\beta+1)q_r} & \theta \approx 1 \\ \frac{1}{T_r}\sqrt[\theta]{\frac{1}{\beta q_r}} & \theta > 1 \end{cases} \tag{24}$$

Proposition 1. If the demand function of a congestion control protocol satisfies the relation (25), the protocol results in the bandwidth allocations *weighted ρ-fair*[2].

$$x_r = \left(\frac{\omega}{q_r}\right)^{1/\rho} \tag{25}$$

If ωr =1,r∈R, the cases ρ→0, ρ=1 and ρ→∞ correspond respectively to an allocation which achieves maximum throughput, is proportionally fair or is max-min fair. It is easily deduced that the scalable TCP protocol satisfies proportionally fair if θ≤1 and is weighted θ-fair otherwise. The relation (12) shows that if flows passing through a single bottleneck link receive the same congestion probability, one with smaller θ obtains higher bandwidth. And with decrease of θ, the available bandwidth of the flow increases to a maximum value which explains the overlapping curves in Fig.3.

4.3 Bandwidth Efficiency

Consider the scenario that a single flow passes through a single link with bandwidth of B packet per second. We review the change of the window W at intervals of the round trip time T. Then W can achieve the maximum value of BT. Suppose that at time t-2, W(t-2) is equal rightly to BT. After the time of T, W(t-1) continues to increase such that the congestion occurs. After the time of T again, the feedback congestion signal is received by the source, which begins to decrease W to alleviate the congestion. Hereafter W increases step by step at intervals of T until the congestion signal is received again. So the W oscillates periodically, referred to Fig.4 and Fig.5 corresponding to the AIMD and MIMD mechanisms respectively. The area of s2 denotes the number of packet sent actually by the source in a period; and the area of s1+s2 denotes the maximum number of packet which the source is allowed to send by the link capacity in a period. So the area of s1 denotes the wasted resource in a period. The bandwidth efficiency of the bottleneck link is given by

$$\eta = \frac{s2}{s1 + s2} \tag{26}$$

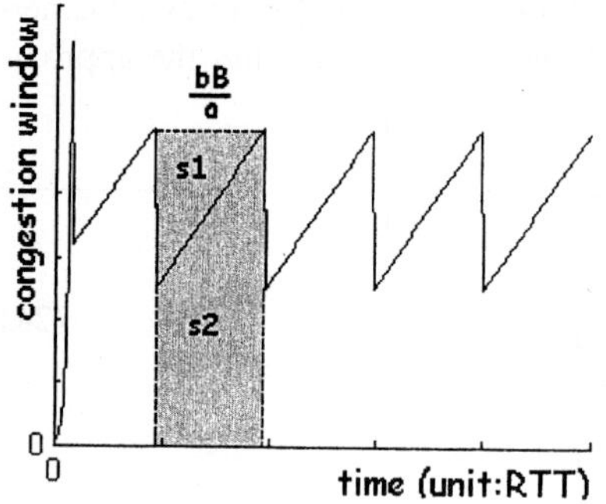

Fig. 4. Congestion window change of AIMD

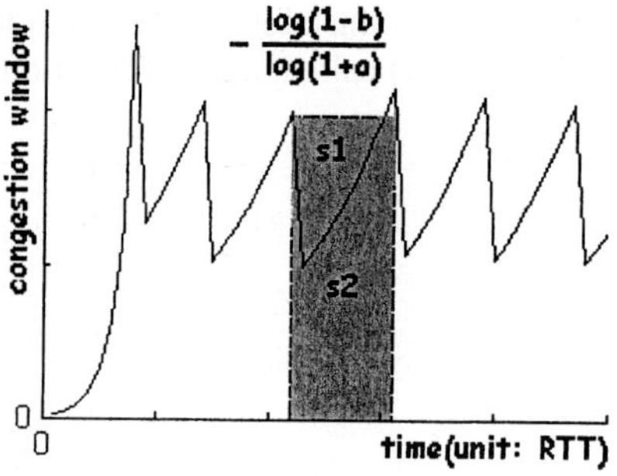

Fig. 5. Congestion window change of MIMD

Theorem 2. The bandwidth efficiency of the AIMD mechanism can achieve the maximum value of about (2-b)/2; the bandwidth efficiency of MIMD mechanism can achieve the maximum value given by

$$\eta = \frac{(1+a)^N - 1}{Na}(1-b) \tag{27}$$

where

$$N = -\frac{\log(1-b)}{\log(1+a)} \tag{28}$$

Proof: Firstly we review the bandwidth efficiency of the AIMD with n=0 and m=1. Supposed a<<BT and at time t-1 the window is about BT in the sense that W(t-1)≈W(t-2). Then at time t0, W decrease to (1-b) BT, thence increase a packets step by step at interval of T. It takes bBT/a RTTs for W to achieve BT again. Referred to Fig.4, the bandwidth efficiency of the AIMD is given by (2-b)/2.

Secondly we review the bandwidth efficiency of the MIMD with n=1 and m=1. Similarly, W(t-1)≈BT and W(t0)≈ (1-b)BT. After the time of i RTTs, MI mechanism increases aW(ti-1) packets in the sense that W(ti)=(1-b)BT(1+a)i. So it takes N RTTs for W to achieve BT again, where N is given by relation (28). The total packets sent in a period are close to the area of s2 in Fig.5.

$$s2 = \int_{t_0}^{t_N} cwnd(t)dt \approx \sum_{n=0}^{N-1} (1+a)^n BT(1-b) = \frac{(1+a)^N - 1}{a} BT(1-b) \tag{29}$$

Based on Fig.5, it is easily to deduce the relation

$$s1 + s2 = NBT \tag{30}$$

■

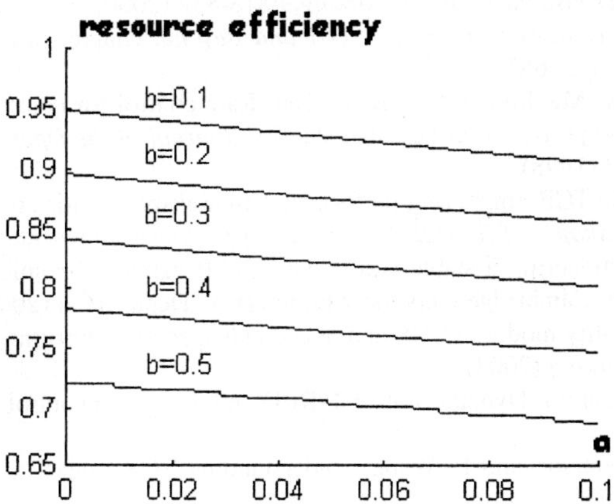

Fig. 6. The impact of the increase and decrease parameters on bandwidth efficiency of MIMD

We review the impact of the increase parameter a on the bandwidth efficiency under the condition of the invariable decrease parameter. Fig.6 shows that the corresponding efficiency curves of the MIMD and that the impact of increase parameter a of both AIMD and MIMD on the bandwidth efficiency is very weak. However the decrease parameter b plays a very important role on the bandwidth efficiency. In general, the bandwidth efficiency is in inverse proportion to the decrease parameter.

5 Conclusion

In this paper we reviewed recent work on end-to-end congestion control. We have described the dynamic model of the scalable TCP protocol on the RTT level time-scale, proved a sufficient condition for stability, and analyzed its fairness and efficiency properties. In particular, we have showed that there are conflicts among these performances. An ideal congestion control protocol must make trade-off between these performances.

References

1. Carpenter B (ed): Architectural principles of the Internet. Network Working Group RFC-1958 (1996)
2. F. P. Kelly: Fairness and stability of end-to-end congestion control. Available via http :// www .statslab .cam .ac .uk (2003)
3. G. Vinnicombe: On the stability of networks operation TCP-like congestion control. In *Proc. of the 15th IFAC World Congress on Automatic Control,* Barcelona,Spain, (2002)
4. G. Vinnicombe: Robust congestion control for the Internet. Available via http://www-control .end.cam.ac.uk/gv/internet/index.html.(2002)

5. G. Vinnicombe: On the stability of end-to-end congestion control for the Internet .Technical Report CUED/F-INFENG/TR.398, Cambridge University Engineering Department.(2000)
6. R. Johari, D. K. H. Tan: End-to-end congestion control for the Internet: delays and stability. *IEEE/ACM Transactions on Networking*,9:818-832 (2000)
7. F. P. Kelly.*Mathematics Unlimited – 2001 and Beyond*, chapter Mathematical modelling of the Internet , pages 685-702.(2000)
8. F. P. Kelly, A. K. Maulloo, and D. K. H. Tan: Rate control for communication networks: shadow prices, proportional fairness and stablity. *Journal of the Operational Research Society*, 49:237-252 (1998)
9. T. Kelly: Scalable TCP: improving performance in highspeed wide area networks. *First International Workshop on Protocols for Fast Long-Distance Networks* (2002)
10. T. Kelly: On engineering a stable and scalable TCP variant. Technical Report CUED/F-INFENG/TR.435, Cambridge University Engineering Department (2002)
11. S. H. Low: A duality model of TCP and queue management algoritms. *IEEE/ACM Transactions on Networking* (2003)
12. S. H. Low, F. Paganini: Dynamics of TCP/RED and a scalable control. In *Pro. of IEEE Infocom* (2002)
13. S. H. Low, L. Peterson and L. Wang: Understanding TCP Vegas: a duality model. *J. of ACM*, 49(2):207-235 (2001)
14. F. Paganini, Z. Wang , S. H. Low and J. C. Doyle: A new TCP/AQM for stable operation in fast networks. In *Proc. of IEEE Inform* (2003)
15. C. Jin, D. X. Wei, S. H. Low: FAST TCP: motivation, architecture, algorithms, performance. In *Proc. of IEEE Inform* (2004)
16. J. Wang, L. Li, S. H. Low: Can shortest-path Routing and TCP maximize utility. In *Proc. of IEEE Inform* (2003)
17. S. Floyd: Highspeed TCP for large congestion windows. RFC3649 (2003)
18. S. Floyd, S.Ratnasamy:Modifying TCP's congestion control for high speeds. http:// www.icir.org /floyd/notes.html (2002)
19. N. Dukkipati, M. Kobayashi: Minimizing the duration of flows.*Stanford HPNG technical report TR04-HPNG061604* (2004)
20. John C. Doyle, S. H. Low: Robustness and the Internet:theoretical foundations. In *Proc. of the ACM SIGCOMM NREDS workshop*(2002)
21. D. Clark, J. Wroclawski: Tussle in Cyberspace: defining tomorrow's Internet. In *Proc. of the ACM SIGCOMM* (2002)
22. D. Alderson, J. Doyle: Toward an optimization-driven framework for designing and generating realistic Internet topologies. In *Proc. of the ACM SIGCOMM* HotNets-I,(2003)
23. T. Ott : ECN protocols and the TCP paradigm. In *Workshop on Modeling of Flow and Congestion Control Mechanisms* (2000)
24. X. Zhu, J. Yu, and J. C. Doyle: Heavy tails, generalized coding, and optimal web layout. In *Pro. of IEEE Infocom* (2001)
25. T. Bonald and L. Massoulie: Impact of Fairness on Internet Performance. In *ACM SIGMETRIC* (2001)

Appendix

Consider the linear system

$$T_r \frac{d}{dt}\delta x_r(t) = -\gamma_r \delta x_r(t) - \kappa_r x_r \delta v_r(t) \tag{31}$$

for r ∈R, where

$$\delta v_r(t) = \sum_{j\in J} A_{jr} K_j \sum_{s\in R} A_{js} \delta x_s (t - T_{sj} - T_{jr}) \tag{32}$$

Theorem 3. Suppose that γ_r, κ_r, $x_r \geq 0$ for $r \in R$; $K_j \geq 0$ for $j \in J$; A_{js}, T_{jr}, $T_{rj} \geq 0$ for $j \in J$, $r \in R$, and the relation (5) is satisfied. Then the system (31) (32) is stable if

$$\kappa_r \sum_{j\in J} A_{jr} K_j \sum_{s\in R} A_{js} x_s < \frac{\pi}{2}, \quad r \in R \tag{33}$$

An Active Measurement Approach for Link Faults Monitoring in ISP Networks*

Wenwei Li, Dafang Zhang, Jinmin Yang, and Gaogang Xie

[1] College of Computer and Communication, Hunan University, Changsha 410082, China
liww@hnu.cn
[2] School of Software, Hunan University, Changsha, 410082, China
{dfzhang, rj_jmyang}@hnu.cn
[3] Institute of Computing Technology, Chinese Academy of Science, Beijing, 100080, China
xie@ict.ac.cn

Abstract. Link failures are common in IP networks. In this paper, we develop a technique for diagnosing link failures in Service Provider or Enterprise IP networks using active measurement. The technique attempts to minimize both the monitoring infrastructure costs as well as the additional traffic due to probe messages. Both the station selection problem and the probe message assignment problem are NP-hard, and we propose approximation algorithms for these problems. We also apply our algorithms to existing ISP networks using topologies inferred by the Rocketfuel tool. The results can be used by ISP operators to trade off between accuracy of diagnosis and monitoring costs.

1 Introduction

Now, more and more Internet Service Providers (ISPs) offer their customers services that require more quality of service (QoS) guarantees and more dependability guarantees than "Best Effort" service; and the ISP networks become increasingly large and complex. For keeping a leading position in the competition, the ISPs need to monitor their network status, especially link faults and performance. However the family of Internet protocols collects and distributes only a limited amount of information on the topology, connectivity and state of the network [1]. Hence information of interest for ISPs, such as link failures or link delays, has to be inferred from other tools or methods.

Using SNMP/RMON tools, ISPs can only get partial network statistical information from routers or switches, for monitoring the performance and status of individual network device. Consequently, active measurement tools such as ping, traceroute, become an effective method for monitoring network link fault and performance. While, a node with such active measurement tools, termed a monitoring

* This work was supported by National Natural Science Foundation of China under grant 60273070 and 60403031, the National High-Technology Program of China (863) under grant 2005AA121560, the Hunan Provincial Natural Science Foundation of China under grant 05JJ30116.

H. Zhuge and G.C. Fox (Eds.): GCC 2005, LNCS 3795, pp. 1066 – 1071, 2005.

station, is able to monitor link faults and measure latencies for only a limited set of links in the node's routing tree. Thus, several monitoring stations are deployed at a few strategic points in the ISP or Enterprise IP network to compose a monitoring infrastructure so as to monitor all network link faults and delays.

The IP packets sent by monitoring stations for the purpose of link faults monitoring are termed probe message. To detect link failures, the path that each probe message actually follows is compared with the path that the probe should follow according to the current network topology information. If the two paths are different, at least one link in the path determined by the current topology has failed. Then a set of probe messages sent from monitoring stations that traverse all links in the network is sufficient to diagnose any link failures.

Considering the deployment and maintenance costs, a practical active measurement based link fault monitoring system must solve two problems: minimizing the infrastructure and maintenance costs associated with monitoring stations, and minimizing the additional network traffic due to probe messages. Minimizing the latter is especially important when information is collected frequently in order to continuously monitor the state and evolution of the network. In this paper, we find that these two problems are NP-hard, we also give algorithms for them separately. At last, we verify our algorithms on existing ISP networks.

The remainder of this paper is organized as follows. Section 2 describes related works. Section 3 introduces the network model. Section 4 presents the minimum monitoring stations placement problem, and Section 5 describes the minimum probe messages assignment problem. Section 6 contains experiment studies of our algorithms on existing ISP networks. Finally, we conclude the paper in Section 7.

2 Related Work

For monitoring the Internet end-to-end performance and fault, projects such as NIMI[2], AMP[3], PingER[4] build distributed measurement systems. These projects provide experimental platforms to investigate the end-to-end performance characteristic and evolution of the Internet. However, the monitoring stations of these projects are often placed in universities and other organizations that are willing to host the software or hardware required, there is no policy on location selection.

In other recent work on monitoring, [5] proposes to solve a linear system of equations to compute delays for smaller path segments from a given set of end-to-end delay measurements for paths in the network. Similarly, [6] considers the problem of inferring link-level loss rates and delays from end-to-end multicast measurements for a given collection of trees. [7] studies ways to minimize the monitoring communication overhead for detecting alarm conditions due to threshold violations. The problems studied in [8] are most closely related to our work. It considers the problem of fault isolation in the context of large multicast distribution trees. The authors of [9] propose an algorithm that identifies link faults by analyzing BGP routing update information. However, using active measurement to pinpoint network faults is routing protocol agnostic; as a result, they can be used with a wide range of protocols like BGP, OSPF, RIP, etc.

3 Network Model

The Service Provider or Enterprise IP network can be modeled by an undirected graph $G(V,E)$, where the graph nodes, V, denote the network routers and the edges, E, represent the communication links connecting them. The number of nodes and edges is denoted by $n=|V|$ and $e=|E|$, respectively. Further, we use $P_{s,t}$ to denote the path traversed by an IP packet from a source node s to a destination node t. We assume that packets are forwarded using standard IP forwarding. For every node $x \in P_{s,t}$, $P_{x,t}$ is included in $P_{s,t}$. In addition, we also assume that $P_{s,t}$ is the routing path in the opposite direction from node t to node s. This, in turn, implies that, for every node $x \in P_{s,t}$, $P_{s,x}$ is a prefix of $P_{s,t}$. As a consequence, it follows that for every node $s \in V$, the subgraph obtained by merging all the paths $P_{s,t}$, for every $t \in V$, must have a tree topology. We refer to this tree for node s as the routing tree (RT) for s, and denote it by T_s. Note that tree T_s defines the routing paths from node s to all the other nodes in V and vice versa.

In case a link f in the network fails, the IP routing protocols define a new delivery tree, $T_{s,f}$, for every node $s \in V$. The new tree $T_{s,f}$ has the property that every path $P_{s,t}$ in T_s, $t \in V$, that does not contain link f is also included in the tree $T_{s,f}$. The reason for this is that the failure of link f only affects those routing paths in T_s that contain f. Thus, it may be possible to infer the topology of a significant portion of $T_{s,f}$ directly from T_s without any knowledge of the route computation algorithms followed by the routers. Note that if $f \notin T_s$, then $T_{s,f}= T_s$. We associate a positive cost $c_{s,t}$ with sending a message along the path $P_{s,t}$ between any pair of nodes $s, t \in V$.

4 The Monitoring Station Selection Problem

As discussed previous, a practical active measurement based link faults diagnoses system must minimize the number of deployed monitoring stations under the condition that ensure every link in the network has been monitored by one or more monitoring stations. This problem is defined as follows.

Definition 1. (The Station Placement Problem - SP): Given a graph $G(V,E)$ and a RT, T_ψ for every node $v \in V$, find the smallest subset $S \subseteq V$ such that $\cup_{\psi \in \psi} T_\psi = E$.

The SP problem is similar to the *minimum set cover* (MSC) problem, and we show that under a shortest path model this problem is NP-hard.

Theorem 1. *The Station Placement Problem is NP-hard.*

Proof. First observe that given a set of k nodes that form a candidate set and a description of the network and its routing policy one can readily verify that the set of k nodes is a monitoring station set, which shows that the Station Placement problem is within the NP class.

To prove hardness we construct a transformation from Minimum Set Cover Problem which is known to be NP-complete [10]. In this problem an instance is a collection of sets $S_1, S_2, \ldots, S_m \subset U = \{x_1, \ldots, x_n\}$ and the objective is to obtain a sub-collection T of k sets or less, such that jointly they contain U, i.e. $\cup_{S_i \in T} S_i = U$.

The transformation is as follows: for each $x_i \in U$, define an edge $e_i = \{v_i, u_i\}$ of weight 1. For each S_j, define a node n_j. Connect the edges $\{n_j, v_i\}$ and $\{n_j, u_i\}$ if and only if $x_i \in S_j$. Let these edges have weight 2. Add three more nodes n_0, n_{m+1}, and n_{m+2}. Join n_0 to all the n_j for $j = 1, \ldots, m+2$. The nodes n_0, n_{m+1} and n_{m+2} form a triangle with edges weighted 1.

Routing is under a shortest path first policy. It follows then that edges in the n_0, n_{m+1} and n_{m+2} triangle can only be tested if one of those nodes is a monitoring station. Since n_0 is the only node connected to the rest of the network and the triangle is otherwise symmetric then the optimal placement of a monitoring station in that triangle is n_0. With a monitoring station thus placed we have that all edges (n_0, n_i) for $1 \leq i \leq m + 2$ are testable. Edges (n_i, u_j) and (n_i, v_j) are also testable from n_0 by means of sending a message to u_j or v_j through the link to n_i.

The only edges that remain to be tested are then having the form $\{v_i, u_i\}$ corresponding to a set element x_i. These edges are part of a triangle composed by v_i, u_i and a node n_j. Therefore they can only be tested by placing a monitoring station at any of these three points. Lastly, if in each triangle we move the monitoring station from a node u_i or v_i to n_j the testability of the network remains the same, and moreover, the collection of monitoring stations on the nodes n_j, with $1 \leq j \leq m$ form a covering set on the minimum covering set problem. Then $n_0 \cup \{n_j / S_j \in T\}$ is a monitoring station set if and only if T is a set cover of U. □

We now present an efficient algorithm for solving the SP problem. The algorithm maps the given instance of the SP problem, involving graph $G(V, E)$, to an instance of the MSC problem, and then uses a greedy heuristic for solving the MSC instance. In the mapping, the set of edges E defines the universe of elements U, and the collection of sets S includes the subsets $S_v = \{e \mid e \in T_v\}$ for every node $v \in V$. The greedy heuristic algorithm is an iterative algorithm that selects, in each iteration, the set S with the maximum number of uncovered elements. The steps of the SP algorithm are as follows.

Step 1: Initialize $COVERED=\{\phi\}$, $COVER=\{S_1, S_2, \ldots, S_m\}$;

Step 2: If there exists a set $S_i \in COVER$, it satisfies that $S_i = U$, then $COVERED= COVERED+\{S_i\}$,end.

Step 3: If there exists $e \in U$, and e only belong to one set S_i in $COVER$, then $COVERED= COVERED+\{S_i\}$, $COVER= COVER-\{S_i\}$, $U=U- S_i$;

Step 4: If there exists two sets $S_i \subseteq S_j$, then $COVER= COVER-\{S_i\}$;

Step 5: Selects set S_i that has maximum element from $COVER$, $COVERED= COVERED+\{S_i\}$, $COVER= COVER-\{S_i\}$, $U=U- S_i$, return to *Step 2*.

5 The Probe Message Assignment Problem

Once we have selected a set S of monitoring stations, we need to compute a probe message assignment A for monitoring link faults in network. A feasible probe message assignment is a set of probe messages $\{m(s, u) \mid s \in S, u \in V\}$, where each $m(s, u)$ represents a probe message that is sent from station s to node u. Further, for every edge $e = (u, v) \in E$, there is a monitoring station $s \in S$ such that $e \in T_s$ and A contains the probes *m(s, u)* and *m(s, v)*. The cost of a probe messages assignment *A* is $COST_A = \sum_{m(s,u)\in A} c_{s,u}$ and the *optimal probe assignment(PA)* is the one with the minimum cost.

Theorem 2. *Given a set of stations S, the problem of computing the optimal probe assignment is NP-hard.*

Proof: The probe assignment problem can be reduced from the *vertex cover* problem, which is a well-known NP-complete problem. For space limitation, we do not prove it here. □

We now describe a simple probe assignment (PA) algorithm that computes an assignment whose cost is within a factor of 2 of the optimal solution. Consider a set of monitoring stations *S* and for every edge $e \in E$, let $S_e = \{s \mid s \in S \wedge e \in T_s\}$ be the set of stations that can monitor *e*. For each edge $e = (u, v) \in E$, the algorithm selects as the monitoring station of *e* the node $s_e \in S_e$ for which the cost $c_{s_e,u} + c_{s_e,v}$ is minimum. In case of ties (that is, multiple stations have the same cost), it selects s_e to be the station with the minimum identifier among the tied stations. Then, it adds the probe messages $m(s_e, u)$ and $m(s_e, v)$ to *A*.

6 Experimental Study

We apply our algorithms on ISP topologies that are inferred by the Rocketfuel tool [11]. We investigate the number of monitoring stations and the number of probe messages required for link faults diagnosis by our algorithms on three backbone ISP topologies with sizes ranging from small (Exodus: 80 nodes and 147 links) to medium (Telstra: 115 nodes and 153 links), and large (Tiscali: 164 nodes and 328 links). For the sake of simplicity, we assume that all the ISPs use shortest path routing to route traffic.In our experiments, the number of nodes that be can be used as monitoring stations (station candidates) $|S'|$ is varied from *n/100* to *n*. For space constraints, we only present the results for the Tiscali topology here. Similar results are obtained for the two other topologies. In Fig.1, we plot the percentage of nodes that are actually used as monitoring stations for link failures diagnosis. We also plot the percentage of useful probe messages returned by the PA algorithm in Fig. 2.

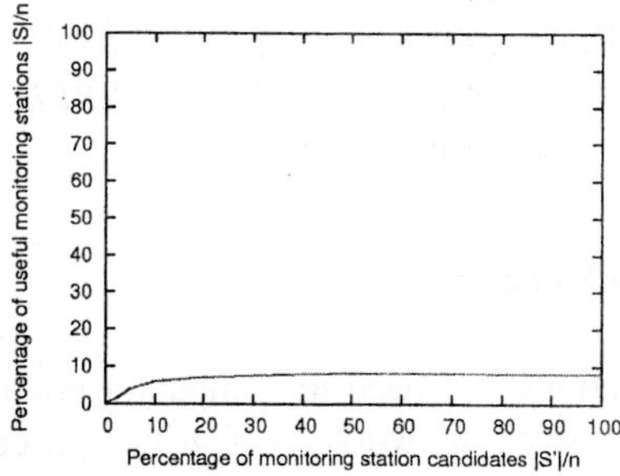

Fig. 1. The number of monitoring stations for link faults diagnosis (Tiscali)

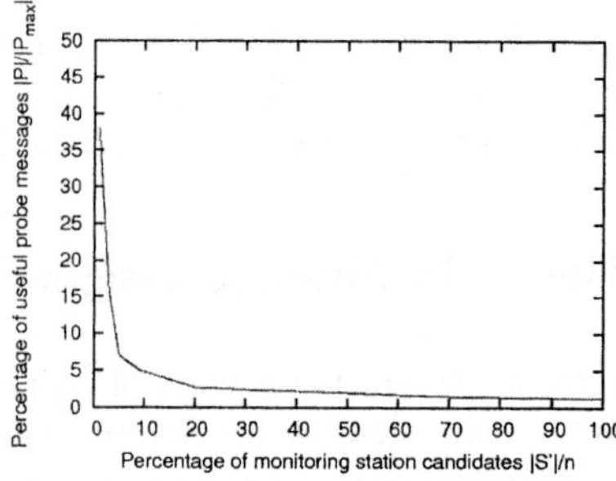

Fig. 2. The number of probe messages for link faults diagnosis (Tiscali)

The number of useful monitoring stations $|S|$ for link failures diagnosis is notably smaller than the number of possible monitoring stations for all sizes of the set $|S'|$ of monitoring station candidates. Furthermore, it increases very slowly, as probes from even a small set of monitoring stations are enough to detect and locate link failures.We observe that for all sizes of the set of monitoring station candidates, the number of useful probe messages $|P|$ is less than a half of the total number of possible probe messages $|P_{max}|$ that can be sent in the network. The percentage of useful probe messages also decreases rapidly as the number of monitoring stations increases.

7 Conclusions

In this paper, we have investigated the use of active measurement for link failure diagnosis in ISP networks. Our studies show that there is a great reduction in the number of monitoring stations and probe messages that are actually useful for link failures diagnosis. These results can be used by ISP operators to trade off accuracy of diagnosis for probing costs.

We are working on various extensions of the present work. The next step is to determine the failure detection capacity of the optimal sets. We are also investigating how an active measurement scheme can cope with missing and false probe messages. The challenge is to improve the robustness of the active measurement scheme to probe errors without much increasing in the measurement costs.

References

[1] D. Clark. The Design Philosophy of DARPA Internet Protocols, In Proceedings of ACM SIGCOMM'88, Stanford, CA. Aug, 1988.

[2] V. Paxson, A. Adams, M. Mathis. Experience with NIMI. In proceedings of PAM2000. Hamilton, New Zealand, 2000.

[3] T. McGregor, H. Braun, J. Brown. The NLANR Network Analysis Infrastructure. IEEE Communications Magazine, 38(5): 122-128 2000.

[4] Matthews W., Cottrell L. The PingER Project: Active Internet Performance Monitoring for the HENP Community. IEEE Communication Magazine, 38(5): 130-136 2000.

[5] Y. Shavitt, X. Sun, A. Wool and B. Yener. Computing the Unmeasured: An Algebraic Approach to Internet Mapping. In Proceedings of INFOCOM'2001, Alaska, April 2001.

[6] T. Bu, N. Duffield, F. Lo Presti, D. Towsley. Network Tomography on General Topologies. In Proceedings of the ACM SIGMETRICS2002, 2002.

[7] M. Dilman, D. Raz. Efficient Reactive Monitoring. In Proceedings of the INFOCOM'2001, Alaska, April 2001.

[8] A. Reddy, R. Govindan, D. Estrin. Fault Isolation in Multicast Trees. In Proceedings of the ACM SIGCOMM2000, 2000.

[9] M. Lad, A. Nanavati, D. Massey, L. Zhang. An Algorithmic Approach to Identifying Link Failures. In Proceedings of 10th IEEE Pacific Rim International Symposium on Dependable Computing(PRDC10),2004.

[10] M. Garey, D. Johnson. Computers and Intractability: a Guide to the Theory of NP-Completeness. W.H.Freeman, 1979.

[11] N.Spring, R. Mahajan, D.Wetherall. Measuring ISP topologies with Rocketfuel. In Proceedings of ACM SIGCOMM2002.

GT-Based Performance Improving for Resource Management of Computational Grid*

Xiu-chuan Wu[1,2], Li-jie Sha[1], Dong Guo[2], Lan-fang Lou[1], and Liang Hu[2]

[1] Institute of Computer Science & Technology, Yantai University,
Yantai, Shandong Province 264005, China
wxc225@126.com

[2] Institute of Computer Science & Technology, Jilin University,
Changchun, Jilin Province 130012, China

Abstract. Resource providers and resources users in the computational grid system are composed of the two parties for gaming in fact. A multi-auctioneers prototype system based upon game theory (GT) for grid resource management is designed and implemented in this paper. The prototype system improves throughput of system in high throughput computing. Furthermore it prevents from the fraud actions, which come from dishonest auctioneer's fraud action and user's cahoots fraud action. The prototype system improves the performance and QoS for resource management of computational grid system greatly.

1 Introduction

Grid computing is emerging as a new paradigm for solving large-scale problems in science, engineering and commerce [1, 2, 3]. Resource management is one of the most important contents for computational grid. Because the dynamic performance behavior as well as heterogeneity of resource of the computational grid, system have no integrity information about resource, resource management is a well-known difficult problem. It also refers to other important problems.

There are many methods for resource management for computational grid [4]. Just like in a real world market, there exist various economic models for setting the price of services based on supply-and-demand and their value to the user. In these economic models the most important use is GT.

This paper analyzes and researches deeply the economic models for resource management, and then designed and implemented the prototype system of the multi-auctioneers that is based upon GT. Simulating experimental results shows the prototype system eliminates the bottleneck of job scheduling and as a result improves the management performance for grid system. Furthermore users can select an auctioneer from multiple-auctioneers so prevents from the dishonest auctioneer's fraud action. On the other hand it also can prevent from user's fraud action.

* This work was supported by the National Natural Science Foundation of China under Grant No. 60473099.

H. Zhuge and G.C. Fox (Eds.): GCC 2005, LNCS 3795, pp. 1072–1077, 2005.

2 The Uses of GT in Resource Management of Computational Grid

Resource providers and users in the computational grid system both are composed of the two parties for gaming in fact. Literature [2~[13] and so on bring forward the concept of the computing commerce i.e. G-commerce or computing economy. It uses economy principle that comes from the human being market to fulfill the management and scheduling of resources in the processes of computing. The computational grid is as the product-oriented computing environment. Computational grid environment takes different resources as interchangeable commodities. The result is both of providers and requesters of the resources drive the price of the resources. The model based on the economy has distinct advantages. The main characteristic is adjusting the contradiction of the supply and demand. In this way the processes of deciding the stratagem of resources scheduling is distributed to the users and the resources owners. Furthermore it can also help the developer to develop scheduling stratagem and to come into begin the high extensible system.

At present there are many of economic models are used for resources scheduling in the computational grid. Most common used economic model is auction model that is based upon GT. For in auction model comparatively small price information is needed and on the other hand it is also implemented easily relatively. An auction is a market institution with an explicit set of rules determining resources allocation and prices on the basis of bids from the market participants. Auctions are stylized markets with well-defined rules, modeling them is very appropriate. Besides the mundane reasons such as velocities of sale that make auctions important, auctions are useful for a variety of informational purpose. Often the buyers know more than the seller about the value of what is being sold, and the seller, not wanting to suggest a price first uses an auction as a way to extract information.

Auctions can be differentiated across many parameters including, but not limited to, those concerning: matching algorithm, price determination algorithm, event timing, bid restrictions, and intermediate price revelation and so on [2,4,12,13].

3 The Design and Implementation of the Multi-auctioneers System Model Based Upon GT

High throughput computing is a kind of important computing type in grid computing. It is different from traditional high performance computing. It emphasize particularly on the utilization of the whole system, that is to say how much service can be provide and how many tasks can be completed which is concerned in this kind of computing.

At present there are a lot of resources management systems that based upon auctions model. But all the systems are based upon single-auctioneer. This kind of systems exist two distinct faults. Firstly it becomes a bottleneck in this case when lots of jobs are needed to schedule. Secondly auctioneer may cahoots with some one bidder to fraud other bidders in order to get the maximum profit. The multi-auctioneers system we designed and implemented can overcome these two defaults.

The architecture of the system is as illustrated in Figure 1.

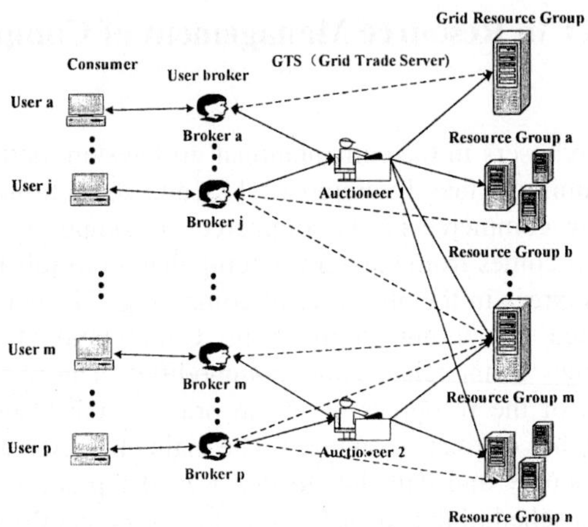

Fig. 1. The architecture of multi-auctioneer for resources management of grid system

In the figure GTS (Grid Trade Server [2,4,11]) is in fact the auctioneers. Its main function is to enable resource trading and execution of consumer requests. Between the auctioneer and user is user broker, it contacts auctioneer on behalf of the user. Resource providers, auctioneers and users brokers mentioned above are composed of three key parts in the auctioning model prototype system.

Resource broker's main function is to contact auctioneer for users. Auction strategy can be optional. In this paper double auction is used and users are grouped in the way of odd number users for auctioneer1and even number users for auctioneer2.

For an auctioneer it must provide about resources information provided by some provider. At the same time it also must obtain the demand information provided by bidder and finally to decide the auction strategy. Certainly it must control the process of the auction process and maximize the profit for both provider and consumer.

Firstly based on formula (1) to decide the reserve price [2, 11]:

$$\text{Reserve\_Price}=[\sum_{i=1}^{No\_of\_Res} (\text{resource\_set[i].No\_of\_PEs*resource\_set[i].} \\ \text{PE\_SPEC\_Rating*resource\_set[i].Cost\_Per\_Sec})]/\text{No\_of\_Res+P\_adjust} \tag{1}$$

Secondly calculating valid resources and according to the resources amount as well as resources description so as to obtain calculating formula 2[2,11]:

$$\text{Res\_Available}=[\sum_{i=1}^{No\_of\_Res} (\text{resource\_set [i]. No\_of\_PEs}) \\ \text{*resource\_set [i]. PE\_SPEC\_Rating}] \tag{2}$$

Based on GT for the double auction model following formula (formula 3) makes resource providers and resource consumers both sides reaching the maximum payoffs. This is Bayesian Nash equilibrium for this case [12,13].

$$p_s(c) = \frac{1}{4} + \frac{2}{3}c$$
$$p_b(v) = \frac{1}{12} + \frac{2}{3}v \qquad (3)$$

Thereinto P represents price, c represents cost of resources and v represents the value evaluated for resources by the consumers. S is denotation of seller and b stands for buyer of resources.

When $P_b \geq P_s$, there is a business takes place each other and the trading price is: P= (P_b+ P_s)/2 and then this P is as new P. According to the price P given the estimated price as V, V= P* stochastic number and calculating P_b= (2/3)*V+1/12.

Bargain each other on the price P= (P_b+ P_s)/2 and P is as new P for next P.

If several bidding price are same, auctioneer selects one user to submit his job to the system according to some kind of rules such as the bid time stamp and so on.

4 Simulation Results Analysis and Performance Comparing

As described in section 3, the prototype system eliminates the bottleneck of job scheduling when there are abundant jobs that are needed to submit to the grid system so that can improve the performance of the resource management system.

In the prototype system GridSim [11] is used to simulate the resources in the grid environment and in the simulating process also used the results provided by [14]. Being the focus of this paper on the performance improving of the resource scheduling, we do not simulate different kinds of resources but they are the same machines and the price of these resources all are the same. Moreover we limited the jobs that are submitted to the system are also same. They all do the same work and these works are very simple. They are neither quality-sensitive nor price-sensitive.

Experimental results are shown in Figure 2. In single auctioneer system when few jobs are submitted to the system the resources using rate of the resources is higher. There are many idle resources that cannot be allocated when numbers of jobs increase. Comparatively multi-auctioneer system can effectively use computing re-

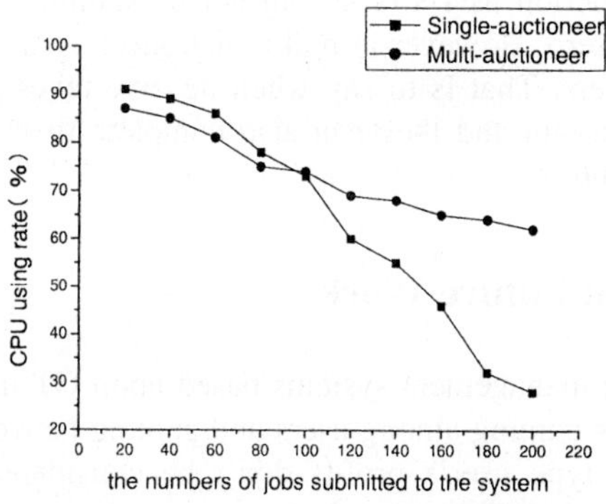

Fig. 2. Resource using rate of comparing single auctioneer and multi-auctioneer system

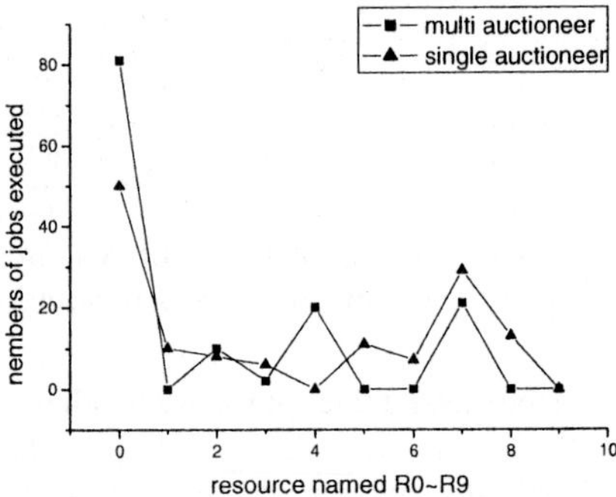

Fig. 3. Distributing case of jobs in resources

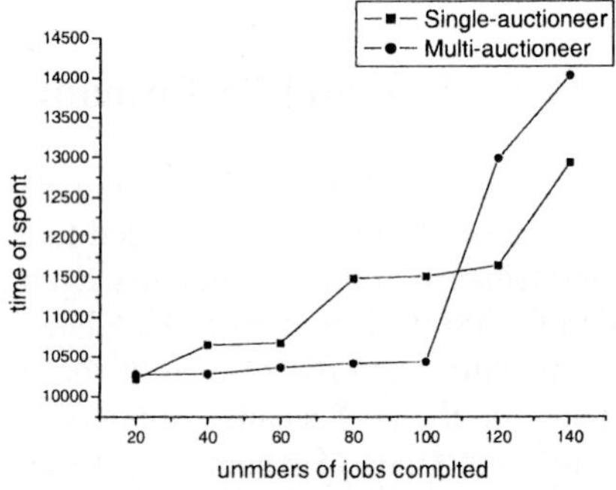

Fig. 4. System performance when auctioneer's deceiving takes place

sources. As the result resource using rate are heightened and performance of resource scheduling are improved greatly.

Comparing multi-auctioneer system and single-auctioneer system, jobs that are submitted to the system are distributed nearly all resources. It is showed in Figure 3.

When one of the auctioneers deceives users to use high price to purchase resources, in the case of single auction user's tasks can not be submitted to the system so the payoffs both sides are zero. However in multi-auctioneer system users can turn theirs steps to other auctioneers. That is to say when deceive takes place users can select other auctioneers to bargain and they can also complete their tasks in the end. The case is as shown in Figure 4.

5 Conclusions and Future Work

At present the resource management systems based upon GT mainly have two types. They are respectively is gaming among users and gaming between users and resource providers. In the first type user's profits don't be considered in fact. The multi-auctioneers prototype system for resource management for computational grid system is designed and implemented in this paper. It is belonging to the second type mentioned above. The system has at least two advantages. In the case that there are many jobs are submitted to the grid system it delimits the bottleneck of submitting section. Another advantage is prevents from the fraud actions, which come from dishonest auctioneer's fraud action and user's fraud action. In fact the prototype system improves the performance and QoS of resource management for computational grid.

In future works some other factors include job deadline, cost as well as budget restriction and QoS of network and so on would be considered. Such as in the mechanism adopted in the prototype system at present job deadline priority will be considered firstly and then the system would become more consummate.

References

1. I. Foster and C. Kesselman (eds.) The Grid: Blueprint for a New Computing Infrastructure, Morgan Kaufman, San Francisco, 1999.
2. Rajkumar Buyya. Economic-based Distributed Resource Management and Scheduling for Grid Computing. Ph.D thesis. School of Computer Science and Software Engineering Monash University, Melbourne, Australia. April 2002.
3. Peter R. Wurman, Michael P. Wellman, William E. Walsh. Specifying Rules for Electronic Auctions. AI Magazine (2002), 23(3), pages 15-23.
4. Klaus Krauter, etc. A Taxonomy and Survey of Grid Resource Management Systems. Software Practice and Experience, Vol. 32, No. 2, Feb. 2002, pp. 135-164.
5. R. Wolski, J. Plank, and J. Brevik. G-Commerce--Building Computational Marketplaces for the Computational Grid (UT Tech. Rep. #CS-00-439).
6. R. Wolski, J. Plank, J. Brevik, and T. Bryan. Analyzing Market-based Resource Allocation Strategies for the Computational Grid (UT Tech. Rep. #CS-00-453).
7. R. Wolski, etc. G-commerce-market formulations controlling resource allocation on the computational grid. Technical Report UT-CS-00-450, University of Tennessee, 2000.
8. Paul Klemperer. Auction Theory: A Guide to the Literature. Journal of Economic Surveys. 1999 Vol.13, no.3.
9. Armstrong, Mark. Optimal Multi_Object Auctions. Review of Economic Studies. 2000 (67), 455-481.
10. Rajkumar Buyya, etc. The Journal of Concurrency and Computation: Practice and Experience, Volume 14, Issue 13-15, Pages: 1175-1220, Wiley Press, USA, 2002
11. Rajkumar Buyya, Nimrod/G Problem Solving Environment and computational Economics, Grid Computing Environments Community Practice (CP) Document, Global Grid Forum (GGF)/First GGF Workshop, Amsterdam, The Netherlands, March 4-7, 2001.
12. Shi Xi-quan, Game Theory. SUFEP. 2000. ISBN 7-81049-398-1/F. 334, In Chinese.
13. Zhang wei-ying, Game theory and information economics. SHANGHAI RENMIN CHUBANSHE 1996. ISBN 7-208-02432-4.
14. http://www.specbench.org/osg/cpu2000/results/cpu2000.html

The PARNEM: Using Network Emulation to Predict the Correctness and Performance of Applications*

Yue Li[1], Depei Qian[2], Chunxiao Xing[1], and Ying He[2]

[1] Research Institute of Information Technology, Tsinghua University, 100084 Beijing, P.R. China
yueli@tsinghua.edu.cn

[2] School of Computer, Beihang University, 100083 Beijing, P.R. China
depeiq@263.net

Abstract. Internet is characterized as a uncontrollable, variable and unpredictable infrastructure, this brings the difficulty of developing, debugging and evaluating network applications. Network emulation system constructs a virtual network environment which has the characteristics of controllable and repeatable network conditions. This makes it possible to predict the correctness and performance of proposed new technology before deploying to Internet. In this paper we present a methodology for predicting the correctness and performance of applications based on the PARNEM, a parallel discrete event network emulator. PARNEM employs a BSP based real-time event scheduling engine, provides flexible interactive mechanism and facilitates legacy network models reuse. PARNEM allows detailed and accurate study of application behavior.

1 Introduction

Network emulation provides a controllable and repeatable environment over which real application can exchange data units among each other. If the *interactive mechanism* of emulator offers the same communication interface to the application processes and the data units to be transmitted between application processes were delayed or dropped in a realistic way, it would be hard to recognize on application level whether communication functionality is performed by a real network or by a network emulator. Furthermore, network emulation avoids the burden of modeling the application to be evaluated, while this difficult and time-consuming task is necessary under pure simulation scenario. Emulation must run in real-time. Otherwise, it will lead to inaccurate results. Sequential emulation of the virtual network may be sufficient for small models, but as the size and/or

* This work was supported by the National Key Basic Research Program of China (G1999032710), the Specialized Research Fund for the Doctoral Program of Higher Education of China (20020006011), and National Natural Science Foundation Major Program of China (90412011).

H. Zhuge and G.C. Fox (Eds.): GCC 2005, LNCS 3795, pp. 1078–1083, 2005.

traffic volume of the model increases, the ability to maintain real-time execution is quickly hindered. Parallel discrete event simulation techniques (PDES) can be used to simulate different portions of the virtual network concurrently.

The goal of PARNEM [1] project is to develop and implement a flexible and scalable network emulator that provides a vehicle for study of application correctness and performance issues. If the behavior of application is hard to model accurately, the use of direct application execution enables accurate experimental results.

2 Related Work

A common approach to network emulation involves the kernel extension technology that allows packets to be intercepted between layers of protocol stack. Some emulators that use this approach are ModelNet [2] and NistNet [3]. Kernel extension based network emulators lack a representation of traffic that would be present in a real network. The widely used NS sequential network simulator has been extended to allow for emulation capability [4]. In the previous work we have pointed out three main deficiencies of NS emulator and a scheme for improving the deficiencies is presented [5].

A multi-paradigm network modeling framework called MAYA [6] provides an environment where discrete event simulators, analytical based fluid simulators and interfaces to real networks can interact. The Georgia Tech dynamic network simulation backplane [7] is used to provide interaction between the different simulators through the use of High Level Architecture (HLA) techniques. These systems employ PDES technology to improve real-time capability, but they all require users to learn new languages to describe their models, so none of them has been widely used. By contrast PARNEM provides a simple way to reuse a large number of existing NS based models. These models can run on parallel platform with minor changes to the input script. In addition, the emulators above do not provide a flexible interactive mechanism, this may bring inconvenience to the design of experiment for the variety of applications.

3 PARNEM Architecture

The basic functionality of PARNEM allows network researchers to directly execute their applications over a virtual network environment. PARNEM employs PDES technique to achieve scalable network emulation. BREEN, a BSP based real-time event scheduling engine runs on MPI-connected cluster system to achieve scalable performance. Interactive mechanism acts as an essential middle layer between the emulator and the applications. PARNEM presents two interactive modes (e.g. host mode and process mode) for different kinds of applications. One can choose a more appropriate interactive mode to design and conduct the experiment. More flexibility can be achieved.

3.1 BREEN - A BSP Based Real-Time Event Scheduling Engine

BREEN is designed based on the bulk synchronous parallel model (BSP), its execution cycles through following two steps: firstly, a global synchronization is employed to compute T_b, a lower bound on time stamp of messages that might be received later; secondly, the events with time stamp not exceeding T_b can be safely processed. It is clear that BREEN conforms to the conservative synchronization in nature. To achieve real-time execution all emulation processes must share a common notion of real-time. Typically, we use local wall-clock time (Lwct) as the reference for real-time after calibration at the initial stage, ignoring any skew among local clocks.

T_b computation cost is an important performance factor. The T_b computation algorithm guarantees that the number of messages for synchronization will never exceed $2n \log n$ despite of the amount of transient messages, n denotes the number of emulation processes. High performance communication infrastructure (LAN for example) ensures that messages transmission has an upper bound to communication latency. So it can be concluded that T_b computation cost also has an upper bound.

3.2 Flexible Interactive Mechanism

Usually we hope to conduct a small-scale experiment on a single machine for decreasing cost and configuration complexity. If the traffic volume generated by the application is limited, sequential emulation is sufficient for maintaining real-time execution. While large-scale applications, especially distributed cooperative systems usually generate large amount of traffic volume, the experiment should involve more hosts for enhancing scalability of emulation. PARNEM presents two interactive modes: process mode and host mode to meet the need of different experiments. Process mode is more suitable for small-scale experiment, host mode adapts to large-scale experiment.

Host Mode. A main issue in host mode is how to route IP packets generated by real application through PARNEM. Our resolution is to allocate a virtual IP address for each application host respectively, and set the routing table on application hosts to route the traffic flow with virtual IP destination through emulation host. It ensures that only the traffic involved in experiment will pass through the emulation host. We use the portable packet capture library (PCAP) for packet reading, PCAP provides a set of simple API for kernel filter programming. The filter is configured as accepting the packets with IP destination within the preset virtual address range. So only one filter is needed, and the burden for scripting network model can be greatly alleviated[5]. The usual raw API can be used for writing IP packets back to network, because IP header has been appropriately modified in PARNEM and no additional operations to TCP and IP headers is needed by protocol stack of OS.

Process Mode. In process mode application acts as a process and resides on the same host as emulation process. FSI is a hybrid communication mechanism between processes, it combines communication between system module and user space process with normal socket communication. System module is loaded at IP layer of OS protocol stack, its main function is to do packet filtering in kernel space. System module communicates with emulation process through Netlink.

4 Applications

In this section we describe two typical applications for case studies: bottleneck bandwidth measurement and distributed cooperative web caching system. We will use PARNEM to predict the correctness of IGI/PTR [8], a tool for characterizing and measuring the available bandwidth on a network path, and to evaluate the performance of a novel neighborhood hierarchical cooperative web caching system NHCW.

The two applications are very representative. The IGI/PTR tool is characterized as a small-scale application, client and server residing at two ends of a path communicate by TCP or UDP traffic and carry out corresponding computations. Further, IGI/PTR generates limited traffic volume for minimizing the impact on the accuracy of measurement results. Based on the analysis above we found that process mode is suitable for the experiment of IGI/PTR correctness prediction. While the NHCW system is more complex than IGI/PTR in nature, it is a large-scale distributed system and may generate large amounts of traffic volume. So host mode is a better choice for the experiment of NHCW performance evaluation.

5 Experiments

In this section we describe experiments we performed using the PARNEM. We have validated the delay model, bandwidth model and loss model in PARNEM, and proved that PARNEM yields almost the same output as NS under uniform experimental scenario. This means that the emulation results of PARNEM are trustworthy. We also use the two applications described in the previous section as case studies to demonstrate how PARNEM can be used to predict the correctness and performance of applications.

5.1 Case Studies

Bottleneck Bandwidth Measurement. Bottleneck link bandwidth on a network path is an important network performance parameter. In practice it is hard to conclude whether the values obtained by a measurement tool are accurate because the real network is uncontrollable and variable. So it is very necessary to predict the correctness of these measurement tools. The objective of this set of experiments is to validate the correctness of IGI/PTR under various network conditions.

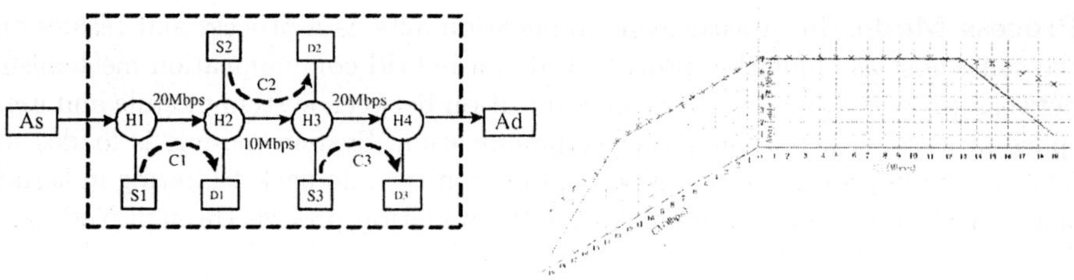

Fig. 1. Model (left) and experimental results (right) of bandwidth measurement experiment. The solid curve illustrates the real bandwidth values, "x" stands for values measured by IGI/PTR.

Network model used is shown in Fig. 1, capacities of three links are 20Mbps, 10Mbps, 20Mbps respectively, competing loads consist of CBR traffic (constant bit rate) C1, C2 and C3. As and Ad are source and destination of IGI/PTR. In the first set of experiments, we set C2 to 3Mbps, C3 to 0, and change C1 from 1Mbps to 19Mbps, measurement results are shown in Fig. 1. When C1 is in the range 1-13Mbps the bottleneck bandwidth is the available bandwidth of link 'H2-H3', namely 7Mbps. When C1 is in the range 13-19Mbps the bottleneck bandwidth is the available bandwidth of link 'H1-H2'. Experimental results indicate that measurement values are of considerable accuracy when C1 is less than 13Mbps, while errors appear when C1 is larger than 13Mbps. In the second set of experiments, we set C2 to 3Mbps, C1 to 0, and change C3 from 1Mbps to 19Mbps, experimental results are similar to the first, also shown in Fig. 1.

Distributed Cooperative Web Caching System. Web caching technology is considered as an important approach to enhance the performance of WWW. This set of experiments aim at providing a performance comparison between NHCW and the classical hierarchical caching scheme.

Mean response time (MRT), global hit rate (GHR), cooperative cost (CC) and server load (SL) are used as metrics for performance evaluation. The experiment employs a trace-driven methodology, we uses trace file from NLANR. A benchmark model which is designed for performance comparison of the two caching schemes is described as follows.

- The two caching schemes employs the same network model;
- The same number of caching proxy servers (12) and clients (36) are involved for the two caching schemes;
- The total cache size is the same (72Mbyte);
- All caching proxy servers employ the same document replacement algorithm (LRU);
- The corresponding client is loaded with the same trace file and utilize uniform access pattern.

Fig. 2 shows the performance data of two caching schemes for mean response time, global hit rate, cooperative cost and server load respectively. Experimental

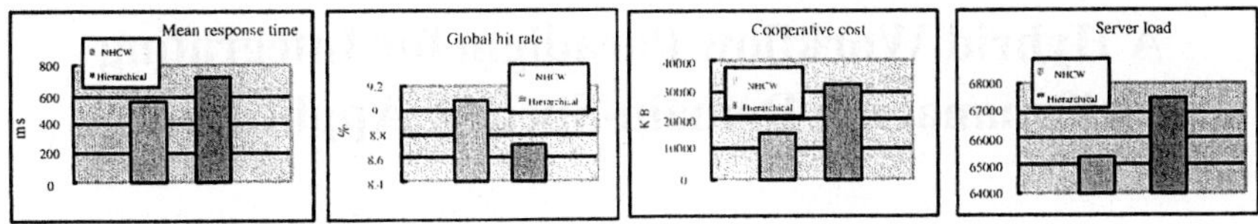

Fig. 2. Performance data of NHCW and hierarchical scheme for mean response time, global hit rate, cooperative cost and server load

results demonstrate that the NHCW has the advantage of the classical classical hierarchical caching scheme for smaller response time, higher global hit rate, lower cooperative cost and server load.

6 Summary

The rapid development of network technology accelerates increasing demands for an improved understanding of the correctness and performance of applications. The dynamic characters of Internet and application adaption introduce new complexity to the situation. We have described a new tool, the PARNEM, and both its validation and demonstration of the methodology it enables for studying correctness and performance issues. These capabilities open a wide range of new opportunities for understanding the behavior of applications.

References

1. Yue Li, Depei Qian. A Practical Approach for Constructing a Parallel Network Simulator. Lecture Notes in Computer Science. Vol.2869 pp.739-746, 2003
2. A.Vahdat, K.yocum, K.Walsh, P.Mahadevan, D.Kostic, J.Chase and D.Becker. Scalability and Accuracy in a Large-scale Network Emulator. In Proceedings of the 5th Symposium on Operating Systems Design and Implementation. 2002. pp.271-284
3. M.Carson and D.Santay. NIST Net: a Linux-based Network Emulation Tool. ACM SIGCOMM Computer Communication Review. 33(3):111-126, 2003
4. K.Fall. Network Emulation in the VINT/NS Simulator. In Proceedings of the fourth IEEE Symposium on Computers and Communications. pp.244-250. 1999
5. Yue Li, Depei Qian, Chunxiao Xing, Ying He. A Scheme for Improving the Deficiency of NS Emulator. Journal of System Simulation, 17(11):555-559, 2005
6. J.Zhou, Z.Ji, M.Takai, and R.Bagrodia. MAYA: Integrating Hybrid Network Modelling to the Physical World. ACM Transactions on Modeling and Computer Simulation, 14(2):149-169, 2004
7. G.F.Riley, M.H.Ammar, R.M.Fujimoto, A.Park. A Federated Approach to Distributed Network Simulation. ACM Transactions on Modeling and Computer Simulation. 14(2):116-148, 2004
8. Ningning Hu, Peter Steenkiste. Evaluation and Characterization of Available Bandwidth Probing Techniques. IEEE Journal on selected areas in communications, 21(6):879-894, 2003

A Hybrid Workflow Paradigm for Integrating Self-managing Domain-Specific Applications

Wanchun Dou[1,2,3], S.C. Chueng[3], Guihai Chen[1,2], J.Wang[4], and S.J. Cai[1,2]

[1] State Key Laboratory for Novel Software Technology
douwc@nju.edu.cn
[2] Department of Computer Science and Technology, Nanjing University, Nanjing, China, Post Code 210093
[3] Department of Computer Science, Hong Kong University of Science and Technology, Hong Kong
[4] Department of Civil and Environmental Engineering, Stanford University, Stanford, CA 94305, USA

Abstract. A hybrid workflow system could be treated as a domain-across infrastructure by incorporating different workflow systems and WfMSs engaged in the complex business processing. For enacting a hybrid workflow system, the self-managing discipline employed in autonomic computing is imposed on domain-specific applications. By classifying the data issues engaged in a domain-specific application into process data and application data and for enhancing the incorporation among the self-managing domain-specific applications from global view of point, the foundation of self-governing management is discussed based on behavior logic and control logic analysis. To conclude, a case study is presented for illustrating the scenarios and the characteristics of hybrid workflow paradigm are summarized.

1 Introduction

To gain and retain competitive advantages in a competitive business arena, an enterprise must continuously strive to offer new services and remain competitive. Currently, an increasing number of enterprises make use of workflow systems to orchestrate their business processes and improve productivity [1]. A workflow is the representation of a business process in a machine-readable format. From a semantics perspective, a WfMS is a computerized organizational system, which integrates heterogeneous information systems and automates applications access to those information resources, for streamlining complex business processes [3]. In [5][6], conventional WfMS and its applications are classified into four classes: production workflow systems, administrative workflow systems, ad hoc workflow systems and collaborative workflow systems, according to the nature of the business processes they are able to support; the workflows in the two former classes are structured and the workflows in the two latter classes are unstructured. Production workflow systems are characterized by a high volume of transactions, several thousand or more per day, and by the need for accuracy, reliability, efficiency, short processing cycles, security, and privacy. Credit and loan applications, or insurance claims are typical examples of production workflow systems. Administrative workflow systems have those features but have

H. Zhuge and G.C. Fox (Eds.): GCC 2005, LNCS 3795, pp. 1084 – 1095, 2005.

less stringent throughput requirements. Production and administrative WfMSs are suitable for routine, clerical situations that demand efficient, consistent and accurate execution of standard processes. They are not suitable for the increasingly important area of knowledge work, where processes cannot be defined precisely beforehand and there is a need for dynamic communication and collaboration between workers. Ad hoc workflows address exceptions and unique situations. Collaborative workflow is mainly characterized by the number of participants involved and their interactions. Unlike other types of workflow that assume continual forward progress, a collaborative workflow might involve several iterations over the same step until the participants reach some agreements; it might even involve going back to an earlier stage. A good example is when several authors write a paper. Ad hoc workflow systems and collaborative workflow systems are more flexible, and are suitable for spontaneous, user-controlled business processing or task routing. Engineering design, planning for marketing campaigns, brainstorming, and knowledge sharing are typical applications of ad hoc workflow systems and collaborative workflow systems. From the underlying criteria of the workflow category presented above, we could find that the execution path or execution logic of a structured workflow system could be prescribed or defined definitely as a whole in advance, while the execution path or execution logic of an unstructured workflow system could only be determined on the fly.

With the development and maturity of infrastructures and solutions that support distributed applications, large-scale workflow systems are being developed to satisfy the advent and evolution of complex business processing, which may consist of some conventional workflow systems executed independently. The engaged organizations are often supervised under a conventional WfMS. They are often integrated loosely through web-based interaction interfaces and engaged workflow systems, as well as the WfMS deployed inside an individual organization, could be enacted in a different style. Typically, when a complex business processing relies on incorporating some conventional workflow systems as well as some conventional WfMSs, it often leads a new workflow deployment fashion or workflow execution manner, which would be characterized into a hybrid workflow system in this paper [7].

In this paper, the extracted workflow constituents are represented by ***domain-specific application***. Accordingly, a hybrid workflow system could be treated as a collection of domain-specific applications integrated across application frameworks. The conventional workflow system executed inside a domain-specific application would be treated as a sub-workflow system and the corresponding WfMS would be treated as a sub-WfMS in this paper, while the global workflow system and global WfMS supporting hybrid workflow system execution is often enacted across multi-platforms in a heterogeneous environment against sub-workflow and sub-WfMS.

In this paper, some approaches of ***self-managing*** exploited in Autonomic Computing (AC) [8][9][10] would be employed to better deal with these management issues. The paper is organized as follows. In section 2, the data engaged in workflow execution is classified into application data and process data, source-specific data management is explored for facilitating the interaction among domain-specific applications from a data perspective. In section 3, taking advantage of concepts of *HyperSet* and Nested *HyperSet*, behavior logic and control logic are discussed, respectively. In section 4, a hybrid workflow instance is put forward to illustrate the scenarios presented in this paper. Finally, we conclude the paper and propose some future research issues in section 5.

2 Source-Specific Data Management for Supporting Domain-Specific Application from Data Perspective

Consistency, rationality and correctness are often treated as basic research issues related to workflow modeling and execution [11][5]. In [11], the authors believe that workflow rationality and correctness analysis should be carried out from four aspects, that is, process control logic, timing constraint logic, resource dependency logic, and information dependency logic. Accordingly, we use a Petri-net formulation [12] to explore hybrid workflow-related resource dependency logic in this section, and process control logic in section 3. Typically, the resource referred here would be instantiated into data resource. Typically, data are passed into and out of domain-specific applications through interaction or interoperability interfaces. The consistency of data shared and manipulation should be kept during domain-across workflow execution. Facilitating further discussion, basic data elements of process data and application data are defined as follows for underlying source-specific data management.

(1) The process data are the static data related to process specifications underlying workflow enactment, or some dynamic process specifications produced during process execution for perfecting its execution or satisfying some exceptions.
(2) The application data are those data that depict the target of process execution from different dimensions. It is stored in a persistent database as the outcome after the workflow execution, and could be exploited by other processes later.

Essentially, process data and application data are the data issues related to the internal behavior of a self-managing domain-specific application. Here, how to identify the *AD* and *PD*' is a key factor to deploy the framework. In this paper, the *PD*' is often the dynamic process specifications produced during execution.

According to the scenarios presented above, a hybrid workflow system composed of domain-specific applications could be formalized as follows.

$$Hybrid\_Wf\_System = D\_S\_Application\ \boldsymbol{R}\ D\_S\_Application$$

Where, *D_S_Application* stands for the set of self-managing domain-specific applications; ***R*** is associated relations among *D_S_Application*, that is, ***R***: $D\_S\_Application \times D\_S\_Application \rightarrow \{T, F\}$, T and F are the Boolean values, true and false.

In view of its self-governing management, the domain-specific application could be treated as a black box with a definite application interface associated with certain input and output parameters. Satisfied the hierarchical infrastructure, mechanism of workflow engine should be altered in architecture to adapt to the domain-specific application with different control scope. Typically, routines of a domain-specific application are under control of the local conventional workflow engine set up inside it. A global workflow engine driven by incorporating disciplines would take charge of defining the input and output parameters, and answer for managing the interactions or interoperability among domain-specific applications from global view of point.

For interactions among domain-specific applications are often realized through data transfer, so ***R*** are often instantiated into **Routes&Rules** piloting data accessing based on certain dynamic behavior logic. **Routes&Rules** consists of source-specific location approach, data access control strategies, temporal dependency, or data invocating disciplines. It steers both data flow and control flow in logic. In Fig.1, the workflow system consists of four domain-specific applications (indicated with T_i), and there are some interactions (indicated with long dash dot arrowhead-lines, that is, **Routes&Rules**) among them. A domain-specific application is formalized by extending notations of place and transition defined in Petri-net from data perspective, which aggregates three kinds of data resource, that is, *PD*, *PD*' and *AD*. By specifying all the execution-related data elements, a domain-specific application could be put into the global workflow execution under certain data flow control. Source-specific data managements provide the data infrastructure for intermediating global and local workflow supervision from resource configuration. Please note that the interaction illustrated in Fig.1 is implemented around both *PD*' and *AD*'; and there also could be a situation that the interaction is implemented only around *AD*' in practice.

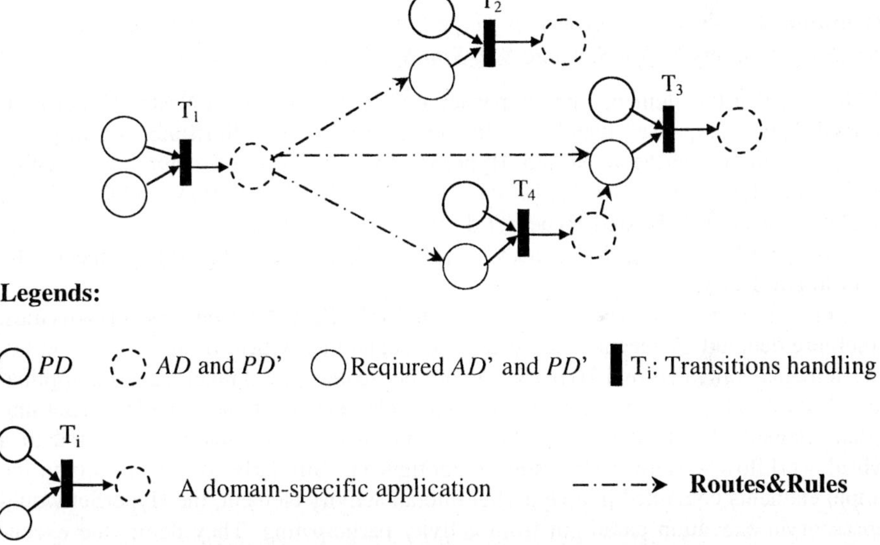

Fig. 1. A typical workflow paradigm composed of domain-specific applications

Up to now, we have discussed the domain-specific application from an interaction view of point. From a self-managing view of point, each application concentrates on managing both internal behavior and external behavior. In practice, internal behaviors are often driven by a task or by subcontracts indicated from others. How to integrate self-managing and domain-specific applications into a hybrid workflow system depends on interaction logic determined by the specifications of the task or subcontracts, which pilots the external behaviors of domain-specific applications. Exploring the associations among external behaviors is indispensable for integrating the self-managing domain-specific application into a hybrid workflow system.

3 Foundation of Self-governing Management Based on Behavior Logic and Control Logic Analysis

In this section, the execution paradigm is depicted from behavior logic and control logic. The behavior logic is realized mainly through resource deployment or activity organization. The control logic concentrates on the execution control according to the self-governing manner scenario. More specifically, the foundation of self-governing management is explored in this section by taking advantage of the concepts of HyperSet and Nested HyperSet [4].

Definition 1. (HyperSet). A HyperSet S is a set whose elements are either simple elements or hyper-elements.

Here, a HyperSet S is a flat set if S has no hyper-element, that is, any $S_i \in S$ is a simple element. S_i, which may be a simple element or a hyper-element, is a sub-element of a HyperSet, denoted as $S_i \in S$, iff $S_i \in S$ or $S_i \in S_j$ for some $S_j \in S$. The set of base elements of HyperSet S, denoted as base(S), is a flat set which contains all the simple sub-elements of S.

Definition 2. (Nested HyperSet). A HyperSet S is said to be nested if base(S_i) $\cap$ base(S_j) = ϕ for any S_i, $S_j \in S$, where $S_i \notin S_j$ or $S_j \notin S_i$.

Observe that the elements in a HyperSet are not disjoint; and a Nested HyperSet is derived from a HyperSet, which has disjoint elements. Fig.2 illustrates a transportation paradigm to derive a Nested HyperSet from a HyperSet. More specifically, Fig.2.a is a HyperSet $S = \{a, \{c, \{b, d\}, \{d, f\}\}, \{e, \{d, f\}, \{g, h\}\}\}$, and Fig.2.b and Fig.2.c represent two Nested HyperSet derived from S, which can be indicated by $S1 = \{a, \{c, \{b, d\}\}, \{e, f, \{g, h\}\}\}$ and $S2 = \{a, \{b, c\}, \{e, \{d, f\}, \{g, h\}\}\}$, respectively, according to Def.1.

In [4], the concept of HyperSet is exploited to reflect the groupings of activities, which are denoted as execution blocks or conceptual activities. In this paper, the hyper-elements contained in a HyperSet would be treated as a domain-specific application. Accordingly, if we instantiated the simple elements contained in a HyperSet into a data element, the HyperSet would represent an execution paradigm related to a hybrid workflow system from resource configuring. Similarly, if we instantiate the simple elements contained in a HyperSet into an activity element, the HyperSet would represent an execution paradigm from activity participating. They depict the execution state of a hybrid workflow system in the form of behavior logic [13].

Specifying the controlling object and the controlled object related to a shared issue in logic is the precondition for enacting a self-governing manner inside a hybrid workflow system. A HyperSet could depict the global behavior logic corresponding to a hybrid workflow execution, but it could not indicate the control logic related to its behavior logic clearly. For example, let $\{b, d\}$ and $\{d, f\}$ as shown in Fig.2.a stand for a certain domain-specific application, respectively; we could find that there has a part folded among them, that is the shared element of d belongs to both (b, d) and (d, f). If the shared element is instantiated into a data issue, which domain-specific application plays the role of data authorization, and which domain-specific application plays the

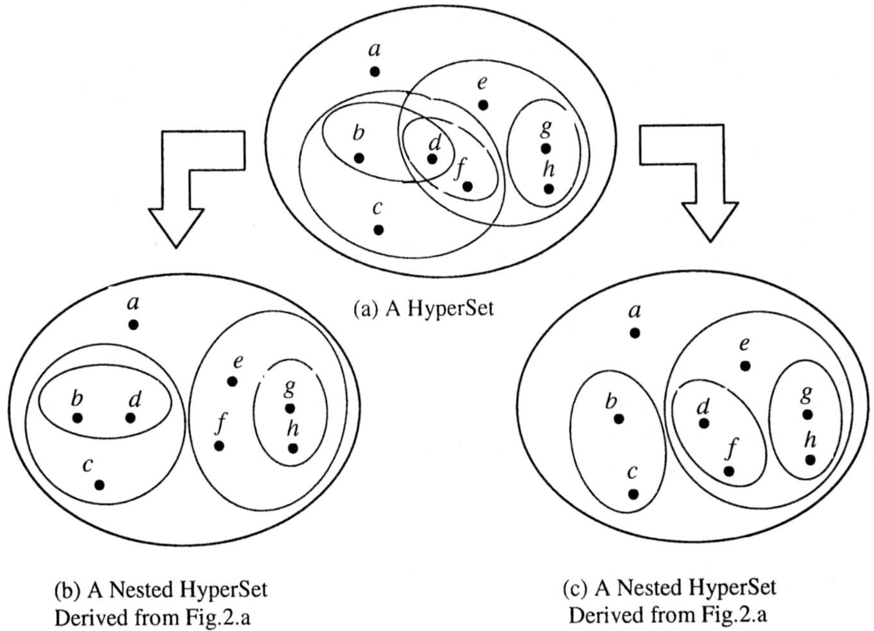

Fig. 2. Rationale of Domain-Specific Control and Interaction

role of data consuming should be defined in advance to support the execution of the self-managing domain-specific applications.

From source-specific view of point, the shared data element must belong to a source-specific DB in control logic. Typically, source-specific data management is a typical self-governing paradigm supporting domain-specific applications. Additionally, if the shared element is instantiated into an activity issue, the associated activity should also be under the control of a definite control subject of domain-specific application in control logic. Here, the associated activity is an activity, which is implemented by more than one activity entity. The engaged active entities expend their efforts in a cooperative way for the same expected goals. Contract negotiation, cooperative design, or service of UEMSC (Urban Emergency Monitoring and Support Centre) is often completed by more than one entity and they are the typical associated activities.

Fig.2.a demonstrates execution-focus behavior logic. The shared issues engaged in different domain-specific applications have no definite control object; therefore, it does not indicate the control logic piloting the executions according to the self-governing discipline. By redefining domains as shown in Fig.2.b and Fig.2.c, we find that all the element is belong to a definite domain that could be either a domain-specific application or data domain of source-specific DB. Therefore, Nested HyperSet derived from a HyperSet satisfies the control requirements for assigning every shared simple element into a definite control domain. Consequently, if the simple element stands for a data element, a Nested HyperSet derived from a HyperSet indicates a control paradigm from source-specific data management corresponding to the behavior logic indicated by the HyperSet. Similarly, if the simple element stands for an activity element, a Nested HyperSet indicates an efficient control paradigm from decision-making privilege during execution. The control logic represented by Nested HyperSet constitutes the foundation of the self-governing management facilitating a hybrid workflow execution.

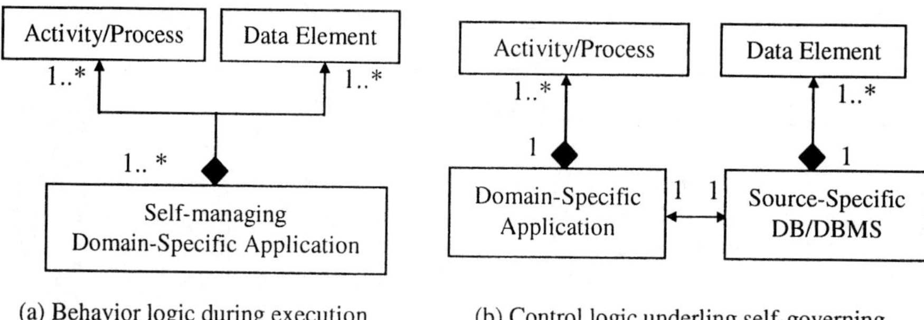

(a) Behavior logic during execution (b) Control logic underling self-governing

Fig. 3. Behavior Logic and Control Logic Corresponding to the implementation of a hybrid workflow system

In structure, Fig.2.b or Fig.2.c represents respectively a domain-specific paradigm that is different from the paradigm as shown in Fig.2.a. In this paradigm, a domain-specific application is covered by another one, or it has no folded part with others at a flat level. An application interface is indicated by domain's definition in nature without interweaving. Besides, if the element is instantiated into an activity issue, every activity belongs to a definite control object of a domain-specific. The logical structure of domain organization is isomorphic with the source-specific data management, that is, the source-specific data management matches the domain-specific application in organizational structure, which is very helpful for improving the management of a hybrid workflow system.

Please note that the domain referred to in Fig.2.a is in practice an activity domain, while the domain referred in Fig.2.b and Fig.2.c is logically a control domain. Besides, by masking the detailed data flow inside its hyper elements, Nested HyperSet also indicates an efficient hierarchical formalization in domain-specific control in a layered structure. Data flow among domains indicates the logical path of data access from origination domain to destination domain without intervening domain's private data flow enacted inside it, which is the basic requirement for self-management.

To depict a hybrid workflow from a different perspective, a HyperSet is used to extract the behavior logic corresponding to the execution of a hybrid workflow system in practice. The behavior logic derived from a HyperSet could be depicted by Fig.3a. A Nested HyperSet is used to represent the control logic supporting a self-governing management supporting a hybrid workflow execution. The control logic extracted from a Nested HyperSet could be extracted by Fig.3.b, which indicates not only a source-specific logic in data management but also domain-specific control logic for governing the behavior logic of a hybrid workflow system.

By regrouping the elements into a self-governing domain in control logic, a hybrid workflow system could manage the netlike domain-oriented data interaction during execution through a treelike domain-specific supervision mechanism in control logic. In practice, the business processing logic among the domain-specific application is the key factor related to determining the self-governing control paradigm. It is discussed in our case study in section 4.

4 Case Study

In this section, a case study is put forward, the background of which is similar to the case recruited in [2]. In [2], it was exploited to demonstrate workflow view driven cross-organization interoperability in a web service environment. Here, we employ it with some modifications to illustrate the self-governing rationale and disciplines presented in this paper.

The presented example demonstrates a cross-organizational workflow based on a supply chain with e-service scenario under web-based environment, as depicted in Fig.4. The workflows are specified as UML activity diagrams. Note that incoming (outgoing) transitions connected to a synchronization bar, which is represented as a thick line in UML, follow the semantics of AND-joins. Other transitions follow the semantics of XOR-join. There are three types of organizations involved, viz., end-users, system integrators, and parts vendors. The interactions between them are enacted in the form of web-service.

The end-user goes through an acquisition workflow, say, for an advanced server system. First, quotation enquiries are sent to a number of system integrators. The received quotations containing price and product information are evaluated. A purchase order is then issued to the selected system integrator. The server system is then received and checked. Finally, payment is arranged.

A system integrator's workflow starts when a quotation request is received. The first step is to check from its parts vendors the lead-time and the updated prices of major parts, especially those with a large price fluctuation (for example, CPU and memory). After the evaluation, a quotation is sent to the end-user. While the end-user evaluates the quotation, the system integrator may need to provide additional or updated information for the bid. After a purchase order is received, the successful system integrator orders any necessary parts, which are out of stock, and estimates a delivery schedule. When all the parts are ready, the system integrator assembles, conducts tests and delivers the server. Finally, the workflow terminates after the payment is received.

A parts vendor's workflow also starts when a quotation request is received. Assuming this is the end of the supply chain, the vendor has all the necessary information to reply to the system integrator with up-to-date parts information and prices. If B2B orders on standard parts are performed together with the payment, this workflow ends after the delivery of the ordered parts.

Fig.4 demonstrates the behavior logic of a hybrid workflow system that supports complex business processing. Once the control subject of the shared data is defined definitely, the individual organization could be treated as a Nested HyperSet, and the hybrid workflow system is degraded into three domain-specific organizations in form of Nested HyperSet. According to the rationale of Nested HyperSet, each self-managing domain-specific application is nested inside a definite application interface based on source-specific data management. This structured control framework facilitates the implementation of self-governing and domain-specific application from control logic.

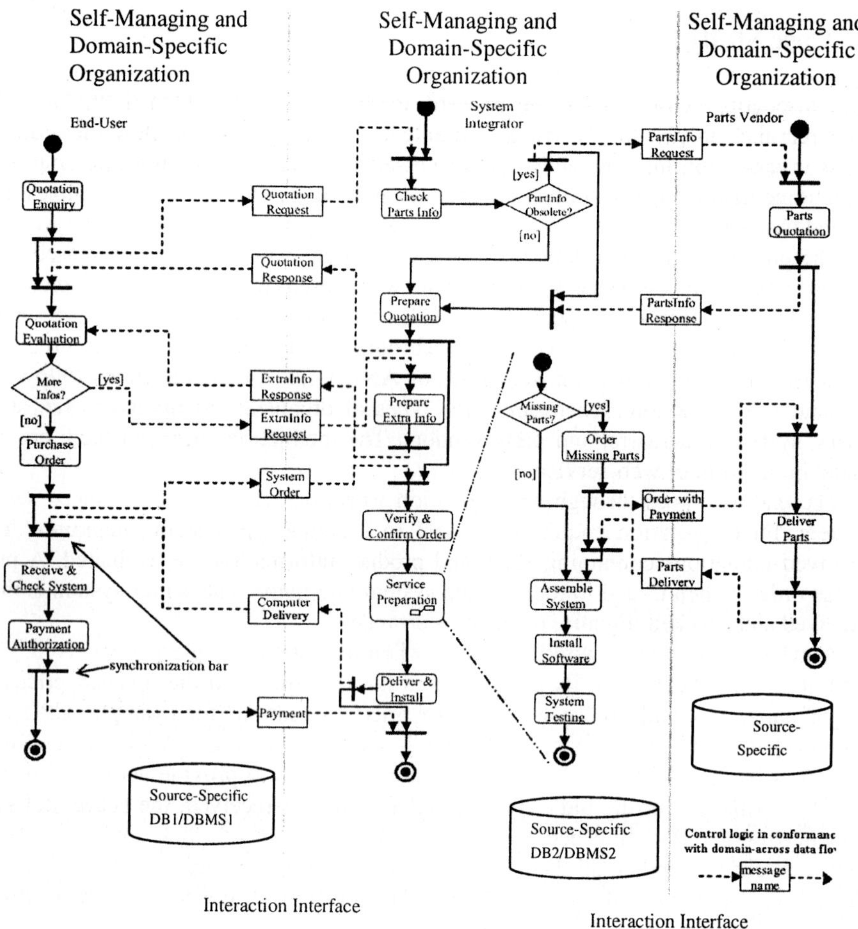

Fig. 4. A hybrid workflow paradigm composed of domain-specific organizations in self-governing fashion

In view of service processes, a service consumer often cares little how the service provider implements the service items. What he pays attention to is the service targets and the related QoS[14]. For example, in this case, the end user often chooses a system integrator collaborator according to the received quotations that contains price, product information and other QoS. How to order missing parts, project the assembling schedule, and carry other operational metrics related to a product is up to the system integrator while the end user is only concerned with the QoS. Similarly, there is the same relation between system integrator and parts vendors; providing the precondition to enact in a self-managing execution manner.

Moreover, the composition process of a hybrid workflow system for modeling service-oriented applications differs from the design process of traditional workflows, whether in task assignment method, heterogeneous execution environment, or self-managing properties [34]. Therefore, the interaction and interoperability between domain-specific applications should be discriminated as another kind of workflow paradigm. For example, process interaction or data transfer engaged in data flow or control flow inside an organization is under control tightly up to a conventional WfMS. Workflow management is often organized in a hierarchical manner under a united environment. The domain-across process interaction or data transfer is jointly supervised by different organizations, while the cooperation often unfolds in a flat way at the same level. Furthermore, privacy of organization in resource access often makes it difficult to tightly integrate all the data and process issues engaged in domain-across applications into a united workflow system. How to develop an incorporative infrastructure under a heterogeneous environment often challenges traditional workflow technology. In light of an organization's function and goal-independence at the system level, it is more reasonable to put the minutia into the individual domain it belongs to for handling, and indicate the controlling object and controlled object of the shared issues engaged in interaction or interoperability. These features make self-governing execution manner more suitable for domain-across interaction management.

In practice, the style of sub-WfMS enacted inside a domain-specific application and between domain-specific applications may be different:

(1) The sub-WfMS support ender user's division making and order process could be viewed as an administrative WfMS that often has consistent clerical processing routines.
(2) The sub-WfMS support domain-across interaction is often a production WfMS that centralizes on accuracy, reliability, security, privacy, short processing, and so on. It also may be an ad hoc MfMS for meeting some dynamic requirements during interaction.
(3) The sub-WfMS support system integrator could be an ad hoc or a collaborative application enactment according to the requirements from the end user, which is unstructured without rigid process definitions. Similarly, the sub-WfMS support parts vendor is also an ad hoc or a collaborative application.

Upon a domain-across management, security is often a key issue for incorporating self-managing domain-specific applications, since web-based interaction is often threatened by hackers, viruses, or other insecurity factors. Besides, with the pervasive application of e-commerce, some public services could be invoked and integrated into a domain-across WfMS. For example, some functions of domain-across WfMS could be taken over by a third party or certain agency such as service for financial processing provided by a bank. The processing function is independent of a domain-specific application and is often integrated loosely. The research issues about it underlie the agile workflow system or large distributed autonomous cooperation system, and could play a positive function in promoting workflow techniques.

In the hybrid workflow system demonstrated in Fig.4, each organization has its own individual workflow system and its own control and execution policies enacting inside it. Besides, they are also engaged in a associated sub-WfMS for interaction management, which is enacted by incorporating the three organization entities and is maintained jointly by them. So, there are two kinds of data flow and control flow management that is, domain-across data/control flow management and domain-inside data/control flow management. Domain-inside data flow management and control flow management are conventional workflow issues and could be implemented well by existed workflow techniques, which could be treated as the internal behavior logic. The domain-across interaction management is an incorporating process among different workflow systems, it is often enacted under a heterogeneous environment and often causes some challenges to the conventional workflow technology. It stands for the external behavior logic indicating the interaction relation among self-managing domain-specific applications. It is the motivating research issues we pay attention to in this paper. Characteristics of a hybrid workflow system are summarized below in detail:

(1) Source-specific data management is one of the key factors for supporting the hybrid infrastructure related to a complex business processing.
(2) Behavior logic and the control logic inside and outside the domain-specific application should be treated in different ways.
(3) Different style WfMSs are often engaged in a hybrid workflow system, which are often enacted in a self-managing manner in behavior logic.
(4) Distributed autonomous cooperation characterizes the execution of a hybrid workflow system. The engaged organizations are often incorporated into a self-governing manner in control logic.
(5) A hybrid workflow system often integrates domain-specific applications loosely, and a domain-specific application often integrates its composed factors tightly.
(6) The sub-WfMS responsible for managing the interaction among domain-specific applications is a typical associated mechanism and should be enacted jointly by them.

5 Conclusion

In this paper, the hybrid workflow system is explored from data and control perspectives. A hybrid workflow system could be treated as a cross-organization infrastructure for incorporating different workflow systems and WfMSs engaged in complex business processing. A self-governing approach for supporting self-managing domain-specific application presented in this paper provides an efficient technology for incorporating heterogeneous WfMS engaged in hybrid workflow systems. Some advantages, such as improved fault tolerance, scalable organization, enhanced flexibility, and enhanced security, can be achieved by incorporating domain-specific application in a self-governing manner. Through extracting the control logic from the behavior logic, our contribution is that the self-governing and domain-specific approach could degrade the complexity of hybrid workflow modeling and execution without losing the control of supervision. For future research, we will apply the self-governing workflow execution paradigm and the prototype to the implementation of a self-governing, intelligent and adaptive web-service oriented workflow system.

Acknowledgement. This paper is based on the Project 60303025 supported by NSFC, and Jiangsu Provincial NSF research funds (No. BK2004411 and No. BK2005208). Besides, it is partially supported by a grant of the Research Grants Council of Hong Kong (Project No. HKUST6167/04E).

References

1. P.W.H.Chung, et al., "Knowledge-Based Process Management—An Approach to Handling Adaptive Workflow," Knowledge-Based Systems, vol.16, no.3. (2003) 149-160
2. Dickson.K.W.Chiu, S.C.Cheung, et al. "Workflow View Driven Cross-Organization Interoperability in a Web Service Environment," Information Technology and Management, vol.5, no.3-4, pp.221-250, 2004.
3. D.Hollinsworth, "The Workflow Reference Model," Workflow Management Coalition, Tech. Report, WfMC-TC-1003, Dec. 1994 [Online].Available: http://www.wfmc.org/standards/standards/model.htm
4. B.I.Arpinar et al., "Formalization of Workflows and Correctness Issues in the Presence of Concurrency," Distributed and Parallel Databases, vol.7, no.2, pp.199-48, 1999.
5. E.A.Stohr and J.L.Zhao, "Workflow Automation: Overview and Research Issues," Information System Frontiers, vol.3, no.3, pp.281-296, 2001.
6. G.Alonso, et al., "Enhancing the Fault Tolerance of Workflow Management Systems," IEEE Concurrency, vol.8, no.3, pp.74 –81, 2000.
7. R.Fierro and F.L.Lewis, "A Framework for Hybrid Control Design," IEEE Transactions on System, Man, and Cybernetics—Part A: System and Human, vol.27, no.6, pp.765-773, 1997.
8. J.O.Kepbart and D.M.Cbess, "The Vision of Autonomic Computing," IEEE Computer, vol.36, no.1, pp.41-50, 2003.
9. John J.Ritsko, Alfred G.Davis, et al., "Preface," IBM Systems Journal, vol.42, no.1, pp.4-5, 2003.
10. A.G.Ganek and T.A.Corbi, "The Dawning of the Autonomic Computing Era," IBM Systems Journal, vol.42, no.1, pp.5-18, 2003.
11. J.Q.Li, Y.S.Fan, and M.C.Zhou, "Timing Constraint Workflow Nets for Workflow Analysis," IEEE Transactions Systems, Man, and Cybernetics, vol.33, no.2, pp.179-193, 2003.
12. K.Salimifard and M.Wright, "Petri net-based Modelling of Workflow Systems: An Overview," European Journal of Operational Research, vol.134, no.3, pp.664-676, 2001.
13. J.H.Son, et al., "GM-WTA: An Efficient Workflow Task Allocation Method in a Distributed Execution Environment," Journal of Systems and Software, vol.67, no.3, pp.165-179, 2003.
14. Jorge.C, Amit.S, et al, "Quality of Service for Workflows and Web Service Processes," Web Semantics: Science, Services and Agents on the World Wide Web, vol.1, no.3, pp.281-308, 2004.

Supporting Remote Collaboration Through Structured Activity Logging

Matt-Mouley Bouamrane[1], Saturnino Luz[1], Masood Masoodian[2], and David King[2]

[1] Department of Computer Science,Trinity College, Dublin, Ireland
{Matt.Bouamrane, Saturnino.Luz}@cs.tcd.ie
[2] Department of Computer Science, The University of Waikato, Hamilton, New Zealand
{M.Masoodian, dnk2}@cs.waikato.ac.nz

Abstract. This paper describes an integrated architecture for online collaborative multimedia (audio and text) meetings which supports the recording of participants' audio exchanges, automatic metadata generation and logging of users editing interaction and also information derived from the use of group awareness widgets (gesturing) for post-meeting processing and access. We propose a formal model for timestamping generation and manipulation of textual artefacts. Post-meeting processing of the interaction information highlight the usefulness of such histories in terms of tracking information that would be normally lost in usual collaborative editing settings. The potential applications of such automatic interaction history generation range from group interaction quantitative analysis, cooperation modelling, and multimedia meeting mining.

1 Introduction

In ordinary meetings, much of the information needed to understand how the group arrived at a particular outcome is contained in verbal interactions which took place during the meeting itself. In online synchronous collaborative scenarios, explicit communication will usually be conveyed via audio but also through group awareness widgets, such as pointing and gesturing. These can therefore be considered as an integral part of the interaction history [11], [12].

In [10] a model of interaction history is proposed which integrates audio and text activity events and supports information visualisation and retrieval from histories. In this model, the relevant abstract data unit with respect to timestamping and history maintenance is the paragraph. Paragraphs are natural text segments that often hold self-contained information items which can be independently linked to speech segments. Unlike individual characters and words, paragraphs have histories that persist when the segment is moved or altered. Paragraph histories also differ from sentence and line histories in that paragraphs tend to be less dependent on their surrounding contexts. One could, for instance, compare our model based on tracking paragraph history to the one adopted in [6] which attaches interaction information to lines of text and displays quantitative interaction feedback ("wear marks") on special visualisation scrollbars. While this kind of interaction history can be quite effective in highlighting positional "hot spots" of activity in documents where the context surrounding a line is more relevant than the individual line itself, such as computer programs, its

H. Zhuge and G.C. Fox (Eds.): GCC 2005, LNCS 3795, pp. 1096–1107, 2005.

usefulness would be limited with respect to indexing and retrieving data external to the document, in our case: speech.

In order for a post-meeting information retrieval model based on temporal and contextual relationships between text and audio media to be effective, detailed logging of textual events is needed. The system must be able to record and timestamp not only editing operations (insertions, deletions, etc.) but also all actions that meaningfully relate to the time-based medium, including pointing, highlighting, and feedback about each user's focus of attention at various points in time. The last three types of actions are usually implemented in real-time collaborative editors through *awareness widgets*. In what follows we present a shared editing environment designed to support capture of user interaction metadata at the paragraph level (RECOLED), discuss the complexity of maintaining such metadata as the document evolves and its implications with respect to the implementation of basic editing operations, and present the solutions we have implemented. Post-meeting processing demonstrates the usefulness of such histories in terms of group interaction quantitative analysis, cooperation modelling, and multimedia meeting mining.

2 Design and Architecture of RECOLED

In synchronous collaborative work over a shared workspace, audio has been shown to be the most efficient communication medium [7]. As such, RECOLED [1] was designed explicitly to be used in conjunction with an audio channel. It is assumed that the co-authors will use the audio channel provided by the conferencing tool for their explicit verbal communication, while the implicit communication and awareness will be supported (and recorded) through the shared editor.

RECOLED employs a semi-centralised architecture which consists of a single server and several clients, as shown in Fig. 1. Text and workspace awareness are

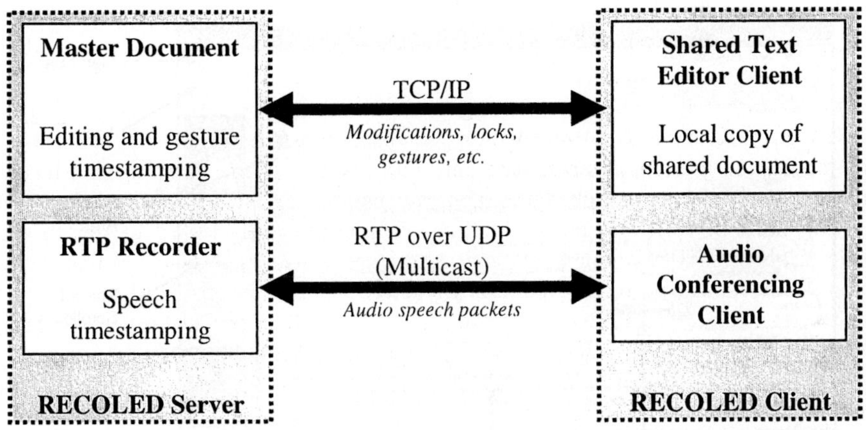

Fig. 1. Audio and text editing history recording architecture of RECOLED

through TCP-IP connections while audio is multicast over UDP sockets. The audio tools used by the clients transmit audio in RTP (Real-time Protocol) packets and the server records these packets directly, keeping the original RTP timestamps and adding arrival timestamps to the recorded data. These timestamps are essential for profiling speech activities and linking them to text segments. In addition, all editing and gesturing operations performed by co-authors are automatically recorded by the central timestamping mechanism of the server. This mechanism is subordinated to the locking mechanism and is described in further detail in the following sections.

2.1 Document Consistency and Concurrency Control

Due to the synchronous and distributed nature of the collaborative writing scenario targeted by RECOLED, concurrency and consistency mechanisms are critical to ensure effective use of the editor. Concurrency control is a well researched area in groupware and a number of approaches have been proposed, including: turn-taking, locking, serialization and operational transformations [3], [4], [13]. We opted for a paragraph-based locking scheme for its relative simplicity of implementation and because it suited best our system's architecture and central paragraph-based timestamping need. In order to maintain consistency between the copies of the document, we use a document implementation based on paragraphs, so that modifications are made on these rather than on the document as a whole. This segmentation of the document into paragraphs permits concurrent modification of distinct paragraphs, while a locking scheme ensures that a single paragraph can only be modified by one client at a time. This locking scheme is optimistic so that local responsiveness can be maintained. In order to reduce the likelihood of conflicting editing operations, RECOLED uses a number of group awareness mechanisms. A paragraph currently locked by another participant will have its margin highlighted in that participant's colour (Fig. 2). A usability study carried out on RECOLED showed that overall, this locking scheme did not hinder the co-authoring task.

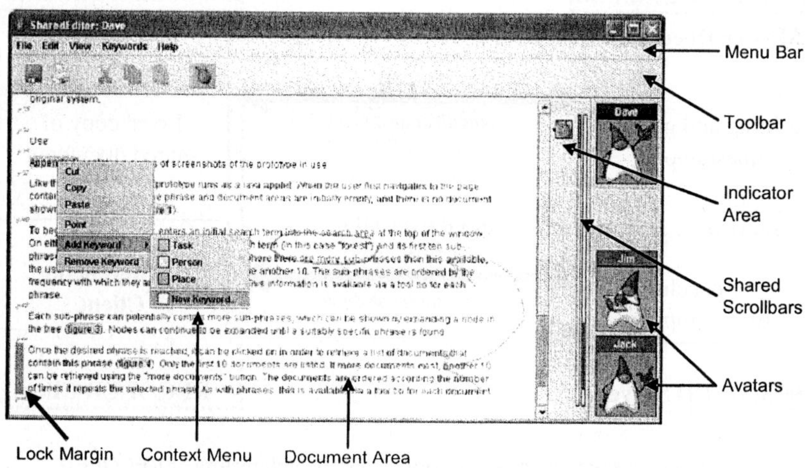

Fig. 2. RECOLED client application interface

The lock manager is the cornerstone of our collaborative writing module. On the client side, the lock manager is responsible for checking if a participant's edit can proceed. If the participant is already holding the lock, the edit is carried out and sent to the server, which it then broadcasts the update to the other clients. However, if the participant does not yet hold the lock for the particular paragraph, then the lock needs to be requested from the server. On the server side, the lock manager grants or denies a lock depending on the current paragraph's status. Since it is the lock manager's responsibility to permit editing operations, it is also at the centre of the timestamping process. If an update is allowed to go ahead, the lock manager identifies the exact type of operation being performed and triggers the appropriate timestamping operations, generating action and paragraph timestamps, merging or mapping timestamps lists, according to the model described in details in the following sections.

Although updates in RECOLED are character-based to allow high responsiveness, generating a separate timestamp for each character typed or deleted would be rather expensive. Furthermore, one of our main design goals is to identify and highlight semantic clusters in the document writing process. As such, a character-based timestamping mechanism would be pointless. Therefore, for timestamp generation purposes, a participant's consecutive edits are buffered, and the timestamping is subordinated to the locking mechanism. This means that a timestamp is generated only when the paragraph lock is released (currently this is set to 3 seconds of user's inaction).

2.2 RECOLED Shared Text Editor

Designers of existing groupware applications such as synchronous shared editors have often focused on incorporating interface components which provide means of group awareness, particularly workspace awareness (e.g. use of tele-pointers, shared scrollbars, etc.) and social awareness (e.g. video links, participant lists or images, etc.). These types of group awareness mechanisms are clearly important in supporting the collaborative work process, and indeed the usability and effectiveness of groupware depends largely on the extent to which it supports group awareness [2], [5].

In most synchronous shared editor software, however, the group awareness information is only used to support the collaborative work activity during the synchronous session itself, after which such information is not recorded and largely ignored. Although some systems record information such as the names of the participants, session duration, and other particulars, the information relating to specific user actions such as text insertion, deletion, focus of attention, and pointing is lost.

In order to address this, RECOLED not only provides the users with important awareness information during the collaborative writing and editing sessions, but also extracts and records the information derived from the awareness components of the interface such as pointing, gesturing and word highlighting for post-meeting access to document history.

Successful collaborative writing essentially involves communication, argumentation and negotiation. Audio communication seems to be a natural choice for coordination in real-time collaborative work. RECOLED's collaborative functionality has therefore been implemented in a way that takes into account the fact that speech will in general form a significant part of the interaction history.

3 Metadata Generation

One of our design assumptions is that when writing text, co-authors often naturally use text segmentation to structure their document into semantic units. Our aim is to attempt to keep track of these semantic units from their creation, and follow their evolution during the co-writing process. In RECOLED, it is assumed that the appropriate granularity of the text unit for this purpose is the paragraph; defined as a segment of text followed by a blank line. Metadata generated is stored with the document content in a XML format for convenient post-meeting processing.

3.1 Editing Primitives

RECOLED is primarily designed to accurately capture editing operations. The original set of editing operation primitives defined was designed to be as general as possible, and included:

- *Insertion:* insertion of a single character
- *Deletion:* deletion of a single character
- *Gesturing:* use of a tele-pointer or other deictic widgets used on one or more text segments.

However, trials of earlier prototypes quickly showed that these were clearly insufficient. In particular, insertions or deletions of new lines are highly significant operations in that they modify the structure of the document. To address these particular cases, two new primitives were added to the previous set:

- *Paragraph_Insertion:* insertion of a new line
- *Paragraph_Deletion:* deletion of a new line

Finally, someone using a single editor would naturally expect to be able to cut and paste text. These operations, supported by RECOLED, are also significant because once again, their use can possibly modify the structure of the document. As such, two further primitives were also defined:

- *Paste:* insertion of strictly more than on character in a single editing operation
- *Cut:* deletion of strictly more than on character in a single editing operation

3.2 Timestamping

The timestamping mechanism used in RECOLED generates two distinct sets of timestamps. The first set consists of **paragraph timestamps**, as illustrated in Fig. 3, whose purpose is to describe the nature of editing operations performed on every single paragraph. These contain information on the *agent* who performed the operation, the type of *action* (i.e. one of the editing primitives previously described) the *start* and *end time* of the action, as well as a reference to a unique **action timestamp.** In the XML representation of the document, text segments consist of the paragraph content and the paragraph timestamps which were generated on that particular paragraph. If the document is structurally modified, RECOLED ensures that these paragraph timestamps are handled accordingly. We later describe the design choices that were made to handle these timestamps.

<segment id="16">
<timestamp id ="137" agent="1" action="Insert" start="1153" end="1155"/>
<timestamp id ="138" agent="1" action="Paste" start="1155" end="1155"/>
<timestamp id ="139" agent="1" action="Delete" start="1157" end="1158"/>
<timestamp id ="142" agent="1" action=" Gesture " start="1167" end="1167"/>
Staying in Western N. Hotel. </segment>

Fig. 3. Paragraph timestamps of RECOLED

The second set of timestamps consists of **action timestamps,** as illustrated in Fig. 4. Action timestamps accurately describe editing or gesturing operations performed on the document. The information they contain are: a unique *identifier*, the *type* of operation performed, the *start* and *end time* of the operation, the *list of paragraphs* which were affected by this operation, the *offset* (within the first paragraph affected by the operation) at which the operation started, and in the case of gesturing the *positions* of the gesturing. In addition, they contain the exact text content of the operation performed (e.g. what text was added or deleted), and in the case of gesturing the text which was pointed at.

<actions>...
<action id="137" type="*Insert*" startT="1153" endT="1155" paragraphs="16" startOffset="0"> **Staying in** </action>
<action id="138" type="*Paste*" startT="1155" endT="1155" paragraphs="16" startOffset="11"> **Western N. Hotel double** </action>
<action id="139" type="*Delete*" startT="1157" endT="1158" paragraphs="16" startOffset="32" endOffset="33"> **double** </action>...

Fig. 4. Action timestamps of RECOLED

4 Document Structure and Timestamping Model

The final version of a document text follows a linear path from start to end. Such document can be represented by the familiar tree structure of Fig. 5. This, however, fails to describe the often laborious process by which the text was produced. For instance, words might have been written or deleted in arbitrary locations, or paragraphs might have been merged, split and moved in many different ways. Although representing the structure of a text at a given state is a straightforward operation, attempting to make a structured representation of a document as the sums of its editing operations can quickly become extremely complex and intractable.

In RECOLED, the actions timestamps describe completely the evolution of the document, and applying these actions at their time of appearance would in effect replay the process by which the document was created. The paragraph timestamps, on the other hand, attempt to describe as accurately as possible the evolution of the text segments. As such, some paragraph timestamps might no longer be reflected in the actual text content, and instead might describe an operation which was performed when the paragraph was in an earlier state.

4.1 Moving Paragraphs

Fig. 5 illustrates the evolution of the structure of a plain style text document, when its first paragraph was removed and its content was appended to the end of the document. The paragraphs "Par" represent positions within the document structure and make no reference to textual content. The actual text content is represented by the "*text\n*" boxes.

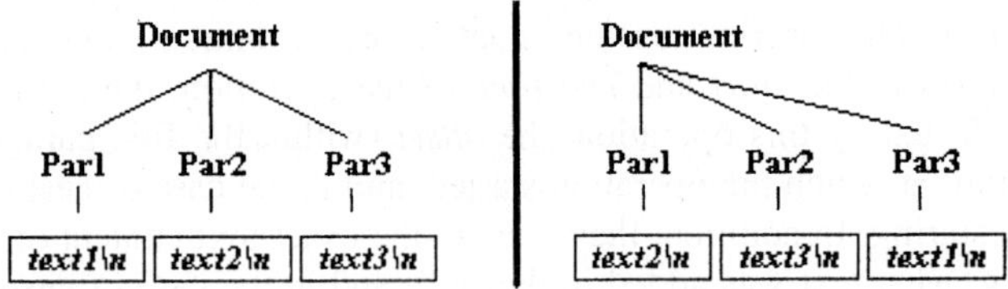

Fig. 5. a. Original state of document b. Text1\n has been cut and appended

In this scenario, the list of timestamps which described the operations performed on the content of *text1* prior to its move will follow the paragraph to its new position (illustrated in Fig. 6). In order to achieve this, the paragraph timestamps lists are mapped to paragraphs contents. Action timestamps will record both the paste and cut operations, and in addition, in the paragraph pasted, a newly generated "paste" timestamp will be appended to the previous list of paragraph timestamps.

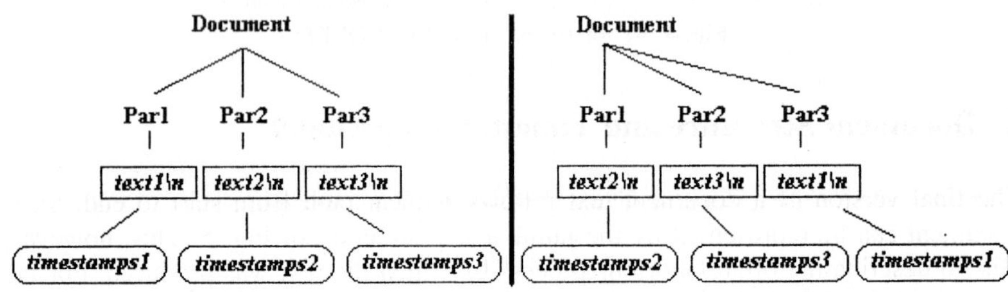

Fig. 6. Effect of paragraph content manipulation on paragraph timestamps

4.2 Merging Paragraphs

Steps similar to those taken when a paragraph is moved are also taken when paragraphs are merged. In Fig. 6 the deletion of the new line at the end of *text3\n* will merge paragraphs 2 and 3 (illustrated in Fig. 7). In this case, an action timestamp will record the operation as a *Paragraph_Merge*. However, as paragraph 3 disappears, its list of timestamps is appended to that of paragraph 2. In this context, the timestamps which recorded operations on the content of *text1\n* are not necessarily relevant to the content of *text3\n*. This however models the fact that paragraph 2 is a merge of two separate text segments, and therefore, its timestamps describe operations which were performed on earlier states of these two separate text segments and eventually led to the current state of paragraph 2.

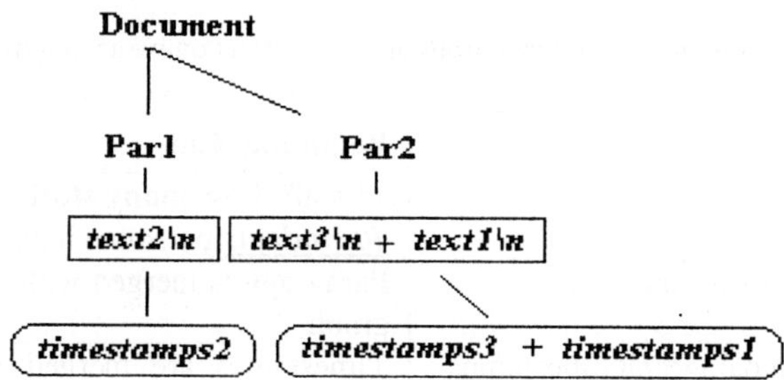

Fig. 7. Effect of paragraphs merging on paragraph timestamps

4.3 Examples of Timestamps Manipulation

The timestamping model which has just been outlined is useful for describing "clean cut" operations, where paragraphs are manipulated as atomic units. However, our experience from using RECOLED in co-authoring situations shows that text operations are often rather complex, and therefore require a more advanced timestamping model. In what follows we propose a taxonomy of cut operations and their effects on paragraph timestamps (Table 1). In the examples, the cut corresponds to the text in bold and the portion of the paragraph described by the cut operation taxonomy is underlined. The other paragraph is there to illustrate the relative position within the document.

5 Post-Meeting Processing

5.1 Analysing Shared Editor Usage and Group Interaction

Analysing and building models of group interaction is a large and well documented research area of Computer Supported Collaborative Work (CSCW) and Computer Supported Collaborative Learning (CSCL) [8]. Analysing how people use computer as a communication medium is the key to building successful and viable groupware systems. Many of the approach have focused on qualitative evaluations of group behaviours, and user interfaces and artefacts usage, while seeking a systematic quantitative and automatic approach to collecting interaction data has often been overlooked.

While this was not the original motivation behind the design of RECOLED, the automatic interaction history capture provides valuable information about the collaborative writing task, users' interactions and the shared editor's usage. An example of this is gesture information. The significance of group awareness information can be evidenced by the frequency with which users utilize awareness mechanisms in the course of a typical collaborative writing session. Table 2 shows data collected during our early user trials illustrating the fact that users tend to employ the pointing awareness mechanism frequently and extensively. This confirms the importance of gesturing as a group awareness tool, as demonstrated in previous groupware awareness studies [5].

Table 1. Taxonomy of Cut Operations and their effect on paragraph timestamps

Title	**Beginning Cut**
Example	15 staff, **how many students?** ***40 students*** but some have their...
Effect on Document Structure	Paragraph is merged with previous paragraph
Action taken on paragraph timestamps	Timestamps are merged with previous paragraph timestamps
Title	**Middle Cut**
Example	15 staff, how many students? 40 students ***but some*** have their...
Effect on Document Structure	No change to paragraph in document structure
Action taken on paragraph timestamps	No action taken on paragraph timestamps
Title	**Whole Cut**
Example	15 staff, how many students? ***40 students but some have their...***
Effect on Document Structure	Paragraph disappears
Action taken on paragraph timestamps	paragraph timestamps are mapped to paragraph content
Title	**End Cut**
Example	15 staff, ***how many students?*** **40 students** but some have their...
Effect on Document Structure	No change to paragraph in document structure
Action taken on paragraph timestamps	No action taken on paragraph timestamps

Table 2. Editing and awareness actions in four separate meetings

Total editing operations	**Total pointing operations**	**Pointing mean duration (in s)**
268	54	8.5
64	22	6.4
128	36	5.7
84	22	6.2

People adopt a variety of approaches to collaborative writing. RECOLED's paragraph based logging mechanisms enables us to develop a clear-picture of the co-authoring task in terms of collaboration behaviour and participants priorities during the collaborative meeting. During the usability study carried out on RECOLED, one set of participants (24 students in 12 separate dyadic groups) were asked to arrange the organization details of a fictional week-end away for final year students and staff. The tasks they were requested to perform included booking a hotel, a restaurant, organizing travel arrangements, proposing day time and night time activities, assessing costs, etc. Upon starting the session, a basic plan was loaded on to the editor with a number of outstanding issues to be resolved. An extremely interesting point was that participants almost never addressed these points in the order in which they appeared on the initial document. In fact, we observed a wide variety of approaches in tackling the various tasks. Participants overall did not try to physically reorder these points within the document. The various groups did however address them in totally different orders from each other, according to their own views of priorities (cost, travel arrangements, etc.) It other words, it would be impossible to infer how each group decided to approach the overall tasks by solely looking at the final document. Therefore, the users' perceptions of priorities are typically something which would be lost in the document's final outcome in traditional shared-writing scenarios. One of our assumptions is that, by capturing time and nature of participants' actions, post-meeting processing of timestamps generated by RECOLED will allow to emphasize different groups' sense of priorities when working on a similar task. In this case, editing history is useful to identify "clusters" of activity within each meeting.

5.2 Interaction History for Meeting Mining and Information Retrieval

We have shown elsewhere [9], [11] that document histories can support effective retrieval of information from multimedia (audio, text and gestures) recordings of collaborative activities. One of our assumptions is that when writing text, co-authors naturally structure their documents into semantic units. The data collection framework described in this paper was designed so as to enable us to keep track of these semantic units from their creation, and follow their evolution during the co-writing process. The most interesting aspect of the paragraph-based editing history recording lies in using the timing of editing operations performed on each paragraph in order to provide temporal entry points to an otherwise sequential audio file. A similar approach was used in FILOCHAT [14] where hand-written notes on a portable device is used as temporal indexing to collocated meeting audio recordings.

Editing timestamps captured on each paragraph during the co-writing tasks provide temporal entry points to the meeting audio recording by exploiting concurrency of actions and speech segments. These audio segments might in turn point to another set of editing actions performed on different paragraphs. Therefore, interactions on the space-based artefacts (segments of text) is used in order to uncover not only non-sequential temporal links with the continuous medium (audio), but also links to other non-contiguous space-based artefacts. In this scenario, the timing properties of the various data units are not used as the underlying structure of our data representation but rather as a means of linking these various data units. A paragraph's *retrieval unit* is based on the notion of temporal intervals and uses concurrency of editing and gesturing actions performed on each paragraph of the text document and participants speech exchanges. The algorithm used to generate a paragraph's retrieval unit is as follows:

- retrieve all editing and gesturing actions performed on a paragraph
- use the timing information of these actions to find all concurrent speech exchanges
- use the duration of these speech exchanges to find all concurrent editing actions not previously uncovered
- iterate through the 2 previous steps until no new actions or audio intervals can be found

The retrieval algorithm stops when no more concurrent editing operations or audio segments can be found. A paragraph's retrieval unit then consists of the set of audio speech exchanges and text interactions retrieved by this algorithm.

6 Conclusion

This paper presented a real-time multimedia meeting architecture that integrates traditional editing and awareness functionality with mechanisms designed to implicitly capture document history. We presented a formal model for the automatic document history generation, based on a textual artefact (a paragraph and its interaction history) by defining editing and gesturing action primitives and presenting our proposed solutions for these artefacts manipulation (splitting and merging) relating to a number of common editing operations such as cutting and pasting. We highlighted a number of possible applications of this history tracking in terms of group interaction quantitative analysis and meeting mining. The model for history capture and retrieval presented here can easily be extended to any mix of space-based artefacts and continuous medium by defining a set of legal operations on the space-based artefact and defining rules for their manipulation in terms of history tracking. Future work will involve the integration of speech recognition for keyword spotting and text mining for contextual clustering of the multimedia meetings and the formal definition of the above model to any combination of space-based artefacts and continuous medium.

References

1. Bouamrane, M., King, D., Luz, S., Masoodian, M.: A Framework for Collaborative Writing with Recording and Post-Meeting Retrieval Capabilities. Special issue on the 6th International Workshop on Collaborative Editing Systems, IEEE Distributed Systems Online (2004).
2. Dourish, P., Bellotti, V.: Awareness and Coordination in Shared Workspaces. In: Proceedings of the Conference on Computer-Supported Cooperative Work, Toronto, ACM Press (1992) 107–114.
3. Ellis, C.A., Gibbs, S.J.: Concurrency Control in Groupware Systems. In: Proceedings of the ACM SIGMOD International Conference on the Management of Data, Seattle, Washington, USA (1989) 399–407.

4. Greenberg, S., Marwood, D.: Real Time Groupware as a Distributed System: Concurrency Control and its Effect on the Interface. In: Proceedings of the ACM CSCW'94 Conference on Computer Supported Cooperative Work (Chapel Hill, N. Carol., Oct. 22–26). ACM Press (1994) 207–217.
5. Gutwin, C., Greenberg, S.: The Effects of Workspace Awareness Support on the Usability of Real-Time Distributed Groupware. ACM Transactions on Computer-Human Interaction 6(3), (1999) 243–281.
6. Hill, W. Hollan, J., Wroblewski, D., McCandless, T.: Edit Wear and Read Wear. In: Proceedings of the SIGCHI conference on Human factors in computing systems, CHI 1992, ACM press (1992) 3–9.
7. Jensen, C., Farnham, S., Drucker, S., Kollock, P.: The Effect of Communication Modality on Cooperation in Online Environments. In: Proceedings of CHI'00 (The Hague, Netherlands). ACM Press (2000) 470–477.
8. Komis, V., Avouris, N., Fidas, C.: Computer-Supported Collaborative Concept Mapping: Study of Synchronous Peer Interaction. Education and Information Technologies, vol. 7, No.2, Kluwer Academic Publishers, Hingham, MA, USA (2002) 169–188.
9. Luz, S., Masoodian, M.: A Mobile System for Non-Linear Access to Time-Based Data. In: Proceedings of Advanced Visual Interfaces AVI'04, ACM Press (2004) 454–457.
10. Luz, S., Masoodian, M.: A Model for Meeting Content Storage and Retrieval. In: Proceedings of the 11th International Conference on Multi-Media Modeling, ed. Yi-Ping Phoebe Chen. IEEE Computer Society (2005) 392–398.
11. Masoodian, M., Luz, S.: COMAP: A Content Mapper for Audio-Mediated Collaborative Writing. In: Usability Evaluation and Interface Design, Proceedings of HCI International, eds. M. J. Smith, G. Savendy, D. Harris, and R. J. Koubek. Lawrence Erlbaum (2001) 208–212.
12. Moran, T.P., Palen, L., Harrison, S., Chiu, P., Kimber, D., Minneman, S., van Melle, W., Zellweger, P.: "I'll Get that off the Audio": A Case Study of Salvaging Multimedia Meeting Records. In: Proceedings of ACM CHI 97, Atlanta, Georgia, USA (1997) 202–209.
13. Sun, C., Jia, X. Zhang, Y. Yang, Y., Chen. D.: Achieving Convergence, Causality Preservation, and Intention Preservation in Real-Time Cooperative Editing Systems. ACM Transactions on Computer-Human Interaction., 5(1) (1998) 63–108.
14. Whittaker S., Hyland P., Wiley M.: Filochat: Handwritten Notes Provide Access to Recorded Conversations. In: Proceedings of the ACM Conference on Human Factors in Computing Systems, ACM Press (1994) 24–28.

The Implementation of Component Based Web Courseware in Middleware Systems

Hwa-Young Jeong

Faculty of General Education, Kyunghee University,
1, Hoegi-dong, Dongdae-mun-gu, Seoul 130-701, Korea
hyjeong@khu.ac.kr

Abstract. Web-Based Instruction(WBI) system offers many advantages to those seeking to advance their education using internet. And WBI system embodied according to traditional process until present. But, this process has inefficiency in system development and gives trouble of operation and administration after development. Therefore, It needs induction of component based development in Web-Based instruction system. In this paper, I implement web-courseware system by component composition in middleware system. For this application, I embody component by Enterprise Java Beans(EJB) and use Prism-MW architecture at the composition method, a middleware platform intended to support software architecture-based development. In this result, I show in application possibility of component based development in Web-Based instruction system as to construct whole score processing system through composition of each component.

1 Introduction

The World Wide Web opens new ways of learning for many people. Now, educational programs and learning materials installed and supported in one place can be used by thousands of students from all over the world[1]. Most systems of web-based learning areas including web course-ware have followed traditional development process because of application environment and characteristic of web server language which is development language. But these existing development processes have long development time and complicate operating process and, after the system was developed, give difficulty in operation and administration of system. Also, it could not cope with various requirements for additions and modifications of learning contents and functions. Therefore, also in web-based system development process, the changeover from static system development to dynamic system development is required. As alternative technique for this purpose, component based development technique is being proposed. Component based development paradigm is the development technique that creates another new component or constructs completed software through creation, selection, assembly/composition and evaluation of software module which is reusable component. In order to precisely composite and operate components, architecture-

H. Zhuge and G.C. Fox (Eds.): GCC 2005, LNCS 3795, pp. 1108–1118, 2005.

based component generation and composition process must be achieved. Several architecture-based technologies exist: Pipe-and-filter architecture of UNIX, Blackboard architecture[2] that has been widely used over the years in general applications, Style-based Unicon[3], Aesop[4], C2[5,7], Symantec-model based Wright, Rapide, middleware based Prism-MW[8, 9] and Domain Spec based ROOM[6].

I implement web courseware using Prism-MW[8,9]. Prism-MW provides highly efficient and scalable implementation-level support for the key aspects of Prism application architectures, including their architectural styles. I say that the middleware is architectural because it provides programming language-level constructs for implementing software architecture-level concepts such as component, connector, configuration, and event. Applied component model is EJB, the server side component model. And I use UML for system design. In this system, I use the item difficulty method for more educational effect. And then I show that this system is applicable by assembling and operating the component which was implemented in web courseware.

2 Relate Work

2.1 Component Based Software Development(CBSD)

System development using the CBSD approach becomes selection, reconfiguration, adaptation, assembling and deployment of encapsulated, replaceable and reusable, building blocks with hidden interior called components, rather than building the whole system from scratch[10]. That is, These improvements result from reuse: building software from existing well tested building blocks is more effective than developing similar functionalities from scratch[11]. That is, CBSD is a state-of-the-art software development paradigm and is the technique that makes it possible to develop high quality software rapidly and efficiently. Java beans, EJB, CORBA and .NET are good examples as representative component platform. Developed components have interface to connect each other and they are assembled and composed according to the architecture-based composition specification. Unicon, C2, Aesop, ACME, Prism-MW and Wright are software architectures to assemble and composite components. Software architecture provides design-level models and guidelines for composing the structure, behavior, and key properties of a software system. An architecture is described in terms of software components (computational elements), software connectors (interaction elements), and their configurations (also referred to as topologies). An architectural style codifies architectural composition guidelines that are likely to result in software systems with certain desired properties. One component (the client) obtains on runtime a handle to another (the server), and then uses it to invoke operations via interfaces.

2.2 Prism-WM

Several aspects of architecture-based development(component-based system composition, explicit software connectors, architectural styles, upstream

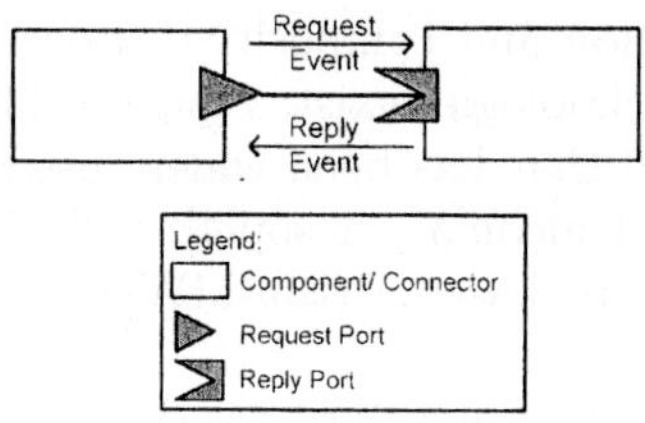

Fig. 1. Link between two ports in Prism-MW

system analysis and simulation, and support for dynamism) appear to make it a good fit for the needs of Prism. Fig 1 show the simple architecture of Prism-MW.

Prism-MW[8,9] should provide native support for designing and implementing architectural abstractions(components, connectors, communication events, and so on). And it should impose minimal overhead on an applications execution and should be scalable in order to effectively manage the large numbers of devices, execution threads, components, connectors, and communication events present in Prism systems. Prism-MW should be extensible and configurable in order to accommodate the many and varying development concerns across the heterogeneous Prism domain. These include multiple architectural styles, but also awareness, mobility, dynamic reconstruction, security, real-time support, and delivery Guarantees.

2.3 The Item Analysis for E-Education

Susan[12] said that the item analysis investigates the performance of items considered individually either in relation to some external criterion or in relation to the remaining items on the test. One of the facts of life in testing is that examines will get items correct by guessing. Birnbaum[13] modified the two-parameter logistic model to include a parameter that represents the contribution of guessing to the probability of correct response. Nevertheless the resulting model has become known as the three-parameter logistic model, high, middle and low, even though it technically is no longer a logistic model. The equation for the three-parameter model is item difficulty parameter, item discrimination parameter, item guessing parameter[14]. Item analysis is an important technique for perfecting norm-referenced tests that discriminate between high and low scorers. For example, high scorers - students with test scores in the top 1/3 of the class, and low scorers - students with test scores in the bottom 1/3 of the class[16]. Sachon[17] had divided 3 class(high scoring, middle scoring, and low scoring). The high and low achievers are comprised of (approximately) the top 27 percent of raw scores and the bottom 27 percent of raw scores. Item difficulty (or easiness) (P) is the share of correct answers per each question. It is set after the test by calculating the percentage of correct answers[15].

Easiness = total number of correct answers / number of students who took the test

Difficulty = 1 - easiness.

3 Component Based Web Courseware

3.1 Selecting Question by Item Difficulty

In this research, I applied the relative difficulty to each question considering the relative correction of item difficulty containing Item guess parameter. Let learner be able to study by choosing question according to the pertinent relative-difficulty in learning level to increase studying effect. That is, when learner selects learning level and the number of questions to study before studying then pertinent questions produced according to the relative correction of item difficulty are provided as many as the number of selected items in multiple-choice type followed by selection of 5 class.

Table.1. Evaluation standard by the relative correction of item difficulty

Learning level	Relative correction of item difficulty	Remark
Expert	0 ~ 0.2	Very difficult
Expert-middle	0.21 ~ 0.40	Difficult
Middle	0.41 ~ 0.60	Normal
Middle-beginner	0.61 ~ 0.80	Easy
beginner	0.80 ~ 1	Very easy

3.2 Design and Implementation of Web Courseware

This system was designed with UML and constituted with dispersed server having main and middleware server, include EJB components. EJB component part

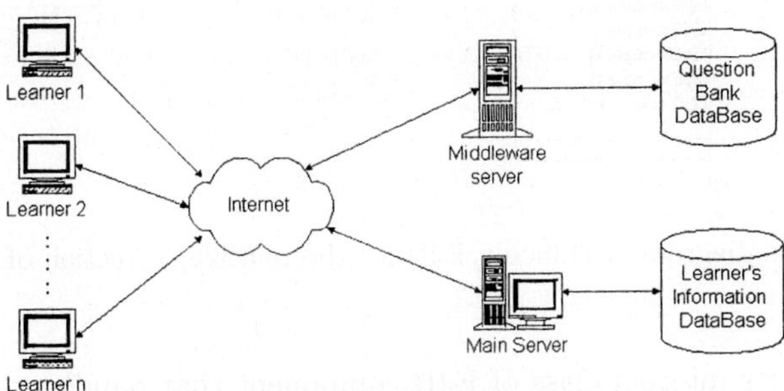

Fig. 2. Deployment of web courseware

was implemented with stateless session bean. And it has been process learning request, learning response and business logic for setting-question. Functions of main server implemented view logic with HTML and JSP controlled learners information. I was constructed database using Cloudscape of Informix Company built in J2EE. The structure diagram of this system is as like Fig 2. Fig 3 show internal structure of middleware server by Prism-MW. And each component, such as WebcoursewareEJB, DifficultyEJB, QuestionselectEJB and Learnerin-formationEJB, was composed by Prism-MW.

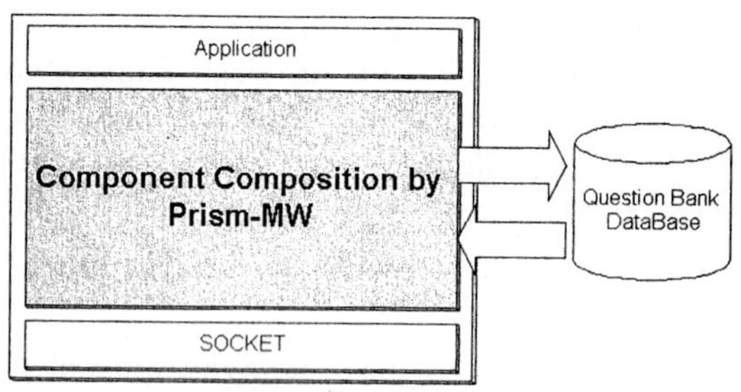

Fig. 3. Internal structure of middleware server

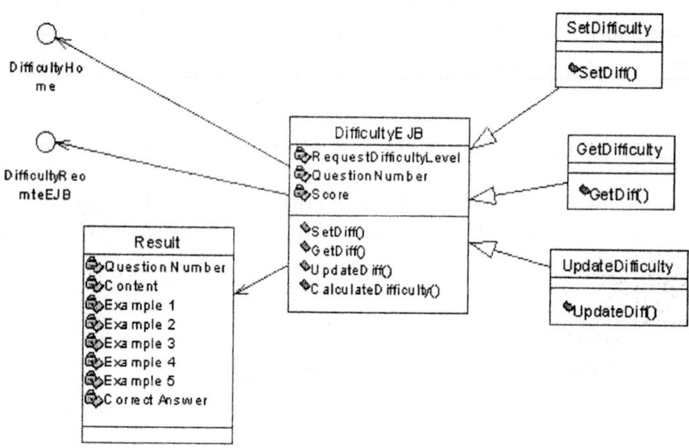

Fig. 4. Class diagram of DifficultyEJB for the relative correction of item difficulty

Fig 4 shows internal class of EJB component that handles the relative correction of item difficulty and sets questions. DifficultyHome is home interface to register component from the outside. DifficultyEJB class has the relative correction of item difficulty and actual business logic to set questions. Difficulty method, such as SetDifficulty( ), GetDifficulty( ) and UpdateDifficulty( ), process item difficulty. Questions corresponding to learning level chosen by learner are extracted randomly according to the relative item difficulty collection from question bank database. Extracted questions have information of each items set in Result class and provide learners questions. Fig 5 shows sequence diagram in this system. Registration of component and creation of object come through DifficultyHome(home interface) then internal methods of EJB component can be called out through DifficultyRemote(remote interface).

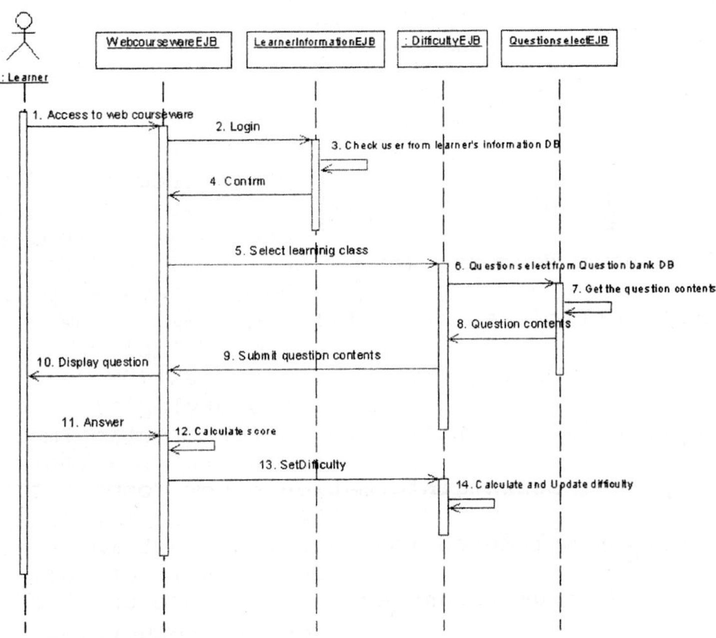

Fig. 5. Sequence diagram. It shows Sequence diagram between EJB components in middleware for the relative correction of item difficulty.

Calculation of the relative correction of item difficulty is requested according to learning result of learner and then, in DifficultyEJB, the relative item difficulty is calculated first through ItemDifficulty.

3.3 EJB Component Composition Using Prism-MW

This system is constructed with EJB component composition using Prism-MW. Fig 6 shows the Prism-MW based component composition using connector.

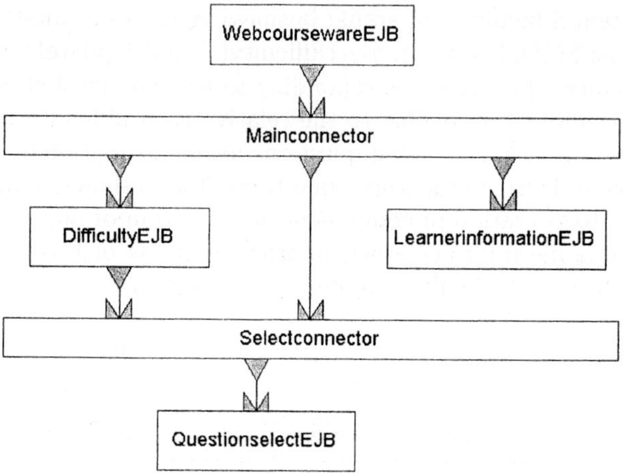

WebcoursewareEJB

Mainconnector

DifficultyEJB

LearnerinformationEJB

Selectconnector

QuestionselectEJB

```
class WebcoursewarePrimMW {
  static public void main(String argv[]) {
     Architecture arch = new Architecture("
                             Webcourseware");
     AbstractImplementation WebcoursewareImpl = new
                             WebcoursewareImpl();
     Component Webcourseware = new Component("Wd",
                             WebcoursewareImpl);
     AbstractImplementation DifficutyImpl = new
                           DifficutyImpl();
     Component Difficulty = new Component("Di",
                           DifficutyImpl);
     AbstractImplementation LearnerinformationImpl = new
                           LearnerinformationImpl();
     Component Learnerinformation = new Component("Li",
                           LearnerinformationImpl);
     AbstractImplementation QuestionselectImpl = new
                           QuestionselectImpl();
     Component Questionselect = new Component("Qs",
                           QuestionselectImpl);
     Connector Main = new Connector("Mainconnector");
     Connector Select = new Connector("
                             Selectconnector");
           :   :
   Port portWebcoursewareRequest=new Port(REQUEST);
   Port portMainConnRequest=new Port(REQUEST);
   Port portMainConnReply=new Port(REPLY);
   Port portDifficultyRequest=new Port(REQUEST);
   Port portDifficultyReply=new Port(REPLY);
   Port portLearnerInformationReply=new Port(REPLY)
   Port portSelectconnRequest=new Port(REQUEST);
   Port portSelectconnReply=new Port(REPLY);
   Port portQuestionReply=new Port(REPLY);
```

```
    Webcourseware.addPort(portWebcoursewareRequest);
    Difficuty.addPort(portDifficultyRequest);
    Difficuty.addPort(portDifficultyReply);
    Learnerinformation.addPort
                      (portLearnerInformationReply);
    Questionselect.addPort(portQuestionReply);
            :  :
    arch.weld(portWebcoursewareRequest,
                       portMainConnReply);
    arch.weld(portMainConnRequest,
                       portDifficultyReply);
    arch.weld(portMainConnRequest,
                       portSelectconnReply);
    arch.weld(portMainConnRequest,
                       portLearnerInformationReply);
    arch.weld(portDifficultyRequest,
                       portSelectconnReply);
    arch.weld(portSelectconnRequest,
                       portQuestionReply);
    arch.start();
  }
}
```

Fig. 6. Component composition using Prism-MW

4 Application of Sample System

In this research, I make English question-learning a model system. Learner can access learning system through login. After login, he can select the relative dif-

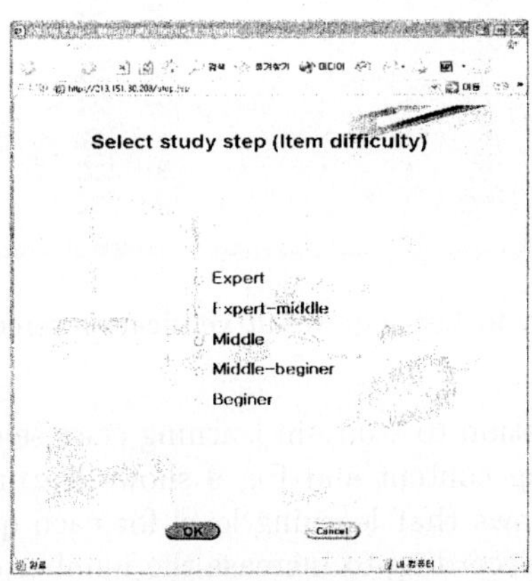

Fig. 7. Learning level selecting screen

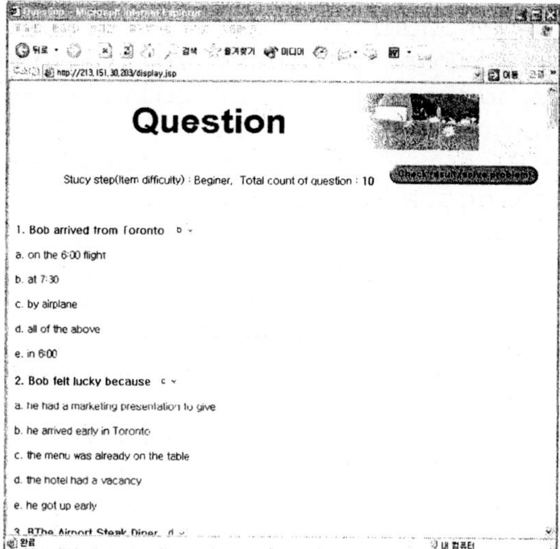

Fig. 8. Learning contents screen

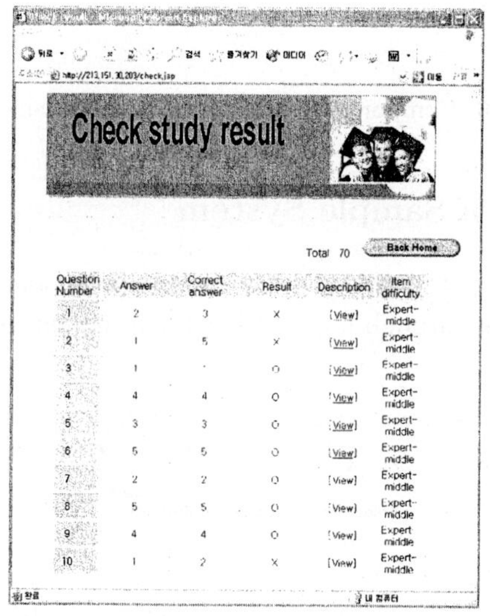

Fig. 9. Learning result verification screen

ficulty of presented question to study in learning class selecting screen as Fig 7. Fig 8 shows the learning content and Fig 9 shows learning result. From these results, this research shows that learning level for each question is reset by reflecting learning result according to increase the number of times of learning of various learners on the relative correction of item difficulty continuously. Therefore, more relevant items can be presented in learning level selected by learner.

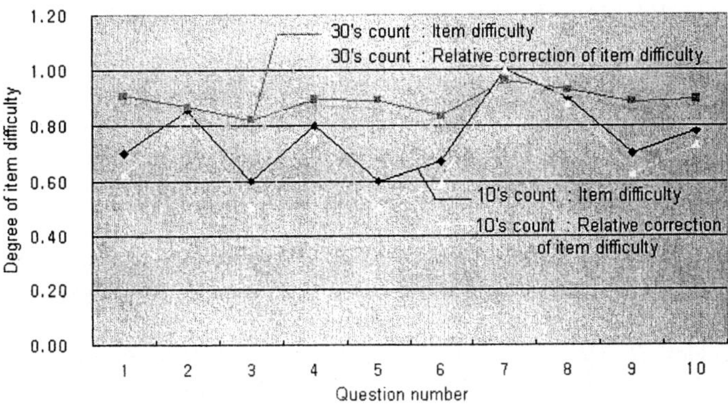

Fig. 10. Question and correct answer state by testing

According to this, Fig 10 shows result that applied item difficulty and relative correction of item difficulty each other.

5 Conclusions

In this paper, I constructed web courseware system by component composition. For this purpose, I embodied business logic of grade processing with EJB and completed whole system by composing embodied components on the basis of Prism-MW architecture. Compared to existing web-based learning systems constructed by traditional development techniques, this technique has lots of advantages as follows. First, the efficient development is possible. As business logic is embodied with component which can be processed independently and connected by composition specification, whole process can be divided easily and simultaneous embodiment of each component is possible. That is, we can embody each functional module of score processing system separately and at the system construction time, make whole system by composing these. Second, the substitution of functional module is easy. If changes of grade level calculation standards or methods are required in this web courseware system, I can modify or embody just the corresponding component and substitute it in that part of whole composition structure. Third, the reuse is convenient. When new system requires same functional module, each score processing component can be adopted without modification to new composition structure. In the web courseware system, I provide learners select the relative difficulty by themselves according to 5 learning levels, such as expert, expert-middle, middle, middle-beginner and beginner, by the relative correction of item difficulty and can expect more appropriate learning effect.

As a further research subject, it is necessary to prepare the theoretical basis to verify objectivity about the relative difficulty which is set at the first question registration by examiner. Also, with running parallel with detailed classification works such as learning chapter and so forth, learner should be able to choose not only learning level but also learning chapter and subjective questions should be applied in company with objective multiple-choice questions followed by 5 levels.

References

1. P. Brusilovsky, E. Schwarz and G. Weber, A Tool for Developing Adaptive Electronic Text-books on WWW , proc of WebNet-96, Association for the Advancement of Computing in Education (AACE), (1996)
2. R. N. Taylor, N. Medvidovic, K. M. Anderson, E. J. Whitehead, Jr., Robbins, J. E., Nies, K, A., Oreizy, P. and Dubrow, D. L., A Component and Message-Based Architectural Style for GUI Software, IEEE Transactions on Software Engineering, Vol.22. No.6, June, (1996)
3. M. Shaw, R. DeLine, D. V. Klein, T. L. Ross, D. M. Young, and G. Zelesnik, Abstractions for Software Architecture and Tools to Support Them, IEEE Transactions on Software Engineering, Vol. 21, No. 4, April (1995)
4. D. Garlan, R. Allen, and J. Ockerbloom, Exploiting Style in Architectural Design Environments, Proceedings of SIGSOFT '94 Symposium on the Foundations of Software Engineering, December (1994)
5. N. Medvidovic, P. Oreizy, and R. N. Taylor, Using Object-Oriented Typing to Support Architectural Design in the C2 Style, Symposium on the Foundations of Software Engineering (FSE4), San Francisco, CA, Oct. (1996)
6. B. Selic, G. Gullekson, and P. T. Ward, Real-Time Object-Oriented Modeling, John Wiley and Sons, Inc., (1994)
7. The C2 Style, http://www.isr.uci.edu /architecture/c2.html, Information and Computer Science, University of California, Irvine. (2003)
8. Nenad Medvidovic, Marija Mikic-Rakic, Nikunj Mehta, Sam Malek, Software Architectural Support for Handheld Computing, Computer, IEEE Computer Society, September, (2003)
9. Nenad Medvidovic, Sam Malek, and Marija Mikic-Rakic. Software Architectures and Embedded Systems, Proceedings of the Monterey Workshop on Software Engineering for Embedded Systems (SEES 2003), Chicago, IL, September 24-26, (2003)
10. Z. Stojanovic and A. Dahanayake, Components and Viewpoints as integrated Separations of Concerns in system Designing, International Conference on Aspect-Oriented Software Development, April (2002)
11. Miguel Goulao, CBSE: a Quantitative Approach, Proceeding of ECOOP (2003)
12. Susan Matlock-Hetzel, Basic Concepts in Item and Test Analysis, Texas A and M University, January. (1997)
13. Birnbaum, A., Some latent trait models and their use in inferring an examinees ability, Addison and Wesley. (1968)
14. Frank B. Baker, The basics of item response theory, ERIC Clearinghouse on Assessment and Evaluation. (2001)
15. Item Analysis after the Test, and Before the Results, http://www.carnet.hr/referalni/obrazovni/en/spzit/theory/analize. (2004)
16. Test diagnostics, http://www.edtech.vt.edu/edtech/id/assess/diagnostics.html. (2004)
17. Michael Sachon, Program grade: test scoring and item analysis, http://www.odu.edu/af/occs/opscantest/gradeprogram.htm, January. (2002)

A Single-Pass Online Data Mining Algorithm Combined with Control Theory with Limited Memory in Dynamic Data Streams

Yanxiang He[1], Naixue Xiong[2,1], Xavier Défago[2,3], Yan Yang[4], and Jing He[5]

[1] The State Key Lab of Software Engineering, Computer School, Wuhan University, P.R. China
yxhe@whu.edu.cn
[2] School of Information Science, Japan Advanced Institute of Science and Technology (JAIST), Japan
naixue@jaist.ac.jp
[3] PRESTO, Japan Science and Technology Agency (JST)
defago@jaist.ac.jp
[4] Computer School, Wuhan university of science and technology, P.R. China
Y.Yang@mail.ccnu.edu.cn
[5] Department of Computer Science, Utah State University, Logan UT 84322-4205, US
jinghe@cc.usu.edu

Abstract. This paper addresses a fundamental problem that arises in data streaming scenarios, namely, today's data mining is ill-equipped to handle data streams effectively, and pays little attention to the network stability and the fast response [36]. To the question, we present a control-theoretic explicit rate (ER) online data mining control algorithm (ODMCA) to regulate the sending rate of mined data, which accounts for the main memory occupancies of terminal nodes. The proposed method uses a distributed proportional integrative plus derivative controller combined with data-mining, where the control parameters can be designed to ensure the stability of the control loop in terms of sending rate of mined data. We further analyze the theoretical aspects of the proposed algorithm, and simulation results show the efficiency of our scheme in terms of high main memory occupancy, fast response of the main memory occupancy as well as of the controlled sending rates.

1 Introduction

Situations abound in which data arrives and is processed in a continuous data stream. The unique characteristic of such streams is "you only get one look", and therefore these transient data streams rarely stored in persistent relations. Examples of such applications include financial tickers, performance measurements in network monitoring and traffic management, call detail records in telecommunications, online queries, log records or click-streams in Web applications, data feeds from sensor networks, e-mail messages, and others. In the stream

H. Zhuge and G.C. Fox (Eds.): GCC 2005, LNCS 3795, pp. 1119–1130, 2005.

model mentioned above, data arrives continuously and needs to be processed in real-time algorithm whose memory is insufficient to store all the data, so the algorithm must process and then discard each data element. The algorithm maintains a summary data structure whose storage requirement is considerably smaller than that of the data streams [1]. Therefore, the processing rate must match the arrival rate.

Nowadays, two trends contribute to the emergence of data streams model. First, scientific simulations and increasing numbers of high precision data collection instruments are generating data continuously, and at a high rate. The second, it is the rapid improvements of Wide Area Networking (WAN) technologies, which is evidenced by the National Lambda Rail (NLR) proposal and the interconnectivity between the TeraGrid and Extensible Terascale Facility (ETF) site. As a result, often the data can be transmitted faster than it can be stored or accessed from disks within a cluster.

Streaming or one-pass algorithms have been studied in different areas. In algorithms, streaming models have been studied in [2], [3], [4], [5], [6], [7], where methods have been developed for comparing data streams under various L^p distances or clustering them. Within the database community, one-pass algorithms have been designed for obtaining median, approximate quantiles [8], and other order statistics [9], [10], [11], correlated aggregate queries [12], mining [13], [11], [42], [43].

Recently, there is an effort to study the general principles behind monitoring statistics over streams [14] and continuous queries over data streams in the database community (e.g., [15], [16], [15]). The problem of summarizing a data stream to provide point and range estimates was first considered in the conference version of this article [17]. Furthermore, conventional OLAP and data mining models have been extended to tackling data streams, such as multi-dimensional analysis [18], clustering [6, 19-20], and classification [21-22]. Problems related to frequency counting include approximate frequency moments [23], L1 differences [24], bit counting [14], frequent items [25-27], hot items in dynamic data stream model [28], stream evaluation [20, 29-31], iceberg queries [32], and top-k queries [28, 33-34]. A sketch-based architecture for collecting and processing distributed network measurements is discussed in [3, 35].

The need for processing data streams is beginning to be understood and it is highly desirable to have an approximate, but reasonably accurate, representation of the data stream that can be stored in a small amount of space [21]. Within the database community, it is understood that "...Today's database systems and data processing algorithms (e.g., data mining) are ill-equipped to handle data streams effectively, and many aspects of data management and processing need to be reconsidered in the presence of data streams [36]."

The main contribution of this paper presents a theoretic analysis and designing method of a data mining control system. In particular, it shows how to design a PID controller for achieving the required sending rate of the router matching with the receiver's main memory size. Relevant pseudocodes for implementation are presented. Simulations under a variety of load conditions have been carried out in the LAN and the WAN case respectively. Simulation results demonstrate that the proposed online data mining control algorithm (ODMCA) performs well, in the sense that it leads to high main memory occupancy, fast response of the main memory occupancy as well as of the controlled sending rates.

The rest of this paper is organized as follows. In Section 2, we present the network computation model and definitions for data streams. Section 3 discusses the ODMCA algorithm to ensure the receiver's memory occupancy stabilized at the target. In Section 4, we analyze the stability of the ODMCA and develop the guidelines for choosing the proportional integrative plus integral parameters to achieve system stability at the target, based on the theoretic analysis. Section 5 provides various simulation results to verify that our algorithm works as analyzed. Finally, we conclude our work and discuss further work in Section 6.

2 The Network Computation Model

To analyze the performance and characteristic of the proposed online data mining control algorithm (ODMCA), we focus on the following network computation model for dynamic data stream in Fig. 1.

In this model, the dynamic data stream is an infinite sequence of data items that may be seen only once. Data mining control algorithm is located at the router. These transaction data flows are sent to the router, and we are interested in finding the change of the sending rate from the router based on transaction data streams requested by customers in a specific time. Note that the main memory in the receiver can be optionally set for temporary storage of recent transactions from the transaction data streams.

We focus on two resources: the workspace (in bits) required in main memory, measured as a function of the input rate λ, and the processing rate P of data streams in a sampling time.

And the considered data streams service is described as follows:

The network is connection-oriented and time is slotted with the duration $[n, n+1)$, equals to T. The associated data is transferred by a fixed size packet.

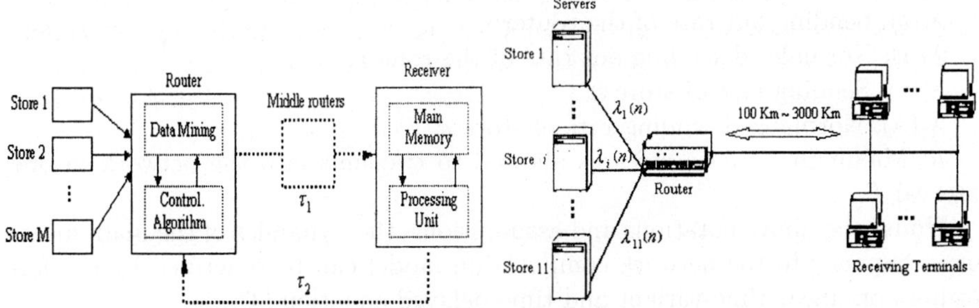

Fig. 1. Network computation model for dynamic data streams

Fig. 2. A simulation model of multiple stores and one router node

The router generates forward control packet (FCP) that is passed by the middle routers and finally is received by the receiver. After receiving data streams coming from the network, the receiver constructs backward control packet (BCP) well, including the occupancy of the main memory, and sends them back to the network.

The middle routers, between the router including the control algorithm and receivers, transfer each data packet including FCP (or BCP) to its downstream (or upstream).

After the router, including the control algorithm, receives the BCPs passed by the middle routers, the required rate of the receiver is computed by control algorithm and is sent to data mining algorithm.

The ODMCA mines the appropriate data from all the data in the stores. The data with the higher degree of similarity is sent out at the computed rate by control algorithm and those with the lower degree of similarity are discarded.

The feedback delays are usually constant since the control packets have higher priority in data processing and transmission.

We assume that all the data in the stores are massive datai.e., all the sum of the data streams arriving at the router is an order of much larger than the sending rate of the router.

Unless otherwise specified, the following notations pertain to the remainder of the paper.

τ_1': Link forward delay from the router to the receiver;

τ_1: Normalized link forward delay from the router to the receiver;

τ_2': Link feedback delay from the receiver to the router;

τ_2: Normalized link feedback delay from the receiver to the router;

τ: Normalized round trip time (RTT) between the router to the receiver, i.e., $\tau = \tau_1 + \tau_2$;

P': Processing rate of the receiver;

P: Data streams processed by the receiver in one sampling time interval T ;

K: Main memory size of the receiver;

$x(t)$: Main memory occupancy of the receiver at time t;

$x(n)$: Normalized main memory occupancy of the receiver node at time $t = nT$;

M: Total number of store nodes;

$\lambda'(t)$: Sending out rate of the router;

$\lambda(n)$: Normalized sending out rate of the router;

$\lambda_i'(t)$: Sending rate of store i;

$\lambda_i(n)$: Normalized sending rate of store i;

μ: Maximum of data streams allowed to transmit into the network in one interval T .

Under the above notations and assumptions, the dynamics of the main memory occupancy in the network computation model can be described by the following non-linear time-variant and time-delayed equation [37-38].

$$\dot{x}(t) = Sat_K\{\lambda'(t - \tau_1') - P'\} \tag{1}$$

where

$$Sat_K\{x\} = \begin{cases} K, x > K; \\ x, 0 \le x \le K; \\ 0, x < 0. \end{cases}$$

And $\lambda'(t) = f(\sum_{i=1}^{M} \lambda'_i(t))$, $f(\bullet)$ denotes the data mining function for all the data in the stores.

Now assume that the router sends data to the main memory of the receiver every T seconds, i.e., the signals get sampled every T seconds, and τ'_1, τ'_2 are exactly integral multiples of T. This is reasonable because one can always add a small delay to these delays so that they are a multiple of T when timing, i.e., $\tau'_1 = \tau_1 T$, $\tau'_2 = \tau_2 T$, and τ_1, τ_2 are integers. Therefore we get $\tau = 2(\tau_1 + \tau_2)$, which includes the propagation, queuing, transmission and processing delays. Let $\lambda(n) = T\lambda'(nT)$ denote the amount of data streams flowing out of the router during the nth interval of T. The component $P = TP'$ denotes the amount of data streams that is processed and removed in the main memory during the nth interval of T.

After lifting the saturation restriction, equation (1) can be written into [38]

$$x(n+1) = x(n) + \lambda(n - \tau_1) - P. \tag{2}$$

3 The ODMCA

The key component of the proposed ODMCA in the router is the way to compute the required sending rate matching with the receiver's main memory size. The PID controller [39] is proposed and described in equation (3). The sending rate of the router $\lambda(n)$ is computed and updated upon every T epoch by ,

$$\lambda(n) = \mu + a(x(n-\tau_2) - \overline{x}) + \sum_{j=1}^{\tau} b_j \lambda(n-j) + c(x(n-\tau_2) - x(n-\tau_2-1)), \tag{3}$$

where $\overline{x}$ is the target main memory occupancy and a, b_j $(j = 1, 2, ..., \tau)$, c are proportional, integral and derivative control gain respectively, which are to be determined from the stability criteria.

In (3), the main memory occupancy of the receiver is measured at the instance $n - \tau_2$. After the feedback delay τ_2 , the router receives the BCP and then takes the main memory occupancy from BCP at time $t = n$.

There is a single FIFO (first-in-first-out) queue to multiplex streams traveling through the outgoing link. The router issues or transmits a FCP in the forward direction repeatedly upon every T epoch, in order to communicate the related flow-control information in the routers of the network. The receiver sends these BCP back to the router as soon as it receives FCP. We assume in the paper that the forward paths and the backward paths are identical respectively.

4 Stability Analysis and Control Gain Selection

The stability analysis and control gain selection are essential for the system. In order to avoid sharp oscillation of the main memory occupancy and the loss of data in main memory, the ODMCA computes the expected sending rate of the router based on main memory occupancy and history sending rate of the router. The system has fast response of the main memory occupancy and of the controlled sending rates. This way, the scheme improves the utilization of the memory and the system's performance. These coefficients are used to locate all the poles of the closed-loop equations (2) and (3) within the unit circle to ensure the stability.

We use a rate-based rather than a window-based adaptation algorithm to achieve the required sending rate matching with the receiver's main memory size. Besides its simplicity, the main advantage of rate-based method is its friendliness to the network [40]. On the contrary, a window-based scheme exposes extra complexity to maintain and synchronize the manageable window across all receivers. It usually generates data bursts periodically. In our PID control scheme, the rate adaptation takes into account the receivers' main memory occupancies as well as the variation of RTTs. The controller parameters are designed to guarantee the stability of rate, which ensures a smooth dynamic of the required sending rate adaptation to minimize the data streams loss rate. This in turn brings an obvious advantage of the proposed scheme over the widely adopted AIMD (addictive increase and multiplicative decrease). For example, see [40]. In AIMD, it is difficult to choose the appropriate increase and decrease factors to guarantee the system's stability and then to obtain smooth and healthy rate adaptation.

In this section, we analyze the stability of the proposed PID congestion control scheme.

If z-transformation is applied to equation (2), one can easily arrive at

$$(z-1)X(z) = z^{-\tau_1}\lambda(z) - P \cdot D(z), \tag{4}$$

where the z-transformation of $x(n)$, $\lambda(n)$ are described by $X(z) = \sum_{n=0}^{+\infty} x(n)z^{-n}$, $\lambda(z) = \sum_{n=0}^{+\infty} \lambda(n)z^{-n}$ and $D(z) = \sum_{n=0}^{+\infty} z^{-n} = \frac{z}{z-1}$.

Taking the z-transform of equation (3), one yields:

$$\lambda(z) = \mu D(z) + a(z^{-\tau_2}X(z) - \bar{x}D(z)) + \sum_{j=1}^{\tau} b_j z^{-j}$$

$$\cdot \lambda(z) + c(z^{-\tau_2}X(z) - z^{-\tau_2-1}X(z)), \tag{5}$$

from equation (4) and (5), one has

$$[(1-\sum_{j=1}^{\tau} b_j z^{-j})(z-1) - az^{-\tau} - c(z^{-\tau} - z^{-\tau-1})]\lambda(z)$$

$$= a(-P \cdot D(z)z^{-\tau/2} - \bar{x}D(z)(z-1)) - c(P \cdot D(z)$$

$$\cdot z^{-\tau/2}(1-z^{-1})) + \mu D(z)(z-1),$$

i.e.,

$$\Delta(z)\lambda(z) = a(-PD(z)z^{-\tau/2} - \bar{x}D(z)(z-1)) - c(PD(z) \cdot z^{-\tau/2}(1-z^{-1})) + \mu D(z)(z-1), \quad (6)$$

where we have denoted

$$\Delta(z) = (1-\sum_{j=1}^{\tau} b^{-j}z^{-j})(z-1) - az^{-\tau} - c(z^{-\tau} - z^{-\tau-1}). \quad (7)$$

The component Δz is the *CharacteristicPolynomial* (CP) of the network system given by equations (2) and (3). The CP (7) is closely related to the stability of the controlled network system. From a control-theoretic point of view when all the zeros of (7) lie within the unit disc, the original network system (2) with the controller (3) is stable in terms of the rate.

With regard to CP (7), one has

$$\Delta(z) = z[1-(b_1+1)z^{-1} + (b_1-b_2)z^{-2} + ... + (b_{\tau-1}-b_{\tau}) \cdot z^{-\tau} + (b_{\tau}-a-c)z^{-\tau-1} + cz^{-\tau-2}],$$

where we denote

$$\Delta_1(z) = 1-(b_1+1)z^{-1} + (b_1-b_2)z^{-2} + ... + (b_{\tau-1}-b_{\tau}) \cdot z^{-\tau} + (b_{\tau}-a-c)z^{-\tau-1} + cz^{-\tau-2}.$$

It is sufficient to ensure the stability if all the roots of $\Delta_1(z)$ lie inside the unit circle for $\Delta(z)$ has all roots of $\Delta_1(z)$ together with a root $z=0$, which is obvious inside the unit circle. Based on Schur-Cohn criterion theory, we set

$$b_j = j\varepsilon - 1; (j \le \tau). \quad (8)$$

$$a = (\tau+2)\varepsilon - 1. \quad (9)$$

$$c = -\varepsilon. \quad (10)$$

In this case, the CP is reduced to the following form

$$\Delta(z) = z\{z^{-\tau-2}[z^{\tau+2} - \varepsilon(z^{\tau+1} + z^{\tau} + ... + 1)]\}. \quad (11)$$

In summary, we have discussed the above two cases under which the control parameters can be chosen so that the CP is reduced to the specific form of equation (11). With regard to the above polynomial, we have the following theorem [41].

Theorem 1: For the coefficients a, b_j and c specified by (8), (9) and (10), the CP (11) is stable iff $\varepsilon < \frac{1}{\tau+2}$.

5 Performance Evaluation

Without loss of generality, we assume that the forward and the backward delay of all links are identical in simulation.

To evaluate the performance of the proposed control method based on network computation model for data streams, we focus upon the following simulation model with eleven stores and one router node (Figure 2), and assume that the stores always have massive data. The controller is used to achieve the required sending rate of the router matching with the receiver's main memory size. The data-mining algorithm based on the computed rate of the control algorithm mines the appropriate data from all the data of the stores. The data with the higher degree of similarity is sent out, and data with the lower degree of similarity is dropped. Here we suppose that the data mining function $f(\bullet)$ follows rectangular distribution based on the degree of similarity β. Then the required sending rate of the router should be the function $\beta f(\sum_{i=1}^{N} \lambda_i(n))$, where $N = 11$.

We are mostly interested in analyzing the transient behaviors of the network computation model for data streams. In the performance analysis, the duration of response time and steady state of main memory occupancy are the main concerns. Simulations were carried out over a wide range patterns and propagation delays between the sending router and the receiver including a LAN (Local Area Network) setting and a WAN (Wide Area Network) setting.

As shown in Figure 3, the router starts to receive data from the stores at time $t = 1msec$ together. We assume that the network bandwidth is sufficient. The sampling time T is $1msec$ and the main memory occupancy threshold is set as $x_0 = 250Kb$. During the simulations, those nodes reasonably close time delays. Then we set $P = 20msec$, $\bar{x} = 235Kb$.

To investigate the performance between the sending router and the receiver node in the LAN case, we assume the distance to be $100Km$ with a delay $\tau_1 = \tau_2 = 1msec$. Therefore the sum of delay in the RTT is $\tau = 2msec$.

We assume that the link delay RTT is dominant compared to other delays such as processing delay and queuing delay, etc.

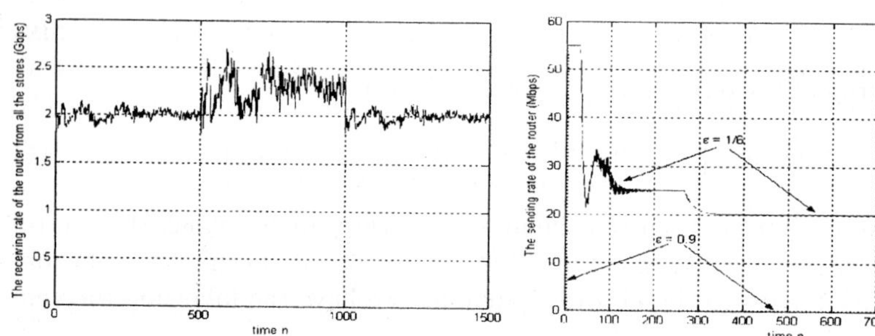

Fig. 3. The receiving rate of the router from all the stores

Fig. 4. The sending rate of the router in the LAN case

We separately set ε to be $1/6$ and 0.9. The former is stable in the system, and the latter, $\varepsilon = 0.9$, makes the system unstable. When $\varepsilon = 1/6$, then $a = -2/3$, $c = -1/6$, $b = [-5/6, -2/3]$; and when $\varepsilon = 0.9$, then $a = 0.8$, $c = -0.9$, $b = [-0.1, 0.8]$.

Figures 3-6 demonstrate the dynamic change of the simulation results in the LAN case. The receiving rate of the router from all the stores is shown in Figure 3. The rate is dynamic and changes with time. Figure 4 indicates the sending rate of the router after the ODMCA process, and Figure 5 shows the dynamic change of the main memory occupancy. It can be seen that, although the sending rate of the router and the main memory occupancy fluctuate at first, they become be stable quickly, and near to the target $20Mbps$ and $235Kb$ respectively.

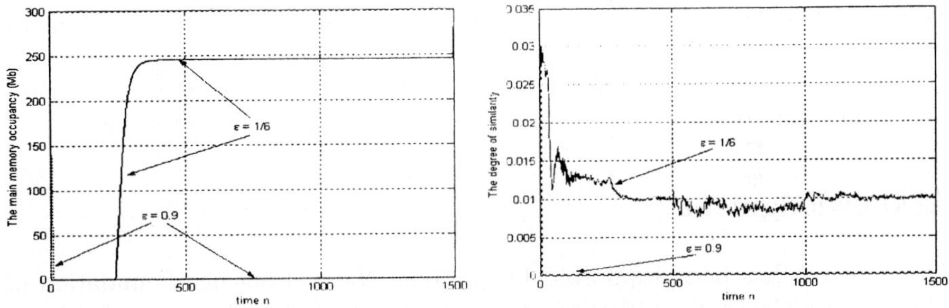

Fig. 5. The main memory occupancy in the LAN case

Fig. 6. The degree of similarity β in the LAN case

Figure 6 shows the change of the degree of similarity β in the LAN case. We can find that the degree of similarity β fluctuates greatly at $500ms$ and $1000ms$ with the great change of the receiving rate of the router from all the stores. From these figures we can find that the presented scheme achieves a short response time, good stability and fine robustness.

Data mining and control method with short response time has following advantages: when the main memory occupancy is close to the threshold, one may inform the router node to reduce the sending rate and prevents the loss of packets as soon as possible; while once the distributed main memory space increases, the router node quickly increases the sending rate and enhances the utilization rate of the main memory. The control scheme corresponding to $\varepsilon = 1/6$ is acceptable and efficient. However, the one corresponding to $\varepsilon = 0.9$ is not acceptable, for it always fluctuates dynamically with the sending rate of the router and the main memory occupancy.

Subsequently, the router uses the ODMCA to adjust the sending rate of the router so as to make the main memory occupancy and sending rate of the router node become steady gradually.

6 Conclusion and Future Work

This paper presents a theoretic analysis and designing method of a data mining control system to design a PID controller for achieving the required sending rate of the router matching with the receiver's main memory size. The control parameters of PID controller can be designed to ensure the stability of the control loop on the basis of control theory. This results in no mined data streams being lost in steady state. Relevant pseudocodes for implementation have been developed. We have shown how the data mining PID controller can be designed to adjust the sending rates of the router based on the feedback mechanism. Simulation results demonstrate that the proposed data mining PID controller performs well in the sense that it leads to high main memory occupancy, fast response of the main memory occupancy as well as of the controlled sending rates. The proposed scheme also supports multiple sessions. We believe that our work is a valuable foundation for the data streams scheme, which can be deployed in the real relevant networks.

The future work will be interesting to attempt to use the proposed scheme to compute the frequency change patterns with sliding windows techniques.

Acknowledgment

This research has been supported by National Natural Science Foundation of China under Grant No. 90104005, by COE (Strategic Development of Science and Technology) foundation in Japan.

References

1. S. Parekh, N. Gandhi, J. Hellerstein, D. Tilbury, T. Jayram, and J. Bigus: Using control theory to achieve service level objectives in performance management. Journal of Real-time Systems, 23 (1/2), July 2002
2. B. Babcock, S. Babu, M. Datar, R. Motwani, and J. Widom, "Models and issues in data stream systems," Proceedings of 21st ACM Symposium on Principles of Database Systems (PODS 2002), Madison, WI, June 2002.
3. N. Alon, Y. Matias, and M. Szegedy, "The Space Complexity of Approximating the Frequency Moments," Proceedings ACM Symp. Theory of Computing (STOC), pp. 20-29, 1996.
4. Hua-Fu Li and Suh-Yin Lee, "Single-Pass Algorithms for Mining Frequency Change Patterns with Limited Space in Evolving Append-only and Dynamic Transaction Data Streams," Proceedings of the 2004 IEEE International Conference on e-Technology, e-Commence and e-Service (EEE'04), pp.215-222, 2004.
5. J. Feigenbaum, S. Kannan, M. Strauss, and M. Viswanathan, "Testing and Spot-Checking of Data Streams," Proc. ACM-SIAM Symp. Discrete Algorithms (SODA), pp. 165-174, 2000.
6. P. Indyk, "Stable Distributions, Pseudorandom Generators, Embeddings and Data Stream Computation," Proc. IEEE Symp. Foundations of Computer Science (FOCS), pp. 189-197, 2000.

7. S. Guha, N. Mishra, R. Motwani, and L. O'Callaghan, "Clustering Data Streams," Proc. IEEE Symp. Foundations of Computer Science (FOCS), pp. 359-366, 2000.
8. N. Alon, P. Gibbons, Y. Matias, and M. Szegedy, "Tracking join and self-join sizes in limited storage," In Proceedings of the Eighteenth ACM Symposium on Principles of the Database Systems (PODS'99), pp. 10-20, 1999.
9. J. M. Hellerstein, P. J. Haas, and H. Wang, "Online aggregation", In Proceedings of the ACM SIGMOD International Conference on Management of Data, pp. 171-182, 1997.
10. R. Agrawal and A. Swami, "A One-Pass Space-Ecient Algorithm for Finding Quantiles," Proceedings of COMAD, Pune, India, December 1995.
11. G. Manku, S. Rajagopalan, and B. Lindsay, "Random Sampling Techniques for Space Efficient Online Computation of Order Statistics of Large Datasets," Proc. ACM SIGMOD, 1999.
12. A. Gilbert, Y. Kotidis, S. Muthukrishnan, and M. Strauss, "How to Summarize the Universe: Dynamic Maintenance of Quantiles," Proc. Very Large Data Bases Conf., pp. 454-465, 2002.
13. J. Gehrke, F. Korn, and D. Srivastava, "On Computing Correlated Aggregates over Continual Data Streams," Proc. ACM SIGMOD Conf., pp. 13-24, 2001.
14. V. Ganti, J. Gehrke, and R. Ramakrishnan, "Mining Very Large Databases," Computer, vol. 32, no. 8, pp. 38-45, 1999.
15. M. Datar, A. Ginois, P. Indyk, and R. Motwani, "Maintaining stream statistics over sliding windows," In Proceedings of 13th Annual ACM-SIAM Symposium On Discrete Algorithms, Jan. 2002.
16. S. Babu and J. Widom, "Continuous Queries over Data Streams," SIGMOD Record, vol. 30, no. 3, pp. 109-120, 2001.
17. S. Madden and M.J. Franklin, "Fjording the Stream: An Architecture for Queries over Streaming Sensor Data," Proc. Int'l Conf. Data Eng., 2002.
18. A. Gilbert, Y. Kotidis, S. Muthukrishnan, and M. Strauss, "Surfing Wavelets on Streams: One-Pass Summaries for Approximate Aggregate Queries," Proc. VLDB Conf., pp. 79-88, 2001.
19. Y. Chen, G. Dong, J. Han, B. W. Wah, and J. Wang, "Multi-dimensional regression analysis of timeseries data streams," In VLDB'02, Hong Kong, China, Aug. 2002.
20. C. C. Aggarwal, J. Han, J. Wang, and P. S. Yu, "A framework for clustering evolving data streams," In Proceedings of the 29th VLDB Conference, Berlin, Germany, 2003.
21. B. K. Yi, N. Sidiropoulos, T. Johnson, H. V. Jagadish, C. Faloutsos, and A. Biliris, "Online data mining for co-evolving time sequences," In Proceedings of the 16th International Conference on Data Engineering, pp. 13-22, 2000.
22. P. Domingos and G. Hulten, "Mining high-speed data streams," In Proceedings of the 6th International Conference on Knowledge Discovery and Data Mining (KDD'00), pp. 71-80, Aug. 2000.
23. G. Hulten, L. Spencer, and P. Domingos, "Mining time-changing data streams," In Proceedings of the 7th International Conference on Knowledge Discovery and Data Mining (KDD'01), pp. 97-106, Aug. 2001.
24. N. Alon, Y. Matias, and M. Szegedy, "The space complexity of approximating the frequency moments," JCSS: Journal of Computer and System Sciences, 58, 1999.
25. J. Feigenbaum, S. Kannan, M. Strauss, and M. Viswanathan, "An approximate L1-difference algorithm for massive data streams (extended abstract)," In FOCS: IEEE Symposium on Foundations of Computer Science (FOCS), 1999.

26. M. Charilar, K. Chen, and M. Farach-Colton, "Finding frequent items in data streams," In Proceedings of the International Colloquium on Automata, Languages, and Programming (ICALP), pp. 693-703, 2002.
27. E. Demaine, A. Lpez-Ortiz, and J. I. Munro, "Frequent estimation of internet packet streams with limited space," In Proceedings of the 10th Annual European Symposium on Algorithms, volume 2461 of Lecture Notes in Computer Science, pp.348-360, 2002.
28. R. Karp, C. Paradimitriou, and S. Shenker, "A simple algorithm for finding elements in sets and bags," ACM Transactions on Database Systems, 2003.
29. G. Cormode and S. Muthukrishnan, "What's hot and what's not: Tracking most frequent items dynamically," In PODS'03, June 2003.
30. G. Dong and J. Li, "Efficient mining of emerging patterns: Discovering trends and differences," In Proceedings of the 5th International Conference on Knowledge Discovery and Data Mining (KDD'99), pp. 43-52, Aug. 1999.
31. V. Ganti., J. Gehrke, and R. Ramakrishnan, "A framework for measuring changes in data characteristics," In PODS'99, pp. 126-137, 1999.
32. V. Ganti., J. Gehrke, and R. Ramakrishnan, "Mining data streams under block evolution," SIGKDD Explorations, 3(2), pp. 1-10, 2002.
33. M. Fang, N. Shivakumar, H. Garcia-Molina, R. Moteani, and J. D. Ullman, "Computing iceberg queries efficiently," In Proceedings of the 24th International Conference on Very Large Data Bases, pp. 299-310, Aug. 1998.
34. B. Babcock and C. Olston, "Distributed top-k monitoring," In Proceedings of ACM SIGMOD, 2003.
35. P. B. Gibbons and Y. Matias, "Synopsis data structures for massive data sets," In Proceedings of the Tenth Annual ACM-SIAM Symposium on Discrete Algorithms, Jan. 1999.
36. A. Gilbert, Y. Kotidis, S. Muthukrishnan, and M. Strauss, "QuickSAND: Quick Summary and Analysis of Network Data," DIMACS Technical Report 2001-43, Nov. 2001.
37. http://www-db.standford.edu/stream.
38. Xi Zhang, Kang G. Shin, Debanjan Saha and Dilip D. Kandlur, "Scalable Flow Control for Multicast ABR Services in ATM Networks," IEEE/ACM Transactions on Networking, vol.10, no.1, pp 67-85, 2002.
39. Yanxiang He, Naixue Xiong and Yan Yang, "Data Transmission Rate Control in Computer Networks using Neural Predictive Networks," The 2004 International Symposium on Parallel Processing and Applications (ISPA 2004), LNCS 3358, pp. 875-887, 2004.
40. B. R. Barmish, "New Tools for Robustness of Linear Systems", MacMillan, New York, 1994.
41. S. Shi and M. Waldvogel, "A rate-based end-to-end multicast congestion control protocol," in Proceedings of Fifth IEEE Symposium on Computersand Communications (ISCC 2000), 2000.
42. Liansheng Tan, Yan Yang, Chuang Lin, Naixue Xiong and Moshe Zukerman, "Scalable Parameter Tuning for AVQ," IEEE Communications Letters, vol. 9, no.1, Jan. 2005.
43. Anna C. Gilbert, Yannis Kotidis, S. Muthukrishnan, and Martin J. Strauss, "One-Pass Wavelet Decompositions of Data Streams," IEEE Transactions on knowledge and data engineering, Vol. 15, No.3, May 2003.

An Efficient Heuristic Algorithm for Constructing Delay- and Degree-Bounded Application-Level Multicast Tree*

Feng Liu, Xicheng Lu, and Yuxing Peng

School of Computer,
National University of Defense Technology, Changsha, China
richardlf@21cn.com

Abstract. In this paper we first investigate the problem of finding a delay- and degree-bounded maximum sum of nodes ALMT. We proved the problem is NP-hard, and testify its relationship with the well-studied degree-bounded minimum maximum-delay ALMT problem. We proposed a greedy algorithm FindOverlayTree with SRPF heuristic. The simulation results show that our design solution is a valid and cost-effective approach where compared to other three modified classic heuristics under several performance metrics.

1 Introduction

This paper considers the problem of how to construct delay- and degree-bounded ALMT (application-level multicast tree) for live video streaming from a source node. Although IP multicast is another method for webcasting, it is not suitable for video multicast [17]. Key wherefore is that IP multicast has deficiency in scalability. However, by organizing all the end hosts into an ALMT, multicast can be achieved through relaying data stream among each parent-child node pair via unicast. Each end host not only receives stream from its parent node, but also tries its best to relay stream through its access network. With the perfect cooperation of host nodes, data stream would overcast a large number of users.

Designing a practical ALMT constructing algorithm should consider the fundamental characteristics of live streaming application itself in the following aspects: (1)delay sensitive, where every participant hope to view the content as earlier as possible, as if at the actual locale of the media source. Therefore source-to-destination OPD(Overlay Path Delay) along the ALMT is the most important QoS requirement;(2)real-time, where each continuous media logical data unit (video frames or audio samples) must be delivered in a given time-span and be presented at end host by a well-determined deadline [1]. By using constrained system resources involved in continuous media data processing (access network, CPU, etc.), each end host can only deliver to a fixed number of nodes accordingly. Thus degree bounded constraint is

* The research work was supported by NSF project no. 60433040 and 973 project no. 2005CB321801.

H. Zhuge and G.C. Fox (Eds.): GCC 2005, LNCS 3795, pp. 1131 – 1142, 2005.

straightforward; (3)lots of concurrent and continuous user requests. Hence requires us to do our endeavor to deliver the stream to hosts as many as possible.

Accordingly, this optimum problem can be informally stated as follows: Given a data source s and a set of nodes, where form a complete undirected overlay graph with a delay weight on each edge and a degree bound weight on each vertex, design a algorithm to construct ALMT rooted at s in the graph that maximizes sum of nodes on the tree, but also satisfies the delay- and degree-bounded constraints. However, this problem is NP-hard. And as far as know, this is the first time to study on the problem.

To address the problem above, we propose a greedy algorithm FindOverlayTree with an efficient heuristic SRPF. The contributions of this paper are as follows:

- Proved that the proposed problem is NP-hard.
- Proved that the proposed problem is equal to the well-studied minimum maximum-delay multicast tree problem under a condition.
- Proved that the FindOverlayTree with SRPF is $O(1/N^{R+1})$ algorithm for the NP-hard problem.

The rest of the paper is organized as follows: in the next section, we formulate the proposed problem and prove that it is NP-hard. Section 3 provides detail of the FindOverlayTree algorithm with the SRPF heuristic. Section 4 presents the simulation results and discussion. Section 5 discusses other ALM algorithms and protocols that are related to our work. Finally, we present our conclusions in Section 6.

2 Problem Formulation

This section we describe the network model and state our solution objectives formally.

The physical network consists of routers connected by links. The end hosts are connected to this network at different points through access links.

The ALM overlay network is the network induced by the host nodes on this physical topology. It can be modeled as a complete undirected graph G = (V,E) , where V is the set of vertices and E=V×V is the set of edges. The delay of edge (u,v) in G represents the unicast path delay from node u to node v in the physical topology, which is denoted by $d(u,v)\in R^+$. The data delivery path will be a directed tree of G rooted at the source node, with the edges directed away from the root. Delay(s,v) represent the OPD from s to v along the delivery tree.

Leaving user's donating inclination out of account, only consider the real-time requirement of live streaming, the host is degree-bounded since the resources involved in continuous media data processing are constrained. Especially, we don't consider the cooperating scheme that multi-nodes serve one node [27][28]. Then each node only receives a stream from its father on the tree. Therefore we assume $f_{max}(v)$ only denotes the maximal out degree of node v. In the following paragraphs, the degree bound only means the out degree bound for simplicity.

Then the optimization problem can be defined as follows:

Definition 1: *Delay- and degree-bounded maximum sum of nodes multicast tree (MSNMT) problem.*

Given an undirected complete graph G=(V,E), a degree bound weight $f_{max}(v) \in Z^+$ for each vertex $v \in V$; a delay weight $d(e) \in R^+$ for each edge $e \in E$; a OPD bound Δ. Find a multicast tree T in G such that the total sum of nodes on T is maximized, where for each $v \in T$, $Delay(s,v) < \Delta$, $f(v) \leq f_{max}(v)$.

Now we prove MSNMT problem is NP-hard.

Theorem 1: MSNMT problem is NP-hard.

Proof: Clearly, the problem is in NP, since we can verify in polynomial time if a candidate solution satisfies both delay- and degree-bounded constraints. Suppose the special case that $f_{max}(v)=1(\forall v)$, $d(u,v)=1$ ($\forall u,v \in V$), and $\Delta=|V|-1$. Then the problem is the same as the Hamiltonian Path (HP) problem. We reduce from the HP problem for the general case where $f_{max}(v)>1$. Let G'=(V',E') be the graph of a HP instance. We transform G' to G''=(V'',E'') by adding $k=f_{max}(v)-1$ vertices $u_1,\ldots,u_k$ for each $v \in V$. We join each of these new vertices u_i to v with an edge length of 0; All other of edges from u_i have length $\Delta+1$, so G'' is still a complete graph. Now the MSNMT instance in G'' has a spanning tree of delay bound Δ if and only if the NP instance in G' has a path joining all the vertices of length V.

We investigate MSNMT problem for the first time. However several studies concentrate on the minimum maximum-delay multicast tree problem [6]-[8]. The MMDMT problem is defined as follows:

Definition 2: *Degree-bounded minimum maximum delay multicast tree (MMDMT) problem.*

Given an undirected complete graph G=(V,E), an degree bound weight $f_{max}(v) \in Z^+$ for each vertex $v \in T$; a delay weight $d(e) \in R^+$ for each edge $e \in E$. Find a multicast tree T including all vertexes in G such that the maximum OPD, Delay(s,v), is minimized, where for each $v \in T$, $f(v) \leq f_{max}(v)$.

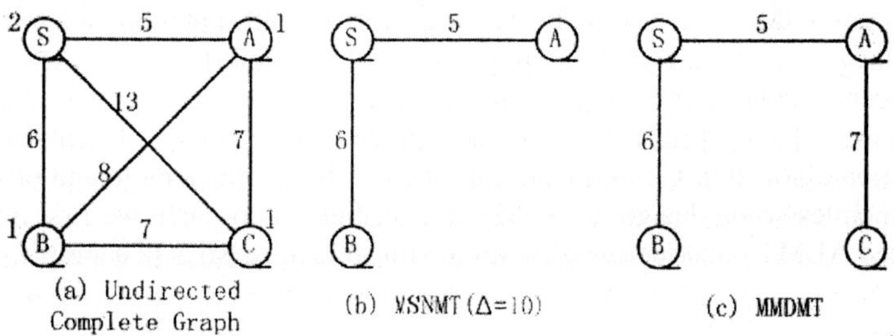

Fig. 1. Constructing ALMT on undirected complete graph of four nodes

We observe that what does the user more care about is the delay to the source node in live streaming application. Giving user a delay bound is more practical in mental satisfaction than tell him what the minimum maximum-delay is. Nevertheless what does the system designer more care about is how many users' request would be satisfied under such a delay bound. That is why we appreciate investigating MSNMT problem more than MMDMT problem.

Figure 1 illustrates the constructed MSNMT and MMDMT on an undirected complete graph of four nodes. S is the source node. The degree bound $f_{max}(v)$ of node v and the delay d(u,v) of edge (u,v) are signed beside it respectively. If the delay bound is 10, then node D is excluded from the MSNMT. The minimum maximum-delay of MMDMT is 12. And now we prove that the two problems are equal under a condition.

Theorem 2: The MSNMT problem is equal to the MMDMT problem when Δ is equal to the minimum maximum-delay.

Proof: (MSNMT<=MMDMT) Suppose in graph G, T is the degree-constrained minimum maximum delay multicast tree, where $Delay_{max}$ = max(Delay(s,v)), $v \in V$. For any delay bound $\Delta = Delay_{max} - \varepsilon$, $\varepsilon \in R^+$, it is impossible to construct a tree while contain all of the nodes in V. When Δ is increased to $Delay_{max}$ just in time, the maximum sum of nodes for MSNMT problem is actually equal to the sum of nodes in graph G at this time, where is |V|.

(MSNMT=>MMDMT) Suppose constructing MSNMT in graph G, the maximum sum of nodes is neither more nor less than |V| when the delay bound is Δ, and for any $\Delta' = \Delta - \varepsilon$, $\varepsilon \in R^+$, the maximum sum of nodes is less than |V| . Consider the MMDMT problem on the same graph G. The minimum maximum-delay must be less than or equal to Δ. And also it must be more than Δ-ε, or else the maximum sum of nodes will be less than |V|. Therefore the minimum maximum-delay is equal to Δ.

Studies to date in the area of ALM have been mostly investigated in nature. There are two main constructing approaches [13], namely centralized and distributed. Many works investigate in distributed approach [5],[6],[9],[10],[14],[16]-[20],[22],[24],[26]. However, the constructed ALMT by many protocols are not optimal where overlay delay along the tree is rather bearable only for the upper layer nodes of the tree. They are incapable of finding some simple and efficient heuristics when father nodes choose topology-optimal son nodes and vice versa. Well matching accuracy between the overlay topology and underlay physical topology would make the tree more scalable. A centralized approach refers to adopt a central server to answer for overlay construction [3],[4],[7],[25]. The main advantage is the great simplification of the tree construction algorithm. Consequently, in order to find some simple and efficient heuristic principles when design an ALMT in distributed approach, we first implement a centralized ALMT construction algorithm with some heuristics in a simple style.

3 Problem Solution

In this section, we focus on the implement of FindOverlayTree with SRPF heuristic for the MSNMT problem.

3.1 FindOverlayTree Algorithm

We now describe FindOverlayTree(G,s,Δ,f_{max}) in its attempt to build a ALMT from source node s , where the delay bound is Δ and degree bound is f_{max} for each node. Based on host-level network topology graph, we first run the well-known Floyd-Warshall algorithm to compute shortest paths between all-pair of vertices so as to acquire a complete undirected graph, G=(V,E). Then we run FindOverlayTree.

```
Algorithm FindOverlayTree(G,s,Δ,f_max)
foreach v∈V
   father[v]=null
   delay[v]=0
   LMW[v]=null
Get LMW[s] from GetWtMap(s, Δ)
T = (S_Full={},S_Work={s},S_Free=V-{s})
While |S_Full|+|S_Work|<|V|
   Let u∈S_Work be a node with global maximal weight
        from LMW,let v∈S_Free be the corresponding node
   if u=NULL then break;
   father[v]=u
   delay[v]=delay[u]+d[u,v]
   Get LMW[v] from GetWtMap(v, Δ)
   if LMW[v] = null
   then S_Full = S_Full ∪ {v}
   else S_Work = S_Work ∪ {v}
   degree[u] = degree[u]+1
   If degree[u] > f_max then
        remove u from S_Work to S_Full
   foreach w∈S_Work
        Update LMW[w] to nodes only in S_Free
```

During execution, the algorithm maintains three sets of nodes:

- S_{Full} is the set of nodes that have been attached to the tree but would no longer accept additional children because of degree constraint or delay constraint. Initially, $S_{Full}=\{\Phi\}$.
- S_{Work} is the set of nodes that have been attached to the tree and satisfy the delay- and degree-constraint. Initially, $S_{Work}=\{s\}$.
- S_{Free} is the set of nodes to be attached. Initially, $S_{Free}=V-\{s\}$.

Through the duration of the running of the algorithm, S_{Full}, S_{Work}, S_{Free} remain mutually exclusive sets with $S_{Full} \cup S_{Work} \cup S_{Free} = V$.

Initially, for s, we adopt ComputerWeightMap procedure to compute its weight array from it to all other nodes in S_{Free}, where the weight is calculated by the following heuristics. And also hold the local maximal weight in LMW array and its corresponding node.

At each cycle, a sender from S_{Work} and a receiver from S_{Free} are chosen. For each node $n \in S_{Work}$, compare the local maximal weight among all these nodes, and select node u that holds the global maximal weight as the node ready to send. At the same time, select corresponding node v in S_{Free} as the node ready to receive.

Finally, for each the node w in S_{Work} except v, recomputes its local maximal weight because new node has been attached to the tree, and S_{Free} set become smaller.

```
PROCEDURE GetWtMap (u, Δ)
LMN = null
LMW[u] = NULL
foreach v∈SFree
    if Delay[u]+d[u,v]> Δ
        WeightMap[u,v]=null
        continue
    WeightMap[u,v] = Heuristic
    if(WeightMap[u,v]>LMW[u])
        LMW[u]=WeightMap[u,v]
        LMN=v
```

In the GetWtMap procedure, we try to get weight map for u. If the sum of the OPD from s to u and from u to v exceeds the delay bound, then WeightMap[u,v] is set to null. Then compute the heuristic weight from u to v, where v is only in S_{Free}. If the weight is greater than LMW[u], record it and register the node holding it in LWN. If for each node v in S_{Free}, WeightMap[u,v] is null, then LMW[u] is null.

The complexity analysis for this algorithm is straightforward. The all pairs shortest path computation requires $O(n^3)$. Each iteration require O(n) time to find a father node in S_{Work} who hold the global maximal weight, O(n) time to computer weight array for the corresponding son node, and $O(n^2)$ time to update the local maximal weight for nodes in S_{Work}. The total running time of the algorithm is $O(n^3)$.

3.2 Heuristic

We draw two observations from many theoretical and experimental results in previous works [3]-[8].It is beneficial to have nodes with high degree closer to the root of the tree. However, it is also beneficial to keep overlay delay of nodes near the root small since edges near the root affect a larger fraction of receivers than do their descendants. A dilemma arises when there are a class of nodes with high degree connected to edges with large delay and another class of nodes with low degree connected to edges with small delay. We now present the SRPF heuristic to balance between these two classes of nodes.

From the definition of MSNMT, we suppose that the node which may bring maximal sum of offspring nodes should be first selected as father node. Hence we suggest that the reproduce power of v is defined as

$$H(u,v)=\begin{cases}\dfrac{f(v)^{l(u,v)}-1}{f(v)-1} & f(v)>1\\ l(u,v) & f(v)=1\end{cases}\qquad l(v)=\left\lfloor\frac{\Delta-Delay(s,u)}{d(u,v)}\right\rfloor \tag{1}$$

As we know, the OPD from s to any node should not exceed Δ. If v hopes to attach to the tree via u, then the remaining time is Δ-Delay(s,u). Since the reproduce power of any offspring node of v should not exceed that of itself, we suppose that the delay of any offspring node to its father is smaller than that of v and the degree bound of it is lower than that of v. Therefore the possible sum of layers below v is no more than l(v). Obviously, the total offspring sum of nodes below v is supposed to be no more than H(u,v).

Suppose the total sum of nodes N=|V|. Let N_{SRPF}, N^* denote the maximum sum of nodes constructed by SRPF heuristic and an optimal solution, respectively.

Theorem 3: If the total degree distribution satisfies power law relationship [32], the source node has the maximum degree, the maximum delay between any node pair is d_{max}, ML=$\lfloor \Delta / d_{max} \rfloor > 1$, then $N_{SRPF} > \varepsilon N^*$, where

$$\varepsilon = \begin{cases} f(\Delta, N) & f(\Delta, N) < 1 \\ 1 & f(\Delta, N) \geq 1 \end{cases} \tag{2}$$
$$f(\Delta, N) = (((ML-1)^{\Re+1} - 1)/(N^{\Re+1}(\Re+1)) - (ML)/N)$$

Proof: The total degree distribution satisfies power law relationship, $f_{max}(v) = r_v^{\Re} / N^{\Re}$, where $\Re$ is the rank exponent and is almost equal to -0.8 in the three inter-domain instances as we see in [32].So the total out degrees of the front K nodes are

$$T(K) = \sum_{r_v=1}^{K} (r_v^{\Re} / N^{\Re} - 1) > \int_1^K x^{\Re} dx / N^{\Re} - K > (K^{\Re+1} - 1)/(N^{\Re}(\Re+1)) - K \tag{3}$$

Suppose the DDF (Degree Depth-First) tree constructing algorithm is as follows: Firstly, choose the source node as the root node. Secondly, choose node in S_{Free} that has the maximum out degree to be the son of the last chosen node in turn, until reach ML level. Thirdly, fill the residual out degree in $ALMT_{DDF}$ with the nodes in S_{Free}. Therefore, the total sum of nodes in $ALMT_{DDF}$ are

$$N_{DDF} = \begin{cases} T(ML-1)+1 & T(ML-1)+1 < N \\ N & T(ML-1)+1 \geq N \end{cases} \tag{4}$$

Obviously, FindOverlayTree algorithm is better than DDF. Then

$$N_{SRPF} > N_{DDF}(N^* / N) > \begin{cases} f(\Delta, N) N^* & f(\Delta, N) < 1 \\ 1 N^* & f(\Delta, N) \geq 1 \end{cases}, \text{ where} \tag{5}$$
$$f(\Delta, N) = (((ML-1)^{\Re+1} - 1)/(N^{\Re+1}(\Re+1)) - (ML)/N).$$

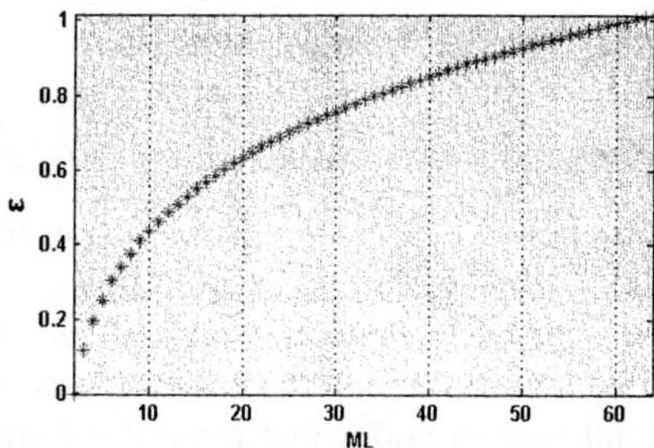

Fig. 2. The relationship between ε and ML

Figure 2 show that the relationship between ε and ML when N=10000, $\Re$ =-0.8. Along with the increasing of ML, ε is approaching toward 1. When ML>64, ε=1, because the out degree of the front ML nodes are greater than ML.

4 A Simulation Study

4.1 Experiment Setup

In this section we analyze the performance of the proposed algorithm. We carried out a simulation- based study. Besides the maximal sum of nodes metric, we also consider stretch and stress [19]. An ALM scheme should have small stretch and stress to keep the end-to-end delay small and the network bandwidth efficiently utilized.

Over the past few years a better method has been devised independently by the authors for generating graphs that reflect the hierarchical domain structure and locality that is present in the Internet [29]. Three levels of router-level hierarchy are modeled corresponding to transit domains, stub domains and LANs attached to stub nodes, where LANs are modeled as star topologies with a router node at the center of the star and the host nodes each connected to the center router.

In order to the run the proposed algorithm under different topology size, we used the GT-ITM Generator to create 10,100,1000-nodes transit-stub graph as router-level network topology [30]. Then use BRITE proposed Top-Down hierarchical topologies model to create LAN-level network topology [31]. Then modify BRITE to create host-level network topology, where LANs are modeled as star topology and each router connect to random number of host node in between 1 and 100. We assure that this kind of generation method would truly reflect the Internet topology.

4.2 Other Heuristics

In order to compare the performance of SRPF to other related research works objectively, we now present HODF, LRTF, LRF heuristics. HODF heuristic is modified from FNF heuristic [11][12]. At each step, firstly, select node u in S_{Work} for the time it receives the stream is the earliest possible time. Then select node v in S_{Free} whose degree is highest. LRTF heuristic is proposed by E.Brosh [7] ,where LRF is proposed by Naceur [3].

4.3 Performance Evaluation

Figure 3 and figure 4 plot the performance of the ALMT constructed by the four heuristics under several metrics. Figure 2 plot the case that there are hundreds of LANs, and in each LAN there are almost 10 requests. Figure 3 plot the case that there are tens of LANs, and in each LAN there are almost 100 requests. In each sub-figure, the value of the x-axis is the total sum of nodes that request the stream. The value of the y-axis is the performance metrics such as satisfied sum of nodes, expectation of stretch, expectation of stress. Each point plotted is the average of 25 runs.

We see that whether the expectation of stretch, or the satisfied node number under the two cases, the performance of our proposed SRPF heuristic is optimal. Although

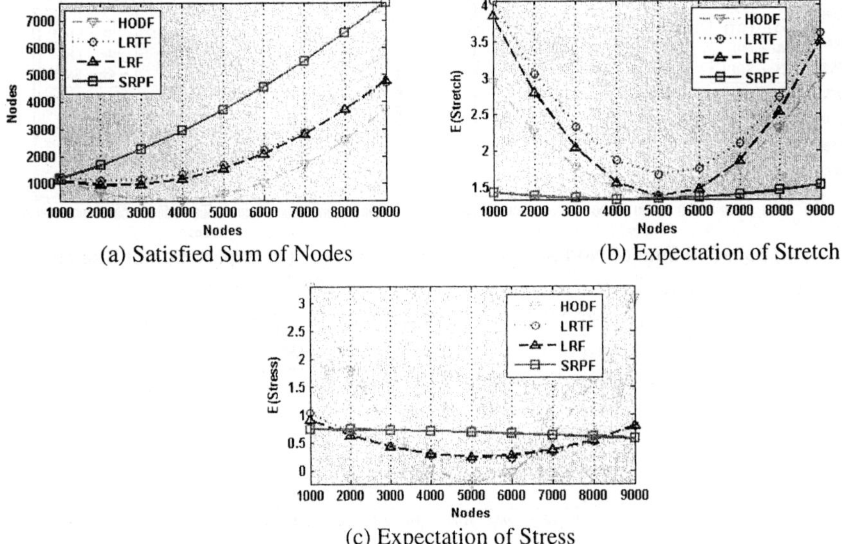

(a) Satisfied Sum of Nodes

(b) Expectation of Stretch

(c) Expectation of Stress

Fig. 3. Δ=30,10 requests/LAN

the performance of SRPF is not optimal under the expectation of stress metric, the curve of it is smoother than other heuristics, we should know that SRPF satisfies much more requests than the other three, so it may bring more stress on the under network.

5 Related Works

As we proved in section II, the MSNMT problem is equal to the MMDMT under a condition. MeshTree [6], OMNI [8] concentrate on MMDMT problem. The overlay built of MeshTree is in the form of a degree-bounded mesh which is based on two main structures: i.) a backbone tree; and ii.) the delivery tree. Extra links are added on top of the backbone tree to form the mesh. The backbone tree is used in the optimization process while the delivery tree is derived from the mesh using a path-vector routing protocol. OMNI allows a multicast service provider to deploy a large number of MSNs without explicit concern about optimal placement. Once the capacity constraints of the MSNs are specified, OMNI organizes then into an overlay topology. OMNI only concerns MMDMT problem on the MSNs' overlay topology. Whatsoever they are distributed construction protocols, (strictly speaking, OMNI is a hybrid protocol,) and our proposed approach is centralized.

Algorithm Approx-MDM [7] is a multicast algorithm for the optimal multicast tree problem (MDM). MDM is almost the same as MMDMT, except the definition of the delay. The delay is composed of two elements: (a) Communication delay –which represents the delay of the unicast path. (b) Processing delay –which represents the delay of processing a message at the sender host. Therefore the MDM problem is even harder than MMDMT problem.

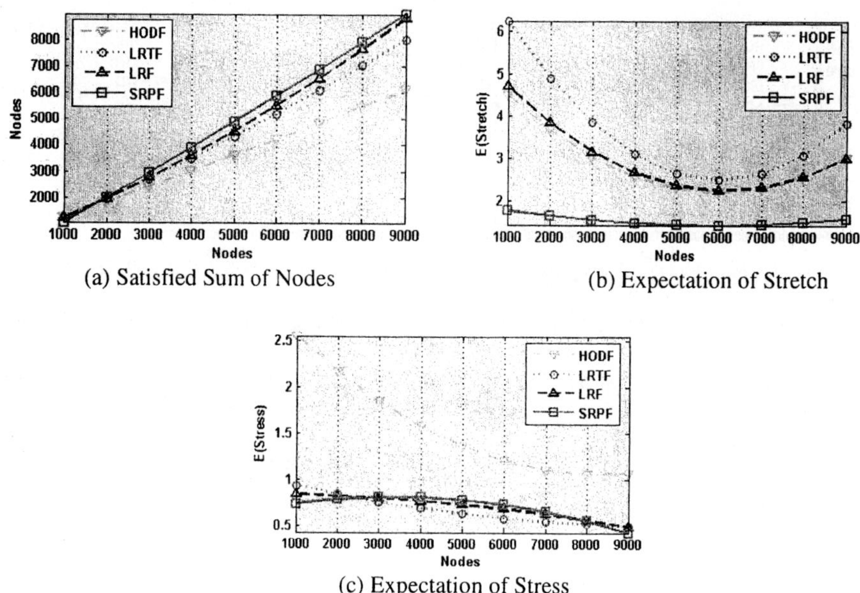

(a) Satisfied Sum of Nodes

(b) Expectation of Stretch

(c) Expectation of Stress

Fig. 4. Δ=30,100 requests/LAN

S.Y.Shi [4] concentrates her study on minimum diameter, degree-bounded spanning tree (MDDBST) problem. It is different from MMDMT problem since the diameter means the distance between any two nodes in N, whereas maximum delay means the distance between root s and any node in N, namely radius. And also it is NP-hard. If the ratio of edge weights is bounded by $\varepsilon \in Z^+$, and the degree constraints satisfy $2<d_{min}<d<d_{max}$ for a constant $d<|V|-1$, then the heuristic algorithm proposed has $\lambda_{Greedy}<O(k)\lambda^*$, $k = 2\varepsilon \log_{d_{min}} d_{max}$,where λ_{Greedy} and λ^* denote the tree diameter constructed by the greedy heuristic algorithm and an optimal solution, respectively.

The algorithm FindMinCost proposed by Naceur [3] finds the degree- and delay-bounded minimum proxy cost legally connected tree in time $n\log^2 n$ under the fully connected, uniform edge overlays condition, where n is the total number of nodes include all host and proxy. Uniform edge means the end-to-end delay between all pairs of nodes is uniform. Obviously it is a hybrid approach, and also we concentrate on the assumption that edge is non-uniform.

6 Conclusion Remark

In this paper, we have taken a systematic approach for designing an overlay network for ALM. We first proved that the MSNMT problem is equal to the MMDMT under a condition, and proved MSNMT problem is NP-hard. Then propose FindOverlayTree algorithm and several heuristics, namely HODF, LRTF, LRF, SRPF. Through simulation, we evaluated the performance of the algorithm and heuristics.

As part of future work, we would apply our research to design a distributed protocol, so as to make it more efficient in building optimal overlay.

References

1. Steinmetz, R. and Nahrstedt, K.: Multimedia: Computing, Communications and Applications," Prentice Hall, Inc 1995
2. Cormen, T. H., Leiserson, C. E. and Rivest, R. L.: Introduction to Algorithms,MIT Press, 1997
3. Malouch, N.M., Liu, Z. , Rubenstein, D. and Sahu, S.: A Graph Theoretic Approach to Bounding Delay in Proxy-Assisted, End-System Multicast. in Proceedings of the Tenth International Workshop on Quality of Service (IWQoS'02)
4. Shi, S.Y. , Turner, J.S. and Waldvogel, M.: Dimensioning Server Access Bandwidth and Multicast Routing in Overlay Networks. in the 11th International Workshop on Network and Operating Systems Support for Digital Audio and Video(NOSSDAV'01),June 25-27,2001
5. Riabov, A., Liu, Z. and Zhang, L.: Overlay Multicast Trees of Minimal Delay. in Proceeding of the 24th International Conference on Distributed Computing Systems(ICDCS'04)
6. Tan, S.W., Waters, G. and Crawford, J.: MeshTree: A delay-optimised Overlay Multicast Tree Building Protocol. Submitted to proceeding of IEEE INFOCOM'05
7. Brosh, E. and Shavitt, Y.: Approximation and Heuristic Algorithms for Minimum Delay Application-Layer Multicast Trees. in Proceeding of IEEE INFOCOM'04
8. 8. Banejee, S., Kommareddy, C., Kar, K., Bhattacharjee, B. and Khuller, S.: Construction of an Efficient Overlay Multicast Infrastructure for Real-time Application. in Proceeding of IEEE INFOCOM'03
9. Cui, Y., Xue, Y. and Nahrstedt, K.: Max-Min Overlay Multicast: Rate Allocation and Tree Construction. in Proceeding of IWQoS2004
10. Yang, M. and Fei, Z.: A Proactive Approach to Reconstructing Overlay Multicast Trees. in Proceeding of INFOCOM'04
11. Bhat, P.B., Raghavendra, C.S. and Prasanna, V.K.: Efficient Collective Communication in Distributed Heterogeneous Systems
12. Banikazemi, M., Moorthy, V. and Panda, D.K.: Efficient collective communication on heterogeneous networks of workstations. In Proc.Intl.Conf.Parallel Processing,pages 460-467,1998
13. Yeo, C.K., Lee, B.S. and Er, M.H.: A survey of application level multicast techniques. ELSEVIER Computer Communication 27(2004) 1547-1568
14. Castro, M., Druschel, P., Kermarrec, A.M. and Rowstron, A.. SCRIBE:A large-scale and decentralized application-level multicast infrastructure. JSAC,vol.20,NO.8,OCTOBER 2002
15. Castro, M., Druschel, P. Kermarrec, A.M., Nadi, A., Rowstron, A.: and .Singh,.A Split-Stream:High-Bandwidth Multicast in Cooperative Environments. in Proceeding of SOSP'03, OCTOBER 19-22
16. Ratnasamy, S., Handley, M., Karp, R. and Shenkar, S.: Application-level multicast using content addressable networks. in Proceeding of the Third International Workshop on Networked Group Communication(NGC), 2001,pp.14-29

17. Chu, Y.H., Rao, S.G, Seshan, S., Zhang, H.: A Case for End System Multicast. SIGMETRICS'00, June 2000
18. Banerjee, S., Bhattacharjee, B., Kommareddy, C.: Scalable Application Layer Multicast.SIGCOMM'02 August 19-23,2002
19. Tran, D.A., Hua, K.A., Do, T.T.: Peer-to-Peer Streaming Using A Novel Hierarchical Clustering Approach. ACM-MM'02
20. Jannotti, J., Gifford, D.K. and Johnson, K.L.: Overcast:Reliable Multicasting with an overlay Network. in Proceeding of OSDI'00,October(2000) 197-212
21. Francis, P.: Yoid:Extending the Internet Multicast Architecture.http://www.icir.org/yoid/ March 2001
22. Kim, M.S., Lam, S.S. and Lee, D.Y.: Optimal Distribution Tree for Internet Streaming Media. ICDCS'03
23. .Sasabe, M, Wakamiya, N., Murata, M., Miyahara, H.: Scalable and Continuous Media Streaming on Peer-to-Peer Networks.Osaka University.P2P'03
24. Liebeherr, L., Nahas, M. and Si, W.: Application-layer multicast with Delaunay triangulations. IEEE J.Select. Areas Communication. 20(8)(2002)
25. Pendarakis, D., Shi, S., Verma, D. and Waldvogel, M.: ALMI: an Application Level Multicast Infrastructure. in Proceeding of the Third Usenix Symposium on Internet Technologies and Systems(USITS),March 2001
26. Chawathe, Y.D.: Scattercast:an architecture for Internet broadcast distribution as an infrastructure service. PhD thesis, Stanford University, September 2000
27. Hefeeda, M., Habib, A., Xu, D., Bhargava, B., Botev, B.: CollectCast: A Peer-to-Peer Service for Media Streaming. Submitted to ACM/Springer Multimedia Systems Journal, October 2003
28. Hefeeda, M., Habib, A., Botev,B., Xu, D., Bhargava, B.: PROMISE: Peer-to-Peer Media Streaming Using CollectCast. In Proc.of ACM Multimedia 2003, pages 45--54, November 2003
29. Calvert, K.L., Doar, M.B., Zegura, E.W.: Modeling Internet Topology. IEEE Communications Magazine 1997
30. Calvert, K. and Zegura, E.: Gt internetwork topology models(gt-itm). http://www.cc.gatech.edu/fac/Ellen.Zegura/graphs.html, 1997
31. BRITE project. http://www.cs.bu.edu/brite/
32. Faloutsos, M., Faloutsos, P. and Faloutsos, C.: On Power-Law Relationships of the Internet Topology. In SIGCOMM'99 Cambridge, MA, USA

The Batch Patching Method Using Dynamic Cache of Proxy Cache for Streaming Media

Zhiwen Xu, Xiaoxin Guo, Xiangjiu Che, Zhengxuan Wang, and Yunjie Pang

Open Symbol Computation and Knowledge Engineering Laboratory of State Education Department, Jilin University,
Changchun City, 130012, Jilin Province, China
xuzhiwen@public.cc.jl.cn

Abstract. The proxy cache for streaming media is the important method to economize the resources of the Internet. The cache policies influence the effect for proxy cache. In this paper, based on the client's request rate, cached the video based on segmentation, we proposed that the method for batch, patch and batch patching using dynamic cache. The policies of batch and batch patching using dynamic cache based on segmentation enlarge the width of the batch and patching. It combines dynamic cache based on segmentation with the excellence of patching. Presented that allocation relation between the segmented cache and dynamic cache in the batch and patching, and assured that batch patching using dynamic cache of proxy for streaming media based on segmentation is optimal.

1 Introduction

Streaming media, simply speaking, is dynamic media information that can be viewed while being downloaded by clients, transmitted through Internet. With the emergence of the Internet as a pervasive communication medium, and a mature digital video technology, streaming media is applied in more and more fields, such as distance education, VoD, live video broadcast, corporate broadcast, video conference and so on. However, video clips are usually so large that the transmission of streaming media consumes a great amount of Internet resource, prolongs startup latency and threats the playback continuity. Till now, one of the solutions is to set up one or several proxy cache between client cloud and origin streaming media server. It's indirectly from the proxy, instead of directly from the server, that clients receive pertinent data. The proxy cache takes advantage of certain cache policies. Thus redundant transmission on Internet decreases while transmission efficiency increases.

2 Related Work

2.1 Prefix Cache

The theoretical and experimental study of streaming media is still in the developing period. In order to solve such problems as startup latency and unsteady

H. Zhuge and G.C. Fox (Eds.): GCC 2005, LNCS 3795, pp. 1143–1154, 2005.

transmission, Sen. S et al proposed prefix cache [1,4], which means the early part of media is cached in the proxy during the process of transmission. That is, when a client request is issued, the proxy cache immediately transmits the video prefix to the client and contacts the server for the suffix that is transmitted only after the prefix is exhausted, prefix cache presents an effective solution to the startup latency. The literatures [3,4,5,6] introduce organization and server connection schemes of proxy caching based on prefix cache and the schedules of batch and patch and so on.

2.2 Cache Based on Segmentation

According to the client request rate, the proxy caches different video data. The higher the requests' rate is, the longer the proxy cache is. Wu. Kun-Lun et al explore the segmentation-based proxy cache method [2], taking into consideration both the importance of the early part of most of media and the necessity of segmentation of video objects, the video objects received by the proxy, are segmented on the volume basis, according to the request rate. The size of segmentation is the increasing index from the initial segmentation. Simply, it goes like this, the size of segment j consists of 2^{j-1} chunks which are respectively marked with 2^{j-1}, $2^{j-1}+1,\cdots,2^{j-1}$ $(j \in 1,2,\cdots,M)$.

2.3 The Cache Policy of Batch Patching

The batch patching algorithm is an effective policy based on prefix cache. Its purpose is to minimize the transmission between the server and the proxy, in order to reduce Internet loads. The cache scheme of batch patching enables clients to acquire video clips via proxy, instead of directly from the server, i.e. all the video clips have to be cached in the proxy, via which they are then transmitted to clients. Batch patching algorithm is a more effective transmission method among the optimal cache schemes. Each batch of requests within every b units of time is served one or two channels. All the data is transmitted to the proxy from the server and then is transmitted to the client cloud. A regular channel delivers the full video from start to finish, while a patching channel delivers only the missing part of the video from the start until the point at which the clients join the regular channel. The client receives both the patch and the ongoing stream and buffers the latter while playing back the former. Once the patch is used the client of the buffered regular channel. On special occasion, the proxy can reduce transmission cost by using of cache for certain special clients. The literatures[7, 8, 9]give a introduction to the research in such areas as the dynamic management and organization of proxy cache.

3 The Dynamic Cache Method for The Batch Patching

The segmentation-based and prefix cache are both pre-fetching cache methods. This paper puts forward a high efficient dynamic cache algorithm, which carries out real time dynamic cache using at the batch patching algorithm for the proxy cache and makes the dynamic cache transmitted and proxy cached by the server, deal with the requests of more than one clients within a relatively short period of time. Therefore, the web resources used by patching channel and regular channel and release the network burden of the server.

3.1 The Dynamic Cache for Batch Patching Based on Prefix

We take the case of single video for example, the same with the case of multiple videos. Proxy cache is set up between the server and clients. The proxy cache divides the time axis into intervals of duration of b units of time and caches the first b units of time in advance. That is, the proxy permanently caches video of b units of time that is called prefix. When the first request arrives at the proxy, the proxy immediately starts regular channel to support the video transmission. At the same time, the proxy creates a patching window of w units of time (W=N b. N is multiple of b), during which a patching is transmitted through patching channel. At each b-length interval boundary, the proxy commences service of each batch and links it to the multicast of the regular channel.

The batch patching scheme is illustrated in Fig1. Assume a request arrives at the proxy at time $t_1 \in [t_{k-1}, t_k]$, the proxy cache immediately starts to stream the cached video of b units of time to clients. Suppose the most recent regular channel was started at time t_s. With $t_s < t_1$, is an integral number of b units of time.

Case 1: if t_k is such that $t_k < t_s + \mathrm{W}$, i.e. The request is within the patching window of W window of time. At time t_k, the proxy cache joins the regular channel and begins streaming the batch patching data to the clients who, at the same time, plays back the prefix of b units of time. At this time, the proxy requests to cache data of duration $t_k - t_s$ for future use.

Case 2: if $t_k \geq t_s$+W, i.e. The request is after the patching window of w units of time. At this moment, content in the patching window has been exhausted, so a new channel of duration T-b (T is the length of single video) is started by server at time t_k. The policy involved here is confined to prefix cache.

3.2 The Dynamic Cache for Batch Based on Segmentation

Batch ensures multiple requests within certain interval to be batch successfully. During the transmission, the smaller the occupancy size of proxy cache is, the larger the length of batch is, and the more efficient the proxy cache is. Those requests accumulated within b units of time are only batch once. In the context of segmentation-based proxy cache, we using dynamic cache to let the length of segmentation-based proxy cache length equals U_i; Thus we can let the maximum batch width be U_i+b, which is right the proxy cache duration. Assume a client issues a request for a video, if the request arrival time is within duration U_i+b, the request is satisfied by prefix cache and segmentation cache; if the arrival time is after duration U_i+b, the request is met directly by regular channel. The duration of regular channel is T-U_i-b and it is available from the point of time

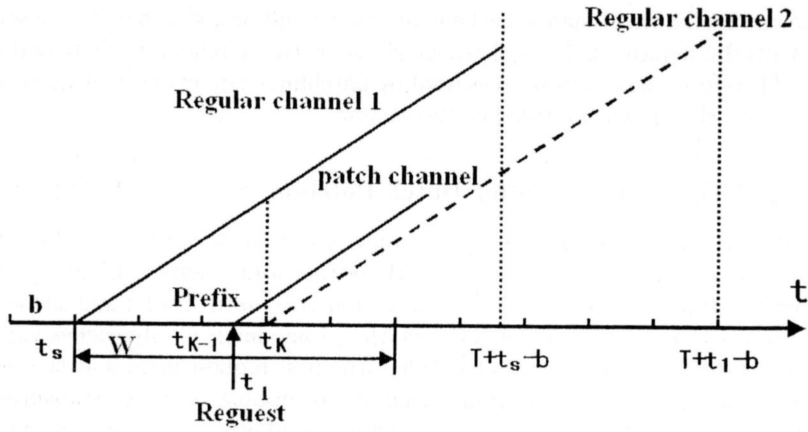

Fig. 1. The process of dynamic cache

U_i+b until the transmission end. Each batch only occupies regular channel of duration T-U_i-b. All the streaming data in batch will be linked to the regular channel, which is buffered by clients for a period of time, which is less than U_i+b. The batch width is based on the request rate and it affects the transmission efficiency, with its maximum being U_i+b. The batch effectively upgrades the width b of batch cache for prefix into the width U_i+b of segmentation-based cache, and it also ensures the batch-efficient transmission with duration of U_i+b.

3.3 The Dynamic Cache for Patching Based on Segmentation

In the prefix cache scheme, the patching window is length W, the video duration is T and p is the possibility of batch.$p = p(0) = e^{-\lambda}$,the length W [6] of the patching window processed in the server end, is given by.

$$W = \frac{-b + \sqrt{pb^2 + 2(1-p)bT}}{b(1-p)} \tag{1}$$

In the server, a client issues a request right within W length time after the regular channel. The server transmits the early part of data to him via patching channel while joining the rest of data to the regular channel. The employment of proxy cache in the video transmission can ensure a dynamic storing of patching window as well as achievement of patching transmission. Specifically, assume a request arrives at time t_k (as Fig1.), if $t_k < t_s$+W, that is the request arrives within the patching window, the request is to be patch; requests before time t_k are transmitted via patching channel while those after t_k apply to the regular channel. In fact, the time t_k request consumes resource by joining the regular channel.

In the segmentation-based patching, the length of segmentation-based cache is determined by the request rate. Segmentation-based cache can handle contents of the patching channel, if the time length of segmentation-based cache is longer than the patching window W, it handles all the patching contents; if the former is shorter than the latter, the less part is handled by the patching window. To be more concrete, if the length of segmentation-based cache $U_i + b > W$, the proxy doesn't start the patching window, because the segmentation-based cache transmits the patching data; if the former length $U_i + b < W$, the proxy patching data of length W-U_i-b. If $t_k \geq t_s + W$, that is the request arrives after the length W, the proxy, instead of starting the patching channel, has to start a new regular channel of duration T- U_i -b (T is length of video). The starting time is the time point U_i+b right after the request. Thus it ensures the temporal agreement between patching and prefix cache, In this case, the segmentation-based cache portion doesn't need to be supported by the server. At this moment, though, the previous regular stream has finished just because the data in the patching channel has been exhausted, this new started channel repeats transmitting the whole regular channel.

3.4 The Dynamic Cache for Batch Patching Based on Segmentation

Batch patching based on prefix is a more effective cache policy. Whose working process can be generalized as requests within b units of time are batched while those within the patching window are patched. The simultaneous employment of batch and patching is batch patching. So it's evident that segmentation-based batch patching is the simultaneous use of segmentation-based batch and segmentation-based patching. To be concrete, it means a process during which requests are firstly analyzed, then segmentation-based batch and finally segmentation-based patching using dynamic cache. The segmentation-based batch width is U_i+b, within which all the requests are transmitted by the proxy, while the server satisfies the first request, which applies to the server the regular channel, lasting from the point U_i+b of video till the video finish, with its length being T-U_i-b. In the segmentation-based batch, the video cached within the period U_i+b is transmitted by using dynamic cache of the proxy cache, and the regular stream within this period is also cached. Though segmentation-based batch saves all the resources within duration U_i+b, it always occupies this period of cache.

W_i is the length of patching window (as Fig.2). The proxy starts patching. Assume a request arrives at time t_1 if $t_1 - t_s < W_i$, a regular channel is started. In fact, the increase of the patching window W_i of the proxy cache can also economize both server and network resource, by saving, to be specific, the resource of the regular channel. The patching channel is employed only within time W_i after the regular channel. Compared with segmentation-based cache, it saves less resource and occupies less cache.

As it is known, the proxy cache capability is limited, so optimal cache allocation is much concerned. Cache allocation is determined by the request rate and this allocation actually the total of segmentation-based cache and patching

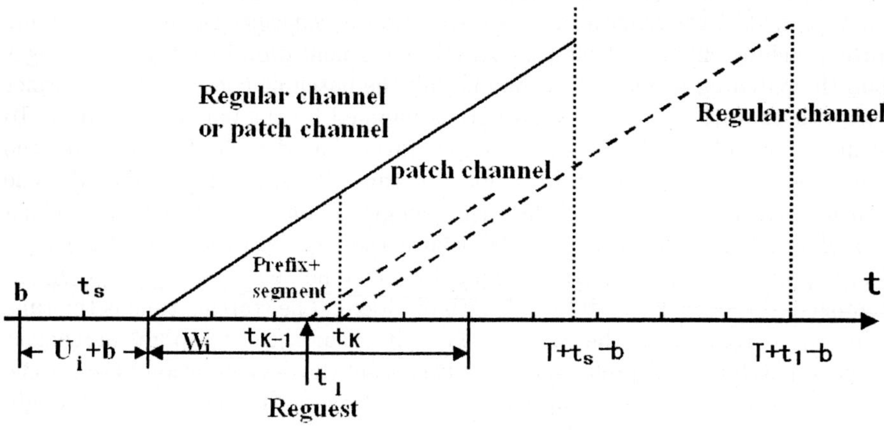

Fig. 2. The process of dynamic cache

using dynamic cache. How to balance and perfect the allocation relation directly affects the efficiency of segmentation-based batch patching.

In segmentation-based cache, the average request interval is T/λ_i and the average interval of regular channel is $U_i + W_i + T/\lambda_i$; if the patching using dynamic cache isn't started, only the segmentation-based cache with its length being W_s, is started the average interval of regular stream is then $W_s + T/\lambda_i$, if the segmentation-based cache isn't started while only the patching window of length W_p is done, the average interval is then $W_p + T/\lambda_i$. The segmentation-based batch patching using dynamic cache saves more server and backbone network resource than either the prefix batch patching or the simple segmentation-based cache. W_p is given by;

$$W_p = W_s + \frac{T}{\lambda_i} \tag{2}$$

$W_s \leq W_i + U_i \leq W_s + \frac{T}{\lambda_i}$; where $0 \leq W_i \leq W_s + \frac{T}{\lambda_i}$; $0 \leq U_i \leq W_s$;if

$$\frac{T - U_i}{W_i + U_i + \frac{T}{\lambda_i}} \geq \frac{T - W_s}{W_s + \frac{T}{\lambda_i}} i.e. U_i \leq W_s + W_i \frac{W_s - T}{T - \frac{T}{\lambda_i}} \tag{3}$$

$$and \frac{T - U_i}{W_i + U_i + \frac{T}{\lambda_i}} \geq \frac{T}{W_p + \frac{T}{\lambda_i}} is U_i \leq \frac{W_p T - W_i T}{T + W_p + \frac{T}{\lambda_i}} \tag{4}$$

More efficient than either the simple segmentation-based cache or the patching cache. From (2) and (4), we have

$$U_i \leq \frac{W_s T - W_i T - \frac{T^2}{\lambda_i^2}}{T + W_s + \frac{T}{\lambda_i}} \tag{5}$$

Assure (3) and (5), segmentation-based batch patching is better than segmentation-based cache and batch patching of prefix.In order to further discussion, let the length of every video be T, the average cache for the video i assigned by the proxy be S_i, and the total cache needed by the proxy to handle every regular channel, then equation is given by,

$$S_i(U_i + W_i + \frac{T}{\lambda_i}) = U_i(U_i + W_i + \frac{T}{\lambda_i}) + W_i^2 \tag{6}$$

What we are discussing is, in effect, that how much should U_i and W_i be respectively, so as to assure the maximum of $U_i + W_i$. From (6), we have,

$$\frac{2}{3}S_i - \frac{T}{\lambda_i} - \frac{2}{3}\sqrt{S_i^2 + \frac{3T^2}{\lambda_i^2}} \leq U_i + W_i \leq \frac{2}{3}S_i + \frac{T}{\lambda_i} - \frac{2}{3}\sqrt{S_i^2 + \frac{3T^2}{\lambda_i^2}} \tag{7}$$

When Ui+Wi reaches its maximum, and $W_i \geq 0$,then,

$$W_i = \frac{1}{3}S_i - \frac{1}{3}\sqrt{S_i^2 + \frac{3T^2}{\lambda_i^2}} + \sqrt{\frac{T^2}{3\lambda_i^2} + \frac{2TS_i}{3\lambda_i} + \frac{2T}{3\lambda_i}\sqrt{S_i^2 + \frac{3T^2}{\lambda_i^2}}} \tag{8}$$

$$U_i = \frac{1}{3}S_i - \frac{T}{\lambda_i} + \sqrt{S_i^2 - \frac{3T^2}{\lambda_i^2}} - \sqrt{\frac{T^2}{3\lambda_i^2} + \frac{2TS_i}{3\lambda_i} + \frac{2T}{3\lambda_i}\sqrt{S_i^2 + \frac{3T^2}{\lambda_i^2}}} \tag{9}$$

From (7) we can see that $U_i + W_i$. Realizes its maximum when segmentation-based batch patching using dynamic cache is ensured in the proxy cache and further (8) and (9) present the optimal answer, that is the optimal assign relation between segmentation-based batch patching U_i and dynamic cache W_i.

3.5 The Analysis of Dynamic Cache Method for Batch Patching

For simplicity, we ignore the transmission delay of network. In order to give our scheme a qualitative analysis, we first make the following summary. The streaming media is a video, whose length is T and with the request rate λ_i. The length of the prefix cache in the proxy is b, while the length of segmentation-based cache in the proxy is U_i, so the total cache length cached in the proxy is $b + U_i$. Supposing the request rate of media object m is represented by a Poison process with the parameter λ_i, namely $P = e^{-\lambda_i(U_i+b)}$ is a vacant request rate, with a duration $b + U_i$.Supposing that x_{ij-1} represents the requests, arrived within the (j-1)th batch interval.Supposing $x_{i0}, x_{i1}, \cdots, x_{iN}$ is an independent random variable sequence with popularized probability distribution. Whether the proxy need to obtain patching data at t_i through extra patching channel depends on the value of $x_{i0}, x_{i1}, \cdots, x_{iN}$ and x_i. If $x_{i0} = x_{i1} = \cdots = x_{iN} = 0$ or $x_{i0} = x_{i1} = \cdots = x_{iN} \neq 0$, then the proxy does not need to apply to the server for any patching data. If the proxy applies to the server for the patching data, whose size is η at the start window, it is obvious that η is probably any value among 0,$(b+U_i)$,2$(b+U_i)$,$\cdots$,(N-1)$(b+U_i)$. Similarly, we may use P_i to represent the probability of $\eta = k(b+U_i)$, namely, $P_k(\eta = k(b+U_i)) = P_k, k = 0, 1, 2, \cdots, N-1$. According to Poison distribution, we may make the conclusion: $P_0 = 1, P_1 = e^{-\lambda_i(U_i+b)}, P_2 = e^{-2\lambda_i(U_i+b)}, \cdots, P_{N-1} = e^{-(N-1)\lambda_i(U_i+b)}$.

According to these assumptions, we can get the request patching channel number μ of N-1.

$$\mu = \sum_{k=1}^{N-1} P_k \tag{10}$$

The batch patching channel resources saved is R.

$$R = (U_i + b \sum_{k=1}^{N-1} kP_k \tag{11}$$

We process the patching channels through dynamic cache of proxy. Under case 1 of dynamic cache algorithm, there is no need to process the patching; under case 2, the transmission of patching channel is needed and the transmission length equals the longest patching channel and all the other patching procession is substituted by dynamic cache. Then we will analyze the performance of dynamic cache algorithm from the point of view of value needed by the system to transmit streaming media. T is the length of streaming media. C_s and C_p represent respectively the value modulus transmitted from the server to the proxy cache and from the proxy cache to the client. b is the length of prefix cache. The media segmentation [b, T] needs to be made from the original server. $C_i(b)$ is the average value of video transmitted by using prefix cache.

$$C_i(b) = (C_s \frac{T-b}{1+\lambda_i b} + C_p T)\lambda_i B_i \tag{12}$$

U_i is segmented cache length. Media segmentation $[b+U_i, T]$ needs to come from the original sever and $C_i(b, U_i)$ is the average value of video transmitted by using segmented cache.

$$C_i(b, U_i) = (C_s \frac{T-b-U_i}{1+\lambda_i(b+U_i)} + C_p T)\lambda_i B_i \tag{13}$$

When using dynamic cache, under case 1, the average request addition is 1+μ, then the transmitted value $C_{id}(b, U_i)$ is.

$$C_{id}(b, U_i) = (C_s \frac{T-b-U_i}{1+\lambda_i(b+U_i)} \frac{1}{1+\mu} + C_p(T + \mu(b+U_i)))\lambda_i B_i \tag{14}$$

When using dynamic cache, under case 2, the average request addition is 1+μ, W is the average length of patching channel, then the transmitted value $C_{id}(b, U_i)$ is.

$$C_{id}(b, U_i) = (C_s \frac{W}{1+\lambda_i(b+U_i)} \frac{1}{1+\mu} + C_p(T + \mu(b+U_i)))\lambda_i B_i \tag{15}$$

The former item represent the transmission value between content server and proxy server, and the later item is the transmission value between proxy server and the client. Our major objective is to reduce the resources of backbone network, and that is the smaller the first item, the better. We considered if two or more applicants apply for the same video within time $b + U_i$, we may save the resource of the backbone network for μ times on average, and improve the byte hit ratio of proxy cache, by making those latter applicants not take up network resources of the backbone.

4 Performance Evaluation

4.1 Methodology

We utilize an event-driven simulator to stimulate the proxy cache service and furthermore to evaluate the algorithm of the dynamic cache based on variable-size segmentation. Let's suppose that the media objects are videos and the size of these videos are uniformly distributed between 0.5 B and 1.5 B blocks, where B represents video size. The default value of B is 2,000. The playing time for a block is assumed to be 1.8 seconds. In other words, the playing time for a video is between 30 minutes and 90 minutes. The size of cache is expressed on the basis of the quantitative description of media blocks. The default cache size is 400,000 blocks. The inter-arrival time distributes with the exponent λ. The default value of λ is 60.0 seconds. The requested video titles are selected from a total of the distinct video titles. The popularity of each video title M accords to the Zipf-like distribution. The Zipf-like distribution brings two parameters, x and M. the former has something to do with the degree of skew. The distribution is given by $p_i = C/i^{1-x}$ for each i∈ (1,$\cdots$,M), where $C = 1/\sum_{i-1}^{M} 1/i^{1-x}$ is a normalized constant. Suppose x = 0 corresponds to a pure Zipf distribution, which is highly skew. On the other hand, suppose x = 1 corresponds to a uniform distribution with no skew. The default value for x is 0.2 and that for M is 2,000. The popularity of each video title changes with time. It is very likely that a group of users may visit different video titles at different periods of time and the users' interest may be different. In our simulations, the distribution of the popularity changes every request R. The correlation between two Zipf-like distributions is modeled by using a single parameter k which can be any integer value between 1 and M. First, the most popular video in the first Zipf-like distribution finds its counterpart, the r_1-th most popular video in Zipf-like distribution 1, where r_1 is chosen randomly between 1 and k. Then, the most popular video in the second Zipf-like distribution finds its counterpart, the r_2-th most popular video. r_2 is chosen randomly between 1 and min (M, k+10), except r_1. The rest may be deduced by analog. When k represents the maximum position in popularity, a video title may shift from one distribution to the next. k = 1 expresses perfect conformity, and k = M expresses the random case or unconformity.

4.2 Impact of Cache Size

For a fairly wide range of cache size, the dynamic cache method has the highest byte hit ratio and the lowest fraction of requests with startup delay, whose byte hit ratio is higher than the variable-sized segmented approach and the prefix schemes with the same startup delay. Fig.3 shows the impact cache size imposes on the byte hit ratio. Fig.4 presents the impact imposed by cache size on the fraction of requests with startup delay. The full video approach and the prefix have comparable byte hit ratio, with the full video approach having a slight advantage over the prefix scheme. For a smaller cache size, the advantage of byte hit ratio managed by the variable-sized segmented approach is quite evident. The dynamic cache method proves to have the highest byte hit ratio. Even though the full video and the prefix approaches perform almost equally in byte hit ratio, they differ dramatically in the fraction of requests with startup delay. The full video approach has a significantly higher fraction of requests with startup delay. For example, for a cache size of 400,000 blocks, 0.61 of the requests cannot start immediately using the full video approach. However, only 0.161 of applicants encounter startup delay using dynamic cache, variable-size segmentation and prefix approaches. Within the whole range of cache size, the effect of the dynamic cache approach, variable-size segmented method and the prefix strategy are basically the same.They all effectively solve the problem of startup delay.

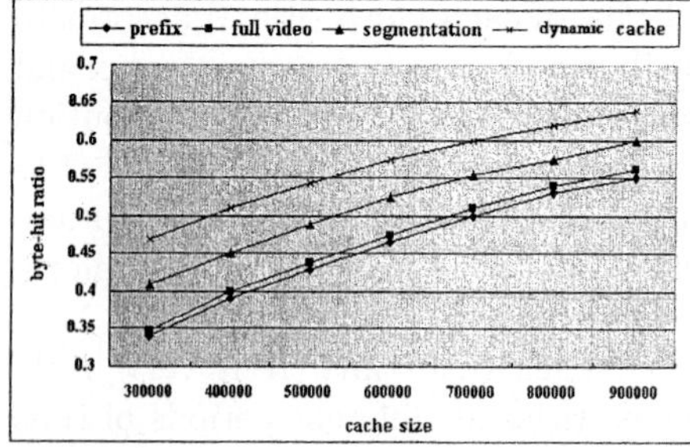

Fig. 3. impact of byte-hit ratio

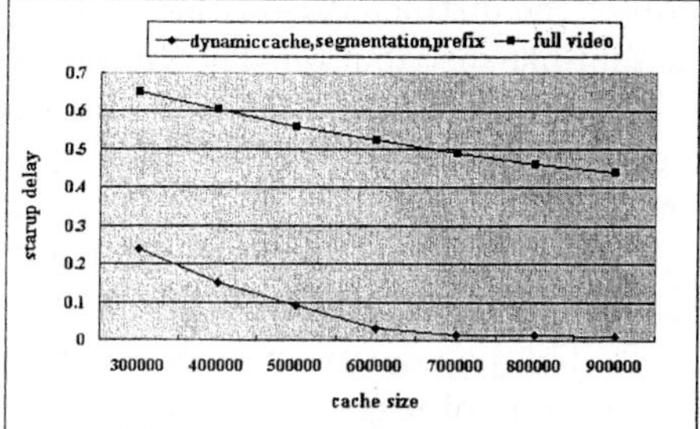

Fig. 4. impact of startup delay

4.3 Impact of Video Popularity

Let us examine the impact that the video popularity imposes on the byte hit ratio and startup delay. The dynamic cache method has the highest byte hit ratio when the video popularity makes changes of wide scope. The dynamic cache approach, the variable-sized segmentation and the prefix schemes all have the same fewest request time with startup delay, which is superior to the whole video. Fig.5 shows the impact of skew in video popularity on byte hit ratio, while Fig.6 shows its impact on the startup delay. In addition to the parameter of Zipf, x, we also studied the changes of the popularity distribution and the impact of

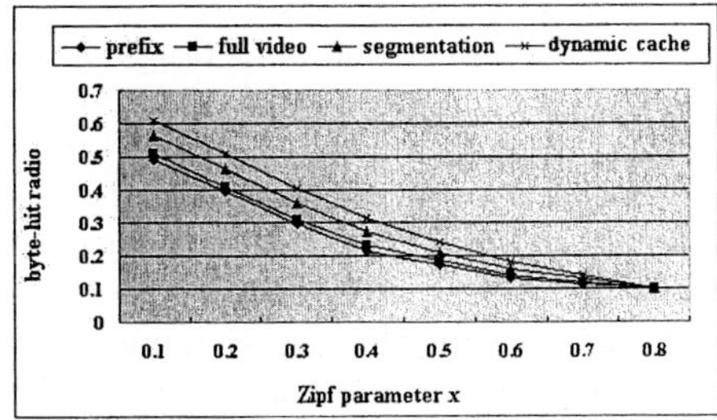

Fig. 5. impact of byte-hit radio

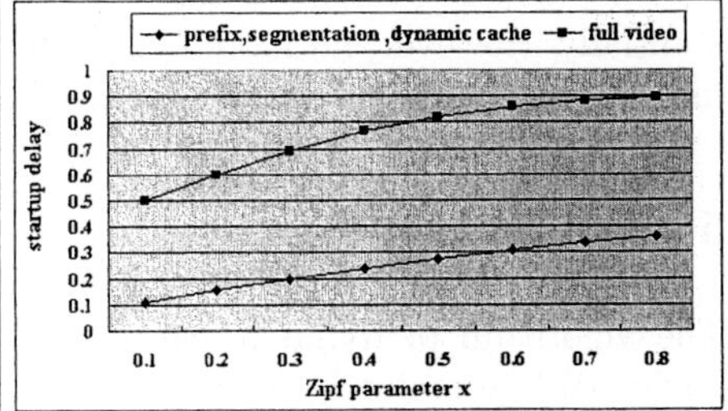

Fig. 6. impact of startup delay

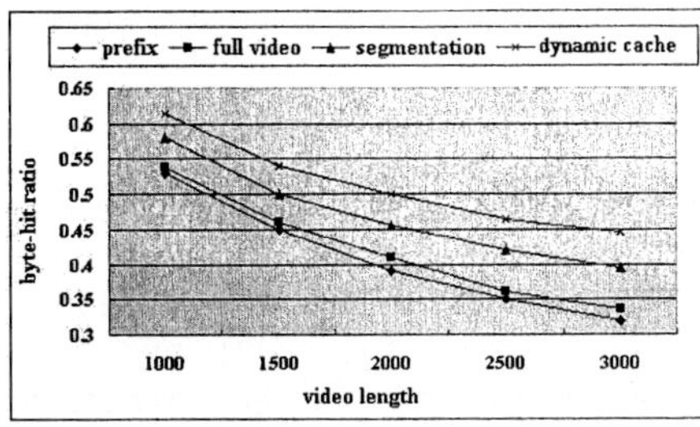

Fig. 7. impact of video length

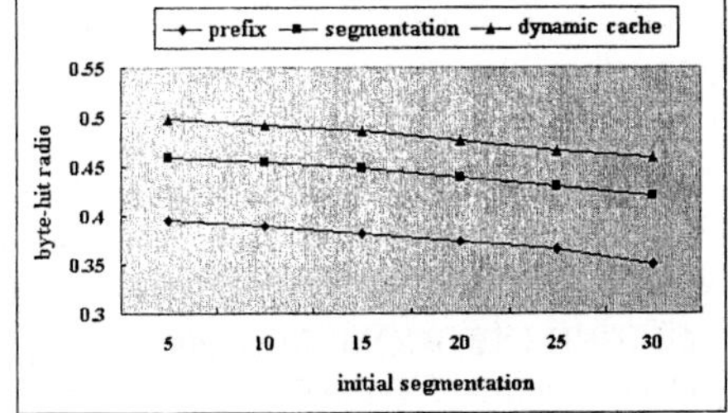

Fig. 8. impact of initial segmentation

the maximum video shifting position k. The request R of the video shift was set to be 200.

4.4 Impact of Other System Parameters

Fig.7 shows the impact of video length imposes on the byte hit ratio. In general, as the size of the media file increases, the byte hit ratio will fall, this is true for all the four approaches. When the size of a media file is very large, the dynamic cache algorithm can ensure higher byte hit ratio than the segmentation and other two approaches. As to a video with the length of 3000 blocks, the byte hit ratios of dynamic cache strategy and variable-sized segmented strategy are respectively 0.331 and 0.284. If the length falls to 1000 blocks, the byte hit ratios may reach 0.634 and 0.589 respectively. No matter which approach we use, dynamic cache strategy or variable-size segmented approach, caching large media will cause the byte hit ratio in proxy cache to fall. However, dynamic cache strategy is better than variable-sized segmented strategy.

Fig.8 examines the percentage of cache dedication for storing the initial segmentation. Because the cache for the suffixes is reduced, the byte hit ratio falls with the increase in using initial segmentation. This slight decrease in byte hit ratio can be offset by increasing benefits substantially by the means of reducing start delay. For example, let us compare these two cases,0.0516 and 0.151. The byte hit ratio is barely decreased, but the fraction of delayed startup drops substantially. However, no more benefits can be derived once the percentage of the initial segmentation cached increases beyond 0.18.

5 Conclusion

The algorithm of dynamic cache considers adequately the users' request behavior. While maintaining the advantage of the variable-sized segmentation, it provides the multi-user within a period of time with the same media they request by using dynamic cache. The algorithm of cache greatly saves traffics resource on the backbone of network, and enhance the byte hit ratio and efficiency of the proxy cache.

References

1. S. Sen, J. Rexford, and D. Towsley, "Proxy prefix caching for multimedia steams." in Proc. of IEEE Inforcom'99, New York, USA, no.3, pp.1310-1319, 1999.
2. K.L.Wu and P.S.Yu, Segment-Based Proxy Caching of Multimedia Streams In Proc. Of IEEE INFOCOM ,May, 2001.
3. O.Verscheure,C.Verkatramani, P. Froassard, and L. Amini, "Joint server scheduling and proxy caching for video delivery", Computer Communications, vol.25, no. 4, pp.413-423, Mar. 2002.
4. B. Wang, S. Sen, M. Adler, and D. Towsley. "Optimal proxy cache allocation for efficient streaming media distribution," IEEE Trans. on Multimedia, vol.6, no.2, April 2004.
5. Pascal Frossard and Olivier Verscheure, Member, IEEE ."Batched Patch Caching for Streaming Media," IEEE COMMUNICATIONS LETTERS, VOL. 6, NO. 4, APRIL 2002.
6. White PP, Crowcroft J. "Optimized batch patching with classes of sevice". ACM Commum. Rev., 2002, 6(4).
7. Zhiwen Xu, Xiaoxin GuoZhengxuan Wang, Yunjie Pang; "The Dynamic Cache-Multicast Method for Streaming Media". In proceeding of 3rd European Conference on Universal Multiservice Networks, Porto, Portugal, October, 2004,pp. 278-290.
8. Zhiwen Xu, Xiaoxin Guo, Yunjie Pang, Zhengxuan Wang; "The Strategy of Batch Using Dynamic Cache for Streaming Media". in proceeding of IFIP International Conference on Network and Parallel Computing, October, 2004, China; pp. 508-513.
9. Zhiwen Xu, Xiaoxin Guo, Yunjie Pang, Zhengxuan Wang; "The Transmitted Strategy of Proxy Cache Based on Segmented Video". in proceeding of IFIP International Conference on Network and Parallel Computing 2004, October, Wuhan, pp. 502-508.

A Rule-Based Analysis Method for Cooperative Business Applications*

Yonghwan Lee[1], Eunmi Choi[2], and Dugki Min[1,**]

[1] School of Computer Science and Engineering, Konkuk University, Hwayang-dong, Kwangjin-gu, Seoul, 133-701, Korea
(yhlee, dkmin)@konkuk.ac.kr
[2] School of Business IT, Kookmin University, Jeongneung-dong, Seongbuk-gu, Seoul, 136-702, Korea
emchoi@kookmin.ac.kr

Abstract. The existing CBD development methods deal with the analysis phase in a superficial manner. Applying such a superficial analysis to cooperative business applications with a number of distributed sub-components makes analysis models be inconsistent with levels and styles, only depending on experiences of the analysts. In this paper, we propose a rule-based analysis method that provides an analysis template for cooperative business applications. This method analyzes the concepts of cooperative business applications by using external events and internal rules that process the events. Employing this method, a huge business application can be developed by a couple of co-analysts who work together in a consistent and systematic manner. This paper also provides an efficient way to apply the rule-based analysis method to UML Component development methods.

1 Introduction

The recent software development processes deal with the analysis phase in a superficial manner, while they emphasize design and implementation phases[1, 2]. Applying such a superficial analysis to cooperative business applications with a number of distributed subsystems and components makes analysis models be inconsistent with levels and styles, only depending on experiences of the analysts[3].

To address this problem, many researchers in software engineering suggest analysis methods, called analysis patterns, which have domain specific features[3, 4]. Fowler identified several patterns that might be used during the analysis phase to represent conceptual models of business process, such as abstractions from accounting, trading, and organizational relationships[5]. There have been object analysis patterns specified for embedded system and security systems[6, 7].

In this paper, we propose an analysis method that provides a rule-based template pattern for analyzing cooperative business applications. This analysis method is called

* This work was supported by the Korea Science and Engineering Foundation (KOSEF) under Grant No. R04-2003-000-10213-0. This work was also supported by research program 2005 of Kookmin University and Kookmin research center UICRC in Korea.

** Corresponding author. This paper was supported by Konkuk University in 2005.

H. Zhuge and G.C. Fox (Eds.): GCC 2005, LNCS 3795, pp. 1155 – 1160, 2005.

the rule-based analysis pattern in this paper. The rule-based analysis pattern can be used for extracting core concepts and for defining relationship among the core concepts in terms of external events and reactive rules to process the events. When domain analysts analyze business processes, this analysis pattern can helps him/her modeling business conceptual models in a systematic way and making artifacts understandable and agreeable among the analysts in detailed level[8].

The remainder of this paper is organized as follows: Section 2 describes the proposed rule-based analysis pattern. Section 3 explains how to apply the rule-based analysis pattern to the UML Component development method. Finally, a conclusion is given in the last section.

2 Rule-Based Analysis Pattern

Figure 1 shows the architecture template of the rule-based analysis pattern we propose in this paper. By using this architecture template, a cooperative business application is able to develop its own component model, so that different distributed subcomponents can have consistent and effective models with the same aspect. We mainly extract the concepts that are closely related to the information to be maintained during the lifecycle of the system and to business rules to be applied.

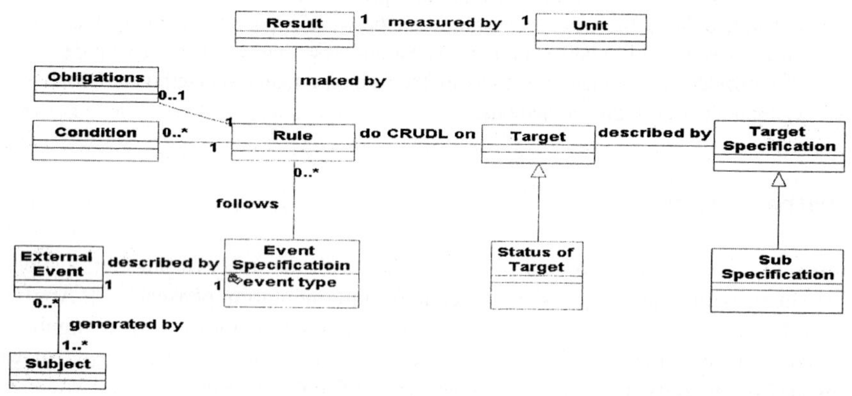

Fig. 1. Architecture Template of Rule-Based Analysis Pattern

Suppose that a bank customer tries to deposit some money through an ATM machine. When he/she makes a deposit service request, the ATM machine identifies what kind of the request happens and searches for rules that are set up for the request event. If the rule conditions are satisfied, then a service action is taken to the target account according to the rule. This action may perform some operations with the target and generate results of the operations. The target can change the bank account according to the results.

In figure 1, the Subject generates ExternalEvents to activate services. An ExternalEvent is described by an EventSpecification. Each EventSpecification has zero or

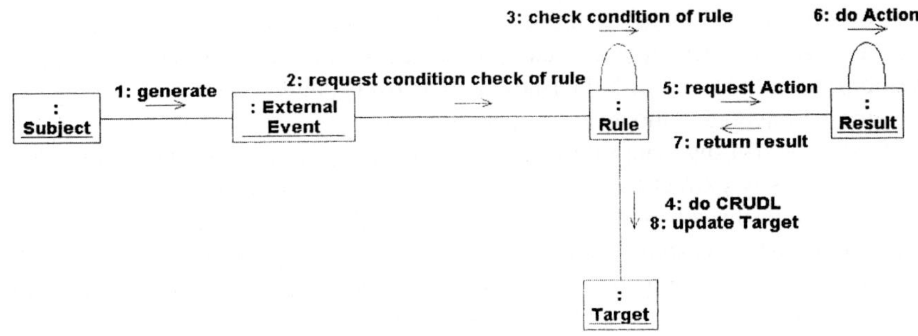

Fig. 2. Course of Event Processing

more Rules that should be applied during business processing. Each Rule has Conditions and Obligation. When the rule's Condition is satisfied, the Obligation is performed for the rule. After processing the Obligation, the rule performs one of the following two actions. The first one is to perform CRUDL (Create, Read, Update, Delete and List) action on the Target. The second one is to perform actions beyond CRUDL, such as computing algorithms, and to update the action results to the Target resource consequently. Figure 2 shows the sequence diagram of the second case of action, which requires extra computation or action beyond CRUDL. If the Target needs extra computational action, the Rule delegates the action to the Result and the Result returns the result back to the Rule and the Target. In our pattern, the Result contains appropriate actions and handles the results from action. It is because we focus on the information and the relationship between information of those cooperating components, which makes the developers easily reduce the complexity of their real component tasks.

The Unit is used to measure the target quantitatively by applying the Quantity Pattern to the rule-based analysis pattern. The Target is an entity or thing, which a rule action is applied to. The Target is specified by the TargetSpecification. Also, the status of target reflects the current identity of resource in its life cycle (for example, a normal account or a specific purpose account of a banking account), which is managed by the StatusOfTarget.

The rule-based analysis pattern that we propose has the following characteristics. First, it provides an analysis template of business concepts to process events according to business rules. Second, it can add an additional event and target types easily by separating operation concepts from knowledge concepts. Since this pattern employs the quantity pattern with the Unit concept, we can measure the target in various units.

3 Applying to the UML Components Development Method

In this section, we describe a mechanism of applying the rule-based analysis pattern to the UML Components development method. The rule-based analysis pattern proposed in this paper is related to the requirements and component specification workflows in RUP[9] method. In this section, we show the business conceptual modeling, interface identification and component identification of the UML components development method[10] with the rule-based analysis pattern.

Business conceptual modeling is one of the major activities in the requirement specification workflow. The rule-based analysis pattern provides a conceptual analysis frame to easily extract the core concepts and their relationship. Accordingly, this pattern provides the advantages of helping the independent modelers to create the standardized and consistent business conceptual models for the different distributed sub-components of complicated business applications. Figure 3 presents an architecture framework employed in the UML Component development method.

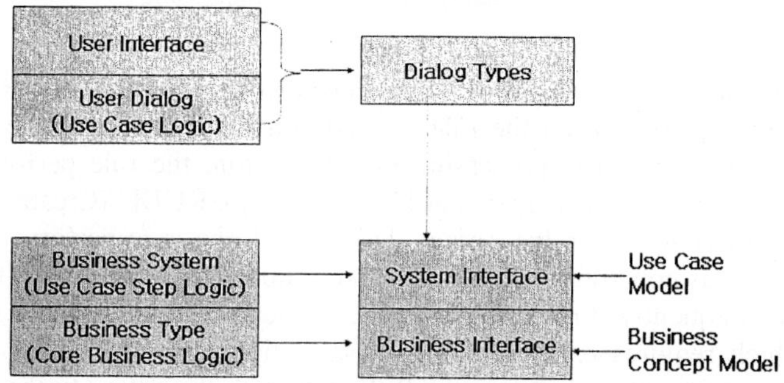

Fig. 3. Application Architecture

In this application architecture, there are two types of interfaces: the system interfaces and the business interfaces. The system interfaces are extracted from interaction scenarios between the users and the system. An External Event generated by a Subject is mapped to various business transaction types according to the Event Specification. A business transaction type is also mapped to a use case of the use case model. Thus, the use case model contains Subject, External Event, and Event Specification provided by the rule-based analysis pattern, and also identifies the system interfaces and their operations. The system interfaces take two roles: one is a façade role toward the external system and the other is a business workflow role such as interaction with another cooperative subsystem's system interface. In order to have a component changeable and reusable, it is necessary to perform interaction with other cooperative subsystem components only through the system interfaces, but not through the business interfaces.

As the second types of interfaces in the application architecture of the UML Component development method, the business interfaces provide the core logics of the business application in the system in view of users. The business interfaces are extracted from the business type models that are refined from the business conceptual models. The business interfaces are built from the core types that identify core business information. It means that UML Components development process uses information dependency to identify business interfaces. In general, a core type is mapped to a business interface one-by-one in a business type model. In the rule-based analysis pattern, the core information types are the Rule, Target, and Result. Because the Condition and Obligation types are dependent on the Rule, these are all interconnected. The Result is the result of some actions as the core type, shown in the Unit. The Target Specification is the specification for the Target and the Sub-Specification inherits from the Target Specification. Thus, the Target can be the core type. Each core type builds up a corresponding business interface as in Figure 4 of the Interface Responsibility Diagram.

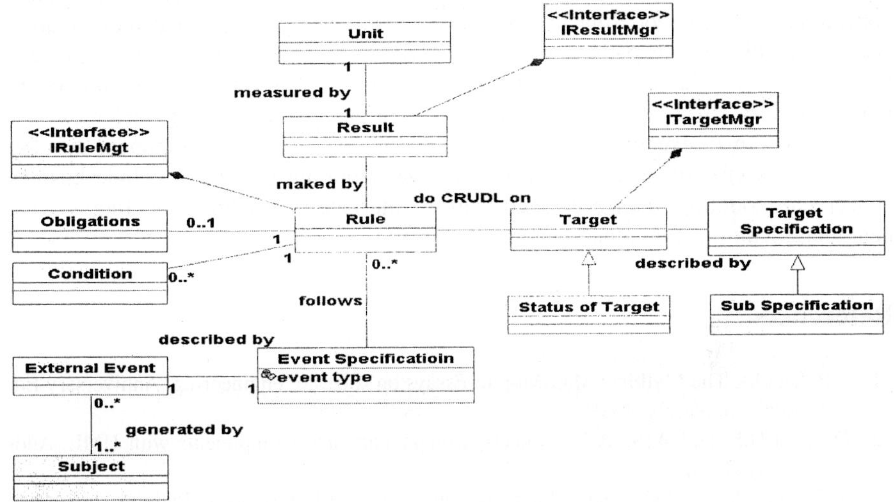

Fig. 4. Interface Responsibility Diagram of Rule-Based Analysis Pattern

The Target interface can be divided into a number of sub-interfaces according to the component usages, such as usages for Target types, Target information, and Target management. This division is considered when the application is complicated and the relationships among components are complex with a number of usages.

Once the interfaces are determined, we need to build the components in terms of component development process. The Rule, Result, and Target become components. When components are identified from the identified interfaces, the major consideration is in deciding how to map interfaces and components. There are a number of possible mappings between interfaces and components. The first mapping is that one interface is mapped to one component. In other word, one component has one interface. The second mapping is that m interfaces is mapped to one component. That means that one component has m interfaces. The third mapping is that one interface is mapped to m components. This means that one interface is implemented by several components independently. The fourth mapping is that one interface is mapped one component but there are internally m components within the outer component. In this mapping, we have the common logic be in a common component that connects to the external interface.

In rule-based analysis pattern, Rule and Result are the cases that one business interface is mapped one business component. In case of Target, Target Specification and

Sub Specification, however, various mappings are possible between business interfaces and business components.

4 Conclusion

In this paper we propose the rule-based analysis pattern that can be used for developing cooperative CBD business applications. The rule-based analysis pattern provides a conceptual analysis modeling to easily extract the core concepts and their relationships. Accordingly, this pattern provides benefits for independent modelers to develop the standardized and consistent business conceptual models for the different cooperative subsystems of complicated business applications. Component modeler can also use this pattern to execute the important activities of the UML component development process effectively and consistently. The important activities include business conceptual modeling, interface identification, interface interaction modeling, component identification, and component architecturing.

References

1. F.P. Brooks. The Mythical Man-Month: Essays on software engineering, Anniversary Edition. Addison-Wesely, 1999
2. D'souza D.F. and Wills A.C., Objects, Components, and Components with UML, Addison-Wisely, 1998
3. S. Konrad, Betty H.C. Cheng, Laura A, Campbell, "Object Analysis Patterns for Embedded Systems", IEEE Transaction on Software Engineering, vol. 30, no. 12, pp.970-992, December. 2004
4. S. Konrad, Laura A. Campbell, Betty H.C. Cheng, and Min Deng. A requirements patterns-driven approach to check systems and specify properties. In Thomas Ball and Sirom K. Rajamani, editors, Model Checking Software, number 2648 in LNCS, pages 18-33. Springer Verlag, May 2003
5. M. Fowler, Analysis Patterns: Reusable Object Models. Addison-Wesley, 1997
6. 6 A. Geyer-Schulz and M Hashler, "Software Engineering with Analysis Patterns." 2001, http://wwwai.wu-wien.ac.at/~hahsler/research
7. E.B. Fernandez and X. Yuan, "Semantic Analysis Patterns." Proc. 19th Int'l Conf. Conceptual Modeling(ER 2000), pp. 183-195, 2000
8. E. Gamma, R. Helm, R Johnson, J. Vlissides, "Design Patterns: Elements of Reusable Object-Oriented Software", Addison-Wesley, 1995
9. Philip Kruchten, The Rational Unified Process, Introduction, Addison & Wisely, 1998
10. Sterling Software Component-Based Development Method, http://www.sterling.com

Retargetable Machine-Description System: Multi-layer Architecture Approach

Dan Wu, Zhiying Wang, and Kui Dai

Computer School, National University of Defense Technology,
Changsha, Hunan, 410073, China,
86-731-4575963
Alavender1979@yahoo.com.cn

Abstract. This paper describes a methodology for machine-description, intended to help develop processor specific tools in a generic and reusable way. It is based on our work about retargetable compiler for embedded processors and is contributed to Architecture Design Language (ADL). The processor described in our machine-description system is modeled in UML class diagram in 3-layer architecture. The resulting machine-description is reusable for developers to create retargetable compilers.

1 Introduction

Retargetable compilation has been the subject of some study over the years[1, 2]. In order to reduce the amount and complexity of the machine-dependent code and to increase the retargetability, machine-level software tools should be retargeted much more easily if the machine-dependent parts were generated from machine descriptions, rather than written by hand. In this paper, we focus on the machine description system and aim at improving it to be reusable for embedded processors. The retargetablity and the reusability are realized to distinguish our own work from others.[4, 5, 6]

In section 2, we describe our methodology of building the multi-layer machine description system. In section 3, we give specification and analysis of this machine description system, modeling with UML class diagrams[3]. In section 4 we summarize our conclusions and give our view on the possibilities for improving the methodology for application specific processors.

2 The Machine-Description System with 3-Layer Architecture

The bottom layer is Machine Independent Description (MID). The middle layer is Machine Specific Description (MSD). And at the exit of this system is the final md file, which can be used to create retargetable compiler. We specify the processor models in this system and the models thus developed are parsed, checked for the errors and converted to the final md (machine description) file. Result from each lay is a file with intermediate form (IR). IR files in different layer are connected by the mapping mechanism, including matching MID with MSD and transformation from MSD to md file. It is fairly simple for compilers to read the information from the md file. Fig. 1 presents the machine description system.

H. Zhuge and G.C. Fox (Eds.): GCC 2005, LNCS 3795, pp. 1161 – 1166, 2005.

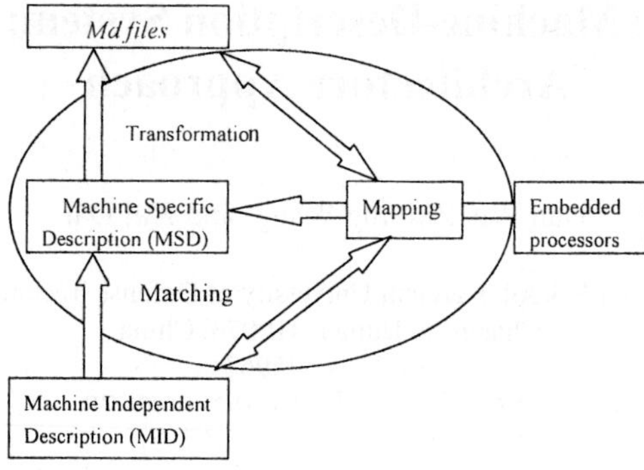

Fig. 1. Architecture of the machine description system

2.1 MID

A machine independent description is a view of description from the machine independent viewpoint. MID exhibits a specified degree of machine independence so as to be suitable for use with a number of different machines of similar type. The machine-independence focuses on the architectures of a type of machines while hiding the details necessary for a particular machine. Machine-independent means the descriptions are those about the general characteristics of general-purposed processors and are not limited to any particular embedded processor. Machine-independent descriptions show that part of the complete specification that does not change from one machine to another. We develop Machine Independent Description as a database with generic descriptions about general-purposed processors with clean architectures, from database to sub-database to meta-database to table, as shown in Fig. 2.

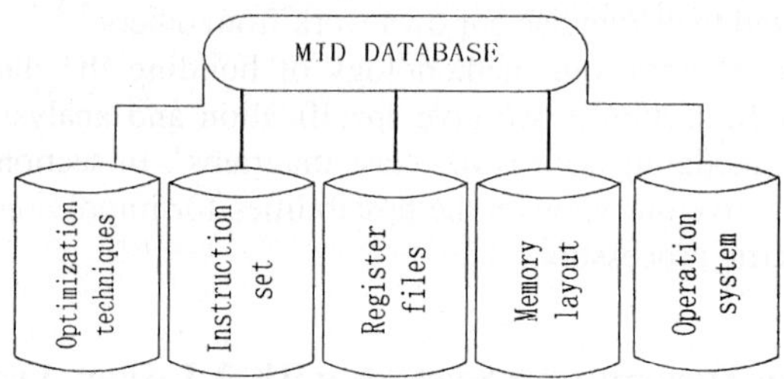

Fig. 2. Outline structure of MID

2.2 MSD

A machine specific description is a view of description from the machine specific viewpoint. A MSD combines the specifications in the MID with the details of an embedded processor requires. We select RISC-like processor to test. Fig.3 illustrates the development process from MID to MSD.

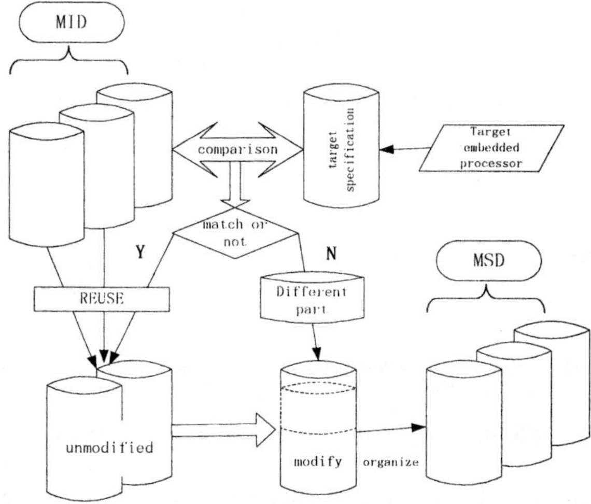

Fig. 3. Development of MSD

2.3 MD

After the construction of MID and MSD, md file is acting as an interface connecting compiler and the machine description system. According to target processor's MSD, the md file is created. The data structure of md file is a large table with many entries and one export. The entries are different description components extracted from MD and the export is the assembly code. Each component in the md file table is corresponding to the descriptions in MSD.

The compiler will explore in the table, through three interfaces-query, schedule and allocation. The three interfaces are actually three functions interfacing with compiler. The md file query interface allows compiler to get the requisite details about the descriptions of the target processor. The md file query interface supports scheduling and register allocation. It also provides some basic information about machine operations. The md file schedule interface realizes the scheduling of instructions, providing latencies for dependence edges in a data dependence graph, presenting a resource usage controller to a scheduler to support allocation and de-allocation of resources to operations during scheduling. The md file allocation interface provides information about the structure of register files and their capacities to the compiler.

3 Formal Specifications and Development of MDS

We use Unified Modeling Language (UML) to model the development of MID to MSD. The reason is that visual modeling can promote reusability and the architecture of MDS can be modeled by elements of UML. The MDS class diagrams shown in Fig. 4 illustrate the existence of classes and their relationships in the logical view of the machine description system.

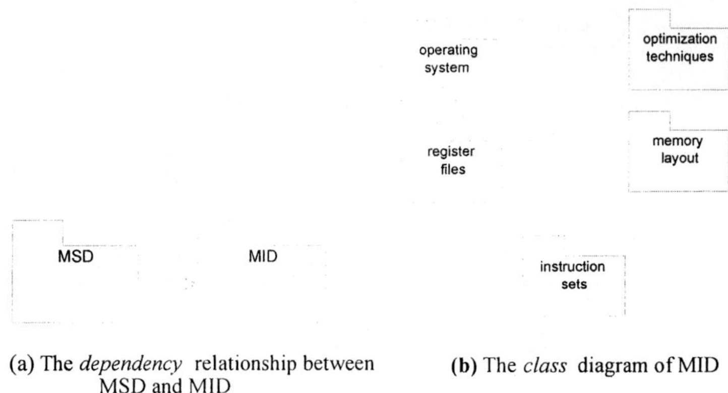

(a) The *dependency* relationship between MSD and MID

(b) The *class* diagram of MID

Fig. 4. Examples of UML class diagram for MDS

Fig.5 shows an example of instruction semantics specification with the particular operation declaration. We take the instruction sets *package* as an example, to illustrate the construction of *class* and *attribute* about processors' instruction sets, as shown in Fig. 6.

After the specification of MID, we can create the model of MSD by using class diagram similarly. We use Binary-Search-Tree algorithm[7] to realize the transformation from MID to MSD. This algorithm creates the class diagram of MSD. The worst-case complexity is linear in the level of tree. For a chain-like tree structure with n nodes this amounts to *O(n)*. If the BST is as balanced as possible this amounts to *O(logn)*.

We use Rational ROSE toolkit to realize visual modeling of MID and MSD. After the model of MSD is refined, it can be transferred into high-level language programs. Thus, the final md file written in high-level language is created.

```
action {
        temp_src =src;
        temp_src=dst;
        action;
        dst =temp-st;
        }
        op num_action = add | sub|······
        op add ()
        action = {
             temp_dst = temp_dst + temp_src

        }.....
```

(a) An example of instruction semantics specification

```
(Operation declaration
 {exception_handle (user_mode, programmer_mode):
  {ENTRY(page_fault)//page fault entry
      push $ SYMBOL_NAME(do_page_fault)
      jmp error-_code
      ......
  error code:
      ......
  ret_from_exception: //return from exception
  }
 }
{instruction_operation(integer, float):
......
 BEQ < CBR NI>        (jmpt  CL_cbr);
 BNE <CBR NI>         (jmpf  CL_cbr);
 RTS <RTS NI>         (jmpi  ((IOI_ubri RL_Ibr Lat)));
 JSR <JSR NI>         (call  ((IOI_call RL_Ibr Lat)));
 JSR <JSR NI>         (calli  ((IOI_calli RL_Ibr Lat)));
 ADD                (add  CL_Std_Ialu )
 SUB                (sub  CL_Std_Ialu)
 EXCEPT LOAD          (load  CL_Load)
  EXCEPT STORE         (store  CL_Store)
 }
......
)
```

(b) MID *operation* declaration

Fig. 5. Instruction semantics specification with the particular operation declaration

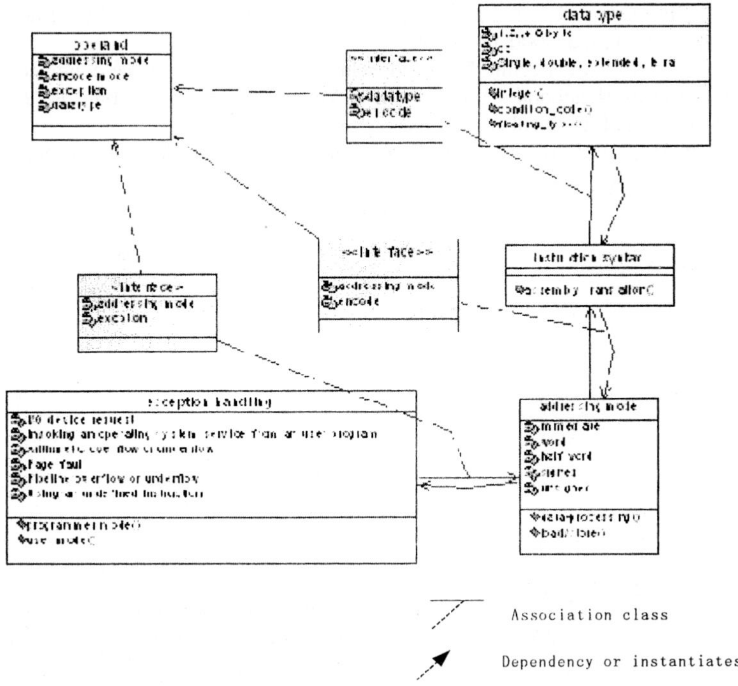

Fig. 6. The *class* diagram of instruction set descriptions in MID

4 Conclusions

The design of machine description system with multi-layer is to realize machine independence and compiler independence. Our approach absorbs UML's visual modeling method. As a result, the retargetablity and the reusability are realized to distinguish our own work from others. At the same time, we are the innovators to combine software engineering method with processor architecture design. We believe this approach is of high efficiency and is important for the free development of embedded processors. Of course, there are still many works need to be further explored in the future.

References

1. Richard M Stallman. Using and Porting Gnu CC, (Supplied in electronic format with the source code). Free Software Foundation 1998. ISBN 1-882114-37-X
2. Rainer Leupers. Compiler Design Issues for Embedded Processors. IEEE Design & Test of Computers 19(4): 51-58 (2002)
3. UML 2.0 Draft Specifications, http://www.uml.org/
4. John Christopher. A Machine Description Language for Compilation. Master's thesis, Department of Electrical. and Computer Engineering, University of Illinois, Urbana, IL, 1994

5. Moona R. Processor Models For Retargetable Tools. Proceedings of IEEE Rapid Systems Prototyping 2000 June. 2000, pp 34–39
6. W. Qin, S. Malik. Architecture Description languages for retargetable compilation, in The Compiler Design Handbook: Optimizations & Machine Code Generation, CRC Press, 2002, Y. N. Srikant and Priti Shankar, Editors.
7. T. H. Cormen, C. E. Leiserson, R. L. Rivest, and C. Stein. Introduction to Algorithms. MIT Press/McGraw-Hill, 2nd edition, 2001

An Unbalanced Partitioning Scheme for Graph in Heterogeneous Computing*

Yiwei Shen[1,2] and Guosun Zeng[1,2]

[1] Department of computer Science and Technology, Tongji University, Shanghai 200092, China
realityshen@citiz.net
[2] Tongji Branch, National Engineering & Technology Center of High Performance Computer, Shanghai 200092, China
gszeng@mail.tongji.edu.cn

Abstract. Most existing graph partitioning algorithms produce equivalent partitions. It means the partitioned subsets have equal number of vertexes. However, in heterogeneous computing, the computing power of different processors varies, so that the size of the tasks to be scheduled should not be the same as well. In order to meet the need of the load balance for heterogeneous computing, we present a novel algorithm that partitions the original task graph into unbalanced subsets according to the arbitrarily given conditions. Generally, the number of the partitions is equal to that of the processors and the size of each partition is set according to the computing power. Our algorithm contains three phases. Coarsen the original graph, then partition the coarsest graph, and finally project it back to the original graph and conduct refinement. We test our algorithm using Greenwich Graph Partitioning Archive and get good experimental results.

1 Introduction

Graph partitioning is an important technology in many areas including scientific computing, task scheduling and VLSI design. The graph partitioning problem is NP-complete. There are two kinds of graph partitioning schemes according to the size of the partitioned subsets: balanced and unbalanced partitioning. Most researches focus on the balanced partitioning and many heuristic algorithms have been developed to find a feasible partition, such as spectral partitioning methods[5] and geometric partitioning algorithms[6]. Another class of graph partitioning schemes is called multilevel partitioning schemes. It reduces the size of the graph, partition the smaller graph, and then uncoarsen it to construct a partition for the original graph[3][4]. However, these kinds of algorithms all emphasize that the size or weight of each partitioned subset is roughly equal. So far, there are not many achievements on unbalanced partitioning. We take parallel task scheduling for example. In heterogeneous environment[1][2], the computing power of processors or workstations varies so greatly that the size of the corresponding tasks should be different accordingly. For the reasons mentioned above, it is essential to study an algorithm which partitions the vertexes of a graph into arbitrary subsets with unequal size or weight. Moreover, the edge-cuts of the graph produced by the algorithm are as small as possible.

* Supported by the 863 High-Tech Project under grant of 2004AA104340.

H. Zhuge and G.C. Fox (Eds.): GCC 2005, LNCS 3795, pp. 1167 – 1172, 2005.

The rest of this paper is structured as follows. Section 2 presents the basic concepts of the unbalanced partitioning. Section 3 describes the algorithms in detail. Section 4 presents the experimental evaluation of the algorithms.

2 Problem Description

Definition 1 (Computing power). In heterogeneous computing environment, the computing power of a processor is a concentrated reflection calculated as follows:

$$CP = \frac{\frac{f_{i/o}}{\bar{t}_{i/o}} + \frac{f_{r/w}}{\bar{t}_{r/w}} + \frac{f_{comp}}{\bar{t}_{comp}} + \frac{f_{comm}}{\bar{t}_{comm}}}{f_{i/o} + f_{r/w} + f_{comp} + f_{comm}}$$

$f_{i/o}$, $f_{r/w}$, f_{comp} and f_{comm} is the frequency of occurrence of each type of operations: I/O, memory Read/Write, computation, and communication. $\bar{t}_{i/o}$, $\bar{t}_{r/w}$, $\bar{t}_{comp}$ and $\bar{t}_{comm}$ are the average execution time of program segment on the underlying machine.

Definition 2 (Distribution vector). Distribution vector $A = (\alpha_1, \alpha_2, \ldots, \alpha_k)$, k is the number of the elements in A, and $\sum_{i=1}^{k} \alpha_i = 1$. If A is the distribution vector of heterogeneous task[2], then $\alpha_i = \frac{CP_i}{\sum_{j=1}^{k} CP_j}$, where CP_i is the CP of the i_{th} processor. If A is the one of partitioned graph, α_i is the ratio of the size of the partition i.

Definition 3 (Unbalanced partitioning). Given a graph $G = (V, E)$, V is the set of vertexes and $|V| = n$. E is the set of edge. A distribution vector $A = (\alpha_1, \alpha_2, \ldots, \alpha_k)$. The unbalanced partitioning problem is to partition V into k subsets, $V_1, V_2, \ldots, V_k$, such that $V_i \cap V_j = \phi$, $i \neq j$, $|V_1| : |V_2| : \ldots : |V_i| = \alpha_1 : \alpha_2 : \ldots : \alpha_k$, $\bigcup_i V_i = V$, and the number of edges of E whose incident vertexes belong to different subsets is minimized.

We use a vector P of length n to record the partitioning result for graphs. $\forall v \in V$, $P[v] = p$, $p \in \{0, \ldots, k\text{-}1\}$.

Definition 4 (Edge-cuts). Given a graph $G = (V, E)$, suppose a partition result P, the edge-cuts of P is defined as $EC_p = \sum_{P[v] \neq P[u]} w(v, u)$, where $v, u \in V$, $(v, u) \in E$, $w(v, u)$ is the weight of edge (v, u).

3 Unbalanced Partitioning Algorithm

The basic structure of unbalanced partitioning scheme consists of three phases. Coarsen down the graph G_0, and then compute an unbalanced partitioning. Last this partition is projected back towards the original graph.

3.1 Coarsening Phase

During this phase, a sequence of smaller graphs $G_i = (V_i, E_i)$ is constructed from the original graph $G_0 = (V_0, E_0)$ such that $|V_i|<|V_{i-1}|$. Generally, a set of vertices of G_i is combined to form a single vertex of the next level coarser graph G_{i+1}. Let V_i^v be the set of vertices of G_i combined to form vertex v of G_{i+1}. In order for a partitioning of a coarser graph to be good with respect to the original graph, the weight of vertex v is set equal to the sum of the weights of the vertices in V_i^v. Also, in order to preserve the connectivity information in the coarser graph, the edges of v are the union of the edges of the vertices in V_i^v. In the case where more than one vertex of V_i^v contains edges to the same vertex u, the weight of the edge of v is equal to the sum of the weights of these edges. Thus, the edge-cuts of the partitioning in a coarser graph are equal to the edge-cuts of the same partition in the previous level of graph. The coarsening method can be defined in terms of matching[7].A matching of a graph G_i is a set of edges no two of which are incident on the same vertex. We illustrate it as M_i. Thus, the next level coarser graph G_{i+1} is constructed from G_i by finding a M_i of G_i and collapsing the vertices being matched into multinodes. The unmatched vertices are simply copied over to G_{i+1}.

Heavy Edge Matching Algorithm
Let $W(E)$ be the sum of weights of all the edges belonging to E. We know that $W(E_{i+1}) = W(E_i) - W(M_i)$. In order to minimize the edge-cuts, we should select a M_i whose edges have large weights. The vertexes are visited in random order. We match a vertex u with one of its adjacent unmatched vertexes v such that the weight of the edge (u, v) is maximum over all valid incident edges.

Our heavy edge matching does not end until the number of vertexes of graph G_i is less than ck, while k is the number of the partitions and c is a constant. In our experiment[4], c is between 15 and 20. We also end the coarsening phase if the reduction in the size of successively graphs is less than a factor of 0.8, that is, $|V_{i+1}| / |V_i| > 0.8$. After coarsening phase, the original graph is coarsened down to a much smaller graph. We can conduct faster partitioning phase on the smaller graph.

3.2 Unbalanced Partitioning Phase

Our partitioning algorithm is a k-step cycle. On each step it produces one of the k partitions on the graph we get from coarsening phase.

Unbalanced Partition Growing Algorithm
Given a distribution vector $A = (\alpha_1, \alpha_2, \ldots,\alpha_k)$, let wgt be the sum of weights of vertexes of G_i. We start from a vertex and grow a region around it in breadth-first fashion to construct the partition until the total weight of this partition is equal to $\alpha_i{*}wgt$. Then we continue the process on the remaining vertexes. Because we must ensure the connectivity of the partition, it's hard to avoid the situation that when searching unpartitioned vertexes in breadth-first fashion, we can not get enough large partition for there is no vertex in the queue. The current region is called fragment. Our algorithm is to solve the problem and get enough large partitions.

After the process of growing region, it begins to deal with fragments if there are vertexes unpartitioned. On the other hand, if all the vertexes have been partitioned but the number of subsets is less than k, it sets the closest fragments to be these partitions. Next, it switches the vertexes of the fragments into adjacent partitions whose actual weight compared to the preferred weight is the smallest. After unbalanced partitioning phase, we get an initial partition P. Partition i is roughly equal to α_i*wgt.

3.3 Uncoarsening Phase

This phase consists of two steps. First, project back the partitions to the graph of previous level. Second, conduct refinement. Since each vertex of G_{i+1} contains a distinct subset of vertexes of G_i, obtaining P_i from P_{i+1} is done by simply assigning the set of vertexes V_i^v collapsed to $v \in G_{i+1}$ to the partition $P_{i+1}[v]$(i.e., $P_i[u] = P_{i+1}[v]$, $\forall u \in V_i^v$). We find that even though there is no further improvement in the weights of P_{i+1}, the projected partition P_i may not be like this. Since G_i is finer, it has more degree of freedom to improve P_i. For this reason, after projecting a partition, a refinement algorithm is used. We should pay attention to the following two aspects when conducting refinement. Making the actual weights of partitions close to preferred weights and decreasing the edge-cuts as much as possible. We achieve this goal by swapping vertexes from one partition to another without destroying the connectivity of the former partition and the idea of decreasing edge-cuts is based on KL refinement[8].

Refinement Algorithm

Let $Adj(v)$ be the set of adjacent vertexes of v. We define $N(v) = \cup_{u \in Adj(v)} P_i[u] - \{P_i[v]\}$. Note that if v is an interior vertex of a partition, $N(v) = \phi$. $\forall p \in N(v)$, we define $ED(v)_p = \sum_{P_i[u]=p} w(v,u)$, $ID(v) = \sum_{P_i[v]=P_i[u]} w(v,u)$, $gain(v)_p = ED(v)_p - ID(v)$. If $gain(v)_p$ is positive, the total edge-cuts will be decreased by the amount of $gain(v)_p$.

Given an unrefined Partition p, if $w(p)$ is smaller than preferred weight $W(p)$, first we get q from adjacent partitions of p such that $w(q)$-$W(q)$ is the largest, then we swap the vertex v from q to p whose $gain(v)_p$ is the largest. If $w(p)$ is larger than $W(p)$, we do it similarly. After refinement, we begin to project it back to the previous level of the graph.

3.4 Algorithm Analysis

The coarsening phase is tended to reduce the size of the original graph. The complexity of heavy edge matching algorithm is $O(|E|)$. The unbalanced partition growing algorithm is a kind of variation of breadth-first searching algorithm. It takes into account the problem of fragments. Its complexity is also $O(|E|)$. The information of adjacent vertexes of each vertex should be clear in the refinement process which indicates that the complexity is $O(|E|)$ all the same. So, the complexity of the whole scheme is linear to the number of the edges.

4 Experimental Results

Our testing cases all come from Greenwich Graph Partitioning Archive[9]. It is open. Table 1 shows the attributes of these graphs to be tested.

Table 1. Various graph used in the experiments

Name	No. of V	No. of E	Description
3elt	4720	13722	2D finite element mesh
add32	4960	9462	32-bit adder
brack2	62631	366559	3D finite element mesh
crack	10240	30380	2D nodal graph
cs4	22499	43858	3D dual graph
data	2851	15093	Map data
fe_sphere	16386	49152	Sphere graph
uk	4824	6837	2D dual graph
whitaker3	9800	28989	2D finite element mesh

For simplicity, we take graph 'data' and 'uk' for example to show the result of the size of each partition. The two graphs are divided into 4 partitions. The distribution vector $A = (0.1, 0.2, 0.3, 0.4)$ and $\varepsilon = 0.02$. The weight of 'data' is 2851. The sizes of the partitions are 290, 581, 862 and 1118 respectively. The weight of 'uk' is 4824. The sizes of the partitions are 492, 946, 1476 and 1910 respectively. For experiments show, the size of each partition of the graphs is in the range of error.

Table 2 shows the edge-cuts produced by balanced partitioning and unbalanced partitioning. The data of the edge-cuts of balanced partitioning is from reference [3][4]. The distribution vectors we use for unbalanced partitioning are listed below.

$A_1 = (0.2, 0.2, 0.3, 0.3)$;

$A_2 = (0.05, 0.05, 0.1, 0.1, 0.15, 0.15, 0.2, 0.2)$;

$A_3 = (0.025, 0.025, 0.025, 0.025, 0.05, 0.05, 0.05, 0.05, 0.075, 0.075, 0.075, 0.075, 0.1, 0.1, 0.1, 0.1)$;

A_4 is a 32-dimension vector with identical value of elements, which equal 0.03125.

Table 2. The comaprison of edge-cut. EC refers to edge-cut

Name	EC of Unbalanced				EC of Balanced
	A_1	A_2	A_3	A_4	
3elt	373	647	1092	1424	972
add32	27	96	161	304	234
brack2	17071	19239	33120	32568	22451
crack	788	1067	1868	2680	1768
cs4	2436	3411	5331	5668	3110
fe_sphere	1594	1963	3728	3903	2567
whitaker3	685	1068	1581	2466	1719

For experiments show, the edge-cuts produced by unbalanced partitioning with A_4 are larger than that of balanced partitioning with 32 partitions. The reason is that unbalanced partitioning can not emphasize much on the *gain* of the vertexes in order to ensure the size of partitions sticking to the distribution vector.

5 Conclusions

The unbalanced partitioning scheme for graph in heterogeneous computing is the one based on the idea of multilevel partitioning. It partitions the graph with a distribution vector to adjust the size of each subset. The algorithm is applicable in the field of the load balance of parallel task scheduling in heterogeneous environment and other similar problems. We have done a lot of experiments on this algorithm to verify its substantial result. The result shows that the algorithm is accurate. Our future work will focus on how to further reduce the edge-cuts of the partitions.

References

1. R. F. Freund, H. J. Siegel, Heterogeneous processing, Computer, June 1993, 26(6): 18-27.
2. G. Zeng, X. Lu, Load Sharing in Heterogeneous Computing, Journal of Software, 2000, 11(4):551-556.
3. G. Karypis, V. Kumar, A Fast and High Quality Multilevel Scheme for Partitioning Irregular Graphs, SIAM J. Sci. Comput., 20(1):359-392, 1998.
4. G. Karypis, V. Kumar, Multilevel k-way Partitioning Scheme for Irregular Graphs, J. Parallel Distrib. Comput., 48(1):96-129, 1998.
5. Bruce. Hendrickson, Robert. Leland, an improved spectral graph partitioning algorithm for mapping parallel computations, SIAM J. Sci. Comput., 16(2):452-469, 1995.
6. Gary L. Miller, Shang-Hua Teng, Stephen A. Vavasis, A unified geometric approach to graph separators, In Proceedings of 31st Annual Symposium on Foundations of Computer Science, pages 538–547, 1991.
7. Bruce Hendrickson, Robert Leland, A multilevel algorithm for partitioning graphs, Technical Report SAND93-1301, Sandia National Laboratories, 1993.
8. B. W. Kernighan, S. Lin, An efficient heuristic procedure for partitioning graphs, The Bell System Technical Journal, 49(2):291–307, 1970.

A Connector Interaction for Software Component Composition with Message Central Processing

Hwa-Young Jeong

Faculty of General Education, Kyunghee University,
1, Hoegi-dong, Dongdae-mun-gu, Seoul 130-701, Korea
hyjeong@khu.ac.kr

Abstract. Recently, software development method supporting CBD has been adopted widely, and there have been many studies on composition and application of architecture that can effectively use CBD. C2 architecture has been popular because of its composition of message-driven components. However, when you have classified sequence in component and want to use method-call method in server component, modification of component in C2 architecture is inevitable. In this paper, I propose connector interaction method with central message processing. This allows us to use the component without any modification (Plug-and-Play) even when method-call method is in use. More flexible message handling can be achieved by having a parallel composition of components that are free of classified sequence.

1 Introduction

Component-based development (CBD) technology has been developed to allow us to build system through composition of components that I can Plug-and-Play[1, 2]. CBD requires an architecture where all the components can assemble seamlessly[3]. To do this, component composition method must fix any mismatch of interfaces between components and it also should be able to compose components without individually modifying the component [12]. Several architecture-based technologies exist: Pipe-and-filter architecture of UNIX, Blackboard architecture[4] that has been widely used over the years in general applications, Style-based Unicon[5], Aesop[6], C2[7], Symantec-model based Wright, Rapide, and Domain Spec based ROOM[10]. Among these, C2 style architecture is one of the architectures that support asynchronous interaction through messages instead of using direct method-call method among components. C2 style has limitations in that I cannot check the result right away and it has to go through multiple steps of connector port or has to go down to the lowest level component through Notification to get the result due to C2 styles hierarchical structure of components that have a defined top and bottom.

In this paper, I present connector interaction method utilizes Message Central Processing (MCP) for advanced connector interface between components. MCP

H. Zhuge and G.C. Fox (Eds.): GCC 2005, LNCS 3795, pp. 1173–1178, 2005.

delivers messages to each component from one message space as opposed to directly handling messages among components. This is achieved by having parallel structure with message space in the middle in stead of having hierarchical structure of components. For memory space, this only requires three: one for Message Name Vector, the other two for Request/Notification message space. Implementation and test were done in multi-server environment where I have two EJB servers for database and another main server system that handles the two EJB servers.

2 C2 Based Connector Interaction

The main characteristics of C2 style architecture[14] are: communication among components, multi-thread, independence between layers, composition of components through Message Routing Connector, and capability to meet GUI software requirements. C2 style architecture is also suitable for distributed or heterogeneous environment, applying component in an environment free of divided address space, multi-user and multiple tool kit, and dynamic structure that changes in real-time[4]. All communication between components is achieved solely by exchanging messages. Request message is sent to upper level through top port and Notification message is received from upper level through bottom port of the upper level. Central to the architectural style is a principle of limited visibility or substrate independence: one component within the hierarchy can only be aware of components above it, and is completely unaware of the components beneath it. Fig 1 shows the C2 style architecture frame-work.

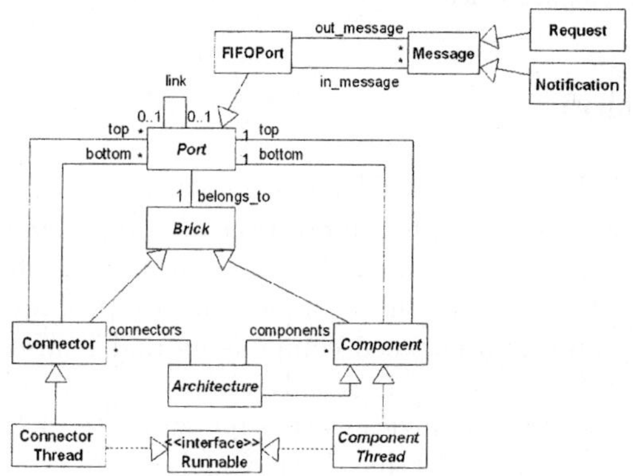

Fig. 1. C2 style architecture framework

3 Connector Interactions with Central Message Processing

3.1 Composition Structure with Message Central Processing

Despite this sequential structure, more often than not, I get result from intermediate component and need to process the result. Also, existing C2 style is not

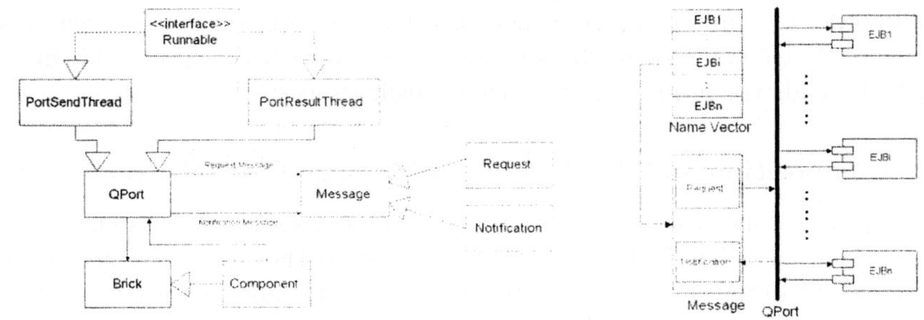

Fig. 2. Proposed modified C2 style framework and Message Central Processing

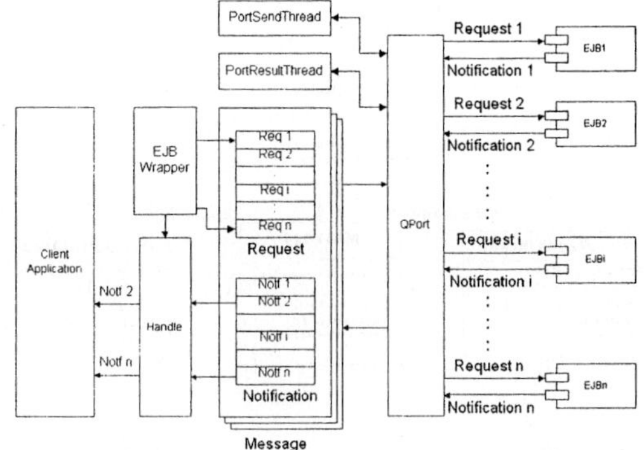

Fig. 3. Component composition framework with message central processing

truly Plug-and-Play. In case of server side component model, EJB, existing C2 style uses direct method-call method among components. With this style, I cannot start, stop, or restart Thread at EJB, which is why considerable modification is required. To solve this problem, I need to substitute method-call method with message-call method and also need to make changes to Component Thread and Connector Thread. I propose a modified C2 style framework, which is shown in Fig 2. Under modified style, message handling among components is done within the message itself with Thread instead of handling messages at the stages of component or connector. Component message is saved in message area through Qport and message is handled at PortSendThread and PortResultThread, which allow us to compose and apply components without modification.

Component composition framework with message central processing is shown in Fig 3. EJB Wrapper contains information of components that will be assembled, and through this it initializes request method of each component. Based on component information from Wrapper, Handle saves request methods in Request area of Message space and in Name Vector. Saved Request Messages can be checked through Port-SendThread. It calls method messages according to assembly order of components, and then checked result messages are saved in Notification. PortResultThread checks messages saved in Notification and through Handle it sends the requested component result to user.

3.2 Composition and Application of Message Central Processing

Modeling was done with UML. Fig 4 shows the class diagram. Assembly component is initialized at EJBWrapper and request method of each component is transformed to request message and then saved in Handle. After this, Notification message is sent to Client.

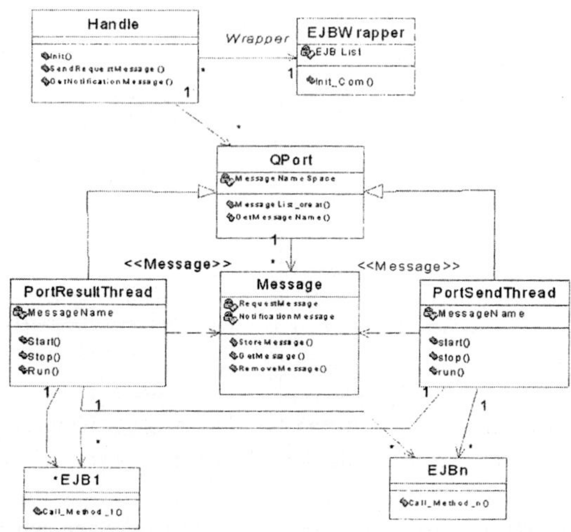

Fig. 4. Class Diagram

4 Connector Interactions with Central Message Processing

Fundamental structural difference between original C2 architecture and modified architecture is shown in Table 1. Where C2 architecture needs Threads in both

Table 1. Fundamental difference between C2 and modified architecture

Item	C2 architecture	Modifed architecture
Component	2	0
Connector	2	0
Message	1	1
Port	2	3
Threads needed for Message handling	2	2

Table 2. Functional difference of the two architectures

	C2 architecture	Modifed architecture
Structure	Sequential hierarchical structure	Parallel structure with Message List
Sequential handling of messages	Yes	Yes
Parallel handling of messages	Requires multiple steps	Easily done
Check result from Intermediate level component	Requires multiple steps	Easily done
Number of places to save message	4	3

component and connector, modified architecture places massage handling part within message itself and allows us to use component without any modification.

Functional difference between C2 architecture and modified architecture is given in Table 2. For parallel handling of messages for checking result from intermediate level component, I need to use Port of connector, which takes multiple steps.

5 Conclusions

In this paper, I presented modified C2 architecture that uses method-call method among components and that is also suitable for parallel component structure. Message-handling part of C2 architecture has been placed on the message as opposed to on components and connectors. Plug-and-Play is possible by getting rid of In/Out Vectors and having one Message Name Vector, which allows us to use components without modification. For the case where I have server components with method-call method, C2 architecture requires modification on components and connectors, whereas proposed new architecture has Qport that handles message and thus allows us to Plug-and-Play. More flexible Plug-and-Play of components is possible due to parallel structure of components with message in the middle and not having sequenced hierarchical structure. I can now check results regardless of composition order of component. For application example, I used database server loaded with Cloudscape and one Handle server between EJB servers to implement and test this new architecture.

For more efficient composition and application, I may consider using hybrid of C2 and proposed modified architecture. Future work may include developing more efficient handling part among components after evaluating the result of new architecture.

References

1. F. Brosard, D. Bryan, W. Kozaczynski, E. S. Liongorari, J. Q. Ning, A. Olafsson, and J. W. Wetterstrand, Toward Software Plug-and-Play, in Proc. of the 1997 Symposium on Software Reusability, (1997)
2. P. C. Clements, From Subroutines to Subsystem : Component-Based Software Development, Component Based Software Engineering, IEEE CSPress, (1996)

3. Dong-ik Shin, etc, Development of an ADL tool set that supports the description of C2-style architecture, Korea Information Processing Society, Vol. 8-D, No 6. (2001)
4. Taylor, R. N., Medvidovic, N., Anderson, K. M., Whitehead, E. J., Jr., Robbins, J. E., Nies, K, A., Oreizy, P. and Dubrow, D. L., A Component and Message-Based Architectural Style for GUI Software, IEEE Transactions on Software Engineering, Vol.22. No.6., June, (1996)
5. M. Shaw, R. DeLine, D. V. Klein, T. L. Ross, D. M. Young, and G. Zelesnik, Abstractions for Software Architecture and Tools to Support Them, IEEE Transactions on Software Engineering, 21(4):314-335, April (1995)
6. D. Garlan, R. Allen, and J. Ockerbloom, Exploiting Style in Architectural Design Environments, Proc. of SIGSOFT '94 Symposium on the Foundations of Software Engineering, December (1994)
7. N. Medvidovic, P. Oreizy, and R. N. Taylor, Using Object-Oriented Typing to Support Architectural Design in the C2 Style, Symposium on the Foundations of Software Engineering (FSE4), San Francisco, CA, Oct. (1996)
8. R. Allen and D. Garlan, Formalizing Architectural Connection, Proc. of 16th Int l Conference on Software Engineering, Sorrento, Italy, May (1994)
9. D. C.Luckham and J. Vera, An Event-Based Architecture Definition Language, IEEE Transactions on Software Engineering, Vol. 21, No 9, pp. 717-734, Sept. (1995)
10. B. Selic, G. Gullekson, and P. T. Ward, Real-Time Object-Oriented Modeling, John Wiley and Sons, Inc. (1994)
11. The C2 Style, http://www.ics.uci.edu/pub/arch/c2.html, Information and Computer Science, University of California, Irvine. (2003)
12. You-hee Choi, Oh-cheon Kwon, Gyu-sang Shin, An Approach to Composition of EJB Component Using the C2 Style, Korea Information Processing Society, Vol. 8-D, No 6. (2001)
13. Sun Mircosystems Inc, Enterprise Java Beans Specifications, at URL:http://java.sun.com
14. Nenad Medvidovic and Richard N. Taylor, A Classification and Comparison Framework for Software Architecture Description Languages, IEEE Transactions on Software Engineering, Vol. 26, No. 1, pp. 70-93, January (2000)

Research on the Fault Tolerance Deployment in Sensor Networks

Juhua Pu and Zhang Xiong

School of Computer Science, Beijing University of Aeronautics and Astronautics, Beijing, China, 100083
{Pujh, Xiongz}@buaa.edu.cn

Abstract. In this paper, we consider the problem of how to place redundant sensor nodes in an arbitrary sensor network to establish multi-connectivity. Specifically, after exploring the existing general *k*-connectivity algorithm, this paper proves that its approximation ratio is upper-bounded by only $O(k^3\alpha)$, asymptotically one order of *k* lower than that presented before. Since establishing *k*-connectivity is not cost-efficient for many applications, this paper further relaxes *k*-connectivity to partial *k*-connectivity and upper-bounds the approximation ratio of partial *k*-connectivity with $O(k^4\alpha)$.

1 Introduction

Wireless sensor network is an emerging technology that is typical of coordination and cooperation and that has a wide range of potential applications including environment monitoring, smart spaces, medical systems and robotic exploration [1]. Such a network normally consists of a large number of distributed sensor nodes that organize themselves into a multi-hop wireless network, where the *multi-hop* style means that the nodes may cooperate with and route message for each other [2].

Usually a sensor node has one or more sensors, embedded processors, and low-power radios, and is normally battery-operated, but in order for sensor networks to be cost efficient, the onboard processing and wireless communication capabilities and the battery power of each node are highly limited. Consequently, the nodes are prone to both damages from their environment and inner failures such as battery demise. Moreover, in most applications, the networks are deployed in either hostile or inaccessible environments, and it is impractical or infeasible to repair or replenish energy via replacing batteries on these sensors. As a result, to prolong the network lifetime and prevent loss of connectivity, fault-tolerant strategies are needed to deploy sensor networks initially or to deploy additional sensor nodes to repair the networks [3,4,5]. A simple but efficient method is to deploy the sensor networks with significant node redundancy so that multi-connectivity is guaranteed [3,4,6].

Given an integer *k*, *k*-connectivity means that each pair of the nodes is connected by at least *k* node-disjoint paths, therefore providing additional bandwidth. In the worst case, a *k*-connected sensor network requires *k* node failures to disconnect the network. Thus, multi-connectivity is favorable for both fault tolerance and communication capacity. In this context, many researchers [7, 8] have focused on attaining *k*-connectivity through power assignment, which aims to assign the sensors' communication power to

H. Zhuge and G.C. Fox (Eds.): GCC 2005, LNCS 3795, pp. 1179 – 1184, 2005.

ensure k-connectivity and minimize overall power consumption. However, this paper concentrates on another natural approach that improves connectivity through adding additional sensors. Hence, the target problem, called k-connectivity problem hereunder, can be informally expressed as follows: how to add as few as possible nodes to a sensor network such that the resulting network is k-connected?

Interestingly, seldom has this problem been considered in the research community. G. Lin et al.[9] first proved that solving it with a minimum number of additional sensors is NP-hard, so only approximate algorithms are promising to be developed in practice. Then in 2001, D. Du et al.[10] managed to find an algorithm with 5/2 as its approximation ratio (the ratio of the number of additional nodes added by the algorithm to the minimum number of additional nodes that should be added), but they only considered the special case $k = 1$. The next breakthrough is contributed by J. Bredin et al. [3], who designed a k-connectivity-repair algorithm for an arbitrary integer k. Based on any algorithm computing α-approximate minimum-weight k-connected spanning sub-graph of a weighted complete graph, the algorithm establishes the k-connectivity of an input sensor network with the approximation ratio upper-bounded by $O(k^4\alpha)$.

To the best of our knowledge, J. Bredin et al. are the first to propose general algorithms for k-connectivity problem, and $O(k^4\alpha)$ is the first general upper bound of approximation ratio for any integer k. However, evidence implies that the approximation ratio is likely not tight [3]. Starting with this intuition, this paper makes an effort to show that in fact the approximation ratio of the algorithm in [3] can be upper-bounded by $O(k^3\alpha)$, asymptotically one order of k lower than the original one.

The rest of this paper is structured as follows. Section 2 presents necessary preliminaries and accurately formulates the problems to be solved. In section 3 we prove that the approximation ratio of J. Bredin's algorithm is no more than $O(k^3\alpha)$, one order of k lower than the ratio presented in [3].We briefly discuss the partial k-connectivity in section 4, and section 5 concludes this paper.

2 Preliminaries

In this section we establish the formal models for sensor networks, and formulate our problems accurately.

As illustrated in section 1, every sensor node uses low-power radio to transmit message, thus its transmission distance is finite.

Like [3], we only consider static symmetric multi-hop sensor networks with omni-directional fixed- power transmitters. That is, the sensor network considered in this paper has the following characteristics: 1) all sensor nodes are stationary; 2) all sensor nodes have the same maximum transmission distance r; 3) a sensor node u can transmit messages to another node v if and only if the distance between u and v is at most r; 4) each sensor node can route message for other sensor nodes.

Given these assumptions, we can model our sensor network as a unit-disk graph in Euclidean plane, $G = (V, E)$, where each vertex represents a sensor node and is assigned two-dimensional coordinates. Two vertices are connected by an edge if and only if their distance is at most the maximum transmission distance r. For simplicity of exposition, we normalize the coordinate assignment so that $r = 1$.

In terms of this model, the k-connectivity problem is: How to add as few as possible vertices to a unit-disk graph such that the new unit-disk graph is k-connected?

To clarify the meaning of "as few as possible", we define approximation ratio of algorithms. Given a unit-disk graph G and a property P, let n denote the least number of new vertices that should be added to G for it to satisfy P, and n' denote the number of the new vertices added by an algorithm to G for it to satisfy P. Then, the ratio of n' to n is called the approximation ratio of the algorithm. The k-connectivity problem is translated into finding an algorithm with the smallest approximation ratio.

Based on this model, J. Bredin et al presents a general algorithm for k-connectivity, and proves that the approximation ratio of this algorithm is upper-bounded by $O(k^4\alpha)$. Now we use this model to re-analyze the approximation ratio of this algorithm.

3 Re-analysis of the Approximation Ratio of *k*-Connectivity Problem

Based on any α-approximate algorithm computing minimum-weight k-connected spanning sub-graph of a weighted complete graph, J. Bredin et al. developed an algorithm establishing the k-connectivity of an input sensor network, with the approximation ratio upper-bounded by $O(k^4\alpha)$. But this approximation ratio isn't tight as the authors conjectured in [3], and we prove a much tighter one in our Theorem 1.

***Theorem* 1:** In the case $n \geq k$, the algorithm is an $O(k^3\alpha)$-approximation on the minimum number of added sensor nodes to attain vertex k-connectivity of the entire unit-disk graph.

Remark: Proving this theorem is almost the same as that of Theorem 6 in [3], except that Lemma 4 in [3] is replaced by an improved version. Hence, we first prove the improved version and formulate it as our Lemma 7.

Convention: This paper follows [3] by calling the added sensors Steiner sensors.

By Lemma 1 of [3], for any set of original and Steiner sensors, there is a sub-graph G' of the induced unit-disk graph G such that: (1) for each edge of G' incident to at least one Steiner sensor, we can assign it to one of its Steiner endpoints such that each Steiner sensor is assigned at most $6k$ edges, and (2) for any set S of less than k vertices, two vertices are connected in G-S if and only if they are connected in G'-S.

For convenience of exposition, Steiner components in [3] are also introduced here. With G' as above, we can construct the Steiner component rooted at a Steiner sensor node s by growing a set of vertices and edges in G' starting with $\{s\}$, and stopping after we reach any original sensors. That is, Steiner component is a connected component of the induced sub-graph of G' on the Steiner sensors, together with the edges connecting these Steiner sensors to original sensors and these original sensors.

Every Steiner component C of G' has a spanning tree $T(C)$ in which the original sensor nodes are leaves of $T(C)$.

***Lemma* 2.** The number of edges in $T(C)$ is no more than $6kn$, where n denotes the number of Steiner sensor nodes in C.

Proof: each edge in $T(C)$ is incident to at least one Steiner sensor, and by Lemma 1 of [3], there are at most $6kn$ edges in $T(C)$.

Given a Steiner component C, the set of original sensors in it is named the border of C, denoted by Border(C). Now we proceed to explore the properties of Steiner components and their borders. Firstly we sort the border sensors of $T(C)$ by the order they appear in the process of depth-first traversal of $T(C)$, as illustrated in Figure 1. where stars represent Steiner sensor nodes and dots represent border sensor nodes.

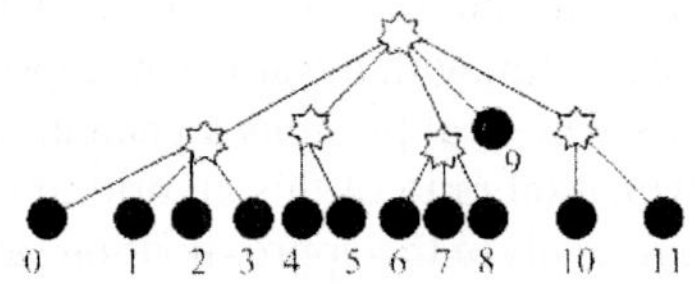

Fig. 1. Sorting the border sensors of $T(C)$

Assume that the sorting result is $v_0, v_1, \ldots, v_p$. If $x>p$, we identify v_x with v_y where $0 \le y \le p$ and $y \equiv x \pmod{p+1}$. For each i and j, since $T(C)$ is a tree, there is a unique path in $T(C)$ that connects v_i and v_{i+j} and whose vertices are pair-wise different, and the path is denoted by $P(i, j)$ hereunder. Define $ne(i,j)$ to be the number of edges in $P(i, j)$. Given an edge uv, if v is a child of u in $T(C)$, define the number of leaves of the edge uv, denoted by $nl(uv)$, to be the number of leaves in the sub-tree of $T(C)$ rooted at v. Some properties of $P(i, j)$, $ne(i,j)$, and $nl(uv)$ will be shown in the following lemmas.

***Lemma* 3.** Given an integer j such that $j \ge 1$, if $nl(uv) \le j$ then there are at most $2nl(uv)$ integers i such that $P(i,j)$ contains the edge uv, otherwise there are at most $2j$ integers i such that $P(i,j)$ contains the edge uv.

Proof: Without loss of generality, assume that v is a child of u in $T(C)$. Assume that the leaves in the sub-tree of $T(C)$ rooted at v are $v_s, v_{s+1}, \ldots, v_t$. Obviously, only when $((i<s) \wedge (s \le i+j \le t)) \vee ((s \le i \le t) \wedge (i+j > t))$ holds, can $P(i,j)$ contain the edge uv.

Hence, in the case that $nl(uv) \le j$, i.e. $t-s+1 \le j$, $P(i,j)$ is possible to contain uv only if $s-j \le i \le t-j$ or $s \le i \le t$. Since $[(t-j)-(s-j)+1]+(t-s+1)=2(t-s+1)=2nl(uv)$, the lemma holds.

In the case that $nl(uv)>j$, i.e. $t-s+1>j$, $P(i,j)$ is possible to contain uv only if $s-j \le i < s$ and $t-j < i \le t$. Since $[s-(s-j)]+[t-(t-j)]=2j$, the lemma also holds in this case.

Given an edge uv in $T(C)$, it's named an exterior edge if one of its vertices is a leaf, and otherwise it's named an inner edge.

***Corollary* 4.** If uv is an exterior edge, for any integer j such that $j \ge 1$, there are at most 2 integers i such that $P(i,j)$ contains the edge uv.

Proof: The corollary immediately follows from Lemma 3.

Define $L_j = Num(0,j) + Num(1,j) + \ldots + Num(p,j)$ for every integer j such that $j \ge 1$.

***Lemma* 5.** Given an integer j such that $j \ge 1$, we have $L_j \le 2jm + 12km$, where m is the number of Steiner sensors in the Steiner component C.

Proof: Let n_1 and n_2 denote the number of exterior edges and that of inner edges of $T(C)$ respectively.

L_j is the sum of the number of the edges in $P(i,j)$, $0 \leq i \leq p$. By lemma 3, given an inner edge uv, there are at most $2j$ integers i such that $P(i,j)$ contains uv, and by corollary 4, given an exterior edge uv, there are at most 2 integers i such that $P(i,j)$ contains uv. Consequently, there are altogether at most $2n_1+2jn_2$ edges in all $P(i,j)$ for $0 \leq i \leq p$, i.e. $L_j \leq 2n_1+2jn_2$.

Note the following three facts: (1) the number of the exterior edges equals to the number of the leaves of $T(C)$, (2) the number of the exterior leaves of $T(C)$ is no more than $6k$ times the number of the Steiner sensors, and (3) the number of the inner edges is no more than the number of the Steiner sensors. Then we have $n_1 \leq 6km$ and $n_2 \leq m$. As a result, $L_j \leq 2n_1+2jn_2 \leq 2jm+12km$.

***Lemma* 6.** $L_1+L_2+\ldots+L_{\lceil k/2 \rceil}=O(k^2m)$, where m is the number of Steiner sensors in the Steiner component C.

Proof: By Lemma 5, $L_1+L_2+\ldots+L_{\lceil k/2 \rceil} \leq 2m(1+2+\ldots+\lceil k/2 \rceil)+12km \times \lceil k/2 \rceil \leq O(k^2m)$.

Given each Steiner component C of G', assuming that its sorted bound nodes are v_0, v_1, …, v_p, we first construct Harary graph $H_{k,p+1}$ using $v_0,\ldots, v_p$ as its vertices, and then follow the procedure in [3] to replace C with this graph, resulting a sub-graph of the weighted complete graph K which is defined in the algorithm 1 in [3]. Lemma 6 may be employed to estimate the total weight of the new edges for replacing C.

***Lemma* 7.** The total weight of the edges of K that replace a Steiner component C is at most $O(k^2)$ times the number of Steiner sensors in C.

Proof: The lemma is in fact an improvement of Lemma 4 in [3], so their proofs are almost the same except that in this paper $ne(i,j)$ is used as an upper bound of the Euclidean distance between vertex v_i and v_{i+j}. Hence, the total weight of the new edges is upper-bounded by $L_1+L_2+\ldots+L_{\lceil k/2 \rceil}=O(k^2m)$.

Sketchy Proof of Theorem 1: The proof is almost the same as that of Theorem 6 in [3] except that Lemma 4 in [3] is replaced by Lemma 7 above. As a result, the weight of a minimum-weight k-connected spanning sub-graph of the weighted complete graph (K, ω) in [3] is no more than $O(k^2)$ times the least number of Steiner sensors to make the original graph k-connected. Note that in [3], this upper bound is as high as $O(k^3)$. Then it's easy to show that Theorem 1 holds. Interested readers please refer to the proof Theorem 6 in [3] for detail.

That is, we prove a much tighter approximation ratio of the k-connectivity algorithm proposed in [3].

4 Brief Discussion of Partial k-Connectivity

In Algorithm 1 in [3], if only one sensor node is placed at position $(1-t)v+tw$ and none sensor node is placed at v and w, then it guarantees k node-disjoint paths between each pair of original nodes, which is called partial k-connectivity. Partial k-connectivity is also very important in sensor network deployment, so we extend Theorem 1 to this case, to establish $O(k^4)$ as an upper bound of its approximation ratio. Because of the space limitation, we ignore the detail of the proof.

5 Conclusion

As sensor networks are prone to failures, this paper considers deploying and repairing algorithms for fault tolerance. As far as we know, J. Bredin's *k*-connectivity repair algorithm is the first general algorithm in this field, whose approximation ratio is $O(k^4\alpha)$ in [3]. However, evidence implies that the approximation ratio is likely not tight, as is stated in [3]. Thus, this paper proves that the approximation ratio of the algorithm in [3] can be upper-bounded by only $O(k^3\alpha)$. We also discussed partial k-connectivity, finding that its approximation ratio is no more than $O(k^4\alpha)$.

Intuitionally, the upper bound of *k*-connectivity and that of partial *k*-connectivity may not be tight, and how to further reduce these ratios is our future work.

Acknowledgement

The authors wish to thank Dr Xingwu Liu for his many technique suggestions.

References

1. Akyildiz I., Su W., Sankarasubramaniam Y., Cayirci E.: Wireless Sensor Network: A Survey. Computer Networks (2002) 393–422.
2. Tilak S., Abu-Ghazaleh N., Heinzelman W.: A Taxonomy of Wireless Micro-Sensor Networks Models. Mobile Computing and Communications Review (2002) 1–8.
3. Bredin J., Demaine E., Hajiaghay M., Rus D.: Deploying Sensor Networks with Guaranteed Capacity and Fault Tolerance. Proceedings of the 6th ACM international symposium on Mobile ad hoc networking and computing. ACM Press, New York (2005) 309–319.
4. Cheriyan J., Vempala S., Vetta A.: An Approximation Algorithm for the Minimum-cost k-vertex Connected Subgraph. SIAM J. Comput. (2003) 1050–1055.
5. Bruck J., Gao J., Jiang A.: Localization and Routing in Sensor Networks by Local Angle Information. Proceedings of the 6th ACM international symposium on Mobile ad hoc networking and computing. ACM Press, New York (2005) 181–192.
6. Blough D., Leoncini M., Resta G., Santi P.: The K-neigh protocol for symmetric topology control in ad hoc networks. Proceeding of 4th ACM International Symposium on Mobile Ad Hoc Networking and Computing (2003) 141–152.
7. Wattenhofer R., Li L., Bahl V., Wang Y.: Distributed topology control for power efficientoperation in multihop wireless ad hoc networks. Proceedings of twentieth Annual Joint Conference of the IEEE Computer and Communications Societies (2001) 1388–1397.
8. Hajiaghayi M., Immorlica N., Mirrokni V.: Power optimization in fault-tolerant topology control algorithms for wireless multi-hop networks. Proceedings of the 9th Annual International Conference on Mobile Computing and Networking, ACM Press, New York (2003) 300–312.
9. Lin G., Xue G.: Steiner tree problem with minimum number of Steiner points and bounded edge-length. Inform. Process. Lett. (1999) 53–57.
10. Du D., Wang L., Xu B.: The Euclidean bottleneck Steiner tree and Steiner tree with minimum number of Steiner points. Lecture Notes in Computer Science, Springer-Verlag, Berlin Heidelberg New York (2001) 509–518.

The Effect of Router Buffer Size on Queue Length-Based AQM Schemes

Ming Liu, Wen-hua Dou, and He-ying Zhang

Computer College, National University of Defense Technology,
Hunan, 410073, P.R. China
liutomorrow@hotmail.com

Abstract. AQM is an effective method to improve the performance of end-to-end congestion control. The behavior of various AQM schemes with respect to buffer capacity issues has not been studied in much detail. In this paper, we show the effect of router buffer size on AQM schemes based on queue length and present the reason: the buffer saturation will make the input and output of AQM schemes conflicting. We also propose a saturation compensator which can improve the performance of AQM schemes when routers have small buffer. At last, using PI as an example we propose PI with saturation compensator whose performance is evaluated through NS2 simulations.

1 Introduction

An important Internet router design question is how large a buffer should be. If buffers are too large, it may lead to excessive packet delay. Buffers being too small may cause excessive packet loss and inefficiencies. TCP/AQM systems are also relevant to the router buffer size. The popular TCP Reno congestion control mechanism reacts to congestion (packet loss) by halving its congestion window. If buffers are small, such reaction to congestion often empties the queue and creates a situation whereby the system does not work conserving, this means under-utilization of resources. Internet routers nowadays may be designed with large buffer size, but it is not a good idea for two reasons. First, it increases end-to-end delay in the presence of congestion, large buffers conflict with the low-latency needs of real time applications. Second, it complicates the design of high-speed routers, leading to higher power consumption, more board space.

AQM performance can be significantly affected by the buffer size of router. RED, as the originally proposed one, is the best known and recommended by IETF. RED can only achieve an ideal operating point when it has a sufficient amount of buffer space and is correctly parameterized [1, 2]. PI[3], as the most popular one, outperforms RED in regulating steady state queue length to a desired reference value with changing levels of congestion. But its' performance is very sensitive to buffer space, in case of small buffer at routers, the transition period before the queue converges to the target value is quite long in our ns2 experiments.

The rest of the paper is organized as follows. In section 2, we show the effect of router buffer size on AQM algorithms based on queue length and deduce the possible reason by analyzing the control system model of AQM. The proposed compensator is presented and analyzed in Section 3. Simulation study is given in Section 4, and the conclusions are drawn in Section 5.

H. Zhuge and G.C. Fox (Eds.): GCC 2005, LNCS 3795, pp. 1185 – 1191, 2005.

2 Buffer Saturation in AQM

Most of the AQM schemes use drop (or mark) probability to regulate the queue length, some calculate it periodically, others do it when packets arrive. The drop probability (AQM output) in real systems should belong to 0~1.

$$\begin{cases} p = 1 & p > 1 \\ p = p & 0 \le p \le 1 \\ p = 0 & p < 0 \end{cases} \tag{1}$$

It is a burden for high speed routers to calculate drop probability when packets arrive, many AQM schemes do this at every sampling instant. We suppose the sampling time is T, the arrival packets number is A during one sampling period. q_old is the last time sampling queue length. $q_{\max}$ is the router buffer size. The queue length (AQM input) in real systems should belong to 0~ $q_{\max}$

$$\begin{cases} q = q_{\max} & q\_old + A - C*T > q_{\max} \\ q = q\_old + A - C*T & 0 \le q\_old + A - C*T \le q_{\max} \\ q = 0 & q\_old + A - C*T < 0 \end{cases} \tag{2}$$

Furthermore, when $q = q_{\max}$, in despite of the value p that calculated by AQM schemes, the arrival packets will be lost, that means $p = 1$.

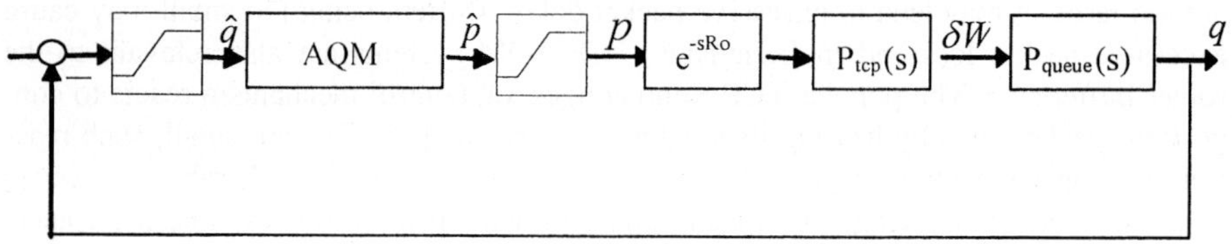

Fig. 1. TCP/AQM system model

The TCP/AQM system model can be depicted as Fig1. Internet is a rather complex huge and nonlinear dynamic system, number of TCP sessions and round trip time are very changeable, so it is unavoidable that TCP/AQM systems run into buffer saturation, that means $q \ne \hat{q}$ or $p \ne \hat{p}$. For example, when $q\_old + A - C*T > q_{\max}$, the sampling value $\hat{q} = q_{\max} \ne q$, it can not indicate the severity of congestion; the drop probability $p = 1$, it is not the output of AQM controller. These make the input and output of controller conflicting, even make the system out of control.

3 Proposed Algorithm

From Section 2, we know the plant input and the controller output will be conflicting in TCP/AQM systems as the result of buffer saturation. When this happens, the control loop is broken and the controller output does not drive the plant. Thus the states of the controller are updated incorrectly, resulting in serious performance deterioration. A well-known and successful method is using compensator during saturation to improve the performance of the closed loop system. The method using in this section can be depicted as fig2.

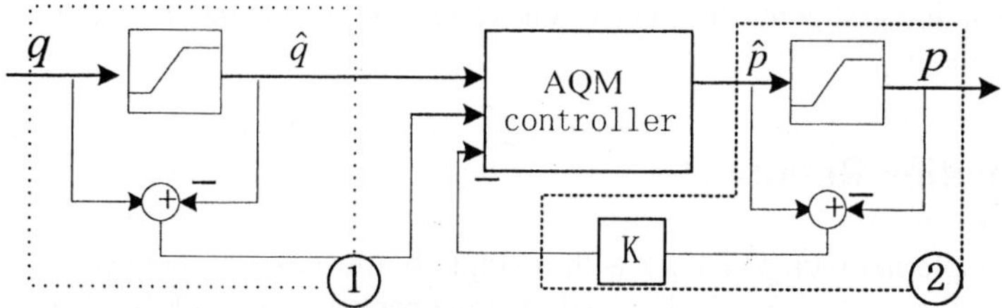

Fig. 2. AQM with a saturation compensator

We use PI controller for AQM as our example, its transfer function is:

$$C_{PI}(s) = K_{PI}\frac{s/\omega_g + 1}{s} \tag{3}$$

the drop probability can be calculated as follows:

$$\Delta p = a*(q - q\_ref) - b*(q\_old - q\_ref) \tag{4}$$

$$a = K_{PI}(1/\omega_g + T), \qquad b = K_{PI}/\omega_g$$

We suppose the sampling time is T, the arrival packets number is A during the sampling period, then we have:

$$q = q[n-1] + A - C*T, \qquad q\_old = q[n-1] \tag{5}$$

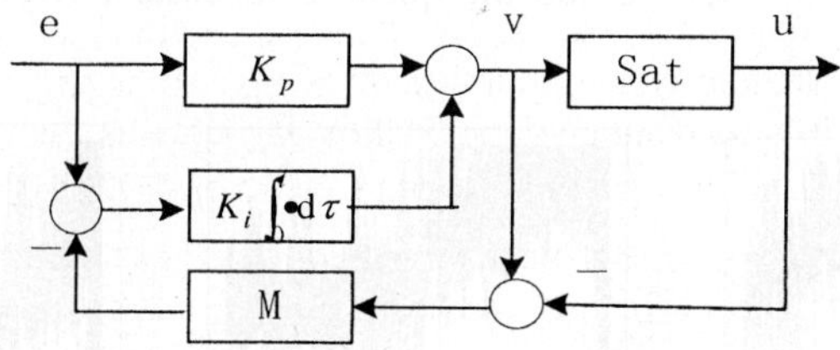

Fig. 3. PI controller with the proposed anti-windup compensator

When $q\_old + A - C*T > q_{\max}$, the drop probability $p \neq \hat{p}$, we suppose $K = K_i T / K_p = \omega_g T$ and use the compensation $-\omega_g T(p - \hat{p})$ to decrease the difference between p and $\hat{p}$.

It is shown in [4] that when a PI controller is used for AQM, the "windup" phenomenon of the integral action can cause performance degradation because the packet drop probability is limited between 0 and 1. To compensate the saturation, [4] apply an anti-windup scheme to the conventional PI controller. The transfer function is $K_p + k_i / s$, $M = 1 / K_p$, PI controller with the proposed anti-windup compensator can be depicted as fig3. This kind of problem is known as the "windup" phenomenon of a position integral controller, but when we use the increment, an integral controller can overcome it.

4 Simulation Results

We use simple network topology with a single bottleneck link between r1 and r2 as depicted in Figure 4. C is 15Mbps and average packet size is 500B. Connections are established between s_i and d_i. The delay ranges between 40ms and 220ms, the buffer size is 200 packets, target queue length is 100 packets. r1 runs PI and supports ECN marking, while the other router runs Drop Tail.

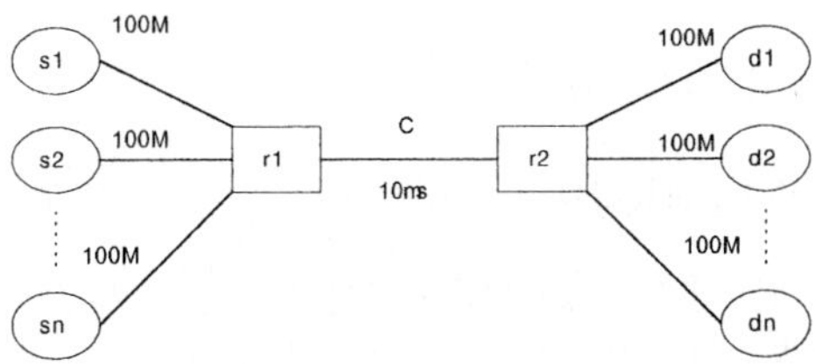

Fig. 4. Simple network topology

A. Experiment 1

In this experiment, we show the effect of the compensator. The results of PI are depicted in Figure 5a; after we add the queue compensator (fig2(1)), the results are depicted in Figure 5b; after we add the queue compensator (fig2(1)) and the drop

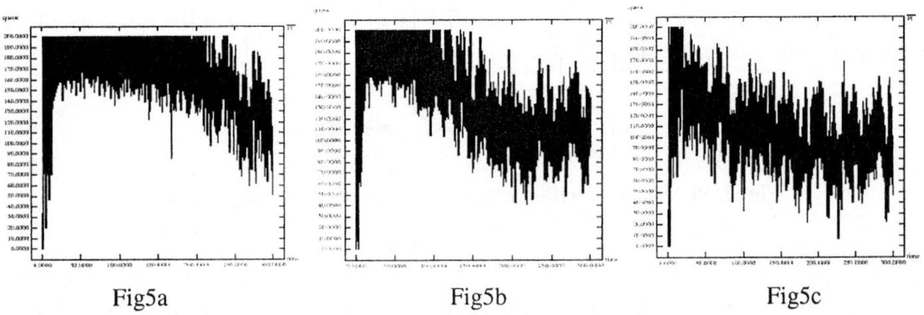

Fig. 5. Evolution of the queue length with FTP flows

probability compensator (fig2(2)), the results are depicted in Figure 5c. From fig5b and fig5c, we know the queue compensator make the controller responds much more quickly. During the experiment of fig5c, the link utilizations are near 100% and few packets are dropped (using ECN). We call this algorithm PI Controller with a Saturation Compensator (SCPI).

B. Experiment 2

In this experiment, we evaluate the performance of SCPI under varying traffic load. We compare the responsiveness and queue size of SCPI and PI in the presence of long-lived FTP flows only. The number of FTP flows is 200 at the beginning, 100 FTP flows leave the link 500 seconds later, they join the link again when t=1000s. The total simulation lasted for 1500s.

As shown in figure6, under varying traffic load and small buffer, SCPI can regulate queue length to the desired reference value quickly, on the contrary the queue length of PI climbs to the highest point and last for a while when the number of FTP flows increases from zero to 200, it lasts small when the number of FTP flows decreases from 200 to 100, once the number of FTP flows increases suddenly, the queue length increases and converges slowly once again.

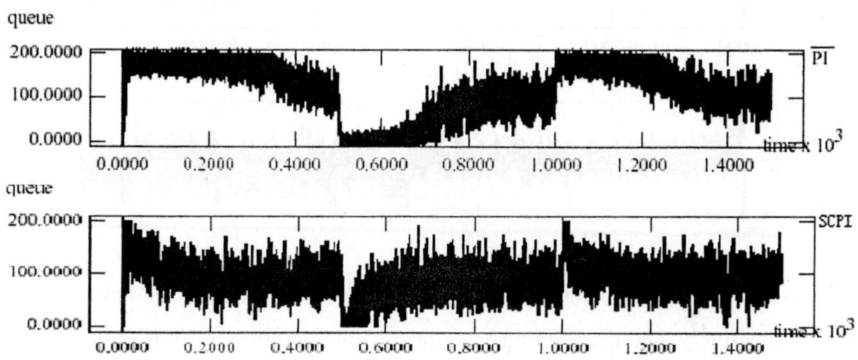

Fig. 6. Evolution of the queue length with FTP flows

When the queue length becomes very small, the link is under utilization, so SCPI has higher link utilization than PI in this experiment.

C. Experiment 3

In this experiment, we analyze the performance of SCPI when unresponsive flows and short lived TCP flows exist. Here, we use three mixtures: FTP flows, HTTP flows and ON/OFF flows. The number of FTP flows is 100 at the beginning, 50 CBR flows and 300 HTTP flows arrive at the link 500 seconds later. Among them, HTTP flows are short-lived with an average page size of 10240B and an average request interval of 5s. The burst and idle times of the ON/OFF service model are 0.5s

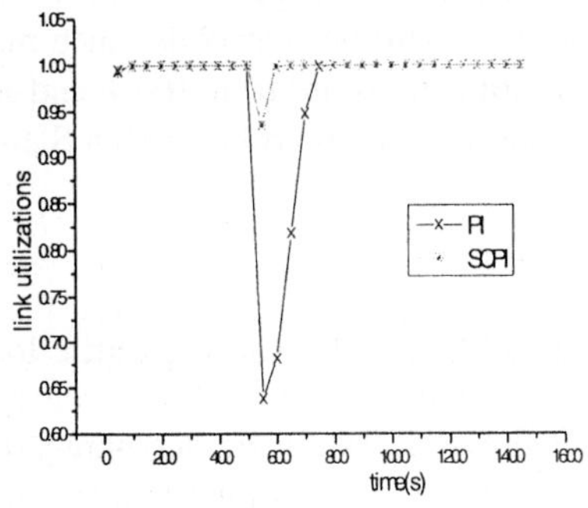

Fig. 7. Link utilizations

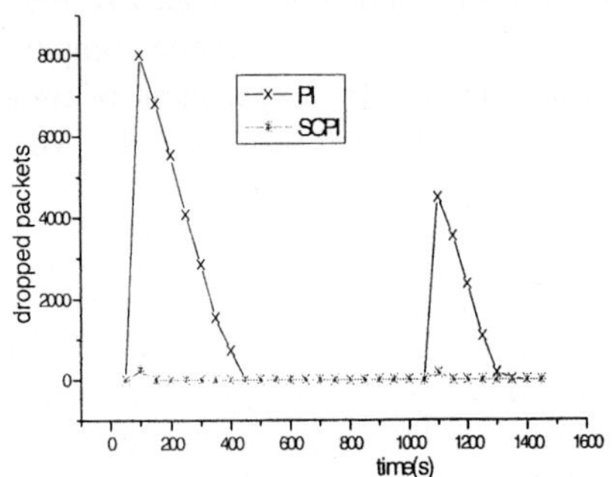

Fig. 8. The number of dropped packets

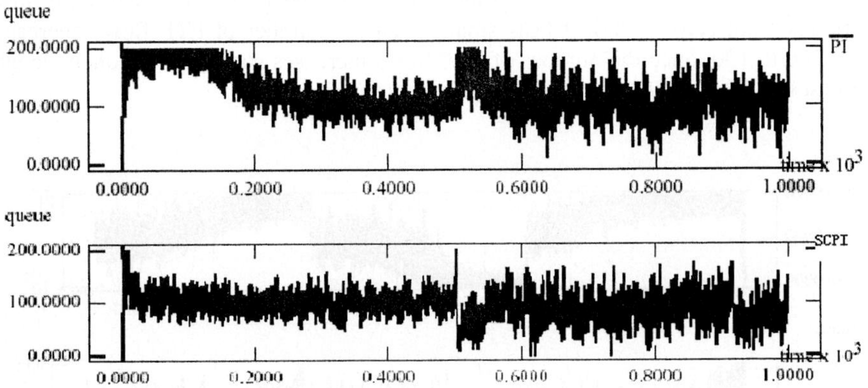

Fig. 9. Evolution of the queue length with FTP, HTTP and ON/OFF flows

and 1s respectively, and the sending rate during "on" duration is 200Kbps. The queue length, plotted in Figure 9, show that SCPI is robust when unresponsive flows and short lived TCP flows exist.

5 Conclusion

If routers continue to be built using the current rule-of-thumb, it will become very difficult to build line cards from commercial memory chips, and so in the end, necessity may force buffers to be smaller. In this paper, we analyze the effect of small router buffer size on AQM algorithms based on queue length and recognized saturation compensator as a potential solution. Using PI as an example, we propose a saturation compensator. The performance of SCPI is evaluated by simulations and compared with PI. The results under a variety of network and traffic situations indicate that the proposed scheme exhibits robust behavior. It is our future work to study the effect of router buffer size on variable TCP/AQM systems.

References

1. C. Villamizar and C. Song.: High performance tcp in ansnet. ACM Computer Communications Review, 24(5):45-60, 1994 1994
2. S. Doran.: RED Experience and Differentiated Queueing. In NANOG Meeting. June 1998.
3. C. Hollot, V. Misra, D. Towsley, and W. Gong.: On designing Improved Controllers for AQM Routers Supporting TCP Flows. Infocom2001, 2001.
4. Hyuk Lim, Kyung-Joon Park, Eun-Chan Park, and Chong-Ho Choi.: Proportional-Integral Active Queue Management with an Anti-Windup Compensator. Conference on Information Sciences and Systems, Princeton University, March, 2002
5. Guido Appenzeller, Isaac Keslassy, Nick McKeown.: Sizing Router Buffers. SIGCOMM 2004, 2004

Parallel Web Spiders for Cooperative Information Gathering

Jiewen Luo[1,2], Zhongzhi Shi[1], Maoguang Wang[1,2], and Wei Wang[2]

[1] The Key Laboratory of Intelligent Information Processing,
Institute of Computing Technology, Chinese Academy of Sciences,
PO Box 2704-28, Beijing, 100080, China
[2] Graduate School of Chinese Academy of Sciences
luojw@ics.ict.ac.cn

Abstract. Web spider is a widely used approach to obtain information for search engines. As the size of the Web grows, it becomes a natural choice to parallelize the spider's crawling process. This paper presents a parallel web spider model based on multi-agent system for cooperative information gathering. It uses the dynamic assignment mechanism to wipe off redundant web pages caused by parallelization. Experiments show that the parallel spider is effective to improve the information gathering performance within an acceptable interaction efficiency cost for controlling. This approach provides a novel perspective for the next generation advanced search engine.

1 Introduction

As the size of the Web grows, it becomes more difficult to retrieve the whole or a significant portion of the Web using a single spider in the search engine. Therefore, many search engines often run multiple processes in parallel to perform the task. We refer to this type of spider as a parallel spider. This approach can considerably improve the collection efficiency. However, it also takes great challenges in how to control the redundant pages by parallel spiders and minimize the efficiency cost [1,2,4,6].

In order to investigate this problem, we explore to design the parallel spiders as a multi-agent system. A multi-agent system is one in which a number of agents cooperates with each other to achieve a global objective in a complex and distributed environment. With the cooperation, spider agents can coordinate information collection actions, which effectively avoid the page redundancy caused by parallization. To test the performance of this approach, we implement a parallel spider prototype based on multi-agent platform MAGE [3] and conduct a series of experiments. Experiment results demonstrate it is effective to improve the search performance within acceptable efficiency cost.

2 Parallel Web Spider Model

Based on the framework of MAGE, we construct a parallel model for web information gathering. Figure 1 shows the model's architecture. It contains three kinds of

H. Zhuge and G.C. Fox (Eds.): GCC 2005, LNCS 3795, pp. 1192 – 1197, 2005.

agents: managing agent (Facilitator), spider agent and index agent. They all inherit the generic Class Agent and can correctly run on the MAGE platform.

As mentioned above, MAGE provides the multi-agent environment support for the whole system. It includes white page service, message transmission service and agent life cycle management service etc. With this software, we need not consider the agent run-time environment and can focus our work on the function implementation of the parallel Spider.

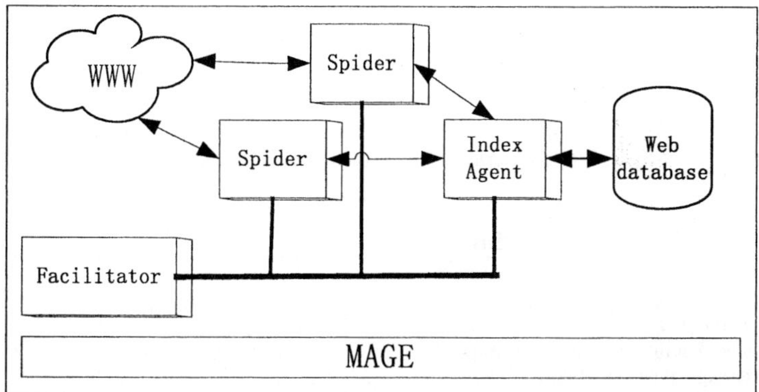

Fig. 1. Architecture of parallel Web Spider

Facilitator is the center of management and communication in the system. It is a special agent that is used to manage the seed URL resources and other agents. Hence, facilitator mainly acts as the server between agents, affording the services including query of addresses and coordination of multi-agent actions. Spider agent starts its work after receiving the allow information from the facilitator. It fetches web pages according to URL and parses their hyperlinks. In our parallel model, we apply the FIPA ACL as the standard communication language for spider agent and facilitator. Through dynamic assignment process of the facilitator, spider agents can effectively avoid the redundant pages.

3 Dynamic Assignment Process

In this section, we discuss how to avoid redundant pages in the parallel spider system. When multiple spiders download pages in parallel, different spiders may download the same pages multiple times. The overlap situation is demonstrated by figure 2.

In order to deal with this problem, we implement the dynamic assignment using multi-agent coordination mechanism. A central facilitator logically divides the Web into different domains (e.g. sina.com and yahoo.com) and dynamically assigns each domain to a spider as the seed URL to download. When MAGE initiates a new spider and assigns it a seed URL, it first checks the facilitator's URL domain to check whether the seed URL has been assigned to other spiders. If not, the new spider adds the seed URL and correctly registers to the facilitator. When facilitator agent receives the registration message, it records the seed URL to its domain in order to avoid redundant allocation in the future.

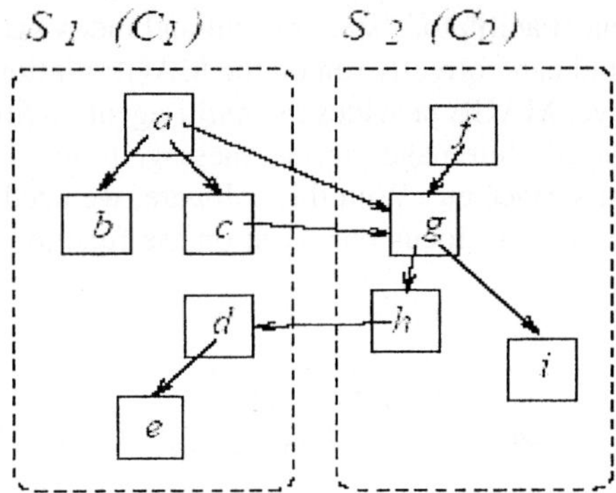

Fig. 2. Site S_1 is crawled by C_1 and site S_2 is crawled by C_2

Dynamic Assignment Procedure

```
Procedure FacilitatorDynamicAssignment ;
 Begin
  Facilitator ();
  Message=Facilitator.WaitForMessage ();
  If (Message. type= = "Registration")
    Record (SpiderName, IP, seedURL);
    Put (seedURL, DomainLibrary);
    Else If (Message. type= = "CheckSeedURL")
          url=Message.url; //get the spider's seed url from the message
          flag=Check (url); //check whether the url is existent in domain library
          If (flag= = true)
          SendMessage (Spider, Refuse," The seed URL is existent");
          Else SendMessage (Spider, Allow," You can use the seed URL");
  Wakeup (Spider);
 End
```

```
Procedure SpiderDynamicAssignment ;
 Begin
  Spider (SpiderName, IP)
  seedURL=Spider.getSeedURL ();// Get the seed URL from user Input
  SendMessage (Facilitator, "CheckSeedURL");
  Message=WaitForMessage (); //Get the response from facilitator
  If (Message. type= = Refuse)
    System.out.println (Message. Content);
    Else SendMessage (Facilitator, "Registration") ;
 Do
  url=Search (seedURL);
 If (url is not consistent with seedURL)
  SendMessage (Facilitator,"CheckSeedURL");
  Message=WaitForMessage ();
 If (Message. type= =Refuse)
  seedURL=FindBrotherNode (url); // Call back and Find the Brother Node
  Else New Spider (SpiderName, IP) // Generate a spider for the new seedURL
       SendMessage (Facilitator, "Registration");
  Until (NumOfSite>MaxOfVisitedSite|| SearchDepth> MaxOfSearchDepth)
 End
```

Fig. 3. Pseudocode of Dynamic Assignment

4 Implementation and Experiments

4.1 Implementation

We have implemented the parallel spider system based on our multi-agent platform MAGE. All programs are written in Java to be independent with operating system. Every spider inherits **Agent** Class in MAGE and has the basic functions such as communication using FIPA ACL message and life cycle.

Figure 4 demonstrates the spider agent screenshot. A Spider thread runs in a separate thread to conduct the Web search. Separate threads are used so that the main GUI frame can continually update the search tree and process the stop search request. As the Spider runs, it continually adds hyperlink nodes to the display tree. When the search completes, users can view the site's vital statistics, including the keywords present, total text characters, total images, and total links.

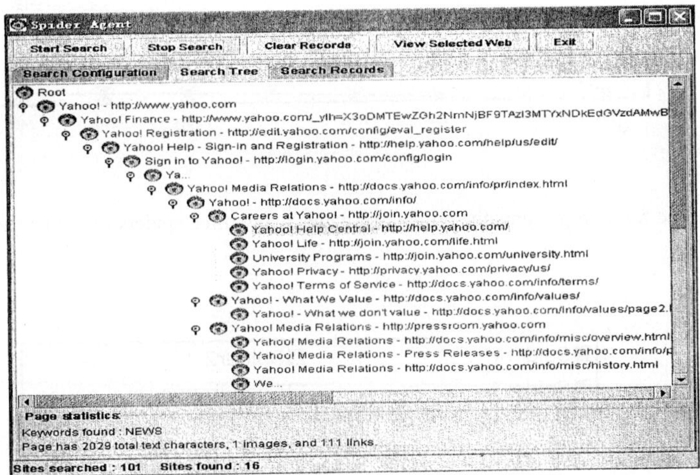

Fig. 4. Screenshot of Spider Agent

4.2 Experiments

In order to test the performance, we conduct a series of experiments. In the first experiment, the three spiders run independently. That means we permit the redundant web pages and the facilitator agent does not work as the coordinator. We record the number of search pages and redundant pages every 30 seconds. The experiment results are showed in figure 5. The average redundant rate of the parallel web paper is 4.1 %. Because most search engine has to collect millions pages in its tasks, this redundant rate should be seriously considered in order to save a mount of storing space.

In the second experiment, we adopt the dynamic assignment mechanism and make the spiders can coordinate with each other to wipe off the redundant pages phenomenon. We can completely avoid the web page repetition through the facilitator's coordination. However, although avoiding redundancy, it takes efficiency cost at the interaction process. This effect is reflected by the decrease of search number at a fixed time scope.

The experiment result is showed in the figure 6. From the result ,we find in most time area, the efficiency cost are between 1% and 5%.That means we have to sacrifice some effiency if we want to wipe off the redudant pages in the parallization process. However, it is worthy to adopt the dynamic assignment since we can control the efficiency cost in a proper scope, which will be made up by the upgrade of hardware.

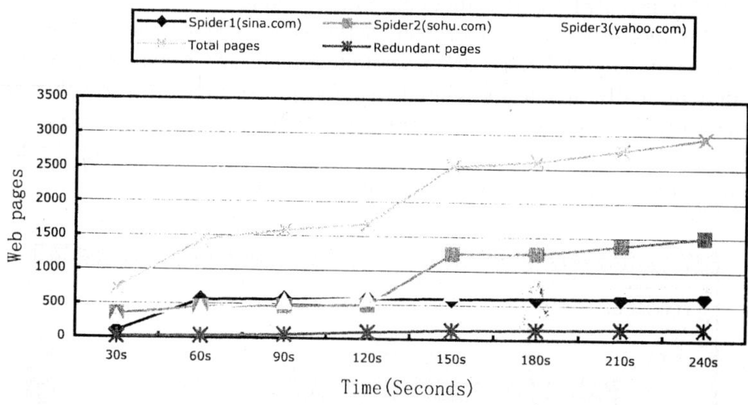

Fig. 5. The figure represents the number of pages when three spiders run independently

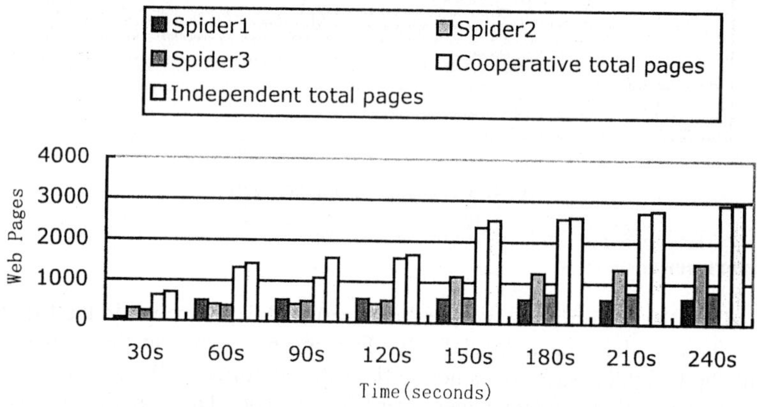

Fig. 6. Comparison of cooperative run and independent run

5 Conclusions and Future Work

Experiment shows that it costs about 4%-6% storing space for redundant web pages caused by parallelization if we do not adopt some effective measures to avoid it. In this paper, we construct a parallel spider based on multi-agent paradigm. Experiment result shows the spider model is effective in eliminating redundancy and improving the search although it takes some cost. In future work, we plan to integrate post-processing in the parallel spider system. In this case, mature data mining technology can be applied to acquire the useful information hided in the tremendous web pages.

Acknowledgements

The research work in this paper is supported by the National Basic Research Priorities Programme (No.2003CB317004), the 863 Project (2003AA115220) and National Natural Science Foundation of China (No. 60435010).

References

1. J. Michael Chau. Design and evaluation of a multi-agent collaborative Web mining system Decision Support Systems 35 (2003) 167– 183
2. Junghoo Cho, Hector Garcia-Molina. Parallel Crawlers Proc. of the 11th International World--Wide Web Conference
3. Zhongzhi Shi MAGE: An Agent-Oriented Programming Environment Third IEEE International Conference on Cognitive Informatics (ICCI'04) pp. 250-257
4. Zhuge, China's E-Science Knowledge Grid Environment, IEEE Intelligent Systems, 19(1) (2004) 13-17
5. Marian Nodine, Jerry Fowler, Tomasz Ksiezyk, Brad Perry, Malcolm Taylor and Amy Unruh. Active Information Gathering in InfoSleuth In International Journal of Cooperative Information Systems 9:1/2, 2000, pp. 3-28.
6. Dong, Shaohui Liu, Haijun Zhang, Zhongzhi Shi, Parallel Web Spider Based on Intelligent Agent, In: Proceedings of The 5th Pacific Rim International Workshop on Multi-Agents (PRIMA2002), Tokyo, 2002

Author Index

Lecture Notes in Computer Science

For information about Vols. 1–3702

please contact your bookseller or Springer

Vol. 3835: G. Sutcliffe, A. Voronkov (Eds.), Logic for Programming, Artificial Intelligence, and Reasoning. XIV, 744 pages. 2005. (Subseries LNAI).

Vol. 3814: M. Maybury, O. Stock, W. Wahlster (Eds.), Intelligent Technologies for Interactive Entertainment. XV, 342 pages. 2005. (Subseries LNAI).

Vol. 3807: M. Dean, Y. Guo, W. Jun, R. Kaschek, S. Krishnaswamy, Z. Pan, Q.Z. Sheng (Eds.), Web Information Systems Engineering – WISE 2005 Workshops. XV, 275 pages. 2005.

Vol. 3806: A.H. H. Ngu, M. Kitsuregawa, E.J. Neuhold, J.-Y. Chung, Q.Z. Sheng (Eds.), Web Information Systems Engineering – WISE 2005. XXI, 771 pages. 2005.

Vol. 3805: G. Subsol (Ed.), Virtual Storytelling. XII, 289 pages. 2005.

Vol. 3799: M. A. Rodríguez, I.F. Cruz, S. Levashkin, M.J. Egenhofer (Eds.), GeoSpatial Semantics. X, 259 pages. 2005.

Vol. 3795: H. Zhuge, G.C. Fox (Eds.), Grid and Cooperative Computing - GCC 2005. XXI, 1203 pages. 2005.

Vol. 3793: T. Conte, N. Navarro, W.-m.W. Hwu, M. Valero, T. Ungerer (Eds.), High Performance Embedded Architectures and Compilers. XIII, 317 pages. 2005.

Vol. 3792: I. Richardson, P. Abrahamsson, R. Messnarz (Eds.), Software Process Improvement. VIII, 215 pages. 2005.

Vol. 3791: A. Adi, S. Stoutenburg, S. Tabet (Eds.), Rules and Rule Markup Languages for the Semantic Web. X, 225 pages. 2005.

Vol. 3790: G. Alonso (Ed.), Middleware 2005. XIII, 443 pages. 2005.

Vol. 3789: A. Gelbukh, Á. de Albornoz, H. Terashima-Marín (Eds.), MICAI 2005: Advances in Artificial Intelligence. XXVI, 1198 pages. 2005. (Subseries LNAI).

Vol. 3785: K.-K. Lau, R. Banach (Eds.), Formal Methods and Software Engineering. XIV, 496 pages. 2005.

Vol. 3784: J. Tao, T. Tan, R.W. Picard (Eds.), Affective Computing and Intelligent Interaction. XIX, 1008 pages. 2005.

Vol. 3781: S.Z. Li, Z. Sun, T. Tan, S. Pankanti, G. Chollet, D. Zhang (Eds.), Advances in Biometric Person Authentication. XI, 250 pages. 2005.

Vol. 3780: K. Yi (Ed.), Programming Languages and Systems. XI, 435 pages. 2005.

Vol. 3779: H. Jin, D. Reed, W. Jiang (Eds.), Network and Parallel Computing. XV, 513 pages. 2005.

Vol. 3777: O.B. Lupanov, O.M. Kasim-Zade, A.V. Chaskin, K. Steinhöfel (Eds.), Stochastic Algorithms: Foundations and Applications. VIII, 239 pages. 2005.

Vol. 3775: J. Schönwälder, J. Serrat (Eds.), Ambient Networks. XIII, 281 pages. 2005.

Vol. 3773: A. Sanfeliu, M.L. Cortés (Eds.), Progress in Pattern Recognition, Image Analysis and Applications. XX, 1094 pages. 2005.

Vol. 3772: M. Consens, G. Navarro (Eds.), String Processing and Information Retrieval. XIV, 406 pages. 2005.

Vol. 3771: J.M.T. Romijn, G.P. Smith, J. van de Pol (Eds.), Integrated Formal Methods. XI, 407 pages. 2005.

Vol. 3770: J. Akoka, S.W. Liddle, I.-Y. Song, M. Bertolotto, I. Comyn-Wattiau, W.-J. van den Heuvel, M. Kolp, J. Trujillo, C. Kop, H.C. Mayr (Eds.), Perspectives in Conceptual Modeling. XXII, 476 pages. 2005.

Vol. 3768: Y.-S. Ho, H.J. Kim (Eds.), Advances in Mulitmedia Information Processing - PCM 2005, Part II. XXVIII, 1088 pages. 2005.

Vol. 3767: Y.-S. Ho, H.J. Kim (Eds.), Advances in Mulitmedia Information Processing - PCM 2005, Part I. XXVIII, 1022 pages. 2005.

Vol. 3766: N. Sebe, M.S. Lew, T.S. Huang (Eds.), Computer Vision in Human-Computer Interaction. X, 231 pages. 2005.

Vol. 3765: Y. Liu, T. Jiang, C. Zhang (Eds.), Computer Vision for Biomedical Image Applications. X, 563 pages. 2005.

Vol. 3764: S. Tixeuil, T. Herman (Eds.), Self-Stabilizing Systems. VIII, 229 pages. 2005.

Vol. 3762: R. Meersman, Z. Tari, P. Herrero (Eds.), On the Move to Meaningful Internet Systems 2005: OTM 2005 Workshops. XXXI, 1228 pages. 2005.

Vol. 3761: R. Meersman, Z. Tari (Eds.), On the Move to Meaningful Internet Systems 2005: CoopIS, DOA, and ODBASE, Part II. XXVII, 653 pages. 2005.

Vol. 3760: R. Meersman, Z. Tari (Eds.), On the Move to Meaningful Internet Systems 2005: CoopIS, DOA, and ODBASE, Part I. XXVII, 921 pages. 2005.

Vol. 3759: G. Chen, Y. Pan, M. Guo, J. Lu (Eds.), Parallel and Distributed Processing and Applications - ISPA 2005 Workshops. XIII, 669 pages. 2005.

Vol. 3758: Y. Pan, D.-x. Chen, M. Guo, J. Cao, J.J. Dongarra (Eds.), Parallel and Distributed Processing and Applications. XXIII, 1162 pages. 2005.

Vol. 3757: A. Rangarajan, B. Vemuri, A.L. Yuille (Eds.), Energy Minimization Methods in Computer Vision and Pattern Recognition. XII, 666 pages. 2005.

Vol. 3756: J. Cao, W. Nejdl, M. Xu (Eds.), Advanced Parallel Processing Technologies. XIV, 526 pages. 2005.

Vol. 3754: J. Dalmau Royo, G. Hasegawa (Eds.), Management of Multimedia Networks and Services. XII, 384 pages. 2005.

Vol. 3753: O.F. Olsen, L.M.J. Florack, A. Kuijper (Eds.), Deep Structure, Singularities, and Computer Vision. X, 259 pages. 2005.

Vol. 3752: N. Paragios, O. Faugeras, T. Chan, C. Schnörr (Eds.), Variational, Geometric, and Level Set Methods in Computer Vision. XI, 369 pages. 2005.

Vol. 3751: T. Magedanz, E.R. M. Madeira, P. Dini (Eds.), Operations and Management in IP-Based Networks. X, 213 pages. 2005.

Vol. 3750: J.S. Duncan, G. Gerig (Eds.), Medical Image Computing and Computer-Assisted Intervention – MICCAI 2005, Part II. XL, 1018 pages. 2005.

Vol. 3749: J.S. Duncan, G. Gerig (Eds.), Medical Image Computing and Computer-Assisted Intervention – MICCAI 2005, Part I. XXXIX, 942 pages. 2005.

Vol. 3748: A. Hartman, D. Kreische (Eds.), Model Driven Architecture – Foundations and Applications. IX, 349 pages. 2005.

Vol. 3747: C.A. Maziero, J.G. Silva, A.M.S. Andrade, F.M.d. Assis Silva (Eds.), Dependable Computing. XV, 267 pages. 2005.

Vol. 3746: P. Bozanis, E.N. Houstis (Eds.), Advances in Informatics. XIX, 879 pages. 2005.

Vol. 3745: J.L. Oliveira, V. Maojo, F. Martín-Sánchez, A.S. Pereira (Eds.), Biological and Medical Data Analysis. XII, 422 pages. 2005. (Subseries LNBI).

Vol. 3744: T. Magedanz, A. Karmouch, S. Pierre, I. Venieris (Eds.), Mobility Aware Technologies and Applications. XIV, 418 pages. 2005.

Vol. 3740: T. Srikanthan, J. Xue, C.-H. Chang (Eds.), Advances in Computer Systems Architecture. XVII, 833 pages. 2005.

Vol. 3739: W. Fan, Z.-h. Wu, J. Yang (Eds.), Advances in Web-Age Information Management. XXIV, 930 pages. 2005.

Vol. 3738: V.R. Syrotiuk, E. Chávez (Eds.), Ad-Hoc, Mobile, and Wireless Networks. XI, 360 pages. 2005.

Vol. 3735: A. Hoffmann, H. Motoda, T. Scheffer (Eds.), Discovery Science. XVI, 400 pages. 2005. (Subseries LNAI).

Vol. 3734: S. Jain, H.U. Simon, E. Tomita (Eds.), Algorithmic Learning Theory. XII, 490 pages. 2005. (Subseries LNAI).

Vol. 3733: P. Yolum, T. Güngör, F. Gürgen, C. Özturan (Eds.), Computer and Information Sciences - ISCIS 2005. XXI, 973 pages. 2005.

Vol. 3731: F. Wang (Ed.), Formal Techniques for Networked and Distributed Systems - FORTE 2005. XII, 558 pages. 2005.

Vol. 3729: Y. Gil, E. Motta, V. R. Benjamins, M.A. Musen (Eds.), The Semantic Web – ISWC 2005. XXIII, 1073 pages. 2005.

Vol. 3728: V. Paliouras, J. Vounckx, D. Verkest (Eds.), Integrated Circuit and System Design. XV, 753 pages. 2005.

Vol. 3726: L.T. Yang, O.F. Rana, B. Di Martino, J.J. Dongarra (Eds.), High Performance Computing and Communications. XXVI, 1116 pages. 2005.

Vol. 3725: D. Borrione, W. Paul (Eds.), Correct Hardware Design and Verification Methods. XII, 412 pages. 2005.

Vol. 3724: P. Fraigniaud (Ed.), Distributed Computing. XIV, 520 pages. 2005.

Vol. 3723: W. Zhao, S. Gong, X. Tang (Eds.), Analysis and Modelling of Faces and Gestures. XI, 4234 pages. 2005.

Vol. 3722: D. Van Hung, M. Wirsing (Eds.), Theoretical Aspects of Computing – ICTAC 2005. XIV, 614 pages. 2005.

Vol. 3721: A. Jorge, L. Torgo, P.B. Brazdil, R. Camacho, J. Gama (Eds.), Knowledge Discovery in Databases: PKDD 2005. XXIII, 719 pages. 2005. (Subseries LNAI).

Vol. 3720: J. Gama, R. Camacho, P.B. Brazdil, A. Jorge, L. Torgo (Eds.), Machine Learning: ECML 2005. XXIII, 769 pages. 2005. (Subseries LNAI).

Vol. 3719: M. Hobbs, A.M. Goscinski, W. Zhou (Eds.), Distributed and Parallel Computing. XI, 448 pages. 2005.

Vol. 3718: V.G. Ganzha, E.W. Mayr, E.V. Vorozhtsov (Eds.), Computer Algebra in Scientific Computing. XII, 502 pages. 2005.

Vol. 3717: B. Gramlich (Ed.), Frontiers of Combining Systems. X, 321 pages. 2005. (Subseries LNAI).

Vol. 3716: L. Delcambre, C. Kop, H.C. Mayr, J. Mylopoulos, Ó. Pastor (Eds.), Conceptual Modeling – ER 2005. XVI, 498 pages. 2005.

Vol. 3715: E. Dawson, S. Vaudenay (Eds.), Progress in Cryptology – Mycrypt 2005. XI, 329 pages. 2005.

Vol. 3714: H. Obbink, K. Pohl (Eds.), Software Product Lines. XIII, 235 pages. 2005.

Vol. 3713: L.C. Briand, C. Williams (Eds.), Model Driven Engineering Languages and Systems. XV, 722 pages. 2005.

Vol. 3712: R. Reussner, J. Mayer, J.A. Stafford, S. Overhage, S. Becker, P.J. Schroeder (Eds.), Quality of Software Architectures and Software Quality. XIII, 289 pages. 2005.

Vol. 3711: F. Kishino, Y. Kitamura, H. Kato, N. Nagata (Eds.), Entertainment Computing - ICEC 2005. XXIV, 540 pages. 2005.

Vol. 3710: M. Barni, I. Cox, T. Kalker, H.J. Kim (Eds.), Digital Watermarking. XII, 485 pages. 2005.

Vol. 3709: P. van Beek (Ed.), Principles and Practice of Constraint Programming - CP 2005. XX, 887 pages. 2005.

Vol. 3708: J. Blanc-Talon, W. Philips, D.C. Popescu, P. Scheunders (Eds.), Advanced Concepts for Intelligent Vision Systems. XXII, 725 pages. 2005.

Vol. 3707: D.A. Peled, Y.-K. Tsay (Eds.), Automated Technology for Verification and Analysis. XII, 506 pages. 2005.

Vol. 3706: H. Fukś, S. Lukosch, A.C. Salgado (Eds.), Groupware: Design, Implementation, and Use. XII, 378 pages. 2005.

Vol. 3705: R. De Nicola, D. Sangiorgi (Eds.), Trustworthy Global Computing. VIII, 371 pages. 2005.

Vol. 3704: M. De Gregorio, V. Di Maio, M. Frucci, C. Musio (Eds.), Brain, Vision, and Artificial Intelligence. XV, 556 pages. 2005.

Vol. 3703: F. Fages, S. Soliman (Eds.), Principles and Practice of Semantic Web Reasoning. VIII, 163 pages. 2005.